Warman's
English &
Continental
Pottery & Porcelain

Second Edition

Susan and Al Bagdade

Wallace-Homestead Book Company
Radnor, Pennsylvania

Encyclopedia of Antiques and Collectibles
Harry L. Rinker, Series Editor

Warman's Americana & Collectibles, 5th Edition, edited by Harry L. Rinker
Warman's English & Continental Pottery & Porcelain, 2nd Edition, by Susan and Al Bagdade
Warman's Oriental Antiques, by Gloria and Robert Mascarelli

ACKNOWLEDGMENTS

Harry L. Rinker has guided us through every step of planning and preparing this book. Without his advice, prodding, and encouragement, it would not have come to fruition.

Al's partner in dentistry, Burton Turek, must be thanked for taking on the lion's share of work at the office, and for his infinite patience while Al made innumerable phone calls, did research, and delved through auction catalogues.

Our children, David and Felicia, have been very understanding when we spent hour after hour attached to the computer.

A special debt of gratitude must go to Rich Kleinhardt for drawing the pottery and porcelain marks required for the manuscript.

This book would not have been possible without the cooperation of hundreds of antiques dealers who allowed us to gather information and photograph their wares at antiques shows and in their shops.

A special thank you goes to the auction houses in the United States, England, and the Continent, which provided subscriptions to their extensive catalogues and access to their photographs. The authors express grateful appreciation to auctioneers Leslie Hindman of Chicago and Terry Dunning of Elgin, Illinois, who allowed us to photograph auction properties.

Mary and Dudley Pierce of Wisconsin Rapids, Wisconsin, were exceptionally generous in inviting us to their home for a private photo session. Sotheby's in London was kind enough to send photographs from their auction catalogues for difficult categories.

Additional thanks to Randi Schwartz, who once again allowed us to invade her private collection of majolica and her shop, The Raven and Dove, to photograph examples for this book's cover.

Front Cover. *Clockwise from top left:* Strawberry dish, 10¾" l, 10" w, majolica, c1870-80, imp English Registry mark, George Jones **1800.00**; Vase, 11⅛" h, c1880, "blue Poquier-Beau" mark, Quimper **900.00**; Plate, 12¼" d, Delft, shaped rim, 1790, "blue claw" mark, Holland **375.00**; Teapot, 9 " l, 7 " h, majolica, c1880, raised English Registry mark, Fielding **900.00**; Tobacco Jar, 9" h, bisque, c1890, German **900.00**.

Published in Radnor, Pennsylvania 19089, by Wallace-Homestead,
a division of Chilton Book Company

Manufactured in the United States of America

Library of Congress Catalog Card Number: 91-50430
ISBN 0-87069-577-0 paperback
ISBN 0-87069-617-3 hardcover

1 2 3 4 5 6 7 8 9 0   9 8 7 6 5 4 3 2 1

CONTENTS

PREFACE TO THE SECOND EDITION

For the second edition, decisions were made concerning certain categories that needed to be added, changed, or amended. Readers will be pleased to find the Blue Onion Pattern, Relief Molded Jugs, Staffordshire Blue and White, as well as additional Sevres information.

Imperial St. Petersburg has been incorporated into Russia—General, Plymouth now resides in England—General, and Zurich is at home in Switzerland—General. Bernard Moore has been retired.

More importantly, users of our first edition should note that this edition contains *entirely new* pottery and porcelain examples, more than twelve thousand in total. All the photographs are *new for this edition,* and additional marks have been added, along with dates for all the original marks.

As with the first edition, we invite readers to send their comments to us in care of our new publisher, the Wallace-Homestead Book Company.

We appreciated the generous remarks from readers of our first edition, and think they will be pleased with this new and improved effort.

Susan and Al Bagdade
Northbrook, Illinois

PREFACE TO THE FIRST EDITION

For the past few years we have been writing "Answers on Antiques," a column that appears in The *Antique Trader Weekly.* We realized that many of the questions we received related to English and Continental pottery and porcelain. Our readers wanted to know: What is it? When was it made? How much is it worth?

As we did our research, we realized how little information was available from American publishers about English and Continental pottery and porcelain. The books that did exist were published by European firms, most notably the Antique Collectors' Club in England. They were expensive, difficult to obtain, and focused on the European market. The English antiques price guides reflected foreign prices and did not contain helpful introductory material to a collecting category that is now the hallmark of the American antiques price guides.

A void existed, and we decided to fill it.

This book represents a true division of labor. Al was in charge of the sixteen thousand data entries and their prices. Susan wrote over two hundred histories of the companies and categories listed in the guide. Both weathered the numerous crises involved with writing one's first book on a brand new computer.

Everywhere we turned in gathering information for this book, whether it was to a member of the staff of a large auction house or to a small antiques shop owner, we found encouragement for our efforts. We also queried these individuals about what type of information they felt should be included. This book is not only a response to their needs but to their numerous requests as well.

When we started to work on this book, Harry L. Rinker, our editor, suggested that a book has a far longer gestation time than a child, involves more work, and is much harder to deliver. We wish we could say that he was wrong. But, alas, he was right. We only hope that the final product brings you as much joy as our two real children and this adopted child in book form does to us.

Susan and Al Bagdade
Northbrook, Illinois

Part One: How to Use This Book

ORGANIZATION OF THE PRICE GUIDE

Listings: More than two hundred categories dealing with English and Continental pottery and porcelain are listed alphabetically in this price guide. Most categories refer to a single manufactory. A general category by country includes smaller firms that are not dealt with individually.

Every effort has been made to make the price listings descriptive enough so that specific objects can be identified by the reader. Emphasis has been placed on examples being sold in the marketplace today. Some harder to find objects were included to provide a full range in each category.

History: Every category has a capsule history that details the founding of the company, its principal owners, the nature of the wares, the patterns utilized, and general information available on the specific company. Notes about marks are included in the history or collecting hints.

References: Reference books are listed whenever possible to encourage the collector to learn more about the category. Books are listed only if there is a substantial section on the specific category being considered. Included in the listing are author, title, publisher, (if published by a small firm or individual, we have indicated "privately printed"), and date of publication or most recent edition.

Many of the books listed may be out of print, no longer available from the publisher; these will usually be available in public libraries or through inter-library loan. Readers also may find antiques book dealers at antiques shows, flea markets, and advertising in trade papers and journals. Many book dealers provide mail order services.

Periodicals: In addition to publications of collectors' clubs, there are numerous general interest newspapers and magazines that devote much attention to pottery and porcelain. A sampling includes the following:

Antique Monthly, P.O. Drawer 2, Tuscaloosa, AL 35402
Antique Review, P.O. Box 538, Worthington, OH 43085
Antique Showcase, Amis Gibbs Publications, Ltd., Canfield, Ontario, Canada, N0A 1C0
Antique Trader Weekly, P.O. Box 1050, Dubuque, IA 52001
Antique Week, P.O. Box 90, Knightstown, IN 46148
Antiques and Collecting Hobbies, 1006 S. Michigan Avenue, Chicago, IL 60605
Antiques and The Arts Weekly, 5 Church Hill Rd., Newtown, CT 06470
Antiques (The Magazine Antiques), 551 Fifth Avenue, New York, NY 10017
Collector News, Box 156, Grundy Center, IA 50638
Maine Antique Digest, P.O. Box 645, Waldboro, ME 04572
New York-Pennsylvania Collector, Fishers, NY 14453
Southern Antiques & Southeast Trader, P.O. Box 1550, Lake City, FL 32055
West Coast Peddler, P.O. Box 5134, Whittier, CA 90607

Museums: Museums are listed if significant collections in the category are on display. Many museums have large collections of pottery and/or porcelains, but did not provide a listing for inclusion in this book.

Collectors' Clubs: All collectors' clubs have been verified to be active. Addresses are listed for membership information. Some clubs have regional and local chapters. English clubs welcome American members.

Reproduction Alert: Where reproduction alerts are listed for a particular category, the collector should be extremely careful when purchasing examples. Some reproductions are unmarked; the newness of their appearance is often the best clue to identification as a reproduction.

Collecting Hints: This section calls attention to specific hints if they are applicable to a category. Clues also are given for spotting reproductions when known.

Additional Listings: When more than one category is covered by a specific listing, other listings are added to help the reader find additional information.

Marks: When pottery and porcelain wares are marked, we have included representative marks for that manufactory. However, to see the full range of marks used by a firm, one must consult one of the marks books listed in the bibliography.

DERIVATION OF PRICES USED

The prices in this book were derived from a variety of sources. Antiques shows, antiques shops, and flea markets representing all parts of the country were important sources. The prices listed reflect what the collector would have to pay for an item, i.e., the retail price.

Auction houses in the United States, London, Geneva, and Amsterdam were a valuable source of prices, not only for the upper level pottery and porcelain examples, but also for many of the middle and lower range price levels. Prices realized are noted with an (A) at the end of the listing preceding the price to denote an auction price. This price represents the actual hammer price plus the buyer's premium where applicable.

Antiques magazines, trade papers, and journals were an additional source for what is available currently on the market. They also indicate what is being sold and what is sitting on the shelf.

Specialized price lists featuring collections of one specific type of ceramics were invaluable. These lists included all ranges of prices in a particular field.

Where conflicting prices occurred for similar pieces, an additional source was sought which included consulting with specialists to confirm or reject a specific item's value.

It is unlikely that the collector will be able to match exactly a specific piece with listings in the price guide. Each category represents a range of prices; use as a guide rather than an absolute determination.

CONDITION OF WARES

Condition plays an important role in determining the value of ceramics. Porcelain and pottery from the early periods, i.e., 16th to 18th century, and rare pieces are less affected pricewise by condition than the more recent ceramic examples. One would be less concerned about missing fingers on a figure by the Meissen modeler Kaendler than by the same damage found on a 19th or 20th century Dresden "lace" figure. Availability is the key word.

Middle and lower priced pieces that are damaged should not be overlooked completely. In some cases they may act as a "filler" piece for a collection until a better example becomes available. However, these damaged pieces should reflect a lower price than a fine example. The price should be directly proportional to the extent of the damage. As an example, tin-glazed earthenware often shows signs of wear along the rim. Glaze flakes in this area are to be expected. However, glaze flakes affecting the central design are less acceptable, even if they are smaller in diameter.

Outright chips also should be reflected by a lower price. Under-the-rim chips are more tolerable than those on the surface or at a margin. Major defects such as breaks, cracks, fades in the design, pieces missing (knobs, handles, covers, etc.) or heavy cuts in the glaze greatly diminish the value of a piece. Remember that an age crack is still a crack and should be treated as such. It is wiser to spend extra dollars to purchase the best example available.

Repaired examples should be evaluated critically. A reglued handle detracts considerably from the value of a piece. A professionally restored handle may be more acceptable to the collector. Casual examination of a piece may not show the location or extent of a repair.

Changes in the glaze, brilliance and texture, and slight variations in the decorative colors are often signs of a repair. By examining the inside of a hollow figure, a repaired fracture may be quite visible since inside cosmetics often were overlooked during inferior restorations. It behooves the buyer to examine a piece carefully under a strong light or blue light before purchasing the piece since repaired merchandise is difficult to return when discovered at a later time.

THE CARE AND FEEDING OF CERAMICS

Ceramics by nature are fragile and should be treated with the utmost care. Dirt and dust are natural enemies to all ceramics and should be removed whenever encountered. The natural impulse is to plunge the dirty object into a sinkful of hot, sudsy water and give it a good "once-over." This is the wrong procedure to follow. Care was used in selecting the piece; and care should be used in the cleaning process.

Visual examination of the piece is the first step. Check for obvious repairs, hairline cracks, and crazing, as these factors require additional care when cleaning the piece. It is important to know what the piece is made of, as this also controls the method of cleaning. Unglazed ceramics are washed differently than glazed examples.

Set aside a work area that is uncluttered and near running water. A textured towel makes a good work surface and adds support for the piece. Remove loose dirt and dust with a soft brush, such as an artist's brush. Never use a stiff brush since this can disturb surface decorations. Proceed slowly and carefully, especially around projections and handles. A good portion of the grime can be removed in this manner. In addition, pieces with hairlines will less likely soak up dirt when the washing process starts.

A solution of mild soap in lukewarm water with ammonia (1 oz. of ammonia to 10 ozs. of water) is an ideal working solution. Enough soap should be added to bring forth suds. Cotton swabs or balls dipped into the solution and applied gently to the surface will loosen and remove years of grime. Stains, such as grease and unknown stains, should be approached with caution.

On vertical pieces such as figures, begin at the top and work towards the base. Constantly change the wash water as it tends to become dirty with use. Continually rinse away the soapy solution using clean water and cotton swabs. Never use abrasive materials such as scouring or soap pads or harsh detergents. Unglazed ceramics such as earthenware and bisque should be wiped with moist, soft swabs.

Though the dishwasher is a handy device for commercial dishware, it is not a friend to early ceramics. Hot water and strong detergents can dissolve water soluble glue joints and remove surface decorations. Pieces with metal bases should not be immersed in water. This is true especially for ormolu.

Never use bleach. This material is harmful to certain types of decoration. In addition, bleach can cause a stain to spread rather dramatically. Dry pieces with equal care using cotton swabs or linen towels. A hair dryer can be a handy tool for getting into hard to reach areas. If stains are persistent, are of unknown origin, or if a glue joint separates, it is wise to consult a professional restorer.

Once the pieces are clean, storage is the next consideration. Certain precautions apply. All pieces must be dried thoroughly before storing. When stacking plates, always keep the same sizes and shapes together. Tissue or felt should separate each plate. Cups should be hung from plastic coated hooks or stored individually. Never stack cups or bowls since this tends to damage surface decorations.

Plate hangers serve a purpose, but should be used with discretion. Always use the proper size. Too large a hanger will not support a piece properly. Hangers that are too small put excessive pressure on a piece. Wrap the wire projections in plastic tubing. This helps protect the rim glaze.

For additional hints on the care of ceramics, consult one of the following books: Frieda Kay Fall, *Art Objects: Their Care and Preservation,* Museum Publications, 1967; Albert Jackson & David Day, *The Antiques Care & Repair Handbook,* Alfred A. Knopf, 1984; Judith Larney, *Restoring Ceramics,* Watson-Guptill Publications, 1975; V.P. Wright, *Pamper Your Possessions,* Barre Publishers, 1972.

STATE OF THE MARKET

The dozing ceramics field of the late 1980s has slipped into a deep sleep in the early 1990s. Whether it is the sluggish economy or the lack of interest in these antiques, dealers are finding it more and more difficult to sell articles that were recently in demand.

Auction houses are also experiencing tough times; many items fail to reach their opening minimum bids and go unsold. A perusal of "prices realized" sheets show many "N/S" or not sold items, something that was quite unthinkable in the early 1980s.

Porcelains from Meissen, Vienna, Wedgwood, Worcester, and Sevres continue to fill the auction catalogue pages, but only the unique or rarer pieces arouse much interest. These continue to bring top prices from the few players who are still involved in the ceramics auction scene. Additionally, we see that ceramics sold in the 1980s are reappearing in the auction catalogues in the 1990s as collectors streamline their holdings and turn these antiques into ready cash.

The new "darlings" of the late 1980s and early 1990s are the Art Nouveau and Art Deco designs of Clarice Cliff, Susie Cooper, Turn-Teplitz, Amphora, and Moorcroft, and the highly styled studio lines of Doulton, Meissen, and Wedgwood. However, the key word is "style," and those pieces that show artistic merit are finding favor with collectors. Flow Blue, Historic Staffordshire, Quimper, and KPM porcelain plaques are holding their own, with exceptional pieces bringing exceptional prices.

Several items brought record prices at auction, indicating that the "rare" or "outstanding" is not being overlooked by the serious collector. These items rarely come across the block, and when they do, they are actively bid to the upper levels.

The Brunner Collection of Gaudy Dutch and spatterware sold by Wolf's in Cleveland, Ohio, brought some outstanding prices. A Gaudy Dutch "Butterfly" coffee pot sold for $10,000, and the same price was recorded for a "Butterfly" wash bowl. A rare set of six fish design spatterware cups and saucers soared to $36,000. A Minton "cat and mouse" majolica teapot sold at Skinner's rooms in Boston for $13,000, and an unusual Paris pitcher featuring Grant and Farragut portraits—thought to be available for $1000—went for an astounding $23,000.

Single subject auctions continue to draw collectors. The Arman auctions of the Ritt Quimper collection drew international attention and strong prices. Much the same can be said for the Historic Staffordshire, majolica, and Flow Blue auctions where unusual shapes and styles continue to sell well.

Collectors with available funds can be successful in today's market. As large holdings reach the auction houses or dealers' shelves, the collector has the opportunity to add to his holdings or start new ones at very competitive prices. Happy hunting!

Part Two: Pottery and Porcelain Listings

Abbreviations Used in the Listings

C	century
circ	circular
d	diameter
dbl	double
dtd	dated
emb	embossed
ftd	footed
ground	background
h	height
H-H	handle to handle
hex	hexagonal
horiz	horizontal
irid	iridescent
irreg	irregular
l	length
med	medium
mtd	mounted
mts	mounts
#	numbered
no.	pattern number
oct	octagonal
pr	pair
prs	pairs
rect	rectangular
sgd	signed
SP	silver plated
sq	square
vert	vertical
w	width

ABC AND MAXIM WARE

Staffordshire, England and Continental
19th Century

History: Nineteenth century English ABC plates from Staffordshire are not considered great works of art, but are quite collectible. They were made by many potteries, most of whom did not mark the plates with a factory mark.

ABC plates were designed to teach a child letters and numbers. In addition, knowledge of important people, places, or things also was transmitted via these plates at mealtimes.

ABC plates were made in forty-four different sizes, ranging from 4″ to the large size of approximately 9″. Usually the alphabet was on the rim of the plate, either applied (transferred) or embossed (raised). The center of the plate usually had a scene of a person, animal, or some type of design transferred onto it.

When the picture was transferred to the plate and fired, the basic color was added as well. When additional colors were used, the plate had to be fired one or more additional times depending on the number of colors.

ABC plates also were made in braille for the blind child. These are quite rare today.

Benjamin Franklin's *Poor Richard's Almanac* was the source for many of the maxims and moral lessons used on maxim ware. Biblical passages and nursery rhymes also were used on these plates to present a message to the child.

Plates are most frequently encountered. But teapots, cups, bowls, and porringers also carried lessons for the young. Most of the maxims were illustrated with transfer printed pictures that helped make the lesson more palatable. Some were hand painted, but most were multicolored transfers. The same maxim or rhyme frequently was illustrated by various manufacturers, each using a slightly different drawing.

Reference: Mildred & Joseph P. Chalala, *A Collector's Guide to ABC Plates, Mugs & Things*, Pridemark Press, 1980.

Collecting Hints: Interest in ABC plates has increased dramatically in the past five to ten years. Make certain the transfers are in good to very good condition. Avoid pieces that are cracked or crazed.

Baby Dish, 7¾″ d, Mickey Mouse in center, red pants, yellow shoes, playing guitar, printed black alphabet border, "Made in Bavaria" mark	140.00
Bowl, 8½″ d, multicolored transfer of little girl having doctor taking pulse, gold alphabet, scalloped edge	70.00
Mug	
2⅜″ h, "G" for goose, "H" for horse, black transfer with red and green accents, 19th C (A)	175.00
Franklin's Maxims	
Boys chopping tree, maxim, unmarked	225.00
Woman at spinning wheel, maxim, unmarked	225.00
2½″ h	
"None are wise or safe but they who are honest," blue transfer, c1840	137.00
Pink transfer of "K" and "L" with blue and yellow, c1840	150.00
Purple transfer of "C" and "D" with orange, yellow, and blue, c1840s	285.00
Red transfer of "N" and "n" with nest of eggs, c1840	165.00
2⅝″ h	
Black transfer of two Franklin Maxims, "Keep thy shop . . ." (A)	121.00
"P" man with flag and approaching train and "is the careful policeman, who stands, to guard us from danger, with flag in his hand," black transfer, iron-red int rim, age cracks, rim chip	95.00
2¾″ h, "P" and "p" with pigeon and "H" and "h" and horse, red transfer	145.00
3″ h	
"C" for cat, "D" for dog, mulberry transfer	58.00
Printed alphabet, three scenes of children at play, iron-red transfer	125.00
Red transfer of two Franklin Maxims, "Plough deep . . ." (A)	132.00
Transfer of Nightingale scene, printed alphabet	110.00
Plate	
4½″ d, multicolored scene of farmer, cow, and sheep, raised alphabet border, imp "J.& G. Meakin" mark	150.00
4¾″ d, oct shape, "Three Removes Are As Bad As A Fire" and "A Rolling Stone Gath-	

Left, dish, 7½″ d, "Ride a Cock Horse to Banbury Cross," dk blue transfer, "Swinnertons Hanley, Made in England" mark, $65.00; center, plate, 7″ d, brown transfer, c1840, unmkd, $195.00; right, plate, 7″ d, "Marine Railway Station, Manhattan Beach Hotel," brown transfer, unmkd, $165.00

ers No Moss, Franklin's Proverbs," blue
transfer, purple luster border **110.00**
5" d, raised alphabet border
"Exhibition Prized Fowl-White Cockingham
. . . ', blue, yellow, green, and red...... **115.00**
Goat herder leaning on fence, with goat,
dog, and horse, black transfer with polychromes **150.00**
Franklin's Proverbs, colored transfer of two
children at play, mother in kitchen, "Silks
and satins scarlets and velvets put out the
kitchen fire," imp "J.& G. Meakin" mark **190.00**
"Harvest Home" in red, blue, green, and
yellow transfer...................... **50.00**
Mother with child in cradle and angels,
"Hush My Dear Lie Still & Slumber-Holy
Angels Guard Thy Bed. Heavenly Bless-
ings Without Number Gently Falling On
Thy Head" **125.00**
Puzzle, black figures on front with "What
fruit does our sketch represent?" answer
on reverse......................... **225.00**
"The Graces" in black transfer, burgundy
rim, imp "Godwin" mark **175.00**
"The Late Sir Robert Peel Bart," bust of Bart,
pink transfer....................... **125.00**
5⅛" d, raised alphabet border
Boy sailing boat in pond, mother and farmhouse in ground, black transfer with polychromes **135.00**
Franklin's Maxim, "Poor Richard's Maxim's-
He that by the plough," black transfer.. **125.00**
General McClellan, black transfer, hairline. **155.00**
5³⁄₁₆" d, woman on spotted horse with fruit
basket on head, horse led by man, black
transfer with polychromes, raised alphabet
border **95.00**
5¼" d, raised alphabet border
Sheep and cow, black transfer with polychromes, "Everybody Bids . . . " around
scene, red line rim **85.00**
Two soldiers, one with trumpet, another at
attention, "Quartermaster and Trum-
peteer" **165.00**
5¼" d, Franklin's Maxim, blue transfer of Masonic compass and motto "Keep within the
Compass/And you shall be sure to avoid
many troubles which others endure," emb
floral rim accented with pink luster, red,
blue, yellow, and green enamels (A)..... **110.00**
5⅜" d, "Constant Dropping Wears Away
Stones" and "Little Strokes Fall Great
Oaks," multicolored transfer, raised floral
border **145.00**
5⁷⁄₁₆" d, "That girl wants the pup away," two
boys, girl, dogs and puppy, black transfer,
blue, green, and red accents, raised alphabet border.......................... **145.00**
5½" d
"Gathering Cotton," multicolored scene of
black men, women, and children picking
cotton, raised alphabet border......... **195.00**
"Old Mother Hubbard," brown transfer of
Mother Hubbard and dog at cupboard,
polychrome accents, printed alphabet
border **145.00**
5¾" d, "The Blind Girl" in colored transfer,
raised alphabet border................ **180.00**
6" d, raised alphabet border
Boys playing banjo, blue transfer........ **45.00**

Newsboy peddling papers in red, yellow,
brown, and green, imp "Edge Malkin &
Co." mark.......................... **125.00**
Riddle plate, three black men and "Why are
these boys wrong in their arithmetic," answer on reverse, multicolored transfer.. **225.00**
"The Blind Child," blue, red, green, brown,
and yellow transfer, Staffordshire, unmarked **110.00**
Two black elephants and tiger in jungle, imp
"Meakin" mark **65.00**
6" d
Boy and girl Kewpies in center, gold alphabet
border, sgd "Rose O'Neill Germany"..... **210.00**
Three cats, one in bowl, black transfer, blue
rim **165.00**
Three deaf children in burgundy transfer,
wreath of hand signals for deaf, "H. Aynsley & Co., England" mark **210.00**
Two cats in cherry tree, black transfer, dbl
blue rim **165.00**
Two kittens skipping rope in green transfer,
wreath of hand signals for deaf, "H. Aynsley & Co., England" mark **195.00**
6⅛" d, raised alphabet border
"The Guardian," black and white transfer,
imp "Elsmore and Forster" mark....... **150.00**
Zebra, black transfer with polychrome
enamels, stains, "Powell and Bishop"
mark (A) **94.00**
6⅛" d, "Rebus," three black persons in boat
fishing, "Why is this geometrical fishing" . **165.00**
6³⁄₁₆" d
"Crusoe Making a Boat," printed alphabet
border, pink transfer................. **110.00**
"The First Nibble," multicolored scene of
boy and two girls fishing, raised alphabet
border **135.00**
6¼" d, "Administration Building-World's
Columbian Exposition," blue transfer, raised
alphabet border...................... **225.00**
6⅜" d
Nursery Rhyme, Miss Muffet, printed alphabet, blue transfer, unmarked........... **75.00**
"See-saw Margery daw . . . ," green transfer,
raised alphabet border................ **75.00**
6½" d, raised alphabet border
"American Sports, The Baseball Pitcher,"
black transfer....................... **225.00**
Three children playing leap frog, black transfer with polychrome accents **145.00**
6½" d, center scene of sailing ship and "The
Staffordshire Potteries/And Free Trade.
With All the World," brown transfer with
blue, yellow, and green enamel highlights,
brown printed alphabet border (A)....... **170.00**
6⁹⁄₁₆" d, two men working at hearth, green
transfer, raised alphabet border on stippled
ground............................. **175.00**
6¹¹⁄₁₆" d, raised alphabet border
"A Sioux Indian Chief," brown transfer ... **95.00**
"The Candle Fish," two Indians fishing in
canoe, brown transfer **165.00**
6¾" d, seated bulldog with "My face is my
fortune," brown transfer, raised alphabet
border **125.00**
6⅞" d, raised alphabet border
Boy and girl on brick wall, pink transfer,
"Staffordshire, England" mark **95.00**
Fox hunt scene, brown transfer, unmarked **150.00**

6¹⁵/₁₆" d, raised alphabet border
"The Drive," polychrome accents........ 125.00
"The Village Blacksmith" in colors 175.00
7" d
Cobalt transfer of mother and father drinking, child playing on floor, pawn ticket shelf, "The Jug and Glass Were Filled Again-and Now We Have No Money," raised and cobalt alphabet borders..... 145.00
Dr. Franklin's Maxim, green transfer, "Want of Care Does Us More Damage than Want of Knowledge," raised animal border, green rim 150.00
7" d, raised alphabet border
"Boys Playing Cricket," dark red transfer.. 55.00
Seal hunters, red, blue, yellow, and brown transfer, Elsmore 135.00
"The Baker," worker placing loaves in oven............................. 135.00
"The New Pony," black transfer with polychromes, blue-green rim............. 100.00
"The Pretty Child On Tiptoes Stands To Reach The Piano With Her Hands," transfer of little girl at piano in blue, black, green, and red, unmarked............ 125.00
Young man carrying basket, resting against fence, church in ground, colored transfer, imp "Edge Malkin & Co." mark........ 110.00
7¹/₁₆" d, raised alphabet border
Blue, brown, red, green, and black transfer of mother sitting with daughter on knee and "Mother & Daughter Dear to Each With a Love Surpassing Speech," imp "Ellsmore & Forster" mark 195.00
"Hamoc-Hammock," three girls sitting on hammock, black transfer with polychromes, rim chip................... 100.00
7¹/₈" d
"Make Hay While the Sun Shines," Franklin's Proverbs, black and white transfer, raised floral and leaf border........... 185.00
Raised alphabet border
"Incidents of the War," 'Arrival of the Post in the Army Before Sebastopol," soldiers lying about, brown transfer with polychromes, iron-red inner and outer rim, hairline................. 150.00
"Keep Thy Shop & Thy Shop Will Keep Thee," Franklin's Proverbs, black transfer with polychromes of man in store, dark red rim, imp "J.& G. Meakin" mark....................... 150.00
"Kingfisher," brown transfer with polychromes, "E. M.& Co." mark........ 100.00
"The eye of the master will do more work than both his hands," green transfer . 95.00
"The Necklace," black transfer with green accents, inner and outer blue line rims 185.00
"The Young Sergent," polychromed.... 165.00
7³/₁₆" d, "Nations of the World-Wallachian," brown transfer, blue accents, printed alphabet 165.00
Raised alphabet border
Multicolored transfer of children drawing caricature of seated soldier, unmarked 145.00
"Silks and Satins Scarlet & Velvets Put Out the Kitchen Fire," Franklin's Proverbs, kitchen setting, black transfer with

polychromes, imp "J.& G. Meakin" mark........................... 150.00
7¹/₄" d
Printed alphabet border
Black transfer of horse with horseshoes, "W. Adams & Co., Tunstall, Eng." mark........................... 135.00
"Crusoe at Work," brown, orange, and blue 95.00
Raised alphabet border
"Niagara, From the Edge of the American Fall" 125.00
"Plough deep while sluggards sleep," brown transfer, green line rim....... 150.00
Punch and Judy, pink transfer, unmarked 185.00
"Shuttlecock," black transfer with polychromes, dark red rim, imp "J.& G. Meakin" mark 150.00
7⁵/₁₆" d
"A Fishing Elephant," blue transfer, raised alphabet border..................... 95.00
Bird and flowers, blue transfer with polychromes, raised and printed alphabet border 145.00
Boy with guitar eating lunch on fence, purple transfer, raised alphabet border 125.00
7³/₈" d
"Crusoe Viewing the Island," brown transfer with printed alphabet, "B.P.& Co." mark........................... 175.00
Dutch canal scene with windmill, printed and raised alphabet border, green transfer................................. 135.00
"Famous Places," scene of "Capital at Washington" in sq, "Washington's Tomb" in circle, printed alphabet and flowers in red, green, and brown, "B.P.& Co. and Eng Reg" marks............. 125.00
"Old Mother Hubbard," Nursery Rhymes, blue transfer, printed alphabet border .. 145.00
Raised alphabet border
"A Timely Rescue," man with ax and tiger rescuing lady, blue-gray transfer 135.00
Multicolored transfer of boys playing baseball, unmarked................. 42.00
7⁷/₁₆" d, raised alphabet border
"Doe's Thou Love Life?" brown transfer, green line rim...................... 185.00
Franklin's maxim, "Lost time is never found again," black transfer 175.00
7¹/₂" d
"Nations of the World-Greek," brown transfer, printed alphabet, "Tunstall, England" mark 145.00
Victorian girl in bathing suit, four Teddy bears, multicolored, dbl ABC border ... 205.00
7¹/₂" d, raised alphabet border
Blue transfer of man and boy on donkey, "C.A.& Sons, England" mark 125.00
Brown and white transfer of horse race, unmarked 225.00
"Evening Bathing Scene at Manhattan Beach," polychrome transfer 85.00
Man and dog sliding down hill, two lovers walking on beach, brown transfer with polychromes, "C.A.& Sons England" mark........................... 135.00
"Niagara From the Edge of the American Fall," polychrome transfer............ 85.00

Two men carrying dead deer, brown transfer.................................... **145.00**

7⅝″ d, clock face with Roman numerals, months and days around border, printed alphabet border, pink transfer **100.00**

7¾″ d, "F is for Frank who a sailor would be-so in a new hat and jacket he starts for the sea"................................ **125.00**

8″ d

"Brighton Beach Bathing Pavilion," red, brown, green, and blue, raised alphabet border............................ **95.00**

"Cottage Girl," little girl with basket, brown transfer with polychromes, pink rim **145.00**

"Evening Bathing at Manhattan Beach," brown, red, blue, and green, raised alphabet border **95.00**

"The Stable Yard," horse, pony and barn, raised alphabet border................ **135.00**

Transfer of three black men raising glasses, banner with "Rule of Three," alphabet border.............................. **195.00**

8¼″ d, raised alphabet border, brown and white transfer of man painting landscape scene, unmarked...................... **185.00**

8¼″ d

"Crusoe and his pets," brown transfer with yellow, blue, and green, printed alphabet border............................. **70.00**

"Crusoe on the raft," blue, red, brown, and orange, printed alphabet border **139.00**

Red, brown, green and blue transfer of bird on left, alphabet on right.............. **85.00**

8⁵⁄₁₆″ d, tumbled cart with scattered children and animals, brown transfer, red and green accents, raised alphabet border.......... **145.00**

8⅜″ d, raised alphabet border, brown and white transfer of people in yellow boat, imp "Edge Malkin & Co." mark.............. **175.00**

8½″ d, black transfer, maxim, "They Took It Away to the end of the Field," raised wreath border **145.00**

1826 - 20TH CENTURY   1804 - 1840

ADAMS

Burslem, Staffordshire, England
1770 to Present

The Adams family established themselves in Burslem. The first potter was William Adams, but this name was used repeatedly throughout the Adams' history. Eventually there were Adams potteries in seven different locations. Most of the potteries, if they marked their works, simply used the name "Adams."

WILLIAM ADAMS

Brick House, Burslem and Cobridge, 1770–c1820

He produced blue-printed wares with chinoiserie patterns early in the 1780s. They were probably not marked. Two of his potteries were lent to other potters among whom were James and Ralph Clews in 1817.

WILLIAM ADAMS

Greengates, Tunstall, c1779–1805 (1809)

Blue-printed wares were made. They were the first pottery in Tunstall to do so. William died in 1805, but the works were continued by trustees. Benjamin, his son, took over in 1809.

WILLIAM ADAMS

Stoke-on-Trent, 1804–1819

Large quantities of blue and white transfer wares were made both for the home market and for export to America. In 1810, William, his son, joined the partnership and three other sons joined soon after. The company was then called "William Adams & Sons."

BENJAMIN ADAMS

Greengates, Tunstall, 1809–1820

Benjamin used the impressed mark "B. Adams." He continued making blue-printed wares.

WILLIAM ADAMS & SONS

Stoke-on-Trent, 1819 to Present

William Adams died in 1829; and William, his eldest son, took over. In 1834, the Greenfield pottery was added to the firm. The Stoke factory was closed in 1863. The Greengates pottery was added to the group in 1858.

William Adams joined the Wedgwood Group in 1966.

ADAM'S ROSE

1820s–1830s

This pattern was named for its maker William Adams & Sons of Stoke-on-Trent. It consists of a border of large red roses with green leaf sprigs on a white ground.

G. Jones & Son, England, produced a variation known as "Late Adam's Rose." The colors are not as brilliant. The background is a "dirty" white.

References: A.W. Coysh, *Blue-Printed Earthenware 1800–1850*. David & Charles, 1972.

Bowl

5½″ d, Titianware, hp green rings, brown lines, blue leaf band, onion center, ivory ground............................... **5.00**

Coffee Pot, 11½" h, pastoral scene, red transfer, imp "Adams" mark, (A) $50.00

8½" d, American Forest Scene series, "Maple Sugaring" 45.00
10" d, "Cries of London-Strawberry's Scarlet Strawberries" design................... 68.00
10" H-H, molded hex shape, "Chinese Bird" pattern, blue transfer, blue twisted handles, c1875 .... 225.00
11" d, Currier & Ives series, Yosemite Valley, Calif-'The Bridal Veil Falls" 55.00
Bowl, Ironstone
11¼" l, 3¼" h, "Cattle Scenery," blue and white, pedestal, silver luster ruffle edge, "Adams" mark...................... 250.00
Blue oriental transfer, "Adams" mark (A).... 71.00
Bread and Milk Set, "Bamboo" pattern, red transfers, "W. Adams & Sons" mark........ 95.00
Cheese Dish, Cov, 4½" h, 7" l, "Chinese Bird" pattern, blue transfer, blue handle, sq base, c1875.................................. 225.00
Creamer, 5¾" l, scene of man and two women near farmhouse on sides, blue transfer, imp "Warrented Ironstone Adams" mark 325.00
Cup and Saucer
Calyxware, rose center, mustard rim and border, twisted rope in black border, pale green ground, repaired 15.00
"Sharon" pattern in brown transfer......... 10.00
Mug, Oliver Twist design, "Oliver's Reception" 70.00
Plate
6⅝" d, emb floral rim, blue feather edge, imp "Adams" mark (A) 65.00

6⅞" d, Adam's Rose, two purple luster bands on border...................... 55.00
7½" d
Adam's single rose, rust and green florals, raised basketweave border, two purple luster bands on border 115.00
St. Petersburg, Florida, flow blue transfer . 40.00
7¾" d, fisherman by stream, dark blue transfer, imp "Adams" mark (A).............. 150.00
8" d
Dark blue "Wild Rose" pattern, "Wm Adams & Co." mark.................. 45.00
"Italian Scenery" design in green, red, and yellow, cream relief border............ 38.00
9" d
Adam's Rose design in red, green, and black 65.00
English scene of two fishermen on shore, boat on river, castle in ground, dark blue transfer, imp "Adams" mark (A) 72.00
9¼" d, center with girl in blue and red dress on green ground with bushes, relief border of yellow flowerheads, small red and blue flowers with green and brown leaves.............................. 210.00
9½" d
Adam's Rose design in red, green, and black, imp "Adams" mark (A) 105.00
Oct, "Cries of London, Match Seller" in colors 28.00
10" d, "SS Grand View Hotel—A Steamboat in the Allegheny Mountains," cobalt transfer.................................... 40.00
10½" d
Adam's Rose design in red, green, and black 150.00
"Etruscan" pattern, two maidens with horses and chariots on black ground, gold rim, c1900 (A)..................... 5.00
Platter
11½" l, Titianware, hp green rings, brown lines, blue leaf band, onion center, ivory ground............................... 18.00
12¾" l, open red rose in center, open roses with black leaves on border, black line rim 135.00
16" l, "Regent" pattern................... 85.00
Soup Plate, 10¼" d, Adam's Rose design.... 165.00
Teacup and Saucer, "Beehive" pattern, blue and white, c1810–25, William Adams, pr 150.00

Plates, left to right: 9" d, Adam's Rose pattern, green and maroon flowers, imp "Adams" mark, $125.00; 10" d, Oliver Twist series, "Oliver Amazing at Dodger's Mode of Going to Work," gray center, orange and brown bands on border, (A) $25.00; 10½" d, Cupid center, floral and bow knot border, med blue transfer, c1840, $100.00

Teapot, 10¾" l, wide open florals, med blue
transfer, floral knob, early 1800s **425.00**
Toddy Plate, 6" d, English scene with single
masted sailboat, floral border, dark blue trans-
fer, imp "Adams" mark (A) **72.00**

AFTER 1892

AFTER 1892

AMPHORA

Turn-Teplitz, Bohemia
1892 to Present

History: Riessner and Kessel started the Amphora Porzellan Fabrik in 1892 for the manufacture of earthenware and
porcelain. This pottery was established at Turn-Teplitz, Bohemia (now Czechoslovakia). It produced mostly porcelain figures and Art Nouveau styled vases were widely
exported. Many of the wares were hand decorated. They
marked their wares with a variety of stamps, some incorporating the name and location of the pottery with a shield
or a crown. Before WWI, Bohemia was part of the Austro-
Hungarian empire so that the name "Austria" may have
been used as part of the mark. After WWII, the name
"Czechoslovakia" may be part of the mark.

The Amphora Pottery Works was only one of a number
of firms that were located in Teplitz, an active pottery
center at the turn of the century.

Museum: Antiken Museum, Basel, Switzerland.

Basket
6⅛" h, tan village scene on cobalt ground on
front, tan stars, sides with jewels and green
and blue stars on light blue ground, cobalt
overhead handle, yellow int **275.00**
8" h, 4" w, band of flowers in light red, white,

**Bud Vase, 6½" h, Art Nouveau bust on front,
florals on reverse in gold, matte finish, "blue
Amphora Turn" and "red R. St. K, Turn Teplitz"
mark, (A) $154.00**

Vase, 8½" h, hp colored jewels and swirls, gold
accents, white pearlized finish, c1900, imp "Amphora" mark, $2750.00

Vase, 9¼" h, caramel color, dripping candle
design, c1900, "Amphora, Turn-Teplitz" mark,
$6500.00

and light blue, stylized green leaves, relief of
abstract earth in green enamel below, tan
and light brown matte stippled ground, red,
blue, and green dots on foot, cobalt rim and
foot, int with luster finish, "Amphora Made
in Czechoslovakia" mark **135.00**
Ewer
10½" h, stylized owl in tree branch, turquoise lip and handle, "Amphora, Czecho-
slovakia" mark **225.00**
13" h, matte gold sponged ground, matte
mauve molded water lily handle and top . **1500.00**
14" h, Art Nouveau style green and gold irid
leaves on cream ground, flower form neck,
dbl handle **495.00**
Figure
17½" h, peasant woman carrying baskets,
soft tans and brown shades, "Amphora
Austria" mark **575.00**
21" h, young woman in wispy garments,
standing on shell, shawl on shoulders, soft
colors (A) **2700.00**
Humidor, 9" h, hp owls in colors **175.00**
Jar, 7" h, ovoid with four loop handles, raised

enamel iris on beige ground, imp "Amphora, Austria" mark (A)........................ **200.00**

Pitcher

5 1/2" h, bulbous shape, incised and over-glazed flowers and leaves in red, yellow, blue, and green, matte green and white mottled glazed ground, "Amphora Made in Czechoslovakia" mark (A).............. **30.00**

6 1/4" h, four brown figural chicks on base, pink and green jewels, matte ground, figural rooster head spout in tan, green, and dark green enamels **150.00**

Planter, 12 1/2" l, 11" h, figure of boy in short pants and coral cap, basket on ground **595.00**

Plate, 9 1/2" d, two horses pulling man in sleigh in enamels, brown dogs chasing, white enameled snow, tan matte sky, border of blue stars with pink centers and green diamonds **145.00**

Vase

3 1/2" h, 8" w, center band of flowers in cobalt, light red, light blue with light green leaves, reverse with large brown butterfly with light yellow wings and blue dots, upper and lower purple bands, shiny cobalt foot, rim, and handles, lustered int glaze, "Amphora Made in Czechoslovakia" mark.... **110.00**

4" h, green with colored circ patterning, "Amphora Austria" mark (A) **55.00**

4 1/2" h, Art Nouveau type woman's head, raised gold and enameled flowers **375.00**

5" h, blown out design with raised gold jewels.................................... **125.00**

5 1/2" h

Campana shape, enameled hummingbird in pale orange, blue and white head, blue back with brown wings, light brown and tan pebble ground, cobalt bands top and base, shoulder band of blue, red, white, and light orange stylized flowers with green leaves, band of blue oblique shapes at neck, "Amphora Made in Czechoslovakia" mark............... **135.00**

Enameled stork-type bird in green, black, and orange enamels, tan mottled ground, black bands at top and base, two small handles **135.00**

Gold and bronze Art Nouveau bust of woman with flowers, flowing hair, forest ground, blue "AMPHORA TURN" mark **600.00**

6" d, squat shape, pink flower pattern, imp "Amphora, Austria" mark (A)............ **250.00**

6 1/2" h, cobalt bands top and base, multicolored raised parrot in blue dot and flower border, beige mottled satin ground, two small handles on rim, sgd "Campina," imp "Austria and Amphora" marks.......... **175.00**

7" h

Art Deco style bird and flowers in high gloss on matte ground, "Amphora, Czechoslovakia" mark **85.00**

Brown incised designs on light tan ground, eight circ jewels in blue, red and green in band on neck, four large oval jewels below, enameled red and green ovals, cobalt foot and neck, "Amphora Made in Czechoslovakia" mark............... **85.00**

Multicolored enameled parrots on branch, enameled circles, matte brown ground, imp "crown Amphora Austria" mark (A) **90.00**

Ovoid with everted rim, painted profile of young woman, "Turn Teplitz, Amphora" mark (A) **750.00**

Urn shape, mottled brown-gold with green leaves, dbl handles **95.00**

8 1/2" h, bulbous, raised design on top and lines to base, cobalt ground with mottled crystalline splotches **225.00**

9" h, irid gold and yellow floral encrusted vines, blue-green Tiffany ground **245.00**

9 1/8" h, 6 1/2" d, floral band in center in rose, blue, white, tan, and green emb enamels, cobalt top border, soft gray satin ground with shadow flowers, "Amphora Czechoslovakia" mark....................... **175.00**

10" d

Blue-green floral basket hanging from purple floral chain, green and gold salamander handles, imp "Amphora, Austria, red St. K/Bohemia" mark................ **350.00**

Rose, green, and blue jeweled matte shell design **85.00**

10" h, hp vase with flowers, open dbl handles.............................. **150.00**

10 1/4" h

Brick red irises, green leaves outlined in gold, turquoise beading, cream to beige ground, serpent handles, fluted rim **195.00**

Red, green, and blue oval stones on gray textured ground, green and red jeweled rim **275.00**

10 1/2" h, blue-green floral baskets hanging from floral chains, green-gold ground, modeled salamander handles, c1890–1900, red "St. & K." and incised "Amphora, Austria" marks **350.00**

10 3/4" h, emb pink flowers and green leaves, light green ground, dark green trim, tan and green dbl handles, "Made in Czechoslovakia Amphora" mark **175.00**

11" h

10 3/4" w, modeled dog standing on ground next to vase, bronze finish, imperial mark **695.00**

Art Nouveau bronze finish, applied handles................................. **575.00**

Lustrous pearlized beads on body, gold trim, two heavy gold dragon handles, crown mark **295.00**

11 1/2" h, enameled geometric design...... **275.00**

12" h

Enameled stylized flowers, two handles... **355.00**

Modeled as woman holding seeds in apron, leaning on tree trunk, or man holding firewood and lantern, pastel colors, dtd 1903, pr **695.00**

Multicolored peacock, cobalt ground..... **195.00**

12 3/16" h, figural baluster shape, molded with three parrots in full feather with crests curling over short cylindrical neck, glazed in muted shades of tan, ecru, and green, c1900, imp "AMPHORA/AUSTRIA/ 11986/46" and company marks, pr (A).... **1375.00**

14" h, swelled cylinder shape, multicolored enameled potted tree with geometric flowers and grapes.................... **285.00**

16" h, hp florals on heavy gold panel, cream ground, turned down pierced flared lip fuses to handle on shoulder............ **475.00**

17" h, figural basket with applied figures of

three putti climbing floral vines in colors, c1900 (A) 550.00

17½" h, baluster shape, blue-green with applied foliage (A) 150.00

29" h, baluster shape, blue-green ground with relief of spider webs on top, enameled and jeweled moths on lower section, mtd on four bronze lion's paw feet, restored, "Amphora 02049 D" mark 4500.00

Wall Pocket, 9" h, blue band with flowers on basketweave ground 110.00

ANGELICA KAUFFMANN

Switzerland
1741–1807

History: Marie Angelique Catherine Kauffmann (1741–1807), a Swiss artist, worked primarily in a neo-classical style. Many artists copied her original paintings and used them on hand decorated porcelains during the 19th century.

Bowl

9¼" d, center transfer of classical maidens in colors, hairline, sgd "Angelica Kauffmann," Austria 65.00

9½" d, 4 classic maidens in colors, sgd "A. Kauffmann" 65.00

Cabinet Plate, 9⅝" d, center painted with Cupid reaching for bow and arrow held by draped woman, pierced gilded blue ground border, c1880, "blue X'd swords and script Cupid u. Elphrosine, Angelica Kauffmann" mark (A). 2000.00

Charger, 13½" d, scene of ladies and cherub, eggshell shaded to tan ground, green border with gilt, Austria 75.00

Chocolate Pot, 9½" h, center scene of classical maidens in garden setting, tan and white with gold trim, Silesia Germany 150.00

Cup and Saucer, multicolored mythological scene in center, lime green ground, ornate gold handle, raised center on saucer, sgd "Kauffmann, Victoria Austria" mark 25.00

Demitasse Cup and Saucer, multicolored classical scene on front, chartreuse panel and gold flowers on back of cup and saucer, gilt trim, 1891–1918, sgd "Kauffmann, Victoria, Austria Carlsbad" 110.00

Ewer, 9½" h, classical center scene, aqua ground with gold tracery, gold handle, "Victoria Carlsbad Austria" mark 90.00

Milk Pitcher, multicolored classical scene of Cupid and figures, pink luster trim 75.00

Plate

9" d, multicolored classical scene, cobalt border 45.00

9½" d, multicolored transfer of classical scene in center on blue ground, green and gold border, sgd "A. Kauffmann," Royal Vienna 135.00

10" d, classical center scene in colors, green scalloped border with gold tracery, "Victoria Austria" mark 85.00

10½" d, "The Young Achille," center scene of warrior with helmet, woman holding baby, maiden, mountainous ground, wide burnished gold inner border, magenta border with gold designs, raised white dots and green dashes, sgd "Angelica Kauffmann" on front, blue beehive mark 85.00

13" d

Center scene of three classic ladies dancing, seated boy with lyre, green and gold border, sgd "Kauffmann," Germany 125.00

Three maidens and cherubs in center, six hp floral panels, gold trim, "Kauffmann, Bavaria" mark (A) 50.00

Tea Set, pot, 10" h, cov sugar bowl, creamer, classic scenes in gold curved medallions, med blue ground, scattered gold sprigs, gold and pink handles, "Kauffmann" on teapot, "Victoria Carlsbad, Austria" marks 365.00

Tray, 17" d, multicolored transfer of classical scene, "Angelica Kauffmann, Austria" mark . 99.00

Vase

10½" h, classical scene in colors on front, blue and pearlized ground 95.00

12" h, urn shape, classical scenes in colors, sgd "Kauffmann" 275.00

Water Pitcher, 10¼" h, 8" d, A. Kauffmann scene of nymphs and florals, gold floral trim, bulbous shape, pr 350.00

Plate, 9½" H-H, multicolored center scene, green inner border, cream rim and handles, gold trim, sgd "Kauffmann" on front, "Victoria, Carlsbad, Austria" mark, (A) $50.00

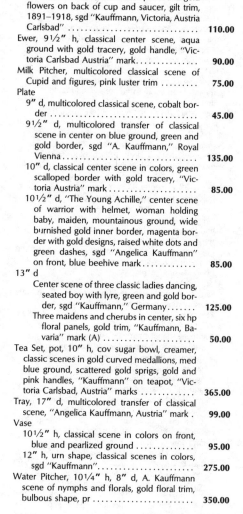

AUSTRIA

16th Century to Present

History: Salzburg was the center of peasant pottery or pottery stove making during the 16th and 17th centuries. These wares were similar to those being made in Germany at the same time. Sometimes they were colored with tin enamels. Factories in Wels, Enns, and Steyr also made this type of pottery ware.

Peasant pottery, known as "Habaner ware" or Hafner ware, was decorated in an unsophisticated style with flowers, animals, and figures. These faience wares were made in Salzberg and Wels during the late 17th century. Most was used locally.

The only porcelain being produced in the early eighteenth century was made by a Vienna factory founded by Claudius I Du Paquier in 1718 with assistance from Meissen workers. This was the second factory in Europe to make hard paste porcelain. The factory was sold to the Austrian State in 1744.

Many of the later Austrian porcelain factories such as Schlaggenwald, Klosterle, Prague, Dallwitz, Pirkenhammer, and Elbogen are classified with Bohemia porcelain because of their location.

A number of porcelain factories originated in the nineteenth and twentieth centuries to make utilitarian and decorative porcelains. These included Brux, Frauenthal, Turn, Augarten, Wienerberger, Spitz, and Neumann.

In 1897 the Vienna Secession Movement provided a stimulus to Austrian ceramics. A group of young painters, sculptors, and architects desired to overthrow conservatism in the arts and design and revolutionize taste. Moser and Peche were designers of tableware and decorative porcelains associated with this movement.

In 1903 Moser and Peche founded the Wiener Werkstatte, an association of artisans, along with porcelain maker Joseph Bock. They made innovative designs in both shape and pattern.

Michael Powolny and Berthold Loffler founded the Wiener Keramik Studio in 1905 which produced advanced tablewares and figure designs in earthenware and porcelains. Products include black and white majolica, generally decorated with Cubist inspired geometrical patterns from designs by J. Hoffmann, D. Peche, and Powolny. Figures were modeled by Loffler and Powolny. Art Nouveau and Art Deco designs were utilized. The products of the Wiener Keramik Studio became the foundation for the international Modern Movement that developed after World War I.

References: George Ware, *German & Austrian Porcelain.* Lothar Woeller Press, 1951.

Museums: Osterreiches Museum fur Angewandtekunst, Vienna, Austria; Vienna Kunsthistoriches Museum, Vienna, Austria.

Bone Dish, white, scalloped edge, "M.Z. Austria" mark, set of 7 . . . . **75.00**
Bowl
  7" d, hp pine cones and needles on int and rim, shaded chocolate brown to cream ground, sq gold handles, gold rim. "M.Z. Austria" mark **28.00**
  7½" d, emb figures of deer, birds, and running boys, mottled blue glossy glaze **30.00**
  10" d, 2½" h
    Blue and gold Art Nouveau stylized design, "M.Z. Austria" mark **35.00**
    Square
      Pink, green, rust, and blue scene of maidens with strings of flowers, green, ivory, and maroon ground, fluted rim **95.00**
      Scene of couple dancing next to table, pink sides, white ground, "Victoria, Austria" mark **35.00**
  10½" d, red, pink, and white roses in seven

Pitcher, 12" h, purple grapes with white and green flowers, lt green to brown shaded ground, gold rim, brown handle, "Vienna, Austria" mark, (A) $170.00

Vase, 13" h, molded leaf neck in beige and gold, c1900, "red Vienna, Austria" mark, $7500.00

panels, six florals molded in scalloped and fluted rim, gold border, c1891, "M.Z. Austria" mark (A) **70.00**
Box
  4" l, 3" w, 2" h, red and yellow roses on shaded gold ground, gold relief trim **18.00**
  6¼" l, 5½" h, shaped rect, black and white with yellow birds, c1905, Gemuncher Keramik, black painted mark **2200.00**
Butter Pat, small green and white rose garlands, set of 6 . . . . **15.00**
Cake Plate
  9½" d, pink roses, green border, "M.Z. Austria" mark **27.00**
  11" d, overall small pink roses and green leaves with gilt on white ground, relief scroll and molded pointed rim, "M.Z. Austria" mark (A) **20.00**
  11½" d, center portrait of Marie Louise, Hortense, Mdm Recamier, and Josephine on rim, scalloped and fluted rim, c1910, "M.Z. Austria" mark (A). **30.00**

11¾" d, hp blueberries and leaves on cream ground, gold rim, c1895, "M.Z. Austria" mark (A) **20.00**

Cake Set, cake plate, 10" H-H, 4 plates, 6½" d, pearlized rose decor on white and green ground, pointed zig-zag rims, chips, "M. Z. Austria" marks **65.00**

Candlestick, 3⅛" h, 3¼" d, pink roses, green ground, gold handle and ball feet, "Vienna, Austria" mark **65.00**

Canister Set, 5 jars, 7½" h, 5 jars, 4¼" h, English names of condiments on front, band of red roses and green leaves on top, center medallion of open pink and purple flowers, swags of green leaves and blue flowers, "Victoria, Austria" marks **325.00**

Centerpiece, 10¼" h, porcelain figural, open vessel with lengths of drapery, maiden reclining on one side, stylized blossoms and leaves, glazed in white and shaded with umber and gilt, c1900, blue underglaze marks **550.00**

Chocolate Set, pot, 10¼" h, 4 cups and saucers, yellow flowers with orange centers outined in gold, black ground, handle, and finial with gold stripes, cups, white int with border of orange and yellow flowers, gilt rims, Austria mark **150.00**

Cracker Jar, dbl handles, blue and gold Art Nouveau design on white, c1910, "M.Z. Austria" mark (A). **30.00**

Creamer, 4½" h, porcelain, figural moose.... **38.00**

Cream and Sugar
   Garlands of white roses, gold trim, "Austria" marks **35.00**
   Hex shape, small florals on light blue ground, gold trim and knob.................... **20.00**

Cup and Saucer, porcelain, tan panels with Secret and Discretion, gilt edged, white ground, blue beehive mark....................... **160.00**

Dish
   7" l, modeled animal with dish on back, pink and green **50.00**
   14¾" d, armorial, yellow, ochre, manganese, and blue with quartered armorial bearing, broad rim, shallow well, 17th C, Habaner (A)................................. **2880.00**

Ewer
   8" h, hp yellow, pink, and purple roses, gold spout and handle, "Vienna Austria" mark. **145.00**
   12" h, hp violets, matte finish **75.00**
   14½" h, floral decor, cream and melon green ground, latticework handle, crown shape spout **115.00**

Figure
   7¾" h, porcelain, female in flapper type costume, blue beehive Wien Austria mark (A) **170.00**
   13¾" h, standing woman in lilac bodice, crinoline with indian flowers, one Pug dog under arm, another on base (A) **950.00**
   15" h, porcelain, Dante modeled as standing man in red robe with book clutched at chest.................................. **275.00**
   25" h, figural vessel, ceramic, modeled as giant bulbous lotus pod, leaves continuing to form the neck, spout, and handle, sinuous female figure leaning at side of long neck wearing revealing robes, flowing flower strewn hair, glazed in metallic gold tinged with green, c1900, imp "MADE IN AUSTRIA".................................. **3575.00**

Fish Set, tray, 24" l, 12 plates, 9" d, multicolored fish in various positions, white ground **225.00**

Humidor, 7" h, porcelain, melon ribbed body, green, red, and purple grapes, pink florals, gold accents, c1900, "M.Z. Austria" mark (A)................................... **90.00**

Jardinaire
   8" l, rect, 9½" l, arc shape, white porcelain, molded ribbed body with swags, 1840–50, stamped "Neo-classical Austrian," imp beehive and crown mark, set of 4........... **1400.00**
   12½" H-H, purple, pink, and yellow flowers, raised gold dot centers, green leaves, reverse with florals, molded light green with gilt border and handles, cream ground, "EW Turn Wien, Crown, Made in Austria" mark **195.00**

Mug, 4½" h, hp red-orange poppies with green foliage, white ground, artist sgd, "Austria" mark................................. **20.00**

Pitcher
   4" h, multicolored scene of Princess Street, Kingston, Ontario, ornate gold trim, "Victoria, Austria" mark.................... **15.00**
   12" h, hp purple wisteria, green leaves, gold handle **115.00**

Plaque
   7⅜" d, multicolored castle scene, molded gold-brown border, "Austria" mark (A) ... **87.00**
   8" h, multicolored scene of young girl under floral arbor, "Victoria, Austria" mark...... **35.00**
   12" d, young girl in blue dress holding flowers, gold trim, wine red border **135.00**
   13" d, black and white portrait of dog, cream, green, and blue ground, gold rococo border, pierced for hanging **225.00**

Plate
   7¼" d, porcelain, two seated Classical figures in garden landscape, maroon border with gilt curvilinear design, Juno blue beehive mark (A) **80.00**
   7⅜" d, hp poppy and cornflower design in colors, "Victoria Austria," set of 6........ **120.00**
   8½" d, hp swimming carp in blue-green with burgundy............................. **25.00**
   9½" d
      Hp country snow scene, marked......... **18.00**
      Lavender flowers with tan leaves, scalloped rim, "Austria China, crown and circle" mark............................. **8.00**
      Large grape clusters with florals.......... **37.50**
   11¼" d, hp large clusters of green and purple grapes, sgd "Sufottner, Vienna, Austria" mark................................. **110.00**

Platter, 16½" l, large pink roses, white ground.................... **40.00**

Powder Box, 4½" l, 2¼" h, hex shape, porcelain, white, blue, yellow, and green florals, gilt trim, white ground, M.Z. Austria mark **45.00**

Salt and Pepper, 2½" h, hp roses on rust and green sprayed ground, gold beading around top **12.00**

Sardine Box, 4¾" l, pink flowers, white ribbed, white and black fish on top, gilt trim, Victoria, Austria **95.00**

Tray, 19" l, 6" w, butterfly and floral design in colors, marked.......................... **175.00**

Urn, Cov, 12" h, enamel floral design with medallions of birds on base, fluted border, gilt outlined and jeweled, sq pedestal base, dbl handles, c1900 (A) **385.00**

Vase

5¾" h, multicolored portraits busts in period clothes, brown ground, gold rim, red "AUSTRIA" marks...................... 45.00

6¼" h, bulbous shape, melon-ribbed, narrow neck, handles at waist, hp red, yellow, pink, and green flowers on cream medallion, rose-beige ground...................... 28.00

6½" h, blue florals, raised gold, satin ivory ground, reticulated top, "E.W. Turn, Vienna" mark......................... 75.00

9" h, hp red and yellow roses with green foliage, light blue ground, gold trim, scrolled foot, ribbed scalloped neck, red "RH/Made in Austria" mark 55.00

11" h

Medallion with transfer of portrait of lady, green with gold detail 85.00

Singing birds with branches in yellow, green, and gold, serrated top, dbl handles................................. 55.00

12" h

Framed portrait of Bohemian girl, lavender and blue floral design, ornate gold handles, Victoria, Austria mark 275.00

Gold outlined medallion of woman and Cupid on turquoise ground, two ornate gold handles, "Victoria, Austria" mark .. 65.00

14" h, hp scattered florals in colors 300.00

14½" h

Enamel decor of fuchsias in natural colors, cobalt and gold handles 335.00

Large hp flowers, dbl handles, "Royal Wettina, Austria" mark 175.00

19" h, oval tapered form, shaped top, applied leaf sides, hp central floral bouquet, gold decoration, c1850 (A) 275.00

20ᵀᴴ CENTURY

1898-1943

HJC
BAVARIA
c1906

Bavaria

JC
1902

BAVARIA

Bayreuth, Bavaria
c1713–1852

History: By the eighteenth century many factories were established in the Bavarian region. Bauscher at Weiden produced utility wares, some of which featured cobalt blue ornamentation. J.N. Muller at Schonwald supplied painted and unpainted utility wares. Other factories operating in Bavaria included Schuman, Thomas, and Zeh, Scherzer and Company.

J. G. Knoller founded the Bayreuth factory in Bavaria and produced faience and brown glazed wares with silver, gilt, and engraved decorations. The finest work was done from 1728 until 1745. Bayreuth brown glazed wares were a lightly fired reddish earthenware covered with a manganese brown or red glaze. Yellow glazed wares were lighter in body and were covered with a buff or pale yellow glaze. About 1745 Frankel and Schrock took over and started to make porcelain. J.G. Pfeiffer acquired the firm, later selling it in 1767.

After 1728, the pottery and porcelain pieces were marked frequently. The mark consisted of the initials of the place and the owner, along with the painter's mark.

Museum: Sevres Museum, Sevres, France.

TIRSCHENREUTH

1838 to Present

The Tirschenreuth Porcelain Factory was established in 1838 and made tablewares, utilitarian and decorative porcelains, figures, and coffee and tea sets. In 1927 the company was acquired by the Porcelain Factory Lorenz Hutschenreuther in Selb.

Additional Listing: Hutschenreuther.

Basket, 5¼" l, 3¾" w, 3⅜" h, hp roses with gold trim, luster pearl int, entwined branch handles, "Z.S.& Co. Bavaria" mark 75.00

Bowl, 10¾" H-H, white, yellow, and green florals, bluish ground, gold rim, Tirschenreuth mark, $45.00

Plate, 9" d, white and pink dress, peach flower bouquet, jewels in hair, lt and dk blue ground, molded rim with gold trim, (A) $45.00

Bottle, 6″ h, figural elephant in orange, "Bavaria" mark **95.00**

Bowl

5½″ d, scene of Prospect Point, Niagara Falls, reticulated border, gold trim, "Schwartzenburg, Bavaria" mark **30.00**

7½″ d, Dresden type flowers in center, pierced sides, scalloped rim, "Schumann, Bavaria, U.S. Zone" mark **45.00**

8″ sq, hp water lilies on shaded green ground, ornate gold handles, sgd "Renault" **50.00**

8½″ sq, multicolored parrot and cockatoo, blue reticulated border, "Schumann, Bavaria" mark **25.00**

10″ d

2½″ h, hp light green Calla Lily design, gold scalloped and reticulated border .. **95.00**

Ext hp grapes, peaches, and cherries on green leaves, black outlined scrollwork, black and gold border, white int, c1900 (A) **20.00**

White and purple grapes and vines, pearlized satin ground, gold accents and rim (A) **20.00**

10½″ d

Black rasberries and vines, gold trim, scalloped light green border (A)........... **13.00**

Blue and orchid roses, shell design on rim, "TSL Bavaria" mark................... **95.00**

Light yellow acorns and oak leaves on white ground, gold rim, single handle, artist sgd, c1912 (A) **38.00**

Red strawberries and flowers on green ground, heavy gold trim, c1900 (A) **50.00**

Cake Plate

10½″ H-H

Multicolored flowers, reticulated border, scalloped rim, "Schumann, Arsberg" mark...... **65.00**

Repeated small green, gold, and salmon floral medallions, gold trim, scrolled handles................................. **15.00**

11¼″ H-H, three large red roses in center, white ground, pale gold trim **22.00**

12¼″ l, oval shape, hp, tree with oranges, yellow int, rust feet..................... **65.00**

Candy Dish, 5″ d, tricorne shape, hp violets, rainbow irid int, gold handle and trim **20.00**

Celery Tray

12¼″ l, basket of orange and yellow fruits, green leaves, magenta ground, gold edge, marked................................ **45.00**

13″ l, light lavender flowers, cream ground . **35.00**

Cheese Dish, 9″ d, 2½″ h, hp yellow flowers, green leaves, gold trim..... .... **45.00**

Chocolate Set, pot, 6 cups and saucers, blue luster, Bavaria marks.................... **47.50**

Coffee Service, Part, pot, 6¾″ h, 5 cups and saucers, gold and lavender leaves, "Royal Heidelberg, Winterling Bavaria Germany" marks **50.00**

Compote, 5½″ h

7½″ d, hp delicate flowers, reticulated border, Schumann....................... **125.00**

8¼″ d, multicolored fruit in center, reticulated border.......................... **30.00**

Cookie Jar, 7½″ h, light and dark pink roses, green leaves, green, yellow, and white ground, gold trim **100.00**

Creamer, 4″ h, pink roses with yellow and green ground, gilt accents (A) **15.00**

Creamer and Sugar, hp, pink and green florals,

white and pink ground, irid int, matte gold handles, pr **65.00**

Cruet, 6¼″ h, violets on body and stopper, "R.A.K. Bavaria" mark.................... **300.00**

Cup and Saucer, pink roses on light blue ground, gold handle and rim, "J.& C. Bavaria" mark, set of 9..................................... **95.00**

Cup and Saucer, ftd, turquoise band with gold florals and leaves, latticework, white body .. **8.00**

Dinner Service, Part

6 dinner plates, luncheon plate, 5 soup bowls, cov vegetable bowl, tureen, platter, gravy boat, teapot, coffee pot, creamer, sugar bowl, "Summer" pattern, Heinrich **75.00**

12 dinner plates, 14 salads, 10 bread plates, 11 bowls, 21 saucers, 10 dbl handled bouillon cups, 8 coffee cups, gravy boat, undertray, 7 fruit dishes, open vegetable bowl, 2 cov bowls, relish dish, 2 oval platters, cream pitcher, cov sugar bowl, floral bouquets with emb gold bands, "Thomas Bavaria" marks (A)............................. **510.00**

Dish

5½″ sq, multicolored floral center, reticulated border, "Schwarzenhammer Bavaria Germany, U.S. Zone" mark **8.00**

8″ l, oval, overall small buds in colors, open handles, "Z.S. & G. Bavaria" mark **10.00**

12½″ l, 8½″ w, four shell lobes, hp enameled medallion with scene of castle, trees, snow, and moon, gold trim, pink shaded ground, Oscar Schaller & Co............. **75.00**

Dresser Set

4 piece, tray, 11″ l, 7½″ w, pin tray, 4½″ l, 3″ w, cov powder dish, hair receiver, hp white roses on shaded green ground, "Bavaria" marks........................... **85.00**

6 piece, tray, 12″ l, 9″ w, 2 perfume cruets with stoppers, 6½″ h, cov box, 3¼″ d, cov box, 2¾″ d, dish, 4¾″ d, pink and yellow ground, purple violets, green and white ground, gold trim................. **225.00**

Gravy Boat, "Wild Rose" pattern, Schumann .. **45.00**

Hatpin Holder, 5″ h, 2½″ d, irid luster on white ground, wrap around gold handles, "H.& C. Selb Bavaria" mark **55.00**

Pitcher

3⅝″ h, rose garlands design.............. **12.00**

5¼″ h, bulbous, pink and yellow roses, pearl luster at top **30.00**

6½″ h, 9″ w, large purple grapes and green leaves, overall shaded green body, gold outlined shaped rim, 'Jaeger & Co." mark.... **215.00**

11¼″ h, tankard shape, bunches of green and purple grapes with gold trim, green to cream shaded ground **110.00**

Plate

6″ d, large peach roses, gold lattice and leaf swag trim, scalloped rim, set of 5 .... **30.00**

7½″ d

Gold tulips on black and white ground ... **15.00**

Pink roses, clustered leaves and stems, gold border, artist sgd..................... **10.00**

8″ d

Five red roses, green leaves, green ground, gold scalloped border, "J.Braun" mark . **30.00**

Hp mossy, aqua blue figures, thorns, mauve flowers, artist sgd **16.00**

Oranges with yellow peaches and flowers, gold edge "R.C. Kronach Bavaria" mark **15.00**

8 1/2" d

Center bunch of violets and green leaves, three bunches of violets on border joined to center with green stems, "Z.S.& Co., Bavaria" mark **20.00**

Floral center, old rose border, Tirschenreuth **50.00**

9" d

Center floral spray, gilt and rose banding, set of 15 (A)....................... **600.00**

Center portrait of young girl in colors, maroon border with lacy gold tracery **65.00**

10" d, white ground, gold rim, "Thomas, Bavaria" mark........................... **10.00**

Platter

11 3/4" H-H, repeated small green, gold, and salmon floral medallions, gold trim, scrolled handles **18.00**

13" d, white irid nymph and fish in waves, sea green and rose, gilt highlighted gilt waveform edge, "Kronach" mark (A)......... **190.00**

Relish Dish, 12 1/4" l, white and yellow roses.. **30.00**

Salt and Pepper

2 3/4" h, purple and yellow pansies, cream ground, gold tops **25.00**

Hp pink poppies on light blue ground, gold colored tops, "Z. S.& Co., Bavaria" marks. **20.00**

Sugar Bowl, Cov, 5 7/8" h, purple and green florals, white ground, gold bands and handles, green "BAVARIA" mark.................. **40.00**

Toothpick Holder, 2 1/4" h, violets at top, front and back, white ground, gold design band around rim and middle, two small handles .. **40.00**

Tray, 12 1/2" l, center castle garden scene with couple seated on marble bench, multicolored florals, gold trim, slotted and reticulated rim (A).................................... **33.00**

Vase

4 1/2" h, overall gold flowers and leaves on red ground, "Bavaria Germany U.S. Zone" mark................................... **9.00**

7" h, figural girl in red dress, red trim on upper arm, elbow length sleeves with white ruffles, holding fan next to skirt, gray pompadour hair **60.00**

Vase, Cov, 12" h, multicolored large floral spray on white ground, gold trim, "Waldershof Bavaria Handarbeit" mark **70.00**

1751-96

BELGIUM—GENERAL

1751–1891

History: Belgium's principal pottery and porcelain manufacturing center was Tournai. When Francois J. Peterinck came from Lille to Tournai in 1751, he took over a faience factory belonging to Carpentier. Empress Maria-Theresa gave him a grant to make porcelains. The early decorations were done in underglaze blue. Oriental patterns, mostly derived from Chantilly, and some Meissen-style decorations were used.

In 1763 Duvivier joined the factory as chief painter and

added Sevres-style decorations, adopting the Louis XVI style in 1780. The principal background colors were bleu de roi and yellow. Figures and groups also were made in biscuit and glazed porcelain.

When Peterinck died in 1799, the factory experienced difficulties. Peterinck's descendents continued production until 1815 when the firm went bankrupt. Henri de Bellingnies reopened the factory in 1817 and managed it until 1850. Porcelains with a blue ground, similar to earlier styles, were made. The Boch brothers of Luxembourg purchased the factory in 1850. They made creamwares until 1891.

Francois Peterinck's son Charles established a second factory for stoneware production at Tournai that operated from 1800 to 1855.

Another smaller porcelain center in Belgium was in Brussels and its suburbs. Several factories operated on a small scale, mostly as decorating workshops utilizing in the Paris style of decoration.

Museums: Chateau Mariemont, Brussels, Belgium; Musee du Cinquantenaire, Brussels, Belgium.

Basin, 12 15/16" l, oval, harvest scene in center painted in shades of brown, blue, yellow, ironred, and puce in gilt edged elongated panel, cobalt blue ground, int marbleized in gold, sides with gilt edged oval panels with pr of perched birds on sepia landscape, ext with gilt foliate entwined vine border, gilt bands at rim and footrim, c1795, script "brown L. Crette a Brux, incised f" mark (A)................. **2475.00**

Coffee Pot, 10 3/8" h, pear shape, sepia and yellow birds perched on gilt leafy branches, gilt edged rim and foot, gilt foliate vine border, fluted spout and handle with gilding, c1795, Brussels (A)............................. **330.00**

Dessert Service, Part, 18 dessert plates, 9 3/4" d, 5 circ dishes, dbl handled sauceboat, spirally molded and painted with pendent swags of flowers enclosing central floral spray, c1770, Tournai, blue stork mark, 24 pcs (A)....... **4211.00**

Figure

4 1/2" h, seated frog in green wash with black markings and yellow chest, ochre mound, late 18th C, Brussels................... **1100.00**

Vase, 11" h, Art Nouveau cobalt, brown, orange, and gold design, green int, c1913, imp "Belgium" mark, $250.00

5³/4" h, white, farm boy in broad hat, jacket, breeches, and boots, holding radishes, bowl and rooster on sq base, c1770, Tournai .. **925.00**

7" h, faience

Seated cat, manganese patches on white body, tail curled over front paws, flat blue base, c1770, Brussels (A) **4453.00**

Seated spaniel, manganese patches on white body, green flat base, c1770, Brussels (A) **4453.00**

8¹/4" h, white seated grayhound with yellow edged manganese collar, manganese accents, yellow and manganese edged blue washed rect base, c1790, "Fabrique Hors la Porte de Laeken," pr **8500.00**

13¹/2" h, white faience, girl with basket of flowers standing on rocks, men at sides, putti and girl holding flowers or drinking, restored, c1770, Tournai **650.00**

Ice Bucket, 2³/8" h, painted with three rows of panels of birds, insects, or classic medallions and trophies in colors or en grisaille, bleu de roi ground with gilt swags and foliage, horiz raised ribbing between panels, gilt foliate handles, c1790, Tournai, pr (A)............... **9500.00**

Plate, 9³/8" d, center in green and mauve with chinoiserie scene of man and girl with bird and hoop seated by arbor, shaped rim edged with feathering, Tournai (A) **180.00**

Soup Plate, 9¹/4" d, molded ogee panels painted with floral swags and sprays, Dutch decorated, Tournai, set of 8 (A) **925.00**

Sugar Bowl, Cov, 4³/4" h, gold edged reserves of painted named birds and insects on bleu de roi ground with gilt trellis, gold acorn knob, c1787, Tournai (A) **10,900.00**

Tureen, Cov, faience

9¹/4" h, modeled as cabbage with green and turquoise wash, veins outlined in olive, turquoise and blue, applied ochre caterpillers, dog finial, four leaf shaped straps, restored, mid 18th C, Brussels (A) **4506.00**

14¹/16" l, turkey shape with ochre beak, eyes and wattles, green delineated mottled blue and turquoise plumage, sitting on brown heightened yellow basket with green grasses, int in pale green glaze, restored, late 18th C, Rue de Lauken Factory (A) **4675.00**

Vase

8" h, 7" w, electric blue crackle finish, raised turquoise, burnt orange, and white designs, two scalloped attached handles, "R/V LAROUTE BELGE" mark **395.00**

12" h, Art Nouveau, yellow drip on matte blue ground **125.00**

17" h, oct, tin glazed variegated blue flowers, leaves, insects, and scrolls on white ground, c1850, "Bock Bros." mark **245.00**

Vinegar and Oil, 6⁷/8" h, two pear shaped jugs and stand with loop handle, blue, yellow, and ochre snails and butterflies on green mottled ground, hinged pewter covs, mid 18th C, Brussels (A)...................................... **1518.00**

Wet Drug Jar, 10³/4" h, ovoid body, blue inscription "S.BISANTINUS" on songbird label flanked by carnations, tall cylindrical stem, spreading foot, ribbed strap handle, knopped spout, chipped spout, early 18th C (A) **658.00**

BESWICK

Staffordshire, England
Early 1890s to Present

History: James Wright Beswick and John, his son, acquired the Gold Street Works in Longton, Stoke-on-Trent in 1896. They made utilitarian and ornamental wares, but are best known for their series of figures of horses and domestic pets. All of their animals are created with utmost accuracy and attention to details. In 1918, the Beswicks added the Warwick China Works in Longton.

After James Beswick died in 1920, John took over the firm. In 1934, John was succeeded by John Ewart Beswick, his only son. John Ewart worked along with Gilbert Ingham Beswick. They expanded the firm and increased their reputation for excellent equestrian figures. The firm was called John Beswick Ltd. from 1936.

The firm continued to expand by acquiring the site of Williamson & Son's factory in 1945 and Thomas Lawrence's site in 1957. They were converted to a public company in 1957.

Since neither Ewart or Gilbert had a successor to take over, they sold the firm to Royal Doulton Tableware Ltd. in 1969. Their reputation for figures of animals continues to the present day.

Beswick's best known models of horses are part of the "Connoisseur Series." Though the "Connoisseur Series" was developed in the early 1970s, it incorporated figures that had been made many years before. Cats, dogs, farm animals, birds, wildlife, and figures identified with children's literature such as "Winnie the Pooh," "Alice in Wonderland," and the works of Beatrix Potter have been modeled by Beswick.

The Beswick name is stamped on most pieces, but the earliest examples are unmarked. Every item made since 1933 is assigned a model number.

Reference: Harvey May, *The Beswick Collectors Handbook,* Kevin Francis Publishing Ltd., 1986.

Collecting Hints: It is usually best to start a collection by selecting a specific theme or subject.

Ashtray, 6¹/2" l, rust colored dogs, green base, "Beswick 869" mark, $95.00

Figure, 3″ h, Beatrix Potter's "Mrs. Tiggy Winkle," brown face, red and white top, c1948, #14, $65.00

Figure

2½″ h, Winnie the Pooh................	**18.00**
3¼″ h, collie, #1814	**45.00**
4½″ h	
Jemima Puddleduck, multicolored, Beatrix Potter.............................	**55.00**
Owl, multicolored, #2026..............	**35.00**
5¼″ h, Bobwhite quail in earthtone colors.	**55.00**
5½″ h, German Shepherd	**40.00**
5¾″ h, collie, Lochinvar of Ladypark, #1791	**50.00**
6″ h, two spaniels, white with luster trim ...	**65.00**
7″ h, Sussex Rooster, c1899, "Beswick England" mark	**60.00**
8¼″ h, standing duck, pastel colors, #317, sgd "Greaves"........................	**38.00**
10″ h	
Hunter on stallion in colors	**95.00**
Sheep Dog, #1378/3	**110.00**
Jug	
3¼″ h, Mr. Micawber in colors..........	**25.00**
10″ h, Winston Churchill in colors	**36.00**
Plaque, 12″ d, pheasant scene in colors	**25.00**
Teapot, 6″ h, Peggoty, #1116	**40.00**
Vase, 10″ h, multicolored landscape scene....	**38.00**

20 TH CENTURY

BING AND GRONDAHL

Copenhagen, Denmark
1853 to Present

History: The Bing and Grondahl Porcelain Factory was established in Copenhagen in 1853 when Frederich Grondahl left the Royal Copenhagen Porcelain Manufactory due to an artistic disagreement and joined with M. H. and J. H. Bing. The Bing brothers provided the business expertise, while Grondahl was the artistic force.

About one and one-half years after the company started, Grondahl died. The Bings hired top designers and decorators to continue fabricating utilitarian and art wares. In 1886 the firm first used underglaze painting. Previously, the firm manufactured pieces with "biscuit" or overglaze porcelain decorations.

In 1895 the first Christmas plate was issued. A seven inch blue and white plate utilizing the underglaze technique is made every year with the molds being destroyed after Christmas to prevent later restrikes. From 1910–1935 Easter plaques also were issued.

Several great artists were employed by the company such as J.F. Willusmen, Effie Hegermann-Lindercrone, Fanny Garde, Haus Tegner, Kai Nielsen, and Jean Gauguin. In 1914, stoneware was made for the first time. Soft paste porcelain began in 1925. In 1949 a new factory was built for producing dinnerwares.

Every piece of Bing and Grondahl work is signed with either the artist's name or initial. While today's collectors know Bing and Grondahl primarily for their figurals and annual Christmas plates, the company still produces a porcelain line.

Reference: Pat Owen, *The Story of Bing & Grondahl Christmas Plates*, Viking Import House, Inc., 1962.

Museums: The Bradford Museum, Niles, Illinois; Metropolitan Museum, New York.

Ashtray, 7⅛″ w, gray and brown figural squid head, pale blue squid arms in tray.........	**295.00**
Cake Plate, blue and white flying seagulls, open handles	**80.00**
Cream and Sugar, "Seagull" pattern, gold trim.	**115.00**
Cup and Saucer	
"Seagull" pattern	
With gold trim,.......................	**60.00**
Without gold trim	**40.00**
Cup and Saucer, demitasse, small multicolored flowers on front of cup, gold leaves on body and saucer, blue and gold line rims	**25.00**
Dish	
7⅜″ l, leaf shape with handle, "Blue Lace" pattern on white ground, marked	**48.00**
9½″ l, 7″ w, leaf shape with handle, "Seagull" pattern..........................	**45.00**
Figure	
Boston Terrier, 7½″ h, #2330	**178.00**
Cat	
2″ h, white, #2527...................	**50.00**

Figure, 6½″ h, blue and cream, "B. & G. Made in Denmark" mark, (A) $120.00

Vase, 14¼" h, "Eskimo" design, blue-green seal killing scene, blue bands, c1925, "B. & G. Denmark" mark, $1275.00

4¾" h, #2466	55.00
7¼" h, #2256	110.00
4¾" h, monkey family, #1581	135.00
5" h	
"Ear ache," white, B & G mark	30.00
"One Drop," #1745	225.00
"Stomach ache," white, B & G mark	30.00
"Tooth ache," white, B & G mark	30.00
"Victor," #1713	175.00
6" h, white dog with gray spots and ears, B & G mark	130.00
7" h	
Girl kissing boy	135.00
Grouse (A)	100.00
"Little Mother," #1779	225.00
7½" h, "The Whittler," #905	295.00
8" l, Pekinese dog, #2114, B & G mark (A)	80.00
8¼" h, young soldier hiding in tree stump and witch, polychrome (A)	350.00
8¾" h, Girl with milkcan, #2181	375.00
9" h	
Boy playing accordion, #1661SV	175.00
Chimney sweep kissing young girl, polychrome (A)	350.00
10½" h, shepherdess	470.00
11" h, mandolinist on stool, #1600	325.00
11⅞" h, bisque, John Milton holding scroll, leaning on pile of books on column (A)	115.00
Gravy Boat, with attached undertray, "Seagull" pattern, gold trim	150.00
Plaque, 6½" d, shell design with Art Nouveau style "Exposition Universelle, Paris 1900" on front	500.00
Plate	
9½" d, blue and white butterfly cartouche, scale border with flowers surrounding blue circles on outer border, scalloped edge, gilt rim, green "B & G Denmark" mark	38.00
9⅝" d, "Seagull" pattern	
With gold trim, 40.00	
Without gold trim	40.00
Platter, 16" l, 11" w, "Seagull" pattern, with gold trim	175.00
Vase, 8" h, enameled flowers and silver overlay,	

two cherubs on side of neck, gray ground, c1852–72, pr **195.00**

BISQUE

English/Continental
1750 to Present

History: Bisque, or biscuit china, is white, marble-like, unglazed hard porcelain or earthenware that has been fired only once. The composition of the body and the firing temperature are most important to achieve the matte, porous surface of the figure. Since there is no glaze or decoration, the surface has to be completely free of imperfections. Razor-sharp modeling of details is made possible by the absence of glaze.

Bisque figures first were produced around 1751 at Vincennes and Sevres in France. They became very fashionable. Many French porcelain factories during the latter part of the 18th century added them to their product lines. Bisque figures also were made at Meissen in Germany.

Beginning in 1773 Derby was the principal manufacturer of bisque figures in England. Bisque figures in soft paste porcelain have a great smoothness to the touch and a warm soft tone.

About 1850 German factories produced bisque dolls. Delicacy of coloring and realism of features could be achieved with this material. In the late 1850s France also started producing bisque dolls. Both French and German factories manufactured bisque dolls in the image of children rather than ladies during the 1880s. They were called "bebes" even though they depicted girls from about eight to twelve years old.

Most bisque examples are unmarked.

Museums: Bayerisches National Museum, Munich, Germany; Victoria & Albert Museum, London, England.

CONTINENTAL

Box, Cov, 4" d, ovoid shape, two pink lovers on cov with raised rose border in pink, tan ground, raised pink roses on base	130.00
Candleholder, 8" h, figure of German girl leaning on bridge in woods, dbl candleholders	55.00

Figure, 12" h, Virgin Mary, white, France, $125.00

Vase, 9" h, green and violet clothes, green bow, molded house scene, bird with envelope, gilt trim, Unger Bros, (A) $25.00

Figure

2" h

Red suited elf sitting next to golliwog jack-in-the-box, "Germany" mark **69.00**

Young girl in wide brimmed hat seated on brick wall in colors **3.00**

3½" l, reclining girl in mauve swim suit and cap, Germany......................... **65.00**

4¼" l, white recumbent spaniel, incised coat, rect base, c1830, imp "griffin and ROCK-INGHAM WORKS BRAMELD" marks (A) . **600.00**

7½" h, boy standing with hands clasped in front, basket of flowers at side, rockwork base, c1755, Sevres **1850.00**

9" h, group of young sailor and maiden being watched by older man, naturalistic molded base, late 18th C (A) **495.00**

9½" h, male and female nodders in period clothes, beige, white and gold, France.... **385.00**

10" h, busts of Spring and Autumn as young children, floral wreaths on heads, round bases, sgd "L. Kley," France **275.00**

10½" h

Boy or girl carrying baskets over shoulders, scythe in hand, pastel colors, France, pr **300.00**

Girl and kitten playing with ball of thread, soft pastel colors, c1870, Germany **45.00**

Man carrying violin, woman with pitcher, pastel green and lavender with raised gold dots, German, pr **245.00**

Peasant boy or girl in colors, France, pr... **300.00**

11" h

Bust of young woman in pastel flowered hat, orange dress, pastel flowered blouse, oct base with flowers, "M & B" mark .. **295.00**

Maiden standing with right hand at breast, clad in long flowing dress, sq base, c1921, imp "RAOUL LARCHE" and factory marks........................ **1100.00**

12½" h, girl holding umbrella in blue outfit trimmed in gilt, boy holding bird on stick in blue outfit, both have loosely worn black framed eye glasses, pr **310.00**

13" h

Classical maiden in rose, blue, and cream, turned stand, pr..................... **100.00**

Standing figures of young lovers in period clothes, holding hands, glazed floral highlights, Germany **275.00**

13¼" h, girl leaning on vase on tree stump counting money, two seated boys, one with flute, another with spoon, circ pedestal base, c1800, imp "Niderviller" mark (A) .. **800.00**

13½" h

Peasant man in red lined blue jacket and buff trousers, green hat, holding bowl and leash, female peasant in red skirt, white and black bodice, holding puppy in apron, brick wall backdrop, pr........ **325.00**

Standing gentleman in blue tricorn hat and lavender coat...................... **150.00**

14½" h, standing girl holding kitten, white blouse with blue lapels, pink trim, blue and hat with pink bow, c1920............... **250.00**

14½" h, 14" w, group of revelers, gilt bronze base, French (A) **1600.00**

15" h

Boy and girl with cobalt and gilt accents on clothes, boy with cigar, pr............ **900.00**

Nobleman in coral and aqua with gold beaded trim **75.00**

17½" h, white bust of Emile Loubet, rect base, c1907, Sevres................. **247.00**

18¼" h, standing blond woman, swirling white gown with gold flowers, Cupid at feet, gold flowers and trim on base, France, pr. **425.00**

21" h, girl in light blue flowing dress, wide gold belt, pink sash, man in blue striped trousers, long tan coat, pink jacket, France, pr **1150.00**

24" h, man or woman in 18th C costume, multicolored, late 19th C, pr **400.00**

25" h, bust of Duchesse de Lambelle, dressed in mid 18th C draped bodice and tresses at shoulders, chip on base, late 19th C (A) .. **550.00**

30" h, bust of Marie Antoinette, medallion on chest, blue circ socle on sq base, France (A)........................... **770.00**

36" h, gentleman in 18th C costume, one hand resting on threshing implement, other under chin, multicolored enamels and gilt, restored hairline, Germany (A).......... **2750.00**

Half Doll, 5⅛" h, gray hair, arms raised at elbows, incised "5275 German" mark **125.00**

Plaque

11" l, oval shape, raised female nude with pale blue drapery, gold accents, c1895, French **545.00**

12" d, bas relief with neoclassical figures, late 19th C, Royal Copenhagen, pr (A) **247.00**

ENGLISH

Figure

5½" h, white, young girl holding bird and garland above basket of flowers, repairs, late 18th C (A)........................ **180.00**

6⅞" h, Hannah Moore in bonnet and long dress, seated in armchair, foot on cushion, scrolling base, Minton (A)............... **380.00**

9" h

Standing milkmaid in yellow dress, holding pitcher, glazed trim................... **60.00**

Vineyard worker carrying basket of grapes, ivory finish, Robinson and Leadbetter .. **75.00**

9½" h, bust of Duke of York, shoulder draped with ermine, socle base, c1827, "H. Chamberlain & Sons" mark............. **400.00**

11¾" h, little blond girl in blue dress and white pinafore, large brown dog at side,

"Don't Be Greedy" on front, "R.& L."
mark................................. **395.00**
Hen on Nest, 7¾" l, polychrome top, white
base (A)................................. **275.00**
Urn, 6¹³/₁₆" h, white, shield shape, applied
floral garland pendants from loop handles,
fluted neck and foot, incised "crowned X'd
batons and D" mark, chips (A)............ **175.00**

AFTER 1882

BLUE ONION

German
c1730 to Present

English/Continental
1800s to Present

History: The Blue Onion or bulb pattern was started in Meissen, Germany about 1728 and was based on a Chinese aster pattern from the late Ming dynasty. After Horoldt perfected the underglaze blue paint technique in 1739, the onion pattern took on its more familiar form. This pattern really had nothing to do with onions. The flower in the center has been described as a chrysanthemum, peony, or aster. The bulbs or fruits on the border were not onions either, but resembled pomegranates and peaches. In later years, they resembled onions more closely.

More than sixty European and Oriental manufacturers copied the onion pattern and called it by a variety of names. In German, the pattern is called "Zwiebelmuster."

The pattern underwent various changes and was produced in tremendous numbers. It was less expensive to make and could be painted by less experienced workers.

The Royal Prussian Manufactory in Berlin was one of the most serious competitors utilizing the onion pattern from the 18th to the 20th century. They utilized the sceptor mark.

Popularity increased in the second half of the 19th century, and the onion pattern appeared on other items such as pots, boxes, tablecloths, and napkins.

Most of the onion pattern pieces available today were made after 1865. Some examples have a gilt edge, or the fruits and plants are heightened with gold or red contours.

Some of the European manufacturers produced blue onion stoneware in addition to their porcelain examples. Since the pattern was not copyrighted, it could be used by any factory. To protect the actual Meissen examples, the factory utilized the crossed swords mark in the lowest part of the bamboo cane about 1888. Pieces without this mark date before 1888.

Carl Teichert's factory combined with Melzer's as the Meissen Stove and Fireclay Factory and copied the Meissen onion pattern exactly. They hand painted their copies. In 1882 they registered a trademark with the name "Meissen" that caused much confusion. Other factories were established that used similar marks to add to the confusion. There were disputes with Meissen over the

marks. Another popular producer of the onion pattern was L. Hutschenreuther who printed the pattern rather than hand painting it since they produced it in quantity for everyday use.

The Meissen Stove and Porcelain Factory acquired a factory in Eichwald Bohemia which later became B. Block's factory. He continued to produce the onion pattern.

Additional changes in the factory and borders put the Block factory in Czechoslovakia after 1918 but they still utilized marks that caused confusion. With WWII more changes occurred and the factory came under German jurisdiction.

After WWII, the factory returned to Czechoslovakia and with other factories became Duchsovsky Porcelain. This Dubi branch continued to make the onion pattern.

After 1900 Meissen added "MEISSEN" to its mark impressed into the piece before firing and then glazed over it. "Made in Germany" was printed in blue under the glaze for export pieces.

Other factories in Germany and abroad also copied the onion pattern in both porcelain and stoneware. Examples are available from English, French, Japanese, Austrian, and Czechoslovakian manufactories.

Basket, 11⅞" l, pierced waisted oval, underglaze blue flowers and foliage, branch handles leading down to form scroll feet, c1890, Meissen (A)............................. **768.00**
Bowl
5½" d, "Meakin" mark................. **10.00**
8⅝" sq, "blue X'd swords" mark (A)...... **25.00**

Coffee Pot, 9" h, applied rose finial, "blue X'd swords" mark, (A) $125.00

Teapot, 4" h, 6½" w, "TK Czechoslovakia" mark, (A) $20.00

Tray, 12" l, "blue arrow" mark, (A) $88.00

Vegetable Bowl, Cov, 12" l, 7⅛" h, "Meissen and star in oval" mark, (A) $125.00

9" d, "Cauldron" mark 48.00
9½" sq, hairline, unmarked (A) 33.00
Candlestick, 6½" h, unmarked, pr 22.00
Chocolate Cup, Cov, and Stand, 5¾" h, underglaze blue decoration, early 20th C, "X'd swords" Meissen mark, 17 pcs (A) 2217.00
Cream and Sugar, "Germany" mark 20.00
Cup and Saucer, Hutschenreuther............ 25.00
Cup and Saucer, Demitasse, "blue X'd swords" marks 68.00
Dish
    3½" l, leaf shape with handle, "blue X'd swords" mark...................... 76.00
    4" sq, "Meissen, star in oval" mark 45.00
Fish Platter, 25" l, "blue X'd swords" mark.... 250.00
Funnel
    3" l, unmarked......................... 35.00
    4¼" l, unmarked (A) 60.00
Gravy Boat
    10" l, 4" h, two side handles, attached undertray, two pouring spouts, "blue X'd swords" mark (A) 27.00
    "Germany" mark......................... 45.00
Invalid Feeder, 7" l, imp "Germany" mark 225.00
Letter Opener, "Germany" mark 30.00
Meat Platter, 21½" l, oval, shaped border ... 525.00
Mustard Pot, "Germany" mark.............. 35.00
Nappy, 6¼" d, saw tooth edge............. 38.00
Oil and Vinegar Bottles, Germany marks...... 300.00
Oil Lamp, 8½" h, overall blue onion design, unmarked 45.00
Pap Boat, unmarked 45.00
Plate
    7" d, "Meakin" mark.................... 5.00

7½" d, unmarked...................... 25.00
7¾" d, porcelain, "blue X'd swords" mark (A)................................. 25.00
8" d
    Plain border, "blue X'd swords" mark, set of 9 (A)............................... 275.00
    Reticulated, "blue X'd swords" mark 20.00
9" d, "blue X'd swords" mark 15.00
9½" d
    "Blue X'd swords" mark 10.00
    "Ridgway England" mark............... 15.00
9¾" d, "Meissen, star in oval" mark 45.00
10" d
    "Blue X'd swords" mark 10.00
    "Meakin" mark 8.00
12" d, "Meissen" mark (A).............. 25.00
Platter
    9" l, oval, "blue X'd swords" mark........ 45.00
    10½" l, imp anchor mark 68.00
    11" l, oval, "blue X'd swords" mark....... 50.00
    13" l, oval, "blue X'd swords" mark....... 55.00
    13½" d, ftd, SP rim (A) 125.00
    13¾" d, "blue X'd swords" mark 25.00
    16¼" l, 11¾" w, "blue X'd swords" mark (A)................................. 210.00
    18" l, oval, "blue X'd swords" mark....... 100.00
    18½" l, 13½" w, unmarked............. 125.00
    19" l, with drain, "blue X'd swords" mark .. 275.00
    21⅝" l, 9¾" w, oval, "blue X'd swords" mark (A) 225.00
    23¼" l, 17½" w, mid 19th C, "blue X'd swords" mark (A) 330.00
Salt and Pepper Shakers, "Meakin" marks..... 25.00
Sauce Dish, 5½" d, "blue X'd swords" mark, set of 14 (A) 980.00
Sauce Tureen, 6½" h, with underplate, "Germany" mark 75.00
Seafood Bowl, 5" d, shell form, "blue X'd swords" mark, set of 6 (A) 420.00
Serving Dish
    10" l, dbl oval form, Germany (A) 83.00
    11¼" l, oval shape, "blue X'd swords" mark................................. 25.00
    12½" l, modeled reclining male or female in period clothes holding pierced oval dish with blue onion design on int, serving bowl, 22¾" h, mtd on stand with modeled male and female in period clothes around trunk, scrolled ftd base, pierced bowl at top with blue onion design on int, late 19th C, "blue X'd swords" marks, pr (A).............. 4700.00
Serving Dish, Cov, 13" l, rect, tab handles, scroll foliate finial 225.00
Soap Dish, with drain, unmarked............ 98.00
Soup Plate
    9½" d, "blue X'd swords" mark 75.00
    10" d, unmarked....................... 75.00
Sugar Bowl, 3" h, "Thurn, Kloesterle" mark ... 65.00
Tea and Coffee Set, teapot, 6" h, coffee pot, 10" h, creamer, 4" h, cov sugar bowl, 4" h, "blue X'd swords" marks (A).................... 770.00
Tray
    8" sq, unmarked....................... 14.00
    10½" l, paneled border, scalloped rim (A) . 55.00
Tureen, Cov
    8" h, circ foot, scrolled finial, unmarked 450.00
    11" h, oval, allegorical finial, restored, "blue X'd swords" mark...................... 575.00
    14½" l, acanthus handles, domed cov with scrolled foliate finial 600.00

Vegetable Bowl, 13 1/4" H-H, 9 1/8" w, "blue R
   and X'd swords" mark **125.00**
Vinegar Bottle, 5 1/2" h, with stopper **150.00**

c1900

BOCH FRERES KERAMIS

La Louviere, Belgium
1841 to Present

History: The Boch Freres factory at La Louviere, called
Keramis, was founded in 1841 by Victor and Eugene Boch
and Baron J. G. Nothomb. Previously, the Boch brothers
were associated with the Villeroy and Boch concern.

The designs of Alfred William Finch, an English artist,
and Marcel Goupy, a French artist, were produced at the
Keramis factory. Finch signed vases, dishes, jugs, and candlesticks featuring a rough, red earthenware body covered
with slip and glazed in ochre, blue, bottle green, or fawn
along with incised linear decoration and dots of light colored glaze in the Art Nouveau style.

Marcel Goupy made earthenware services decorated in
ochre and blue for the Keramis factory. His pieces usually
were signed.

Tiles were made from the 1880s at a branch factory in
France. The Keramis factory also produced earthenware
and stoneware similar to Staffordshire wares. Imitations of
Delft china were produced along with Rouen and Sevres
copies.

Museum: Museum voor Sierkunst, Ghent, Belgium.

Figure, 17" h, 17 1/2" l, lady in blue riding habit,
   black hat, riding gray and black horse jumping
   stump, "Keramis" mark **395.00**
Jardinaire, 8 1/4" l, "Delft's" pattern **80.00**
Jug, 10" h, stylized Art Deco penguin shape,
   metallic black glaze, c1937–39 (A) **275.00**

Vase, 9 3/4" h, turquoise, yellow, and iron-red
florals, white crazed ground, blue rim, "Boch F.
Made in Belgium" mark, **$310.00**

Vase, 10" h, 9" d, enameled yellow, black, and
gray flowers, orange ground, crazed crackle finish, c1926, "Keramis Made in Belgium" mark,
$450.00

Lamp
   7 1/2" h, enameled blue, green, and orange
      flowers, sgd "Ch. Catteau" **285.00**
   8 1/2" h, lime green, rust, and blue design on
      white ground, sgd "Chas. Catteau" **375.00**
   12" h, oct, alternating panels of yellow with
      orange and black flowerheads and rays,
      crackle glaze, c1920s (A) **135.00**
Vase
   5" h, narrow neck, Art Deco geometric floral
      design in colors, high gloss glaze, sgd
      "Lison" **150.00**
   6 1/4" h, white flowers with dark red and
      green centers, yellow ground on shoulder,
      white base with vert green stripes, yellow
      and green banded neck **200.00**
   8 1/2" h, frieze of yellow with geometric de-
      sign in cream, green, black, and rose, black
      vertical lines with black dots, cream ground,
      "Boch Freres Made in Belgium" mark **65.00**
   9 1/2" h
      Baluster shape, Art Deco polychromed, yel-
         low panels separated by black outlined
         green designs with magenta forms with
         black centers, c1928, "Boch Freres Olga"
         mark **550.00**
      Grazing gazelles in med and dark blue
         enamels, white crackle ground, sgd "Cat-
         teau" **1700.00**
      9 3/4" h, ovoid shape, overall floral designs in
         shades of blue, yellow, gold, and green, tur-
         quoise int, gold rim and base, applied gold
         ribbon handles, crackle blue ground,
         marked **395.00**
   10" h
      Bottle shape, gloss yellow flambe glaze drip-
         ping over bluish-green ground, light blue
         int (A) **170.00**
Flambe glaze, marked **60.00**
   12" h, streaky tan, brown, shading to black,
      gold rope trim around neck, gold rim and
      base, turquoise int, marked **450.00**
   12 1/2" h, ovoid shape, yellow crackle glaze. **150.00**
   13" h, baluster shape, orange and black
      flowerheads, crackle finish, marked (A) ... **100.00**
   13 1/2" h, oviform, yellow panels separated by
      bands of rust, white, black, and blue, c1928,
      "Boch Freres" mark **650.00**

MODERN MARK

BOHEMIA—GENERAL

Germany
Late 1700s to Present

History: Franz Anton Haberditzel pioneered the Bohemian porcelain industry. In 1789, along with twenty-five partners, he established a factory in his native Rabensgrun near Schlaggenwald. Johann Gottlieb Sonntag of Rudolstadt was the technical director. When Haberditzel died in 1792, Sonntag carried on. The company disbanded in 1793 due to the unsatisfactory nature of the porcelain.

The first successful porcelain factory in Bohemia was started by Johann George Paulus and Georg Johann Reumann at Schlaggenwald. Production initially was limited to earthenware because their patent to produce porcelain was refused in 1793 as a means of protecting the porcelain production in Vienna. Louise Greiner acquired the firm in 1800, enticed workers to move from Meissen in 1808, and received a regional patent in 1812. After 1876 the firm became Haas and Czizek.

Johann Nikolas Weber established a porcelain factory at Klosterle in 1794. This firm was rented by Christian Noone in 1799 to distribute Volkstedt porcelain. In 1820 Count Thun assumed management of the factory. Karl Venier, as director, improved the quality of the porcelain and produced examples that were gilded richly. Important sets, such as the "Empire" set (1851) and the "Thun" service (1856), and fine figures were made during his tenure.

Christian Noone set up a new factory near Carlsbad. After Noone died in 1813, Anton Hladik took over. There was a succession of owners. The factory eventually was sold to Johann Schuldes.

Johann Wenzel, Karl Kunerle, Josef Longe, and Josef Hubel started a factory in Prague in 1795. At first stoneware was made. Later the plant became the largest porcelain factory in Bohemia. In 1800, the firm was called Hubel and Company. It was sold to J.E. Hubel in 1810 who took in his son in 1820. Many figures were made during the 1840s for the wealthy bourgeois of Prague.

Friedrich Hocke established the Pirkenhammer factory in 1803 near Carlsbad. He sold out to Johann Fischer and Christof Reichenbach in 1811. By 1830, this was a fine Bohemian porcelain factory. All kinds of subjects were used on their porcelains: views, flowers, mythological, antique, and allegorical themes. Lithophane bedside lamps, dessert dishes, vases, and figures were made.

Christian Fischer became managing director in 1831. Fischer bought out Reichenbach in 1846. From that date until 1853, Reichenbach was the sole proprietor. In 1853 Ludwig von Mieg, Reichenbach's son-in-law, entered the business. The name was changed to Fischer and Mieg from 1857 to 1918 and used after both Fischer and Mieg died. After 1875 the wares became less important artistically and more practical. In 1918, the firm operated at Branch Pirkenhammer by Opiag. The name eventually was changed to Epiag and existed until 1945.

By the mid-19th century, there were thirty new porcelain factories in Bohemia. Forty-three factories existed by the end of the century.

Reference: E. Poche, *Bohemian Porcelain*, Artia, 1954.

Museums: Industrial Art Museum, Prague, Czechoslovakia; Museum of Bohemian Porcelain in the State Castle, Klosterle, Czechoslovakia.

Centerbowl, 11" d, shell shape with applied Cupids and flowers, four coral feet, pearlized finish **195.00**
Coffee Service, pot, 9⅝" h, milk jug, cov sugar bowl, 5 cups and saucers, Biedermeier style, painted oval panels of peasants in everyday pastimes, half white and puce ground, gilt scrolling foliage, c1820, "blue S" marks (A) **11,545.00**
Compote, 9" h, 7" d, ftd, floral center, reticulated base and top, gold tracery **245.00**
Creamer, 3⅜" h, pink and gray flower and leaf cluster, melon ribbed body, fancy handle, scrolled edge and foot **6.00**
Cup and Saucer, flared cylindrical shape with scroll handle, finely painted continuous band of flowers on black ground, gilt borders, fluted foot, c1815, incised "S" mark (A) **1210.00**
Dinner Service, Part
  12 dinner plates, 12 salad plates, 11 bread and butter plates, 12 compote bowls, 11 bouillon cups, 10 teacups, 11 saucers, creamer, sugar bowl, 4 serving dishes, foliate spray design on white ground, "Pirkenhammer" marks **475.00**
  18 dinner plates, 12 soup plates, 10 salad plates, 3 platters, 2 vegetable dishes, 12 cups and saucers, cov tureen, white with gold border decorations **550.00**
Kettle, 8¾" h, Vienna style gilt painted birds and flowers, gilt metal mtd overhead handle, scroll molded dolphins connecting body to porcelain handle, late 19th C, Pirkenhammer **950.00**
Match Holder, 4" h, 5" w, figural boy dressed in blue, standing with dog, c1890, Elbogen **125.00**
Plaque
  5¾" d, painted center portrait of gentleman in black suit and yellow vest, wide gilt border, c1815, "blue S" mark **1500.00**
  11½" l, 8½" w, two fairies seated on grassy band between snowdrops looking at old man resting on rock before them, tall conifer trees in distance, c1880, sgd "A.M.C.E." imp "CF" for Christian Fischer, Pirkenhammer, framed (A) **1000.00**

Box, 5¾" l, 2¼" h, multicolored romantic picnic scene on cov, magenta and dk green bands, raised gold trim, multicolored florals on int of box and cov, Pirkenhammer, $145.00

Plate, 9 1/2" d, daffodils, daisies, and pansies with
green foliage and black details, gilded pierced
basketweave border, c1840, imp mark and
black "27," Schlaggenwald (A)............ **1122.00**
Vase
7" h, panels of poppies, drip enamel cobalt
ground, gold trim, four handles fused to
pierced rim.......................... **250.00**
9" h, Portland design, relief of classic figures
accented with applied black enamel, red-
brown ground, dbl handles, imp "W.S.& S."
mark (A) **137.00**
10 1/4" h, waisted flared form, pierced with
panels of stylized flower heads, blue and
green enamels on white ground, two dolphin head feet, waisted sq base, gilded
details, 2nd half 19th C, imp "V. Portheim'
(A)................................... **1776.00**
Vase, Cov, 22 3/4" h, ovoid body, lobed panels
of 18th C lovers or castles in wooded landscapes between raised gilded scroll borders,
flared necks with pierced rims, domed covs
with pinecone finials, flared circ foot on oct
base, gilded scroll handles, c1870, Pirkenhammer, printed hammers mark, missing piece of
rim, pr (A) **3292.00**

BOW

1760 - 76

East End of London, England
c1741–1776

History: The Bow factory, one of the earliest English porcelain factories, was located in what is now the East End of
London from c1741–1776. Mostly utilitarian wares that
imitated the imported Chinese porcelains were made; un-
derglaze-blue designs also were made. Bow's porcelains
were the soft paste variety, incorporating a high percentage of bone ash in the paste mixture.

In the 1760s and 1770s numerous decorative figures
and animal models were made. The back usually had a
square hole to hold a metal candle holder. Bow figures
were press molded and thick walled.

Bow pieces of the 1760s are not marked with a true
factory mark. They usually have the painter's mark or a
reference number painted under the base. Later pieces
often have an anchor and dagger mark painted in red
enamel.

Bow porcelains found a willing audience in American
buyers. Many pieces were exported. American clay also
was utilized to manufacture some of the wares.

References: Elizabeth Adams & David Redstone, *Bow Porcelain*, Faber & Faber, 1981; Anton Gabszewicz & Geoffrey Freeman, *Bow Porcelain*, Lund Humphries, 1982;
Egan Mew, *Old Bow China*, Dodd, Mead & Co., 1909; H.
Tait, British Museum Catalogue of the 1959 Bow Exhibition, Faber & Faber.

Museums: British Museum, London, England; Victoria &
Albert Museum, London, England.

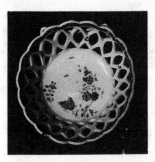

**Basket, 6" d, multicolored Kakiemon pattern
with partridge, reticulated sides, unmkd, pr,
$1000.00**

Bowl
4 3/4" d, white, applied prunus branches,
shaped rim, chips, c1755 (A) **385.00**
5 7/8" d, Famille Rose palette with flowering
peonies from rockwork (A)............. **290.00**
Bowl, Cov, 5 1/2" d, white, applied dbl prunus
sprays with blossoms, C-scroll handles, rustic
finial, c1755 (A)......................... **3460.00**
Box, 4 11/16" l, figural duck, shaded purple plumage, green accents on white crested head,
black eyes, yellow bill, cracks, c1756 (A)... **20,900.00**
Candlestick
9 3/8" h, two yellow birds perched on flower
encrusted tree with nest of fledglings,
seated dog, puce, yellow, and red edged
nozzle on leafy metal branches (A)....... **1525.00**
11 3/8" h, modeled brown spotted retriever
chasing two grouse around tree with red,
blue, and yellow modeled flowers and
green leaves, supporting red, blue, and yellow scroll molded nozzle and drip pan,
puce, gold, and turquoise scroll molded
base set on four feet **3500.00**
Coffee Can, 2 3/8" h, Famille Rose colors of peonies from rockwork...................... **185.00**
Cream Jug, 3" h
Painted birds in flowering branches in Kakiemon colors, brown rim, c1760 (A) **975.00**
Sparrow beak, blue and white gnarled yellow
tree and flowers, small chips, c1760–65
(A)................................... **170.00**
Cup and Saucer, white, molded applied prunus
branches, shaped rim, chips, c1750 (A) **495.00**
Dish
4 15/16" d, blue, puce, yellow, green, and iron-
red sprays and flower sprigs, brown edged
pierced rim with applied yellow flowers and
puce scrolls, c1765 (A) **1430.00**
6 5/8" d, "Quail" pattern in Kakiemon colors,
iron-red and gilt foliate border, c1758 (A). **330.00**
7 7/8" w, oval, "Quail" pattern in Kakiemon
colors, gilt trim, shaped rim, c1758 (A) ... **1320.00**
8" d, leaf shape, painted fruiting vine, natural
stalk handle, c1760–65 (A)............. **405.00**
8 1/4" l, oval, molded and blue painted overall
fruit, vines, and insects, c1765 (A) **385.00**
10 1/2" l, center with painted spray of fruit,
flowers, and foliage, border relief molded
with fruiting vines accented in puce, green,
and yellow, gilt shaped wavy rim, c1765,
"red anchor and dagger" mark (A)....... **2580.00**

Egg Cup, 2 1/2" h, painted flowers in circ and half panels, powdered blue ground, c1760 (A) ..   **565.00**

Figure

3" h, seated cat in purple-gray coat, yellow eyes, mouse in paw, rocky mound, puce and yellow accented scroll molded base, restored, c1758–60 (A) **3235.00**

4" h, white, seated lion with paw on tree stump, shaped oval base, cracks, chips, c1755 (A) **2640.00**

4 3/8" h, hen and cock with brown, yellow, iron-red, and black markings, oval mound base with applied flowers, repairs, c1760 (A). **6600.00**

4 3/4" h

Harlequin, seated, playing bagpipes, black pointed hat, purple, pale yellow, and white outfit decorated with playing cards, florets and checker pattern, frilled ruff at neck, mound base and stump, c1755, some damage to fingers and pipe (A) ..   **3179.99**

Sphinx, leonine body draped with tasseled saddle cloth, tasseled headdress, beaded necklace, cuffed forepaws crossed beneath bare breasts, muddy enamels, gilding over chocolate brown, scrolling base, c1750 (A) **6170.00**

4 7/8" h, saltbox player seated on stump with box resting on knee, lilac hat over striped bandeau, yellow jacket with gilt buttons, orange breeches (A)......................   **1080.00**

5 1/8" h, Autumn, boy seated on tree stump holding bunch of grapes, purple jacket, blue waistcoat, yellow breeches, basket of grapes at side, flowering plants on purple scroll edged base, restored, c1756 (A)....   **1084.00**

5 3/4" h

Seated monk, white habit, purple lined black hooded cloak, black scapula, reading breviary, gilt details, left hand damaged, c1755–60 (A) **650.00**

White, seated nun in hooded cowl, flowered scapula and tunic, book in hand, restorations, finger missing, c1755 (A)..   **935.00**

Young man wearing puce hat, floral jacket, yellow knee breeches, standing beside tree trunk, playing recorder, reclining dog on flower encrusted pad base, c1755 (A) **3590.00**

5 7/8" h, putto with puce edged wings and yellow sash, lamb in arms, bocage tree stump, pink and gold edged mound (A) ..   **795.00**

6" h, Shepherdess, young girl in turquoise bodice over flowering skirt and apron, ring of flowers in raised hand, lamb at feet, scroll molded base, c1765, "iron-red anchor and dagger" mark (A)......................   **1645.00**

6 1/2" h, white glaze, nun holding book, mound base, c1755–60 (A) **615.00**

6 5/8" h, Blackamoor Attendant, purple faced pale yellow jacket, blue skirt, pink hose, yellow boots, carrying salver supporting bowl and saucer, tripod puce scroll edged base, tree stump support, head restuck, c1760 (A).........................   **1625.00**

7 1/4" h, seated woman wearing black hat with green bow, green lined lavender vest, multicolored bows on sleeve, floral skirt with yellow apron, hurdy gurdy on knee, puce lined scroll base with applied flowers, four scroll feet, repairs, c1760–65 (A) **1650.00**

8" h, bust of Mongolian with curly mustache, goatee, ruffled cap, beaded lacy collar, open coat molded with frogging, mtd on ebonized wooden base, c1750 (A) **4125.00**

8 1/4" h, "Air," Juno wearing flowered purple dress, flower paneled underskirt, holding billowing yellow-lined orange cloak, brown and yellow eagle at feet, rocky base, eagle repaired, c1760 (A)......................   **3290.00**

10" h, "Flora," standing lady wearing flowered shirt, purple sash, pale blue skirt, pale pink underskirt, left breast exposed, nosegay in one hand, other resting on potpourri vase on flower encrusted pedestal, restored, c1758–60 (A)...................   **1309.00**

11 3/8" h, "Air," as Juno in white dress sprigged in iron-red, blue, and gold, petticoat with rose scalework, wide floral border alternating with stripes, brown and yellow eagle at side, pink and lilac mound applied with clusters of flowers and green leaves, pierced scrollwork base in green, rose, and gold, c1765, "iron-red anchor and dagger" mark (A) **330.00**

Jug, 2 7/8" h, houses, trees, and rockwork in blue, sparrow beak, clip handle (A).............   **468.00**

Mug

3 1/2" h, campana form, white with applied flowering prunus branch on front, double scroll handle with kick terminal, early 1750s (A)....................................   **860.00**

4 1/4" h, baluster shape, one large and several small plum and rose-pink chrysanthemums with green stems from pale lavender root, green and turquoise foliage, other lavender and blue flowers, green diaper border on rim with plum, turquoise, and blue flowerheads, grooved handle, heart shaped terminal, rim chip repair, c1755 ....   **950.00**

4 7/8" h, baluster form, Imari style, painted in underglaze blue, iron-red, and gilding, flowering shrubs growing from pierced rockwork in fenced garden, iron-red diaper and demi-floret border, grooved handle with heart shaped terminal, small chips to rim, c1749–52, "31" in underglaze blue mark (A) **1122.00**

5 3/4" h, bell shape, rim with border of white flowerheads on crossed-hatched ground enclosing three panels of flowers, base with two bands of cell diaper borders, grooved strap handle, heart shaped terminal, base hair crack, 1760–62 (A)................   **531.00**

6" h, bell shape

Enameled with exotic birds and large butterfly amongst berried branches, iron-red loop and dot border, dentil gilt rim, ribbed handle with heart shaped terminal in iron-red, inscribed on base "Rd, & My, TIDSWELL 1772" (A)...................**13,156.00**

Painted sprays of flowers and insects, cell diaper borders, grooved strap handle with heart terminal, c1760–65 (A) **730.00**

Mustard Pot, Cov, 3" l, cylindrical, blue and white chinoiserie island scene below diaper and demi-floret paneled border, early 1750s (A) ..   **4725.00**

Pail and Ladle, 2 7/8" h, 3 5/8" l, circ body, painted between three lightly molded horizontal ribs with blue floral sprays, blossoms, and insects, back of rim forms handle, painted on front and reverse with floral sprig, ladle with circ bowl with floral sprig, scrollwork border, dbl scroll stem, c1760 (A) **2200.00**

Plate,

6⅝" oct, ribboned emblemed circ panel of blue and white seated oriental lady, boy flying overhead, diaper and demi-floret border, c1755–60 (A). **715.00**

7" d, oct, central circ panel of dwelling on an island, smaller circ and fan shaped panels of landscapes and flowers, c1760, pseudo character mark (A) **425.00**

8½" d

Famille Rose style flowering prunus, chrysanthemum, and peony sprays, border molded with sprays of white prunus branches alternating with scattered sprigs and insects (A). **912.00**

"Manchu Lady Purchasing Haberdashery," groups of figures and objects, printed in sepia, enameled, molded brown edged scalloped rim, c1765, "iron-red anchor and dagger" mark (A) **540.00**

Oct, "Two Quail" pattern, Kakiemon style with two birds, one iron-red, one blue, eyeing insects, prunus tree with blue trunk, blossoms of iron-red and gilt, iron-red leaf border on rim with gilt flowerheads and scattered blossoms below, c1760 . . . . **750.00**

Pot, Cov, 2⅝" h, cylinder shape, iron-red, blue, and green "Quail" pattern, gilt accents, flower finial with iron-red and gilt floral border, repairs, c1758, pr (A). **5600.00**

Salt, 4½" h, modeled triangular shell, pink edge with Famille Rose style painted flowering branches and rocks on int, supported on modeled colored shells, coral, and seaweed, chips, c1750 (A) **625.00**

Sauceboat, 7¾" l, underglaze blue with sprays of oriental flowers, within molded panels entwined with flowers on fluted ground, int with diaper border reserving tulip-like flowerheads, handle with heart shaped terminal, c1760–65 (A). **523.00**

Spoon Tray, 10⅜" l, oval Imari colors of loose peonies from rockwork, gold accents, lobed and notched rim (A) **690.00**

Sugar Bowl, Cov, 4¼" d, "Quail" pattern in Kakiemon iron-red, blue, and green, gilt accents, crack in bowl, c1755, "iron-red G" mark (A). **770.00**

Sweetmeat Dish

4⁹⁄₁₆" w, heart shape, blue and white, man riding donkey and 2 men on foot crossing bridge before cottage in wooded landscape within blue band border, wavy rim, c1753, underglaze blue pseudo Chinese six-character mark (A) **605.00**

5" w, six sided star shape, blue painted chinoiserie figure seated on mat playing instrument, garden ground, blue feathered border, three scroll feet, c1754–58 (A) . . . **1540.00**

7⅛" w, triple circ scallop shells, int in rose, blue, yellow, turquoise, and green, large floral cluster beneath purple edged rim, pierced trefoil base encrusted with shells, russet coral, and green moss, central larger shell and coral cluster, 1760–65 (A). **1540.00**

Teabowl and Saucer

"Island" pattern, muted colors with open sided pavilion flanked by trees on island surrounded by rocks, mid 1750s, painter's numeral "3" (A). **530.00**

"Jumping Boy" pattern, runny underglaze blue with Chinese lady seated on pierced rocks beneath tree, watching little boy jumping, int of teabowl and int rim on saucer with four ribbon tied scrolls and other precious objects, 1755–60, underglaze blue 1 on bowl, 43 on saucer (A) **440.00**

Tea Caddy, 5½" h, ovoid, painted flower spray and scattered sprigs with winged insects, repaired, c1765 (A) **715.00**

Teapot Stand, 4½" w, scalloped corners with applied prunus branch and three flowers and four buds on int corners, white, c1752–55 (A). **1760.00**

Tub of Flowers, 6¾" h, painted with floral spray and scattered sprigs, surmounted by foliate stem with brightly colored flowers, restored, c1760–65 (A). **600.00**

Tureen, Cov, 11" d, Imari colors and gilt flowering shrubs from blue rockwork in floral borders, lower rim with radiating lappets of flowers and diapering, branch handle on cov, loop handles with mask faces, c1750 (A) **6600.00**

Vase, 6¼" h, flared shape, applied colored flowers, pierced basketwork rim, mask handles, pr (A) **700.00**

Washbowl, 10⅞" d, circ, oriental buildings on islands by river, rim with sprays of peonies, ext with floral sprigs (A) **990.00**

3

1770-81

BRISTOL

Bristol, England
c1749–1752, soft paste
c1770–1781, hard paste

History: Soft paste porcelain called "Lund's Bristol" was made in Bristol, c1749–52. Pieces show a strong Chinese influence. There usually was no factory mark. Hence, it is easily confused with early Worcester porcelains. In 1752 the Worcester Porcelain Company, under Dr. John Wall, purchased the Bristol soft paste factory and relocated it at Warmstry House in Worcester.

In 1770 a second porcelain factory at Bristol was established by William Cookworthy. This venture made hard paste porcelain, rather than soft paste. Richard Champion continued the factory between 1774 and 1778. A group of Staffordshire potters bought Champion's patent for hard paste porcelain and formed the New Hall Company, closing the Bristol factory in 1781.

Bristol porcelains of the 1770–78 period are rare. Tea services, dessert services, and dinner wares were made with simple floral patterns. Some gilding was used. Figures and vases were decorated with florals too. The factory is best known for its oval biscuit floral encrusted plaques.

Much Bristol porcelain was unmarked. Sometimes a cross in blue was accompanied by a painter's or gilder's mark. Copies of Dresden crossed swords also were used on some Bristol pieces.

References: F.S. Mackenna, *Cookworthy's Plymouth & Bristol Porcelains*, F. Lewis, 1947; F. Severne, *Chapmion's Bristol Porcelain*, F. Lewis, 1947; Dr. B. Watney, *English Blue & White Porcelain of the 18th Century*, Faber & Faber, rev. ed, 1973.

Museum: Gardiner Museum of Ceramic Art, Toronto, Canada.

Collecting Hints: Fake Bristol porcelains often bearing the cross mark with a date are in the marketplace.

Chamber Pot, 3⅜" h, miniature, painted blue, red, and green stylized insects over shrubs and grasses, white ground, iron-red key pattern on neck, blue rim, flat loop handle, c1715 (A). .**11,220.00**
Charger
  11¾" d, three tulips and stylized foliage in center in yellow, iron-red, cobalt, and gray-green, concentric blue and yellow line border, blue dash rim, c1700 (A) **2387.00**
  12½" d, polychrome, light and dark blue, yellow, and rust figure and gate in center, crosshatch and blue design border with green and brown, c1750. . . . . **600.00**
  13" d, "Adam and Eve" in polychromes, blue and yellow line border, blue dash rim, repaired, early 18th C (A). **1315.00**
  13¼" d, central green and yellow leaf surrounded by four others divided by stylized fruit in blue and manganese, pierced for hanging, early 18th C (A) **3700.00**
  13⅜" d
    Cockerel strutting before a basket of flowers, blue, red, and green, border of paneled floral sprigs, hairlines, 2nd qtr 18th C, Delft (A). **1025.00**
    Three tulips and stylized foliage issuing from mound in blue, green, yellow, and red, blue and yellow line borders, "blue dash" rim, c1700 (A). **1850.00**
  13½" d, painted center tulip and stylized flowers in yellow, green, blue, and iron-red, border of zig-zag leaves and striped fruit, blue hatched rim, c1730–45 (A) **4453.00**
Cup and Saucer, flower sprays in looped purple and gilt borders, floral swags, gilt scrollwork and laurel wreathes, gilt dentil rims, c1775, "blue X'd swords" mark (A) **1245.00**

Charger, 12⅞" d, blue, rust, and yellow, green accents, c1750, $600.00

Dish
  8⅝" d, border to border blue painted scene of lion among sponged trees, white ground, c1700, Delft. **1385.00**
  11½" d
    Blue painted central flowering branch in blue edged cushion shaped reserve, powdered manganese ground with four leaf shaped floral panels, mid 18th C (A) **365.00**
Central bunch of grapes in blue, squirrels in gourd vine on rim, c1740 (A). **225.00**
  13" d
    Long tailed bird perched on oriental shrub from edge of cliff, pavilion in ground, blue, gray-green, iron-red, and yellow, border of stylized buds reserved on diaper ground, c1730–40 (A) **815.00**
    Yellow, green, reddish-brown, and blue with three chinoiserie figures seated on rocks in mountainous landscape, group of low buildings beyond, reverse with grases, c1730, "blue 4" (A) **2480.00**
  13⅛" d, radiating geometric pattern in blue, gray-green, iron-red, and yellow (A) **645.00**
  13⅜" d, blue, red, green, and yellow cockerel strutting before basket of flowers, border of paneled floral sprigs on rim, minor hair cracks to rim, 2nd qtr 18th C (A) **750.00**
  13½" d, polychrome, Chinese boy skipping in stylized landscape, rim chips, c1750 (A) **1240.00**
  13⅝" d, manganese, gray-green, blue, and yellow flowering shrubs from pierced rockwork, scalloped rim (A) **645.00**
Inkwell, 3¼" d, cylindrical form, grayish blue with broad border of foliage and berries, top pierced with large central well encircled by four smaller openings with blue flowerheads, minor chips, c1740 (A) **673.00**
Jar, 5⅛" h, Delft, dbl ogee shape, blue painted band of flowers reserved on dotted ground, decorative borders, two applied handles, early 18th C **645.00**
Mug, 4" h, baluster shape, blue seated figure in mountainous Chinese style landscape, wavy line borders, blue dash loop handle, rat tail terminal, rim crack and chips, late 17th C (A). **3187.00**
Pickle Dish, 3⅞" d, leaf shape
  Blue painted floral spray in whorl and zig-zag borders, mid 18th C, pr (A) **1018.00**
  Underglaze blue painted chinoiserie scene of Sage standing in garden of shrubs, c1755, Lund, pr (A) **545.00**
Plate
  8⅝" d, dark blue oriental type floral in center, pale blue ground, raised white enamel leaves and pineapple border, c1735. . . . . . . **450.00**
  8¾" d, polychrome, peacock standing among stylized sponged trees in yellow, iron-red, manganese, and blue, c1740 (A) **1328.00**
  8⅞" d, polychrome, three iron-red fish above "M.T. 1744" in manganese, rim with wide border of manganese circles with three fish, c1774, rim chips (A) **3542.00**
  9" d, half length portrait of King George I in blue wearing full bottomed wig, flanked by initials "G R" within concentric line borders, chips, c1720 (A) **2685.00**
  11⅞" d, blue painted with two Chinese men in boat, another fishing from bridge near

English houses, pine cone, leaves and
flowers on border, chips, c1755–65...... **250.00**
Porringer 5 1/8" d, blue painted stylized bud on
int, dentil border, ext with row of buds, heart-
pierced lobed lug handle with radiating blue
lines, cracks, c1730 (A) **1120.00**
Posset Pot
5 1/4" h, blue painted flowering plants, flared
neck with scrollwork, two applied strap handles, S-shaped spout with blue dashes,
c1720, Delft.......................... **365.00**
6 1/4" h, blue painted views of Cupid with
bow and arrow in garden of trees, scroll
devices on neck, strap handles, blue dash
spout, chips, cov missing, c1700–30 (A).. **1795.00**
Potpourri Jar, 4 1/2" h, 7 1/2" d, blue and white
florals and design, holes in top, c1740...... **1500.00**
Punch Bowl, 10 1/4" d, painted blue, red, and
green flying birds in flowering shrubs, looped
border, int with blue floral sprig, blue edged
rim, c1730 (A) **2645.00**
Puzzle Jug, 7" h, painted iron-red, blue, and
green gabled twin houses on islands, cylinder
neck pierced with florets and hearts outlined
in red and blue, tubular handle with blue and
red dashes, three nozzles (A)............. **12,210.00**
Sauceboat, 6 1/2"l, oval shape, colored flower
sprays within scroll molded cartouches, foot
and rim with purple line borders, scrolling handles, c1775, "blue cross and II" mark (A)... **331.00**
Scent Barrel, 4 3/8" h, pearlware, inscribed "JCS
1835" around center hole, flanked by two lg
floral bouquets, pink and blue conc banding
outlined in brown (A).................... **185.00**
Strainer Dish, 4 1/16" d, center pierced with pinwheel pattern of small holes, painted in underglaze blue with floral spray within a trellis diaper border on rim, c1775, underglaze "blue
X" mark (A)............................ **440.00**
Teapot, 5 1/2" h, barrel shape, colored sprigs and
flower sprays, gilt scrollwork borders, ear
shaped handle, curved spout, flower knob,
c1775, "blue cross" mark (A)............. **1145.00**

PARAGON

BY APPOINTMENT

FINE CHINA
MADE IN ENGLAND
REG?
1932

BRITISH ROYALTY COMMEMORATIVES

**Staffordshire, England
1600s to Present**

History: British commemorative china dates from the
1600s, although the early pieces were rather crude in form

and design. When transfer printing was developed about
1780, the likeness of the king or queen was much improved.

With coronations or jubilee celebrations of England's
royalty, a great number of souvenir wares appeared on the
market to commemorate the occasion. This practice
started in earnest with the coronation of Queen Victoria
and has been in use ever since.

The bulk of these wares were manufactured in the Staffordshire district of England. Many small potters, finding a
ready market for these souvenir products, produced them
well in advance of any upcoming celebration. At times this
was premature. The number of pieces prepared for the
coronation of Edward VIII is an excellent example. With
his abdication of the throne, the coronation ware quickly
became abdication ware. Since large quantities were produced and sold previously, wares for this event that never
happened are not scarce.

It was not long before the major houses such as Minton,
Royal Doulton, Aynsley, and Wedgwood began producing commemorative wares. Plates, jugs, pitchers, and tea
sets were the popular pieces.

Transfers and decals that often featured busts of the
king or queen and the consort graced most pieces. Other
royal symbols used on the pieces include: crowns, dragons, royal coats of arms, national flowers, swords, scep-
tres, dates, messages, and initials.

Some items were issued in limited quantities and are
very desirable, but the bulk of materials prepared for coronation and jubilee celebrations were mass produced and
are readily available.

References: Josephine Jackson, *Fired for Royalty*, Heaton
Moor, 1977; John May, *Victoria Remembered, A Royal
History 1817–1861*, London, 1983; John & Jennifer May,
Commemorative Pottery 1780–1900, Heinemann, 1972;
David Rogers, *Coronation Souvenirs & Commemoratives*,
Latimer New Dimensions Ltd, 1975; Sussex Commemora-
tive Ware Centre, *200 Commemoratives*, Metra Print En-
terprises, 1979; Geoffrey Warren, *Royal Souvenirs*, Orbis,
1977; Audrey B. Zeder, *British Royal Commemoratives
With Prices*, Wallace-Homestead, 1986.

Collectors' Clubs: Commemorative Collectors Society, 25
Farndale Close, Long Eaton, United Kingdom, NG 10 3PA,
$25.00 per year, *Journal of the Commemorative Collectors
Society.*

Museums: Brighton Museum, Brighton, England; London
Museum, Kensington Palace, London, England; Victoria &
Albert Museum, London, England.

Collecting Hints: Some collectors specialize in just one
monarch while others include several different ones. Another approach is to collect only pieces for special occa-
sions, such as coronations, jubilees, marriages, investi-
tures, births, or memorials. Others specialize in one
specific form such as mugs, teapots, spoons, etc.

Since the marriage of Prince Charles in 1981 to Lady
Diana Spencer and the birth of their two sons, a whole
new area of collecting emphasis has begun.

EDWARD VII

Bonbon Dish, 7" d, Coronation, busts of Edward
and Alexandra, pleated edge **58.00**
Candlestick, 2 1/2" h, 6 1/2" d, Coronation, color
portraits with lion and unicorn and arms on
base, hairline............................ **125.00**
Cup and Saucer, Coronation
Busts of Edward and Alexandra **75.00**

Multicolored crown in wreath with flags, gold
trim, unmarked......................... 59.00

Dish, Coronation
5" l, 4½" w, leaf shape, color royal crest, gilt
rim 39.00
6¾" H-H, color design of English crest, gilt
trim, fluted border, "Foley" mark 65.00

Milk Jug, 3½" h, Coronation, color portraits of
Edward and Alexandra and trim, cobalt and gilt
at top and handle 89.00

Mug, 2¾" h, Coronation
Color cipher with crown, "1902" below,
lithophane of Edward or Alexandra, pr . 235.00
Lion and Unicorn with Royal Arms and
crown in color, "Johnson Bros. Semi-porcelain" mark.......................... 55.00

Plaque
4¾" d, raised white profile bust of Alexandra, black wood frame, "Bauerrichter &
Co." mark............................ 245.00
9⅝" h, oval, printed multicolored bust of Edward or Alexandra, crown overhead, cipher
under bust, Royal Doulton, pr (A)........ 225.00

Plate
6½" d, oct, "England's Future King" in black
transfer with polychrome highlights, emb
floral border, red rim 825.00
7" d, Coronation, sepia portraits of Edward
and Alexandra, color flags and crown, "William Whiteley, Ltd" mark................ 69.00
7¼" d, Coronation, portrait of Queen Alexandra, scalloped gold rim, "Doulton Burslem, England" mark 135.00
9" d, gold printed view of University of Aberdeen, commemorating Edward VII opening
Extension, Paragon (A)................. 300.00
9¾" d, Proclamation-Queen Victoria Memorial, sepia portraits of Edward, Alexandra,
and Victoria in beaded frames on blue
ground, color trim, gold rim 275.00

Teapot, 3½" h, 7" l, Coronation, multicolored
royal crest on side, gold trim, Hammersley .. 175.00

Teapot Stand, 7" d, Coronation, color portraits in
flags and seal, gold rim, "Borough of St. Hel-
ens" 82.00

EDWARD VIII

Cookie Jar, 9" h, 6½" l, caravan shape, Coronation, sepia portrait of Edward, color wreath,

**Edward VIII cup, 3¼" h, Coronation, multicol-
ored, design by Dame Laura Knight, lion handle,
"Myott Son, Made in England" mark, $60.00**

blue and red trim, rattan handle, Parrott and
Co. 195.00

Cup and Saucer, Coronation, color portrait of
Edward, St. George slaying the dragon, ci-
pher, and "1937" on reverse of cup, Royal
Doulton................................ 79.00

Dish, 5" d, triangular, Coronation, sepia portrait
of Edward with multicolored flags at top,
crossed flags at base, gold rim, "Made in England" mark 42.00

Mug
3½" h, Coronation, sepia portrait of Edward,
color flags on each side, cipher and "1937"
on reverse, gold trim 59.00
3¾" h, Coronation, sepia bust facing right,
color flowers on rim, blue trim, "G.W.S.
Longton" mark........................ 55.00
4" h, Coronation
Framed color lion and crown, sepia portrait
of Edward, "LONG LIVE OUR KING" on
top, Coronation date on reverse, "Alma
Ware" mark 49.00
Sepia portrait of Edward, multicolored
flags and crown, blue trim, cipher and
crown on reverse, "J.& G. Meakin Pottery" mark 43.00
4¼" h, "H.R.H. King Edward VIII" and sepia
portrait bust on front, sepia flags on reverse,
gold trim 115.00
4½" h, Coronation, sepia portrait of Edward,
multicolored flags and crown, modeled orb,
crown and scepter handle with gold trim . 79.00

Plaque, 5" d, emb bust of king, Royal Worcester.................................... 85.00

Plate
7¼" d, Coronation, portrait in center, scalloped gold rim, "Doulton Burslem, England," mark.......................... 135.00
8" sq, blue profile of Edward, Myott 38.00
9" d, Accession, color portrait of king flanked
by flags, blue band and emb rim, "Ruwaha
Belgium" mark........................ 175.00
10¼" d, Coronation, blue transfer of bust of
Edward in royal seal, floral border, "With
Compliments of Lawleys Regent Street" on
reverse, Copeland Spode 95.00

Tankard, 4½" h, Coronation, raised profile of
Edward in wreath, ribbon, and crown,
wreathed cipher and crown on reverse, green-
orange mottled ground, "Arthur Wood &
Son" mark............................ 95.00

ELIZABETH

Beaker
4" h, Coronation, sepia portrait of Elizabeth in
wreath, color decorations, cipher and
crown on reverse, yellow rim band, Royal
Doulton.............................. 45.00
4½" h, 25th Anniversary of Coronation,
color decoration of Royal coach and horses,
crown above, gold lion's head handles, gold
trim................................. 95.00

Bell, Silver Jubilee
5¼" h, raised flowers with silver trim, commemoration around base, "Crown Staffordshire" mark 29.00
7½" h, black and white portrait of Elizabeth,
color decorations, silver trim, wood handle,
"Royal Grafton" mark 69.00

Bowl, 8″ d, Coronation, burnt brown crown, "E.R." and crown in center, color rings on border, "Poole Pottery" mark................. **45.00**

Box, Cov

3″ d, 60th Birthday, color portrait of Elizabeth in floral wreath on cov, commemoration on side, gold trim, "Coalport" mark......... **25.00**

4″ d, 5″ h, Coronation, orb shape, hp color jewels on gold ground, gold commemoration, purple and gold crown finial, "Wedgwood & Co. Ltd" mark **89.00**

5″ w, heart shape, Silver Jubilee, white bust of Philip or Elizabeth on blue jasper ground, floral wreath, Wedgwood, pr **110.00**

Cup and Saucer

Coronation

Sepia portrait of Elizabeth, color decorations, cipher, crown, and commemoration on reverse, gold trim............. **59.00**

Queen in Scottish attire, Alfred Meakin... **40.00**

Sixtieth Birthday, color portrait of Elizabeth, floral border, gold trim, "Coalport" mark . **43.00**

Dish, 4½″ sq, Coronation, sepia Marcus Adams portrait of Elizabeth, Prince Charles, Anne, color decorations, gold trim **43.00**

Jar, Cov, 4½″ h, Silver Jubilee, white profile of Elizabeth on front, Duke of Edinburgh on reverse on red ground, national flowers, crown and cipher on sides...................... **35.00**

Jug, Coronation

3½″ h, sepia portrait bust of Elizabeth, color flags, cipher and crown on reverse, gold trim, "Made in England" mark........... **35.00**

4½″ h, black bust of Elizabeth with angel overhead holding crown, wreathed cipher and crown on reverse, commemoration on inside lip, mask spout, Royal Worcester... **95.00**

5¼″ h, raised tinted portraits of Elizabeth, color bands, gold trim, musical base, Crown Devon **135.00**

5¾″ h, raised profile of Elizabeth on reverse, ivory color, musical base, "Royal Winton" mark **125.00**

Loving Cup

3″ h, photo transfer of Elizabeth and Duke in colors, commemoration on reverse, gold trim, "Coronet" mark................... **39.00**

3¼″ h, 5½″ H-H, 25th Anniversary of Coronation, color decoration of information regarding Coronation, State coach and commemoration on reverse, gold lion handles, "Paragon" mark....................... **113.00**

4″ h, 7″ H-H, Silver Jubilee, black silhouette portrait of Elizabeth, gray and gold highlights, Drury Lane theater on reverse, "Coalport" mark **85.00**

Mug

Coronation

3″ h, sepia portrait of Elizabeth, color lion and unicorn frame, crown and cipher on reverse, gold trim, "Shelley" mark...... **37.00**

4¼″ h, sepia portrait of Elizabeth, color flowers and designs, Royal Arms and commemoration on reverse, gold trim, "Royal Albert" mark................. **35.00**

Shelley mark........................ **30.00**

3¾″ h, 25th Wedding Anniversary, color decoration of Westminster Abbey, commemoration band on inside rim and reverse, gold trim, "Aynsley" mark........ **59.00**

Plaque

6″ h, 4¼″ w, Silver Jubilee, black profile portrait of Elizabeth with gray and gold highlights, "Coalport" mark **39.00**

6½″ h, 4¼″ h, white bisque profile bust of Elizabeth, blue velvet ground, with hanger **49.00**

7½″ d, Silver Jubilee, color portrait of Elizabeth on black ground, gold trim, commemoration on reverse, pierced for hanging, "Crown Staffordshire" mark **49.00**

Pin Tray, 4½″ l, Silver Jubilee, Wood and Sons..................................... **15.00**

Plate

4″ d, 25th Anniversary of Coronation, color design of symbols of event, "HER MAJESTY QUEEN ELIZABETH II CORONATION" on rim, commemoration on reverse, "Coalport" mark **24.00**

Coronation

8¾″ d, sepia portrait of Elizabeth in gold frame with red and gold crown above, gold lion and unicorn, dark red border with gold overlay, "Coalport" mark **115.00**

9″ d

Bust of queen, Johnson Bros.......... **25.00**

Sepia portrait of Elizabeth in lion and unicorn frame, color floral border, gold trim, "Weatherby" mark **42.00**

9″ d, Silver Jubilee, sepia portrait of Elizabeth, turquoise border **35.00**

9″ sq, queen in Scottish attire Alfred Meakin **30.00**

Tankard, 2″ h, sepia portrait of Elizabeth, gold trim, name on reverse, "Coronet" mark..... **22.00**

Teapot, 5″ h, 8½″ l, Coronation, raised light brown profile of Elizabeth on dark brown ground, raised arms on reverse, crown finial, "Dartmouth Potteries" mark.............. **95.00**

GEORGE V

Ashtray, 4¼″ d, Silver Jubilee, color portraits of George and Mary with flag between, silver trim, "Made in England" mark **40.00**

Beaker, 4″ h, Coronation, black and white portraits of George and Mary surrounded by color flags and seal, crown and "IN COMMEMORATION" at top, birth, marriage, and Coronation dates, gold rim, "S.Fielding & Co." mark................................... **69.00**

George V cup, 4½″ h, black transfers of George and Mary, multicolored flags, crown, and "Long May They Reign, June 22, 1911," "Samual Ford & Co." mark, $65.00

Egg Cup, Silver Jubilee, portrait busts of George and Mary and 1910–1935 .... **50.00**

Jug
4³/4" h, black and white portrait of Duke of York, reserved on puce and white ground, Germany **135.00**
6" h, figural bust of George or Mary, hp highlights, named on base, pr **275.00**

Milk Jug, George in blue uniform, gold trim, emb body, hairline **39.00**

Mug
3" h, Coronation, green and blue slip decoration with royal portraits in terra cotta relief, Borough of Poole **95.00**
3¹/2" h, Coronation, color portrait of George in blue uniform and Mary, gold decorations and trim............................ **59.00**
4¹/4" h, Silver Jubilee, black and white portraits of George and Mary, color trim, "Diamond China" mark.................... **55.00**

Plate
7" d, Coronation
Color portraits of George and Mary with Edward between, crest below, gold rim **69.00**
Portrait of George in red uniform, Mary in colors, brown swags on border, Royal Doulton............................... **125.00**
7¹/4" d, Royal Wedding, brown toned portraits and designs on left side of plate **175.00**
7¹/2" d, Royal Wedding, color crest at top, crown at base, gold rim, "Foley" mark ... **135.00**
8¹/2" d, Visit to Canada, black and white portraits with crown between, gold emb border, Austria........................... **235.00**
9" d, brown and yellow printed bust of George or Mary, gilt border, Ridgways, pr (A)..................................... **85.00**

Vase, 6¹/4" h, color portrait of Mary, gilt handles, "Russell & Sons" mark................... **75.00**

GEORGE VI

Ashtray, 4" d, Coronation, raised cipher and crown in gold, color wreath on border, gold rim, Foley............................... **45.00**

Beaker
3¹/2" h, Coronation, sepia family portrait, color trim, names of family on reverse, blue rim, "Made in England" mark........... **65.00**
4" h, Coronation, sepia portraits of George and Elizabeth, color flags surround portraits, cipher on reverse, gold rim, Crown Ducal **52.00**

Cup and Saucer
Coronation, sepia portraits of king and Elizabeth **30.00**
Family portrait, Royal Albert **45.00**

Dish
5" d, Coronation, sepia portrait busts of George and Mary, color flags and crown, gold trim **25.00**
5³/4" h, 5¹/4" w, Australia Visit, raised bust of George in light green, Sylvae Ware **65.00**

Loving Cup, 3¹/4" h, Coronation, sepia portraits of George and Elizabeth, cipher and crown on reverse, gold handles **78.00**

Mug
3" h, Coronation, multicolored decal of royal crest, "George and Elizabeth" on rim, lion handle, Paragon...................... **125.00**

3¹/4" h, 80th Birthday, color floral decoration with silver commemoration and trim, "Made for the National Trust by Boncath Pottery" mark........................ **39.00**

George and Elizabeth coronation, Moorcroft **125.00**

Pin Tray, 4³/4" l, 3¹/2" w, Coronation, multicolored flags in center with G.R. at top, gold rim, Hammersley............................... **59.00**

Pitcher, 4¹/4" h, portrait of George and Elizabeth **48.00**

Plate
6¹/2" d, portrait of George and Elizabeth, Meakin............................... **38.00**
7" d, Coronation, G.R. and date at top, crossed flags at base, gold rim, Hammersley................................. **75.00**
9¹/4" d, Coronation, gold intertwined initials and date in center, border of orange and black squares, Charlotte Rhead **75.00**
9¹/2" H-H, Coronation, sepia portraits in center, color decoration, maize yellow handles and band around portraits, Shelley **65.00**
10¹/2" d, Canada visit, 1939, color portraits of George and Elizabeth, black and white shields of provinces and maple leaves, gold rim, Royal Winton...................... **99.00**

Tea Plate, 6¹/4" d, Coronation, multicolor crest in center, gold rim, Paragon **42.00**

Tankard, 5¹/2" h, Coronation, busts of George and Elizabeth, brown glazed stoneware, silver luster rim and handle, Ridgway **65.00**

ROYALTY, MISCELLANEOUS

Bowl, 5¹/2" d, Princess Charlotte in Memoriam, portrait on tomb, angels above, Britannia weeping next to tomb, black and white with pink luster trim.......................... **145.00**

Jug
4¹/2" h, creamware, sepia portrait of Queen Caroline and "Her Majesty Caroline" and "Virtue Triumphant," reverse with loyal verse, copper luster line borders, c1820 (A)..................................... **425.00**
6" h, King William IV Coronation on one side, Queen Adelaide on reverse, purple transfer, flowers inside rim, restored.............. **795.00**

Pitcher, 5¹/2" h, raised bust of Queen Caroline in colors, flowers above and "Success to Queen Caroline" below, blue trim, restored. **825.00**

Plate
5¹/2" d, oct, maroon transfer of Queen Adelaide with name in center, emb floral border **775.00**
6⁵/8" d, inscribed "Coronation WA at Westminster September 1831," for William and Adelaide, border of birds, dogs, and flowers, rim with three bust portraits, flowers, and beaded loops (A)...................... **600.00**
7¹/2" d, relief molded profile of Queen Caroline in green plumed yellow hat, blue coat, border relief molded and colored crowns, Prince of Wales feathers, and insignias (A)..................................... **495.00**
8¹/2" d, molded center with titled bust of George III in naval uniform or Queen Caroline in feathered hat, molded rim with crowns, thistles, roses, and Prince of Wales feathers, colored enamels with pink luster trim, c1820, pr (A) **1395.00**

Vase, 4⅞" h, pearlware, tapered cylinder shape, black printed bust of "His Sacred Majesty, King George III," reverse with bust of Duke of Wellington...................... 750.00

VICTORIA

Bowl, 6½" d, multicolored scene of standing Albert and seated Victoria in center, pink luster swag border......................... 155.00
Cup and Saucer
   Diamond Jubilee, color decoration of commemoration information in beaded gold frame, flags and crown above, three groups of beaded crowns on saucer, "W.L. Lowe" marks................................... 137.00
   Royal family, Albert flying kite on cup, royal family on saucer, pink luster trim......... 145.00
Jug
   6⅝" h, puce printed portraits of Victoria and Albert on yellow ground, copper luster body (A)............................. 200.00
   9⅜" h, brown stoneware, molded relief of Royal Coat of Arms, portraits of Queen Victoria and Duchess of Kent, relief of florals on neck, handle repaired (A).............. 285.00
Jug, Diamond Jubilee
   6⅝" h, stoneware, tan relief busts of young and old Queen on tan ground, white raised medallions, white inscriptions on dark brown neck, Doulton Lambeth (A)....... 350.00
   7" h, 1897, color decoration of commemoration information, gold beaded frame, blue rim and spout, "W.L. Lowe" mark........ 145.00
   7⅜" h, brown stoneware, green collar, sterling silver rim, Doulton.................. 475.00
Mug, 3" h, Gold Jubilee, multicolored decal of jubilee information with flags and crown, unmarked................................. 111.00
Plaque, 7¹/₁₆" d, black printed portrait of young Victoria, seated in chair, Windsor castle in ground, yellow and black border (A)....... 420.00
Plate
   7" d, Coronation, brown printed bust of Victoria, inscribed "Victoria Regina, Crowned

28th of June 1838, Born 24th of May 1819, Proclaimed 20th of June 1837," floral molded border (A)..................... 250.00
8" d, portrait of Victoria in center, Jubilee plate, silver luster scalloped edge, "M & B, Made in Austria" mark.................. 125.00
8¼" d, Diamond Jubilee, black portrait of Victoria in center, puce emb border, "Made in Austria" mark...................... 65.00
9" d
   Color decal of Victoria and Albert, pink luster border, scalloped rim.............. 85.00
   Portrait of Victoria in colors, floral border, gilt trim, emb rim.................... 66.00
9¼" d, Diamond Jubilee, color scene of Windsor Castle in center, crown and banner above, banner below, gilt rim, unmarked . 145.00
9½" d, Diamond Jubilee, color center portrait of Victoria, four royal residences, unmarked................................. 149.00
9⅝" d, oct, 1887 Jubilee, black printed bust of Victoria in rect panel, flanked by thistle, rose, and leaves, "Wallis Gimson & Co." mark (A)............................. 285.00
Tankard, 4½" h, porcelain, relief of Victoria in cartouche, flanked by busts of Victoria 175.00

c1760 - EARLY 20ᵀᴴ C

CAPODIMONTE

Near Naples Italy
1743–1759
Buen Retiro, near Madrid, Spain
1760–1812

History: Capodimonte was a royal palace in Naples where a porcelain factory was established in 1743. Charles III, the Bourbon King, and his Queen, who had brought quantities of porcelain from Meissen, were the founders. The factory produced primarily soft paste porcelain in a milky white color for the court.

Guiseppe Gricci was the chief modeler. His specialties included religious subjects (madonnas, pietas, and holy water stoups,) snuff boxes, and mythological figures. Gricci was in charge when the factory created an entire room for the king that featured porcelain panels in high relief decorated in chinoiserie and which can be viewed today at the Museo di Capodimonte in Naples. Pieces usually were marked with the armorial fleur-de-lis of the Bourbon family.

When Charles inherited the throne of Spain and became king in 1759, he moved the factory and workers to Madrid with him. Gricci, now signing his works Jose Gricci also made the transition. The new factory, located on the palace grounds was called Buen Retiro. They continued to make soft paste porcelains similar to those made at

Victoria, figure, 13" h, parian, 1897 Jubilee, imp "Turner and Wood, Jubilee" mark, (A) $220.00

Capodimonte including elaborate tablewares, centerpieces, flowers, and figures. Sometimes the factory used the Bourbon fleur-de-lis mark. An attempt to make hard paste porcelains was made shortly before the factory closed.

When Ferdinand IV governed Italy in 1771, he revived the royal factory. Styles were influenced by a classical revival, inspired by the unearthed treasures at Pompeii. Best known are the pieces decorated with mythological reliefs.

After 1807 the factory declined and closed several years later. In 1821 the molds and models were sold to the Ginori factory at Doccia.

Museums: Metropolitan Museum of Art, New York; Museo di Capodimonte, Naples, Italy; Woodmere Art Museum, Philadelphia, PA.

Collecting Hints: Many factories in Hungary, Germany, France, and Italy copied Capodimonte examples. Many of the pieces on the market today are of recent vintage.

Beaker, 2³⁄4" h, everted rim, painted bouquet of garden flowers and peony in puce, yellow, blue, and green tones, bluebell spray on reverse, short foot, c1745, "blue fleur-de-lys" mark (A).. **1650.00**
Bell, 4³⁄4" h, relief of cherubs in trees, fancy handle **28.00**

Cup and Saucer, Cov, 5¼" h, classical scenes in colors, "blue crowned N" mark, pr, (A) $120.00

Jewel Box, 8" l, 6" w, 6" h, 6 panels of classical scenes in colors, "blue RE" mark, (A) $275.00

Bowl, 12" d, relief scene of Capri San Michele in center, semi-nude cherubs on rim, pierced for hanging, "Capodimonte, Crowned N" mark.. **85.00**
Box, Cov
3¼" h, 7" l, 6½" w, relief of putti at various pursuits **175.00**
4½" h
7" d, relief figures of children and trees, fruit finial, three paw feet, round shape..... **75.00**
10" l, 7" w, relief scene of Aphrodite and attendants, "crowned N" mark (A)..... **80.00**
4³⁄4" l, emb and polychromed frolicking cherubs, "crowned N" mark (A)............. **145.00**
Casket
9½" l, oval, molded high relief of classical figures, gilded borders, gilt metal mts, c1880, "blue crowned N" mark........ **1150.00**
9³⁄4" l, oval, relief of warriors at rest, mythological medallions, hinged domed cov with relief of classical warriors in battle, gilt scroll borders, "blue crowned N" mark (A)................................... **1287.00**
10¼" l, rect shape, molded with scenes of revelry with naked maidens and bacchicalian figures dancing and feasting, late 19th C, underglaze "blue crowned N" mark (A)................................... **1122.00**
Centerpiece
4" h, 10" l, relief of cherubs and children on ext, floral int, gold scalloped rim......... **285.00**
8" h, oval center bowl mtd with gilt floral swags and putti surrounded by three figures of dancing maidens in gilt robes......... **600.00**
Clock, 17" h, 10" w, charioteer at top, classical women at base, olive green griffin feet, pink faux marble top and base, French movement.................................... **1600.00**
Coffee Cup and Saucer, trembleuse saucer, molded relief of rococo scrolls, foliage, and berried sprays in light ochre, yellow, light and dark green, and light and dark crimson, c1745–50, underglaze "blue fleur-de-lys" marks (A)............................. **14,245.00**
Cup and Saucer, Demitasse, relief of harvest scenes in colors, set of 12................. **200.00**
Cup and Saucer, oversize, molded classical nude male and female figures in colors.......... **95.00**
Figure
6½" h, girl reading, white net dress with applied flowers, blue ruffle edge, blue bodice, gilt scalloped edge, tree behind with applied pink flowers, green leaves, "crown N, Made in Italy" mark........................ **295.00**
8" h
10" l, "Chestnut Vender," old woman in front of copper stove roasting chestnuts, ragged urchin at side, multicolored, sgd "G. Armani"......................... **250.00**
"Dandy," in long blue coat, striped trousers, floral vest, posies in right hand, Baroque base.............................. **160.00**
8¼" h, man in pink trimmed dark green long coat, holding top hat and bunch of posies **160.00**
8½" h, 9½" l, boy kneeling taking photograph of girl on brick wall, multicolored, "crowned N" mark..................... **125.00**
8½" h, "Pan," mythological half man-half goat, gold horns, seated on sq pyramid

plinth, raised bat head on front, gold
trim.................................... **325.00**
9½" h
"Beauty," young girl in wide brim hat, carrying
bouquet of roses, basket of flowers at feet,
sgd four places **150.00**
"Pearl Fisherman," captain in blue trousers,
pink shirt, holding bag with shell and
pearl, shell at foot, sgd Bonalberti...... **185.00**
10" h, standing lady in period clothes holding
flowers, c1900, France.................. **85.00**
10½" h, 10½" l, "Fisherman," man in red
tassel cap, smoking pipe, holding net to
be mended, sea shell at base, sgd "G. Armani"................................... **225.00**
12" h, 6" l, "Buccaneer," man on rocky base,
green trousers, red cape, feathered hat,
right hand drawing, sword, sgd "A. Colle" **175.00**
14" h, "African Crowned Crane," one foot in
water, other held up in the air, water plants,
sgd G. Armani **175.00**
Garniture, 3 piece, 2 urns, cov, 15" h, oval center bowl, 17" l, neoclassical style figural frieze
(A).. **165.00**
Jar, Cov, 7½" h, painted continuous scene of
crusaders battling Mohammedens, cov with
gold pointed knob and painted crusader camp
scene, restruck knob, c1755, Carlos III...... **9000.00**
Jewel Box, 7½" d, 8½" h, molded bouquet of
brown and ivory flowers, four curved feet, int
with yellow and red rose bouquet **80.00**
Plaque, 10½" d, bust of Josephine Bonaparte in
relief in gold center, multicolored enamels,
pierced for hanging, c1850 (A) **38.00**
Plate, 10½" d
Floral spray in center, border relief of putti in
colors, set of 12 (A) **820.00**
Relief of figures in enamels on border, heavy
gold trim, c1850 (A)................... **40.00**
Snuff Box, 3" w, lid and base modeled as shells
and coral, int lid painted with "Education of
Cupid by Muse" in colors, gilt int, silver gilt
mts, c1745, G. Gricci (A)................ **24,420.00**
Tea Set, teapot, 8" h, ftd, creamer, 3½" h, ftd,
sugar, 5" h, ftd, cup and saucer, handleless
cup, 3" h, "First Love," molded cherubs in
various scenes with trees, raised multicolored
florals, raised dot borders, gilt rims, "R.
Capodimonte with shield and crown, Italy in
gilt," marks **175.00**
Urn
8½" h, raised classical ladies, flower swags in
colors, loop handles **50.00**
13½" h, molded semi-nude men and
women with grapes and jugs, blue and yellow pedestal, floral leaf base and top, two
gold loop handles **325.00**
16" h, baluster shape, relief of putti in garden,
ribbon twist handles, pr................. **450.00**
Urn, Cov
15" h, molded bodies of cherubs and grapes,
Bacchus head handles, floral leaf cov, pr.. **375.00**
19" h, baluster shape, relief decoration of
putti, dbl entwined handles, round foot, pr
(A)..................................... **880.00**
20" h
Multicolored relief of nudes, blue and pink
diapering, geometric design on cov with
raised banding, fruit finial, pr (A)....... **522.00**
Winged cherub handles, panels of nymphs

and cherubs in dolphin boat with two
molded heads and girls, baroque floral
relief................................. **650.00**
20½" h, molded cherubs on body, cherub
and wreath finial, two gold loop handles,
four feet sq base...................... **550.00**

c1883

CARLSBAD—GENERAL

Bohemia, now Czechoslovakia
1848 to Present

History: Carlsbad and the vicinity surrounding it was the
center of the Bohemian porcelain industry. Many factories
used the name Carlsbad in their marks despite the fact that
they were not located in the city itself. The factories manufactured household and decorative porcelains and gift
items.

Opiag, Austrian Porcelain Industry AG changed its
name to Epiag after Bohemia was removed from the Austrian Empire at the end of WWI to become part of the
newly created state of Czechoslovakia. Epiag was nationalized after WWII.

Bone Dish, pale pink and green flowers, white
ground, set of 9........................... **75.00**
Bowl, 12" d, cobalt with three maidens, cherubs,
and doves in center panel, heart-shaped
reticulations around rim, c1895 (A)........ **60.00**
Cake Plate, 11" d, pink poppies with leaves,
white ground, emb gilt rim, pierced handles,
"Austria Imperial Carlsbad" mark **65.00**
Candy Dish, 7½" l, purple open iris, fluted
white satin ground, rolled gold perforated handles..................................... **38.00**
Celery Dish, 11¾" l, 5½" w, multicolored
fruits and flowers, gold wavy edge **35.00**

**Relish Dish, 8½" l, purple flowers, green leaves,
cream ground, matte gold trim, "red Carlsbad"
mark, $22.00**

Charger, 13½" d, hp landscape scene with three maidens dancing, cherub with harp and five additional maidens in colors, pierced for hanging (A) **20.00**

Chocolate Set

Pot, 6 cups, overall floral design in colors, chips on 2 cups **165.00**

Pot, 10½" h, sugar, 5" h, creamer, 3¼" h, Angelica Kaufmann classical transfers in gold dotted cartouches, blue ground with gold leaf designs, gold handle with purple luster trim, gold borders **365.00**

Coffee Service, coffee pot, 8¾" h, creamer, sugar, 12 cups and saucers, navy blue and gilt decorated border, off-white ground, "Carlsbad Bohemia" mark, 22 pieces (A) **500.00**

Cup and Saucer, hp classical scene of four women with urn and fruit, maroon with gold fleur-de-lys design **38.00**

Cup and Saucer, Demitasse, Victorian classical scenes of women, fuchsia ground, gold trim   **65.00**

Dish

7¼" d, flower shape, blue-green irid, "Carlsbad, Made in Austria" mark (A) **55.00**

10" d, shell shape, rose and lavender flowers on pink ground **38.00**

Ewer, 6¼" h, panels of flowers and figures in colors, gold trim, "Victoria Carlsbad" mark, pr **135.00**

Oil Lamp Base, 12" h, iris design **285.00**

Pitcher

7½" h, large gray and green leaves, white ground with mauve windswept leaves, "Marx and Gutherz" mark **65.00**

9" h

Horn shaped, "Victoria, Carlsbad" mark . .   **45.00**

Hp small flowers, ivory ground **55.00**

Salt, Dbl, 3¾" l, 1¾" h, white body joined in center by handle, gold wash int, flowers on front **30.00**

Sauce Bowl, 5½" d, small pink flowers, green foliage, gold trim, sculptured scrolls, "L.S. & S Carlsbad Austria" mark **3.00**

Sugar Bowl, Cov, 6" h, 5" d, small pink flowers with green foliage, gold trim, scalloped base, leaf scroll handles and finial, "L.S. & S. Carlsbad" mark **20.00**

Sweetmeat Dish, hp multicolored florals on cream to white ground, gold geometrics and swirls, single handle, c1895 (A) **18.00**

Tea Caddy, 5½" h, signed portrait of woman, raised design on shoulders, "Victoria Carlsbad Austria" mark **75.00**

Tray

11¾" l, 7½" w, center scene of three draped women and cherub, cobalt ground, scalloped border, gold tracery, sgd "Larren" **95.00**

17" l, oval, pink, blue, and orchid flowers, gold decorations **95.00**

Tureen, 7½" h, 11½" l, tan mum design, gold trim **45.00**

Vase

7½" h, 5" w, bulbous shape, curved split top, blue clouds with flying cherubs with bow and arrows, coiled snake handle, "Victoria, Carlsbad, Austria" mark **150.00**

9½" h, center panel of four Grecian figures in cream and dark blue-green, ornate handles **48.00**

c 1894

CARLTON WARE

Stoke-on-Trent, Staffordshire, England
c1890 to Present

History: Staffordshire porcelain and earthenware were produced at the Carlton Works, Stoke-on-Trent, by a firm that traded as Wiltshow and Robinson from about 1890 until 1957, after which its name became Carlton Ware Ltd.

The background color most often used on the wares was black. Ornamental wares, including porcelain vases, with luster decorations in Oriental designs were made during the 1920s. Some pieces were decorated with bright enameled and gilt flowers in Art Deco designs.

Most products are marked with a circular printed mark with W & R/STOKE ON TRENT enclosing a swallow and topped by a crown.

Ashtray, Rouge Royale oriental scene **24.00**

Biscuit Jar

7" h, multicolored flowers, green leaves, and gold accents on satin cream ground, SP top, rim, and handle **110.00**

8¼" to handle, circle of white cameos of dancing women holding hands, floral band at top, gold beaded base, green jasper ground, SP top, rim, and handle **285.00**

9½" to handle, pottery, multicolored florals on front and back, cobalt trim at top and bottom **110.00**

Bowl

7" d, Art Deco stylized black tree with orange flowers on yellow ground **280.00**

Pitcher, 8" h, Art Deco design in blue, pink, and yellow stripes and florals, rose-beige satin ground, artist sgd, c1928, $295.00

9" d, green ground, applied yellow and brown banana feet............................ **48.00**

9¼" d

Gold, green, orange, and mauve enameled Indian temple and palm trees on int, cobalt ground, gold cross-hatched border, white enameled birds on ext.......... **275.00**

Multicolored phoenix bird in flight with oriental swirled motif on int and ext, matte pink ground........................ **225.00**

9½" l, leaf ground, red flowers......... **40.00**

10" d, ftd, int with white, blue, and pale red ducks in flight, marsh flowers and reeds, cobalt irid ground, gold rim and foot, pr (A)................................... **200.00**

Charger, 15½" d, Art Deco style girl with hoop skirt and parasol in bright colors........... **1500.00**

Dish

5" l, yellow figural leaf, marked............ **25.00**

8½" H-H, "Australian" design, orange and green molded flowerhead in center, yellow-cream ground, hairline................. **85.00**

9½" d, Rouge Royale, raised triangle in center with curved borders, orange, green, and blue enameled and gilt pagoda scene, maroon ground......................... **110.00**

10½" l

"Australian" design, small red and green leaves and branches on border, yellow-cream ground...................... **85.00**

Green molded cabbage and lettuce ground, hp red tomatoes.................... **55.00**

Oval, Rouge Royale, Art Deco style gold trim, "Wiltshaw and Robinson" mark... **115.00**

Feeding Dish, 7½" d, center multicolored scene of children on "See-Saw," 'BABY'S DISH" in black on rim............... **104.00**

Flower Frog, 5" h, purple irid glaze, marked... **20.00**

Ginger Jar, Cov, 14¾" h, painted Egyptian motifs and hieroglyphics, Egyptian in horse drawn chariot, winged maidens, gilt borders, powder blue ground, domed cov with gilt molded Isis figural knob (A)............. **3228.00**

Jar, Cov, 20" h, white, blue, and pale red ducks in flight, multicolored marsh flowers and reeds on base, irid cobalt ground, gold rims, modeled Foo dog finial, c1920 (A)............. **210.00**

Jardinaire, 13" l, oriental pagodas on islands with trees, figures and birds in enamels and gold on cobalt ground, pearlized irid int, four small feet, dbl gold handles, c1920 (A).......... **130.00**

Mug, 3¾" h, man in black hanging from brown wooded support, green grass, black hat on ground, chartreuse handle, cream ground, reverse in black "There are several Reasons for Drinking" etc........................ **35.00**

Mustard, Cov, 1¼" h, drum shaped, cream with orange base and top, black lines and drum sticks on cov....................... **195.00**

Pitcher, 3¾" h, squat shape, bands of green, blue-green, orange, gray, purple, and black, black handle....................... **125.00**

Salad Bowl, 10½" d, 4" h, red tomatoes and molded leaf green border, three lobster claw feet, unmkd....................... **95.00**

Salad Set, bowl, 9¾" d, 6¼" h, fork and spoon, 11½" l, multicolored flowers on int and ext, beige ground, SP rim............. **385.00**

Sugar Shaker, 5" h, yellow, green, and gold sheaves of wheat, orange and green top.... **40.00**

Tea Service, magenta and gilt cup and saucer,

scalloped edge, fitted case, set of 6, marked (A)...................................... **200.00**

Vase

5¼" h, Rouge Royale, hp oriental birds and trees in orange, yellow, and green enamels, ribbed bottom, matte gold handles, gold trim, raised dots on trees............... **150.00**

5⅜" h, Rouge Royale, hp enamels in oriental scene with bridge and pagoda, matte gold trim, purple ground, luster int, gold border **350.00**

5⅞" h, bulbous shape, stacked enameled hollyhocks with butterflies, cobalt ground. **225.00**

6" h, flared cylinder shape, hummingbirds and flowers in enamels and gold on cobalt ground............................. **195.00**

7" h

Gold and enamel bird and flower design, maroon luster ground, pearl int, shaped rim................................ **240.00**

Rouge Royale, pale pink luster int, gold handles, "Wiltshaw and Robinson" mark... **175.00**

10¼" h, gold and enameled pagodas, boats, bridges, and figures, blue ground, luster finish, pr.............................. **225.00**

1775-90   **c 1775-1790**

CAUGHLEY

Royal Salopian Porcelain Manufactory

Shropshire, England
c1775–1799

History: Thomas Turner, who received his training at the Worcester porcelain factory, converted an existing pottery at Caughley in Shropshire in 1772 to make possible the manufacture of porcelain products. He developed a uniformly smooth, transparent glaze that lent itself well to the transfer printed decorations. Basic Caughley porcelain has a white soapstone body.

Blue and white ware with printed transfer decorations in a Chinese design was the chief item of manufacture. The "willow pattern," c1780, and the "Broseley dragon" were two of the most characteristic and popular Caughley patterns. Sometimes the Caughley blue and white china was painted in underglaze blue as well as transfer printed. The china often was enriched with bands of gilding.

Turner established a London warehouse called the "Salopian China Warehouse" in 1780 for the sale of Caughley chinaware. Tablewares, tea and coffee services, and other utilitarian items were the chief Caughley products. Few decorative pieces were made.

In 1870 Turner brought back several French china decorators leading to a greater variety in decoration. Turner sent some of his porcelain pieces to be gilded and enameled at the Chamberlain factory at Worcester. By 1796 hard paste porcelain was introduced.

The factory was taken over by John Rose of nearby Coalport in 1799 and continued to offer whiteware for decoration at London and Coalport until its closing in 1814.

References: G.A. Godden, *Caughley & Worcester Porcelains, 1775–1800*, Herbert Jenkins, 1969.

Museums: Clive House Museum, Strewbury, England; Metropolitan Museum of Art, New York; Victoria & Albert Museum, London.

CAUGHLEY

Basket, 11⅝" l, oval, pierced sides, printed "Pine Cone" pattern on int, ext with applied florets at intersections, twisted handles and floret terminals, hairline, c1770–75, "hatched C" mark................................. 365.00

Butter Tureen, Cov, Stand, 7⅛" H-H, 4¼" h, oval shape, blue and white printed "Fench" design, applied handles on stand, tureen, and cov, c1785–90, "blue printed C" mark 1250.00

Coffee and Tea Service, Part, teapot, cov sugar bowl, saucer dish, bowl, 4 teabowls, 4 coffee cups, 4 saucers, rose sprigs on white ground, dark blue border with gilt cable, "blue S" marks (A)............................... 912.00

Coffee Cup and Saucer, Miniature, transfer printed in "Fisherman" pattern, c1785 (A) .. 290.00

Dish
8¼" d, oriental coastal village scene, blue transfer, gilt trim, "blue S" mark (A) 180.00
12" d, center painted in underglaze blue with Prince of Wales feathers accented in gilt, gilt framework of C-scrolls and lambrequins, dark blue border with gilt panels of rope twists, scrolls, and diapering, c1775–90, "blue S" mark (A)..................... 637.00

Can, Caughley, 5¾" h, blue transfer of fruit and florals, c1790, "blue C and S" marks, $450.00

Teapot, Caughley, 4½" h, blue transfer of fruit clusters, c1790, "blue S" mark, $350.00

Jug, Caughley, 9" h, dk blue chinoiserie transfer on molded cabbage leaf body, mask spout, c1790, "blue S" mark, $1200.00

Creamer, Salopian, 4¾" h, green monochrome transfer, c1820, $275.00

Teabowl and Saucer, Caughley, blue printed oriental scene, gilt rim, "blue S" mark, $185.00

Plate, Salopian, 7" d, multicolored Bird of Paradise transfer, unmkd, $225.00

Jug

3 15/16" h, blue printed "Three Flowers" pattern, sparrow beak (A)................. **456.00**

6" h, globular, blue printed rose sprays and flower sprigs, scroll molded handle and spout, "black S" mark (A)385.00

8 1/2" h, cabbage leaf molded, blue printed scene of Chinese figures fishing, chips on foot rim, c1765 (A).................... **330.00**

Jug, Mask

5 7/8" h, underglaze blue floral decoration, emb body, blue printed rim (A).......... **500.00**

6 7/8" h, cabbage leaf molded, printed with large thorny rose spray flanked by fruit sprigs, mask lip with crossed over beard, unglazed base with "S" mark (A) **720.00**

7 1/4" h, garlands of flowers enclosing gilt "TC," molded with leaves below ribbed neck, foot and rim with blue and gilt borders, c1780, underglaze "blue S" mark (A) **1275.00**

7 3/8" h, Cabbage leaf Molded

Front in blue with gentleman seated in chair holding jug, smoking pipe, sprig of vines hanging above, each side printed with view of Iron Bridge over River Severn at Broseley, int with printed Fitzhugh border, "S" mark (A) **4320.00**

Vase initial "B" with floral swags, within border of gilt scrollwork, flanked by strawberry arrangements with gilt foliage, band of pink roses at neck below gilt border, scrolling handle, decorated in Chamberlain studio at Worcester, chips to spout, c1785–90 (A)....................... **1309.00**

7 1/2" h, baluster shape, underglaze blue "Parrot Pecking Fruit" pattern, scrolling handle, c1775–80, small chips, underglaze "blue C" mark (A) **673.00**

Mug

4 3/8" h, blue printed "Fisherman" pattern, "HC" monogram, cell and dagger border, spurred loop handle (A)................. **225.00**

5 5/8" h, cylindrical, transfer printed with "La Peche," looped strap handle, c1775, "C" mark (A) **525.00**

Pickle Dish, 3 1/8" l, leaf shape, blue painted foliate motif, blue serrated rim, pr (A) **608.00**

Plate

1 3/4" d, miniature, blue painted oriental scene of pagodas on island **175.00**

8" d, scalloped, oriental scenes in circ and fan shaped panels, powder blue ground, pseudo Chinese mark, imp "salopian" (A). **540.00**

8 3/8" d, shield shaped coat-of-arms in center over banner with hawk on perch, gilt flowering branches tied with ribbon on blue border edged with gilt spear and flower design, chips, c1770, pr (A) **528.00**

Saucer Dish, 8 1/2" d, molded flutes with gilt accents (A) **35.00**

Tankard, 4 3/4" h, blue printed with "La Promenade Chinoise" and twice with "La Peche," scrolled strap handle, c1780, underglaze "blue S" mark (A) **496.00**

Taster, 2 9/16" d, blue printed "Fisherman" pattern, cell and dagger border, angular handle, "blue S" mark (A) **266.00**

Teabowl and Saucer

Blue and gilt cartouche and int rim, ribbed ext with florals and gilt, c1760–80, "blue crescent" mark **55.00**

Blue oriental transfers, gilt trim, "blue S" mark (A)................................. **93.00**

Peony and fence beside river, two birds in flight, blue and white ground, blue rims, c1770, "blue crescent" mark (A)........ **165.00**

Miniature, chinoiserie island scenes, underglaze blue, c1785 (A) **290.00**

Tea Caddy, 5" h, circ shape, "Fence" pattern, blue design, c1780–85................. **700.00**

Teapot, 9" h, ovoid, molded flutes, painted line of gilded foliage joined by blue dots (A) **100.00**

Tea Service

Miniature, teapot, jug, 3 teabowls, 4 saucers, blue printed "Fisherman" pattern, "blue S" marks (A)............................. **1250.00**

Teapot, cov, stand, sucrier, cov, jug, cake plate, 12 teabowls, 11 saucers, 12 coffee cups, fluted shapes, printed in underglaze blue with "Temple" pattern of Chinese riverscape within Fitzhugh type border edged in gold, some pieces with "S" mark, 421 pcs (A)........................... **1080.00**

Vase, 4 1/2" h, ovoid, blue transfer of chinoiserie floral motif, c1770 (A) **40.00**

Waste Bowl

5 5/8" d, underglaze blue and red enamel continuous oriental scene, "blue S" mark (A). **110.00**

6 3/4" d, reserves of flowers on blue scale ground, int painted with rose bud, c1770, "blue crescent" mark (A) **250.00**

SALOPIAN

Bowl, 7 3/4" d, milkmaid milking cow in meadow scene, panels of men at work separated by florals, brown-black transfer with polychromed enamels (A)...................... **242.00**

Creamer

3" h, deer and cottage design, brown-black transfer with polychromed enamels (A)... **49.00**

4 1/2" h, black and green transfer of Chinese family, blue rim, c1790 .... **263.00**

6" h, black transfer of maiden with urn, yellow and burnt orange accents, black and white frieze, black, white, orange, and yellow florals around rim border, c1790........ **225.00**

Cup and Saucer, deer pattern in blue, black, yellow and green transfer, chip on rim **250.00**

Cup and Saucer, Handleless

Britannia, black transfer with polychromed enamels, emb ribs (A) **40.00**

Deer in foliage in green, amber, yellow, and blue (A).............................. **55.00**

Eagle and shield design, brown-black transfers with polychromed enamels (A) **280.00**

Overall floral design, black transfers, blue rims (A)................................. **93.00**

Miniature

Youth and sheep, black transfer with polychrome enameling (A)................ **82.00**

Milk Jug, 5" h, black transfer of castle and cows, yellow-gold and blue accents, black and white geometrics on int, blue rim, c1790........ **338.00**

Pickle Dish, 5 1/2" d, shell shape, underglaze blue in "Fisherman" pattern, cell diaper border, c1780 imp "Salopian" mark (A) **224.00**

Plate, 7 1/4" d, white stag center, floral border, black transfer with polychrome enamels (A). **110.00**

Posset Pot, 4" h, brown transfer of large and small flowers highlighted by light blue, orange, yellow, and green (A)..................... **302.00**

Teabowl and Saucer
  Britannia and Columbia with floral borders in
    polychrome brown transfers, emb ribs and
    scalloped edge (A) **80.00**
  Brown transfer with polychrome of farm scene
    (A)................................ **150.00**
  Floral pattern in black transfer with poly-
    chromes, hairline on cup (A) **75.00**
  Green transfer of woodchopper on cup, barn-
    yard scene on saucer (A) **110.00**
Tea Caddy, 4" h, black transfer of deer and cot-
  tage, pink and yellow accents, missing lid ... **225.00**
Teapot
  5³⁄₈" h, milkmaid milking cow in meadow
    scene, floral lid, brown-black transfer with
    polychrome enamels (A) **137.00**
  6⁷⁄₈" h, Castleford-type shape, Nelson's Vic-
    tories at Nile, Copenhagen, and Trefalger in
    scalloped shell, flanked by two half serpents
    blowing trumpets, green-black transfer with
    red, yellow, flesh, green, and ochre accents,
    applied ochre border, swan finial, restored
    (A)................................. **550.00**
Waste Bowl, 5" d,
  2½" h, Britannia, black transfer with poly-
    chrome enamels, emb ribs (A).......... **115.00**
  Classical cartouches in brown transfers with
    three maidens, cobalt blue, yellow, green,
    and ochre flowers, int with brown transfer
    with florals **185.00**

**Plate, 10" d, gold center with cobalt ring, border
of raised gold on cobalt, set of 12, (A) $925.00**

Cup and Saucer, gold leaf and vine decoration,
  white ground, Royal Cauldon, 32 pcs....... **200.00**
Dinner Service, Part
  12 dinner plates, 12 salad plates, 11 dessert
    plates, 11 bread and butter plates, 8 soup
    bowls, 12 fruit bowls, 12 teacups and sau-
    cers, 11 demitasse cups, 10 saucers, cov
    gravy dish, 2 cov tureens, serving bowl, 2
    platters, white ground with gold rims..... **750.00**
  13 dinner plates, 8 bread and butter plates, 9
    salad plates, 13 soup bowls, 15 saucers,
    oval tray, vegetable server, 5 teacups, gilt
    Greek key banding on cream ground (A) . **165.00**
Plate
  10" d
    Cobalt blue border, extensive gold filigree,
      set of 12 (A)........................ **840.00**
    Gilt neoclassical borders, set of 10 (A).... **142.00**
    Multicolored floral design, marked **10.00**
  10½" d
    Crested with motto "Dictis Factisque Sim-
      plex," claret rim, c1920, printed marks
      "Cauldon China, England," set of 12 (A) **475.00**
    Spaniel, fronds, sky-like ground, sgd "G Pe-
      dersen," 'Cauldon England" mark...... **60.00**
  10¾" d, bone china, "Consort" pattern, red
    rim with gold designs, "Royal Cauldon Bone
    China" mark, set of 8 (A) **40.00**
Platter, 12¾" d, scene of Washington at Valley
  Forge, blue shades **395.00**
Vase, 14" h, painted seated young lady in woodland setting, gilded border, applied loop handles on shoulder, repaired, c1900, pr (A) ... **1255.00**

CAULDON ENGLAND
1905-20

CAULDON

Shelton, Hanely, England
1905–1962

History: This Staffordshire pottery, a direct descendant of
the Ridgway potteries, operated from 1905 to 1920 at
Cauldon Place, Shelton, Hanely. After John Ridgway dissolved his partnership with William, his brother, in 1830,
he operated the Cauldon Place Works. A wide variety of
china and earthenware were made including utilitarian
and decorative pieces.

  Ridgway sold to T.C. Brown-Westhead, Moore & Company in 1855. Brown-Westhead, Moore & Co. (1862–
1904) became Cauldon Ltd. in 1905. From 1920 to 1962
the firm operated as Cauldon Potteries, Ltd., at which time
it became known as Cauldon Bristol Potteries, Ltd. It was
eventually acquired by Pountney & Co. Ltd. of Boston in
1962.

Bouillon Cup and Saucer, ftd, pink roses and
  forget-me-nots, set of 6 .... **110.00**
Cabinet Plate, 8½" d, four Mallard ducks in
  flight over marshland in colors, border of
  raised scrolls and dots in gilt, blue scalloped
  rim with gilt, c1890...................... **425.00**
Cup and Saucer, Demitasse, gold designs on
  white ground **20.00**

1725 - 1800

CHANTILLY

Chantilly, France
1725–c1860

History: The Chantilly factory, established in 1725 in the
Chantilly district of France, produced soft paste porcelain.
The first manager of the works was Ciquaire Cirou who
worked under the guidance and influence of the Prince de

Conde. The factory's original purpose was to copy old designs rather than initiate new ones.

Conde's love for Japanese porcelain dictated that the first products assume the form and color of the classic Japanese porcelains. In order to achieve the strong colors of the Japanese palette, a milky glaze was developed to present a satisfactory surface for decoration.

In addition to the Japanese designs, many of the popular Meissen designs and decorations were imitated. The factory also made soft paste of old silver pieces. A lobulated body form characterized Chantilly porcelain of this period.

By the mid-18th century, the opaque glaze was replaced with a more transparent type. The decorative style now shifted to imitating the porcelains from the Sevres factory. This second glaze gave a softer look to the finished products. "Chantilly Sprig," a sketchy type blue floral motif, appeared about this time. Table services, statuettes, writing paraphernalia, and boxes and jars for the ladies dressing table were the staple products of the factory.

About 1800 the factory ceased operation. Several other factories in the area picked up the production of the most popular Chantilly designs in hard paste porcelain. These pieces were characterized by a soft pastel coloring and dull surface finish, contrasting with the early products of the original factory. They are classified under the general heading of "Chantilly."

References: W.B. Honey, *French Porcelain of the 18th Century*, Faber & Faber, 1950; George Savage, *Seventeenth & Eighteenth Century*, Hamlyn Publishing Co., Ltd., 1969.

Museums: J. Paul Getty Museum, Malibu, California; Musee Conde, Chantilly, France; Musee des Arts Decoratifs, Paris, France; Victoria & Albert Museum, London, England.

Basket
  10¼" d, blue painted flower sprays, pierced sides, undulating rim, "hunting horn" mark, pr (A) **685.00**
  11" l, oval, pierced sides and base with stylized foliage outlined in puce with panels of colored flowers, brown rim, puce and blue accented twin ribbon tied handles with acanthus leaf terminals, c1770, "hunting horn and D" mark **2200.00**

Dish, 6⅞" l, 2 applied manganese washed branches with green washed leaves, iron-red and yellow buds, mid 18th C, "red hunting horn" mark, (A) $1200.00; Teabowl, lobed body, green and yellow accented leaves, "red hunting horn" mark, (A) $525.00

Figure, 13¾" h, purple, blue, green, and pink ribbons on white ground, pink cloak lined in lt blue, gold edge, pink shoes with blue bows, gold trimmed bagpipe, mottled green and gold base, mkd, $1495.00

Bowl, 7¼" d, Kakiemon colors of iron-red, turquoise, blue, yellow, and black on front of ext with flowering plant growing behind stylized rock, reverse with three small sprigs, int with long flowering branch, three sprigs, and insect beneath brown edged petal shaped rim, hair cracks, 1735–40 (A) **2475.00**
Box, 4¼" d, Kakiemon style painted fruiting pomogranate branch, reverse with clumps of bushes, crouching rabbit finial, silver mts, cracks, c1735–45, "red hunting horn" mark. **1025.00**
Cache Pot
  5½" h, Kakiemon style and colors of seated Oriental man being served teas by three attendants, reverse with two ladies and man reading, flowered border, blue and green dragon handles, c1735 (A) **17,300.00**
  6¼" d, squirrel on hedge eating grapes, reverse with flowering prunus, Kakiemon colors, dbl branch handles ending in flowers and leaves, c1735 (A) **1080.00**
Chamber Pot, 4⅜" h, bulbous shape, orange, yellow, green, lilac, and blue florals, scrolling strap handle with trailing scroll, c1740–50, "orange enamel hunting horn" mark (A).... **2992.00**
Dish
  6⅞" l, leaf shape, two applied manganese washed branches with green washed leaves and iron-red and yellow buds extending to form handle, flowering branch over firing crack, mid 18th C, "red hunting horn" mark (A)................................. **1000.00**
  7½" d, underglaze blue floral design, emb rim (A) **38.00**
Egg Cup, 3⅜" h, lobed form, fluted bowl painted with blue flower sprigs, spirally entwined branch stem, dry blue accents, c1750................................. **1245.00**
Figure
  6¾" h, seated fat oriental man wearing white robe with pencil painted Kakiemon flowers,

fluted potpourri jar painted with squirrel and grape vine pattern, flower knob, green washed base, c1735 (A) **27,750.00**
7" h, elephant with raised trunk, white with Kakiemon decorations on rust and blue blanket across back, c1760, "red hunting horn" mark......................... **2950.00**
Finger Bowl, 4" h, lobed, fluted body, painted sprays of flowers and insect in Kakiemon colors and style, brown line rim, c1735, "brown hunting horn" mark (A) **810.00**
Flower Pot, 4" h, circ shape, Kakiemon palette with peonies growing from behind a bamboo fence, reverse with bush on oriental flowers and blades of grass, rim with flowerheads within Chinese scrolls, everted petal shaped rim, chip to rim, c1730, erased mark (A).... **1850.00**
Jar, 2¾" h, green and red painted wheat sheaves, blue and red flowerheads, c1735, "iron-red hunting horn" mark, pr (A)975.00
Jar, Cov, 3¼" h, applied branches in iron-red, blue, green, and purple, c1740, "horn" mark (A)...................... **690.00**
Master Salt, 6¼" l, oblong shape, three compartments, green, yellow, iron-red, and blue scattered flowers, raised blue and yellow scroll shaped ornament, iron-red loop border, cov missing, c1740, "red hunting horn" mark ... **1675.00**
Mug, Handleless, 2¾" h, two floral sprays in pink, purple, and blue, green leaves, brown rim, white ground, c1770 .... **225.00**
Pitcher, Cov and Bowl, pitcher, 5" h, fluted bodies, painted insects and flowers in Kakiemon colors, flower knob, silver mts, c1735, "horn" marks (A)............................. **9535.00**
Platter
6¾" H-H, blue florals, blue feathered rim, blue handles, white ground, c1755–80, 1st Period, "blue M. Migory" mark.......... **650.00**
9" l, blue florals, blue feathered rim, white ground, c1802, 2nd Period............. **550.00**
Pot de Creme, iron-red and green florals with wheat sheaf, molded floral and leaf knob, ivory ground, c1740, "iron-red hunting horn" mark.......................... **2500.00**
Potpourri
5½" w, white, modeled as melon-reeded vase beside tree trunk, applied vines and three Chinese figures, shaped base, cov missing, c1735 (A) **3872.00**
5¾" h, applied blue, green, iron-red, and purple flowering branches, draped pavilion drapery on shoulder, crack, c1740 (A).... **1133.00**
7½" h, 12⅛" l, figure of Chinese lady wearing yellow collared robe painted with Kakiemon floral sprays, reclining on yellow, turquoise, and brown mottled mound, supporting on lap spherical jar pierced with enamel edged floral, foliate, and circ openings, rococo scrollwork ormolu base, 1735–49, "crowned C" mark, repaired (A) ... **29,700.00**
8¾" h, seated naked girl with puce drape on lap, bird on hand, pierced urn at side with applied colored flowers and green leaves, tree trunk at side, rocky base, c1755..... **3700.00**
Sweetmeat Dish, 6" h, figural seated woman in yellow bodice and puce flowered dress, shell bowl on each side with brown edges and puce ext lining, green and brown washed rockwork base, c1750, "red hunting horn and L" mark **1850.00**

Table Salt, 6¼" h, baroque silver shape, three compartments, Kakiemon style with flowers, birds, and pagodas, central well with molded scroll borders in blue and yellow, hinge restored, c1740, "red hunting horn" mark (A). **1110.00**
Teabowl
1⅞" h, painted Kakiemon style of panel of flowering prunus from rockwork, reverse with lily, brown line rim, "red horn" mark (A)..................... **950.00**
Lobed body molded in green and yellow with spiraling leaves, haircrack, mid 18th C, "red hunting horn" mark (A)................ **723.00**
Tea Bowl and Saucer, lobed hex, Kakiemon enamels with prs of quails and storks with flowers, brown rims, c1730, "iron-red hunting horn" mark (A)........................ **5610.00**
Teapot, 4¼" h, bullet shape body, pastel shades of rose, yellow, blue, purple, and green with floral spray, rims edged in yellow, handle, spout, and knop with yellow blossoms, domed cov, cracked, c1755, "black hunting horn, incised J and D" marks (A).................. **495.00**
Tobacco Jar, 4" h, cylinder shape, Kakiemon colors of birds and insects in flowering plants, borders of trailing branches, c1740, "hunting horn" mark (A)........................... **3576.00**
Wine Cooler, 5⅝" h, front with Kakiemon palette of iron-red, yellow, turquoise, blue, and black with squirrel nibbling grapes from vine growing between banded hedges, reverse with kylin biting tail of shou-medallion kite, black stippled border of flowering manganese branches on lower body, manganese growling bear head handles, open mouths with yellow int and iron-red protruding tongues, 1735–40, "iron-red hunting horn" mark, pr (A) **10,450.00**

c1752-1769 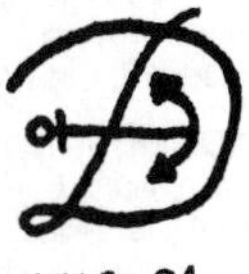   1769-84

CHELSEA

London, England
c1745–1769

History: As early as 1745, soft paste porcelains were being manufactured at Chelsea in London, one of the most famous English porcelain factories. Nicholas Sprimont, originally a silversmith, was manager of the factory for most of its history. Chelsea porcelains were the most richly decorated of English 18th century ceramics. Pieces were ornate and made for the higher class market.

Various periods of Chelsea porcelain are classified according to the anchor-like mark. But before these were used, there was an incised triangle mark, c1745, and a painted mark of a trident piercing a crown.

From 1749 to 1752, a "raised-anchor" mark was used. This mark was relief molded on a small applied oval pad. Porcelains of this period have the tin-added glaze and mostly are decorated with Oriental motifs or simple, floral designs.

The "red-anchor" period (1752–56) has the anchor

painted directly on the porcelain. Small light colored "moons" can be seen on these porcelains when held up to the light. Animal fables and botanical studies were characteristic of this period along with florals and Oriental motifs.

The Chelsea "gold-anchor" period dates between c1786 and 1769. Porcelains of this era were richly decorated and ornately gilted. The glazes tend to be thickly applied.

The anchor period dates are only approximations. More than half of all Chelsea porcelains had no mark at all.

William Duesbury of the Derby factory purchased the Chelsea factory in 1770. The wares of the 1770–1784 period are called "Chelsea-Derby." Because of the interaction of these two factories and the interchange of molds, clay, and workmen, it is difficult to distinguish between the Chelsea and Derby porcelains of this period. Further complications resulted when Duesbury used the Chelsea gold anchor mark on some Derby pieces. A "D" and anchor mark also was used, as was a crowned anchor mark. By 1784 the last of the Chelsea works were demolished and the molds and workers transferred to Derby.

References: John C. Austin, *Chelsea Porcelain at Williamsburg*, Colonial Williamsburg Foundation, 1977; John Bedford, *Chelsea & Derby China*, Walker & Co., 1967; Yvonne Hackenbroch, *Chelsea and other English Porcelains, Pottery and Enamel in the Irwin Untermyer Collection*, Harvard University Press, 1957; William King, *Chelsea Porcelain*, Benn Brothers, 1922; F. Severne Mackenna, *Chelsea Porcelain, The Triangle & Raised Anchor Wares*, F. Lewis, 1948; F. Severne Mackenna, *Chelsea Porcelain, The Red Anchor Wares*, F. Lewis, 1951; F. Severne Mackenna, *Chelsea Porcelain, The Gold Anchor Period*, F. Lewis, 1952.

Museums: Colonial Williamsburg Foundation, Williamsburg, Virginia; Fitzwilliam Museum, Cambridge, England; Gardiner Museum of Ceramic Art, Toronto, Canada; Henry E. Huntington Library & Art Gallery, San Marino, California, (gold anchor); Museum of Fine Arts, Boston, Mass.; Seattle Art Museum, Seattle, Wash.; Victoria & Albert Museum, London, England; Wadsworth Atheneum, Hartford, Ct.; Walters Art Gallery, Baltimore, Maryland.

REPRODUCTION ALERT: Samson made copies of Chelsea pieces, but these were generally marked as copies. Many forgeries and imitations are seen every year bearing red or gold anchors.

Bowl
    6⅜" d, cabbage leaf, ext molded with overlapping leaves shading from dark green to yellow, puce midribs rising from puce and yellow footrim, int painted in pastel shades of rose, yellow, blue, purple, green, iron-red and gray with floral bouquet and six scattered sprigs, c1755, "red anchor" mark (A) 7700.00
    7" d, puce int and ext with sprays and scattered sprigs of garden flowers, ext molded with overlapping petals, 1752–58, "red anchor" mark (A)....................... 956.00
Box, Cov
    3⁷/₁₆" h, 3³/₈" d, molded as rose with overlapping petals feathered in shaded pink, rising from green calyx forming foot, cov with rose colored center beneath pink rosebud sprig knop, green and white stem with gray veined green leaves, c1755, red anchor period (A) 6600.00
    3½" h, 4⁵/₁₆" l, lobed yellow melon fruit

Scent Bottle, 3⅛" h, "Girl in a Swing," yellow bodice, white shirt, purple apron, rose sprigged skirt, green tree stump support with leafy pink roses, gold mtd neck and rose stopper, inscribed "J'AIME LA DOUCEUR," original case, c1755, (A) $5700.00

molded with veining, shaded and mottled in green, short green stem on bowl, cov with brown snail knob with white shell striped in black and maroon, c1755, red anchor period (A) 12,100.00
Box, Cov, and Stand, 5⅛" d, 9" l, sunflower head forms box, shaded green leaf base, yellow and white petals, cov of developing seeds in brown shading to plum, leaf knob, stand is open blossom with stem handle and two attached leaves, knob repaired, c1755, "brown anchor" mark on stand 12,500.00
Cream Jug, 4½" h, molded fluted int, Kakiemon style flowering prunis branch with insects, scalloped rim with wavy iron-red hatched and turquoise dot border on int over iron-red and gilt flowerheads, c1752 (A)............... 6700.00
Dish
    6" d, sunflower shape, open purple brown centered flowerhead of yellow edged petals, ribbon tied green stalk handle with spray of colored flowers and foliage, c1755, "red anchor" mark (A) 4594.00
    6¼" d, ten sided, blue, yellow, and iron-red bird perched on blue rock, iron-red and salmon phoenix above, flowering branches at sides, border of iron-red and gilt flowerheads, brown line rim, c1753 (A) 715.00
    6⅝" d, ten sided, Kakiemon style, painted in shades of iron-red, salmon, blue, turquoise, pale yellow, and black with flying fox above squirrel nibbling grapevines growing on banded hedges, brown edged rim with border of colorful florettes, 1753–55, "brown anchor" mark (A) 880.00
    6¹⁵/₁₆" d, green and yellow with sprig of mulberry leaves with two bean pods, two iron-red, blue, puce, brown, and gray insects, two ladybirds, brown edged fluted rim, 2

hair cracks, c1755, "Hans Sloane, red anchor" mark (A)........................ **3025.00**

7⅛" d, lobed circ, floral spray, sprig, leaf, floret, and fly, brown edged rim, restored rim chips, c1752 (A).................... **650.00**

8⅝" d, painted naturalistic flower bouquet with scattered flower sprays, cartouche molded rim lined in gilt and puce painted with four groups of exotic birds, c1760, "gold anchor" mark, pr (A)............. **825.00**

9" l, leaf shaped, overlapping purple veined leaves attracting winged insects and caterpillars, applied green twig handles with curling tendrils, white ground, c1755, pr (A). **11,814.00**

9¼" l, leaf shaped, center with spray of flowers in rose-pink, blue, yellow, amd ironred, stem and veining in two shades of rosepink, rim shading fom yellow to green, c1755, "red anchor" mark.............. **1250.00**

9⅝" l
Oval, center with bouquet and scattered flowers in border of molded trailing vine and green leaves, purple accents, grape bunches in shaped chocolate brown rim, c1760, "red anchor" mark (A)........ **935.00**

Silver shape, painted flower branches and floral bouquet, scattered flowerheads, brown lined molded rim, scalloped handle, c1752–56, pr.................... **1500.00**

9¾" l, oval, painted flower sprays and scattered sprigs, shaped rim with brown line border, c1756, "red anchor" mark (A).... **855.00**

10¾" d, 10⅝" d, scalloped, painted in shades of rose, yellow, mauve, green, ironred, and gray with floral bouquet, scattered sprigs, and single butterfly or three shaded insects, brown edged rim, c1754, "red anchor" marks, pr...................... **1400.00**

11³⁄₁₆" l, cabbage leaf, rose colored mid rib with molded ribbing, continues to form curled stem handle, shades of rose, yellow, blue, green, iron-red, mauve, and black, crimped rim shading from dark green to yellow, c1756, red anchor period (A)....... **6050.00**

11⅜" l, kidney shape, painted in shades of purple, rose, iron-red, turquoise, yellow, blue, green, brown, and gray with bird in flight above three exotic birds perched on branches of small tree growing from rock and ground shrubbery, gilt rim, 1760–65, "gold anchor" mark (A)................. **1650.00**

11¾" l, oval, molded basketweave body, molded chartreuse stemmed yellow wheat shaded in purple, scattered puce, purple, and tan feathers, brown edged rim, c1756, "red anchor" mark (A).................. **1045.00**

Egg Cup, 2⅛" h, miniature urn form, spray and sprigs of colored flowers, brown rim, c1755, "red anchor and 5" mark (A)............. **2150.00**

Figure
4" h, two children playing with cards, blue and white (A)............................. **123.00**

5⅛" h, Winter modeled as old man in fur lined yellow peaked cap, white overcoat, purple tunic, black shoes, holding basket of coal, circ base with applied leaves, c1756, "red anchor" mark (A)................. **1430.00**

5¾" h
Boy playing flute, black tricorn hat, blue neckerchief, yellow coat and red

breeches, pouch on shoulder, seated on tree stump base with gilt scroll molding, c1755, "red anchor" mark (A)........ **2200.00**

Chinese musicians modeled as boy playing piccolo (missing) in puce flowered robe with black cuffs seated on flowered encrusted stump, girl playing drum (beater missing) in yellow lined flowered coat, green trousers, c1755, "red anchor" mark, pr (A) **4950.00**

5¾" l, white Sphinx wearing soft cap over hair tied in chignon and falling over shoulders, lightly covered in drapery clasped at one side, tail curling under left leg, recumbent on rect mound base, unglazed int, 1749–52, raised anchor period (A)...... **11,000.00**

6" h, finch in green, yellow, purple, and puce plummage, perched on white tree stump with painted scattered flowers, c1752 (A). **10,120.00**

6⅝" h, Cupid holding heart on tasseled cushion or holding pr of doves, tree stump support, raised scrolling base, repairs, c1765, "gold anchor" mark, pr (A)............. **920.00**

6⅞" l, "Spring" as two putti seated on rockwork, one holding upturned basket spilling colored flowers, other holding flower, partially covered with gilt edged white drapery, applied colored flowers and foliage to base, restored, c1754 (A).................... **1600.00**

7" h
Actor in pale yellow cloak with floral sprigs, plumed pink hat, white shirt, blue shoulder knot, green breeches with blue bows, oval basket, restored, c1755, Meissen style (A)............................ **1645.00**

Five children dancing around well, blue and white (A)............................. **124.00**

Tyrolean dancers, girl with puce bodice, white apron, purple skirt, man in plumed hat, mask, white vest, green sleeves, yellow breeches, gilt scroll molded base with applied flowers, repairs and chips, c1756, "red anchor" mark (A)............... **2200.00**

7½" h
Boy in yellow lined pink vest and red breeches seated on overturned basket of vegetables, eating from bowl on yellow keg, girl in yellow lined pink hat, green bodice, pink skirt, basket at feet, cherry tree in ground, scroll molded base with gilt accents, chips, c1759, "red anchor" mark (A) **3080.00**

Seated nurse in white cap, gray bodice, flowered apron and pink skirt, nursing baby wrapped in red ribboned blanket, rect base with gilt scrolls, cracks, c1752, "red anchor" mark (A)............... **5500.00**

7⅝" h, Mars wearing plumed helmet, brightly colored tunic, long cloak, scroll molded mound base, c1756, "red anchor" mark (A) **1338.00**

7¾" h, masquerader as a bird-catcher in yellow straw hat and jacket, purple waistcoat, turquoise breeches, holding birdcage, bag slung over shoulder, gilt scroll edged base applied with flowers and foliage, chips to leaves and flowers, c1760 (A) **4862.00**

8" h, white owl perched on rockwork base, c1750 (A) **22,000.00**

8⅝" h, two children struggling with fish

shaded in green and puce, one boy standing, one lying beside him on rocky base with blue flower and leaf sprigs, "red anchor" mark (A) 1350.00

Finger Bowl, 2⅝" h, with underdish, 6" d, painted peony and honeysuckle bouquet with scattered sprigs, brown line scalloped rims, c1755, "red anchor" mark (A) 1760.00

Ice Pail, bombe shape, molded purple grape bunches and green vines, two painted flower bouquets, gilt line and gadrooned rim, shell molded handles, crack in handle, c1755, "red anchor" mark, pr (A) 4950.00

Jug, 5⅜" h, silver shape, lobed baluster body, bright colored flowering branches, foot applied with trailing fruiting strawberry plant, restored, 1745–49, incised "triangle" mark (A) 6170.00

Plate
8¼" d
Figs and cob nuts in naturalistic shades, wavy rim edged in brown, "brown anchor" mark (A) 612.00

Scattered moths and insects in center, three panels with exotic birds, puce scrolls, feather molded edge in turquoise and gilding, c1760, "gold anchor" mark 1875.00

8½" d
Hans Sloane, painted yellow flowers with green leaves, insects and butterfly, brown edged shaped rim, crack in rim, c1755, "red anchor" mark (A)................ 2100.00

James Giles style brightly painted center of red and yellow exotic bird perched on rock with leafy bough, two birds on feather molded border lined in brown and green, c1760–65, "brown anchor" mark (A) 550.00

Painted leafy stem with purple flowers and buds, three floral sprigs, feather scroll molded rim accented in brown and turquoise, c1755–60, "brown anchor" mark (A) 1110.00

8⅝" d, Hans Sloane, two painted pears with brown and green leafy branch, scattered insects and flower sprays, brown line shaped rim, c1755, "red anchor and J.O." mark (A) 2530.00

8¾" d, iron-red, turquoise, blue, yellow, and lilac with oriental flowers growing from rockwork, butterfly above, shaped rim with smaller insects between flowering branches, brown-line border, chips, 1752–58, "red anchor" marks, set of 5 (A) 2125.00

8⅞" d, botanical, shades of puce, yellow, blue, green, brown, and black, three insects beside large floral sprig, brown edged rim, c1759, gold anchor period (A)........... 3025.00

9" d
Flowers issuing from rockwork and butterfly painted in Kakiemon colors, shaped border with flowering branches and insects, shaped brown rim, c1755, "red anchor" mark (A) 1650.00

Multicolored floral sprays and sprigs, scroll molded rim accented in blue and gilt, c1765, "gold anchor" mark (A)........ 400.00

Painted center bouquet and scattered flower sprigs, green and brown feather molded border, c1756, "brown anchor" mark, pr (A) 550.00

9¼" d, center arrangement of flowers and fruit, rim molded with scroll edged panels of colorful bouquets alternating with insects, scalloped edge, c1765, "gold anchor" marks, pr (A)......................... 895.00

Relish Tray, 9½" l, leaf shape, green, yellow, and iron-red butterflies, insects, and leaves, white ground, c1770, pr (A) 605.00

Salt, 6¾" h, modeled as actor in pink plumed hat, yellow floral cape, green breeches, seated on rockwork base, open basket as salt holder, chips, 1756 (A) 605.00

Sauceboat
7⁵⁄₁₆" l, leaf shaped body, molded at base with pale puce strawberry vine with iron-red berries, two purple centered yellow and blue blossoms, three leaves shading from green to yellow, int with bouquet and sprigs of flowers and leaves, four short feet, brown edged rim, c1755, "red anchor" mark (A) 550.00

7½" l, with underdish, 9" l, strawberry leaf spray and two buds on int, painted flower bouquet and scattered sprays on ext, green stalk handle with applied foliage and flowers, four feet molded and painted with flowers and buds, stand with green branch handle painted with flower bouquet on puce molded veining, brown line rims, c1752, "red anchor" marks (A)......... 2750.00

Saucer Dish
4⁷⁄₁₆" w, oct, "Lady in a Pavilion" pattern, Kakiemon palette of iron-red, turquoise, blue, black, and gold with bird flitting above seated Japanese lady looking toward large jar beneath draped and tasseled roof of pavilion, 1750–52, raised anchor period (A). 1430.00

8¼" d, 8⅜" d, Hans Sloane, painted with large shaded green leaf sprig surrounded by puce, yellow, blue, pale iron-red, and gray insects, scalloped rim, edged in brown, in Meissen manner, c1754, red anchor period, pr (A)..............................10,450.00

Scent Bottle
3⅜" h, "Girl in a Swing" harlequin, brightly colored checkered costume, black mask, holding slapstick and beaker, pale yellow ground flowered barrel at his side, part of base missing, early 1750s (A)........... 2431.00

3½" h, Orpheus standing before flowering tree stump, sash inscribed "MELODIE AMOUREUSE," lyre supported on head of lion, wolf and dog at feet, squirrel on branch behind, underside with gilt flower spray, pink rose stopper, c1765 (A) 7190.00

Soup Plate, 9⅛" w, oct, Kakiemon style, iron-red and gold phoenix in flight above yellow, blue, and iron-red ho-ho bird perched on turquoise-green rock amidst flowering shrubbery in center, brown-edged rim with four iron-red and gold blossoming black prunus branches alternating with flowering branches, c1754, "red anchor" mark (A).................... 2750.00

Sugar Bowl, 4" d, iron-red, blue, green, and yellow "Quail" pattern, fluted body, rim chips, c1752 (A) 2200.00

Sweetmeat Dish, 5¾" w, "Blind Earl" pattern, gray-veined chartreuse and yellow leaves, gilt edged scalloped rim, two green and puce rosebuds, smaller spray of leaves, twig handle, c1755, "red anchor" marks, pr (A) 4125.00

Teabowl, 2 1/8" h, sprig of pink flowers on front with gray veined and yellow shaded green leaves, reverse with sprig of iron-red buds and green leaves, center of int with traces of blossom, scalloped rim, gilt dentil edge, c1756, "red anchor" mark (A).................... **660.00**

Teabowl, Oct

Painted Kakiemon style alternating panels of flowering plants in iron-red, blue, and turquoise, c1750–52 (A)................... **1150.00**

Scene of figures, a church, and buildings on riverbank, reverse with floral sprigs, brown rim, chip, wear to int, c1752 (A)........ **1215.00**

Teabowl and Saucer

Exotic birds in parkland, array of insects hovering above, c1755, "red anchor" marks, pr (A)..................................... **2431.00**

Fluted, gilt scroll edged panels reserving colored flowers, claret ground with ribboned flower festoons in tooled gilding, c1770, Chelsea-Derby, "red conjoined anchor and D" mark (A)........................... **740.00**

Teacup and Saucer, oct, "The Lion and Mouse" in continuous river landscape in brown, green, yellow, blue, and black, scroll handle, int with brown beetle and blue, yellow, and green floral sprig, saucer with "The Fox and Grapes" within iron-red roundel surrounded by yellow, purple, blue, and green floral sprigs, reverse with yellow ground, rim in chocolate brown, c1752, painted by Jefferyes Hamett O'Neale, raised anchor period (A) **11,000.00**

Teapot, 4 3/4" h, hex, "Lady in a Pavilion" pattern, Kakiemon style with oriental lady seated by a bird cage in pavilion, continuous chevron border, cov with song bird going towards cage, knobbed finial, c1750–52, "raised anchor" mark inside cov **56100.00**

Tureen, Cov

4 7/8" l, lettuce shape, molded as overlapping leaves ribbed in puce, edged in chartreuse shading to pale yellow, cov with leaf curled to form knob, c1755, "red anchor" mark (A) **9900.00**

5 5/16" l, 5 1/8" h, cauliflower shape, modeled with white florettes enclosed by ribbed leaves shaded in spring-green, hair cracks, c1755, "red anchor" mark (A)..........**14,300.00**

Vase

5 3/4" h, hex, pear shape base with slender neck, Kakiemon colors and style floral sprays and prunus branches, border of scrollwork and floral lappets, c1750–52 (A)................................... **8140.00**

7 3/8" h, seated shepherd playing bagpipes to his lass, keg at his feet, reverse with bouquet of flowers, swelling neck with pierced rococo handles with gilding, rect foot, turquoise ground, neck restored, c1765, "gold anchor" mark (A) **765.00**

Wine Cooler, 7 7/16" h, 7 9/16" h, painted in shades of iron-red, blue, puce, mauve, yellow, green, and gray on front and reverse with floral bouquet, sides and stepped circ foot with small sprigs, chartreuse shaded branch form handles terminating in sprays of brown and yellow centered blue forget-me-nots and leaves, brown edged rim, bottom int with traces of floral decoration, c1756, "red anchor" marks, pr (A)...................... **9350.00**

CHILDREN'S WARE

English/German
Late 17th C to Present

History: Initially miniature English china dinnerware sets were made primarily to furnish miniature decorative rooms. By the late 19th century the emphasis shifted. Most of these dinnerware and tea sets now were made as children's playthings. They served a dual purpose, first as playthings and second as a means of teaching the social graces to children in families of means.

Children's dinnerware sets were made in two basic sizes. One size was used by children to entertain their friends. A smaller size was used when playing with dolls. Various designs were used on these sets, including historical scenes, moral and educational phrases, botanical lessons, and art works of famous illustrators.

Children's feeding dishes, often divided into sections, were made during the late 19th and early 20th century, and used for children's meals. Many have a unit to hold hot water to keep the food warm during the meal. These dishes were designed with colorful animals, nursery rhymes, and children's activities to make mealtime fun for the child.

German children's dishes also were designed with rhymes, animals, children, and florals. Paints, decals, and lusters were used in abundance on these dishes. Among the leading German manufacturers was the R.S. Prussia factory of Schlegelmilch.

References: Doris Anderson Lechler, *Children's Glass Dishes, China, & Furniture,* Collector Books, 1983; Doris Anderson Lechler, *English Toy China,* Antique Publications, 1990; Lorraine May Punchard, *Child's Play,* published by the author, 1982; Margaret & Kenn Whitmyer, *Children's Dishes,* Collector Books, 1984.

Butter Dish, "Asiatic Pheasant" pattern, blue transfer................................. **145.00**

Cake Plate, 7 1/2" H-H, gray, brown, and blue scene of seven mice on branch, yellow roses and shadow leaves, black trim and handles, Bavaria................................. **55.00**

Chamber Pot

5 1/2" d, "Athens" pattern, med blue transfer, "H.H.& M." mark **150.00**

Pitcher and Bowl Set, pitcher, 7 3/4" h, bowl, 10 3/4" d, transfer of alternating brown and green vines with red and green fruit, raised English Reg mark, $75.00

Plate, 6½" d, black transfer with orange and yellow accents, raised flowerhead border, unmkd, $115.00

6½" d, 4½" h, printed with "Little Red Riding Hood" and "Jack and Jill" rhymes, inscribed "Morning Exercise" on bottom, spatter trim (A)............................. 165.00

6⅞" d, circ body, blue and white with three vignettes of birds or insect in flight above pavilions or cottages amongst trees and shrubbery at river's edge, loop handle with heart shaped terminal, blue ground border of stylized demiflowerheads on rim, int with central peony sprig, c1765, Bow (A) 495.00

8¾" d, multicolored florals in garden scene transfer, gilt trim, white ground, "Royal Staffordshire Pottery Dickinsen Ltd, England" mark................................. 60.00

Chocolate Set

Pot, 6" h, creamer, sugar, 5 cups and saucers, shaded irid blue to purple, black handles, white int, c1920, "Rudolstadt B, Made in Germany with crown" mark............. 140.00

Pot, 6¾" h, sugar, creamer, 6 cups and saucers, irid white, blue, pink, and green birds, blue feet, finials, and handles, c1890–1900, Germany mark.......................... 450.00

Condiment Set, 6 small containers, 4 large containers, vinegar cruet, cov salt box, red, purple, and yellow flowers on front, gold name and outline trim, "GERMANY" marks........... 275.00

Creamer, tea leaf ironstone on lily of the valley blank.................................... 195.00

Crockery Set, bean pot, coffee pot, roaster, and plate, brown and tan glazes 155.00

Cup and Saucer

Children playing with toys, multicolored scene on paneled and scrolled body, "Bavaria, Germany, U.S. Zone" mark 10.00

Multicolored scene of children marching with infant, "One Foot Up and One Foot Down, That's the Way to London Town" on cup and saucer, "Germany" mark............. 75.00

Swirl mold with multicolored cherubs, pink luster trim, figural bird whistle handle, "Germany" marks 125.00

Handleless, tea leaf ironstone on lily of the valley blank............................. 125.00

Cup Plate, 4⅝" d, "Constant dropping wears away stones and little strokes fall great oaks," green transfer with polychromes (A)........ 71.00

Dinner Service

15 piece, "Humphrey's Clock," blue transfers, Ridgway............................... 395.00

16 piece, cherubs in center, fruit and floral border, "E.S. Prov. Saxe" marks.......... 295.00

19 piece, "Fishers" pattern, brown transfers, Malkin 360.00

22 piece, floral design in purple transfers, c1860, Morley......................... 550.00

26 piece, leaves and vines in black transfers with pink, green, and yellow accents, pink rims, c1860, Dimmock................. 550.00

35 piece, cov soup tureen with ladle and tray, pr of cov gravy tureens and trays, pr of cov oval vegetable dishes, ftd compote, pr of gravy boats, pr of oval open vegetable bowls, 5 graduated platters, 5 luncheon plates, 5 soup bowls, 6 dinner plates, brown "Dart" design transfer border, imp "Copeland" marks (A)........................ 357.00

36 piece, "Maidenhair Fern" pattern, green transfers on white ground............... 275.00

51 piece, teapot, sugar bowl, creamer, waste bowl, 4 cups and saucers, soup tureen, 2 gravy tureens with trays, 2 gravy boats, ftd compote, 4 small plates, 4 med plates, 8 large plates, 4 soups, 6 graduated platters, 2 open vegetable dishes, 2 plates, "Blue Bands" pattern, Dimmock (A) 1000.00

Dinner Service, Part

5 piece, 2 sq cov vegetable dishes, 2 oct platters, rect vegetable, blue "English Scenes" pattern, Minton 700.00

10 piece, cov gravy tureen, 2 sq vegetable dish bases, platter, 2 small plates, 3 large plates, soup bowl, blue "Kite Flyers" pattern (A)................................. 550.00

16 piece, soup tureen with tray, ftd compote, gravy boat, rect vegetable dish, 3 graduated platters, 4 med and 4 large plates, blue seaweed design (A) 520.00

Dish, 6¼" d, multicolored house in center and "This is the House Jack Built," border of cannon, puppy on cushion, baker, "red Germany" mark 20.00

Feeding Dish

6" d, mother duck and ducklings in wheelbarrow, verse, sgd "Mabel Attwell," Shelley.. 45.00

7" d, scenes of Dutch children in colors, "JMW-England Falcomaware" mark 25.00

7½" d, blue transfer of five children at fence, green "BABY'S DISH" on rim, green rims, Royal Doulton 85.00

Mug

2⅛" h

"A Present from the Potteries" flanked by brown and yellow bands, 19th C (A)... 165.00

Creamware, black transfer of two girls and "A Present for my dear Girl," red border (A) 247.00

2¼" h

"Boys at Play" in blue-gray transfer (A)... 60.00

Mother with children scene, black transfer, c1840 .... 135.00

"VICTORIA," transfer of girl on prancing horse (A)........................... 230.00

2⅜" h

"PEACEABLE KINGDOM" and biblical saying, child with lion, red transfer (A)..... 100.00

"The Little Plunderer" in multicolored transfer................................. 165.00

2½" h

"A Token of Respect," green, red, and yellow wreath........................ 90.00

Boys with sailboat, boys on fence, brown transfer, c1840 .... **135.00**

Brown transfer of two children, cat, and dog (A) **33.00**

"Deer Stalking," black transfer.......... **185.00**

"For a Good Boy," blue floral cartouche, c1840 .... **250.00**

Gilbert and Sullivan "H.M.S. Pinafore" transfer **165.00**

"Henry" in wreath, black transfer (A)..... **165.00**

"He who rides may fall," boy riding a dog, rust transfer, pink luster border (A)..... **132.00**

"Hickory, Dickory, Dock" transfer........ **24.00**

"Jolly Sailor," black transfer with blue, green, and yellow, c1840–60.......... **250.00**

Maypole, couple standing in woods, blue transfer with red, green, and yellow accents (A).......................... **100.00**

Multicolored scene of two women, man, and doves, c1820.................... **195.00**

Scalloped cartouche on girl on swing and girl pushing, brown transfer, burnt orange int rim, c1840 .... **135.00**

Spatterware, peafowl in yellow, blue, and red, medallion on front with brown "A Present for Charles' (A).............. **1017.00**

Tea leaf ironstone, unmarked, England.... **250.00**

"The Seasons-February," black transfer ... **175.00**

"Willow Root" pattern of Chinese man sailing boat past a fenced garden with rockwork and trees, blue and white, ribbed loop handle, 1751–55, Worcester (A) **4605.00**

2⅝" h, multicolored decal of Humpty Dumpty on wall and gold "Humpty Dumpty Sat on a Wall, Humpty Dumpty Had a Great Fall" **42.00**

2¾" h

"Field Sports No. 2", gray transfer of hunting dogs, floral transfer on int rim, c1850s, Edge Malkin **235.00**

"Playing With Pompey," girl and puppy, black transfer with red, yellow, and green enamel accents **120.00**

2⅞" h, white scene of "THE KILL" on blue ground, handle crack (A)............... **55.00**

3" h

"Going to market," 'Come away Pompey," green transfer, c1850–70 .... **75.00**

"Poultry Feeding," green transfer, c1840 . **135.00**

Plate

3" d, "Indian Chief's," brown transfer, emb rim (A) **125.00**

3¼" d, red, black, and green enameled sprig in center, emb lily pad shoulder, blue feather edge (A) **77.00**

4" d, Willow pattern, blue.................. **8.00**

4¾" d, "Hey Diddle Diddle" nursery rhyme, brown transfer, "Hanley, Great Britain" mark................................ **30.00**

4⅞" d, "Columbia Shape," ironstone, 1855, imp "Joseph Goodwin, Ironstone China" mark.................................. **28.00**

5" sq, oct, green transfer of young girl with lyre, emb border (A)................... **55.00**

5½" d

"Little May," red transfer............... **35.00**

"Punch & Judy" design in colors, Allerton **30.00**

5⅝" sq, oct, black transfer with polychromes of boy with two dogs, emb border, purple luster rim (A) **93.00**

5¾" sq, oct, black transfer with polychromes of "Robinson Crusoe," emb border (A)... **82.00**

7" d

Jesus with scriptures, c1850, Staffordshire. **40.00**

Scene of children hanging out wash, Germany **24.00**

9" d, multicolored scene of man playing flute, pig dancing, verse, "Fenton" mark **15.00**

11" d, "Landscape" pattern, divided, blue and white, "M.R. Midwinter" mark.......... **20.00**

Platter

12" l, multicolored decal of Dutch children, blue line rim...................... **20.00**

15½" d, Aesop's Fable, "Fox and Sick Lion," brown transfer, Copeland and Garrett, 1833 .... **85.00**

Tea Service

3 piece, teapot, creamer, sugar, "Southern Belles" pattern....................... **150.00**

4 piece

Teapot, creamer, sugar, cup and saucer, "Stag" pattern, pink transfers.......... **90.00**

Teapot, 3⅛" h, cov sugar bowl, creamer, waste bowl, blue applied floral sprigs on gray ground **250.00**

Teapot, 3⅜" h, creamer, cov sugar bowl, cup and saucer, blue, green, and yellow floral design, gilt trim (A)............. **375.00**

Teapot, 4¼" h, sugar bowl, 2 cups and saucers, "Red Star" transfers, Staffordshire (A) **170.00**

5 piece, teapot, 2⅞" h, creamer, sugar, 2 cups and saucers, red oriental transfer with polychrome enameling and purple luster trim, Staffordshire (A).................. **275.00**

6 piece

Teapot, cov sugar, creamer, 3 cups and saucers, pink luster "Merry Christmas" design, "Leuchtenburg, Germany" marks . **165.00**

Teapot, creamer, sugar bowl, 2 cups and saucers, tray, dark blue and white "Maiden Hair Fern" pattern, England... **275.00**

Teapot, cov sugar, creamer, 3 cups and saucers, blue and white, child with dog cartouche, birds, and flowers............ **245.00**

7 piece

Teapot, 4½" h, sugar bowl, creamer, 4 cups and saucers, "Tracery Type," ironstone, bulbous body style, embossed scallops, 1890s, unmkd............... **195.00**

Teapot, 5¼" h, creamer, sugar bowl, 4 cups and saucers, R.S. Prussia mold #517, pink and yellow roses......... **450.00**

8 piece

Teapot, cov creamer, 2 cups and saucers, 4 plates, Happifats design, Royal Rudolstadt............................. **325.00**

Teapot, creamer, sugar, 5 cups and saucers, brown and white spatterware, Staffordshire............................. **260.00**

9 piece

Teapot, cov sugar bowl, waste bowl, 2 plates, 4 cups and saucers, oriental scenes on Farm Scotland blanks, "John Carr" marks **195.00**

Teapot, 4 cups and saucers, 4 plates, blue, green, red, and gold brush stroke design, Davenport.......................... **195.00**

10 piece

Teapot, 4¾" h, creamer, cov sugar bowl,

waste bowl, plate, 5" d, 5 cups and saucers, "Stag" pattern, blue transfers 325.00
Teapot, 5 1/4" h, creamer, 3" h, cov sugar, 4 3/4" h, plate, 5 1/2" d, 6 cups and saucers, "Punch and Judy" design, brown transfers, Allerton 325.00
11 piece, teapot, 5 1/4" h, creamer, 3 1/4" h, cov sugar bowl, 4 1/2" h, 4 plates, 5 1/2" d, 4 cups and saucers, "Little Mae" design blue transfers, "Staffordshire England" marks 255.00
13 piece
Teapot, 3" h, wastebowl, creamer, sugar, 5 cups, 4 saucers, black transfer decorated with neoclassical figures on cream ground with maroon highlights, 2nd qtr 19th C (A) 247.00
Teapot, 3 1/2" h, creamer, 3" h, cov sugar bowl, 2 3/4" h, 5 plates, 3 1/4" d, 5 cups and saucers, "Dutch Children" design, c1900 .... 150.00
16 piece, teapot, creamer, cov sugar bowl, slop bowl, 6 plates, 6 cups and saucers, brown stick spatter design with brown bands, white ground, England 485.00
17 Piece, teapot, 5" h, sugar bowl, 3 3/4" h, creamer, 2 5/8" h, waste bowl, 3" d, 6 plates, 4 7/8" d, 4 handled cups, 2" h, 3 saucers, 4 1/2" d, "Chelsea Type," ironstone, sprays of lavender violets and gold luster trim, 1880s, unmarked 185.00
18 piece, teapot, creamer, sugar, waste bowl, 6 cups and saucers, 2 plates, 6 spoons, Chintz pattern in black transfers on white ground, Ridgway 440.00
Tea Service, Part, 14 piece, sugar bowl, 4 3/4" h, creamer, 3 3/8" h, 6 cups and saucers, 6 plates, 4 1/4" d, "Washington Shape" with rope embossment, ironstone, unmarked, John Meir & Son 265.00
Tea Set, teapot, sugar bowl, creamer, Willow pattern, blue transfers 30.00
Trio, cup, saucer, and bowl, red boy and girl playing in garden, red floral border, "Crownford Ironstone, Staffordshire England" marks 22.00

Black transfer prints were used with occasional touches of color. After 1860 more relief work was used, and some pieces were glazed with brilliant colors. Majolica wares were made with careful glazing and naturalistic colors. Other works included tiles and *trompe l'oeil* pieces in the form of ducks, pigs, and plates of asparagus or oysters.

Beginning in 1836 the factory traded as Hautin and Boulanger. Marks incorporate Choisy, or Ch le Roy, or HB & Cie. The factory still remains in operation.

Cake Set, majolica, ftd cake stand, 12 plates, 8" d, pansy design in colors, marked 375.00
Compote Set, 2 compotes, 1 1/2" h, 11 3/4" d, 2 compotes, 4" h, 11 3/4" d, majolica, Greek key design, sq handles, multicolored (A) 440.,00
Figure, 9" h, 9" w, bust of woman in 18th C costume, yellow coiffe with dark green dots, light blue blouse, rose gown with white and brown sprigs, dark brown base, "HB Choisy" mark (A) 258.00
Fish Platter, 13 1/2" l, oval, applied fish in center, sea creatures on sides, natural colors, late 19th C (A). 275.00
Plate
7 1/2" d, Queen of Clubs and Jack of Diamonds, "HB Choisy" mark 35.00
7 7/8" d, black transfer of "Photographie" in center, blue-purple border of dancing men, "H.B. & Cie" mark 35.00
8 1/2" d
Bust of General Moreau and "Ne en 1763, Mortle 6 September, 1813" border of military trophies, black transfers 140.00
"Delgorquet Gal Del Dri Soldads," military scene, black transfer, yellow ground, "P & H Choisy" mark in shield 295.00
"Le Defaut," hunting scene, black transfer, yellow ground, "P & H Choisy" mark in shield 495.00
8 5/8" d, "Vue de l'hotel Roy. des Invalides," black transfer, yellow ground, "P & H Choisy" mark in shield................ 450.00
8 3/4" d, majolica, green game cock, shaped edge, c1870, "H.B. & Cie France" mark .. 30.00
Vase, 11 3/4" h, bottle shape, heavily stippled body with green transluscent glaze, brown spearhead neck, hairline, "Hautin and Boulanger" marks, pr (A) 220.00

c 1836 -1900

CHOISY-LE-ROI

Seine, France
1804 to Present

History: This French factory produced porcelain and white earthenware at Choisy-le-Roi in Seine, France from 1804. First, table services and toilet sets that featured French views or classical scenes printed in red or black were made here. Later, relief decorative motifs were added.

The factory began making earthenware about 1830.

Plate, 8" d, en grisaille transfer of period scene, molded floral border, "HB Choisy le Roi" mark, set of 6, (A) $132.00

WILKINSON LTD
ENGLAND

c1930

CLARICE CLIFF

**Burslem, England
1925–1963**

History: Clarice Cliff, 1899–1972, began her training at Stoke-on-Trent at age 13 when she joined the staff at A.J. Wilkinson, Ltd.'s Royal Staffordshire Pottery at Burslem. They acquired the adjoining Newport factory along with a huge supply of undecorated bowls and vases that were assigned to Clarice Cliff to decorate. She utilized vivid colors and eccentric Art Deco designs with chunky, angular shapes that contrasted sharply with the flowing lines of the earlier Art Nouveau period. Cliff became art director of A. J. Wilkinson, Ltd. in 1930.

Cliff's earthenwares were gay, colorful, and all hand painted. Circles, squares, colored bands, diamonds, conical shapes, and simple landscapes were incorporated in the designs. Pattern names included: Applique, Bizarre, Fantasque, Gay Day, Latonia, Lodore, Ravel, and the most popular Crocus. These patterns were all mass produced and achieved tremendous popularity in both England and America.

Shapes also had special names such as: Athens, Biarritz, Chelsea, Conical, Daffodil, Iris, Lotus, Lynton, Stamford, and Trieste. A customer could order the shape that he wanted decorated with the pattern of his choice. Many novelty pieces such as flower holders, vases, inkwells, candlesticks, cruet sets, bookends, umbrella stands, and even a ceramic telephone cover all were made in Clarice Cliff designs.

Clarice Cliff used several different printed marks, each of which incorporated a facsimile of her signature and usually the name of the pattern.

In 1965, Wilkinson was bought by Midwinter. Midwinter merged with J & G Meakin in 1968. In 1970 Meakin was absorbed by the Wedgwood Group.

References: Leonard Griffin & L & S Meisel, *Clarice Cliff: The Bizarre Affair*, Adams, 1988; Howard Watson, *Collecting Clarice Cliff*, Kevin Francis, 1988; Peter Wentworth-Shields & Kay Johnson, *Clarice Cliff*, L'Odeon, 1976.

Collectors Club: Clarice Cliff Collectors Club, Leonard R. Griffin, Fantasque House, Tennis Drive, The Park, Nottingham NG71AE, England.

Museum: Brighton Museum, Brighton, England.

Collecting Hints: Unmarked pieces of Clarice Cliff china are rare. The large number of back stamps that were used leads to confusion in dating examples.

Biscuit Jar
   7½" h, "Celtic Harvest" pattern, orange feet,
      tan ground, silver top, c1935 . . . . **225.00**
   9½" to handle, Bizarre ware, "My Garden"
      pattern, rattan handle **355.00**
Bone Dish, 7" l, "Tonquin" pattern
   Blue **12.00**
   Green **20.00**

Bone Dish, 6¾" l, "Tonquin" pattern, brown transfer, "Royal Ironstone" mark, $12.00

Dish, 9" l, 7¾" w, "The Biarritz" design, brown, orange, and tan stripes, cream ground, "The Biarritz, Bizarre Ware" mark, $50.00

Pitcher, 7¾" h, raised fruit and berries, brown and yellow leaves, twisted rope band, green int, $425.00

Tray, 13" l, 5¼" w, raised fruit and berries, brown and yellow leaf, lt green ground, "Newport Pottery Co." mark, $175.00

Vase, 9 1/4" h, blue and red edged raised flowers, green leaves, purple accents, cream ground, lt blue int, "Newport Pottery, England" mark, $550.00

Bowl
5" d, "Tonquin" pattern, plum transfer 6.00
5 3/4" d, Bizarre Ware, "Crocus" pattern, crocus florals in orange, blue, and purple, green grass, tan band, green base on ext, int with bands of yellow, cream, and tan separated by green lines 225.00
7 3/4" d
   Bizarre Ware, yellow, orange, and brown flowers, gray leaves, cream ground, yellow int with orange and brown flowers.   500.00
   Bizarre Ware, purple and orange triangles separated by cream bands outlined in black on ext, int with green, cream, and orange bands separated by black, black base 750.00
8 1/4" d, spiral fluted body, "Harvest" pattern, red transfer 15.00
9" d, "Tonquin" pattern, purple transfer 20.00
Candlestick, 2 1/2" h, Bizarre Ware, orange, blue, green, rust, and yellow geometrics 325.00
Coffee Pot
7 1/2" h, "Gay Day" pattern, orange, purple, blue, and green flowers, yellow-cream and brown ground 195.00
8 1/2" h, "Indian Canada" pattern, teepee shape, figure handle, Indian spout, orange top, tan ground, made for Canadian market, c1950 . . . .   125.00
Coffee Set, Bonjour pot, creamer, sugar, 6 conical cups and saucers, rust and gold bands . .   1800.00
Compote, 8" d, 3 1/2" h, "Celtic Harvest" design, metal pedestal. 95.00
Condiment Set, "Cabbage Flower" pattern, conical form 295.00
Cream and Sugar
Creamer, 3 3/8" h, sugar bowl, 2 3/8" h, 5" d, Art Deco pink and green flowers, green band, cream ground 65.00
Bizarre Ware, ovoid, hp landscape scene with gold stars in sky 250.00
Cup and Saucer, "Crows" pattern 75.00
Dinner Service
"Coral Fir" pattern, service for six plus candleholders 1850.00
"Tonquin" pattern, brown transfer, 8 dinner

plates 10" d, 8 dessert plates, 7 salad plates 6 1/2" d, 6 cups, 8 saucers, cream and sugar, round bowl, oval platter, 46 pieces 125.00
Gravy Boat, with undertray, "Tonquin" pattern, purple transfer 23.00
Honey Pot, "Crocus" Bizzare ware, figural bee knob 125.00
Jam Jar, 5" h, "Celtic Harvest" pattern, emb wheat on cream ground, chrome handle and spoon 55.00
Jug
6" h, "Gay Day" design in colors 575.00
8 1/4" h, emb orange flowers with green and yellow trim, light gray ground, brown branch handle, green int, "Clarice Cliff, Newport Pottery Co. England" mark 85.00
9 1/2" h, "My Garden" design, streaky yellowbrown glaze, purple flower handle ending in green leaves 245.00
12" h
   Bizarre Ware, border of orange and yellow nasturtium and circ green leaves, brown speckled ground 575.00
   "Latona," wide blue geometric bands dividing pink and blue stylized flowerheads .   950.00
Pitcher
5 1/4" h, Bizarre Ware, bulbous shape, three bands, yellow, blue florals, and blue separated by green lines 500.00
6 1/4" h, "Gay day" pattern, ribbed body, yellow and floral band separated by black lines, orange, purple, rust, blue, and green florals, brown band, narrow green band, cream ground and handle 595.00
6 1/2" h, "Delicia" pattern, hp, yellow, rust, blue splashes, molded body, raised dotted top, white ground 600.00
8" h, Bizarre Ware, "Delicia Pansies" pattern, ribbed, hp green base and top, green splashed on top int, pink, yellow, and rose florals, brown stems, cream ground 675.00
9" h, "My Garden" pattern, brown and orange on gray, floral handle 355.00
9 1/2" h, "Celtic Harvest" pattern, fruit handle in green, orange, and yellow, tan ground, c1935 . . . .   225.00
11 1/4" h, cylinder shape, Bizarre Ware, pastel pink, green, and yellow "Rhodanthe" pattern (A) 200.00
Plate
6 1/4" d, "Autumn Crocus" pattern with four crocuses in colors 75.00
6 1/2" d, "Tonquin" pattern, pink transfer . . .   5.00
8" d
   "Celtic Harvest" pattern, emb painted fruit and wheat sheaves on border, honey glaze ground, chrome foot, "Newport Pottery" mark 75.00
   "Tonquin" pattern
      Blue transfer 5.00
      Pink transfer 6.00
8 3/4" d, "Celtic Harvest" pattern, raised colored fruit, tan ground, c1935 . . . .   95.00
9 3/4" d, landscape scene with aqua and brown tree, gray ground, aqua rim, "Clarice Cliff Wilkinson England" mark 85.00
10 1/2" d
   Buckingham Palace design 15.00
   Portrait of Gainsborough in colors 36.00
10 3/4" d, Spanish explorer and monk discovering Niagara Falls in center, border with

oak leaves in feathered design, scalloped rim, "Royal Staffordshire Ceramics, Burslem, England" mark 140.00
11" d, center scene of Trafalgar Square, marked 50.00
Platter
11½" l, "Tonquin" pattern, purple transfer.   22.00
12" l, "Tonquin" pattern, red transfer 15.00
Sauceboat, with undertray, "Tonquin" pattern, brown transfer 20.00
Soup Plate, 8" d, "Tonquin" pattern, pink transfer 20.00
Sugar Bowl, Cov, 4½" h, ribbed body, Bizarre Ware, brown lines and green swag line on cream ground 145.00
Sugar Shaker
5" h, Bizarre Ware, orange, gold, and brown flowers on cream and yellow ground 100.00
5½" h, Bizarre Ware, "Crocus" pattern, blue, orange, and purple crocuses 225.00
6¼" h, Bizzare Ware, red poppies with green and cream, black outlines, silver top 650.00
Toothpick Holder, 2½" h, figural toby in colors   60.00
Tray, 11¼" l, 8¼" w, oct, pink and yellow flowers, pink and gray shading to green base, cream ground, marked 350.00
Trio, cup, saucer, and plate, 6½" d, Art Deco pink and green flowers, green band, cream ground 35.00
Vase
7" h, 5" d, "My Garden" pattern, pink melon sectioned scalloped top, emb painted flowers at base 95.00
8" h, "Inspiration," turquoise lotus flowers outlined in tan, sponged blue ground 550.00
8¼" h, trumpet shape, brown, orange, tan, and cream bands 525.00
8½" h, tapered shape, raised leaves and branches in colors, "Newport Pottery, #989" mark 245.00
8¾" h, 4¾" d, emb blue and pink flowers, green leaves on light gray ground, ribbing at middle, molded handle, blue int 88.00
9½" h, emb large green, yellow, and gray leaves, green ground, "Newport Pottery" mark 95.00
10½" h, Bizarre Ware, "My Garden" pattern 1200.00
12¼" h, multicolored lovebirds on light yellow ground 225.00
Vegetable Bowl, 11½" d, "Celtic Harvest" pattern, raised colored fruit forms handles, tan ground, c1935 . . . .   225.00

They were known for the fine quality of their blue transfer-printed earthenwares, mostly made for the American market. American views used on their wares were taken from contemporary prints. In addition designs were taken from books, e.g., the Clews series of Dr. Syntax and Don Quixote. Plates also were made from the comic pictures drawn by Sir David Wilkie. The company's English views consisted chiefly of castles, abbeys, and cathedrals.

Reference: N. Hudson Moore, *The Old China Book,* Charles E. Tuttle Co., second printing, 1980.

Museums: Cincinnati Art Museum, Cincinnati, Ohio; Metropolitan Museum of Art, New York.

Collecting Hints: The two most famous patterns by Clews are "Landing of Lafayette" and the "States." The "Landing of Lafayette" pattern contains an extremely large number of accessory pieces.

Creamer, 5¼" h, gaudy floral design, emb band, repairs, imp "Clews" mark (A) 45.00
Dessert Dish, 14½" l, oval, "Doctor Syntax Copying the Wit of the Window," med blue transfer, tied ribbon handle, molded border, imp "circle, crown and Clews" mark (A) 360.00
Plate
3¼" d, ivy design blue transfer, imp "Clews" mark 75.00
5" d, oriental scene, dark blue transfer, scalloped edge, imp "Clews" mark 135.00
7" d, oriental fishing scene, dark blue transfer, c1850, imp "Clews" mark. 150.00
7½" d, "Sancho Panza and the Priest and the Barber," dark blue transfer 78.00
8" d, "Moral Maxims," red transfer 34.00
8¾" d
"Doctor Syntax Reading His Tour," dark blue transfer, imp "Clews" mark 145.00
Pearlware, blue feather edge, emb floral rim, imp "Clews" mark (A) 137.00
9" d, "Christmas Eve," floral border, dark blue transfer, c1819–35, imp and printed "James & Ralph Clews" mark 490.00
10" d
"Doctor Syntax Disputing his Bill with the Landlady," blue transfer, c1818–34, imp "Clews" mark 325.00
"Doctor Syntax Drawing After Nature," blue transfer, second period, imp "Clews" mark (A) 50.00
"Doctor Syntax Taking Possession of His

c1818-1834

CLEWS

Cobridge Works, Staffordshire, England 1818–1834

History: James and Ralph Clews were Staffordshire potters who operated the Cobridge Works from 1818 to 1834.

Plate, 10½" d, "Doctor Syntax Taking Possession of His Living," blue transfer, c1840, $100.00

Living," blue transfer, second period, imp "Clews" mark (A) **50.00**

"Knighthood Conferred on Don Quixote," dark blue transfer (A) **187.00**

"The Valentine," Wilke's Designs Series, dark blue transfer, imp "Warrented Staffordshire" with crown mark **385.00**

Platter, 18 1/2" l, 15" w, "Sancho Panza and the Duchess," dark blue transfer, c1820 .... **650.00**

Serving Dish, Open, 12 1/4" l, 10 1/4" w, "The Escape of the Mouse," imp "Clews" mark (A) **660.00**

Slop Bowl, 4 5/8" d, 2 5/8" h, "Coronation" pattern, dark blue transfer (A) **66.00**

Soup Plate
8 3/4" d, blue and yellow ochre gaudy floral design, blue emb rim, imp "Clews" mark, pr (A) **350.00**
9 7/8" d, scene of Windsor Castle, dark blue transfer, imp "Clews" mark (A) **132.00**

Sugar Bowl, Cov, 6" h, gaudy floral design with dbl handles, repairs, imp "Clews" mark (A) . **126.00**

Teabowl and saucer, "Coronation" pattern, dark blue transfer **250.00**

Teapot, 7 1/2" h, "Neptune" in dark blue transfer, cracks, finial reglued, imp "Clews" mark (A) **300.00**

Toddy Plate, 4 1/2" d, landscape with fisherman, dark blue transfer, hairline, imp "Clews" mark (A) **125.00**

A.D. 1750.
c 1891

ENGLISH PORCELAIN
CO-ALPORT
1830 - 50

COALPORT

Severn Gorge, Shropshire, England
c1796 to Present

History: After John Rose completed his apprenticeship at Caughley, he established a pottery at Coalport in Shropshire in 1796. Rose expanded his original factory with the purchase of Caughley in 1799. His original soft paste formula eventually was superseded by bone china ware.

By 1822 molds, models, and some key personnel were acquired from the South Wales porcelain manufacturers at Swansea and Nantgarw and incorporated into the Coalport factory. In 1820 John Rose won a Society of Arts medal for his lead-free glaze.

The most characteristic type of Coalport porcelains are the distinctive Rococo style flower-encrusted decorative pieces called "Coalbrookdale." "Indian Tree," first made in 1801, and "Hong Kong," made c1805 are two tableware patterns that are still popular to this day.

John Rose died in 1841. Production at Coalport continued under Thomas Rose, his son, W.F. Rose, his nephew, and William Pugh. The influence of Sevres is reflected in the style and decoration of table and ornamental wares made during the mid-nineteenth century.

In 1885 the Bruff family took over. The Coalport firm was sold to Cauldon Potteries Ltd. in Staffordshire in 1923

and moved to the Staffordshire area in 1926 along with many of the workers.

By 1936 both Coalport and Cauldon became part of Crescent potteries at Stoke-on-Trent. In 1958 Coalport was acquired by Brain of Foley China and preserved its separate identity. Many traditional patterns and lines were revived. In 1967 Coalport became part of the Wedgwood group. The Coalport name continues on a line of modern china products.

References: G. Godden, *Coalport and Coalbrookdale Porcelains*, Praeger, 1970; Compton MacKenzie, *The House of Coalport, 1750–1950*, Collins, 1951; Michael Messenger, *Coalport 1795–1926*, Antique Collector's Club, 1990.

Museums: Cincinnati Museum of Art, Cincinnati, Ohio; Coalport China Works Museum, Ironbridge Gorge Museum Trust, Shropshire, England; Victoria & Albert Museum, London, England.

Bell, 3 1/4" h, molded large leaves, beading at top, green open handle, "Coalport, Made in England" mark **18.00**

Bowl, Cov, 3 1/2" h, enamel decorated floral bouquets, gilt accents, blue encrusted flowers and leaves, branch handles, ftd, Coalbrookdale (A) **125.00**

Box, Cov, 3" l, 2" w, oval, applied yellow flowers on lid **35.00**

Bulb Pot, Cov, D-shape
8 5/8" l, colorful basket of flowers on marbleized table on tan ground with gilt edge in rect panel on front, floral bouquets on sides on lozenge shaped panels on gilt diamond trelliswork ground, fluted columns with flowering vines and gilt borders of entwined foliate vines on base, beadwork on rim, yellow ground, four gilt ball feet, cov with four pierced openings around three gilt edged bulb holders, 1805–10 (A) **6600.00**
9 1/8" h, central panel with full blown summer flowers resting on pillar, side panels with wide rose sprigs, gilt columns, bracket base, yellow ground cov with three bulb holders, restored, early 19th C (A) **1900.00**

Candlestick, 5 1/2" h, white, relief scrolls, baluster standard, scalloping **8.00**

Plate, 8 1/4" d, stoneware, "Canton" pattern in yellow, red, and green, "Kingsware, Canton" mark, set of 9, (A) $151.00

Urn, Cov, 10" h, multicolored landscape scene in cartouche, gilt swirls, cobalt ground, dbl gilt handles, late 19th C, "green England Coalport, AD 1760" mark, (A) $165.00

Chocolate Pot, 6" h, multicolored birds and
flowers on white ground **65.00**

Clockcase, Stand, 13" h, swag molded body applied with flowers and foliage, four feet, bright enamel colors, brass dial, Roman numerals, French bell striking movement, c1835, script mark to stand (A) **1589.00**

Cream and Sugar, small pink and blue flowers,
marked **85.00**

Cup and Saucer

Alternating floral and bird cartouche on cobalt ground with scrolled gilt border, 1st qtr 19th C, 4 pcs (A) **110.00**

"Countryware" pattern **10.00**

Gold starburst in center, cobalt band, raised tooled gold rims **65.00**

"Mandarin" pattern...................... **30.00**

"Ming Rose" pattern **20.00**

Miniature, landscape panels reserved against gilt ground enameled with blue studs in various sizes, loop handle, c1910, printed crown mark and T294 and T288 marks (A)................................... **840.00**

Mossy fern-like fronds and shells on int, fronds on ext, white and cobalt, gold trim, scalloping, ftd............................... **15.00**

Dessert Dish, 8¼" d, shell shaped, "Japan" pattern, cobalt, burnt orange, and green with gilt, white and gilt ground, hairline, c1800 unmarked.................................. **550.00**

Dessert Plate, 7¾" d, rounded sq shape, light yellow alternating border panels with trellis and foliate designs, "Coalport Kingsware England" mark, set of 11 (A)................ **50.00**

Dessert Service

2 circ sauce tureens, covs, stands, 7½" w, chamfered rect fruit stand, 2 chamfered sq dishes, 2 oval dishes, 26 plates, 18 berry dishes, center with fable scene of either figures or animals in landscapes, berry dishes and sauce tureen covs with colorful floral sprigs, green and gray shaded checkered border within inner edge of rococo gilt scrollwork with small floral sprigs, outer gilt dentil edge, gilt scroll handles molded with spears of green asparagus and cauliflower, covs with apple sprig knobs, 1810–15, iron-red or olive green pattern nos. 53 pcs (A) **4400.00**

12 plates, 9" d, 3 shaped sq dishes, 3 oval dishes, 2 comports, large oval dish, still life of fruits on woodland bank, rim with gilt foliate scrolls and formal borders, royal blue ground, c1910, sgd "F.H. Chivers," printed crown mark, painted no. 5351R, imp "8K21", 21 pcs (A) **9537.00**

12 plates, 9½" d, 2 lozenge dishes, 2 circ dishes, 2 shaped sq dishes, tazza, botanical, each painted with different specimen between gilded swag borders, reserved with floral panels on dark blue ground, c1839–45, 19pcs (A)..........................**11,616.00**

12 plates, 10" d, 12 soup bowls, 11 dessert plates, 11 side plates, 5 shaped rect meat dishes in sizes, soup tureen, cov, stand, 2 sauce tureens, covs, stands, salad bowl, botanical, bright colored flower sprays and foliage between raised floral borders with gilding, dark blue ground on border, some cracked, c1820, some imp "2," 61 pcs (A) **14,108.00**

Dinner Service, Part

16 dinner plates, 16 salad plates, 10 butter plates, 16 cups and saucers, "Sandringham," multicolored floral sprays in centers, pink borders between gilt scrolling forms . **450.00**

Oval soup tureen, cov, 12½" l, oval sauce tureen, cov, stand, oval vegetable dish, cov, liner, sq vegetable dish, oval platter, 16⅜" l, platter, 15" l, platter, 11¼" l, 3 oval platters, 10⅜" l, 10 soup plates, 10 dinner plates, 10 dessert plates, colorful scattered floral sprigs within gilt edged wide floral border on scalloped rim, scroll handles and knobs gilded, some cracks, c1815, 42 pcs (A)..................................... **4125.00**

Dish

9¼" H-H, painted view of Dunster Abbey reserved on blue and gilt ground, c1900, sgd "J.H. Plant' (A) **390.00**

11¹¹⁄₁₆" l, lozenge shape, "Japan" pattern, center of iron-red, gold, pink, and green with jardiniere of peonies and flowering prunus branches of fenced terrace, gilt edged rim, border of iron-red, salmon, and gold prunus panels alternating with underglaze blue ground panels with iron-red, salmon, and gold birds on flowering branches, c1805, pr (A)................ **880.00**

Egg Cup Stand and Six Cups, 8" d, "Imari" pattern with alternating panels of flowers and foliage in underglaze blue, iron-red, green, and gilding, stand with gilded ring handle, domed foot, slightly waisted cylindrical form, circ foot, c1820 (A) **1505.00**

Ewer

13" h, molded panels with summer flowers between gilded borders, blue ground, two scroll feet, pierced lip with scroll molding, multiple scroll handles, c1830 (A)........ **420.00**

13¾" h, ovoid body, encrusted with two

panels of flowers and foliage on green ground, gilt shaped lip, scroll handle, sq foot, c1830, Coalbrookdale (A) **345.00**

14½" h, globular body, brightly colored summer flowers on body, neck and foot in turquoise with gilded details, scroll handle flanked by serpents, terminating at base with mask, three cracks, 1860–80, printed mark, pr (A) **1411.00**

Ewer, Cov, 4⅛" h, sides with applied colored flowers and painted butterflies, gilt accents, scroll handle and spout, c1830, Coalbrookdale (A) **400.00**

Figure

3½" l, green open pod of cream peas, c1830 (A). **675.00**

8¼" h, "Stella," swirled green and lavender gown **75.00**

Flask, 10½" h, moon shape, Chinese style lotus flowers and scrolling foliage in yellow, maroon, orange, and pink, gilt dot ground, dbl gilt loop handles, c1870, pr (A) **1925.00**

Fruit Cooler, Cov

10⅛" h, 10⅜" h, "Bengal Tiger" pattern, iron-red, green, blue, pink, yellow, black, and gold around body with arched panels with front and reverse with dragon on plateau, gilt scroll handles, sides with vases on tables, green and iron-red dentil border, iron-red and green cell diaper border, gilt scrolling loop knob, molded leaves, liners missing, 1805–10, pr (A). **11,000.00**

10½" h, "Japan" pattern, iron-red and gold chrysanthemums and panels of yellow dragons, beasts, and birds within blue and gold scroll band borders, iron-red and green triangular vignettes, cobalt blue ground, gilt scroll handles, cov with gilt double scroll knob, gilt band borders on rims, liner missing, c1810 (A) **1375.00**

Goblet, 11" h, large panel of painted exotic birds, small panel of summer flowers, gilt scroll borders, dark blue ground, domed foot with small panels of painted insects, three gilded handles and rim, white int with gold flecks, c1910 (A) **1045.00**

Gravy Boat, liner, "Beverly" pattern, white Cupids on blue band, gray feathery lines, gold trim **25.00**

Ice Pail, Cov, Liner, 10½" h, "Church Gresley" pattern, circ panels of floral sprays reserved on ground of yellow and gilt lozenge diaper interspersed with pink rose heads, early 19th C, pr (A). **21,659.00**

Inkwell, 6¾" l, Empire style, footed oval vessel, brown monochrome on either side with classical figures, yellow ground top with neoclassical trophies and foliate scrolls, gilt edged foot with gilt acanthus border, gilt eagle's head handles, two removable inkpots flanked by pierced quill holes, covs missing, early 19th C (A). **700.00**

Jar, Cov, 9¼" l, D-shape, panels of colorful water birds in natural habitat separated by columns molded with gilt wreaths and drapery, S-scroll feet feathered in gilt, single scroll foot at back, turquoise-green ground, gilt feathered fluted dome, budding sprig knob, gilt chain border rims, c1865, "gold CSN ampersand" marks, pr (A). **9350.00**

Jardinaire, 5¹⁵⁄₁₆" h, 6⅛" h, cylindrical form,

front painted in shades of brown and gold with mythological scene with warrior in chariot or Venus in water chariot drawn by sea horses within gilt edged oct panel, gilt Greek key border above foliate scrolls on reverse, gilt molded ring mock handles, central pierced hole in base, brown band on footrim, rim edged in gilding, stands missing, c1810, pr (A). **1650.00**

Jug, 8¼" h, pear shape, armorial, youth wearing black hat and shoes, iron-red sashed rose jacket and breeches, with three brown hounds in lavender, mauve, and yellow landscape, blue and salmon sky, within gilt edged oval surrounded by iron-red edged gilt foliate scrolls and bell flower swags, foliate molded scroll handle, cylindrical neck with iron-red, black, white, and tan arms of City of Worcester on gold luster ground, reverse with gilt roundel monogrammed in gold "JED', spout and foot gilded, 1796–1800 (A) **770.00**

Letter Rack, 6¼" h, Feldspar, rect trough with relief molded sawtooth rim, four peg feet, painted basket of flowers blown off table, flanked by foliate gilt panels, back painted with flower sprays in gilt frame, pierced and gilt leaves, c1820 . . . .   **550.00**

Plate

8" d, "Imari" pattern, pr (A). **88.00**

8½" d

Dragon pattern, cobalt blue center dragon outlined in gilt, orange florals, green leaves, four panels of brown and gilt leaves with cobalt and gilt outlines, slightly scalloped edge, set of 6, c1825, unmarked **895.00**

Floral centers in pink, iron-red, purple, and olive green on white ground, four floral panel inserts on border with gilt leaf decorations on either side, scalloped edge, c1830, unmarked, pr. **540.00**

Lobed form, orange with large spray of flowers and foliage on burnished gilt ground, c1805 (A) **1881.00**

9" d, painted cherub surrounded by flowers, pastel ground with raised gold flower garland, scroll gold edge, dtd 1893 . . . .   **395.00**

9¼" d, tromp-l'oeil of postcard, crossed pencils, and books on gilt ground, border of gilt and pink S-scrolls, c1808 (A) **2580.00**

9⅜" d, iron-red, sepia, and gold in center with goat's head crest within roundel, encircled by florette chain borders, gilt striated panels, three panels of trophies of war, three gilt scale patterned panels with iron-red classical figures, c1810, pr (A) **1210.00**

9½" d, center with lemons on grained wood table against stippled brown ground, gilt Greek key band inner border, lobed rim with gilt border of leafy branches alternating with palmettes and anchors within bands and lines, sgd "T Baxter 1808,' (A). **3575.00**

9⅞" d, painted en grisaille of classical figures, red ground, dark blue and scrolling gilt border, set of 9 . . . .   **3800.00**

10½" d, blue transfer of bust of Admiral Dewey, Manila, May, 1898 in center, border of laurel wreaths with ships names, gold rope border **95.00**

10⅝" d, blue printed commemoration of Captain Matthew Webb, gold line rim (A)   **245.00**

Platter, 24" l, oval, cornflowers and poppy center, poppy and trailing vine border, mid 19th C (A).................... **990.00**

Scent Bottle, 4½" h, molded sq shape, four scroll feet, painted and encrusted flowers, chips, c1830 (A) **345.00**

Soup Plate, 10⅜" d, green, yellow, and brown with elm tree, crest of Ellames of Allerton Hall near Liverpool, within cobalt blue border edged and inscribed in gold with motto "NEC.SPERNO.NEC.TIMEO," cobalt blue ground scalloped rim bordered with gilt dentil band, c1825, imp 2 marks, set of 12 (A).... **770.00**

Tea Kettle, Cov, Stand, Globular Body
  8" h, colorful flower sprays, encrusted with colored flowers, cov with pink rose finial, waisted scrolling triangular stand, overhead strolling handle in green and gilding, some restoration, c1820, underglaze "blue C Dale" Coalbrookdale (A)................ **1600.00**
  8¼" h, encrusted with colored flowers, painted with floral sprays and insects, Coalbrookdale (A)........................ **756.00**

Tea Service, Part, teapot, cov, stand, 6⅞" h, oval shape, cov sugar bowl, milk jug, waste bowl, 10 teacups and saucers, wide border of flowers and foliage above narrow diamond band, heavily gilded, center of teapot stand and saucers with gold ground floral medallions, int of waste bowl and teacups gilded, c1810, John Rose, imp "5" on teapot, 25 pcs (A)................................ **6600.00**

Tete-a-Tete Set, coffee pot, cov, 7" h, cov sucrier, cov cream jug, 2 cups and saucers, painted with cherubs at festive pursuits, leisurely activities, and artistic pursuits, floral garlands between gilded borders, egg-shell body, 1851–1861, blue enamel painted mark, 10 pcs (A)................................ **2400.00**

Vase
  3½" h
    Cylindrical, "Hong Kong" pattern in colors **24.00**
    Spider web and leaves with spider, cobalt and gilt ext, white int, c1890, marked .. **250.00**
  5¾" h, "jeweled," ovoid with waisted neck and flared foot, triangular panel with enamel beading and tooled gilded scrolling foliage, turquoise beading on body, neck, and foot, pierced scroll handles, c1900, "crown" mark (A) **5016.00**
  7⅝" h, baluster shape with slender flaring neck, circ foot, gilt designs on pink ground, beaded turquoise and white beading, applied gilt scrolling dbl handles (A) **770.00**
  8¼", 9⅓" h, encrusted flowers and leaves, gilt accents, molded and pierced leafy rim, scalloped base, Coalbrookdale, pr (A) **165.00**
  8¾" h, "Church Gresley," wide band of flower sprays reserved on yellow ground, gilt lozenge diaper interlaced with pink roseheads, foot restuck, c1800 (A).......... **1050.00**
  9½" h, painted with sprays of colored garden flowers, applied modeled blooms trailing from leafy handles, molded with foliate motifs, scale pattern panels, green ground, c1835, pr (A) **1027.00**
  9⅞" h, baluster shape, encrusted multicolored flowers and foliage, dark blue ground, c1830, Coalbrookdale, pr **600.00**
  11⁹⁄₁₆" h, brown oval panel with rural couple with two children, gilt checked ground, foli-

age borders around tapering cylindrical body, waisted neck, circ foot with colorful floral border, gilt borders of striped and leaf patterned triangles, gilded sq base, cov missing, c1802, sgd "T. BAXTER" **900.00**

12¼" h, cartouche of flowers and birds surrounded by encrusted flowers and leaves, molded leafy handles with green trim, mid 19th C, Coalbrookdale, pr (A) **1100.00**

14¼" h, ovoid body, large panel painted with hens, cockerels, and other birds before a river in wooded landscape, or sprays of summer flowers, necks and shoulders molded with gilded hanging braid, gilded swag and floral borders, circ foot in sq base, pink ground, cov with twisted circles, 1861–75, John Rose, "gilt ampersand" mark, pr (A).................................... **4114.00**

24¼" h, panel with head and shoulders portrait of smiling girl, one with basket of apples, reverse with musical and rustic trophies with fruiting vine or foliage, within ribbon tied beaded borders, azure ground, turret handles and knobbed neck entwined with serpents curling through rings, circ foot, shaped sq base, formal borders, cov, repairs, sgd "Ch. Palmere, gilt ampersand," retailers mark and 1871, pr (A) **7261.00**

Vase, Cov, 16" h, ovoid form, painted with panels of fruit and summer flowers between gilded scroll borders on dark blue ground, circ foot on sq base, domed cov with foliate finial, 1861–75, cov with printed "ampersand" mark, printed "English Coalport Porcelain" (A) **1505.00**

1833 - 47

COPELAND
1850 - 67

COPELAND
1851 - 55

COPELAND-SPODE

London and Stoke-on-Trent, England
1833 to Present
(see Spode for early history)

History: William Copeland died in 1826, and Josiah Spode II died in 1827. In 1833 William Taylor Copeland bought the Spode share in the London showroom and warehouse as well as the Spode Factory. Copeland took Thomas Garrett, a London colleague, as a partner and the firm was known as Copeland & Garrett from 1833 to 1847.

About 1842 Copeland's statuary porcelain body was developed and achieved success. Statuary porcelain, a major new art product, was sponsored by the new Art Unions. Many competitors adopted it, renaming it "Parian." Copeland statuettes, portrait busts, and other objects dominated the market until 1914. Production was halted after that date.

The name Spode was subordinated to that of Copeland after 1847, but the high standards of quality in all its products both in design and execution were maintained. The Spode Factory has held Royal Warrants from 1806 to the present time. The Spode Factory survived many difficult times, constantly striving to maintain its reputation as the producers of fine ceramic wares.

In 1966 the Copeland family sold the firm to the Carborundum Company Ltd., who injected much needed capital to help the firm compete with the other English pottery and porcelain companies. In 1970 the bicentenary year of the firm's establishment, the name of the company was changed back to Spode to honor the founder. In 1976 Spode joined with the Worcester Royal Porcelain Company to form Royal Worcester Spode.

Up to 1833 the name "Spode" refers to the period during which the two Josiahs controlled the company. From 1833 onwards "Spode" refers to the Spode Factory irrespective of ownership. From about 1842 to 1880 the name Spode seldom appears on its products. Remember all Copeland & Garrett and Copeland wares are Spode factory productions.

Copeland & Garrett 1833–1847
Copeland c1847–1970
Spode 1970–Present

References: see Spode.

Museums: see Spode.

Asparagus Server, 13" l, 10" w, 6¾" h, rect curved top, four feet, "Spode Bridge" pattern, blue transfer **1250.00**

Bone Plate, 9" l, black transfer of classical scene with man on horse statue, fruit and flower border, ribbed ground, "Copeland Spode England" mark **30.00**

Bowl, 8" d, "Spode's Tower" pattern, blue transfer, set of 8 . . . . **120.00**

Pitcher, 5½" h, relief molded cherub and grape scene, gilt rim and branch handle, "Copeland's China, England" mark, $150.00

Plate, 9" d, romantic country scene of man and woman, mandolin on ground, floral swags, blue transfer, scalloped rim, c1844–67, $45.00

Butter Pat
    Blue, yellow, and purple pansy design, c1878 . . . . **75.00**
    "Wickerdale" pattern **8.00**

Candle Snuffer and Stand, 4½" h, figural bishop's miter edged in gilt, imp "Copeland" mark **100.00**

Candlestick, 4" h, multicolored butterflies and dragonflies on brown, green, and white leaf pattern ground, pr **110.00**

Cream and Sugar, "Florence" pattern **65.00**

Creamer, "Fitzhugh" pattern, green and white . **36.00**

Cup and Saucer
    "Blue Geisha" pattern **40.00**
    "Chelsea Wicker" pattern **14.00**
    "Knightsbridge" pattern **15.00**
    "Old Colony Rose" pattern **50.00**
    "Rosalie" pattern **8.00**
    "Spode's Trophies" pattern, blue transfer . . . **10.00**

Cup and Saucer, Demitasse
    Bird of Paradise design in colors **38.00**
    "Mayflower" pattern, mulberry flowers and

Game Set, platter, 20½" l, 12 plates, 10" d, stoneware, each transfer printed with game, enameled floral borders, "Copeland Late Spode and boat" marks, (A) $2420.00

scrolls on ext, hp red flowers on int, gadrooned rim, fancy handle **65.00**
"Rosalie" pattern......................... **45.00**
Dessert Dish, 11½" l, shaped rect, "Tobacco
Leaf" pattern, white ground, molded handles,
c1833–1847, "Copeland-Garrett Late Spode"
printed and imp marks.................... **350.00**
Dinner Service, 29 plates, 10" d, 6 soup bowls,
2 vegetable tureens, covs, 2 sauce tureens,
covs, stands, large serving dish, 7 kidney
shaped dishes, salad bowl, printed and
painted with pendant leaves in tones of green,
gadrooned border with gilding, c1892, printed
marks, date codes and Retailer's mark for Daniell, Wigmore St, London, 54 pcs (A) **1710.00**
Dinner Service, Part
8 dinner plates, 8 soup bowls, 7 waste bowls,
8 dessert plates, 7 saucers, 7 egg cups, oval
platter, "Bridal Veil" pattern **150.00**
8 soup plates, 8 lunch plates, 11 salad plates,
11 bread and butter plates, 6 cups, 8 saucers, 16 dessert dishes, tureen (damaged),
shaped borders with blue and gold designs
(A)................................... **225.00**
12 dinner plates, 7½" d, 11 luncheon plates,
apple green and gilt borders (A) **715.00**
Dish, 10" d, "Japan" pattern in colors, deep well,
"Copeland & Garrett" mark (A)............ **55.00**
Figure, 6¼" h, two standing hunting dogs supported by tree stump, blue and white, oval
base (A)................................ **467.00**
Loving Cup, 5⅜" h, multicolored portrait of Admiral Lord Nelson, flanked by scenes of Britannia on sea chariot and H.M.S. Victory, rim
with "To Celebrate the Centenary lest we for-
get of the Battle of Trafalgar, Oct. 21, 1805,"
three handles **95.00**
Pitcher
4" h, cream cameos of hunters, dogs, and
fallen moose on dark blue ground, c1900 **50.00**
4¾" h, cream cameos of golfers on dark
green drab ground, cream cameo leaf border, imp marks (A) **468.00**
7⅛" h, stoneware, applied white relief
scenes of "THE KILL," light green-blue
ground, imp "COPELAND ENGLAND"
mark (A) **82.00**
9½" h, ewer shape, sprays of blue flowers on
body and handle...................... **85.00**
Plaque, 27½" h, 18½" w, oval, painted shepherd and shepherdess seated on hill with
pipes, sheep seated at feet, wall with fountain
and lion's head statue at side, framed, late
19th C, imp "COPELAND" mark........... **7800.00**
Plate
6" d, Audubon bird design in colors **12.00**
7⅝" d, brown transfer of sheep, imp "COPE-
LAND" mark, set of 9 (A).............. **89.00**
7¾" d, "Spode's Tower" pattern, red transfer.................................. **10.00**
8" d, "Tobacco Leaf" pattern, pale blue
ground, blue and orange Copeland Spode
printed mark, 1875, pr................. **275.00**
8¼" d, dark blue geometric design, light
gray/blue border, scalloped, imp mark.... **48.00**
Basket of flowers in center, blue ground
with gilt border **40.00**
"Italian" pattern, blue transfer, "Copeland-
Spode" mark **20.00**
8⅜" d, blue and white oriental bridge scene,

two men fishing, birds, floral border,
c1833–1847, "Copeland & Garrett Late
Spode" mark **185.00**
9" d
"Boston State House," black transfer..... **40.00**
"Chinese Rose" pattern................. **10.00**
Dark blue transfer, romantic courting scene
with man and woman, mandolin on
ground, overall designed border with
floral swags, scalloped shape, white
ground, 1844–67, "Copeland Late
Spode" mark **45.00**
"Old Concorde" pattern............... **18.00**
"Spode's Jewel" pattern, green phoenix
bird in center, imp lace overall design,
cream ground, scalloped rim, "Spode's
Jewel, Copeland Spode, England" mark. **11.00**
9¼" d
"Ermine" pattern...................... **9.00**
Felspar, painted view of Eltham Bridge in
center, lime green ground, gilt rococo
border panels........................ **150.00**
9¾" d, center gold snowflake pattern, white
ground, pink border with gold rim and designs, set of 8 (A) **80.00**
10" d, divided, "Italian" pattern, blue transfer.................................. **50.00**
10½" d
"Chinese Rose" pattern................. **12.00**
Hunting scene of hunter in red coat with
hounds in green forest setting, red and
purple floral border on green leaves,
printed mark......................... **30.00**
"Fairy Dell" pattern.................... **18.00**
"Rosalie" pattern...................... **8.00**
"Rose Briar" pattern................... **12.00**
"Spode's Tower" pattern, blue transfer ... **34.00**
Platter
12" d, brown "Fleur de Lis" pattern........ **25.00**
13" l, 9½" w, "Spode's Tower" pattern, red
transfer............................. **75.00**
14" l, "Billingsley Rose" pattern **85.00**
14½" l
10" w, pierced, Imari pattern in typical colors, c1847–67 .... **150.00**
10¾" w, oct shape, oriental type floral
center in blue, yellow, rose, and green,
florals on border, geometric rim, white
ground, c1912, "Copeland Late Spode,
Made for Harrods" mark.............. **85.00**
"Shanghai" pattern.................... **45.00**
15" l
"Blue Geisha" pattern, oval **80.00**
"Cowslip" pattern...................... **40.00**
"Spode's Tower" pattern, blue transfer ... **65.00**
16" l, "Billingsley Rose" pattern **125.00**
17" l, "Reynolds" pattern **95.00**
Rouge Pot, Cov, 4" h, gilt with floral borders,
center circ panel of flowers on cov, c1840
(A).................................... **470.00**
Serving Plate, 9" H-H, "Old Colony Rose" pattern................................... **25.00**
Soup Bowl, 10" d, "Imari" pattern, floral center
and paneled border in green, brown, red, cobalt and gold, c1875 (A) **30.00**
Soup Plate
7¾" d, "Spode's Tower" pattern, red transfer.................................. **12.00**
9" d, "Spode's Tower" pattern, blue transfer **31.00**
Teapot, 6½" h, multicolored hunt scene **85.00**

Tea Set, pot, creamer, sugar bowl, "Mayflower" pattern **320.00**

Tureen, Cov, 11" l, 9" w, 6" h, "Spode's Tower" pattern, red transfer **75.00**

Vase, 6 1/4" h, triangle shape, three floral multicolor gilt outlined cartouches with "August," "September," and "July," chartreuse ground, three scroll feet in white and gilt, white and gilt molded indented shells on top border, scalloped, 1833–47, green "Copeland Garrett Felspar Porcelain late Spode" mark **495.00**

Vase, Cov
12 1/2" h, painted figures, buildings, river with mill in landscape, scroll and ring handles, circ foot on sq base, sgd "W. Yale," pr (A) **835.00**

15" h, painted band of dancing and playing children, turquoise pierced domed cov, bud knob, pierced base, flared foot, knob restored, c1880, sgd "L. Besche" (A) **3000.00**

Vegetable Bowl
10" sq, "Cowslip" pattern **40.00**
"Spode's Tower" pattern, blue transfer **47.00**

Wine Cooler, 9 1/4" h, brown and blue variegated solid agate body, c1840, Copeland and Garrett **750.00**

Covered, 7" h, black sponging, white ground, multicolored milk maid, c1850, $500.00

COW CREAMERS

**Staffordshire, England
2nd half 18th C to mid 19th C
Delft, Holland
c1755**

History: Cow creamers are cream jugs in the shape of a cow. There is an oval hole opening in the top of the back of the cow for filling the creamer. The spout is the mouth with the curved tail serving as a handle. Historically, most filling holes had lids. Today they frequently are missing.

Some cow creamers have a seated milkmaid alongside the creamer. The earliest earthenware cow creamers were made in Staffordshire during the second half of the eighteenth century.

English cow creamers were made in Whieldon ware, creamware, Prattware, and many others. Large size versions often are called cow milk jugs. Cow creamers in tin-glazed ware, c1755, were made at Delft, Holland.

Museum: City Museum and Art Gallery, Stoke-on-Trent, Hanley, England.

COVERED

5 1/8" h
Dark brown, milkmaid in brown dress seated on hummock of grass, translucent green flat base, repaired, c1770, Whieldon type **3500.00**

Sponged raspberry-pink and black patches, seated milkmaid, shaped green sponged base **650.00**

5 1/4" h, dark brown and ochre sponging with brown swags, suckling calf, fluted rect base (A) **1148.00**

5 1/2" h
Pearlware, brown sponged cow standing on molded rect base with pink luster border,

Open, 5 1/2" h, 7" l, orange-rust spots, black mouth, gold horns, green splashed base, unmkd, $350.00

seated milkmaid, green stopper, Staffordshire (A) **912.00**

Pink luster spotting, tail arched over back, rect green base, Cambrian (A) **722.00**

Sponged in brown and ochre on dark cream glaze, nursing calf, sq cov with flower knob, stippled base imp with florets, repair to horns and cov, c1760 . . . . **1900.00**

6 1/4" l
Dark brown sponging on body, dark green base **375.00**

Gray and ochre sponged patches, shaped green washed base, seated milkmaid, c1800 (A) **1018.00**

Iron-red and black trefoil spots, green rect base, cracks, c1840 . . . . **300.00**

Pearlware, black and puce sponging on cow and milkmaid, rect green sponged base, chamfered corners, c1830 . . . . **500.00**

Red-brown spotting on body, green base . . . **375.00**

6 1/2" l
Black and yellow sponged body, milkmaid kneeling under cow, gray-green washed canted base, repairs, late 18th C (A) **575.00**

Blue, gray, yellow and ochre sponged body, seated milkmaid, shaped flat base, restored (A) **575.00**

Blue willow design, c1840, Staffordshire **650.00**
Sponged in raspberry pink and black, green
sponge shaped rect base, kneeling milkmaid
at work to one side, chips, c1800, Staffordshire (A)............................. **650.00**
6⅝" l
Black and puce sponging, seated milkmaid in
blue dress, green rect base, cov replaced,
c1820 .... **500.00**
Pink and black sponging, green sponged
canted rect base, seated milkmaid, early
19th C (A)........................... **1018.00**
6¾" l, 4⅝" h, lg orange-red spots, pink luster horns, black hooves, muzzles, and eyes,
white body, oval green base with pink luster
line (A)............................. **209.00**
7" l, 5⅝" h, red-brown spotting, purple luster
horns, green base outlined in purple luster,
mid 1800s............................ **375.00**
7½" l, mottled brown and ochre body, eyes
blue, tail curled over, canted rect green
washed and brown edged base, restored, late
18th C (A)............................ **1850.00**

OPEN

5" h, seated orange-brown cow, black horns and
tail, circular "Made in Czechoslovakia" mark **49.00**
5¼" h, coat sponged in rasberry-pink, blue, and
gray, milkmaid seated to one side, shaped
green base, repairs, early 19th C (A)....... **708.00**
5½" l, blue harbor scene, white ground, Germany **78.00**
6" l, burnt orange body, gray feet........... **30.00**
6¼" l, mottled manganese body, seated milkmaid in blue skirt, stepped canted rect base,
horns damaged c1800 (A)................ **675.00**
6½" l, 4" h, blue and white, "SCH over X'd
swords" mark......................... **195.00**
6¾" l, blue Delft, windmill and sailboats, unmarked.............................. **79.00**
7¼" l, runny manganese spots, shaped green
washed rect base, tail restored, late 18th C, St.
Anthony.............................. **925.00**
7½" l, gray with black markings, Germany ... **30.00**

CREAMWARE

English/Continental
c1740 to Present

History: Creamware (cream-colored earthenware) provides a fine form and thin body in addition to a clean and
brilliant glaze. Creamware made no pretense to imitate
porcelain in color, form, or decoration. Yet, it found a
ready acceptance in the market place.

Creamware was made from the beginning of the 18th
C. The materials were identical to those used to make salt
glaze. The principal difference is that creamware is fired at
a lower temperature and glazed with lead.

In 1740 Enoch Booth of Tunstall in Staffordshire invented a fluid glaze that provided a brilliant, transparent
cream color. Thomas Whieldon and Josiah Wedgwood
both used this glaze. By 1760 enameled decoration was
being added to the creamware glaze. Derbyshire, Liverpool, Yorkshire, and Swansea also produced creamware
products.

Creamware was improved in 1768 by introducing china
clay and china stone from Cornwall into the body and
glaze. This resulted in creamware that was paler in color,
plus lighter and more brilliant in the glaze.

Since there was much interchange and copying of
ideas among a number of potteries, similarities in both the
body and glaze are found. Hence, it is quite difficult to
assign early creamware to a particular factory since most
creamware was unmarked prior to that manufactured by
Wedgwood.

Creamware was the main product in England between
1760 and 1820. It supplanted the manufacture of white
salt glaze by c1780. Creamware's prominence during
these years provided the death blow to tin-glazed earthenware in England and on the continent. From c1760 English
creamware was exported to nearly every European country.

Many Staffordshire potters left England and established
factories in France, thus threatening the faience factories
and undercutting the sale of porcelains. The European
factories turned to the manufacture of creamware in self
defense.

Reference: Donald Towner, *Creamware*, Faber & Faber,
1978.

Museums: Castle Museum, Norwich, England; Cincinnati
Art Museum, Cincinnati, Ohio; City Museum & Art Gal-
lery, Hanley, Stoke-on-Trent, England; Victoria & Albert
Museum, London, England.

**Plate, 9" d, en grisaille ship design, early 19th C,
England, $150.00**

**Plate, 10" d, en grisaille scene of baptism of
Christ, shaped border with floral sprays, c1780,
unmkd, England, $500.00**

CONTINENTAL

Chestnut Basket, 11 3/8" l, with stand, oval shape with pierced basketweave sides, Germany .. **375.00**

Coffee Cup, 2 3/4" h, painted building landscape in colors, stylized border, "Lodi and A.M." marks, Italy **190.00**

Compote, 10 3/4" l, boat shape on pedestal base, emb leaf design outlined in purple (A) **522.00**

Inkstand, 9 3/4" l, upper tier with two pewter cov wells, lower pen tray with shaped gallery, lion paw feet, late 18th C (A)................. **440.00**

ENGLISH

Basket
6" l, oval, loop handle, brown rope border, Wedgwood (A) **88.00**

8 1/4" l, 3" h, yellow and black enameled design, reticulated body, imp "E. Mayer" mark (A)................................. **302.00**

9 3/4" H-H, reticulated, raised molded heads on either side, molded rim swags, twisted handles, minor repairs, c1780 .... **850.00**

Basket, 10 7/8" l, Cov, Stand, completely pierced, latticework stand, strips molded with roping in low relief, cov surmounted by crawling infant with flower pot, basket with acanthus-molded handles, hairlines, c1780 .... **6100.00**

Basket, Stand, 9 3/16" l, oval, reticulated, pierced around lower body of baskets and rim of stands with border of blue edged oval beneath blue edged scalloped rim, iron-red and black arms of Beaumont or Fleming, loop handled with blue florettes and dots, 1815–20, one imp "Spode F," others imp "SPODE 40" marks, pr........................... **500.00**

Berry Dish, 11 1/4" l, 9 1/2" w, shaped diamond shape, pierced center, four feet, c1780–1800 .... **795.00**

Bowl
9 3/4" l, oval, basketweave center, reticulated sides with turquoise and brown enameling (A)................................. **522.00**

11" d, black and orange enameled anthemiom border, "WEDGWOOD" mark (A) **50.00**

Bowl, Cov, Stand
6" h, 3 fish stand, cov with pierced linear design (A) **140.00**

7" h, 8" H-H, urn shape, salmon panels with black leaves, black lines, cream and black finial, c1790 .... **795.00**

7 3/4" h, bowl molded with band of vertical flutes, cov with band of piercing, circ stand pierced, turquoise and black feathered borders, cov has rose finial, late 18th C (A) .. **1870.00**

Candlestick, 10 5/8" h
Corinthian capitals surmounted by sq nozzles edged in gadrooning, shafts with stopped fluting, flared bases with concave panels molded with ram's heads with garlands, c1785, pr **3850.00**

Ionic capitals on columnar shaped fluted shafts, stepped circ base, repaired chips, c1790 .... **1200.00**

Coffee Cup and Saucer, painted in green florals outlined in black with trailing floral sprays, scattered springs, dbl entwined handle, c1780 (A)................................. **615.00**

Coffee Pot, 9" h, baluster body, painted in red and black with couple having tea alfresco, man in yellow waistcoat, reserve with pagoda in landscape, restored spout, c1782, "iron-red J*D' (A) **935.00**

Cradle, 4 1/2" l, basket molded, rockers, baby in bonnet and dress propped up on pillow, blanket with crimped edge, dotted in light and dark brown scallops, one rocker restored, c1765. **750.00**

Cruet Stand
7 1/2" h, circ stand with intertwined ribbon base, center handle with knob, two oil bottles with Greek key design on neck, three shakers with basketweave bands at neck, early 19th C, Wedgwood (A)........... **825.00**

8" w, central upright dbl rope twist handle, two containers pierced with trellis work, border of continuous raised berried foliage, four feet, two glass cruet bottles and stoppers, late 18th C (A).................... **1028.00**

Cup and Saucer, rose, green, and blue florals, brown rim and int of cup, dbl entwined handles, c1760 .... **425.00**

Cup and Saucer, Handleless, polychrome rose design (A) **50.00**

Cup, Handleless, 2 1/4" h, mustard butterfly int, green feather line on ext, c1790–1800 ..... **95.00**

Cup, Miniature, olive green lines, rust feathered design border, c1790, Wedgwood **110.00**

Decanter Stand, 5 1/4" h, pierced work, c1780–90.. **395.00**

Dessert Dish, 11" d, lobed panels each molded in a stylized tulip motif with piercing, rim with rope border, c1785...................... **1500.00**

Dessert Service, 6 plates 9 1/8" d, 2 tazzas, 9 1/4" d, 3 1/2" h, hp scenes in French style signed by Emile Lessore, center cartouches with figures in countryside, pink borders with purple leaves and florals, mustard rim, tazzas in green, mustard, and white feet, butterflies and florals on undersides, shaped edges, sgd "Emile Lessore, WEDGWOOD" mark.................... **4650.00**

Dish
5 3/4" l, leaf shape, green glazed edge, late 18th C (A)........................... **55.00**

6" l, oval shape, basketweave inner border, looped outer border, c1770–90 .... **195.00**

10" l, 8" w, leaf form, "Ferrara" pattern, dark blue, "WEDGWOOD" mark **225.00**

11 1/8" l, 9 1/2" w, open lattice border, hairline, late 18th C (A) **100.00**

Egg Beater, Cov, 4 1/4" h, cylindrical walls applied with converging spikes, spikes inside cov missing, c1800, Wedgwood, incised numerals (A)................................. **1683.00**

Figure
3" h, bird with double ruff, splashed in green, ochre, and brown, repaired, c1765....... **850.00**

3 1/2" h, recumbent cat with brown and tan spots, striped base, cracked, c1800 (A)... **575.00**

5 1/8" h, seated cat, deep cream color body splashed in manganese brown, rect base incised with zig-zag border, mid 18th C (A)................................. **2550.00**

5 3/4" h, youth in ruffled collar, coat, and knee breeches, holding a bunch of flowers, repaired, c1785........................ **1450.00**

6 1/4" h, girl with "Marmalade Cat," yellow bodice, dot design on skirt, sq base, brown line, c1780–90....................... **1500.00**

Fish Trowel, 10½" l, pierced with decorative
design, handle molded with acanthus, c1785 **3250.00**
Fruit Basket, Stand
   10" d, rims lobed and decorated with piercing
    alternating with sprays in green enamel,
    twisted reed handles ending in green flow-
    ers and foliage, c1775 .... **4100.00**
   11" l, oval shape, pierced with openwork pan-
    els, molded with winged-angel masks, dou-
    ble entwined handles with flowering termi-
    nals, feathered edges, some chips, late 18th
    C (A) **1120.00**
Jug
   5½" h, barrel form, painted with rose spray
    attracting butterfly, beaded blue line bor-
    ders, mask spout, cracks, late 18th C (A) . **400.00**
   8¼" h, ovoid body, printed in black and
    painted in colors, scene of Iron Bridge on
    one side, Sailor's Farewell verse on reverse,
    neck with flowers, pink luster line borders,
    early 19th C (A)...................... **748.00**
Master Salt, 2¼" h, med blue band flanked by
   two narrow brown bands, 19th C.......... **100.00**
Milk Jug, 4⅞" h, silver shape, grapes vines,
   cream glaze, crabstock handle, three mask and
   paw feet, repaired, c1760, Whieldon type.... **1850.00**
Mug, cylindrical form
   2" h, miniature, c1790................... **150.00**
   3⅜" h, black cartoon transfer of Napoleon
    and Cossack, "THE NARROW ESCAPE OF
    BONEY THROUGH A WINDOW," green,
    yellow, red, brown, and black accents, early
    19th C (A).......................... **110.00**
   3¾" h, "Ann Buck Danby Mill" in black,
    brown line rim and base, 1790–1800 ..... **275.00**
   4⅝" h, cylinder shape, "John and Ann Jack-
    son" with crossed tools and foliage, polych-
    romed (A).......................... **214.00**
   4¾" h, painted with a stylized flower spray
    reserved in a multi-lobed panel, red and
    black chintz ground, pink washed dbl en-
    twined reeded handle applied with flower-
    ing terminals, hairlines, c1775 (A)........ **1540.00**
   5¾" h, transfer printed in black, hp colors of
    East India man in full sail with oval husk
    bordered medallion, flanked by figures of
    Peace and Plenty, rhyme below, engraver's
    initials "W C," c1802, Dawson & Co. (A). **510.00**
Mustard Jar, 6" h, shaker shape, c1790....... **275.00**
Pap Boat, oval body imp with rows of roundels,
   two side handles applied with shell thumb
   pieces, molded mask spout, rear handle in
   form of dog's head, pierced for suspension,
   restored, late 18th C (A) **1435.00**
Pepper Pot, 4¾" h, plain body, c1790 ...... **195.00**
Pipe, 10" l, modeled as scaly snake with ribbed
   bowl issuing from its mouth, repaired, c1785 **900.00**
Pitcher
   4⅛" h, 4 med blue bands in descending size **125.00**
   4½" h, globular shape, olive green base,
    cream spout, green, rust, and cream border,
    c1810 .... **695.00**
   5⅛" h, verse on front in rust, green and rust
    florals on either side of verse, rust border,
    blue designs, c1780 .... **950.00**
   5¼" h, ovoid shape with flared scalloped
    rim, entwined ribbed handle with emb floral
    ends, polychrome enameled floral design,
    hairlines and chips (A) **150.00**
   7" h, center panel "Peter-Jackson Minchall

Mill 1780" outlined in green, rust windmill,
   rust and green designs, green border..... **850.00**
10½" h, figural bust of Lord Nelson with
   uniform and medals in relief, white (A) ... **275.00**
Plate
   7¼" d
    Floral center in rust, green, and purple,
     green border, brown edge, c1770 ..... **130.00**
    Seal of the United States in green, ochre,
     and brown in center, green feather edge
     (A) **1040.00**
   7⅜" d, deep cream color, strawberry molded
    shaped rim, c1765 (A).................. **411.00**
   7¾" d, center design of agricultural imple-
    ments in browns, "WEDGWOOD" mark
    (A)................................. **50.00**
   8" d, basketweave inner border, looped bor-
    der and soft green edge, c1770–80...... **195.00**
   8⅝" d, emb basketweave body, pierced rim,
    gilt edge, imp "WEDGWOOD/AFG" mark,
    set of 18 (A)........................ **440.00**
   9" d, woman in purple dress, standing on
    green, mustard, and black base, swag bor-
    der in purple, green, and mustard, message
    commemorating the French Revolution,
    c1793 .... **295.00**
   9⅛" d, blue floral decoration, molded edge,
    c1780 .... **295.00**
   9¼" d, exotic bird in center, six birds in land-
    scape settings on border, black transfer,
    shaped rim (A)....................... **150.00**
   9½" d
    Blue-gray sponging with areas of green, late
     18th C (A) **336.00**
    Center vignette of figure in chinoiserie land-
     scape, blue and white with feather leaf
     border, hairline **265.00**
   9¾" d
    Black armorial transfer of Royal Crest of En-
     gland, scalloped rim, scattered florals on
     rim (A)............................. **275.00**
    Black transfers of scenes of male and female
     peacocks in landscapes, peacocks and in-
     sects on borders, late 18th C, set of 6.. **450.00**
    Molded feather edge, "Wedgwood" mark
     (A) **25.00**
   10⅛" d, center scene of orange tree in tub,
    man and woman in profile, scalloped rim
    (A).................................. **467.00**
Platter, 19¾" l, blue feather edge (A)....... **110.00**
Porringer and Stand, miniature, dbl handles (A) **100.00**
Puzzle Jug, 8" h, quarter moon piercing, extra
   four holes, c1780 .... **900.00**
Sauceboat
   6" l, paneled body, loop handle, c1790 .... **295.00**
   6¾" l, duck form, c1780................. **1800.00**
Sauce Tureen, 7" h, with attached stand, boat
   shape, trailing foliage and vine border, domed
   cov, early 19th C (A) **330.00**
Soup Bowls, 9½" d, black transfers, monogrammed armorials, initials in two places on
   border, blue rims, c1825, set of 8.......... **850.00**
Sucrier, Cov, 4" h, fluted body and cov, rose-
   pink garlands on neck and cov, dbl entwined
   ribbed handles with flower and foliage terminals, opening fruit knob with thistles and foliage, beading on cov and footrim, c1780.... **600.00**
Sugar Caster
   4" h, egg shape, footed base, c1780....... **190.00**
   5¼" h, plain body c1780 .... **190.00**

Sweetmeat Basket, stand, 4⅞" l, lower body molded with ribbing, band of piercing above, twisted reed handles, stand pierced, c1780, "WEDGWOOD" mark................... 1200.00

Tea Caddy
3⅝" h, cylinder shape, wide band of indented flutes around body accented in light green vert stripes (A) 250.00
4⅜" h, thin black and white checkerboard band between two wide med blue bands, 19th C.................................. 175.00
4⅝" h, plain body c1780–90............. 395.00

Tea Canister, 6⅝" h, green stripes, concave neck, sides and neck outlined in raised bands of contiguous ovals and florets, replacement top, c1770 .... 2250.00

Tea and Coffee Service, Part, miniature, baluster coffee pot, 3½" h, cylindrical teapot, kettle, milk jug, cov sugar, slop bowl, 6 teabowls and saucers, white (A) 2100.00

Teapot
4½" h
Globular shape, painted with leafy sprays of flowers and cherries in iron-red, green, and yellow, green knotted crabstock handle and spout, minor repair to spout, c1765 (A).......................... 3085.00
Iron-red transfer printed scene of figures drinking tea, reverse with shepherd seated under tree in landscape, cabbage molded spout, interlaced strap handle, floral finial, handle crack, c1770 (A).... 770.00
4¾" h
Blue oriental design of house with fence and clouds, intertwined handle with emb ends, flower finial, repairs (A) 350.00
Polychrome enameled rose design, ribbed spout and handle (A) 350.00
5" h
Bulbous, red, green, purple, and yellow exotic flowers, applied entwined dbl strap handle 450.00
Oriental scene of woman pouring tea in red enamel, ribbed spout, ribbed intertwined handles with floral terminals, flower finial, repairs (A)......................... 1160.00
Panels of iron-red overpainted with floral sprays in black alternating with panels of cream painted with sprays of flowers in iron-red, green, and black, matching teabowl and saucer, c1775 .... 9750.00
5¼" h
Cylindrical, diaper pattern of iron-red and black with bands of yellow, green, and iron-red, ribbing on lower body, beading about shoulder and cov rim, twisted spout, dbl strap reeded handle, flower and foliage terminals, flower knob, hairline in neck, c1775................... 7500.00
Painted sprays of red, green, and black flowers, dbl entwined strap handle applied with molded and colored flowering terminals, c1770, Wedgwood (A)...... 1645.00
Ribbed and fluted body striped in green, dbl strap reeded handle, foliate terminals, foliage molded spout, spreading foot, high domed cov, flower finial, pierced gallery, repair, hairline in body, c1775......... 3600.00
6" h, oviform, painted oriental garden scenes,

rust, black, and gray, pale blue flower finial, handle restored, c1770, Staffordshire..... 1750.00
6¼" h, exotic flowers in red, green, black, and yellow enamels, molded spout, late 18th C............................... 450.00
10" h, "The Tea Party" on one side, "The Shepherd and Sheep" on reverse, black transfers, c1780 (A) 247.00

Tea Service, teapot, 6¼" h, creamer, cov sugar bowl, waste bowl, 10 handleless cups and saucers, center gaudy florals in polychromes, purple luster rims, repairs (A) 852.00

Toddy Plate
3¾" d, green design and rim, scalloped border, c1790–1800, pr.................... 150.00
4½" d, rose, green, and blue florals, scalloped edge, pr....................... 325.00

Tray, 10" l, oval shape, one with pierced border, one with raised architectural relief border, c1850, imp "WEDGWOOD" mark (A) 180.00

Tureen, Cov
7½" H-H, 6" h, underplate, raised molded design, scalloped edge, c1770–80 .... 995.00
8⅝" h, melon shaped, pierced cov with melon knob coming from branch, vein molded leaf with serrated edge forming attached stand, small repaired rim chips, late 18th C, incised numerals (A) 1190.00
10" l, molded with shell and leaf pattern, rims feathered, dbl entwined reeded handles, briar terminals, four lobed with spreading foot, cov with pomegranate finial resting on leaves and buds, c1775, incised "O" in cov.................... 3850.00
10½" h, 7½" d, blue painted decoration of vines, floral sprays, chinoiserie figures, dbl handle on top, raised molded leaf border, c1790–1820............................. 995.00
12" H-H, with underdish, molded leafy handles, sunflower finial, "WEDGWOOD" mark (A) 200.00

Vase, 9¾" h, urn form body, putti in relief in runny green and manganese brown, dbl dragon handles, canted rect plinth, repaired, c1780 (A) ....:........................ 450.00

Wall Pocket, 8¾" l, cornucopia shape, molded cherubs, grapes and vines on rim, 18th C... 650.00

Wash Pitcher, 12½" h, helmet shape, acorns and oak leaves design, black transfer, green and ochre accents, imp "WEDGWOOD" mark (A)................................. 310.00

CREIL
IM& CIE
MONTEREAU
1841 - 1895

CREIL

Seine-et-Marne and Oise, France
1784–1895

History: About 1784 the Englishman Bagnad in association with M. de St. Cricq-Cazeaux established a factory for the manufacture of English style earthenware. These two founders united with Montereau during the early 19th century, forming a firm that continued until 1895.

The Creil factory was the first French pottery to use transfer printing on earthenware. Transfer views of Paris, French chateaux, portraits of important people, English country houses, fables of La Fontaine, and painted with religious or allegorical subjects in monochrome graced white or cream colored ware. Porcelain never was made.

Marks were either stamped in the paste or stenciled. They included Creil et Montereau or LM & C.

Coffee Service, Part, pot with molded dragon spout, sugar bowl, 10 coffee cups and saucers, black transfer colonial scenes, canary ground, c1810, imp "Creil" marks (A).............. **1870.00**

Plate, 8" d, "le Peiroquez No. 5", orange, white, and green dress, yellow, orange, and green tree, yellow cottage, blue, rust, and yellow floral border, imp "Creil" mark, (A) $50.00

Plate, 8" d, polychrome transfer of int domestic scenes, floral borders, mid 19th C, stamped "Creil et Montereau Porcelaine Opaque L & B" mark, set of 7, (A) $275.00

Dish, 9½" l, oval, "La Temperance," black transfer, c1820, imp and transfer mks (A) ... **400.00**
Pate Pot, 2¼" h, blue and white cow on lid with "L.T. Piver" Paris, cow scenes on bottom, L & M Montereau Market, c1820............. **275.00**
Plate
  6" d, crane with floral design, black transfer, cream ground, "Creil et Montereau" mark **75.00**
  7¼" d, cow scene, yellow and black
    Castle in ground, imp mark............. **485.00**
    Girl with cows, imp mark **475.00**
  7⅝" d, polychrome scenes of two women working in garden, yellow house in ground, c1820s, set of 4...................... **495.00**
  7⅞" d
    Black transfers of cartoons of French life, set of 9 (A)........................... **95.00**
    Puce printed buildings in rustic landscape in scroll-shaped panel, pr (A) **495.00**
  8" d, polychrome scenes of children with blue, salmon, and yellow florals, white ground, c1820, set of 6, imp "CREIL" mark................................. **1500.00**
  8⅛" d
    "L'Aveugle de Bagnolet" with verse, yellow and black, imp "CREIL" mark.......... **465.00**
    "Le Bon Vieillard," animated discussion, with verses, yellow and black, imp "CREIL" mark....................... **475.00**
    "Le Vieux Sergent," man pushing baby in swing, woman with spinning wheel, with verses, imp "CREIL" mark............. **475.00**
  8¼" d
    "La Double Chasse" and "Beaucoup d'Amour," poems of love, black transfers, white ground, imp "CREIL" mark, pr ... **295.00**
    Transfers of various characters and vices, c1840, set of 8 (A)................... **360.00**
  8⅜" d
    "La Bourse" scene, green/black transfer, yellow border, white ground **225.00**
    "St. Sulpice" scene, green/black transfer, yellow border, white ground **225.00**
  8½" d
    Creamware plates with various French scenes, c1850, set of 4 .... **650.00**
    "Lord Byron A La Tete D'un Detachment Grec," yellow and black transfer, c1830, imp "IL Mont" mark.................. **275.00**
    Black transfer, yellow ground
      PORT ST. DENIS, imp "MONTREAUX" mark (A)...................... **350.00**
      PORT ST. MARTIN, imp "MONTREAUX" mark (A)...................... **350.00**
    Scene of people on lawn in front of large house with gate, yellow and black, floral border, c1830 .... **295.00**
  8⅝" d, LE CHAT BOTTE, seated man in period clothes feeding monkey, windmill in ground, black transfer, floral wreath on border, yellow ground, imp "MONTREAUX" mark (A) **187.00**
  9½" d, black transfer of bust of "Alexander es Empereur de Tuetes les Russies," floral border, imp "CREIL" mark **350.00**
Tureen, 13" w, cov molded with leaves and decorated with blue flowering branches in border of scrolls and fans, scroll handles, bird finial, cracks, early 18thC (A)................... **715.00**

c1890   1878-90

CROWN AND ROYAL CROWN DERBY

Osmaston Road, Derby, England
1876 to Present

History: Edward Phillips, formerly of the Royal Worcester Company, established the Royal Crown Derby Porcelain Company, on Osmaston Road in Derby in 1877. This new company had no connection with the original Derby works. By 1878 the new factory was producing earthenwares called "crown ware" in addition to porcelains.

The new Derby porcelain was richly decorated in the old "Japan" patterns featuring reds and blues along with rich gilding very much in the manner of the earlier Derby porcelains. Additionally, the new Derby company produced ornamental forms including figures and highly decorated vases and services.

1890 marked the beginning of the Royal Crown Derby period began when the company was appointed manufacturers of porcelain to Queen Victoria and "Royal Crown Derby" was added to the trademark.

Desire Leroy was the most distinguished artist employed by Royal Crown Derby. He trained at the Sevres factory, went to Minton in 1878, came to Royal Crown Derby in 1890, and stayed until his death in 1908. His most successful contribution was the use of white enamels painted over rich dark blue ground in the style of Limoges enamels. He exhibited a great versatility of design and remarkable use of colors. His lavish designs usually featured birds in landscape, fruits, flowers, and occasional figures. He also added gilt embellishments.

In 1904 toy shapes were produced that attracted the attention of miniature collectors. Figures were made in the late 1920s and early 1930s. During the post-war period, Arnold Mikelson modeled lifelike birds and animals.

In 1935 the Royal Crown Derby company purchased the small King Street works which had been established by some former Derby workers in 1848. This provided a link with the original Derby factory founded by William Duesbury in the mid 18th century.

References: F. Brayshaw Gilhespy, *Crown Derby Porcelain*, F. Lewis Ltd., 1951; F. Brayshaw Gilhespy & Dorothy M. Budd, *Royal Crown Derby China*, Charles Skilton Ltd., 1964; John Twitchett & Betty Bailey, *Royal Crown Derby*, Barrie & Jenkins, Ltd., 1976.

Museums: Cincinnati Art Museum, Cincinnati, Ohio; Gardiner Museum of Ceramic Art, Toronto, Canada; Royal Crown Derby Museum, Osmaston Road, Derby; Derby Museums & Art Gallery, The Strand, Derby; Victoria & Albert Museum, London, England.

Collecting Hints: Royal Crown Derby continues production to the present day as part of Royal Doulton Tablewares Ltd. From 1882 onwards, all Crown Derby can

be dated. A year cypher appears under the trademark, the key for which can be found in Geoffrey A Godden's *Victorian Porcelain*, (Herbert Jenkins, 1961).

Bone Dish, "Imari" pattern in cobalt, iron red, and gold, Royal Crown Derby	**48.00**
Cache Pot, 3¾" h, central panel on each side painted with spray of flowers, gilt framework, mottled blue ground, stepped, shaped oval base, gilt rims, c1907, sgd "C. Harris"	**1000.00**
Candlestick, 10½" h, "Golden Aves" pattern, Royal Crown Derby, pr	**1200.00**
Cream and Sugar, "Imari" pattern #2451	**325.00**
Creamer, 3⅛" h, bone china, blue and white oriental figures in landscape, gold trim, Royal Crown Derby	**25.00**
Cup and Saucer	
Imari pattern	**95.00**
"Pinxton Roses" pattern	**25.00**
Cup and Saucer, Demitasse	
"Olde Avesbury" pattern, set of 6, Royal Crown Derby (A)	**25.00**
"Vine" pattern, emb gold grapes and vines, light green ground, Royal Crown Derby	**24.00**
Dessert Plate, 8¾" d, floral motif, blue border with scalloped gilt edge, white center, set of 12 (A)	**375.00**
Dinner Service, 12 dinner plates, 12 luncheon plates, 12 dessert bowls, 12 coffee cups, 12 bread and butter plates, 14 tea cups and saucers, teapot, cov sugar, creamer, waste bowl, coffee pot, cov sugar, 2 creamers, waste bowl, sweet meat dish, "Red Aves" pattern, 84 pcs (A)	**1540.00**
Dish, 10½" sq, "Imari" pattern, "Royal Crown Derby, Made in England" mark	**50.00**
Ewer	
7½" h, raised gold floral and arabesque design on Chinese red ground, hairline, c1880	**195.00**
8¾" h, Imari pattern of flowers and foliage in	

Cup and Saucer, oriental scene, blue transfers, gilt rim, Royal Crown Derby, (A) $25.00

Mug, 4" h, Domino, molded face in colors, late 19th C, $100.00

underglaze blue, iron-red, and gilt, garlic neck, scroll gilded handle, c1891 .... **450.00**

11" h, panels of hanging floral garlands with pink roses and forget-me-nots above oval panel with musical trophies, royal blue and turquoise ground, raised gilt borders, c1900, sgd "Leroy," printed crowned initials mark, incised 448 (A) **6124.00**

14" h, overall gold design on yellow ground, dtd 1896 .... **350.00**

Figure, 5" l, pig in colors **45.00**

Inkwell, 4" h, footed, modeled sq shape, multicolored florals, gilt trim **75.00**

Jar, Cov

4" h, gold enameling on bright yellow ground, c1894 .... **135.00**

5½" h, white, yellow, and blue flowers on green and gold ground, jeweled lid, dtd 1892, Royal Crown Derby **275.00**

Molded and gilt decorated flowers on red ground, late 19th C, Royal Crown Derby (A) **440.00**

Pitcher, 9" h, multicolored flowers on ivory satin ground, gold handle, Royal Crown Derby ... **395.00**

Plate

8" d, "Red Aves" pattern **22.50**

9" d, cobalt, rust, and gold Imari style florals and swirls, six section rim, c1894, pr **180.00**

9¼" d, man standing beside sailing boat smoking pipe on seashore, naturalistic colors, wide pink border, gilt edges, beaded in blue and turquoise, c1883, sgd "W.N. Statham," printed mark, imp "DERBY (A) ... **1161.00**

10½" d, "Mikado" pattern, blue and white, Royal Crown Derby **35.00**

10¾" d, white center, gold encrusted rim on white ground, Crown Derby, set of 8 (A) . **262.00**

Platter, 19" l, "Imari" pattern in typical colors, Royal Crown Derby (A) **495.00**

Potpourri Jar, Cov, 11½" h, lobed bulbous body, enameled florals, gilt leafy ground, neck and pierced cov with gilt design on dark red ground, dtd 1889 (A) **1870.00**

Spill Vase, 4⅜" h, painted landscape panel reserved on blue ground, gilt borders, dtd 1918, sgd "W.E.J. Dean" (A) **395.00**

Teapot, 2¾" h, miniature, white, gold, red, and cobalt "Imari" pattern on cobalt ground, Royal Crown Derby **110.00**

Tea Service, pot, creamer, sugar bowl, 6 cups and saucers, orange, cobalt, and gold oriental design................................. **950.00**

Teaset, 6 cups and saucers, 6 side plates, bread and butter plate, sugar bowl, milk jug, Imari pattern of formal panels of stylized flowers and foliage, gilded details, 1910, printed "crowned interlaced L's," date code, pattern no. 2451, 21 pcs (A) **561.00**

Tray, 19" l, 12½" w, red, gold, blue, and green Japanese motifs, dbl handles, Royal Crown Derby................................. **750.00**

Urn, 6½" h, Japanese type florals in gilt floral band, blue ground, marked (A) **140.00**

Urn, Cov, 5" h, gold butterflies and leaves on yellow ground, molded mask handles, 1887. **295.00**

Vase

6½" h

Bulbous shape, gold leaf, fruit, and flowers on mottled cobalt ground, gold swags on shoulder, c1890 .... **450.00**

Ornate gold design on red ground, two handles, dtd 1890 .... **95.00**

6¾" h, oval body, panels of summer flowers within ornate tooled gilt foliate borders, royal blue ground, supported by two figures, pierced scroll handles, domed cov with crown knob, c1903, painted by Leroy, printed crown mark, incised shape no. 1362 & date code (A)...................... **4488.00**

7" h, panels of birds in green, blue, and gold on white ground, sgd "Darlington," pr ... **495.00**

9" h, gold morning glories, buds, vine, butterfly, two floral knob handles, yellow ground, Royal Crown Derby mark **250.00**

9¼" h, painted sailing boats reserved on blue ground between gilt beaded and scroll borders, gilt pierced handles, flared foot, waisted shaped neck, dtd 1902, sgd "W.E.J. Dean" (A) **965.00**

11½" h, multicolored flowers on bulbous body, gold and green designs on neck and pedestal foot **155.00**

Vase, Cov

5¾" h, one side decorated with spray of pink roses, flowers and foliage enclosed by tooled gilt scroll border, cov with smaller panels with pink roses and foliage, bud finial, scrolling foliate handles, whole reserved on dark blue ground with gilding, c1900, sgd "Leroy', printed "crown initials" mark, incised numerals, pattern no. "7461/1326, pr (A)............... **8025.00**

8¼" h, enamel and gilt dragonflies and bees in floral and leaf panels, pierced cov and finial, hairline, c1884, pr (A) **275.00**

10¼" h, shouldered ovoid body, trails of summer flowers above ornate gilt scrolls, white ground, blue borders, two handles, c1900, sgd "C. Gresley," printed "crowned initials" mark (A) **5280.00**

12¼" h, Persian style, three leaf shape panels of stylized foliage in pink, gray, green, and gilt, reserved on blue ground molded with scrolling foliage with gilt accents, pierced handles, domed cov, hex foot, pierced crown finial, c1884, printed "crown initials" mark, Crown Derby, pr (A)............. **2790**

STOKE ON TRENT
ENGLAND
c1917-1930

CROWN DEVON

Stoke-on-Trent, England
1870 to Present

History: S. Fielding and Co., Ltd. established a pottery at Stoke-on-Trent, England in 1870. This Staffordshire factory produced a wide variety of products including majolica wares, terra cotta wares, and earthenwares for domestic use.

Their "majolica argenta" was a white body and glaze introduced in the early 1880s. The wares were decorated with high temperature colors and designs in relief. From 1913 lustre wares were sold under the trade name Crown Devon, including works done in the Art Deco style.

Marks used were an impressed "FIELDING" and "SF & CO" printed with the title of the pattern.

Biscuit Jar, 7½" h, panels of multicolored flowers on cream and green ground, SP top **125.00**

Coffee Pot, 7¾" h, two pheasants in colors,

Bowl, 9" d, "Delph" pattern, purple, brown, mint green, and rust, cream shaded ground, blue ext border, "Crown Devon Delph Patchwork, Fielding Stoke on Trent" mark, $165.00

Vase, 9" h, horiz ribbing, gold oriental scene with green, orange, blue, purple, and turquoise enamels, maroon ground, gold handles, cream irid int, "Crown Devon Made in England" mark, $175.00

pastel ground, gold handle and trim, sgd "J. Coleman" **145.00**

Dish
5¼" l, 3¾" w, leaf shape, emb pink and purple fuchsia flowers, green leaves, light gray ground **20.00**
12" l, 5¾" w, two green molded leaves joined by figural red tomato handle **65.00**

Jug
7" h, emb colored figures of woman and two men toasting by fireplace on cream ground, bust of Robert Burns and Auld Lang Syne verse on reverse, musical base.......... **195.00**
8" h, John Peel hunt scene, fox handle, musical base **150.00**

Mug
6" h, emb colored figure of John Peel on cream ground on front, verse on reverse, figural riding crop handle, musical base... **165.00**
6¾" h, woman and two men dancing in colors on cream ground, figural musical instrument handle, musical base **165.00**

Pitcher, 6⅞" h, emb pink and purple fuchsia flowers, green leaves, veined light gray ground................................ **45.00**

Sugar Bowl, 4" h, hp columbines, floral handle, "Crown Devon, Made in England" mark (A) **15.00**

Sugar Shaker, 4¾" h, multicolored flowers on tan ground **85.00**

C. TIELSCH—GERMANY

Silesia, Germany; now Walbrzych, Poland 1845–1945

History: Beginning in 1845, the C. Tielsch and Company factory located at Altwasser made household, hotel, and decorative porcelain, along with coffee and tea sets. The C.M. Hutschenreuther Company in Hohenberg acquired most of the stock of Tielsch in 1918 and merged the factory with its own. Hutschenreuther continued using the C. Tielsch name until after WWII.

Berry Set, master bowl, six serving bowls, pink roses design, "C. T. Germany" mark........ **50.00**

Bowl
6" d, relief scrolls, rim shades to yellow, wide multicolored floral band, gold rim band, "green C.T. Germany" mark............. **4.00**
9" d, rect, enameled winter cabin scene in colors, gold trim, unmarked (A) **18.00**
10" d, multicolored hp florals in three panels on apricot to white shaded ground, ribbed and fluted body, c1880 (A) **18.00**
11" d, hp multicolored florals in four panels on lightt pink and aqua ground, gold outlining, border and edges, c1900, "C.T. Germany" mark (A)...................... **33.00**

Vase, 10¼" h, multicolored scene of man reading paper, dk brown ground shaded to lt brown, "CT Altwasser Silesia" mark, $85.00

12" l, 9" w, oval, hp rasberries with green and yellow leaves on white ground, light fuchsia border, ribbed and beaded rim, c1860, unmarked (A) **25.00**

12½" d, three dainty floral panels, three bright pink panels, heavy gold trim, relief of vines and leaves on reticulated border, c1880, "C.T. Germany" mark (A) **45.00**

12¾" d, floral center, pierced leaf border. . **125.00**

14" l, 9" w, large red and yellow roses on blue to green shaded ground, pierced handles, "C.T. Tielsh, Altwasser" mark **60.00**

Cake Plate

9" d, hp large multicolored floral spray, light gray spray, c1870, unmarked (A)........ **5.00**

10½" d

Hp center floral panel with gold trim, light pink and green ground, "C.T. Germany" mark (A) **13.00**

Iris and buttercups in colors, heavy gold trim, c1900, "C.T. Germany" mark (A) **15.00**

Three multicolored florals, hp gold border, c1893, "C.T. Germany" mark (A) **35.00**

Yellow and pink roses, green vines and birds in center, gold rim and handles, c1880, "C.T. Germany" mark (A) **20.00**

11" d

Small multicolored center flowers, light green and pink border, gold trim, c1900, "C.T. Germany" mark (A) **25.00**

Yellow and green bullthistle leaves and blue blossoms on rose-pink ground, gold accents, c1870 (A) **20.00**

Chocolate Set, pot, 6 cups and saucers, large pink roses on brown and white ground, c1900................................ **300.00**

Cup and Saucer

Gold luster "Friendship" design, marked.... **18.00**

Large pink roses on white ground, "C.T. Altwasser" mark........................ **75.00**

Pitcher, 4" h, blue and gray florals with gold

leaves, gilt trim, bamboo handle, white ground, "C.T. Germany" mark **40.00**

Plate

6" d, roses and scattered flowers, green and pink Greek key border, gold trim, "C.T. Altwasser" mark....................... **5.00**

7½" d

Gibson girl design, "C.T. Altwasser, Germany" mark........................ **75.00**

Small wild rose sprays, relief leaf clusters, scalloped gold rim, "C.T. Germany" mark, set of 11 .... **75.00**

8" d, plain gold bands, "C.T. Altwasser" mark................................ **6.00**

8¼" d, grapes, peaches, and foliage in colors, "C.T. Altwasser" mark **14.00**

9⅛" d, multicolored center transfer of two women and man in classical dress with Cupid, garden setting, mauve border, gold trim, lime green shaped rim **75.00**

10½" d, center with four multicolored fruit, relief of trumpet vine, leaves, and bloom, c1880, marked (A) **18.00**

12" d, blue with pink roses, "C.T. Altwasser" mark................................ **47.00**

Platter

13" l, three gold bands, off white ground, marked............................... **15.00**

22" l, 9" w, oval, center with multicolored pike type fish swimming in weeds, shaped rim **195.00**

Ramekin, pink roses, scalloped rim, "Altwasser, C.T. Germany" mark, set of 3............. **30.00**

Relish Dish, 13½" d, dbl, hp flowers, gold with pink rim, curved handle................... **90.00**

Sauce Dish, 5½" d, enameled cottage scenes in centers, pink, white, and gold rims, "C.T. Germany" mark, set of 4 (A)................. **10.00**

Serving Dish, 11" l, 8½" w, 5½" h, divided, multicolored bunches of flowers on white ground, two pink and blue applied leaves at gold center handle, pink luster edge........ **135.00**

Sweetmeat Dish

14" l, 10" w, blue and white flowers, lobster handle, c1880 (A)...................... **35.00**

Leaf relief border, multicolored hp florals, gold trim, single handle, c1880, "C.T. Germany" mark (A) **15.00**

Tray

12" l, hp multicolored fruit in center, relief of vines and leaves on border, heavy gold trim, c1880, "C.T. Germany" mark (A) **28.00**

12½" l, multicolored scene of cottage, bridge and water in white center oval, pink and gilt hp border, "C.T. Germany" mark (A)................................... **10.00**

13" l

Hp floral center panel, gold border (A) ... **7.00**

Iris and dogwood on light pink ground, heavy gold trim, relief of leaves and vines on reticulated border (A) **25.00**

Relief of wheat heads and florals on handles, multicolored florals in center, gold trim, c1860 (A) **15.00**

14" l, light pink and green florals, sprayed gold border, ruffled edge, c1910 (A).......... **8.00**

Vase, 9" h, multicolored garden scene with two cherubs and young girl, dbl handles, green "C.T. eagle" mark **175.00**

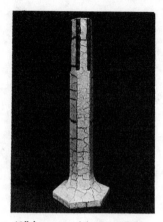

Vase, 12" h, green veining on yellow ground, orange stripes at neck, c1930, $185.00

CZECHOSLOVAKIA— GENERAL

1918 to Present

History: In 1918 the Czechs and Slovaks became free of Austro-Hungary domination and were granted their own country, Czechoslovakia. Portions of the regions of Bavaria, Bohemia, Moravia, and Austrian Silesia made up the new country. Bohemia, now the metropolitan area of Czechoslovakia, was the chief ceramic producing area in the Astro-Hungarian empire in the 19th century.

A variety of china wares were made by the many Czechoslovakia factories, among which are Amphora in Egyptian and Art Deco styles and Erphila Art Pottery. Decorative items such as flower holders and wall pockets in the form of birds were produced. Creamers, salt and peppers, and napkin rings were made in interesting shapes. Kitchen or cereal sets and complete dinner sets, with pattern names such as Iris, Royette, Royal Bohemia, Ivory Rose, etc., kept factory production high.

The Karlsbad Porcelain Factory "Concordia" Brothers Lew & Co. operated from c1919 until 1937. From 1939 until 1945 the factory was operated by Winterling & Co. It was nationalized in 1945 and merged with the former Count Thun's Porcelain nationalized factory in Klosterle. Several other factories such as Meierhofen, Alp, and Altrohlau merged with Epiag in Karlsbad about 1939. This merged firm was nationalized in 1945.

Between 1871 and 1940 B. Bloch & Company made table, household, and decorative porcelain and earthenware, some in the onion pattern. After 1920 the name was changed to the Eichwald Porcelain and Stove Factory Bloch & Co., then to the Eichwald Porcelain Stove and Tile factory for the period from 1940 until 1945.

Most items are stamped "Made in Czechoslovakia" with an ink stamp.

Reference: Ruth A. Forsythe, *Made in Czechoslovakia*, Richardson Printing Corp., 1982.

Ashtray
Hp small flowers in colors, set of 4.	**15.00**
Relief of lizard in colors	**20.00**

Bell, 5" h, figural comical man's head in natural colors, brown hair finial handle **35.00**

Box, Cov, 5 1/8" h, triangle shape with clipped corners, terra cotta ground, orange, green, and blue enameled relief classical scenes of elephants and attendants, pinecone knob, "Erphila Czechoslovakia" mark **115.00**

Candlestick
4 1/2" h, blue and yellow flowers, green leaves, black outlines, one handle, cream ground. **30.00**

5 1/2" l, Art Deco style, checkered black and white border on yellow ground **35.00**

9 3/4" h, hp multicolored swirling geometrics **45.00**

10" h, dark turquoise and cream swirls, flared petal base **10.00**

Condiment Set
5 cov jars, 7 1/2" h, 5 cov jars, 3 1/2" h, 2 vinegar and oil bottles, upper and lower bands of multicolored flowers, black lettering, "Made in Czechoslovakia" marks **238.00**

Flour, 8" h, vinegar and oil, 8 3/4" h, cloves, pepper, nutmeg, allspice, 4 1/4" h, salt box, 8" h, orange flowers with green, blue, and purple accents, yellow ground, wooden top for salt box **325.00**

14 canister and spice jars, orange, magenta, rust, green, and yellow floral bands with black borders, irid ground **325.00**

Creamer
3" h, red and blue checkerboard body, orange luster rim bands, hairline **5.00**

4 1/2" h, figural parrot in yellow, orange, and green **30.00**

5" h, multicolored hunt scene **30.00**

Cup and Saucer
Blue luster ext, orange luster int, black trim . **6.00**

Multicolored pheasant on cup **30.00**

Cup and Saucer, demitasse, silver luster ext, gold int, set of 6 . . . . **50.00**

Dinner Service, 12 dinner plates, 12 luncheon plates, 12 soup bowls, 12 bread and butter plates, 12 sauce bowls, 7 saucers, 4 cups, creamer, sugar bowl, oval vegetable bowl, oval platter, cov vegetable dish, gravy boat, blue and gold banding (A). **231.00**

Dish, Cov, 4 3/4" l, red figural crab, set of 4 . . . **55.00**

Ewer, 16" h, turquoise and cream mottled glaze, brown streaks, marked **65.00**

Feeding Dish, 7" d, multicolored decal of two girls with umbrella, stork with baby in beak, "Eipig, Czechslovakia" mark **78.00**

Figure
7 1/2" h, multicolored Art Deco woman's head, "Erphila Czechoslovakia" mark **135.00**

8 1/8" h, bust of Art Deco woman, orange and yellow curls, red lips, gray-tan crackle face, turquoise sq base **185.00**

17" h, orange and yellow cockatoo, marked **135.00**

Flower Frog

3" h, 4 1/2" d, basket, pearlized finish, black handle, "Made in Czechoslovakia" mark. . **15.00**

4 5/8" h, bird in brown, tan and rust, blue breast, yellow bill, seated on green stump, "Made in Czechslovakia" mark **16.00**

5 1/4" h, red, blue, and green crested parrot, seated on green tree trunk, "Made in Czechoslovakia" mark **12.00**

Honey Pot, Cov, 5 1/4" h, raised forget-me-nots in form of hanging chain, blue with green leaves, orange basketweave ground **50.00**

Jar, Cov, 6 1/8" h, orange painted poppies, blue tulips, turquoise and brown leaves, black rims.................................... **95.00**

Mug, 3" h, multicolored transfer of dancing peasant couple in village scene, Czech saying in black, red "Czecho" in red circle mark ... **18.00**

Mustard Jar, Cov, 2 3/4" h, purple figural grape cluster, handled **7.00**

Perfume Bottle, 9" h, figural girl in colonial dress, pompadour hair, head forms lid **75.00**

Pin Tray, 7" l, Art Nouveau bust of woman in relief.................................... **32.00**

Pitcher

3" h, green dots on white ground **15.00**

5" h, figural moose head, red-brown top, cream base........................... **40.00**

7" h, purple grapes, orange-red apple raised design, green leaves, shaded cream to green ground, bright red upper part and handle.................................. **65.00**

7 1/4" h, orange luster with bubble designs, black key border...................... **85.00**

8 1/2" h, stylized figural rooster, red comb and wings, black eye and beak, white ground . **145.00**

9 3/4" h, bulbous shape, narrow top, purple shapes with yellow, green, and black int, red dots, white int, black ground **75.00**

Planter, 5" h, ftd, gold and brown silhouette of gypsy campfire scene, "Erphila Czechoslovakia" mark.............................. **45.00**

Plate

7" d, red trim on white ground, marked **4.00**

9" d, multicolored classical scene in center, marked.................................. **27.00**

10 3/4" d

Polychrome floral center, gold encrusted rim, "Czechoslovakia" mark, set of 12 (A) **200.00**

"Royal Ivory" pattern, set of 8 .... **150.00**

White center, gold encrusted rim, "Czechoslovakia" mark, set of 10 (A) **132.00**

11" d

Center bouquet of flowers with gold trim, border of flower bunches separated by med blue quadrants with gold tracery, shaped rim, "OMECO CZECHOSLOVAKIA" mark......................... **25.00**

Cobalt and cream bands with gold tracery around center of pink and blue flowers, set of 14 .... **280.00**

Platter, 17 3/4" l, 12 1/4" w, oval with sq corners, lavender, pink, and blue birds and flowers in center and on cream and gold border **95.00**

Sauce Dish, figural red lobster **10.00**

Teapot, hp figural Dutch girl in blue trimmed dress, holding large basket of flowers **85.00**

Tea Service, teapot, sugar bowl, creamer, 6 cake plates, 6 cups and saucers, blue luster ext, peach luster int **185.00**

Tea Set, teapot 3 3/4" h, creamer, sugar, Art Deco style, panel with blue leaved trees, blue clouds, yellow sky, green and pink ground, reverse with circ design in same colors, burnt orange ground........................ **110.00**

Trivet, 7 1/2" d, oct, center scene of man on camel, gold and cobalt border **45.00**

Vase

4 3/4" h, decal of vert hanging flowers amd scrolls, yellow ground, two tiny handles .. **40.00**

5 3/8" h, stylized florals with raised black and blue enameled outlines, yellow shoulder to rim handles, artist sgd.................. **28.00**

6" h, three raised black stripes outlined in gilt, orange ground, white int, two handles.... **35.00**

6 3/4" h, five panels with magenta flowers, blue/green leaves, black lines and stems, cream ground....................... **35.00**

7" h, fan shape, red, green, black, and blue Art Deco design, cream ground **30.00**

7 1/8" h

Black honeycombed ground with small orange three leaf pattern, black swirls on front with small green leaves, blue and yellow bands on base **110.00**

Painted blue violets, red flowers, green leaves, black scroll on upper 1/3, lower 1/3 in caramel yellow, raised black stick design and dots on int rim **110.00**

7 1/2" h

Front panel of emb black flowers, tan and rust crackle glaze, handles rim to base, marked **22.00**

Mottled yellow ground, multicolored spatter.................................. **45.00**

8 3/8" h, striped body in yellow, mustard, orange, terra cotta, cobalt, and black, black lines separate panels, two yellow handles with black designs...................... **85.00**

9 1/2" h, yellow hp, orange and yellow flowers outlined in black with raised blue dots in center of flowers, green leaves, two handles **48.00**

10 1/2" h, purple luster finish (A).......... **20.00**

Wall Pocket, 6 1/2" h, orange and yellow modeled bird, pierced for hanging, "Made in Czechoslovakia" mark **45.00**

DAVENPORT
STONE CHINA
1805-20

DAVENPORT
LONGPORT
STAFFORDSHIRE
1870-1886

DAVENPORT

Longport, Staffordshire, England
1794–1887

History: John Davenport and family established the factory in 1794. Earthenware, ironstone, porcelains, cane ware, black basalt, and glass were made. Few of the early examples were marked. Porcelains were not manufactured until 1805–1810. The earliest Davenport porcelains were marked with the word "Longport" in red script.

About 1825 Davenport teawares and dessert services came under the influence of the Rococo revival. The shapes of pieces resembled the Coalport forms of this period. Landscape decorations were used frequently.

Porcelain painted plaques were decorated both at the factory and by independent artists about 1860–1880. Earthenware table services for use on ships became a specialty product. Colorful Japan patterns were produced in the Derby manner in the 1870s–1880s. These were a specialty of the Davenport factory. The firm ceased operation in 1887.

References: T.A. Lockett, and Geoffrey A. Godden, *China, Earthenware & Glass, 1794–1884,* Random Century, 1990.

Museums: British Museum, London, England; Cincinnati Art Museum, Cincinnati, Ohio; Hanley Museum, Stoke-on-Trent, England; Liverpool Museum, Liverpool, England; Victoria & Albert Museum, London, England.

Bowl, 5⅝" d, "Imari" pattern (A) **100.00**
Cake Set, cake plate, 4 serving plates, pink flowers on white ground, marked **225.00**
Compote, 9" h, "Nectorine" pattern, blue-gray

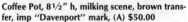

Coffee Pot, 8½" h, milking scene, brown transfer, imp "Davenport" mark, (A) $50.00

Pitcher, 5½" h, blue, iron-red, and pink florals, white ground, printed "Davenport" mark, $75.00

Tankard, 6½" h, figures in landscape, blue transfer, c1835, $200.00

open flowers, white center, magenta border with molding. **410.00**
Cup and Saucer, white and gilt center, orange and gilt trim, c1815, "blue anchor" mark . . . **195.00**
Cup Plate, 4" d, "Villaris" pattern, black transfer. **45.00**
Dessert Service
  2 high comports, 4 low comports, 12 plates, iron-red, blue, and gold with flowering rockwork and stylized floral sprays, stone china, blue printed marks, 18 pcs (A). **900.00**
  Teapot, creamer, sugar, 6 plates, 6 teabowls and saucers, multicolored transfer and painted floral sprays with bird, peacock eye borders, imp "anchor" marks. **750.00**
Dinner Service
  12 plates, 10¼" d, tray, 12½" l, tray, 20¼" l, ironstone, "Imari" pattern of large iron-red flower from cobalt leaves with gold trim, orange, cobalt, and green floral border. **2500.00**
  39 plates, 9⅞" d, 22 soup bowls, 22 dessert plates, 4 vegetable tureens, covs, 2 soup tureens, covs, 4 sauce tureens, covs, stands, ftd bowl, 2 oval meat serving dishes, 14 oval serving dishes in sizes, strainer, "Imari" pattern in underglaze blue, iron-red, and gilding with peony and bamboo within alternating border of stylized leaves and sprigs of flowers, 1810–20, underglaze blue printed mark, gilt pattern number 135, 125 pcs (A) **18,000.00**
Dish
  9–9¼" l, shell shape, each with botanical specimen within gilt edged wide matte green border, gilt fluted handle, 1820–25, botanical inscriptions, underglaze "blue DAVENPORT LONGPORT" marks, 4 pcs (A). **1925.00**
  10¾" H-H, oval, "Chinese River Scene," med blue transfer, repaired hairlines, marked (A) **88.00**
Pitcher
  6½" h, stoneware, red-brown enameled band on neck, relief of fox hunting scene, dbl emb coiled rope around base, imp "DAVENPORT and anchor" mark (A) **88.00**
  8⅛" h, stoneware, dark brown band around neck with thin gold band, relief of tavern scene with pipe smokers around body, bas-

ketweave relief around base, imp "DAVEN-
PORT and anchor" mark (A) **231.00**

Plaque

8⅝" l, 6⅜" w, ratter chasing a rat which
goes through a hole in wooden fence, two
cottages amongst trees in ground, mid 19th
C, imp "DAVENPORT PATENT" mark (A). **1181.00**

8⅝" l, 6½" w, "The Raising of Lazarus,"
c1850–70, framed (A) **1317.00**

Plate

7¼" d, creamware, brown toned center design of musk ox in mountainous setting,
openwork rim accented in brown, imp
"DAVENPORT and anchor" mark (A) **88.00**

8½" d

Armorial with crest in center, raised shaped
gilt border, white ground, c1850. . . . . . . **295.00**

"Cyprus" pattern, black transfer, c1860,
imp "anchor" mark **60.00**

White ground with green feather edge, imp
"anchor" mark (A) **35.00**

9⅞" d, armorial, iron-red, gold, blue, and
green center with arms of Claxson of East-
gate House and Wotton Lodge, Gloucester-
shire, motto "SAPERE AUDE INCIPE," dot,
leaf, and bud border, royal blue ground rim,
raised gold floral sprays, c1820, "gray DAV-
ENPORT LONGPORT STAFFORDSHIRE"
mark, 265 in gold, set of 6 (A). **1210.00**

10" d

Italian village with beached boat, floral border, light purple transfer, imp "Davenport
and anchor" mark. **35.00**

Multicolored floral center, wide fuchsia border, gilt inner rim, white and gilt rim, white
ground, c1830, imp "Davenport anchor"
mark, pr. **540.00**

Platter

16½" l, "Chinoiserie High Bridge," blue and
white, 1793–1810. . . . . **895.00**

16¾" l, 12¼" w, with strainer, landscape
scene with English manor in ground, two
men seated by pond, branch border, med
blue transfers, early 19th C (A) **400.00**

17¼" d, "Tyrol Hunter," brown transfer . . . **100.00**

19" l

15" w, "Bride of Lammermoor" in ma-
roon. **225.00**

Figures in forest and meadow setting, estate
in ground, floral border, dark blue transfer
(A) **495.00**

Potpourri Basket, 4⅛" h, caneware, oval shape,
molded basketweave sides, pierced top, rope
twist handles, early 19th C, imp "Davenport
and anchor" mark, pr (A) **1150.00**

Potpourri Vase, Cov, 13½" h, waisted globular
body, panels and sprays of roses and foliage
between foliate gilt borders, twisted vine
branch handles extending to encircle the lip,
pierced gilded cov with pinecone knob, cov
restored, c1835 (A). **3179.00**

Soup Plate, 8⅛" d, multicolored floral design,
green feather edge, imp "Davenport and an-
chor" mark (A). **160.00**

Tea Service, 11 cups and saucers, 11 plates,
etruscan shape, Harlequin, bright sprays and
panels of roses, tulips, and daisies, gilded,
1822–26, pattern no. 741, 33 pcs (A) **2805.00**

Wine Cooler, Caneware, Relief Molded
9¼" h, deep U shape, fruiting vine on either

side with applied satyr mask handles,
c1810, imp "Davenport and anchor"
marks, pr (A). **3643.00**

10" h, bust of Nelson, reverse with naval trophies, fish head handles, imp mark (A) . . . **1330.00**

Wine Pitcher, 14" w, 11¼" h, white with cobalt
blue twisted rope handle and rim, blue leaves
on spout and under lip, blue lines around mid
section and base, 18th C, imp "Davenport"
mark. **3850.00**

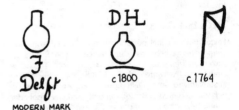

MODERN MARK   c 1800   c 1764

DELFT, DUTCH AND ENGLISH

Holland
c1613 to Present
Bristol, Lambeth, and Liverpool, England
1690–1790

DUTCH

History: Tin enamel ware was first manufactured in Delft
about 1613 as a result of Italian potters immigrating to
Holland and bringing the techniques with them. Prior to
this the Dutch relied heavily on the Dutch East India Company's importing Chinese porcelains to fulfill their china
need.

When the imported supply was reduced, through dis-
ruption of the trade routes, the local Dutch pottery industry thrived. Idle breweries were refitted as potteries. By the
mid 1600s more than thirty pottery manufacturers were
operating out of the defunct breweries making imitations
of Chinese and Japanese porcelains in blue and white tin
glazed wares. A transparent lead glaze was added as a
"flashing" or overglaze to make the tin enamel copies
closely resemble Chinese porcelain.

Two types of blue and white wares were made. The first
type featured blue and white motifs in the monochrome
Chinese style. The blue and white motifs of the second
type included Dutch subjects such as landscapes, windmills, sailing ships, portraits, Bible stories, views of towns,
and other "series" plates. The prime period of production
for both types of blue and white wares was 1640–1740.
Other towns in Holland also produced blue and white in
addition to Delft. Few pieces are found with identifying
maker's marks.

After 1700 more polychrome wares were produced in
tones of copper green, iron red, and yellow. Japanese
Imari wares were the source of inspiration for the polychrome wares. In addition to plates, tiles, vases, and other
dishes, Delft potters also specialized in novelties such as
shoes, cow milk jugs, violins, and small figures especially
of animals.

The decline of Dutch delft was accelerated by the introduction of Wedgwood's creamware in the second half of

the 18th century. In addition, the works of Meissen and Sevres surpassed the tin glazed wares from Delft. By the beginning of the 19th century, the number of pottery manufacturers in Delft was reduced to three.

Today only one of the original producers of Delftwares remains in operation. De Porceleyne Fles began producing pottery in 1653. This firm was saved from bankruptcy in 1870 by Joost Thooft. To make the company competitive, Thooft made some changes in the manufacturing process, among which was importing white baking clay from England. Each piece is marked with the logo of De Porceleyne Fles, Joost Thooft's initials, and the initials of the decorator.

ENGLISH

History: Tin enamel pottery came to England from Antwerp in the Netherlands in the 16th century. At first the tin glazed earthenware was called "galley-ware." The name changed to Delftware in the mid-18th century because of its similarity to Dutch Delft products. English delft production was centered in Bristol, Lambeth, and Liverpool after strong beginnings in London in the mid-17th century.

At Lambeth, apothecary wares, barber basins, and puzzle jugs were among the most popular forms produced. In Bristol, the glaze had a more bluish tone. Plates, bowls, and flower holders with a naive treatment predominated. Liverpool delft with its harder body resembled Chinese porcelains more closely than that made elsewhere. By 1790 tin enamel glaze wares fell into decline in England due to the rise of Wedgwood's creamware.

References: John Bedford, *Delftware*, Walker & Co., 1966; Frank Britton, *London Delftware*, Jonathan Horne, 1987; Carolene Henriette De Jonge, *Delft Ceramics*, Praeger, 1970; H.P. Fourest, *Delftware*, Rizzoli, 1965; F.H. Garner & Michael Archer, *English Delftware*, Faber & Faber, 1972; Ivor Hume, *Early English Delftware from London and Virginia*, The Colonial Williamsburg Foundation, 1977; Diana Imber, *Collecting European Delft and Faience*, Praeger, 1968; Anthony Ray, *English Delftware Pottery in the Robert Hall Warren Collection*, Boston Book & Art Shop, 1968.

Museums: Ashmolean Museum, Oxford, England; Fitzwilliam Museum, Cambridge, England; Gemeente Museum, Arnhem, Holland; Gardiner Museum of Ceramic Art, Toronto, Canada; Henry Ford Museum, Dearborn, Michigan; Hius Lambert van Meerten Museum, Delft, Holland; Musees Royaux d'Art et d'Historie, Brussels, Belgium; Prinsenhof Museum, Delft, Holland; Rijksmuseum, Amsterdam, Holland; Royal Factory "De Porceleyne Fles" Collection, Delft, Holland; Sheffield City Museum, Sheffield, England; Victoria & Albert Museum, London, England; William Rockhill Nelson Gallery of Art, Kansas City, Mo.

Reproduction Alert: The old Dutch wares have been copied as souvenirs and are quite popular with the foreign traveler. Be careful not to confuse these modern pieces with the older examples.

DUTCH

Albarello, blue "C Hamech." and "U Desiccat. Rub" within songbird and fruit basket cartouche, ftd, mid 18th C (A)............... 350.00
Ashtray, 6 1/2" d, blue and white florals, three rests, "De Porcelyne" mark30.00
Barber Bowl, 9" d, blue painted stylized flowering plants, formal leaf border, pierced for hanging, c1780 (A)..................... 300.00
Bowl
  6 1/4" d, melon-ribbed body, blue and white

stylized leaf and scroll design, tab handles, "De Porcelyne" mark.................. 60.00
9 3/4" d, blue and white, chinoiserie, ext with three different vignettes of Chinamen, separated by bobbin shaped blue ground panels of flowerheads and foliage, int with "1687" between squiggles within dbl circle, crack, chips (A)............................ 550.00
Butter Tub and Stand, 7 1/2" w, oct, blue overall chrysanthemums in scrolling foliage, shell finial, c1710 (A)......................... 495.00
Candlestick, 8 1/2" h, polychrome, molded as rococo tree stumps overlaid with scrolls and foliage, green, blue, ochre, manganese, and red, scroll molded bases, manganese "JVDH," c1760, Young Moor's Head factory, pr (A). .11,814.00
Charger
  12 1/4" d
    Blue oriental figure in landscape, floral border, yellow line rim, pierced for hanging, 18th C (A) 360.00
    Center with open florals, serrated inner rim, border with stylized flowerheads separated by arrowheads, blue and white (A)........................... 220.00
    Vase with flowers in center, scattered sprigs on border, line rim, blue and white (A). 77.00
  13 1/4" d, overall dark blue with white panels housing designs in blue, c1720.......... 695.00
  13 1/2" d, portrait in center in blue, yellow, and green, molded and scalloped, c1690. 3000.00
  13 3/4" d, blue and white central floral panel, four smaller floral designs on border, yellow rim, "HB" mark (A)..................... 275.00
  16" d, blue and white scene of woman with children, floral border, imp "Thoeft & Labouchere" mark, pr (A)............... 385.00
  16 3/4" d, polychrome parrot on branch, compartment type border (A) 1100.00
Dish
  6 1/2" d, equestrian group of man in red cloak riding spirited horse in landscape of stylized sponged trees, polychrome, pierced for hanging, c1730 (A)..................... 1378.00
  8 5/8" d, molded rib body, center stylized flowerhead, vert rays, border of dashes, blue and white with black trim, rim chip (A)..... 165.00
  8 3/4" d
    Fluted, oriental standing in rocky setting painted in blue, outlined in black, border of radiating tassels and demi- florets, hairline, late 17th C (A) 350.00
    Green, iron-red, blue, and manganese with panels of single flowers in blue lines radiating from central flower, c1700, pr (A)...................... 275.00
  12 1/4" d, blue peacock design in yellow line rim, c1680, "De Porceleyne Claeuw" mark (A)................................... 350.00
  13 1/2" d, circ, blue portraits of William and Mary, titled in English, rim with florettes and scrollwork (A)........................... 516.00
  13 1/2" d, blue, yellow, and green portrait of William or Mary with tulips at sides, border of trailing tulips and flowers, fluted body, cracks, chips, c1700, pr (A) 2420.00
  13 5/8" d
    Blue stork in center with flowers from rockwork, pagoda in ground, rim with five pagodas on hills, c1730 (A).................. 440.00
    Yellow, iron-red, green, and blue with fe-

male figures of Plenty holding cornucopia amongst sponged trees, rim chips, c1750 (A) **648.00**

14½″ l, 5″ w, blue relief of fish in center, floral and fan leaf border, "De Porcelyne" mark **65.00**

Drug Bottle, 9⅞″ h, blue inscription "A Ru-thae" within cartouche surmounted by two birds and basket of fruit, winged putto's head beneath (A) **270.00**

Ewer, 9″ h, blue and white windmill scene, raised rococo trim, handle on shoulder with thumbrest **80.00**

Ewer, Cov, 17½″ h, flask shape on ovoid foot, blue and white cherubs, insects, and leaves, sides with applied satyrs, c1780–83, "blue crowing cock" mark (A) **413.00**

Figure

3⅛″ l, recumbent spaniel, polychrome, manganese eyes, nose, and spotted coat, green shaped oval base, mid 18th C, pr (A) **1210.00**

3¾″ h, 4″ l, standing cow with head turned, blue and white floral design, "Delft de Porcelyne Fles" mark **30.00**

6″ l, tortoise, shell molded with overlapping plates in red and yellow with green splashes, edged in blue, head and legs in manganese, c1760, "red 5,O" mark (A) **2360.00**

6¼″ h, resting parrot in blue and manganese feathers, wings and tail in yellow, green, and brown, c1760 "red APK" monogram (A) . **2165.00**

7¼″ h

Seated puppy with manganese splotches, yellow padlock collar, blue dotted green washed base, yellow washed border, repairs, c1760 .... **1300.00**

Woman in local costume with yellow straw hat, carrying storage jar and bottle, man in manganese hat, carrying baby in swaddling clothes on back, sq blue-edge base, baby repaired, c1780 (A) **1500.00**

7½″ h

Pierrot as young boy, dotted yellow suit with manganese ruff, purse in right hand, left hand missing, c1770 (A) **1279.00**

White standing elephant, puce outlined ears and tail, yellow tusks, orange tongue, manganese toenails, "blue JVDH" mark **1530.00**

8⅞″ h, polychrome parrot, perched on blue washed tree stump, red head, blue speckled chest, yellow legs, plumage in blue, yellow, green, and manganese, restuck, mid 18th C (A) **1050.00**

9½″ h, recumbent horse, muzzle, mane, tail, and horseshoes in manganese, marbled yellow, green, orange, and manganese high base, c1760, "manganese claw" mark for De Porceleyne Claew factory (A) **10,285.00**

9½″ h, 9⅝″ h, milking group, cow with iron-red nose, manganese markings, floral garlands around neck and back, milked by maid in manganese costume and hat, chamfered rect base, green top, manganese border of shells, scroll, and triangles, c1760, "manganese claw" and 9 or 6 marks, pr (A) **2475.00**

Fruit Dish, 9″ d, with stand, pierced, blue design of central flowerhead on scrolling foliage in blue bands, border with panels of scrolling foliage, shaped rims, c1720 (A) **132.00**

Jar, Cov, 8½″ d, blue peonies and willow on

fenced terraces, loop handles with blue scrolls, button finial, c1720 (A) **440.00**

Jug, 9″ h, green, yellow, and blue exotic birds on rocks with lush flowering plants below a scale border, c1700, "blue V" mark (A) **1300.00**

Pitcher, Dutch, 3⅜″ h, 6″ d, Art Nouveau style, brown leaf on tan ground, $375.00

Pitcher, 8″ h, blue painted scene of whale ship "Charles W. Morgan" at sea, white ground, "Made in Holland" mark (A) **100.00**

Plaque

3¾″ l, rococo shape, shepherd watching two goats, canal lock with two sailing boats in dockland, oriental pagoda in ground, painted in blue, polychrome scroll, shell, and foliage molded rim, pierced for hanging, late 18th/early 19th C (A) **2057.00**

9¹³⁄₁₆″ w, 9¹¹⁄₁₆″ w, blue and white, dog chasing parrot in flight amidst insects near long tailed bird perched on flowering tree above small pagoda and banded hedge in fenced garden, molded cartouche shaped frame, border of trellis diaper panels alternating with panels of stylized blossoms edged with leaf scrolls, surmounted by shell device, pierced for hanging, c1740, pr (A) **4950.00**

10″ l, 12⅝″ w, rect shape, young mother and child playing with cat painted in blue, stepped manganese border as frame, pierced for hanging, 2nd half 18th C (A) .. **4500.00**

11¾″ d, blue design of flowers in ftd vase, scattered floral border, crosshatched rim, hairlines, 18th C (A) **360.00**

12¾″ l, 14⅞″ w, rect form, blue and white, four travelers in riverscape fringed by trees and arcaded building, early 18th C (A) ... **4600.00**

13¼″ h, molded asymmetrical scrolled form, blue painted insects in flight above pierced rocks and flowering plants in fenced garden, scrolled rim in brown, yellow, manganese, and green, mid 18th C (A) **3540.00**

Oval, blue and white group of mounted horsemen playing cards and drinking outside inn, pierced for hanging, reverse with "Junius, 6/51657″ (A) **2834.00**

Plate

6½″ d, manganese carnation, yellow flower, four bud sprigs on pie crust rim, turquoise ground, rims restored, 3rd quarter 18th C, pr (A) 650.00

8¼″ d, blue painted man with ax over head (A) **385.00**

8¾″ d, center with polychrome vase of

flowers with dbl dash ring, border of single dashes (A).......................... **440.00**

8⁷⁄₈" d, blue and white oriental figure with pagoda in landscape setting, paneled border, pr (A)............................ **330.00**

9" d, blue peacock, yellow line rims, restored rim, c1690, "blue B:P" mark (A)......... **198.00**

9¹⁄₈" d, blue and white center scene of bird perched on fence, pecking at basket of fruit, peacock eye feathered border design (A). **160.00**

9¹⁄₄" d, blue and white

Center vase of flowers in ten sided cartouche, border of five panels of kites on diaper ground, early 18th C, "blue PAK" mark (A).......................... **132.00**

Dancing couple in period clothes, ruins at side with tree branches, stylized clouds overhead, hairlines, pr (A)........... **33.00**

Open summer flowers in center, scattered florals on border, pr (A).............. **275.00**

11⁷⁄₈" d, blue and white with figures in landscapes with buildings and sponged trees, haircrack, late 17th/early 18th C, underglaze "blue 12" mark, pr (A)........... **1619.00**

Posset Pot and Cov, 8" h, blue panels of flowering plants below border of fungus and foliage, domed cov with similar decoration, two strap handles, c1730 (A)..................... **1531.00**

Shoe, 4" h, molded and painted with elaborate buckles in blue, scrolling carnations, tongues with parrot perched in a ring, c1710, pr (A). **1350.00**

Strainer, 16¹⁄₂" w, blue and white, oriental cottage beside stylized rockwork issuing pendent leafy boughs within a border of scrollwork panels, foliage and demi-flowerheads at rim, whole pierced with pattern of circ holes, rim with two blue dashed loop handles, underside with three stump feet, 1760–80 (A)....... **990.00**

Teabowl and Saucer, painted oriental style scrolling foliage in orange-red, green, and blue, fluted bodies, pr (A)..................... **195.00**

Tea Caddy

4¹⁄₄" h, rect, blue European genre scenes and geometrics, pewter cap, early 18th C (A) . **880.00**

4¹⁄₂" h, hex, blue, green, red, and manganese scene of two oriental figures in landscape, metal cap, restorations, late 17th C (A) ... **880.00**

Tobacco Jar, 9¹⁄₂" h, blue and white pipe smoking Indian seated beside cargo including a tobacco jar inscribed "TONKA" and parcel with "VOC," two Dutch ships in distance, late 18th C, blue "BP" mark (A).................... **600.00**

Tureen, Cov

10⁵⁄₈" h, lobed form, manganese stem finial spills over cover and continued over bowl with blue and orange flowers, yellow ground, hair crack, 3rd quarter 18th C, "blue 3 Astonne" mark (A).............**18700.00**

12¹⁄₂" h, modeled as a blue goat reclining on mossy ground, ochre horns, little boy in blue jacket, yellow breeches, black hat, climbing on back of goat, restored, late 18th C, "blue axe" mark (A) **12,345.00**

Urn, Cov

13¹⁄₂" h, ovoid shape, blue willow tree and flowering foliage, early 19th C........... **250.00**

18¹⁄₂" h, baluster body, center cartouche with courting couple surrounded by floral spray, cov with bird finial, 19th C, pr (A).. **1320.00**

Vase

5¹⁄₂" h, flared rim, narrow waist, circ foot,

scroll handles, blue and white central bird surrounded by floral sprigs, hairline, 18th C (A).................................... **605.00**

6" h, blue and white scene of Dutch woman carrying basket, three figural dragon handles.................................. **240.00**

Vase, Dutch, 6³⁄₈" h, gold and black Aztec design, lt green ground, c1901, "Delft W" mark, $1875.00

7" h, bottle shape, green, iron-red, blue, and yellow Chinese figures in fenced garden with rockwork, band of stylized leaf tips, c1710, "iron-red PAK" mark (A)......... **462.00**

9" h, paneled shape, blue painted Chinese man at table with teapot, in molded cartouche, molded shell at top, c1800, pr ... **1275.00**

9¹⁄₂" h, paneled shape, two oriental men in boat, bridge in ground with house, trees, birds, in raised cartouche, c1750–95 ..... **675.00**

10¹⁄₂" h, blue and white floral design, flared top and base **195.00**

11¹⁄₂" h, polychrome, Chinese export style with sailor's farewell scene within rococo border of scrolling foliage, reverse with Chinese boy chasing butterfly within vignette of flowering peonies, touches of gilding, rim damaged, mid 18th C (A).............. **1337.00**

13¹⁄₈", 13³⁄₈" h, oct bottle shape, blue painted alternating panels of bird on branch or diapering, border of stiff leaves on neck, florals below rim, spherical knob, c1725, pr (A).................................... **550.00**

19⁵⁄₁₆" h, oct baluster body, blue and white Chinese warriors in continuous hilly landscape, wide border of still leaves, flaring rim, c1710, cobalt blue 20, pr (A)........... **9350.00**

Blue Dutch woman carrying basket, three dragon handles **245.00**

Vase, Cov, 13¹⁄₄" h, oct baluster body, blue and white, molded scroll edged cartouche on front with sailing ships within oval surrounded by flowers, reverse with cluster of grasses, cov molded with cartouche painted with floral sprig beneath seated kulin knob, crack, c1780, De Porceleyne Bijl Factory, "blue axe and backward 7" mark (A).................... **495.00**

Vegetable Bowl, Cov, 8¹⁄₂" H-H, Blue "Parsley" pattern, "Royal Delft de Porcelyne Fles" mark.................................. **60.00**

ENGLISH

Barber Bowl, 10½" d, blue painted razor, shears, and comb, stylized foliage on rim, pierced for hanging, cracked, c1760 (A) **4975.00**

Bottle, 7⅝" h, globular shape, blue "Sack 1641" on white ground, ringed neck, loop handle **3700.00**

Bowl
  4" d, blue, green, yellow, and manganese with chinoiserie island scene and birds flying in formation, mid 18th C (A)............... **1110.00**
  9" d
    Circ, lakeside scene of church and cottages nestling among trees, tones of blue, linked comma border, pierced sides outlined in blue, reverse with flowering branches and "K," crack, 1760–70 (A) . **2440.00**
    Scattered floral sprays in rust and green, pie crust rim with blue V's and dashes, early 18th C (A) **1045.00**

Brick
  5¾" l, 2⅜" w, 3½" h, blue and white oriental scene of man on bridge and coastal village, sides with floral sprays, top with rect hole and 12 small holes, 18th C (A)...... **605.00**
  5⅞" l, rect, blue painted European figures in landcapes before ruins, sponged trees, top perforated with rows of blue petal edged holes, restored, c1740 (A)............... **1025.00**
  6¼" l, oriental island scenes in blue, top with two sq apertures, three rows of perforations, bracket foot, damage, c1760 (A) ... **350.00**
  6½" l, 2¾" w, 3¼" h, blue and white coastal scene with fence and florals, water and boat in center, pierced top, 18th C (A). **600.00**

Caudle Cup, 2⅝" h, white, squat baluster shape with applied loop handle, mid 17th C (A) ... **1625.00**

Charger
  8¼" d, sm, blue, manganese-purple, and copper-green with radiating geometric pattern, reverse with straw colored lead glaze, chips, late 17th C, drilled for hanging (A) . **8096.00**
  11¾" d
    Yellow, blue, and green leaves, central leaf and four radiating leaves, scattered berries on ground, concentric blue line borders, blue-dash rim, c1700 (A)........ **2992.00**
    Three tulips and stylized foliage from a mound in yellow, blue, and green, concentric blue line borders, blue-dash rim, repaired, c1700 (A) **925.00**
  12" d, blue, turquoise-green, and yellow single tulip flanked by leaves issuing from mound, triple blue line border, repaired, 1680–90 (A)...................... **1110.00**
  13" d, blue fox flanked by turquoise-green cloud-like trees in circ panel reserved within border of leaves and fruit in yellow, ochre, blue, and green, concentric line borders, blue-dashed rim, c1670–80 (A)........ **64,977.00**
  13⅛" d
    Blue painted stylized plant, border of demiflorets in manganese arcs and blue dashes, late 17th C.................. **1000.00**
    Vase of flowers and flying bird in blue paint outlined in manganese, dbl line border, hairline, chips, late 17th C **1000.00**
  13¼" d
    Adam and Eve in center with apple tree and

serpent, flanked by foliage, blue and yellow dash rim, cracked, rim chips, early 18th C (A) **2200.00**
Center with bird and florals in shades of blue, yellow-gold, and iron-red with two blue bands, border leaves in same colors with blue band, c1760............... **975.00**
  13⅜" d, polychrome of oriental fisherman and companion by flowering bamboo on a riverbank, figure in sampan in distance, mid 18th C (A)........................... **1430.00**
  13½" d, blue, iron-red, ochre, and yellow with group of tulips, gillyflowers, and leaves growing from fenced mound, yellow line rim, blue-dash border, reverse with greenish lead glaze, pierced for handing c1690, Lambeth (A) **1950.00**
  13⅝" d, turquoise-green, blue, yellow, and ochre oak leaf and stylized fruit sprigs within blue roundel, surrounded by four oak leaves and fruit motifs and floral sprigs within blue-dashed yellow band at rim edge, c1680 (A) **3300.00**
  14" d, radiating geometric pattern in blue, sage green, mauve, and yellow, rim chips, early 18th C (A)....................... **1000.00**
  19" d, press molded, white, foliate border around central design, saw tooth edged rim with molded radiating triple row border, pierced for hanging, mid 17th C (A)...... **6000.00**

Collander, 8½" d, pierced top, overall blue bird and floral design, white ground, mid 18th C (A)............................ **715.00**

Dish
  8⅞" d, lobed, yellow and manganese-purple bird perched on leafy stem, molded rim with manganese tasseled demi-floret border, late 17th C, Bristlington (A) **385.00**

Dish, English, 11½" d, blue florals and geometrics on white lobed ground, pr, $1400.00

  11⅞" d, circ, blue chinoiserie island scene within diaper border reserving panels of ribboned leaves, flowering scrolling branches and flower heads on shaped rim, c1760 (A).......................... **300.00**
  12⅜" d
    Blue and white central fence and floral garden, floral border, mid 18th C (A) **235.00**
    Blue painted Oriental seated in rocks and shrubs, dbl line border (A) **2105.00**
  13" d, polychrome Adam and Eve outlined and painted in blue, flanking blue trunked tree with green sponged foliage and

striped fruit, red and yellow striped serpent entwined in bough, mid 18th C, Lambeth (A) **2631.00**
13 3/8" d, manganese, blue, iron-red, and yellow stylized pinwheel in center, spokes terminating in stylized tassel, border with alternating trellis and flowering branches, rim chips, c1750 (A) **495.00**
13 5/8" l, blue, red, green, and yellow with parrot perched on branch from rock, rim with pine sprays, restored crack, 2nd half 18th C, Lambeth (A). **700.00**
Drug Jar, 5 1/2" h, squat cylindrical, blue horizontal band of erect and inverted patterns of various sized arcs within multiple line borders, glaze restored, early 18th C (A). **1646.00**

Figure, English, 6 1/4" h, polychrome floral and scroll decoration, restored, early 19th C, pr, (A) $660.00

Fuddling Cup, 3 1/4" h, three cups joined by three dbl twist handles, blue painted floral sprig on each cup, blue dash handles, c1640, Southwark (A) **4020.00**
Head Flask, 4 1/8" h, child's head with dark blue curly hair, floret below vertical spout, flared base with gadroons, pale blue ground, damaged, c1680 (A). **2431.00**
Jug, 5 5/8" h, globular, ribbed cylindrical neck, blue and manganese chinoiserie seated figure in mountain landscape, blue dash loop handle, c1690, Lambeth. **4550.00**
Mug
3 5/8" h, cylindrical, two oval panels with oriental style buildings and willow tree on rocky island, panel with "SL," powder blue ground, glass bottomed (A) **1260.00**
5 1/2" h, baluster shape, blue flowering branch, blue-dash looped handle, c1760 (A) **680.00**
Oil Jar, 4 5/8" h, inscribed "O:COMMUN" on songbird label, spouted, mid 18th C (A) **1193.00**
Plate
7 5/8" d
Oct shape, blue painted Chinese style with seated figure in mountainous landscape, other figures on rim in garden settings, crack, c1690, Lambeth (A) **805.00**
Spray of three thistles in blue, dbl line border, c1750 (A) **385.00**
8" d, oct, tones of blue with Oriental seated on rocky landscape, border of stylized tasseled flowerheads, late 17th C (A) **607.00**

8 1/2" d, blue painted crown and "G R" in sunburst cartouche, concentric line border, c1715, London (A) **1725.00**
8 5/8" d, tones of blue with bird standing on rock by stylized plants, border of concentric lines and linked ovals, small repair to rim, early 18th C, London (A). **810.00**
8 3/4" d
Blue crested cartouche on body and border with crown, winged animals, tassels, and scrolls, dtd 1706 and CCC in cartouche (A) **770.00**
Oriental designed florals in medium blue, yellow, iron-red, and brown, design continued on border, c1760, Lambeth. **395.00**
8 7/8" d
Blue bust portrait of William Augustus, Duke of Cumberland, flanked by initials "D W," concentric line borders, c1746–50 (A) **2805.00**
Blue swan swimming in pool among green rushes, rim with border of manganese lozenges and blue lines, c1750, Lambeth, pr (A). **5135.00**
Delicate blue and rust florals and leaves encircled in blue, blue and rust curved line on border, blue rim, c1750, Lambeth . .   **650.00**
9" d
Blue and white coastal landscape scene, leaf border (A) **235.00**
Blue, green, yellow, and manganese with balloon floating over a house by fenced terrace and trees, border of stylized swags, blue feathered rim, c1785, Lambeth (A) **2024.00**
Blue, rust, yellow, and blue-green simple floral center, petals on border, c1720, Lambeth **695.00**
Blue "Union," thistle and rose below crowned "GR" cipher within blue borders, crack, c1715, Lambeth (A) **1416.00**
Five stylized flowers and foliage from mound painted in manganese, green, blue, and red, looped border, mid 18th C, pr (A). **1221.00**
Long tailed bird perched amongst flowering shrubbery attracting winged insect in blue, greenish-gray, and yellow, outlined in manganese, chipped, c1760, Liverpool (A) **475.00**
13 1/2" d, polychrome scene of Chinese boy seated in fenced garden, rim with pendant flower sprays in red, blue, and green, pr (A). **1235.00**
Platter, 17 1/16" l, rect, blue painted oriental river landscape with pagoda and tree on one bank, fenced garden on opposite, foliate scroll border with orange rim, hairlines, c1760–70, Irish (A). **2090.00**
Posset Pot
4 1/4" h, cylindrical shape, two blue painted seated orientals flanking blue-dashed upright spout, reverse with standing figure, rocky landscape, stylized shrubbery, scrolling handles, late 17th C (A) **1235.00**
5 1/8" h, blue painted bird on rock, flowering shrubs, scrolling border on neck, blue dashes on strap handles and spout, early 18th C (A). **765.00**
8" h, baluster shape, birds perched on flower-

ing branches, neck with whorl pattern border, blue-dash handles, cov with mushroom knob, restored, early 18th C (A) 2400.00

8¼" h, baluster shape, blue flowering branches, blue-dash strap handles and spout, cov with mushroom finial, early 18th C, "blue 3" mark (A) 3272.00

Punch Bowl

9⅞" d, ext with half length portrait of Frederick the Great in blue above ribbon inscribed "The King of Prussia," putto holding victor's wreath, reverse with figure of Fame blowing trumpet amongst military trophies, int with halberd and flag, c1760 (A) 4331.00

10⅛" h, blue peony sprays below looped trefoil border, int with florals, mid 18th C (A). 595.00

10⅜" d, blue ext scene of pavilion by rock flanked by flowering shrubs, int with floral sprigs, mid 18th C (A) 400.00

Puzzle Jug

7¹/₁₆" h, spherical body, blue and white, "I.P" between running Chinaman and vignette of two gazebos in oriental landscape, scalloped and barbed circ foot bordered with blue lines repeated around ankle and shoulder, pierced and knobbed neck edged in blue, supporting tubular rim, three spouts, loop handle, 1680–90, London (A). 18,700.00

7½" h, globular shape, blue and white, "Here Gentlemen come try your skill" on one side, reverse with flowering plants, pierced cylindrical neck, tubular rim has three nozzles, mid 18th C (A) 2805.00

Salver, 8½" d, circ, iron-red and gray-green with stylized floral sprigs within shaped panels, blue ground with iron-red motifs, upturned fluted rim, pierced for hanging, early 18th C, numerals in blue (A) 700.00

Shoe, 6⅝" l, high heel and buckled, simulated lacework and flowers in runny cobalt blue, restored, early 18th C (A) 750.00

Soup Plate

8⅝" d, soft blue scene of taking of Portobello, three English ships in foreground, rim with border of pendant berries and foliage, brown enamel edge, 1740–45, Liverpool (A). 2125.00

8¾" d, house scene in center, blue and white paneled border with lines, dots, and designs, 18th C 185.00

Vase

6½" h, cartouche of water landscape with boat, scattered florals on body, blue and white (A) 192.00

6⅞" h, baluster shape, blue washed and outlined landing bird and butterfly in flowering shrubs (A) 1045.00

7¼" h, bulbous body, trumpet neck, flared lip, blue painted stylized flowerheads and sprigs, stiff leaf border on neck, restored, early 18th C 500.00

Wall Pocket, 7" h, twisted rib shape outlined in blue shading, 18th C (A) 206.00

Wet Drug Jar

8" h, dark blue songbird label ins "S:5 RADIC" for Syrup of Five Roots, above a winged angel-head and pendant tassels, early 18th C (A) 2260.00

1872–1881    1882–1898   1898–1907

1888–1897

DE MORGAN, WILLIAM

Chelsea, England
1872–1881
Merton Abbey, near Wimbledon, England
1882–1888
Sand's End Pottery, Fulham, England
1889–1907

History: William De Morgan, 1839–1917, was primarily a designer and decorator, not a potter. He purchased many tile blanks from commercial firms, e. g., Architectural Pottery Company to decorate with his own designs. In 1872 De Morgan established a pottery in Chelsea to produce his own underglaze blue tiles while experimenting with other colors such as red luster. In the mid-1870s he used the Persian colors purple, blue, and green for decorating tiles and ornamental vases. William Morris, De Morgan's friend, influenced his design motifs in areas such as flowers, birds, fish, ships, or mythical beasts.

In 1882 De Morgan moved to Merton Abbey near Wimbledon. He still made tiles, but increased his output of jugs, bowls, and globular vases. In partnership with Halsey Ricardo, an architect, he moved to Sand's End Pottery at Fulham in 1888. Together they produced pottery, tiles, panels, and murals. De Morgan's pottery body was lightly fired, rather granular, and well suited to the ornamental nature and broad designs of his work. Vases were decorated in the "Isnik" style with the strong Persian colors. Although some pieces showed an Art Nouveau influence, De Morgan was associated with the Arts and Crafts Movement during the Sand's End Pottery period. The more important decorators to work for De Morgan were: Charles and Fred Passenger, James and John Hersey, and Joe Juster. Their initials usually appeared with the standard factory marks on their works.

De Morgan was the first English potter to rediscover the secrets of older luster decoration. Later lusters used by Pilkington (see Tiles) are related to De Morgan's successful experiments in the 19th century.

After 1892 De Morgan lived much of the time in Italy due to illness. In 1898 his partnership with Ricardo ended; and, the showroom closed. De Morgan reorganized and took into partnership the artists Charles and Fred Passenger and his kiln master, Frank Iles. The factory stopped making its own pots and bought biscuit wares from Carter and Co. of Poole. The factory closed in 1907. De Morgan gave permission to the Passengers to continue using his designs.

References: Julian Barnard, *Victorian Ceramic Tiles*, Mayflower Books, 1972; John Catleugh, *William DeMorgan Tiles*, Van Nostrand Reinhold Company, 1983; W. Gaunt & M.D.E. Clayton Stamm, *William De Morgan*, N.Y. Graphic Society, 1971.

Museums: Art Institute of Chicago, Chicago, Illinois; Battersea Old House, London, England; Castle Museum, Norwich, England; City Art Gallery, Birmingham, England; City Museum & Art Gallery, Stoke-on-Trent, England; Fitzwilliam Museum, Cambridge, England; Leighton House, Kensington, England; William Morris Gallery, Walthamtow, England; Victoria & Albert Museum, London, England.

Charger 14″ d, Ruby Luster
   Rearing antelope in pinks and red, scrolling foliage, white ground, reverse has four foliate scrolls from central circle, rim with wide horiz band of foliage, c1888–1895 (A) ... **4224.00**
   Seated winged creatures in pink and red, styl-

Dish, 14½″ d, lustered, winged lions accented in yellow and pink, c1888–97, "FP" mark, (A) $1500.00

Vase, 11½″ h, "Persian," ruby, salmon, and yellow stylized flowerheads and foliage, c1890s, "W. DE.M. & Co." mark1025.00

ized foliage, cream ground, reverse with circ motif in middle, horiz band border with leaves, c1880 (A) **5702.00**
Stylized dolphin-like creatures in pink and red, dense scolling foliage, white ground, reverse with horiz scale border, c1888–1895 (A) .. **7392.00**
Stylized flowers in vase, border of inlocking semi-circles, reverse painted with wide band of orange foliage, c1898–1911 ..... **1050.00**
14⅛″ d, ruby luster, two fantasy dolphins in iron-red underglaze on ground of scrolling arabesques, ground lustered over in pink, reverse decorated in iron-red concentric bands, centering dots, dashes, and squiggles, Early Fulham Period, 1888–97, unsgd (A) .. **3300.00**
Dish
   9″ d, ruby and salmon-pink with galleon in full sail at sea, crew silhouetted against skyline, flying fish in foreground at evening sun sets, c1898–1911, imp "BODLEY & SON" mark (A)................................... **1599.00**
   10¼″ d, ruby, salmon, and gold lustered design of gallion with rolling clouds, spiked waves, white ground, red luster, salmon, and gray bands and foliate band border on reverse, c1888–97, "W.D.M. FULHAM" mark (A) **4115.00**
   11⅞″ d, seated stag in center in ruby, surrounded by stags amongst foliage, center inscribed "Cervus," reverse painted with foliage, cracked, c1898–1911 (A)......... **800.00**
   14⅛″ d, ruby luster coiled scaley snake on scrolling leaf foliage ground, c1880 ...... **1950.00**
   14⅜″ d, ruby luster painted winged creature, gold luster sun motif, c1880............. **1975.00**
   14½″ d, seated winged lions facing each other in yellow and pink lusters, c1888–97 (A)................................... **1500.00**
Plaque, 9⅞″ d, ruby luster large and small carp swimming in weeds, white ground, reverse with white and ruby luster concentric circles, c1900 (A) **2600.00**
Tile, 5½″ sq, green foliage with turquoise and blue flowers, c1882–88 (A)............... **860.00**
Vase
   8⅝″ h, ovoid, cylindrical neck, painted black swimming fish in weeds, reserved on turquoise ground, 1921–23 (A) **700.00**
   11½″ h, "Persian," ruby, salmon, and yellow stylized flowerheads and foliage, c1890s, script "W.DE.M.& CO." mark........... **1000.00**

1903

COPENHAGEN
c 1925

DENMARK—GENERAL

1759 to Present

History: Louis Fournier, a Frenchman, made soft paste porcelain in Denmark from 1759 to 1765. These wares had a yellow tone with a dull glaze and were decorated with flowers and cupids in the French style. The principal products were tableware.

Franz Muller made the first hard past porcelain in Denmark in 1773. From 1779 until his death, Muller managed the Royal Porcelain Manufactory in Copenhagen. Furstenberg and Meissen models were copied. Anton Carl Luplau, master modeler, came from Furstenberg to work in Denmark. His strawflower pattern in underglaze blue achieved tremendous popularity.

Neo-classical decorations were used on the majority of Copenhagen porcelains. Gustav Hetsch served as managing director of the Royal Porcelain Manufactory about 1815. During the 1830s many state services were designed for the royal residences. Denmark's national sculptor Berthel Thorwaldsen made numerous sculptures and reliefs during the 1840s. Copies of his works were made in biscuit porcelain and these statuettes sold extensively. Christian Hetsch continued his father's Neo-classical style at the Royal Porcelain Manufactory, but enhanced the pieces with colorful decorations, relief, and gilt.

Financial problems occured after 1850. By 1868 the factory was Royal in name only. It was privately owned. In 1882 the firm regained some prominence when it merged with the Faience Alumina factory which had been established in Copenhagen in 1863. Philip Schou served as manager.

Arnold Krog became artistic director in 1885. He reinstituted the original strawflower ornamentation and designed new tableware shapes. Krog's revival of underglaze blue decoration utilizing the strawflower and other patterns started a prosperous period for Copenhagen. Animal sculptures were introduced by Carl Liisberg in 1888.

The Bing and Grondahl factory was the second factory established in Copenhagen. Starting in 1852 the sculptor Hermann Bissen produced biscuit statuettes and reliefs based on the same models as the Royal Porcelain Manufactory. Harold Bing became managing director in 1885. He appointed Pietro Krohn as artistic director in 1886. Krohn's greatest design was the "Heron Service" where the heron appeared on each piece.

Museum: Royal Porcelain Factory, Copenhagen, Denmark.

Bowl, 4" d, high gloss harlequin portrait in colors in center, circ devices on ext and int, white speckled ground, Bjorn Wiinblad (A) **95.00**
Dish
    4" d, stoneware, hp, muted fruit center, black border, terra cotta ground, imp mark "L. Hjorth" **30.00**
    8" d, art pottery, three seals on rust red ground (A) **80.00**

Bowl, 8½" l, 5" h, burnt orange ground, black seal, green edge, "crown PIE" mark, (A) $192.00

Figure, 3¾" h, blue dress, white flowered cap, brown bucket, "crown DJ Copenhagen Denmark" mark, (A) $176.00

Vase, 6⅛" h, Art Nouveau style, applied dragonflies, hand cut openwork, maroon and black glaze, $1200.00

Figure
  2¾" h, Pomeranian in colors, #1148, Dahl Jensen **50.00**
  3½" h, boy with butterfly wings, white, #01161, Dahl Jensen **200.00**
  4" h, Australian wren, #1315, Dahl Jensen mark **150.00**
  5" h, seated desert fox, #01236, Dahl Jensen **335.00**
  5½" h
    Faun with grapes in colors, #01173, Dahl Jensen **395.00**
    Standing wirehair fox terrier, #1009, Dahl Jensen mark **190.00**
  7½" h, boy in winter clothing, #1064, Dahl Jensen **145.00**
  8" h
    Sculptor, #1244, Dahl Jensen mark. **750.00**
    Standing cat with tail raised, gray coat, Dahl Jensen **265.00**
  10½" h, cow grazing, barefoot woman standing at side, Dahl Jensen **450.00**
Needle Case, 5¼" l, figural fish in gray and brown, fins accented in salmon pink, silver mts, c1770–80 (A) **1620.00**
Vase
  2" h, terra cotta body, glossy small white stars and ext, white int **5.00**

3½" h, stoneware, hp band of fruit, terra
cotta ground, imp mark "L. Hjorth" **35.00**
3¾" h, florals on front, crackle ware, matte gold
rim, "DJ Copenhagen Denmark" mark. **50.00**
5" h, stoneware, hp, bird in muted tones,
leaves and berries, black border, terra cotta
ground, imp mark "L. Hjorth" **125.00**
5½" h, art pottery, toad stills on rust red
ground (A) **88.00**
8" h, vert stripes hung with small portraits in
Art Deco style, "Nymolle, Denmark" mark **85.00**
9½" h, stoneware, hp, four fruit clusters, geometric band at top and bottom, terra cotta
ground, imp "L. Hjorth". **125.00**

1782- 1825   1820-40

DERBY

Derby, England
1755 to Present

History: William Duesbury I opened the Derby works at
the Nottingham Road factory in 1755. Tablewares and
ornamental wares were produced. Chinoiserie designs,
exotic bird paintings, and blue and white patterns were
the favorite design motifs. Derby had no factory mark
before Duesbury purchased the Chelsea factory.

In 1769 Duesbury acquired the Chelsea factory and
transferred some of the extremely skilled craftsmen from
Chelsea to Derby. 1770 witnessed the production of the
first biscuit or unglazed porcelain and figure groups. Originally developed at the Sevres factory about 1752, biscuit
figures were to make Derby famous.

In 1784, Duesbury closed the Chelsea works, moving
the remainder of the craftsmen to Derby. Duesbury died
in 1786, and William Duesbury II, his son, assumed control.

Between 1786 and 1797, under the guidance of Duesbury II, the Derby factory became a major British pottery.
Great advances were made in body, glaze, potting, and
decoration. A tremendous variety of lavishly decorated
objects were made. Added to the popular floral patterns
were landscapes, maritime subjects, and hunting scenes.
Duesbury's group of painters and craftsmen were among
the finest in England during the eighteenth century.

In 1795 Duesbury took Kean as his partner. Duesbury
died in 1791. Kean continued to produce landscape and
marine subjects, but the quality of the body and the glaze
deteriorated. Robert Bloor leased the factory in 1811 and
then took over completely. The shapes tended to be
larger, utilizing flamboyant gilded decoration as a reflec-
tion of the current tastes. The Japan or Imari patterns with
their rich colorings and lavish use of gold typified of the
period. Imari patterns that started about 1770 are still
being produced. Many figures were also modeled during
the Bloor period. Bloor experienced a long illness during
which the factory declined. He died in 1846. In 1848 the
factory was sold.

The Nottingham Road factory closed. Several of the
potters and painters began manufacturing china at King

Street, trading as Sampson Hancock until the eventual
merger with Royal Crown Derby in 1935. Utilitarian wares
were made with an emphasis on the popular Japan and
Imari designs. This small factory is the link to the claim of
continuous china production in Derby.

References: F.A. Barrett & A.L. Thorpe, *Derby Porcelain
1750–1848*, Faber & Faber, 1971; H. Gilbert Bradley, ed,
Ceramics of Derbyshire, 1750–1975, privately published,
1978; F.B. Gilhespy, *Derby Porcelain*, Spring Books, 1961;
Dennis Rice, *Derby Porcelain - The Golden Years, 1750–
1770*, Hippocrane Books, 1983; John Twitchett, *Derby
Porcelain*, Barrie & Jenkins, 1980.

Collectors Club: Derby Porcelain International Society,
The Honorary Secretary, in care of 31 Beaumont, Oxford,
OX1 2NZ, England; £25 membership, quarterly newslet-
ter, journal, occasional essays.

Museums: see Crown & Royal Crown Derby.

Basket
7" d, circ, underglaze blue with pavilion,
fence, and pine tree in oriental riverscape,
borders with painted flowerheads and
fishroe, tapering sides pierced with trellis
and applied with florettes, double ropetwist
handles with flower terminals, c1760–65,
patch marks, pr (A). **1404.00**
8¾" l, reticulated yellow open lattice weave,
red flowerheads at junctions, red and yellow twist handles with floral and leaf termi-
nals, Chelsea-Derby, pr (A) **3875.00**
Basket, Stand, 7⅛" l, 9¹³⁄₁₆" l, oval, center in
shades of yellow, iron-red, puce, green, and
brown with cluster of fruit surrounded by purple, yellow, iron-red, puce, and black insects
repeated on basket molded ext of basket,
brown edged rim, basket rim with turquoise
twisted dbl loop handles terminating in yellow
centered white floral clusters with green
leaves, 1760–65 (A) **1650.00**
Berry Dish, 6¹³⁄₁₆" d, botanical, each with dif-
ferent floral specimen in center, gilt edge rim,
c1815, iron-red botanical identifications and
"crowned X'd batons, D marks, puce 29
painter's mark," set of 8 (A) **2475.00**
Bough Pot, Cov, Bombe Body
6⅞" h, painted with summer flowers flanked
by decorative gilt bands reserved on dark

**Urn, 8" h, baluster form, landscape and figural
frieze, cobalt and gilt banding, dbl bracket handles, c1800, pr, $1000.00**

blue ground, sides with gilt edge foliate handles, four gilt scroll feet, pierced cov, c1830, Bloor Derby, "red circular" mark (A) **1772.00**

8" h, lobed, painted with named "View in Kent" of fisherman on promontory, bridge in distance, gilt arabesque borders, acanthus molded handles, pierced cov in gilding, c1825 (A) **815.00**

Bowl, 9 5/8" w, blue, iron-red, and gilt "Old Japan" pattern, angular gilt handles, c1805, "puce crown, X'd batons and D" mark **200.00**

Box, 7 1/2" l, figural nesting dove in purple and white, nest encrusted with tan and brown foliage, c1800 (A) **880.00**

Candlestick

6" h, figures of putti scantily draped with pale purple cloak, seated on tree stump, "Spring" wearing flowers and holding nosegay, "Autumn" with fruiting vine and holding bunch of grapes, scrolling bases encrusted with flowers or grapes, foliate molded nozzles, restorations, c1765, pr (A) **785.00**

10" h, Venus in turquoise lined flower sprigged pink robe with Cupid at side, Mars in turquoise skirt with gilt tipped red tassels, before trophies of war, flower entwined tree stumps surmounted by foliate nozzles, scrolling bases with applied colored flowers, repaired, c1765 (A) **2362.00**

Caudle Cup and Saucer, multicolored birds in naturalistic plumage, standing or perched in landscapes scattered with exotic insects, lobed double ogee shape with gilt scroll handles, "red crown, X'd batons, and D" marks, gilders 2 (A) **810.00**

Creamboat, 4 3/4" h, blue painted chinoiserie scene of islands and trees, scrolling rim and handle, c1760–65 (A) **450.00**

Cup, 2 1/2" h, rust, green, and gilt classic design, gilt panel outlines, white base, late 18th C, crown mark, pr **140.00**

Dessert Plate, 9" d, cluster of purple grapes, iron-red and yellow apple, three green plums, four rose strawberries and branch of white currants in center in gilt band and berried foliate roundel, gilt husk and dot inner border, fluted rim with branches of autumnal foliage in brown, orange, yellow, and green within gilt border, c1790, painted by George Complin, "crowned X'd batons and D" mark, pattern no. 140, gilder's no. 8 (A) **990.00**

Dessert Service, Part, fluted lozenge shaped fruit stand, 11 13/16" l, 2 circ sauce tureens, cov, stand, 2 scalloped lozenge shaped dishes, 3 smaller fluted lozenge shaped dishes, 4 sq dishes, 19 plates, printed in gold, center with lion rampant crest, gilt edged rim, gilt foliate vine border entwined with gilt dot-edged iron-red ribbon, 1795–1800, "pink crowned X'd batons, D" marks, 35 pcs (A) **3300.00**

Dinner Service, Part

2 rect cov veg dish, 2 oval sauce tureen, cov, stand, oval platter, 19 7/8" l, 4 oval platters, 14 1/8" l, 4 oval platters, 13 1/8" l, 3 oval platters 10 3/4" l, 19 soup plates, 41 dinner plates, 20 small plates, painted in two shades of underglaze blue, iron-red, green, and gold, "Derby Rose" pattern, central stylized oriental floral sprig surrounded by trailing sprays with gilt edged panel, four similar panels alternating with underglaze blue panels patterned with gilt foliate scrolls and cell diaper vignettes, gilt edged rim, 1820–25, "crowned X'd batons and D" mark, iron-red painters' numerals, platters with incised size numerals, 98 pcs (A) ... **13,200.00**

Oval platter, 16 3.8" l, oval platter 14" l, rect cov veg dish, 10 1/2" l, oval sauce tureen, cov, stand, 8 soup plates, 8 dinner plates, 8 small dessert plates, "King's" pattern, underglaze blue, iron-red, and gold with central prunus tree amidst peonies and other flowers within border of cell diaper vignettes and iron-red ground panels of white scrolls within underglaze blue and gilt foliate scrolls, gadrooned rim edge with underglaze blue and gold zig-zag border, some cracked, c1825, "iron-red crowned X'd batons and D" marks, various numbers, 28 pcs (A) **2420.00**

Dish

6 5/16" l, molded as brown centered yellow rose blossom striated in puce, sprays of green-veined spring green leaves, three rose buds on turquoise-green and yellow stem form handle, yellow ground, central leaf in iron-red, purple and yellow, and butterfly, 1756–60, pr (A) **13,200.00**

8 1/2" l, lobed oval, transfer printed in underglaze blue with two scenes of classical ruins, rim with four floral sprigs, c1765–70 (A) .. **1279.00**

9 1/8" l, oblong oct, bifurcated foliate rose stem with purple buds attracting winged insects, turquoise edged rim, underside with green florets, c1775, Chelsea Derby (A) **1279.00**

9 3/8" d, oct, "Imari" pattern, cobalt, iron red, and green stylized fruit branches, gilt accents, c1770, "blue Chinese characters" mark, pr (A) **715.00**

9 9/16" l, oval, iron-red and yellow apple with purple twig with three shaded green leaves, large and small insects in puce, purple, yellow, iron-red, pale green, brown, and black, russet-edged scalloped rim, c1760 (A) **2337.00**

10" l, gold putto feeding goose in center, border of gold putti at various pursuits in gold bands, white ground, shaped handle accented in gold, Chelsea-Derby **95.00**

10 13/16" l, lozenge shape, "Lilies of the Valley" in gray and green, gilt design border on fluted and scalloped rim, 1795–1800, botanical inscription, "crowned X'd batons and D" marks, pattern no. 115 in blue enamel (A) **962.00**

11 1/4" l, leaf shaped, purple veined green edged leaf painted with floral spray and scattered sprigs, resting on gilt edged basket molded dish with purple florets, c1760 (A) **945.00**

Ecuelle, Cov, and Stand, circ, continuous friezes of colorful garden flowers, rims edged in gold, dbl twisted handles, ring scroll finial, "red crown, X'd batons, and D" mark, gilder's 9 (A) **594.00**

Figure

2 1/4" h, seated pug dog, shaded tan coat, black muzzle, iron-red mouth, black eyes,

gilt collar with bell and iron-red rosette, green grassy top on low mound base, pink scrollwork on sides, gilding, c1795 (A).... **550.00**

2½" h, charging bull with brown markings on white body, grassy stump under belly, raised oval base with painted flowers, restored, c1760 (A) **5060.00**

3¼" h, squirrel, seated, nibbling nut, red and brown, wearing gilt collar, grassy mound base, restored at base, c1770, incised "2" (A)...................................... **615.00**

3¾" h, cherub holding yellow flower basket, pink drapery, flowered crown, multicolored florals, green on base, c1770, "pad" period **350.00**

4¼" h, putti, scantily clad, multicolored flowers on heads and shoulders, holding baskets of flowers, c1758, pr............ **1250.00**

4⅜" h, russet and brown recumbent stag on flower encrusted base, c1765 (A)........ **825.00**

4½" h

Bird with yellow, green, and purple plumage, perched on flowering tree stump with nut in beak, rocky mound base encrusted with colored flowers, restored, c1760–65 (A)........................ **1150.00**

Seated fox in natural colors, gilt collar, gilt bordered grass topped rect base, repairs, early 19th C, pr (A) **2488.00**

5⅛" h, gallant, pale turquoise jacket, flowered waistcoat, spotted breeches, pug at side, tricorn hat at feet, c1775, Chelsea-Derby, incised "N 51" (A) **850.00**

5⅜" l, recumbent whippet, white with brown spotted coat, gray shaded nose and paws, black eyes, iron-red outlined mouth, gilt collar, brown and turquoise mottled rect base with gilt band, c1870, "puce X'd crossed batons, S,H and D, 11" marks.......... **660.00**

5⁹⁄₁₆" h, Harlequin, broad brim black hat, green jacket patterned with salmon, white, and gilt scrolls, pale yellow tights striped with purple dots, black slippers, yellow belt, leaning against brown, ochre, and green mottled tree stump, gilt edged low mound base, 1815–25, unmarked (A) **2200.00**

6" l, setter, brown and tan curly coat, green mound base with brown, yellow centered white, iron-red and blue floral clusters, green leaves and moss, c1795, "brown painter's 5" (A) **770.00**

6⅛" h, 6¼" h, children, girl in gilt-edged pink and white bodice, bustled turquoise skirt, yellow underskirt with purple and gold sprigs, recumbent lamb by feet, boy in blue-lined pink jacket, gilt-edged yellow flowered waistcoat, turquoise breeches, brown spotted dog at feet, each seated before flowering bocage, pierced scrollwork base in turquoise and gold, c1780, incised No "81 g or G" marks, pr (A) **1100.00**

6½" h

"America" modeled as Indian youth wearing wreath and apron of puce, iron-red, yellow, and turquoise feathers trimmed in gilding, gilt edge white skirt and quiver of arrows, gray bow, standing before green tree stump, purple crocodile, green mound base, 1770–75 (A) **440.00**

Bullfinch in iron-red and puce markings, perched on tree with applied multicol-

ored flowers and leaves, restorations, c1765 (A)........................... **990.00**

Farm girl in pink-lined hat, turquoise coat and iron-red flowered skirt, green washed mound base, c1780 (A)....... **1300.00**

7¼" h, shepherd seated on tree stump playing bagpipe, dog at side, shepherdess playing mandolin, sheep at side, multicolored, scrolling base, c1770–75, pr (A) **2300.00**

7⅜" h, singer, upraised hands holding music, gown and coat painted with floral sprays, base with applied flowers, c1775, pr **6650.00**

8" h, bunting perched astride flowering tree stump, yellow and iron-red plumage with grayish-purple patches, purple edged scrolling base, restored, c1760–65 (A) **1130.00**

8⅝" h, Neptune, billowing white drapery with colorful floral sprays and lined in yellow, holding metal trident, gilt edged crown, standing on yellow scallop shell before turquoise, yellow, and puce scaly dolphin spouting steam of pale blue water, pierced base encrusted with colorful shells, iron-red coral and green and turquoise moss, 1765–70 (A)........................... **1210.00**

8¾" h, sportswoman wearing a white-plumed turquoise hat, fur-lined pink jacket, pale yellow waistcoat, turquoise striped flowered red skirt, holding bird in one hand, dog seated beside her, turquoise and gilt scroll edged base with flowers and foliage, bird's head restored, c1765 (A)......... **1476.00**

9" h, "Europe," crowned girl holding orb, flowered robe and yellow-lined turquoise drapery, applied with emblems of the Arts, flower encrusted mound base, repair to crown, c1765–70, (A) **1084.00**

9⅜" h, gardener wearing turquoise-lined purple cloak belted at the waist, red trimmed white shirt, pale yellow breeches, watering can at sandaled feet, flower encrusted base with molded scrollwork edged in turquoise and gilding, restoration, c1770 (A)..................................... **795.00**

10¼" h, shepherd, pink hat, blue vest, yellow waistcoat, iron-red breeches reserved with puce flowers, flowering tree stump and fruit basket at side, lamb under arm, gilded scroll molded base, c1770 (A) **1045.00**

11⅜" h, Mercury holding caduceus and purse in pink cloak over red-lined flower sprigged pale yellow robe, supported on a cloud, mound base molded with turquoise and gilt edged scrollwork, restoration, c1765 (A)........................... **450.00**

11½" h, Milton with one arm resting on pile of books supported on pedestal molded with The Expulson from Eden, wearing pink-lined white cloak, gilt detailed costume, scrolling base edged in turquoise and gilding, c1765 (A) **1279.00**

11⅝" h, Shakespeare in white costume with pink-lined cloak, leaning on pedestal with pile of books and "Tempest" scroll, scrolling base, c1770 (A)........................ **1052.00**

Fruit Cooler, 9" d, cobalt banding with gilt borders, ducal coronet, collared lid, early 19th C, pr (A) **330.00**

Inkwell, 6" d, cylinder shape, dbl spouts, loop handle, center well, scrolling gilt design on cobalt ground, mid 19th C (A) **330.00**

Mug, 3⅝" h, barrel shape, molded horiz bands, painted large flower spray on each side, scattered sprigs, brown line rim, ribbed loop handle, c1760 (A) **2132.00**

Plaque
  7⅝" l, 5⅝" w, rect, "Daniel in the Lions' Den," bearded prophet kneeling amongst a pride of lions, framed c1830 (A) **3150.00**
  12" h, 7¾" w, Venus holding water in cupped hands which she offers to Cupid, Venus in long flowing pink robes, c1878–90, sgd "J. Platts', reverse inscribed in red "AT THE FOUNTAIN AFTER AUBERT," 'crowned interlaced L's," framed (A) **4857.00**

Plate
  8⅞" d
    Blue, green, and yellow scattered cornflowers, border of interlaced cornflowers and gilt lines, cracks, c1815, "iron red crown, X'd batons, and D" mark, pattern #60, pr (A) **5500.00**
    Ichthyological, turbot, sprat, and sea carp against background of weeds, gilt borders, one with hairline, c1810, named on reverse, "crown, red X'd batons and D," set of three (A) **1150.00**
  10¼" d, "Blue Mikado" pattern **30.00**
Platter, 20¼" l, oval, center spray of full summer flowers, six other floral sprays on border, gilt edged rim, early 19th C, "red crowned" mark (A)............................... **785.00**
Potpourri Holder, 4½" h, hp purple and gilt decorations, claw feet on pedestal, two gilt handles, c1830, "orange X'd batons" mark.. **275.00**
Potpourri Vase, Cov
  5¾" h, circ shape, gilt scrolling foliage on dark blue and white ground, four paw feet, four Bacchus masks on rim, acorn finial, cov and rim pierced, c1820 (A)............. **400.00**
  11" h, lobed baluster form, butterflies and other winged insects below pierced shoulder, shell like foliage, pierced domed cov, bird finial, flower encrusted female mask handles, c1765 (A) **1053.00**
Serving Dish, 11⅜" l, "Kings" pattern, iron-red, cobalt, and gilt flowering tree, stylized trailing vine border, shaped rim molded with flowerheads on beaded band, c1780, "iron-red X'd batons" mark (A)....................... **145.00**
Sweetmeat Stand, two tiers of three scallop shells
  5⅞" h, 9" w, shading on int from pale pink to pale cream, ext from light yellow to iron-red or brown, openwork stand of yellow and green moss encrusted with iron-red and white coral, brown, purple, salmon, puce, and rose heightened shells, surmounted by white spotted turquoise kingfisher with iron-red breast and purple legs, c1765 (A) **2750.00**
  10⁷⁄₁₆" h, beneath single scallop shell at top, each painted with pink and green rose sprig within cell diaper border on int rim, pierced stand encrusted with green moss, iron-red coral, and puce, iron-red, yellow, and black small shells, green washed circ base, c1765 (A)................................... **1430.00**
Tulip Vase, 5¾" h, open orange striated tulip above stems and foliage in tones of green, closed bud to side, brown base applied with three flowers and foliage, repairs, early 19th C (A)................................... **6545.00**

Tureen, Cov, 6⁹⁄₁₆" h, melon shape, lobed oval fruit with rough skin striped in green and yellow, network of purple veining, short turquoise-green stem with two gray veined leaves, leafy stem on cov, with leaves and tendrils, 1756–59 (A)...................... **5225.00**
Urn
  6½" h, cobalt and blue decorations, titled "In Wales" and "Near Aston Upon Trent," panels with rural scenes, gilt handles and rim, c1820, Derby mark, pr................. **2500.00**
  14" d, squat waisted body, painted with flowers below border of molded rose sprays, burnished gilt entwined vine branch handles, continuous band of gilt vine tracery hung with grape clusters in relief, c1820 (A) **1151.00**
Vase
  6" h, figural tulip with yellow petals accented in orange and puce, small bud and green leaves on natural colored base, c1800–20 (A).................................... **2131.00**
  7⅜" h, trumpet form, arrangement of colorful flowers in basket on ledge, within gilt border oct panel reserved on dark blue ground with feathery gilt scrollwork, dbl handled stand, early 19th C, "red crown, X'd batons, and D" (A)................. **1650.00**
  7⅞" h, ovoid body, panel on front in green, yellow, purple, iron-red, brown, blue, and gray with scene of ladies washing clothes near ducks swimming in stream beside cottage, reverse with similar panel with two birds perched on small tree and surrounded by butterflies, flaring neck with two gilt foliate panels, gilt dentil edge, scroll handles heightened in turquoise-green and gold terminating in colorful florettes and gilt trimmed white leaves, runny blue ground, 1758–60 (A)......................... **990.00**
  8" h, compressed baluster shape, landscape panel on gros bleu ground, pr (A)....... **770.00**
  9" h, rococo scroll molding accented in green and puce, painted birds in landscape on front, spray of flowers on reverse, applied flower swags and ribbons on sides, c1765, pr (A)............................... **3925.00**
  11¾" h
    Campana shape, spray of colorful summer flowers in gilt edged oct panel reserved on apple green ground, applied with looped gilt serpent handles, one handle restored, c1835, "red crown" marks, Bloor Derby, pr (A).................. **3938.00**
    Shield shape body, view of Loch Tummil with two sportsmen and retriever in foreground in gilt edged oct panel on dark blue ground with gilt scrollwork, acanthus leaf molded scrolling handles with gilt mask terminals, one handle repaired, c1830, "red crowned D," view named, Bloor Derby (A)..................... **795.00**
  12½" h, 12¹¹⁄₁₆" h, campana shape, front oct panel with colorful flowers on white ledge against tan-brown ground, panels surrounded by gilt neoclassical palmettes, foliate scrolls, and leaf sprays, mid section with gold and white border of foliate motifs, foliate molded handles, sq base, cobalt blue ground, c1825, "iron-red crowned X'd batons, D," marks, pr (A)................. **5500.00**

18" h, ovoid body, applied summer flowers, apple blossom handles with birds, cov with floral cluster finial, royal blue ground, chips, c1840, Bloor Derby (A) **980.00**

Vase, Cov, 17½" h, bottle shape, vert panels of chrysanthemums and oriental flowers in iron-red, purple, and green on alternating green and iron-red grounds, Bloor-Derby (A) **1235.00**

Vegetable Tureen, Cov, 11¾" l, "Imari" pattern in iron-red, cobalt, and gold, c1890 .... **195.00**

Watering Can, Cov, 3½" h, miniature, cylindrical form, pink body encrusted with flowers and foliage, pierced spout encrusted with flowers, floral cluster finial, c1830, Bloor Derby, printed mark (A) **514.00**

Wine Cooler, 10½" d, painted spray of summer flowers, rim and foot gilded, c1815, "red X'd batons and D" mark (A) **670.00**

Wine Glass Coolers, 4" h, wide grape-vine border of shaded purple and green fruit clusters, brown shaded green leaves, gilt tendrils, gilt foliate scroll handles, gilt band borders on rim, mid-section, and circ foot, c1815, "iron-red crowned X'd batons and D" marks, pr (A) .. **1760.00**

'PETRUS PAULUS
MANCINUS DE DIRUTA'
17ᵇ C.

DERUTA

Near Perugia, Italy
Late 15th Century to Present

History: A large pottery industry was established at Deruta near Perugia, Italy. Metallic luster decorations in a golden mother-of-pearl iridescence and ruby colors were used on the polychrome wares utilizing special firing techniques. Deruta also was known for the excellence of its border patterns usually encircling a central motif of a bust or heraldic arms.

At first yellow colored pieces outlined in blue were prominent at Deruta. Later wares included olive green shades. Large dishes were made, some with raised decorations.

Today Deruta produces souvenir wares for tourists.

Museums: Gardiner Museum of Ceramic Art, Toronto, Canada; Victoria & Albert Museum, London, England; Wallace Collection, London, England.

Albarello

7½" h, dbl ogee shape, blue and yellow painted scrollwork panel of mask and pelicans drinking from goblet, front with "ZUCo ROSSi," reverse with ribbon and "1632" (A) **1330.00**

8½" h, cylindrical shape, majolica, green, ochre, and manganese with large foliate scrolls on blue ground, panel inscribed "Ung. Egitiaco'(Egyptian ointment) (A).... **306.00**

8¾" h, painted ribboned laurel wreath cartouche enclosing label with drug name, late 16th C **1300.00**

Drug Jar, 8"–8⅝" h, center scroll painted with drug name, shield with putto below, scrolling foliage border, dated "1611" on reverse, cracks, set of 3, (A) $3750.00

Dish

15" d, center with ochre armorial shield on blue ground, blue and ochre border, outer band of diamonds and circles with line borders, rim painted with blue flowers and green and ochre leaves (A) **535.00**

19⅞" d, blue, mustard, yellow, green, and black kitchen int showing servants in bakery kneading and forming bread, two dogs, caldron, and oven in ground, rim with broad border of fruit and lush foliage in blue washed ground, 17th C (A) **13,398.00**

Drug Jar, 5½" h, urn shape, inscribed "TROC. ALANDOLI" in lozenge, ochre ground painted with blue and manganese scrolling foliage, small twin handles, cracks, mid 16th C (A)..................................... **1325.00**

Jar

7¾" h, "Pine Cone," scale molded ovoid body in blue, green, yellow, and ochre, knopped foot with blue lappets, foot restored, early 16th C (A)................**16,456.00**

8¼" h, waisted neck painted with blue and yellow luster panels of stylized foliage in dotted borders, bands of laurel and pseudo gadroons, dbl loop handles, restored, c1515 (A) **2035.00**

Panel, 16⅞" h, 13¼" l, rect, molded with Madonna and Child flanked by cherubs heads against yellow ground, robes in blue and brown, veil with blue scrollwork, border with blue zig-zags, inscribed "Alma Redentores Mater Q. Pvia Celi," mid 17th C (A)........ **990.00**

Plaque

13¼" d, baroque cartouche shape, center oval panel molded with Sacred Monogram over emblem of Virgin Mary, winged cherub masks at each end, painted in yellow, ochre, green, and blue, accented in manganese, dtd 1760 (A) **1620.00**

17⅜" h, 13½" w, rect, relief molded bust of Madonna in yellow and ochre robe with green-lined cloak, infant in lap, yellow halos, blue, green, and yellow ground, framed in lozenges and circles......................... **3800.00**

Stand, 16⅛" l, center painted with building in landscape in manganese and yellow on turquoise-green ground, wreath molded border, radiating molded lappets extending to molded scrollwork outer border **750.00**

Syrup Jar, 8½" h, blue painted trailing leaves and "S ROS. SOL." and multicolored armorial on stippled ground, dbl serpentine handle, straight spout (A)........................ **1620.00**

Tazza

9¾" d, blue painted radiating compartments of birds in spreading plants, flared foot, late 17th C............................... **415.00**

10¼" d, blue and yellow luster painted stylized foliage around central flowerhead, restored, c1525 (A)........................ **855.00**

10½" d, ochre and blue with central medallion of birds and stylized rabbits among flowering foliage within broad border, raised on short stem, domed circ foot, 1620–40........................ **555.00**

Vase, 9¾" h, globular shape, everted rim, blue, yellow, ochre, and green stylized scrolling foliage, gadrooned border, dbl loop handles, 16th C................................ **1000.00**

Wet Drug Jar

8" h, painted cherub with cross under spout, border of trailing foliage, white ground, entwined loop handle, late 16th C........ **1125.00**

12¾" h, majolica, polychrome armorial bearing, manganese inscription on label "A.D. BORRAGINE," stylized foliage, reverse manganese 1689 on medallion, one handle and spout restored (A).................. **1122.00**

c 1902-1929

DOULTON AND ROYAL DOULTON

1880-1902

DOULTON OF LAMBETH

Lambeth, near London
1815–1956

History: In Lambeth, near London, John Doulton founded the Doulton Lambeth pottery in 1815. Utilitarian salt glazed stonewares were the mainstay. When John Watts joined the firm, it became known as Doulton and Watts (1820–1853). Stoneware barrels, bottles, spirit flasks, and jugs were produced in vast quantities.

Henry Doulton, John's second son, joined the firm in

1835. His inventiveness led to the application of steam to drive the potter's wheel, placing Lambeth Pottery ten years ahead of the other potteries. Architectural terracotta and garden ornaments were added to the catalog. Production of stoneware drainpipes, conduits, and other sanitary wares also began.

The Lambeth School of Art, under John Sparkes' direction, became associated with the Doulton wares. Through Sparkes, George Tinsworth began working with Doulton in 1866. Hannah and Arthur Barlow, students at the school, joined Doulton in 1871. They made pots with incised decorations worked directly into uncoated clay. During the next twenty years, the number of artists and designers grew; 250 artists were at work by 1885. The monogram, initials, or signature of the artist appeared on the piece; often the assistants' initials appeared too. In 1887 Queen Victoria knighted Henry Doulton for his achievements in the advancement of ceramic art.

Sir Henry died in 1897; Henry Louis Doulton succeeded his father. In 1899 the family company became Doulton & Co., Ltd. During the 20th century, reductions took place in the production of artist signed pieces from Doulton Lambeth. By 1925 only 24 artists were employed. Leslie Harradine did excellent stoneware figures of Dickens' characters. He also modeled spirit flasks of comtemporary politicians.

During the 1920s and 1930s, collectors' pieces in simple shapes, subtle colors, and uncluttered decorations were made. A large range of commemorative wares also were produced. Agnete Hoy, working at Lambeth from 1951–1956, achieved fame for her cat figures. She used salt glaze techniques and developed a new transparent glaze. In 1956 production ceased at the Doulton Lambeth pottery.

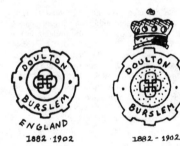

ENGLAND
1882·1902

1882 - 1902

DOULTON OF BURSLEM

Staffordshire, England
1877 to Present

History: In 1877 Henry Doulton acquired the Nile Street pottery located in Burslem, Staffordshire, from Pinder, Bourne & Co. The name was changed to Doulton & Co. in 1882. Beginning in 1884 porcelains of the highest quality were manufactured. Simple, inexpensive earthenware tablewares also were made. A large group of artists under the direction of John Slater assembled at the Burslem factory.

Doulton's china was exhibited at the Chicago Columbian Exposition in 1893. Charles Noke, who joined the company in 1889 and became one of the most important workers at Burslem, exhibited his vases. Many Noke figures portrayed contemporary people as historical personages. His early achievements included Holbein, Rembrandt, and Barbotine wares plus a popular range of flasks, jugs, and other shapes in subdued colors. Rouge Flambe was perhaps the most important ware introduced by Noke. He became art director in 1914.

At the Burslem factory, a tremendous amount of tablewares were produced. In addition to the earthenwares, fine bone china ornamented in gold and frequently exhibiting elaborate designs also was manufactured. In 1901 King Edward VII granted the Royal Warrant of appointment to Doulton. From that point on they used the word "ROYAL" to describe their products.

ROYAL DOULTON FIGURES

Nearly all of Royal Doulton figures are made at the Burslem factory. Three basic ingredients, china clay, Cornish stone, and calcined bone ash, are blended together with water to make a fine body able to withstand the high temperature firings needed to produce a superfine, yet strong translucent ceramic body. Figurine subjects include child studies, street sellers, and historical, literary, or legendary characters in large and miniatures sizes.

In 1913 Royal Doulton began marking each new figurine design with an "HN" number. Harry Nixon was the artist in charge of painting the figures. The "HN" numbers refer to him. "HN" numbers were chronological until 1949 after which blocks of numbers were assigned to each modeler. Over two thousand different figures have been produced. New designs are added each year. Older ones designs are discontinued. Currently there are approximately two hundred designs in current production.

CHARACTER AND TOBY JUGS

Character jugs depicted the head and shoulders; Toby Jugs feature the entire figure either standing or seated. Noke revived the old Staffordshire Toby tradition in the 20th century by modeling characters based on songs, literature, legends, and history. The first jugs were produced by Noke in 1934. Large jugs measure 5 1/4" to 7 1/2", small jugs 3 1/4" to 4", miniatures 2 1/4" to 2 1/2", and tinies 1 1/4" tall or less. The shape and design of the jug handle aids in establishing the age of a jug. For a brief period all seated Tobies were discontinued. Production of the seated Tobies began again in 1973.

SERIES WARE

Series Ware, created by Charles Noke, used a large number of standard blank shapes decorated with a selection of popular characters, events, illustrators. A series ranged from two to three to as high as twnety scenes.

A variety of printing techniques were used on Series Ware. Transfer printing from engraved plates and lithography supplemented with hand coloring was one technique. The block printing and silk screening techniques produced denser, more colorful images. A photographic process captured famous views and characters.

Series Ware production was interrupted by WWII. However, a revival of decorative plate production led to the Collectors International plates during the 1970s, featuring plates for special holidays such as Valentine's Day and Christmas and designs by international artists.

Today Doulton and Company is the largest manufacturer of ceramic products in the UK. Minton, Royal Crown Derby, Ridgeway, Royal Albert, Royal Adderley, Colclough, Paragon, John Beswick, and Webb Corbett are all part of the company.

References: Richard Dennis, *Doulton Character Jugs,* Malvem Press, 1976; Desmond Eyles & Richard Dennis, *Royal Doulton Figures Produced at Burslem,* Royal Doulton Tableware Ltd., 1978; Desmond Eyles, *The Doulton Burslem Wares,* Royal Doulton & Barrie Jenkins, 1980; Desmond Eyles, *The Doulton Lambeth Wares,* Hutchinson, 1975; Louise Irvine, *Royal Doulton Series Ware,* Vol. 1 & 2, Vol. 3 & 4, Richard Dennis, 1980, 1984; Ralph & Terry Kovel, *The Kovels' Illustrated Price Guide to Royal Doulton,* Crown, 1980; Katherine Morrison McClinton, *Royal Doulton Figurines & Character Jugs,* Wallace-Homestead, 1978; Kevin Pearson, *The Character Jug Collectors Handbook,* 3rd Edition, Kevin Francis Publishing Ltd., 1986; Kevin Pearson, *The Doulton Figure Collectors Handbook,* Kevin Francis Publishing Ltd., 1988.

Gallery: Sir Henry Doulton Gallery, Doulton Fine China Nile Street Pottery, Burslem, England.

Collectors Club: Mid-American Doulton Collectors, Box 2434, Joliet, IL 60434. Annual membership: $20 per year. Newsletter: 6 per year; Royal Doulton International Collectors Club, P.O. Box 6705, Somerset, NJ 08873. Annual membership: $22 per year, quarterly magazine.

Newsletter: Character Jug Report, Box 5000, Caledon, Ontario, L0N1C0, Canada.

DOULTON OF BURSLEM

Bowl
    9 1/2" d, raised floral decoration, tapestry finish **395.00**
    10 1/2" l, green leaves with raised gold veins, four gold rococo feet, c1886–88 . . . . **255.00**
    15 3/4" d, blue and white flowered body . . . **100.00**
Centerpiece, 9" l, 5 1/2" h, swirl mold with applied silver and gold flowers **350.00**

Pitcher, Burslem, 6 5/8" h, cobalt flower and butterfly, gilt trim, off white ground, cobalt handle and panel under rim, "Doulton Burslem" mark, (A) $150.00

Charger, 13 3/4" d, center scene of horses, hounds, and hunters, grapevine border (A) . . **55.00**
Cup and Saucer, demitasse, multicolored flower with gold trim, matte finish, c1888 . . . . **80.00**
Dessert Service, 12 plates, 9" d, 2 sq ftd dishes, 2 leaf shaped ftd dishes, 2 shaped oval ftd dishes, botanical, orchids and other flowers in pastel colors and gilding, c1890, sgd "D. Dewsberry," printed marks, registered no. and pattern no. 2581, 18 pcs (A) **1496.00**

Ewer

6" h, small floral design, gold trim **175.00**

6¾" h, blue crocus, cobalt trim with gold. . **150.00**

Figure, 12⅝" h, theatrical portraits, Ellen Terry as "Catherine of Aragon," Sir Henry Irving as "Cardinal Wolsey," Cardinal holding scroll, Queen in embroidered dress, tones of ivory tinted with pale greem, c1895, printed marks, pr (A) **890.00**

Pitcher

5" h, floral decor, turquoise jewels, cream ground. **195.00**

9" h, blue and white horseshoe with two does on one side, doe and stag on other **350.00**

Plate

8¾" d, pink and yellow flowers in center, gold tracery around edge with white enamel . . . **120.00**

9" d, multicolored berry blossoms on spiney vines, light peach to white shaded ground, gold ruffled edge (A). **23.00**

9¼" d

Leaves outlined in gold, emb floral design on irregular rim **105.00**

Yellow daisies outlined in gold, gold tracery, open work on edge **170.00**

Platter, 22" l, oval, footd with drain channels, multicolored small florals on white ground, tan border (A) **28.00**

Pot, 6½" h, yellow and purple floral spray, cream ground, pewter lid and handle, brown Burslem mark (A). **110.00**

Punch Bowl, 12" h, 17¾" d, "Watteau" pattern, blue and white, designs inside and out, c1882, imp "Ivory" mark. **3500.00**

Tea Service, trefoil tray, 18" d, teapot, creamer, cov. sugar, 3 cups and saucers, green and brown oriental designs, bamboo handles, silver hallmarked rims, dtd 1882 . . . . **995.00**

Tea Set, teapot, creamer, cov sugar bowl, pink and blue flowers, gold scrolls, c1902 . . . . . . **175.00**

Tray, 8½" l, hp large and small fish in coral bed, fluted sides, scalloped handle, dtd 1884 . . . . **120.00**

Vase

3⅛" h, porcelain, blue fruit trees and irises around body, scalloped gold top. **65.00**

4¼" h, pottery, florals and leaves on beige ground, vert designs on sides, fluted top edge, gold feet. **100.00**

4½" h, wild rose decoration, three molded gold feet extending up sides, irregular shaped rim, chip on back foot **125.00**

5½" h, multicolored flowers outlined in gold, dbl handles **105.00**

11" h, painted with cattle drinking from stream, misty woodland landscape, early 20th C, sgd "C.B. Hopkins" **475.00**

11½" h, multicolored flowers outlined in gold on bottom, gold handles **235.00**

DOULTON OF LAMBETH

Ashtray, 3¾" d, 4½" h, blue, gray, and brown figural bird, royal blue ground, ext with green leaves. **275.00**

Biscuit Jar, 7¼" h, impressed ferns and plants, brown leaves highlighted in gold, blue and beige ground, silicon glaze **280.00**

Charger, 17⅜" d, faience, brown and cream flowers and foliage, green ground, lined semicircular border in red, brown, and orange,

1878–1884, painted by M. Challis, printed and imp marks (A). **374.00**

Figure

4⅜" h, stoneware, mouse group, three mice, larger with tall conical hat, each holding implements, ribbed oval base, inscribed "I SEE NO REASON WHY GUNPOWDER TREASON SHOULD EVER BE FORGOT', damaged, c1885, modeled by George Tinworth, imp mark and incised monogram (A) **1122.00**

7¾" h, stoneware, plump owl, molded and slip decoratoed with flowers, long wings tucked behind, circ base with claw feet, blue, white, and brown, detachable domed head, raised eyebrows, c1900, by Bessie Newbery, imp "DOULTON LAMBETH ENGLAND," incised "BN' (A) **1052.00**

11¾" h, stoneware, Boer War soldier, full military uniform standing before large rock, waisted socle base in green and brown, metal gun, c1901, imp mark and incised "J. Broad Sc' (A) **748.00**

Fountain, 17⅛" h, stoneware, three pelicans standing back-to-back with three toads standing on lily pads by their large feet, flared upper reservoir support molded with bull rushes, white birds with brown markings, green and brown base and neck, repair, 1874–1883, imp "Doulton Lambeth," incised monogram (A) . **700.00**

Jardinaire

9" d, painted cinque foil hearts, "Doulton Lambeth Slater's Patent" mark **250.00**

37" h, circ ribbed and fluted body with acanthus leaves, winged griffin feet, baluster column shaped base, brown, green, and turquoise, imp "Doulton Lambeth" marks . . . **775.00**

Jug

6½" h, figural rugby ball inscribed "The More the Merrier" **135.00**

7¼" h, 5" d, stoneware, embossed cupids, grapes and leaves and "Good is not good enough, the best is not too good," brown to tan shading **175.00**

8" h, stoneware, globular body, incised with running horses before trees, stiff leaf borders and incised foliage in browns and greens, loop handle, 1874, decorated by Florence Barlow, imp marks and incised monogram (A) **400.00**

8½" h, brown stoneware, "Hollyroob Castle', c1870. . . . . **95.00**

Pitcher

6⅜" h, stoneware, green and blue bands with vine and geometric design, brown edges and handle, imp "Doulton Lambeth England" mark (A). **110.00**

7¼" h, tan and brown with applied white "Glasgow" shield and "This is the tree..This is the Bird..This is the bell..This is the fish," c1880 . . . . **175.00**

7½" h, relief figures of man on barrel drinking beer, family of five around table, hunting scene with trees, tan and brown ground, SP rim **350.00**

Teapot, 5" h, turquoise and white flowers, light brown ground, tapestry finish, "Doulton Lambeth and Doulton Slater" mark. **145.00**

Tea Service, pot, creamer, sugar bowl, hot water pitcher, milk jug, dark brown-tan and dark blue with applied flowers, c1890 . . . . **720.00**

Vase

5" h, blue and white enameled daisies on stippled gold ground, Slater's Patent........ **125.00**

5½" h, small gold scrolls, applied cream leaves with small aqua flowers at top, blue-green base and rim..................... **125.00**

6" h, emb blue and white flowers, med brown ground, Silicon ware.................. **70.00**

7" h, bowl shape, chocolate brown glaze with cream overlay of Japanese style floral motif, Slater's Patent (A) **200.00**

Vase, Lambeth, 7½" h, incised cat design, rust, dk green, and mustard tones, lt green int, Hannah Barlow, $850.00

10" h, bulbous base, slender neck, incised and raised floral designs on gray-blue ground, stamped enameled floret decoration, sgd "Louisa Davis and Eleanor Burrell" (A) **357.00**

10½" h, overall reticulated design, Silicon . **625.00**

10⅞" h, stoneware, incised and beaded scrolling foliage accented in blue and white, reserved on slip trailed cell pattern ground, c1880, George Tinworth (A)............ **450.00**

11½" h, faience, overall blue flowers and green leaves on dark green ground, raised blue band on neck, mottled blue int **495.00**

11¾" h, raised relief bands of blue ovals and teardrops, Art Deco earthenware, imp "Doulton Lambeth" mark (A)............ **110.00**

13¾" h, stoneware

Ovoid body, incised with wide band of horses, cattle, and dogs, one with cat seated in a large tree with dog looking up, blue and green borders incised with scrolling foliage and stiff leaf design, shoulder with band of florets, 1885, decorated by Hannah B. Barlow and Emily E. Stormer, imp marks, date, incised no. 529, artist's monograms, pr (A)........ **2250.00**

Pate-sur-pate with birds against stippled ground between slip-trailed borders in form of stylized clouds, neck and body molded with branches of apples and leaves from tall trunk, green and brown glazes, c1880, decorated by Mark V. Marshall and Florence E. Barlow, imp marks and incised monograms (A) **935.00**

14" h, Art Nouveau style green flowers and leaves with mottled blue and brown ground, molded lacy rim, c1895, pr (A)... **880**

15¾" h, flambe, ovoid body, horse and rider,

another horse at watering hole, 1920s, printed lion, crown, and circle mark (A) .. **561.00**

17½" h, stoneware, ovoid, incised band of horses in green and brown, Art Nouveau bands of foliage at top and base, c1890–1910, Florence E. Barlow............... **1000.00**

18" h, faience, bright yellow and brown flowers with green foliage, shaded green ground, brown line rim, 1874–1893, decorated by Mary Butterton, imp marks and painted monogram (A).................. **1683.00**

22⅝" h, faience, dbl gourd shape, Persian style blue, green, mauve, and red scrolling foliage on cream ground, dtd 1879, imp "Lambeth Doulton Faience" mark (A) **2060.00**

ROYAL DOULTON

Ashtray

3⅝" d

Series ware, "Dutch People," three Dutchmen **35.00**

Series ware, "Welsh Ladies," sgd "Noke". **40.00**

3½" d, series ware, "Witches," witch with caldron, caramel brown ground......... **30.00**

Biscuit Jar

6" h, pastoral scene with sheep **295.00**

7¾" h, pottery, bunches of multicolored flowers, cream ground, embossed green and cobalt design at top and base, SP rim, top, and handle...................... **165.00**

8½" h, blue scenes of mountains, castles, and lakes with boats, white ground, SP handle, rim, and lid **155.00**

Bowl

4½" d, blue border with stylized flowers, brown and blue ext, Art Deco, imp mark (A).................................... **30.00**

9⅛" d, red and orange flowers, blue ground, scalloped edge, brown border (A)........ **55.00**

9¼" d, series ware, "Romeo" **65.00**

Bud Vase, 12" h, Romeo figure on one, Juliet on other, pastel shaded ground, pr........... **425.00**

Candlestick

5¾" h, multicolored tiny flowers on white ground, pr........................... **225.00**

6½" h, series ware, "Shakespeare-Juliet" in colors.............................. **85.00**

Chamberstick, 6" d, series ware, "Under Greenwood Tree," c1914...................... **180.00**

Character Jugs

Ann Boleyn, small, D6650................. **32.00**

Aramis

Large, D6441........................ **55.00**

Mini, D6508 (A) **30.00**

Small, D6454........................ **32.00**

'Ard of Earing, mini, D6594................. **975.00**

'Arry

Large, D6207........................ **175.00**

Mini, D6250......................... **65.00**

Athos

Large, D6439........................ **55.00**

Mini, D6509......................... **28.00**

Small, D6452........................ **32.00**

Auld Mac

Large, D5823........................ **65.00**

Small, D5824........................ **30.00**

Bacchus

Large, D6499........................ **55.00**

Small, D6505........................ **32.00**

Beefeater
  Large, D6206 . . . .   55.00
  Mini, D6251 . . . .   45.00
  Small, D6233 . . . .   60.00
Blacksmith
  Large, D6571 . . . .   80.00
  Small, D6578 . . . .   60.00
Bootmaker
  Large, D6572 . . . .   80.00
  Mini, D6586 . . . .   38.00
  Small, D6579 . . . .   60.00
Cap'n Cuttle, small, D5842 . . . .   95.00
Captain Ahab, small, D6506 . . . .   45.00
Capt Henry Morgan
  Large, D6467 . . . .   075.00
  Small, D6469 . . . .   45.00
Capt Hook, large, D6497 . . . .   425.00
Cardinal
  Large, D5614 . . . .   126.00
  Mini, A, D6129 . . . .   45.00
  Small, D6033 . . . .   60.00
Catherine of Aragon, small, D6657 . . . .   32.00
Cavalier
  Large, D6114 . . . .   145.00
  Small, D6173 . . . .   57.00
Cleo, large, A mark, D6728 . . . .   95.00
Clown, white hair, large, D6322 . . . .   800.00
Crocket/Santa Anna, large, D6729 . . . .   95.00
Dick Turpin, gun handle, small, D5618 . . . . .   60.00
Don Quixote
  Large, D6455 . . . .   55.00
  Small, D6460 . . . .   32.00

Royal Doulton Character Jug, Falstaff, large size, D6287, (A) $45.00

Falconer, small, D6540 . . . .   32.00

Royal Doulton Character Jug, The Falconer, large size, D6533, (A) $55.00

Falstaff, large, D6287 . . . .   55.00
Fat Boy
  Small, D5840 . . . .   110.00
  Tiny, D6142 . . . .   90.00
Fortune Teller
  Large, D6497 . . . .   425.00
  Mini, D6523 . . . .   300.00
Friar Tuck, large, D6321 . . . .   399.00
Gaoler
  Large, D6570 . . . .   80.00
  Smaller, D6577 . . . .   60.00
Gardener
  Large, D6630 . . . .   175.00
  Mini, D6638 . . . .   30.00
  Small, D6634 . . . .   60.00
Gladiator
  Large, D6550 . . . .   475.00
  Mini, D6556 . . . .   375.00
Golfer, large, D6623 . . . .   55.00
Gone Away
  Large, D6531 . . . .   80.00
  Small, A mark, D5638 . . . .   36.00
Granny
  Large, A mark, D5521 . . . .   76.00
  Small, D6384 . . . .   30.00
Guardsman, large, D6568 . . . .   80.00
Gunsmith, small, D6580 . . . .   60.00
Jarge, large, D6288 . . . .   295.00
Jester, small, D5556 . . . .   95.00
Jockey, large, D6625 . . . .   260.00
John Barleycorn
  Large, D5327 . . . .   135.00
  Mini, D6041 . . . .   45.00
Johnny Appleseed, large, D6372 . . . .   310.00
John Doulton, small, D6656 (A) 60.00
John Peel
  Large, A mark, D5612 . . . .   135.00
  Small, A mark, D5731 . . . .   85.00
Long John Silver
  Large, D6335 . . . .   80.00
  Mini, D6512 . . . .   28.00
  Small, D6386 . . . .   32.00
Lumberjack, large, D6610 . . . .   95.00
Mad Hatter
  Large, D6598 . . . .   95.00
  Small, A mark, D6602 . . . .   75.00
Mephistopheles, large, D5757 . . . .   2375.00
Merlin, large, D6529 . . . .   55.00
Mikado, large, D6501 . . . .   499.00
Mine Host, small, D6470 . . . .   60.00
Monty, large, D6202 . . . .   55.00
Mr. Micawber, small, D5843 . . . .   95.00
Mr. Pickwick, small, D5839 . . . .   60.00
Neptune, small, D6552 . . . .   32.00
North American Indian
  Large, D6611 (A) 70.00
  Small, D6614 . . . .   45.00
Old Charley
  Large, D5420 . . . .   80.00
  Mini, A, D6046 . . . .   30.00
  Small, D5527 . . . .   35.00
  Tiny, D6144 . . . .   90.00
Old King Cole, large, D6036 . . . .   245.00
Old Salt
  Large, D6551 . . . .   65.00
  Small, D6554 . . . .   60.00
Oliver Twist, tiny, D6677 . . . .   30.00
Paddy
  Large, D5753 . . . .   125.00
  Mini, A, D6042 . . . .   40.00

Small, D5768	50.00
Tiny, D6145	90.00
Pied Piper, small, D6462	60.00
Poacher	
Large, D6429	60.00
Small, D6464	32.00
Porthos	
Large, D6440	80.00
Mini, D6516 (A)	35.00
Punch and Judy Man, large, D6590	545.00
Rip Van Winkle, small, D6463	60.00
Robin Hood	
Large, D6205	100.00
Mini, D6252	40.00
Sairey Gamp	
Large, D5451	295.00
Mini, A mark, D6045	35.00
Small, D5528	30.00
Tiny, A mark, D6146	100.00
Sam Weller	
Small, D5841	45.00
Tiny, D6147	100.00
Sancho Panza	
Large, D6456	95.00
Small, D6461	60.00
Santa Claus, large	
Doll handle	90.00
Reindeer handle	100.00
Toy handle	100.00
Scaramouche, large, D6558	690.00
Sergent Buz Fuz, small, A mark, D5838	110.00
Simple Simon, large, D6374	475.00
Simon The Cellarer	
Large, D5504	126.00
Small, D5616	60.00
Sleuth, small, D6635	45.00
Smuggler	
Large, D6616	75.00
Small, D6619	60.00
The Apothecary	
Large, D6567	75.00
Small, D6574	60.00
Toby Philpots, A, D6043	40.00
Tony Weller	
Mini, D6044	50.00
Small, D5530	57.00
Touchstone, large, D5613	221.00
Trapper	
Large, D6609	95.00
Small, D6612	45.00
Ugly Dutchess	
Large, D6599	380.00
Small, D6603	300.00
Uncle Tom Cobbleigh, large, D6337	425.00
Vicar of Bray, A mark, D5615	125.00
Walrus and Carpenter, small, A mark	75.00
Coffee Pot, 6¾" h, series ware, "Moorish Gate"	145.00
Comport, 5⅜" d, 3⅜" h, green, orange, and gold shaded sunset cottage scene, gold pedestal, sgd "H. Morrey"	165.00
Cream and Sugar	
"Malvern" pattern	65.00
"Prelude" pattern	100.00
"Spindrift" pattern	22.00
Cup and Saucer	
"Chatsworth" pattern, #4794	40.00
"Chivalry" pattern	95.00
Dickensware, relief of Sam Weller and Fat Boy	

on cup, Pickwick and Mrs. Cluppins on saucer	150.00
Medallion of fruit, yellow and white stripes, black trim	25.00
"Ormonde" pattern	40.00
Cup and Saucer, Demitasse, "Melrose" pattern	28.00
Dish, 5" d, three footed, Little Boy Blue design	70.00
Figure	
6" h, 14" l, Rouge Flambe, tiger with open mouth in charging position, black stripe in fur, flambe veined, Doulton logo mark	975.00
9" h, 17" l, Rouge Flambe, rhinoceros, half seated position, head and horn raised, mottled green-red bottom hide and feet	950.00
12¼" h, 6" l, Rouge Flambe, horned owl, claws on limb, mottled green and red body, flambe veined, Doulton logo mark	750.00
14" l, 6" h, Rouge Flambe, tiger, black stripes	1150.00
Rouge Flambe, lying fox	36.00
Rouge Flambe, rabbit with ears	51.00
Abdullah, HN 1410	775.00
A Courting, HN 2004	395.00
Adrienne, HN 2152	120.00
Airdale with pheasant, HN 1022	400.00
Affection, HN 2236	121.00
Afternoon Tea, HN 1747	225.00
A La Mode, HN 2544	215.00
Alexandra, HN 2398	140.00
Alice, HN 2158	95.00
Alison, HN 2336 (A)	120.00
Angela, HN 1204	1050.00
Ann, HN 2739	95.00
Antoinette, HN 2326 (A)	70.00
Apple Maid, HN 2160	285.00
A Polka, HN 2156	225.00
Ascot, HN 2356 (A)	150.00
At Ease, HN 2473	215.00
Autumn Breezes, red dress, HN 1934	110.00
A Winters Walk, HN 3052	150.00
Babie, HN 1679	85.00
Baby Bunting, HN 2108	250.00
Bachelor, HN 2319	225.00
Ballerina, HN 2116	300.00
Ballon Man, HN 1954	120.00
Bather, HN 687 (A)	561.00
Bed Time, HN 1978 (A)	30.00
Bedtime Story, HN 2059	246.00
Belle, HN 754, "Potted by Doulton"	1150.00
Betsy, HN 2111	200.00
Biddy, HN 1445	145.00
Blithe Morning, HN 2021	175.00
Bonnie Lassie, HN 1626	260.00
Boy From Williamsburg, HN 2183 (A)	75.00
Bride, HN 2166	140.00
Bridget, HN 2070	295.00
Broken Lance, HN 2041	425.00
Buddies, HN 2546	225.00
Bunny, HN 2214	130.00
Calumet, HN 1469	1500.00
Carmen, HN 2545	215.00
Cavalier, HN 2716	120.00
Celeste, HN 2237	190.00
Cellist, HN 2226	300.00
Centurian, HN 2726	165.00
Chesnut Mare with Foal, HN 2522	950.00
Child From Williamsburh, HN 2154 (A)	70.00
Chloe, miniature, M10	245.00
Choir Boy, HN 2141	70.00

Chow, K15	55.00
Christmas Time, HN 2110	285.00
Cissie, HN 1809	75.00
Cleopatra, HN 2868	1200.00
Clockmaker, HN 2279	250.00
Cobbler, HN 1706	275.00
Cocker Spaniel	
Brown and white, HN 1036	145.00
Black and white, HN 1078	65.00
Columbine, HN 1439	575.00
Constance, HN 1511, "Potted by Doulton"	1350.00
Coralie, HN 2307 (A)	100.00
Corgi	
HN 2557	200.00
K16	55.00
Cup of Tea, HN 2322	120.00
Dachshund, "CH Shrewd Saint", HN 1127	375.00
Dancer of the World, Philipines, HN 2439	700.00
Day Dreams, HN 1731	175.00
Debutante, HN 2210	360.00
Deidre, HN 2020	275.00
Delight, HN 1772	160.00
Diana, HN 1716	285.00
Dinky Do, HN 1678	53.00
Dorcas, HN 1558	320.00
Easter Day, HN 2039	225.00
Elegance, HN 2264 (A)	80.00
Elfreda, HN 2078	550.00
Eliza, HN 2543	165.00
Elyse HN 2429	170.00
English Setter with pheasant, HN 2529	400.00
Ermine Coat, HN 1981	200.00
Esmeralda, HN 2168	380.00
Eve, HN 2466	500.00
Fair Lady	
Coral pink, HN 2835	149.00
Green, HN 2193	85.00
Falstaff, HN 2054	157.00
Family Album, HN 2321	325.00
Farmer's Wife, HN 2069	400.00
Fiddler, HN2171	850.00
Fiona	
HN 2349	285.00
HN 2694	140.00
First Dance, HN 2803	203.00
Fleur, HN 2368 (A)	120.00
Flirtation, HN 3071	115.00
Foaming Quart, HN 2162	231.00
Fortune Teller, HN 2159	395.00
Forty Winks, HN 1973	225.00
Genevieve, HN 1962	225.00
Giselle, HN 2139	325.00
Good Friends, HN 2783	125.00
Good King Wenceslas, HN 2118	260.00
Good Morning, HN 2671	140.00
Grace, HN 2318 (A)	75.00
Grandma, HN 2052	240.00
Granny's Treasure, HN 2031 (A)	250.00
Gud Grey Mare, HN 2567	285.00
Gwynneth, HN 1980	245.00
Gypsy Dance, HN 2230	200.00
Harlequin, HN 2737	510.00
He Loves Me, HN 2046	140.00
Henrietta Maria, HN 2005 (A)	300.00
Her Ladyship, HN 1977	295.00
Hilary, HN 2335	135.00
Honey, HN 1909	322.00
Hornpipe, HN2161	595.00
Huntsman, HN 2492	200.00

Ibrahim, HN 2095	435.00
Innocence, HN 2842	125.00
Invitation, HN 2170	145.00
Ivy, HN 1768	87.00
Jack, HN 2060	116.00
Jack Point, HN 2080	1300.00
Jacqueline, HN 2001	575.00
Janet, HN 1537 (A)	90.00
Janice, HN 2165	410.00
Jean, HN 2032	235.00
Jersey Milkmaid, HN 2057	275.00
Jill, HN 2061	120.00
Jolly Sailor, HN 2172	600.00
Jovial Monk, HN 2144	170.00
Judge, HN 2443	95.00
Kate Hardcastle, HN 1719	485.00
King Charles, HN 2084	1020.00
Ko-Ko, HN 2898	650.00
Lady Anne Nevill, HN 2006	650.00
Lady April, HN 1958	259.00
Lady Fayre, HN 1557	430.00
Lady Jestor, HN 1285	1800.00
LaSylphide, HN 2138 (A)	250.00
Laurianne, dark blue overdress, HN 2719	195.00
Leisure Hour, HN 2055	438.00
Lilac Time, HN 2137	260.00
Linda, HN 2106	135.00
Little Boy Blue, HN 2062	85.00
Little Bridesmaid, HN 1433	120.00
Little Child So Rare and Sweet, HN 1542	475.00
Long John Silver, HN 2204	380.00
Lori, HN 2801	70.00
Love Letters, HN 2149	300.00
Lunchtime, HN 2425	195.00
Lucy Locket, HN 524	525.00
Make Believe, HN 2225	85.00
Mallard Duck, HN 2556	150.00
Margery, HN 1413	475.00
Marie, HN 1370	58.00
Marigold, HN 1555	450.00
Mary Had a Little Lamb, HN 2048	100.00
Mary Jane, HN 1990	235.00
Mask Seller, HN 2103	125.00
Masquerade, HN 2259	250.00
Master Sweep, HN 2205	495.00
Matilda, HN 2011	550.00
Maureen	
HN 1770	275.00
M 85	275.00
Melody, HN 2202 (A)	130.00
Memories, HN 2030	250.00
Mendicant, HN 1365	220.00
Miss Demure, potted, HN 1402	140.00
Miss Muffet	
HN 1936	165.00
HN 1937	325.00
Modina, HN 1846, pr.	1995.00
Monica, HN 1467	110.00
Mr Pecksniff, HN 1891	285.00
Mrs Fitzhubert, HN 2007	625.00
My Pet, HN 2238	185.00
Nell Gwyn, HN 1882	950.00
Nina, HN 2347 (A)	110.00
Officer of the Line, HN 2733	200.00
Old Mother Hubbard, HN 2314	240.00
Olga, HN 2463	190.00
Omar Khayyam, HN 2247	125.00
One of Forty, brown hat, HN 497	1800.00
Organ Grinder, HN 2173	750.00

Owd Willum, HN 2042	**200.00**
Paisley Shawl, HN 1987	**195.00**
Patchwork Quilt, HN 1984	**260.00**
Patricia, HN 1414	**475.00**
Paula, HN 2906	**165.00**
Pearly Boy, HN 2035	**165.00**
Pearly Girl, HN 2036	**175.00**
Peggy, HN 2038	**80.00**
Pekinese	
HN 1040	**225.00**
K6 (A)	**60.00**
Penelope, HN 1901	**260.00**
Perfect Pair, HN 581	**850.00**
Persian Cat, white, HN 2539	**150.00**
Premiere, HN 2343	**250.00**
Pretty Polly, HN 2768	**140.00**
Professor, HN 2281	**150.00**
Proposal Lady, HN 715	**850.00**
Prue, HN 1996	**235.00**
Punch and Judy Man, HN 2765	**295.00**
Puppet Maker, HN 2253	**385.00**
Rag Doll, HN 2142	**82.00**
Reclining Rabbit, HN 2593 (A)	**90.00**
Reverie, HN 2308	**225.00**
Rhapsody, HN 2267	**190.00**
River Boy, HN 2128	**195.00**
Romany Sue, HN 1757	**950.00**
Roseanna, HN 1926	**279.00**
Rosebud, HN 1983	**325.00**
Royal Govenor's Cook, HN 2233	**350.00**
Sabbath Morn, HN 1982	**239.00**
Sailor's Holiday, HN 2442	**275.00**
School Marm, HN 2223	**185.00**
Scottish Terrier, "Champion Albourne Arthur', HN 1015	**225.00**
Seashore, red shorts, HN 2263	**195.00**
Sea Sprite, HN 2191	**335.00**
Secret Thoughts, HN 2382	**145.00**
Serenade, HN 2753	**150.00**
Spaniel with pheasant, HN 1029	**100.00**
Spook, HN 50	**2500.00**
Spring Flowers, HN 1807	**185.00**
St. George and the Dragon, HN 2856	**3995.00**
Stayed at Home, HN 2207	**175.00**
Stitch in Time, HN 2352	**135.00**
Summertime, HN 3137	**140.00**

Sunday Best, yellow dress, HN 2206	**250.00**
Sunshine Girl, HN 1344	**1950.00**
Susan, HN 2056	**310.00**
Sweet and Twenty, HN 1298	**215.00**
Sweet Anne	
HN 1496	**179.00**
M 5	**250.00**
Sweet Lavender, HN 1373	**675.00**
Sweet Suzie, HN 1918	**750.00**
Symphony, HN 2287	**285.00**
Taking Things Easy, HN 2677	**145.00**
Tall Story, HN 2248	**165.00**
Tea Time, HN 2255	**189.00**
Thanks Doc, HN 2281	**200.00**
The Bather, HN 687	**750.00**
The Bridesmaid, HN 2148 (A)	**150.00**
The Chief, HN 2892	**245.00**
The Ermine Coat, HN 1981	**225.00**
The Flower Seller's Children, HN 1342	**455.00**
The Gossips, HN 2025	**345.00**
The Lady Anne Neville, HN 2006	**600.00**
The Last Waltz, HN 2315 (A)	**130.00**
The Lobster Man, HN 2317	**203.00**
The Master, HN 2325	**200.00**
The Pied Piper, HN 2102 (A)	**330.00**
The Polka, HN 2156 (A)	**140.00**
The Puppet Maker, HN 2253	**400.00**
The Shepherd, HN 1975 (A)	**100.00**
The Young Master, HN 2812	**280.00**
Tiger, 9¼" l, crouching, flambe	**400.00**
To Bed, HN 1805	**145.00**
Tom Brown, HN 2941	**50.00**
Tom Tom the Piper's Son, HN 3032	**75.00**
Tootles, HN 1680	**80.00**
Top of the Hill, red dress HN 1834	**275.00**
Town Crier, HN2119	**231.00**
Treasure Island, HN 2243	**125.00**
Twilight, HN 2256	**165.00**
Uncle Ned, HN 2094	**300.00**
Valerie, HN 2017	**115.00**
Victorian Lady	
Miniature, M2	**235.00**
Potted, HN 728	**375.00**
Vote For Women, yellow coat, HN 2816	**325.00**
Wardrobe Mistress, HN 2145	**350.00**
Willy-Won't He, HN 2150 (A)	**295.00**
Windflower, HN 2029	**150.00**
Wistful, HN 2396	**322.00**
Young Miss Nightingale, HN 2010	**575.00**
Yum-Yum, HN 2899	**650.00**

Royal Doulton Figures, left, Lady Ann Nevill, HN 2006, (A) $340.00; right, The Blacksmith of Williamsburg, HN 2240, (A) $90.00

The Old Balloon Seller, HN 1315, repairs, (A) $45.00

Figure, flambe finish
Fox, Lying 36.00
Rabbit with ears up...................... 51.00
Rhinoceros, 17" l, half seated, mottled green
and red 950.00
Tiger, 14" l, 6" h, 4 black stripes 1150.00
Ink Pot, 3½" h, modeled as baby in brown
dress, puffy sleeves, white bib, "Vote For
Women" on front (A).................... 415.00
Jardinaire
7" h, "Welsh Ladies" series ware, ladies and
children going to church............... 335.00
8" h, 9½" w, Babes in Woods, lady and child
with basket picking flowers............. 595.00
Jug
6⅛" h, "Eglington Tournament', dark green
knights and horse, lustered brown and gold
bands, wide aqua band................ 145.00
7" h, man in red jacket toasting others,
"Here's to the man who is pleased with his
lot and never sits sighing for what
he has not," blue and white with gold
trim.................................. 175.00
7½" h, Dewars Scotch, "Bonnie Prince
Charlie" in colors 175.00
8" h, stoneware, brown with applied relief designs, c1922......................... 245.00
10½" h, Shakespeare, molded face of Shakespeare forms spout, theatrical mask handle,
molded Shakespeare characters on sides,
1938, sgd "Noke".................... 875.00
Pitcher
6" h
Brown floral transfer with underglaze blue,
polychrome enamel and gilt (A) 33.00
"Room For One," motor series 175.00
"The Castle Inn at Marlborough," blue and
white 95.00
6½" h, scene of Oliver Goldsmith's house. 98.00
7" h, hp sailboats 85.00
11" h, blue and green decorative band with
stylized flowers, brown earthenware, imp
mark (A)110.00
Plate
4½" d, Jack and Jill design, unmarked..... 30.00

6½" d, Little Boy Blue design 70.00
7¼" d, series ware, "Shakespeare's Country-
Beggarly Broom"...................... 75.00
8½" d
Dickensware, Sam Weller 60.00
Little Boy Blue design.................. 85.00
8¾" d, Babes in Woods
Mother and child with basket, shades of
blue 235.00
Two girls with pixie.................... 320.00
9½" d, "Kirkwood" pattern, set of 10..... 125.00
10" d
"Babes in Woods" design, three girls look-
ing at light in forest, blue transfer 435.00
Gibson Girl, "She Decides to Die in Spite
of Doctor Bottles" in black and blue
transfer 125.00
10¼" d, series ware, "The Admiral" 55.00
10½" d
"Airship" design, men in airplane, dirigible,
and balloons........................ 195.00
Banff National Park, Bow Valley 35.00
"Cambridge" pattern 8.00
Castles-Rochester Castle
Blue and white 35.00
Polychrome transfer.................. 45.00
"Dickensware," 'Artful Dodger," ruffled
edge, sgd "Noke".................... 105.00
"Jackdaw of Rheims" series ware, "And Off
That Terrible Curse He Took" 95.00
"Old English Coaching Scenes" series ware,
"Coach Unloading at Inn" 165.00
"Shakespeare's Country" series ware, "Beg-
garly Broom" 75.00
"The Squire" series ware, D6284 .... 45.00
10¾" d, Golfing, "Give Losers Leave to
Speak and Winners to Laugh".......... 400.00
13½" d, series ware, "Treasure Island," Long
John Silver with parrot, men loading boat in
ground............................... 165.00
Platter, 18" l, eight bunches of dainty florals on
white ground, hp gold rim (A) 10.00
Sugar Shaker
6¾" h, series ware, "The Jackdaw of Rheims,
But No-Then Can't Find the Ring," SP
top 175.00
7¼" h, English country scene of thatched
cottage and country church in green, pink,
and blue, SP top 135.00
Teapot, 9½" h, "Gold Lace" pattern, H4989. 95.00

Pitcher, 7" h, stoneware, gold Greek figures,
matte black ground, silver hallmarked rim, imp
"Royal Doulton" mark, (A) $240.00

Teapot and Stand, 5" h, "Gaffers" series ware,
D4210, "Royal Doulton Gaffers Made in England" mark, (A) $200.00

Tea Set, pot, creamer, sugar bowl, "Sairy Gamp"
design. **2000.00**

Toby Jugs
7" h, head with wreath of grapes and leaves,
twisted vine handle. **80.00**
Cap'n Cuttle, D6266 . . . . **155.00**
Cliff Cornel, large, blue. **325.00**
Fat Boy, D6264 . . . . **175.00**
Mr. Micawber, D6262 . . . . **180.00**
Mr. Pickwick, D6261 . . . . **180.00**
Old Charlie, D6069 . . . . **175.00**
Regency Beau, D6559 . . . . **800.00**
Sairy Gamp, D6263 . . . . **175.00**
Sam Weller, D6265. **175.00**

Tray
5½" l, flambe, cottage scene, sgd "Noke". **95.00**
8½" l, 7¼" w
Red and pink poppies, royal blue trim **175.00**
Roses on dark blue ground, green lion mark **125.00**
9¼" l, rect, red and orange flowers, blue
ground, brown border (A). **55.00**
9⅜" l, 6½" w, series ware, "Zunday
Zmocks" **95.00**
11" l, 5" w
Series ware, "Cecil Aldin's Dogs" **135.00**
Series ware, "Zunday Zmocks," man in black
top hat with hollyhocks, sgd "Noke" **85.00**
Trivet, 6½" d, blue portraits of monks and la-
dies on buff ground **45.00**

Vase
2½" h, raised blue flowers, blue and gray
glossy glaze **70.00**
4½" h, Arabian scenes, jewels on rims and
bases, pr **150.00**
4¾" h, "Bunnykins," family at table on front,
reverse with bunnies kissing under mistle-
toe, sgd "Barbara Vernon" **100.00**
5¼" h, stoneware, bulbous shape, enamel
decorated stylized flowers on white band,
blue glazed lower section, c1925, imp
"UBW," pr (A). **110.00**
5½" h, sq, Robin Hood series, "Robin Slays
Guy of Gisborne" **95.00**
6" h, rouge flambe, scene of farmer, plow, and
horses **95.00**
6½" h, Babes in Woods, snow scene of lady
with child walking down lane. **425.00**

7" h, rouge flambe, country cottage scene,
sgd "FM" **185.00**
8" h, flambe, hex lobed, gourd decorated at
shoulders with shoal of flying fish in black
over mottled orange-red ground, c1910,
sgd "Noke," black printed "Flambe," black
painted "Sung," signature and 1219/E
marks (A). **2000.00**
8¼" h
Flared cylinder form, purple and light green
flowers around rim, blue glaze (A) **100.00**
"Pressed Leaves" design, dark brown leaves
on mottled light brown glossy ground . . **165.00**
8½" h, decorative band with stylized rose
bouquets, wide base, Art Deco style, imp
Doulton mark (A) **100.00**
9½" h, flowing blue English cottage in trees
. . . . **110.00**
10" h
Bulbous shape, young man in purple and
rose with tree and hills, cream ground. . **135.00**
Stylized flowers on cobalt ground, pr **250.00**
10¼" h, flambe, baluster form, single exotic
firebird in flight over deep red ground with
scattered orange bubbles above curling
waves in speckled blue glazes, squat red
rim, mottled blue int, c1905, sgd "Noke,"
black printed "Flambe," imp marks, painted
"Sung," signature, 1182 marks (A) **2732.00**
14" h, baluster shape, raised flowers on tex-
tured beige ground, pr. **1000.00**
16" h, green reserves of stylized flowers, bul-
bous shape with tapering neck, short base,
blue ground, incised mark, pr. **450.00**
16½" h, cylinder shape, "Chang," gray and
blue veined glaze, runny scarlet, green, and
yellow over crimson and green ground,
c1930, painted "Royal Doulton, Noke, and
Chang" marks (A) **1825.00**

DRESDEN
1927

Dresden
1883-93

DRESDEN
1905

1883

DRESDEN

Germany
1694 to Present

N
Dresden
MODERN MARK

**Tobacco Jar, 5" h, with tamper, stoneware, white
raised figure on tan ground, dk brown neck and
lid, imp "Royal Doulton" mark, (A) $450.00**

History: Two men, working for Augustus II Elector of Saxony rediscovered the technique to make hard paste porcelain of the Oriental type. Count Tschimhaus, who began

his research in 1694, was joined by Johann Bottger, an alchemist, in 1701. At first they produced a red stoneware. By 1709 Bottger was producing white porcelain. Tschimhaus did not live to enjoy their success, having died in 1708. The king established the Royal Saxon Porcelain Factory in Dresden in 1710 and then moved it to Meissen one year later.

During the 18th century, Americans and English used the name "Dresden china" for the porcelain ware produced at Meissen. This has led to much confusion. Dresden, the capitol of Saxony, was better known in 18th century Europe than the city of Meissen, fifteen miles away. In addition Meissen products were sold in Dresden. Hence, Dresden became a generic term for all porcelains manufactured and decorated in the city of Dresden and its surrounding environs, including Meissen.

In the mid-19th century, about thirty factories were operating in the city of Dresden producing and decorating porcelains in the style of Meissen wares. Marks adopted which were similar to the crossed swords of the original Meissen factory. Many simply faked the Meissen mark.

Helena Wolfson and her successors imitated AR Meissen porcelain between 1843 and approximately 1949. Her firm had a large staff of painters trained to imitate the 18th century porcelain. Wolfson also purchased "white" china blanks from the Meissen factory and had them decorated by her own staff of painters and gilders. After much litigation, Wolfson was forced to abandon the AR mark. About 1880 the firm adopted a mark using the word "Dresden" with the letter "D" surmounted by a crown.

Meyers and Son was the greatest rival of Wolfson in the production of imitation Meissen porcelains. They used the crossed swords with an "M" to mark their examples. Franziska Hirsch, another copiest, used a mark similar to that of Samson, the French potter, on her Meissen and Vienna imitations made between 1894 and 1930.

The porcelain factory of Carl Thieme of Potschappel produced Rococo imitations of Meissen pieces from 1872 until 1972 often marketing them as Meissen 18th century figures. They also produced household, table, and decorative porcelains, knickknacks, souvenirs, and gift articles, all decorated in the Meissen and Vienna styles.

A "Dresden style" came into being when four decorators, Richard Klemm, Donath and Co., Oswald Lorenz, and Adolph Hamann, all registered the same mark in 1883. The mark was a crown with "Dresden" underneath in blue. Later this group altered their marks. Eight other decorators then used the "Dresden" and the crown mark.

Donath and Co. produced porcelain in the Meissen and Vienna styles from 1872 until 1916. The company merged with Richard Klemm's decorating workshop for three years. In 1918 the firm became the Dresden Art Department of C.M. Hutschenreuther, continuing in that relationship until 1945. Adolph Hamann, another member of the "Dresden style" group, operated a porcelain decorating workshop from 1866 until 1949. It was acquired by Heinrich Gerstmann in 1933 and continued with its earlier name.

Franz Junkersdorf, A. Lamm, Henfel and Co., Anton Richter, Max Robra, Wilhelm Koch, and others had decorating workshops from the last quarter of the 19th century and extending into the 20th century. All of these firms imitated of Meissen porcelains.

Museums: Bayerishes Nationalmuseum, Munich, Germany; Kunstgewebemuseum, Berlin, Germany; Museum fur Kunst und Gewerbe, Hamburg, Germany; Staatliche Porzellansammlung, Dresden, Germany.

See: Hutschenreuther.

Tankard, 7 1/2" h, porcelain, painted birds, silver mts, c1840, (A) $1100.00

Vase, 9 1/2" h, shaded brown and tan scene of monk holding candle, tankard and jug, gold trim, c1916, "blue Donath & Co." mark, (A) $385.00

Basket, 7" l, 4 1/2" h, reticulated body, applied blue and pink flowers, floral loop handle, four baroque feet............................. 150.00
Berry Set, pitcher, 6" h, 6 cups, 5" h, purple berries with green leaves, raised dot handles edged in purple, gilt rims, Dresden china mark.................................... 180.00
Bonbon Dish, 5 1/2" h, pastel flowers, reticulated border, Schuman........................ 125.00
Bowl, 10 1/2" H-H, hp flowers in center, reticulated body with relief of flowers 150.00
Box, 6" d, Sevres style painted cov with classical figures in wooded setting reserved on gilded blue ground, "crowned D" mark (A) 1310.00
Cake Stand, 5 1/2" h, 7 1/2" d, reticulated with floral design 125.00
Candelabra, 10 1/2" h, three branches, modeled with vintner groups with children at revelry drinking wine or crushing grapes, flower sprigs, scroll molded base, chips, late 19th C, underglaze "blue R," pr (A) 1200.00
Center Bowl, 17" l, boat shape on four sq feet, hp floral int, applied florals on front and back, sgd "Frulauf" 325.00
Centerpiece, 19 1/2" l, base modeled with four

rustic figures resting after harvest, sheafs of wheat around them, mound base and pierced basket applied with colored flowers and foliage, gilding, late 19th C (A) **1267.00**

Clock Garniture, 24½" h, clock base supporting white bust of Pan mounted on plinth, surrounded by putti and fauns seated on barrel resting on leopard-skin covered cart, holding bunches of grapes, base with four scroll molded feet, encrusted with flowers, two 9 holder candelabras, column with dancing faun, repair and damage, mid 19th C, underglaze "blue X'd swords," pr (A) **3850.00**

Compote, 5" h, 8½" d, polychrome floral design, reticulated bowl and foot, gilt accents, "Dresden" mark (A) **94.00**

Dessert Service, Partial, 7 plates, 9½" d, 2 dishes, 9⅞" d, figures on horseback before ruins, tents, and buildings, pierced borders enameled with flowers in bright colors, late 19th C, underglaze "blue crowned D," Helena Wolfsohn mark (A) **1589.00**

Dresser Tray, 9" d, 8 panels of turquoise, light green and gold florals, cream ground, c1890 (A) **8.00**

Ecuelle, Cov, Stand
   9½" d, scenes of 18th C figures in wooded landscape within gilt cartouches, purple scale ground, stand with central spray of summer flowers, cov and ecuelle with branch handles, c1870, underglaze "blue AR" (A) **1400.00**
   10¼" h, quatrefoil, lovers in landscape vignettes alternating with burnished gilt panels with floral bouquets, scrolling foliage between, cov with lemon finial, c1880, underglaze "blue AR" mark (A) **1975.00**

Ewer, 12" h, center scene of two ladies and Cupid in garden, reverse with four children playing blind man's bluff with rabbits, maroon and gold trim top and base, ornate gold accented handle, c1890, Wissman **795.00**

Figure
   4" h, monkeys dressed in band suits, polychrome (A) **425.00**
   6" h, boy and girl in period clothes, multicolored on base **255.00**
   6¼" h, 12" l, seated Russian wolfhound in colors, "Unterweiss Bach" mark **300.00**
   6½" h
      Man in red coat, woman in blue and gold dress with lace applied flowers, chess table and pieces **450.00**
      Young girl in white lace dress with applied flowers, red bodice and shoes, arms outstretched **250.00**
   7" h, red haired ballerina in pink and white lace dress with applied flowers, pink shoes **225.00**
   8" h
      Boy and girl with floral basket and game, pedestal base **215.00**
      Lady "Marquise de Vereuil, 1667" in long blue gown, gold trim, high fan collar, holding fan, 1875, "Carl Thieme" mark. **350.00**
   8" h, 8" l, lady seated in chair with vase of flowers, yellow hat, lace skirt, greyhound at feet **325.00**
   8¼" h, 7" w, lady in period lace dress seated,

man standing holding violin, cobalt coat, gold outlined rococo base, c1925 .... **250.00**
   9" h, man in pink coat, blue flowered breeches, white stockings holding floral bouquet, woman in floral period dress with blue waist with basket and tray of flowers, Carl Thieme, pr **750.00**
   9½" h, 11" l, man seated in blue coat holding violin, standing man in red coat holding violin, woman seated in lace dress playing piano, gold outlined footed base **1050.00**
   10½" h, 8" w, seated gypsy lady with goat, multicolored, "crowned Dresden" mark .. **450.00**
   10¾" h, tropical bird perched on tree trunk in colors and gilt accents, late 19th C, "blue Carl Thieme" mark (A) **605.00**
   11" h, seated mother cat with two kittens at feet, white fur with brown markings, blue collar with bells, late 19th C, incised 817 (A) **3198.00**
   12" h, tailor riding billy goat carrying scissors and iron on horns **350.00**
   12½" h, male or female in 18th C costumes in dancing poses, multicolored, scalloped oval base, "Dresden Germany" mark, pr.. **350.00**
   13½" l, man playing piano, woman playing cello, period lace dress, molded scroll base with gilt accents, c1930s **395.00**

Fruit Bowl
   5" l, 8½" d, multicolored florals, gold trim, open lattice work, pedestal base, "Crown Dresden Germany" mark **350.00**
   9½" l, 7" w, 4" h, reticulated sides, blue, white, and yellow applied flowers on ext, painted flowers on int, four curved feet .. **225.00**

Lamp, 18" h, four lithophane shades, three cherubs on base **1895.00**

Plaque
   3½" h, 3" w, Queen Louise in colors, sgd "Gerzer' (A) **175.00**
   6" h, 4" w, bust of semi-nude woman with flowing hair and thin gown trailing from shoulders, sgd "Gaylon" **2500.00**
   7½" h, 5" w, painted gypsy girl with tambourine, c1900, sgd "Wagner," gilded frame (A) **3000.00**

Plate
   9" d, hp gray and brown birds with yellow butterfly, pink clouds, blue ground, lattice pierced border with floral bouquets, c1875, "AR" mark **295.00**
   9½" d, center floral painting, gold trim, scalloped edge **125.00**
   10¼" d, couples in arcadian landscape, pierced borders in blue and gilt, applied florets, late 19th C, underglaze "blue crossed lines, gilt crown" mark, pr (A) **1161.00**
   10½" H-H, multicolored overall design of flowers, gold rococo border............. **20.00**
   10¾" d, pale multicolored flowers, gold border **25.00**

Salt, 11½" h, modeled with seated lady and gentleman before shaped oval baskets with flowers, molded gilt scroll base, early 20th C, blue line mark, pr (A) **1693.00**

Tea Service, hp rose decor, floral motif, molded head on pot, creamer, sugar, 6 cups and saucers, 15 pcs, 1875, "Carl Thieme" mark **850.00**

Urn, 12" h, 6½" d, floral decor, two panels of lovers in garden scene, red ground, c1860–1900, "R. Klemm" mark **550.00**

Urn, Cov., 24½" h, medallion of multicolored dancing nymphs, maroon ground, two gold branch handles, "AR" mark 650.00

Vase

7½" h, ornate floral decor in colors, three handles 175.00

8" h, scenic period medallion in colors, cobalt ground with gold decor and beading..... 325.00

20½" h, trumpet shape, painted peony, chrysanthemum, and prunus in pink, orange, blue, green, and iron-red, yellow ground, gilt rims, late 19th C (A).................. 1600.00

Vase, Cov

10¼" h, shield shape body, classical scene panels between gilded foliate borders, dark blue ground, undulating border molded as serpent on fluted circ base, foliate handles applied at shoulder, domed cov with molded pineapple knob, c1885, underglaze "blue crowned D," pr (A).............. 1900.00

14½" h, ovoid form, alternating yellow ground floral panels and courting couples in woodland landscape, domed cov, gilded borders, Meissen style, late 19th C, enameled "blue R," pr (A) 1028.00

13¾" h, double gourd shape, trumpet neck, both sides with stag hunting scenes or figures at revelry enclosed within gilded swag molded borders, yellow ground, rim chip, late 19th C, underglaze "blue AR" mark, pr (A)............................. 1100.00

18" h, waisted ovoid form, scenes of lovers in parkland and sprays of flowers, molded foliate handles, pierced foliate bases studded with florets and two cherubs, domed cov with flower finial, bases restored, late 19th C, pr (A) 1870.00

22" h, ovoid body, applied overall with ground of florets and branches trailing to leaves and balls of flowers, applied birds, domed cov with large bird finial, repair, late 19th C, incised numerals (A) 2916.00

23½" h, four shaped panels with painted period courting scenes reserved on blue ground accented with gilt scrolls, domed cov with small panels, gilt tear finial, "blue AR" mark, pr (A)...................... 5435.00

26¼" h, painted scene of courtly lovers in classical landscape, applied flowers and berries, reverse with painted flower sprays on white ground, modeled nymph head handles, relief molded waisted socle base, domed cov with painted flowers sprays, flower cluster knob, late 19th C (A)...... 6150.00

Vase, Cov, Stand

24" h, ovoid body, Watteau type panels of lovers or sprays of summer flowers, shoulders modeled with females holding flowers of baskets, stand, cov, shoulder, and foot molded with flowers and foliage, domed cov with cherubs supporting crown and armorial shield, late 19th C, pr (A) 4862.00

34¾" h, waisted globular form painted with classical maidens or sprays of summer flowers, shoulder applied with two prs of cherubs, pierced cov with seated female, encrusted with fruit and flowers, c1880, imp numerals, underglaze "blue crossed mark and T' (A)...................... 2822.00

ENGLAND—GENERAL

Porcelain
1700 to Present

History: Before the 1740s porcelains available in England were of Chinese or Japanese origin and were imported by the British East India Company. Many early English pottery manufacturers tried to duplicate oriental porcelains and the continental porcelains of Meissen and Sevres, but achieved only limited success.

The earliest English porcelains date about 1745 and were made at the Chelsea factory. This porcelain was the soft paste type. By the mid 18th century production of soft paste porcelain was well established at Bow and Chelsea. Other factories, including Bristol, Longton Hall, Derby, Worcester, Liverpool, and Lowestoft soon followed. The English factories were private enterprises, not subsidized by royal families or princely households as were those on the Continent.

Soft paste was fragile. Hot liquids could crack it. Sometimes it collapsed or lost its shape in the kiln. Efforts were mounted to find a material that was more stable in the kiln and durable. The Bow factory tried adding ash of calcined bones. Bristol and Worcester incorporated a soapstone paste to their mix to strengthen their porcelains.

Many credit William Cookworthy of Plymouth with the rediscovery of the Chinese method of hard paste porcelain manufacture in England about 1768. He made hard paste type porcelain at Plymouth for only two years, 1768–70. In 1771, he moved to Bristol.

Pieces from the Plymouth pottery have an Oriental influence. Some under-the-glaze blue designs are enhanced with over-the-glaze enamels. Figurines and animal and bird groups also were made. The second Josiah Spode of Stoke developed bone china by adding bone ash to the ingredients of hard paste porcelain. This "bone" china led to the development of cream colored earthenware. Based on the hard paste rediscovery and Spode's bone china, England became a major supplier to the world wide market.

Pottery
17th Century to Present

History: Early pottery wares in England included stoneware, Delftware, slipware, and salt glaze ware. Potters such as Thomas Toft, John Dwight, and the Elers were among the principal manufacturers.

During the early 17th century, Staffordshire became the center of the pottery industry due to an abundant supply of coal, availability of clays and adequate transportation to the marketplace. Astbury, Whieldon, and the Woods experimented with all forms of earthenwares from figure groups with colored glazes to numerous types of vessels and dishes. Earthenware production dominated the first half of the eighteenth century.

As the newly perfected cream colored earthenwares introduced by Josiah Wedgwood in the 1760s came to the forefront, Staffordshire salt glazed wares started to go out of fashion. Numerous Staffordshire makers such as the Turners, Elijah Mayer, Palmer and Neale, Wilson of Hanley, Leeds, William Adams of Tunstall, and Josiah Spode of Stoke copied Wedgwood's cream colored earthenwares. They also imitated Wedgwood's black basalt, jasper, and cane colored stoneware. Spode introduced the manufacture of blue printed earthenwares.

During the 1800s lusterwares became popular with the

Staffordshire potters. New techniques in the early 19th century included overglaze transfer printing and ironstone china. Underglaze blue printing was developed in the first half of the 19th century.

Figures, depicting all sorts of people and animals, were made during the 1800s by John Walton, Ralph Salt, and Obadiah Sherratt. During the reign of Queen Victoria, earthenware cottage mantelpiece figures were decorated in enamels and some gilding. Underglaze blue was the most important color used. Sampson Smith was the principal manufacturer. Pot lids were another 19th century product with decorations in polychrome underglaze.

Other pottery firms making utilitarian and decorative wares during the 19th century included H. & R. Daniels, Miles Mason, W. Ridgway & Co., Cauldon Place Works, John Davenport, Job Meigh, Lakin & Poole, Mintons, and Doulton of Lambeth.

Since the late 1800s the studio potter has become important in England. This movement is a reaction against the emphasis on mass produced pieces. The studio potter usually throws his own wares with the glazing and decorating done either by himself or under his supervision. The first of the studio potters were William de Morgan and the Martin Brothers. Bernard Leach of the St. Ives Pottery made stoneware influenced by early Chinese and Japanese wares. The studio potters use many traditional methods of manufacture such as tin glaze, salt glaze, slipware, agate ware, and sgraffito work.

Patent Office Registration Marks: From 1842 until 1883 many manufacturers' wares were marked with the "diamond mark" which was an indication that the design or form of the piece was registered with the British Patent Office and protected against piracy for three years. The mark could be applied by either printing, impressing, or applying a molded piece of clay. Pottery and porcelains were in Class IV. In the diamond the numbers or letters in each corner were keyed. A ceramic marks book is necessary to decipher the mark and discover the date the design was registered with the Patent office. After 1884 the diamond mark was replaced by a registry number.

References: Cyril G.E. Bunt, *British Potters & Pottery Today,* F. Lewis Publishers, 1956; J.P. Cushion, *English China Collecting for Amateurs,* Frederick Muller, 1967; B. Watney, *English Blue & White Porcelain,* Faber & Faber, rev. ed., 1973.

Museums: British Museum, London, England; City Museum & Art Gallery, Stoke-on-Trent, England; Cranbrook Academy of Art Museum, Bloomfield Hills, MI; Gardiner Museum of Ceramic Art, Toronto, Canada; Victoria & Albert Museum, London, England.

Collectors Clubs: English Ceramic Society, Membership Secretary, 5 The Drive, Beckenham, Kent BR3 1EE, England. Membership: 19 pounds. *Transactions* published annually. Northern Ceramics Society, Membership Secretary, Bramdean Jacksons Lane, Hazel Grove, Cheshire, England SK75JW. Membership $30.00 USA. Newsletter four times a year, journal yearly.

Additional Listings: Adams, Beswick, Bisque, Bow, Bristol, Carlton Ware, Caughley, Cauldon, Chelsea, Clews, Coalport, Copeland-Spode, Creamware, Crown & Royal Crown Derby, Davenport, Delft, De Morgan, Derby, Doulton, Flow Blue, Ironstone, Jackfield, Leeds, Liverpool, Longton Hall, Lowestoft, Lusterware, Majolica, Martin Brothers, Mason, Meakin, Meigh, Minton, Mocha Ware, Moorcroft, Nantgarw, New Hall, Pot Lids, Pratt, Ridgway, Rockingham, Royal Worcester, Salt Glaze, Slipware,

Spode, Staffordshire, Stoneware, Swansea, Wedgwood, Whieldon Ware, Willow Ware, Enoch Wood, Ralph Wood, Worcester.

Biscuit Jar
  6½" h, pottery, three multicolored birds on branch with gold leaves, cream ground, SP top 135.00
  9¾" to top of handle, pottery, emb gold leaf design, multicolored florals, SP lid and bail, Eng Reg mark......................... 255.00
Bowl, Porcelain
  6" d, scallop trimmed panels alternating in enamel decorated oriental floral and figural scenes between rust scalloped wheel designs, early 19th C (A) 110.00
  8" d, small purple and green thistle flowers, gilt trim (A) 227.00
Cheese Dish, Cov
  6½" h, 9¼" l, 7¼" w, pottery, pink, white, orange, and yellow flowers with green leaves, gold trim, cream ground......... 118.00
  8" h, "Imari" pattern in typical colors (A)... 65.00
Clock, 12" h, pottery, polychrome transfer of Middle Eastern scene with gilt, mauve ground, "Made in England" mark (A) 61.00
Coffee Can, 2½" h, painted scene of Chinese man crossing bridge with trees and rockwork, blue and iron-red, loop handle, Plymouth ... 195.00
Creamer, 3¾" h, raised hound panel on bottom, green trim, raised floral border around spout, hound handle, white ground, c1790, Yorkshire, David Dunderdale & Co., manufacturer 585.00
Cup and Saucer
  Handleless, porcelain, pink and purple house pattern (A) 28.00
  House of Parliament, Victoria, B.C., black transfer, cream ground, "Royal Winton, Made in England" mark................. 9.00
  Pink floral design (A) 10.00
  Polychrome floral design (A)............... 10.00
  Red and blue floral design (A) 15.00
  Reserves of landscapes in colors (A)........ 44.00
Dessert Service, porcelain, large compote, 2 sq compotes, 3 pr of oval compotes, 18 plates, 9" d, shaped borders with large cobalt band interspersed by floral reserve panels, gilt enhancements, early 19th C (A)............. 1760.00

Mug, 4" h, porcelain, Domino, molded face in colors, late 19th C, $150.00

Dish

8" d, emb multicolored flowers, cobalt ground, Mailing **85.00**

12⅝" d, painted scene of hunter in bush, white setter in foreground, mountains in ground, c1840 . . . . **3000.00**

Ewer, 7½" h, gold flowers and blue leaves on shaped peach to eggshell ground, molded griffin handle **150.00**

Figure

5¼" h, seated woman playing hurdy gurdy, scrolled base, late 18th C (A) **302.00**

6⅛" h, rabbit seated on haunches, med brown coat, white underbody, oval base with applied flowers, repairs, c1770, Plymouth (A) **5291.00**

10" h, porcelain, standing woman in flowered skirt and green cape (A) **220.00**

Flower Pot, 3¼" h, olive tan clay body with applied acanthus leaves and foxglove in green, yellow and pink enamels, repaired saucer (A) **148.00**

Milk Jug, 5½" h, black basalt, putti with fleur de lis and swag decoration (A) **100.00**

Milk Pitcher, 6½" h, vert ribbed body, slate blue flowers, buds, and leaves, white ground, scalloped spout, unmarked **42.00**

Mug

4¼" h, campana shape, famille verte colors and style, "Dragons in Compartments" pattern, cell diaper and demi-floret border, c1769–70, Plymouth (A) **3256.00**

5" h, Wellington as Prime Minister, Walmer Castle Kent, Duke at Waterloo, black transfers, hairline, mid 19th C (A) **165.00**

Pen Tray, 10⅛" l, porcelain, painted scene of Oriental carrying birdcage on stick, leaf molded rim, gilt accents, four lion mask and paw feet, early 19th C (A) **285.00**

Pitcher

4⅝" h, "Imari" pattern in cobalt, iron red and gold, ribbed body, cobalt handle, "England" mark (A) **35.00**

5" h, black transfer of European country scene on white ground in oval, brown glazed body (A) **110.00**

6¾" h, porcelain

Bust of Lord Hill, purple transfer with blue, flesh, red, and gold accents, gold oval frame, early 19th C (A) **405.00**

Oriental scene in polychrome enamels (A) **85.00**

Pitcher, Cov, 10" h, painted scene of DYREFJIORD ICELAND in lavender, brown, green, and gray, gilded crouched lion on handle, 19th C (A) **187.00**

Plaque

6⅕" l, 12⅛" w, porcelain, three cherubs reclining on bank of clouds in blue and gray tones, c1868, script title "Group of Cupids by W.P. Simpson, 1868" mark (A) **630.00**

7½" l, 5⅝" w, porcelain, rect, painted loose bouquets of summer flowers on ledge with bird's nest and eggs, giltwood frame, c1830, pr (A) **2860.00**

11⅝" h, 8⅝" w, oval, sprays of pink roses and green leaves on white marble table top, c1880, framed **3500.00**

12¼" l, 6¼" w, rect, porcelain, painted scene of three putti floating on clouds, blue sky, c1868, sgd "W.P. Simpson' (A) **2300.00**

Plate

7¾" d, polychrome enamel rose design, emb rim with purple luster stripe (A) **34.00**

8½" d

Black transfer of GENERAL WILLIAM BOOTH/SEPTEMBER-NOVEMBER/ 1907, gray-blue border (A) **20.00**

Painted flower specimen named on reverse, gilt enriched border molded with continuous vine, set of 11 (A) **1980.00**

9½" d, porcelain, blue, iron-red, green, salmon, and gilt "Japan" pattern, early 19th C, pattern #820, set of 12 (A) **4117.00**

10" d, Queensware, polychrome enameled floral design with black enameled bust of man and woman, unmarked (A) **155.00**

Platter

11¼" l, pottery, oval, polychrome scenes of ruined abbeys, emb floral border, gold bands on inner and outer rim, pr (A) **187.00**

20½" l, 16" w, well and tree, brown table with urn, yellow, rust, pink, violet, and green florals, four floral urns on border, white ground, c1830, "Saxon China" **850.00**

Sauce Tureen, 6¼" h, with stand, painted pink roses divided by molded flowers, satyr head handles, gilt line borders (A) **340.00**

Spirit Barrel, 13" h, porcelain, oval, painted stag and bird in landscape, marked "PORT," brass tap, late 19th C **250.00**

Sugar Bowl, Cov

6¼" h, porcelain, oriental flowers and scrolls in blue, red, and gold, late 19th C (A) **55.00**

6½" h, basalt, two relief medallions, one of Nelson Victories with PATRIOTS in banner, reverse with monument flanked by Britannia and angel holding tablet inscribed "HOWE" and "NELSON," early 19th C (A) **467.00**

Tankard, 7¼" h, "Imari" pattern in cobalt, iron red, and gilt, pewter top, flake on base (A) **85.00**

Teabowl and Saucer, porcelain, oriental coastal village scenes, blue transfers, shaped gilt edges, 18th C, set of 4 (A) **180.00**

Teapot

6" h, porcelain, red and blue sprig decoration (A) **100.00**

6¼" h, porcelain, polychrome enameled oriental design, molded applied floral finial, hairline on spout (A) **770.00**

6¾" h, black transfer of two women with baby on ground, polychrome enamel accents, "H.&S." mark (A) **70.00**

11¼" h, redware, tooled body, emb leaf handle, dome top lid, mismatched lid (A) **150.00**

14¾" h, Bargeware, red, green, and black applied flowers and birds, brown ground, imp "A Present for a Friend 1874," rim restored, 19th C (A) **410.00**

Tea Service, porcelain, teapot, creamer, cov sugar, 6 cups and saucers, gilt oak leaves and blue acorns on white ground, late 19th C (A) **247.00**

Toothbrush Holder, 5½" h, Victorian design, pink roses with green floral swags, scalloped

edge with gilt trim, c1911, "Winkle & Co. Ltd"
mark................................... **195.00**
Urn, 6 1/4" h, multicolored floral cartouche outlined in gilt, raised white dot lines, white int,
med blue panels, gilt base and rim, c1815 .. **535.00**
Vase
   8 1/2" h, pottery, relief of English country
   scene, cream, brown, and black, c1883,
   Bretby **60.00**
   10 1/2" h, ovoid body, porcelain, decorated
   with reserves of exotic birds with molded
   acanthus handles, apple green ground, gilt
   highlights, pierced flaring rim, mid 19th C, pr
   (A)................................ **330.00**
   11" h, underglaze green floral design on yellow ground, Ruskin..................... **525.00**
   15" h, porcelain, figural reserves on blue
   ground, late 19th C, pr (A) **110.00**

FAIRINGS AND TRINKET BOXES

Locket, Elbogen, Germany, now Czechoslovakia c1860–1890

Staffordshire, England

History: Fairings, common during the Victorian era, were
small porcelain groups of gaily colored human and animal china figures designed to catch the eye with their
humor and sentimentality. One figural, captioned "The
last in bed to put out the light," shows a man and
woman bumping heads as they jumped into bed while a
lighted candle stands on a table nearby. "Five o'clock
tea" features humanized cats at a tea party. Fairings
were made to be given away as prizes or purchased at
English fairs.
   Although fairings were associated with England, they
were actually made by Springer and Oppenheimer of
Locket, Elbogen, Germany, now Czechoslovakia. Themes
included courtship and marriage scenes, events in the lives
of the people, war, politics and the law, children at work
and play, and animals behaving like people. Most fairings

Box, left, 5 1/2" h, gold mirror frame, lt brown hair on
child, blue shoes, white dress with green florals, brown
dog, "Conta & Boehme Thuringia Germany" mark,
$345.00; Fairing, right, "The Welsh Tea Party", magenta
dresses, striped aprons, black hats, open tree trunks, gold
trim on base, c1870, $65.00

had inscriptions written in English. Often the inscriptions
were naive or intended to be risque.
   Colors mainly were shades of pink and blue with the
inscriptions in black. Early examples were usually 3 1/2 to
4 1/2" high with plain, undecorated bases. Gilt was used
sparingly. After 1890 the colors became more garish.
   Fairings are made of white heavy paste. Most have
numbers incised or impressed beneath their bases, though
the earliest and best examples have no numbers.
   Small English Staffordshire porcelain trinket boxes
were sold at fairs and seaside resorts. They range in size
from about 3"-5" in length and usually are several
inches tall. The lids were decorative and featured subjects similar to the fairings from Germany. Many had animals or children on them. Most were white and had gilt
trim.

References: W.S. Bristowe, *Victorian China Fairings*, Ta-
plinger Publishing Co., Inc., 1965.

FAIRINGS
2 3/4" h, 5 1/2" l, "Tug of War," baby and dog
   pulling at doll, baby in green and white, gold
   trim.................................. **175.00**
3" h, Ben Franklin in red vest, light black hair
   on grass pedestal base, Staffordshire **65.00**
3 1/4" h
   "For Heaven's Sake Maria, Give Us Rest,"
   woman standing over man in bed, pale
   blue blanket, white with gold trim, German mark.......................... **200.00**
   "Returning at One O'Clock in the Morning," wife spanking husband, blue, red,
   and brown, "Made in Germany" mark
   (A) **121.00**
   "The Last in Bed to Put Out the Light" ... **295.00**
   "Twelve Months After Marriage," blue, purple, and green **195.00**
3 1/2" h, "Looking Down upon his Luck,"
   young man and wife looking down at twins,
   purple, blue, and red, "Made in Germany"
   mark (A) **93.00**
3 3/4" h
   Blond child in mint green nighty with orange candle, looking at doll in bed, unmarked **68.00**
   "The Wedding Night," man on knee,
   woman with back to him, mantel with
   clock, chair with blanket, gold trim, German mark.......................... **165.00**
   "Will We Sleep or How?," couple in bed,
   light blue, red, gold, and brown, "Made in
   Germany" mark (A) **121.00**
4" h
   One girl playing concertina, another playing
   tamborine, multicolored, Germany **20.00**
   "The Last in Bed to Put Out Light," German
   mark................................ **225.00**
   4 1/4" h, open basket style in rare green color,
   applied girl on one, boy on other, crusted
   white and rust flowers and leaves in one
   corner, gilt trim, pr **285.00**
4 1/2" h
   "Let us do Business together," two boys
   sitting on chamber pots, green, gold,
   flesh, and red (A) **148.00**
   Pocket watch holder, two kneeling children
   holding wreath, green and gold (A) **154.00**
4 1/2" l, Craigneil House Bognor, white and

salmon, green and rust trim, gray roof Staffordshire 85.00

TRINKET BOXES

2½" h,

Black cat on blue cushion, pitcher, and book, gilt trim........................ 155.00

Fruits on top, basketweave bottom, blue line trim, matte finish 125.00

Sleeping baby on orange pillow, rose bows on blanket, ruffle edge, gilt trim........ 225.00

Three little boys seated wearing light blue jackets, pink pants, white stocking caps, brown log base, gilt trim 150.00

2½" l, white deer lying down, blue edge .. 75.00

3" h, white parian box with molded leaves and berries on top, rope handle, basketweave base, minor damage.................. 110.00

3¼" h, reclining angel with blue draped skirt, yellow wings, rose and bird, pale turquoise base with raised design 155.00

3½" h

Deer head in center on white ground with gilt trim, flat base with ladies leg, ftd, gilt trim............................... 155.00

Dresser

Coiled rope, anchor, and cannon on top, gold highlights, anchor repaired (A) 11.00

Pitcher, sword, and bugle on top, gold and orange (A) 27.00

Matte finish lion on green ground, white base with raised leaves and gilt trim.... 175.00

Passenger pigeon with blue beak, package around neck, brown and yellow on wings, matte finish, white base with blue band, gilt trim........................ 185.00

3 3/4" h, pirate in black boots, rust jacket, and yellow gloves, white ground 75.00

4" h

King and Queen in white, matte finish ... 175.00

Urn shaped tureen with gilt trim, gilt ram's head handles 135.00

4¼" h, fireplace with small boy sitting on mantle, gold, tan, and red (A)........... 93.00

4½" h

Dresser set on top, mirror with gilt trim, four green leaves........................ 145.00

Fireplace with mirror and large cat playing with frog on mantle, black, brown, green, red, and gold, unmarked (A) 176.00

Harlequin with basket and green crusted florals, raised green leaves on base with gold circles and rim 185.00

Tea set on top with mirror space, fireplace bottom, white and gold............... 135.00

White with gilt trim, pitcher and bowl with mirror space, ftd 85.00

4¾" h

Fireplace with mirror, small boy with chicken on mantle, gold, red, orange, and tan, restored (A) 148.00

Piano with mirror and open book, gilt trim.................................. 125.00

Table with two chairs and tea set on top, gilt mirror, base with blue center medallion with raised figures, white with gilt trim.................................. 145.00

5" h

Blue fireplace with girl on top with dishes, gilt edge 145.00

Male and female figures, basketweave center with applied florals, mirror frame, white base with blue and gilt trim...... 225.00

"Paddling His Own Canoe," baby rowing in tub on top, mirror frame, gilt trim, "Made in Germany" mark 185.00

Watch top with ring, open mirror, white with gilt trim and blue bands 60.00

5½" h

Dresser tray, mirror in green with orange and purple flowers, pink trim, gilt trim.. 35.00

Gilt mirror frame on lid, applied rose with pink insert, molded shaded green leaf, cobalt panels on base 145.00

Matte finish swan with orange beak on top with pale green trim, ribbed base with black dots and orange handles 225.00

FISCHER

MF
1880

Herend, Hungary
c1839 to Present

History: Moritz Fischer established a porcelain manufactory at Herend, Hungary about 1839. His factory was noted for the high quality of its reproductions of Chinese porcelains and 18th century European porcelains from Meissen, Vienna, Capodimonte, and Sevres. Reticulated vases, ewers, and chimney ornaments also were made in very bright enamel colors, almost majolica like in appearance. Oriental patterns such as famille rose, famille verte, and Imari decorations were imitated by Herend craftsmen. They employed no independent designers, only craftsmen. Every piece was hand painted.

When the Imperial Vienna factory closed in 1864, Fischer received the right to use the patterns and models selected by Emperor Franz Joseph for continued use. These old Vienna molds and patterns were marked with a beehive. Many wares were exported to the United States.

Fischer was raised to the nobility and used the name Farkashazi in 1865. Fischer was succeeded by his sons. The factory failed in 1874 and then underwent a series of changes in ownership.

New prosperity was achieved under Jeno Farkashazi, the grandson of Moritz. The factory was taken over by the state in 1948. The factory continues to produce hard paste porcelain dinnerware, vases, and figures similar to those of Meissen and Sevres.

Herend porcelain is still produced today. Although figures are very popular, Herend is most known for its tablewares. Patterns are never discontinued, so it is always possible to order replacements.

Museum: Victoria & Albert Museum, London, England.

Center Bowl, 7½" h, 9" l, oval, gilt bordered reserves of birds on cobalt ground, four putti and floral swags, gilt bronze mtd, early 19th C, Herend. 700.00

Vase, 14½″ h, triangular shape, multicolored florals, protruding reticulated roudels, "blue Fischer Budapest" mark, (A) $248.00

Ewer
12″ h, overall blue, rose, and gold lustered reticulated surface, large loop handle, "Fischer, Budapest" mark, pr 300.00
15¾″ h, bold multicolored florals with gold trim, long spout and handle with florals 350.00

Figure
2¾″ h, gray elephant standing on ball, Herend 75.00
5¼″ h, rooster in colors, dtd 1943, Herend   48.00
7″ h, peasant child holding two piglets, Herend 225.00
11½″ h, folk dancer in colors, #5491, Herend 395.00
14″ h, hp Madonna and child in colors, Herend mark 350.00
15″ h, seated nude fixing her hair, white glaze   250.00
Peasant woman with fish in colors 200.00
Plaque, 11½″ h, 8¼″ l, seated lady wearing 18th C costume with low cut bodice, rose in one hand, leans on table with open book and glove by side, two figures in distance in grounds of formal garden, c1860–80, script title "Mondespan C. Netscher, Dresden Museum," imp "CF" for Christian Fischer, framed (A) . . . 8424.00
Plate, 9½″ d, overall reticulated medallions in gold, rose, and turquoise, "Budapest, Hungary" mark, pr 300.00
Potpourri Desk, 6¾″ h, 4¾″ l, shaped rect, raised molded body, multicolored florals, scroll feet, cobalt border, gilt edges, holes in top lined in gold with shades of blue and pink raised dots, fleur-de-lys on ends, 1895, "J. Fischer Budapest" mark 595.00
Puzzle Jug, 13″ h, brown transfer of three gentlemen, polychrome and gilt accents, "Fischer, Budapest" mark (A) 125.00
Vase
7″ h, multicolored flowers on alternating panels of brown and crusted gold, "Fischer-Budapest" mark. 130.00
8″ h, bulbous body with pinched and crimped rim, four feet, dark blue glaze with granular overlay in cream and gilt (A). 40.00
10½″ h, red, blue, and yellow stylized flowers, gold accents on neck and base, "Fischer-Budapest" mark, pr. 310.00

STOKE POTTERY
GRIMWADES
c1900

COLONIAL POTTERY
& W Co
STOKE ENGLAND

1890-1925

THOMAS FURNIVAL
& SONS
c1871-1890

COBRIDGE STAFFORDSHIRE

ALLERTONS

ENGLAND
c1890

FLOW BLUE

Staffordshire, England
Early Victorian 1835–1850s
Mid Victorian 1860s–1870s
Late Victorian 1880s, 1890s, and the early 1900s

History: "Flow" or "Flowing" Blue was developed for commercial consumption in the 1820s by Josiah Wedgwood. Other well-known makers include W. T. Copeland, Samuel Alcock, and William Davenport. Flow Blue was being marketed in many countries including France, Germany, Holland, and the U.S. The peak production period was from the mid-1800s to the early 1900s.

The Flow Blue process occurs when a transfer printed design, originally in cobalt oxide, receives volitizing agents such as lime of chloride or ammonia causing the pattern to "bleed" during the glaze firing stage. The cobalt when first applied was brown in color and changed to a deep blue during the firing. The degree of flowing varies considerably with some designs barely discernable while others show a slight hazing of the pattern.

The earliest patterns were Oriental in style named in most cases by the manufacturer. These names are often found incorporated with the maker's mark. Scenics and florals were popular during the Victorian period. Some Art Nouveau designs were produced. Most designs were applied by transfers. In some cases, hand painted designs were done.

Though some of the designs were registered, it is not unusual to find the same name used by two different companies for two entirely different designs. Manufacturers also had a habit of changing design names. Over 1,500 patterns were manufactured during the peak years of Flow Blue production.

Early Flow Blue is characterized by a dense coloration. Later pieces had a softer look to them. By the mid-Victorian era, colors as well as gold embellishments were added to enhance the designs.

Many early examples are made of stoneware, but porcelain and semi-porcelain also served as bodies for the Flow Blue patterns. By the later half of the 19th century, semi-porcelain was the material of choice. The designs of this period usually are sharper and cleaner. The body design is more elaborate.

Back stamps usually provide the pattern name and initials or name of the maker. Often the location of the factory is included. Transfer marks out number all other types. Marks with a pattern name date after 1810.

References: Sylvia Dugger Blake, *Flow Blue*, Wallace-Homestead, 1971; Robert Copeland, *Spode's Willow Pattern and Other Designs After the Chinese*, Rizzoli, 1980; Mary Gaston, *The Collector's Encyclopedia of Flow Blue China*, Collector Books, 1983; Veneita Mason, *Popular Patterns of Flow Blue China with Prices*, Wallace-Homestead, 1982; Petra Williams, *Flow Blue China, An Aid to Identifications*, Fountain House East, 1971; Petra Williams, *Flow Blue China II*, Fountain House East, 1973; Petra Williams, *Flow Blue China & Mulberry Ware*, Fountain House East, rev. ed., 1981.

Collectors' Clubs: Flow Blue International Collectors Club, David Seal, Membership Chairman, P.O. Box 205, Rockford, IL 61105. Newsletter "Blueberry Notes."

Museums: Margaret Woodbury Strong Museum, Rochester, NY.

Reproduction Alert: New Flow Blue has been manufactured by Blakeney Pottery Limited in Stoke-on-Trent since 1968. Objects are termed "Victorian Reproductions" and are made with large blue roses in many forms. Evidence shows that some of these items have been sold as old.

Collecting Hints: The center for collecting Flow Blue is in the United States. Even though the vast majority of Flow Blue was made in England, the English do not attach much antique value to Flow Blue since it was mass produced, transfer decorated, and inexpensive. Since most was exported to the U.S. during the 19th century, it is not prevalent in the English market.

Miniatures and children's dishes are scarce in Flow Blue since not many examples were made. Art or decorative items are harder to find than ordinary table and utiliarian wares.

Gravy Boat, "Chapoo" pattern, 8" l, unmkd, $395.00

Cup and Saucer, "Jewel" pattern, "Johnson Bros. England" mark, $55.00

"Abbey" pattern
Bowl
  6" d, ftd, "Petrus Regout Holland" mark .   55.00
  8" d, "George Jones" mark 85.00
  11" d, "George Jones" mark 68.00
Breakfast Set, coffee pot, teapot, jam pot, 4 cups and saucers, 4 side plates, 4 single and 4 dbl shredded wheat dishes, cake plate, "G. Jones" marks 825.00
Coffee Pot, "George Jones" mark 255.00
Cup and Saucer. 45.00
Pitcher and Bowl, "George Jones" marks . . .   475.00
Plate
  6" d 20.00
  10 1/2" d 28.00
Relish Tray, 10 1/2" l, 5 1/2" w, "G. Jones & Sons" mark 120.00
Teapot, 5" h, "George Jones" mark 225.00
"Alaska" pattern
Berry Dish, 5 1/4" d, "W.H. Grindley" mark .   30.00
Bowl, 10" d 90.00
Plate
  6" d 25.00
  6 1/2" d 28.00
  8" d 38.00
  10" d 65.00
Platter, 14" l 125.00
Soup Plate, 9" d, "W.H. Grindley" mark 49.00
"Albany" pattern
Cup and Saucer, gold trim 55.00
Gravy Boat 75.00
Platter, 14" l, "W.H. Grindley" mark 100.00
Vegetable Bowl, 9 1/4" H-H, "W.H. Grindley" mark. 85.00
"Albion" pattern
Plate, 8" d. 50.00
"Aldine" pattern
Butter Pat, "W.H. Grindley" mark 12.00
Platter, 18" l, 13" w, "W.H. Grindley" mark   225.00
"Alhambra" pattern
Bowl, 10" d 56.00
Chamber Set, pitcher, bowl, soap dish, chamber pot, "Meakin" marks. 975.00
Vegetable Bowl, 10 1/2" d. 48.00
"Alton" pattern
Creamer, 3 1/2" h, "W.H. Grindley" mark . . .   95.00
Soup Plate, 9 7/8" d, "W.H. Grindley" mark. 95.00
"Amerilla" pattern
Sauce Tureen, ladle and undertray, "P.W.& Co." mark. 735.00
"Amoy" pattern
Cup Plate, 4 1/8" d, Davenport 35.00
Plate
  7" d, 12 sided 75.00
  7 1/4" d 55.00
  8 1/2" d 65.00
  9" d 95.00
  9 1/4" d 85.00
  9 1/2" d 90.00
  10 1/2" d, Davenport 83.00
Platter
  10" l 150.00
  12" l 450.00
  16" l 425.00
  18" l 325.00
Sauce Dish 65.00
Teapot 350.00
"Arabesque" pattern
Plate, 10 1/2" d 95.00

"Arabic" pattern
Plate, 8" d, "W.H. Grindley" mark 17.50
"Arcadia" pattern
Plate, 10" d 58.00
Platter, 16" l. 175.00
"Argyle" pattern
Gravy Boat, 8" l, with undertray 150.00
Plate, 10" d
Ford 55.00
"W.H. Grindley" mark 75.00
Platter
12¾" l, 8¾" w, "W.H. Grindley" mark   165.00
15" l, 10½" w, gold trim, "W.H. Grindley"
mark. 150.00
17" l, "W.H. Grindley" mark 275.00
Relish Dish, 8½" l. 35.00
Soup Bowl, 7½" d 55.00
"Ashley" pattern
Plate, 10½" d, c1879–1900, "Smith & Binall"
mark 65.00
"Atlanta" pattern
Plate, 9" d, "Petrus Regout & Co." mark . . .   45.00
"Ayr" pattern
Plate
7" d, "W.& E. Corn" mark 45.00
9" d, "W.& E. Corn" mark 55.00
"Baltic" pattern
Plate, 10" d 79.00
"Basket" pattern
Pitcher, 8½" h, corset shape, Swinnerton . .   95.00
"Beatrice" pattern
Plate, 10" d 55.00
"Beaufort" pattern
Plate, 8½" d 42.00
Platter
14"l, 10" w, "W.H. Grindley" mark. 135.00
16⅛" l, 10" w, "W.H. Grindley" mark . .   175.00
"Beauties of China" pattern
Plate, 8½" d 75.00
"Beauty Rose" pattern
Pitcher, 6" h. 95.00
"Begonia" pattern
Plate, 9" d, "Johnson Bros." mark 25.00
"Bell" pattern
Platter, 10¼" d 125.00
"Belmont" pattern
Bread and Butter Plate, 5" d 45.00
Butter Pat 15.00
Plate, 6¾" d, "A. Meakin" mark 30.00
"Bentick" pattern
Plate
6" d. 22.00
10" d, "A. Meakin" mark 65.00
"Beryl" pattern
Gravy Boat 120.00
"Beufort" pattern
Bowl, 10" d 90.00
"Bisley" pattern
Gravy Boat with undertray, "W.H. Grindley"
mark. 145.00
"Bluebell" pattern
Compote, 12" l, Ridgway 95.00
"Blue Rose" pattern
Bowl, 6¼" d, "W.H. Grindley" mark 40.00
Plate, 8½" d, gold edge, crazing. 45.00
"Bohemia" pattern
Platter, 20" l, Dimmock. 475.00
"Bolingbroke" pattern
Bone Dish, Ridgway 45.00

"Brooklyn" pattern
Plate, 10" d, semi-porcelain, gold trim, "John-
son Bros." mark (A) 45.00
"Burleigh" pattern
Plate, 6" d, "Burgess & Leigh" mark. 40.00
"Burma" pattern
Pitcher, 8" h, tankard shape, Ford. 275.00
"Burmese" pattern
Plate, 8⅝" d. 35.00
"Byzantine" pattern
Butter Pat, "Wood & Sons" mark 30.00
"Cambridge" pattern
Bowl, 7½" d. 45.00
Plate, 9" d
Meakin. 60.00
"N.W.P." mark. 80.00
Platter, 14" l, Meakin 185.00
"Camellia" pattern
Charger, 12½" d, Wedgwood 395.00
Platter, 18½" l, Wedgwood 475.00
"Candia" pattern
Pitcher, melon ribbed
5⅜" h, Cauldon 165.00
8⅜" h, Cauldon 165.00
"Canton" pattern
Bowl, 10" d 265.00
Creamer, Maddock. 295.00
Cup and Saucer, "James Edwards" mark. . . .   140.00
Plate
6" d. 20.00
7" d. 48.00
10" d, Ashworth 65.00
Platter, 17¾" l, 13¾" w, Maddock 595.00
Soup Plate, 10½" d, Maddock 145.00
"Carlton" pattern
Plate
9" d, "F.W. Winkle" mark 17.00
9½" d, "Samuel Alcock" mark 60.00
10¼" d 125.00
10½" d 115.00
Platter
13½" l. 195.00
15½" l, 12" w, Samuel Alcock 225.00
"Cashmere" pattern
Cup and Saucer. 125.00
Milk Pitcher, 7⅝" h, chips, "Morley" mark.   625.00
Plate, 10⅝" d, "Morley" mark. 130.00
Platter, 18" l. 795.00
Vegetable Bowl, Open, 10¾" l, 8¾" w . .   495.00
"Catherine" pattern
Bowl, 9" d 49.00
Plate, 10" d 38.00
"Cavandish" pattern
Vase, 12" h 325.00
"Celeste" pattern
Cup and Saucer, handleless 60.00
Plate, 10½" d, unmarked 130.00
"Celtic" pattern
Vegetable Tureen, Cov, "W.H. Grindley" mark   225.00
"Chang" pattern
Soup Plate, 8½"d 25.00
"Chapoo" pattern
Cup and Saucer. 150.00
Plate
9" d. 58.00
9⅜" d 90.00
Platter
13½" l, 10¼" w. 350.00
15" l, Wedgwood.   475.00
15¾" l. 375.00
Teapot, 9½" h, chips on base 325.00

'Chatsworth" pattern
Platter, 11" d............................ **145.00**

"Chen-Si" pattern
Cup and Saucer, handleless, restored, c1835,
"John Meir" mark...................... **125.00**
Plate, 8¾" d, Meir **68.00**

"Chinese" pattern
Cup and Saucer....................... **145.00**
Plate, 9" d, "Allerton" mark............... **28.00**
Platter, 17" l, 14" w, "W.H. Grindley" mark **325.00**
Sauce Tureen, shell finial, Dimmock........ **395.00**

"Chusan" pattern
Compote, 6¼" h, 10" d, Morley **550.00**
Creamer, shell shape.................... **250.00**
Plate
6¼" d............................. **50.00**
7¼" d, "J. Clementson" mark.......... **45.00**
8½" d............................. **65.00**
9¼" d, Ashworth **140.00**
10¼" d, "Royal Doulton" mark **125.00**
Platter
15½" l............................. **345.00**
16" l, "P.W.& Co." mark............... **350.00**
Teapot **495.00**

"Circassia" pattern
Soup Plate, 10½" d **45.00**
Sugar Bowl **150.00**

"Claremont" pattern
Dresser Tray, 11" l, 8" w, "Johnson Bros."
mark................................. **75.00**
Plate, 10" d, scalloped edge.............. **50.00**
Platter, 16¼" l, 11¼" w, scalloped edge,
shell handles, gold trim **195.00**
Syrup Pitcher, 6½" h, pewter top......... **95.00**

"Clarence" pattern
Bowl, 9" d, "W.H. Grindley" mark......... **55.00**
Butter Pat **30.00**
Platter, 13" d......................... **75.00**

"Clarissa" pattern
Butter Pat, set of 6 .... **105.00**
Plate, 10" d, "Johnson Bros." mark **60.00**

"Clayton" pattern
Bone Dish............................ **60.00**
Cup and Saucer, Demitasse **55.00**
Plate, 10" d, "Johnson Bros." mark **25.00**
Platter, 14½" l, "Johnson Bros." mark..... **155.00**

"Clover" pattern
Bowl, 7¾" d........................... **35.00**
Cup and Saucer, "W.H. Grindley" mark **60.00**
Plate,
5¾" d, "W.H. Grindley" mark.......... **30.00**
9" d, "W.H. Grindley" mark **45.00**
Platter
14¼" l, "W.H. Grindley" mark **150.00**
16½" l, "W.H. Grindley" mark **160.00**
Relish Dish, 7½" l, ... **65.00**
Soup Bowl, 7¾" d, "W.H. Grindley" mark.. **40.00**
Vegetable Bowl, Cov., 11" l, oblong, "W.H.
Grindley" mark **250.00**

"Cluny" pattern
Pitcher, 7" h.......................... **140.00**

"Coburg" pattern
Pitcher and Bowl...................... **1750.00**
Plate, 10½" d **95.00**
Platter
17" l, 12" w **450.00**
17⅞" l, Edwards..................... **345.00**

"Colonial" pattern
Plate, 8" d, "Meakin" mark **25.00**

"Constance" pattern
Butter Pat **20.00**
Plate, 9" d............................ **26.00**

"Conway" pattern
Bowl, 9⅛" d. "N.W.P." **70.00**
Plate, 10" d **75.00**
Platter, 10½" l, 7¾" w, scalloped edge,
c1891, "N.W.P." mark.................. **135.00**
Sauce Dish, 5½" d **25.00**
Soup Plate, 9" d, "N.W.P.".............. **45.00**
Vegetable Bowl, Open, 9" d **60.00**

"Corey Hill" pattern
Cup and Saucer........................ **90.00**
Ladle, 9" l............................ **250.00**
Sugar Bowl **175.00**

"Corinthian Flute" pattern
Plate, 9¾" d, c1905.................... **72.00**

"Crossed Bands" pattern
Dish, 11" l, 8" w, heart shape, cut out handle,
imp "Ridgway" mark **225.00**

"Crumlin" pattern
Plate, 9" d............................ **70.00**
Soup Plate, 9" d **70.00**

"Cyprus" pattern
Cake Plate, 12" d, ftd.................. **395.00**
Plate, 10¾" d, "Davenport anchor" mark.. **55.00**
Toothbrush Holder, Booth................ **250.00**

"Dainty" pattern
Butter Pat **30.00**
Egg Cup.............................. **100.00**
Plate, 7" d............................ **16.00**

"Dartmouth" pattern
Platter, 14½" l........................ **35.00**

"Davenport" pattern
Creamer, "Wood & Sons" mark **75.00**

"Delft" pattern
Plate
8½" d, "Minton" mark **50.00**
9" d, "Minton" mark.................. **40.00**

"Delmar" pattern
Platter, 12" l.......................... **50.00**

"Del Monte" pattern
Vegetable Bowl, 9½" d, gold trim, "Johnson
Bros." mark.......................... **55.00**

"Delph" pattern
Plate, 10" d, "Wood & Sons" mark **27.00**

"Denton" pattern
Bowl, 5½" d, "W.H. Grindley" mark **20.00**

"Devon" pattern
Butterpat, Meakin **45.00**
Plate, 7¾" d, Meakin................... **58.00**

"Dog Rose" pattern
Jardinaire, 12" h, 12½" d, dbl handles, gold
trim, Ridgways **350.00**

"Doreen" pattern
Toothbrush Holder, hairline.............. **120.00**

"Dorothy" pattern
Platter, 17" l.......................... **135.00**

"Dover" pattern
Plate, 5⅞" d, "W.H. Grindley" mark **25.00**

"Dresden" pattern
Plate, 7" d............................ **20.00**
Platter, 14" l, "Villeroy & Boch" mark **85.00**

"Duchess" pattern
Bone Dish............................ **40.00**

"Dundee" pattern
Gravy Boat, Ridgways................... **95.00**

"Ebor" pattern
Gravy Boat **95.00**

"Empress" pattern
Plate, 10½" d **90.00**

"Erie" pattern
Plate, 9½" d. **17.50**
Tureen, Cov, 9" d **70.00**
"Excelsior" pattern
Plate, 10½" d, "T. Fell" mark **115.00**
Teapot **550.00**
"Fairy Villas" pattern
Bowl, 10" d **68.00**
Butter Pat, Adams **28.00**
Pitcher, 7¾" h **295.00**
Vegetable Dish, Cov, 12½" l, 10" w, 7½"
h, ftd, dbl handles, Adams **350.00**
"Fairy Villas II" pattern
Butter Pat, c1891, "W. Adams & Co." mark. **28.00**
Plate
9" d **45.00**
10" d, "W. Adams & Co." mark **75.00**
"Farm" pattern
Plate, 10" d, "Ford" mark **58.00**
"Fleur-De-Lis" pattern
Sauce Tureen, undertray **250.00**
"Florence" pattern
Bone Dish **35.00**
"Florida" pattern
Bowl
6" l, oval, "W.H. Grindley" mark **35.00**
7½" d, "W.H. Grindley" mark **20.00**
10" d, "W.H. Grindley" mark **125.00**
Butter Pat, "Johnson Bros." mark **20.00**
Plate
7" d, ... **50.00**
8" d, "Johnson Bros." **48.00**
8⅞" d, "Johnson Bros." **55.00**
10" d
"W.H. Grindley" mark **40.00**
"Johnson Bros." mark **50.00**
Platter
10⅛" l, "W.H. Grindley" mark **125.00**
14" l, 10" w, "W.H. Grindley" mark **145.00**
Soup Plate, 7½" d, "Johnson Bros." **50.00**
Vegetable Bowl, Open, 10" l, 7" w, "W.H.
Grindley" mark **65.00**
"Formosa" pattern
Compote, 9" h, oct, two handles, "Ridgway"
mark **950.00**
Plate
5" d **45.00**
6" d, Ridgway **55.00**
7" d **60.00**
9¾" d, "Mayer" mark **115.00**
10" d, "Mayer" mark **150.00**
Platter, 13¼" l, "Mayer" mark **295.00**
"Fortuna" pattern
Plate, 10" d, "Johnson Bros." mark **95.00**
"France" pattern
Soup Plate, 10¼" d, c1868, Brown, West-
head **45.00**
"Gainsborough" pattern
Chamber Pot, Cov., 9½" d, 5½" h, fancy
finial, "Ridgways" mark **275.00**
"Gem" pattern
Platter, 16½" l, Hammersley **165.00**
"Geneva" pattern
Pitcher and Bowl Set, Doulton **900.00**
"Georgia" pattern
Berry Dish, "Johnson Bros." mark **30.00**
Plate
7" d, "Johnson Bros." mark **32.00**
10" d, "Johnson Bros." mark **53.00**
Platter, 14" l, 10½" w, "Johnson Bros." . . . **145.00**

"Gipsy" pattern
Gravy Boat **120.00**
"Gironde" pattern
Bone Dish **50.00**
Bowl, 11" H-H **110.00**
Butter Pat, "W.H. Grindley" mark **35.00**
Cup and Saucer, "W.H. Grindley" mark **110.00**
Plate
6" d **27.50**
7½" d, "W.H. Grindley" mark **40.00**
8½" d, "W.H. Grindley" mark **50.00**
9½" d, "W.H. Grindley" mark **65.00**
Platter
14" l, "W.H. Grindley" mark **170.00**
15" l, "W.H. Grindley" mark **185.00**
17" l, "W.H. Grindley" mark **200.00**
18" l, "W.H. Grindley" mark **185.00**
Soup Bowl, 7½" d **30.00**
Vegetable Bowl, 10" l, oval, "W.H. Grindley"
mark **85.00**
Vegetable Tureen, 9½" d, oct, "W.H. Grind-
ley" mark **350.00**
Vegetable Tureen, Cov, 10" l, oct, "W.H.
Grindley" mark **350.00**
Waste Bowl, 5¾" d, 3" h, "W.H. Grindley"
mark **95.00**
"Gladys" pattern
Plate, 9¾" d, scalloped edge **45.00**
"Glenmore" pattern
Cream and Sugar, "W.H. Grindley" mark . . . **185.00**
Cup and Saucer, "W.H. Grindley" mark **50.00**
Plate
6" d, "W.H. Grindley" mark **20.00**
8" d, "W.H. Grindley" mark **30.00**
Platter
10½" l, "W.H. Grindley" mark **55.00**
12" l, "W.H. Grindley" mark **85.00**
Soup Bowl, 8" d, "W.H. Grindley" mark **35.00**
Vegetable Bowl, Open, 8¾" l, oval, "W.H.
Grindley" mark **55.00**
'Glentine" pattern
Berry Dish, "W.H. Grindley" mark **25.00**
Cream and Sugar, "W.H. Grindley" marks . . **175.00**
Cup and Saucer, "W.H. Grindley" marks . . . **55.00**
Gravy Boat, "W.H. Grindley" mark **85.00**
Plate,
6" d, "W.H. Grindley" mark **25.00**
8" d, "W.H. Grindley" mark **30.00**
9" d, "W.H. Grindley" mark **40.00**
Soup Plate, 7¾" d, "W.H. Grindley" mark . **40.00**
"Glenwood" pattern
Chamber Pot, 8½" d **170.00**
"Gothic" pattern
Plate, 8" d, Furnivals **110.00**
"Grace" pattern
Butter Pat, "W.H. Grindley" mark **30.00**
Pitcher, 6" h, "W.H. Grindley" mark **170.00**
Plate, 10" d, "W.H. Grindley" mark **68.00**
Platter, 21" l, "W.H. Grindley" mark **345.00**
"Granada" pattern
Coffee Cup and Saucer, Alcock **75.00**
Teacup and Saucer, Alcock **65.00**
"Hague" pattern
Tureen, 8¼" l, 6½" h, with underplate,
"Johnson Bros." mark **245.00**
"Halford" pattern
Sauceboat, "Burgess and Leigh" mark **20.00**
"Hampton Spray" pattern
Plate, 9" d, "W.H. Grindley" mark **30.00**

"Hanley" pattern
  Charger, 11½" d, pierced for hanging, Meakin mark **135.00**
"Hindustan" pattern
  Cup and Saucer......................... **65.00**
  Platter, 16" l, Maddock **475.00**
"Holland" pattern
  Egg Cup................................. **50.00**
  Plate, 10" d, "Johnson Bros." mark **80.00**
  Platter
    12" l **85.00**
    14" l, "Johnson Bros.".................. **145.00**
  Vegetable Bowl, Open
    9" l, oval............................. **110.00**
    9¾" l **75.00**
"Hong" pattern
  Plate
    6" d.................................. **25.00**
    8" d.................................. **75.00**
    9" d, copper luster trim, c1850.......... **70.00**
"Hong Kong" pattern
  Cup and Saucer, Handleless............... **125.00**
  Plate
    9" d.................................. **85.00**
    10¼" d **125.00**
  Platter
    16" l, 12" w **425.00**
    18" l, 12" w **650.00**
"Hops" pattern
  Cup and Saucer, Royal Bonn **25.00**
"Hudson" pattern
  Berry Bowl, 5¼" d, "J.C. Meakin" mark ... **27.50**
"Idris" pattern
  Platter, 14" l, 10" w, "W.H. Grindley" mark **75.00**
"Indiana" pattern
  Platter, 18½" l, 14½" w, "Wedgwood & Co. Tunstall" mark **75.00**
"Indian" pattern
  Cup and Saucer, "Pratt" mark **100.00**
  Plate
    7¼" d **35.00**
    9" d.................................. **60.00**
  Soup Plate, 10½" d **110.00**
"Indian Jar" pattern
  Creamer, 6" h, Furnivals **225.00**
  Plate
    7" d, Furnival......................... **95.00**
    10¼" d **100.00**
    10½" d **115.00**
  Platter
    13" l **225.00**
    22" l **1150.00**
  Sauce Dish **50.00**
"Irene" pattern
  Plate, 10" d, "Wedgwood & Co." mark **55.00**
"Iris" pattern
  Berry Dish, 5¼" d, c1907, Wilkinson...... **10.00**
  Butter Pat **18.00**
  Gravy Boat, "W.H. Grindley".............. **85.00**
  Plate, 10" d, crazing, c1907, Wilkinson..... **38.00**
  Platter, 12" l, oval...................... **95.00**
  Vase, 9½" h, "Doulton Burslem" mark **195.00**
"Ivanhoe" pattern
  Plate, 10¼" d **95.00**
"Janette" pattern
  Bowl, 10" d............................ **90.00**
  Plate, 8¾" d, "W.H. Grindley" mark **45.00**
  Platter, 10" d.......................... **70.00**
  Vegetable Bowl, 6" l, 4¼" w, "W.H. Grindley" mark **30.00**

"Japan" pattern
  Plate
    9" d, c1860, "T. Fell" mark **75.00**
    9¼" d, "T. Fell" mark **58.00**
  Soup Plate, 9½" d, "B.W.M. Co. Cauldon" marks, set of 4......................... **220.00**
"Jeddo" pattern
  Relish Dish, 7½" l, 5" w, Adams......... **50.00**
"Jenny Lind" pattern
  Bowl, 7½" d, c1895, Wilkinson........... **165.00**
"Jewel" pattern
  Vegetable Bowl, Open, 10" l.............. **65.00**
"Keele" pattern
  Platter, 9" l............................ **70.00**
'Kelvin' pattern
  Butter Pat, "Alfred Meakin" mark **30.00**
  Gravy Boat and undertray, small knick, "Alfred Meakin" mark **150.00**
  Plate
    6¾" d, "Alfred Meakin" mark......... **35.00**
    7" d, "Alfred Meakin" mark............. **22.50**
    8" d, "Alfred Meakin" mark............. **46.50**
    9" d, "Alfred Meakin" mark............. **56.50**
  Platter, 12½" l, 8½" w, "Alfred Meakin" mark................................... **150.00**
  Vegetable Bowl, Open, 8½" l, 6¾" w, "Alfred Meakin" mark **110.00**
"Kenworth" pattern
  Berry Bowl, "Johnson Bros." mark **40.00**
  Bowl, 7½" d, "Johnson Bros." mark....... **57.50**
  Cup and Saucer, "Johnson Bros." mark..... **60.00**
  Gravy Boat, "Johnson Bros." mark **70.00**
  Plate
    7½" d, "Johnson Bros." mark **39.50**
    9" d, "Johnson Bros." mark............. **50.00**
  Platter, 14" l, 11" w, "Johnson Bros." mark. **175.00**
  Vegetable Bowl, Open, "Johnson Bros." mark................................... **80.00**
"Kin Shan" pattern
  Platter, 15½" l, "Challinor" mark **395.00**
"Kirkie" pattern
  Plate
    10" d................................. **70.00**
    10½" d................................ **135.00**
"Knox" pattern
  Plate
    8" d.................................. **25.00**
    9" d.................................. **48.00**
'Kyber' pattern
  Bowl, 9" d **75.00**
  Cup & Saucer, handleless **135.00**
  Honey Dish, 6" d, hex, "Adams" mark, set of 6................................... **245.00**
  Plate
    7" d, "W. Adams & Sons" mark........ **58.00**
    8" d, Adams.......................... **35.00**
    9" d.................................. **40.00**
    10" d, Adams **50.00**
  Platter
    10" l, 7¼" w......................... **58.00**
    14½" l, 11" w, hex, Adams............ **235.00**
  Soup Plate, 9" d **45.00**
"LaFrancais" pattern
  Bowl, 8½" d.......................... **20.00**
  Cup and Saucer......................... **15.00**
  Platter
    12½" l, 9½" w...................... **60.00**
    15" l **100.00**
"Lahore" pattern
  Plate
    8½" d, "Phillips & Sons" mark **120.00**

9" d, "Phillips & Sons" mark **130.00**
9½" d **110.00**
Platter, 16" l, 12" w **395.00**
"Lakewood" pattern
  Cup and Saucer **55.00**
  Platter, 12¼" l **90.00**
"Lancaster" pattern
  Cup and Saucer **65.00**
  Plate, 9" d
    "Corn" mark **55.00**
    "New Wharf Pottery" mark **55.00**
  Platter, 12½" l, 9¼" w, c1890–94, "New
    Wharf Pottery" mark **95.00**
  Sauce Dish **30.00**
"Larch" pattern
  Plate, 10½" d, "Hancock & Sons" mark . . .   **80.00**
"Lawrence" pattern
  Butter Pat, "Bishop & Stonier" **32.00**
"LePavot" pattern
  Bone Dish **20.00**
  Soup Tureen, 12" l, "W.H. Grindley" mark .   **265.00**
"Leicester" pattern
  Vegetable Dish, 12½" l, 8" w, gold accents
  . . . .   **130.00**
"Lily" pattern
  Coffee Pot, 9" h **125.00**
"Limoges" pattern
  Cup and Saucer, "Till & Son" mark **70.00**
  Platter, 10¼" l, Woodson **100.00**
"Linda" pattern
  Bone Dish **60.00**
  Plate, 10" d, "John Maddock & Sons" mark   **45.00**
"Lobelia" pattern
  Pitcher and Bowl set **450.00**
  Sugar Bowl **125.00**
"Locarno" pattern
  Vegetable Bowl, Cov, 9" d, "Gibson & Son"
    mark **70.00**
"Lonsdale" pattern
  Plate, 7⅞" d, "Ridgway" mark **34.00**
  Tray, 10" l, 8" w, "Samuel Ford & Co., En-
    gland" mark **85.00**
"Lorne" pattern
  Butter Pat **28.00**
  Egg Cup **60.00**
  Gravy Boat **85.00**
  Plate, 10" d **65.00**
"Lorraina" pattern
  Bone Dish **25.00**
"Louise" pattern
  Plate
    7" d, "N.W.P." mark **16.00**
    9¾" d, c1891, "New Wharf Pottery"
      mark **50.00**
  Soup Plate, 9" d, c1891, "New Wharf Pot-
    tery" mark **45.00**
"Lucerne" pattern
  Chamber Pot **90.00**
"Ludgate" pattern
  Plate
    7½" d, "Keeling & Co." mark **15.00**
    9½" d, "Keeling & Co." mark **15.00**
"Lynnhurst" pattern
  Plate, 10" d, "W.H. Grindley" mark **60.00**
"Madras" pattern
  Bowl, 5" d, Doulton **22.00**
  Milk Pitcher, 8" h, Doulton **345.00**
  Pitcher
    5" h **110.00**
    7" h, Doulton **95.00**
    7⅞" h, Doulton **325.00**

Plate
  6½" d, Doulton **28.00**
  8½" d, Doulton **30.00**
  8¾" d, Doulton **70.00**
  9¼" d, Doulton **32.00**
  9½" d, "Doulton & Co." mark **85.00**
  10" d, "Doulton & Co." mark **95.00**
Platter
  11" d, "Doulton & Co." mark **140.00**
  13½" l **195.00**
  15¼" l, 12½" w, Doulton **195.00**
  18" l, 15" w **325.00**
Vegetable Bowl, Open, 9¾" d, "Doulton &
  Co." mark **150.00**
"Malta" pattern
  Plate, 8¼" d, c1891, "F.A. Mehlem" mark .   **28.00**
  Trivet, 6⅞" d **60.00**
"Mandarin" pattern
  Plate, 10" d, "Pountney" mark **55.00**
  Platter, 12¼" l, 9½" w **60.00**
"Manhatten" pattern
  Bowl, 9" d, flanged **48.00**
  Butter Pat, Alcock **28.00**
  Cup and Saucer **50.00**
  Plate
    7⅞" d, c1900 . . . .   **45.00**
    9" d, c1900 . . . .   **55.00**
  Soup Plate, 9" d, c1900 . . . .   **50.00**
  Teapot, 7½" h, "Henry Alcock" mark **200.00**
"Manilla" pattern
  Berry Bowl, 6" d **48.00**
  Cup and Saucer **125.00**
Plate
  8" d **50.00**
  9½" d **75.00**
  10" d **75.00**
Platter, 16" l **395.00**
Teapot **625.00**
"Maréchal Niel" pattern
  Butter Pat, "W.H. Grindley" mark **30.00**
  Creamer **150.00**
  Plate, 10" d, "W.H. Grindley" mark **65.00**
  Platter
    12" l, "W.H. Grindley" mark **65.00**
    12½" l, 9" w, "W.H. Grindley" **90.00**
    18" l **125.00**
  Soup Bowl
    8" d, "W.H. Grindley" mark **40.00**
    9" d, "W.H. Grindley" mark **45.00**
"Marie" pattern
  Butter Pat **25.00**
  Pitcher, 6½" h, "W.H. Grindley" mark **75.00**
  Plate
    8" d, "W.H. Grindley" mark **40.00**
    9" d **37.00**
  Platter
    12" l **95.00**
    16" l **150.00**
  Vegetable Bowl
    Cov
      11" l, 8" w, "W.H. Grindley" mark **245.00**
      Lacy handles **155.00**
    Open **65.00**
"Marlborough" pattern
  Plate, 9¾" d **65.00**
  Platter, 14" l **225.00**
"Marguerite" pattern
  Bone Dish, "W.H. Grindley" mark **65.00**
  Platter, 18" l, "W.H. Grindley" mark **120.00**

"Marquis" pattern
Cup and Saucer, "W.H. Grindley" mark 65.00
Plate, 6" d............................... 28.00
'Martha" pattern
Bone Dish........................... 25.00
Bowl, 9" d 55.00
"May" pattern
Plate, 7½" d, "Till & Sons" mark......... 35.00
"Mayfair" pattern
Plate, 8" d, "T. Rathbone & Co." mark 35.00
"Medieaval" pattern
Plate, 9½" d,........................ 95.00
"Meissen" pattern
Berry Dish, 5½" d, c1891, "Libertas Prussia"
mark............................ 15.00
Bowl, 6¼" d, Ridgway.................. 15.00
Plate
8" d, Ridgway 15.00
9½" d, Ridgway 25.00
"Melbourne" pattern
Cup and Saucer......................... 50.00
Gravy Boat, "W.H. Grindley" mark........ 120.00
Plate, 10" d 35.00
Platter
11" l................................. 85.00
18" l, 12" w, "W.H. Grindley" mark..... 245.00
"Melrose" pattern
Plate, 9⅛" d, gilt rim, c1891, Doulton..... 65.00
Platter, 18" l, 12" w, Doulton 245.00
"Melsary" pattern
Tureen, Cov, 8" l, with underplate and ladle,
Booth............................... 150.00
"Merion" pattern
Bone Dish, "W.H. Grindley" mark 40.00
"Messina" pattern
Platter, 18" l........................... 350.00
"Mikado" pattern
Platter, 16" l, 12" w, Corn 250.00
"Milan" pattern
Butter Pat, "W.H. Grindley" mark.......... 20.00
"Mongolia" pattern
Bowl, 8½" d, "Johnson Bros." mark....... 70.00
Platter, 12" l........................... 120.00
"Morning Glory" pattern
Soup Tureen, 9" d, 9" h, scalloped rim and
cov, trimmed in gold, scalloped raised base,
fancy handles, "Wood and Hughes" mark 295.00
"Moyune" pattern
Platter, 16" l, 12" w, oct, Ridgway........ 245.00
"Nankin" pattern
Pitcher, 7½" h, Doulton 175.00
"Navy" pattern
Bone Dish........................... 40.00
Cup and Saucer....................... 55.00
Plate
7" d................................. 30.00
9" d................................. 40.00
Relish Dish, 8¾" d 65.00
"Neopolitan" pattern
Creamer............................. 125.00
"Ning-Po" pattern
Plate, 9½" d.......................... 100.00
"Non Pariel" pattern
Cake Plate, 11" H-H, gilt trim, c1891, "Bur-
gess & Leigh" mark................. 185.00
Charger, 13½" d, "Burgess & Leigh" mark. 350.00
Creamer............................. 150.00
Plate
8½" d 55.00
9" d, "Burgess & Leigh" mark.......... 50.00
9⅞" d, c1891, "Burgess & Leigh" mark . 110.00

Sugar Bowl, Cov, "Burgess & Leigh" mark .. 175.00
Vegetable Dish, Cov, 12" l, 8½" w, 6½" h,
ftd, dbl handles, flower finial, "Burgess &
Leigh" mark 350.00
"Norbury" pattern
Pitcher, 6" h........................... 55.00
"Normandy" pattern
Butter Dish, Cov 285.00
Butter Pat, "Johnson Bros." mark 28.00
Cup and Saucer....................... 78.00
Gravy Boat, 4¼" h, 7½" l, attached under-
tray................................ 95.00
Plate
8" d, "Johnson Bros." mark............. 45.00
10" d, "Johnson Bros." mark............ 85.00
Platter
8" l................................. 85.00
12" l................................. 125.00
14" l................................. 175.00
16" l, 12" w, "Johnson Bros. " mark..... 175.00
Sauce Dish
5¼" d.............................. 30.00
6" d................................. 25.00
"Olympia" pattern
Butter Dish, Cov, "W.H. Grindley" mark 105.00
Cup and Saucer, "W.H. Grindley" mark 45.00
Sugar Bowl, "W.H. Grindley" mark........ 90.00
"Ophir" pattern
Plate, 9" d............................. 15.00
"Oregon" pattern
Plate
7" d................................. 60.00
9½" d, "Mayer" mark................. 115.00
10" d................................. 100.00
12" d................................. 90.00
Platter
10½" l, Mayer........................ 225.00
13½" l................................. 250.00
Sauce Dish, 5" d, Mayer................. 55.00
Sugar Bowl 225.00
Soup Plate, 9½" d 100.00
Teapot 595.00
"Oriental" pattern
Compote, 5" h, 8½" d, "Ridgway" mark .. 350.00
Creamer, 4½" h, "Ridgway" mark 45.00
Cup and Saucer, Ridgway................ 40.00
Plate
5¾" d, "Ridgway" mark................ 28.00
7" d, "Ridgway" mark................. 35.00
9" d, "Ridgway" mark................. 38.00
"Osborne" pattern
Egg Cup............................. 65.00
Gravy Boat, c1905 .... 90.00
Milk Pitcher, 7⅝" h, c1905 .... 345.00
Plate, 9¾" d, c1905.................... 55.00
Sauce Dish, 5" d, c1905................. 22.00
Soup Plate, 9" d, crazing, c1905........... 45.00
Vegetable Bowl, 9" l, 6¾" w, c1905...... 48.00
"Ovando" pattern
Butter Pat, Meakin..................... 30.00
'Oxford" pattern
Berry Bowl, 5" d, "Johnson Bros." mark 20.00
Cup and Saucer, "Johnson Bros." mark..... 40.00
Plate
6¼" d, "Johnson Bros." mark 20.00
7" d, "Johnson Bros." mark............ 28.00
8¾" d, "Johnson Bros." mark 45.00
Platter
10½" d, "Johnson Bros." mark 50.00
11½" l, 8½" w, "Ford & Sons" mark .. 125.00
12½" l................................. 78.00

14" l
11" w, "Ford & Sons" mark **195.00**
"Johnson Bros." mark **188.00**
"Paris" pattern
Bowl, 7" d **35.00**
Plate
9" d, "N.W.P" mark **50.00**
10" d **79.00**
Platter, 14¼" l, 11" w, "Edge Malkin & Co."
mark **130.00**
"Peach" pattern
Plate, 7" d **32.00**
"Pearl" pattern
Cake Stand, 10" d, ftd **245.00**
"Pekin" pattern
Bowl, 9½" d **80.00**
Cup and Saucer, lg, yellow and orange clob-
bering, c1901, Wilkinson **185.00**
Pitcher, 6½" h **75.00**
Plate, 11½" d, c1908, "Albert & E.J. Jones"
mark **110.00**
Platter, 14½" l, 11" w, c1845 . . . .   **305.00**
Toothbrush Holder **195.00**
Warming Dish, 10½" d, original stopper,
scalloped rim, c1844, Davenport **440.00**
"Pelew" pattern
Cup and Saucer, Handleless, "Challinor" mark
. . . .   **75.00**
Plate
9½" d, "Challinor" mark **55.00**
9¾" d, "Challinor" mark **75.00**
10¾" d, "Challinor" mark **85.00**
"Penang" pattern
Plate, 9¼" d, c1840, "Ridgway" mark **70.00**
"Persian" pattern
Bowl, 9" d **80.00**
Platter, 18½" l, 13½" w **375.00**
"Petunia" pattern
Dresser Set, tray, 12½" l, 9" w, pin tray, 5"
l, 2⅜" w, oval handled trinket box, 3½"
l, candlestick, 6⅞" h **375.00**
"Poppea" pattern
Dessert Stand **165.00**
"Poppy" pattern
Plate
9" d, "W.H. Grindley" mark **35.00**
10" d, "W.H. Grindley" mark **10.00**
Soup Plate, 9" d **35.00**
"Portman" pattern
Butter Pat **26.00**
Cup and Saucer **65.00**
Plate, 8" d, "W.H. Grindley" **46.00**
Vegetable Bowl, Cov, 12" l, 8" w, "W.H.
Grindley" **210.00**
"Primrose" pattern
Pitcher, 7½" h, "Wood & Sons" mark **140.00**
"Raleigh" pattern
Berry Bowl, "Burgess & Leigh" mark **22.00**
Butter Pat, "Burgess & Leigh" mark **17.50**
Cup and Saucer, "Burgess & Leigh" mark . . .   **38.00**
Plate
6" d, "Burgess & Leigh" mark **18.00**
8½" d, "Burgess & Leigh" mark **40.00**
8¾" d, "Burgess & Leigh" mark **30.00**
9½" d, "Burgess & Leigh" mark **40.00**
9¾" d, "Burgess & Leigh" mark **42.50**
Platter
13½" l, 10¼" w, "Burgess & Leigh" mark   **125.00**
17¾" l, 13½" w, "Burgess & Leigh"
mark **195.00**

Soup Bowl, 8¾" d, "Burgess & Leigh" mark.   **28.00**
Vegetable Bowl, Cov, "Burgess & Leigh" mark   **225.00**
"Regent" pattern
Platter, 15" l **135.00**
Vegetable Bowl, Cov, 12" d, ...   **185.00**
"Renoun" pattern
Platter
10½" l, "Arthur Wilkinson" mark **32.00**
15" l, "Arthur Wilkinson" mark **75.00**
"Rheims" pattern
Platter, 15", 17", 19" l, nested set of 3 . . . .   **295.00**
"Rhine" pattern
Milk Pitcher, 7" h, "Thos. Dimmock" mark. .   **240.00**
"Rhone" pattern
Plate, 7" d **39.00**
'Richmond" pattern
Butter Pat **24.00**
Cake Plate, 10" H-H, c1900, "Alfred Meakin"
mark **245.00**
Dish, Cov, 11" l, gold accents, "Johnson
Bros." mark (A) **120.00**
Plate
6⅛" d, Meakin **30.00**
6¾" d **30.00**
9" d, Meakin **50.00**
10" d, "Johnson Bros." mark **55.00**
"Rock" pattern
Plate, 7½" d **60.00**
"Rose" pattern
Serving Bowl, 9" d, "W.H. Grindley" mark. .   **85.00**
"Rosette" pattern
Plate, 9" d, "Burgess & Leigh" mark **48.00**
"Roseville" pattern
Cup and Saucer, Demitasse **55.00**
"Savoy" pattern
Soup Plate, 9" d **20.00**
"Scinde" pattern
Creamer, "P.W.& Co." mark **325.00**
Cup and Saucer **130.00**
Dish, 5" d **45.00**
Gravy Boat **475.00**
Pitcher, 12½" h **850.00**
Plate
7" d, twelve sided **75.00**
8" d **80.00**
8½" d **65.00**
9" d **95.00**
9½" d, "T. Walker" mark **65.00**
9¾" d **105.00**
10½" d **110.00**
Platter
16" l
10¼" w, Alcock **465.00**
12" w **425.00**
17¾" l, "P.W.& Co." mark **495.00**
18" l, 15" w, "Henry Alcock" mark **450.00**
Sauce Tureen, with ladle and undertray, "Al-
cock" mark **1195.00**
Soup Plate, 10½" d **110.00**
Vegetable Bowl, Open, "Samuel Alcock" mark   **350.00**
"Seville" pattern
Platter, 14¾" l, 11½" w, "Royal Crown
Staffordshire" mark **65.00**
"Shanghai" pattern
Plate
6" d, "W.H. Grindley" mark **25.00**
7" d **38.00**
8½" d **70.00**
9⅛" d **75.00**
9¾" d **70.00**

10" d.................................. **75.00**
10½" d................................ **125.00**
Platter, 12½" l, 8¾" w, "W.H. Grindley"
mark.................................. **95.00**
Vegetable Bowl, 9" l, oval, "W.H. Grindley"
mark.................................. **95.00**
"Shapoo" pattern
Plate, 8½" d, c1842, "T.& R. Boote" mark. **75.00**
Sugar Bowl, 9¼" h, c1860, Hughes....... **225.00**
"Shell" pattern
Cup Plate, 4" d, c1860, "Challinor" mark... **75.00**
Plate
8½" d, "Challinor" mark............... **70.00**
9¾" d, "Challinor" mark............... **90.00**
"Simla" pattern
Cup and Saucer, Handleless, c1860........ **85.00**
"Singan" pattern
Plate, 8¼" d, "T. Goodfellow" mark...... **60.00**
"Sobraon" pattern
Platter, 16" l......................... **425.00**
Vegetable Dish, Cov, 6½" h, 12⅛" l, 9½"
w, rect with concave corners, chips and
hairline, c1850....................... **400.00**
"Spinach" pattern
Ale Mug, 4⅛" h, crazing, c1890s......... **195.00**
Bowl, 4¼" d.......................... **65.00**
"Stafford" pattern
Soup Bowl, 8½" d, "B.& L." mark........ **125.00**
"St. Louis" pattern
Platter, 16" l, small chip under rim........ **140.00**
"Surrey" pattern
Cup and Saucer, "Bishop & Stonier" mark.. **50.00**
"Sydney" pattern
Platter, 14" l.......................... **150.00**
"Sylph" pattern
Plate
10" d.............................. **85.00**
10½" d, Pountney................... **85.00**
"Temple" pattern
Cup & Saucer, Handleless, "P.W.& Co.".... **13.00**
Pitcher, 8" h.......................... **295.00**
Plate
7¾" d, "P.W.& Co." mark............. **50.00**
8" d, "P.W.& Co." mark............... **65.00**
8⅝" d, "P.W.& Co." mark............. **90.00**
8¾" d, "P.W.& Co." mark............. **75.00**
9" d, "P.W.& Co." mark.............. **70.00**
9¼" d, c1850....................... **75.00**
9¾" d, "P.W.& Co." mark............. **90.00**
9⅞" d, "P.W.& Co." mark............. **110.00**
10" d, "P.W.& Co." mark............. **125.00**
Platter
12½" l............................. **295.00**
16" l, 12" w....................... **395.00**
Sugar Bowl, Cov, 8" h.................. **250.00**
"The Duchess" pattern
Platter, 18" l, scalloped edge.............. **225.00**
"The Hofburg" pattern
Bowl, 10" d.......................... **90.00**
Butter Pat, set of 4..................... **80.00**
"The Holland" pattern
Butter Pat............................ **17.50**
Gravy Boat, "A. Meakin" mark........... **160.00**
Platter
12½" l, "A. Meakin" mark............. **125.00**
16" l, "A. Meakin" mark............. **175.00**
"Timor" pattern
Bowl, 6" d........................... **20.00**
"Tivoli" pattern
Gravy Boat........................... **160.00**

Platter, 10" d......................... **85.00**
Teapot............................... **625.00**
"Togo" pattern
Bowl, Cov, 16" l, "F. Winkle & Co." mark.. **130.00**
Butter Pat............................ **24.00**
Cup and Saucer........................ **35.00**
Plate
7" d, "F. Winkle & Co." mark.......... **24.00**
9¾" d.............................. **65.00**
10" d.............................. **60.00**
Platter
10" d.............................. **55.00**
12" d.............................. **60.00**
16" l, "F. Winkle & Co." mark.......... **175.00**
Sauce Dish, 5" d, "F. Winkle & Co." mark.. **18.00**
"Tokio" pattern
Bowl, 5" d........................... **13.00**
Platter
12½" l, 9½" w, "Johnson Bros." mark. **140.00**
14½" l, 10¾" w, "Johnson Bros."
mark............................... **200.00**
"Tonio" pattern
Plate, 9" d........................... **55.00**
"Tonquin" pattern
Cup and Saucer, Handleless, "Heath" mark. **140.00**
Plate
7½" d, Adams...................... **55.00**
9" d, 1861, John Carr & Sons.......... **95.00**
9½" d.............................. **80.00**
"Touraine" pattern
Berry Bowl........................... **45.00**
Bone Dish............................ **38.00**
Bowl
8½" d, "Henry Alcock & Co." mark.... **60.00**
9" l, oval.......................... **85.00**
10" d, tab handled.................. **75.00**
Butter Pat............................ **36.00**
Creamer.............................. **165.00**
Cup and Saucer, "Stanley" mark........... **75.00**
Pitcher, 8" h.......................... **450.00**
Plate
6½" d, "Stanley" mark................ **30.00**
7¾" d.............................. **55.00**
8⅝" d, "Stanley" mark................ **58.00**
8¾" d.............................. **65.00**
9" d............................... **60.00**
10" d.............................. **80.00**
Platter
10½" l............................. **100.00**
12½" l............................. **125.00**
13" l.............................. **140.00**
14⅝" l, "Stanley" mark............... **137.00**
Soup Bowl, 7½" d, "Stanley" mark....... **38.00**
Vegetable Bowl
9½" l............................. **100.00**
10" d.............................. **135.00**
10½" l............................. **125.00**
"Troy" pattern
Plate, 8¼" d, c1845, Meigh............. **45.00**
"Tulip" pattern
Bone Dish............................ **40.00**
Pitcher
6" h............................... **225.00**
8" h............................... **225.00**
"Turin" pattern
Casserole, Cov, 11" l, "Johnson Bros." mark **150.00**
Plate
9" d, "Johnson Bros." mark............ **35.00**
10" d, "Johnson Bros." mark........... **45.00**

Platter
- 12½″ l, 9½″ w, "Johnson Bros."
  mark.............................. **110.00**
- 14½″ l, 10½″ w, "Johnson Bros." mark **135.00**
- 16¼″ l, 12″ w, "Johnson Bros." mark... **150.00**

Tureen, Cov, "Johnson Bros." mark **155.00**

"Tyne" pattern
- Pitcher, 6″ h, "Ford & Sons" mark **175.00**

"Venetia" pattern
- Vase, 8½″ h, hex, "Barker Bros. Ltd-Meir
  Works Longton" mark **235.00**

"Venice" pattern
- Butter pat, "Johnson Bros." mark **25.00**
- Plate, 7″ d, "Johnson Bros." mark.......... **25.00**
- Toothbrush Jar, 5⅜″ h, Grimwades **80.00**

"Venus" pattern
- Soup Plate, 10″ d **30.00**

"Vermont" pattern
- Butter Pat **25.00**
- Cup and Saucer, "Burgess & Leigh" mark... **65.00**
- Cup and Saucer, Demitasse, "Burgess &
  Leigh" mark, set of 6 .... **275.00**
- Plate
  - 7¾″ d, "Burgess & Leigh" mark **32.00**
  - 9″ d, "Burgess & Leigh" mark **65.00**
  - 10″ d.............................. **48.00**
  - 10½″ d, "Burgess and Leigh" mark **65.00**
- Sauce Dish, 5″ d, "Burgess and Leigh" mark **22.00**
- Soup Plate
  - 8¾″ d, "Burgess & Leigh" mark **40.00**
  - 9″ d.............................. **45.00**

"Verona" pattern
- Butter Pat, "Wood & Son" mark **45.00**
- Cup and Saucer, "Wood & Son" mark **115.00**
- Pickle Dish, 8½″ l, 5″ w, Ridgway **50.00**
- Plate
  - 8″ d, "Wood & Sons" mark............. **35.00**
  - 10″ d.............................. **60.00**
- Platter, 11¾″ l, 9½″ w, "Wedgwood &
  Co." mark........................... **125.00**

"Victoria" pattern
- Bowl, 10″ d, "Wood & Son" mark **120.00**
- Plate, 8″ d............................. **30.00**

"Vincennes" pattern
- Bowl, 14½″ d, c1870, "John Alcock" mark **240.00**

"Vine" pattern
- Plate, 8″ d, "Wedgwood" mark **34.00**

"Virginia" pattern
- Butter Pat, "John Maddock" mark, set of 10
  (A)................................. **110.00**
- Plate
  - 6″ d, "John Maddock" mark, set of 7 (A). **98.00**
  - 8″ d, "John Maddock" mark, set of
    12 (A) **228.00**
  - 9″ d, "John Maddock" mark, set of 9 (A). **157.50**
- Platter
  - 12″ l, "John Maddock" mark (A) **105.00**
  - 16¾″ l, "John Maddock" mark.......... **120.00**
  - 18″ l, 15″ w, emb handles............. **325.00**
- Vegetable Dish, "John Maddock" mark (A) . **60.00**

"Waldorf" pattern
- Bowl, 9″ d **125.00**
- Plate
  - 9″ d.............................. **46.00**
  - 9¾″ d, "N.W.P." mark **88.00**
  - 10″ d.............................. **60.00**
- Platter
  - 10½″ l, 7½″ w..................... **75.00**
  - 18″ l **300.00**

"Watteau" pattern
- Beaker, 4″ h, Doulton **65.00**

Bowl
- 5″ d, ... **45.00**
- 7″ d, Doulton **45.00**
- 12½″ d, flanged, Doulton............... **125.00**
- Cereal Bowl, 6¼″ d, "N.W.P." mark **35.00**
- Chamber Pot, 8½″ d, Doulton **125.00**
- Fruit Compote, 4¾″ h, 9¾″ d, pedestal, dbl
  handles, Doulton..................... **300.00**

Plate
- 6″ d, unmarked........................ **45.00**
- 6½″ d, Doulton........................ **35.00**
- 7½″ d, Doulton........................ **42.00**
- 8″ d, scalloped, Doulton................ **55.00**
- 8½″ d, Doulton........................ **47.00**
- 9″ d **40.00**
- 9½″ d, Doulton........................ **55.00**
- 10″ d **48.00**
- 10¼″ d, Doulton **125.00**
- 10½″ d **45.00**

Platter
- 10¾″ d, "N.W.P." mark **95.00**
- 11″ l, 8″ w............................ **68.00**
- 12″ d **110.00**
- 12½″ d, scalloped edge, Doulton....... **110.00**
- 13¼″ l, 11″ w, Doulton **250.00**
- Meat Server, 12¾″ l, oval, meat well, two
  cutout handles, domed lid.............. **395.00**

Soup Plate
- 9¼″ d, Doulton....................... **70.00**
- 10¼″ d, gold rim, Doulton............. **75.00**

Vegetable Bowl, Open
- 8¼″ d, Doulton....................... **75.00**
- 9¼″ l, Doulton **85.00**

Waffle Cup, 6½″ h, three handles, "Royal
  Doulton" mark....................... **395.00**

"Waverly" pattern
- Bread and Butter Plate, 7″ d, "W.H. Grindley"
  mark................................ **50.00**
- Cup and Saucer......................... **45.00**

"Warwick" pattern
- Tea Tile, 7″ d, raised gold gadrooned border **110.00**

"Weir" pattern
- Gravy Boat, "Ford & Son" mark **120.00**
- Meat Platter, 12″ l, 9″ w, "F.& Sons" mark . **85.00**
- Vegetable Tureen, 11″ l, 7″ w, "Ford & Sons"
  mark................................ **110.00**

"Wentworth" pattern
- Bone Dish............................. **40.00**
- Butter Pat, Meakin...................... **9.00**
- Cup and Saucer......................... **75.00**
- Gravey Boat, with undertray, Meakin **50.00**
- Plate, 9″ d............................. **75.00**

"Whampoa" pattern
- Mug, 4⅛″ h **295.00**
- Plate, 7½″ d, "Mellor & Venables" mark .. **55.00**
- Platter, 17″ l........................... **385.00**

"Wild Rose" pattern
- Plate, 10½″ d, c1910, "George Jones"
  mark................................ **45.00**

"Willow" pattern
- Bowl, 10¼″ l, 7½″ w, scalloped edge,
  c1891, Minton........................ **145.00**
- Plate, 7¾″ d, c1886, Keeling............. **58.00**

"Windsor Scroll" pattern
- Creamer............................... **295.00**

"Yeddo" pattern
- Plate
  - 8⅜″ d, c1862, "Ashworth" mark **65.00**
  - 9¼″ d **65.00**
  - 9½″ d, gold band on rim, c1862, "Ash-
    worth" mark........................ **80.00**

10" d	55.00
10³⁄₈" d, c1862, "Ashworth" mark	95.00

Platter, 15³⁄₈" l, 12½" w, gold band on rim, c1862, "Ashworth" mark

Soup Plate, 10¼" d, c1862, "Ashworth" mark	110.00
Vegetable Tureen, Cov, 11⁵⁄₈" l, 6" h, pedestal base, c1862, "Ashworth" mark	235.00

"York" pattern

Gravy Boat and Undertray, Meakin	120.00

PILIVITE

PORCELAINES A FEU
PILLIVUYT & Cⁱᴱ
MEHUN FRANCE
1853

FRANCE—GENERAL

Rouen
1673–1696

Louis Poterat, a faience maker, was granted a patent to make the earliest French soft paste porcelain at Rouen in 1673. The decorations were dark blue in the style of faience ware with lambrequins and gadroons. Relief work appeared on the body of pieces such as salt cellars, mustard pots, and vases. Poterat died in 1696.

Lille
1711–1817

Barthelemy Dorenz and Pierre Pelissier established a soft paste porcelain factory in Lille in 1711. Pieces were decorated with Chinese designs. Leperre Ducot began manufacturing hard paste porcelains in 1784. The French Dauphin became a patron of the factory in 1786. The dolphin was chosen as the factory's mark.

Strasbourg
1721–1781

Charles Hannong, who started a porcelain factory in Strasbourg in 1721, manufactured clay pipes and stoves that were decorated in relief and glazed. For a short time he was a partner with Johann Wachenfeld who came from Meissen. Together they made faience and porcelain wares. In 1724 a second factory was established in Haguenau.

Hannong transferred the factories to his sons, Paul Antoine and Balthasar, in 1732. Between 1745 and 1750 hard paste porcelains were produced that were decorated in

red and pale gold. Adam Lowenfinck arrived from Hochst in 1750 and became co-director of the porcelain factory. He brought the Rococo style and introduced flower painting to Strasbourg.

By 1753 Paul Hannong assumed control of both factories. When Louis XV of France ordered him to dismantle his porcelain factory and demolish his kilns, Paul Hannong went to Frankenthal. As a result, early Strasbourg ware and Frankenthal ware resemble each other.

By 1766 Joseph-Adam, Hannong's son, tried to reestablish a hard paste porcelain factory in Strasbourg. Opposition by the authorities forced its closure in 1781.

Sceaux
1748–1795

Under the patronage of Duchess de Marne, the architect de Bay established a porcelain factory that was managed by Jacques Chapelle. The firm's soft paste porcelains were decorated with exotic birds, flowers, and cupids in the fashion of the Louis XVI period. The factory closed in 1795.

Niderviller
1754–1827

Baron Beyerle faience established a faience factory in 1754. Porcelains were produced by 1765. When opposition arose from the Sevres potters, Beyerle took Count de Custine into partnership in 1770 because of his influence at the French Court. On Custine's death, the factory was sold to Claude-Francois Lanfrey and continued until 1827. Tea sets, tablewares, and services were made and decorated in the manner of Sevres.

PARIS AREA

The majority of French hard paste porcelains available in today's market were made at numerous small factories in the Paris area. Production of porcelain began in the early eighteenth century.

Museums: Frick Collection, New York, NY; Louvre, Paris, France; Musee des Arts Decoratifs, Paris, France; Musee des Beaux-Arts et de la Ceramique, Rouen, France; Musee National de Sevres, Sevres, France; Victoria & Albert Museum, London, England; Wadsworth Atheneum, Hartford, CT.

Additional Listings: Chantilly, Choisy-le-Roi, Creil, Faience, Limoges, Malicorne, Mennecy, Old Paris and Paris, Quimper, Saint Cloud, Sevres, Vincennes.

Basket, 10" H-H, 3½" h, porcelain, reticulated, small blue and green flowers inside, blue and green lines outside, two handles, c1820, Niderville, France blue mark	550.00
Box, Cov, 4³⁄₄" l, rect, Sevres style, courting figures in landscape in turquoise and red jeweled borders, gilt scroll and trellis, dark blue ground, late 19th C (A)	1028.00

Bowl

5¼" d, redware body, green vert drips, cream horiz lines, brown ground, cream int	125.00
15" l, oval centerpiece, gilt floral swag design, curvilinear handles, blue ground, gilt metal, white int (A)	675.00
Bowl, Cov, 8½" d, porcelain, lovers in woods scene with falls, green ground, bronze handles, feet, and acorn, sgd "Rene"	175.00

Plate, 8" d, multicolored hunting reserves, floral and trellis border, mid 19th C, "Gien Porcelaine Opaque" mark, $80.00

Cabinet Tray, 17" l, oval, Sevres style, portraits of Louis XVI and Marie Antoinette below the Royal cipher, jeweled border, blue ground, late 19th C (A)........................... 2805.00

Cache Pot, 9" h, lobed panels of summer flowers, reserved on pink and gilt trellis ground . 300.00

Cake Set, master plate, 13" l, 10" w, rect, 6 plates, 6 1/4" d, centers with hp bird, butterfly, water scene, wide cobalt borders with gold overlay, c1880 (A)...................... 80.00

Centerpiece

17 1/4" h, Bacchus supporting pierced basket, high base modeled with scroll feet alternating with female and rams masks, piece of basket missing, c1880, underglaze "blue X'd swords and dot" mark (A).......... 1223.00

19" d, oval section on front of harbor scene reserved on gilded blue ground, gilt metal handles and ftd base, late 19th C (A)..... 2620.00

Charger, 14" d, 10 hp peacocks, border of multicolored fruit and foliage, artist sgd, c1911 (A)............................. 25.00

Clockcase, 13" h, porcelain, pierced scroll case in bright green with gilded details enclosing panels of summer flowers, enameled clock dial with Roman numerals, c1880, key (A) .. 752.00

Coffee Can and Saucer, porcelain, multicolored painted sprays and garlands of flowers, painted pearl and gilt borders, Nyon, pr (A)................................... 1140.00

Coffee Pot, 9 5/8" h, Cov, oval baluster body, agate, gadrooned, mask spout, brown and red glaze, three paw feet, cov with fruit knob, foliate handle, feet, knob in white, one foot restored, 1790–1800 (A)................... 598.00

Coffee Service, 12 coffee cups and saucers, 6 plates, coffee pot and cov, cov sugar bowl, milk jug, 2 sauce boats and stands, 4 boat shaped cups and 2 saucers, handles and spouts modeled as swans necks, body as feathers, gilded stripes and iron-red coral branch handles on boat shaped pieces, late 19th C, printed Dagoty mark, 45 pcs (A)................................14,960.00

Cup, 3 3/4" h, Jaspe-white circles on brown glaze at base, green upper portion (A).......... 33.00

Cup and Saucer, miniature, Jaspe-brown and white checkerboard design (A)............ 38.00

Dish, 8 3/8" d, porcelain, lobed, multicolored painted rural landscape with figures, border of butterflies and insects, gilt rim, "brown script N" mark............................... 150.00

Dresser Box, 5 1/2" h, 8" l, bow front chest type, three drawers, top lid, flower and leaf design, top with lovers in meadow with trees, bridge, and house, aqua body, sgd "Menuit"....... 250.00

Figure

5 1/4" h, standing Turkish gentleman holding covered pitcher, lacy trim, polychrome enamels, "E & C X'd swords" marks (A) .. 220.00

6 3/4" h, white, young girl in wide brimmed hat, flowers in apron, flower in left hand, beehive on mound base, c1760 (A)...... 2420.00

7 1/2" h, porcelain, shepherd lad, arms folded over open mauve jerkin and breeches, dog at feet, naturalistic base, c1760, Strasbourg (A)................................. 225.00

8" h, porcelain, man in blue tunic, woman in floral dress with floral basket and tray, c1890, crossed feathers mark............ 395.00

11" h, terra cotta, embracing cupids, sgd (A)................................. 990.00

21" h, porcelain, woman in floral decorated dress with apron holding rose, man in pink long coat, floral vest, holding rose in right hand, pr............................. 1150.00

22" h, terra cotta, bust of smiling woman with long braided hair to shoulder, circ base, repaired, inscribed "Charles Breton, 1916" (A)................................. 715.00

26" h, lady holding jug, man with two doves on one arm, enamel colors, late 19th C, printed "black anchor" mark, pr (A)...... 3574.00

Jewel Box, 5" l, 3" h, porcelain, enameled raised gold shells and blue flowers.............. 165.00

Mortor and Pestle, 3 3/4" d, 2 1/8" h, hp rose buds, gold leaves on int, cranberry red band with gold leaf rim on ext, pestle in white, gold, and cranberry red........................ 65.00

Mug, 3" h, Jaspe-marbleized band (A)........ 22.00

Plaque

21 1/4" l, 14" w, earthenware, "La Seduction" and "La Perdition," scenes of scantily clad Venus, late 19th C, painted by E. Poitovin, pr (A)................................. 3762.00

26" l, 17 3/4" h, painted harbor scene with wooden bridge, windmill on hill, c1860–80 (A)................................. 5010.00

Plate

9 1/2" d

Hp center medallions in multicolored flowers, raised leaf border in tan and yellow, pr.................................. 40.00

Sevres style, jeweled, center portrait medallions of Cardinal Richelieu and "Le Grand Conde," borders of garlands and scrolls in gilding, shaped and molded rims with floral wreaths, 19th C, letter dates for 1779, script titles, pr (A)............. 748.00

12" d, large yellow and red roses on dark green to light green ground, relief of lilies on rim, gold trim, unmarked (A)............ 10.00

Pomade Pot, 3 1/2" h, 3 1/2" d, porcelain, purple and blue floral cartouche on front with green leaves, floral cartouche on reverse, scale purple ground, white int, gilt base and two knob handles, 18th C........................ 350.00

Pot de Creme, Cov, 4" h, blue pattern with farm animals, acorn finials, c1875, set of 4. . . . . . **1200.00**

Soup Tureen, 8" h, with undertray, 18" l, porcelain, gilt band decoration, early 20th C (A). **100.00**

Teapot, 8 1/2" h, 4" d, porcelain, multicolored cornflower design, ribbed body, "Porcelain de Paris," crossed arrows, 1774 mark **180.00**

Tete-a-Tete Set
Tray, 11 1/2" l, teapot, cov, milk jug, cov sucrier, 2 coffee cans, saucers, Sevres style, painted vases overflowing with colorful summer flowers, tooled and gilded scroll and foliate borders, dark blue ground, lobed two handled tray, first half 19th C, incised nos, "interlaced L's" mark, 10 pcs (A). **4862.00**

Tray, 16 1/2" l, scalloped edge, teapot, creamer, 2 cups, saucer, white porcelain with cherub heads, floral scrolls and birds in pink, green, blue, and yellow, gilt accents (A). **110.00**

Trinket Box, 5 1/4" sq, porcelain, hp floral design on turquoise ground, gold trim, brass mts, hinges, and feet, c1925 . . . . **245.00**

Urn
17" h, porcelain and gilt, panel with courting couple, human head gilt handles, painted gilt curvilinear decoration, blue ground . . . **400.00**

22 1/2" h, baluster shape, porcelain, reserve of putti and maidens, rust ground, pr **500.00**

Urn, Cov
8" h, Sevres style, lady in period dress, green ground, ormolu mts **325.00**

17" h
Center oval panel of lovers on front, bouquet of summer flowers on reverse, gilt twig and floral design on blue ground, dbl gilt handles, mid 19th C, pr (A). **1045.00**

Sevres style, maidens gathering water with Cupids in lavender, green, blue, and purple, gilt accent, gilt metal mts, sgd "R. Pent," pr. **1000.00**

26" h, Sevres style, gadrooned floral painted body, cobalt ground, gilt musical trophies and scrolls on neck and lid, gilt bronze base (A). **385.00**

29" h, tapered ovoid body painted with young woman and putto by stream, cobalt cov, spreading base with gilt foliage, repaired cov, late 19th C, sgd "Lheri' (A) **2530.00**

Vase
3" h, enameled band of florals on cobalt ground, irid overspray, sgd "Barol Cannes" **850.00**

5" h, porcelain, armorial with crest in blue, yellow, and brown, two handles, scalloped top, c1800 . . . . **495.00**

6" h, porcelain, castle scene with multicolored bird on tree limb, floral reserves, gold butterfly, four curved feet. **95.00**

7" h, porcelain, figure of woman in red kimono, blue sash, holding gold fan, butterflies, ovoid shape, black ground **150.00**

10" h, baluster form, porcelain, relief spiral body and floral decoration, late 19th C, pr (A). **220.00**

10 1/2" h, porcelain
Baroque open work base with three tulip shaped flower holders molded at sides, lavender and gold colors, unmarked . . . **125.00**

Two children with instruments on baroque base, ornate floral top with applied flowers, c1860–90, unmarked. **175.00**

11" h, Sevres style, hp bird scenes in cartouches on front and reverse, dark rust ground (A) **60.00**

11 1/2" h, lady in gown and plumed hat in panel, deep aquamarine with black trim, relief of flowers and leaves, scroll handles . . **95.00**

12" h, porcelain, cobalt blue with gold leaf and vine, gold panels of green and purple grapes. twisted vine handles and feet. **180.00**

13 1/2" h, oval urn shape, panels with courting couples, pierced Greek key handles and border, gilt trim, turquoise ground, pr (A). **275.00**

17 1/2" h, flaring form, porcelain, foliate molded rim, floral bouquet on handles, late 19th C (A). **220.00**

Vase, Cov, 10" h, stylized florals and enameled jewels on turquoise ground, ormolu mts and ram's head handles (A) **605.00**

Vase, Cov, Stand, 27" h, globular body, courting couple in wooded landscape, reverse with spray of summer flowers, dark blue ground, gilded handles, late 19th C (A). **1881.00**

FRANKENTHAL   1762-1793

Palatinate, Germany
1755–1799

History: Paul Hannong established the Frankenthal hard paste porcelain factory in 1755 with the consent and patronage of the Prince Elector Karl Theodor of Palatinate. Previously Hannong worked at Strasbourg, France, 65 miles south of Palatinate.

Dinner services and accessory pieces were marketed along with biscuit and decorated figures, some of which were excellent artistically. The Rococo style dominated and was similar to that appearing on Vincennes-Sevres pieces. Frankenthal decorators used a full range of colors along with the Vienna style of raised gilt work. Classical and natural themes proved the most popular.

Despite high quality pieces, the company suffered from financial difficulties. In 1762 Karl Theodor purchased the factory and personally supervised its operation. Luck and Melchior, modelers, fashioned figural pieces of note. Nevertheless, the company failed in 1799. Nymphenburg acquired the Frankenthal molds to reproduce the old forms. The Nymphenburg factory used the blue lion mark and "CT" with a crown on their pieces made from Frankenthal molds.

Frankenthal's forty-four years of production are the shortest production period experienced by a major German porcelain manufacturer. However, Frankenthal's high quality and variety of products produced during this brief period are enough to rank it among the greatest of the German factories.

Reference: George Ware, *German & Austrian Porcelain,* Crown, Inc., 1963.

Museums: Bayerisches Nationalmuseum, Munich, Germany; Museum fur Kunst und Gewerbe, Hamburg, Germany; Schlossmuseum, Berlin, Germany; Victoria & Albert Museum, London, England.

Basket, 8¹⁵⁄₁₆" d, reticulated basketweave body, painted center with floral bouquet and sprigs in puce, purple, yellow, green, iron red, and blue, loop handles, gilt edged, flared foot with rope edging, c1765, "crowned CT" mark (A)...................................... 1045.00

Charger, 14½" d, center in shades of brown, iron-red, green, blue, purple, and yellow with small figures and Italianate buildings in landscape, iron-red, green, and purple floral sprigs on border, gilt rim, 1759–62, underglaze "blue lion rampant, JAH monogram imp JHI" marks, pr (A).................................. 3850.00

Coffee Pot, 4⅝" h, painted scene of lady sitting by monument, young man playing lute, scattered flowers, puce and gilt accented handle and right angle spout, flower knob, "blue crowned CT and puce 70" marks (A) 3867.00

Cup and Saucer, Handleless, multicolored enameled chinoiserie lady with bird on shoulder and telescope on cup, lady with caged parrot on saucer, rims with inverted bells and parasols in pink and gilt, c1771–72, "blue crowned CT" mark (A) 6105.00

Dish, 11¾" d, chinoiserie scene of man in puce jacket, iron- red trousers, standing on rock in landscape with palm tree, scattered insects and leaves in floral molded rim quartered and alternating with painted exotic birds and flower sprays, c1759, "blue rampant lion" mark, pr (A) 3300.00

Ecuelle, Cov, 6½" l, panels of figures in landscapes, birds on branches, scattered flower

Figure, 9⅛" h, Goddess, yellow drapery with green flower sprigs, gilt edged base, repairs, c1759–62, "blue rampant lion and JAH" mark, (A) $1590.00

sprays within gilt flower and chain link borders, shell knob, scrolling foliate handles, molded with flower and fruit sprays, 1759–62, underglaze "blue rampant lion and monogram, incised H" marks (A)............... 5513.00

Ewer, 13½" h, baluster shape, shell form lip, neck with mermaids, figural and landscape reserves on floral pattern ground, pedestal base 250.00

Figure

4⅛" h, putto with black tricorn, flower sprigged drape over pink shorts, container on back, stick in hand, purple and gilt edged scroll base, c1755–56, imp "PH" mark ... 750.00

4¼" h, gallant in puce breeches and orange jacket, giving grapes to seated woman in yellow skirt with green sprigs, holding grapes in puce apron, grassy pierced scroll base, c1759–62, "blue lion and J.A.H." mark (A) 1120.00

4⁵⁄₁₆" boy on sled, dark gray tricorn, yellow-lined pink jacket patterned with rose trellis work, orange waistcoat and breeches, fur edged yellow mittens, seated on light brown sled, 1759–62, modeled by Johann Friedrich Luck, underglaze "blue rampant lion, JAH" monogram for Joseph Adam Hannong (A) 3575.00

4⅜" h, "Spring," boy draped in puce lined cloth, holding bouquet of flowers, green mound on gilt edged scroll base, c1765, modeled by K. Linck, "blue crowned CT" mark................................. 475.00

5" h, Chinaman, wide tricorn hat, iron-red and black striped costume with blue stripe sash, yellow scarf and shoes, opening striped parasol, scroll edged mound base, modeled by C.G. Luck, restored, c1775, underglaze "blue crowned CT" mark (A)........... 1496.00

5½" h, poultry girl, pale yellow hat with blue florette and puce ribbon, gilt edged white bodice laced in puce, white skirt with puce and iron-red stripes and iron-red sprigs, yellow shoes, black apron filled with grain, black and iron-red rooster and three chicks at feet, moss encrusted green mound base with gilt scrolls, 1784, modeled by Adam Bauer, underglaze "blue crowned Carl Theodor and "84" marks (A)........... 1650.00

5⅝" h, peasant group, woman resting on walking stick, carrying bucket of apples on back, youth in wide brimmed black hat who swings ax, green washed mound scroll base, modeled by C.G. Luck, some restoration, c1771, underglaze "blue crowned CT and 71" mark (A) 2618.00

6⅛" h, lovers, young man presenting flowers to a girl seated with flower basket in lap, shell and scroll molded base in puce and gilding, modeled by J.W. Lanz, some restoration, c1765, "iron-red crowned CT and I" mark (A) 2244.00

6¼" h, allegorical group, "Summer," girl in yellow straw hat, white blouse, purple flowered skirt under blue-lined apron, seated on pile of sheaves making wreath, young man wearing black hat, puce breeches, white jacket with gilt buttons, standing beside her holding sheaves, green-washed mound base edged in gilt scrolls, restored, c1770, modeled by C.G. Luck, underglaze "blue crowned CT" mark (A). . . . **1589.00**

6³⁄₈" h, allegorical group, "Autumn," young man in yellow waistcoat under puce pants and jacket, young girl in yellow jacket and pale blue flower sprigged skirt holding grape vine in left hand and bunch of grapes in right, gilt edged shell and scroll base, modeled by I.W. Lanz, 1759–62, underglaze "blue rampant lion and JAH monogram' (A). **6919.00**

6¹⁄₂" h, Pantaloon, theatrical pose, one arm raised to pointed beard, other holding back black cloak, deep red suit, purple and gilt rococo molded scrolling base, from Italian Comedy, dagger missing, c1755–59, modeled by J.W. Lanz, underglaze "blue rampant lion, imp PH and incised 3" marks (A). **10,829.00**

7⁵⁄₈" h, hunting group, huntsman in green costume with white, gilt edged jacket, high white boots, blowing hunting horn, standing beside dead stag bound to tree, hound seated to one side, gilt edged scroll molded base, some damage and restoration, ec1756, modeled by J.W. Lanz, underglaze "blue rampant lion, imp PH, N, 6" marks (A) **3700.00**

9¹⁄₈" h
Goddess, half-naked body covered with yellow drapery with green flower sprigs, crown in hair, standing on pierced rococo base edged in gilding, repaired, 1759–62, underglaze "blue rampant lion, JAH" mark (A) **1589.00**

Hercules, standing classical bearded man wearing lion's skin, leaning on club, gilt edged scroll base, "blue crowned CT and AB" mark (A). **1730.00**

9³⁄₄" h, chinoiserie potpourri group, man in gold and white turban, pink cape, iron-red and green striped white coat, yellow breeches, supporting large green artichoke form potpourri vase, pierced around rim, companion in iron-red, yellow, and green sprigged white cape fringed in gold, yellow apron, gilt edged rococo scroll molded base in green on top, cov missing, cracks, 1765–70, modeled by Johann Friedrich Luck, unmarked (A) **2200.00**

10¹³⁄₁₆" h, "Summer" as young lady wearing white cap with iron-red ribbons, iron-red dress patterned with russet diaperwork, seated with basket of apples and pears, male companion wearing black hat with green ribbon, white shirt, gilt edged jacket and breeches patterned with gray trellis diaperwork, brown and green tree, sheaf of yellow wheat, scroll molded base with puce and gilding, restored, 1756–59, modeled by Johann Wilhelm Lanz, underglaze "blue rampant lion, imp PH6" twice for Paul Anton Hannong (A) **6050.00**

Plate
9¹⁄₄ d, painted bouquet of flowers, shaped rim with alternating molded and painted flower sprigs, gilt trellis border, 1759–62, underglaze "blue monogram of Joseph-Adam Hannong, rampant lion" marks (A). **1870.00**

10" d, central loose flower spray with roses

and carnation among scattered "flowers, gilt striped ground, 1770–75, "interlaced CP, incised AL & H" marks (A) **925.00**

10⁵⁄₈" d, shaped decagonal form, central loose flower spray of roses, carnation, and tulip, laurel molded rim, striped gilt ground, monogram "CP" in purple on rim, 1770–75, underglaze "blue crowned CT" incised marks (A). **1250.00**

Potpourri Vase, 9" h, pear shaped body, battle scene and travelers on horseback at rest, scrolling acanthus and shell handles, four feet, pierced cov in puce and gilding, repaired, 1759–62, underglaze "blue rampant lion" mark (A). **14025.00**

Salt Cellar, 5⁹⁄₁₆" h, figural of "Spring" as young lady wearing blue flowers in brown hair, pearl necklace, iron-red laced yellow bodice, iron-red and blue striped skirt, seated beside rococo urn rising from pierced scrollwork base, c1765, modeled by Johann Friedrich Luck, underglaze "blue crowned Carl Theodor and B" mark (A) **3850.00**

Slop Bowl, 3¹⁄₈" d, lady holding a fan, musician playing violin, both seated next to monument in landscape, well with large tulip, puce edged rim, c1762, painted by A. Le Grand, "crowned CT monogram, incised IH, painter's G" marks (A). **2460.00**

Soup Plate, 9" d, center floral bouquet in puce, purple, iron- red, yellow, blue, and green, scattered sprigs, ozier molded border with four floral sprigs, gilt rim, c1756, "blue rampant lion and imp PH" marks (A). **300.00**

Spoon Tray, 7⁵⁄₁₆" l, yellow, blue, puce, iron-red, green, and brown painted scene of two long tailed birds perched on branched tree, scattered sprigs, ozier molded border with gilt rim, c1770–75, "blue crowned CT" mark (A) **770.00**

Tea and Coffee Service, Part, Teapot, 4⁷⁄₁₆" h, 2 teacups, 4 coffee cups, 7 saucers, iron-red, yellow, and purple with travelers in landscape before distant buildings, scattered floral sprigs, iron-red scrollwork border, gilt edged rim, cracks, underglaze "blue crowned Carl Theodor: 74 or 75" date marks, 14 pcs (A). **3850.00**

Tureen, Cov, 9¹⁄₄" h, circ ogee shape, bouquet of roses, carnation, and tulip on each side, ornate gilt striped ground, domed cov, artichoke finial, double mask and acanthus handles, 1770–75, underglaze "blue crowned CT, inc L2" mark (A) **4114.00**

Vase, 9¹⁄₄" h, 9⁷⁄₈" h, vase formed as Chinese cabbage with shaded green leaves, modeled with chinoiserie figures of ladies and men, brown, yellow, and green mottled mound base with applied moss and small plants, restored, 1773, modeled by Konrad Link, underglaze "blue crowned Carl Theodor" mark and 73, pr (A). **6325.00**

Wine Cooler, 6¹¹⁄₁₆" h, 10¹⁄₄" w, ogee shape body, front and reverse in puce, purple, yellow, green, blue, and iron-red spray of flowers above molded floral border on lower body, panels of landscapes or perched birds on top portion, gilt borders, scalloped rim with gilt star border, rococo scrollwork handles, c1760 porcelain, c1780 decoration, underglaze "blue lion rampant, JAH incised "JH" and imp II" marks (A). **2475.00**

1738-c1790

1758-1788

c1827

1740-60

FRENCH FAIENCE

Nevers
c1632–1800
Rouen
1647–c1800
Moustiers
1670–1800
Marseilles
1677–c1800
Strasburg
1721–1780

History: Faience, a porous pottery, is lightly fired earthenware that is painted and then covered with an opaque stanniferous glaze. Tiny particles of tin oxide suspended in the glaze provide the characteristic white, opaque nature of the pottery.

Italian potters migrated to France in the 1600s, first to Nevers, and later to Rouen, Moustiers, Marseilles, and other pottery centers. In **Nevers** the potters transformed the Italian majolica tradition into something distinctively French. The Nevers potters developed a Chinese style employing Oriental subjects and the Chinese blue and white color scheme. They also added a richly intertwining border pattern of leaves and flowers. Nevers was the leader during the 17th century.

In the third-quarter of the 17th Century, four main schools - Rouen, Moustiers, Marseilles, and Strasburg - developed. **Rouen** faience was characterized by "decor rayonnant," a richly intricate pattern of stylized leaves and florals which adorned the outer border, cascading in swags around a central flower burst that was adapted from the delicate lace and iron work of the mid-18th century Rococo patterns. Polychrome chinoiserie styles also were introduced.

Moustiers derived its early system of decoration from Nevers. The pioneer was Pierre Clerissy (1679–1739). The Chinese influence is in evidence in pattern design, form, and the blue and white palatte. The use of "grotesques,"—fantastic human or animal figures in scenes of wild vegetation, added excitement to the pieces.

In 1677 Joseph Clerissy came from Nevers to **Marseilles**. The Marseilles potters used border patterns that were heavier than at Moustiers. Landscape panels, acanthus leaves, or birds with foliage followed the Nevers style.

Strasburg faience was influenced by the Rococo motifs

from Rouen. In 1748–1749 a group of artists, who had worked at Meissen, arrived in Strasburg from Hochst. They applied enamel painting techniques, giving the wares a more German than French appearance.

Before the French Revolution, faience factories were thriving. After the revolution and the treaty of commerce between England and France, English potters flooded the market with their industrial pottery that was cheaper to make, lighter in weight, easier to transport, and less liable to chip or crack under heat. This pottery appealed to both wholesale dealers and the public. The French factories experienced great difficulties competing. Many factories closed. By 1850 the French pottery industry was practically extinct.

References: Diana Imber, *Collecting European Delft and Faience*, Frederick A. Praeger, 1968; Arthur Lane, *French Faience*, Faber and Faber, 1970; Millicent S. Mali, *French Faience*, United Printing, 1986.

Museums: Musee Ceramique, Rouen, France; Musee des Arts Decoratifs, Paris, France; Victoria and Albert Museum, London, England.

Reproduction Alert: Collectors of French faience should be very wary of imitations being made in large quantities in modern day Paris. Genuine French faience is rare and only is offered for sale when a famous collection is dispersed.

Albarello, 5¼" h, manganese "EX 1 De Bourrac" within reserve of entwined snakes in blue, ochre, and manganese, c1750 (A) **650.00**
Ashtray, 4½" d, multicolored porcupine in cen-

Charger, 13½" d, Art Nouveau style, enameled in gray, iron-red, and tan, "Corbillan" mark, $6500.00

Inkwell, 5¼" l, black ground, pink, green, rust, and blue florals, gilt pages, "Aladin France" mark, $75.00

Plate, 8" d, multicolored florals, late 19th C, $75.00

Tea Service, Part, pot, sugar bowl, cov, 2 cups and saucers, molded basketweave borders, multicolored florals, mid 19th C, "blue CM" marks, $500.00

ter, fleur-de-lys and florals on border, loop and dot shaped rim, Desvres (A).............. 55.00

Basin, 17 1/8" l, shaped oblong form, blue trellis band enclosing reserves of female busts, scroll and foliate borders, well with grotesques and arabedques, three canted sq feet, lion mask handles, late 18th C (A).................. 1295.00

Basket
  11 1/2" H-H, oval, int painted with green, manganese, blue, turquoise, yellow, and brown flower spray, basketweave border with applied florets, ropework handles with florets, c1760, Sceaux........................ 950.00
  14 3/4" l, pierced body, center painted in colors with bouquet of spring flowers, ext with purple edging and blue flowerheads at intersections, rope twist handles, restored, early 19th C (A)...................... 880.00

Bowl, 7 3/4" l, scallop shell form on flared foot, molded in relief with nude woman bathing, holding painted towel, leg raised, shades of yellow, ochre, blue, and manganese, mid 18th C, Nevers (A).......................... 555.00

Cache Pot
  7 5/8" d, 4 1/2" h, ftd, shaped pink, rose, and white with pink lions' heads, pink and rose

rim and feet, 1871, "rose Gien castle" mark................................. 675.00
  12 1/8" d, 9 3/4" h, cobalt glazed, white int, 19th C, pr........................... 950.00

Candle Snuffer, 5 1/2" h, pyramid shape, enamel and gilt decorated tobacco leaf design, powder blue ground, "St. Clement" mark (A) ... 82.00

Candlestick
  5 1/2" h, blue, yellow, rust, green Rouen style pattern with florals, scalloped raised base, c1885, pr 350.00
  7 1/4" h, male peasant lighting pipe on body, fleur-de-lys and ermine tail ground, coat of arms on circ base, loop and dot border, crazed glaze (A) 470.00
  7 3/4" h, blue, yellow, rust, green Rouen style pattern, eight sided base, c1890, pr 495.00
  9 1/4" h, triangular stem, green, red, yellow, and blue small flowers, leaves, and scrolls, scroll-shaped tripod feet, repaired, Rouen (A)................................. 100.00

Caster and Cov
  7 5/8" h, cylindrical body, blue and white, four panels of stylized pineapple devices, blossoms, foliate scrolls, and shells beneath foliate lambrequins, separated by narrower blue ground panels of blossoms and leaf scrolls, domed cov with dots, wheels, stars, ladders, and leaves, pierced with small circles and blossoms, dbl knobbed finial, c1720, "Rouen, boue 5 0r 2" on int (A). . 3300.00
  8 1/4" h, sugar, silver form, blue and rust with band of geometric and foliate motifs, trefoils around base, pierced screw cov with blue and brown sprigs, acorn finial, c1730, Rouen (A)............................. 2834.00

Chamberstick, 3" h, 9 3/4" l, blue, green, terra cotta, and yellow swirled Rouen style pattern with salamander on base, handle repaired, "Blois Fait Main" mark (A) 60.00

Charger, 15 5/8" d, purple, blue, yellow, and green bouquets in center, stylized flowers on molded border, hairlines and chip, c1770, incised "JH" mark (A) 275.00

Clock, Mantel, 10" h, blue and white with country landscapes (A) 385.00

Cruet, 8" h, blue, green, red, and purple chinoiserie design of birds, flowers, and foliage with black accents, unmarked, pr (A)........... 28.00

Cruet Stand, 5 3/4" h, two circ pots joined by loop handle in blue with stylized flowering foliage within line borders, cracks, panel with incised letters and "1756" mark (A)........ 650.00

Dish
  9" l, shell shape, shades of rose, yellow, blue, and green with tulip among large floral spray and smaller floral sprays and sprigs, ruffled rim edged in brown, footrim pierced for hanging, c1770, Strasbourg, "blue JH monogram" marks and 775, pr (A)....... 3575.00
  11 7/8" d, stylized flower, cracked, mid 17th C, Nevers (A).......................... 200.00
  12 1/8" d
    Buildings within wreath of formal foliage and fruit, cracked, mid 17th C, Nevers (A) 225.00
    Rect, convex sides, rounded corners, ribbed rims, bright colors with tulip sprig and sprays of oriental flowers, brown edged rims, "iron-red fleur-de-lys" mark (A)... 1110.00

12 1/4" D, lobed form, blue, manganese, yellow, bust portrait of woman encircled by border of scrolls, mid 17th C, Nevers (A) . **236.00**
14 3/4" l, shaped oval form, branch of flowers and a bird in blue within stylized border of scrolls, flowers, and foliage, "blue G" painter's mark, c1750, Strasbourg (A) **675.00**
15 3/4" l, silver shape, painted sprays and scattered sprigs of flowers on white ground, reeded and shaped rim, Niderville (A) **278.00**
16 1/4" l, shaped oval form, purple and yellow shaded tulips, scattered florals, dark brown rim, c1763–70, "blue IH" mark (A) **3815.00**

Figure
6 1/2" h, seated lion on haunches with tail curled around back, rect base washed in blue, head turned to side, coat with blue and iron-red splashes, pierced ears, 18th C, Rouen (A) **11,100.00**
15" h, putto and swan, naked young boy scratches head, holding swan between his legs, wings raised, plumage in blue and yellow, blue, yellow, and manganese stepped base, late 18th C (A) **3938.00**
17" h, Madonna and child in blue, green, and ochre, robe with fleur-de-lys splashed with green, shaped oval base, cracks, c1740, Nevers (A)............................ **880.00**

Garniture, 2 vases 6 5/8" h, hex bottle shape, center piece of dbl ogee form in flared foot, continuous band of pagodas set in fenced garden behind flowering plants, fruiting trees and rockwork in green, blue, ochre, and manganese, formal borders, mid 18th C, Rouen (A) **7400.00**

Inkwell, 4 1/4" sq, 2 1/2" h, blue, red, yellow, and green florals and scrolls, four small feet, glass insert, Rouen (A) **77.00**

Jar, Cov, 11 1/2" h, large yellow scrolls forming four panels of multicolored fruit and flowers, blue cross-hatching on shoulder (A) **49.00**

Jardinaire
11 1/2" l, 5" h, oval shape, rose and white, floral sprays on int sides, rose color rim, scroll feet and handles, 1871, "rose Gien castle" mark......................... **675.00**
12 1/2" l, 9" w, 7 1/4" h, Rouen style birds, quivers of arrows and criss-cross borders in terra cotta, yellow, green, and blue, modeled quarter moon feet at each corner in yellow, painted moon faces, "green C" mark (A)......................... **1430.00**

Jug, 7 3/4" h, silver shape, relief molded fleur-de-lys and armorials, turquoise glaze, stepped circ foot, scrolled angular handle, late 17th C, Nevers (A) **1525.00**

Jug, Figure, 11" h, naval officer in blue sponged jacket and tricorn hat, astride dark blue sponged barrel, carafe and goblet in hand, yellow waistcoat, green sponged base, late 18th C (A).................................. **1020.00**

Jug, Hot Water, Cov, 9 7/8" h, globular body, cornucopia full of flowers and scattered insects, flared foot with Buddist symbols, cov with flowers and butterfly, straight neck, pinched spout, loop handle, pewter mts with shell thumbpiece, restorations, c1770, "green D" Rouen mark (A)...................... **1295.00**

Knife Rest, 3/3/8" l, blue, yellow, rust, green Rouen style pattern, mid 19th C, pr **120.00**

Lavabo, 27" h, 18" w, multicolored bird and scroll decoration, dbl handles, brass spigot .. **475.00**

Pincushion, 2 3/4" h, 2 1/2" w, molded face of child, fleur-de-lys on each side, velvet cap for cushion, pierced for hanging, "CA" mark (A) **495.00**

Pitcher
5 1/2" h, bulbous body, pinched spout, golden dog on front with gray marbled scrolls and stones, orange-yellow fleur-de-lys and black ermine tails, blue and red border and handle, "CA 382" mark (A) **66.00**
6 1/4" h, 9 1/8" w, three cartouches with coats of arms or florals on terra cotta and blue criss-cross ground, Rouen designs between cartouches and on handle, "Chocolate de royal" on bottom (A) **550.00**

Plate
7 3/4" d, Funeral of Napoleon in 1840, black transfer, "Gien/porcelaine/opaque" mark, set of 12 (A).......................... **330.00**
8" d, green dragon under gold crown in center, "CHAMBORD" under dragon, two orange-yellow fleur-de-lys at sides, black ermine tails above and below, loop and dot border with fleur-de-lys and ermine tails, shaped rim, pierced for hanging (A)...... **38.00**
8 1/4" d
Center armorial in yellow, orange, and black, green foliage, black ermine tails, blue and red loop and dot border, crackled glaze, pierced for hanging, "CA" mark (A) **71.00**
Transfer of Napoleonic wars, invasion of Moscow, flower, drum, eagle, flag, and cannon border, "Louis LeBeuf Montereau" mark **145.00**
9" d, large open bouquet of flowers in polychromes, red vert dash border, Strasbourg (A)................................... **61.00**
9 1/4" d
Birds and flowering branches in yellow, ochre, and white, blue ground, white line rim, c1660, Nevers, pr (A) **2860.00**
Birds perched on flowering branches, quiver of arrows, torch, and cornucopia, shaped diaper border edged with C-scrolls and foliage suspending flowerheads, blue, green, iron-red, and yellow, c1765, Rouen (A).................... **440.00**
Flowering plant in fenced garden, encircled by border of alternating compartments of trellis and stylized flowers, blue, yellow, green, and iron-red, c1740, Rouen, "blue GB" mark (A)....................... **1110.00**
Stylized flowers in center, diaper border reserved with four panels of flowering branches, blue, green, iron-red, and yellow, c1730, Rouen (A) **1430.00**
9 3/8" d, scene of Chinese pavilions in garden, bird and insect above, diaper border with four panels of flowering branches, blue, green, iron-red, and yellow, c1730, Rouen (A)..................................... **1980.00**
9 1/2" d
Bouquets and scattered flowers painted in colors, brown line shaped rim, late 18th C, Niderville, pr (A).................. **1320.00**
Central flower spray and scattered sprigs in muted colors, brown edged shaped rim, restored, c1765, set of 6 (A) **1518.00**
Painted carnation in center, three small scattered flowers on rim, white ground, shaped rim, c1760, Strasbourg **500.00**

9⅝" d

Lobed silver shape, loose scattered sprigs and butterfly in yellow, blue, and shades of green and purple, cracks, set of 3 (A)   **775.00**

Shaped circ form, crouching half tiger-half dragon creature below flowering tree growing from rockwork in front of prunus orchard in blossom, pr of parrots perched on branch, rim with flowering twigs, rim chips, 1740–50, Rouen, "blue GB" mark (A) **1480.00**

9¾" d, coat-of-arms in palm frond cartouche at top, scenes of Chinese men in landscapes, c1660, Nevers, pr (A) **3960.00**

9⅞" d, silver shape, enamels with flowers, peony, rose, brown edged rims, 1754–62, Paul Hannong, Strasbourg, "blue PH," pr (A). **5667.00**

10" d, two ducks in shallow water, framed by rockwork and flowers growing from trees on each side, scattered insects, wavy rim, blue, yellow, green, and iron-red, 1750–60, Rouen (A) **1850.00**

Puzzle Jug, 7½" h, blue and yellow flower spray with brown, waisted neck with pierced florets for decoration, c1800, Le Croisic (A) **708.00**

Salt, Dbl, 3½" w, loop and dot border, black ermine tails, center loop handle, "Caite-de-Carcasonne" mark (A) **15.00**

Sauce Boat, 3¾" l, silver shape, continuous blue-ground band reserved with quatrefoil panels of Dutch landscapes within oriental flower sprays, flared foot, branch handle, restored, c1730, Rouen (A) **1480.00**

Teapot, 5⅝" h, pear shape body, blue, iron-red, green, and yellow Kakiemon style with birds and insects in flight above oriental flowers growing from banded hedges, scattered floral sprigs, rims with border of iron-red-dotted blue circles, fluted mushroom knob, animal head spout, foliate molded handle, restored, c1750, Sinceny (A) **770.00**

Tureen, Cov

6⅝" l, molded asparagus bunch of cream colored stalks with purple scales, shaded green tips with purple, bound with two brown cords, repaired, 1755–60, Sceaux, Jacques Chapelle Period, "brown fleur-de-lys" mark (A) **4950.00**

12¹¹⁄₁₆" l, green and pink painted rose sprig, purple and green carnation on reverse, scattered insects, purple accented foliate scroll handles, brown edged rims, figural yellow lemon knob with raised green leaves, cracks, c1765, Niderville (A)............   **935.00**

13½" l, painted bouquets and scattered flowers in colors, brown line rims, lemon finial, Niderville (A) **2860.00**

Vase

6⅝" h, ogee form, white slip of two Chinamen under pine tree and with palm trees, conifers, and rocks, straight neck, scrolling border, foot with trailing foliage, blue ground, late 17th C, Nevers (A).........   **1110.00**

8" h

Narrow body, flaring mouth with emb scrolls and rim, crest of Francois I in green, yellow, orange, red, and blue, black ermine tails, reverse with large orange-yellow fleur-de-lys, cream crackled ground, "CA 376 B" mark, pr (A) **220.00**

Three brown and yellow sailing boats, black birds, blue clouds, Rouen (A).........   **175.00**

9½" h, cobalt, yellow, green, and orange florals and scrolls, white ground, Boulogne-sur-Mer (A)..........................   **33.00**

Vegetable Tureen, Cov, 13½" l, canted rect oct shape, blue, yellow, green, and iron-red cornucopias and floral lambrequins pendent from lappets and shells, int with flower basket within blue ground band reserved with flowers and floral panels, domed cov with flower swags, pie crust rims, twin angular handles, looped snake knob, knob and one handle restored, 1720–25, Rouen (A)..............   **5550.00**

Wall Pocket, 13" h, bagpipe shape, molded blue bow at top, two dancing couples on front in colors, "AUVERGNE" in ribbon below, "AR" mark (A).................................   **410.00**

Wet Drug Jar, 8¼" h, inscribed in manganese "S. NYMTH." on label within band of trailing laurel in green and manganese, early 18th C (A)...................................   **654.00**

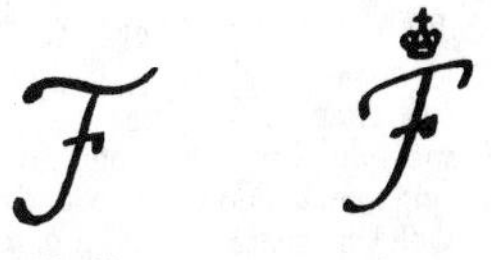

1753 - 70   1922-58

FURSTENBERG

Brunswick, Germany
1747–1859 Royal-State
1859 to Present-Private

History: The Furstenberg factory was founded in 1747 in the castle of Karl I, Duke of Brunswick, primarily to satisfy his vanity. Six years past before porcelain was produced in 1753. The technique came from artists who left Hochst. Raw materials for the paste and glaze had to be imported from a great distance. By 1770 the porcelain paste closely approximated that made at Meissen.

Many figures were modeled, but the amount of production was not great. The figures imitated figural molds and decorations produced at Meissen and Berlin. English styles—Bow, Wedgwood, Chelsea, and Sevres—also were copied. After 1760, Frankenthal vases became famous. China services and various utilitarian and decorative wares were competitive with those produced by other 18th century factories.

The period of 1770 to 1790 was the golden age at the Furstenberg factory. Materials improved considerably, additional enamel colors were utilized, and gilding was employed in the border patterns. After 1775 Neo-classical influences appeared.

During the French occupation, Brunswick was part of the Kingdom of Westphalia ruled by Napoleon's brother, Jerome Bonaparte. The factory became the Royal Porcelain Manufactory from 1807 to 1813. After Napoleon's defeat, Brunswick regained its independence. In 1813 the former name was restored. The factory continued to produce tablewares, decorative porcelains, figures, and coffee and tea sets.

In 1859 Furstenberg was leased by the Brunswick government. Private ownership took over again in 1876. The company was reorganized as a joint stock company and named Furstenberg Porcelain Factory AG. Today, the factory still manufactures a great variety of vases, tablewares, and other porcelains.

Reference: George A. Ware, *German & Austrian Porcelain*, Crown, Inc., 1963.

Museums: Museum fur Kunst und Gewerbe, Hamburg, Germany; National Museum, Stockholm, Sweden; Victoria and Albert Museum, London, England.

Candleholder, Dbl, 5" h, 7" l, molded baroque base outlined in gold, applied pink and yellow roses, raised stem at each end, marked, pr . .   **250.00**

Chocolate Pot, Cov, 7⅛" h, cylindrical body, blue and white, spray of flowers on front, small sprigs on reverse, shoulder and cov with floral garland, blue-tipped ranunculus-sprig knob, molded spout, turned wood handle with gilt metal band, 1770–75, underglaze "blue F and 2, imp Bo" marks (A) **550.00**

Coffee Pot, 4⅞" h, cylindrical shape, shades of brown, green, blue, turquoise, and iron-red with scenes of travelers in rural landscapes on front and back, spout molded with gadrooning, 1785–90, underglaze "blue F, 2, imp Bo 2" marks (A) **660.00**

Coffee Pot, Pear Shape
8¼" h, one side with lady seated at rustic table talking to man and youth in landscape, reverse with lady seated on mound, sewing and listening to companion in rural landscape, foliate molded spout and handle dashed in purple, cov with two purple floral sprigs, bud form knob, c1755, underglaze "blue F, incised P Z" mark (A) **2475.00**

9¾" h, "Chintz" pattern in colors, flower finial, scrolling handle accented with gilt, finial crack, chips, c1765, "blue script F" mark (A) **440.00**

Cup and Saucer, Cov, tapered cylinder shape, painted butterflies in oeil de perdrix borders, dbl handles, bud finial, c1780 (A) **810.00**

Dish
6½" d, overlapping leaf shape, branch handle, painted center flower spray, gilt edge, c1770–90, "blue script F" mark, set of 8 (A) **1818.00**

10¼" l, oval, molded scroll edged panels, painted flower sprays and sprigs, chip on rim, "blue F" mark (A) **285.00**

Candy Box, 5½" h, turquoise, rust and white stripes and panels, "blue crowned F" mark, $125.00

Ecuelle, Cov, 7⅜" d, circ, underglaze blue and white with unfinished pattern of strapwork forming cartouches on front and reverse, entwined foliate scrolls form handles, ranunculus sprig knob, c1775, underglaze "blue F, 3, imp 3, Bo" marks (A) **770.00**

Figure
6" h, girl in black hat, iron-red bodice, striped skirt with white apron, holding goat with violet scarf, rocky base, early 19th C, "blue F" mark (A) **1460.00**

6¼" h, biscuit group, young mother with bonnet on head instructing baby seated on lap, scroll molded base, late 18th/early 19th C, "blue F, incised 252, imp F" (A) **555.00**

7½" h, 7 " l, seated lady in white dress, brown bodice, brown hair, holding a rose, green sofa, c1860–90 . . . .   **550.00**

7⅝" h, group of Neptune, bearded man with laurel wreath and horns in gray hair, sitting on overturned vase, flowing water, putto and triton, scroll edged base with gilt, repaired, c1775, modelled by Desoches, underglaze "blue F and incised, imp shape no.112" marks (A) **4930.00**

8¼" h, Venus standing next to Cupid riding dolphin, pastel colors, gilt lined slab base, late 19th C, "blue F" mark **375.00**

Milk Jug, Cov, 5⅝" h, pear shape, shades of iron-red, green, blue, yellow, puce, and purple with two exotic birds perched on flowering branches, insects and small floral sprigs, flat cov with stylized flowering branch, insect, two leaf sprigs, blue bud knob, gilt rims, S scroll handle, c1767, underglaze "blue F" mark (A) **3025.00**

Plate
10¼" d, sepia painted scene of Aenaes rescuing Anchises from burning Troy, formal foliate borders, gilt rim, c1805–10, "blue F" mark **475.00**

11" d, multicolored romantic country scenes, gold inner border with designs, yellow outer border with five blue floral cartouches with Cupid in each one, overlaid sculptured gold border, Furstenberg mark, set of 8 . . . .   **1400.00**

Plaque, 8" l, rococo rect form, pastoral scenes of shepherd playing flute to young girl resting in grass, cows, goats, and sheep resting next to them, pierced scroll and foliage corners, gilt frames, c1765, underglaze "blue F, incised j and S" marks, pr (A) **22,264.00**

Potpourri Vase, Cov
9³⁄₁₆" h, 9½" h, 12½" h, neoclassical style, each painted on front and reverse with shaded rose ground roundel bordered with iron-red berried green laurel garland, painted with sepia bust portrait of classical personage, large vase with "SOCRATRES." and "PLATO." smaller with "ARISTOLELES." "HERACLITIS." and "ARCHITAS." "ARISTIPPUS." elaborate gilt trims and bases, c1795, underglaze "blue F" mark, set of 3 (A) **7150.00**

10¹⁄₁₆" h, pear shape, shades of brown, green, blue, yellow, and black with continuous scene of men in and near boats with distant buildings, molded around neck and foot, cov with pierced leaves, artichoke knob, gilt edge, c1765, underglaze "blue F" mark (A) **3575.00**

Snuff Box, 2 1/8" d, bombe shape, sides and lid molded with shell and scroll cartouches with military battle scenes in colors, int cov with two commanders on horseback, ormolu mtd, c1760–65 (A).......................... **4975.00**

Spoon Tray, 6 5/8" l, painted period couple seated by monument in landscape, shaped rim with gilt scrolling foliage and pendant flower swags, c1770, "blue F" mark (A).......... **3238.00**

Tea and Coffee Service, Part, drum shape teapot, 4 7/8" h, coffee pot, 6 1/8" h, cov sugar bowl, waste bowl, 9 coffee cups and saucers, front or center with different bust-length portrait of men wearing turbans, ladies, European gentlemen, and peasants, shaded brown ground, within gilt roundel, bow knotted on saucers, gilt edged rim entwined with green ribbon, berry cluster knobs, 1780–85, underglaze "blue F" mark, 22 pcs (A)................**19,800.00**

Teacup and Saucer, chinoiserie design in shades of iron-red, blue, purple, pale yellow, brown, green, and black, front of cup and center of saucer with two figures conversing amidst shrubbery on plateau beneath border of gilt striped pale pink panels alternating with gold and salmon fan shaped devices, gilt rims, C scroll handles in salmon and gilding, 1765–70, "F and imp 3" marks, pr (A).............. **5500.00**

Waste Bowl, 6 3/4" d, ext with European and Turkish cavalry skirmish, reverse with hussars and mounted soldier in river landscape, sides with floral sprigs, gilt scroll edged green scalework border, gilt dentil edge, 1770–75, underglaze "blue F, incised S" mark (A)......... **1925.00**

Watchstand, 6 1/8" h, kneeling putto with yellow lined blue sprigged cloth, supporting rococo watched stand made of scrolls and shells in light green and purple, one finger missing, c1765, incised 1Zc (A).................. **3179.00**

GALLE

1846-1904

Nancy, France
1874–1904

History: Emile Galle, a leading designer and manufacturer of art glass, first made faience in Nancy, France in 1874. Later he experimented with both stoneware and porcelain. Galle's decorations included heraldic motifs and scenes that resembled Delft ware. A series of souvenir dishes was made to commemorate the Franco-Prussian War.

Glazes used were flowing and opaque in nature. Sometimes several colors were mixed together. Most of the forms were simple in design.

Victor Prouve, an artist friend of Galle, provided designs for figures of bulldogs and cats. The most popular figures were painted yellow with blue hearts and circles, black and white with pale indigo blue, or beige with pink and green decorations of naturalistic flowers. Green glass eyes were used. Prouve's designs were used for candlesticks of heraldic lions and grotesque and fantastic ducks, fox, owls, swans, and parakeets. Plant designs of dandelions, chrysanthemums, and orchids were used in Art Nouveau style decorations that duplicated Galle's work on glass.

All of Galle's ceramics were marked with the impressed initials E.G., Em. Galle Faiencerie de Nancy, or some version of his signature.

Museums: Bowes Museum, Barnard Castle, Durham, England; Musee des Arts et Metiers, Paris, France.

Collecting Hints: Galle faience now is prevalent in the American antiques market. Cat, parrot, and dog figures are seen in various colors and sizes. Sets of plates, three sectioned dishes, tureens, wall vases, and inkwells are eagerly sought. Large candlesticks with figures of lions are ammong the most expensive pieces.

Basket, 8" h, Egyptian style, portraits, scarabs, and florals painted and modeled on sides in colors (A)............................. **3500.00**

Bowl, 4 1/4" d, blue crest on front and back, paneled blue rim, "blue Galle Nancy S.C." mark.................................. **225.00**

Candlestick
  8 1/2" h, baroque style, glazed in white, overpainted with burnt umber and gray enhancements, "Galle Nancy" mark, pr (A) . **440.00**
  10" h, blue ground with Chimera, scrolling shapes, and "Rien Sans Amour" on rim, handle modeled as face of bearded man, "E Croix de Lorraine G. Deposes Emile Galle a Nancy' (A)........................... **500.00**

Centerpiece
  12" l, sleigh shape, purple, pink, and green scattered flowers, gilt accents, cream ground, "E G deposes Emile Galle a Nancy" mark (A) **500.00**
  14" l, Egyptian style, molded as large wing with enameled scarab and dragonfly in colors, gilt accents, "Emile Galle/Nancy, Modele at Decor deposes, Croix de Lorraine" mark (A) **3900.00**

Dish, Cov., 10" d, 6 3/4" h, Delft style lowland scenes in shades of blue, ftd, "E. Galle/Nancy" mark.................................. **1000.00**

Inkstand, 12" l, black scenes of cherubs, turquoise and gold florals and trim, (A) $800.00

Ewer, 8" h, free form body, romantic minstrel
scene in colors........................... **1250.00**
Figure, 15" h, seated pug in yellow crackle glaze,
blue hearts and circles, blue collar, "E. Galle
Nancy" mark (A)......................... **1500.00**
Gravy Boat, 4" h, figural French hen with overall
decor in colors........................... **950.00**
Planter, 13½" l, 5¾" h, faience, canoe shape,
multicolored scene of boats on sea with castles in ground, brown ground, raised scrollwork on reverse accented in gold, "E.G. De-
posse, E. Galle, Nancy" mark.............. **1350.00**
Plate, 9½" d, scalloped shape, gold color florals
with dark blue stems, gold and blue border,
pale blue ground, "E. Galle/Nancy" mark ... **295.00**
Vase
6½" h, amphora shape, enameled purple, yellow, pink, and green wildflowers, gilt accents,
blue ground, applied lion's paw handles, "E.
Galle Nancy" mark (A).................... **275.00**
9" h, gray to brown five sided bulbous leafy
base molded with gilt flowers on branches **350.00**
15" h, sq and flared, white tin glaze decorated
in relief with polychrome insects, butterflies,
and blossoms, applied blossom handles, restored, "Galle/Nancy/St Clement" mark, pr
(A)..................................... **2200.00**
Wall Pocket, 14" h, fan vase shape, olive green
leaves, cobalt blue borders with gilt design,
matte gilt trim, yellow/green ground, sgd "ElG
Depose E. Galle Nancy" mark............. **1200.00**

GAME PLATES AND SETS

English/Continental
c1870–1915

History: Game plates and sets, usually including a large
platter, serving plates, and a sauce or gravy boat, were
popular between 1870 and 1915 both in England and on
the Continent. They are specially decorated plates used to
serve game and fish. Subjects utilized by the makers included all types of game birds, e. g., quail, snipe, pheasants, mallards, etc., and fish.

Among the principal French manufacturers were Haviland and firms in Limoges. Makers in England included
Crescent and Sons, Mason, Royal Doulton, Wedgwood,
and Royal Worcester. Factories in Bavaria, Villeroy and
Boch in Germany, and Royal Vienna in Austria also made
game plates and sets.

Fish Set
7 pieces, tray, 23" l, 6 plates, 8⅜" d, swimming fish in colors, green borders with gold
shaped rims, imp "J.S. Germany" marks .. **295.00**
9 pieces, platter, 24" l, 8 plates, 9" d, hp fish
designs in light blue ground, gold rims, dbl
marks................................ **595.00**
13 pieces
Platter, 23" l, 12 plates, hp fish centers, gilt
and blue waved patterned border, scalloped edge, "J. McD & S Limoges France
with crown, and Limoges V.F. France"
marks.............................. **450.00**
Tray, 19¼" l, 12 plates, 8½" d, each with
different fish in colors, pink and gold
floral borders, shaped rims, blue "L.S.& S.
Carlsbad Austria" marks, c1915 .... **325.00**

**Charger, 13½" d, hp game birds in colors,
wooded setting, gold rim, artist sgd, "Blakeman
& Henderson, Limoges France" mark, (A)
$100.00**

Tray, 23½" l, 12 plates, 9" d, gray fish with
blue and green seaweed, molded shaped
rims, each plate with slightly different fish
and muted tones, "Royal Copenhagen, 3
waves" mark **2750.00**
15 pieces
Platter, 24¾" l, cov tureen, sauce boat, 12
plates, each painted with different specimen fish in seaweeds, c1900 (A) **1150.00**
Tray, 24" l, 12 plates, sauce boat on undertray, different fish on each piece, Limoges
(A) **410.00**
Plaque
10" d, hp pheasants, scalloped rim, artist sgd,
pr **65.00**
11¼" d, game bird in forest setting, gold
border, green "E.S. Germany" mark...... **295.00**
11½" d, two fish swimming in purple flowers, pastel colors, gold rococo border, artist
sgd **125.00**
13¼" d, multicolored hanging dead birds,
scalloped gold rococo border, sgd
"Dubois".............................. **295.00**
16" d, multicolored mallard in center, gold
rococo edge, Limoges **185.00**
Plate
8¼" d, multicolored grouse in natural setting,
sgd "C.J. Weaver," Copeland............ **115.00**
8½" d, hp long billed birds, "Royal Munich"
mark................................. **65.00**
8¾" d, hp fish with different fish on each
plate, sea weed decoration, pink, purple,
and green with turquoise, gray-green or tan
ground, white ground around fish, scalloped edge in gilt, c1891, imp "George
Jones" mark, set of 6 .... **1200.00**
8⅞" d
Dead game bird in colors, hanging from
branch, shaped gold outlined rim,
"C.F.H." mark, set of 4 .... **300.00**
Hp wild ducks in tans and greens, gilt edge,
"France" mark....................... **55.00**
9" d
Border with oval panels of painted game
birds on light yellow ground, gilt rim,
c1900, sgd "A.H. Wright," Minton, set of
12 (A) **5240.00**
Enamel and gilt underwater scenes of fish,

raised beadwork border, dtd 1889, sgd
"E. Salter," Worcester, set of 3 .... **300.00**
Raised enamel pheasant, flowers and grain
border, gilt trim, "Crown Derby, Tiffany
Co." marks **100.00**
9¼" d
Fish out of water in white, green, and black,
artist sgd, "red J.P.L. France, green
Limoges" mark **165.00**
River, game, and sea fish swimming among
weeds, named, border in raised gilding
with seaweed, three cracked, c1909, sgd
"A.H. Wright," Minton, printed
"crowned globe," date codes
"P.A.7762." Retailer's mark for Spaulding
& Co., Chicago, set of 10 (A) **940.00**
Scenic landscape in yellow, green, and
white, trees without leaves, artist sgd,
"red J.P.L. France, green Limoges" mark **165.00**
Two turkeys in white, black, and brown,
naturalistic ground, gilt edge, artist
sgd, "red J.P.L. France, green Limoges"
mark **165.00**
9⅜" d, central enameled fish subjects, red
printed floral border, gilt framed trim,
c1880, Derby, set of 6 (A) **305.00**
9½" d, multicolored duck in center, gold
border, sgd "Marc," Limoges **85.00**
9¾" d, Basketweave Border, Naturalistic
Tones, Hp, Gilt Trim
Birds on water's edge **65.00**
One duck flying, one swimming **65.00**
Wild birds **65.00**
9⅞" d, different fish in naturalistic colors,
shaped gilded rim, c1900, underglaze "blue
scepter, printed red orb, KPM" and imp numerals marks, set of 11 (A) **900.00**
10" d
Buffalos in color, gold trim, "Coronet
Limoges" mark **75.00**
Game bird
In flight, gold rococo border, artist sgd,
"Coronet Limoges" mark **105.00**
Woodland setting in colors, gold scalloped rim, Limoges................ **45.00**
Hp pheasant in wooded setting in colors,
ornate gold border, artist sgd, Limoges . **125.00**
Multicolored painted duck, gold rococo
border, sgd "Max, Coronet Limoges"
mark **95.00**
Partridge on plum to green ground, pierced
for hanging, "B.& H." mark **50.00**
Running deer with antlers and hunting dog
barking, green foliage, purple distant
ground, emb border, scalloped edge, artist sgd "Pradet, Coronet Limoges" mark **95.00**
10¼" d, hp standing bird, cerise, yellow, orange, turquoise, embossed ground in aqua,
blue, light green, moss, scalloped edge,
pierced for hanging, "B & M Limoges,
France" mark **135.00**
10½" d
Hp pheasants on one, quail on other, woodland setting, gold rococo border, pierced
for hanging, pr.................... **350.00**
Multicolored quail in center, burgundy border with gold trim, Bavaria **28.00**
Pheasant in center, yellow, gray, and mauve
ground, "B & H Limoges" mark **75.00**
12½" d, hp long tailed birds pecking at snow
cov, large fox behind slight rise, trees, holly-

like foliage, heavy gold rococo scalloped
and emb, artist sgd, "Limoges" mark **135.00**
13" d, transfer of pheasant in grassy setting,
gold rococo edge, pierced for hanging, unmarked.............................. **195.00**
13¾" d, hp quail in natural setting, pastel
colors, emb beaded scroll border, gold trim,
pierced for hanging, sgd "Day," Limoges . **225.00**
Platter
15" l, multicolored scene of pheasant in forest
setting, gold edge, "L. Sazaret Limoges"
mark (A) **60.00**
16" d, multicolored mallard in center, gold
rococo edge, Limoges **185.00**
18⅛" l, painted marten in tree, named on
reverse, serrated border accented in light
green and gilt, "green Royal Copenhagen
and blue wave" mark (A) **700.00**
19" l, 13" w, multicolored scene of two dogs,
one with rabbit in mouth, birds in flight,
shaped rim, sgd "Muville".............. **580.00**
Set
7 pieces, platter, 17½" l, two black ducks in
flight, 6 plates, 8½" d, 3 plates with two
woodcocks in forest setting, 3 plates with
partridges in wooded setting, shaded pink
to aqua ground, "Carlsbad Austria" marks **335.00**
13 pieces, platter, 18¼" l, three ducks in
flight in pastel colors, 12 plates, 9" d, various game birds in meadows and woodlands, aqua borders with gold tracery,
"Theo. Haviland" marks............... **1350.00**
15 pieces, platter, 17" l, 11 plates, cov sauce
tureen with undertray, each with different
bird, deer head handles on undertray,
sculpted bird handles on platter, late 19th C,
Worcester (A)........................ **1980.00**

ΓΑΡΔΗΕΡΖ

EARLY 19ᵀᴴ CENTURY

GARDNER

Verbiki, near Moscow, Russia
1766–1891

History: Francis Gardner founded his factory in 1766. He
brought experienced European potters and decorators to
Russia. Utilitarian wares, artistic objects, and articles for
sale at fairs comprised the production.

Floral motifs and pastoral scenes were favored. Many
dinner sets were made on commission. The Gardner family controlled the factory until 1891 when it was acquired
by the Kuznetsov family.

The initial "G" or name "Gardner" was used as the
mark.

Reference: Marvin Ross, *Russian Porcelains*, University of
Oklahoma Press, 1918.

Museum: Hermitage, Leningrad, Russia.

Bowl, 7¾" d, ext with alternating bands shaded
from red-orange to white, int with white
ground and alternating bands of red-orange

Basket, 12" l, 4 transfer printed medallions of classical busts, lt green molded vines with pink bowknot handles, "green Gardner" mark, (A) $660.00

and floral design, c1880s, bottom with large Arabic plaque with "127 Lash El Man," imp "St. George & Dragon and Gardner" marks. 265.00

Cup and Saucer
Floral reserves on cobalt ground, early 19th C, marked.............................. 250.00
Intricate geometric pattern in red and blue with gilt highlights and white floral designs, white tendril design on handle, c1900, "red Imperial eagle, St. George & the Dragon, and Made in Gardner in Moscow" marks. 175.00
White plaque with wild flower bouquet in red, yellow, pink, and green with gilt, gilt rims with gilt bands on int, tendril style handle in gilt, c1900, "red Imperial eagle, St. George and the Dragon and "Made by Gardner in Moscow" marks 195.00

Figure
6¾" h, man in peach cape, flowered shirt, black boots and cap, seated on bench, playing accordian, sq green textured base with brown edge, marked 450.00
7⅞" h, road sweeper in tall black hat, gray jacket and boots, holding broom and spade, leaf pile on circ base (A)............... 1140.00
9" h, colored biscuit, inebriated husband escorted by wife carrying child and one of his boots, printed and imp marks (A) 468.00
9⅞" h, colored biscuit, three revellers, one man playing concertina, one flourishing bottle, one putting on greatcoat, printed and imp marks (A) 990.00
10¼" h, Finn in traditional costume of brown hat, gray jacket and breeches, black boots, hands on hips, tree stump on base, marked (A). 610.00

Plate
7¾" d, alternating concentric bands of geometric and floral designs in red-orange glaze with gilt, center bands with white grounds and red-orange flowers with gold, c1880s, black Arabic plaque on bottom with "127 Lash El Man," imp "St. George & Dragon and Gardner" marks, pr 365.00
9⅛" d, "St. Vladimar" service, center painted with Star of the Order, border with ribbon and Badge of the Order, lobed and gilt rim, "blue G" mark (A) 750.00
Slop Bowl, 7" d, 3¼" h, powdered red ground, multicolored florals in circ reserve, "iron-red

Fabrika·Gardner, St. George and Tsarist eagle" mark................................... **150.00**

J & R. Riley
1802-1828

GAUDY DUTCH
Staffordshire, England
c1810–1830

History: Staffordshire pottery with a Gaudy Dutch motif was made for the American trade and experienced wide popularity from c1810–1830. White earthenwares, mostly plates and teawares, were made by a number of Staffordshire potters among whom were Riley and Wood. Painted patterns include: Butterfly, Grape, King's Rose, Oyster, Single Rose, Strawflower, Urn, War Bonnet, etc. Dominant colors are cobalt blue, bright yellow, green, red, and pink.

References: Eleanor J. Fox and Edward G. Fox, *Gaudy Dutch*, privately printed, 1970, out of print. Sam Laidacker, *Anglo-American China Part I*, Keystone Specialties, 1954, out of print; Earl F. Robacker, *Pennsylvania Dutch Stuff*, University of Pennsylvania Press, 1944, out of print; John A. Shuman, III, *The Collector's Encyclopedia of Gaudy Dutch & Welsh*, Collector Books, 1990.

Museums: Henry Ford Museum, Dearborn, Michigan; Philadelphia Museum of Art, Philadelphia, PA; Reading Art Museum, Reading, PA.

Reproduction Alert: Cup plates, bearing the impressed mark "CYBRIS," have been reproduced and are collectible in their own right. The Henry Ford Museum has issued pieces in the Single Rose pattern, although they are of porcelain and not soft paste.

Bowl
6¼" d
"Butterfly Variant" pattern (A) 660.00
"Dahlia" pattern (A).................... 357.00
6⅜" d, "Butterfly Variant" pattern (A)..... 880.00
6½" d, "Grape" pattern, lustered rim (A).. 385.00
Coffee Pot
9½" h, "Sunflower" pattern (A) 1650.00

Teabowl and Saucer, "Single Rose" pattern, blue, rust, yellow, and green florals, blue border with yellow leaves, $525.00

11⅛" h, "Single Rose" pattern, domed cov
(A)................................. 5720.00
11½" h, domed cov
"Butterfly Variant" pattern (A)..........11,000.00
"Oyster" pattern (A)................... 2090.00

Creamer
3½" h, "Butterfly Variant" pattern (A)..... 660.00
3⅝" h, "Double Rose" pattern (A)........ 632.00
3¾" h
"Butterfly Variant" pattern (A).......... 1320.00
"Oyster" pattern, handle restored (A) 137.00
"Sunflower" pattern, handle restored,
stained (A) 110.00
4⅛" h, "War Bonnet" pattern (A)......... 605.00
4¼" h, "Dove" pattern, squat shape (A)... 412.00
4½" h
"Butterfly Variant" pattern, barrel shape
(A) 990.00
"Dove" pattern, barrel shape (A) 715.00
"Single Rose" pattern (A) 605.00
"Sunflower" pattern (A)................. 852.00
"Urn" pattern (A) 880.00
4¾" h
"Carnation" pattern (A)................. 605.00
"Double Rose" pattern (A).............. 935.00
5¼" h, "Double Rose" pattern (A)....... 633.00

Dish, Deep Well
7⅜" d, "Single Rose" pattern 350.00
8¼" d, "Butterfly Variant" pattern (A)..... 467.00
9½" d, "War Bonnet" pattern (A) 825.00
9⅝" d, "War Bonnet" pattern (A) 1540.00
9¾" d, "War Bonnet" pattern (A) 1540.00
9⅞" d, "Butterfly Variant" pattern (A)..... 990.00
10" d
"Butterfly Variant" pattern (A).......... 1320.00
"Single Rose" pattern (A) 660.00
10⅛" d, "Single Rose" pattern, imp "RILEY"
mark (A) 660.00

Jug
6¹/₁₆" h, "Double Rose" pattern, mask spout
with dark beard (A).................... 1705.00
6¼" h, "Double Rose" pattern, mask spout
with light beard (A).................... 550.00

Pitcher
5¾" h, "War Bonnet" pattern, rim repair
(A)................................. 220.00
8" h, "Grape" pattern (A)................. 2420.00
8¼" h, "Double Rose" pattern (A)........ 1430.00

Plate
4¾" d
"Primrose" pattern (A)................. 412.00
"Strawflower" pattern (A) 370.00
5⁵/₁₆" d, "Urn Variant" pattern (A) 383.00
5½" d
"Strawflower" pattern (A) 370.00
"War Bonnet" pattern 400.00
5¾" d, "Carnation" pattern (A)........... 412.00
7³/₁₆" d, "Urn Variant" pattern (A)........ 413.00
8⅛" d, "Dove" pattern (A)............... 632.00
8¼" d
"Single Rose" pattern (A) 330.00
"Urn Variant" pattern (A) 660.00
"War Bonnet" pattern (A).............. 410.00
8⁷/₁₆" d, "Dahlia" pattern (A)............. 2310.00
8½" d, "Single Rose" pattern (A) 220.00
9⅝" d, "Grape" pattern (A)............. 633.00
9¾" d
"Butterfly Variant" pattern (A) 715.00
"Carnation" pattern (A)................ 467.00

"Dove" pattern (A).................... 715.00
"Grape" pattern (A) 495.00
"Single Rose" pattern (A) 1045.00
"Sunflower" pattern (A)................. 1155.00
"War Bonnet" pattern (A).............. 470.00
9⅞" d
"Butterfly Variant" pattern (A) 935.00
"Carnation" pattern (A)................ 550.00
"Dove" pattern (A).................... 742.00
"Oyster" pattern (A)................... 633.00
"Primrose" pattern (A)................. 2640.00
"Single Rose" pattern, repair to edge (A) . 110.00
"Strawflower" pattern, imp "RILEY" mark
(A) 2750.00
"Sunflower" pattern (A)................. 1045
"Urn Variant" pattern (A) 660.00
10" d
"Butterfly Variant" pattern (A) 578.00
"Carnation" pattern, deep well (A)....... 1210.00
"Double Rose" pattern (A).............. 715.00
"Dove" pattern (A).................... 770.00
"Strawflower" pattern, imp "RILEY" mark
(A) 2860.00
"Zinnia" pattern, imp "RILEY" mark
(A) 660.00

Platter
10½" l, "Double Rose" pattern (A) 2970.00
11⅝" l, "Double Rose" pattern (A) 3630.00
15" l, "Double Rose" pattern (A) 3630.00

Soup Plate, 8⅜" d, "Carnation" pattern
(A)................................. 467.00

Sugar Bowl, Cov
5" h, sq shape, "Double Rose" pattern (A) . 1100.00
5¼" h, "Dove" pattern (A).............. 632.00
6½" h, "Urn" pattern, round shape, lip and
base restored (A)..................... 275.00

Teabowl and Saucer
"Grape" pattern, hairline on saucer (A)..... 275.00
"Single Rose" pattern (A) 275.00
"Urn" pattern........................ 300.00
"War Bonnet" pattern 500.00

Teapot
5¾" h, rect, "Butterfly Variant" pattern (A) 1320.00
6" h
"Butterfly Variant" pattern, restored lid,
handle, and spout (A) 358.00
"Sunflower" pattern, restored spout and
body (A) 247.00
6¼" h
"Butterfly Variant' (A).................. 605.00
Rect, "Double Rose" pattern (A)......... 1980.00
6½" h
"Butterfly Variant', spout and handle repaired (A) 330.00
"Carnation" pattern (A)................ 660.00
7" h, "Butterfly" pattern, repair to spout (A) 715.00
7½" h, "Dove" pattern (A).............. 660.00
"War Bonnet" pattern 2500.00

Wash Basin, 13¾" d, "Butterfly Variant" pattern, "Adams" mark (A).................. 11,000

GAUDY IRONSTONE

Staffordshire, England
1850–1865

History: Gaudy Ironstone was produced in the Staffordshire district between 1850 and 1865. Edward Walley's

Jug, left, 7" h, blue, iron-red, green, and copper luster, unmkd, $325.00; Plate, center, 9½" d, blue with copper luster trim, unmkd, $155.00; Teapot, right, 10¼" h, "Strawberry" pattern, green and cobalt leaves, rust strawberries, luster trim, (A) $200.00

"wagon wheel" was a popular Gaudy Ironstone design similar to the design of Gaudy Welsh. Walley, who worked at Villa Pottery in Cobridge, utilized bright colors and floral designs to give a country or folk character to his pieces.

While some of the examples used the same colorations as Gaudy Welsh, other pieces used varying shades of red, pink, and orange with light blue and black accents. Some designs utilized copper luster, while others did not. The flow blue technique also was used on some Gaudy Ironstone pieces.

Cup and Saucer, "Seeing Eye" decoration in colors.	145.00
Cup and Saucer, Handleless	
Floral decoration (A)	66.00
"Morning Glory" decoration, underglaze blue with polychrome enamels, hairline (A)	82.00
Strawberry decoration (A)	88.00
Jug, 7½" h, yellow, red, white, and blue tulips on sides, light blue pebble ground, luster trim and rim outline.	295.00
Plate	
8" d, "Urn" decoration in colors	110.00
8½" d, "Strawberry" design, twelve sided .	95.00
9¼" d	
"Blackberry" pattern, twelve sided, 1850s	165.00
Oriental decoration in underglaze blue with orange and yellow enameling (A)	60.00
9⅜" d, "Morning Glory" pattern, underglaze blue, red and green enamels (A)	132.00
9¾" d, "Strawberry" pattern, shaped rim . .	175.00
10½" d, pink, red, green, brown, and yellow gaudy florals, wide cobalt border, c1851, Ashworth, set of 6 (A)	80.00
Platter	
11¾" l, "Oriental" pattern in underglaze blue with orange and yellow enameling (A).	65.00
12⅜" l, floral design in underglaze blue and red, purple and blue enamels (A)	145.00
15⅛" l, "Strawberry" pattern.	525.00
15½" l, 12" w, yellow, green, brown, red, and gold gaudy flowers, wide cobalt border, "Ashworth" mark (A)	13.00
Soup Plate, 9½" d, "Blackberry" pattern, mid 19th c.	185.00
Sugar Bowl, 4" h, red, blue, and green floral design, stripes on rim, unmarked (A)	71.00
Vegetable Bowl, Open, 10" l, 7½" w, "Strawberry" pattern.	385.00

GAUDY WELSH

England, Wales
1820–1860

History: Gaudy Welsh, manufactured between 1820 and 1860, was produced for the working class people in England and Wales. It traces its decorative motifs to Japanese Imari. Gaudy Welsh is identified by its colors of underglaze cobalt blue (often in panels), rust (burnt orange), and copper luster on a white ground, plus its decoration which most often is floral, although trees, birds, or geometric forms are sometimes used. The body can be earthenware, creamware, ironstone, or bone china.

Swansea and Llanelly were the two areas in Wales where the Gaudy Welsh motif began. At least four firms in Newcastle and two Sunderland firms copied the design to their wares. However, it was the Staffordshire potteries at Stoke-on-Trent that produced the greatest amount of Gaudy Welsh.

Grape leaves, panels, cartouches, fences, and flower petals appear repeatedly in Gaudy Welsh designs and reflect the Oriental influence. Many patterns have names indicative of the design, e. g., "Tulip," "Sun Flower," 'Grape," or "Oyster," while other names are more fanciful and bear little resemblance to the decorative motif. True Gaudy Welsh has the cobalt portion of the design under the glaze and the additional enamel colors including the lusters over the glaze. In addition to the bold colorations of cobalt, orange, and luster decorations, pieces can be found with shades of green and yellow highlights added. As many as 300 designs have been identified.

Tea cups and saucers were made more than any other forms. Most Gaudy Welsh designs are painted on the inside of the cups. Tea sets, jugs, bowls, and miniatures were produced in smaller quantities.

Much of the Gaudy Welsh is unmarked. Design and techniques allow some pieces to be traced to specific companies.

References: John A. Shuman, III, *The Collector's Encyclopedia of Gaudy Dutch & Welsh*, Collector Books, 1990; Howard Y. Williams, *Gaudy Welsh China*, Wallace-Homestead, 1978.

Museums: Royal Institution of South Wales, Swansea, Wales; St. Fagen's Welsh Folk Museum, near Cardiff, Wales; Welsh National Museum, Cardiff, Wales.

REPRODUCTION ALERT: Gaudy Welsh has been reproduced during this century by several Staffordshire potteries. The most prolific was Charles Allerton & Sons (1859–1942) who specialized in jugs in the "oyster" pattern. The orange-red pigment, often streaked and uneven, is the sign of a reproduction.

Biscuit Plate, 9¾" H-H, "Tulip" pattern	60.00
Bowl	
6" d, "Oyster" pattern, unmarked	30.00
6¼" d, "Tulip" pattern	85.00
Childrens Tea Service, "Wagon Wheel" pattern, teapot, creamer, sugar bowl, 6 place settings	900.00
Cockle Dish, 4½" d, "Grape" pattern, mid 1800s	35.00
Compote, 8⅛" d, Ftd, "Aberystwyth" pattern, blue, burnt orange, green, and luster	375.00
Creamer, 3¼" h, central pink flower with blue and green floral garland	85.00
Cup and Saucer	
"Buckle" pattern	85.00
"Drape" pattern	75.00
Ftd, "Japan" pattern	75.00
"Grape" pattern	45.00
"Honeysuckle" pattern, unmarked (A)	100.00
"Japan" pattern	85.00
"Oyster" pattern, unmarked	35.00
"Sunflower" pattern	65.00
"Tulip" pattern, unmarked	57.50
Egg Cup, 2½" h, "Tulip" pattern, c1840	145.00
Jug	
2¼" h, "Oyster" pattern, c1800	75.00
5" h, "Grape" pattern, mid 1800s	125.00
Mug	
2" h, "Grape" pattern, c1840	145.00
2½" h, "Chinoiserie" pattern, c1840	95.00

Mug, 3½" h, "Grape" pattern, unmkd, $170.00

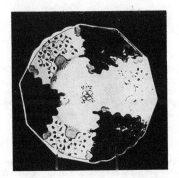

Plate, 8¾" d, "Tulip" pattern, unmkd, $155.00

3¼" h, "Grape IV" pattern, c1840s	150.00
4⅛" h, "Oyster" pattern	225.00
Pitcher	
3" h, "Sunflower" pattern, c1840	115.00
3⅞" h, "Grape" pattern (A)	90.00
4" h, "Oyster" pattern, unmarked	45.00
4¼" h, "Anglesey" pattern, unmarked (A)	90.00
5" h, "Oyster" pattern	175.00
5½" h, "Sunflower" pattern, Allertons (A)	66.00
6" h, "Sunflower" pattern, c1840	295.00
7" h, "Strawberry" pattern, repaired	75.00
7½" h, "Hanging Basket" pattern, early to mid 1800s, small crack	225.00
Pitcher and Bowl, Miniature, "Geometric" pattern, c1840	275.00
Plate	
7" d, "Oyster" pattern, unmarked	18.00
8½" d, "Grape" pattern	55.00
8¾" d, "Flower Basket" pattern	65.00
9" d	
"Oyster" pattern, unmarked	25.00
"Urn" pattern, c1840	80.00
10" d, "Oyster" pattern, "Allerton" mark	65.00
Teapot, 7¼" h, "Flower Basket" pattern	325.00
Waste Bowl	
5¼" d, "Columbine" pattern	85.00
6⅜" d, "Oyster" pattern (A)	225.00
Water Jug, 10½" h, "War Bonnet" pattern (A)	302.00

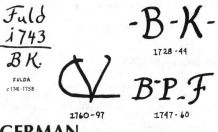

GERMAN FACTORIES—MAJOR

History: Many small, but highly important factories were established in the German provinces during the last half of the 18th century. Some were started by princes, but the majority were private commercial enterprises.

ANSBACH
Hesse, 1758–1860

Under the patronage of Hohenzollern Margrave Alexander of Brandenburg and with the help of workers from Meissen, this porcelain factory was established in 1758 in connection with an old faience works. In 1762 the firm moved to a hunting castle at Bruckberg. Fine pieces were made during the Rococo period, c1775. The factory was sold to private interests in 1807 and continued to make a variety of wares until 1860.

Wares imitated those made at Berlin, Meissen, and Nymphenburg. Exotic groups and figures, white and painted decorative and utilitarian wares, especially coffeepots, souvenir plates, monogrammed cups and saucers, and silhouette medallions were made. The principal mark in the c1760 to 1785 period was an "A" of varying sizes and shapes.

BAYREUTH
Bavaria, Germany
1899–1920

Siegmund Paul Meyer's factory produced utilitarian and hotel porcelains. The firm changed its name to First Bayreuth Porcelain Factory in 1920, continuing to make oven-proof pots and coffee machines.

FULDA
Hesse, 1765–1790

This factory was established for the Prince-Bishop of Fulda in 1765. The predominant decorative style was from the late rococo period. The products resembled those manufactured at Frankenthal. The main subjects of the figures were shepherds, children, ladies, cavaliers, and comedians positioned on Rococo trellises. The factory mark in underglaze blue was a double "F" with or without a crown. A few pieces were marked with a cross.

GOTHA
1757–1782

Wilhemn von Rotberg established this factory in 1757. His cream colored paste had a translucent glaze. Products included coffee sets, tea sets, and decorative porcelain figures. At first, the Rococo style was predominant. Later the Louis XVI and Neo-classical styles were used. Underglaze blue marks were first an "R" and then "R-g" and "G." The factory survived until 1782.

KASSEL
Hesse, 1766–1788

Friedrich II founded the factory. It made attractive tablewares with underglaze blue decoration and some simple figures. The mark was a lion or "HC" in underglaze blue.

KLOSTER VEILSDORF
1760 to Present

The factory was established in 1760 under the patronage of Friedrich Wilhelm Eugen. Tablewares and decorative porcelains, coffee sets, tea sets, and figures were made. The typical decorations were large freely painted purple, red, and yellow flowers evolving from thread-like stems. The underglaze blue monogram "CV" was used, occasionally supplemented with a coat of arms. After 1799, the mark became a three leaf clover.

LIMBACH
1772 to Present

Gotthelf Greiner established this factory in 1772. Porcelains were decorated primarily in blue and purple tones. Figures were rustic subjects and small town people. The marks "LB" or crossed "L's were applied on the glaze in red, purple, or black. About 1787 an underglaze blue clover leaf mark was used. Later clover leaf marks were purple, black, or red.

Greiner and his five sons acquired other factories such as Grossbreitenbach in 1782 and Kloster Veilsdorf in 1791. From 1797 to 1850 G. Greiner's Sons made utilitarian and decorative porcelains and figures.

THURINGIAN FACTORIES
From 1757

Nine hard paste porcelain factories were established in the Thuringian region. The three main ones were Gotha, Kloster Veilsdorf, and Volkstedt-Rudolstat. (see Volkstedt)

WALLENDORF
1764–1833

Johann W. Hammann established this factory in 1764. The first products had Rococo style decoration. Later dinner services were made in formal styles. Pastoral and street scenes in monotones of purple, brown, black, and gray tones featured figures of rural characters. The factory's mark was underglaze blue "W's. In 1833 the factory was sold to Hutschenreuther, Kampfe, and Heubach.

Reference: George W. Ware, *German & Austrian Porcelain*, Crown, Inc., 1963.

Museums: Bayeriches Nationalmuseum, Munich, Germany; Gardiner Museum of Ceramic Art, Toronto, Canada; Museum fur Kunst und Gewerbe, Hamburg, Germany; Schloss Museum, Berlin, Germany; Victoria & Albert Museum, London, England.

Tankard, Bayreuth, 5" h, sponged manganese trees, c1745, (A) $500.00

Bowl, Frankfort, 6½" h, continuous chinoiserie scene of figures in mountainous landscape, blue painted, restored, c1700, (A) $1625.00

ANSBACH

Chocolate Pot, Cov, 4⅞" h, cylindrical body, front with multicolored rooster and gray fowl flanking small trough amidst brown rocks on yellow and brown plateau before flowering plant, gilt edged spout molded with lady's mask, reverse with gold and puce trimmed scroll handle, two small floral sprigs, puce and green floal sprig knob, gilt rim and foot, 1780–85, unmarked (A) 4125.00

Coffee Pot, 6⅝" h, baluster shape, painted fruit arrangement with walnuts, flowers, and scattered sprigs, Dutch decorated (A) 925.00

Cup, painted village landscape with mountains in ground, flanked by flower sprigs, scrolling handle, painted "A" mark (A) 345.00

Cup and Saucer, porcelain, vignette of colorful garden bird perched in branches of tree among scattered flowers, c1770, underglaze "blue eagle and A" mark (A) 1200.00

Figure
4½" h, porcelain, gallant leaning on staff holding nosegay of flowers, turquoise lined hat, flowered yellow ground coat lined in purple, checked waist coat, orange breeches, staff restored, c1775, incised "3" (A) 1600.00

5½" h, porcelain, allegorical putto as "Smell," standing in drapery, holding flower, natural skin tones, brown hair, flat sq base, c1775, incised "S * 2" marks (A) 765.00

Jug, 14¼" h, ovoid body, faience, ring turned neck, decorated in blue on pale blue glaze with small birds perched on floral sprgs amidst further sprigs, clusters of dots, diamond band border, braided handle with blue herringbone dashes, hinged pewter cov, 1730–50 (A) 5225.00

Teacup and Saucer, shades of brown, green, blue, iron-red, yellow, and puce, front of cup with ruins of distant church and houses in hilly river landscape, center of saucer with fisherman seated on rock near two men in skiff on river with cottages and church on opposite bank, small floral sprigs beneath gilt edged rim, loop handle with gilt husks and dots, c1770, underglaze "blue A, black 5, cup imp 2, saucer incised 5" marks (A) 1320.00

Vase, 7" h, bulbous shape, faience, blue painted chinoiserie figures and pavilions in continuous stylized landscape, c1770 . . . . 435.00

Vase, Cov
8" h, baluster shape, faience, blue, iron-red, and gilt panels of pagoda and rockwork in oriental garden, knob missing, c1730 . . . . . 695.00
15⅜" h, blue and red panels of chinoisere landscapes, covs molded with fruit and scrolling knobs, c1730, pr (A) 2953.00

BAYREUTH

Dish, Faience
11¾" d, two blue birds perched on jardinaire of fruit in landscape, scrollwork and foliage border, blue-tinted ground, 2nd quarter 18th C, "blue i" (A) 984.00
12" d, fluted, blue pr of birds perched on rim of fruit bowl within Chinese style scale, feather, and foliate borders, haircracks, c1755, "blue B.P." (A) 1148.00

Tankard
6⅝" h, yellow, blue, and green stylized bush and flowers, two manganese-sponged trees, strap handle striped in blue, cracked, mid 18th C (A) 280.00
9¼" h, faience, chinoiserie man wearing green hat, yellow buttoned and belted blue costume, smoking pipe, standing on manganese, yellow, green, and blue glassy plateau between blue sponged trees, rims with blue bands, broad handle striped in blue, hinged pewter cov initialed "IA" and pewter footrim, late 18th C (A) 990.00
9⅞" h, Saint George fighting the dragon in hilly landscape flanked by two palm trees, pewter cov incised "F.G.S. 1806," knobbed thumb piece, c1760 (A) 1309.00

Teabowl and Saucer, ribbed body, dark brown glaze, c1730–40 . . . . 460.00

FRANKFORT

Bowl, 6½" h, bell shape, faience, blue continuous chinoiserie scene of figures in mountainous landscape, restored, c1700 (A) 1627.00

Charger, Faience
15" d, blue central group of orientals in landscape with rockwork, alternating panels of chinoiserie figures in conversation and stylized chrysanthemums, restoration, early 18th C (A) 708.00
18⁹⁄₁₆" d, blue and white chinoiserie, center with beast leaping hedgerow before two seated and three standing Chinamen in stylized landscape, rim with panels of recumbent beast snarling at two Chinamen at top and bottom, three Chinamen in garden at sides alternating with four panels of flowerheads and scrolling foliage, 1680–1700 (A) 5775.00

Dish
8" d, center with yellow and blue painted stylized flowering plant, demi-florets on rim, c1700 . . . . 500.00
10" d, spirally lobed shape, faience, blue and manganese panels of figures in Chinese landscapes alternating with scrolling flowers, c1700 (A) 700.00
12⅛" d, center painted with Chinese man in stylized architectural setting, four panels of seated Orientals sitting on rocks with trees, c1680 . . . . 835.00
13¼" d, lobed, center with Oriental holding fan, chinoiseries in manganese and yellow 800.00
13½" d, blue painted with doe and stag standing in Chinese garden, four Chinese men sitting on rocks around border with stylized trees, c1680 (A) 1710.00
15½" d, faience, blue bushes of lotus and peonies encircled by border of birds perched in flower sprays on wide rim, underside with crosses and circles, c1680 (A) 3179.00

Jug, 6³⁄₈" h, pear-shaped body, faience, blue and manganese large baroque flowers, front with carnation flanked by spray of anemones and peonies, birds in flight, blue and manganese brush strokes, twisted handle, silver-gilt cov embossed with foliage, dog-tooth footrim, hairlines, c1690, maker's mark in heart-shaped shield (A)..............................**14025.00**

Plate, 13¹⁄₂" d, molded lobed body, faience, central boss and border painted with Chinese figures in yellow and blue, c1700.......... **1250.00**

Salt, 4¹⁄₄" h, oct body, faience, molded with flowerhead well, blue continuous chinoiserie landscape, boy seated among rocks on one side, four stub feet, c1710 (A)............. **1440.00**

Vase, Faience

8¹⁄₄" h, squat baluster form, blue Chinese style with birds on rocks and in flight amongst lush dotted foliage, haircracks, c1700 (A)............................ **1148.00**

9⁷⁄₈" h, manganese and blue figures, recumbent horse in stylized landscapes in Chinese style, sloping shoulders, foliate borders, c1700 (A)............................ **2559.00**

14" h, baluster form, blue and white oriental figures in rocky garden terraces with coconut trees and exotic plants, scrollwork and stiff leaf borders, late 17th C (A)......... **3643.00**

FULDA

Coffee Pot, 6¹⁄₈" h, pear shape, enamel painted travelers in land and riverscapes with houses and church, triple scroll handle, brown accented scroll molded spout, domed cov with artichoke finial, c1767 (A)................ **7733.00**

Cup and Saucer, painted scene of river landscape on cup, two fishermen in boat near large building on saucer in green, blue, brown, gray, tan, and iron-red, c1780, "blue X and FF" marks (A).............................. **2420.00**

Figure

5¹¹⁄₁₆" h, young savoyard wearing black hat with yellow ribbon, tattered brown coat, olive green breeches, black shoes, gray box strapped to back, holding brown stick, on tree stump, grassy mound base, two applied leaf clusters, repaired, c1780, underglaze "blue crowned FF" mark (A)............ **4400.00**

5¹³⁄₁₆" h, vintager as young man in black hat with yellow and iron-red plumes and blue ribbon, white jabot, green jacket tied with sash, puce breeches, standing beside brown banded white container filled with green and purple grapes, scroll edged mound base with maroon trim, c1770, modeled by Georg Ludwig Bartholome, underglaze "blue X" mark (A)...................... **7700.00**

6⁹⁄₁₆" h, "The Sleeping Shepherd," young shepherd in green hat with yellow ribbon, white jacket with blue, puce, iron-red, yellow, and green floral clusters, puce breeches, napping against mottled brown, olive, and lavender tree, yellow horn on lap, brown spotted cream lamb, female companion in white blouse, green bodice, white skirt with colorful floral clusters, kneeling beside shepherd, applied green leaf clus-

ters, mottled green, brown, and lavender rocky mound base, chips, branch reglued, c1780, modeled by Georg Ludwig Bartholome, underglaze "blue crowned FF" mark (A)............................**37,400.00**

10³⁄₈" h, "The Apple Pickers," youth in black hat, pink jacket, yellow breeches, standing in brown apple tree, handing fruit to lady companion in black hat and ruff, puce dress and apron, another youth in black hairbow, white-lined iron-red jacket, green waistcoat and breeches, grassy mound base edged at front with yellow, puce, iron-red, and gray marbleized rocks, repaired, c1778, modeled by Wenzel Neu, underglaze "blue X" mark (A)............................**22,000.00**

Salt, 3³⁄₄" h, rococo shape, bunch of flowers and scattered sprigs, puce accents, four scroll feet, c1780, "blue crowned FF" mark (A)................................... **1415.00**

Spoon Tray, 6¹³⁄₁₆" l, puce, iron-red, yellow, blue, and green bouquet of flowers in gilt oval with berried laurel, puce bowknot and three small gilt floral sprigs in puce, blue, and green flowering vine border, gilt edged rim, c1785, "blue crowned FF" marks (A)............. **1100.00**

Teapot, 5¹⁄₂" h, globular, painted roses and tulips in ribbon and laurel swag medallion on each side, pinks and forget-me-nots on shoulder and cov, pine cone finial, dbl scroll handle, painted animal spout, c1785, "blue crowned FF" mark (A)............................ **2225.00**

GERA

Oval Stand, 11⁵⁄₈" l, reticulated, center in rose, orange, blue, yellow, and green floral bouquet, pierced basketwork rim with yellow centered blue forget-me-nots and green leaves with brown edge, 1790–1800, underglaze "blue G, iron-red 42" marks (A)................... **275.00**

GOTHA

Cabaret Set, tray, coffee pot, cov milk jug, cov sucrier, 2 coffee cans, panels of figures in landscapes framed with gilt line borders and foliage, "blue R" marks, 8 pcs (A)............. **1350.00**

Plate, 11³⁄₄" d, painted with view of Gotha or Reinhardsbrunn between scroll molded gilded border, c1880, "red PORZELLAN MANUFACTUR GOTHA," named in script marks, pr (A)..................................... **950.00**

KASSEL

Tea and Coffee Service, teapot, cov and stand, coffee pot, cov hot water jug, cov tea caddy, cov sugar bowl, cov circ tureen, 11 large teabowls and saucers, 3 small teabowls and saucers, purple vignette of exotic birds in branches on trees, within purple border of entwined laurel and foliate bands, gilt rims, broken scroll handles, flower knobs, some restoration, one bowl cracked, c1770, underglaze "blue ranpant lion, incised L1, L2 and a1," 41 pcs (A)................................**13,500.00**

Kloster Veilsdorf

Basket, 11" l, oval, molded sides, painted fruit and flowers on int and ext, pierced border, entwined branch handles with flower terminals, repaired and damaged, c1770–75, "blue CV" mark, pr (A)....................... 2430.00

Figure

3½" h, fish setter seated on tub leaning on staff, floppy brown hat, green jacket, white breeches, barrel of fish and tankard of ale at feet, brown wash base, staff restored, c1770, modeled by Pfrnger jun (A) 1531.00

3⅝" h, Dutch peasants, each in black hats and shoes, one with turquoise jacket, tan belt and apron, lavender breeches, gray sheath of knives, holding gray jug, seated on brown wood chair, other in yellow-lined tan jacket, light brown breeches, seated on overturned white bucket bound in gray, 1769–75, modeled by Ludwig Daniel Heyd, unmarked (A)........................ 3850.00

4⅝" h, "Summer," young man in yellow hat, puce striped jacket and breeches, caressing girl seated on stack of corn stalks, white skirt with iron-red floral border, yellow top, puce bow-tied ribbon in hair, scroll molded base, c1770 .... 1100.00

4⅞" h, putto as Mars in iron-red lined gray helmet, white quiver of arrows on puce strap, russet drapery, iron-red edged gray shield, gray cannonball, reglued, c1769 (A) 770.00

5⅛" h

Sultana wearing jeweled linen head dress, ermine lined green cloak, lilac and gilt scrolled robe, purple underskirt, hand restored, c1770, modeled by F.W.E. Doll, incised "Kaiserin" (A)................ 1722.00

Turk in fur lined iron-red and puce patterned robe, turban on head, one hand resting on hip, restored, 1770–75, inscribed "black Bostangi Bachi" on base (A) 740.00

5¼" h, sultan with jeweled turban and belt, ermine lined green cloak, gilt scrolled robe, head restored, c1770, modeled by F.W.E. Doll (A) 1627.00

Sugar Bowl, Cov, 3⅞" h, sides painted with chinoiseries of old man and boy with bird or dancing Oriental, cov with flying dragon, pear knob, bowl restruck, c1770, "blue CV" mark (A)..................................... 780.00

Tea and Coffee Service, coffee, pot, teapot, cov milk jug, cov sugar bowl, tea caddy, 4 coffee cups, 3 tea cups, 8 saucers, bright earth tone enamels, ducks, turkeys, and chickens, scroll molded, restored, c1770, underglaze "blue CV" mark, 24 pcs (A)................... 30,800.00

LIMBACH

Figure

4¾" h, muscial couple, gentleman standing to sing from sheet music, companion sits on cabriole chair playing lute, puce rococo molded flat base, restored, c1775 (A) 1900.00

5³⁄₁₆" h, man with dish of flowers in white cravat, green lined coat and waistcoat, iron-red breeches, dish of yellow centered iron-red and puce flowers and green leaves, mauve and gray mottled tree stump, green mound base with scrolls, chips, 1780–85 (A)................................... 770.00

5½" h, gallant, puce cloak, flowered waistcoat, striped breeches, hatful of flowers, puce scrolled base, c1775 (A) 984.00

5¾" h, Autumn modeled as standing man in puce edged frock coat, checkered breeches, flat hat with iron-red rim, long gray pigtail with black ribbon, holding cluster of grapes, puce accented scroll-molded base, c1780 (A)...................... 2024.00

NUREMBERG

Ewer, 10¾" h, faience, front and reverse with panel painted with stylized buildings above borders of dashed triangles, scallops on lower body and foot, horiz reeded neck, gray monochrome with dots, pinwheels, and leaf scrolls, handle formed as braided loop, pewter foot, pewter cov, 1730–50, black mark (A) 3575.00

RAUENSTEIN

Coffee Pot, 4⁷⁄₁₆" h, cylindrical, colorful equestrian soldiers in hilly river landscape on either side, black edged oval bordered in gilt floral sprays, ribbon tied laurel boughs, shoulder with yellow scroll edged border of rose scalework below gilt band, spout and angular handle edged in rose, cov missing, 1790–1800, "rose R and incised 3" marks (A).......... 275.00

WALLENDORF

Coffee Service, coffee pot, 8⅝" h, cov cream jug, cov sugar bowl, 12 cups and saucers, ribbed bodies, gold "G.A.C." in puce medallion with floral garlands, scattered flower sprigs, repairs, c1790, "blue W" marks (A).. 4415.00

Cup and Saucer, painted flower decorated urn in landscape, scattered gilt flower sprigs, gilt rims, c1790, "blue X'd swords and star" mark (A)...................................... 850.00

Figure, 5⅛" h, doctor in high wig, puce coat, flowered waistcoat, red breeches, outstretched hand, purple scrolled base, c1775 (A)...................................... 984.00

Tureen, Cov, Stand, 8" h, modeled as cabbage with overlapping leaves in light green and edged and ribbed in gold, center with shades of rose, iron-red, blue, green, turquoise, and gold with spray of tulips and other flowers, 1785–1800, underglaze "blue X'd swords, star, and incised 1" marks (A)............. 5500.00

WURZBURG

Figure, 6⅞" h, pensive man, white, curly hair, hat with gilt dentil border beneath brim, long beard, fur lined and gilt sprigged cloak, standing cross legged beside gnarled tree stump, rocky mound base molded with gilt scrollwork, 1775–80 (A)...................... 4950.00

1907   1914   1895

GERMANY—GENERAL

Pottery
15th Century to Present

History: Some of the earliest forms of German decorative pottery were made by the Hafner or stove-makers. The stove tiles of the 15th century were covered with a green lead glaze. Later 16th century stoves contained tiles of yellow, brown, and white clays or with tin-glaze over red clay bodies. Hafner wares also include large vessels or jugs made in Nuremberg.

In 1712 Marx and Hemman first made tin-glazed earthenwares. They continued in a series of partnerships until 1840. Most of the wares were decorated in blue with Baroque style scrolls, foliage, or strapwork. Subjects encompassed landscapes, heraldic shields, and biblical or mythological scenes.

Hamburg faience falls in the period of the second quarter of the 17th century. Pear shaped jugs decorated with a coat-of-arms in a blue motif were best known.

The most prolific center of German faience was at Hanau, near Frankfort-am-Main, from 1661 until 1806. The wares imitated Delftware. Many Chinese forms were copied. At first only blue decoration was used. By the early 18th century wares were decorated with landscapes and biblical scenes in a variety of colors. Naturalistic flowers in enamel colors dominated the mid-18th century wares.

Ansbach, Bayreuth, Cassel, Erfurt, Frankfort-am-Main, Proskau, and Schrezheim were other areas where faience factories were established.

Porcelain
16th Century to Present

History: In Germany there were many small principalities which competed with each other in establishing porcelain factories. Each developed an individual style. There was no royal monopoly in Germany as there was in France since there was no unified Germany.

In addition to the major German factories of Berlin, Frankenthal, Furstenberg, Hochst, Ludwigsburg, and Meissen, at least twenty minor manufactories were established in the German provinces during the last half of the 18th century. Some of these include Ansbach, Fulda, Gera, Gotha, Grossbreitenbach, Gutenbrunn, Ilmenau, Kassel, Kelsterbach, Kloster Veilsdorf, Limbach, Ottweiler, Rauenstein, Volkstedt, and Wallendorf.

Though some of these factories were established by princes, most were formulated as private commercial enterprises to make wares that could be sold competitively. For the most part, these wares copied works of the major German factories, such as Frankenthal and Meissen, etc.

The majority of the minor factories were able to continue operation despite changes in ownership, economic disruptions, and competition from larger firms, especially those established in the 19th and 20th centuries that were close to the source of raw materials.

Independent painters developed soon after the establishment of the Meissen factory about 1720. Porcelains painted by these independent decorators in their homes or studios are known as Hausmalerei. The painters are designated as Hausmaler. Hausmalers were experienced painters of faience and other ceramics. The large porcelain factories feared their competition. Hausmalers obtained Meissen and Veinna blanks and painted them as they wished. Ignaz Bottengruber of Breslau was best known of the independent decorators. Hausmalers were active for about forty years during the mid-18th century.

A smaller group of factories were in operation during the last half of the 18th century. These included Baden-Baden, Blankenhain, Eisenberg, Ellwangen, Hanau, Hoxter, Schney, and Tettau. Only Tettau still operates today.

Germany was in the forefront of the hard paste porcelain industry. Many new factories, making high quality utilitarian and decorative porcelains, were established during the 19th and 20th centuries. Most of these 19th and 20th century factories, approximately two hundred of them, are concentrated near the source of porcelain's raw materials, i. e., the central and eastern regions of Germany, (mainly North Bavaria, Thuringia, Saxony, and Silesia). Among the dominant factories are Sitzendorf, Rosenthal, Schumann, Hutschenreuther, and Heinrich. Factories located at Altwasser, Passau, Plaue, Potschappel, Rudolstadt, and Selb concentrate on the production of utilitarian and decorative porcelains.

Reference: William B. Honey, *German Porcelain*, Faber & Faber, 1947.

Museums: Arts & Crafts Museum, Prague, Czechoslovakia; Bayerishes Nationalmuseum, Munich, Germany; Kunstgewerbemuseum, Berlin, Germany; Metropolitan Museum of Art, New York, NY; Museum fur Kunst und Gewerbe, Hamburg, Germany.

Additional Listings: Bavaria, Bohemia, Carlsbad, C.T. Germany, Dresden, Frankenthal, Furstenberg, Heubach, Hochst, Hutschenreuther, KPM, Ludwigsburg, Major German Factories, Meissen, Nymphenburg, Rosenthal, Royal Bayreuth, Royal Dux, Rudolstadt, Schlegelmilch, Sitzendorf, Volkstedt.

Basket, 3″ w, 3″ h, porcelain, hp red roses on int, applied flowers on sides and handle, "Made in Germany" mark.......................... **10.00**
Basket Set, 7″ d, white woven basket with applied pink and yellow roses, small blue flowers on rim, gilt scalloped edge, six smaller baskets, 3¼″ d, three with blue flowers, three with multicolored flowers, 1875, Schierholtz mark **875.00**
Biscuit Jar, 6″ h, violets design, figural lady's head handles **75.00**
Bowl
    6¼″ d, five Kewpies, one standing on ladder looking out window, sgd "Rose O'Neill Germany".......................... **135.00**
    7″ d, swans on blue ground, three feet..... **33.00**
    8¼″ d, large rose in center, scattered roses on int, gold rim **40.00**
    9″ d
        Large pink, yellow, and rust roses with hp gold, shadow maple leaves, pearlized

Candy Dish, 4½" h, applied pink and yellow roses, green leaves, painted floral int, gold trim, white ground, "blue shield and 3 leaves" mark, C.G. Schierholz and Sons, $275.00

Figure, 8½" h, 7½" l, pink, white, turquoise, and lavender, gilt trim, "blue X'd swords" mark, (A) $1050.00

Vase, 15½" h, pink and white roses, yellow buttercups, purple asters, gold trim, "blue X'd swords" mark, (A) $550.00

ground, beaded and scrollwork border (A) 10.00
Multicolored nasturtium center, olive leaf luster band, "3 Crowns China, Germany" mark............................... 22.00
Small pink roses on int and ext, pearlized irid ground, three feet, c1900, Silesia (A) 90.00
9¼" d, multicolored parrots in center 65.00
10" d
Hp poppies in center, gold border with black scrolling, "3 Crown Germany" mark (A) 40.00
Multicolored small florals in center, four white side panels, wide dark green border with heavy gold accents, c1890 (A) 23.00
Red, pink, and white roses with green leaves, sponged and spattered gold, scalloped rim with scroll relief 26.00
Roses with gold trim on int, gold beaded rim 20.00
10½" d
Blue and white petunias and yellow rose on white center, light tan, green, and yellow rim with gilt accented relief scrollwork (A) 80.00
Chrysanthemums in colors on white center, hp iris in relief on turquoise and yellow rim, gold accents (A) 100.00
Flowers and ferns in relief, pink roses in center, gold accents (A).................. 45.00
Large roses in center, luster rims with gold tracery wreath of flowers 85.00
Multicolored small florals on white ground in center, hp daisies and molded stems on pearlized aqua ground, relief molded florals and leaves on ruffled rim, gold accents, c1880 (A) 45.00
Porcelain, yellow, white, pink, and apricot roses in center on light pink ground, relief of grapes, vines, and leaves, gold rim, sgd "Loubart' (A) 65.00
Yellow roses, green and red leaves in center, satin finish, gold emb ribbed border, emb flowers on ext, unmarked 145.00
11" d
Gooseberries and snowball florals and leaves, relief scrollwork on fuchsia irid rim (A) 25.00
Grapes design on pearlized green to lavender ground, relief of beads on notched rim, c1885 (A)...................... 25.00
Red, yellow, and pink roses in center, three borders of gold, cobalt, or fuchsia, relief scrollwork panels c1895 (A).......... 35.00
13" d, porcelain, large spray of fuchsia, purple, and pink florals, hp gold on rim with relief florals, white ground (A) 10.00
Box, Cov, 3¾" h, faience, recumbent pug form, fur with sponged manganese patches, blue and yellow collar, curled tail, snout in dark blue, base in blue with flower sprigs, one ear restored, mid 18th C, blue "K" mark (A).... 1683.00
Bread Tray, 13" H-H, blue and green floral center, reticulated border..................... 125.00
Cabinet Tray, 20¼" l, shaped oval form, scene of courting couple and shepherdess in wooded country landscape, border molded with scrolls, ormolu mtd, 2nd half 19th C (A) 3010.00
Cache Pot, 6½" h, porcelain, figural African man and woman beside basket with floral dec-

oration, naturalistic base, mid 19th C, pr
(A). **1100.00**

Cake Plate

9" d, lg chrysanthemums in center, light pearl
luster rim, scrolled open handles. **20.00**

10½" d, center with red and green currents,
strawberries, peaches and pears, green
leaves, c1900 (A) **10.00**

11" d, porcelain

Large white lilies and green leaves outlined
in gold, light green pearlized ground, re-
lief border, scalloped edge (A). **40.00**

Multicolored florals on light green to white
shaded ground, relief of leaves and scrollwork on border, gold rim, c1880 (A). . . **8.00**

Pink roses in center, six heart-shaped light
green florals on dark fuchsia and pink
ground, gold accents, six relief florals on
rim, c1880 (A) **20.00**

Candlestick, porcelain, magenta floral enamel-
ing, "blue X'd swords," pr (A) **150.00**

Celery Dish

12" l

Hp green holly leaves and red berries on
white ground, gold highlights, c1900 (A) **23.00**

Multicolored iris and yellow roses, gold
beaded edge (A). **35.00**

12½" l, relief of acorns and oak leaves and
blossoms, hp gold trim (A) **13.00**

Centerpiece

16¼" h, three cherubs linking hands around
a tree stump stem on a circ column, molded
with ram's heads, floral garlands, supporting
pierced basket studded with florets, late
19th C, "blue pseudo X'd swords," pr (A) **1309.00**

17" l, 9¼" h, porcelain, figural maiden sitting
between two shell bowls with Cupids, ap-
plied fruits and flowers **395.00**

Charger, 19" d, circ, blonde haired maiden
wearing blue and white dress with pink ties,
gold necklace, hair surmounted by laurel
leaves, gilt rim, c1890, sgd "H. Corner,"
framed (A). **3415.00**

Chocolate Pot

5½" h, scattered florals in polychrome, pur-
ple trim, three small feet, pear finial (A). . . **55.00**

9" h, lg yellow daisies design, "Germany"
mark. **25.00**

Clockcase, Stand, 20½" h, landscape panels
between florally encrusted borders, top surmounted by three putti amd bird on each side,
three scroll feet on clock, shaped rect base on
four scroll feet, encrusted with flowers, base
cracked, late 19th C, Carl Thieme (A). **2244.00**

Coffee Set, pot, creamer, sugar bowl, tray, cobalt
ground with gold swirl pattern, c1880, "HEN-
NEBERG" marks (A) **170.00**

Cologne Bottle, 8½" h, applied pink roses and
greenery, green luster ground, Elfinware **55.00**

Compote

16⅝" h, basket bowl with reticulated and
pierced sides and applied fruits and flowers,
tree form pedestal base, mtd with male and
female figures, restored, early 20th C,
Schierholz. **450.00**

21" h, oval bowl with reticulated flaring border, flower encrusted, supported by figural
Cupid on naturalistic base, multicolored . . **450.00**

Condiment Set, sugar, barley, coffee, 8½" h,
cloves, nutmeg, 4½" h, oil and vinegar, 10"

h, salt, 11" h, blue geometric designs on white
ground, salt box missing lid. **425.00**

Cream and Sugar, pink and white roses, peach
luster ground **30.00**

Dish

4" d, multicolored floral center, reticulated
border with orange luster **6.00**

5" d, hp, Old State House, New Haven, Conn,
beaded rim. **6.00**

8½" d, faience, tromp l'oeil design of group
of six walnuts in brown shades and black,
trail of forget-me-nots around center, rim
restored, c1770 (A). **1150.00**

10½" H-H, multicolored flowers in center,
magenta border with gold overlay, pierced
handles **15.00**

14½" d, faience, shaped form, flowering
branch of peonies and bird with flower in
beak on one end in manganese, yellow,
ochre, blue, and green, butterfly above, rose
sprig on rim, c1740 (A). **2431.00**

Dresser Set, 12" h, porcelain, two bath salt bottles, cov bowl, overall green leaf and pink
flowers, pointed stoppers, 3 pcs **125.00**

Dresser Tray, 11½" l, irreg shape, rose design,
green border, unmarked **28.00**

Figure

3" h, Snow Babies riding snow bear **165.00**

4"-5½" h, monkeys dressed in period band
uniforms with instruments, multicolored,
c1900, set of 12 . . . . **495.00**

4½" h, 4" l, porcelain, young girl in pink
hat, floral decorated trousers, arms around
goose and flower basket, imp "shield"
mark. **75.00**

5" h, Dalmation dog in colors, "Erphila, Ger-
many" mark **32.00**

5⅛" h

Girl in ribboned bonnet and spotted gray
apron, trail of flowers applied over shoulder, basket of flowers overturned at feet,
puce and gilt rococo scrolled base, re-
stored, c1770, Thuringia (A). **861.00**

White, lamb and ewe on rect base, c1900,
shield mark. **150.00**

5½" h, man with lute, woman and man in
cream and gold, baroque plinth, c1920,
"W.C.K. Germany" mark. **75.00**

6" h

Girl as spring standing with basket of flowers under arm, orange lined lime green
bonnet, yellow bodice, flowered skirt,
butter churn at feet, late 18th C, Thuringia
(A) **1722.00**

Lady with red bodice, green bustles, flowered dress, hands extended, man in lavender coat, white vest, striped breeches,
applied ruffles, gold trim, "blue X'd
swords" mark, pr **12.00**

6" l, porcelain, polar bear and baby seal
on stand, gray and white, "Germany"
mark. **65.00**

6¼" h, faience, seated spaniel with yellow-
belled collar, features and fur patches in
manganese, curled yellow tails, oval base
with blue scroll border, restored, 2nd quar-
ter 18th C, pr (A) **1028.00**

6¾" h, porcelain, standing male in period
clothes, seated maiden, lamb at feet, poly-
chrome, crown mark (A) **135.00**

7" h, porcelain, "Begger Lady" or "Musical Vagabond" in bright colors, pr........... **245.00**

8" h
Porcelain, "Beauty" in brown hair wearing a lavender floral toga with mallet and chisel, bust of man, tinted pedestal..... **275.00**

Young girl wearing winged hat, butterfly wings on back, carrying three floral baskets, blue mark **350.00**

10½" h, group of 18th C maiden playing lyre, man with guitar, two children dancing, multicolored **475.00**

12" h, porcelain group of Europa in blue drapery and the bull, gilt scalloped form decoration (A) **800.00**

13" h, young boy resting on broken branch of tree trunk, multicolored, hairline (A)..... **35.00**

14½" h, 11" l, young girl in green bodice and red dress holding fan in right hand, loop of pearls, c1907, Schierloz **750.00**

15" h, maiden giving flower to man on horseback or footman helping woman on horseback, multicolored, pr.................. **650.00**

20" l, porcelain, carriage group, maiden seated on floral decorated carriage drawn by four horses (A)..................... **660.00**

26½" h, Meissen style, vulture perched on large tree stump, wings in brown and black, gray neck with red, black, and yellow details around face, cracked, late 19th C (A) **3500.00**

Flower Holder
7" h, 5" l, boy with tassel cap, girl with Dutch bonnet, standing on rustic log with applied flowers and pink leaves, imp "shield" mark........................ **150.00**

8¼" h, nude lady with arms out holding lavender cape across back................. **40.00**

8¾" h, Art Deco style dancing nude woman, holding scarf, crackle ivory glaze......... **42.00**

Food Mold, 8½" l, turtle shape, blue and white (A).................................. **80.00**

Goblet, 5" h, beehive shaped bowl, putti allegorical of The Arts within billowing cloud panels, burnished gilt ground, stem with figures enacting allegorical scenes, gilt int and circ base, mid 19th C, imp "I and 4" with gilt leaf, pr (A) **1881.00**

Jar, 3½" h, applied fruit on lid, polychrome decoration, "crowned Germany" mark (A) **120.00**

Match Holder, 2¼" h, figural red devil's head, two black horns, pointed chin, striker on reverse.................................. **45.00**

Nodder, 3¼" h, black boy in white turban, red clothes, yellow flute, pierced head, cork in base **75.00**

Pitcher
6" h, figural baby chick, yellow with black trim................................... **45.00**

7½" h, tankard shape, foxhunters with horses and dogs in blue and gray, c1910, "WITTELSBACH, Germany" mark (A)..... **35.00**

Plaque
6" l, porcelain, Madonna della Sedia in muted palette, gilded wood frame, late 19th C, printed mark and "Firenze' (A) **903.00**

6¾" h, 5⅛" w, oval form, seated young boy with long hair, holding pipe, white shirt, burgundy waistcoat, leather breeches, late 19th C (A) **700.00**

8⅝" h, 5¾" w, "The Thread of Life," The

Three Fates, the young Clotho spinning the thread of life, accompanied by Lachtsis holding flowers and sprig of bay, aged Atropos holding shears to cut the thread, c1880, framed (A)..................... **3950.00**

9⅝" h, 5¾" w, porcelain, Psyche walking in lush green undergrowth, ray of light coming through trees in distance, framed, c1880 (A)........................... **5049.00**

12½" d
Porcelain, overall hp lilies in red, yellow, orange, and blue, green enameled rim, c1880 (A).......................... **10.00**

Pottery, six heart shape, six round reserves in multicolor florals, center panel of town "Zweisimmen" between mountains, porcelain insert on back with "S, Bourne" mark............................... **250.00**

13" d, river and mountain landscape scene in colors, fuchsia and gold border, c1890, sgd "DANILO' (A) **20.00**

13½" d, relief molded monks drinking beer at table, multicolored, "Mustershutz/JM/ 5231" mark **450.00**

14" d, pottery, Arab girl bust in high relief wearing scarf and necklace, buildings in tan and cream, green trees at top, brownleaf and branches in bottom half, "Musterschutz/JM(J. Maresch-1841)............ **350.00**

15" d, pottery, relief of woman dancing with tambourine and man playing mandolin or man buying fruit from woman at market, multicolored, gold and black borders, Musterschutz, pr......................... **295.00**

15" h, 10" l, young boy in white suit with lace collar, hat with white feathers, c1880, framed (A)...........................**10,246.00**

Plate
7" d, 3 Kewpies on branch, four smaller Kewpies around border, "Copyright Rose O'-Neill Wilson, KEWPIE, Germany" mark ... **75.00**

7½" d, green and white flowers, ivory ground, scalloped edge................. **62.00**

8" d, bone china, multicolored center scene of cabin in mountain with pine trees, border of shadowed oak leaves, "3 Crowns Germany" mark (A)....................... **25.00**

9½" d
Center portrait of dog, burgundy and gilt paneled border with animal scenes (A). **450.00**

Central tulip and flower sprigs around rim, c1780, Proskau, pr (A)............... **1250.00**

Gold "Give us this day our daily bread" in center, large red and white roses with green leaves, gold tracery leaves and stems on border, open handles, "Germany" mark........................ **24.00**

Head and shoulders portrait of young girl against burnished gilt ground, wide blue border, gilded scroll motifs, late 19th C, printed marks, pr (A) **1035.00**

"Meditation," center portrait of young woman, gilt curvilinear and floral decoration, green border, sgd "Wagner' (A)... **1600.00**

Silver shape, faience, lightly painted scattered flowering branches and insects, c1750, "manganese K" mark (A) **383.00**

"Solitude," center portrait of female, blue and gilt border with floral design, scalloped edge, sgd "Wagner' (A)........ **1600.00**

Vienna style, "Echo" dressed in red robe and sheer white cloak, hand cupped to ear, misty mountainous landscape, green paneled border with gilding, late 19th C, painted marks and script title (A) **1589.00**

Young woman in center, gilt flowering vine pattern in burgundy border, sgd "Wagner' (A) **1300.00**

Young woman with floral wreath in hair in center portrait, gilt curvilinear border, green ground, artist signed (A)........ **1300.00**

Waitress in red outfit carrying three steins, blue luster border with scrolling, "Altenburg China, Germany" mark **9.00**
9¾" d

Faience, scattered sprays of flowers and flying insects in turquoise, green, yellow, blue, and manganese, 1745–48, "blue A" painter's mark (A).................... **800.00**

Vienna style, "Louise" wearing Empire-style white dress tied with pink sash, blue cloak trimmed with ermine, hair tied with white scarf, gold tiara, blue and green ground with thistles and foliage, shell molded rim, late 19th C, painted shield and printed marks, script title (A) **1589.00**

10" H-H, hp bird, butterfly, and florals with thistle blooms, white ground, unmarked (A)..................................... **10.00**

10⅛" d, faience, rose sprig in center, pierced basketwork rim outlined in green and manganese, 1765–70, Kiel, pr (A)...........**14960.00**

11¼" d, 4 large roses and foliage, shaded brown rim, pierced for hanging **20.00**

11½" d, two ladies with wings on back, sitting on morning glories, flower and leaf border, openwork border **65.00**

12" d, 4 hp enameled floral panels on white ground, wide cobalt border, c1880, "blue X'd swords" mark (A).................... **80.00**

Powder Box, 4½" h, figural child in blue dress with dark blue trim, white blouse, blue bow in short brown hair, incised rabbits on skirt, ball in left hand **90.00**

Relish Set, 2 master bowls, 7" d, 12 salts, 4½" d, hp fruit design **70.00**

Scent Bottle, Pear shape
2⅞" h, two molded leaves, natural colors, gilt metal rim and stopper mts, restored, c1770 .... **880.00**

11" h, applied flowers, leaves, and buds in colors, flower finial, chips **250.00**

Snuff Box, Cov
3" l, cartouche form, bright enamels with scenes from life of Sarah and Abraham, cov with banishment of Hagar, sides with scarifice of Issac, int of lid with three angels announcing birth, int of base with flowers, insects and ornament in Chinese style, reeded silver mts, mid 18th C (A)............... **2837.00**

3⅛" l, porcelain, each piece with putti among clouds with puce lattice borders, int with half length portrait of young woman in wooded landscape, base with flying putto, gold mtd, c1755 (A)................... **7482.00**

Solitaire Set, pot, 5½" h, creamer, cov sugar bowl, cup and saucer, tray, 12" H-H, orange ground with black chain of leaves on white band, white luster ints, "S in house," Schoenau, Swaine & Co. mark **175.00**

Tankard
9½" h, faience, hunter in black tricorn hat, green jacket, yellow breeches, rifle strapped to manganese dog, blue plateau between green sponged trees, blue and manganese knolls, loop handle with manganese dashes, pewter mounted, cov with "C.F.D.," mid 18th C, Thuringia (A) **2090.00**

10¼" h, tin glazed blue and white sprig and bird decoration, crimped top, pewter base and hinged cov, hairline (A)...... **715.00**

Tazza, 8½" d, faience, blue with crowned armorial marriage bearing of Schmidburg of Bohemia and Wacker of Saxony, within border of stylized foliage and seeded panels, conical foot, c1740 (A) **1723.00**

Tea Caddy
4⅝" h, rect body, faience, molded in relief in Chinese style, blue flowering prunus branches on each side, two stylized florets on edges of shoulders, short screw neck, 18th C (A)............................. **550.00**

5" h, porcelain, polychrome loose bouquet on front and reverse, polychromed draped shoulder, "X'd swords and star" mark (A). **715.00**

Teapot, 9" h, figural cat in black, cream, and gray, tail handle, paw spout, "U.S. Zone Germany" mark **40.00**

Tea Service, teapot, creamer, sugar bowl, 2 cups and saucers, tray, 18¾" l, en grisaille landscapes of "Schloss Nymphenburg," blue and gilt trim (A) **605.00**

Tray
13¼" d, hp fuchsia, white, yellow, and green florals on light tan and cream ground, gold highlights, c1880 (A).................... **23.00**

13½" l, purple plums with green leaves in white oval, pink border with hp relief gold florals and edgework, c1870 (A)......... **13.00**

Tureen, Cov, 5⅝" h, with stand, duck form, faience, head turned back touching feathers in yellow and manganese, fixed stand with blue, green, manganese, yellow, and ochre flower sprigs, shaped rim, mid 18th C (A) **3100.00**

Urn
6" h, applied flowers and cherubs in colors, pr **150.00**

19" h, Meissen style decoration of rose cluster, dbl scroll handles, pedestal base with gilt banded highlights (A).................. **770.00**

Vase
4¼" h, pinched neck, high dbl handles, souvenir, hp medallion of Life Saving Station, South Haven, Mich., cobalt ground, "Made in Germany" mark **8.00**

7½" h, tapestry, country scene in blue shades **230.00**

9" h, pansies in shaded lavender, rose, light gold, and pale green, "Royal Vienna, Germany" mark **150.00**

9½" h, porcelain, young lady in pink with white bonnet, two sheep, man with rake, dark brown and gold ground........... **135.00**

13¾" h, curved shell supported by mermaid or triton, brown washed shell encrusted mound on baroque two cornered bases, applied with beared masks in blue and gilding, late 19th C, pr (A)..................... **700.00**

15½" h, baluster shape with applied climbing roses, restored, 19th C, pr **1000.00**

Vase, Cov, 14⅝" h, fluted body, baluster oct form, faience, peacocks in blue amongst flowering bushes, formal vertical borders, high domed cov, bud, knob, c1740, Berlin (A) ... **400.00**

Wall Bracket, 7⅛-8" h, earthenware, white throated brown stag's head with matte black antlers, black muzzle and eyes, pale turquoise lined ears, gilt edged cartouche form backplate pierced for hanging, supporting shaped sq shelf, late 19th C, pr (A) **2200.00**

Watering Can, 3⅛" h, 2½" d, 2 black cats with colored bows, one with cane, other with umbrella, "Bon Jour" on front, green trim ... **65.00**

Wine Cooler, 8" h, oval form, porcelain, continuous scene of Venus surrounded by putti in springtime ancient Greek landscape reserved on dark brown ground, molded foliate strapwork, pierced and flared gilded base, c1900, printed mark (A) **1215.00**

GINORI

1847 - 73

GINORI

DOCCIA
LATE 19ᵗʰ C.

Doccia, near Florence, Italy
1737 to Present

History: In 1737 the Ginori family established a factory to manufacture porcelain and earthenware at a villa in Doccia, a few miles from Florence. Marquis Carlo Ginori, the founder, operated the factory until 1757. Carlo Ginori's management is known as the "first period."

Stencil decorated dark blue plates, teapots, coffeepots, and cups were the earliest wares. Ginori produced many examples of snuff boxes, extremely popular in the 18th century, in a variety of shapes and decorations. Sculptures and large reliefs depicting mythological or religious subjects also were made.

In 1757 Lorenzo, his son, took over. This is the "second period." Lorenzo introduced an imitation Sevres blue ground, and strong use of colors. He continued making figurals in the Rococo style.

Anton Maria Fanciullacci served as director from 1791–1805, the "third period," changing the designs to reflect the Empire style. In 1792 the manufacture of creamware helped subsidize the production of porcelain.

Doccia was the only Italian pottery that survived and prospered during the 19th century. It remained in the control of the Ginori family. Around 1821 the Doccia factory acquired Capodimonte molds from the Naples factory and continued production. Ginori used the Old Naples mark on these examples.

Lorenzo Ginori II took charge in 1848. The firm started to make lithophanes, majolica, and egg-shell porcelains. A large number of pieces were decorated with urban scenes enclosed within a shield shaped reserve on a white ground in the classical style. The crowned "N" mark was used on some of the wares. Industrial ceramics for the electrical industry also were manufactured on a large scale.

In 1896 the firm incorporated with Societa Ceramica Richard in Milan to become Societa Ceramica Richard-Ginori. The Art Nouveau style was introduced. In addition to modern forms and decorations, some traditional motifs such as cockerels, narrative reliefs, and tulip motifs continued to be used.

Early Ginori porcelains were frequently not marked. During the Third Period, the "F" or "PF" incised marks appears. In the 19th century, "G', "Ginori', or a "N" crowned and impressed was used. The present mark is "Richard-Ginori" with a crown.

References: Arthur Lane, *Italian Porcelain*, Faber & Faber, 1954; Francesco Stazzi, *Italian Porcelain*, G.P. Putman's Sons, 1964.

Museums: Doccia Museum at Sesto Fiorentino, Florence, Italy; Fitzwilliam Museum, Cambridge, England; Metropolitan Museum of Art, New York; Victoria & Albert Museum, London, England.

Bottle, blue hp scenes on front and reverse of youth with damsel, gold trim, white ground, "crown and Richard Ginori" mark......... **18.00**

Bust, 2⅜" h, female with hair pinned up, green drapery over puce-lined blouse, bald-headed man with puce drapery on shoulders, supported on waisted circular plinth, c1770, Doccia, pr (A)......................... **525.00**

Cabaret Set, coffee pot, milk jug, two dbl handled cups and saucers, shaped rect tray, 15¼" l, relief molded classical figures in landscapes, c1850, imp "crowned N" marks, Doccia (A)............................. **2300.00**

Coffee Pot
9⅞" h, baluster shape, painted flower sprays on sides, scattered sprigs, loop handle, bird's head spout with scrolling bridge to body, Doccia (A)...................... **465.00**

10" h, pear shape, puce painted naturalistic wooded landscapes and buildings, spout and handle outlined in puce lines and dots, white tin glazed ground, c1780, Doccia .. **1200.00**

10½" h, baluster shape, circ reserves of ruins in gilt borders, elongated dolphin handle with gilt, c1800, Doccia................ **450.00**

Dish
11" l, oval, center painted with architectural view of Italian town, pierced border with blue ribbon, c1790, pr (A) **1290.00**

11⅛" l, oval, purple painted feathered trees and buildings in landscape vignette, gilt branch of grapes on side, rim with four small

Vase, 4¾" h, 7½" d, hp orange, purple, and magenta flowers, cream ground, green lower section, gilt trim, artist sgd, "red crowned Ginori" and "green Ginori" marks, $275.00

landscape vignettes, gilt borders, c1780, Doccia.................................. **750.00**

11⅝" d, silver shape, painted stylized tulips and flowers, sprays on rim, c1760, Doccia, pr **925.00**

15⅛" d, Chinese famille rose flowering peonies and wild cherry tree growing from stylized rocks, fungi on reverse, c1760, Doccia.............................. **1500.00**

Figure

3⅞" h, miniature bust, lady wearing black spotted yellow drapery suspended from gilt strap across shoulder, naked man with brown beard, each on waisted circ socle marbleized in rose, yellow, and blue, bombe shaped sq pedestal with molded rococo cartouches with iron-red, purple, yellow, and gold, 1765–70, Doccia, "rose 6," pr (A)............................ **3025.00**

5" h, bearded old man in yellow and brown drapery, c1760, Doccia (A)............. **1914.00**

5¼" h, Pulcinella, tall hat, white-frilled ochre jacket, striped pantaloons, basket over right arm, marbled sq base, c1760–70, Doccia (A)..................................... **2805.00**

Ice Cup, 3½" l to 3⅝" l, leaf shape, int in iron-red, puce, green, and yellow with floral spray, green enameled leaf molded ext, green twig handle, c1770, set of 12 (A) **1100.00**

Pickle Dish, 3½" l, leaf shape with stalk handle, center painted with flower sprays, Doccia, pr............................ **175.00**

Plate

8" d, multicolored poppies in center, red border... **8.00**

8¾" d, underglaze blue, iron-red and gilding with flowering branches and butterfly, cell border reserved with flower panels and rosettes, c1770, Doccia (A) **486.00**

9" d, Chinese Export style with ribbon tied spray of flowers within formal foliage border on milk white tin glazed ground, c1770, Doccia, pr (A) **536.00**

Salt, 5¼" h, modeled naked putto holding seashell on head, perched on scrolling blue and puce wave, repaired, c1775, pr............ **800.00**

Snuffbox, Cov, 3 1/16" l, "The Arts," allegorical classical figures in shades of purple, blue, green, yellow, brown, and iron-red, "Music," 'Painting," 'Sculpture," and "Architecture," ext rims with cobalt blue borders, cont gold mount, 1790–1800, Doccia (A)...........**11,000.00**

Sucrier, Cov, 3⅞" h, quatrelobed shape, painted flower sprays and sprigs, yellow rose finial **145.00**

Teabowl and Saucer

Meissen style, chinoiseries in landscapes with trees and house, gilt scrollwork accented with purple and iron-red, c1770, Doccia (A)............................ **485.00**

Quatrelobed piece, panels of elegant couples in Italianate landscapes against yellow ground, int with gilt borders, int of bowl with spray of Kakiemon style flowers, c1745, Doccia (A)............................. **4594.00**

Teapot, 5⅛" h, globular body, spray of flowers on each side, dbl scroll handle, spout and handle with gilt scrolls, cov with pagoda knob, hairline, 1770–80, Doccia (A)............. **300.00**

Tray, 12½" l, 9" w, hp poppies, artist sgd ... **55.00**

Tureen, Cov, 9¾" d, lobed, oval shape, enameled scattered flowers, entwined green and puce ribbons, dbl handles, c1770, Doccia .. **1295.00**

Vase

2⅝" h, miniature, shield shape, painted multicolored flowers with light blue border to sq foot, leaf scroll handles with female mask................................ **325.00**

8" h, peonies in green and white, ftd, sgd "Dants".............................. **160.00**

12¾" l, ovoid shape, majolica, painted on side with female nude figure holding shell, drapery about hips, body supported by looped and festooned cords with tasseled drops, reverse with cords and tassles, shades of beige, blue, and yellow against deep maroon sponged ground, c1927, underglaze "brown Gio Ponti/1927/Italia/ Ginori/1031, incised X" mark (A) **8250.00**

18⅞" h, ovoid form, majolica, underglaze rugged mountainous landscape with buildings and trees bordered by river, beneath giant olive trees at either side with intertwining branches adorned with ropework patterns, shell form handles, inscription at neck "A J. W Lieb-al culture di Leonardo-all' amico sincero dell'Italia," thick rolled rim decorated with rope patterns, shades of blue, green, brown, and yellow, underglaze Ginori marks (A) **3520.00**

Vase and Cov, 21" h, Venus riding on shell with attendants, foliate and stiff leaf borders, rams' mask handles, Capodimonte style, late 19th C, underglaze "blue N under coronet" mark (A) **1505.00**

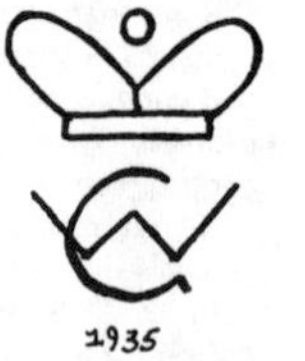

GOEBEL   1935

Rodental, Bavaria, Germany
1871 to Present

History: In 1871 Franz and William Goebel, father and son, applied for a permit to manufacture porcelain in the village of Oeslau near the city of Coburg. When Duke Ernst II of Saxe-Coburg intervened, the permit finally was granted in 1879. The firm, F. D. & W. Goebel Porcelain Works, began manufacturing dinner services, milk pitchers, beer steins, and egg cups.

When Franz died in 1909, William expanded the porcelain dinnerware and figurine business into an export-oriented concern. Max-Louis, William's son, took over in 1912 when William died. Max-Louis introduced many new porcelain figurine designs and added a ceramic figurine line as well. Frieda, wife of Max-Louis, Franz, son of Frieda and Max-Louis, and Dr. Eugene Stocke, Frieda's brother, assumed control when Max-Louis died in 1929.

Franz Goebel first saw Sister Maria Innocentia Hummel's sketches in 1934. In March 1935 the first "M. I.

Hummel" figure was made. These were an immediate success, especially in America.

During WWII the Goebel works concentrated on the manufacture of dinnerware for the domestic market. A few figurines were made. When the United States Military Government of Germany lifted the wartime embargo and gave permission for production and exportation of "M. I. Hummel" figurines and other objects in 1946, a rapid recovery followed by the firm.

When Franz died in 1969, the management of the company transferred to Wilhelm, his son, and Ulrich Stocke, Eugene's son. They continued expansion of the company and acquisition of other factories.

Today the Goebel factories manufacture high quality porcelain dinnerware for the home and export markets. In addition to the popular Hummel series, they manufacture figurine series that include Disney characters, birds, animals, and Friar Tuck monks. A collectors plate series also is made.

References: Eric Ehrmann, *Hummel,* Portfolio Press Corp., 1976; John F. Hotchkiss, *Hummel Art II,* Wallace Homestead, 1981; Thomas E. Hudgeons, III, ed., *The Official Price Guide to Hummel Figurines and Plates,*House of Collectibles, 1980; Carl F. Luckey, *Hummel Figurines and Plates,* 5th Edition, Books Americana, 1984; Robert L. Miller, *M. I. Hummel: The Golden Anniversary Album,* Galahad Books, 1989.

Collectors Clubs: Goebel Collectors' Club, 105 White Plains Road, Tarrytown, NY 10591. Membership: $17.50. *Insight,* quarterly newspaper; "Hummel" Collectors Club, P. O. Box 257, Yardley, PA 19067. Membership: $20.00. Quarterly newsletter on M. I. Hummel Figures. The "Hummel" Collectors Club is not affiliated with W. Goebel Porzellanfabrik.

Museum: Goebel Museum, Tarrytown, NY.

Beer Mug, 8" h, figural friar with toes showing   **250.00**

Creamer, Figural
2½" h, Friar Tuck in brown robe, stylized bee
mark..................................   **30.00**
4" h, Friar Tuck **35.00**
4½" h, musician **30.00**
5½" h, Friar Tuck **30.00**
Black boy with turban, red and blue clothes,
imp mark...........................   **59.00**
Clown head, blue with red hearts, imp mark   **59.00**

Egg Timer, Friar Tuck......................   **45.00**
Figure
2" h, cat in colors.......................   **10.00**
2¾" h, bird in olive green, black, brown,
cream, and blue......................   **35.00**
3" h
5½" l, Cinderella coach with two horses,
multicolored, c1934.................   **350.00**
Bathing girl seated on scalloped shell, dbl
crown mark **130.00**
Standing Bulldog in colors..............   **15.00**
3½" h
Long tailed Titmouse, white bisque, TMK5   **20.00**
Owl in colors........................   **25.00**
4½" h, 6" l, sitting Boxer dog in colors....   **65.00**
5" h
Seagull..............................   **35.00**
7" w, Goldfinch birds in colors, stylized bee
mark..............................   **75.00**
6½" h
Barn owl, marked **35.00**
Praying Madonna, #HM147, stylized bee
mark..............................   **22.00**
11½" h,
Madonna in blue gown and pink robe ...   **40.00**
Black poodle **8.00**
Jug
2½" h, figural friar in colors..............   **25.00**
4" h, figural cardinal in colors, stylized bee
mark...............................   **175.00**
Lemon Reamer, 4½" h, green and yellow body,
cream top, brown handle, crackle finish, registered 1927, imp mark, 2 pc **135.00**
Mug
1½" h, figural head of Great Dane dog in
brown shades, black trim..............   **45.00**
4" h, Friar Tuck figure **40.00**
5" h, Friar Tuck figure **75.00**
Mustard Pot, 3¾" h, figural friar in colors, stylized bee mark **75.00**
Pitcher
7½" h, figural clown **42.00**
8¼" h, Friar Tuck **92.00**
Salt and Pepper, 2¾" h,
Figural cardinals in colors, stylized bee marks   **250.00**
Figural Friars, #SB¹⁵³/₁, ...   **30.00**
Sugar Bowl, 4½" h, figural friar with toes showing in colors **35.00**
Vase, 8" h, figure of Japanese child with bamboo
stems, marked **95.00**

Pitcher, 4" h, brown robe, "bee and V Goebel" mark, $65.00

1845 - 1897   1927

GOLDSCHEIDER

**Vienna, Austria
1885 to Present**

History: Friedrich Goldscheider founded the Goldscheider Porcelain and Majolica Factory in 1885. Goldscheider's family owned a factory in Pilsen, Czechoslovakia, along with decorating shops in Vienna and Carlsbad. Decorative earthenwares and porcelains, faience, terra cotta, and figures were made.

Regina Goldscheider and Alois Goldscheider, her brother-in-law, ran the firm from 1897 until 1918. They made figures along with sculptured vases in the Art Nouveau style. Regina's sons, Walter and Marcel, took control in 1920 and adopted styles prevailing in Vienna during the 1920s.

The factories experienced several name changes both before and after World War I and II. Following Hitler's invasion of Austria, the family left and settled in Trenton, New Jersey, in the early 1940s. They established a factory in Trenton and made art objects and tablewares.

After World War II, Marcel Goldscheider established a pottery in Staffordshire, England, to manufacture bone china figures and earthenware. The company's mark was a stamp of Marcel's signature.

Figure
5¾" h, Madonna, cobalt wrap, green blouse,
    headpiece, and wings, black sq base **110.00**
6" h, 9" l, seated shepherd dog in colors,
    "Goldscheider, Wein" mark **165.00**
7" h, Madonna and child in colors, sgd "Pierre
    Fumers"............................   **75.00**
7½" h
    Art Deco style standing woman holding
        sides of black and white lace dress,
        Austria...........................   **225.00**
    Madonna and Child, Austria.............   **200.00**
19" h
    Bust of Arab man, terra cotta with poly-
        chromes, chips (A) **770.00**
    Gibson type girl seated on Greek chair, left
        hand on cheek, lyre in right hand, cloth
        draped on knee, imp "Friedrich Gold-
        scheider Wien" mark.................   **750.00**
Lamp, 23" h, pottery, three holders for lights in
    green, yellow, and brown checked trim, cream
    circle with Art Deco nude figure in center,
    artist signed, "Thomasch," marked **1500.00**
Wall Mask
11¼" h, Art Deco style woman's face with
    curly brown hair, red lips, aqua scarf **175.00**
    Terra cotta face, silver curls, marked........   **750.00**

Figure, 9" h, green dress, rose ribbon, tan base, "F.G. Wien" mark, $20.00

GOSS AND CRESTED WARE

W. H. GOSS
c1862

Stoke-On-Trent, England
1858–1930

History: William Henry Goss founded the Goss China Company in 1858 at Stoke-on-Trent. Goss began producing a fine grade parian which was used for figural groups, busts of famous people both past and present, pierced baskets, and a variety of other items. Terra cotta tobacco jars and wine vases decorated with transfers also were produced. Goss developed a method of imbedding colored glass into the parian body to make "jewelled" vases, patenting the technique in 1872. Fine tea services appeared in his catalog by 1880.

In 1883 Adolphus, William's son, joined the firm. William's aggressiveness helped launch the company into new and profitable fields. It was William who introduced crested china.

Victorian England had increased leisure time and great accessibility to the seacoast and resort areas. These vacation sites were perfect for the introduction of inexpensive souvenir items. Adolphus, much to the chagrin of William, produced and marketed the now famous white glazed souvenir pieces complete with enameled decorations and coats of arms of various towns and resorts. The technique was simple. A paper transfer was applied to the glazed body, and the colors hand painted in the design. These heraldic souvenirs were an instant success. Shops were established in the resort areas to sell Goss crested china. Other factories quickly imitated the Goss crested ware.

In 1893 Goss China began producing miniature full color buildings, duplicating every detail of the original buildings from which they were modeled. Expansion was necessary to meet the demands for the Goss products. Victor and Huntley, Adolphus's sons, became partners in 1900. Goss china even published its own journal, "Goss Records," to promote its products.

The company suffered during the Great Depression. Its assets were sold to Cauldon Potteries in 1929. Cauldon began the manufacture of figurines of young girls similar to the Royal Doulton figurines. Coalport China Co. purchased the rights to Goss in 1945; Ridgway and Adderly took control in 1954. The company currently is part of the Royal Doulton organization.

Other manufacturers of crested ware in England were: Arcadian, Carlton China, Grafton China, Savoy China, Shelley, and Willow Art. Gemma in Germany also made crested wares.

References: Sandy Andrews, *Crested China,* Milestone Publications, 1980; Sandy Andrews & Nicholas Pine, *1985 Price Guide to Crested China,* Milestone Publications, 1985; John Galpin, *Goss China,* 1972, published by author; John Magee, *Goss for Collectors - The Literature,* Milestone Publications; Nicholas Pine, *Goss China: Arms, Decorations & Their Values,* Milestone Publications, 1982, revised ed.; Nicholas Pine, *The Concise Encyclopedia & Price Guide To Goss China,* Milestone Publications, 1989.

Collectors Club: Goss Collectors Club, The Secretary, 4 Khasiaberry, Walnut Tree, Milton Keynes, MK77DP, England. Membership 18 pounds. Monthly newsletter; The Crested Circle, 42 Douglas Road, Tolworth Surbiton, Surrey KT6 7SA, England. Membership: 7 pounds. Bimonthly magazine, and *Crested Circle Annual Magazine*. This circle covers the products of W. H. Goss, Arcadian, Carlton, Grafton, Shelley, and Savoy factories and commemoratives from the different factories.

Collecting Hints: Early Goss pieces tend to be heavier and less perfectly rounded than later pieces, gilding tends to come off easily if rubbed, and a heavy mold line is often apparent. By 1890–1900 the molding technique was improved, and resulted in a thinner, more precise mold. Gilding also was of better quality and did not rub off easily. Greater color and more precision was used in the application of the coats of arms transfers.

Aberdeen Bronze Pot, Cardinal Woolsey crest, Goss	22.00
Abergavenny Jar, Basingstoke crest, Goss	18.00
Antwerp Oolen Pot, Dorthy Vernon, Duke of Devonshire, Buxton crests, Goss	30.00
Bag Plate, 5″ d, Hastings crest, Goss	22.00
Ball Vase, small, Sandwich crest, Goss	18.00
Basket, 2²/₃″ h, Ftd, Craignez Honte crest, gilt trim, center handle	15.00
Bath Roman Ewer, Ambleside crest, Goss	15.00
Bideford Mortar, Folkstone crest, Goss	55.00
Bowl	
Tiny, Chippenhs Ancient crest of Unity and Loyalty in orange, yellow, and blue	7.00
2″ d, Arms of Stratford on Avon, Shakespeare crest, gilt trim, Foley China mark	30.00
Bristol Puzzle Cider Cup, St. George, William the Conqueror, Andover, Hampshire crests, Goss	65.00
Caerleon Lamp, Bath Abbey crest, Goss	32.00
Canary Covered Jarre, Sandgate crest, Goss	32.00
Canary Jarre, Bergen crest, Goss	28.00
Carlisle Salt Pot	
Huddersfield crest, Goss	15.00
Leicestershire crest, Goss	15.00
Carnarvon Ewer, See of Wells crest, Goss	24.00
Channel Isle Lobster Trap, Luton crest, Goss	40.00
Chester Roman Ewer, Cork crest, Goss	18.00
Colchester Famous Vase	
Hornsey crest, Goss	18.00
Manor of Bramber crest, Goss	15.00
Walton-on-Naze crest, Goss	18.00

Pitcher, 2³/₄″ h, "The Arms of the City of London," gold rim and outline on handle, "Foley" mark, $28.00

Cone Extinguisher, Warminister crest, Goss	22.00
Creamer	
Basalt, enameled crest of Onterio, Canada and trim, "Wedgwood, England" mark	45.00
Hawick crest, six flutes, Shelley	15.00
2¹/₄″ h, City Arms London crest, white, rust, and gilt	15.00
Cup, 2¹/₂″ h, three handles, yellow, orange, and brown City of London crest, white ground, gilt trim, "crown, shield, GEMMA" mark	8.00
Cup and Saucer	
Braemer crest, Shelley	30.00
Masonic Crest in colors, Shelley	30.00
Dart Sack Bottle, Floreat Etone crest, Goss	22.00
Devon Oak Pitcher, Warwick crest, Goss	15.00
Dorchester Jug, Fowey crest	15.00
Eddystone Lighthouse, Shoreham crest, Goss	60.00
Eddystone Spanish Jug, City of London crest, Goss	15.00
Egyptian Mocha Cup, Tonbridge crest, Goss	18.00
Figure	
4″ h, pedestal, Margate crest in orange, turquoise, and green with dragons, reverse "To the memory of William Philpott and Charles Etroughton, gilt trim, Arcadian China mark	30.00
4¹/₄″ h, bust of Shakespeare, black vest over dark brown shirt	85.00
13¹/₂″ h, parian, standing pensive maiden holding folds of tunic in hand, circ base, imp "W.H. Goss" mark	495.00
Fountains Abby Cup, Sheringham crest, Goss	18.00
Glastonbury Jack	
Gloucester crest, Goss	16.00
Selby crest, Goss	18.00
Glastonbury Vase, Tonbridge Wells crest, Goss	15.00
Glouster Jug, Battersea crest, Goss	15.00
Goodwin Sands Carafe	
Hastings crest, Goss	15.00
Royal Arms of Scotland, Goss	18.00
Hatpin Holder, Turnridge Wells crest, Shelley	50.00
Herne Bay Ewer, See of York crest, Goss	18.00
Highland Cuash, See of Lincoln crest, Goss	28.00
Horsham Mediaeval Jug, Brighton crest, Goss	15.00
Irish Mather, Glasgow crest, Goss	25.00
Irish Wooden Noggin	
Bromsgrove crest, Goss	25.00
Hitchen crest, Goss	23.00
Oakham crest, Goss	25.00
Itford British Urn, Great Yarmouth crest, Goss	23.00
Japan Ewer, See of Exeter crest, Goss	35.00
Jersey Fish Basket, 4″ l, "W.H. Goss" mark	25.00
Kettering Urn, Quebec crest, Goss	18.00
Lanlawren Celtic Sepulchral Urn, Nurnberg crest, Goss	18.00
Lewes Roman Vase, Ramsgate crest, Goss	10.00
Lichfield Jug	
Eastbourne crest, Goss	15.00
York crest, Goss	15.00
Lincoln Jack, Boulogne-Sur-Mer crest, Goss	18.00
Looe Ewer, Falmouth crest, Goss	15.00
Loving Cup, three handled, Henry of Navarre, Ramsgate, and Kent crests, Goss	30.00
Melon Cream Jug, small, City of Leicester crest, Goss	20.00
Melon Cup and Saucer, small	
Farnham crest, Goss	22.00
Faversham crest, Goss	22.00
Margate crest, Goss	22.00

Melon Plate
   4⅛" d, Sussex crest, Goss 18.00
   6" d, Flintshire crest, Goss 22.00
Mini Mug, one handle, Battersea crest, Goss .. 15.00
Model
   3" h, "Oven in Which Goss Was Fired,"
     brown ground with gray trimmed win-
     dows 100.00
   4¼" h, Centopath, erected on Whitehall
     London, London crest on front in black and
     brown with green wreaths, reverse "In
     memory of the falled in the great war 1914–
     1919" 30.00
   5½" l, Worcester Cathedral with crest, Ar-
     cadian 100.00
Newbury Leather Bottle, Southend-on-Sea crest,
   Goss 15.00
Newcastle Roman Jug
   Abergele crest, Goss..................... 16.00
   New Zealand crest, Goss 18.00
Norwich Urn
   Bishop Aukland crest, Goss.............. 15.00
   Ealing crest, Goss....................... 15.00
   Nurnberg crest, Goss.................... 16.00
   Southampton crest, Goss................. 15.00
   Wolverhampton crest, Goss 15.00
Ostend Bottle, Egham crest, Goss 22.00
Ostend Tobacco Jar, Paddington crest, Goss .. 15.00
Ostend Vase, Preston crest, Goss 15.00
Painswick Roman Pot, Walton-on Naze crest,
   Goss 15.00
Penmeanmawr Urn
   Bishops Strotford crest, Goss 15.00
   Las Planches Montreux crest, Goss........ 15.00
   Seal of Leominster, Goss 15.00
Pitcher, 3⅞" h, white cameo of coat of arms
   and "Dominion of Canada," grape border,
   dark blue jasper ground, "Wedgwood, En-
   gland" mark 78.00
Plate, 9⅜" d, multicolored crest of "Dominion
   of Canada" 20.00
Portland Vase
   Bodian crest, Goss 15.00
   Great Yarmouth crest, Goss 15.00
Pot, 1⅝" h, multicolored crest of Margate,
   horiz ribbed alternating panels, "green crown,
   shield, GEMMA" mark................... 12.00
Pourer, 2¾" h, green, orange, and green crest,
   gilt trim, Coronet Ware, crown mark 25.00
Reading Vase, Skegness crest, Goss 15.00
Scuttle Mug, 3" h, Craignez Honte crest, gilt
   rim 15.00
Sea Shell, 4" l, Clacton on Sea crest, orange and
   yellow with blue, molded body, gilt trim, "Flo-
   rentine China" Made in England mark...... 25.00
Shakespeare's Jug, Shakespeare's Arms,
   Goss................................... 50.00
Shoes, transfer scenes, "Prince's Parade Bridling-
   ton" and "Brindlington, The Childrens Cor-
   ner', green, blue, and brown, pr 30.00
Southwold Jar, Glasgow crest, Goss 18.00
Staffordshire Tyg
   Single handle
     Ancient Port of Minehead crest, Goss 18.00
     Earl of Cromarte crest, Goss.............. 18.00
     Interlaken crest, Goss................... 18.00
   Double Handles, Norfolk crest, Goss 18.00
Sugar Bowl, Crest of Quebec, Wildman....... 8.00

Swan, 2" h, molded, Hastings Stoke on Trent
   crest, cobalt, gold, and orange, gilt trim..... 25.00
Swindon Vase
   Walton-on-Naze crest, Goss.............. 15.00
   Waterlooville crest, Goss................. 15.00
Swinton Vase, Large, Swindon crest, Goss 50.00
Swiss Vinegar Bottle, Eastbourne crest, Goss .. 28.00
Tea Set, teapot, creamer, sugar bowl, New
   Brunswick coat of arms in colors........... 55.00
Toothpick, 2" h, St. Asaph crest, Clifton mark . 22.00
Tresco Brazier, Clacton-on-Sea crest, Goss 45.00
Trinket Tray, 9⅜" l, 7¾" w, Keswick crest,
   Goss................................... 62.00
Vase
   2¼" h, Craignez Honte crest, two handled 15.00
   2½" h, Craignez Honte crest, triangle shape,
     blue shield, gilt trim 15.00
   2¾" h, Craignez Honte crest, globular
     shape.............................. 15.00
   3½" h, Henry of Navarre crest 30.00
Wall Pocket, 2¾" h, South end-on-Sea crest
   with ship 25.00
Walmer Roman Vase
   Harrogate crest, Goss................... 18.00
   Kingston-on-Hill crest, Goss 18.00
   Yorkshire crest, Goss 18.00
Wareham Roman Bottle, Hoylake and West
   Kirby crests, Goss 15.00
Weymouth Roman Vase, Marblethorp crest,
   Goss................................... 20.00
Wide Taper Vase
   Lewes crest, Goss 22.00
   Manor of Shrewton crest, Goss............ 22.00
York Roman Ewer, Morecomb crest, Goss 18.00

MADE IN

Zuid Holland

c 1897

GOUDA

Gouda, Holland
17th Century to Present

History: Gouda and the surrounding areas of Holland
have been producing Dutch pottery wares since the 17th
century. Orginally Delft-type tin glazed earthenwares
were manufactured along with the clay smokers' pipes.

    When the production of the clay pipes declined, the
pottery makers started producing art pottery wares with
brightly colored decorations. These designs were influenced by the Art Nouveau and Art Deco movements.
Stylized florals, birds, and geometrics were the favorite
motifs, all executed in bold, clear colors. Some Gouda
pieces have a "cloisonne" appearance.

    Other pottery workships in the Gouda region include:
Arnhem, Plazuid, Regina, Schoonhoven, and Zenith. Utilitarian wares, vases, miniatures, and large outdoor garden
ornaments also were included in the product line.

REPRODUCTION ALERT. With the recent renewal of interest in Art Nouveau and Art Deco examples, reproductions of earlier Gouda pieces now are on the market.
These are difficult to distinguish from the originals.

Candlesticks, 15″ h, multicolored swirl and flame design, satin black ground, "house and Gluck Plazuid Holland" mark, pr, (A) $350.00

Ashtray, 5 1/4″ l, shoe shaped, black, white, blue, yellow, and red swirls, matte finish, "Regina Osiris Gouda Holland" mark 55.00
Biscuit Jar, 5 1/4″ h, gold outlined orange, brown, and blue flowers on black and cream ground, SP lid, rim, and handle 145.00
Bowl
  5″ d, gilded pink and turquoise geometric Art Deco design on matte black ground, scalloped edge, "Zward, Gouda Holland house" mark (A) 15.00
  8″ d, blue and orange flowers in band with cream ground, black ground, "Lacon Plaxuid Holland" mark (A) 60.00
  13″ d, mustard, magenta, and blue mums, other flowers in rust, blue, and mustard, olive green leaves, cross-hatch orange border, cream ground, pierced for hanging, "Ranonco Gouda Holland" mark 395.00
Candy Dish
  6 3/4″ H-H, blue, mustard, and rust designs on int, olive green ext, two handles, "Gouda Holland Louanae" mark................. 65.00
  7 1/4″ l, rust, blue, and gold geometrics and swirls, olive green base and ring handle, matte finish, "Metz, Royal Zuid Holland, House" mark 73.00
Candlestick
  3 3/4″ h, green, rust, cobalt, and ochre geometric design, "Candis, #1137, house" mark................................. 50.00
  7 1/4″ h, turquoise leaves and trim, large yellow flowers, black satin ground, house mark, pr............................ 145.00
  8″ h
    Cobalt, tan, and green geometrics, brown ground, stem with raised rings supported by four arms, brown ground, matte finish, "Damascus Holland" mark................. 265.00
    Rust, blue, and green designs, green ground, four handles, marked 250.00
  10″ h, twisted black stem, geometric designs on base and top in rust, blue, green, and gold, blue rim, "Beek Gouda, Made in Holland" mark 145.00

Chamberstick
  3 1/2″ h, turquoise, dark blue, orange, and yellow leaf design, black trim, matte finish, ring handle, house mark 88.00
  4 1/8″ h, turquoise, red-brown, and orange leaf design, cream ground, dark brown nozzle and rim, light brown handle, satin finish, house mark.......................... 195.00
Compote, 7 3/4″ d, 3 1/4″ h, three orange and blue open flowers with yellow and brown buds on cream ground on int, dark brown body, foot, and dbl handles, house mark.... 195.00
Decanter, Stoppered
  2 1/2″ h, Delft-type scene of house, windmill, and fence in three shades of blue, "BOLS" & legend, white ground, gloss glaze, "Zenith Gouda" mark (A) 20.00
  10 1/2″ h, black pedestal base, orange, brown, and ochre florals, "Nadra Gouda" mark .. 150.00
Dish
  7 1/2″ d, 2 1/2″ h, ftd, orange, blue, and cream open center blossom, olive ground with blue sectional stripes, "Unsaro house" mark 95.00
  7 5/8″ d, 4 1/4″ h, three section, gold, orange, green, and blue flowers, cream ground, black handle and trim, satin finish........ 88.00
Figure
  Dutch Shoe
    3″ l, multicolored Art Nouveau design on black matte ground, pr 90.00
    4″ l, turquoise, orange, and yellow designs outlined in gold, black int, marked 45.00
Humidor
  5 1/4″ h, dark and light blue, brown, gold, and lavender flowers and scrolls, black trim, cream ground, matte finish, house mark................................. 135.00
  6″ h, high gloss islander scene with palm tree, banana skirt, sailing ship, packing crate, tobacco plants, two men, one smoking pipe, floral border with crown at top, brass lid incised "Octr. Aangevr. Kon. Goedewaagen," 'Royal Goedewaagen Potteries, Gouda Holland" mark (A).............. 35.00
Jar, Cov, 10″ h, large stylized berries in panels, turquoise and olive ground, matte finish, "Dec, Gouda Holland" mark (A).......... 175.00
Jug, 11 1/4″ h, pastel geometrics, pinched body, light gray ground, gold-orange borders, turquoise int, "Rhodesia, Royal Zuid Holland, house" mark........................... 350.00
Match Holder, 2″ h, aqua, blue, gold, and red Art Deco design, black ground, matte finish, striker under base, house mark 40.00
Nappy, 6″ d, red berries with green and gold leaves, black ground, scalloped rim, "Zwaro Gouda" mark........................... 55.00
Pedestal Dish, 3 1/4″ h, 5 3/4″ d, blue and rust designs with purple flowers and green leaves, black ext, "Silken Gouda, Made in Holland" mark.................................... 80.00
Pitcher
  4″ h, high gloss mottled dark green drip glaze over light green ground, "Royal Gouda Holland" mark (A).......................... 20.00
  6″ h, open yellow, brown and purple flowers, gray ground, green int, "Karo Gouda Holland, Royal Zuid Holland, house" mark... 195.00

6¾" h, finely painted brown, yellow, and purple tulips, cream ground, olive green handle, turquoise int, "Irene Royal Z. Holland, house" mark...................... 155.00

7" h, white with gold flowers, rust and blue decoration, satin black ground, "Zenith" mark.................................. 95.00

9½" h, orange, ochre, and turquoise stylized animals on ivory ground 195.00

Multicolored swirling florals.................. 230.00

Pitcher, Cov, 9⅛" h, large open purple flower, orange, green, and brown swirled ground, high gloss finish, "Regina crown" mark 225.00

Plate, 12" d, orange, brown, and ochre florals, "Nadra Holland" mark.................. 110.00

Popouri Jar, 5" h, stylized orange, blue, yellow, and mint green flowers, three brown rect feet, satin finish, brass perforated cov 155.00

Tumbler, 4⅜" h, green, gold, blue, orange, pink, and yellow flowers and leaves, cream ground, black trim, satin finish, house mark 55.00

Tray, 11⅛" d, rust flowers, green and brown leaves, royal blue and gold trim, cream ground, green edge, satin finish............ 110.00

Vase

2½" h, orange berries on brown-beige speckled ground, "Zenith Gouda" mark .. 28.00

3¼" h, colored florals, glossy crackle glaze, pr 65.00

4¼" h, urn shape, rust, orange, gold, cream, and shades of blue designs, two black handles, black ground, matte finish, "Regina', Gouda Holland marks 275.00

4½" h, stylized open flowers in yellow, gray geometrics below, brown ground, black dots at rim, glossy glaze, "E.A. Gouda, Made in Holland, Catma" mark.............. 210.00

5¾" h, yellow and white florals, olive green leaves, green int, tan ground, "2564 Dena Gouda Holland" mark 85.00

6" h, Delft-like scene of windmill, boat, lake, ducks and house, reverse with "Saint Nicholas Society, Anniversary Dinner, December, 6, 1937," two shades of blue on light blue ground, "Royal Goedewaagen Gouda, Made in Holland' (A) 30.00

7¼" h, yellow, blue, red, and orange flowers on gray ground, marked 75.00

8" h

Art Deco style, red stylized flowers and leaves, brown and gold bands......... 40.00

Sq shape, florals in purple, yellow, olive green, and blue, rust on top, olive green on base, turquoise green int, white crackle ground, shiny glaze, "Berzina-Royal" mark........................ 275.00

8¼" h, blue, mustard, and rust designs on int, olive green ext, "Gouda Holland Louanae" mark................................ 120.00

8½" h, multicolored swirls on black ground, black int, matte finish, "Regina Holland" mark................................ 140.00

9" h, sq base, dark multicolored floral motif, four handles, gloss finish, "Zuid Holland" mark................................ 249.00

9½" h, shapes of rust, green, blue, with black base, brown ground, shiny glaze, "Zenith, Gouda Holland" mark 475.00

10" h

Rust, light purple, and olive green flowers and leaves, gold dots and dark green accents, black ground, gloss finish, Regina, Gouda............................ 125.00

Rust, orange, gold, cream, and shades of blue designs, two overhead black joined handles, black ground, matte finish, "Regina, Gouda Holland" marks....... 375.00

10¾" h, Art Nouveau pattern of overall flowers, stylized iris in lilac, green shades, and yellow, mustard trim around neck, off white ground, "Zuid Holland Gouda" mark........................ 250.00

20½" h, large parrot seated on foliage in orange, green, brown, blue, and yellow, c1918–32, "Zuid-Holland, Gouda" mark (A)................................. 1775.00

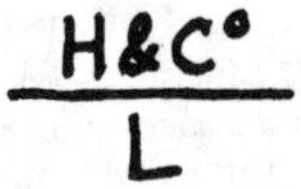

H&Cº
L
c1885

CFH
GDM
FRANCE
c1891

HAVILAND

Limoges, France
1842 to Present

History: David and Daniel Haviland, two brothers, had a china import business in New York. When traveling to France in search of china, David decided to remain in Limoges, the leading center for the manufacture of pottery. By 1842 David and his family were firmly established in Limoges. David supervised the purchasing, designing, and decorating of stock for export from several Limoges companies. In 1865 he acquired a factory in Limoges to produce porcelains directly. Instead of sending whiteware to Paris to be decorated, David established studios at his own factory. He hired and trained local decorators.

In 1852 Charles Field Haviland was sent by Robert Barclay Haviland, his father, to learn the business from Uncle David. Charles Field married into the Alluaud family who owned the Casseaux works. When Charles Field took over, the mark used on the whiteware was "CFH."

Charles Edward and Theodore, sons of David Haviland, entered the firm in 1864. By 1878 the Haviland factory was the largest in the Limousin District. When David died in 1879, the firm passed into the hands of his two sons. A difference of opinion in 1891 led to the liquidation of the old firm. Charles Edward produced china under the "Haviland et Cie" name. After Charles died in 1922, his firm lost its significance and went out of business in 1931. Theodore started his own factory, "La Porcelaine Theodore Haviland," that produced china until 1952.

In 1875 Charles and Theodore Haviland founded a faience studio in Paris that was headed by Bracquemond, the famous engraver. This Auteuil Studio gathered together the greatest artists and decorators of the period. The entire French china production at the end of the 19th century was influenced by this studio's output.

William David, son of Theodore, took over in 1919. William David's three sons, Theodore II, Harold, and Frederick, eventually became involved. Members of the Haviland family, all direct descendants from the founder David Haviland, always have directed the French firm in Limoges. Each has chosen to retain their U.S. citizenship.

Marks: Until 1870 only one back mark was used for the "H & Co." or the Haviland & Co. After that time, two back marks were used - one for the factory where a piece was made and the other for the factory in which the piece was decorated. Department stores, hotels, railroads, and restaurants that placed special orders received individual marks.

All the whiteware marks are under the glaze. The decoration back marks are over the glaze. Various colorings used in the back marks designate different periods in the Haviland factory production. Pattern names often appear on many older sets between the whiteware and decorating marks.

References: Jean d'Albis & Celeste Romanet, *La Porcelain de Limoges*, Editions Sous le Vent, 1980; Mary Frank Gaston, *Haviland Collectables & Objects of Art*, Collector Books, 1984; Mary Frank Gaston, *The Collector's Encyclopedia of Limoges Porcelain*, Collector Books, 1980; G.T. Jacobson, *Haviland China: Volume One & Volume Two*, Wallace-Homestead, 1979; Arlene Schleiger, *Two Hundred Patterns of Haviland China, Books I-V*, published privately, Omaha; Harriet Young, *Grandmother's Haviland*, Wallace-Homestead, 1970.

Collectors' Club: Haviland Collectors Internationale, Dave Herwynen, Treasurer, 1716 S. Rustin, Sioux City, Iowa 51106. Membership: $20.00. Quarterly newsletter.

Collecting Hints: The term "blank" refers to the whiteware piece before any pattern decoration has been applied. A blank can be a simple, all white finished glazed piece. Blanks can be smooth or have embossed edges and designs in the whiteware itself. Decorations and gold trims were applied later.

One must know both the blank number and the pattern number to make an exact match of a Haviland piece. The width and placings of the gold trims also exhibited tremendous variety and must be checked carefully.

Haviland matching services use Arlene Schleiger's reference books to identify patterns. Xerox a plate on both sides and indicate colors of the patterns when sending a sample to a matching service.

Monsieur Jean 'Albis, Haviland & Company historian, believes that more than 20,000 patterns were created and produced by artists of the company. Many old patterns have been discontinued, but Haviland Limoges porcelain dinnerware still is being made and sold in department and specialty stores.

In addition to the popular floral pattern tablewares, collectors of Haviland also should be alert for the art objects and richly decorated tableware and the unique non-tableware items that the company also manufactured.

Bone Dish, "Rose" pattern, set of 12 . . . .   **75.00**
Bowl, 8 1/2" l, 7 1/2" w, fuchsia and orange
 flowers in side, white ground, c1880 (A). . . .   **15.00**
Cake Plate
 9 1/2" d, "Forget-Me-Not" pattern, "Charles
  Field Haviland" mark **35.00**

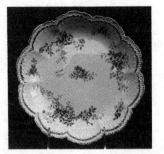

Bowl, 9" d, pink roses, blue and green florals, raised border with gold trim, "green GDA France Haviland Limoges" and "orange CH Field" marks, $85.00

11" H-H, pink and blue flowers, gold ac-
 cented handles, "Theo. Haviland" mark . .   **45.00**
13" d, small blue and pink flowers **75.00**
Candlestick, 7" h, small blue forget-me-nots,
 Marseilles blank, dbl mark, pr **250.00**
Chamber Set, bowl, pitcher, cov, chamber pot,
 cov, waste jar, toothbrush holder, soap dish,
 small pitcher, mug, "Moss Rose" pattern,
 "H.& Co." marks **1200.00**
Charger, 13 1/2" d, border of blue peacocks. . .   **50.00**
Chocolate Pot
 9 1/2" h, rose and gilt decoration, "Rouen"
  mold, "H. Haviland, France" mark **125.00**
 11" h, pink flower sprays, gold trim, "Haviland
  & Co." mark **175.00**
Chocolate Set
 Pot, 10" h, ribbon handle, 5 cups and saucers,
  floral design **400.00**
 Pot, 11 1/4" h, 5 cups and saucers, small pink
  roses. **325.00**
Chop Plate
 10" d, "Autumn" pattern, gold handles. **55.00**
 12" d, "Clover" pattern. **100.00**
Coffee Pot
 6 1/2" h, Sandez, pelican shape in colors. . . .   **500.00**
 10 1/2" h, clusters of bluebells, gold ribbons,
  ribbed body, gold scalloped base **175.00**
Creamer, "Rajah" pattern, Theo. Haviland. **8.00**
Cream and Sugar, "Louise" pattern, "Theo. Havi-
 land" mark **35.00**
Cup and Saucer
 "Blue Garland" pattern, ftd **7.00**
 "Crimson Mosaic" pattern **10.00**
 Light pink florals and leaves, embossing and
  deep gold, "Theo. Haviland Limoges" mark,
  set of 6 . . . .   **90.00**
 "Strasbourg" pattern.   **8.00**
Cup and Saucer, Demitasse
 "Garden Flowers" pattern. **25.00**
 Small pink flowers, emb blank, gold trim on
  handle, "C.F.H." mark **20.00**
Dinner Service, 12 dinner plates, 10 salad plates,
 8 bread and butter, 12 teacups and saucers,
 teapot, creamer, sugar, platter, sauce boat, cov
 vegetable bowl, service bowl, "Paradise" pat-
 tern (A) **300.00**
Ice Cream Set, master plate, 9 1/2" w, 14" l, 12
 plates, 7" sq, folded napkin shape, hp winter

scenes with enamel accents, wide coral
shaded borders, c1876–89 . . . . 850.00
Meat Platter, 11" l, 9" w, "Montreaux" pattern,
"Theo. Haviland" mark. 38.00
Oyster Plate
  8³⁄₄" d, 5 wells, seaweed and fish design,
  gold scalloping. "Haviland & Co." mark . . 45.00
  9" d, blue and pink florals, "Haviland & Co."
  mark. 80.00
Pitcher
  3¹⁄₂" h, rust and blue flowers, gold trim and
  handle 35.00
  7" h, pink flowers and green leaves, gilt han-
  dle, "Portia" blank 115.00
  10¹⁄₄" h, melon ribbed with floral sprays,
  gold trim, scalloped base, "Theo. Haviland"
  mark. 55.00
Plate
  7¹⁄₂" d
  "Coromandel" pattern, "Theo. Haviland"
  mark. 12.50
  Entwined roses, gilt edge, "Theo. Haviland,
  France" mark, set of 4 . . . . 45.00
  "Louise" pattern 12.00
  8" sq, painted peaches, gold trim, "Haviland,
  Limoges" mark. 50.00
  8¹⁄₂" d
  Hp pansies, pastel ground, artist sgd 48.00
  "Rosalinde" pattern 24.00
  Six long stem pink roses in center, apple
  green and gold border, set of 12 . . . . . . 185.00
  Swags of pink roses, gold rim. 12.00
  8³⁄₄" d, pink and green roses 10.00
  9" d
  Art Nouveau style, yellow poppies, gilded
  accents, sgd "K. Florenze" 30.00
  Napkin shape, hp butterflies and grasses,
  set of 6 . . . . 150.00
  9¹⁄₄" d, Hotel Astor logo, emb gold edge,
  "Theo. Haviland, France" mark 55.00
  9¹⁄₂" d, autumn leaves design, wide peach
  colored scalloped border. 25.00
  9³⁄₄" d, overall large pink roses, gold beaded
  edge 22.00
  10" d, "Glendale" pattern 10.00
  11" d, multicolored swallowtailed bird and
  butterflies 40.00
Platter
  11¹⁄₂" d, pink flowers with gold stalks, white
  ground. 55.00
  13¹⁄₂" l, small green and pink flowers 22.00
  13³⁄₄" l, "Clover" pattern. 55.00
  14" l
  "Albany" pattern. 25.00
  "Princess" pattern. 25.00
  16¹⁄₂" l, 11¹⁄₄" w, small pink and green
  flowers, white ground, gold and white
  bows 45.00
  18³⁄₄" d, pink, blue, and gray florals, "Havi-
  land & Co." mark 78.00
  19" l, small pink and red roses on rim, molded
  drain channels, c1910 (A). 20.00
Serving Bowl, 10¹⁄₂" d, oct, with handle, "Montreaux" pattern, "Theo. Haviland" mark. 28.00
Soup Bowl, 7¹⁄₂" d, "Eden" pattern, "Theo.
  Haviland" mark 15.00
Sugar Bowl, "Wedding Ring" pattern 45.00
Tankard, 12" h, melon ribbed body, large pink
  roses, buds, and leaves on front, gold trim,
  "Haviland & Co." dbl mark. 185.00

Teapot, 10¹⁄₂" h, hp pine cone design, gilt ac-
  cents (A) 15.00
Vegetable Bowl, Cov
  8" d, two gold handles, pink roses, green and
  yellow trim, "Theo. Haviland, Limoges"
  mark. 25.00
  9" l, oval, small blue flowers, Theo. Haviland 50.00

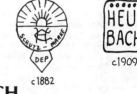

c1882

HEUBACH

Thuringia, Germany
1840s to Present

History: Christoph and Philip Heubach founded the Heubach factory to manufacture decorative and household
porcelains, figures, dolls heads, and dolls. Their dolls
heads, animals figures, and piano babies are their most
famous products. There is no connection between this
factory and the Ernst Heubach factory in Koppelsdorf.

After World War II, the company was nationalized and
experienced several name changes. The present company
name is VEB United Decorative Porcelainworks Lichte.

Figure
  3¹⁄₄" l, child lying on back holding large blue
  egg, marked 110.00
  4¹⁄₄" h, seated bisque dog with black muzzle,
  white with tan head and rust ears, un-
  marked. 85.00
  4¹⁄₂" h, little girl seated with hands folded,
  multicolored, marked 95.00
  5" h, seated girl with large orange bonnet,
  pulling on socks. 200.00
  5³⁄₄" h, seated Dutch girl in white bonnet,
  green bodice, orange skirt, head tilted to
  side. 85.00
  6" h, 7" l, sitting dog with bib and bonnet with
  blue ribbons, marked 275.00
  6¹⁄₂" h, seated gray and white rabbit, pink
  ears and eyes, marked 135.00
  6³⁄₄" h
  Dutch boy on sq base, blue shirt, tan pants
  and hat 110.00
  Little boy with net and fish, cap on head, or
  little girl with oval basket, ruffled bonnet,
  white with blue trim, unmarked, pr 295.00
  7" h, "The Fat Boy" from Pickwick series, multicolored, marked 85.00
  7¹⁄₄" h, 4³⁄₄" d, Dutch boy and girl standing
  back to back, red, green, and white 145.00
  8" h
  Girl with bird on shoulder. 165.00
  Sitting baby holding toes. 375.00
  10" h, children dressing in adult clothes, girl in
  lavender shawl and plumed hat, boy in pink
  dunce cap, looking in hand mirror, pr 735.00
  11" h, girl holding dove to breast in colors,
  marked. 550.00
  11¹⁄₂" h, dancing girl in aqua dress, pink bow,
  white lace collar, multicolored base 510.00

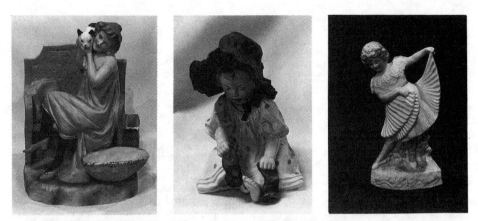

Cigar Holder, left, 7" h, lime green dress, black stockings, blue ground with yellow trim, gold accents, unmkd, $550.00; Figure, center, 6" h, white dress with blue dots, orange hat, gray socks, printed and imp marks, $350.00; Figure, right, 6³⁄₄" h, white dress, blue stockings, lt green base with florals, imp sunburst mark, $125.00

12¹⁄₂" h, man with ax wiping forehead, woman holding baby and jug, pastel colors, imp marks, pr......................... 725.00

16" h, little girl in bathing outfit and cap with blue bow, holding shovel and pail with wire bale, placing toe in water 855.00

Flower Holder, 5¹⁄₂" h, seated Dutch boy or girl in orange, green, and white, baskets on back, marked, pr............................. 165.00

Planter, 4" h, 10³⁄₄" l, figural shepherdess tending flock, marked......................... 195.00

Tray, 8¹⁄₂" l, 5" w, painted sailboats, molded seagulls on border....................... 75.00

Vase

3¹⁄₈" h, 5" l, 3¹⁄₂" w, oval, incised white iris and green leaves, outlined in white, dark mottled blue-green ground, green "HB and rising sun" mark 70.00

4" h, scene of Dutch boy................. 48.00

6" h, painted woman near stream, sage green ground, marked...................... 115.00

8³⁄₄" h, pink roses on blue, yellow, and green 48.00

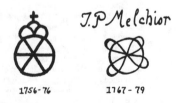

1756-76   1767-79

HOCHST

Hesse, Germany
1746–1796

History: Though in existence for a short time, the porcelain factory at Hochst produced a high quality product. Johann Goltz and Johann Clarus, his son-in-law, founded the porcelain factory together with Adam Friedrich von Lowen-

finck, a decorated, who came from Meissen. The group did not work well together and soon split up. By 1750 Johann Benchgraff from Vienna joined Glotz and Clarus to produce porcelains.

After Benchgraff left in 1753, Goltz had financial difficulties. The Prince-Elector, Friedrich Carl von Ostern, from Mainz, took over. Johann and Ferdinand Maass were appointed managers of the factory, now known as the Prince-Electoral Privileged Porcelain Factory, from 1756 to 1776. Tablewares, decorative porcelains, coffee and tea sets, and figures were made. Oriental, Rococo, and Neoclassical decorative themes were used. Piercing and fretwork were common design elements.

Hochst porcelain is probably best known for the figurals that were modeled under the supervision of Johann Melchior. These painted and biscuit figures showed a high degree of artistic ability. Religious and pastoral groups, figures of children, and mythological characters were modeled with special attention to detail. Pinks and light rose tones were most prominently used by Melchior on his figures of children.

The new Prince-Elector, Breidbach-Burresheim, converted the company into a joint stock company in 1776. The factory was renamed to Prince-Electoral Fayence Manufactory. With the departure of Melchior to the Frankenthal factory in 1779, a gradual decline in quality occurred, although attempts at modeling continued. The factory ceased operations in 1796.

Reference: George Ware, *German & Austrian Porcelain*, Crown, Inc., 1963.

Museums: Metropolitan Museum of Art, New York, NY; Museum fur Kunsthandwerk, Frankfurt, Germany; Schlossmuseum, Berlin, Germany; Seattle Art Museum, Seattle, WA.

Reproduction Alert: Following the closing of the Hochst factory, many of the molds were sold in 1840 to the Muller factory 1840 at Damm near Aschaffenburg. Muller produced many of the more popular items including the figures. The Hochst mark was used, but these new copies lacked the subtle coloration of the earlier Hochst originals.

The Fasold & Stauch Company of Bock-Wallendorf and Dressel, Kister & Co. of Volkstedt employed a mark which often is confused with Hochst. The quality of their products differs significantly from the high quality of the Hochst material.

Basket, 10" l, oval form, basketweave bases, pierced lattice sides, edges entwined with gilt ribbons, c1770, underglaze "blue wheel" marks, one incised "HM," pr (A).......... **740.00**

Bough Pot, 3¾" h, semi-circ ribbed shape, floral spray on front with rose, tulip, forget-me-nots, scattered flowers on sides, top and back pierced with holes, brown rim, c1755, "brown enamel wheel, imp 3" mark (A)........... **2040.00**

Box, Cov, 7" l, rococo bombe form, birds on branches on rustic fences in shell and feather cartouches, cov with reclining putto finial, restored, c1765, modeled by Laurentius Russinger, "blue crowned wheel, imp I.H." marks (A)............................... **1430.00**

Chocolate Pot, Cov, 4⁹⁄₁₆" h, cylindrical body, gold seated chinoiserie figure conversing with bearded man while attendant approaches with parasol, spout and handle flanked by floral sprays, cov with fruit sprig knob, handle in turned wood terminal, repaired, 1755–65, incised "NI" mark (A)..................... **1540.00**

Figure

3⅞" h, allegorical group of "Spring," gallant in puce hat, waistcoat, and striped breeches, approaches seated girl in tree stump holding loose flowers in apron of puce dress, yellow hat, mossy scroll edged base in puce and gilding, restored, c1765, underglaze "blue wheel, inc iw, ii, 94, MG" marks (A)............................. **1589.00**

4" h, sleeping children, boy with black tricorn hat seated on mossy pile of rocks, head and arm resting on marmot cage, girl leaning towards tree stump, rests elbow to support head, hurdy-gurdy in grass beside her, restored, c1780, modeled by J.P. Melchior,

Figure, 4¾" h, white scarf, dotted puce skirt, green underskirt, mossy green base, c1785, (A) $1120.00; figure, 5⅜" h, flower-sprigged dress, gilt embroidered bodice, green underskirt, grassy rocky base, c1770–75, "blue crowned wheel" mark, $650.00

underglaze "blue wheel, incised and R2" marks, pr (A)......................... **2431.00**

4¼" h

Beggar boy, yellow neckerchief, open white shirt, tattered blue and turquoise jacket, gray breeches, brown peg-leg, brown crutch under left arm, gray satchel, standing before green mottled brown tree stump, white mound base molded with gilt heightened scrolls, repairs, c1755, "iron-red wheel, incised IH" marks (A) . **1210.00**

Little girl, white head scarf, yellow bodice, puce skirt, striped underskirt, carrying large jug with both hands, handle missing, c1775, modeled by J.P. Melchior, "blue wheel, incised MH" mark (A)......... **1122.00**

Jesus and Mary with hands tied and wearing crown of thorns, incised 318 and 320, pr (A) **650.00**

4⁷⁄₁₆" h, young blacksmith wearing turquoise cap, pale blue neckerchief with puce and white stripes over white shirt, pale orange and tan apron, yellow breeches, black slippers, raising brown handled hammer, black anvil, standing on gray marbleized and brown stone base, c1770, modeled by Johann Peter Melchior, underglaze "blue wheel, incised HM" marks (A).......... **1980.00**

4½" h

Boy wearing white pointed cap, embroidered waistcoat, puce breeches, carrying large water jug, c1775, modeled by J.P. Melchoir, underglaze "blue wheel, incised, and 95" marks (A) **1870.00**

Girl crying over spilled milk, drying eyes with left hand, other lifting skirt, milk jug at feet with milk pouring over edge of base, restored, hand missing, c1775, modeled by J.P. Melchior, underglaze "blue wheel, incised No 86,M" marks (A) **748.00**

4⅝" h, young man in black hat, pink jacket with white collar, striped knee breeches, playing flute, puce scroll bordered base, modeled by Melchior, "blue wheel" mark (A)................................... **798.00**

4¾" h

Girl in dotted puce dress, holding grape vine, hair tied with white scarf, c1785, underglaze "blue wheel mark, incised PN, 238" marks (A)................. **1122.00**

Young flautist, dark gray peaked cap, white scalloped ruff, yellow cape and sash over puce and green striped white jacket edged in gilding, dark gray breeches and puce shoes, playing pale yellow flute, standing before mauve and green mottled tree stump on mound base molded with puce and gilt heightened scrolls, repaired, c1755, "iron-red wheel, incised I" marks (A) **1320.00**

4⅞" h

Boy with dog, black hat, puce coat with dotted cuffs, yellow breeches, seated on pile of rocks patting dog, holding flower in left hand, grassy base, restored, c1775, underglaze "blue wheel" mark (A)..... **1496.00**

Young girl in white scarf, green bodice, purple trimmed white skirt, carrying flower-sprigged jug, or boy in yellow scarf, purple waistcoat, blue breeches, pitcher at

side, grassy bases, repairs, modeled by
J.P. Melchior, c1770, "blue wheel" mark,
pr (A).............................. **3645.00**
5" h, young trumpeter, black tricorn with
green bows, puce cape, turquoise lined
jacket patterned with puce floral diaperwork and edged in gold, white shirt, pale
yellow breeches and iron-red shoes, blue
buckles, playing gilt trumpet, standing
before mottled green and brown tree
stump, mound base molded with gilt heightened scrolls, chips, cuff reglued, c1755,
"iron-red wheel, incised IH" marks
(A)................................... **2090.00**
5³⁄₈" h, peasant girl, one hand on hip, right
arm stretched out to point, flower sprigged
dress, gilt embroidered bodice, green underskirt, grassy rocky base, 1770–75, underglaze "blue crowned wheel mark, 4 incised
H's" mark (A)....................... **750.00**
5¹⁄₂" h, two children with rabbit, girl in yellow
hairband, pink apron over white dress with
brown dotted yellow stripes and flower
sprigs, boy wearing gilt-edged white hat
with turquoise ribbon, turquoise lined pink
jacket, gold and green dotted waistcoat, yellow breeches striped in puce, ochre, and
green, patting tan rabbit, grassy green,
ochre and gray rockwork base, c1780, unmarked (A)........................... **2475.00**
5³⁄₄", 6" h, man holding gun, green jacket,
rose shoulder strap, yellow breeches,
brown satchel, woman holding gun, black
tricorn hat, brown purse on hip, rose shoulder strap, puce and gold scroll molded
bases, restored, c1755, "gold wheel" mark,
pr (A)............................**10,771.00**
5⁷⁄₈" h, group of Leda and swan with Cupid,
young woman wearing gilt patterned hairband and scant rose drapery, brown tree
stump behind her, white swan by left hand,
Cupid with puce heightened wings hands
her iron-red heart, gray bow at feet, gilt
quiver of iron-red feathered arrows tied
with puce ribbon, green grassy mound
base, 1765–70, underglaze "blue crowned
wheel" mark (A)....................... **1320.00**
6" h
Bust of Shakespeare in colors, c1775–80 . **285.00**
Standing girl in pink bonnet and shoes, yellow bodice, light blue skirt, outstretched
arm scattering seeds from apron, repairs,
c1770, modeled by J.P. Melchior, "blue
wheel" mark (A).................... **1012.00**
6¹⁄₄" h
Boy with finger to lips, puce jacket, ribboned waistcoat, light yellow breeches,
repairs, c1770, "blue wheel" mark..... **925.00**
Woodcutter, young lad with peaked cap,
leather apron, leaning on ax, against tree
stump, tools on grass on rocky base, restored, c1770, modeled by J.P. Melchior,
underglaze "blue wheel, incised M No 3,
M.H. script" mark (A)................ **1309.00**
6¹⁄₂" h, gardener, as young boy standing
barefoot with one foot on rock beside
marbled pedestal, puce hat, turquoise long
jacket, blue and red striped breeches,
pointing to flower pot in right hand,
mossy base, restored, c1765, modeled by

J.P. Melchior, underglaze "blue crowned
wheel" mark (A)...................... **1215.00**
7¹⁄₂" h, Chinese boy with goat in colors (A)   **120.00**
9⁷⁄₈" h, group of Venus and Amor, slender
figure draped with yellow scarf, turning towards Amor, holds hand, curly hairstyle,
green rocky base, restored, c1765, modeled by J.P. Melchior, underglaze "blue
wheel" mark (A)...................... **1402.00**
10¹⁄₄" l, "The Adorned Hat," young shepherdess in pink and blue striped white
apron over yellow bodice and white dress,
seated tan dog and black spotted white
lamb at feet, young man in pink coat with
gold buttons, iron-red striped jacket and
breeches, green grassy mound, olive green
and tan hollow stump and base, basket of
flowers at feet, 1765–70, modeled by Johann Peter Melchior, underglaze "blue
wheel," incised triange mark (A)........ **3575.00**
10¹⁄₄" h, 14¹⁄₄" l, group of Amynthas and
Sylvia, young shepherd wearing yellow
lined white tunic striped in iron-red and
green, sprigged in gold over iron-red striped
white breeches, gilt edged black horn and
pink drapery tied at waist kneeling on hummock to untie naked Sylvia from tan, brown,
and green mottled tree trunk behind her,
flowers in hair, scant gilt edged white drapery, green grass covered brown and green
rocky mound base, chips, c1770, modeled
by Johann Peter Melchior, underglaze "blue
wheel, incised HM" marks (A).......... **4400.00**
Mustard Pot, 3³⁄₈" h, oviform barrel shape,
painted with three horiz bands with flower
sprigs in colors, divided by lilac line borders,
dbl scroll handle accented in lilac.......... **375.00**
Plate
9¹⁄₄" d
Center in shades of iron-red, yellow, turquoise, blue, black, and puce with three
birds perched on small tree above green
and brown grassy plateau before distant
woods, scalloped rim molded with
pierced basketwork and edged in gilding,
hair cracks, c1770, underglaze "blue
wheel" marks, one incised "SR," pr (A) **1650.00**
Kakiemon style "Hob in the Well" pattern,
painted scrolling foliage border, c1750–
60, Dutch decorated, incised "Z" mark
(A) **2035.00**
9³⁄₄" d, painted loose bouquet of flowers and
scattered sprays, molded floral border,
shaped brown rim, c1765–70, "blue
crowned wheel" mark, set of 6......... **900.00**
Tea Caddy
4⁹⁄₁₆" h, rect, shades of puce, iron-red, blue,
yellow, and green on front and reverse with
floral spray, sides and shoulders with small
sprigs, cov missing, 1760–65, "iron-red
wheel, incised IH" marks (A)........... **302.00**
5¹⁄₂" h, rect, arched shoulders, painted scene
of woman feeding bird in landscape, reverse with seated gallant, sword in lap, scattered flowers on sides, shoulder, and cov,
artichoke knob, c1765................. **1850.00**
Teacup and Saucer
Green, blue, purple, and brown chateau on
front of cup, center of saucer with carriage
approaching tower building, each with

black edged green rococo trellis entwined with blue, puce, iron-red, and yellow flowers and green leaves, scattered sprigs, gilt edged rim, 1760–65, "iron-red wheel mark and C, incised NI on cup, W2" on saucer marks (A)............................ **1650.00**

Puce painted scene of figures in landscape with buildings, gilt line rims, "red wheel" mark (A) **750.00**

Teapot, bullet shape, painted with two scenes of mtd soldiers in landscapes, scattered sprigs, rococo scroll molded handle and spout with gilt, gilt acorn finial, c1760 (A)............ **1100.00**

Tureen, Cov
7¹/₈" h, 9" l, figural woodcock with black eyes and beak, brown feet, sepia speckled breast and back, rose, speckled brown, and sepia plummage, base of applied moss and mushrooms with leafy branch in colors, repairs and cracks, c1750 (A)............ **10,450.00**

11" h, fluted oval shape, puce painted landscape scenes and scattered flower sprigs, molded border, puce and green accents, four scroll and foliate feet, ribbed and scalloped cov with artichoke knob, c1755, "blue wheel" mark (A)................. **4775.00**

24¹/₂" h, blue, manganese, and brown, sitting bird modeled with wings folded under body, restored, 1748–53, "black wheel and IZ" marks (A)....................... **26,796.00**

Waste Bowl, 6¹/₂" d, ext in shades of green, brown, gray, turquoise, yellow, iron-red, and blue, front with two turkey hens, two chickens, and four chicks near trough in barnyard, reverse with pr of ducks by stream, sides and center of int with small gilt sprigs, gilt edged rim, c1770, underglaze "blue wheel" mark (A) **1430.00**

1755 · 1773

HOLLAND—GENERAL

PORCELAIN

1757–1819

Porcelain by Dutch manufacturers is not as well known as the country's Delftware. Dutch porcelain factories at Weesp, Oude Loosdrecht, Amstel, and The Hague produced some wares, although production was limited and frequently imitated styles from other areas.

Hard paste porcelain was made at the **Weesp** factory near Amsterdam beginning in 1757. The factory was sold to Count Diepenbroick in 1762. The factory used French and German styles for inspiration, e.g., white porcelains decorated with flowers and other motifs in relief. Perforated baskets were made along with Rococo relief decorated wares featuring landscapes in cartouches or adorned with birds or flowers. The factory did not prosper and was sold in 1771. The mark used by Weesp was a copy of the Meissen crossed swords in underglaze blue

with the addition of three dots between the points of the blades and on either side.

De Moll bought the factory, and the company moved to **Oud Loosdrecht** between Utrecht and Amsterdam. The wares exhibited more Dutch characteristics. Landscapes were especially popular. The mark used at Loosdrecht was "M.O.L." either incised or in underglaze blue, black, or colored enamels.

The company moved again in 1784 to **Ouder-Amstel** and was taken over by Frederick Daeuber. The wares now imitated the Empire style wares from Sevres.

In 1800 the factory belonged to the firm George Dommer and Co. It was moved to **Nieuwer-Amstel** in 1809 and was closed in 1819. Sometimes the "M.O.L." mark was used with the word Amstel. Other wares were marked "Amstel" in black.

Lynker, a German, established a porcelain factory in 1775 at **The Hague.** It produced hard paste porcelain similar to Meissen. The pieces were decorated with landscapes, seascapes, and birds. The factory also decorated china from other sources. It closed in 1786. The Hague mark was the stork from the city arms in blue underglaze. When other blanks from other firms were decorated, the mark was painted on the glaze.

POTTERY

The earliest pottery in Holland was made before 1609, long before Holland became an independent nation state. Tin glazed wares of the early sixteenth century that were made in Antwerp, Haarlem, Rotterdam, and Amsterdam were similar to Italian wares known as majolica. Mid 16th century dishes made in Antwerp utilized the "blue-dash" around the edges that was later a design element found on 17th century English wares. Drug jars and spouted drug pots painted in high temperature blue tones similar to Italian wares were quite popular in the Netherlands.

With the founding of the Dutch East India Company in 1609, trade flourished with both China and Japan. As the Dutch potters became familiar with Far Eastern porcelains, they imitated the Oriental designs on the earthenware. By the early 17th century, Delftware had developed.

When English salt glazed stonewares and cream colored earthenwares were imported from England in large quantities about the 1760s, Dutch potteries experienced a decline. Customers prefered the English goods over the tin glazed wares made in Holland.

Museums: Gemeente Museum, The Hague, Holland; Municipal Museum, Amsterdam, Holland.

Additional Listings: Delft, Gouda, Maastricht, Rozenburg.

Albarello
11" h, cobalt, ochre, turquoise, and rustbrown painted berried scrolling foliage, blue-dash and line borders, cracks, early 17th C, Antwerp **1200.00**

11³/₄" h, waisted cylinder shape, blue painted inscription "C.CITRI.COND" on cherub and grotesque mask label, holed, cracks, c1630 .... **1480.00**

Dish
6¹/₂" d, blue, manganese, iron-red, and yellow cavalier on prancing horse, rim chips, c1730 (A)............................ **154.00**

12¹/₂" d, blue center with flowers from rockwork, border of half flowerheads and foliage, c1730, Makkum (A)................ **275.00**

Drug Jar, 9¹/₂" h, blue inscription of contents, blue scrolling foliage and hare, leaves and

Vase, 7¼" h, faience, open purple flowers, lt blue centers, green leaves, tan and red-brown ground, "Purmerende, Holland" mark, $1500.00

flowers accented in yellow, ochre, and green, early 17th C, Antwerp (A) 5500.00

Plaque

4¾" w, 6⅛" h, blue and white canal and sailboat scenes, raised framing borders, pr   310.00

15" w, 22" h, porcelain, blue and white canal with boat, house, windmill, and trees, gold leaf frame 450.00

Plate

7⅞" d, creamware, painted bust of Prince of the House of Orange (A) 75.00

12½" d, green, yellow, blue, and iron-red ferns and flowers, border with five gourd shaped diaper panels alternating with flower sprays, pierced for hanging, c1740, Rotterdam (A) 400.00

Snuffbox and Cov, 3¾" l, puce, iron-red, yellow, blue, green, and brown clusters and sprigs of flowers and fruit in cartouches on either side, int of cov with large cluster of flowers and fruit, rims mtd with later gilt metal hinged mount, 1775–80, Oude Loosdrecht (A). 1320.00

1743 - 1826

HUNGARY—GENERAL

Holitsch
1743–1827

History: The Holitsch pottery factory was established in 1743 by Francis of Lorraine, consort of the Empress Maria Theresa. Decorative motifs followed the popular Strasbourg style. Tureens were made in the form of birds. Most of the painting favored a Hungarian peasant pottery style. When the firm started to produce English style earthenwares in 1786, they used workers from the Vienna factory. It continued in operation with State support until 1827.

The early faience wares were marked with the "HF" monogram for "Holitscher Fabrik." Later creamwares bear the full name "HOLICS" or "HOLITSCH."

Reference: Tivadar Artner, *Modern Hungarian Ceramics*, Art Foundation Publishing House, 1974; Gyorgy Domanovszky, *Hungarian Pottery*, Corvina Press, 1968.

Additional Listings: Fischer, Zsolnay.

Bowl, 7½" d, 4" h, "Blue Garden" pattern, Herend. 75.00

Centerpiece, 12" h, molded three tier fountain shape with green feathered creatures, puce, blue, yellow, and iron-red, c1750, Holitsch. . 1850.00

Charger, 16⅛" d, faience, large flower vase on table in puce luster, green, manganese, and blue, floret scattered ground, border of stylized foliate motifs on trellis ground, early 19th C (A). 475.00

Dish

10¼" l, leaf shape, molded with ribs, painted polychrome bouquet and scattered flowers, c1760, "black HH" Holitsch mark 750.00

12¼" l, oval, faience, center painted with rose, shaped puce border painted with sprigs and scattered flowers, c1760–65, "black H" mark (A). 1415.00

Holy Water Font, 8¾" h, modeled as Veronica in white dress with puce slashes, holding puce edged shroud of Christ, cracks, feet missing, c1755, "blue HF" Holitsch mark. 850.00

Jug, Cov, 12⅜" h, figural parrot in orange, yellow, green, blue, puce, and manganese, tasseled collar, mound base, puce entwined strap handle, screw top head cov, c1760, "manganese HH" Holitsch mark (A). 2442.00

Plate, 7" d, emb decoration of little boy carrying cane, walking with duck, castle and trees in ground, multicolored glazes 25.00

Soup Tureen, Cov, Stand, 7⅝" h, fluted silver form, purple landscape scenes with buildings within molded sprigs and flowers, pear knob, double scroll handles, hairline, 1760–70, "manganese HP," purple painter's mark (A).   450.00

Sweetmeat Stand, 8" h, two tiered flower molded bowls painted in puce, blue, yellow, and iron-red sprigs of flowers in shaped borders, four scroll supports on shaped pad base, c1760–75, "black HH" Holitsch mark (A). . . 2430.00

Teabowl and Saucer, faience, teabowl with con-

Sweetmeat Dish, 5¾" h, man with blue jacket, puce breeches and hat, woman in puce bodice, yellow apron, blue skirt and hat, green mound base, partitioned bowl, repairs, c1760–65, Holitsch, pr, $2500.00

tinuous scene of cows watering in river landscape, saucer with mounted huntsman and mastiff fighting wild boar in mountainous landscape, c1750, "manganese H.F." mark (A) ..   **650.00**

HUTSCHENREUTHER

Hohenberg, Bavaria, Germany
1814 to Present

History: Carl Magnus Hutschenreuther established a German porcelain factory, Hutschenreuther A.G. at Hohenberg, Bavaria in 1814. When Carl Magnus died in 1845, he was succeeded by Johanna, his widow, and Christian and Lorenz, his sons. Lorenz was not satisfied simply to carry on the family business. He was bought out by his partners and established his own porcelain factory in Selb. The Lorenz Hutschenreuther and Carl Magnus Hutschenreuther porcelain factories co-existed as two totally independent businesses. When Lorenz Hutschenreuther died in 1856, Viktor and Eugen, his sons, took over his company.

The Lorenz family enlarged their firm through acquisitions and the creation of new factories during the first part of the 20th century. In 1906 they acquired the porcelain factory Jaeger, Werner & Co. in Selb. In 1917 Lorenz Hutschenreuther bought the Paul Muller Porcelain Factory in Selb. In 1927 they purchased the Tirschenreuth Porcelain Factory and Bauscher Brothers Porcelain Factory in Weiden. The following year the Konigszelt Porcelain Factory was added.

Both branches of the Hutschenreuthers were noted for the high quality of their tablewares and figures. In 1969 all branches of the Magnus and Lorenz firm were united under the group name Hutschenreuther AG.

A merger with Porzellanfabrik Kahla AG of Schoenwald in 1972 brought the Arzberg and Schonwald brands of porcelain along with two earthenware factories into the Hutschenreuther group of enterprises. The company is still in business today producing limited edition plates, figures, dinnerware, and other china. Distribution companies have been established in France, the United States, Canada, Scandinavia, Belgium, and Italy.

Bowl, 7½" d, white figural Cupid flower frog in center.....................   **275.00**
Bowl, Cov, 7½" l, 8" d, alternate panels of multicolored florals, light blue ground with silver design, three baroque feet.............   **90.00**
Cake Plate, 11" H-H, hp grapes, oranges, pears, and pineapple in center, clusters of grapes and leaves on rim, gold trim, open handles, "Hutschenreuther Selb Bavaria" mark...........   **75.00**
Cup and Saucer, pink ground, gold trim **15.00**
Figure
  4" h, two cherubs fighting **100.00**
  5" h, white cherub holding mask **70.00**
  6" h, Madonna and child in colors.........   **95.00**
  6" l, reclining white cat with gray eyes, holding ball, sgd "Achtziger"....................   **165.00**
  7" h
    Seated white cat with green eyes, striped

Tray, 12¾" d, "Charlottee" pattern, red hp poppies, gold rim, "circ HR Bavaria" mark, $75.00

body and tail, Hutschenreuther Germany mark...............................   **285.00**
White Dachshund standing on hind legs..   **165.00**
8¼" h
Art Deco style man and woman entwined, male in purple, female in light yellow and coral, sgd "Werner".................   **345.00**
"Brennertown Band," woman in medieval dress seated on donkey, multicolored ..   **345.00**
8½" h, kneeling lady in yellow blouse and coral skirt, holding child in air...........   **275.00**
10" h, Art Deco, nude woman in flesh tones, holding gold ball, sgd "C. Werner".......   **395.00**
Nappy, 5¼" d, multicolored floral sprays, gold trim, scrolled rim **5.00**
Plaque
5⅛" w, 7" h, young girl in red skirt and low cut chemise, holding candlestick, shielding flame with hand, 1185.00 (A) **1185.00**
6" l, 4" w, two children beside a well, steps and wall of building in ground, late 19th C, sgd "Wagner," imp mark and no. (A) **510.00**
7" h, 5⅛" w, "Good Night," young maid wearing red skirt, low-cut chemise, smile illuminated by glow of candle, c1860, Carl Magnus, imp "circ" mark (A)...........   **1000.00**
7⅝" h, 5½" w, Madonna and Child, angels looking down, reserved on glowing orange ground, c1875–90, sgd "K. Muller," imp "crowned shield" mark (A).............   **1400.00**
Plate
8" d, "Argarette" pattern, yellow, red, and blue daisies, gold trim **8.00**
8½" d, multicolored fruit design **24.00**
9½" d, Vienna style, young girl with golden hair, white dress covered by yellow coat, green lustrous ground, gilded border, late 19th C, sgd "Wagner," script title "Summer," underglaze "blue shield" mark, imp mark (A) **1776.00**
9⅝" d, Vienna style, "Reverie" and "Schwermuth," head and shoulders portrait of young girl, borders in red and blue glazes, gilded with stylized foliage, 1857–99, sgd "Wagner," imp mark to one, script titles and numbered 3676/229 40F, pr (A).........   **3179.00**
9⅞" d, portrait of "Alexandra Prinzessin von Bayern" in green dress, brown hair in tight curls with rose, formal gilded border reserved with panels of classical vases, c1900,

sgd "painted by J. Tadra," printed marks and named title (A) **1099.00**
10¾" d, wide gold leaf design, Selb Bavaria **20.00**
Platter, 15" l, 11" w, "Kensington" pattern ... **80.00**

MADDOCK&CO.
BURSLEM ENGLAND
TRADE MARK
1906

INDIAN TREE

English
Mid 1800s to Present

History: Indian Tree is a popular dinnerware pattern that was made by English potters, e. g. Burgess & Leigh, Coalport, John Maddock & Sons, S. Hancock & Sons, and Soho Pottery from the middle of the 1800s until the present. The main theme is an Oriental landscape with a gnarled brown branch of a pink blossomed tree. The remainder of the landscape features exotic flowers and foliage in green, pink, blue, and orange on a white ground.

Bowl
6¼" d, "Alfred Meakin" mark **6.00**
7¾" d, Copeland-Spode **20.00**
Bouillon Cup and Saucer, scalloped edge, Coalport **40.00**
Butter Pat, Minton, set of 8 .... **85.00**
Cream and Sugar
Coalport **65.00**
"Johnson Bros." mark **30.00**
Creamer, blue and white, "J. & G. Meakin" mark **10.00**
Cup and Saucer
"Alfred Meakin" mark **10.00**
Blue and white, "J.& G. Meakin" mark **7.00**
Coalport **20.00**

Copeland-Spode **10.00**
Minton **10.00**
Myott **12.50**
Cup and Saucer, Demitasse, Copeland-Spode . **24.00**
Dinner Service, service for 8, coffee pot, teapot, creamer, sugar, serving pieces, Copeland-Spode **650.00**
Dish, 8" l, oval, "Johnson Bros." mark **10.00**
Fruit Compote, 9½" d, 3" h, pedestal, scalloped edge, Coalport **150.00**
Gravy Boat
Copeland-Spode **25.00**
"Johnson Bros." mark **25.00**
Ladle, unmarked **45.00**
Plate
6" d, "Alfred Meakin" mark **3.00**
6¾" d, scalloped edge, Coalport **20.00**
7½" d, oct, "Johnson Bros." mark **10.00**
8" d
"Alfred Meakin" mark **8.00**
Maddock **10.00**
9" d, scalloped border, set of 12 (A) **275.00**
9" sq, two small handles, Coalport **45.00**
9¾" d, Maddock **11.00**
10" d, "Alfred Meakin" mark **10.00**
Platter
11" d, Copeland-Spode **25.00**
12" l, "Johnson Bros." mark **25.00**
13½" l, "Johnson Bros." mark **30.00**
14½" l, Copeland-Spode **30.00**
15" d, "Czechoslovakia" mark **25.00**
16" l, "Johnson Bros." mark **35.00**
Sauce Tureen, with undertray, cracks on rim, Minton, pr **350.00**
Soup Bowl, 8" d
"Alfred Meakin" mark 10.00
"Johnson Bros." mark **8.00**
Teapot, "Johnson Bros." mark **45.00**
Tray, 10½" H-H, scalloped edge, Coalport ... **85.00**
Vegetable Bowl, 9" sq, Copeland-Spode **30.00**

FIRST MARK 1863-90

Second Mark
1891-1926

THIRD MARK
1926-46

IRISH BELLEEK

County Fermanagh, Ireland
1857 to Present

History: Pottery production using native clay deposits began in 1857 in Belleek in County Fermanagh, Ireland.

Plate, 9" d, "J. & G. Meakin Hanley" mark, (A)
$15.00

Although David McBurney and Robert Armstrong, the founders, started with earthenwares, they soon produced Belleek parian china a fine porcelain. William Bromley brought some workers from the Goss factory at Stoke-on-Trent when he moved to Belleek about 1860.

Native marine motifs, such as seashells, corals, marine plants and animals, seahorses, and dolphins were the subjects of early Belleek pieces. The Irish shamrocks also were a favorite subject. Many of these motifs continue in production. From its beginning, the factory produced both utilitarian and decorative wares.

Belleek porcelain is extremely thin and light with a creamy ivory surface and iridescent luster. Probably its most distinctive quality is its delicate cream or pastel tone with a pearl like luster. All pieces are hand crafted.

William Henshall's introduction of basketwork and flowers in 1865 gave Belleek porcelains a world wide audience. Each basket is woven out of fine rods of clay, not cast; and, each leaf and flower is made by hand. These intricate and highly decorative pieces are most sought after by collectors. Belleck baskets are dated according to whether they are 3 strand or 4 strands. Also, the pieces are identified with strips of Belleek parian with various impressed wording to give the date.

Irish Belleek parian china still is hand crafted, just as it was more than one hundred years ago. Each piece is made by one craftsman from start to finish; there is no assembly line technique.

References: Richard K. Degenhardt, *Belleek*, Portfolio Press, 1978; Walter Rigdon, *Illustrated Collectors' Handbook*, Wilkins Creative Printing, 1978.

Museums: National Museum, Dublin, Ireland; Ulster Museum, Belfast, Ireland; Victoria & Albert Museum, London, England; Visitor's Center, The Belleek Pottery, Belleek, Co. Fermanagh, N. Ireland.

Collectors Club: The Belleek Collectors' Society, 144 W. Britannia Street, Taunton, MA 02780. Membership: $20.-00. "The Belleek Collector" is the quarterly newsletter.

Collecting Hints: Belleek pieces are marked with the Belleek backstamp consisting of an Irish Wolfhound, a Harp, a Round Tower, and Sprigs of Shamrock. This first mark was used from 1863 to 1890. The marks were either printed or impressed into the china. Early marks are usually black, but can also be red, blue, green, or brown.

With the second mark, 1891 to 1926, "Co. Fermanagh, Ireland" was added along with a ribbon. The third mark was used from 1926 to 1946; the fourth mark in green from 1946 to 1955; the fifth mark in green from 1955 to 1965; and, the sixth mark in green from 1965 to c1980. Brown/Gold mark has been used to stamp pieces made since 1980 to the present time.

Specialty shops and department stores usually carry contemporary Belleek wares. These are good sources for comparing the new examples with the older ones. In the modern pieces, the paste has a creamy white appearance and the high, brilliant glaze has a yellowish color tone. Modern pieces usualy have more color used in the design than their older counterparts. Every genuine Belleek piece carries the company crest. Christmas collector plates were started in 1970. Reed and Barton is now exclusive distributor of Belleek products in the United States.

Basket
    5" d, heart shape, four strand, applied pastel
       flowers on rim, green mark (A) **225.00**
    8½" l, 6" h, "Urne" pattern, shamrock,
       basketweave, green rope trim, 2nd black
       mark. **500.00**

Basket, 7¾" sq, pink flowers, turquoise trim, ribbon mark, $950.00

Pitcher, 5½" h, "Shell" design, 1st black mark, $775.00

10¼" H-H, four strand, applied flowers,
   c1900, applied ribbon mark "Belleek Co.
   Fermanagh Ireland" mark **1850.00**
Three strand, shamrock shape, three applied
   flowers on edge, three small shamrocks . . **532.00**
Basket, Cov, Oval, Three Strand
   8½" l, buds and flowers on cov **4800.00**
   12⅞" l, rim and cov applied with roses,
    shamrock, and thistles, shape no. D113, imp
    "Belleck Co. Fermanagh" mark (A) **4680.00**
Bowl
   3¼" l, oval, shell and coral design, 1st black
    mark. **175.00**
   5" d, shell mtd on figural flying fish, pearl
    finish, 1st black mark **650.00**
   6¾" d, gold trimmed shells, pink coral, 1st
    black mark **275.00**
Bread Plate, 11¼" d, "Shell" pattern, pink trim,
   1st black mark **525.00**
Breakfast Set
   Cup and saucer, plate, 7" d, "Tridacna" pattern, c1861, 1st black mark **120.00**
   Cup and saucer, plate, "Pine Cone" pattern,
    pink edge, 1891–1926, 2nd black mark . . **350.00**
Butter Plate, Open, leaf shape, 3rd black mark. **37.00**
Candelabra, 14½" h, parian boy seated on
   rockwork base with ring of beads, supporting
   coral stem with three sea urchin sconces,
   c1870, pr (A) **2277.00**
Centerpiece, 12½" h, marine design, three tall
   open vert shells of different hts, shell and coral
   base, pearl glaze, 1st black mark **1900.00**
Coffee Pot
   7" h, "Shamrock" pattern on basketweave
    ground, twig handle, 3rd black mark **250.00**
   "Limpet Ware" pattern, molded body, gilt

decorated handle, finial and trim, 3rd black
mark (A) **250.00**
Cream and Sugar
"Artichoke" pattern, 1st green mark........ **45.00**
"Shamrock" pattern, 2nd black mark....... **155.00**
"Snail" pattern, pink edges and handles, 2nd
black mark **185.00**
Creamer
4" h, "Mask" pattern, green handle, c1890,
2nd black mark **86.00**
"Ampanida" pattern, pink trim, dbl handle,
2nd black mark **210.00**
Cup and Saucer
"Limpet" pattern, 3rd black mark **81.00**
"Mask" pattern, 3rd black mark............ **85.00**
"Neptune" pattern, shell feet, 2nd black
mark................................. **81.00**
"Shamrock" pattern, harp handle, 3rd black
mark................................. **100.00**
"Shamrock" pattern, twig handle, 3rd black
mark................................. **81.00**
"Shell" pattern, 3rd black mark **85.00**
"Snail" pattern, pink edges and handles, 3rd
black mark **125.00**
"Tridacna" pattern, pink trim, 2nd black
mark................................. **50.00**
"Tridacna" pattern, 3rd black mark........ **80.00**
Dejeuner Set
"Echinus" pattern, tray, 15" l, 12 1/4" w, teapot, 4" h, open sugar bowl, 3 1/8" h,
creamer, 3 3/8" h, cup and saucer, pink trim,
1st black mark **1750.00**
"Neptune" pattern, tray 17" d, teapot 5 1/4"
h, creamer 3 1/2" h, sugar bowl, 2" h, 2
cups and sacuers, green edges, shell feet,
1st black mark **2100.00**
Dessert Plate, 9 1/4" d, pierced basket shape,
turquoise center and rim, imp and printed 1st
black mark........................... **600.00**
Dish
4 1/2" d, shell shaped, 1st green mark **20.00**
4 3/4" d, "Shell" pattern, 1st black mark **250.00**
8 1/4" l, shell shaped, pink trim, 1st black
mark................................. **395.00**
10" d, 4 1/2" h, "Shell" pattern, pedestal, pink
trim dolphin base, 1st black mark **700.00**
Heart shaped, c1890, 2nd black mark **64.00**
Egg Set, 6" h, 6 1/2" d, six egg cups in holder with
handle and ring in center, 1st black mark ... **1295.00**
Ewer, 8 1/2" h, embossed designs and mask face
under handle, green with gold trim, 2nd black
mark................................. **795.00**
Figure
4 1/2" h, Swan
1st black mark........................ **120.00**
3rd black mark........................ **110.00**
5 1/2" h
Leprechaun on mushroom, 3rd black
mark.............................. **295.00**
Swan, 3rd black mark.................. **155.00**
8 1/4" h, crouching Venus modeled as naked
woman seated on scallop shell, band on
arm, rocky base with sea grass, restored,
c1863–91, 1st black mark (A) **3000.00**
8 5/8" h, boy and girl basket holders, girl holding skirts high showing petticoats, balancing
woven basket on shoulder, boy wearing
waistcoat and lustrous pink tie, one basket
restored, 1863–1890, black printed marks,
pr (A)................................ **550.00**

11" h, lighthouse and cov, tapering brick
tower with slit windows, rockwork and
wave molded shaped base, cylindrical cov
with conical finial, c1873, imp "Belleek,"
black printed mark, reg # for 1873
(A).................................. **500.00**
11 3/4" h, "Clytie," bust of young woman,
curled leaf edge, circ base, 1st black mark **1995.00**
14" h, "Meditation," 3rd black mark **1500.00**
"Irish Greyhound," 3rd black mark........ **615.00**
"Leprechaun," 3rd black mark............ **190.00**
"Pig," med size, 2nd black mark.......... **222.00**
Flower Pot
3 1/2" h, "Diamond" pattern, 2nd black
mark................................. **142.00**
5" h, molded flowers, coral feet, 2nd black
mark................................. **250.00**
10 5/8" h, "Naiads," relief molded babies with
dolphins in reeds and bullrushes, coral border, three scrolled shell feet, luster glaze, 1st
black mark (A) **650.00**
Frame, 10 5/8" h, oval, molded basketweave with
four applied sprigs of lily of the valley in green,
beaded borders, late 19th C (A) **720.00**
Hot Water Pot, 7 1/4" h, "Neptune" pattern,
green trim and handle, shell feet, 2nd black
mark................................. **875.00**
Ice Pail and Cov, 18" h, cylindrical body, parian,
molded with armorini playing amongst dolphins and rushes between coral and shell borders, cov with cherub blowing conch, three
mermaids supporting body, one finial missing,
1868–72, printed and imp marks "P.O.D.R.,"
pr (A)................................. **6440.00**
Jug
5 1/2" hm "Tridacna" pattern, pink trim and
handle, 2nd black mark................ **600.00**
7 1/2" h, "Florence," enamel and gilt garlands
and ribbons, face mask spout, sq handle, 1st
black mark (A) **605.00**
10" h, dbl gourd shape, molded lappet and
triangular design with green accents,
flared wavy neck, loop handle, 2nd black
mark (A) **920.00**
Milk Pitcher, 6" h, shamrocks on basketweave
ground, branch handle, 2nd green mark **75.00**
Mug, 6" h, "Shamrock" pattern, 3rd black
mark................................. **94.00**
Pitcher, 5 1/2" h, "Shell" pattern, 1st black
mark................................. **775.00**
Plate
6 1/2" d, "Shell" pattern, pink trim, 1st green
mark................................. **54.00**
7" d, "Shamrock" pattern on basketweave
ground, 3rd black mark................ **60.00**
8 1/4" d
"Grass" pattern, with luster, 1st black
mark.............................. **350.00**
"Shamrock" pattern on basketweave
ground........................... **77.00**
8 1/2" d
"Shamrock" pattern, 3rd black mark **48.00**
"Shell" pattern, green tint, 3rd black mark **90.00**
9" d, leaf plate, 2nd black mark **200.00**
Platter, 11 1/4" H-H, "Ring Handle Ivory" pattern, orange handles with gilt trim, printed and
imp 1st black mark **950.00**
Salt, "Shell" pattern
1 7/8" h, ftd, 2nd black mark **125.00**
5 1/8" l, supported on raised mound of shells

and coral, 1863–90, printed mark and imp
"BELLEEK CO. FERMAMAGH', pr (A)..... **475.00**
3rd black mark......................... **45.00**
Spill Vase
6½" h, "Lily" design, 3rd green mark **75.00**
Small size, sea horse, c1890, 2nd black mark **180.00**
Sugar and Creamer
"Clearey" pattern, 2nd black mark **110.00**
"Lotus" pattern, 3rd black mark........... **78.00**
"Shamrock" pattern, large hairline, 3rd black
mark............................... **65.00**
Teacup and Saucer
"Grass" pattern, tiny floral spots in pink and
orange, blue-green grass, gilt trim, 1863–91,
1st black mark....................... **400.00**
Hex, hp orange poppies, 2nd black marks .. **210.00**
Teapot
4" h, "Shamrock Ware" pattern, enamel colored flowers, green handle, spout, and finial
(A)................................. **150.00**
5" h, enamel colored leaf and berry vine,
molded ring handle and finial........... **175.00**
5¼" h, "Mask Ware" pattern, molded face of
Bacchus on side with grapevines, grapes
finial, 3rd black mark (A)............... **250.00**
7½" l, "Bamboo" pattern, McBirney lid with
instructions printed inside, 1st black mark. **600.00**
"Neptune" pattern, shell feet and finial, green
trim, 2nd black mark **299.00**
"Tridacna" pattern, gold trim, 2nd black
mark................................. **334.00**
Tea Service, teapot, 5¾" h, sugar bowl, milk
jug, 5 cups, 10 saucers, molded with branches
of flowering prunus in green, orange, brown,
pink, blue, and turquoise with gilded details,
c1878, imp Reg mark, printed and some imp
marks, 14 pcs (A) **2822.00**
Tea Set, teapot, 5¼" h, sugar, 2" h, creamer,
2¼" h, "Hexagon" pattern, green twisted
rope handles, 2nd black mark **800.00**
Tete-a-Tete Set
Teapot, creamer, sugar bowl, 2 cups and saucers, tray, 16" l, 14" w, "Tridachna" pattern, 1st black mark **2000.00**
Teapot, creamer, sugar bowl, 2 cups and saucers, tray, 14½" l, "Neptune" pattern,
molded shell shapes with pink tints, c1860–
1926 (A) **840.00**
Toy Sugar and Creamer, "Shamrock" pattern,
3rd black mark......................... **99.00**
Tray, 17½" d, "Erne" pattern, yellow trim, 2nd
black mark............................. **550.00**
Tumbler, 2nd black mark **110.00**
Vase
3½" h, 5" l, seahorse, 1st black mark **595.00**
6" h
Corn figurals, 1st black marks, pr **385.00**
Frog figural with black outlined eyes, 2nd
black mark **1375.00**
6¼" h, tree trunk, worn purple luster trim, 1st
black mark **400.00**
7" h, "Aberdeen" pattern, ewer shape with
ribbed body and raised floral relief, loop
handle, 3rd black mark, pr (A)........... **495.00**
7½" h, "Sunflower" design, 3rd green
mark.................................. **50.00**
8¼" h, lizard curling around vase stem,
mushrooms on base, pearl finish, 1st black
mark................................. **1500.00**
9" h, "Princess," flowers in yellow, pink, blue,
and white, 2nd black mark **795.00**

10" h, "Aberdeen" pattern, overall applied
flowers, 2nd black mark **495.00**
11" h, "Hippiritus Centre," four places for
flowers, slightly yellow edge, c1863–91, 1st
black mark **1500.00**
13" h, modeled tree trunk with flowers and
birds, 2nd black mark.................... **1200.00**
13⅛" h, "The Nile" design, protruding lilies
at fluted neck, raised leaves on base, 2nd
black mark **595.00**
14" h, Calalily, 3rd black mark............. **1200.00**
Typha Spill, green ribbon at center, bows front
and back, 2nd black mark............... **88.00**

1857

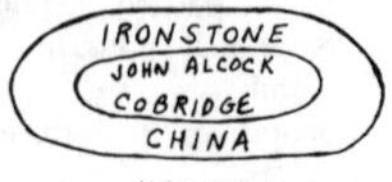

ROYAL   PREMIUM
SEMI PORCELAIN
T. & R. BOOTE.
ENGLAND.
1890-1906

ROYAL STONE CHINA
WEDGWOOD & CO
ENGLAND
1891-1900

IRONSTONE, PATTERNED AND WHITE

Staffordshire, England
Early 1840s–c1891

History: White ironstone in Gothic shapes was first produced from Staffordshire in the early 1840s. Gothic
shapes already had been used by Staffordshire potters for
cobalt and mulberry transfer wares. Roses, lilies, and
human profiles comprised the finials or the trim under the
handles.

The firm of James Edwards of Burslem made a tremendous variety of designs in white ironstone. T.J. & J. Mayer
designed "Prize Puritan" and "Prize Bloom." "Adam's
Scallop," "Line Trim," and "Scalloped Decagons" by J.
Wedgwood and Davenport all used scallops in the pottery
design. "Fluted Pearl" by J. Wedgwood and "Fig" by J.
Wedgwood and Davenport are among the most collectible patterns.

William Adams, John Alcock, E. Challinor & Co., Davenport, C. Meigh & Son, and J. Wedgwood were some of the
firms making white ironstone in the 1840s and 50s.
Thomas and Richard Boote's "Octagon Shape" in 1851
was the forerunner of the famous "Sydenham Shape"
from 1853. Many potters proceeded to copy these popular shapes.

'President' by James Edwards and "Columbia," made
by six different companies, were registered in 1855. The
potters of "Columbia" used the same borders on the
plates and platters, but used varied finials and foliage
decorations. "Dallas," "Mississippi," and "Baltic Shapes"

also were registered in that year. Many other shapes appeared from the Staffordshire Potteries during the 1850s.

Many white ironstone patterns used corn, oats, and wheat in the design such as "Corn & Oats" manufactured by J. Wedgwood and Davenport from 1863, "Wheat & Blackberry" by J. & G. Meakin from 1865, "Prairie Shape" from 1862, and "Ceres" by Elsmore and Forster from 1859.

During the 1860s gardens and woods inspired the designers of white ironstone. Patterns such as "Sharon Arch," "Hanging Arch," "Winding Vine," and "White Oak and Acorn" are just a few that developed. Flowers also influenced the Staffordshire potters during the 60s in such patterns as "Morning Glory" by Elsmore & Forster, "Moss Rose" by J. & G. Meakin, "Bordered Fuchsia" by A. Shaw, and "The Hyacinth" by J. Wedgwood.

Ribbed patterns also were popular as in Meakin's "Ribbed Raspberry with Bloom" and Pankhurst's "Ribbed Chain" during the 1860s. A classical revival was seen in "Athens Shape" by Podmore Walker & Co. and "Athenia" by J.T. Close.

Rectangular shapes became popular during the 1870s and 1880s. After 1891 ironstone diminished as the demands for porcelains increased.

References: Jean Wetherbee, *A Look at White Ironstone*, Wallace-Homestead, 1980; Jean Wetherbee, *A Second Look at White Ironstone*, Wallace-Homestead, 1984.

Plate, Patterned, 9" d, multicolored floral and vine design, gilt highlights, c1875, England, (A) $30.00

Sauce Tureen, White, 9" h, 8" l, "1851 Shape," imp "T. Boote" mark, 225.00

PATTERNED

Cake Stand, 11¾" d, 3" h, light blue fruit and basket design, c1845, "Francis Morley & Co." mark **175.00**

Cheese Dish, 8½" l, 6" h, rect, oriental style pink, rust, green, and blue florals, bridge scene, fluted edge, blue gilt handle, c1850, unmarked **225.00**

Cup and Saucer, Handleless, "Flora" pattern, "FLORA-WEDGWOOD" mark, set of 4 . . . . **90.00**

Dinner Service, 48 plates, 18 soup bowls, 36 dessert plates, 12 oval serving dishes in sizes, 4 cov vegetable tureens, 2 cov soup tureens, stands, 2 cov sauce tureens, stands, ftd bowl, strainer, printed and painted with "Two Temples" pattern with figures crossing a bridge and boats in an island setting, 1862–80, Ashworth, printed and imp marks, pattern no. "B3345," 136 pcs (A) **9029.00**

Dish, 8" l, leaf shape with stem handle, green feather edge, imp "W. Daniel" mark (A) **220.00**

Dish, Cov, 10" d, ftd, four yellow and brown birds, multicolored florals, gilt rim, c1900, "Alfred Meakin" mark (A) **18.00**

Jug, 6⅞" h, black printed and colored with port scene, reverse inscribed "Our bread untaxed, our commerce free," grotesque handle (A). . **200.00**

Mug, Cylindrical
  2⅞" h, applied glazed white reliefs of the "THE KILL" on center blue band, sq handle (A) **77.00**
  5" h, colored enamels with flowering foliage in shades of green, puce, orange, and blue, loop handle, early 19th C, pr (A) **1693.00**

Mustard Pot, 2⅞" h, green feather edges, emb leaf handle (A) **165.00**

Pitcher
  4½" h, floral design highlighted with pink, blue, yellow, green, and red, "Fielding and Co." mark **50.00**
  7¾" h, black transfer of Oddfellows motif, applied lavender scenes of dogs ans scrolls, 19th C (A) **220.00**
  8⅜" h, emb green leaf design, mask spout, repairs (A) **660.00**
  9" h, gaudy floral designs in poychromes, "Allerton's Persian Ware, England" mark (A). . **37.00**

Plate
  6¼" d, "Our Union Forever Centenial" in center, Liberty Bell, flags and 1776–1876 on border, "Edge Malkin & Co." mark **50.00**
  7" d, "Moss Rose" design, gold decor, "EDWARD BROS." mark (A) **10.00**
  9½" d, rect scenic center, blue Imari style floral design, "Patent Ironstone China" mark, set of 10 . . . . **195.00**
  9¾" d, cobalt, orange, iron-red, and gold flowers, green leaves, flowerhead border, "blue Ironstone China" mark **185.00**
  10" d
    "Chinese Chinc" in blue, pink, green, and tan, scalloped edge, c1860, "W. Adams & Co, England" mark **145.00**
    Hp multicolored florals and bird on branch on border, white ground, "Alfred Meakin" mark (A) **10.00**
    "Progress" pattern, blue transfer, "W.H. Grindley" mark **22.00**
    "Royal Blue" pattern, blue floral center,

white ground, spiral relief border, platinum rim, "Wedgewood, Ironstone" mark, set of 6 .... 45.00
White center panel with cobalt, pink, yellow, and rust florals, cobalt rim with gilt and cartouches with chinese figures and flowers, printed and imp "Ashworth" mark 295.00
10 1/8" d, oct, green feather edge (A) 55.00
10 1/4" d, "Chinese Landscape" pattern with green, salmon, red, and dark green highlights, "Ashworth Brothers" mark 75.00
10 3/8" d, black underglaze berry design (A) 50.00

Platter
11" l, "Phileau" pattern, pink transfer 22.00
13" l, 9 1/2" w, rect, moss rose design with gilt accents, white ground, Meakin (A) 5.00
13 1/4" l, underglaze blue floral design with polychrome enamels, unmarked (A) 165.00
13 5/8" l, oct, blue, red, green enameled seaweed design, luster accents, crazing (A) .. 75.00
14 1/4" l, white body, blue feather edge (A). 60.00
15 1/4" l, 12 1/4" w, oval, "Imari" pattern with central mons in cobalt, iron red and gilt, c1887, Ashworth 200.00
16 1/2" l, "Alsager Rose" pattern, "John Maddock & Sons" mark 45.00
19" l, blue and white floral transfer decoration, last qtr 19th C (A) 357.00
21" l, 17" w, "Apple Blossom" pattern, blue and white transfer, mid 19th C (A) 525.00

Punch Bowl, 18" d, multicolored flowers on red ground (A) 66.00
Sauce Tureen, 7 1/8" l, with ladle, green feather edges, floral knob, hairlines (A) 550.00
Soup Bowl, 9" d, "Alhambra" pattern, green transfer, "Henry Alcock" mark 20.00
Soup Plate, 10" d, green feather edge (A) 55.00
Soup Tureen, Cov, and Stand
11 1/2" h, oval body, blue underglaze and polychrome floral decoration, twig handles, foliate finial on domed cov, broken handle (A) 375.00
15" H-H, 16" l, oval, "Chinese Chinc" pattern, blue, pink, green, and tan florals, c1862, imp "ASHWORTH" mark 695.00
16 3/4" d, painted panels of roses, lilacs, and passion flowers, gilt floral scroll borders, dbl handles with gilt leaf terminals, orange pumpkin knob (A) 1045.00

Sweet Meat Dish, 11" H-H, oriental garden scene with building and fence, brown, pink, rust, and green florals and leaves, paneled border, scalloped edge, c1830, unmarked 250.00
Teapot, 8 3/4" h, paneled, blue floral transfer with polychrome enamels (A) 105.00
Toothbrush Holder, 4 1/2" h, "Diana" pattern, Meakin 35.00
Vase, Cov, 31" h, oct, printed and painted sprays of colored flowers and foliage on iron-red ground, twin dolphin handles, entwined dolphin finial, c1835–50, pr (A) 10,450.00
Vegetable Bowl, Cov, 11" d, "Savoy" pattern, "T.& R. Boote" mark 78.00

WHITE

Baking Dish, 13" l, 10 1/8" w, 3" d, "Gothic Shape," eight sided rect, 1840s-1850s, imp "J. Edwards, Dale Hall, Opaque China" mark... 45.00
Chamber Pot, Cov, "Corn and Oats" pattern, 1863, imp "Ironstone China, Wedgwood" mark 130.00
Compote, 7 1/2" h, pedestal, "Gothic Shape," ten sided, handled, 1840s-1850s, "black Ironstone China, I. Meir & Son" mark 95.00
Creamer, 5 1/2" h, bulbous shape, "Cable and Ring," 1870s, "black Stone China, H. Burgess, Burslem" mark 35.00
Cup and Saucer, "Wheat," 1860s
"Black Pearl White, Baker & Co. LD" mark 25.00
"Black Robert Cochran & Co., Glasglow, Imperial Ironstone China" mark 30.00

Cup and Saucer, Handleless
"Athens Shape," 'Wedgwood & Co." mark 28.00
Tea size, "Ceres Shape," 1859, imp "Elsmore & Forster, Ceres Shape, Tunstall" mark 45.00
"Vintage Shape," Grape and Medallion, 1865, imp "Ironstone China, E & C Challinor" mark 35.00
"Wheat," 1860s, imp "J & G Meakin" mark. 27.00
"Wheat," 1860s, "black Royal Ironstone China, Mellor, Taylor & Co., England" mark 27.00

Cup Plate, 4 3/4" d, "Prairie Shape," 1862, imp "J. Clementson, Hanley" mark 18.00
Dessert Plate,
6 5/8" d, "Prairie Shape," 1862, imp "Clementson, Hanley" mark 10.00
7 1/4" d, "Sydenham Shape," round, 1853–54, imp "T & R Boote, Sydenham Shape" mark 17.00

Gravy Boat,
5" h, "Wheat and Blackberry," 1860s, unmarked 40.00
5 1/4" h, "Fuchsia," bulbous, 1860s 25.00
5 1/2" h, "Ceres Shape," 1859, imp "Elsmore & Forster, Ceres Shape" mark 40.00

Milk Pitcher, 8 1/2" h, "Ceres Shape," 1859, imp "Elsmore & Forster, Ceres Shape, Tunstall" mark 60.00
Nappie, 5" d, "Mocho Shape," 1863, imp "T & R Boote, Ironstone" mark 8.00
Pitcher
9" h, "Wheat and Blackberry" pattern, "Taylor and Hanley" mark 65.00
11" h, "Ceres Shape," ewer body style, 1859, imp "Elsmore & Forster, Ceres Shape, Tunstall" mark 250.00

Plate
9 1/4" d, "Scalloped Decagon," 1852, imp "Davenport, Ironstone China" mark...... 2.00
9 1/2" d
"Fluted Pearl," twenty sides, 1847, imp "Registered October 9, 1845, J. Wedgwood," 'black Ironstone China, Pearl, J. Wedgwood" mark 15.00
"Sydenham Shape," oct shape, 1853–54, imp "T & R Boote, Sydenham Shape" mark 20.00

9 3/4" d
"Bell Flower," 1860s, imp "J & J Edwards, Manufacturers, Fenton" mark 15.00
"Ceres" shape, "Elsmore & Forster" mark. 22.00

Platter, 16" l, "Sydenham Shape," oval, 1853–54 .... 50.00
Relish Dish, 8 1/4" l, 5 1/8" d, "Wheat," 1860s. 20.00

Sauce Dish
    4" l, cov, ladle, "Baltic Shape," 1855 imp "T.
    Hulme, Baltic Shape," **85.00**
    6⁷/₈" l, 2⁷/₈" d, ladle, "Cable and Ring,"
    1870s.............................   **45.00**
Sauce Tureen, Cov, 7⁷/₈" H-H, underplate, "Co-
    lumbia Shape," 1855, imp "Joseph Goodwin,
    Ironstone China" mark...................   **110.00**
Sauce Tureen, Cov, Underplate, Ladle
    6¹¹/₁₆" h, "Ribbed Bud," oval shape, 1860s   **220.00**
    8" h, "Prize Bloom," eight sided round shape,
    1851, "black Prize Medal 1851, T.J.& J.
    Mayer, Dale Hall Pottery, Longport, Im-
    proved Berlin Ironstone" mark..........   **220.00**
Shaving Mug
    3¹/₄" h, "Athens Shape," 1842, unmarked .   **70.00**
    3³/₈" h, "Wild Flower," 1860s **85.00**
    3³/₄" h, "Ceres Shape," 1859, unmarked...   **35.00**
Soap Dish, Cov, Insert, 4¹/₄" h, "Bordered Hya-
    cinth," 1860s, "W. Baker & Co." mark **140.00**
Soup Plate
    8³/₈" d, "Sydenham Shape," round, 1853–
    54, imp "T & R Boote, Syndenham Shape"
    mark............................   **12.00**
    9¹/₂" d, "Fig," ten sided, 1856, imp "Daven-
    port, Ironstone China" mark..........   **25.00**
    9⁵/₈" d, "Ceres Shape," 1859, "black War-
    rented Stone China, Elsmore & Forster," imp
    Elsmore & Forster, Tunstall, Ceres Shape"
    mark............................   **25.00**
Soup Tureen, 8³/₈" h, 9³/₄" d, cracker tray,
    ladle, "Sydenham Shape," replaced finial,
    1853–54, imp "T & R Boote & Co., Sydenham
    Shape" mark........................   **395.00**
Sugar Bowl, Cov, 7¹/₄" h, "Ceres Shape," 1859,
    imp "Elsmore & Forster, Ceres Shape, Tun-
    stall" mark.........................   **60.00**
Syrup Pitcher, 5" h, "Panelled Columbia,"
    1850s, unmarked.....................   **60.00**
Teapot, 10" h, "Ceres Shape," 1859, "black
    Royal Patent Ironstone, Turner Goddard &
    Co." mark.........................   **225.00**
Toothbrush Holder, 8¹/₈" l, 2⁵/₈" d, lid, "Wheat
    and Blackberry," 1860s, unmarked........   **70.00**
Tray, 9" H-H, "Moss Rose" design, gold decor,
    "Wedgwood" mark (A) **15.00**
Vegetable Dish, Open,
    5" d, individual, "Vintage Shape," Grape and
    Medallion, 1865, imp "E & C Challinor"
    mark.............................   **8.00**
    8⁵/₁₆" l, "Prairie Shape," 1862, imp "Prairie
    Shape, Clementson, Hanley" mark **22.00**
    9¹/₈" l, "Boote's 1851 Octagon," imp "T & R
    Boote & Co." mark..................   **55.00**
    9³/₈" l, "Hebe Shape," 1853, imp "John Al-
    cock, Hebe Shape" mark **40.00**
    11³/₄" l
       6¹/₂" h, "Memnon Shape," 'John Meir &
       Son" mark **115.00**
       7³/₄" h, "Tiny Oak and Acorn," "J.W. Park-
       hurst" mark **110.00**
Vegetable Tureen, Cov
    6¹/₄" h, 9⁵/₈" l, "Ivy Wreath," oval, 1857,
    imp "Ivy Wreath. John Meir & Son," 'black
    Stone China, John Meir & Son, Tunstall"
    mark.............................   **70.00**
    7³/₈" h, 8¹³/₁₆" d, "Boote's 1851 Octagon,"
    imp "T & R Boote" mark...............   **85.00**

ITALIA
1901

ITALY—GENERAL

Venice
1727–1812

Hard paste porcelain was made by Francesco and Guiseppe **Vezzi** in Venice with workers brought from Meissen
between 1720 and 1727. The products resembled the
early Meissen and Vienna wares. Teawares were the most
popular form. The oldest pieces have black and gold coloring. Later Venetian red was used. Porcelains were marked
with various forms of the word Venice: VENEZIA, VEN, or
Va in either gold, underglaze blue, or red.

After the Vezzi factory closed, a new factory was established by Friedrich Hewelke in 1758. His china was
marked with the letter "V." The factory failed in 1763
during the Seven Years War.

A more successful factory to manufacture hard paste
porcelain was established by Geminiano **Cozzi** from 1764
until 1812. Both utilitarian and ornamental wares were
made and exported throughout Europe. Cozzi's wares
featured pouring spouts on coffeepots molded with leaf
decorations. Figures from the Italian Comedy were made
along with colored and white tea sets, services, and vases.
Pieces were marked with an anchor in red, blue, or gold.

Le Nove
1750 to Late 19th Century

Pasquale Antonibon established a porcelain factory in
Le Nove in 1750. He took Francisco Parolini as a partner
in 1781. The painter Giovanni Marconi was the factory's
most prolific decorator. He signed several Meissen type
examples of harbor scenes and rural romances. The factory was leased to Baroni in 1802, reverted to the Antonibon family in 1825, and continued to produce until the
late 19th century. Its principal production was tablewares.
Special pieces included fish shaped tureens. The Sevres
influence was strong. The mark used was a comet or a star
in red, blue, or gold.

Naples
1771–1807

King Ferdinand IV, son of Charles IV, established the
Royal Naples Factory in Naples in 1771 to manufacture
porcelain and fill the gap left by the transfer of Capodimonte to Buen Retiro in Spain in 1759. Neo-classical
wares were made along with the rococo styles formerly
used by the Capodimonte workers. Domenico Venuti became director from 1779 until 1807. Filipo Tagliolini modeled figures of people from Naples in the fashions of the
day. The factory was taken over by the French in 1807 and
then closed in 1834.

The marks used were "FRF" under a crown until 1787
and then a crowned "N" impressed or painted in underglaze blue.

Vinovo
1776–1840

Gian Brodel from Turin and Marchese Birago of Vische, assisted by Peter Hannong, established a hard paste porcelain factory in Vinovo in 1776. It went bankrupt after a few years. Dr. Victor Gioanotti and Tamietti, a modeler, reopened the factory in 1780. They made mythological figures in colored and white porcelain, services with rococo decorations, vases with rural landscapes, groups and statuettes in the Capodimonte style, and busts of famous people in biscuit ware. The factory remained in operation until 1815 when Gioanotti died.

Giovanni Lamello, after working there as a sculptor from 1798, bought the factory in 1815. The factory marks imitated those of Sevres and the Meissen swords. The marks were either impressed or painted in underglaze blue or in red, gray, or black on the glaze.

Maiolica or Faience
1400 to Present

The earliest maiolica was produced by potteries located near Florence at Orvieto, Faenza, Siena, and Arezzo and used manganese purple and copper green decoration on pieces made for everyday use. These wares were inspired by earlier Spanish examples. Early in the 15th century, a cobalt blue was introduced from the Middle East. About 1450 new colors of yellow, turquoise, and orange appeared.

The rise of Faenza coincided with the brilliant colors used in the istoriato or pictoral style of Urbino. The entire surface of the piece was covered with historical, classical, mythological, or biblical scenes. Subjects included heraldic lions, birds, portraits, and foliage designs. Large drug jars with strap handles were made. Grotesques and arabesques were introduced in the 16th century. Faenza wares were at their finest from about 1480 until 1520.

Pictorals in the istoriato style were done at Castel Durante and Urbino. Venetian maiolica exhibited an Oriental influence due to trade with the East. Large globular jars were a favorite shape.

Savona in Liguria made maiolica in the 17th and 18th centuries. A wide variety of wares were made including teawares and figures. Castelli near Naples, made maiolica in the 17th and 18th centuries, reviving the Istoriato style.

During the 17th and 18th centuries, many factories produced maiolica wares. Eventually they turned to the production of lead glazed earthenwares in English style. Manufacturing of tin enamel wares still continues in Italy. Some of the production directed toward making souvenirs for tourists.

Cantagalli
1878–1901

Cantagalli, an Italian potter, opened his faience factory in Florence in 1878 and used the crowing cock as its mark. The firm traded as Figli di Giuseppe Cantagalli. This factory manufactured imitations of early Italian maiolica, similar to pieces from Urbino, Faenza, Gubbio, Deruta, and at the Della Robbia workshop. The factory also imitated tin glazed earthenwares in the Isnik and Persian styles. Art Nouveau style is found in vases decorated with elongated plant motifs. Vases and dishes designed by William De Morgan were manufactured. Among its original products were decorative tablewares.

References: A. Lane, *Italian Porcelain*, Faber & Faber, 1954; B. Rackham, *Italian Maiolica*, Faber & Faber, 2nd Edition, 1963; John Scott-Taggart, *Italian Majolica*, Hamlyn Publishing Group, Ltd., 1972.

Museums: Bargello Museum, Florence, Italy; Birmingham Museum of Art, Birmingham, Alabama; British Museum, London, England; Gardiner Museum of Ceramic Art, Toronto, Canada; Musee National de Ceramique, Sevres, France; Museo Civico, Turin, Italy; National Museum of Wales, Cardiff, Wales; Seattle Art Museum, Seattle, WA; Victoria & Albert Museum, London, England; Wadsworth Atheneum, Hartford, CT.

Additional Listings: Capodimonte, Deruta, Ginori.

Albarello
4¾" h, blue inscription with drug name within linenfold and berry borders in blue and brown, 1480–1500, Siena (A) **15,428.00**
7½" h, painted with drug names "Ell. Teriaia" and Vng. Rosato Mal" on scrolling foliate label below figure of Justice standing on defeated devil, late 17th C, pr (A) **2674.00**
7¾" h, procession of swans and fish passing along a river, mtd troops on opposite bank, reverse plain, mid 18th C, Naples (A) **785.00**
9" h, dumb-bell body, blue inscription " V;ROSATO" on scroll, ground of scrolling shaded foliage, damaged, 16th C (A) **452.00**
9½" h, cylindrical form, colorful flowerheads and leaf scrolls, two circ portrait panels of old bearded man and lady with light blue veil, blue washed ground, late 16th C, Venice (A) **1080.00**

Charger, 12" d, faience, underglaze blue floral decorations, late 19th C, (A) $51.00

Plaque, 6" d, terra cotta, white with blue insert, imp "Cantagalli Firenze, Marco Otto and rooster" marks, pr, $2950.00

10½" h, majolica, portrait medallions within foliate cartouches, sloping shoulders and foot with broad entwined ribbon borders, yellow and blue ground, hair cracks, 17th C, Burgio (A) **1309.00**

11" h, armorial bearing of a rampant lion above blank cartouche, slender waisted form, blue, yellow, and green, cracked, late 17th/early 18th C, Naples, pr (A) **785.00**

Basket, 6" h, boat form, majolica, white glaze, rope form handle and trim (A) **55.00**

Bottle, 7⅝" h, fluted sq shape, blue painted ship, castle, and landscape, leaf and line border, Savona **650.00**

Bowl

7⅝" d, panels of harbor scenes hung with flower garlands, rims edged in gold and platinum, two handles, "blue and incised N" mark (A) **864.00**

9¼" d, with underplate, faience, basketweave with polychrome flowers, "Made in Italy" mark (A) **25.00**

13" l, int and ext painted in blue with putti and other figures among scattered flowers, blue-tinted ground, late 17th C, Bassano, "crown" mark (A) **1234.00**

14¾" l, fluted body, manganese and blue with Adam taking apple from Eve, human headed serpent entwined in tree behind them, bluedash rim and ext, foot damaged, late 17th C, Savona (A) **1722.00**

18" l, oval, majolica, painted floral and leaf decoration **275.00**

Cabinet Cup and Saucer, can shape, colored panels with Temple of Serapis at Pozzouli near Naples, saucer with view of Piazza at Pozzuoli, gold fishscale borders, both scenes titled on reverse, incised workmen's marks, Naples (A) **1530.00**

Centerpiece, 9" h, 7" d, tin glazed, six white merry-go-round horses holding center bowl, brown and green raised base **75.00**

Coffee Cup and Saucer

Comical figure blowing horn in oriental garden, multicolored enamels, leaf and berry border, c1770, Cozzi (A) **2244.00**

Painted in enamels with finely dressed figure on elaborate scrolled and stepped support, monkey on gold lead, rococo style, low set loop handle, small bun thumbpiece, c1765, "red enamel star" marks, Nove (A) **1074.00**

Coffee Pot, 5⅛" h, pear shape, multicolored bunch of flowers and scattered sprigs, sparrow-beak spout, scroll handle, domed cov pierced with two holes, ball finial, 1770–80, incised mark, Cozzi (A) **300.00**

Cup and Saucer, Demitasse

Bright floral design, yellow rim on saucer ... **5.00**

Red and yellow roses on ivory ground, lavender trim, scrolled body................ **5.00**

Dish

9⅜" d, circ, blue, ochre, light blue, and tan with Venus and three putti riding in cockle shell chariot drawn by two dolphins, rim with border of putti and scrolling foliage flanking arms of Galliani of Bologna, c1720, Castelli (A) **14,355.00**

10⅝" d, majolica, Isnik style with spray of tulips, carnations, and bell-flowers among foliage in blue, green, ochre, and manganese, reverse with stylized characters in blue, early 17th C, Padua (A) **1870.00**

11½" d

Istoriato, tones of brown, green, yellow, and blue with prophet and warriors standing before broken statue in river landscape, washed in cream slip, reverse unglazed, ftd, 17th C (A) **2631.00**

Majolica, Fall of Adam, human-bodied serpent handing down an apple from tree round which she is entwined, Eve at foot of river, river god holding cornucopia and pouring water from urn, blue towns and mountains in distance, ochre, green, tan, c1545, repainted flakes, Urbino (A) **52360.00**

13⅜" l, silver shape, majolica, blue and colored flowering plants growing from stylized rococo scrolls, rim with narrow band of trailing foliage, haircrack, c1760, Nove (A) ... **1148.00**

14¼" d, majolica, central circ medallion with animals in landscape, three oriental fan shaped reserves with oriental or European figures within red line borders, blue ground, hairline, mid 18th C, "red script Milano' (A) **3200.00**

16" d, majolica, gray-blue Chinese style spiralling flowers within a barbed line border, barbed rim with seeded diaper border, c1760 (A) **850.00**

Drug Bottle, 10⅜" h, rect form, blue rabbits, deer, and birds amidst flowering foliage, floral and line borders, Savona (A).............. **792.00**

Drug Jar

6½" h, dumb-bell body, inscribed in manganese "Ung:Artanite" within manganese and blue flower and laurel swag borders, lower border with "A.C." c1780, Nove (A)................................ **648.00**

9" h, ovoid body, painted manganese, washed in blue, green, and yellow with overlapping peacock feathers within borders of lines and groups of dots, 17th C, Caltagirone (A)........................ **1748.00**

Ewer, 9½" h, baroque form, multicolored floral sprays, broken scroll handle with stylized sunbursts, 18th C, Nove (A) **1914.00**

Figure

5⁹⁄₁₆" h, innkeeper and wife, man in pink cap, black buttoned pink waistcoat, iron-red sash, maroon striped pink breeches, wife with white apron, maroon dotted pink jacket with yellow cuffs, dark brown bodice, dark brown edged pink skirt, iron-red stockings, mottled tan mound bases, 1790–1800, Naples, pr (A)......................... **14,300.00**

6¼" h, white group of Esther and the King, young woman kneeling in chains before Xeres on throne, feet on tasseled cushion, firing crack, late 18th C (A) **4725.00**

6¾" h, lady, purple dotted yellow scarf, white bodice, blue dotted white skirt, purple sash, green overskirt, black slippers, grassy mound base in mottled green, brown, and ochre, 1790–95, underglaze "blue N" mark (A)............................... **14,850.00**

7⅛" h, gentleman, tall black hat, gold hatband, gilt edged brown coat, yellow collar, yellow breeches, gold buckled black shoes, tan mound base, 1790–1800, Naples (A)................................. **7700.00**

8" h
"Ciabattino," The Shoemaker, multicolored,
sgd "Tiziano Galli' (A) 70.00
Duck, overall floral and vine motif in colors,
pr 65.00
9" h, 5 1/2" l, pottery, boy in brown trousers,
pointed shoes, holding leaves and berries,
two geese, rustic seat, sgd "Maklico" 75.00
10 1/16" h, majolica, bust of Madonna in blue
and green head scarf, ochre dress, green
washed circ socle, 17th C 850.00
11 1/2" h, majolica, group of the Continents,
white, two turbanned Asiatic figures and
seated figure of Minerva, representing
Europe, grouped around tree and accompanied by horse, camel, and lion, c1750, Milan
(A). 5742.00
12" h, "Young Lovers," multicolored, sgd
"Cappe' (A) 250.00
13 3/4" h, young boy with wide floppy hat
atride fountain, seated monkey and dog,
multicolored, damage to hat, early 17th C,
Urbino (A). 3142.00
16" h, 20" l, modeled three allegorical female
figures seated on columnar base, classical
tripod base, tin glazed polychromes (A) . .   900.00
17 1/2" h, Madonna and child in tin glazed
polychromes, "Minghetti, Bologna, Italy"
mark (A) 187.00
40" h, majolica, woman holding fan or man
playing guitar, 18th C style dress, circ base
with acanthus scrolled feet, multicolored,
pr 850.00
55" h, majolica, Blackamoor wearing feath-
ered headress and Moroccan style costume, holding pillow, faux marble pedestal,
multicolored, pr (A). 6600.00
Inkstand, 2 1/2" h, tin glazed, lobed form, floral
decoration (A) 66.00
Jar, 11 3/4" h, globular body, majolica, lion roar-
ing in a domestic landscape, reverse plain,
short neck and foot with blue line borders,
bright colors, 18th C (A) 2244.00
Jar, Oil, 13" h, globular body, majolica, broad
strap handle, short waisted neck, white
ground, inscribed in blue "OGLIO," cracks,
dated 1670 (A) 490.00
Jug
2" h, globular body, blue with scroll inscribed
"salus" among scattered flowers, 18th C,
Savona, "tower" mark (A). 411.00
7 7/8" h, waisted pear shaped body, porcelain,
loose bouquets of garden flowers in colors,
mask spout, formal borders, high handle
molded with lion and female mask terminals, c1790, Naples, imp "ll and crown"
mark (A) 740.00
8 1/4" h, bottle shape, tin glazed, blue with
putto amongst flowers on island, flowering
plants, tied strap handle, entwined terminal,
haircracks, 17th/early 18th C (A). 804.00
15 1/4" h, slender ovoid body, majolica, green
and manganese with stylized plants and
cross-hatched fruit, strap handle, broad rim,
15th C (A). 540.00
Milk Jug, Cov, 4 5/16" h, pear shape, rose, blue,
purple, yellow, and green sprays and sprigs of
flowers, pale green bands around foot and
base, pink shaded yellow pear sprig knob with
tan stem and three green leaves, spout

molded with stylized leaf, 1775–80, Naples,
"blue enamel crowned RFF monogram and
incised S" marks (A) 660.00
Pitcher
9" h, glazed redware, incised and polychrome
animal scene with oak leaves, inscribed
base (A). 245.00
13" h, ovoid body, majolica, blue, yellow,
ochre, and manganese with Turk wielding
scimitar to behead victim, within ladder pattern panel, reverse with blue monogram
"GS" and scroll decoration, damaged, late
17th C (A). 1028.00
Plaque
4 7/8" l, 6 1/2" w, rect shape, Naples style,
molded and brightly colored with bear
scenes, gilt metal mtd, c1880–1900 (A) . .   250.00
7" d, circ, captioned scenes from book of
Genesis, Creation of Man, Formation of Eve,
Adam and Eve at Tree of Knowledge, and
Banishment from Eden, blue, rust, ochre,
green, and brown, c1740, Castelli (A) 5550.00
7 3/4" l, 9 3/4" w, pastoral scene of cows drinking at a pond watched by herdsmen before
village, late 18th C Castelli (A) 800.00
10 1/4" l, 7 3/4" w, Madonna and Child seated,
St. John the Baptist kneeling in front of them
holding cross, blue and ochre tones, mid
18th C, Castelli (A) 2057.00
Plate
8 7/8" d, silver shape, polychrome with flowering plant vignette and dragonfly in flight,
c1760, Savona (A) 612.00
9" d, street traders, one showing tattooist
working on client's arm, other with cobbler
mending boots of customer, rims with formal gilt borders, c1800, Naples, captions in
gilding, incised "J," pr (A) 6699.00
9 1/4" d
Center with girl in yellow and ochre blouse
and blue skirt, blue and green leafy
sprays, classic buildings at side, early 18th
C, Savona 1800.00
Porcelain, girl in Spanish dress standing in
mountainous landscape, panels of
seeded diaper within asymmetrical scrolling foliate border, gilt rim, c1800, Naples
(A) 3544.00
Rococo shape, faience, lobed well with bird
perched beside trellis in garden, molded
rim with shells and scrolls, c1750, Le
Nove (A). 1028.00
Tin glazed, polychrome center of bird and
eel, border of wreath of leaves, line rim
(A) 104.00
9 3/8" d, iron-red and gilt branches of grapes,
border of vines and line in gilt bands, c1790,
LeNove, "gold star" mark, set of 12 (A) . .   935.00
10" d
Majolica, blue, green, and manganese with
stylized flowerhead in center surrounded
by line borders, rim incised with squiggles
and lines on manganese ground, re-
stored, 2nd half 15th C, Florentine (A) .   1645.00
Tin glazed, center with lady wearing white
headband and blouse, pink bodice, green
apron over white skirt, floral patterned
hem, carrying basket of flowers, standing
on stone wharf beside little girl, boat in
distance at sea, distant lavender hills

within roundel edged with gilt foliate border, rim with gilt lyre and sprig border, 1785–88, inscribed "Donna della Ma rine di Pozzuoli," 'iron-red crowned RF" mark, Naples (A) 1320.00

10¼" d, majolica, blue sketch of three putti playing blind man's bluff in landscape within formal foliate borders, reverse inscribed in blue "P.G. 1789," green ground (A) 550.00

13¾" d, 2½" h, redware, sgraffito with polychrome glaze, "Pisa, Italy" mark (A) .. 35.00

Platter, 14" l, oval, polychrome enamel florals, scalloped edge (A) 330.00

Snuff Box, Cov, 3⅞" l, waisted rect form, porcelain, molded in relief with wreath of shells with radiating spiralling ribs, reeded sides, Corinthian columns on corners, inside cov with overflowing flower basket on table in soft colors, c1770 (A) 785.00

Sugar Box, Cov, 5⅛" h, oval, swelled sides, multicolored painted sprays of flowers, rose hip knob, Savona (A) 760.00

Tazza, 11⅝" d, circ, majolica, blue deer and rabbit in hilly wooded landscape, birds perched in trees above, Savona (A) 504.00

Teapot, Cov, Warmer, and Stand, 8⅞" h, puce spots within white sqs on green ground, "gold star" mark, Le Nove (A) 126.00

Tea Service, teapot, cov sucrier, cov jug, 5 cups and saucers, puce monochrome, landscape and water scenes with figures and ships, within gilt diaper designs, gold scroll border, Vinovo, unmarked (A) 1980.00

Tray, 17¾" l, majolica, large flower bouquet with rose, tulip, and sunflower in ochre, yellow, blue, green, and manganese, pierced dbl scallop shaped rococo handles, 2nd half 18th C.. 925.00

Tureen, Cov, 15⅛" h, 15¼" l, earthenware duck, ochre bill and feet, black eyes, dark green head, green ringed olive neck, white breast, olive-green and brown plumage and wings, touches of dark green, rose, and blue, seated on oval mound base mottled in brown, green and rose, 19th C, blue "A.V.Nove*" mark (A).............................. 2860.00

Urn
13¾" h, ovoid body, majolica, two cherubs in drapery flanking monogram above pierced hole for spigot, reverse with bird perched on stylized flowers, knobbed base with medallions of birds and animals, twin tope twist handles, molded caryatid masks at shoulders, mid 18th C (A) 1113.00

19¼" h, majolica, center portrait of Caesar, overall florals and stylized leaves, multicolored, dbl loop handles, 18th C (A) 495.00

Vase
13" h, modeled tulip with three sections, each with four floral spouts, painted summer flowers and foliage, circ foot, c1802–20, Le Nove 525.00

19½" h, baluster body, tin glaze, blue with vignette of rural church scene encircled by multicolored flowers, reverse dated 1764, two foliate handles, mask terminals (A) ... 4210.00

Vase, Majolica
11" h, medallion of missionary saint against ground of white daisies and scrolling foliage, neck restored, early 17th C, Sicily (A) 3085.00

13¾" h, ovoid body, one side with yellow ground portrait of Renaissance nobleman, reverse with scrolling emblems and musical instruments on blue ground, foliate borders, neck and foot restored, 17th C, Sicily (A) . 5348.00

Vase, Cov
11½" h, ovoid, high relief of mythological figures in pastel colors, fruit finial, mid 19th C, "blue crowned N" mark, Naples (A)... 850.00

16½" h, ovoid body with Baccholic figures dancing below floral sash garlands, Bacchus head handles, bright enamels, c1900 ..... 575.00

Wet Drug Jar
7½" h, ins "Syr. De Bettonica" on ribboned and striped ground with yellow, ochre, and green flowers, mid 18th C, Urbana (A) ... 574.00

8¼" h, dark blue with drug label "Mosto Cotto" among scrolling fruiting foliage above figure of female saint flanked by initials "SM," late 16th C, Venice (A) 1450.00

JACKFIELD

Staffordshire and Shropshire, England
2nd half 18th century

History: Jackfield was a generic term used for black glazed earthenware made during the second half of the 18th century. The red clay body was covered with a blackish glossy slip that was ornamented with scrollwork and relief flowers, oil gilding, and unfired painting. Jackfield was named after the Shropshire Pottery center.

From c1750–1775 the Jackfield factory was managed by Maurice Thursfield. John Rose of Coalport assumed control of the firm about 1780. Staffordshire potters such as Astbury and Whieldon also produced Jackfield wares.

References: R.G. Cooper, *English Slipware Dishes, 1650–1850*, Tiranti, 1968; The Jackfield Decorative Tile Industry, pamphlet (12 pages), published by Ironbridge Gorge Museum Trust, England, 1978.

Museum: British Museum, London, England.

Cow Creamer
5" h, 6⅜" l, black glaze 231.00

5½" h, 6½" l, gold enamel eyes and band on oval base (A) 137.00

Creamer, 3¼" h, emb floral design (A) 35.00

Cuspidor, 3¼" h, globular body, flared neck, looped handle, brown glaze (A). 210.00

Milk Jug, 8½" h, center cartouche in dark green, blue and yellow florals, gilt trim, pewter top, c1760–80, Shropshire England. 325.00

Teapot, 4¾" h, 8" l, c1889, unmkd, $125.00

Teapot
2½" h, emb acanthus design, unmarked
(A).. **85.00**
4½" h, globular, twig handle and spout, early
19th C...................................... **100.00**
5¾" h, low bellied body, crabstock handle,
curved spout, chained cov, late 18th C
(A).. **210.00**
Tea Urn, 16" h, olive green panel with pink,
black, gold, flowers and leaves, raised green
berries, gilt trim, brass spigot, c1760–80,
Shropshire England **550.00**

JASPER WARE

Staffordshire, England
Continental
1774 to Present

History: About 1774 Josiah Wedgwood perfected a hard,
unglazed stoneware whose body was capable of being
stained throughout its substance with metallic oxides.
Shades of blue, lavender, sage, olive green. lilac, yellow,
and black could be used. With jasper dip, the color was
applied only on the surface.

Many firms, in addition to Wedgwood, produced jasper
wares. Adams made jasper from the early 1800s into the
20th century. Adams blue jasper is distinguished from that
of Wedgwood because it has a faint violet shade. Initially
Adams modeled many of the designs for his jasper ware.
In 1785 he employed Joseph Mongenot from Switzerland
as a modeler. Together they designed the bas-reliefs and
border decorations that were applied in white jasper to
the colored bodies of vases, urns, tea and coffeepots,
plaques, medallions, and candelabra drums. Most of the
Adams jasper is marked.

Another producer of jasper ware was Spode. Other
Staffordshire manufacturers produced marked jasper
ware. Unfortunately, many examples do not include a
maker's mark. Several continental potters, e.g. Heubach
also manufactured jasper ware.

Museums: British Museum, London, England; Memorial
Hall Museum, Philadelphia, PA; Museum of Fine Arts,
Boston, MA; Victoria & Albert Museum, London,
England.

Additional Listing: Wedgwood jasper ware pieces are
found in the Wedgwood listing.

**Cake Server, 9" h, 11" d, white cameos on med
blue ground, unmkd, (A) $220.00**

**Plaque, 8¾" l, white cameos, blue ground, imp
"Germany" mark, $65.00**

Bank, 5" h, 5½" l, ftd, white cameos of six
Kewpies, one holding "K" flag, border of
flowers, "Koin Keeper" on top, blue ground **450.00**
Bookends, 6" h, white figural colonial man with
cane or woman with basket, blue ground, Germany, pr **120.00**
Box
4¼" l, 2¾" w, 2⅛" h, oval, white cameos
of seated fairy queen and Cupid playing
mandolin, flowers on base, blue
ground.................................... **65.00**
4½" l, 3" w, three dancing cherubs in white,
blue ground, unmarked................. **55.00**
5¼" l, oval, white flower cameos on body,
seated winged nymph with bird on hand
and cherub on cov, blue ground, un-
marked.................................... **35.00**
Chamberstick
3⅞" h, pink figural sphinx with tail forming
handle, olive ground, Art Deco style, unmarked.................................... **85.00**
5¾" d, white swirls on green ground, triangular base **20.00**
Cheese Dish, Cov
10½" h, blue dip, large bell shaped cov applied with ferns and grasses, rope and asparagus knob, base with applied grasses,
c1880 (A)................................. **685.00**
11" d, white classical figures and oak leaf trim
on cov, blue ground, unmarked.......... **325.00**
Creamer
3¾" h, raised white classical scenes, pale
green ground **69.00**
White Kewpies on blue ground........... **165.00**
Cup and Saucer, cup with white cameos of Maria
and Charlotte at Tomb of Werther, engine
turned saucer with white stiff leaf border, blue
ground, "TURNER" mark (A) **345.00**
Dish
4½" d, white cameo of Indiam smoking pipe,
green ground........................... **25.00**
5¾" l, 5" w, white cameos of Indian on
horseback with buffalo, green ground, imp
mark.................................... **115.00**
6" d, ftd, white cameo of Cupid shooting
arrow at seated maiden, floral wreath border, green ground, pierced for hanging ... **50.00**
Hair Receiver
2½" h, 4½" w, heart shape, white nymphs
and winged Cupid with birds and flowers,
green ground, Germany **45.00**
White cameos of horse and hunt scene, dark

blue ground, nickel plate top, imp "Adams" mark.................................. 75.00

Humidor, 5" h, white cameo of Indian chief on cov, Indian accessories on base, green ground, Heubach........................ 165.00

Jug
  5 1/8" h, blue and white, classical figures and putti, silver mounting, imp "William Adams" mark (A) 300.00
  5 1/2" h, tan ground, raised white leaves and berries, pewter lid.................... 200.00
  6" h
    Blue and white, lion's head and swag design, pewter lid, England (A).......... 170.00
    White putti playing musical instruments, brown ground, England.............. 112.00

Match Striker, 3 3/8" h, white cameos of ram's heads and draped garlands, band of acorns and oak leaves on base, blue ground, unmarked................................. 55.00

Medallion, 3 1/4" h, 2 3/8" w, black portraits of man and lady, English, pr (A) 270.00

Perfume Bottle, white Cupid and reclining woman, blue ground, unmarked 38.00

Planter
  4 1/2" h, white tumbling Kewpies, blue ground, sgd "Rose O'Neill" 220.00
  6" d, white cameos of putti at various pursuits in floral medallions, white mask feet, blue ground, Germany 85.00

Plaque
  4" h, 3 1/2" w, heart shape, white Kewpies on green ground, sgd "Rose O'Neill" 135.00
  4 1/2" d, Art Nouveau style white nude with trailing gown on green ground, Germany.......................... 65.00
  4 1/2" l, triangular shape, white cameos of three Kewpies sitting on bench with flowers and butterflies, blue ground, pierced for hanging, sgd "Rose O'Neill"............. 265.00
  5 3/4" d, white cameo of seated woman being caressed by Cupid, white leaf border, green ground, Germany 95.00
  6" d
    Oval, white cameo of Indian stalking tigers, green ground, Heubach 125.00
    White and lavender Indian chief on horse, green ground, unmarked.............. 79.00
    White cameos of knight blowing horn and swan, castle in ground, green ground, molded edge 49.00
  7 1/2" d, 8 3/4" l, oval shape, white cameos of classical figures feeding birds, pie crust edges of four border sections, green ground, unmarked, pr..................... 395.00
  9" w, 10 1/2" h, three white dancing Cupids in relief, white baroque framing, green ground, Volkstedt.......................... 450.00
  12 1/2" l, curved, white cameos of six nudes, elk, and goose on green ground, Germany 225.00

Scent Bottle, 3 1/8" h, white cameos of man and woman on each side, blue ground, silver top 495.00

Tea Caddy, 4" h, cylinder shape, white cameos of putti with animals, border of linked S scrolls and florets, stylized foliate border on shoulder and cov, blue ground, imp "TURNER" mark (A).................................... 1215.00

Toothpick Holder, 2 1/4" h, white cameos of dancing maidens, blue ground, "Dudson, Henley, England" mark................... 35.00

Tray, 4 1/2" l, Cupid, man, and woman on green ground, "Germany" mark 30.00

Tumbler, 4" h, white cameo of hunt scene on horseback, blue ground, Copeland 34.00

Vase
  4" h, intaglio cut to white florals, green body, Germany.......................... 65.00
  5" h, white trailing flowers, green ground, unmarked........................... 11.00
  7 1/16" h, white cameo busts of Lord Roberts and Sir Redvers Buller, blue ground, Dudson, pr (A)....................... 300.00
  8" h, white cameos of dancing cherubs, green ground, unmarked...................... 155.00
  10 1/4" h, white cameos of Diana and Apollo in chariots in clouds, formal borders, upright acanthus leaf scroll handles, blue ground, black basalt base, imp "TURNER & CO." mark (A) 575.00

Wall Pocket, 5 1/4" h, cameo of two maidens dancing, hanging pendants, green ground, unmarked................................ 50.00

JOHNSON BROTHERS

Staffordshire, England
1883 to Present

History: Henry, Robert, Alfred, and Fred, the four Johnson brothers, founded a pottery in 1883 in Staffordshire, England. Although begun on a small scale, it soon expanded. Its principal success was derived from earthenware tablewares that were quite successful in both England and the United States.

By 1914 the Johnson Brothers had five factories scattered throughout Hanley, Tunstall, and Burslem. Some popular patterns include "Granite" made for the overseas market, "Green & Golden Dawn," and "Rose." Johnson Brothers' wares originally were white ironstone. It was replaced by a lighter weight ware known for its uncommon lightness and finish.

Johnson Brothers became part of the Wedgwood Group in 1968.

Bowl
  8" d
    Oval, "Coral" pattern................... 25.00
    "Royal Peach" pattern................. 5.00
  8 1/2" d, "English Chippendale" pattern, large red roses and branches................ 10.00

Cream and Sugar, "Wedding Ring" pattern ... 10.00

Cup and Saucer
  "Coral" pattern 10.00

Platter, 12″ l, 10″ w, "English Chippendale" pattern, rose transfer (A) $20.00

"Fruit Sampler" pattern	6.00
"Rose Chintz" pattern	12.50
Windsorware, "Garden Bouquet" pattern . . .	12.00

Dinner Service, Part, 4 plates, 10″ d, 10 plates, 9″ d, gravy boat, platter, 16″ l, platter, 13″ l, open vegetable bowl, 9½″ l, 6 cups and saucers, "Mikado" pattern **85.00**

Gravy Boat, "Lemon Tree" pattern **30.00**

Meat Platter, 12″ l, ironstone, "English Chippendale" pattern **25.00**

Plate
6¼″ d
  "Historic America-Covered Wagons and the Rocky Mountains," blue transfer, set of 6 . . . . **40.00**
  "Old Britain Castles" pattern in blue **7.00**
7⅛″ d, "Mongolia" pattern, center with two exotic birds, blue-green transfer, set of 4 . **60.00**
7½″ sq, "Devonshire" pattern, brown transfer **5.00**
9″ d
  "Gleaners" pattern, artist sgd, "Tatler Johnson Bros. England" mark **20.00**
"Oxford" pattern, blue transfer **30.00**
10″ d, "Olde Abbey" pattern **12.00**
10¾″ d, "Oregon," scenes and portraits in sepia transfer **20.00**

Platter
11″ l, "Friendly Village" pattern **18.00**
12″ l
  "Encore" pattern, "Johnson Bros." mark . . **10.00**
  "Indies" pattern, blue transfer **20.00**
14″ l
  "Coaching Scenes-Passing Through" pattern, blue transfer **25.00**
  "Oxford" pattern, blue transfer **100.00**
17″ l, 14″ w, Windsorware, "Pomona" pattern **55.00**

Soup Plate, 9″ d, "Fenn" pattern **20.00**

Toothbrush Holder, 5⅜″ h, small pink and blue flowers, brown leaves, gold trim, relief scrolled body, scalloped rim, "Royal Semi Porcelain, Johnson Bros." mark **15.00**

Vegetable Bowl
9″ d, ironstone
  "English Chippendale" pattern **22.00**
  "Old Mill" pattern **20.00**
9¼″ l, oval, "The Forks," farm scene with

---

crossroads, purple transfer, made for Marshall Field & Co. for Century of Progress . . **54.00**

KG
Luzeville
1788 - 19ᵀᴴ CENTURY

KELLER AND GUERIN

Luneville, France
1778 to Present

History: Keller and Guerin bought the old faience factory of Jacques Chambrette from Gabriel, his son, and Charles Loyal, his son-in-law, in 1778. The factory made blue decorated faience similar to that of Nevers and rose and green faience that imitated old Strasbourg motifs.

Schneider was the most celebrated of the potters that worked at Keller and Guerin. The company commissioned designs from sculptors Ernest Bussiere and E. Lachenal among others. Biscuit porcelain figures, especially of large animals, were a specialty.

The company switched from faience to English style earthenware at the end of the 19th century. Majolica and transfer printed wares entered the product line. The company still is in operation.

Bowl, 16″ w, raised leaf design on front, white roses in panels, sea green ground, rose int, rim with roses, "K.& G. Luneville" mark **1200.00**

Plate
7¾″ d, "Ce Bons Chasseurs," black transfer, comic scene, green border, "Luneville, France" mark **55.00**
8⅛″ d, flow blue, floral center and border, "green K & G, opaque, Luneville, France" mark, set of 6 . . . . **175.00**
8½″ d, yellow and orange Pears Woman, skirt in blue and yellow with monkey in relief, green leaves, lavender ground, sgd "Obert, Luneville" mark **37.00**
9½″ d, open pink rose with green foliage in center, floral sprigs on border, white

Plate, 9⅛″ d, multicolored, blue rim, marked, $20.00

ground, shaped pink rim, "K.& G. Luneville"
mark.............................. **40.00**

KPM 1835-44   1870-PRESENT

KPM
1844-1947

KING'S PORCELAIN MANUFACTORY (KPM)

Berlin, Germany
1763 to Present

History: The King's Porcelain Manufactory (KPM) was purchased and controlled by Frederick the Great. He ran the factory according to his own ideas and was responsible for its successes and failures, even though he employed Johann Grieninger as director.

The early porcelains were characterized by a dense, clear glaze over a fine white body. Many of the more talented German painters were employed by Frederick, resulting in products that competed with the highly successful Meissen factory.

The 18th century at KPM was characterized by technically superior figures in the glazed and biscuit state that showed a critical attention to details. However, the mainstay of the company was a line of popular, fine tablewares and ornamental pieces. Large quantities of tablewares were decorated with detailed florals and period and pastoral paintings. These early pieces showed a discriminating use of gilding, often used to highlight rather than to decorate. The later periods saw an increase in the use of gilting to the point of excessiveness. After the death of Frederick the Great in 1786, the factory continued to produce dinner services and other utilitarian and decorative porcelains.

The King's Porcelain Manufactory also was known for the fine miniature plaques in porcelain which featured copies of popular paintings of the period. KPM, along with other major European houses, kept up with the times and changing styles, adopting the Rococo, Neoclassical, and Empire styles as each became fashionable. KPM was among the first to produce lithophanes. During the 19th century, the emphasis shifted to simple, clean designs.

From its beginnings, KPM was under the control of the Prussian monarchy. With the abdication of William II, the last of the kings, in 1918, KPM became the property of the Prussian state. It was renamed the States Porcelain Manufactory Berlin. Severe damage from bombings during World War II resulted in the factory being moved to Selb where it leased the porcelain factory of Paul Muller.

After WWII the factory in Berlin was reconstructed. Since the two factories were in separate occupation zones, both branches remained legally separated until 1949. When the Federal Republic of Germany was established in 1949, the factory in Berlin became the property of the City of Berlin (West Property.) The branch in Selb returned to Berlin in 1957. Products from Selb have an "S" beneath the scepter.

References: Winfred Baer, *Berlin Porcelain*, Smithsonian Institution Press, 1980; George W. Ware, *German & Austrian Porcelain*, Crown, Inc., 1963.

Ashtray, 4¾" d, bisque center medallion of two
masks smoking, white ground **35.00**
Bowl
    5" d, two rope handles, scattered flowers .. **40.00**
    9" l, oval form, int reserved with rect panel of classical females and Cupid in wooded clearing, winged caryatid handles, side molded with cherubs flanking a male mask, crimson and blue ground, heavy gilt, late 19th C, underglaze "blue scepter" mark (A) **450.00**
    12" H-H, small pink roses................ **125.00**
    13" l, 9½" w, hp flowers and butterflies in colors, gold trim, "KPM and scepter" mark............................... **95.00**
Cabaret Set
    Tray, 14" l, teapot, hot water jug, sugar bowl, cream jug, 2 cups and saucers, painted sprigs and sprays of flowers between molded gilded spiral borders, "KPM, scepter and orb" marks (A)................. **3740.00**
    Tray, 16¾" l, teapot, 2 tea cups and saucers, cov sucrier, milk jug, cartouches of courting couples, harbor scenes, and landscapes between raised gilded borders on white ground edged in pink, yellow, and green, c1870, underglaze "blue scepter" and imp numerals marks (A)................... **1693.00**
Cabinet Cup and Saucer
    7⅛" d, relief molded biscuit portrait of Kaiser Wilhelm II within gilded foliate border, wide band of overlapping leaves in tones of green, three paw feet, pierced scroll handle, c1914, underglaze "blue scepter," incised marks, printed "black iron cross," pr (A)..................................... **940.00**
    Panel of knight talking to child sitting on his lap, gilt scrolling foliage, saucer with gilding, beaded scroll handle, flared foot, 1725–30, underglaze "blue scepter, imp II" marks (A) **1214.00**
Cabinet Dish, 24" d, Hotel de Ville with horse drawn procession in foreground pulling gilded rococo chariot, wide border molded with

**Cabinet Cup and Saucer, bisque cameo on gold
tooled ground, burgundy body with gold trim,
2nd quarter 19th C, "iron-red orb, blue sceptor,
black iron cross" marks, (A) $330.00**

gilded scrolls and swags, blue ground, c1880, underglaze "blue scepter," inscribed "Char de Bacchus," retailer's mark Hannes & Wieninger, Munich (A) **7392.00**

Candlestick, 10" h, cobalt and gold porcelain support on shaped foot, gilt bronze candle nozzle, pr (A)........................... **150.00**

Centerpiece
13½" l, rim with reserves of enameled blossoms in gilt borders separated by openwork friezes of blossoms and drapery gilt, incised and enameled decorations below, white ground, four block feet, c1900 (A) **1000.00**

14" h, figural, floral decoration on shell form body mounted with putti and cherubs, 19th C (A) **550.00**

19¼" l, oval shape, panels of ladies and gentlemen at leisure in wooded clearing between gilded borders, white and light green ground, sprays of flowers tied with ribbons, molded body, c1880, underglaze "blue scepter, iron-red KPM and printed orb" marks (A).............................. **9292.00**

Clock Set, clock, 21" h, pr of cov urns, clock mtd on three scrolls, seated woman on top, floral base, urns with painted flowers on body, applied ribbons, foliage, and flowers....... **8500.00**

Coffee Cup and Saucer, classical maiden wearing blue hair ribbon, rose drapery, white skirt, seated and holding distaff beneath inscription in black script, flaring rim, loop handle, dome foot and saucer rim with gilt band borders, c1820, underglaze "blue scepter," orange marks and black painter's marks (A)........ **330.00**

Coffee Pot, 10½" h, scattered rust flowers with blue leaves, rust trim, cream ground, "green crowned KPM" mark **50.00**

Coffee Service, coffee pot, 9½" h, creamer, cov sugar, 2 cups and saucers, Empire style, floral spray in gilt trailing vines, mid 19th C (A) ... **220.00**

Cup and Saucer
4" h, angel amidst clouds, gilt floral decorated ground, 3rd qtr 19th C (A) **77.00**

Painted view of Goethe's house, figures in foreground, gilt scrolls on saucer, "blue scepter and KPM" marks (A) **185.00**

Portrait of nobleman in military dress within oct reserve, borders of matte gilding on burnished gilt ground, scrolling acanthus handle, three paw feet, c1830, underglaze "blue scepter, imp 2" marks (A)........ **911.00**

Trembleuse saucer, painted with two hunting scenes in colors, "blue scepter" mark (A) **412.00**

Dinner, Dessert Service, 26 plates, 9½" d, 10 soup bowls, 6 dessert plates, 2 vegetable dishes, sauce boat, circ dish, oval dish, 2 circ bowls, 3 comports, cov soup tureen, 2 leaf dishes, 16 kidney shaped dishes, colorful summer flowers and insects around larger central spray, basket molded gilt line rims, c1870, underglaze "blue scepter, red orb and KPM', imp factory marks, 72 pcs (A)............... **10,000.00**

Ecuelle, Cov, and Stand, 4⅜" h, panels with playful putti in clouds with musical instruments or bow and arrow, gilt trellis ground, 1775–80, underglaze "blue scepter, imp K3 and K11" marks (A)............................. **6477.00**

Figure
4" h, young fish vendor from "Cris de Berlin" series, black and white cap, blue sprigged shawl, pink blouse, yellow skirt, basket of fish, another basket at feet, c1769, modeled by W.C. Meyer, underglaze "blue scepter," imp workman's marks (A).............. **911.00**

5½" h, boy with basket of grapes in colors, mid 19th C (A)........................ **165.00**

6" h, piper as young boy in gray hat with pink ribbon, yellow shirt, gray suspenders, salmon breeches, holding black banded brown recorder, tan and green treen stump, sq mound base, c1775, underglaze "blue scepter" mark (A) **385.00**

6⅛" h, quail in natural colors, holding ear of corn, perched on rock base, c1765, "blue scepter" mark **1500.00**

6⁹⁄₁₆" h, shepherdess in gray hat with flowers, salmon and yellow edged pink dress, satchel over shoulder, green dotted white apron, holding nosegay tied with blue bow, brown spotted lamb, sq mound base, c1775, underglaze "blue scepter" mark (A) **440.00**

7½" h, standing white bear **65.00**

8¼" h, Endymion and Diana, goddess in light purple dress under flower patterned coat, embracing Endymion sleeping in yellow lined flower patterned robe, dog and Cupid by side, base inscribed "Luna-Endimion," c1780, underglaze "blue scepter" mark (A)........................ **1316.00**

9" h
Man in 18th C costume with sack over shoulder, woman in period dress, carrying hat full of fruit, gilt edged scroll base, late 19th C, "blue scepter" mark, pr (A) **815.00**

Standing woman holding baskets of flowers, apron with flowers, multicolored....... **595.00**

13⅛" h, chinoiserie lady on tray with pale turquoise lined robe patterned with Indian blossoms, blue striped sash, rose sprigged overskirt, oct parasol, standing before gilt edged beaker vase on gilt edged circ base, affixed to angular cartouche shaped tray painted with six chinoiserie figures in gardens amidst floral sprays, gilt rim, finger repaired, c1830, underglaze "blue scepter, imp 2" marks (A) **4125.00**

13½" h, "Tango," dancing couple, lady in long green dress, man in breeches and tails, tones of green and gilding, white oval base, c1913, underglaze "blue scepter, red orb, and KPM" marks, imp "10375, script 140/816" (A)......................... **3590.00**

16" d, bride seated on back of large bull, raised oval plinth, bride holding gold and purple cape, bull with underglaze gray markings, c1910, underglaze "blue scepter, red, and underglaze blue orb and KPM," imp "C 9366, 140/939" (A).............. **3500.00**

18½" h, "Destiny," blindfolded naked young maiden standing on marbled slab, holding book of Fate and quill pen, grasped by warrior, bearded man in armour seated on marble slab, symbols of peace and war strewn around domed circ base, c1880, underglaze "blue cancelled scepter," imp numerals **2300.00**

Goblet, 5⅛" h, bowl painted with two putti painting and sculpting, supported by figures of "Industry," foot and int with burnished gilt, mid 19th C **350.00**

Jar, Cov, 26½" h, faience, baluster body, painted with Chinese figures, landscapes, and pavilions in tones of black and white on red ground, cylindrical neck, domed cov surmounted by cock, early 19th C (A) **1320.00**

Plaque

5¾" h, 42/8" w, oval, young girl in white dress, long garland of flowers in brown hair, c1880–90, imp "KPM and scepter" mark, framed (A) **2956.00**

7" h, 4" w, young girl dressed in native costume in colors, sgd "Wagner' (A) **3300.00**

7" h, 5" w, painted angel on rock, artist sgd **4500.00**

7" h, 5⅛" w, Mary Magdelene gazing heavenwards in blue satin hood, c1880, imp "KPM and scepter" marks, framed (A) **650.00**

7¾" h, 57/8" w, multicolored scene of monk drinking wine in wine cellar, dtd 1865, imp "KPM and scepter" mark (A) **3025.00**

8¼" h, 5¾" w, Egyptian maiden in national costume, holding earthenware jug beside a spring in desert landscape, late 19th C, sgd, imp "KPM, scepter," incised numerals (A) **4114.00**

8½" h, oval, portrait of "Daphine, the Blind Girl," bare shouldered woman wearing crown of laurel leaves, multicolored, imp "K.P.M." mark (A) **6000.00**

9¼" h, 6½" w

"Darling," seated woman in classical clothes with bird on finger, leaning on birdcage, framed, late 19th C (A) **4400.00**

Painted with standing harem girl with fan, another seated on carpet, drape in ground, mid 19th C, imp "KPM and scepter" marks (A) **3650.00**

12½" h, 10¼" w, young lady and gentleman resting in large room, lady holding parasol and bodice, gentleman in tails holding hat, large mirror and marble mantelpiece behind with clock, vase, and figure, c1860, imp "KPM, scepter" and numerals marks (A) **6545.00**

13⅛" h, 8¾" w, maiden in classical dress, embraced by young man in russet robe, seated on rocky step in woodland glade, late 19th C, painted by R. Dittrich, imp "KPM and scepter" marks (A) **4675.00**

Plate

8⅜" d, center painted in shades of brown, beige, blue, and touches of red with young boy holding his ram on table for inspection of judge above black script inscription, wide gilt band inner border, gilt edged rim and gilt foliate border, 1834, underglaze "blue scepter, imp 43 a/" mark (A) **800.00**

9½" d

Center painted with roses and forget-me-nots on burnished gold ground, gilt etched formal rim, c1825, "blue scepter, brown eagle and KPM" marks (A) **5092.00**

Cupids holding bundle of arrows, one standing holding bow and arrow in

brown sepia, white ground with band of gilded scrolling leaves between gilded line borders, c1815, underglaze "blue scepter," painter's, and incised "3 lines" marks (A) **527.00**

9¾" d, "Beverly" pattern, multicolored fruit basket medallions and floral sprays on ivory band, green and gold border, "green crown KPM" mark **10.00**

913/16" d, center in puce and shades of green, turquoise, and gray with spray of full blown roses and buds, rim with three smaller rose sprigs within wavy edge, molded with icicle devices and foliate scrolls, c1780, underglaze "blue scepter" marks, pr (A) **990.00**

10" d, white rose in center on white ground, scalloped gold rim, pierced handles **45.00**

Platter

137/8" l, oval shape, shades of iron-red, rose, blue, purple, yellow, gray, and green with three small insects and floral bouquet, three sprigs within molded rim, c1780, underglaze "blue scepter, imp 22, incised //" marks (A) **220.00**

18" l, 13½" w, floral center in green, white, and pinks, four sprigs on inside border, raised basketweave border, gilt trim and rim, mid 19th C, unmarked **750.00**

Potpourri Urn, Cov, 13¾" h, oviform body, central band painted on either side with figures in rural landscape, two ram mask handles above vine leaves and branches tied by pale blue ribbons, puce scale ground gilt with stars between gilt borders and rims, pierced domed cov, gilt artichoke knob, gilt sq plinth, one knob restored, c1880, underglaze "blue scepter" mark, pr (A) **3301.00**

Salt, 5⅛" h, oval dish painted with birds on branches, pink, turquoise, and gilt scroll base with draped putto, late 19th C, "blue scepter" mark **485.00**

Sugar Caster, Cov, 4¾" h, baluster shape, blue painted flowering lotus between fruit and flower border, bayonet cov, hairline, c1740 . **250.00**

Sweetmeat Dish, multicolored florals on white ground, light pink and gold accented border, c1900 (A) **20.00**

Teapot, 5½" h, globular shape, raised curved lined body, pink, yellow, blue, and purple flowers, basketweave border around neck of pot and cov, white and gilt spout, rosebud finial, c1770–80 .... **850.00**

Tea and Coffee Service, Part, coffee pot, 8" h, teapot, creamer, 4 cups and saucers, 2 side plates, shaded pink borders with floral sprays, late 19th C (A) **220.00**

Tobacco Jar and Cov, 57/8" h, rect form, front and back molded with scrolls enclosing groups of figures in landscape vignettes, sides with flower garlands, cov with flowering knob, front with ormolu mounted keyhole, gilt metal mounted, four scroll feet, two scroll handles, handles and knob restored, c1760, underglaze "blue G" (A) **6,050.00**

Tray, 127/8" l, scalloped oval, center with pink ground oval medallion with four Cupids playing with floral garlands and doves amidst clouds, enclosed in colorful floral garland entwined with rose edged white ribbon, seven floral sprigs, rim with pink ground border with flowering vine within gilt lines and dentil bands, c1780, underglaze "blue scepter" mark (A). 4125.00

Tureen, Cov, 13" h, circ form, panel of garden banquet, gentlemen seated around table, reverse with termination of party, bouquets of summer flowers, flowers on rim, ozier molded rim, cov with scenes around table, surmounted by Bacchic putto holding goblet and ewer, c1880 (A). 1900.00

Urn
14" h, floral sprays on white ground, griffin handles, mid 19th C, "scepter" mark (A). 850.00
27" h, ovoid shape, reserve of Roman palace scene or two cherubs kissing in garden setting, reserves of Cupids on sides, blue ground with neoclassical gold star trim, wine band with neoclassical scenes, late 19th C, pr (A). 14,300.00

Vase
5½" h, peach colored crystalline glaze 175.00
7" h, white with 2 goat heads on side. 65.00
8½" h, campana form, oval panel of Cupid among clouds, white ground, gilt scrolling foliage, burnished gilt neck and base, c1830, underglaze "blue scepter" mark (A). 1700.00
12⁷⁄₁₆" h, ovoid body, scene of chinoiserie figures in garden, above blue and gilt dragon within pale yellow panel edged in salmon, black, and gold, puce scalework bracket edged in gilt scrollwork, reverse with large spray of Indian blossoms, surrounded by scattered insects, flared rim with border of gilt Laub-und-Bandelwerk, c1870, underglaze "blue scepter" marks, other imp marks, pr (A). 18,700.00
13" h, inverted baluster form, sang-de-boeuf, mottled and streaked mauve and flambe glazes, tear finial, two hair cracks to rim, c1885–1895, printed "scepter" mark (A). 1870.00
18⁷⁄₈" h
Campana form body, white biscuit bust length portrait of Friedrich Wilhelm III in military uniform surrounded by tooled gilt oak and laurel branches, in gold oval panel on pinkish-brown luster ground, reverse with tooled gilt cluster of military trophies above cornucopias, circ foot, 1823–32, underglaze "blue scepter" mark (A) 17,600.00
Ovoid body, panel of four putti at play, dark blue ground gilt and embellished with white enamel, serpent handles, oct foot, "orb and scepter" marks (A) 828.00
24" h, ovoid form
Oval panels depicting nymphs, maidens, and cupids holding cabbage roses against blue sky with white clouds, gilded floral border with light green panels against white ground, scroll handles molded with mask heads, circ foot on oct base, c1885–95, sgd "Ludwig C. Frenzel," underglaze "blue scepter and printed orb, red KPM" mark (A) 10,534.00

View of Palais unter den Linden, reverse with castle within tooled gilded floral borders, dark blue ground, flared neck with scrolling foliage, mask handles, splayed foot on shaped wooded oct base, foot damaged, c1870 (A). 4500.00
Vase, Cov, 20" h, circ painted panel of lady and gentleman dancing, tooled gold border, reserved on blue ground, loop handles, fruit finial, "blue scepter, red orb" mark. 2000.00

KING'S ROSE AND QUEEN'S ROSE

Staffordshire, England
c1820–1830

History: The King's Rose pattern, decorated on a soft paste body, is related closely to Gaudy Dutch in form as well as in the colors used in decoration. A large orange or red cabbage rose with green, yellow, and pink leaves surrounding it as accents forms the center of the design. Many plates also featured relief motifs.

The Queen's Rose pattern has a pink rose as the center with the accent colors in more delicate tones.

Coffee Pot, 10½" h, Queen's Rose, large pink roses with green and yellow leaves and flowers, cream ground (A) 330.00
Creamer
4" h, squat shape, King's Rose design in ironred, vine border (A) 92.00
5" h, iron-red rose, yellow circles with ironred, green, and yellow leaves, int with roses and green leaves, handle with iron-red line and dots, rim in iron-red, c1820 . . . .   265.00
Cup and Saucer, 2¼" h, King's Rose design (A)10.00
Cup and Saucer, Handleless, King's Rose design in iron-red, segmented pink border (A). 154.00
Plate
4½" d, pink rose, yellow circles with iron-red and green leaves, pink rose border with iron-red and green leaves, c1820 . . . .   125.00
6¼" d, pink rose with yellow, dark pink and green florals and leaves, yellow cirles with

Plate, 8½" d, creamware, iron-red King's Rose, unmkd, $295.00

pink lines around border with four dots and
X design, c1820....................... **175.00**
6½" d
Creamware, iron-red rose in center, luster
and green leaf border **65.00**
Iron-red rose with yellow centered with
iron-red lines, leaves in light green and
yellow, dark pink border with four dots
and X pattern plus scalloped iron-red line
inside, c1820........................ **165.00**
6¾" d, Queen's Rose in pink, waffle border,
luster bands **145.00**
7⅛" d, King's Rose in iron-red, segmented
pink border (A) **84.00**
7⅜" d
Iron-red rose, small puce flowers and green
leaves on border, creamware body **195.00**
Pink rose, yellow circles with iron-red lines,
iron-red and green leaves, pink border
with white X's plus four insert panels,
iron-red rim, c1820 .... **145.00**
7½" d
Large iron-red flower in center
Pink border......................... **125.00**
Pink diamonds and raised dots on pink
border............................. **225.00**
Pink florals with green leaves on border,
iron-red line rim, unmarked **195.00**
Pink rose, iron-red leaves, yellow circles
with iron- red and green leaves, line
and circle border with pink roses
c1820 .... **145.00**
8" d, large pink rose, unmarked **80.00**
8¼" d, large pink rose, pink, yellow, and
green flowers, scalloped edge, early
1800s............................... **235.00**
8⅜" d, King's Rose, vine border (A)....... **125.00**
9" d, Queen's Rose in pink, c1800 .... **90.00**
9¾" d, iron-red rose with yellow center, iron-
red lines, dark green leaves, dark pink border with four dots and X pattern, two iron-
red lines on rim, c1820 .... **375.00**
10" d, Queen's Rose in pink, dot border,
slightly shaped rim (A) **50.00**
10¼" d, King's Rose in iron-red in center,
pink luster trim (A) **68.00**
Soup Plate, 8" d, shaded pink rose, yellow circles
outlined in iron-red, small green leaves, iron-
red double line border intertwined with roses
and green trailing leaves inside, iron-red rim,
c1820................................. **125.00**
Sugar Bowl, Cov, 5" h, Queen's Rose design in
pink, vine border, emb shell handles, small
hairlines (A)............................. **137.00**
Teabowl and Saucer, iron-red rose, yellow circles
with iron-red lines, green and yellow leaves,
cup with red flower in center, rose outside
with green and yellow leaves............. **285.00**
Teapot
6¼" h, King's Rose in iron-red, vine border
(A).................................... **93.00**
6½" h, King's Rose, iron-red rose with multicolored flowers, solid border, age lines
(A).................................... **247.00**
7" h, large iron-red rose on side with polychrome enameled florals, repairs, hairline
on lip (A)............................. **650.00**
Waste Bowl, 6⅜"h, 3¼" h, Oyster pattern
(A)..................................... **225.00**

HARTLEY GREENS & CO.
LEEDS POTTERY
c1781-1820

LEEDS

Yorkshire, England
c1757–1878

History: The original Leeds factory was located in Yorkshire and was founded by John and Joshua Green about
1757. Among its products were saltglaze, basalt, and
stoneware, plus a very fine pearlware using a bluish glaze
similar to that of Wedgwood. Figures, transferwares, lusters, and mottled wares, similar to Whieldon's, also were
produced.

Probably the most recognized Leeds product was yellow glazed creamware, first produced about 1760. This
creamware was characterized by its soft yellow-cream
color and the extensive use of perforations and open
work, especially evident in the border treatments.

All types of utilitarian and decorative items were made
in creamware from the simplest plate to elaborate, multi-
sectioned fruit coolers and figural groups. The basic body
often was augmented with painted and printed designs.
Floral and fruit finials were a Leeds trademark.

The Green brothers had several different partners in
their enterprises; shortly after forming the company, it
traded as Humble, Greens & Co. Financial difficulties
beset the Yorkshire pottery. After several additional owners and attempts at resurrection, the company failed and
closed its doors in 1878.

Only a small amount of Leeds wares bear factory marks.

References: Heather Lawrence, *Yorkshire Pots and Potteries*, David & Charles, 1947; Donald Towner, *The Leeds
Pottery*, Cory, Adams & MacCay, 1963.

Museums: City Art Gallery, Leeds, England; Everson Museum of Art, Syracuse, NY; Fitzwilliam Museum, Cambridge, England; Museum of Fine Arts, Boston, MA; Victoria & Albert Museum, London, England.

Barber Bowl, 12¾" l, creamware, flattened
scalloped and shell molded rim, pierced for
hanging, c1790, imp "LEEDS*POTTERY, 20"
mark................................... **1150.00**

**Bud Vase, 11" h, creamware, multicolored flor-
als, blue feathered edge, molded rect ft, repaired, c1790, pr, $600.00**

Bowl, Ftd, 1" l, 4" h, creamware, pierced, c1880 .... **575.00**

Butter, Cov, 5 1/2" H-H, oval, pierced top with acorn finial, tab handles with holes, c1790 .. **795.00**

Coffee Pot

8 1/2" h, baluster form, creamware, iron-red chinoiserie maiden and boy in fanciful landscape, cov with flower finial, entwined rope twist handle, acanthus molded fluted spout, cracks, c1770 (A) **1328.00**

9 7/8" h, baluster body, pearlware, blue chinoiserie island scenes, dbl entwined handle with flowering terminals, domed cov with flower finial, restored finial, late 18th C (A) **225.00**

Compote, 4 1/2" h, 11" l, 9 1/2" w, creamware, blue oriental design, man with umbrella on bridge, temple in ground, emb and pierced rim, reticulated foot, imp "Leeds Pottery" mark (A) **800.00**

Creamer, 3 3/8" h, central flower in blue and amber with green leaves (A) **396.00**

Cream Jug

3 1/4" h, ribbed baluster body, green glazed vert bands, circle and diamond pierced neck, brown dentil rim, molded mask spout, grooved handle with floral terminal, c1785 .... **1530.00**

3 7/8" h, creamware, black and red painted building in trees, beaded borders, grooved handle, hairlines, c1770 (A) **775.00**

Cuspidor, 3 1/2" h, blue printed oriental landscape scene on body and rim, interlaced strap handle terminating in flowerheads, c1780... **400.00**

Dessert Plate, 7" d, creamware, arcaded looped border, 1775–80, Yorkshire Leeds.......... **125.00**

Dish, 6 3/4" l, creamware, molded pineapples on border, open border with twisted ropes, c1895, imp "Leeds Pottery' mark **325.00**

Figure

4" h, creamware, child leaning on base, c1780 .... **1660.00**

5 1/4" h, cradle, brown, blue, and yellow stripes on basketweave ground (A) **522.00**

Frog Mug, 5 3/8" h, "A West View of the Iron Bridge at Sunderland" transfer, mottled brown and tan frog inside, hairline, c1800........ **575.00**

Milk Jug, Cov, 6" h, creamware, iron-red, green, and yellow bouquet and sprigs, interlaced reeded strap handle terminating in flowerheads, c1780 (A) **550.00**

Mug

2 1/4" h, green creamware, lined body, c1800–1810 .... **295.00**

4 5/8" h, creamware, mustard, blue, olive green, and green florals, olive green lines on top and bottom, c1810 .... **650.00**

4 3/4" h, pearlware, yellow, blue, green, and brown florals, brown line rim, c1790 ..... **695.00**

Pitcher

3 1/2" h, Paragon design, roses with silver stripes **45.00**

5" h, creamware, paneled shape, brown and yellow bands, green leaves, c1770–90.... **225.00**

Plate

8" d

Blue transfer of oriental pagoda and park scene, shaped rim, c1830.............. **110.00**

Pearlware, blue, mustard, and green floral, brown line stem, blue feathered edge, c1775 .... **300.00**

8 3/4" d, blue florals, scalloped feather edge, c1790 .... **295.00**

9" d, creamware, reticulated border with raised swags, scalloped edge, 19th C, imp "LEEDS POTTERY" mark **295.00**

9 1/2" d, creamware, emb and reticulated rim (A)... **175.00**

Platter, 15 1/4" l, 11 3/4" l, pearlware, center floral cartouche in mustard, blue, green, brown stem line, four scattered floral sprays, blue feathered and scalloped edge, cream ground, c1800 .... **2000.00**

Potpourri Jar, 9 1/2" h, creamware, intricate piercing design, imp "Yorkshire Leeds" mark **1600.00**

Shaker, 4 1/2" h, creamware, blue lines, raised dot panel and base...................... **250.00**

Soup Plate, 9 5/8" d, creamware, blue Chinese figure holding parasol in garden landscape, diaper border edged in blue, c1780, pr (A) ... **418.00**

Strainer, 3" d, creamware, cut out in center, leaf type handle, c1740–60, pr **345.00**

Sugar Bowl

4" h, 9" d, floral decoration in four colors, yellow int edge band (A)................ **550.00**

4 1/2" h, blue and white gaudy floral design, hairlines (A)................................. **137.00**

6" h, gaudy floral design in five colors, emb shell and ring handles, acorn finial, hairline on lid (A)............................. **220.00**

Tea Caddy, 4 1/2" h, creamware, black transfer of man and woman on bench in landscape, shepherd on reverse, c1780 .... **475.00**

Tea Kettle, 7 1/2" h, globular shape, redware, decorated with over all engine-turned wave pattern, dbl entwined overhead handle with flowering terminals, masked spout with silver tip, c1770, imp "pseudo-seal" mark........ **2992.00**

Teapot

4 1/2" h, creamware, painted flower sprays on sides, leaf molded spout, entwined strap handle, iron-red half loop and dot border, applied floral knob, c1770 .... **1020.00**

5 3/8" h, globular shape, creamware, rose colored roses, green leaves, cross-hatch rose panels on cov, c1790.................. **895.00**

5 1/2" h, globular shape, creamware, puce bouquets and scattered sprigs, interlaced strap handle terminating in flowerheads, flower branch finial edged in puce, c1775 (A)... **1430.00**

7 1/2" h, globular, redware, decorated with engine-turned wave pattern, scroll molded spout, basketweave handle, restored, c1770 (A)... **2057.00**

Toddy Plate, 4 1/4" d, creamware, blue feather edge, c1770–90.............................. **95.00**

Vegetable, Cov, 7 1/2" H-H, 6 3/4" h, creamware, applied designs, twisted rope handles, twisted handle on cov, c1780 .... **950.00**

Veilleuse, 11 5/8" h, creamware, pierced dbl ogee body, applied human masks, dbl entwined handles with flowering terminals, opening bordered with foliate scrollwork, cylindrical neck forming rest for the jug, cov with candle nozzle, damage, c1775 (A) **3179.00**

GUERIN-POUYAT-
ELITE, Ltd.
c1895

FRANCE

CHARLES AHRENFELDT
c1894

LIMOGES

FRANCE

J. Granger & Cie
LATE 19TH CENTURY

T & V
LIMOGES
FRANCE

RAYNAUD & CIE
c1919

Limages FRANCE

c1893

DEPOSE
CHARLES MARTIN
&
DUCHÉ
c1875

LIMOGES

Limousine region of France
c1770 to Present

History: Limoges' first hard paste porcelain dates from about 1770 and is attributed to the company of Massie, Grellet, and Fourneira. Permission was granted to make porcelain by the Council of the Court. The company came under the patronage of Comte d'Artois, brother-in-law of King Louis XVI, in 1777. Since the company was financed and supported by the court, the products were marked with the initials "C.D."

Due to financial and technical problems, the company was sold to the King in 1784. He used the factory as a branch of Sevres. Whitewares were made at Limoges and sent to Sevres for decoration.

Grellet served as manager from 1784 until 1788. J. Francoise Alluaud followed as manager and remained until 1794. About 1794 the factory was sold to Joubert, Cacate, and Joly, three of the workers.

At the end of the French Revolution, circa 1796, the progress of porcelain making continued at Limoges with the addition of many new factories. Alluaud, Baignol, and Monnerie were among those establishing their own factories during the 1790s.

Additional factories developed between 1800 and 1830, among which were two factories begun in 1825 at Saint-Leonard the Recollet factory, which remained in production until 1963, and the Pont de Noblat factory, still in production. These factories responded to the growing demands of a large export market for Limoges porcelains,

with America as the largest customer. The mid to late nineteenth century was the golden age for Limoges porcelain.

David Haviland also established himself in Limoges during the 1850s. Many of the other factories imitiated his techniques. Limoges porcelain is usually more bold than Haviland.

With the tremendous amount of porcelain produced, the market could not absorb all the wares. After World War I and the economic crisis of the 1920s and 1930s, many older companies were forced out of business. There was some revitalization after World War II. Today Limoges still is the center of hard paste porcelain production in France.

A wide range of objects were made with vivid decoration of florals, fruit, figural, and scenic themes that were embellished with gold. Decorative pieces included vases, large plaques, trays, tankards, mugs, bowls, plates, paintings, and jardinaires.

Smaller accessory pieces such as dresser sets, trinket boxes, cache pots, candle holders, baskets, and inkwells added variety. In addition, a whole range of dinnerware sets, compotes, coffee, tea, and chocolate sets, and fish and game services bore the Limoges mark.

Early Limoges porcelain whiteware blanks were sent to Paris for decoration over the glaze. Decoration under the glaze did not begin in Limoges until the late 1800s. Transfer decoration was used mostly on tablewares. Hand painting usually appeared on accessory art pieces and decorative porcelain pieces. Mixed decoration, where the transfer outline was filled in or trimmed with hand painting, was used primarily on tablewares. The decoration is found in both over and under the glaze styles.

Floral decor is most prominant on Limoges porcelain. Fruit themes of berries, cherries, and grapes are next. Oyster, fish, and game sets contain birds and marine life subjects. Figurals of either allegorical subjects or portraits also were used, but in a more limited context.

Most of the Limoges colors are deep and vivid. The lavish gold embellishments have a rich patina.

Reference: Mary Frank Gaston, *The Collector's Encyclopedia of Limoges Porcelain*, Collector Books, 1980.

Museums: Limoges Museum, Limoges, France; Musee National Adrien Dubouche, Limoges, France; Sevres Museum, Sevres, France

Additional Listing: Haviland

Collecting Hints: Limoges porcelains are still in production. Marks aid the collector in determining the age of a piece of Limoges.

The quality of the craftsmanship and decoration on the older pieces are superior to the new examples. Less gold decoration is used on newer pieces

The newer marks usually are found over the glaze. Many pieces have factory whiteware marks in addition to marks to indicate whether the piece was decorated at the factory or at another decorating studio.

Ashtray, 4 1/2" d, gold paisley border, cobalt ground, "Porcelain D'Amp, Limoges, France" mark **6.00**
Berry Bowl, 6 1/2" d, molded floral border, large white flower in center with dark red edging, gold shaped rim, "A L Limoges" dbl marks **18.00**
Bowl
    5 1/2" H-H, branch handles, gold raised acorns, brown ground **18.00**

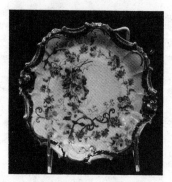

Plate, 6" d, hp int in colors, gold and green border, "Coronet Limoges dbl" marks, set 6, $90.00

10" d, fuchsia, pink, and yellow roses on int, four groups of roses on ext, "Coronet" mark................................. 125.00
10½" d, small roses and greenery on rim, gold rococo border.................... 50.00
12" l, oval, holly pattern in colors, "T & V Limoges" mark....................... 95.00
Salad, 13" d, pink rose pattern on int and ext, gilt edges, white ground, "T & V Limoges France" mark (A)..................... 180.00
Box
  4¼" l, 4" w, white cherubs in relief, blue ground.................... 185.00
  8½" sq, small hp pink and lavender rose garlands, gold trim, artist sgd.............. 55.00
Button, red roses on yellow ground, set of 5..................................... 85.00
Cake Plate
  11" d, hp pine needles, oak leaves and acorns on dark green ground, "T & V Limoges" mark............................... 45.00
  11½" d, gold medallion center, brushed gold scalloped rim, ivory ground, "T & V Limoges" mark...................... 70.00
  12" d, grape design with gold trim, open handles.................................. 75.00
Cake Platter, 15" l, 13" w, yellow, pink, white, and purple chrysanthemums, artist sgd..... 115.00
Candlestick
  5" h, Art Deco design in gold and pastels, handled, pr........................... 95.00
  8¼" h, two bands of small blue flowers and green leaves, cream ground, bordered by wide gold and thin black bands, med blue ground, pr........................... 125.00
Chamberstick, small pink flowers, gold handle............................. 35.00
Charger, 13½" d, gold Egyptian motif....... 185.00
Chocolate Pot
  9½" h
    Panels of red poppies and green buds, green leaf design, sgd "C.P.G."........ 250.00
    Pink and yellow floral design, green leaves, melon rib body, burgundy upper section and handle, gold trim................ 175.00
  12" h, oak leaves and acorns in brown and green shades, "J.P.L." mark.............. 125.00
  13" h, purple violets and green leaves on

cream base, gold handle, spout, and base, "J.P.L. France" mark.................... 325.00
Cider pitcher, 4¾" h, hp apples in foliage on dark green ground, beaded handle, "J.P. Limoges" mark.......................... 80.00
Cider Set, pitcher, 6" h, 3 cups, 3½" h, hp clusters of grapes and leaves on wide border, cocoa brown ground.................... 210.00
Coffee Pot
  10" h, pink and yellow roses on green and white ground, gold spout, handle, and finial.................................. 150.00
  12⅜" h, center painted panel depicting putti and angels with floral swags and drapery, pink and gilt borders with curvilinear designs, gilt handle, Limoges mark (A)...... 310.00
Cologne Bottle, 9" h, red roses on white ground, pr...................................... 75.00
Cream and Sugar
  Burgundy and pink roses, gold dotted circles, gold edges, "D & C. Co." mark.......... 55.00
  Floral border on cream ground, gold handles 65.00
  Red and pink roses on rainbow ground, gold handles and trim...................... 55.00
Cup and Saucer
  Floral decoration, yellow ext, gilt handle and rim, "Limoges France" mark (A)......... 25.00
  Yellow peaches on ivory ground, gold trim, "T & V Limoges" marks.................. 30.00
Dish
  6½" l, large apple blossoms and gold scrolls, relief icicle and scroll rim............. 15.00
  12½" d, three section, pink flowers with small blue flowers, salmon to white shaded ground, gold irreg rim, three part gold handle................................. 135.00
Dish, Cov
  5" d, 5" h, ftd, light and dark pink roses, green leaves, blue and white ground, gold handle, feet, and finial...................... 65.00
  6¾" d, large hp red and pink roses, spiral scrolled and beaded body, gold ribbon loop knob................................. 125.00
Dresser Tray, 9½" d, hp gold flowers, white ground, scalloped rim..................... 45.00
Figure, 25" h, 13" l, two girls with arms entwined, one with basket of flowers and books, other with book and purse, off white and tan ground, "C & V" mark on purse, "L & L" mark on base................................ 450.00
Fruit Bowl, 9⅝" d, 4⅝" h, ftd, purple grapes, autumn colored ground, gold trim, sgd "Bauer, T & V Limoges" mark............. 225.00
Hatpin Holder, 5" h, hp roses and florals, pink and gold top and feet.................... 95.00
Humidor
  6½" h, painted pine cones in light yellow, coral, and brown...................... 125.00
  8" h, white hp pipes and imp tobacco leaves on beige melon ribbed body............ 125.00
Jardinaire, 5" h, 9" d, hp yellow roses, purple flowers, green leaves, four floral baroque feet, "Limoges, France" mark.................. 275.00
Lemonade Pitcher, 6" h, hp grapes on vine, gilt accented lip and handle, sgd "H.T." (A).... 60.00
Mug
  5" h, monk seated at table of food, raised gold "Drink Hearty" at top, "J. P. Limoges" mark...................... 70.00
  5¾" h, pastel flowers on purple, green, and

cream ground, dragon handle, "Pouyat" mark.................................. **55.00**

6" h, burgundy and green grapes, leaves, and vines, figural arched female handle....... **145.00**

Pancake Server, 9¼" d, yellow and pink roses, marked................................. **195.00**

Pitcher

8½" h, hp butterflies and flowers on white ground, "H & C Limoges" mark **95.00**

14½" h, painted poinsettas, salmon and green glaze, dark green dragon handle (A)................................... **80.00**

Pitcher, Cov, 6" h, with underplate, green berries and heavy gold ivy, white ground, gold knob, handle, and trim, marked................. **30.00**

Plaque

5⅛" sq, hp multicolored scene of Annunciation, framed, 18th C (A) **385.00**

6" h, 14" l, multicolored rural scene (A).... **200.00**

7⅝" l, 5¾" w, rect, multicolored scene of four kittens seated in row, c1900, sgd "Agnes A. Neoville," T & V Limoges" mark (A)..................................... **1017.00**

10¼" d, two large apples on light green ground, scalloped rim, artist sgd **48.00**

11" l, 8" h, seascape with icebergs and sailing ships in shades of blue, wood frame, "D.& Co." mark (A)......................... **470.00**

12" d, hp lake scene with boats, gold border, sgd "Hugo" **150.00**

12" l, 8" w, hp scene of European man and woman seated before wall of house, child resting in mother's lap, c1900 (A)....... **600.00**

12½" d, multicolored dancing couple in period clothes, light blue ground, gold scalloped rim, sgd "DuBois" **225.00**

12¾" d, tiger or leopard stalking deer, pastel ground of palm trees and sky, heavy gold rococo border, pierced for hanging, pr ... **495.00**

13" d

Hp landscapes of French buildings, heavy Roman gold border, pierced for hanging, unmarked, pr **395.00**

Soldiers firing cannon in colors, gold scroll border, artist sgd..................... **375.00**

14" h, seated figure of lady dressed in dark blue velvet costume with cuffs and collar embroidered in lace, wearing white hood, c1894, sgd "M. Chanson," framed (A) ... **3415.00**

15" d, enamel relief bust of French girl with blue earrings, high collar jacket, feathered hat with pearls, sgd "A. Dussou" **650.00**

16" d, white, pink, red roses, green leaves and buds, green and yellow ground, T & V Limoges mark......................... **450.00**

Plate

7¼" d, three chateau in colors, burgundy border with ornate gold design **30.00**

8⅜" d, green, caramel, cerise, gold floral with center of gold tracery, streamers and gold trim, scalloped, emb rococo gold, "J.P.L. France 1908" mark **12.00**

8½" d

Pale pink roses on white ground, reticulated border **30.00**

Pink roses in center, green and gold border, "GDA Limoges" mark **40.00**

Scalloped border decorated with polychrome floral bouquets and gilt scrolls

centering floral bouquet, cream ground, set of 8 .... **150.00**

8⅝" d, presidential plate, center decorated with polychrome eagle, inner blue banding with stars, gilt cornstalk border, scalloped rim, "T & V Limoges, Harrison 1892" mark, (A)..................................... **935.00**

9" d

Hp gold webs and spiders on emerald green ground, white moon in center, rococo gold scalloped rim **50.00**

Hp rasberries and leaves, scalloped rim, c1908 .... **40.00**

Multicolored scene of parrots **19.00**

9¼" d, hp yellow and tan flowers, green leaves, sgd "Stafford".................. **40.00**

9½" d, hp berries and holly in colors, "T & V Limoges" mark........................ **40.00**

10" d

Bust of dog in colors in center, dark green ground, sgd "L. Coudet, Coronet Limoges" mark **95.00**

Dutch girl with basket, man on wharf, sgd "Leo" **37.00**

11" d, maroon and tan chrysanthemums, gold accents **48.00**

11½" d

Hp fish with water lilies, gold edge, artist sgd, "J.P.L. France" mark.............. **95.00**

Madame Pompadour in center in colors, "Charles Ahrenfeldt" mark **75.00**

12" d, hp water lily design, artist sgd....... **95.00**

13" H-H, multicolored strawberries, leaves, and blossoms, ornate gold handles....... **110.00**

13¼" d, transfer of gypsy woman playing tambourine or mandolin, pastel ground, gold trimmed scalloped edge, pierced for hanging, pr **395.00**

14" d, hunter and maiden or fisherman and maiden, multicolored, gold rococo border, pierced for hanging, pr.................. **550.00**

Platter

13½" l, 9½" w, white and yellow ears of corn on shaded brown ground **75.00**

15" l, 13" w, yellow, pink, white, and purple mums, artist sgd...................... **115.00**

20" l, small hp flowers in colors, white ground, c1880, "D & Co." mark (A) **13.00**

Large yellow and orange roses............ **145.00**

Pot-de-Creme, 4" h, American eagle transfer below purple band and gilt leaf and dot pattern, white ground (A) **275.00**

Punch Bowl

5¼" h, 12½" d, yellow birds, blue flowers, grapes, leaves, gold band, 1915, sgd "Ada Sagar" **350.00**

6" h, 14" d, center with "B.P.O.E." seal on int, grape motif on ext **550.00**

Sardine Box, 5½" l, 4½" w, undertray, 10" l, 9" w, blue and pink swimming fish, starfish, shells, and seaweed, well for sauce, "T & V Limoges" marks......................... **225.00**

Sauceboat, hp jumping fish on pink and green ground, sgd "Rene," A & D/Limoges, Limoges France" marks (A)....................... **35.00**

Serving Bowl, Cov, 12" l, 7" w, small pink and green garlands, top border of blue asters, gold trim, four feet, dbl handles, entwined finial, "Wm. Guerin & Co." mark **55.00**

Tankard
  10½" h, lavender and white poppies, green
    foliage, green and white ground, gold on
    base and top, gold handle, "T & V Limoges"
    mark................................. **225.00**
  11" h
    Hp berries and leaves, green borders..... **195.00**
    Painted hanging grape clusters, variegated
      ground, "T & V Limoges" mark........ **195.00**
    Purple blackberries and flowers on blue to
      mauve ground, "D.& C. France"
      mark................................ **225.00**
  14½" h, hp portrait of monk with glasses on
    nose looking at wine bottle, rose ground,
    gold trim, "T & V Limoges" mark........ **195.00**
Tea Set, teapot, 8" h, 5 cups and saucers, hp
  pine needles, cones, and tree trunks, gilt accents (A) **50.00**
Toothbrush Holder, 4¼" h, small pink roses
  and green leaves, "GDA Limoges" mark.... **30.00**
Tray
  9" l, 6" w, hp center scene of castle, boat, and
    people in river landscape, open handles,
    sgd "Plinia"........................... **125.00**
  12" l, 8¾" w, palette shape, pierced handle,
    orange poppies, yellow to brown shaded
    ground, scalloped rim, "Guerin" mark.... **65.00**
  13¼" l, polychrome floral center, green and
    gold reticulated border, "Limoges France"
    mark (A) **93.00**
  15" l, pink and yellow roses, stems, and
    leaves, shaded green ground, gold trimmed
    black edging, gold scalloped rim, "Pouyat"
    mark................................. **180.00**
Trinket Box, 8¼" sq, open yellow flowers on
  cov, cobalt trim, flake on side, "T & V
  Limoges" mark.......................... **95.00**
Trivet, 6½" d, hp yellow roses and foliage on
  pastel ground, three button feet, sgd "E. Thau,
  T & V Limoges" mark.................... **55.00**
Vase
  6" h, border of alternating pink and yellow
    roses, cream ground, gold rim, "D & C
    France" mark......................... **125.00**
  7½" h, hp acorns in shades of brown, gold
    trim, artist sgd **95.00**
  8" h, compressed baluster shape, pink and
    yellow roses with leafy stems, green ground,
    two scrolled handles.................. **175.00**
  9" h, scenic, wide gold collar, heavy gold
    dragon handles, "J. Pouyat" mark....... **85.00**
  9½" h, 8½" d, angels, roses, flat sided, ruf-
    fle top, gold handles, pale blue ground, sgd
    "E. Ryland"........................... **350.00**
  12½" h
    Hp yellow and brown birds in flowering
      trees, artist sgd..................... **125.00**
    Pink magnolias on cream ground, dbl en-
      twined handles **235.00**
  12¾" h, birds perched on branch, yellow
    luster ground, wide gold band, "T & V
    Limoges" mark........................ **240.00**
  14" h, pink poppies with green leaves...... **125.00**
  24" h, iris and scene of two women watching
    swans on lake, blue ground, "T & V
    Limoges" mark........................ **900.00**
Vegetable Bowl, 9½" l, 6" w, 3½" h, pink,
  blue, orange-red, and yellow wildflowers and
  butterflies, "D.& C. Limoges" mark........ **45.00**

c 1833-1836   c 1796-1833

LIVERPOOL

City and port of Liverpool, England
c1754–1840

History: During the 18th century, a group of potteries in
Liverpool were producing mostly tin-glazed Delft type
wares and some porcelains. Utiliarian wares usually were
made without distinguishing factory marks. Among the
Liverpool potteries were:

Richard Chaffers & Co.,
c1754–65

Made soapstone-type porcelain. Chaffers' blue and
white and enameled pieces featured Oriental designs.

Samuel Gilbody,
c1754–61

Took over his father's earthenware pottery and
switched production to enameled porcelains.

William Ball,
c1755–69

Used a soapstone body with a glossy glaze that gave
a wet appearance to his Chinese designs in underglaze
blue.

Willaim Reid & Co.,
c1755–61

Also used underglaze blue Oriental motifs on an almost
opaque body.

Philip Christian & Co.,
c1765–76

Took over Chaffers' factory and made soapstone-type
porcelains, mostly with underglaze blue designs.

Pennington & Part,
c1770–99

Produced lesser quality wares decorated with underglaze blue prints. Their enameled pieces exhibited simple
decorations.

Thomas Wolfe & Co.,
c1795–1800

Made hard paste porcelains.

Herculaneum-Liverpool factory at Liverpool, c1796–1840

Established by Samuel Worthington. Most of the workers were brought from the Staffordshire Potteries. At first only earthenwares and stonewares were made. "Herculaneum Pottery" was the name of the factory. Some pieces were marked with an impressed "Herculaneum." About 1800 porcelains were introduced. Some Empire-style vases were manufactured, but the principal production focused on teawares. Extremely large jugs were a specialty.

References: Dr. Knowles Boney, *Liverpool Porcelain of the 18th Century and its Makers*, B.T. Batsford, 1957; H. Boswell Lancaster, *Liverpool and Her Potters*, W.B. James & Co., 1936; Alan Smith, *The Illustrated Guide to Liverpool Herculaneum Pottery 1796–1840*, Barrie & Jenkins, 1970; B. Watney, *English Blue and White Porcelain of the 18th Century*, Faber & Faber, 1936.

Museums: City of Liverpool Museum, Liverpool, England; Henry Ford Museum, Dearborn, Michigan; Potsdam Public Museum, Potsdam, N.Y.

Beaker, 2³⁄₈″ h, hex, underglaze blue with stylized sprig of roses or chrysanthemums on each side beneath trellis diaper border, demiflowerhead panels, c1760, Richard Chaffers' Factory (A) **1650.00**

Bowl
  4¹⁄₄″ d, enameled with oriental priest at altar set with candlesticks and incense burner, reverse with two followers beating drum and tambourine, gilding, c1765–70, Christian's Factory (A)..................... **607.00**
  5″ d, creamware, black transfer of British sailing ship on int, humorous scenes and sayings on ext, early 19th C (A) **470.00**
  6³⁄₁₆″ d, thick underglaze blue and blue wash with chinoiserie figure holding flower and standing before pierced rock, reverse with

Jug, 6¹⁄₄″ h, molded bearded face at spout, vert blue stripes with iron-red stripes on each side, c1820, unmkd, $350.00

youth holding bowl of fruit and standing in fenced garden, int with blue line at rim, c1785, Pennington's Factory (A)........ **200.00**
  9¹⁄₂″ d, creamware, int with scene of brig, inscription "Success to the Griffin, Capt. Grimshaw, 1778," griffin crest, rim with paneled and foliate scroll border, ext with flower sprays and scattered sprigs, cracks, 1778 (A) **2656.00**
  11″ d, black tranfers of ship "Stockport" with American flag, polychrome enameling, repairs (A)............................ **495.00**
Coffee Cup, iron-red, puce, green, and blue bouquet of scattered flowers, c1775, Chaffers' Factory (A) **121.00**
Coffee Cup and Saucer, Miniature, blue and white V-shaped flock of birds in flight between two rocky islands, loop handle, 1762–65, Chaffers' Factory (A)..................... **1210.00**
Coffee Pot
  10³⁄₄″ h, cream and med blue, cream and brown geometric band, ribbed cream bottom, and ribbed cov, acorn finial, c1790 .... **1450.00**
  11″ h, Portobello-type, yellow chinoiserie transfer on brown glazed ground, domed cov (A).................................... **330.00**
Creamer, 5¹⁄₂″ h, Portobello-type, yellow chinoiserie transfer on brown glazed ground (A)...................................... **165.00**
Cream Jug, 3″ h, underglaze blue and iron-red enamel with Oriental walking over bridge between rockwork and plants, hilly handscape beyond, rim with paneled and diaper border, ribbed loop handle, sparrow beak spout, c1760, William Ball (A).................... **885.00**
Cup and Saucer, Handleless
  Center bird in orange, rose, and blue, perched on rust branch with green leaves, rust border, bird also on cup, c1768–75, Pennington's.................................. **450.00**
  "Washington, His Country's Father," black transfer, patriot on reverse (A).......... **55.00**
Dish, 14¹⁄₂″ l, blue chinoiserie landscapes, one with figure seated by fence, other with building amongst rocks and trees, mid 18th C, pr (A).................................... **700.00**
Flower Brick, 5¹⁄₈″ l, sides painted in blue with flower sprays, top pierced with holes, painted with star-shaped motifs within border of dashes, four molded pedestal feet, c1760 (A) **815.00**
Jug
  5¹¹⁄₁₆″ h, baluster shape, painted on either side in rose, purple, iron-red, blue, yellow, and green with a floral bouquet beneath a brown scallop edged yellow border, reeded neck with rose wavy lines, foliate molded spout, S scroll handle trimmed in rose, c1780, "iron-red B" mark (A)........... **275.00**
  7″ h, creamware, polychrome black transfer of "An East View of Liverpool Light House & Signals on Bidston Hill" with list of signals and subscribers, black transfer of British sailing ship on reverse, hairlines, early 19th C (A).................................... **930.00**
  9¹⁄₄″ h, baluster shape, creamware, black transfers with peasants dancing in farmyard, reverse with "The Farmer's Arms," "L.A.R."

and "Winmarlow" below spout, hair crack
in foot, c1800 (A) **531.00**
9⅞" h, ironstone, transfers of two hunt
scenes and intellectual arts with color accents, cream ground, berry and leaf border
(A) **522.00**
Milk Jug, Miniature, pear shape, underglaze blue
monogram "JCH," handle repaired, c1780,
Seth Pennington's Factory (A) **330.00**
Mug
2½" h, Chinese boy in yellow coat and rose
breeches standing before table with iron-
red and green vases of flowers, shaded
green grassy plateau, large urn beneath pine
tree, loop handle with iron-red branch
motif, gray tone glaze, 1758–60, Richard
Chaffers' Factory (A) **990.00**
3½" h, Cylindrical Form
  Creamware, painted with points of compass
  around signed central panel, inscription
  "Come Box The Compass," iron-red line
  borders, loop handle, c1785, sgd "Joseph
  Johnson of Liverpool,' (A) **483.00**
  "The Stag Head" pattern, rose, green, iron-
  red, russet, yellow, and black, one side
  with Chinaman carrying spear and racing
  after hound in pursuit of leaping stag,
  other side with two Chinamen conversing
  near pavilion, each within russet edged
  octafoil panel reserved on ground of
  blossoms and scrolling foliage,
  1758–60, Richard Chaffer's Factory
  (A) **4125.00**
4¾" h, creamware, black transfer of "Song of
Auld Robin Greg-Jemmy's Farewell" **245.00**
4⅞" h, creamware, Nelson after Trafalger,
black transfer (A) **550.00**
5½" h, creamware, "Lord Nelson engaging
the Toulon Fleet off the Mouth of the
Nile," black transfer, "Make-Do" tole
strapping top and bottom rims and han-
dle, c1797 (A) **192.00**
5⅞" h, black transfer of "An East View of
the Iron Bridge" and "Augusta Wilemina
Charlotta Weyda 1797," stains, hairlines
(A) **137.00**
6" h, barrel shape, blue pagoda in mountain-
ous Chinese landscape bellow cell border,
c1760, William Ball (A) **1098.00**
6¼" h, black transfer of "The True Blooded
Yankee," hairline (A) **880.00**
Pickle Dish
3½" w, shell shape, vase of feathers before a
scroll, within ribboned feathers, c1755, Wil-
liam Reid Factory (A) **1214.00**
4¼" w, vine leaf shape, foliate border on
serrated rim with central sprig, c1770, Chris-
tian's Factory (A) **405.00**
4½" w, leaf shape, painted basket of
flowers, bowl of fruit, and flower vase in
oriental style, gilt accents, serrated rim with
iron-red and gilt border, molded veining
on underside, three conical feet, c1765
(A) **3830.00**
Pitcher
7½" h, creamware, printed sailing ship titled
"The True Blooded Yankee," reverse with
compass and "Come Box the Compass,"
black transfers, c1800 (A) **1045.00**

7¾" h, Portobello-type, chinoiserie design in
yellow transfer, honeycomb rim on int,
brown glaze ground (A) **187.00**
8" h, creamware
  "Britannia Weeping o'er the ashes of her
  Matchlefs Hero, Lord Nelson," Masonic
  emblem on reverse, black transfers, red
  enamel border (A) **1320.00**
  Bust of Nelson with Masonic emblem
  around neck, circ cartouche with "ADMI-
  RAL NELSON" and VICTORY" in ribbons
  below, "Free Trade Sailing Ship in re-
  verse, black transfers (A) **1100.00**
8⅛" h, black transfer of "Peace and Proper-
ity to America," old repairs (A) **330.00**
8⅜" h, black transfer of American ship and
"Jack Spritsail," worn transfer (A) **75.00**
9¼" h, creamware, black transfers of Wash-
ington portrait surrounded by names of
states, Washington with Liberty and map of
U.S. on reverse, American eagle and "Herculaneum Pottery" under spout, damages,
c1800 (A) **1430.00**
9½" h, eagle and ship "America," black
transfer, gilt trim, hairlines (A) **2530.00**
10" h, creamware, black transfers of "Poll and
my partner Joe" on one side, British sailing
ship on other, crazed, early 19th C
(A) **495.00**
10¾" h, "Success to America" and "Wash-
ington Memorial-1804" and eagle, purple
transfers, blue edge striping, repairs
(A) **1870.00**
11" h, creamware, black transfer of "Ship
Caroline" on front, "James Leech" cartouche, "The Shipwright Arms" on reverse,
c1820 . . . . **3000.00**
Plate
8¾" d, oct shape, dark blue oriental style
scene of two figures on bridge in landscape
with dwellings, rim with criss-cross border,
c1765, Chaffers (A) **1275.00**
9¾" d, creamware, black transfer of sailing
ship with American flag, polychrome accents, floral sprig border, early 19th C
(A) **385.00**
11⅞" d, blue painted Chinese boy chasing
butterfly, rocky landscape, c1755–65 . . . . . **250.00**
Platter, 18½" l, 15" w, "India Series," view in
the Fort Madura, blue transfer, c1810, imp
"Herculaneum" mark **1250.00**
Sauce Boat
5½" l, oval, white crane perched on iron-red
fence near blue rock amidst green leafed
peonies and gold or white chrysanthemums
in rococo cartouches, molded rows of
scalework, int with vignette of pink dotted
white pigeon, S scroll handle with iron-red
diamond and foliate motif, c1770, Philip
Christian's Factory (A) **605.00**
5¾" l, silver shape, umbrella trees issuing
from fencework and rocks within molded
cartouches, dbl C scroll handle, c1770,
Christian's Factory (A) **400.00**
7⅜" l, underglaze blue fruit and flower
sprays, leaf scroll molded body, scrolling
handle, c1785, Pennington (A) **280.00**
9" l, oval, porcelain, rose, blue, green, tur-

quoise, yellow, iron-red, and black sprays and sprigs of stylized flowers surrounded by tiny black birds, scallop shell molded body, oval foot, 1760–65, "iron-red D" mark (A)..................................... **2310.00**

Soup Plate, 10" d, creamware, black transfer of "Indiaman Taking a Pilot on Board," mid 19th C (A)....................................... **135.00**

Tankard, 6⅜" h, creamware, Battle of Nile in 1798, "The young Alexander of France/May boast of his prowess in vain/When Nelson appears tis confest/That Britannia are Loards of the Main. Lord Nelson engaging the Toulon Fleet off the Mouth of the Nile," black transfer, hairlines (A)............................. **330.00**

Teapot
  5½" h, spherical body, two oriental birds by rock amidst flowering peonies in underglaze blue and iron-red with gilding, shoulder and cov with flowering branches, underglaze blue spout rim and knob, 1770–80 (A)..................................... **220.00**
  6½" h, ovoid body, painted on both sides in shades of rose, yellow, iron-red, blue, turquoise, green, and black with a bird perched amidst leafy branches amongst distant flocks, iron-red band and circlet border at base of neck repeated around cov rim, iron-red and green floral sprig knob, spout and handle with iron-red floral sprigs (A)..................................... **275.00**
  6¹³⁄₁₆" h, ovoid body, two oriental figures near table by tree in garden beneath flocks of birds in rose, iron-red, green, yellow, and black, iron-red scallop and dot border around shoulder and cov rim, 1770–80 (A)......................... **220.00**
  7" w, blue painted Chinese pavilion, next to bridge, flower branches from rocks, diaper border, c1765 .... **150.00**

Teabowl and Saucer, fluted, front and saucer with pink flowering peony and other yellow centered pink and iron-red flowers and green and brown foliage growing aroung blue rock on black stippled green plateau, teabowl with insect above grassy rock on reverse, pink peony sprig on int, brown border of trefoils (A)........................... **2530.00**

Vase, 3⅛" h, ovoid shape, underglaze blue with two Chinamen sailing in sampans between islands with small pavilions amidst bamboo, willows, and pines, 1760–65 (A).................................... **1210.00**

Vase and Cov, 5¾" h, urn shape, blue, green, yellow, rose, gray, and brown with different vignettes of birds in irregularly shaped scroll edged cartouches outlined in gold, circ foot, cov molded on either side with putto supporting fluted knob above two gilt edge cartouches, c1760, William Ball's Factory (A).................................... **1100.00**

Wall Pocket, 4¾" l, cornucopia shape, underglaze blue on four faceted front with butterfly and floral sprig above floral bouquet, two floral sprigs on curving end, pierced for hanging, 1760–65 (A)..................... **2200.00**

Waste Bowl, 6⅝" d, black continuous oriental

river landscape depicting man in sampan sailing toward another man crossing stone bridge, islands and hills in distance, iron-red edged black cell diaper border with three floral panels, int with islet, grayish green glaze, c1765, Richard Chaffers' Factory (A).................................... **990.00**

LLADRO

**Almacera, Spain
1951 to Present**

History: The Lladro brothers, Juan, Jose, and Vicente, started their small studio in 1951 in Almacera, Spain, They built their own kiln and began making small flowers for decorative lamps. All three brothers shaped the porcelains. Only Juan and Jose decorated them, Vicente supervised the firing.

As their business expanded, they formed Lladro Porcelanas in 1958 and produced their first porcelain figurine of a ballet dancer. Their distinctive style emphasizes the elongated look in porcelain sculpture. The figurines are hand painted in a variety of pastel colors.

Salvador Furio is one of the most senior and prolific sculptors at Lladro. His "Clown with Concertina" was the first figurine he designed for Lladro. Furio has become the Lladro sculptor specializing in particular thematic subjects such as historic characters, figures of literature, and personalities in public life.

Today the Lladro complex is located in Valencia, Spain and is known as "Porcelain City."

Musuem: Lladro Museum, New York, N.Y.

Collectors' Club: Lladro Collectors Society, Dept. 1219, 43 West 57th Street, New York, N.Y. 10019–3498. Membership: $25.00.

Figure
  4¾" h, two white turkeys facing each other, pink and gray beaks, pink and black eyes, shiny glaze, marked (A)................. **25.00**
  5¼" h, flying bird, white, green base, shiny glaze, marked (A) **38.00**
  5½" h, crouching girl with slippers........ **80.00**
  6¼" h, girl reclining on rocky base, gray skirt, blue vest, gray ground, matte finish, marked (A)............................. **110.00**
  6½" h, seated
    Ballerina............................. **185.00**
    Lady with bird on stump................ **115.00**
  7½" h, bride and groom, man in gray coat and hat, light gray pants, bride in white and pink dress, holding white bouquet, shiny glaze, marked (A) **185.00**
  7¾" h, girl manicuring nails **125.00**

1749-55

Figure, 13" h, rust and brown shades, c1960s, blue mark, $575.00

8¼" h, white turkey with gray beak, brown eyes, gray-green base, shiny glaze, marked (A)................................. 25.00
8½" h
  Bust of bugle boy 135.00
  Girl in white pajamas with pink trim, seated on gray and blue stool, hands raised, bottle in hand pouring on head, matte finish 220.00
  Girl with mandolin, matte finish, marked (A) 25.00
9" h, seated hunter leaning on stump, gray pants and hat, white vest, white and tan dog, gray-green base, matte finish, marked (A)................................. 110.00
9¼" l, lying ballerina 185.00
9½" h
  Boy carrying flower basket, light blue overalls, gray basket and hat, pink and yellow flowers, gray-green base 325.00
  Girl with rabbit, white skirt, gray bodice, green base, matte finish, marked (A) 55.00
  White angel with gray hair, white wings, shiny glaze, marked (A).............. 55.00
9¾" h, female dancer seated on blue stool, white skirt, green top, brown hair, shiny glaze, marked (A) 55.00
10" h, girl selling balloons, blue-gray dress, brown purse, multicolored balloons 180.00
10½" h, girl feeding goose, tan skirt, gray apron, dark gray bodice, white goose, tan basket with feed, green base, shiny finish, marked (A) 85.00
11" h, girl in long mauve dress, blue tie, holding white hat on head with hands, shiny glaze, marked (A) 60.00
13½" h, cellist with gold bow, matte finish 350.00
16½" h, Romeo and Juliet (A)........... 200.00
31" l, Vatala, gondola on wooden base, sgd "J. Ruiz', #1212..................... 5000.00
Girl with sheep, #4584.................. 90.00
Plate, 8" d, Navidad
  1973, raised white matte scene of children with Christmas tree and toys, light blue border, gilt inside rim 35.00
  1974, raised white scene of children, one with cross, light blue border, gilt inside rim, matte finish 50.00

LONGTON HALL

Staffordshire Potteries, England
c1750–1760

History: Longton Hall existed for the ten year period between 1750 and 1760. There were several different partnerships during the factory's short production period.

Longton Hall porcelains featured an underglaze blue design in the Oriental style. Some pieces exhibit a streaky blue glaze. Most wares were thickly potted and finished in a crude fashion. Some leaf shaped tablewares were produced.

Most Longton Hall soft paste porcelain was unmarked. Although production was brief, the amount of production was large. Many examples survived to attract the attention of today's collector.

Reference: B. Watney, *Longton Hall Porcelain*, Faber & Faber, 1957.

Museum: Walters Art Gallery, Baltimore, Maryland.

Candlestick, 8⅛" h, modeled as two putti playing with goat before tree trunk, multicolored flowers, foliate nozzle, rococo scrolled base with blue and gilding, c1755 .... 4950.00
Coffee Can
  2⅜" h, green, blue, rose, yellow, iron-red, and black painted scene of two large houses on each side of river, ruins on banks, forked twig handle terminating in cluster of maroon veined green edged leaves, c1755–57, "purple C" mark (A) 2300.00
  2½" h
    Iron-red and yellow painted flowering peonies from rocks and two exotic birds (A) 1045.00
    Painted with standing Oriental holding ban-

Basket, 6⅝" l, ext molded with interweaving, painted sprays of colored flowers, turquoise rope twist handles, flower terminals, c1755, $850.00

ner, pierced rockwork and bamboo in
ground, strap handle, c1756 (A) **2630.00**

Dish

6¹⁵/₁₆" w, pinwheel shape, figures in river
landscape with church on far bank in puce,
purple, chartreuse, iron-red, brown, olive,
pale turquoise, one with couple conversing
by tree, one with man seated before an urn
on pedestal, c1755, pr (A) **7700.00**

10¾" l, leaf shape, painted center floral bouquet of pink and purple roses, puce leaf
veining, green and yellow serrated rim,
green stalk handle, c1755 (A) **2750.00**

Figure

4" w, ram or ewe standing with tree stump
support, black and red-brown markings,
oval mound base with applied flowers and
leaves, restored, c1756, pr (A) **2090.00**

4⅝" h, pug, shaded in brown, black collar
around neck, seated on rect green base,
back leg raised to scratch ear (A) **936.00**

4⅞" h, Autumn, seated girl in purple hat and
skirt, yellow bodice, white apron, holding
basket of grapes in lap, scrolling base with
colors and gilt, repaired, c1755 . . . . **850.00**

Leaf Dish, 8½" l, castle and village church in
center, forked tree in foreground, within border of six green edged leaves with purple veining and short stems, one leaf restored, c1755
(A). **4725.00**

Mug

2½" h, cylinder shape, blue painted oriental
style landscape, spur handle. **650.00**

5⅛" h, baluster shape, grayish blue stylized
chinoiserie island landscape with large pine
tree, broken scroll handle, handle cracked,
c1756 (A) **2125.00**

Plate

8¹¹/₁₆" d, center painted with floral cluster,
spray, and two sprigs in rose, purple, green,
blue, and yellow, rim molded with green
and purple stemmed strawberry vines, iron-
red berries and purple buds in rose veined
green leaves, c1755 (A). **2541.00**

9¼" d, painted bouquets of roses in puce,
yellow, and green, molded leaf and straw-
berry border, c1755, pr (A) **5500.00**

Potpourri Vase, Cov, 16" h, rococo scroll
molded body, painted with floral sprays, encrusted with colored flowers and birds,
edged in purple, pierced cov with applied
flowers, birds, cock, hen, and dancing girl,
circular foot with floral sprigs, restored
flowers, c1755 (A) **16,736.00**

Sauceboat

5⅞" l, silver shape, colorful sprays of oriental
style flowers and insects, scrolled handle,
scroll molded spout, oval foot (A). **900.00**

6" l, oval, blue and white with oriental style
landscape with saucer shaped pavilion, int
with boulder, molded lobed foot, c1755,
workman's mark (A). **1027.00**

6⅞" l, shell molded, kingfisher on a tree
trunk, reverse with pelican, dragonfly beneath spout, wasp above, looped handle,
fluted oval foot, hairline in foot, c1755 (A) **5513.00**

7¼" l, molded green edged overlapping lettuce leaves, painted floral sprays and sprigs,
c1760 (A) **575.00**

8" l, scroll molded with pale scattered floral
sprays and sprigs, one side with two oriental
figures, int base with large floral spray,
scrolling handle, restored, early 1750s (A)   **525.00**

Stand, 7⅞" d, circ, painted butterflies and
flower sprays on basketweave ground, brown
rim (A) **1235.00**

Sweetmeat Stand, 8¼" h, three radiating scallop shells supported on bed of coral, seated
figure of Harlequin playing bagpipes, shirt decorated with playing cards, black spotted yellow breeches, checkered socks, ribboned purple hat and ruff, int of each shell with flowers
and ladybirds, blue-green coral base with butterflies and ladybirds, early 1750s (A). **6000.00**

Tureen, Cov

5½" h, cauliflower shape, bowl molded as
white stems and ribbed chartreuse leaves,
int with rose, yellow, and pale green floral
sprig, cov modeled as white florettes with
florette knob, cracked, c1756 (A) **3575.00**

8¼" h, modeled as pigeon sitting on nest
lined with foliage, purple plumage with
touches of pale green, pink, and blue, int
with spray of foliage (A). **1224.00**

LONGWY
20ᵀᴴ CENTURY

LONGWY

Lorraine, France
1798 to Present

History: A French faience factory, known for its enameled
pottery which resembled cloisonne, was established in
1798 at Lorraine. Utilitarian wares were made in addition
to the enameled pieces.

About 1875 Emaux de Longwy introduced wares that
were decorated with Persian inspired motifs. His designs
were first outlined with black printed manganese resist
and filled in with brightly colored glazes, especially the
turquoise color for which the pieces are most famous.
The company achieved its greatest fame for pieces with
Art Deco motifs featuring bold colors and geometric designs.

Marks used on Longwy examples incorporate
"LONGWY" either impressed or painted under the glaze.

Ashtray

5¼" l, center with enameled salmon and
pink open flowers, brown branches, green
leaves, med blue ground, yellow "HOTEL
CONTINENTAL" on dark blue border, imp
and printed mark. **145.00**

6⅜" sq, small pink and white flowers, brown
branches, med blue ground, dark blue line
rim **125.00**

Ashtray and Match Box, 7" l, oval shape, cobalt,
pink, yellow, green, and turquoise flowers, cobalt outline, turquoise crackle int, marked. . . **185.00**

Bowl

5" d, hex shape, Art Deco enameled florals,
bright blue ground, light turquoise int,

Box, 4" d, turquoise and yellow geometrics, white crazed ground, "Longwy France" mark, $275.00

Plate, 8 1/2" d, raised enameled florals in green, iron-red, magenta, and cream, turquoise ground, imp "Longwy" mark, $145.00

"decore a la main, Emaux Longway, Made in France" mark (A) 90.00

6" d, overall floral design in colors, turquoise crackle ground, dark blue banding, "Emaux de Longwy" mark 175.00

Box, Cov

3 1/2" d, oct, red and white flower with green leaves on cov, orchid crackle ground 175.00

5 1/4" l, 3 1/2" h, turquoise, yellow, magenta, and black flowers, cobalt blue outlines, light turquoise lid, four feet, marked 395.00

Bud Vase, 7 1/8" h, enameled dark red open flowerheads, green leaves, yellow branching, bright blue ground, dark blue band on neck, dark red band on foot, imp "LONGWY" mark. 195.00

Candlestick, 8" h, bronze figural griffin holding enameled multicolored candle nozzle, pr . . . 195.00

Clock, 15 1/4" h, printed in brown with foliate designs bordered by strapwork applied with grotesque masks, canted rect base with masks, eight feet, c1884, imp "Longwy, H,2.84" mark (A). 752.00

Cup and Saucer, yellow and red enameled flowers, dark blue rim and handle, med blue ground. 125.00

Dish

4 1/2" d, multicolored enameled flowers on bright blue ground 85.00

5" d, multicolored enameled design, scalloped edge. 65.00

9" d, ftd, center oval medallion of brown bird perched on rock, flowers growing from water, med blue enameled ground with red and white open flowers and brown stems 395.00

Plaque, 14 1/2" d, center scene of three herons in stream in enameled colors, enameled Art Deco floral border, sgd "AK, Emaux de Longwy, France, Decor a la Main" mark (A). 400.00

Shoe, 6 1/2" l, enameled, pink, rose, cobalt, cream, and salmon florals, black branches, pink int, turquoise ground, pr. 175.00

Sugar Shaker, light blue, yellow, tan, green, orange, and white swirls on dark blue ground, SP top, c1890 (A) 75.00

Tile

6" sq, enameled, multicolored bird on bright blue ground 85.00

8 1/8" sq, standing woman in brown dress, leaning on brown tree, blue leaved florals on right, yellow and tan crackle ground, printed mark. 550.00

Tray

7 1/2" l, rect, enameled, rose and pink florals, yellow and green leaves, blue edge, turquoise ground 150.00

11" l, 10" w, rect, multicolored enameled bird with trees and foliage, turquoise crackle ground, raised rim. 200.00

Trivet, 8" sq, ftd, "Primavera," woman in mustard, blue, and purple dress, shades of blue leaves, purple branch, "Longwy France" mark. 750.00

Vase

7" h, cylinder shape, multicolored enameled bird, palm tree and mountain, blue ground 295.00

7 1/2" h, enameled, yellow, salmon, mustard florals, white interior, cobalt edge, turquoise ground. 295.00

9" h, enameled, yellow, orange, and red flowers on blue ground. 325.00

LOWESTOFT   c1775-1790

Bell Lane, Lowestoft, England
c1757–1799

History: Soft paste porcelains were made in Lowestoft beginning about 1757 and ending in 1799. The principal production was ulititarian wares for the local community. Until 1770 all the designs used blue and white Oriental motifs. Sales were direct from the factory.

Later, formal floral patterns were introduced. During the 1770s blue-printed designs, copied from Worcester and Caughley, were produced. Lowestoft's enamelled wares of the 1780s resembled the Chinese export figure and flower painted wares imported by the English East India Company. Rarer examples of Lowestoft have naturalistic flower painting and English views.

No Lowestoft factory marks were used.

References: G. A. Godden, *The Illustrated Guide to Lowestoft Porcelain,* Herbert Jenkins, 1969; W.W.R. Spelman, *Lowestoft China,* Jarrold & Sons, 1905.

Museums: Castle Museum, Norwich, England; Christchurch Mansion, Ipswich, England; Fitzwilliam Museum, Cambridge, England; Lowestoft Museum, Lowestoft, England; Museum of Fine Arts, Boston, Mass.; Victoria & Albert Museum, London, England.

Basket, 5" d, circ, transfer printed and painted in underglaze blue in center with floral spray surrounded by three foliate sprigs, sides formed of open interlocking circlets painted on int with floral sprigs beneath pineapple and scrollwork border on scalloped rim, ext with further foliate sprigs and florettes, 1775–80 (A) **880.00**

Bottle, 4³/4" h, continuous scene of Chinese woman in fenced garden carrying parasol and teapot, another seated at table, pavilion in ground, rose, iron-red, green, turquoise, purple, yellow, brown, and black, iron-red scalloped and banded border, c1770–75 (A) ... **2178.00**

Bowl, 9" w, oval, pierced body with rope twist handles, flower terminals, blue "Pinecone" pattern and diaper border on int, applied flowerheads on ext, c1770 (A)............. **1430.00**

Coffee Cup, 2³/8" h, multicolored painted chinoiserie scene of flowers from rockwork in garden, spurred loop handle (A) **800.00**

Coffee Pot, 8³/4" h, pear shape, enameled vert panels of oriental ladies, quail, chrysanthemums, or flowering prunus, gilt edged blue scale vert panels, mushroom knob, crack, c1770–75 (A)........................... **2475.00**

Creamboat
3⁵/8" h, painted in purple, red, and green floral sprays and sprigs, green rim, entwined dolphin molded spout, c1775 (A)........ **425.00**
4" h, blue painted oriental fishing scene and island in oval molded reserve, rib molded ground, demi-floret border, c1765–70 (A) **495.00**

Cream Jug, 3" h
Blue peony and weeping willow from rockwork and fencing, lattice border, sparrow beak spout, loop handle, c1775 .... **260.00**
Pear shape, painted in rose, purple, iron-red, and green with spray and 2 sprigs of Chinese Export-style flowers beneath brown scalloped border at brown edged rim (A) . **275.00**

Custard Cup, 2³/8" h, painted "Regrave" pattern in colors, egg and flower border, loop handle (A)............................... **278.00**

Teabowl, 1¹/2" h, 2⁷/8" d, blue painted floral, modified berry border, c1775, painter's mark, $250.00

Dish
4⁵/8" d, shell shape, flowering peony, dk underglaze blue, scrolling border, diaper border on thumb piece, white ground, c1770 (A)..................................... **620.00**
5¹/2" l, leaf shape, underglaze blue with crane-like bird perched on flowering tree, rim edged with dashes, reverse relief molded with veining, 3 molded feet, painter's 4 (A) **1800.00**

Eye Bath, 2¹/4" h, oval cup, molded on either side of ext with blossom and foliate scroll edged cartouche painted in underglaze blue with floral spray, molding repeated on top of oval foot around reeded stem, foot and cup int with small sprigs, int rim with scallop and dot border, c1770 (A) **1870.00**

Feeding Cup
2⁷/8" h, bucket shape, blue painted five petal flower with two sprays and moth, spurred loop handle (A) **555.00**
3¹/2" h, flared cylinder shape, straight spout, loop handle, painted flowering Oriental shrubs from rockwork and fencing, c1765–70 (A) **625.00**

Figure, 3¹/2" h, seated brown Pug dog with green collar, green rect base (A) **1100.00**

Flask, 6¹/2" h, spherical form, enamels with spray of flowers, reverse in black with "MH" above laurel branches encircled by iron-red and black flower sprigs, c1798 (A)........ **531.00**

Jug, Cov, 5¹/2" h, ovoid shape, "Mansfield" pattern in underglaze blue, cov with flowering finial, c1775, underglaze blue crescent mark (A)..................................... **841.00**

Milk Jug, Miniature, 1⁷/8" h, pear shape body, blue and white with island pavilion beside tree on front, reverse with cottage on rocky island, sides with small boat, rim with fringed scallop border, loop handle, 1765–70, underglaze blue workman's numeral 2? on footrim (A).. **550.00**

Mug
4¹/2" h
Baluster shape, painted in blue with "Ann Sawyer, 1773" within a scrolling cartouche, flanked by floral sprays attracting winged insects, int with diaper border, S scroll handle, 1773 (A) **5513.00**
Cylindrical form, underglaze blue, iron-red, and gilding with panel inscribed "Jacob & Mary Bray, 1775," flanked by bouquets of flowers, rim with border of ring motifs, scroll handle, underglaze "blue 5" mark, crack below rim chip (A)............. **1328.00**
5⁵/8" h, campana shape, painted bifurcated spray of pink roses, anenomes, and fuschsias, flanked by floral sprigs, butterfly and dragonfly, int rim with 4 sprigs, scrolling handle, c1775 (A).................... **3062.00**
6" h, bell shape, grayish blue exotic bird perched on sm island, reverse with Chinoiserie garden of flowers and pierced rocks, int with border of flower reserves and dotted lattics, scrolled handle, c1765, workman's numeral 5 (A).......................... **1151.00**

Mustard Pot, Cov, 3¹/2" h, cylindrical body, dk underglaze blue with "Mansfield" pattern of peony spray and floral sprigs below pineapple and scrollwork border on shoulder repeated around notched cov rim, floral sprig knop, ear shaped handle with foliate sprig, 1780–85 (A)............................. **1760.00**

Patty Pan, 3³⁄₁₆″ d, runny underglaze blue in center with insect, int and ext sides with smaller insects alternating with flowering branches, fringed scallop border on flat rim, 1770–80, pr (A)........................ **250.00**

Pickle Dish, 2¹¹⁄₁₆″ l, leaf shape, blue and white with cottage on island beneath runny trellis diaper border at rim, underside molded with 3 leaf form feet, 1770–80 (A)............... **250.00**

Sauceboat, 5¹⁄₂″ h, molded floral panels, blue painted "Fisherman and Billboard Island" pattern (A) **266.00**

Spoon, 5″ l, oval bowl painted with peony and cell diaper border, tapered handle with molded floret terminal, c1775 (A).......... **1420.00**

Sugar Bowl, Cov, 2³⁄₄″ h, underglaze blue with island pavilion beside tree on front, reverse with cottage on rocky island, sides with small boat, rim with fringed scallop border, center of ring form knob with grassy rock, 1765–70 (A)....................... **800.00**

Tankard

4¹⁄₈″ h, cylinder shape, blue printed and washed chinoiserie landscape with figure on bridge, loop handle with basal spur and thumbrest (A).......................... **418.00**

4³⁄₄″ h, blue flower sprays and moth, int with flower and scroll border, scrolled handle, c1770, workman's mark (A)............. **815.00**

Teabowl and Saucer

Blue painted "Doll's House" pattern (A) **135.00**

Oriental scene in lavender, gold, blue, green, and iron-red, weeping willow on int of cup, c1770 .... **180.00**

Teapot

3³⁄₈″ h, miniature, globular, blue printed "Three Flowers" pattern, two line border, loop handle (A) **925.00**

3⁹⁄₁₆″ h, spherical body, transfer printed in underglaze blue on either side with butterfly above spray of mixed flowers, cov with floral spray and sprig above dbl line border around rim, loop handle, c1775 (A) **770.00**

5¹⁄₂″ h, globular, multicolored sprays and sprigs of flowers, knobbed cover, chips to cov, c1770–75 (A) **1230.00**

The peak period of production was between 1758 and 1776. Utilitarian wares decorated with birds and ornamental wares, e.q., candlesticks, were produced. Riedel, the major designer and modeler during this period, crafted mythological and classical figures. Berger, another sculptor, made small figural groups comprised of peasants, work and ballet groups. These figures did not match the quality of the figurines from Meissen, Nymphenburg, or Frankenthal.

Initially the Ludwigsburg shapes and decoration were in the Rococo style. The factory changed its forms and designs as tastes changed. Rococo gave way to Neo-classical followed by Empire. Ludwigsburg porcelain started to decline after 1770. The enterprise never really was profitable or highly scuccessful. Duke Karl Eugen died in 1793. Production deteriorated even more after his death. The factory struggled on for thirty more years, it closed in 1824. During the 19th century, the Ludwigsburg molds were sold to Edward Kick, at Amberg in Bavaria. Kick reissued a number of the pieces.

References: George W. Ware, *German and Austrian Porcelain,* Crown Publishers, Inc., 1963.

Museums: Cincinnati Art Museum, Cincinnati, Ohio; Museum fur Kunst und Gewerbe, Hamburg, Germany; Shlossmuseum, Berlin, Germany; Wurttembergishes Landesmuseum, Stuttgart, Germany.

Coffee Pot, Cov, 7³⁄₈″ h, pear shape, front with black-headed green and yellow bird and shaded brown bird flanking large white parrot with iron-red crest and tail, behind iron-red parrot with blue, yellow, and green wings and tail feathers, perched amidst green leaves of small brown tree, reverse with spray two sprigs of puce flowers, S scroll handle, leafy vine beneath green foliate thumbpiece, sprout, rim, and cov rim with gilt and puce scroll work, hatched panels, cov with two songbirds, conical knob, 1760–65, underglaze "blue crowned interlaced C's" mark (A)......... **9350.00**

Cup and Saucer, three birds on branches, raised ridged border with panels and designs, gilt rim, c1758, underglaze "blue interlaced C's" mark........................ **350.00**

Dish

7¹⁄₂″ l, shaped form, enamels with travelers in wooded landscape vignettes supported on rococo scrollwork with shells and garlands, ozier borders with scattered flowers, gilt

MODERN MARK   1756-1824

LUDWIGSBURG

Wurttemberg, Germany
1758–1824

History: Karl Eugen, Duke of Wurttemberg, founded a hardpaste porcelain manufactory in 1758 at Ludwigsburg, twelve miles north of Stuttgart. A faience factory was established two years later. Joseph Jacob Ringler directed the porcelain factory from 1759 to 1799. Initially copies of Meissen wares were made.

Figure, 5″ h, multicolored, soft pastels, restored, early 19th C, (A) $605.00

edged rims, 1765–70, underglaze "blue interlaced C's, crown," marks, pr (A). **1110.00**

8⁵/₈" l, oval shape, shades of puce, iron-red, yellow, blue, and green with spray and small sprigs of German flowers in center and on gilt edged molded rim, 1765–70, underglaze "blue crowned interlaced C's," marks (A). **330.00**

Figure

3" h, tailoring group, tailor seated on table stitching waistcoat while another irons on table, customer watches, c1765, underglaze "blue interlaced C's" mark (A) **1914.00**

4¼" h, boy wearing regional costume, carrying small sack, head to one side, c1770 (A). **700.00**

4⁷/₈" h, man seated on rocks, elbow on barrel, blue lined white jerkin, white shirt, orange trousers and cap, pitcher in one hand, glass in other, dog on puce and gilded scroll edged base, c1765, modeled by J.J. Louis, "blue crowned interlaced C's" mark **1350.00**

5" h, man or woman playing hurdy-gurdys, multicolored, repairs, pr. **450.00**

5¼" h, sportsman and companion, young man in black tricorn, green jacket, yellow breeches, brown sword, holding rifle, standing beside companion in green edged yellow hat, puce jacket, gilt dotted puce and white skirts, holding birdcage, bird perched on right hand, seated on chartreuse and brown mottled tree stump, spotted brown hound at feet, gilt edged chartreuse and tan mottled chamfered rect base, c1775, modeled by Adam Bauer, underglaze "blue crowned interlaced C's, black H," marks (A) **2750.00**

5⁵/₁₆" h, Apollo as youthful god in iron-red drapery, playing brown edged tan lyre, seated on gray and white architectural element with builder's tools, tan and gray mottled base with clusters of green moss, reglued, c1765, underglaze "blue crowned interlaced C's, iron-red B, incised 3.M./W: and 53" marks (A) **660.00**

5³/₄" h, standing dancing female in puce lined lavender jacket and apron, canary yellow skirt edged in iron-red and gilt, tree stump on scroll molded base edged in gilt scrolls, c1765, "blue crowned interlacedd C's" mark (A) **1650.00**

5⁷/₈" h, shepherd seated on rock playing flute, white puce lined jacket, light brown blue lined breeches, dog at side, rocky base, restored, c1768–70, modeled by "J.C.W. Beyer, "crowned interlaced C's and brown W" mark. **1100.00**

6" h, 5" l, lady in floral decorated lace dress, red hair, red bodice, pink bow, seated on green sofa, c1830–50 . . . . **450.00**

6¹/₂" h

Woman with frilled bonnet, pale yellow bodice, striped puce skirt, shaving bald seated man, writing table, c1770, modeled by J.V. Sonnenschein, underglaze "blue interlaced C's" mark (A). **3366.00**

Young man with a wig, long brown jacket, yellow breeches, examining arm of young woman for blood letting, girl sitting on chair supporting head on arm, leaning on

table, marbled grassy base, one hand restuck, c1770, modeled by J.V. Sonnenschein, underglaze "blue interlaced C's (A) **4301.00**

6³/₄" h, shepherd as youth in black hat, yellow lined puce jacket, white shirt, blue breeches, playing brown recorder, seated beside mottled brown and green tree stump, tan rockwork base, gray dog at feet, repaired, c1765, modeled by Johann Christian Wilhelm Beyer, underglaze "blue crowned interlaced C's and S" marks (A) . **880.00**

7³/₈" h, "The Coffee Drinker," young woman in puce drapery, white blouse, blue sprigged yellow skirt, seated on salmon and iron-red cushioned stool, mottled green table supported on entwined tails of three gray dolphins, pouring coffee from pot, gray rect base draped with green carpet, repaired c1766, modeled by Johann Christian Wilhelm Beyer, underglaze "blue crowned interlaced C's," iron-red "B" marks (A). **4400.00**

8¹/₈" h, "Tailoring," tailor in iron-red cap, gilt edged pink waistcoat, pale yellow breeches, scissors over shoulder, clasping beard of gray spotted rearing goat, apprentice in blue edged pink jacket, green apron, iron-red breeches, milking goat into tan bucket, tailor's wife in purple edged lilac jacket, gilt edged yellow bodice, blue and iron-red stripe skirt, seated on goat's back, holding kid in lap, mottled green, brown, and iron-red oval mound base edged in molded scrolls in puce and gold, restored, 1770–75, modeled by Johann Jacob Louis, underglaze "blue interlaced C's," marks (A) **3850.00**

8¹/₂" h, Apollo, naked youth, gilt edged pink drapery, playing tan lyre, seated on two tan rocks encrusted with green moss, instruments on gilt edged white architectural cornice, mottled green, brown, and gray rocky oval base applied with small leafy plants, haircrack, c1765, modeled by Johann Christian Wilhelm Beyer, underglaze "blue interlaced C's, backwards S in green, marks (A) **1100.00**

9" h, seated gardener with shovel and pail, female seated with flowers in apron, basket and watering can at side, rococo style tree trunk, multicolored, c1766 (A). **5125.00**

10¹/₈" h, Venus and a dolphin, goddess scantily draped in white, hair and features in enamel, iron-red and blue dolphin, oct gilt edged base, c1765, modeled by W. Beyer, underglaze "blue crowned interlaced C's and S" mark (A) **1645.00**

10⁷/₁₆" h, Orpheus and Cerberus, as naked youth in puce lined white drapery, fastened with gold and white strap, playing gilt edged white lyre, leaning against moss encrusted mottled brown, black, russet, and green support, three headed Cerberus with black spotted brown coat and black arrowhead tail leashed to support, green and brown mottled sq base, c1765, modeled by Johann Christian Wilhelm Beyer, underglaze "blue interlaced C's" marks (A) **660.00**

Jug, 8³/₄" h, pear shape, faience, manganese, green, blue, and yellow carnation spray amongst scattered flowers and sprigs, scroll handle, cov molded with crowned Bavarian shield incised "F.E.18," pewter mtd, 3rd quarter 18th C, blue "interlaced C's/1" mark (A) **1440.00**

Plate, 9⅛" d, center painted with pr of birds perched in branches, ozier molded borders edged with brown lines and painted with insects, "crossed interlaced C" marks, set of 6 (A)..................................... **1710.00**

Platter, 16" l, oval, multicolored floral sprays, lobed basketweave border **450.00**

Sauce Tureen, Cov, 7½" w, circ, painted on front and reverse in shades of brown, green, blue, gray, tan, yellow, and iron-red with fisherman or couple conversing in river landscape with buildings on opposite bank above gold, puce, and blue rococo scrollwork with green foliate garland, sides with colorful floral spray, gilt edged molded rim with small floral sprigs, scroll handles, cov with figural knob modeled as youth eating grapes from purple cluster, 1765–75, underglaze "blue crowned interlaced C's" mark (A) **3300.00**

Slop Bowl, 7¾" d, painted large and small flowersprays in iron-red, purple, blue, green, and yellow, relief of ribbon swags, scroll molded rim outlined in purple and gilt feathering, restored, c1760–65, "blue crowned interlaced C's" mark (A).......................... **975.00**

Teabowl and Saucer, painted houses in landscapes, scattered flowers on ozier-molded border, c1770–75, "blue interlaced C's" mark (A).................................... **1100.00**

Tea Caddy, 5¼" h, flat rect shape, painted with fisherman in landscape on front, reverse, and cov, scattered flower sprigs, ozier-molded borders, gilt edged rims, c1770–75, "blue interlaced C's" mark (A) **3238.00**

Teapot, 5" h, cylinder body, puce painted battle scenes, three paw feet, heraldic lion knob, scroll handle with gilt lion mask thumbpiece, c1770, "interlaced C's" mark (A) **1831.00**

Tureen, Cov
11⅜" l, sprays of German flowers in purple, iron-red, yellow, blue, and green, gilt accented scroll handles and four feet, brown edged ozier molded rims, cabbage, parsnip, turnip and beans molded knob, c1765–70, "blue crowned interlaced C's" mark (A) .. **880.00**

11½" h, oval molded body, flower sprays and scattered blooms, domed cov with large vegetable knob, scrolling handles and feet in purple, c1765, knob damage, underglaze "blue crowned interlaced C's" mark (A)................................ **3150.00**

Tureen, Cov, 11⅞" l, Platter, 13³⁄₁₆" l, oval, shades of rose, iron-red, blue, yellow, purple, and green with sprays and sprigs of German flowers on brown edged molded rim, scroll molded handles on tureen, cov with knob formed as green cabbage, puce striated parsnip, iron-red turnip, green peapod, 1765–70, underglaze "blue crowned interlaced C's', imp 4 dot mark on platter (A) **2750.00**

Waste Bowl, 7⅛" d, front of ext with small fisherman in Italianate river landscape, reverse with traveler in rural landscape, sides and center with floral sprays, gilt rim, puce ground, 1765–70, underglaze "blue crowned interlaced C's marks (A)...................... **990.00**

LUSTER

English
19th Century to Present

History: The exact beginning of luster decoration on British pottery cannot be dated accurately. The first pieces date from the first quarter of the 19th century; and, the luster process still is used today.

Luster decoration is achieved by applying thin metallic films to earthenware or china bodies. Gold luster comes from gold oxide, copper luster from copper oxide, silver luster from platinum, and pink or purple luster from "purple of cassuis."

All over lustering imitated metallic wares made in gold, silver, or copper. Luster decorations also were used on rims, details, and decorative highlights.

The "resist" process involved keeping parts of the object white through temporarily resisting them with wax or paper cut-outs so that when the luster solution was applied to the object it would not affect the resisted portions. Reserved panels could be left plain, painted, or transfer printed. Stenciling also was used. Overglaze enamels could be added to the lustered ground.

Sunderland or "Splash luster," a mottled type of pink luster used on a white body, was very popular. The splash effect came from spraying an oil on the wet luster that had just been applied to the white ware. The oil expanded in the kiln to form bubbles and splashes. Manufacturers who used this technique were Southwick, Dixon & Austin, and Ball's. A large portion of Sunderland luster was produced at Newcastle-upon-Tyne.

Jugs, mugs, tea, and tablewares were among the most popular luster forms. An enormous variety of jugs were made, some featuring mottled pink with verses and others silver or other colors. Inscriptions on luster ware varied greatly. Events, landmarks in history, and popular sentiments, were commemorated. Plaques had either mottos or verses, sailing ships, or landscapes within painted frames.

Staffordshire and other potteries that made a wide variety of luster ware types include: Spode, Wedgwood, Lakin & Poole, Ralph & Enoch Wood, Davenport, New Hall, and Minton.

References: John Bedford, *Old English Lustre Ware*, Walker & Co., 1965; W. Bosanko, *Collecting Old Lustre Ware*, George H. Doran Co., 1916; Jeanette R. Hodgon, *Collecting Old English Lustre*, Southworth-Anthoensen Press, 1937; W.D. John & W. Baker, *Old English Lustre Pottery*, Ceramic Book co., 1951; J.T. Shaw, *The Potteries of Sunderland & District*, Sunderland Library, 1961.

Museums: Art Institute of Chicago, Chicago, Illinois; Cincinnati Museum of Art, Cincinnati, Ohio; City Museum & Art Gallery, Stoke-on-Trent, Hanley, England; Cleveland Museum of Art, Clevland, Ohio; Laing Art gallery 7 Museum, Newcastle, England; Potsdam Public Museum, Potsdam, N.Y.; Sunderland Museum, Sunderland, England

REPRODUCTION ALERT: Portmeiron Potteries Ltd., a Stoke-on-Trent firm, produces jugs which are reproductions of older luster types in museums and private collections. These new pieces have the maker's mark and are not intended to confuse the collector. Sometimes the mark is removed, and these reproductions are offered as old pieces.

Teapot, Copper Luster, 5½" h, raised scene of girl in red dress playing with brown and white dog, green ground, unmkd, (A) $30.00

Cup and Saucer, Pink Luster, multicolored oriental transfer, pink luster bands, unmkd, $30.00

Creamer, Silver Luster, 3½" h, 5" l, vert ribbing, raised dots at waist, unmkd, $95.00

Figure, Sunderland Luster, 8½"–9½" h, "Four Seasons," Spring, Summer, Fall, and Winter, multicolored, imp "Dixon-Austin" marks, set of 4, $6000.00

COPPER

Bough Pot, Cov, 12" h, cream glaze overglazed in copper luster, white reliefs of classic figures in landscapes, pink luster on lid and dbl handles, restored lid and handles (A) **605.00**

Bowl
  4¾" d, blue band, c1850 .... **75.00**
  5" d, lacework design on luster body **95.00**
  5½" d, polychrome reliefs panels of scenes and flowers on cobalt band, beaded edge, c1825 .... **135.00**

Creamer
  2¾" h, blue band, luster body (A) **44.00**
  3⅝" h
    Green and yellow banding, luster body (A) **35.00**
    White band with "Hope and Faith," purple transfers, luster body (A) **110.00**
  4⅜" h, pink luster house design, copper luster body (A) **80.00**
  4½" h, green band, lustered body (A)..... **44.00**
  4⅞" h, canary band with white reserves of red transfers of woman and child at desk (A)................................... **165.00**
  5" h, applied and polychrome leafy design, blue bands, mask spout (A) **50.00**

Goblet
  4" h, center blue band with raised floral design in colors (A)...................... **35.00**
  4¼" h, enameled red, blue, and yellow flowers in basket on luster body **110.00**
  4⅜" h
    Emb polychrome basket of flowers on olive band (A) **65.00**
    Pink luster house design, copper luster body (A) **81.00**
  4½" h, Sunderland luster on cream bands, copper luster body **45.00**
  4¾" h, pink luster band, red and green florals on white reserves (A)................. **30.00**

Jug
  5" h, kneeling King Henry III, black transfers, luster accents and decoration under spout, repair to spout (A) **165.00**
  5½" h, pearlware, black printed scene of weavers and banner with "Success to the Cotton Spinners," reverse with verse, floral and bird borders, luster band at neck (A) . **800.00**
  5¾" h, 8½" l, blue band with raised white classical figures, c1830 .... **275.00**

Loving Cup, 4⅝" h, polychrome floral band, luster body (A)......................... **44.00**

Mug
  2¾" h
    Wide blue center band **25.00**
    Wide green band, six yellow bands **65.00**
  3" h
    Center blue band, luster body and handle **24.00**
    Polychrome figures, luster body.......... **25.00**
    Wide center mustard band, floral luster design............................... **42.00**
  3¹⁵⁄₁₆" h, pearlware, black printed and colored "Weaver's Union" coat of arms, flanked by figures and weaving, dtd 1824, copper luster band on rim and base (A) .. **300.00**

Pitcher
  2½" h, wide white pebble band with red,

white, and blue Shield of the United States, flanked by American flag (A) **275.00**

3" h
Cream band, pink luster design **25.00**
Yellow band, c1870 . . . . **55.00**

3¹⁄₃" h, cream band with enameled flowers **30.00**

4" h
Blue band, c1865 . . . . **80.00**
Blue and yellow bands. **35.00**
Blue, yellow, and white flowers, luster body. **30.00**
Molded mask spout, luster body **32.00**
White relief plaques of classical cherubs with goat or dog cart and relief of Seal of the United States under spout on light blue band, light blue band on neck, luster body (A) **660.00**
Yellow horse with male rider in copper, green trees, pink trim, copper rim, white ground, "Old Staffordshire, Paragon, England" mark **20.00**

4¹⁄₄" h, enameled rust hound, brown sheep, multicolored flowers on center blue band **195.00**

4³⁄₈" h, white cameos of cherubs, pink luster banding, luster body (A) **150.00**

4¹⁄₂" h
Center band of colored florals, luster body **45.00**
Emb figures of horse, chariot, and driver on dark green band, mask spout **81.00**
Sunderland luster bands (A) **48.00**

4³⁄₄" h
Cobalt bands on luster body **50.00**
Multicolored panels of mother and child at desk on yellow center band **325.00**

5" h
Bulbous body, center blue band **68.00**
Cream band with enameled flowers **30.00**
Two "sanded bands," luster body **55.00**

5¹⁄₄" h
Overall diamond quilt pattern, violet and green enameled violets on neck, molded hound head on handle, luster body (A) **231.00**
Pink luster band with polychrome flowers (A) **44.00**

5¹⁄₂" h, diamond quilted design, "Made in England" mark **75.00**

5⁷⁄₈" h, emb polychrome cherubs and flowers, orange band (A). **90.00**

6" h
Raised enameled basket of flowers, mask spout **95.00**
Sq panels, pink and green enameled flowers. **85.00**

6¹⁄₈" h, polychrome relief spray on peach ground, beading on base, luster body, unmarked. **295.00**

6⁵⁄₈" h, blue band with cherubs, applied polychrome florals (A) **35.00**

6³⁄₄" h, oval medallions of "LaFayette," "Cornwallis," and fruit in black transfers on white ground, reserved on wide red center band, copper luster body with horiz ribbing (A). **930.00**

7" h, revelers in relief, blue enameled scrollwork, luster body (A) **50.00**

7⁵⁄₈" h, relief of deer, blue enameled decorations on spout and collar. **125.00**

7³⁄₄" h
Dancers in relief, turquoise trim. **65.00**

Pot of flowers and butterfly in polychromes on wide blue band, luster body (A) **220.00**

8" h, red transfer of clock face on white ground on one side, reverse with woman carrying cross. **345.00**

8³⁄₁₆" h, center iron-red band, black transfer reserves of Lafayette with muses, Cornwallis with muses on sides, fruit below spout, luster body with horiz ribbing, beading on rim (A). **1925.00**

8³⁄₈" h, black transfers of Lafayette, Cornwallis, or fruit on white ground in brick red medallions on carary yellow center band, copper luster body (A). **990.00**

8¹⁄₂" h, blue, yellow, and white florals, duck handle **145.00**

8³⁄₄" h
Canary band with white reserves of red transfers of woman and child with badminton rackets, hairline on handle (A) . . **300.00**
Wide blue center band with emb copper luster animals and basket of fruit, luster body, pr (A) **550.00**

8⁷⁄₈" h, applied and polychrome basket of flowers, pink luster base, plugged hole in base (A). **577.00**

9³⁄₈" h, wide blue band with applied and polychrome shepherd, mask spout (A). . . . **330.00**

Plate
8¹⁄₂" d, oatmeal ground with green frond leaf chain, rust-brown leaves on border, English "Searl" mark. **10.00**

9¹⁄₄" d, onion and floral center, copper luster border, c1850 (A) **23.00**

9¹⁄₂" d, copper-gold scrolls on oatmeal ground, ten sided **9.00**

Salt, 2" h, ftd, enameled white and pink open blossoms, blue and green leaves on luster body. **125.00**

Teapot
5³⁄₄" h, pear shape, eagle form handle in copper luster banded with yellow, copper luster stylized leaf designs (A) **143.00**

6" h, ginger colored body with blue and luster glazed vines and flowers, c1820 (A) **176.00**

6¹⁄₂" h, round, cobalt blue panels with raised scenes of girl with dog. **165.00**

6³⁄₄" h, paneled body, small pink, yellow, and green florals **175.00**

7" h, 9" l, enameled red, blue, and yellow flowers on luster body **195.00**

Tea Service, teapot, creamer, 6 cups and saucers, cream ground overglazed with copper luster, raised reserves in white of classic figures bordered and rimmed in pink luster, age lines, Shorthose (A) **550.00**

Tumbler, 3" h, tan band, applied polychrome florals (A) **35.00**

Vase, 2¹⁄₄" h, cream band, luster body **20.00**

PINK

Bowl
7¹⁄₂" d, wide open pink flowers, iron-red and green florals, pink luster rim and bands, unmarked. **90.00**

8¹⁄₂" d, pink luster resist with green and yellow enameled florals on int border (A) . . . **94.00**

8³⁄₄" d, polychrome floral design, luster arches and bands, unmarked (A). **198.00**

Coffee Pot, 11 1/4" h
  Cream body, red grapes, pink luster roses and
    vines, domed cov, restored (A) 247.00
  "House" pattern, domed lid 285.00
Creamer
  3" h, pink luster resist floral design (A) 132.00
  4 5/8" h, large roses in pink luster with grapes
    and spiraling vines (A) 302.00
Cup, 2 3/4" h, transfer of hunting dog and rabbit,
    c1820, restored 70.00
Cup and Saucer
  Gaudy floral design in pink with green leaves,
    pink and pink luster borders with pink luster
    overglaze, cream ground (A) 357.00
  "House" pattern, incised "Patterson" mark . 60.00
  Paneled with roses, c1830 .... 50.00
  Pink luster resist with polychrome florals (A) 22.00
Cup and Saucer, Demitasse, orange transfer of
    chinoiserie scene accented with yellow, blue,
    and green enamels, luster rims (A) 25.00
Cup and Saucer, Handleless
  Green and yellow enamel vining pattern on
    pink luster resist (A) 77.00
  Pink luster floral decor 50.00
Figure, 4 1/2" h, white, luster gilt collar, cobalt
    blue base with gilt trim, Staffordshire, pr 600.00
Jug
  4 3/8" h, brown "Bell Forever," blue and pink
    luster floral and band trim (A) 570.00
  5" h
    Mask spout, basketweave bottom with
      florals, luster trim, c1835 .... 275.00
    Relief molded jug with green leaves, luster
      trim, c1830 .... 240.00
  5 3/4" h
    "Mason Free Arms" transfer, farm scene on
      reverse, c1810 .... 285.00
    Puce printed agricultural scene and verse,
      inscribed "Industry Produceth Wealth,"
      luster trim, Staffordshire (A) 160.00
  5 7/8" h, creamware, black printed cartoon of
    scene of Peterloo and bust of Henry Hunt,
    inscribed "The persevering Advocate of
    People's Rights," pink luster bands (A) ... 570.00
  7 1/2" h, 9" d, "Mason's Arms" center car-
    touche, "Here's to You Jack" sea car-
    touche, "When You Remember Me"
    verse 695.00
Jug, Cov, 5 1/4" h, with underdish, blue, red, and
    green flowerheads, pink luster borders with
    squiggles, early 19th C (A) 232.00
Mug
  2 1/8" d, black transfer of "A Shave For a
    Penny," monkey shaving in mirror, pink lus-
    ter rim 345.00
  2 1/4" h, green and pink luster center band of
    flowers, pink luster rim (A) 110.00
  2 3/8" h, orange, violet, red, and green exotic
    birds, luster rim (A) 94.00
  2 1/2" h
    Strawberry design, c1840 .... 185.00
    Transfer of mother and child, government
      building in ground, luster rim band 100.00
  3 3/4" h, black transfer of Farmer's Arms under
    legend "GOD SAVE THE PLOW," luster
    border, 19th C 125.00
  4 3/4" h, vert blue stripes, horiz luster stripes
    (A) 165.00
Pitcher
  4 3/4" h, pink luster resist with vining pattern,

oval medallions with purple transfers of En-
    glish countryside (A) 302.00
  5" h, relief of fox hunt scene of dogs chasing
    fox through forest, figural hound handle
    with pink luster collar and rim (A) 88.00
  5 1/4" h
    "House" pattern 135.00
    Paneled shape, three panels with house
      scenes, one white panel, raised rib de-
      sign, floral rim 235.00
  5 1/2" h, man standing by horse in pink with
    pink luster coat and mane, pink and luster
    spotted hounds on front, luster and green
    raised leaves, basketweave base 350.00
  5 3/4" h, emb ribs, eagle, and flowers in pink
    and purple luster (A) 148.00
  6" h, emb hunting dogs and strawberries in
    pink luster and green enamel (A) 275.00
  6 1/2" h, emb florals around neck and panels
    of large rose and American eagle accented
    in pink luster, buff ground, hairline (A).... 121.00
Plaque
  5 1/2" l, 4 3/4" h, rect, Queen Caroline molded
    with a profile bust portrait wearing plumed
    hat, below crown and "Q C," within
    molded lustered frame, pierced for hanging,
    c1820 (A) 650.00
  9 3/8" l, 8 3/8" h, rect, "The Great Eastern
    Steam Ship," black transfer with poly-
    chromes, pink luster shaped border (A)... 445.00
Plate
  6 1/2" d, "House" pattern, scalloped edge .. 55.00
  6 7/8" d, rust, yellow, blue florals around circle
    in pink border 75.00
  7 1/4" d, "Robinson Crusoe Family Dining,"
    multicolored transfer, eight sided, raised
    border, scalloped edge, c1830 .... 125.00
  7 1/2" d, polychrome enamel open rose in
    center, emb shell rim with pink luster trim,
    pr (A) 66.00
  7 3/4" d
    Green transfer of "Employ time well..,," emb
      floral border with polychrome enamels
      and luster trim (A) 71.00
    Pearlware, emb rim with pink luster
      stripes, polychrome enameled rose in
      center (A) 50.00
  8 1/4" d, iron-red, blue, and green flowers with
    yellow centers, wide pink luster inner band
    and rim band 80.00
  9" d, polychrome enamel open rose in cen-
    ter, emb border with two pink luster
    stripes (A) 30.00
  9 1/2" sq, green enamel dots, relief scroll body,
    pink luster ground 20.00
  9 3/4" d, painted flowers and leaves in pink,
    purple, and yellow, green and red overglaze
    (A) 38.00
Platter, 15 3/4" l, "House" pattern, pink and pink
    luster (A) 18.00
Posset Cup, Saucer, Tray, 5" h, wide luster bands
    flanked by two red bands, 19th C (A) 275.00
Pot-de-Creme, 5 1/2" h, leaf and vine luster pat-
    tern, ram's head handles (A) 44.00
Puzzle Jug
  8 1/4" h, pearlware, black transfers of "The Tea
    Party," polychrome accents, open flower
    on front, pink luster trim, repairs (A) 797.00
  8 1/2" h, reticulated neck with band of five
    knobs above circ body decorated with puce

transfer floral and acorn sprays, hollowed int centering figure of swan on pedestal, early 19th C (A)........................ **495.00**

Sugar Caster, 5″ h, tan band in center, c1810. **95.00**

Tea Cup and Saucer, Adam Buck type print of mother and child, c1810................. **100.00**

Teapot
  6¾″ h, pink luster and applied yellow, red, and green enamel flowers, four small feet (A)................................... **110.00**
  8″ h, pink luster, red, pink, yellow and blue enameled floral, leaf and sprig design, 19th C (A) **121.00**

Tea Service, teapot, creamer, sugar, 2 biscuit plates, waste bowl, 10 cups and saucers, hp leaf and flower pattern, luster trim, c1840 .. **650.00**

Tea Service, Part, teapot, 5½″ h, (restored), creamer, waste bowl (damaged), 2 shallow bowls (damaged), 2 cups and saucers (damaged), luster ground with green leaves and small yellow flowers, 19th C (A) **253.00**

Vegetable Dish, 13½″ l, pink luster with green, blue, and red enamel vert lines with scattered florals, center diamond design, 19th C (A) .. **192.00**

Wine Cup, 4½″ h, pink-purple luster, resist feathering and graduated dots below against background of corkscrew filaments, rim, pedestal, and foot in iron-red, whole in pearlware glaze, c1810............................. **350.00**

SILVER

Coffee Service, pot, 7⅜″ h, cream pitcher, cov sugar bowl, 6 coffee cans and saucers, silver luster grapes and leaves with rust enamel accents, yellow ground (A)................. **357.00**

Coffee Set, pot, 6¾″ h, creamer, sugar bowl, grapes and vines pattern, open heart geometrics at top, MINTON″ marks **150.00**

Creamer
  3″ h, pink leaves outlined in silver, silver bands, white ground, "Lancaster & Bandland Ltd, Handley England" mark **30.00**
  4″ h, 5″ w, ribbed loop base, incised band near top, shaped handle, unmarked **85.00**

Cup and Saucer
  Floral design in polychrome enamels with silver luster trim (A) **72.00**
  Small red and yellow flowers, cream ground, silver luster borders, "Coalport" mark (A). **33.00**

Cup and Saucer, Handless, overall floral band on cup, scattered florals on saucer (A)........ **28.00**

Figure
  11⅞″ l, standing lion with paw on globe, rect base, repaired, early 19th C **900.00**
  12½″ h, bust of Queen Caroline with hair tied back, waisted plinth, c1820 (A)...... **708.00**

Goblet, 4⅜″ h, silver luster grapes and vines on white ground, lustered foot................ **210.00**

Jug
  4½″ h
    Bright enameled bird on branch in circ panel reserved on silver luster floral ground, trellis border (A).............. **450.00**
    Overall geometrics, lines, and dot chains (A) **66.00**
    Silver resist transfer of village scene with sheep (A) **97.00**
  4⅜″ h, bird on branch with scattered foliage on body, rim with dot chain (A) **192.00**

4¾″ h, silver resist floral pattern (A)....... **110.00**

5″ h, overall floral pattern, c1810.......... **225.00**

5¼″ h, white enameled foliage, luster ground, c1815 (A) **175.00**

5½″ h
  Blue printed hunting scene, border of flowers and leaves, luster ground, c1815, Staffordshire (A)..................... **965.00**
  Gray exotic birds and foliage, luster body, c1815 (A)............................ **375.00**
  "Maltster's" poem in silver luster transfer (A) **110.00**

5¾″ h, transfer of Cribb-Molinaux fight, silver resist borders, cream ground, Liverpool (A)................................ **440.00**

6¼″ h, blue and white hunt scene of two men firing flintlocks with three spaniels, neck with hounds chasing fox, luster ground, c1815, Staffordshire (A)........ **1395.00**

6½″ h, puce printed scene of figures and mansion on each side, lustered scrolling foliate ground **350.00**

7⅛″ h, printed sepia medallions of birds perched on branches or bird chased by dog, center medallion of two figures and English cottage, blue highlights, luster body, c1815, Staffordshire (A)...................... **1072.00**

Mug
  2⅝″ h, soft paste body, foliage luster overlay (A)................................... **125.00**
  3″ h, purple oval transfer of sheep in front of lodge, silver luster flowers on body, band of luster leaves at rim, white ground **210.00**
  3½″ h, black printed profile of John Jones of Yestrad in silver luster oval, luster rim and base band (A) **342.00**

Pitcher
  3½″ h, luster grapes and leaves on cream body, "Lawley, England" mark........... **35.00**
  4″ h
    Stylized luster flowers on white ground, "Wedgwood, Etruria, and Barleston" mark................................ **55.00**
    Two birds on branch on front in rust, purple, green, and yellow, c1820 .... **630.00**
  4¾″ h
    Center band of flowers and leaves off branches, rim band of small leaves (A) . **159.00**
    Overall leaf pattern, c1820.............. **525.00**
  5⅛″ h, floral design with blue enameling, crow's foot (A)........................ **242.00**
  5½″ h, squat body with wide lip, overall silver luster, 19th C (A)...................... **71.00**
  5¾″ h
    Bulbous body on circ foot, silver luster reserved in blue and white of hunter with two dogs, foot in white with silver luster band (A) **770.00**
    Pink side, birds and flowers white etched, c1820 .... **595.00**
  6″ h, tan emb design of lions, dog, and man, silver lustered figural lion handle and drape rim, "Arthur Wood" mark............... **90.00**
  6½″ h, small open daisies with leaf branches on body, rim with vert lines (A) **214.00**

Plate, 6½″ d, lustered geometric designs, lustered edge, unmarked **20.00**

Spill Vase, 4⅛″ h, gray marbleized applied vines and fruits accented in silver luster, white int, pr (A)............................. **40.00**

Teapot
 5½" h, 10" l, pear shape, molded fluted pattern, paw feet, bud knob, c1805 . . . . **175.00**
 6⅜" h, porcelain, paneled polychrome
 enameled floral decorations with silver lus-
 ter trim, hairline (A) **165.00**
 9" h, 9" w, red clay body, pear shape, fluted
 body, paw feet, tortoise-like knob **350.00**
 9¾" h, vert ribbing, domed cov (A) **126.00**
 Urn, Cov, 5½" h, overall silver, leaf design, two
 handles, Wedgwood mark. **59.00**

SUNDERLAND

Bowl, 8¼" d, polychrome highlighted black
 transfers of ship and verse panels, pink marble
 luster, hairline, mid 18th C, (A) **125.00**
Creamer, 5" h, "The Sailor's Tear" outlined in
 florals, reverse with sailing ship and "May
 Peace and Plenty..," luster trim **250.00**
Jug
 5⅛" h, black printed and colored portrait of
 "Jack Crawford the Hero of Camperdown,
 Oct. 11th, 1797" (A) **160.00**
 5½" h, ovoid body, Masonic transfer pirnted
 in black with Lord Byron in Masonic regalia,
 sides with rhyme or Masonic emblems between blue glazed and pink luster borders,
 c1820A) **411.00**
 6⅝" h, black printed and colored scenes and
 insignia of alliance of England and France,
 marbled pink luster border (A) **685.00**
 7½" h, black printed bust of Earl Grey and
 inscription "The Choice of the People and
 England's Glory," flanked by verse, view of
 Iron Bridge at Sunderland (A) **1045.00**
 7¾" h, polychrome decorated transfer of
 ship scenes and view of Sunderland Bridge
 and verse, orange luster, c1860, (A) **137.00**
 8" h, pink luster "Cloud" pattern, Dickens
 characters, black transfers **175.00**
 9¼" h, transfers of sailing ship and an ode to
 an English Bark, names and dates of family,
 bubble luster border, cream ground (A) . . **715.00**
 9½" h, pearlware, printed and colored with
 "Hope" and "The Mason's Arms," painted
 "Richard & Hannah Clark 1828" in bands of
 pink luster and painted foliates, Dixon, Aus-
 ton & Co. **1185.00**
Master Salt, "Cloud" pattern, ftd **45.00**
Mug
 2½" h, overall bubble luster (A) **88.00**
 3½" h
  Historical scripture alphabet, black transfer,
  pink luster trim, mid 19th C **175.00**
  Pink transfer of park setting, starbursts on
  sides, bubble luster rim, white ground . . **185.00**
 4¾" h, "Sailor's Farewell," reverse with
  sailor's poem, transfers with red, green, and
  yellow accents, pink luster trim, int with
  black figural frog (A) **138.00**
 5" h
  Black transfer of compass on front, "The
  Sailor's Farewell" on reverse **145.00**
  Hand colored transfer in green, rust, and
  magenta of "A West View of the Iron
  Bridge Over the Wear," early 19th C,
  marked "Dixon" **525.00**
Mustard Pot, 4" h, sheet design, loop handle
 (A). **150.00**

Pitcher
 4¾" h
  Paneled black transfers of "Sailors' Farewell" and female with agricultural sym-
  bols, pink luster, c1850 (A). **125.00**
  Portrait of Victoria Regina on one side, "The
  Mariner's Compass" on reverse, pink luster trim, wide copper luster banding (A) **206.00**
 5½" h, overall bubble luster (A) **65.00**
 7⅛" h, hex panels, black transfers of John
  Wesley on one side, verse on other, pink
  marble luster, c1850 (A) **125.00**
Plaque
 8¹⁄₁₆" d, black printed bust of Adam Clark,
  luster border (A) **100.00**
 8¼" l, 7¼" h, center portrait of William
  Gladstone, luster border **80.00**
 8½" l
  7½" w, "Thou God Seeist Me," luster trim,
  "Dixon" mark **150.00**
  7¾" w, molded sea shell rim, black trans-
  fer of "Job 8.20," pierced for hanging. . **225.00**
 8¾" l, 7¾" h, rect, black transfer of
  "THOU GOD SEEST ME," pink marble
  luster border. **325.00**
 10" h, seascapes and verse in black trans-
  fers, Sunderland luster rim and base, 19th
  C (A) **225.00**
Plate
 9" d, "Dicken's Days" pattern, "Gray's Pot-
  tery" mark. **35.00**
 9¼" d, "House" pattern, c1850 . . . . **80.00**
 10" d, center transfer printed with portrait of
  Pike and "Be Always Ready to Die for your
  Country," pink luster and yellow banded
  border, c1820 (A) **2640.00**
Punch Bowl, 11½" d, polychrome highlighted
 black transfers of Masonic and nautical
 themes, pink zig-zag luster, repairs, mid 19th C
 (A). **125.00**

Petrus Regout & C°
MAASTRICHT

MAASTRICHT

Maastricht, Holland
1836 to Present

History: Petrus Regout founded a glass and crystal works
in 1834 in Maastricht, Holland. In 1836 he expanded his
operation to include the De Sphinx Pottery that had a
work force recruited from England. It was Regout's desire
to introduce the manufacture of ironstone, a ware that had
greatly reduced the market for Delftware.
 From 1836 to 1870 Petrus Regout manufactured dinnerware in the style of English ironstone decorated with
transfer printed patterns with scenic or romantic themes.
Pattern names were back stamped in English for wares
exported to English and American markets. Patterns in-

cluded: "Amazone," 'Mythology," "Pleasure Party," "Plough," "Ruth & Boaz," 'Wild Rose," and "Willow." Until about 1870 Regout's dceorations had been printed only in one color, either blue, black, violet, or red. If a second color was desired the piece was first decorated with a printed black transfer and the second color then hand applied. In 1870 lithographic decalcomania made possible multicolor printing on china. Brightly colored dinnerware became the rage until the end of the century.

When Regout died in 1878, his sons reorganized the company. They adopted the Sphinx trademark. During the 20th century, tastes became more conservative. Today the firm is called "N.V. Konmklijke Sphinx." Since 1974, it has been part of the British conglomerate Reed International.

Pieces usually have a printed back stamp. Most dinnerware was marked with a pattern name. The company also made blanks for others to decorate. The phrase "Royal Sphinx" was authorized in 1959 and used on decorative tiles.

Other potteries in Maastricht during the 1840s and 1850s included N. A. Bosch, W. N. Clermont and Ch. Chainaye, and G. Lambert & Cie who merged with Sphinx in 1958.

References: John P. Reid, "The Sphinx of Maastricht," *The Antique Trader Weekly,* December 20, 1984.

Collecting Hints: Early Regout pottery always had a heavily crazed glaze. After the 1870s, the glaze was free of crazing. The tan luster did not wear well. The quality of the printing varied with the different transfers.

Bowl
  3¼" h, "The Abbey" pattern, "Petrus Regout
    & Co. Maastricht" mark................ 30.00
  5¾" d, red, green, and blue agate pattern,
    "Petrous Regout, Maastricht and lion"
    mark............................... 28.00
  6" d
    "Sana" pattern, black oriental transfer, or-
      ange wash, "Petrous Regout Maastricht,
      SANA" mark 15.00
    "Timor" pattern, "Petrus Regout Sphinx"
      mark.............................. 35.00
  7¾" d, "Panama" pattern, "Petrus Regout &
    Co." mark......................... 55.00
  8¼" d, ftd, windmill with people fishing,
    brown transfer...................... 15.00
Pitcher, 5" h, rooster with iris and leaves, red
  transfer, "Regout & Co. Haan" mark 65.00

Plate, 8¼" d, "Sana" pattern, black and white with salmon border, "Petrous Regout Maastricht" mark, $18.00

Plate
  6" d
    Large red and green flowers with small red
      stick spatter flowers, dark blue and white
      stick spatter border.................. 52.00
    "Timor" pattern in colors, "Petrous Regout,
      Maastricht" mark.................... 55.00
  6½" d
    Design spatter
      Center with red and green flower, wide
        blue and white geometric border,
        "Maastricht, Holland" mark 48.00
      Dark blue and gold flowers, small blue
        flowers on border, "Maastricht, Hol-
        land" mark....................... 62.00
      Flow blue geometric design 60.00
  7" d, "Fruit" pattern, blue transfer, emb
    woven border, "Petrus Regout & Co. Maas-
    tricht" mark 24.00
  8" d, "Elvire" pattern, "Petrus Regout" mark 25.00
  8½" d, blue and white
    Floral design, "P. Regout & Co. Maastricht"
      mark............................. 20.00
    Peacock design 8.00
  8¾" d
    "Ceylon" pattern, blue, "Petrous Regout"
      mark............................. 37.50
    'The Abbey" pattern, "Petrus Regout & Co.
      Maastricht" mark.................... 45.00
  9" d, blue and white Oriental design....... 18.00
  9¼" d
    "Abbey" pattern, purple transfer with poly-
      chromes (A)........................ 12.00
    "Hong" pattern 30.00

1874-1924   1890 - 1939

MAJOLICA

English and Continental
1850 to Present

History: During a visit to Rouen in 1849, Herbert Minton saw flower pots with a green glaze. When he returned to England, Minton instructed Leon Arnoux, his firm's art director, to copy these wares. Arnoux introduced English Majolica, an opaque tin-glazed earthenware, in 1850. The name Majolica originally came from the Spanish island of Majorca. Its popularity in England remained strong through the second half of the 19th century.

Minton's early majolica wares closely imitated Palissy ware, a pottery made by Bernard Palissy at Saintes, France between 1542 and 1562 and later in a workshop on the grounds of the Palais des Tuileries in Paris.

Palissy ware was characterized by relief figures and ornaments that were covered with colored glazes, mainly yellow, blue, and gray highlighted with brown and manganese. Palissy is known for naturalistic designs of leaves, lizards, snakes, insects, shells, and other natural objects in high relief on plates and dishes. He also made vases, ewers, and basins. The reverse of his wares was covered with a mottled glaze in brown, blue, and manganese. Palissy developed the applique technique which consisted of making plaster casts resembling the natural objects separate from the main body and applying these later.

Early Minton majolica wares were modeled by the French sculptors Emile Jeannest, Albert Carrier-Belluse, and Hugues Protat. Protat made the models from which the wares were cast. Leading artists from the Victorian period who decorated the wares included Thomas Allen, Thomas Kirkby, and Edouard Rischgitz.

Early majolica wares by Minton also attempted to emulate Italian Majolica, basic earthenware, that was coated with an opaque white glaze or covering slip. English majolica meant earthenwares that were decorated with deep semi-transparent lead glazes. Typical Victorian majolica examples included large garden ornaments such as seats and jardinaires plus many types of plates and dishes for utilitarian and decorative use.

Daniel Sutherland and Sons of Longton established a pottery in 1863 to manufacture the majolica wares. A tremendous variety of articles were made. Other manufacturers include: Brown/Westhead, W. Brownfield and Company of Cobridge, Holdcraft, George Jones and Sons, Moore and Company, and Wedgwood. George Jones, who was employed by Minton until he established his own Trent Pottery in Stoke in 1861, made lidded vases, ornamental bowls, candelabras, and wall plaques, along with more ordinary everyday majolica wares.

Wedgwood's majolica took the form of molded leaves and vegetables that were decorated with a translucent green glaze. Other Wedgwood majolica wares were covered with colored glazes on a white body that was molded with high quality relief ornamentation. Vases, umbrella stands, wall brackets, candlesticks, compotes, plates, and a variety of dishes were made.

Majolica wares were made on the Continent by Sarreguimes in France, by Villeroy and Boch and Zell in Germany, and by companies in Austria, Bavaria, and Italy. Nineteenth century majolica is different from the earlier Italian majolica wares.

References: Victoria Bergesen, *Majolica: British, Continental and American Wares, 1851–1915,* Barrie & Jenkins, 1989; Nicholas M. Dawes, *Majolica,* Crown Publishers, Inc. NY, 1990; Marilyn G. Karmason with Joan B. Stacke, *Majolica: A Complete History and Illustrated Survey,* Harry B. Abrams, 1989; Alan-Caiger Smith, *Tin-Glaze Pottery in Europe & the Islamic World,* Faber & Faber, 1973.

Collectors' Club: Majolica International Society, 1275 First Ave., Suite 103, New York, NY 10021, Dues: $35.00, quarterly newsletter.

Museums: British Museum, London, England; Cooper Hewitt Museum, NY; Henry Ford Museum, Dearborn, Michigan; Cleveland Museum of Art, Cleveland, Ohio; City Museum and Art Gallery, Stoke-on-Trent, England; Minton Museum, Stoke-on-Trent, England; J Paul Getty Museum, Malibu, California; Strong Museum, Rochester, NY; Victoria & Albert Museum, London, England; Wadsworth Atheneum, Hartford, CT; Wedgwood Museum, Barlaston, England; Wallace Collection, London, England.

ENGLISH

Biscuit Jar, 6 1/4 " h, gray, green, and tan mottled ext, turquoise int, SP center band, top, rim, and handle, Wedgwood...................... **135.00**
Bowl
  9 1/2 " l, shell shape, green agate body, three olive green shell feet, c1870, imp "Holdcroft" mark.......................... **360.00**
  10" l, 5 1/2 " h, boat shaped, molded pink lilies, green leaves, tan and brown ground, blue int...................... **225.00**
  11 3/16 " h, modeled as two putti, "Winter" wearing wreath and swag of yellow-berried green ivy, "Summer" with wreath and swag of yellow and green wheat, holding brown rope handles of brown wooded bucket with turquoise int, green grasses on green mottled mound base, oval foot glazed in cobalt blue, 1862, imp "MINTON," date cipher, and "A,B and O" marks (A)............. **1925.00**
Bread Tray
  12 1/2 " l, 10" w, oval, basketweave in blue and yellow, brown and green border, c1876, Wedgwood (A) **475.00**
  13" l, cobalt center, yellow wheat heads on green and brown rim, "Eat thy bread with joy and thankfulness' (A)................ **150.00**
Butter Dish, Cov, Underplate, 10 1/2 " H-H, 5 1/2 " h, central cartouches on either side of dish with musical instruments in relief, underplate with ribbon draped handles and portrait medallions to border, goat finial on cov with imp leaf decoration, 1867, "Minton," imp mark and date code (A)................... **7700.00**
Butter Pat
  3" d, oriental design, raised turquoise center, rose flowers, blue woven design, mustard rim, Wedgwood....................... **110.00**
  Shell and seaweed pattern, gray shell, white ground, Wedgwood (A)................ **70.00**
Candlestick
  3" h, green frog, turquoise water lily holder, pink leaves on side, brown base **450.00**
  9 1/2 " h, polychrome dolphin with leaf molded sconce on upright tail, rect base with band of shells, restored, dtd 1875, pr (A) **935.00**
  10 1/4 " h, each formed as two dolphins with entwined tails fitted at top with metal nozzle, glazed in tones of blue, green, brown, and ochre, brown shaped oval base with ochre fluted border, 1868, imp "Wedgwood, L, UVW, and 5" marks, pr (A)..... **2475.00**
  16" h, multiple knobbed, molded with rams' masks, strapwork, swags, and floral decoration, vase shaped nozzles on circ drip pan, standing on pedestal base molded with strapwork and fruiting swags between scrolled mask feet, bases pierced and colored in blue, brown, ochre, green, and white, 1863 and 1865, "MINTON," imp mark, date codes, #765, pr (A) **1599.00**
Centerpiece, Oval Bowl
  8 1/4 " h, pink int, shaded yellow rim, blue ext molded with acorns and leaves, supported on trunk ending in oval base with modeled game bird and dog, c1870, "George Jones" mark (A) **2500.00**
  11 1/2 " h, molded with basketweave and supported by laurel garlands held by two maidens kneeling either side of two smaller bowls also strung with garlands, shaped rect base, bright majolica glazes, c1865, imp "Copeland" mark (A)................... **1346.00**
Cheese Dish, Cov
  7 3/16 " h, 10 1/4 " d, molded as turquoise glazed cask encircled by ochre rings en-

twined with green vine with pink-edged white blossoms, int glazed in puce, underside in green and brown tortoise shell glaze, c1875, imp "GJ & SONS crescent mark, 2230, //" in black enamel (A) **1210.00**

8⅝" h, drum shape, bands of oak leaves and acorns in gray, brown, and ochre against cream ground, imp "Wedgwood," date code for 1872 (A) **576.00**

9½" l, domed cov molded with wheat and daisies growing beside wooden fence, branch handle applied with flowering rasberry bush branches, bright colors on blue ground, 2 cracks, c1870, imp "George Jones, 5204" marks (A) **1683.00**

11" h

Brown simulated wood paneled cov with yellow center band and green florets, twisted twig handle, restored, c1875, George Jones (A) **825.00**

Relief of lily of the valley and ferns in yellow and red, yellow rope twists on body and rim, blue stippled ground, dbl rope twist handle, restored, Samuel Lear (A) **1210.00**

Chestnut Dish, 11" l, green and turquoise domed top with brown open chestnut, turquoise int, brown border with green leaves, yellow rim, c1876, "Minton & Co." mark . . .   **1500.00**

Compote, Ftd

3½" h, 8¼" d, turquoise center, cane ext, green feet, "George Jones" mark **495.00**

7¾" h, turquoise dish with green leaves and yellow flowers, brown tree trunk stem, modeled hound chasing rabbit or pheasant in brown, modeled green leaves, restored, c1852, George Jones, pr (A) **5060.00**

Cup and Saucer

Cauliflower shape, blue ground, imp "WEDGWOOD" mark **110.00**

Yellow and green cauliflower, Wedgwood (A) **75.00**

Dessert Set

4 ftd dishes, 9¼" d, 12 plates, 9" d, molded on surface with green horse chestnut leaf, white diamond ground with rose edging, ochre rims, ochre, brown, and blue mottled reverse and feet, c1870, "turquoise molded CJ and STOKE ON TRENT" marks (A) **1100.00**

8 plates, 1 platter, "Argenta" ware, Bonnet(Kate Greenway), straw color ground, Wedgwood (A) **620.00**

12 plates 8¾" d, 2 plates 9¼" d, snail-form feet, compote on dolphin-form stand, 6½" h, 9½" d, variaged green and brown, imp "WEDGWOOD" mark, chips, 15 pcs (A) .   **1300.00**

Dish

3¼" d, yellow butterfly, olive drab trim **90.00**

11" l, oval, green molded leaves, white blossoms with yellow centers, black, yellow, and blue molded butterflies, blue-black stippled ground, c1878, George Jones (A) **1155.00**

Dish, Cov, 7¼" d, molded overlapping lettice leaves, green glaze, Holdcroft (A) **175.00**

Ewer

11⅞" h, ovoid body, one with youth watching two cavaliers playing cards on drum beneath arbor on terrace above river, other with four cavaliers around table raising beakers to cavalry parade, below maroon edged purple gadrooned border, inter-

rupted with three molded cherub's heads, turquoise int, brown and purple handle, circ foot in purple and maroon, 1864, imp "MINTON," cipher for 1864, "A, 1106, 8, //" marks, pr (A) **990.00**

17½" h, ovoid body, swan with open mouth forming spout and handle, dark blue body with green and brown bullrushes connecting to swan, brown and green rockwork base, c1880, "George Jones" mark, pr (A)   **5240.00**

21¾" h, modeled standing heron against reeds and lily pads, fish in beak, multicolored, dtd 1876, imp "H. Protat, MINTON, #1241" marks **2341.00**

Figure

5½" h, putto standing on green and brown mound base holding a basket, imp "Wedgwood," date code for 1862 (A) **270.00**

6" h, naked figure with blue sash, holding basketweave basket, brown, white, and green int, mottled green and brown base, imp "WEDGWOOD" mark **395.00**

6⅛" h, seated white glazed dog with large black spots, leaf molded rect base, c1910, imp "MINTON" mark (A) **605.00**

8½" h, classical putti holding blue shell, white-gray body, brown and green base, turquoise design on rim, c1865, George Jones (A) **1400.00**

10⅞" h, "Vintager," putto swathed in vine, standing on oval base, quiver at feet, holding rope which encircles wicker molded basket applied with fruiting vine, imp "MINTONS, 406, date code for 1865" marks (A) **900.00**

11¼" h, seated dog with collar, tan fur, dark brown face, turquoise cushion with yellow border, c1880, imp shape no. (A) **1129.00**

13¼" h, seated cat, gray body with black stripes, yellow face, glass eyes, red base with yellow sides, dtd 1873, imp "MINTON" mark (A) **5775.00**

15½" h, "Vintager with Baskets," young man in dark purple jerkin over white shirt, green leggings, yellow wicker basket with green glazed int, green and manganese mottled circ base, imp "MINTON, month and date ciphers for April 1864, 375" and potter's marks (A) **2640.00**

24" h, bust of English noble woman in plumed hat and necklace, circ plinth, sq base, multicolored **4500.00**

31" h, seated classical maiden, blue dress, holding scroll, lyre by side, waisted green and brown base molded with flower garlands, c1880 (A) **1252.00**

33½" h, red deer fawn, standing beside hollow tree truck applied with fern leaves, shades of brown and green, turquoise int, one ear missing, c1876, sgd "P. Comolera," imp "MINTONS," shape no. 2077, date code (A) **14,784.00**

Game Dish and Insert, 8½" l, 5½" h, various game animals in mottled green and brown, green leaves, brown ground, rabbit finial, "Wedgwood" mark **1400.00**

Game Pie Tureen, Cov

10¾" H-H, molded dark brown basketweave body, light brown rims, cov with dead deer and other game in dark brown,

green leaves, lavender ground, "George
Jones" mark 1850.00
13³/₈" l, molded basket body with oak leaves,
oak branch handles, hare, duck, and pigeon
lying on cov, green, brown, ochre, and blue
tones, dtd 1871, Minton (A)............. 841.00
14¹/₂" l, basketwork body, glazed in tones of
green, brown, ochre, and blue, molded with
oak branch handles, trailed with foliage, cov
with hare, duck, and pigeon lying with oak
leaves and ferns, c1859, Minton, imp factory marks and date code (A) 1584.00
15" l, oval, sides molded with rabbits amongst
grasses and ferns against blue ground, applied with bound oak branch handles, cov
with quail and two chicks, lilac int, cov restored, c1875, applied reg. mark, imp mark
and "3371 J, George Jones" marks (A) ... 5236.00
Garden Seat
18" h
Cylindrical form, decorated in relief with
stylized flowers and leaf motifs between
formal borders, top with medallion of
leaves and flowers, greens, blues,
browns, ochres, one crack at base,
c1876, Minton, imp marks and date
code, #892, pr (A) 3762.00
Waisted body, Calla Lily, molded in high relief with white flowers and green foliage,
reserved on basketweave light blue
ground, waisted neck with yellow rope
band, top of seat and foot rim glazed in
brown, c1875, imp "George Jones"
mark, script 5329 (A)................ 6758.00
18¹/₄" h, monkey crouching on rush mat,
holding fruits, head supporting buttoned
and tasseled cushion, brown, gold, green,
and blue, repair, c1873, imp "MINTONS,"
one with date code, one imp shape no. 589,
pr (A)............................ 16,896.00
20" h, tree stump in tan and brown, mid 19th
C.................................. 2100.00
Jar, Cov, 6" h, blue leaves and berries, two olive
drab handles, turq int, berry finial, off white
raised ground 325.00
Jardiniere
12¹/₂" h, flared body, molded with turquoise
herons amongst turquoise foliage and
breaking waves, band of stylized clouds
above, dark blue ground, hair crack to base,
imp marks, date code, 1187, Mintons (A). 630.00
17¹/₂" l, yellow, pink, and white straps,
shaded green agate glaze, six paw feet
linked by vert tooled straps to fixed lion
mask handles at shoulder, short neck rising
to everted gadrooned rim, c1871, imp
marks, date codes, shape nos. 1023, Minton, pr (A)......................... 1496.00
20" h, turquoise ground bowl with green leaf
swags and nuts, lion masks at ends, turquoise ground pedestal with three kneeling
male figures with brown drape and cornucopia, restored, c1874, imp "MINTON"
mark, pr (A) 1650.00
Jardiniere and Stand
16¹/₂" d, spirally fluted body applied with two
rams' head handles in brown glaze, multicolored draped swag of fruit and flowers,
turquoise body, c1860, Minton, imp date
code and star mark (A) 903.00

41" h, "Argenta," cylindrical base molded
with vases of flowers alternating with panels
of repeated motifs, jardiniere molded with
circ panels decorated with branches and
pink flowerheads, three feet, yellow, green,
and brown glazes, c1888, date code "OSR"
on stand, imp "Wedgwood, #K3447," jardiniere imp "WXQ" marks (A)........... 3010.00
Jug
12" h, fish head form with biting lamprey handle, shades of green, yellow, turquoise, and
red, resting on turquoise waves, "#497,"
Royal Worcester, imp mark (A) 468.00
12¹/₂" h, body modeled in relief with mermaid and merman holding hands of a
cherub standing on shell above paneled
border, foliate scroll handles with mask
below, tones of blue, green, ochre, and
brown, c1864, imp mark and date code,
Minton (A) 710.00
15" h, body in cask form, glazed in shades of
brown, green, gray, and ochre, branch handle trailing fruiting vine, four Bacchic putti at
shoulder, c1862, Minton, imp mark, 900,
and date code (A)..................... 800.00
Luncheon Tray, 15" l, three shells supported by
three dolphins, entwined tails forming handle,
three shell feet, mauve, green, and brown,
c1880, imp "George Jones," mark (A)...... 1496.00
Pedestal
28³/₄" h, modeled as dolphin with water issuing from mouth, balanced on rocky base
with shells and seaweed fronds, long tail
raising up as support, two cracks, circ top
missing, c1880, imp "T.C. Brown Westhead
Moore and Co.," #1257 (A)............ 1223.00
34" h, raised band of green and white leaves
and berries, rose ribbons holding classical
medallions in turquoise with yellow outlines
and white heads, cobalt ribbed base, turquoise and brown pedestal, c1880,
"WEDGWOOD" mark 7250.00
39" h, triangular form with molded rams head
at corners connected by festoons, decorated with figural reserves on hoof feet and
plinth base, damaged, pr (A) 5170.00
Pitcher
4¹/₂" h, fern and bamboo design, Wardle,
English reg mark 75.00
5" h
Bird and Fan pattern, blue and gray bird,
gray fan, turquoise int, pink trim, white
ground, Wedgwood (A)............... 325.00
Paneled shape, rose, yellow, and cream
shells, olive brown waves, turquoise int,
Wedgwood......................... 145.00
6¹/₂" h, figural standing frog, green back with
mauve spots, yellow belly and feet, mauve
twist handle, green lily pad base 150.00
7" h, Shell and Fishnet pattern, multicolored
shells, brown-black seaweed, raised net-like
ground, Fielding (A) 550.00
7¹/₂" h, Bird and Fan pattern, blue and pink
fans, prunus blossom branches, rough texture, lavender int, white ground, Wardle
(A)................................. 325.00
8" h, figural shell, ocean waves splashing at
base, turquoise handle and leaves, Fielding
(A)................................. 675.00
8¹/₂" h, "What Tho My Gates Be Poor . . . ,"

bands with green beads, panels in mustard, brown, and black, green int, 1869, imp "WEDGWOOD," imp Eng Reg mark..... **590.00**
9½" h
Multicolored blue slip, cut cut back to wide band of dicing, salmon ground, engine-turned borders, imp "Copeland" mark (A) **137.00**
Stork in Rushes design, cobalt, George Jones (A)........................ **1000.00**
Planter, 18" l, 5" h, rect, three raised white swans on front, dark blue water, light blue sky, pink water lilies, brown and tan bullrushes at sides, c1880s **2200.00**
Plaque, 12½" h, 7¾" w, young girl and man with beard, blue ground, imp "WEDG-WOOD" mark, pr (A) **400.00**
Plate
7⅞" d, green leaf with yellow-brown ground, ribbed border, imp "WEDGWOOD" mark **135.00**
8½" d, molded sunflower design, scalloped rim, green glaze, imp "WEDGWOOD" mark, set of 9 (A) **357.00**
8¾" d, central pink, turquoise, and yellow lilies, green leaves, scalloped edge, c1869, set of 8 (A)........................ **385.00**
8⅞" d, leaves in yellow, green, and brown with blue accents, "H.J. Wood England" mark................................ **25.00**
9" d
Fish lying among reeds and ferns, glazed in green, gray, and white, turquoise ground, imp "Wedgwood GNL' (A)........... **360.00**
Oyster plate, cobalt blue oysters, turquoise center, 1867, Minton (A) **450.00**
Strawberries, plums, and melon on turquoise basketweave ground, imp "WEDGWOOD" mark **95.00**
Three lily pads with pink flowers, Eng Reg mark............................. **50.00**
9¼" d, turquoise center, mustard bamboo border with green leaves, mottled brown and green back, "George Jones" mark ... **325.00**
10¼" d, seaweed and oyster design (A)... **150.00**
Platter
10½" l, 7½" w, green holly and basketweave, Wedgwood..................... **120.00**
11½" l, 9" w, Grape Leaf pattern, yellow and green florals, cobalt center, brown border, c1876, Wedgwood (A) **600.00**
13" l, 9" w, pink flowers, rolled inward sides and handles, George Jones **300.00**
20" l, 11¾" w, oval shape, drainer, cream center with alternating bands of geometric designs in green, rust, black, mustard, and white, c1861, sgd "George Jones"....... **650.00**
Punch Bowl, 12" d, lily pads, lotus flowers and ferns in green, brown, and turquoise, imp "Holdcroft" mark (A) **300.00**
Sardine Box
6¼" l, 5¾" h, cobalt box with off white swan finial, tan trim and dolphin feet..... **1045.00**
8½" l
Cov with three flying fish lying amongst seaweed fronds, green leaves against blue ground, c1875, imp "GJ" monogram (A) **638.00**
Dark brown basketweave ground with pink

and white florals, green shell finial and handles, Wedgwood **345.00**
8¾" l, cov surmounted with three fish lying amongst leaves, foliage on stand, tones of deep blue, green, ochre, gray, and lilac, 1875, imp mark, shape no, date code, molded "P.O.D.R." mark (A) **805.00**
Salt, Double, 4¾" l, 3" h, brown shells, pink int, green feet with crusted flowers **295.00**
Stick Stand, 21¾" h, ribbed cylindrical form, modeled with two fish swimming between colorful flowers and reeds in yellow, white, and tones of green, turquoise ground, foot and rim with woven design in gray between yellow borders, cracked, c1875, imp "George Jones" marks (A)...................... **1223.00**
Strawberry Server, 10½" l, 5" h, brown and pink bird, brown and green nest, ochre feet and edge, green leaves for server **1195.00**
Tazza, 9" d, mottled green, brown, and yellow center, scalloped and pierced turquoise border, three paw feet, c1874, Wedgwood (A). **302.00**
Teapot
5¼" h, seated Chinaman body, holding grotesque mask, pigtail forming handle, detachable head and cov, polychrome glazes, spout restored, c1874, imp "Minton" mark and date code (A)..................... **846.00**

Jardinaire, Continental, 9¼" h, 9" d, raised florals and stones, blue circles, gold trim, gold-brown ground, $240.00

7½" h, sad iron shaped body, white figural cat curved around yellow handle, gray figural mouse with carrot on cov, turquoise body with brown and green bands of gray mice, dtd 1881, imp "MINTON" mark (A)................................**14,300.00**
Tea Set, teapot, 6½" h, sugar bowl, 5¼" h, creamer 3" h, Wardle's "Bird and Fan" pattern, brown cane handles, pink int, cream ground................................ **495.00**
Umbrella Stand, 40" h, heron holding a fish in its beak, standing by clump of bullrushes, rocky base with reeds and water lilies, glazed in tones of gray, green, and brown, 1876, imp "Minton," date code, pattern no. 1917 marks (A).................................... **2244.00**
Urn, 6¼" h, three white doves, cobalt ground, geometric design on rim, repair, Minton (A).................................... **850.00**
Vase
6½" h, emb morning glories, stem handles, green, blue, pink, and lavender **75.00**
6¾" h, ftd, urn shape, mottled lions, brown,

yellow, and green base, three brown feet,
pink int, brown ext **375.00**
7½" h, modeled bamboo trunk with leaves,
two figural monkeys and beetle on base and
trunk, yellow-green and brown, 1872, imp
"MINTON" mark (A) **795.00**
12" h, molded as fish in natural colors, Eng
Reg mark. **250.00**
15" h, standing cherub holding upright cornu-
copia terminating in ram's head, green,
brown, and blue glazes, pink int, c1864,
Minton, pr (A) **2150.00**
21⅝" h, ftd, ovoid body, mottled green,
brown, blue, and ochre, two female handles
terminating in masks, c1859, Minton **600.00**
Vase, Cov, 24" h, bulbous body, long flared
neck, applied angel handles connected by fruit
and floral swags, neck and base molded with
stiff fern leaves, domed cov pierced with Janus
head finial, c1875, Staffordshire (A) **1122.00**

CONTINENTAL

Asparagus Pitcher, 8" h, molded in purple,
green, and beige with rose lines, turquoise int,
19th C, France, pr, unmarked. **1800.00**
Cake Plate
10½" H-H, cobalt center, raised blossoms,
leaves and vines in colors on border **45.00**
11" H-H, raised pink flowers, yellow basketweave ground, "Germany" mark **45.00**
Charger
21¾" d, Moses in bull rushes in center in
colors, Renaissance scrolled border, 19th C,
Italy (A) **220.00**
24½" d, Neptune in center, border with cher-
ubs and masks, multicolored, late 19th C . . **450.00**
Compote, 3½" h, 9" d, relief of white flowers,
pink berries, and green leaves on blue ground,
"Zell, Germany" mark **150.00**
Dish
6½" d, white open water lily in center green
leaves, olive green stippled ground. **130.00**
9½" d, gaudy white, pink, and yellow blos-
soms on rainbow leaves, mottled reverse
(A). **110.00**
Ewer, 32¾" h, two parts, molded in high relief
with continuous central panel with Neptune
leading sea horses with various sea nymphs,
dolphins, and sea horses surrounding, handle
modeled with dolphin attached, mid 19th C (A) **1045.00**
Figure
12¼" h, bird sitting on leafy perch in violet,
blue, green, and brown, France **195.00**
26½" h, blackamoors, lady and gentleman
holding oval baskets, male in yellow
trimmed white jacket, white hat, blue trousers, female in long white robe tied with red
sash, white beaded headdress, brown and
green washed bases, one basket damaged,
late 19th C, pr (A). **1200.00**
Flower Bowl, 12" l, 6" h, grassland scene,
molded flower and berry reserve in front of
five trees, boat shape, floral handles, red
ground, France. **250.00**
Humidor, 7" h, three pine cones in green, yel-
low, and brown **145.00**
Jardinaire
9" h, 12½" l, oblong, molded floral panels
on brushed olive drab ground, female head

handles, oval pedestal base, "W.S. & S."
mark (A) **192.00**

**Teapot, English, 7½" h, pink and brown birds
and trees, cobalt ground, tan bamboo handle,
spout and buddha knob, $750.00**

10½" h, bulbous shape, molded floral and leaf
design in colors, blue ground, hairlines **550.00**
Jardinaire, Stand, 60¾" h, large polychrome
flowers on scrolling stems, bright majolica
glazes, dark blue ground, handles formed as
lion's heads, flute waisted cylindrical form
stand molded with stylized lion's heads at center of column, molded foliate acanthus and
palm leaf borders, c1870, Minton style (A) . . **1496.00**
Jug, 7¾" h, relief of men and women in out-
door cooking scene with dogs and children,
high gloss enamels, "W.S.& S." mark, pr **225.00**
Match Holder, 6" h, figural dwarf on crate, holding open barrel, multicolored, Germany. **145.00**
Pedestal, 26" h, stylized molded leaf and florals
on cobalt ground, late 19th C, France (A) . . . **225.00**
Pitcher
6½" h, dark pink flowers on turquoise
ground, brown handle, unmarked. **75.00**
9" h, emb dark rose colored florals, aqua
leaves, green ground, gold handle, rose col-
ored int, France **75.00**
12" h
Faience beak pouring parrot, French (A). . **180.00**
Relief design of rabbits in colors, hound
handle, "W.S & S." mark (A) **375.00**
12½" h, figural parrot in natural colors **275.00**
14" h, hex, molded flower design on rose
ground, three recessed panels outlined in
blue with relief flowers and leaves, tan handle, baroque floral base, Germany **280.00**
Plaque
7" d, raised alligator and two babies on tex-
tured green grass ground **295.00**
13" d, birds in centers facing each other, bor-
ders of colored flowers and open work,
pierced for hanging, France, pr **610.00**
Plate
7" d, raised blackberries and cherries, basketweave ground, "Zell" mark **55.00**
7½" d, "Les Enfants" pattern, raised tur-
quoise center with two children, ochre and
turquoise woven border, gilt edge, imp
French mark **125.00**
8" d, dog chasing deer through brush, fleur-
de-lys border, brown and blue. **75.00**
10" d
Figural crab, sea life, and plants in colors,
unmarked **195.00**

Serpentine and lizzard, heavy relief of creatures in yellow, green, blue, and gray, Palissy (A) **275.00**

10 1/2" d, old man drinking beer in yellow and brown **75.00**

11" d, relief of blackberries and basketweave, mauve and yellow ground (A) **70.00**

11 1/4" d, lg red and green maple leaves in relief, light yellow ground, "Zell, Germany" mark (A) **23.00**

Platter, 11" l, dog and house design, brown, green, and white **135.00**

Serving Set, 11" d, plate, 8" d, cake plate, 6" d, plates, raised colored birds perching on limbs, colored leaves in relief, 8 pcs, Zell/Germany mark................................ **250.00**

Syrup Pitcher, 6 3/4" h, multicolored floral design on basketweave ground, pewter lid, mid 19th C (A)................................. **35.00**

Trivet, 12" sq, central iris on light blue ground, France (A) **275.00**

Urn

13 1/2" h, ftd, polychrome arabesques, mask handles, "W.S.& S." mark (A)........... **450.00**

23" h, caryatid handles connected by festoons above neoclassical figural frieze, Italian, pr (A) **3080.00**

Vase

6" h, acorn design in natural colors, France . **87.00**

9" h

Bowl shape with incised Chinese figures with lanterns, seated Chinese man support, molded serpent handles, restored, "W.S.& S." mark

Molded band of griffins and florals, brushed olive drab ground, shaped loop handles with bird's heads, "W.S.& S." mark **150.00**

12" h, figural woman with fan, standing next to tree trunk, pastel colors **275.00**

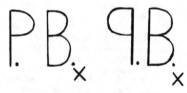

MALICORNE

West of Paris, France
Last Quarter 19th Century to 1952

History: Pouplard established his Malicorne factory in the Sarthe region west of Paris during the last quarter of the 19th century. He was making fine quality reproductions of the typical Quimper patterns, especially those of the Porquier-Beau factory.

To add to the confusion, Pouplard used the "P" from his own name and the "B" from his wife's name Beatrix to form a "PB" mark of his own. Though the design differed from the "PB" mark of Porquier-Beau because the letters were separated and followed by a small "x," Porquier-Beau still brought suit against Pouplard. When the suit was settled in 1897, Malicorne was ordered to cease production and forced to destroy all of his remaining pottery

molds. He continued to sign pieces with the PBx mark, only he no longer used the Breton designs. He ceased doing business in 1952.

References: Sandra V. Bondhus, *Quimper Pottery: A French Folk Art Faience,* privately published, 1981; Millicent S. Mali, *French Faience,* United Printing, 1986.

Museum: Sevres Museum, Sevres, France.

Bowl, 8" sq, two tone blue fleur-de-lys and black ermine tails, white ground, surface scratches, "PBx" mark............................. **150.00**

Creamer, 2 1/2" h, two tone fleur-de-lys and black ermine tails, white ground, blue border, "PBx" mark............................. **125.00**

Figure, 3 1/2" h, shoe, male peasant with bagpipe or female peasant knitting, pink, blue, yellow, and green, cream glaze, blue-dash opening, "PBx" mark, pr (A)94.00

Inkwell, 7 3/4" d, 4 1/2" h, triangle shape, view of peasant man or woman on each side, modeled angel faces at each corner, green decor riche top, "PBx" mark (A) **1320.00**

Mug, 4" h, overall floral, scale and foliage design in blue, green, ochre, and black, hairline on rim, "PBx" mark (A) **165.00**

Pitcher

4 1/2" h

Bagpipe player in charcoal brown pantaloons, blue gaiters and jacket, terra cotta and dark blue flowers, blue banded neck and base, "PBx" mark (A)........ **470.00**

Peasant man playing bagpipe on front, yellow, orange, blue, and green scattered flowers, blue and yellow bands on rim, neck, and base, crazing, "PBx" mark (A) **121.00**

7 1/4" h, peasant man leaning on stick, green, blue, orange, and yellow flowers and butterflies, cream ground, "PBx" mark (A)...... **231.00**

Plate

4 3/4" d, male peasant with whip, cream ground, border with single stroke chain of flowers in blue, green, and orange, "PBx" mark (A) **154.00**

8 1/2" d, male or female Normandy peasant holding umbrella, green, orange, and blue single stroke floral border, unmarked, pr (A)................................. **242.00**

9" d, green, blue, and manganese emb coat of arms in center, floral sprays below, stylized

Plate, 9 1/8" d, multicolored, "P.B.x." mark, $50.00

branching on border, cream glaze, un-
marked (A) **275.00**
9¼" d, center scene of man sitting on rocks
with cane, another standing with vegetable
basket gazing at sea, purple, yellow, green,
blue, and orange, green decor riche border,
shaped rim, "PBx" mark (A) **660.00**
9½" d, walking peasant man, wreath of
florals on border, shaped rim, cream
ground (A) **130.00**
10" d
 Center fleur-de-lys in two tone blue, blue
  shaped rim, "PBx" mark (A) **120.00**
 Multicolored crest of coat of arms in blue,
  green, yellow, and purple, white ground,
  yellow and purple sawtooth border,
  shaped rim, "PBx" mark (A) **225.00**
Relish Dish, 9" l, 5¾" w, peasant woman hold-
ing jug, stylized floral border, shaped rim (A) **130.00**
Snuff Bottle
 3" h, 2½" w, scalloped body, green, orange, and yellow florals, peasant woman
  on front **125.00**
 3¼" d, emb mask face on front in yellow,
  blue, and white, reverse with mask face in
  terra cotta, blue, and white, blue and white
  border banding, blue sponged edge, un-
  marked (A) **800.00**
Wall Pocket, 11" h, bagpipe shape, male and
female peasant standing by fence, half blue
and half yellow fleur-de-lys, brown and orange
bagpipe handles, molded pink bow, "PBx"
mark (A) **495.00**

Martin Bros.
London & Southall

MARTIN BROTHERS

Fulham, England
1873–1877

London and Southall, England
1877–1914

History: Robert, Walter, Edwin, and Charles Martin, the
first of the English "studio potters," were four brothers
who produced salt glaze stoneware called "Martinware."
The Martin tradition evolved around ornately engraved,
incised, or carved designs on salt glazed ware. Glazes
usually were mottled with colors including, gray, brown,
blue, and yellow in muted tones.

Robert initially worked for the Fulham Pottery of C. J. C.
Barley. He and his three brothers established their own
workshop in 1873 at Pomona House in Fulham. They fired
their wares in the kiln at Fulham Pottery. When that kiln
was no longer available, they leased a kiln at Shepherd's
Bush.

Robert, known as Wallace, was the sculptor and director of the Martin team. He received his training at the
Lambeth School of Art. He was an experienced stone
carver and modeler of figures. Wallace modeled grotesques, now eagerly sought by collectors, for over thirty

years. Grotesque birds were called "Walley birds" after
their maker.

Walter was in charge of throwing the large vases, mixing
the clays, and the firing process. Edwin decorated the
vases and other objects with naturalistic forms of decoration. Often he used incised or relief designs of fish, florals,
and birds. Charles handled the business aspects of the
concern.

In 1877 the brothers founded a pottery in Southall and
built their own kiln. They opened a shop in London the
next year. The Southall Pottery declined in 1910 with the
death of Charles Martin. When Walter died in 1912, production ceased.

All pieces of Martinware are signed with their name, the
place of production, and numerals and letters signifying
the month and year. The information was incised into the
soft clay before firing.

Between 1873 and 1883 the pottery was incised "R. W.
Martin" followed by "Fulham" if fired at the Fulham Pottery, "London" if fired at Shepherd's Bush, and "Southall"
if made at their own works. From 1879 when the shop was
operating, the words "and London" were added to
"Southall." From 1883 the full mark was "R. W. Martin &
Bros. London & Southall."

References: C. B. Beard, *Catalogue of the Martinware in
the Collection of F. J. Nettleford*, privately published, 1936;
Malcolm Haslam, *The Martin Brothers Potters*, Richard
Denis, n.d.; Hugh Wakefield, *Victorian Procelain*, Herbert
Jenkins, 1962.

Museum: Victoria & Albert Museum, London, England.

Charger, 15" d, incised stylized foliage accented
in brown and black shades, c1892, "R.W. Mar-
tin & Bros. London and Southall" mark **950.00**
Figure
 8" h, bird, removable head, broad beak, long
  wings tucked under body, large gnarled
  broad feet, partly glazed and matte in tones
  of brown and green, base in blue and gray,
  circ wood base, c1898, cov incised "Martin
  Bros, London & Southall 1–1898' (A) **6336.00**
 9½" h, bird, removable head, slender beak,
  long wings turned behind body, claw feet,
  brown, beige, green, and blue washes, circ
  wood base, c1902, incised "Martin Bros,
  London & Southall" mark (A) **16,850.00**
 9⅞" h, stoneware beast, detachable human-
  oid featured head, one eye half closed,

**Vase, 7¼" h, brown basketweave ground, dtd
1907, "Martin Bros. London and Southhall"
mark, $975.00**

small black pointed beard, sharp scales on top of head, black spotted, straw colored body squatting on ground with froglike feet and bowed front legs, c1884, base and head inscribed "Martin Brothers/London/Southall, 11–1884," marks (A) **25,300.00**

11¼" h, love-bird group, male bird with wing around mate, colored in blue, tan, green, and gray slips, fixed black painted oval wooden base, c1907, base and head inscribed "R.W. Martin & Bros. London & Southall 14–5–1907" mark (A) **17,600.00**

13½" h, wallybird cov vessel, large beaked, full bellied bird, in shades of mottled blue-green and gray, mounted on black painted circ base, restored, c1890, sgd in underglaze pigment, "1–8?/Martin Bros./London & Southall" mark (A) **6050.00**

15" h, bird, removable head, large broad beak forced open by small frog, upright position, wings folded behind back, feathers in tones of blue, brown, gray, and green, web clawed feet spread around circ black wood base, c1885, base and cov incised "R. Wallace Martin S. London & Southall-4.1885," marks (A) **21,631.00**

Flask

6¾" h, sq section, incised with blue flowerheads and green foliage on gray ground, brown spout with vert lines, ring handle, c1892, incised "R.W. Martin Bros London & Southall, 2–1892" mark (A) **887.00**

10⅜" h, sq section, incised with white spring flowers with long brown stems, green foliage, oatmeal ground, loop handle, ins "WHISKY," c1889, incised "Martin Bros London & Southall 9–1889" mark (A) **844.00**

Jug

8⅝" h, incised sparrows on scrolling foliage, accented in shades of green, brown, and blue on light brown ground, loop handle, c1890, incised "R.W. Martin & Bros, London and Southall" mark (A) **1600.00**

8¾" h, tapering cylindrical body, incised with white scrolling foliage, outlined in black, brown ground, loop handle, cracked, c1894, incised "Martin Bros London & Southall, 4–1894" mark (A) **425.00**

9" h, rect, angular handle, incised bird standing in grasses, brown, beige, green, and blue shades, white ground, c1901, incised "Martin Bros, London & Southall" mark (A).... **3950.00**

9¼" h, globular body, dbl sided, mask, grinning face in relief beneath short loop handle, graduated brown glaze with white specks, narrow eyes in white and black, c1897, incised "R.W. Martin & Bros. London & Southall 4–1897" mark (A) **2277.00**

9⅞" h, ovoid body, incised with caricatured monkeys among palm trees in brown and black, cream-oatmeal ground, loop handle, wide lip, c1893, incised "Martin Bros London & Southall, 12–1–93 and 984" mark (A) **4435.00**

10" h, ovoid body, incised on either side with classical maiden playing harp and male companion playing pipe in buff over brown ground framed by pale blue foliate borders between deep blue rims, cylindrical neck incised with band of brown leaves over blue

ground, loop handle, c1876, incised "R.W. Martin London 10–1876" mark (A) **227.00**

Spoon Warmer, 5⅝" h, modeled as a grotesque four legged animal with large ears, bulging eyes, wide open mouth, glazed in brown and tan with blue and white slips. c1888, inscribed "R.W. Martin &/Brothers/London/& SOuthall 6–88," circ mark on side (A)..................................... **9900.00**

Teapot, 7⅛" h, incised flowerheads and foliage accented in brown, blue, and green on mottled brown ground, loop handle, knob finial, c1887, "R. W. MARTIN SOUTHALL" mark (A) **750.00**

Vase

4" h, baluster form, incised flowers and foliage in brown tones, c1881 (A) **100.00**

4¾" h, incised with three birds in bullrushes, accented in shades of brown, orange ground, c1903, incised "Martin Bros' London and Southall" mark (A) **1500.00**

7" h, incised butterflies, bird, and foliage accented in blue, brown, and green on shaded light brown ground, vert striping on neck, c1890, incised "Martin Brothers London & Southall" mark (A)...................... **935.00**

7½" h, ovoid body, modeled on each side with smiling face and pixie ears applied to each side, mottled brown glaze, eyes and details in white, everted rim with two pourers, c1898, incised "R.W. Martin Bors, London & Southall, 10–1898" mark (A) **2960.00**

8¼" h, ovoid body, white orchids and smaller flowers on slender stems with gray foliage, white speckled and mottled brown ground, brown rims with incised vert lines, c1890 incised "Martin Brothers London and Southall, 5–1890" mark (A) **600.00**

8½" h, ovoid body, incised blue, brown, and yellow poppies and chrysanthemums on long stems, green foliage, dragonfly above, oatmeal ground, flared neck incised with vert lines, c1889, incised "R.W. Martin & Bros London & Southall" mark (A) **2006.00**

9" h, ovoid body, incised stylized leaves and foliage on continuous stem, cream and green glazes on mottled brown ground, c1898, incised "Martin Bros London & Southall 5–1898" mark, pr (A).......... **1632.00**

9¾" h, slender elongated faceted form, vert ribs in light and dark green glazes, panels of blue, horizontal lines, c1914, incised "Martin Bros London & Southall, 4–1914" mark (A)................................... **525.00**

10" h, hex, buff body, horiz incised wavy lines with green and black glazes, ribbed borders, everted milled rim, dtd 1898, incised "Martin Bros, London & Southall" mark (A).... **1030.00**

10⅛" h, ovoid shape, fantastic monsters in combat carved in sgraffito, deep brown and cream, flaring collar, c1895, inscribed "Martin Bros./London & Southall" mark, drilled (A)..................................... **2200.00**

10¼" h, ovoid body, ribbed oct section incised with jellyfish swimming against waves formed by vert striations, green glaze, brown rim, c1905, incised "Martin Bros. London & Southall, 9–1905" mark (A).... **2504.00**

15¾" h, dbl gourd shape, central pierced horiz band, incised scrolling foliage ac-

cented in brown and blue, c1875, incised
"R.W. Martin, London" mark **1100.00**

c1829-1845

MASON

**Lane Delph, Staffordshire, England
c1804–1848**

History: Although ironstone is the most familiar product associated with Mason's name, Miles Mason actually began his business career as an importer of china wares, specializing in matching pieces for incomplete sets. After studying the manufacturing methods at Worcester and Derby, Mason joined with Thomas Wolfe in Liverpool in 1780 to manufacture Chinese-style porcelain tablewares.

After the dissolution of the Wolfe-Mason partnership in 1804, Mason started a second concern at Lane Delph in Fenton, Staffordshire. The Fenton factory was devoted to the manufacture of quality blue and white transferware. Within a short time the factory was relocated at Minerva Works and expanded to incorporate the Bagnell factory. The new factory was known as the Fenton Stone Works.

Charles and George, Miles' sons, eventually became the managers. In 1813 they patented the ironstone formula and manufacturing technique. They were not the first to produce this hard and durable earthenware, but they certainly were the most successful. Mason's Patent Ironstone China became dominant in the market. Ironstone, designed to meet the middle class needs for utilitarian, durable china tablewares, was produced at Fenton from 1813 to 1848.

The first designs were Oriental in nature. The most common method of applying the design was by transfer. Areas were highlighted with touches of enamel. Hand painting and gilding of the ironstone blanks was not uncommon, especially in floral and scenic patterns. Every conceivable form was fashioned in ironstone, from common tableware to fireplace mantels.

Economic difficulties beset the works in 1848. Charles was forced to sell the family business to Francis Morley. Morley, in partnership with Ashworth from 1849 to 1862, acquired the Mason designs and molds. Ashworth reissues of Mason's original shapes and decorative patterns are hard to distinguish from those produced at the Fenton works.

For over one hundred years, Ashworth and Brothers,

Ltd, have been selling vast quantities of their Mason's type ware with the traditional Oriental-styled patterns. In 1968 the firm took the new name "Mason's Ironstone China, Ltd." The old mark was reinstituted.

References: Geoffrey A. Godden, *Godden's Guide to Mason's China & Ironstone Wares,* Antique Collectors Club, Ltd., 1980; Geoffrey A. Godden, *The Illustrated Guide to Mason's Patent Ironstone China,* Barrie & Jenkins, 1971; Reginald Haggar & Elizabeth Adams, *Mason Porcelain and Ironstone 1796–1853,* Faber & Faber, 1977; R.G. Haggar, *The Masons of Lane Delph,* Lund Humphries, 1952.

Collector's Club: Masons Collectors Club, Elizabeth Jenkins, Home Farm Cottage, Glenthorne, Countisbury Lynton, North Devon EX356NQ. Membership: 30 pounds. 4 newsletters per year.

Museums: City Museum & Art Gallery, Hanley, Stoke-on-Trent, England; Potsdam Public Museum, Potsdam, N.Y.; Victoria & Albert Museum, London, England.

Collecting Hints: Don't overlook the Ashworth reissue pieces. They qualify as true antiques.

Bowl
  9" d, "Vista" pattern, brown transfer **10.00**
  10" d, ironstone, oriental scene of river, bridge and pagoda **45.00**
  10½" d, 6" h, pedestal base, ironstone, "Vista" pattern, red transfer **35.00**
  10⅞" d, ironstone, gold and pastel enameled butterflies and insects, cobalt ground, gilt rim, gold flowering vines on ext, c1820–25 (A) **495.00**
Bowl, Cov, 7" h, with stand, ironstone, printed and painted "Japan" pattern of landscapes and flowers, acorn knob, c1830, printed "Mason's Patent Ironstone China" mark (A). **412.00**
Cache Pot, 5¼" h, ironstone, oriental type florals in salmon, green, and rust, scalloped, cobalt ground, firing crack on bottom, printed round crown mark **825.00**
Chamber Pot, 9¼" d, 5¾" h, ironstone, "Chinese Landscape" pattern with applied red, pink, green, and orange colors, pr (A) **220.00**
Charger, 13" d, ironstone, blue and white oriental floral design, border with eight panels of stylized brocade baskets, scrolling and reserves of geometric designs, "MASON'S PATENT IRONSTONE CHINA" mark. **165.00**

Platter, 18" l, 14¼" w, blue and white transfer, c1790–1810, $795.00

Compote, 13 1/4" l, 5 1/4" h, center blue and white scene with workers, ships and water, blue scenes underneath, white pedestal with gilt, curly edge in gilt, raised border of pink, orange, and yellow florals, "Symouth North Devon" on base, c1840 .... **1200.00**

Creamer

3 5/8" h, ironstone, orange and blue "Japan" pattern, green handle (A) **110.00**

4 3/8" h, "Juvenile Sports" design in vignettes surrounded by red ground with green, blue, pink, yellow, and salmon accents, int crack **75.00**

Custard Cup, 2" h, blue, pink, rust, florals, int floral border, orange rim, c1820, "Mason's Patent Ironstone China" mark **150.00**

Dish, Shaped

10" l, ironstone, oriental style florals in blue, orange, yellow, and green, scalloped border, "Mason's Patent Ironstone" mark.... **425.00**

11" l, 7 1/4" w, ironstone, oriental pheasant pattern in blue, pink, rust, green, peacock and fowl, molded and ribbed border ends, gilt trim, imp and printed "Mason's Patent Ironstone" mark **595.00**

Ewer, 32" h, ftd, ironstone, Imari style floral motifs, mask cornucopia and merman handles in irid glaze, c1820–25 (A) **2200.00**

Inkstand

5" l, 4 1/2" h, ironstone, dbl, pink shell shape ink holders, gilt trim on cov, mottled green-brown base and handle, applied florals, 1820–25, imp "Mason's Ironstone" mark. **3500.00**

6" l, 3 1/2" h, ironstone, cobalt, orange, rust, and gilt florals, arrowhead border, white ground, rect base, two pen holders, 1813–20, imp "Mason's Ironstone" mark........ **1200.00**

Letter Box, 8 1/2" h, ironstone, small pink flowers, cobalt ground, gilt trim, four feet, 1813–1820, imp Mason's mark.................. **1750.00**

Jug

7 1/4" h, ironstone, rust, yellow, cobalt, iron red, and green florals, two florals on int, iron-red and cobalt rim, cobalt handle with gold line, "MASON'S PATENT IRONSTONE" mark **450.00**

8 1/2" h, ironstone, relief of hunting scene in light and dark green, tree trunk handle, "Mason's Patent Ironstone" mark....... **75.00**

10 3/8" h, oval with waisted neck, ironstone, printed and colored with two oval panels of "sacred objects," lobed borders, blue ground with scrolling flowers, scroll handle (A)................................. **665.00**

Meat Tray

13 1/2" l, ironstone, "Watteau" pattern, brown transfer............................. **45.00**

19" l, "Vista" pattern, pink transfer **250.00**

Pitcher

5 1/4" h, ironstone, green, red, blue, and orange "Chinese Landscape" pattern (A) ... **110.00**

7" h, ironstone, orange and blue "Japan" pattern, green and red serpent handle (A) ... **192.00**

Plate

8" d, "Flying Bird," polychrome florals, c1845, "Mason's Patent Ironstone China" mark.. **110.00**

8 5/8" d, ironstone, white, blue, yellow, and rust florals, paneled border with florals,

white ground, shaped rim, 1845–58, "Mason's Patent Ironstone China, Morley's" mark **110.00**

9 1/2" d, "Willow" pattern, blue transfer with orange, red, and ochre accents, pr (A).... **110.00**

10" d, American marine ship scene, marked **50.00**

10 3/4" d, ironstone, oriental type blue, rust and gray florals in cobalt flower holder in center cartouche, cobalt and pale rust paneled border, scalloped edge, "Mason's Patent Ironstone China" mark **125.00**

Platter

9" l, 6 3/8" w, oct, ironstone, "Table and Vase" pattern, green, cobalt, pink, and orange florals, black and white honeycomb on border, ribbed bottom, c1840, imp and printed "Mason's Patent Ironstone" mark. **290.00**

9 1/2" l, shaped oct, ironstone, "Blue Pheasants" pattern, c1820–40, "Mason's Patent Ironstone" mark **275.00**

Sauce Tureen, Cov

6 1/2" h, 7" H-H, "Blue Willow" pattern, c1815, old repair to handle, Mason's Patent Ironstone China" mark................... **280.00**

7 1/2" h, ladle, tray, 8 3/4" H-H, ironstone, "Fruit Basket" pattern, multicolored fruits, cream ground, shaped edge, pierced handles, "Mason's Patent Ironstone China" mark................................... **275.00**

9" h, with stand, ironstone, hex shape, Imari colors of flowering chrysanthemums and scrolling foliage, flower knob (A)........ **495.00**

Soup Plate, 9 1/2" d, "Vase" design in red, blue, orange, and light yellow, imp mark (A)...... **39.00**

Soup Tureen, 14" l, 9" w, 10" h, with underplate and ladle, "Vista" pattern, pink transfer, int crazing.................................. **75.00**

Tea amd Coffee Service, Part, oval teapot, stand, 6 1/2" h, oval cov sugar bowl, waste bowl, cake dish, 5 teacups, 8 coffee cans, 5 saucers, fluted and painted in underglaze blue, iron-red, and gilding with border of gilt diamond shaped against iron-red diagonal panels edged in foliate trefoils between blue stripes patterned with gilt chains, gilt rim edge, 1805–08, 24 pcs (A)........................... **660.00**

Tray

8 1/2" l, "Stratford" pattern, pink transfer ... **16.00**

13 1/4" l, 10 1/2" w, ironstone, transfer of "Fruit Basket" pattern in red and blue, "MASON'S PATENT IRONSTONE" mark . **150.00**

Tureen, Cov, 12" h, hex, ironstone, enamel painted flowers from blue rock in fenced garden, shaped brown rim, blue and gilt dragon head handles, domed cov with flower finial, pierced spread foot, c1803–25, imp "MASON'S PATENT IRONSTONE CHINA" mark (A)............................... **975.00**

Vase

6 5/8" h, trumpet shape, panel of brightly colored fruit or summer flowers on gray marble table, dark blue ground gilded with leaves and berries, body in gilding with vert stripes, circ foot on sq base, mask handles, c1810, Miles Mason (A) **400.00**

10" h, ironstone, cylinder shape with flared neck, "Imari" pattern with panels of blue, iron-red, and gilt flowers and buildings, dbl

scroll handles with mask terminals, c1815–
25, pr (A) **800.00**
Vase, Cov, Ironstone
8" h, sq, panels with courting oriental men
and women, floral motif panels, gilt trim,
lion's head corners (A) **350.00**
21 3/8" h, oct baluster shape, large gold in-
sects between gilt borders on rim and foot
rim, tall domed cov with gilt butterfly on
front and dragonfly on reverse, seated kulin
knob, cobalt blue ground, 1815–25, pr (A) **4400.00**
21 3/4" h, "Japan" pattern, canted sq section
painted with peony and flowers from
fenced garden in blue, iron-red, and gilt,
pierced dragon handles, Fo dog finial,
domed cov, c1825, pr (A) **4190.00**
24 1/2" h, paneled, green Imari style pattern of
stiff leaves, floral borders, mask handles, lion
finial, c1805–20 (A) **3500.00**
32" h, hex tapered body, chinoiserie style ex-
otic birds on branches of oriental flowers,
domed cov with finial of three entwined
dragons, turquoise, pink, and gilt tones,
c1820–30 (A) **1400.00**
33" h, painted formal floral design in blue, iron
red, green, and gilt, dragon handles and
finial, c1825, pr (A) **5000.00**
Vegetable Bowl, 9" l, ironstone, "Watteau" pat-
tern, brown transfer **35.00**
Watering Can, 3 7/8" h, ironstone, blue, red, and
gold flowering peonies and fence pattern, gilt
handle, blue and gilt spout, marked (A) **386.00**

C. M
Golfe·Jurn·
(A.M)
1845-1917

MASSIER

Golfe-Juan, France
1881–1917

History: Clement Massier, who started work in 1881 in
Golfe-Juan, France, was an artist and potter who produced
earthenware with metallic luster decoration. He used
plant motifs and other nature themes on shapes that were
Art Nouveau in style.

Massier's wares usually are marked with an incised
"Massier" or have his initial or the location of the pottery.

Museums: Museé d'Art Moderne de la Ville de Paris, Paris,
France; Museé d'Orsan, Paris, France; Museé Municipal
de Ceramique et d'Art Moderne, Vallauris, France.

Bowl, 9" d, ftd, threaded body, copper-green irid
finish with fish and seaweed pattern,
c1890s, "Clement Massier Golfe Juan A.M."
mark **12,500.00**
Figure, 19" h, owl, green and blue irid glazes,
Clement Massier **4500.00**
Vase
1 3/4" h, miniature, pale olive irid herringbone
design, c1900, "CM C.J.A.M." mark **325.00**

Vase, 17" h, eel handles, hp irid fish in maroon
and gold tones, c1890, "M. Clement Massier
Golfe Juan" mark, $25,000.00

2 3/4" h, miniature, ruby red ground with dark
blue starbursts, thumbprint indentations on
base, "CM Golfe A.M." mark **525.00**
3 1/4" h, green three petal floral design, gold
ground, c1890s, "Clement Massier Golfe
Juan" mark **975.00**
3 3/4" h
Red and black swirling design, "J. Massier"
mark **95.00**
Ruby red ground with tan overglaze, irid
curlicues, c1900, "C.M.G.J." mark **875.00**
4" h, cylinder shape, irid glaze with three
leafed plant forms in green, purple, and
blue, "Clement Massier Golfe Juan" mark
(A) **275.00**
4 7/8" h, irid green ground with gold curlicues,
c1900, "Golfe Juan A.M. France" mark . . . **1275.00**
5" h, olive, gray, and maroon irid irises, Del-
phine Massier **395.00**
6 1/8" h, round base, sq top, four small handles
in leaf design, dark olive ground, ruby and
tan swirl design, c1900, "Golfe Juan
France" mark **3200.00**
6 3/4" h, irid gold-green swirl design, c1900,
Delphin Massier **2100.00**
8" h, marsh scene in green shades, gold
ground, "Golfe Juan" mark **250.00**
10 1/4" h, tapered body, four handles at base,
green-gold irid finish with cattails and leaf
branches, c1890, "C.M. Golfe Juan A.M."
mark **4500.00**
20" h, squat globular body, intricate foliate
design in gold luster on dark red ground
flecked with turquoise, flared circ foot, long
trumpet neck, script "Jerome Massier"
marks (A) **1425.00**
22 1/2" h, terra cotta, roundels of lions on
brown high glaze ground, lower section in
irid brown with large open flowers,
c1880s, "Clement Massier Golfe Juan
A.M."
mark **18,000.00**

c1891

c1890

MEAKIN

Hanley, England
Alfred Meakin, 1873 to Present

History: Alfred Meakin was a Staffordshire potter who made a wide range of earthenware and ironstone china at his Royal Albert Works in Tunstall starting in 1873. Beginning in 1877 the firm traded as Alfred Meakin Ltd., a name it still uses today.

The earthenware is marked with a crown and "AlFRED MEAKIN/ENGLAND."

J. & G. Meakin, 1845 to Present

History: James Meakin established a pottery in Longton in 1845 and transferred it to Hanley in 1848. When he retired in 1852, James and George, his sons, succeeded him. The firm traded as J. & G. Meakin.

The Meakins built the Eagle Works in 1859 and enlarged it in 1868. Later there were branches of the factory at Cobridge and Burslem. Both earthenware and granite ware were produced. The wares were decorated in the style of French porcelain and made for export to the American market. Meakin also produced romantic Staffordshire and flow blue decorated pieces.

J. & G. Meakin joined the Wedgwood Group in 1970.

Reference: Bernard Hollowood, *The Story of J. and G. Meakin,* Bemrose Publicity Co., Ltd, 1951.

Plate, 7¼" d, black transfer with color accents of "Free Trade With All Nations," raised floral border, green rim, imp "J. & G. Meakin" mark, **$245.00**

Bowl
6½" d, "Stratford Stage," brown transfer, "J.& G. Meakin" mark 7.00
8⅞" d, ftd, busts of J.& G. Meakin and "Presented by J.& G. Meakin, Ltd, 1851–1951," scenes of factory, brown transfers on tan ground, gold rim 175.00
Cream and Sugar, "Fair Winds" pattern, brown transfers 10.00
Cup and Saucer, "Alpine Mist" pattern 8.00
Cup and Saucer, Demitasse, "Medway" pattern, hp flowers, brown transferred leaves 12.00
Dinner Service, Part, 12 plates, 9" d, 8 plates, 6" d, 8 cups and saucers, Audubon Birds of America designs......................... 425.00
Milk Pitcher, 7" h, stoneware, "Tin Turn" on body, "Alfred Meakin" mark.............. 50.00
Plate
6" d, "Rosalie" pattern, "Alfred Meakin" mark................................... 2.00
8" d, "Marigold" pattern, "Alfred Meakin" mark................................... 3.00
8" sq, David Copperfield design, scalloped rim 7.00
9" d, "Moss Rose" pattern................ 12.00
10" d
"Alpine Mist" pattern.................. 6.00
Four small groups of flowers in colors, gold and blue border, "J.& G. Sol" mark 8.00
"Romantic England" pattern, pink transfer 14.00
Platter
12" l, 8¾" w, "Moss Rose" pattern....... 20.00
14½" l, ironstone, "Wheat" pattern, "J.& G. Meakin" mark (A)..................... 35.00
16½" l, "Wheat" pattern 27.00
Trio, cup, saucer, plate, 8" d, "Hastings" pattern, red border, large floral swags on ivory band, scalloped rim with molded scrolls, gold trim, "rising sun" mark........................ 12.00
Vegetable Tureen, Cov, 9¾" H-H, "Washington" pattern, brown transfer, "Parisian Granite, Alfred Meakin" mark 89.00

Stone China 53

c1853

MEIGH

Staffordshire, England
c1805–1834 Job Meigh
1835–1901 Charles Meigh

History: Job Meigh operated the Old Hall Pottery at Hanley in the Staffordshire District beginning around 1805 and ending in 1834. Charles, his son, joined the firm. Charles operated the pottery under his own name between 1835 and 1849. The factory produced earthenwares and stonewares.

Charles Meigh was famous for his firm's white stoneware jugs with relief decorations. The decorations were part of the mold from which the pieces were cast. During the 1840s jugs with Gothic details were made. The "Minister" jug of 1842 was the most famous. Classical jugs featuring designs of sporting events and drinking scenes were produced during the 1840s and 50s.

For two years, 1850 to 1851, the firm operated as Charles Meigh, Son & Pankhurst. For the next eleven years, 1851 to 1861, the company was known as Charles Meigh & Sons.

Museum: Potsdam Public Museum, Potsdam, N.Y.

Dessert Service
  11 hex plates, lobed oval comport, 2 sq dishes, oval dish, ironstone, "Japan" pattern in blue, orange, pink, and green, diaper borders, blue and gold fruiting vine handles, Hicks and Meigh **1295.00**
  12 plates, 8¾" d, 4 shaped oval dishes, 3 shaped sq dishes, ftd comport, cov sauce tureen and stand, ironstone, "Imari" pattern of flowers and foliage in iron-red, blue, gilt, cracks, c1806–22, Hicks and Meigh (A)................................. **2000.00**

Jug, 10¾" h, Apostle design, blue salt glaze, c1842, applied mark, $460.00

Tureen, Soup, 15" l, rect, ironstone, cobalt, iron-red, and gold transfer print design, "Real Stone China" mark, Hicks, Meigh and Johnson, (A) $50.00

Jug, 9" h, modified apostle style, salt glaze finish, hairline on handle, c1842 .... **90.00**
Plate, 9" d, "Susa" pattern, black transfer, "C.M.S.& P." mark **30.00**
Tobacco Jar, 8¼" h, cylinder shape, printed blue overall floral pattern, gilt borders, domed cov with acorn knob, inner cov, marked (A)..................................... **646.00**

Royal Dresden China
1938 - Present

1727

1736   1732   1924-1934

MEISSEN

Saxony, Germany
1710 to Present

History: The history of Meissen porcelain design falls into distinct periods which were determined by the director of the company and the kings who appointed and controlled them. Located in the Saxon district of Germany, the Meissen factory, or Royal Saxon Porcelain Manufactory, was founded in 1710 by Frederich August I and first directed by Johann Boettger. It was Boettger who developed the first truly white porcelain in Europe. His white porcelain was exceptionally plastic and could be molded into a variety of applied decorations. Silver shapes were most popular.

After 1720 Meissen porcelain was decorated with fine enamel painting, even surpassing some of the Chinese porcelains. During this period, most of the Meissen tablewares were of relatively simple form which provided ample backgrounds for the beautiful painted decorations. The original crossed swords factory mark was adopted in 1723.

When Johann Horoldt was manager during the last ten years of the reign of Augustus the Strong (1694–1733), the porcelain was a brilliant pure white. Horoldt did pseudo-Chinese scenes in scrollwork of red, gold, and luster plus other adaptations of Chinese, Japanese, and other Oriental wares and motifs. Johann Kirchner (1727–

1733) made life size figures of animals and birds for Augustus the Strong's Japanese Palace.

When Joachim Kaendler, a modeler, came to Meissen in 1731, he began producing figures, especially the Crinoline figures and groups. About 1738 Kaendler created numerous miniature figures used for lavish banquet decorations for the court of Dresden. He designed the world famous swan set for Count von Bruhl. Kaendler also introduced tablewares with low relief borders in the style of silver.

The Rococo influence occurred after 1740. The famous onion pattern appeared about that time. The factory was severely damaged during the Seven Years' War (1756–1763) and was occupied by the victorious Prussians.

Following a major reorganization, the master modeler Michel Victor Acier came to Meissen in 1764 and became the dominating influence. He moved the factory into the Neo-classical period with emphasis on mythological figures. Pictorial decoration was copied from Sevres. Under the directorship of Marcolini (1774–1813) the style shifted to that of Louis XVI. The Marcolini Period ended with the cessation of the Napoleonic Wars in 1814.

The factory experienced a decline in production under the management of Von Oppel from 1814 to 1833. The wares during this phase often imitated other successful European concerns.

The period from 1833 to 1870 is called the "Kuhn Period," after a director of the factory. The company's fortunes improved, both technically and economically. A revival of production of the great pieces from one hundred years earlier was carried out. Many figures were copied in the Rococo style, which was the popular taste of the times. Sales of the china wares continued to increase. The "New Perid" at Meissen started in 1870 when Kuhn died and Raithel became director. Exports of china to America increased during this time. Utilitarian wares in blue underglaze grew in popularity. Improvements continued to be made in the china production process.

From 1895 to 1901 the factory was managed by Brunnemann. A conflict developed between the supporters of old and new ideas of china manufactory. Between 1901 and 1910 there was increasing success artistically and financially, culminating with the two hundredth anniversary Jubilee year of 1910. Many reforms were carried out. New buildings were constructed for furnaces and studios. A new drawing school was established at the factory.

Following World War II the factory was reorganized. Today it operates as the State's Porcelain Manufactory. New models are made as close as possible to the old shapes. Ornamentation also tends to follow the old models. In addition, some new forms are made. The Meissen factory also manufactures various commemorative wares for coronations, Christmas plaques, and Easter plaques.

References: Dr. K. Berling, Editor, *Meissen China, An Illustrated History,* Dover, 1972; Yvonne Hackenbroch, *Meissen & Other Continental Porcelain Faience & Enamel in the Irwin Untermeyer Collection,* Harvard University Press, 1956; W.B. Honey, *Dresden China: An Introduction to the Study of Meissen Porcelain,* Dresden House, 1946; Ingelore Menzhausen, *Early Meissen Porcelain in Dresden,* Thames & Hudson, 1990; Robert E. Rontgen, *The Book of Meissen,* Schiffer Publishing Co., 1984; Otto Walcha, *Meissen Porcelain,* G.P. Putman's Sons, 1981.

Museums: Art Institute of Chicago, Chicago, Illinois; Cincinnati Art Museum, Cincinnati, OH; Cummer Gallery of Art, Jacksonville, FL; Dresden Museum of Art & History, Dresden, Germany; Gardiner Museum of Ceramic Art, Toronto, Canada; Meissen Porcelain Museum, Meissen, Germany; Metropolitan Museum of Art, New York, NY; National Museum of American History, Smithsonian Institution, Washington, D.C.; Robertson Center for the Arts and Sciences, Binghamton, NY; Schlossmuseum, Berlin, Germany; Stadtmuseum, Cologne, Germany; Wadsworth Artheneum, Hartford, CT; Woodmere Art Museum, Philadelphia, PA; Zwinger Museum, Dresden, Germany.

Collectors Hints: Collectors must distinguish between the productions from the greatest period 1710–1756 and later works. During the 19th century, Meissen reproduced some of its 18th century molds in addition to making new ones.

Numerous Dresden factories also reproduced Meissen wares and figures, some copying the original marks. One should be aware of Helena Wolfsohn's decorating shop in Dresden who used the Augustus Rex (AR) monogram which was not been used by Meissen after 1730 but was applied by Wolfshon to reproductions of much later works. About 1833 the Royal Porcelain Manufactory in Meissen obtained a court decision against Wolfsohn ordering her to cease and desist using the AR mark.

Helena Wolfsohn operated the decorating shop, but probably did not produce her own porcelain. However, most of her AR pieces have the AR mark underglaze. Since this mark was applied before glazing and final firing, Helena Wolfsohn must have ordered the white porcelain blanks with the AR mark from some porcelain factory. The manufacturer is not known. Wolfsohn sold many thousands of pieces with the "AR" mark.

The Meissen factory itself used the "AR" mark in 1873 as a trademark and still uses it on special pieces. Therefore, every "AR" marked piece must be studied very carefully.

Basin, 21 1/4" l, oval, int painted with swimming
fish, ext with sprays of summer flowers,
molded handles, c1880 (A). **5235.00**
Beaker and Saucer
Bell shape, harbor scene with travelers in landscape in shaped reserves, saucer with quay
scene in a gilt and Bottger luster cartouche,
gilt scrolling borders, powder purple
ground, c1730–35, underglaze "blue X'd
swords, gilder's E, incised and imp dots"
marks (A). **1850.00**
Cinquefoil shape, Kakiemon palette of ironred, blue, turquoise, black, and gold with
fruiting pomegranate branch and flowering
peony, saucer with branches of flowering
magnolia and prunus, mocha brown rim on
beaker, dark brown rim on saucer, 1725–
30, underglaze "blue caduceus' (A) **1870.00**
Molded lobe body, iron-red, blue, and green

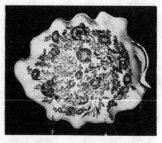

Dish, 9 1/2" l, polychrome enameled flowers, molded gilt rim, Marcolini period, "blue X'd swords and star" mark, (A) $440.00

Salt, 7" h, pastel colors, "blue X'd swords" marks, set of 4, (A) $2090.00

prunus branches and bamboo branches in Kakiemon style, hairline, c1735, "blue X'd swords and incised black #N-342/w" marks (A)............................. **3080.00**

Oct shape, continuous scene of chinoiseries, Chinaman in large flat hat sitting at table below palm tree, bird on dish, reverse with Orientals with hoop, similar decorations on saucer, gilt scroll handles and rims, c1735–40, underglaze "blue X'd swords, incised //, imp 23" marks (A) **3260.00**

Powder purple ground, harbor scene on promontory, c1730–35, "blue X'd swords" marks (A)............................. **1851.00**

Shades of iron-red, purple, green, yellow, brown and black on one side of beaker with Chinese lady holding birdcage, other with Chinaman holding fan and basket, center of saucer with Chinaman holding parasol in cartouches, gilt edged rim, gilt scrollwork border, c1725, 8 on beaker, 1 on saucer (A)......................... **3300.00**

White, molded with flowering prunus branches, c1740, "blue X'd swords" marks (A)............................. **1148.00**

Bouillon Bowl, Cov

3⅜" d, oval, flower sprig decoration, cov with two prs of birds perched on bushes with scattered insects, two scroll handles, ozier molded borders, flower knob restuck, 1765–70 (A)......................... **1402.00**

4⅝" d, scroll mtd spout, baroque handle, blue, iron-red, and gilt swimming birds with water plants and lotus blossoms, domed cov with repeat design and trellis border, repairs, "blue X'd swords" mark (A)...... **1435.00**

Box, Cov, 6³⁄₁₆" h, modeled as large bunch of purple grapes, yellow tipped green forked stem forming knob with three gray veined green leaves, c1785, underglaze "blue X'd swords and star" mark (A) **3025.00**

Bowl

6" d, reserves of purple port scenes in matte gilt cartouches, rust, purple, and yellow florals with green leaves, gilt trim, repaired, "blue X'd swords" mark (A)............. **225.00**

10" d

Shallow, curvilinear relief decoration, gilt highlights, white ground, "blue X'd swords" mark (A) **100.00**

Wreath design floral trellis int, raised on pierced sides, floral swags, gilt border, white ground, "blue X'd swords" mark (A) **140.00**

11" d, relief decorated with foliage in green and gold (A)......................... **140.00**

11½" d, center of two phoenix encircled by dragons and Buddhist symbols, iron-red and gilding, from the Red Dragon Service, c1740–50, underglaze "blue X'd swords, K.H.C. in purple, imp 16" marks (A) **1870.00**

12⅝" d, Kakiemon style decoration, central small iron-red and sea-green floret, flowering and fruiting branches of peony, prunus, and pomegranate, brown edged rim, c1725–30, underglaze "blue X'd swords, incised IX' (A) **2870.00**

Bowl, Cov, 6½" h, 7" l, hexafoil shape, molded basketweave ground, painted insects and floral sprays, gilt trim and rims, green twist handle with blue and white modeled flowerhead, mid 19th C, "blue X'd swords" mark (A) **880.00**

Candelabrum, 22" h, 5 arm, white body with pink and light blue applied flowers and two small children holding flower garlands, gilt accent, tripod scrolled foot, "blue X'd swords" mark (A)............................. **200.00**

Candlestick

5½" h, hex shape, blue floral design outlined in gold, "X'd swords" mark............. **150.00**

5¾" h, cylindrical, panels of couples in wooded landscape, circ foot supported on sq base, shield shape sconce with waisted neck, white ground, gilded details, c1875, underglaze "blue X'd swords" mark, pr (A). **1500.00**

Centerpiece

11" h, two cherubs on scroll and flower encrusted base, flared column supporting pierced scroll basket, c1880, underglaze "blue X'd swords, incised M141," marks (A)................................... **3643.00**

19" h, scroll molded base supporting shepherdess and young gallant playing hide-and-seek around tree trunk encrusted with flowering branches, surmounted by pierced basket applied with further blooms, int painted with bouquets, c1880, underglaze "blue X'd swords, incised 2772" (A) **3553.00**

Charger

11½" d, center floral cartouches, one with fruit, one with floral, three border cartouches with fruit or florals outlined in gilt, wide raised paneled and ribbed border, scalloped edge, gilt trim, early 19th C, "blue X'd swords" mark, pr **625.00**

15³⁄₁₆" d, Kakiemon palette of iron-red, turquoise, blue, green, puce, yellow, black, and gold with stork walking beneath butterfly toward winged tiger entwined around stalk of bamboo among flowering peony branches, rim with scattered sprigs and sprays of Indian blossoms, c1730, underglaze "blue X'd swords' (A) **12,100.00**

Chocolate Pot

5¼" h, baluster shape, two quatrefoil reserves of figures in landscapes, pale turquoise ground, domed cov with similar scenes, ebonized handle, c1740 (A)...... **2975.00**

6½" h, cylindrical, continuous hilly river landscape with figures, blue, iron-red, purple, and gilt foliate scroll molded and fluted spout, gilt edged neck handle with turned wood terminal, shoulder of pot with four sprays of Indian blossoms between gilt bands, flat cov with two figural vignettes flanking central stirring hole, two gilt bands, cov with gilt metal bail handle and sliding cov for hole, c1740, gilder's 37 (A) **4400.00**

6⅝" h, cylindrical, enamels of marriage arms of Albani and Borromeo flanked by two chinoiserie vignettes, one of puppeteers, other of entertainers showing toys to children, flat cov with Kakiemon style florals, wood knob, gilt scroll spout, silver gilt mtd oct hardwood handle, 1730–35, underglaze "blue X'd swords" mark (A) **41,140.00**

Clockcase, 27½" h, circ enamel dial and movement set among rococo scrolls, rockwork, and trails of applied flowers, surmounted by figure of Jupiter and eagle, base with scrolled feet and flowers, figures of Prometheis chained to a rock by Zeus, bright colors, mid 19th C (A) **3750.00**

Clock, Mantel

9½" d, underglaze blue flower painted cylindrical case surmounted by assortment of trophies representing the Arts, putto reading book, rect base, gilt enamels, twin-train movement, one foot restuck, c1880, underglaze "blue X'd swords" mark (A). **2390.00**

23" h, putti as the four seasons with floral swags, white enamel clock face with blue Roman numerals, black Arabic minutes, gilt metal handles, separate three ftd base with floral design, crusted florals, white ground (A). **1000.00**

Coffee Pot, Pear shape

8⅜" h, painted butterflies and insects in brown, black, pink, iron-red, yellow, puce, and light blue, gilt edged ozier molded rim, gilt accented scroll molded spout, gilt checkered handle, green twig knob with pink floral terminals, repairs, c1740, "blue X'd swords" mark (A). **660.00**

9¼" h, molded on each side with flowering prunus branches in gilding, small birds flitting above Chinaman standing over steaming pot, foliate molded spout with gilt, another Chinaman seated before steaming bowls beneath scale molded wishbone handle, bud form knob in gilt, gilt rim, c1750, underglaze "blue X'd swords" mark (A) . . **4675.00**

10¼" h, painted birds perched in branches on grass mounds, scattered insects, scroll handle with flowerhead terminals, floral finial, c1770, "blue X'd swords and dot" mark (A) **605.00**

13" h, two trefoil panels enclosing Orientals at tea ceremony sitting below a tree, domed cov with chinoiseries, scroll handle, gilt ground, c1730, // in luster (A). **3366.00**

Coffee Set

Coffee Pot, 8½" h, cov sucier, cream jug, 6 cups and saucers, iron-red and gilding with dragons and ho-ho birds, white ground, c1900, underglaze "blue X'd swords," imp numerals, 17 pcs (A) **1478.00**

Coffee Pot, 10" h, baluster shape, cov sucrier, baluster cream jug, 6 cups and saucers, 6 plates, sprays of flowers on white ground, other smaller sprigs and insects, shaped gilt rims, c1900, underglaze "blue X'd swords," painted and impressed numerals, 23pcs (A) **2049.00**

Coffee Pot, 10½" h, 14 cups, 14 saucers, 14 dessert plates, teapot, 2 cream jugs, cov sucrier, trailing green ivy between gilded borders, underglaze "blue X'd swords," script numerals, 50 pcs (A) **5806.00**

Tray, 20½" l, 12 cups and saucers, shaped lobed form, underglaze blue with flowers and foliage on composite stem, cups with dbl scroll handle, gilded rims and handles, c1860, underglaze "blue X'd swords" mark, 25 pcs (A). **2040.00**

Compote

6½" h, 9" d, relief floral and beaded center, floral relief rim, gold trim, "blue X'd swords" mark. **450.00**

9" h, gold and green winged lion's heads and floral motifs, white ground, 19th C **400.00**

Condiment Jug, Cov, 6¼" h, pear shape, Indian blossoms, scattered insects, ozier molded border, broken scroll handles, dragon mask spouts, mask terminals, covs with pine cone knobs, c1740, "blue X'd swords" mark, pr (A) **15,420.00**

Cup and Saucer

Bell shape, quatrefoil reserve with harbor scenes, saucer with cartouche of purple trellis and scrollwork with man on horseback near windmill, lilac ground, ear shaped handle, 1740–45, underglaze "blue X'd swords, gilder's K, imp numerals" mark (A) **2057.00**

Birds perched on trees among scattered insects, handle in pale blue and gilding, gilt dentil rims, 1765–70, underglaze "blue X'd swords and dot" imp numerals mark (A). . **1589.00**

Chinoiserie scene of figures with birds and animals in colors in floral scrolls, silver glaze over iron-red ground, c1730, Johann Bottger **850.00**

Cup with painted view of Dresden in gilt swag border, reserved on dark blue ground, saucer reserved with three panels of painted flowers, c1860–80, "blue X'd swords" marks (A). **785.00**

Marcolini painted cup with battle scene of French cavalry soldiers, enclosed by border of ribbons and flowers, saucer with soldiers in battle by a river, gilt rims, c1790, underglaze "blue X'd swords and stars" marks (A). **925.00**

Quatrelobed form, cup reserved with two Watteau scenes of ladies and gallants in park in quatrefoil panels, saucer with lady on horseback in landscape, shell and scrollwork, yellow ground, gilt borders, handle restored, c1740, underglaze "blue X'd swords, gilder's S" marks (A) **1496.00**

Soldiers on horseback in wooded setting, gilded scrolling foliate borders, cell pattern rim, late 19th C, underglaze "blue X'd swords" mark (A) **523.00**

Cup and Saucer, Cov, 4½" h, floral and gilt decoration, saucer with raised pierced base, floral finial on lid, dbl handled, white ground, "blue X'd swords" mark (A) . . . . ./. **65.00**

Desk Set, tray, 10½" l, 7" w, sander, cov inkwell, bell, framed polychrome harbor scenes, puce harber scenes in medallions on border,

gilt trim, late 19th C, "blue X'd swords" marks
(A)..................................... **990.00**
Dish
11" l
  Cobalt ground decorated with gold floral
  relief reserves decorated with painted
  floral sprigs........................ **350.00**
  Quatrefoil shape, central scene of figures by
  walls of house on cliff's edge overlooking
  bay, sepia and gilt floral border, rim with
  oval cartouches and florals, reverse with
  flower studies, insects, and open walnut,
  white ground, c1740–45, underglaze
  "blue X'd swords' (A)............... **1181.00**
  13 5/8" d, Kakiemon palette of iron-red, green,
  turquoise, yellow, lavender, black, and gold
  with bird perched on flowering plant and
  watching another, insect in flight in iron-red
  and green cell diaper border with panels of
  butterflies and iron-red chrysanthemum
  blossoms, gilt edged rim with lotus sprigs,
  underside with two iron-red peony
  branches and insect, c1735, underglaze
  "blue X'd swords" mark (A)...........**14,300.00**
  14 3/4" d, "famille-rose" pattern, large spray of
  flowers in underglaze blue in center, border
  in colored enamels with three groups of
  rocks and flowering branches, underglaze
  blue diaper band on rim, c1725–30, underglaze "blue X'd swords' (A)............. **3544.00**
  16 3/4"d, "Red Dragon" pattern, shades of
  iron-red and gold in center with two phoenix birds among tiny leaf sprigs and insects,
  rim with two dragons separated by clusters
  of trailing ribbons, 1740–50, underglaze
  blue X'd swords, imp 22, puce enamel
  "K.H.C. I.C.46" marks (A).............. **3300.00**
  20" l, oval, central yellow lily and three floral
  springs with bell flowers and pansy, c1820,
  blue "X' swords" mark (A).............. **561.00**
Ecuelle, Cov, Stand, 4 " h, scenes of joyful putti
  playing with flowers, birds, and tools, scattered flower springs on ground, dbl scroll and
  branch handles, flowering terminals, cov with
  bud knob, c1770, underglaze "blue X'd
  swords" mark (A) **1850.00**
Ewer, 26" h, compressed globular shape, allegorical, applied, molded, and painted with
  figures of Diana, Pan, and hunting scenes,
  wheatsheaf handle, c1850, underglaze "blue
  X'd swords, incised 309" marks (A) **1870.00**
Figure
  3 1/4" h, Cupid with garland of flowers,
  c1890 .... **345.00**
  4 3/4" l, "Marriage" group, young child putting
  two birds into bell-shaped pierced bird
  cage, shaped oval scroll molded base, late
  19th C, underglaze "blue X'd swords, incised C99" marks (A)................... **523.00**
  5 1/8" h, seated Dutch boy in gilt edged white
  tunic, fur hat, holding jug and goblet, restored, c1740........................ **1150.00**
  5 1/4" h, Cupid holding wheat and scythe in
  colors, "blue X'd swords" mark....... **450.00**
  5 3/8" h, boy in Turkish costume, tall yellow
  hat and jerkin, flowered waistcoat, purple
  breeches, sword on shoulder, c1745–50,
  "blue X'd swords" mark (A)............ **575.00**
  5 1/2" h
    Seated gentleman writing letter, green and
    brown gilt line molded base, c1860–70,

underglaze "blue X'd swords, incised N"
mark (A) **1593.00**
4 1/2" l, white, goat standing with front paws
on broken bowl...................... **275.00**
Winter as a bearded old man standing,
wrapped in puce drapery, warming one
hand over a brazier, c1755 (A) **470.00**
5 5/8" h, Athena modeled in warrior costume
holding spear, owl at side, Medusa head
shaped shield, multicolored enamels, sq
base, restored, "blue X'd swords" mark (A)   **440.00**
5 3/4" h, allegorical group of summer, three
putti with wheat sheaves around a seated
girl with wreath of flowers in hair, dress
sprigged with Indian blossoms, scroll
molded base, gilded edge, restored, c1760,
imp 16 (A) **1300.00**
6" h, bust of young girl with cap, kerchief at
neck, painted bodice, floral corsage on
shoulder, enamels and gilt, late 19th C,
"blue X'd swords" mark (A)............ **495.00**
6 1/4" h, chinoiserie group, woman with kettle
in one hand, wearing loose flowered jacket
over long white dress, holding jug from
which she pours milk into saucer, boy
kneels at feet holding basket of fruit, late
19th C, underglaze "blue X'd swords," incised numerals (A) **1496.00**
6 1/2" h, hare, black spotted fur in black and
brown, flower applied base, restored,
c1750, by J.J. Kandler (A) **4930.00**
6 5/8" h
  Chariot group, Venus in pale yellow cloak
  with oriental flower sprigs holding flower
  garland and mirror, seated in shell-
  molded chariot, Amor and two doves on
  front of chariot, Neptune with trident in
  puce lined cloak, little triton in shell
  molded chariot, restored, c1765, by J.J.
  Kandler, underglaze "blue X'd swords"
  mark (A) **4300.00**
  Drunken peasant, puce ribboned black hat,
  yellow lined turquoise jacket, white skirt,
  black suspenders, iron-red breeches, gilt
  edged white tankard, seated on white
  tree stump applied with three green leaf
  sprigs, c1740, by Johann Joachim Kandler, imp "50" 3 times (A) **3025.00**
6 3/4" h, pugs in tones of brown, black, and
fawn, female with puppy beneath her,
c1880, underglaze "blue X'd swords" mark,
pr (A)................................ **2163.00**
7" h, "Pagoda," corpulent Oriental seated
cross-legged, wearing loosely tied robe, mid
19th C, underglaze "blue X'd swords' (A). **1496.00**
7 1/4" h, drummer dressed in flowering tunic
and yellow breeches, blowing fife and beating drum, rococo scrolled base with gilt accents, c1750, "blue X'd swords" mark (A) **2680.00**
7 1/2" h
  Child reclining on stool with red checkered
  blanket, feeds dog a biscuit, bright colors,
  canted rect gilt lined base, c1870, underglaze "blue X'd swords, incised E 77"
  mark (A) **2600.00**
  Shepherd with dove on tree stump, letter
  around neck, gilded key-fret circ base
  with standing sheep, late 19th C, underglaze "blue X'd swords" mark (A) **579.00**
7 3/4" h, Bolognese spaniel, tufts of hair in
shades of brown, c1870 (A)............ **2100.00**

8″ h, standing young woman holding garland of flowers draped across urn, man seated, young girl in ground with garland overhead, two doves on base, multicolored, "blue X'd swords" mark........................ **1000.00**

9″ h

Cherub leaning on crutches, holding crumpled hat, waisted circ base, late 19th C, "X'd swords, incised L112" (A)........ **375.00**

Two Freemasons, studying globe, brightly colored and gilded, tricorn hats, pug dog recumbent at feet, c1860–80, "blue X'd swords, incised 376" (A) **1309.00**

9¼″ h, "The Broken Eggs," two women in 18th C costumes, putto climbing underneath dress of standing woman, seated woman grasping shoulder, Cupid kneeling at feet holding broken egg from basket on ground, brown and green rocky base, gilt rim, c1880, underglaze "blue X'd swords, incised F65" mark (A) **2049.00**

9⅝ h, Mercury carrying man and lion skin on back, young boy by their side, bright enamels on green and brown base, gilded details, c1870, underglaze "blue X'd swords" mark................................ **1600.00**

10″ h, dancing girl with scarf............. **595.00**

10¼″ h, cockatoo, perched on tall stump, head with tall orange plumage, gray beak and claws, 20th C, underglaze "blue X'd swords," incised numerals, pr (A) **2323.00**

10½″ h, young boy astride branch in tall tree with lady and gentleman gathering apples below, bright enamel colors on scroll molded gilt lined base, c1870, underglaze "blue X'd swords, incised 2229″ marks (A) **2618.00**

11¾″ h, "The Lessons in Love" group, Cupid reading from book on pedestal, maidens and girls listening nearby, rocky mound base, brightly colored, mid 19th C, underglaze "blue X'd swords, incised F74″ (A) . **4301.00**

13″ h, musician, standing beside vase of foliage playing hurdy-gurdy, birdcage on back, straw hat, fur lined iron-red robes with gilding, circ scroll molded base, late 19th C, underglaze "blue X'd swords, incised 1519″ (A)........................... **490.00**

13½″ h, lion, recumbent on large rock, naturalistic colors, rocky mound washed in tones of brown, ochre, and green, rect base, c1840, underglaze "blue deleted X'd swords, incised M113" (A)............. **2200.00**

14″ h

Juno in robe with sprigs of brightly colored flowers, peacock by side, rockwork base, gilt-lined swag molding to bottom, c1880, underglaze "blue deleted X'd swords, incised 1235" (A) **935.00**

Naked Daphne changing into tree and pursued by Apollo in green robe, gilt lined gilt base, c1870–80, underglaze "blue X'd swords, incised J 9″ marks (A)..... **2390.00**

14½″ h, "Chocolate Girl" in white floral skirt, brown jacket, pink bonnet, carrying tray, c1880, underglaze "blue X' swords, incised F86″ marks......................... **2000.00**

15¾″ h, equestrian falconer group, lady wearing tricorn hat seated on horse with falcon perched on arm, four hounds run on

each side of molded gilt scroll base, green jacket, yellow printed skirt, black and pink hat, gilding, early 20th C, underglaze "blue X'd swords" marks (A)................. **7603.00**

21″ h, magpies, plumage decorated in green, black, white, and blue hues, open beaks, perched on gnarled tree stump applied with foliage, rockwork base, late 19th C, "blue X'd swords," incised marks, pr (A) **710.00**

Gaming Box, Cov, 6¾″ l, four internal division with flower sprigs, cov with deck of cards incl Jack of Hearts, German blossoms, flower finial, repaired, c1760 (A) **1950.00**

Inkwell, 3″ d, molded panel cir body, white lid, yellow base, gilt finial, c1820–40, "blue X'd sword" mark........................... **85.00**

Jug, Cov, 8¾″ h, molded overlapping petals, applied green and gold sprigs of rose foliage, restruck bud knob, c1850 (A) **935.00**

Milk Jug, Cov, 5¾″ h, pear shape body, Oriental seated at table with hammer, child supplied timber board, reverse with oriental family playing with baby, wishbone handle, scrolling border, handle in gilt and purple, pine cone knob on cov, c1740, underglaze "blue X'd swords" marks (A)..............................**13,370.00**

Mirror, 20″ h, oval, scroll molded body applied with foliage, tied curtains on each side, crown on top, bright colors, gilding, c1870, underglaze "blue X'd swords" mark (A)......... **3600.00**

Mug

3¼″ h

Chinaman holding umbrella, carrying food on a plate, following child with flycatcher, oriental garden, iron-red border of scrolling foliage enclosing violet and lilac florets, c1730, "blue X'd swords mark (A). **6580.00**

Cylindrical shape, Kakiemon style with peonies spreading from behind rockwork in turquoise, blue, iron-red and gilding, scrolling border with florets, gilt scroll handle, cracked, c1730, "blue caduceus" mark (A) **2244.00**

Needle Case, 4½″ h, enamel painted lovers and musicians in rococo setting, silver gilt mts, c1760–70 .... **1200.00**

Plaque, 5¹⁵⁄₁₆″ l, oval, white biscuit in relief with three classical maidens, one seated in lion's paw footed chair, facing flaming columnar altar, one kneels with outstretched hand, one stands holding drapery, 1780–90, underglaze "blue X'd swords" mark (A) **330.00**

Plate

8⅛″ d, central rosette, branches of pomegranates, prunus, and peonies, arranged around center, brown edged rim, Kakiemon palette, c1725–30, restored, underglaze "blue caduceus, incised //" mark (A)..... **500.00**

8⅜″ d, shades of iron-red, green, brown, gray, yellow, and turquoise in center with Selene in flight and reaching toward goatskin offered by Pan holding shepherd's crook and standing by goat and tree, draped urn, gilt inner band, rim with four clusters of puce, iron-red, yellow, and green flowers, c1750, Hausmaler, underglaze "blue X'd swords" mark (A) **3300.00**

8½″ d, portrait of three royal children, two King Charles spaniels in gold, white, blue, and orange, blue ground with gold border around portrait, maroon and gold scalloped edge on cream ground **350.00**

8⅝" d, iron-red, green, turquoise, blue, purple, lavender, black and gilding with bird in flight near chrysanthemum plant growing from swirling stylized rocks, iron-red dbl line inner border, rim with three flowering chrysanthemum branches, c1730, underglaze "blue X'd swords" mark (A) **1870.00**

8¾" d, pr of Cupids allegorical of Arts and Victory, pierced borders with applied blue florets, gilded, c1880, underglaze "blue X'd swords," imp numerals, pr (A) **1795.00**

9" d

Armorial, center molded with two swans and crane with bulrushes, crane in flight, radiating shell pattern ground, coat of arms on border, scattered sprays of Indian blossoms, gilt dash rim, from Swan Service modeled by J.J. Kandler and J.F. Eberlein, c1736, underglaze "blue X'd swords" mark (A) **20,570.00**

Scene of boy and girl under tree, blue and gold border, "blue X'd swords" mark . . **125.00**

Three Cupids in Italian country landscape at play or enacting allegorical scenes of seasons, pierced border reserved with gilt cartouches with sprays of summer flowers, c1860, underglaze "blue X'd swords," imp numerals, set of 12 (A). . .**12,672.00**

9½" d, Venus disarming Cupid beside a river bank, pierced shaped border, gilded panels with black details, yellow ground, c1865–75, reverse inscribed "der besiegte Amor, Boucher," underglaze "blue X'd swords" mark (A) **3273.00**

9⅝" d, painted with single bird perched on branch, border painted with butterflies and insects, shaped rim, c1880, "blue X'd swords" mark, set of 6 (A) **1215.00**

9¾" d

Cabinet, Watteau scene of courting couple, gilt and pierced border, "blue X'd swords" mark (A) **180.00**

Leaf on leaf pattern in cobalt, white, and gold **185.00**

10" d, blue and white scene of family carrying Christmas tree on bridge, c1930 . . . . **95.00**

15¼" d, armorial, center painted in enamels and gilding with coat of arms among scattered sprigs of German blossoms, molded borders, shaped rim, 1745–50, underglaze "blue X'd swords, imp 20, incised ////" mark (A) **3740.00**

Platter, 19½" l, oval, multicolored floral decoration, gilt edge, raised border, white ground, "blue X'd swords" mark (A) **270.00**

Plaque, 7½" h, 5⅝" w, scene of young maiden in puce and white drape, hammock suspended between two trees above stream in wooded landscape, peacock stands on grass in foreground, late 19th C, underglaze "blue X'd swords" mark, framed (A) **5464.00**

Pounce Pot, 1⅝" h, sq, flowering peony branches, rockwork, iron-red scrolling foliage border with yellow and light blue florets, c1730, "blue X'swords" mark (A) **500.00**

Sauceboat

5½" h, two quatrefoils reserved with butterfly perched on bouquet of oriental flowers,

S scroll handle, c1735, "blue X'd swords" mark (A) **2618.00**

9¹⁵⁄₁₆" l, oval, ext with Kakiemon palette of iron-red, blue, green, turquoise, yellow, black, gray, and gold with two birds perched on branch and chrysanthemum spray, int with scattered sprigs, molded gilt heighteded acanthus leaves and feathers, shell molded base, gilt dashed foliate molded S scroll handles and feet, scalloped edge, c1740, underglaze "blue X'd swords," mark (A). **3575.00**

Sauceboat, Stand, 8⅝" l, oval, "Imari" pattern, painted in underglaze blue, iron-red, pink, puce, and brown with central vase of chrysanthemums and peonies beneath gilt edged underglaze blue border with iron-red and gold flowering vines, rim edged in gilding, S scroll handle with peony spray, c1740, underglaze "blue X'd swords" on int of sauceboats and undersides of stands, pr (A) **8800.00**

Scent Bottle, 3⅛" h, figural Harlequin in dancing pose, standing before rococo urn mtd and fitted with gilt metal stopper, yellow base with garland of flowers, c1750, underglaze "blue X'd swords" mark (A). **2953.00**

Snuffbox, Cov

3¹⁄₁₆" l, back and cov with amorous couple, sides and base with boy blowing horn or maiden strumming mandolin, cov int in shades of puce, green, blue, iron-red yellow, mauve, lavender, brown, and gray with scene of two children playing harp and mandolin for couple dancing in garden, puce and green floral sprigs, gold mt with rococo scrolls, c1755 (A) **5775.00**

3³⁄₁₆" l, ext and bottom painted in coppergreen, flesh tones, and black with romantic figures conversing or making music in park settings, floral sprigs, int with seven figures playing game around table before trellis, river landscape, contemporary hinged gold mount, 1750–55 (A). **2750.00**

Soup Plate, 8¹³⁄₁₆" d, Kakiemon palette of iron-red, blue, turquoise, black and gold with flowering plants growing from stylized rock, inner iron-red line border, rim with iron-red foliate scroll vine with four gilt flowerheads, c1765, underglaze "blue X'd swords and dot, imp 32" marks (A) **2200.00**

Sugar Bowl, Cov

3¾" h, oct, "Quail" pattern, Kakiemon style decorations in iron-red, blue, sea-green, and gilding, flowering prunus, peonies, brown edged rim, loop handle with gilt scroll, c1730, "Dreher" mark (A) **3700.00**

4⅜" h

Circ bellied shape, two cartouches of figures in river scenes enclosed by gilt scrollwork with iron-red, cov with two scenes of tradesmen beside shores within gilt scroll and shell border, dragon knob in purple, iron-red, and gilding, 1730–35, underglaze "blue X'd swords, gilder's 60, imp Dreher's oo" mark (A). **14,960.00**

Scene of church in front of town in river landscape, painted in green, brown, yellow, iron-red, blue and black, gilt edged cov with puce and green sprig knob, c1745–50, "blue X'd swords" mark (A). **770.00**

Sugar Box, Cov

3³⁄₈" h, oval, sides and cov with coat of arms of Althann and Daun, ducal hat flanked by chinoiserie scenes with gilt scrollwork, luster trellis amongst scattered Indian flowers, gilt scroll borders, cove with burnished gilt crouching hare finial, c1730, underglaze "blue X'd swords" mark (A) **20,000.00**

4¹⁄₂" w, oblong oct, iron-red, pink, and green flowering branches, blue, green, and pink bands, cov crack, c1725, "blue X'd swords and hausmalerei" marks (A) **4400.00**

5³⁄₈" l, oval, chinoiserie figure holding parasol, two holding fan between flowering plants on either side, cov with iron-red and purple trellis diaper border with gilt centered iron-red blossoms with blue leaves, black spotted turquoise frog with salmon feet and iron-red mouth on top, c1730, underglaze "blue X'd swords, incised M" marks (A). **18,700.00**

Sweetmeat Basket, 11³⁄₄" h, figural, young lady and gentleman wearing colorful floral attire, reclining on shaped base with scroll rim, beside two handled, shaped and flower encrusted basket painted on int with scattered sprays of flowers, gilt rims, c1890, underglaze "blue X'd swords, incised 2863, 2858" marks (A) **2390.00**

Tankard, 8¹⁄₄" h, cylindrical body, underglaze blue flowering peonies, chrysanthamum and lotus in fenced garden in Chinese Export style, flying insects below seeded diaper and flower reserve border, pewter mts with ball thumbpiece, strap handle, foliate molded terminal, c1740, underglaze "blue X'd swords" cross mark below handle, imp "20" (A) **4528.00**

Teabowl

Continuous scene of Chinamen playing with balloons, bells, other oriental toys, well has roundel of oriental dignitary holding flag, gilt edged rim, c1735, underglaze "blue X'd swords" mark (A) **925.00**

Two shaped panels with figures in land, riverscapes with boats, int with Kakiemon flower spray within scrolling gilt border, c1730, underglaze "blue caduceus, gilder's E, imp for Meissner senior" marks (A) **650.00**

Teabowl and Saucer, cup reserved with two quatrefoil panels with harbor scenes, scene in well, saucer cartouche with figures looking at classical ruins in a landscape, gilt trellis, shell and scroll borders, yellow ground, c1740, underglaze "blue X'd swords, gilder's Q" mark (A). **1496.00**

Tea Caddy

4¹⁄₈" h, sprays of flowers and tiger lily, arched rect form, c1740–45, "blue X'd swords" mark (A) **1300.00**

4¹⁄₄" h, "Quail" pattern, decorated in Kakiemon style, pair of quails on front and back, flowering prunus, English silver-gilt cov, c1730, "blue X'd swords, Dreher for Schiefer" marks (A). **2050.00**

4³⁄₈" h, painted flowering chinoiserie plants, trellis border on cov, c1735, "blue X'd swords" mark (A) **3636.00**

4³⁄₄" h, painted landscapes with architectural prospects, ladies and men on horseback, shoulders with florals, gilt edged rims, pine cone knob on cov, c1745, "blue X'd swords, gilder's S" marks (A) **12,340.00**

5" h, rect, quatrefoil panel edged in gilt scrollwork on each side with colorful oriental and European quay scenes, arched shoulder and domed cov with sprigs of Indian blossoms within gilt bands, cov encircled by cobalt blue border, gilt artichoke knob, blue ground, 1735–40, unmarked (A) **15,400.00**

Teacup and Saucer

Cup has two quatrefoil cartouches with loose bouquet of German blossoms, gilt edged rims, yellow ground, c1745–50, underglaze "blue X'd swords, imp numerals" marks (A) **820.00**

Shepherdess wearing white scarf, apron over iron-red and lavender dress, tending lamb and white sheep in rocky landscape, int cup with small bouquet and sprig of colorful German blossoms, gilt dentil edged rim, c1780, underglaze "blue X'd swords, star, a /" marks (A). **550.00**

Teapot

3¹⁄₈" h, painted loose bouquets and scattered flowers, molded animal spout, wishbone handle, flower knob, c1760, "blue X'd swords" mark (A) **1122.00**

3⁷⁄₈" h, quatrelobed cartouche with oriental tea ceremony, framed by gilt and iron-red scrollwork with Bottger luster, sprigs of Indian flowers, cov with chinoiseries, oct curved spout, restored finial and spout, c1730, underglaze "blue X'd swords & gilder's 22" marks (A) **2618.00**

4¹⁄₈" h, continuous scene of chinoiseries, figures grouped around tables at leisurely pursuits, gilt scrolling border, purple and gilt wishbone handle, gilt animal spout, pine cone knob on cov, c1740, underglaze "blue X'd swords" mark (A). **13,370.00**

4³⁄₈" h, white, applied flowering rose branches, domed cov with applied branches, spout and cov restored, c1722 (A). **3828.00**

5¹⁄₈" h, ovoid body, decorated in relief above gilt base with border of acanthus leaves and beneath gilt neck with border of bellflowers, cov with gilt conical knob, gilt floral Laub-und-Bandelwerk, loop handle, gilt curving spout from bearded mask terminal, c1723, blue enamel "X'd swords" mark (A) **8800.00**

7⁵⁄₈" h, monkey form, gray and black eyes, iron-red mouth, gray muzzle, salmon face, ears, fingertips, and toes, curly coat heightened in brown on head, shoulders, chest, forearms, feet, and lower end of tail form handle, gilt edged white ruff, modeled seated holding teabowl and saucer, gilt edged spout, head mtd in gilt metal with hinged cov as tricorn, 1735–40, underglaze "blue X'd swords" mark (A) **12,100.00**

7³⁄₄" h, floral sprays, gilt border, gadroon design and finial, "blue X'd swords" mark (A). **230.00**

Tete-a-Tete Set

2 Handled Tray, cov coffee pot, cov hot water jug, cov sucrier, 2 coffee cups, arms of Travagliati of Venice in enamels and gilding on each piece with sprays of fruit, within molded cartouches in puce and gilding, c1755, cov of sucrier restored, underglaze "blue X'd swords" marks (A) **13,783.00**

Tray, 17 3/8" l, teapot, milk jug, cov sucrier, 2 cups and saucers, colorful sprays of flowers over white ground within shaped gilt rim, one cup restored, late 19th C, underglaze "blue X'd swords, incised 8" mark, 10 pcs (A)................................. **3187.00**

Tureen, Cov

7 1/2" h, seated hen with feathers in black and brown, base with six chicks, cov surmounted with single chick, cov restored, c1870, underglaze "blue X'd swords, incised D 9" marks (A)................... **1024.00**

9 3/8" d, circ, four gilt edged quatrefoil panels with coloful quay scenes of European and Turkish figures near boats, cov with artichoke knob, yellow ground, hair cracks, c1740, underglaze "blue X'd swords, imp 1" marks (A) **4950.00**

15" d, stag shape, base as recumbent animal with incised fur markings, face and feet with brown and black details, cov modeled as head and back, applied branch handle, green and orange with leaves and acorn, detachable horns, white ground, c1880, "blue x'd swords, incised E 50, imp 144" marks (A)............................ **5702.00**

Tureen, Cov, Stand, 11 l, vignettes of hunting scenes with wild boar and deer, scattered flowers, domed cov with putto scattering fruit and flowers from a cornucopia, c1760, underglaze "blue X'd swords, B, and imp "D' (A) . **7482.00**

Urn, 11 1/2" h, central floral reserve on cobalt ground, gilt accents, dbl serpent handles.... **550.00**

Vase

8 7/8" h, ovoid body, sprays of brightly colored summer flowers, white ground, dark blue borders, gilded scroll acanthus leaf handles, c1890, underglaze "blue X'd swords" marks, pr (A)......................... **1400.00**

9 3/8" h, cylindrical body, oval panel of courtly lovers in arcadian landscape, reverse with colorful floral arrangement, framed by gilt cartouches, deep blue ground between gilt rims, c1900, underglaze "blue X'd swords, 23" marks, pr (A) **2277.00**

13 3/8" h, ovoid body, encrusted with trails of colorful flowers, foliage, and fruit, body painted with sprays of flowers and insects, white ground, rims gilded, short cylindrical necks, c1880, underglaze "blue X'd swords," mark (A)..................... **6336.00**

16 1/2" h, ovoid body, young girl seated on rock before pond, five birds perched on branch, edge of pine forest, gilded border, white ground, flared neck with gilt band, c1920, underglaze "blue X'd swords" mark (A) ... **3168.00**

18 1/2" h, campana form, panels of 18th C lovers in gardens, sprays of brightly colored flowers within molded and gilt scroll borders, two putti among branches of fruit, rim with sprigs, c1860–70, underglaze "blue X'd swords, incised 2757" marks, pr (A).. **9000.00**

18 3/4" h, neoclassical enamel painted sprays of summer flowers, gilt details, snake handles, late 19th C, "blue X'd swords" mark (A)................................. **1870.00**

19 9/16" h, dbl gourd shape, upper body with two and lower body with three brown edged quatrefoil panels with colorful chinoiserie scenes of figures at various pursuits in gardens, gilt foliate scroll work border on upper

body, gilt borders, tomato red ground, 19th C, underglaze "blue AR" mark (A) **4400.00**

21 1/8" h, baluster shape, blue and white continuous scene on front and reverse of seated chinamen raising beakers before steaming caldron in fenced garden before distant pagodas and gazebos between dbl or triple line borders, 1721–23, unmarked, (A)................................. **23,100.00**

Vase, Cov

11 5/8" h, baluster body, two panels painted with Watteau scenes of gallants and ladies in parkland, applied flowering branches, gilt ground panels, overall molded forget-me-nots, domed cov with flower knob and musicians, scrolling foliage ormolu mounts, c1745, underglaze "blue X'd swords" mark (A)................................. **5236.00**

19 1/4" h, painted in iron-red, purple, green, black, and shades of brown with chinoiserie figures at various pursuits in fenced garden within brown edged quatrefoil panel reserved on front and back, neck with sprays and sprigs of Indian blossoms above gilt band, cov with gilt bands around rim, tear shaped knob, yellow ground, repairs, c1740, underglaze "blue X'd swords" mark in unglazed base (A)................... **10,450.00**

Waste Bowl

6 3/8" d, multicolored chinoiserie ext with continuous scene of oriental figures at various pursuits with animals and children above iron-red dbl line, int with two figures within iron-red dbl roundel, c1739, underglaze "blue X'd swords, 18, incised V" marks (A)............................... **4950.00**

6 5/8" d, ext colorfully painted on front with gallant youth standing beside monument behind seated couple, lady raising glass, reverse with shepherd and sweetheart seated on hummock by brown dog, hazy rural landscapes, sides and int with spray of German flowers, rim edged in gilding, c1745, underglaze "blue X'd swords" mark (A) .. **1760.00**

MENNECY

D·V· 1748-1773

Villeroy, Ile de France
1734–1806

History: In 1734 Louis-Francois de Neufville, Duc de Villeroy, under the direction of Francois Barbin established a soft paste porcelain factory in Paris. The factory was moved to Mennecy in 1748 and to Bourg-la-Reine in 1773. Production was continued by Joseph Jullien and his descendants until 1806.

The porcelain was covered with a "wet-looking" brilliant glaze that absorbed the enamel decoration. Chinese designs were used. Styles used at Vincennes and Sevres soon were copied. Since gilding was forbidden by Louis XV, rose pink or bright blue enamel was used for edging.

Cylinder shapes were used at Mennecy for cups and covered boxes in a variety of sizes. Teapots, custard cups, and shell-shaped sugar basins were popular. Mennecy also produced attractive, but impractical porcelain handles for cutlery.

Reference: Hubert Landais, *French Porcelain*, G. P. Putnam's Sons, 1961.

Museums: J. Paul Getty Museum, Malibu, California; Victoria & Albert Museum, London, England.

Bonbonniere
   2³/₄" h, figural nesting swan with head turned on back, brown toned plummage, silver mts, restored, c1760, pr (A) **1018.00**
   3¹/₂" l, shoe form, pastel floral sprigs and sprays, blue buckle and heel, brown sole, gilt rim, comtemporary silver hinged mt, 1740–50, Paris discharge mark for 1750–56 (A) **1540.00**
Butter Dish, Cov, 8" d, flower bouquets, cov with two loops and flower knob, rims edged in puce, stand fixed, one loop missing, c1750, imp "DV" mark (A) **200.00**
Coffee Can and Saucer
   Exotic birds in landscape, c1760, incised "D.V." mark (A) **275.00**
   Painted sprays of summer flowers, puce edged rim, incised "DSV" mark **185.00**
Cup and Saucer, trembleuse saucer, painted bouquets and scattered flowers in colors, mauve line edges, branch handle with leaf and berry terminals, c1740, incised "D.V." marks (A) **2057.00**
Custard Cup
   3¹/₂" h, painted multicolored flower sprays, white ground, fluted body, incised "DV" mark, pr (A) **1330.00**
   Painted looses bouquets and scattered flowers in colors, puce accented scroll handle, c1745 (A) **62.00**
Dish, 6" l, lozenge shape, painted summer flower sprays, puce edged rim, c1750, incised "D.V." mark, pr **465.00**
Figure
   4³/₄" h, winter as a young boy in white, wearing cloak, warming hands over a brazier, c1750 (A) **500.00**
   5" h, purple, blue, yellow, and green parrot perched in tree stump, c1750, incised "D.V." mark (A) **10,000.00**
   6¹/₂" h, white bisque, two child musicians

seated on rockwork base, facing each other, girl playing drum, boy with cello, incised "D.V." mark (A) **280.00**
8¹/₄" h, dwarf, standing woman with brown hair, mauve hat, flowered white skirt and shirt, mauve belt, yellow knapsack on back, green and brown rocky base, c1770 (A) **14,300.00**
Ice Cup, 2¹/₂" h, campana shape, paneled flower garlands suspended from puce ribbons, waisted socle, puce trimmed rim and scroll handles, blue footrim, c1750, incised "DV" mark, pr (A) **775.00**
Jar, Cov, 2¹/₁₆" h, applied flowering branches between columns of applied florets, cov pierced with stars and circles, rose bud knob **185.00**
Knife Handle, 3" l, scroll shape, puce and painted loose bouquet and rose, scattered sprigs, c1750, set of 6 . . . . **550.00**
Pommade Pot, Cov
   3" h, lobed form, painted with summer flowers, domed cov with berry knob, cov restored, c1750, pr (A) **325.00**
   5¹/₂" h, white, molded with prunus branches, domed cov with flat knob, silver mts, c1730, incised "D.V." mark (A) **850.00**
Sauce Tureen, Cov, 4³/₄" h, oblong, birds on fruiting branches, cov with nesting swan and other birds, berried branch finial, puce rims, fixed stand, bowl restored, c1760, incised "D.V." mark (A) **1000.00**
Sugar Sifter, 6³/₄" l, white, bowl pierced with stars around central floret, shell thumbpiece, c1750 (A) **916.00**
Vase, 2¹/₄" h, lobed campana shape, painted sprays of summer flowers, puce-edged rim, waisted socle, c1750, incised "D" mark (A) . **325.00**

c1843-1872

c1912-1950

MADE IN ENGLAND

EST. 1793

c1860

MINTON

Stoke-on-Trent, Hanley, England
1793 to Present

History: Thomas Minton established his pottery in 1793 in Stoke-on-Trent. During the early years, he concentrated on blue transfer printed earthenware, cream colored earthenware, and plain bone china. By 1810 production expanded to include stoneware, Egyptian black, and printed and painted bone china. A tremendous number of shapes, styles, and decorations with printed, enameled, or gilded designs were manufactured. Many nineteenth century Minton patterns resembled those of Spode, Miles

Snuff Box, sides molded with green enameled vine leaves and black grapes, int painted with leaves and grapes, late gilt mts, hairline, c1750–60, $950.00

Mason, New Hall and Pinxton, the company's principal rivals. Most pieces were unmarked.

Between 1816 and 1824 production at the Minton factory was concentrated on earthenwares and cream colored wares. Bone china production resumed in 1824. A large selection of figures and ornamental wares augmented the tradional tableware line.

Much of Minton's success can be attributed to the decorations applied by the staff of painters. French porcelain artists and ex-Derby decorators were employed by Minton. By the late 1830s Minton had achieved a quality of modeling and decoration on bone china that was unequalled in Europe.

In 1836 Herbert took complete charge when his father died. Herbert Minton, Thomas' son, gradually changed the factory from a small scale producer into one of the greatest Victorian potteries in Europe. By 1858 Minton's employed over 1500 people utilizing new technologies and decorative styles. Encaustic floor tiles and Parian porcelain were developed under Herbert's jurisdiction.

Leon Arnoux became art director at Minton's in 1849. He encourage many French artists move to Stoke-on-Trent and introduced a revival of the Renaissance styles. Arnoux also developed a series of colored glazes for a "majolica" line.

Colin Minton Campbell took control in 1858. The acid gold process was developed, allowing rich gold decorations in bas relief. Louis Marc Solon came to Minton from Sevres in 1870 and brought with him the technique of pate-sur-pate decoration. Pate-sur-pate became a major contribution by Minton to the 19th century English ceramics heritage. After Campbell's death in 1885, Minton continued to be the leading English pottery manufacturer of the 19th century.

In 1968 Minton became a member of the Royal Doulton Tableware Group. Minton china still is being produced today. The company retains its reputation for high quality, hand painted, and gilded tablewares.

References: Paul Atterbury, *The Dictionary of Minton*, Antique Collectors' Club, 1990; G. A. Godden, *Minton Pottery & Porcelain of the First Period. 1793–1850*, Herbert Jenkins, Ltd., 1968; G. A. Godden, *Victorian Porcelain*, Herbert Jenkins, 1961.

Museum: Minton Museum, London Road, Stoke-on-Trent, England.

Basket, 11½" l, rect, painted scene of two women seated in wooded setting, reserved on dark blue ground, gilt swag molded border and overhead loop handle, c1835 (A) **2525.00**

Tray, 10" l, multicolored florals, gold and cobalt border, white center ground, gold accents, c1840, "Felspar Porcelain" mark, $135.00

Bowl, 12" H-H, 9½" w, ironstone, "Oriental Japan" pattern, multicolored and cobalt on white ground **95.00**

Box, 5" d, heart shape, gold etched floral designs, marked **225.00**

Candlestick Group, 12" h, modeled with lad and lass wearing brightly colored clothes, carrying flowers, dark blue foliate stems, scrolling brackets, gilt nozzles and bases, restoration, c1835, pr (A) **2048.00**

Charger
15" d, black with red roses and exotic birds **125.00**
16½" d, bust of young maiden with long brown curling hair, reserved on blue ground with roses, c1870–80, sgd "Rebecca Coleman, Minton's Art Pottery Studio Kensington Gore" mark (A) **1870.00**
22" d, painted blackbird perched on branch with apple blossoms, terra cotta glazed ground, c1878 (A) **920.00**
25¼" d, Urbino style, "The Triumph of Venus," Venus pulled in scallop shell by two dolphins surrounded by bacchanalian figures, Cupid nearby, wide band of figures and grotesques to border, c1858–62, inscribed "E. Lessore and Minton and Co," Retailer's label for Daniell & Son, 40 Wigmore St, London (A).................... **1870.00**

Cup and Saucer
"Dainty Sprays" pattern................... **30.00**
"Minton Rose" pattern................... **35.00**

Cup and Saucer, Demitasse
Blue on black bands of small enameled flowers, cream ground..................... **20.00**
"The Debutante" pattern.................. **35.00**

Dinner Service, Part
10 dinner plates, 10 salad plates, 10 bread and butter plates, 8 soup bowls, 10 cups and saucers, 2 demitasse cups and saucers, gravy boat, 2 serving bowls, creamer, sugar bowl, 2 platters, 12" l, "Ancestral" pattern **500.00**
Ironstone, 12 plates, 10½" d, 12 plates, 9" d, 12 plates, 8" d, 12 soup plates, 2 gravy boats with stands, 2 cov vegetable dishes, 2 cov sauce tureens, cov soup tureen with ladle, 4 graduated platters, well and tree platter, serving bowl, "Vandyke" pattern, transfer printed chinoiserie figural designs in Imari colors, c1863 (A) **2000.00**

Dresser Set, ring tree, cov box, tray, 12" l, 9" w, gold and green flowers on white ground ... **195.00**

Figure
5½" h, bone china flatback equestrian group of Don Quixote and Rozinante, in armour and green cape, named green scroll base, c1828 (A) **561.00**
6" h, Lord Byron in pink lined blue jacket, flowering waistcoat, yellow striped trousers, standing next to rock, rect base with "LD. BYRON at 19 YEARS of AGE" on front, c1830–40, "blue MINTON STOKE" mark (A)................................. **1150.00**
7¼" h, gallant in 18th C costume with tricorn hat, looking through spy glass, floral waistcoat, green stripped trousers, pink jacket, scroll molded base with gilt, c1830, underglaze "blue X'd swords" and incised mark (A)................................. **847.00**
9⅞" h, turquoise peacock pierced for flow-

ers, brown trimmed diamond base, imp
"MINTON" mark **400.00**
Flask
10⁵/₁₆" h, flattened circ body, enameled on
front and reverse in shades of pink, white,
yellow, green, and iron-red with sprays of
roses, poppies, flame vines, and other specimens, cylindrical neck, gilt loop handles
stenciled in brown with stylized palmettes,
gilt rim, oval foot, turquoise ground, imp
"MINTON, 1348" and cipher date for
1870, pr (A)........................... **770.00**
16⁶/₈" h, circ body, cherub seated on apple
branch reserved on brown ground, reverse
with kingfisher flying beside large yellow
irises on green ground, molded ring handles, flared rect foot, 1883, imp marks and
date code (A)......................... **800.00**
Jardinaire, 7⁷/₈" l, U shape body with two panels
painted with exotic birds in branches, turquoise ground, tooled gilt borders, white dbl
shell and scroll handles **475.00**
Pastille Burner, 4" h, thatched cottage with applied vines and multicolored flowers, green
base strewn with flowers and circ forms, repair
to chimney, c1835, 2pcs................. **1950.00**
Pitcher
5¹/₂" h, pink rose decoration, gold trim **25.00**
9" h, white ivy on cobalt ground, dtd 1845,
imp "MINTON" mark **450.00**
Plaque
8¹/₄" l, 15" h, Cherubs at play outside castle,
one with cherubs on pulley rope and young
girl looking at them from window above,
other with four cupids pushing at door, one
in tree above, lady's face looks down
through hole in door, tones of green, blue,
and gold, 1871, imp marks, date code to
one, painted retailer's mark for T. Goode
and Co, artist's monogram to front, carved
wood frames, pr (A).................... **5984.00**
17" d, portrait of classical woman about to
bite into apple, bright colors on turquoise
ground, painted by H.W. Foster, sgd and
dated, painted "MINTON'S 1877" and Re-
tailer's label for T. Goode and Co (A) **1589.00**
19¹/₂" d, circ, two cherubic children in shell
boat, blown across azure main by salmon-
pink scarf, 1871, imp mark and date code,
sgd "W.S. Coleman, printed Minton's Art
Studio" mark (A)...................... **4959.00**
Plate
8¹/₂" d, ironstone, "Oriental Japan" pattern,
multicolored and cobalt on white ground. **35.00**
9" d
Gold band emb with Grecian urns and palm
fronds on white ground, gold band with
ivory flange....................... **23.00**
Molded border with gold scrolls, set of 12 **225.00**
9¹/₁₆" d, iron-red. yellow, blue, russet, and
gray feathers in center cartouche edged in
tooled gilt scrolls and floral sprays, emerald
green ground, rim edged with molded
scrolls and gilding, 1830–35 (A) **385.00**
9¹/₄" d
Enameled head of classical woman, scrolling gilded and enameled borders, c1866
(A) **560.00**
Hp landscape scenes in center, pink and
gold border, imp "MINTONS" mark, set
of 4 (A)........................... **393.00**

9³/₈" d, gilt bird and insect on leafy turquoise
branch, border of gilt cartouches with white
butterflies on turquoise ground, pierced
rim, dtd 1881........................ **475.00**
9¹/₂" d
Painted orchids on cream ground, gilt dentil
rim, c1883, printed "crowned globe"
mark, set of 12 .... **1500.00**
Two gilt and painted birds perched on
branch, turquoise ground, gilt and
painted basketweave border reserved
with oval panel of crowned monogram at
top, c1875 (A)..................... **410.00**
10" d
Bone china, pink border with gilt scrolled
and foliate rim, set of 11 (A) **770.00**
Brown glazed acid etched scene of eagle
grasping rabbit, imp "Minton" mark.... **275.00**
10¹/₄" d, "Clare," classical portrait in center,
paneled border in rust, orange, and black,
1878, "Minton" mark.................. **72.50**
Platter
14³/₄" l, "Hazlemore" pattern **75.00**
15" l, "Vermont" pattern **115.00**
Potpourri Vase, Cov, 10¹/₂" d, painted panel of
elderly lady and man on bridge with cottages,
panel of summer flowers, applied multicolored flowering branches, green entwined
branch handles, c1825–30, "blue X'd swords"
mark (A)............................. **1200.00**
Scent Bottle, 4" h, baluster shape, encrusted with
colored flowers and foliage, gilded bulbous
neck, floral cluster stopper, c1830, pr (A) **1030.00**
Tazza, 9¹/₂" d, 3" h, hp roses on green ground,
gold and brown border **100.00**
Teapot, 3¹/₂" h, miniature, sides with applied
trailing colored flowers, gilt accents, rustic
handle and spout, c1830, "blue X'd swords"
mark (A)............................. **400.00**
Vase
4⁷/₈, 5" h, lily of the valley, formed by overlapping green leaves applied with three sprigs
of yellow centered white biscuit blossoms,
three dark green leaves, scroll molded base
dotted and edged in gilding, c1830, pr (A) **1925.00**
9¹/₂" h, encrusted with painted flowers and
foliage, painted insects, c1830, "blue X'd
swords and M" marks (A)............... **340.00**
10" h, Art Deco stylized vert dripping leaves,
mauve ground **495.00**
11¹/₂" h, painted panels of flowers on ledge,
blue enamel ground, molded stiff leaf borders, c1825, drilled base, pr (A)......... **6935.00**
19⁷/₈" h, painted on front with pink and red
roses, reverse with lilies and berried
branches, turquoise ground, sq base with
gilt pillars at corners with panels of flowers
in colors, Grecian style handles **1150.00**
Vase, Cov
9" h
Enameled white roses connected with gilt
scrolls, pierced neck with applied pierced
scroll handles, gadrooned cov with pine
cone finial, restored, c1895 .... **1100.00**
Waisted cylinder shape, oval medallion with
young girl feeding chicks, reserved on turquoise ground, raised gilt detail, two
pierced scroll handles, domed cov with
knob, c1895...................... **1000.00**
14³/₄" h, oviform body, Sevres style, figures
before ruined castle, within tooled gilt bor-

der, bleu celeste ground, curved scroll handles, supported on waisted stem by sq base,
matching domed cov, c1875, imp "MIN-
TON, incised Minton and shape no. 469"
(A)...................................... **2200.00**
15" h, ovoid body painted with oval shaped
shipping scenes on front, rural river scene
on reverse, green ground, dbl handles with
pierced gilt chain motif, sq base, bud finial,
imp "MINTON" mark, pr **2470.00**
Wall Sconce, 18" h, three scrolling foliate
branches in turquoise and gilding, white
ground, restored, c1878–80, imp "MINTON,"
date code (A)........................... **695.00**

MOCHA WARE

Staffordshire, England
1760–1939

History: Inexpensive utilitarian wares with tree-like,
feather, moss, and worm designs, known as "Mocha"
wares were made during the 19th century. The name
came from the mocha stone or moss agate which the
design resembled.

William Adams made the first examples at his Cobridge
factory in 1799. Since these wares were mainly used in
public houses, jugs, tankards, coffeepots, porringers, and
butter dishes were the principal shapes that were manufactured.

Basically the decorative portion of a piece consisted of
a broad band of colored slip, usually blue, gray, or coffee
colored in tone, upon which was the design itself. To
achieve the "tree" design, mocha ware potters utilized a
mixture called "tea" that was put into the slip while still
damp, thus causing the color to spread out into tree-like
fronds that contrasted with the white earthenware beneath. On some examples, black rings were added.

Mocha ware exhibited a large variety of patterns. Arbo-
ration was made with an acidic solution, forming patterns
such as Tree, Shrub, Fern, Seaweed, and Landscape. Cat's
Eye and Worm patterns evolved from the use of a three-
chambered slip bottle. Marbled and splotched pieces
were made by using a blow pipe.

When the background was green, brown, cream, or
orange the designs usually were brown or black. Ale mugs,
chamber pots, jugs, pitchers, and shrimp and nut meaures
are the forms most frequently found with mocha decoration.

It is rare to find a piece with a maker's mark. Among the
known manufacturers of Mocha ware are Edge and Malkin in Burslem between 1871 and 1890 and T. G. Green
& Co. in Derbyshire from 1864 to 1939. Additional mocha
ware makers include Adams of Tunstall, Cork and Edge of
Burslem, Broadhurst of Fenton, Tams of Longton, MacIntyre of Cobridge, Pinder and Bourne of Burslem, Green of
Church Gresley, and Maling of New Castle-on-Tyne.

Museum: City Museum and Art Gallery, Stoke-on-Trent,
England.

Bowl
4⅜" d, emb green band, black, white, blue,
and orange marbleizing (A)............. **715.00**
6¼" d, gray with emb green band and black
seaweed, crazing (A) **450.00**
7¼" d, orange band with black and white
stripes and black seaweed, emb ribs accented in green, chips and hairline (A) ... **250.00**
7⅜" d, earthworm on white band with black,

Mug, 6" h, worm and cat's eye in shades of
brown, age crack, $1225.00

Pitcher, 5¾" h, brown stripes, mint green incised arrowheads, chip on spout, $475.00

tan, and blue stripes, emb vert rib band accented in blue, chips reglued (A)........ **125.00**
9" d, blue seaweed on yellowware body ... **425.00**
Chamber Pot, Cov, 9" d, 8" h, emb green
band with leaf and cat's eye design in tan,
olive, dark brown, and white, emb leaf handle, hairline (A) **550.00**
Condiment Set, open pot, two pots with hinged
pewter lids, bottle with screw lid, green marbleizing on creamware, repairs (A) **350.00**
Creamer, 4⅛" h, barrel shape, blue, cream, red-
brown, and rust marbleized surface, 19th C
(A)................................... **440.00**
Cup and Saucer, black seaweed on beige
ground, white int on cup (A) **440.00**
Cup and Saucer, Handleless
Emb blue rim with black seaweed on orange
ground, (A)........................... **1430.00**
Gray and white stripes (A)................ **25.00**
Measure, 6¼" h, black seaweed on dark green
band with blue and black stripes, green rim
band, emb leaf handle, metal seal with "V.R."
(A)................................... **150.00**
Mug
2⅝"h, plain grayish band with blue stripes,
embossed leaf handle (A) **40.00**
3¾" h, white band with green seaweed
and gray-black stripes, yellow body, hairlines (A)............................. **165.00**
4¼" h, gray band with dark brown stripes
and earthworm design, emb leaf handle,
hairlines (A)......................... **330.00**
4⅜"h, black seaweed design on a light blue
band with black and blue stripes, marked
"Pint' (A)............................ **150.00**
4¾" h, black, blue, white, and yellow ochre
stripes with white polka dots, emb leaf handle, cracks (A) **275.00**
5⅝" h, emb bands with green, brown, black,
and tan stripes, blue, white, and black

rope squiggles, emb leaf handle, hairlines (A)................................. **880.00**

6" h

Center band of green seaweed on teal ground........................... **350.00**

Emb bands with green, black, white, gray-green, and blue stripes, center band of orange-yellow with white interlocking rings, emb leaf handle, repairs (A)...... **577.00**

Imp checkerboard pattern and earthworm in blue, brown, and ecru (A) **770.00**

6 1/4"h, black seaweed design on a tan band with black and blue stripes (A)........... **75.00**

Mug, Cov, 4 3/8" h, brown and black stripes with black seaweed on orange band, emb leaf handle (A)................................. **770.00**

Mustard Pot

2" h, gray band with black seaweed and stripes, missing lid (A)................... **40.00**

2 1/4" h, earthworm design on blue band with dark brown and orange stripes, emb leaf handle (A)............................ **402.00**

3 7/8" h, blue bands with cat's eyes and stripes in tan, brown, and white, emb leaf handle, repair to lid (A) **1320.00**

Pitcher

4 1/4" h, emb vert ribs with black stripes and green rim, emb leaf handle (A) **85.00**

4 3/4" h, brown and rust fluted and banded decoration (A) **110.00**

5 1/2" h, white band with green seaweed and black stripes, yellow ware body, "Made in England" mark........................ **220.00**

5 3/4" h, black, blue, and white stripes with rope squiggles on wide orange band, emb leaf handle (A) **577.00**

6" h, band of blue earthworms on brown ground, imp bands with green enamel accents, base crack....................... **650.00**

6 1/4" h, black stripes and blue bands with cat's eyes, emb leaf handle (A) **440.00**

6 3/4" h

Blue center band with earthworm, top and bottom brown bands with white curved lines (A)............................. **880.00**

Chocolate brown with white stripes and emb rib bands accented in green, applied leaf decoration on spout, hairlines and chips (A) **525.00**

Earthworm design on wide orange band with brown stripes (A)................ **880.00**

6 7/8" h, gray band with black stripes and black seaweed design, emb ribs accented in blue, emb leaf handle (A) **400.00**

7" h

Blue and black banding with white dots and waves (A) **385.00**

White underglaze with blue and gray banding, brown and white dot pattern (A) **1100.00**

7 1/8" h, herringbone bands with cat's eye at middle, earthworm design top and base, brown, blue, olive, tan, and white, emb leaf handle (A)........................... **1590.00**

7 1/4" h, multiple blue bands with seaweed design (A)........................... **350.00**

7 3/8" h, yellow and ochre with dark brown seaweed, emb ribs on neck accented in green, emb leaf handle, rim hairline (A)... **1100.00**

7 1/2" h, stripes and bands of blue, dark brown and white with white wavy lines and foliage

designs in blue, tan, and dark brown, hairlines (A).............................. **2255.00**

8" h

"Blue and olive green horizontal banding, small foot (A)........................ **275.00**

Ecru center band with earthworm, top and base bands of sienna with earthworms . **1500.00**

Tan bands with cat's eye design and leaf garland, black and white stripes and emb herringbone decorations accented in blue, emb leaf spout and handle, repair to spout (A)............................. **875.00**

8 1/4" h, orange, black, and white tree and dot pattern on center gray band, green and orange imp and banded patterns (A)....... **2530.00**

8 1/2" h, ironstone, wide blue bands with black and white stripes, emb leaf handle (A).... **385.00**

Pitcher, Cov, 5 3/4" h, two broad blue bands with raised white dots, cov repaired, 19th C (A).. **302.00**

Salt, 2 1/8" h, ftd, yellow ware, white band with blue seaweed (A) **275.00**

Shaker

3 3/4" h, black seaweed on center brown band, black, brown, and cream rings **850.00**

4" h, emb green band, blue, white, and brown stripes and foliage on orange band (A) ... **880.00**

4 1/4" h

Emb green stripe with bands and stripes of white, dark brown, and orange (A)..... **700.00**

Gray band with black and white stripes and black seaweed, emb ribbing on shoulder accented in green, cracks (A).......... **200.00**

5 1/4" h, emb blue and white stripes with black and white checkerboard band (A)........ **500.00**

Tankard

4 3/4" h, wide band of blue, gray, tan, and cream, hairline (A)..................... **137.00**

4 7/8" h, creamware, multiple blue banding . **75.00**

5" h, seaweed design on wide blue band (A) . **176.00**

6 3/4" h, broad band of marbled gray, tan, and cream, pewter cov, 19th C.............. **250.00**

7" h, emb bands with white, green, and black stripes, wide orange band with black seaweed, pewtewr lid, hairline on handle (A). **742.00**

Teapot, 4 7/8" h, marbleized brown with emb blue ribs (A) **1130.00**

Waste Bowl

5 1/4" d, earthworm design on gray band with dark brown stripes, emb green rim (A) ... **770.00**

5 1/2" d

Blue and black striping (A) **65.00**

Light orange band with blue stripes and brown and white cat's eyes, hairline (A) **115.00**

6 1/4" d, earthworm design on white band with blue and dark brown stripes (A)..... **880.00**

6 3/8" d, gray-green band and blue stripes with earthworm in brown and white (A) **137.00**

MOORCROFT   c1919

Burslem, Staffordshire
1897 to Present

History: William Moorcroft was first employed as a potter by James Macintyre & Co., Ltd. of Burslem in 1897. Moorcroft's early works included vases, bowls, and biscuit jars that were decorated in blue, red, and gold plant forms called Aurelian ware.

Moorcroft also made Florian ware in a wide variety of shapes and types of decorations. Florian ware featured poppies, violets, or cornflowers applied in relief or portrayed in slip trail outlines. It was marketed under various trade names such as: Claremont, a toadstool design; Hazeldene, a landscape with trees; Honesty; Pansy; Pomegrante; and, Flamminian luster wares. The principal markets were in London, New York, Paris, and San Francisco. The signature "W. Moorcroft" appeared on each piece along with the standard Macintyre printed mark.

In 1913 Moocroft built his own small factory, the Washington Works, at Burslem, employing potters and decorators with whom he worked James Macintyre & Co. Moorcroft continued the floral styles, but now used simpler and bolder designs. Dark colored exotic flowers adorned many pieces. Landscapes were done in the trailed outline technique. Monochrome luster glazes were produced until the 1920s, followed by flambe glazes in the decade that followed. The flambe or transmutation glazes, provided the most interested for Moorcroft.

W. Moorcroft was appointed potter to Queen Mary in 1928. The impressed phrase "Potter to H.M. The Queen" was added to his mark. During the 1930s fruits, fish, birds, and boats joined the traditional decorative motifs. Matte glazes found favor. When Moorcraft died in 1945, Walter, his eldest son, continued the Moorcroft company.

At first Walter used his father's designs. In the 1950s, he developed a more personal style with exotic designs and more dramatic use of color, especially with the eccentric Caribbean and marine life designs. He continued the flambe experiments and increased the range of flambe colors until 1973.

Walter was in charge for more than forty years. Changes during that time included the use of electric kilns, and casting replaced throwing. They still utilized William's styles and basic methods. During the 1970s, Walter designed the magnolia range.

In 1984 Walter's brother John became managing director, and the Moorcroft family sold a controlling interest to the three Roper brothers. This relationship lasted only two years, and the Dennis and Edwards families took over. Walter retired in 1987, but he is still involved in designs.

Marks: Various types of marks include the Moorcroft signature or initials, printed or impressed factory marks, retailers' marks, design registration numbers, and pattern or shape marks. Some paper labels with printed factory marks also were used starting in the 1920s. Rectangular ones were used first. After the awarding of the Royal Warrant in 1928, circular paper labels were used until 1978 when the Royal Warrant expired.

References: Paul Atterbury, *Moorcroft Pottery*, Richard Dennis and Hugh Edwards, 1987; A. W. Coysh, *British Art Pottery, 1870–1940*, Charles E. Tuttle, 1976; Richard Dennis, *William & Walter Moorcroft, 1897–1973*, an exhibition catalog, 1973.

Museum: Everson Museum of Art, Syracuse, N.Y.

Bowl
    3½" h, waisted body, "Tudor Rose," blue and rose circ flowerheads and foliage, light green ground, c1904, "green W.Moorcroft des. printed MADE FOR LIBERTY & CO. Rd. No. 431137" mark (A) **900.00**
    4¾" h, red, purple, green, and yellow toadstools on mottled green ground, restored, 1903–13, "green W. Moorcroft des, MADE

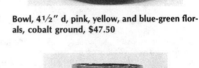

Bowl, 4½" d, pink, yellow, and blue-green florals, cobalt ground, $47.50

Vase, 10½" h, "Fresia" pattern, blue, mustard, and dk red florals, mustard ground, blue int, c1935, signature mark, $1950.00

FOR LIBERTY & Co. Rd. No. 420081" mark (A) **528.00**
5½" d, rose florals on green ground, bluegreen pedestal, imp "Moorcroft" mark . . . **55.00**
5¾" d, light green and red leaves on shaded green ground, blue and green int **145.00**
6½" d, 3" h, Spanish design, iris, cornflower, and tulip, "green W. Moorcroft" mark. . . . **875.00**
7" d, "Pomegranate and Grape" design on dark blue ground on ext and int, imp signature mark **475.00**
7⅜" d, yellow, green, and red orchids, white flowers on dark blue ext ground, imp signature mark **375.00**
8¼" d, flambe, reds, oranges, and yellows leaves and berries, red and blue fruit dividing mottled blue and smoked red ground, hairline, c1930, imp "Royal MADE IN ENGLAND, blue W. Moorcroft" marks . . **540.00**
8¾" d, mauve and yellow freesia in center, green ground, c1935 . . . . **310.00**
9¼" d, "Eventide Landscape," int and ext with large and small trees in hilly landscape in shades of brown, blue, and green with speckled leaves, graduated russet and orange-red sky, c1925, imp "MOORCROFT MADE IN ENGLAND, blue W. Moorcroft" marks (A) **2277.00**
9½" d, "Peacock" flambe, int with peacock

feathers, ext incised with bands and feathers, c1930, imp "MOORCROFT, MADE IN ENGLAND, blue W. Moorcroft" mark (A). **1689.00**

9³/₄" d, dark purple pansies on blue-green ground on int, c1913–16 .... **615.00**

9⁷/₈" d, "Apple Blossom," branches of flowers and berries in tones of green, haircrack, c1914, imp "Moorcroft Burslem 1914, green W. Moorcroft, 1914" marsk (A).... **1138.00**

11" d, pomegrante, purple and red fruit and green leaves, pale green and dark blue ground, two handles, c1920, "green W. Moorcroft, imp MOORCROFT MADE IN ENGLAND" mark (A)........................ **802.00**

Box

3³/₄" h, cylindrical, berry and leaves in dark red, yellow, green, and blue, blue signature and royal mark (A) **440.00**

6" d, red and yellow hibiscus on dark blue ground............................. **250.00**

Candlestick

3³/₈" h, pink and yellow flowers on cobalt ground, script mark, pr.................. **65.00**

7¹/₈" h, "Pomegranate" design, imp "Moorcroft Made in England" marks, pr........ **750.00**

Compote, 7" d, 3¹/₂" h, pink and green flowers on green ground........................ **135.00**

Dish, 7³/₈" d, int with speckled blue and green large tree flanked by two smaller trees in hilly landscape against mottled deep blue sky, raised on plated spreading metal base, c1925, imp "MOORCROFT MADE IN ENGLAND, blue W.M." marks........................ **575.00**

Ginger Jar, 6¹/₂" h, magnolia design **180.00**

Jam Jar, 3" h, "Pomegranate" design, SP lid, c1922................................. **475.00**

Jar, Cov

4" h, raised design of trees on hills, red body, dbl handles, imp "William Moorcroft" mark........................ **175.00**

7¹/₂" h, "Persian," claret, crimson, green, yellow, and blue leaves and palmetes on light green ground, c1914–20, imp "MOORCROFT, BURSLEM ENGLAND', script W. Moorcroft" marks (A).................. **3645.00**

Jardinaire

7¹/₂" h, "Claremont," orange, red, and yellow toadstools reserved on shaded rust and blue ground, two loop handles, c1930 (A) **4865.00**

9¹/₂" h, ovoid shape, "Spanish," red and blue flowers with brown foliage, mottled green and brown ground, c1912–16, imp "1075 and green W. Moorcroft" mark (A) **8448.00**

Jug, 17" h, blue and green tall trees in hills on mottled yellow and blue ground, loop handle, restored, c1903–13, "Made For Liberty & Co. W. Moorcroft" marks (A)................. **2700.00**

Lamp Base, 11³/₄" h, "Fuchsia," ruby floral petals, green toned foliage and stems, reserved on yellow luster ground (A) **3000.00**

Planter, 12¹/₄" l, 8" w, 2³/₄" h, "Claremont" design in rect, purple, green, blue, and yellow **1525.00**

Plate, 10¹/₄" d, two birds in blue, pink, brown, and gray tones, white ground, c1934–38, "blue signature W. Moorcroft" mark (A) ... **1550.00**

Potpourri, 5" h, "Pomegranate and Pansy" design in green, red, yellow, and blue, pierced cov, c1905, "green signature and Made for Liberty & Co." mark (A).................. **1106.00**

Soup Plate, 9³/₄" d, blue and purple orchids on white ground **50.00**

Tobacco Jar, 6" d, pink cornflowers on aquamarine foliate reserves, light green ground, c1900–06 (A)........................... **1775.00**

Vase

3¹/₂" h, "Pomegranate" design, c1922..... **275.00**

4" h, ovoid body, yellow, red, and blue toadstools on green stems over mottled blue ground, c1915–20, imp "M42 C, MOORCROFT MADE IN ENGLAND" mark (A) .. **1252.00**

5" h, "Clematis" design with flame glaze, purple-blue irid highlights **310.00**

5¹/₄" h, large hibiscus on dark blue ground. **250.00**

5¹/₂" h

Columbines on white ground........... **130.00**

Pomegranates, leaves, and berries in cranberry red, mustard, and blue on dark blue ground, imp "W. Moorcroft" mark..... **300.00**

5³/₄" h, poppies on blue ground, c1927 ... **385.00**

5⁷/₈" h, conical body, Macintyre, lilac design, groups of small yellow flowers within oval blue ground panels flanked by pale green leaf forms over white ground between gilt borders, flaring circ foot, swelling neck, short gilt rim, c1905, printed Macintyre mark, black printed retailers mark for Stonier & Co. of Liverpool, "green W. Moorcroft' (A) **1252.00**

6" h

Macintyre, red poppies and blue forget-me-nots, white ground **1320.00**

Yellow, red, green, and blue orchids on blue and flambe ground, imp "Moorcroft Made in England" mark (A) **1310.00**

6¹/₂" h

Baluster shape, incised large flowers and leaves in pink, blue-purple, and green on shaded light green to blue ground, imp "W. Moorcroft" mark **300.00**

Circle of anemones on blue to green ground........................... **250.00**

Florian, green and gold flower and tulip bud design, "green W. Moorcroft" mark.... **1150.00**

6⁷/₈" h, globular body, large red poppies on short buff stems, green foliage, mottled deep blue ground, short flaring cylindrical neck, c1925, imp "MOORCROFT BURSLEM ENGLAND, green W. Moorcroft" marks (A)............................ **1480.00**

7" h

Florian, iris in blue shades, raised slip design................................ **885.00**

Macintyre, red florals, vines, gold trim, white ground, loop handles................. **375.00**

Orange hibiscus on olive green ground... **250.00**

White decorative panels with blue flowers, blue speckled ground, "Moorcroft" mark (A) **250.00**

7¹/₄" h, Macintyre, green and gold Florian tulips, c1903......................... **1010.00**

7¹/₂" h

Blue and red clematis on yellow-green ground, "W. Moorcroft" mark........ **305.00**

Painted and molded large red and green flowers, green and blue ground glaze, imp "MOORCROFT" mark (A)....... **260.00**

8" h

Baluster shape, apples and blueberries in autumn colors, indigo blue ground glaze, imp "MOORCROFT" mark (A)....... **200.00**

Cylindrical form, pale puce and blue cornflowers with green stems and foliage on pale green ground, flaring rim and foot, two flat loop handles, c1910–15, "green MADE FOR LIBERTY & Co. W Moorcroft" marks (A)...................... **2960.00**

Florian, iris, blue flowerheads and foliage outlined in white slip, c1900, incised "W.M des, printed Florian Ware mark, M 705 in blue, & Rd. No. 326689" mark (A)........................... **675.00**

"Pomegranate" design, blue ground, imp "W. Moorcroft Potter to H.M. Queen" mark................................. **375.00**

8¼" h, "Pomegranate and Pansy" design in red, yellow, green, and blue, green signature mark (A) **990.00**

8½" h, forget-me-nots, blue and yellow on cream ground, two handles, "W. Moorcroft" mark........................... **875.00**

9" h, slender waisted tapering cylindrical form, "Hazeldene," tones of green and blue with tall trees in foreground and smaller trees in distance, script "green W. Moorcroft," 1914, and 2037 marks (A) **1411.00**

9¼" h

Baluster body, tree lined landscape in tones of blue and green against a blue sky, flaring rim, c1925–30, imp "W. MOORCROFT," Royal Warrant, blue painted "W.Moorcroft" marks (A)............. **1707.00**

Ovoid body, central band of red and purple fruit and green foliage on deep blue ground, between incised pale blue bands and two narrow bands with stylized foliate scrollwork, deep blue glazed rims, c1925–30, imp "MOORCROFT, MADE IN ENGLAND, blue W. Moorcroft" marks (A) **2277.00**

9¾" h, large berry and leaf design in shades of blue, cream, and brown, blue signature and royal mark (A) **660.00**

10½" h, squat with trumpet neck, Florian, light and dark blue peacock feathers, "Florian Ware, W. Moorcroft des" mark (A) **3275.00**

12½" h, grape and leaf design, light green ground on top to blue base **975.00**

13" h, "Claremont," toadstools in red, blue, and green on mottled yellow and green ground, c1905, "green W. Moorcroft des," printed "MADE FOR LIBERTY & CO. reg #420081" marks (A) **564.00**

13⅜" h, cylindrical, saltglaze, "Dawn," wide horiz band on blue and pink trees, rolling hills, blue, yellow, and white zig-zag borders, c1928, imp "MOORCROFT MADE IN ENGLAND, green W. Moorcroft" mark (A) **1800.00**

16" h, cylindrical body, "Flamminian," flared at neck, bulbous base, three foliate roundels on mottled red ground, sgd "green W. Moorcroft, imp 153, dated 10–1913' (A) . **1693.00**

MULBERRY WARE

Staffordshire, England
1835–1855

History: Mulberry ware was made by many of the same Staffordshire potters that produced Flow Blue. In fact, many patterns with identical design and name are found on both types of wares. The bulk of the Mulberry ware

production occurred during the early Victorian period, i.e., 1835–1855.

The mulberry color was achieved by a chemical combination of red, brown, gray, and purple dyes. Mulberry refered to the color of berries from the English black mulberry trees. Some mulberry patterns on earthenware or ironstone were "flown," producing a soft, hazy effect. Most were presented with a sharp, clear design.

Mulberry ware was a response to the public's need for something new and different. Its popularity did not last. Few pieces were made after 1855.

References: Petra Williams, *Flow Blue China & Mulberry Ware, Similarity and Value Guide,* Fountain House East, rev. ed., 1981.

Collecting Hints: Previously, mulberry prices always had been priced higher than Flow Blue examples. However, in the past few years, there has been a reversal. Mulberry ware now sells for about one-third less than the prevailing price for a comparable Flow Blue piece.

"Abbey" pattern
Platter, 13½" l, 10¼" w, 1850, "W. Adams & Sons" mark......................... **125.00**

"Alleghany" pattern
Plate, 7¼" d, 1850, "Goodfellow" mark... **30.00**

"Athens" pattern
Cup Plate, Adams **45.00**
Plate
8½" d, Adams....................... **48.00**
10" d............................... **39.00**
10½" d **29.00**
Vegetable Bowl, 10" l, 7⅞" w, eight sided rect, 1849, "W. Adams & Sons" mark.... **120.00**

"Balmoral" pattern
Soap Dish, Cov, "S.H.& Co." mark **75.00**

"Bochara" pattern
Platter, 14½" l **100.00**

"Bryonia" pattern
Dessert Dish, 5⅛" l, "Utzshneider & Co." mark.............................. **15.00**
Plate, 9½" d........................... **45.00**
Sauce Dish, 5" d....................... **10.00**

"Calcutta" pattern
Cup and Saucer, handleless **45.00**
Plate, 8½" d........................... **47.00**

"Castle Scenery" pattern
Plate
7¼" d, twelve sides, c1850, Jacob Furnival................................. **22.00**
9 1/16" d **32.00**

Plate, 9¼" d, "Athens" pattern, Charles Meigh, (A) $50.00

"Chusan" pattern
Compote, 10 3/8" l, 9" w, 6 1/8" h, rect,
   c1845, "Podmore, Walker & Co." mark .. **390.00**
Plate, 8 1/4" d, "P.W.& Co." mark **20.00**
Platter
   17" l **185.00**
   18" l **200.00**
Teabowl and saucer **55.00**
"Corea" pattern
Platter, 12 3/4" l, 9 3/8" w, 1840, "J. Clement-
   son" mark **145.00**
"Corean" pattern
Creamer **135.00**
Cup Plate **50.00**
Plate
   7 3/4" d **35.00**
   8 1/2" d, "P.W.& Co." mark **30.00**
   9" d, "P.W.& Co." mark **95.00**
   9 1/2" d **50.00**
   9 3/4" d **60.00**
   10" d **50.00**
Platter
   15 1/2" l **165.00**
   15 3/4" l **250.00**
   18" l, "P.W.& Co." mark **350.00**
Teapot
   9 1/4" h, oct shape, 1850, "Podmore
   Walker & Co." mark **275.00**
   Hex shape, pedestal base, 1850, "Podmore
   Walker & Co." mark **465.00**
Waste Bowl, "Podmore Walker & Co." mark **75.00**
"Corella" pattern
Plate, 6 3/4" d, 1855, "Barker & Son" mark . **28.00**
Plate, 10 1/2" d **25.00**
"Cyprus" pattern
Plate, Davenport
   7" d **30.00**
   9" d **65.00**
Teapot
   9 1/2" h, eight panel, bulbus shape, 1850,
   Davenport **350.00**
   10 1/2" h, Davenport **350.00**
"Dehli" pattern
Plate, 7 3/4" d, "M.T.& Co." mark **30.00**
Relish Dish, 8 1/2" l, 5 1/2" w, "M.T.& Co."
   mark **65.00**
"Dora" pattern
Cup and Saucer, handleless, 1856, "Challinor"
   mark **75.00**
Plate
   9" d **40.00**
   10" d, 1856, "Challinor" mark **45.00**
   10 1/4" d, 1856, "Challinor" mark **45.00**
"Flora" pattern
Cup and Saucer, handleless, 1845, "Thomas
   Walker" mark **75.00**
Plate, 8 3/4" d **40.00**
Soap Dish, 3 pieces, "P.W.& Co." marks **150.00**
Teapot, oct shape, 1845, "Thomas Walker"
   mark **250.00**
"Foliage" pattern
Cup and Saucer, handleless, 1850, "Edward
   Walley" mark **65.00**
Plate, 9" d **40.00**
Teabowl and Saucer, "Edward Walley" mark **65.00**
"Genoa" pattern
Plate, 9 1/2" d, Davenport **30.00**
"Heath's Flower" pattern
Soup Plate, 10 1/2" d **95.00**

"Hong" pattern
Platter, 13 1/4" d **95.00**
"Hyson" pattern
Sugar Bowl **150.00**
"Japan" pattern
Porringer, 5 1/4" d, age stain on rim **35.00**
"Jeddo" pattern
Creamer **125.00**
Cup and Saucer, handleless **50.00**
Cup Plate, 4" d, 1845, "W. Adams & Sons"
   mark **68.00**
Gravy Boat **65.00**
Pitcher and Bowl, c1845, "Adams & Sons"
   mark **695.00**
Plate
   6 1/4" d **28.00**
   7 1/2" d **30.00**
   7 3/4" d **35.00**
   9 1/4" d, 1845, "W. Adams & Sons" mark **45.00**
   9 3/8" d **45.00**
   10 1/4" d **35.00**
Platter
   11 1/2" d **120.00**
   12 3/8" l, 9 1/2" w, 1845, "W. Adams &
   Sons" mark **125.00**
   13 1/2" d **145.00**
   15 1/2" l, 12" w, c1850 . . . . **115.00**
Teapot **195.00**
Vegetable Bowl, 9" d **125.00**
"Kyber" pattern
Teapot, 8 1/2" h, paneled sides, restored,
   1870, "J. Meir & Son" mark **165.00**
"Lozere" pattern
Cup and Saucer, handleless **45.00**
"Madras" pattern
Plate, 8 1/8" d, hairline, 1870, "Wood & Bag-
   galey" mark **18.00**
"Medina" pattern,
Plate, 9 1/2" d **45.00**
"Moss Rose" pattern
Plate, 9 1/2" d **35.00**
"Moultan" pattern
Platter, 22" l, 17" w, 1838, "Wood & Brown-
   field" mark **350.00**
"Neva" pattern
Pitcher, 9" h **200.00**
Plate, 9" d **40.00**
"Ning Po" pattern
Mug **150.00**
"Pelew" pattern
Plate, 9 3/4" d, "Challinor" mark **55.00**
Teabowl and Saucer **55.00**
Teapot, 8" h, eight sides, c1840, "black Chu-
   san, P.W.& Co." mark **225.00**
"Percy" pattern
Cup and Saucer, handleless **78.00**
Toddy Cup, 2 3/4" h, twelve sides, c1850, imp
   "FM" mark, set of 10 . . . . **595.00**
"Peru" pattern
Plate
   7 1/4" d, 1850, "Holdcroft & Co." mark .. **30.00**
   8" d, "Holdcroft & Co." mark **28.00**
"Peruvian" pattern
Cup Plate, 4 1/4" d, 1849, "John Wedge
   Wood" mark **65.00**
Plate
   7 1/2" d, "J. Wedge Wood" mark **30.00**
   9 1/4" d, "John Wedge Wood" mark **50.00**
'Rhone Scenery" pattern
Cup and Saucer **55.00**

Gravy Boat	**120.00**
Plate	
5⅛" d, 1843–55, T.J.& J. Mayer	**20.00**
7¼" d	**30.00**
7½" d	**30.00**
7¾" d, 1843–55, T.J.& J. Mayer	**35.00**
8½" d, "T. J. Meyers" mark	**45.00**
8⅝" d, scalloped rim, "black T.J.& J. Mayer, Rhone Scenery" mark	**20.00**
8¾" d, 1843–55, T.J.& J. Mayer	**40.00**
9½" d	**50.00**
9¾" d, 1850, Mayer	**45.00**
Platter	
12¼" l, 9½" w, 1850, Mayer	**120.00**
13⅜" l, 10¼" w, 1850, Mayer	**160.00**
15¾" l	**125.00**
Tureen, 14" h, Underplate, 16" l, 1843–55, T.J.& J. Mayer	**450.00**
"Rose" pattern	
Cup and Saucer	**55.00**
Plate	
9" d, 1862, "Challinor" mark	**40.00**
10" d, 1862, "Challinor" mark	**65.00**
"Scinde" pattern	
Plate	
7½" d, 1841, "Thomas Walker" mark . . .	**55.00**
10½" d	**95.00**
Platter, 15½" l, "P.W.& Co." mark	**150.00**
Teabowl and Saucer	**52.00**
"Shapoo" pattern	
Plate, 8½" d, 1842, "T & R Boote" mark . .	**32.00**
Waste Bowl	**95.00**
"Singan" pattern	
Coffee Pot	**100.00**
Plate, 9¼" d, "T. Goodfellow" mark	**55.00**
"Susa" pattern	
Cup and Saucer, "Chas. Meigh & Co." mark	**55.00**
"Tavoy" pattern	
Plate, 8¾" d, 1845, "Thomas Walker" mark	**45.00**
"Temple" pattern	
Plate	
7" d, "P.W.& Co." mark	**22.00**
7¾" d, "P.W.& Co." mark	**35.00**
8¾" d, "P.W.& Co." mark	**25.00**
9½" d, "P.W.& Co." mark	**55.00**
Platter, 14" l, 10½" w	**110.00**
Tea Tile, "P.W.& Co." mark.	**75.00**
"Tonquin" pattern	
Plate, 6" d, "J. Heath" mark	**30.00**
Platter, 10¾" l, Heath	**95.00**
Sugar Bowl, Cov, Heath	**165.00**
Vegetable Bowl, Open, 8" l, Heath	**75.00**
Waste Bowl, Heath	**95.00**
"Udina" pattern	
Cup and Saucer, 1850, "J. Clementson" mark	**85.00**
Plate, 9¼" d, 1850, "J. Clementson" mark.	**48.00**
"Venture" pattern	
Vegetable Dish, Cov, 9" l, 7" h, oct shape, tab handles, 1855, "Ralph Hammersly" mark .	**325.00**
"Venus" pattern	
Plate	
8" d, "P.W.& Co." mark	**48.00**
8¾" d, "Podmore, Walker" mark	**50.00**
"Vincennes" pattern	
Cup and Saucer, handleless, 1857, "John Alcock" mark.	**42.00**
Plate	
6" d, "John Alcock, Cobridge" mark	**25.00**

8" d, "John Alcock, Cobridge" mark	**75.00**
9½" d	**50.00**
Platter, 15½" l	**165.00**
Sauce Tureen, 8" h, with underplate, oct shape, 1857, "John Alcock" mark.	**475.00**
Sugar Bowl, oct shape, 1857, "John Alcock" mark.	**210.00**
"Washinton Vase" pattern	
Creamer.	**19.00**
Cup, handleless, 1850, "P.W.& Co." mark . .	**20.00**
Cup and Saucer.	**55.00**
Plate	
8¾" d	**45.00**
9" d	**50.00**
Relish Dish	**85.00**
Sugar Bowl, Cov	**225.00**
Vegetable Bowl, Open, 8" d	**95.00**
"Whampoa" pattern	
Plate, 9½" d, 1840, "Mellor & Vernables" mark	**70.00**
"Wreath" pattern	
Teabowl and Saucer	**55.00**

c1930

LIMOGES
FRANCE
c1895

MUSTACHE CUPS

Germany
c1935

English, Continental
1830 to Present

History: The mustache cup is a Victorian innovation that owes its origin to Harvey Adams, A Stoke-on-Trent potter who introduced the design in 1830. It is a drinking cup used for imbibing tea or coffee, featuring a raised lip guard attached to the rim of the cup to keep the mustache and beard from touching the liquid. Originally called "Napoleons and Saucers" after the small beards popular at the time, mustache cups reached the peak of their popularity in the 1890s when wearing a mustache was the rage.

Mustache cups were first sold singly. Some had matching saucers, most stood alone. As their popularity increased, they were included in dinnerware sets. Gift sets that included a cup with a mustache rim for the gentleman and an identical rimless cup for madam were common. Right and left handed cups were produced. Left handed examples are scarce. Although originating in England, the manufacture of mustache cups quickly spread to other areas including France, Germany, and Austria.

Many different media were used for the body including earthenware, porcelain, and bone china. Free hand painting by artists along with transfer printing and other decorative techniques were used. Heavy raised and burnished decorations and rich gilding proved popular. These are the most frequently encountered pieces. today. Some mustache cups employed several techniques in order to catch the fancy of the buyer.

Many of the major houses produced mustache cups and marked their products accordingly. Crown Derby, Wedgwood, Meissen, and Limoges all provided cups for the mustached gentleman. However, many of the examples found in today's market are unmarked.

The size of mustache cups ranges from demitasse to quart. The eight ounce size is most commonly found.

References: Dorothy Hammond, *Mustache Cups,* Wallace-Homestead, 1972; Thelma Schull, *Victorian Antiques,* Tuttle, 1963.

REPRODUCTION ALERT. Reproduced matching left-handed and right-handed mustache cups have found their way to antique shops. Since matched sets are very rare, collectors should be careful to make sure the matched set is old, not a reproduction.

Collecting Hints: Sayings and mottos are fairly common but do not add significantly to the value of the piece. Advanced collectors seek out Majolica, Imari, Rose Medallion, Sunderland, Luster, and Belleek cups.

Note: All listings are for right handed cups unless indicated otherwise.

CUP AND SAUCER

Autumn leaves and berries, Limoges.	**65.00**
Blue and gold flowers around gold "Be Always Happy," gold bands top and bottom, unmarked.	**30.00**
Bodelwyddan Church on cup, The Promenade on ribbed saucer, gilt trim, Best England China mark.	**125.00**
"Brother" in raised gold, stem of raised gold and white flowers, gold band on lip, top, base, and handle, two raised gold and white branches on lip ledge, "Manufactured in Germany" mark.	**45.00**
Brushed gold rim, "gold "M" and handle, relief scrolled base and guard, "T.& V. France, Depose" mark	**20.00**
Coat of arms of red dragon, shield, yellow ground, blue and white ocean with gray sailing vessel, yellow riibon with "Yr Hafandec Ar Fin Y Don," 'Royal Vale China H J C Longton England" mark	**35.00**
Cobalt band on top of cup and saucer, gold band	

Cup, 3" h, blue and yellow flowers, white ground, "Remember Me" on front, white ground, unmkd, $30.00

at base, saucer and lip, white ground, "Sutherland Art China England #668" mark.	**30.00**
Corrugated white ground with purple and light blue flowers, gold leaves and trim.	**45.00**
Cupid chasing butterflies, pink ground.	**60.00**
"Forget Me Not" in gold old English style, blue pine branches, gold scattered branches, white ground, gold banding, unmarked.	**35.00**
Four bunches of white flowers with yellow centers joined by vines, green leaves with pink and blue accents, garland of gold flowers at top, "A.P. Moore, Elite Limoges France" mark	**45.00**
Garland of black, gray, and gold flowers hanging from top, peach on cream swirl pattern, gold bands top and bottom, unmarked.	**35.00**
Garland of light blue flowers on vine surround cup and saucer, raised gold design around top of cup and saucer, small bouquet in center of saucer, gold band of hearts on cup int, "C.T. Germany" mark.	**65.00**
German poem on side of cup, large bouquets of lavender pansies on each side and base, gold accents, gold banding at top and bottom . . .	**65.00**
Gold design around top with two flowers and two fans, bouquet of white, pink, and green wild roses, white ground, scalloped saucer . .	**35.00**
Green and white band with gold, floral band on bottom, gilt trim, scalloped saucer, "Bavaria" mark.	**115.00**
Green band with red apples, paneled ribbed bottom, gilt trim, left handed	**75.00**
Hp pink roses, gold decor, Bavaria	**42.00**
Lavender clematis vine with green leaves and stems with swirls on one side of cup, two bouquets of clematis on saucer, gold band on bottom, rim, gold accented lip ledge, "C.T. Germany" mark.	**35.00**
Light blue section on top, white bottom, gilt trim and handle, Limoges, France mark	**125.00**
Light green with roses, sgd "Cora Lupton," left handed.	**95.00**
Mint green swirl on white ground with stems of pink and yellow flowers with green leaves on pale green ground, gold rims, unmarked	**35.00**
Multicolored floral spray, scrolled base, lip, and handle, scalloped edge, left handed	**40.00**
Oct ext paneling, white glaze, beaded saucer, "Elite L France" mark	**45.00**
Old Ivory #84 pattern.	**165.00**
Overall floral design in colors, sgd "Louise," left handed.	**65.00**
Oriental branches and flowers in purple, blue, yellow, and rust, gilt trim, white ground.	**45.00**
Pansies in purple, white, and yellow, stem of yellow wheat, white ground, gold band on rim and saucer, gold handle, gold band in center of saucer, "C.T.H." mark	**50.00**
Pedestal shape with scalloped top with heavy gold and white raised design, gold ground, "Made in Germany" mark.	**40.00**
Persimmon with gold, acorn-like florals, leaves, repaired	**20.00**
Pink bleeding hearts and gold flowers on raised gold stems, white ground, gold band top and bottom, angel handle with gold wings, heart, and robe, saucer with two gold branched stems and two gold bands	**65.00**
Pink ground with gold trim	**40.00**
Pink luster design of man and woman on moun-	

tainside, raised design on cup and saucer, "Made in Germany" mark............... 35.00

Portrait of lady in orange and green floral dress on white ground, medallion on pink ground, unmarked............................. 35.00

Presbyterian Church, St. Andrews, N.B. in gray and white ground, pink luster trim, gold bands on lip, rim, and saucer, "Made for Stickney's Wedgwood Store, St. Andrews, N.B." mark............................ 35.00

Purple, brown, light blue flowers and leaves, cup, cream ground, white saucer with leaf sprig, gilt trim, white bamboo handle............... 45.00

Raised gold "AP" and light blue designs on white ground, gold handle, raised center on saucer ... 85.00

Raised leaves and berries on border, floral trim, ribbed saucer, "Weimar, Germany" mark ... 85.00

Red berries, green leaves, and brown stems on one side, white ground, raised design at top and bottom of cup and saucer edge, left handed................................. 70.00

Relief of alpine drinking scene in orange luster with cobalt sky, unmarked................ 10.00

Roman key design in red with band of gold above and below, white ground, lip edge outlined in gold, handle trimmed in gold, hairline on saucer, unmarked.................... 40.00

Royal knight receiving palm crown from child and lady angels, blue shading, Bavaria...... 60.00

Shades of green and gold, roses with leaves, gilt trim, triple crown china, Germany mark..... 125.00

Small red rose bouquets and green leaves all over cup and saucer, green leaf band at cup rim, gold bands at top and bottom, unmarked................................. 35.00

Solid yellow ground with brushed gold band on rim and handle, white saucer and cup int, "H & Co over L" mark...................... 40.00

Swirl pattern of brushed gold at rim, pink, yellow, rose, lavender, and gold straw flowers, gold handle, three floral stems and brushed gold edge on saucer, unmarked............... 40.00

"Thinking of Me" cartouche in pink and purple, ribbed pink saucer, raised gilt trim, "K & L Germany" mark...................... 95.00

Three gold bands on center, vine with two red rasberries and green leaves on one side, pink bleeding hearts and green leaves on opposite, gold rim band, handle and lip outline....... 50.00

Washington Statue, Public Garden, Boston in rust-brown, white ground, gold rims, "Wedgwood" mark........................... 45.00

White and gold tipped tulip design. large gold band at bottom, saucer with gold veined leaves, unmarked....................... 45.00

Yellow and green flowers, scalloped edge on suacer, gilt trim, Limoges mark............ 45.00

Yellow, pink, and blue flowers with light brown vine and green and brown leaves, dbl gold band at top, bouquet on int, gold band and dots on lip, "Marne and crown W" mark ... 45.00

Yellow shading at top, raised swirl and tree design on front, orange, green, white, and brown bouquet on side, small pink and green bouquet on int of cup, brushed gold rim and top of handle, gold lip edge, pink rose and green leaves on orange-yellow ground saucer, unmarked................................. 45.00

Zig-zag pattern in gold and white, pink luster at bottom with raised gold beading, gold band at

top and int, petal shaped design cup, unmarked................................. 45.00

CUP

Boy with donkeys in colors.................. 200.00
Blue water lily design...................... 175.00
Elk trimmed in gold........................ 55.00
Fan design with bird, pink and brown florals, brown cane handle, lavender int, pebbled turq ext, Majolica........................... 325.00
Four emb irises, pink and yellow roses, blue ground, R.S. Prussia red mark............. 295.00
Gaudy pattern in cobalt, rust, yellow, green, gilt trim..................................... 60.00
Gold design of leaves and berries, blank #118, Theo. Haviland........................ 150.00
Man with black mustache and orange tie, orange handle and trim, "Susie Cooper Productions, Crown Works Burslem" mark............. 95.00
Oriental scene of man attending flowers, woman holding staff, black transfer with red, blue, green, and orange-yellow accents, black flowers on int, "E.M.& Co." mark......... 12.50
Raised gold flowers in raised shield, pink luster trim 40.00
Raised white flowers on green ground........ 43.00
Scenes of old Germany separated by raised vert gold bands 45.00
"The Race of the Century" design........... 38.00

DEMITASSE

Four side indentations, raised ripples, small bouquet in green, lavender, orange, and yellow between indentations, bouquet on cup int, raised gold on cup and saucer, two bouquets on saucer 35.00
Gold fleur-de-lys on cup rim, oct shape with small bouquets between sections, each section different color shaded to white, green and pink handle with gold stripe, small rose and bouquet on cup int, "M.Z. Austria" mark ... 65.00
Lattice design in blue, white, and gold with scalloped design in gold and white, gold outlined lip and top and base bands 45.00
Lotus flower in gold, white ground, "Haviland France and Haviland & Co." mark.......... 55.00

NANT GARW
C. W.

c1813 - 1822

NANTGARW

Glamorgan, Wales
1813 and c1817–1820

History: William Billingsley and Samuel Walker started Welsh Nantgarw porcelains in 1813. The cost of operations soon depleted their available funds. Production ceased. The pottery started again about 1817 and survived until 1820. Most pieces from this second period have the company mark.

Nantgarw porcelains were soft, translucent, and usually rather simple in decoration. Many blanks were sold to London decorators. These pieces frequently were more ornate in decoration.

Marked pieces have the impressed mark "Nant-Garw," usually over the initials "CW" (China Works). Sometimes the hyphen was omitted.

References: W. D. John, *Nantgarw Porcelain*, Ceramic Book Co., 1948. Supplement 1956; W. P. John, *William Billingsley 1758–1828*, Ceramic Book Co., 1968; E. Morton Nance, *The Pottery & Porcelain of Swansea & Nantgarw*, Batsford, 1942.

Museum: Glynn Vivian Museum & Art Gallery, Swansea, Wales.

Cake Plate, 9 1/8" l, lobed, puce enamel on pale blue ground, broad border of foliage in gilding, c1813, imp mark (A).................... **175.00**

Dessert Service, Part, rect dish, oval dish, 3 dessert plates, 8 7/8" d, printed central spray of flowers on white ground, bleu celeste border, gilt foliage and suspended flower sprays, shaped gilt dentil rims, c1813–22 (A)....... **3366.00**

Dessert Tureen, 7 1/2" d, with stand, painted bird and floral cartouches linked by gilt scrolls and shells, restored, c1813–22, imp "NANT-GARW C.W." mark, pr (A) **2000.00**

Dish

8" d, sprays and sprigs of summer flowers within gilt line border, C scroll molded rim, c1820, imp "NANT-GARW/C W" mark (A).................................. **935.00**

9 1/2" d,

Selection of flowers including roses and tulips, rim with sprigs of flowers within gilt and molded panels, imp "NANT-GARW C.W. and incised B" mark (A) **1693.00**

Sq, multicolored scattered bouquets, flower sprigs and insects, border of green and black dots, corners molded with ribbon tied flowering branches, gilt lines, c1820, pr (A).............................. **2420.00**

9 3/4" d, shaped sq, bright flower sprays and

Plates, 9 1/2" d; left, center painted with exotic birds in parkland, border with blue ribbon and flowers on biscuit border, shaped gilt dentil rim, c1820, imp "NANT-GARW C.W." mark, (A) $4350.00; right, center painted with bouquet of flowers, border with swags of coral red drapery reserving gilt edged panels of exotic birds, landscapes, and fruits, shaped gilt dentil rim, c1817–18, "NANT-GARW C.W." mark, (A) $3360.00

sprigs within gilt dentil border, c1820, London decorated, imp" NANT-GARW/C/W" mark (A) **374.00**

11 5/8" l, fluted oval form, bouquets of summer flowers and various detached sprigs, dentil gilt rim, c1817–22, imp "NANT-GARW C.W." (A) **750.00**

11 3/4" l, oval, blue and green enamels with scattered cornflower sprigs among stylized foliage, gilt dentil border, c1813, imp mark (A)................................... **175.00**

14" l, shaped oval, scattered brightly colored flower sprays and insects, gilded handles, gilt dentil border, hair crack, c1817–22, imp "NANT-GARW C.W. and incised VI" marks (A)................................... **1100.00**

Ice Pail, Cov, Liner, 8" h, bouquets of summer flowers and sprigs, straight sided body, three bun feet, angular handle, flat cov with flange and entwined scroll handle with bouquets of garden flowers, repairs, c1817–22 (A) **4500.00**

Plate

8 1/4" d, 5 sprays of gray-blue flowers, gilded rim, 1814–22, imp "NANT-GARW C.W." mark (A) **250.00**

8 5/8" d, painted center with three birds on leafy branch, border of bouquets in gilt ovals on gilt oeil-de-perdrix and apple green ground, London decorated (A)........... **2950.00**

8 3/4" d, center with bouquet of summer flowers within gilt line border, turquoise ground with three gilded scroll cartouches with bouquets of summer flowers, shaped rim, c1810–20, imp "NANT-GARW C.W." mark (A) **2069.00**

9 1/8" d, center painted with summer flower arrangement on shelf, gilt border, C scroll molded rim, c1817–22, imp "NANT GARW/C.W." mark (A) **686.00**

9 1/2" d

Bouquet of colored flowers in center, border with swags of coral red drapery reserving gilt edged panels of exotic birds, landscapes, and fruit arrangements, shaped rim with gilt dentil border, from Duke of Cambridge Service, c1817–18, imp "NANT-GARW C.W. mark (A)..... **3347.00**

Brightly colored, large spray of summer flowers among scattered insects, molded border with gilding and vignettes of flowering branches, one with colored bird, C scroll and ribboned flower spray border, c1813, imp mark (A) **1416.00**

Center with single wild rose between wide border with shamrocks in green and gilding, dot and gilt line border, 4 cracked, 1813–20, imp "NANT-GARW C.W." mark, set of 14 (A)................... **2634.00**

9 7/8" d, bright enamels with flower sprays and scattered single blooms, molded with C scroll and ribboned flower spray borders, c1813, imp mark (A) **708.00**

Shell Dish, 8 1/2" l, bouquet of summer flowers and various detached sprigs, gilded dentil rim lip with gilded fan-shaped design, c1817–22, imp "NANT-GARW C.W." mark, set of 4 (A) **2200.00**

Soup Dish, 9 1/2" d, soft blue enamel with formal flower bouquets within molded border of C scroll and ribboned flower sprays, gilt dentil rim, c1813, imp mark, pr (A) **744.00**

1812-35

NEW HALL

Staffordshire Potteries, England
c1781–1835

History: A group of partners purchased Champion's patent to make translucent porcelains. In 1781 they established the New Hall China Manufactory at Hanley in Staffordshire to hard paste porcelains based upon the patent. Tea and dessert sets, along with blue and white wares showing Chinese influences, were characteristic products at New Hall. Gold was used in both simple and elaborate designs. Many early pieces only had elegant gilt borders.

Fidelle Duvivier, who had been employed at Worcester and Derby, worked at New Hall from 1781 to 1790. He did figure and landscape compositions and flower subjects on presentation jugs. Early New Hall teapots were globular in form. Pieces made during the hard paste period were not marked. Pattern numbers were used instead.

About 1812–14 bone china that was lighter and whiter was introduced at New Hall. The pieces were marked "New Hall" in a double lined circle along with a pattern number. Work declined after about 1820. The factory was put up for auction in 1831. Various firms using the original site continued the name until 1836.

References: David Holgate, *New Hall & Its Imitators*, Faber & Faber, rev. ed. 1988; G. E. Stringer, *New Hall Porcelain*, Art Trade Press, 1949.

Museums: City Museum & Art Gallery, Stoke-on-Trent, Hanley, England; Victoria & Albert Museum, London, England.

Coffee Cup and Saucer, painted border of flowers between blue enamel line borders (A). . .   **50.00**
Coffee Pot
    10" h, baluster shape, painted pagoda and ruins under willow tree with flowers and

Sugar Bowl, 6³/₄" h, 6¹/₂" l, sm pink flowers, dk pink outline, cream ground, c1810, unmkd, $240.00

shrubs in Imari colors, gilt floral rim and foot, gilt loop handle and spout, domed cov with gilt knob, hairline, c1800, no.570 . . . .   **500.00**
    11" h, painted central spray of pink and mauve flowers in lobed magenta line frame, border of chains of pimpernels and leaves, large orange-brown markings, c1800, no.449 (A) **700.00**
Creamer, 4³/₈" h, paneled body, small floral bouquets, hanging mauve swags (A) **87.00**
Cup and Saucer
    Adam Buck style black transfer of mother and child, magenta luster borders, c1800 (A). .   **50.00**
    Border of gold and iron-red flowers, purple leaves, c1800 (A) **75.00**
    Shell decoration in polychrome, red borders (A). **40.00**
    Silver luster undulating lines of foliage crossing straight line, silver line borders, c1800 (A)   **85.00**
Dessert Service, bone china, dbl handled oval sauce tureen and stand, 2 rect dishes, 2 heart-shaped dishes, 12 dessert plates, 8" d, central multicolored bat printed landscape scenes in gilt line frame, white relief florals on blue ground borders, shaped gilt line rims, c1822–25, no.1478 . . . .   **1850.00**
Jug, globular, cabbage leaf molded, sprays and sprigs of colored flowers, chocolate brown edge on rim, scrolling handle, cylindrical neck, c1793 (A) **1575.00**
Milk Jug, 4¹/₄" h, painted sprigs of flowers, dot and line borders, c1800 (A) **55.00**
Mug, 4" h, painted bouquet of flowers and sprigs under border of two undulating lines, one of red dots, another with stem of flowers and leaves, black edged rim, molded scroll handle with puce arrow and dot accents, c1790–1805 (A) **960.00**
Plate
    7¹/₄" d, polychrome enameled hanging swag design, blue border (A) **80.00**
    8³/₈" d, polychrome floral design, "N 241" on reverse (A) **90.00**
Slop Bowl
    6" d, painted floral sprigs and puce swags, puce diaper border, no.84 (A) **85.00**
    6¹/₁₆" d, gold decorated dragons and scrolling foliage on dark blue ground, no.761 (A). **150.00**
    6¹/₂" d, painted floral decoration, magenta rim, no. 377 (A). **80.00**
Tea and Coffee Service, Part, oblong teapot, 5⁷/₈" h, cov sugar bowl, milk jug, waste bowl, 2 cake dishes, 10 teacups, 10 coffee cups, 11 saucers, painted with peasant figures at various pursuits within panels alternating with panels of floral clusters, sky-blue and gilt borders, center of circ pieces with colorful floral bouquet, c1820, no.2215, "brown filled incised New Hall Shelton 1799" on teapot, sugar bowl, and milk jug, 37 pcs (A) **2420.00**
Teabowl, 3¹/₂" d, oriental figures in two scenes with orange fence, bands of purple and orange separate scenes, orange design on int base and inside rim, c1780. . . . .   **75.00**
Teabowl and Saucer
    Black enameled central basket of flowers surrounded by floral sprigs, no.308 (A). **100.00**
    Fluted with green and puce floral borders, pr (A). **75.00**

Oriental figures, burnt orange trim, c1795,
no.421 . . . . **185.00**
Painted Chinese design of fenced garden in
multicolored enamels, c1810–20 (A) **50.00**

Teapot
5⅞" h, silver shape, black painted flower
spray and scattered sprigs, no.367 . . . . **175.00**
8¾" d, silver shape, reeded body painted
with sprigs of flowers, mauve undulating ribbon with straight line border, magenta bris-
tles and alternating pink and mauve roses
and iron-red buds above, cracks (A). **100.00**
9" h, three oriental figures seated and standing around table in green shades, c1795–
1805 (A) **200.00**
9¼" h, silver shape, painted central spray of
magenta and iron-red flower and large
green leaf, small sprigs, c1800, no.596 (A) **175.00**
9½" d, with stand, Adam Buck style black
transfer of mother and child, black line borders on rim and stand, restored, c1800,
no.1109 (A) **150.00**
9¾" d, spirally fluted shape, famille rose
enameled painted scattered sprigs below
gold line border and band of blue and puce
petaled flowers, reserved in white ovals and
green trefoils, c1800, no.237 (A). **650.00**

Tea Service
Teapot, 6⅛" h, stand, 4 milk jugs, slop bowl,
8 teabowls and saucers, painted spray of
two pink and mauve roses with green foliage on white ground, scattered blooms
under undulating dotted red line with leaves
and florets, c1790, no.241 (A). **2020.00**
Teapot, 9¾" h, stand, cov sucrier, cream jug,
slop bowl, saucer dish, 6 tea cups, 6 coffee
cups, 6 saucers, underglaze blue, pale blue,
and orange with figures, buildings, and trees
in rocky river landscape in oriental style,
gilding, cracks, spout repaired, c1815–25,
no.1163 on some pcs, one no.1161, 26 pcs
(A). **2400.00**
10⅝" d, with stand, painted central bouquet,
bordered by sprigs, undulating puce border,
c1800, no.130 (A). **150.00**

Tea Service, Part
10 tea cups, 7 coffee cups, 17 saucers, cov
sugar bowl, cream jug, slop bowl, London
shape, painted underglaze blue and iron-
red, green, and gilt "Japan" pattern of
flowering branch from rockwork, c1815,
no.1153 (A) **2857.00**
Teapot, 10¼" h, cov sugar bowl, cream jug,
slop bowl, 2 saucer dishes, 5 cups and saucers, blue, orange, and gilt fruiting palm
trees alternating with large flowers, c1795–
1805, no.484 (A). **2000.00**
Teapot, fluted oval form with faceted curved
spout, milk jug, sugar bowl, slop bowl, 12
teabowls, 13 saucers, painted sprays of pink
and lilac roses, border of iron-red ribbons
and magenta festoons, hairlines, c1787–90,
no.195 (A) **1375.00**

Waste Bowl
4⅝" d, vert ribbed body, small bouquets of
multicolored flowers (A) **85.00**
6⅛" d, large rose decoration, pink geometric
border, hairline (A) **55.00**

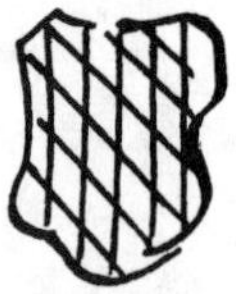

1754 - 65

MODERN MARK

NYMPHENBURG

Near Munich, Bavaria, Germany
1747 to Present

History: The Nymphenburg Porcelain Factory, located in
Neudeck ob den Au, near Munich, was founded in 1747
by the Bavarian Elector. As production increased, the factory was moved to the grounds of Nymphenburg Palace
in Munich.

As with many German porcelain firms, Meissen pieces
strongly influenced the types of wares produced at Nymphenburg. By 1765, under the guidance of the Elector,
Nymphenburg became the most renown hard paste factory in Europe. Shortly thereafter, a series of wars and
economic reversals created a decline in the popularity of
the porcelain. By 1770 the Nymphenburg factory was
hard pressed for markets in which to sell its products.

During the early years at Nymphenburg, production
was devoted to table services, accessory pieces, and
household wares that were painted in a Rococo style
featuring birds, fruits, flowers, and the popular pastoral
scenes. However, it was the modeling of Franz Bustelli, the
Swiss craftsman who worked at Nymphenburg from
1754–1763, that contributed the most to the success of
the company. Bustelli's figures were modeled in a light,
graceful Rococo style and found a ready market with the
gentry.

The Nymphenburg pottery was transferred to the control of the Elector of Palatinate who also owned the Frankenthal factory, a competitor of Nymphenburg. With more
emphasis placed on the Frankenthal pottery, Nymphenburg experienced a period of neglect and subsequent
decline. When the Frankenthal Factory closed in 1799,
many of the workers and artisans were moved to Nymphenburg to revitilize the ailing concern.

Melchoir, who achieved fame at Hochst and Frankenthal, was chief modeler at Nymphenburg between 1797
and 1822. He produced many biscuit portraits and busts.

When Melchoir died in 1822, Friedrich Gartner was
appointed artistic director. He preferred to produce vases
in a variety of decortive motifs. Gartner showed little interest in producing tableware. As a result, the factory declined economically. Royal commissions for Ludwig I
(1825–1848) did result in the manufacture of several outstanding state services.

When Eugen Neureuther assumed control as director in
1848, the factory's finances were poor. Ludwig I ab-
dicated in favor of Maximilian II, his son. Maximilian II had
almost no interest in the pottery factory. Economies were
taken. Popular wares such as paperweights, toothbrush
racks, and cigar holders were made to attract working
capital. Tablewares regained favor. The factory still lost
money. In desperation the factory switched to industrial
porcelains.

In 1862 the Royal Manufactory was leased to a private concern. The new managers produced art porcelain and reissued some of the earlier Rococo figures. The pottery again became profitable.

Albert Keller from Sevres and Louis Levallois, a student from Sevres, developed an Art Nouveau line for Nymphenburg based the underglazed painting of figures. When Theodor Karner, a sculptor, came to Nymphenburg, he introduced a number of successful animal sculptures that were modeled after the animals and birds in Bavaria and the Munich Zoo. Animal motifs also were used on modern tablewares. Other tablewares were produced in the Art Nouveau style that encompassed linear decorations, stylized designs, and angular handles.

The popularity of the Neo-classical, Empire, and Biedermeyer movements that swept across Europe during the late 19th century did achieve the same success at Nymphenburg. In 1887, the Baum family from Bohemia gained control of the company. They still guide its fortunes today. Recently the company reproduced a number of pure white figures from its old models. The company still has not regained the position of prominence it enjoyed in the past.

References: S. Ducret, *German Porcelain & Faience,* Universe Books, 1962; George W. Ware, *German & Austrian Porcelain,* Crown Publishers, Inc., 1963.

Museums: Bayerisches Nationalmuseum, Munich, Germany; Gardiner Museum of Ceramic Art, Toronto, Canada; Metropolitan Museum of Art, N.Y.; Schlossmuseum, Berlin, Germany; Victoria & Albert Museum, London, England.

Beaker, 4³/₄" h, front with gilt edged sq panel in shades of green, brown, blue, lavender, and tan with figures strolling in park before view of Munich, rounded lower body above flaring foot with three gilt bands, c1860, imp "shield beneath star and 8 8" (A) **1100.00**
Breakfast Cup and Saucer, little girl in white dress leaning on knees of seated elder sister in burgundy and white dress, grassy hummock, purple hilly landscape within gilt edged panel, rim, circ foot, and scroll handle with gilt band borders, c1860, imp "shield and incised 3 and 5" marks (A) **330.00**
Butter Dish, 5¹/₂" d, twelve sided, gray domed lid with berry finial, beaded rim **30.00**
Cabinet Cup, conical shape, painted named view of "Tegernsee" with monastery and village, gilt applied scrolled handle, foot, and int, c1820, imp "shield" mark (A) **950.00**
Cabinet Cup and Saucer, Biedermeier style, bell shape with Etruscan serpent handle, bands of

Figure, 8¹/₂" l, gray body, brown muzzle and collar, "green Nymphenburg, W. Germany" mark, (A) $89.00

gilt flowerheads on claret and green ground, gilt int and rim (A) **535.00**
Clock, 17¹/₄" h, rhinoceros in two sections, clock face in high waisted architectural pediment with rococo shell and acanthus molding with laurel wreath with baluster finial, purple hanging saddle flaps molded in high relief with blackamoor heads, rhinoceros with brown bumps simulating leather, rocky base, convex top with flowers, top inscribed "To his Excellency Sir William Gowers in rememberance for all your kindness during my stay in Uganda, Eric R. Miville," c1932, imp "shield and #1826" marks (A) **3010.00**
Coffee Pot, 7¹/₂" h, pear shape, loose cluster of flowers and scattered sprigs, bell shaped cov with apple knob, iron-red rims, dbl scroll handle, 1765–70, imp "shield, 2 and P" mark (A) **925.00**
Cup and Saucer
Mythological scenes of Diana aiming at a bear, water god flirting with a nymph, florals and gilt scroll border, restored, c1765, painted by Cajetan Purtscher, imp "shield, 46, incised 70" marks (A) **1850.00**
Painted view of Marsbach with river in foreground, gilt int and scroll handle, imp "shield" mark (A) **800.00**
Cup and Saucer, demitasse, Art Deco floral design **35.00**
Dessert Dish, 9⁷/₈" d, lobed sq shape, tones of green and puce with riverscape, buildings and trees, flower sprigs, edged in gold, imp "shield, incised 43X" mark (A) **612.00**
Dish, 9⁵/₈" d, mixed bouquet with roses, tulips, forget-me-nots, scattered floral sprigs, gilt edged rim, c1765, imp "shield, W," incised marks (A) **1000.00**
Figure
3³/₄" h, 4" l, deer lying on side in colors. . . **95.00**
4¹/₄" h, white, Pandora modeled as draped putto with box in right hand, flat rococo base, c1758–60, imp "shield" mark (A). . . **650.00**
4³/₈" h, putto as Jupiter with eagle, gilt edged crown, brown hair, yellow lined orange drapery edged in gilding, holding bolt of lightning, brown and tan eagle perched on puce, blue, and yellow mottled cloud, 1755–65, modeled by Franz Anton Bustelli, incised "IX" mark (A). **1430.00**
4¹/₂" h
5" l, bear lying on back, natural colors, sgd "Neuhauser" **185.00**
Two chinoiserie figures in enameled colors **175.00**
5³/₄" h, "Egg Seller," woman in green bodice, yellow skirt, holding puce dotted apron in hand, braided hair tied in black kerchief, crate of eggs on gray washed flat rococo scrolled base, restored base, 1755, modeled by Franz Anton Bustelli (A) **2130.00**
6¹/₂" h, white cherub carrying flowers, pedestal base, c1925 . . . . **175.00**
6³/₄" h, Chinese musician, white stylized figure, draped jerkin, pointed hat, playing string of bells, c1760, modeled by F.A. Bustelli (A) **2585.00**
9" h, 4 cherubs holding cage, setting traps,

chasing birds, holding owl and leaves, tree in center, blanc de chine glaze **350.00**

10⅝" h, Chinese figure, white Oriental squatting on cushion, head shaven except for pigtail and pointed beard, brazier before him, tall corniced pedestal with small flowers, stepped base, facade with buttress with goat mask terminal, c1770, modeled by F.A. Bustelli, impressed "shield and 2" marks (A) **3480.00**

Plate

9" d, twelve sided, multicolored floral center, cut out basketweave with raised gold dots, gilt dot raised rim, set of 8, marked **595.00**

10" d

Center painted with flower spray, scattered flower sprigs, scroll molded rim, c1765, imp "shield and blue hexagram" marks.   **1100.00**

Hp loose bouquet of puce, red, yellow, and blue flowers in center, scattered insects, moth, snails, and flowers on gilt scroll and blue line border, octafoil molded rim with gilt, c1760–65, imp "shield" mark (A) .   **24,684.00**

Large central floral sprays surrounded by scattered sprigs, scroll molded rim, c1765, imp "shield and numerals, underglaze blue hexagram" marks (A) **700.00**

Salt, 4" h, shell shape, pierced rocaille form, green, blue, and purple with gilding, three scrolled feet, white ground, c1755–60, imp "shield and 2 dots" mark (A) **2362.00**

Snuff Box, 3" l, rect, purple painted views of castles and ruins, int with German castle, gilt metal rims, c1763–67, "blue hexagram and imp shield" marks (A) **5667.00**

Sucrier, Cov, 3⅛" h, with saucer, band of gilt relief triangles, borders of garlands of pink and white roses on black ground, gilt rims **285.00**

Tea Caddy, 5⅛" h, waisted rococo silver shape, flower spray on each of the four sides, silver cov, c1765, pr (A) **589.00**

Teapot, 4¹¹⁄₁₆" h, spherical body, shades of brown, gray, blue, green, black, iron-red, and purple on one side with herdsman and companion dangling feet in steam before wading donkey, cattle, and sheep, reverse with piping shepherd and companion beyond recumbent flock and cow, cov with artichoke knob, gilt rims, serpent spout, S scroll handle, 1765–67, underglaze "blue hexagram, imp shield, incised C" marks (A) **1430.00**

Tureen, Stand, 10¼" l, lobed oval shape, large bouquets of flowers and scattered sprigs, gilt edged rims, two scroll handles, c1765, imp "shield and H, incised 26" mark (A). **1020.00**

Vase

6⅜" h, baluster shape, painted panel of "Ruhmeshalle mit der Bavaria," reserved on dark green ground, cylinder neck with applied flowerheads, imp "shield" mark (A) .   **380.00**

11¼" h, urn form, gilt rim, flared foot, sq plinth, applied dbl handles with four gilt female terminals, matte blue ground, c1825, imp "shield" mark, pr (A) **5365.00**

18½" h, reserve of Venus and nymphs clipping wings of sleeping Cupids, reverse with Cupids forging arrows in cave, gilt leaf and keyfret borders, gilt horns crossed and draped with ribbon on cream ground, sq gilt plinth **1500.00**

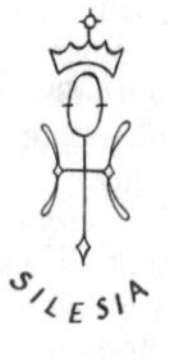

Clairon
LATE 1800s

OLD IVORY

Silesia, Germany
Late 1800s

History: Old Ivory dinnerware was made during the late 1800s in the pottery factories in Silesia, Germany. It derives its name from the background color of the china.

Marked pieces usually have a pattern number stamped on the bottom. The mark also may include a crown and "Silesia."

Bacon Platter, 11½" l, #16 pattern, "Silesia"   **145.00**

Berry Dish

   #15 pattern **15.00**

   #75 pattern **15.00**

Berry Set

   Master bowl, 9½" d, 4 smaller bowls, #113 pattern **250.00**

   Master bowl 10½" d, 6 smaller bowls

     #16 pattern **250.00**

     #73 pattern **195.00**

Bowl

   5" d

     #16 pattern **10.00**

     #84 pattern **22.00**

   5½" d, #32 pattern **10.00**

   5⅜" d, #11 pattern **10.00**

   6¼" d, #84 pattern **40.00**

   6½" d

     #16 pattern **25.00**

     #33 pattern, "Silesia" **35.00**

   8" l, oval, #15 pattern **45.00**

   9½" d

     #16 pattern, "Silesia" **85.00**

Nappy, 6⅝" d, #16 pattern, $68.00

#75 pattern, "Silesia"	85.00
#84 pattern	50.00
#200 pattern	175.00

10" d

#11 pattern	85.00
#16 pattern	125.00
#69 pattern	125.00
#84 pattern	85.00

Bun Tray, 10" l, #84 pattern, "Silesia" 135.00

Butter Pat

#16 pattern, "Silesia"	95.00
#28 pattern, "Silesia"	95.00

Cake Plate

10" d,

#15 pattern, pierced handles	95.00
#16 pattern	70.00
#84 pattern	95.00
10½" d, #75 pattern	110.00
11" d, #16 pattern, "Silesia"	145.00

Cake Set

10" H-H master plate, pierced handles, 6 plates, 6¼" d, #16 pattern	249.00
10" H-H master plate, 6 plates, 7½" d, 6 plates, 6" d, 6 cups and saucers, #32 pattern	995.00
11" master plate, 8 plates, 6 d, #84 pattern, "Silesia"	295.00

Candy Dish, #16 pattern, "Silesia" 45.00

Celery Tray, 11½" d

#11 pattern	60.00
#16 pattern, "Silesia"	125.00
#84 pattern	65.00

Cereal Bowl

6" d, #63 pattern, "Silesia"	45.00
6½" d, #15 pattern	25.00

Charger, 13" d

#15 pattern, "Silesia"	185.00
#16 pattern	175.00

Chocolate Cup and Saucer

#15 pattern	65.00
#33 pattern, "Silesia"	65.00

Chocolate Pot, #84 pattern 285.00

Chocolate Set

#11 pattern	600.00
#15 pattern, 4 cups and saucers	750.00
#16 pattern, "Silesia" 6 cups and saucers	650.00
#73 pattern	595.00
#84, 6 cups and saucers	600.00

Chop Plate, 13" d

#15 pattern	175.00
#16 pattern, "Silesia"	185.00

Cracker Jar

Domed lid, #16 pattern	375.00
Squatty, #16 pattern, "Silesia"	375.00

Cream and Sugar

#11 pattern	120.00
#84 pattern	150.00

Creamer

#15 pattern, "Silesia"	75.00
#32 pattern	29.00

Cup and Saucer

#11 pattern,	60.00
#15 pattern	60.00
#16 pattern	55.00
#33 pattern, "Silesia"	60.00
#53 pattern, set of 6	585.00
#75 pattern, "Silesia"	60.00
#84 pattern	60.00

Cup and Saucer, Demitasse

#84 pattern	55.00
#113 pattern	68.00
#200 pattern	60.00

Egg Cup, #84 pattern, "Silesia" 385.00

Mayonnaise Dish, underplate, spoon, #16 pattern, "Silesia" 195.00

Muffineer, #84 pattern, "Silesia" 395.00

Mustard Pot

#16 pattern, "Silesia" mark	95.00
#84 pattern, "Silesia"	195.00

Oyster Bowl, fluted, #16 pattern, "Silesia" ... 175.00

Plate

6" d

#11 pattern	15.00
#15 pattern	25.00
#16 pattern	25.00
#32 pattern	20.00
#75 pattern	15.00
#84 pattern	25.00

6¼" d

#11 pattern	18.00
#16 pattern	18.00
#73 pattern	18.00
#200 pattern	18.00
6¾" d, #16 pattern	30.00

7½" d

#11 pattern	45.00
#15 pattern	45.00
#16 pattern	45.00
#33 pattern	45.00
#84 pattern	45.00

7¾" d

#16 pattern	20.00
#84 pattern	10.00
8" d, #16 pattern	16.00
8¼" d, #84 pattern, "Silesia"	65.00

8½" d

#16 pattern	25.00
#28 pattern	65.00
#32 pattern	75.00
#84 pattern	65.00

9½" d

#22 pattern, "Holly"	48.00
#28 pattern, round rim	160.00
10" d, #4 pattern	100.00

Platter

11½" l, #16 pattern 50.00

12" l, 8" w

#11 pattern	160.00
#30 pattern	75.00
13" d, #73 pattern	225.00
16" l, #84 pattern, "Silesia"	375.00

Relish Dish

8½" l, #84 pattern	50.00
Thorn handle, #16 pattern, "Silesia" mark	80.00

Salad Plate, 7¾" d, #84 pattern, "Silesia" ... 55.00

Salt and Pepper

#16 pattern, "Silesia"	125.00
#122 pattern	125.00

Salt Shaker, #40 pattern 25.00

Teapot, #84 pattern, "Silesia" 395.00

Tea Tile

#15 pattern, "Silesia"	185.00
#16 pattern	65.00

Toothpick Holder, #15 pattern, "Silesia" 250.00

Tray, 12" l, #84 pattern, "Silesia" 145.00

Vegetable Bowl

9¼" d, #16 pattern, "Silesia"	125.00
9½" d, #84 pattern	125.00

NAST *H. DECK*
a   c1859
PARIS

1782 - MID 19ᵀᴴ CENTURY

J.P
1830-62

OLD PARIS AND PARIS

Paris, France
18th and 19th Centuries

OLD PARIS

History: Old Paris refers to porcelains made in the 18th and 19th centuries by various French factories located in and around Paris. Shapes were usually classical in design, decoration were elegant, and gilding was popular. Although some examples were marked, many were not.

PARIS

History: Most of the early porcelain factories of France were located in and around Paris. Without marks it is difficult to differentiate between the various factories because their shapes and designs were similar. Strewn flower sprigs, especially the cornflower, and lots of gilding were favorite decorative motifs.

Fabrique du Conte d'Artois was founded by Pierre-Antoine Hannong in 1773. Hannong's polychrome flower painting was similar in style to that of Sevres. Coal was used to fire the ovens since the woods around Paris had been depleted by earlier porcelain manufacture. In 1787, Hannong was granted the rights to make figures in biscuit, paint in color, and use gilding. Production ended about 1828.

Hannong used the letter "H" as his mark.

Fabrique de la Courtille was founded by Jean-Baptiste Locre de Roissy, a potter from Leipzig, in 1773. He imitated German porcelains, including those of Meissen. Large vases were a specialty. The factory was taken over by Pouyat of Limoges about 1800. No exact date is known for its closing.

The factory mark was a pair of crossed torches that closely resembled the Meissen crossed swords.

Fabrique de la rue de Reuilly was established by Jean-Joseph Lassia of Strasbourg about 1775. He used an "L" mark. Production ceased in 1784. Henri-Florentin Chanou had a factory nearby from 1779 to 1785. His mark was a "CH"

Fabrique de Clignancourt was founded by Pierre Deruelle in 1771. Porcelains rivalling Sevres were made. The decorative motifs included polychrome flowersprays and landscapes along with gilding. Some figures also were made.

The first mark was a windmill, a tribute to the windmills of Montmartre located nearby. A later mark was "LSX," a monogram for Louis XVIII.

Fabrique de la Reine was organized by Andre-Marie Leboeuf about 1778 under the protection of Marie-Antoinette. Products were called "porcelaine de la Reine."

The decorations included small springs of cornflowers, daisies, and roses, bird paintings, and some gilting. The factory was sold by Guy in 1797.

Fabrique Duc d'Angouleme was established by Dihl in 1780. Guerhard became his partner in 1786. The firm's main pattern was called "Angouleme Sprig," strewn cornflowers. The pattern was copied by many other factories. Biscuit figures were made. Dihl introduced the painting of portraits on porcelain. The favored decorative motif were designs in the Empire style. The factory was transferred to Fabrique rue du Temple in 1796.

Marks include "GA," "Dihl," "Guerhard and Dihl," or "Rue de Bondy'.

Fabrique de la Popincourt, founded by Lemaire, was bought by Johann Nast in 1782. He moved it to Popincourt in 1784. Biscuit porcelains, biscuit clock cases, and Wedgwood imitations were made. The factory's were "Nast a Paris" or "N."

Fabrique du Duc d'Orleans was started by Louis de Villers and Augustin de Montarcy in 1784. Its mark was a monogram "MJ." In 1786 the factory changed hands. The mark became "LP." A single rose, decoration appears on some pieces.

Factory of the "Prince de Galles," the "Prince of Wales" factory, was established in 1789 by the Englishman Christopher Potter. He was the first in Paris to use the transfer printing method. The factory changed hands several times. The first mark was "Potter Paris," then "EB" for E. Blancheron, the manager in 1792, and finally "PB."

Fabrique de Petit rue Saint Gilles was started by Francois-Maurice Honore in partnership with Dagoty about 1785. They made vases in the style of Wedgwood. The names "Honore and Dagoty" are used in the marks.

Fabrique du Jacob Petit was established by Jacob Petit Fontainebleau in 1834. Much of Petit's porcelain was inspired by eighteenth century French and German examples. His animal tureens and figurals all looked to the past for inspirations; he used English shapes for his tea services. Many pieces contained relief ornamentation in the form of flowers, jewels, and fruit. The factory closed in 1866.

Reference: George Savage, *Seventeenth & Eighteenth Century French Porcelain,* Spring Books, 1969.

Museums: Musee National Adrien-Dubouche, Limoges, France; Musee National de Ceramique, Sevres, France; Victoria & Albert Museum, London, England.

Tea and Coffee Service, coffee pot, teapot, cov sugar bowl, creamer, 3 cov coffee cans, 3 cov teacups, gilt and cobalt banding, floral reserves on floral ground, bowknot and wreath handles, 3rd quarter 19th C, Vieux Paris, (A) $990.00

Bottle and Stopper, 13¾″ h, rect section, painted with panels of summer flowers between gilded borders, blue and orange ground, scroll molded waisted neck painted with small flower panels, crown stopper, c1840, Jacob Petit (A) 3907.00

Bowl, 9½″ l, 4½″ h, bird int on pale yellow and black panel with pink roses, geometric panel border inside in gilt and white, gilt designs on ext, c1790–1800 .... 950.00

Box, 8¾″ h, modeled as spiraling seashell, orange coral foot, cov with applied frog, salamander, and seashells on green moss, "blue J.P." mark 1140.00

Candlestick, 8⅝″ h, formed of four separate segments, ext with gilt scrolls and dots, decagonal foot reserved with quatrefoil panels with colorful floral bouquets, black ground, c1845, "brown script Bouchet a Madrid" mark, pr (A) 770.00

Centerpiece, 28″ h, lady and gentleman chasing each other around leaf molded column, supports waisted oval pierced basket with ribbontied handles, four scroll feet on base, all encrusted with flowers and foliage, gilded details, late 19th C, "psuedo X'd swords" mark, Jacob Petit (A) 3553.00

Charger
12½″ d, faience, underglaze blue painted center scene of boy writing on slate from book, border of ivy vines and putto, white ground, c1860–80, imp and enameled "Th. Deck" mark (A) 8650.00
15¼″ d, brown and gilt design in center on white ground, brown tulip border with gilt trim and rim, c1820 .... 375.00

Clock
13¾″ h, modeled as lyre, side panels of lady and male archer, enamel decorated on pink ground with gold trim and beading, hairline (A) 385.00
17″ h, Egyptian Revival, trapezoidal shape with ftd dish on top, polychrome and gilt Egyptian deities and symbols, circ dial with signs of zodiac, c1880, Paris (A) 5500.00

Clock, Mantel, and Stand
14″ h, porcelain, front with shepherdess in wooded landscape, back and sides with brightly colored floral panels, white and green body, waisted rect stand on four scroll feet in gilt, detachable finial in form of leaf and grapes, c1850, "blue J.P." (A) ... 1599.00
17½″ h, swag molded clock painted with sprays of summer flowers between gilded and turquoise borders, c1870 (A) 748.00

Coffee Service, 2 coffee pots, 10¼″ h, milk jug, cov sugar bowl, 5 cups and saucers, Empire shape, painted landscape or riverscape panels in gilt floral borders, blue ground, gilt necks, handles, feet, and int, restorations, early 19th C, Old Paris (A) 3735.00

Coffee Service, Part
Coffee pot, 10″ h, teapot, cov sugar bowl, cov waste bowl, 11 coffee cans, 16 saucers, large coffee cup and saucer, multicolored chickens and birds, gilt patterned ground, gilt highlights, Old Paris 1250.00
Two handled cov sucrier, milk jug, ftd bowl, 10 cups and saucers, Empire Style, central band of flowering pink roses and green foliage

over burnished gilt ground, predominantly gilt and white ground, c1820, 24 pcs (A)................................... 3415.00

Compote, 4½″ h, 8½″ w, delicate multicolored florals in pink, rose, and orange in center and border, gilt trim, pedestal base, hand decorated, late 19th C, pr, marked 450.00

Cooler, 15″ h, globular body, Near Eastern inspiration, spiral decoration of cornflowers alternating with gilded dots, one with pendant floral borders, other with green marbled borders, molded scroll handles, gilded details, flared necks and feet, c1840, pr (A)........ 950.00

Coupe, 13½″ d, 10¾″ h, white glazed and gilded porcelain, open work basket on top, rect base, c1810 .... 1100.00

Cup and Saucer
Bell shape with swan handle, gilded designs, reserved on blue ground, c1835, Paris, pr (A)................................... 1030.00
Large, globular form, band of roses between gilt line borders, pierced scroll floral handle, c1835 (A)........................... 112.00
White body pierced with small holes, coral borders accented with gilt, "H & PL V" marks (A)........................... 560.00
Various insects in enamel and gilt, mid 19th C, set of 4 (A)........................... 82.00

Decanter, 6¼″ h, rect, multicolored florals overall, cross-hatch pattern in gilt on corners, gilt trim, white ground, c1870 .... 525.00

Dessert Service, Part, compote, 9¼″ d, 2 compotes, 8⅜″ d, 1 saucer, 18 plates, each with different colorful bird perched on or near small tree on plateau, compotes with birds on circ foot, gilt foliate border interspersed with stars and sprigs between gilt bands, c1815, underglaze "blue X'd swords" mark, Locre, Russinger, Pouyat Factory, 22 pcs (A) 2750.00

Dish, Radish, 9¼″ l, oblong oct, monogrammed "BD" in green and gold within roundel surrounded by gilt sprigs within borders of red berried green laurel, gilt flowering vine, gilt stippled bands, 1820–30, "iron-red crowned A" for Rue Thiroux Factory (A) 100.00

Eau de Toilette
4″ h, 4½″ h, 5¼″ h, 5½″ h, shaped sq, pink and yellow roses in cartouche of dark cobalt outlined in gilt on front and back, matte gilt bands separate panels, gold designs, c1880, set of 4 .... 650.00
4″ h, 5″ h, 5½″ h, shaped sq, pink, rose, purple, and rust floral panel on front with white ground, fuchsia body, gilt trim, floral lids, c1880, set of 3 .... 550.00
4¼″ h, 4¾″ h, 5¾″ h, shaped sq, pink and blue florals, green lines, rust lines separate panels, white ground, c1880, painted rust mark, set of 3 .... 550.00
4¾″ h, 5½″ h, 7″ h, dainty flowers in rose and green, blue ribbons, gilt trim and dots, white ground, c1880, "Josephine in gilt with eagle" mark, set of 3 .... 550.00

Ewer, Cov, Basin, 10¼″ h, 12⅝″ l, pear shaped body, colorful scene with figures, horses, sailboats near buildings, wide border of floral festoons and swags of gilt beads, chains, and tassels hanging from purple, blue, iron-red, and gold foliate scrolls coming from green bellflowers beneath gilt trimmed salmon triangles, ext of basin with gilt stars and dots beneath foliate vine, cov with gilt cherry knob, handle and cov rim with Louis XVI gilt metal hinged foliate mount and shell form thumbpiece, c1786 (A) **3300.00**

Figure

9½" h, biscuit, Jupiter with eagle by his side, one arm upright, before rockwork, circ base, c1800 (A)........................ **200.00**

12" h, painted parrot resting on rockwork, gilt bronze rococo base, pr, Paris (A) **4675.00**

18¾" h, Napoleon standing in uniform with hand in shirt, decorated gilt, sq base inscribed "Roussel-Bardelle' (A) **660.00**

Fruit Cooler, Cov, Liner, 11⅞" h, 11¾" h, ovoid body, small sprigs of multicolored flowers and gilt leaves beneath gilt foliate garland hanging from gilt edged wide floral border reserved with four gilt oval panels of large floral sprigs, gilt upright scroll handles, cov with central gilt columnar knob, mushroom finial, gilt rim edges, c1785, underglaze "blue X'd swords, incised J.V.B. or C. Heights" mark, pr (A) **2475.00**

Fruit Set, compote, 3 plates, 8" d, fruit centers, burgundy trim............................ **135.00**

Garniture, Cov, 13" h, flared campana form, panels of brightly colored flowers on cobalt blue ground, enriched with gilding, lug handles applied at terminals with bearded masks, waisted socle and sq base, one cov missing, c1840, pr (A) **5610.00**

Ink Stand, 7½" l, 6½" w, 3¼" h, dbl white and gilt with pen tray, unmarked........... **235.00**

Jar, Cov, 5" d, intertwined lines of pink roses and purple flowers in white panel, green panels on base and lid with gilt lines, gold finial, c1810, "blue cursive LR" mark **475.00**

Pitcher

8⅜" h, hp medallion of Farragut or Grant in military uniforms, flanked by gilt leaf and berry branches, shaded ground, Lady Liberty and flag between medallions under spout, gold star ground, gold twist handle, c1862 (A) **23,100.00**

10" h, with undertray, 10" d, light blue and white medallions and flowers, gold trimming, Old Paris **325.00**

Plate

9" d

Crested, one with "Horse Guards London," other "Waterloo," in naturalistic shades, gilt band, gilt edge rim, brown demi-lion rampant and battle-ax crest of Wildman, russet script topographical inscriptions, "Maria Wildman pinx Feb 21 1821 or March 15" marks, pr (A).............. **1210.00**

Pairs of birds perched on or beside branches next to river bank, wide lavender borders, gilded trellis panels, floral garlands, c1830–50, 10 pcs (A)........ **2100.00**

9¼" d, botanical, central flowering specimen within border of tightly bunched roses and violets, pale blue ground, Feuillet, gilt script marks, pr (A)........................... **648.00**

9⅜ d, Hp Young Woman

Classical dress with songbird perched in tree behind her, wide burnished gilt rim tooled with alternating berries and flowerheads on a checkered ground, small crack, 1806–16, Duc d'Orleans factory, gilt inscription "Lefebvre a paris" mark (A) **390.00**

National costume, one in laced green and black bodice and iron-red skirt, tan garden bench, gilt inscription "Costume Suisse," other in brown hat, iron-red and white neckerchief and apron over blue dress, brown garden wall, gilt inscription "Costume Savoyard," gilt borders of neoclassical scrolls, berried vine between bands and lines, 1820–30, "green enamel decorator's Feuillet a Paris" marks, pr (A) **300.00**

9½" d, painted central medallion of different exotic birds, gilt festoons of flowers on rim, c1790, Paris, set of 9 .... **2500.00**

9 9/16" d, different botantical specimen within gilt scrollwork border, cobalt blue ground rim with three floral panels, c1840, decorator's "Feuillet in gold or black" mark, set of 5 (A)................................. **1600.00**

9⅝" d, painted botanical flowers, border with three gilt cartouches of florals on dark blue ground, c1830, "Boyer S. de Feuillet" mark, set of 4 (A) **2871.00**

Pomade Jar, 3" d, 3½" d, 4" d, rust, pink, blue, purple, and yellow floral swags on base, florals on lids, gilt rims and lines, white ground, late 19th C, painted rust mark, set of 3......... **550.00**

Potpourri Vase, Cov

6½" h, shaped panels of Orientals on pagoda terrace, reserved on brown ground painted with colored flowers, four lion paw feet, lion's mask handles, pierced cov, c1850, pr **950.00**

10¼" h, pierced neck modeled with three rams' heads, cov and body painted with panels of summer flowers reserved against blue ground, gilded scrolling foliage, three scroll feet, c1870 (A) **1821.00**

19½" h, lobed bowl, garlands of summer flowers on apple-green ground with gilding, three lion paw and mask feet in burnished gilding, canted triangular base, domed cov, pierced flared neck, detachable flame finial, restored rim, c1860, underglaze "blue JP" mark, 3 pcs (A) **2550.00**

Scent Bottle, Stopper

7⅞" h, pineapple form, orange and yellow fruit heightened in dark orange, pink, purple, and green, serrated green leaves form bottle necks and stoppers, encrusted with spiraling garlands of colorful flowers and green leaves, restored, c1845, underglaze "blue "JP, incised R, green enamel E" mark, pr (A)...............................**12,650.00**

9⅝" h, 9½" h, lily of the valley form, three stalks of yellow centered white blossoms superimposed against pink and yellow shaded leaves rising form gilt heightened rococo scroll molded base, terminating in green leaf tips and gilt veined white smaller leaves forming rim, stoppers formed as leaves surrounding three iron-red tipped white bids, 1835–45, pr (A) **770.00**

Tea and Coffee Service, coffee pot, 7½" h, tea-

pot, cov sugar, creamer, 3 cov coffee cans
with undertray, 3 cov teacups with undertray,
cylindrical form, floral reserves on overall floral
pattern ground, bow knot and wreath handles,
gilt and cobalt banding, 3rd qtr 19th C (A).. **1210.00**

Tea Service
16 cups and saucers, 5 1/8" d, 2 shaped
dishes, sprigs of cornflowers in green, blue
and red enamels, gilded rims and handles,
c1790–1800, "red stenciled crowned A,"
Paris (A).............................. **1000.00**
Teapot, 8 1/2" h, cream bowl, milk jug, 6 cups
and saucers, landscape decorations with
gilding, hairlines, Paris (A).............. **225.00**

Tray
17 3/8" l, lobed oval form, painted in center
with hunt in rural wooded landscape, lake,
small town nestling between trees and hills
beyond, within tooled gilt border, fitted into
gilt metal frame, c1820–50 (A) **4554.00**
18 1/4" l, 13" w, hp multicolored roses and
leaves in center, green and gold border,
molded handles...................... **150.00**

Tureen
10" h, scattered blue cornflowers with green
stems, white ground, circ shape on flared
foot, dbl foliate scroll handles with shell and
palmetto terminals, gilt artichoke knob and
rims, c1810, Old Paris **575.00**
11 1/2" h, 10 1/2" H-H, white and gold decorated, white and gold finial, late 19th C,
marked.............................. **450.00**

Urn
9 1/4" h, white glazed porcelain, two applied
handles with heads, sq base, c1810...... **550.00**
10" h
Green, rust, and gilt classical designs, two
applied gilt handles, dark pink ground,
c1825, pr **2600.00**
Ovoid body, stylized gilt decoration, dbl
scrolled handles, gilt banded neck and
front, 19th C, pr **440.00**
16 7/8" h, unglazed lower section, glazed
brown enameled classical floral design with
acorn border, gilt rims, leaf scrolled handles,
marble base (A)...................... **220.00**
21" h, baluster form, scenic view and figures
in garden, pale yellow ground, gilt metal mts
and handles, c1900 (A)............... **605.00**

Vase
6 3/4" h, urn shape, scene of two lovers, female in blue bodice and pink skirt, male in
blue breeches and purple cloak, reverse
scene of landscape with house, two gilt handles, sq gilt base over white, c1810 ...... **325.00**
7" w, white and gold with gold handles, floral
cartouche on front in pinks, purple, green,
blue, and rust, gilt on base in leaf springs,
scalloped top, imp "JA" mark, pr **325.00**
8 1/2" h, ovoid body, matte blue and painted
with gilded designs, loop handles, flared
neck, sq foot in burnished gilding, c1820, pr
(A)................................. **527.00**
8 3/4" h, rect shape, orange, yellow bird in
flowering landscape, blue ground, Old Paris
mark (A) **110.00**
9" h, center neck, two side necks, painted
panels of flowers in raised gilt borders,

green ground, four scroll leaf feet, c1840,
Jacob Petit, pr (A) **1775.00**
10" h, hp red tulips on white ground, gold
trim, gold outlined leaf molded handles,
shaped rim and foot, c1800, pr......... **1050.00**
12" h, flattened ovoid body, "La Madonna
della Sedia," three figures in colored robes,
burnished gilded ground, oval foot, rect
base, two handles, c1835 (A)........... **1496.00**
13" h, fan shape floral design with extra floral
leaves on sides, multicolor florals **350.00**
13 1/8" h, campana shape, tooled and burnished leaves on lower body, upper body
with continuous Italianate landscape scene
in naturalistic colors with figures and horses
at various pursuits near buildings, gold and
white biscuit ladies' head handles, gilt circ
foot, sq base with white edges, c1815, pr
(A)................................. **4950.00**
13 1/4" h, baluster shape, enameled oriental
figures in stylized trees, flowers, and subjects, soft green ground, damaged, mid 19th
C, pr (A) **440.00**
13 1/2" h, ovoid body, Empire form, central gilt
ground band painted with arrangement of
flowers over vivid blue ground flanked by pr
of gilt loop handles inset with classical
masks, flaring gilt neck, gilt pedestal base,
white glazed sq foot, one restored, c1820,
pr (A)............................... **1024.00**
14" h, flaring floral fan shape, twisted leaves
on sides, tulips in vert panel............. **350.00**
14 3/8" h, flattened urn shape, "La Toilette"
and "La Romance," tooled gilded ground,
winged griffin handles, rect base, four paw
feet, c1820, printed mark, pr (A)........ **2244.00**
14 1/2" h, ovoid body, colorful romantic scene
on front, one with lady presenting singer to
friend, other with lady listening to singing,
gilt edged panel, matte blue ground decorated on reverse with gilt trophies, flowerheads, and scrolls, gilt winged female caryatid handles, gilt trumpet shaped neck, circ
foot, sq base, one damaged, c1840, pr
(A)................................. **2200.00**
15 1/2" h, ovoid body, gilt with emblems of
war and music within laurel borders, applied
biscuit swags of flowers hung from handles
with gilt griffins, burnished gilt necks and
feet, marbled base, green ground, one neck
restored, c1790, pr (A) **766.00**
16" h, center panel of French court scene,
gold and white trim, rose ground, Old
Paris................................. **245.00**
18" h, paneled scenes of lovers in woodland
setting, gilt trim and accents, blue ground,
molded gilt bell flower handles, late 19th C,
pr (A)............................... **330.00**
18 1/4" h, enameled cartouche of male or female figure, heavily gilt raised molded bell
flowers on sides, leafy shaped top, hairlines,
late 19th C, pr (A)..................... **250.00**
Vase, Cov, 17 1/2" h, center scene of children
riding goat, panels of floral bouquets, mint
green ground, molded handles with leaf garlands, ormolu mts, late 19th C, pr (A) **605.00**
Veilleuse, 9" h, cov cup in warming pot set in
container with heating cup, floral and gold design, early 19th C, Jacob Petit (A) **55.00**

1862

PARIAN

English/Continental
Early 1840s to 20th Century

History: Parian has a slightly translucent, natural creamy-white body fired to a matte finish. It was introduced in the early 1840s and remained popular during the entire Victorian era. Parian's strong resemblance to marble appealed to the Victorians since it suggested elegance, opulence, and wealth.

The best parian examples were characterized by the delicacy of the ware's texture. Its excellent molding versatility made it suitable for figures, utilitarian wares, and even floral jewelry pieces.

Among the many firms that have made parian china from the 1840s to the present time is Copeland. Pieces often were marked with an impressed "Copeland." After 1862 Minton impressed its parian with the name of the company and occasionally added the impressed year mark.

Parian also was manufactured by Belleck in Ireland and Coalport, Goss, Robinson and Leadbeater, Wedgwood, and Royal Worcester in England. Gustavsburg and Rorstrand in Sweden carried parian wares as part of their line. Most leading firms marked their parian wares. Smaller firms were less likely to do so.

References: Paul Atterbury, editor, *The Parian Phenomenon*, Shepton Beauchamp, 1989; G.A. Godden, *Victorian Porcelain*, Herbert Jenkins, 1961; C. & D. Shinn, *The Illustrated Guide to Victorian Parian China*, Barrie & Jenkins, 1971.

Museum: Victoria & Albert Museum, London, England.

Candle Snuffer and Stand, 3⅝" h, figural hollow
    arm in puffed sleeve, circ stand (A). **495.00**
Figure
    3⅝" h, standing British lion dressed in
      clothes of period, 18th C **200.00**
    4⅛" h, "The Veiled Bride," bust of maiden
      with veil fastened with floral wreath, waisted
      circ socle, dtd 1861, Copeland (A). **1290.00**
    5¾" h, young Queen Victoria seated on
      throne, wood base, c1839, England (A). . . **440.00**
    6¾" h, bust of Shakespeare (A) **44.00**
    7⅜" h, "Rock of Ages" group, maiden
      dressed in long folding robe, kneeling
      before large cross, oval base molded with
      plants and rocks, cross molded "ROCK OF
      AGES," c1870 (A). **561.00**
    7½" h, bust of Dickens, Scott, Burns, or
      Shakespeare, sq base, c1890s, Robinson
      and Leadbetter, set of 4 . . . . **525.00**
    7¾" h, bust of gentleman with open shirt
      front, circ plinth, "J.&T.B. Burns" mark (A) **65.00**
    7⅞" h, bust of Wagner, "Robinson & Lead-
      beater" mark **175.00**
    8" h, standing youth in jerkin and pantaloons,
      basket of flowers on shoulder, unmarked
      (A). **10.00**
    8⅝" h, bust of Jenny Lind, wearing loose
      tunic, hair tied, waisted socle base, c1847,
      imp "Copeland," molded signature and title
      (A). **320.00**
    9" h
      Bust of sleeping angel, wings tucked under
        chin, c1860, Copeland. **175.00**
      Girl praying, unmarked. **48.00**
    9½" h, German bust of Schiller. **175.00**
    10" h, young boy with bundle of twigs, re-
      paired, Royal Crown Derby **100.00**
    10⅛" h, standing figure of Alexander Hum-
      boldt holding book, sq base (A). **110.00**
    10½" h
      Lady with dove and urn, unmarked **95.00**

**Figure, 11" h, flute missing, imp "interlaced L's
and Paris" mark, (A) $90.00**

**Jug, 9½" h, "Boy and Eagle," white, c1850–59,
Keys and Mountford, $700.00**

"The Death," dog attacking stag on rocky molded base (A) **165.00**

10⅞" h, standing figure of Sir John Peel, scroll in hand, plinth at side, circ base, Minton (A) **750.00**

11" h

Bust of Henry Irving, wearing jacket, waistcoat, wing collar, waisted circ base, c1870 .... **561.00**

Bust of young Queen Victoria, circ pedestal base, c1870, imp "J.&T.B." mark (A) ... **295.00**

11⅜" h, bust of Ophelia, long flowing hair bound with garland of ivy and wheat sheaves, gathered dress, waised socle inscribed "CRYSTAL PALACE ART UNION," c1870, imp "COPELAND," title and sculptor (A) **374.00**

11¾" h, bust of Shakespeare mtd on pedestal base, dtd 1864, imp "F.M. MILLER CO." and "WEDGWOOD AND SONS" on base (A)................................... **880.00**

12" h, seated female nude with draped cloth, molded fish and reeds on base, imp "Marshall Fect SC., Copeland" mark (A)....... **440.00**

12½" h, bust of Albert wearing loose drapery, waisted socle, imp "Marshall Wood Sculp, 1863, Copeland and Crystal Palace Art Union" mark **475.00**

12⅝" h, Florence Nightingale attending wounded soldier with cane, oval base, Copeland (A) **1235.00**

12⅞" h, "Scotland," imp "Josiah Wedgwood & Sons, Published January 6, 1859" mark (A).................................. **675.00**

13" h

"Clorinda," warrior wearing armor, resting against wall, imp "John Bell 1848 Minton" marks (A)...................... **550.00**

"May Queen," modeled as bust of young woman with curly hair, circ base, "May Queen, Ceramic and Crystal Palace Art Union, pub. April 1, 1868 . . . Copeland" mark (A) **121.00**

Queen Victoria, floral garland in hair, waisted circ base, c1870, imp Copeland marks, "pub Aug 1 1864" imp "Crystal Palace Art Union" marks (A) **523.00**

Scantily clad young girl seated on rock, goat on lap, c1870, imp "Turner and Co., Art Union of Great Britian".............. **275.00**

13½" h, "Dorthea," woman seated on rock, bag at feet, 1861, imp "Minton" mark (A) **165.00**

13⅞" h, bust of Nelson in naval uniform, waisted socle, Copeland **195.00**

14" h

"Dying Gladiator," nude male figure semireclined on oval base, sword on ground, c1860, imp "Crystal Palace Art Union" mark (A) **385.00**

Nude woman with draped body, butterfly on shoulder, tinted, c1920 .... **125.00**

14½" h

Ariadne and the Panther, naked maiden with garland of leaves seated on flowing cloak draped on back of growling panther, rocky rect base, c1856, Minton, imp date code, imp "Ermine" mark (A)..... **710.00**

Bust of Milton, imp "WEDGWOOD," titled by E.W. Wyon mark (A).............. **600.00**

14⅝" h, standing child with basket, imp

"Josiah Wedgwood & Sons, Published July 12, 1858" mark (A) **550.00**

15" h

Bust of Lord Byron, "E.W. Wyons" mark.. **500.00**

Nude man and woman in embrace, marble base, artist sgd (A) **50.00**

15¼" h, "The Lion in Love," draped female pulling thorn from lion's paw, glazed base, c1870, imp "Minton" marks

15⅜" h, bust of Admiral Wellington, loose drapery around shoulders, waisted socle base, c1870, imp "E.W.Wyon," Wedgwood (A)................................... **710.00**

15½" h

Bust of Charles Dickens................. **140.00**

Una and the Lion modeled as naked maiden seated on back of lion, holding lion's paw, c1863, Minton (A) **1150.00**

15½", 15¾" h, boy and girl modeled as flower vendors holding baskets, period clothes, circ base, England, late 19th C, pr (A)................................... **605.00**

16" h, girl seated on stool in long lace dress holding rabbit to chest, c1873, imp "Ceramic and Crystal Palace Art Union, Copeland's Copyright Reserved" mark (A)..... **750.00**

16½" h, bust of classical female head, fluted pedestal, c1850 (A) **260.00**

16¾" h, "Venus" by John Gibson, with gilt and tinted borders, c1849, "Copeland, Art Union of Great Britain" marks **3500.00**

16⅞" h, "Go To Sleep," young girl cradling puppy dog in arms, modeled by Joseph Durham, made for Art Union of London in 1862, imp "Copeland' (A)............. **540.00**

17¼" h, Cupid and Psyche, two lovers embracing, dressed in draped robes, caned and curved sq base, c1843, sculpted by H. Bourne, Minton, incised title and sculptor's mark, imp "Ermine" and date code (A) ... **654.00**

19¾" h, Confederate soldier with rifle on right leg, wounded companion at side, imp "Wounded to the Rear, One More Shot," repaired, c1865, imp "John Rogers" mark **525.00**

21½" h, "Beatrice," standing female in classic clothes, imp "Copeland Pub. March 1 1860 Edgar Papworth Jun SC" mark (A).. **440.00**

21¾" h, "Maiden Hood," standing woman with skirt gathered in hands, imp "Pub. Sept. 2 1861 Copeland" mark (A)............. **605.00**

25½" h, classical maiden standing beside pedestal fountain catching water in cup, gilt highlights, c1870, Continental (A)........ **640.00**

Fruit Comport, 21" h, pierced basket supported by Three Graces in classical robes standing back to back, shaped triangular base, still leaf border, minor damage, 1850, imp "Copeland' (A)..................................... **374.00**

Jug

4⅞" h, "Pond Lily" pattern, Copeland (A) . **90.00**

5" h, ribbed design, reg June 5, l852, Minton **295.00**

5½" h, black printed image of Ernest Jones, gilt borders with blue ground (A) **225.00**

6" h, relief of lily of the valley and long leaves on stippled ground **55.00**

7" h, relief scene of slave auction, reverse with mother and child fleeing, dtd January 1, 1838, Ridgway (A) **645.00**

9⅛" h, emb white seaweed design on rose

ground, dtd 1861, "Beech & Hancock" mark.................................. **100.00**

9¾" h, emb lavender classical figures on white ground, bearded face on handle, "black Lion and Unicorn" mark......... **155.00**

9⅞" h, relief profile bust of Prince Albert, reverse with crest and dates, both in laurel leaf medallions, fishscale ground, figural handle of crown, star, and crests (A) **210.00**

Pitcher

4½" h, white roses on green ground...... **65.00**

6½" h, seated classical woman with cherubs and angels overhead, child with book, lamb and birds at feet, robed lady and angel on side, scalloped top **115.00**

8" h, ribbed design with two bands of geometric orange designs with gold outlines, registry mark, Minton................... **275.00**

8½" h, three cartouches with historic scenes, scene of Chicago fire under upper rim, applied vignettes on blue ground, designed for Chicago, "#343 Copeland Late Spode England" mark.......................... **650.00**

9" h, three eagle head spouts and flagstaff handles, shields with "1876 Centennial Memorial," Washington Father of our Country, and 1776 Declaration of Independence," repairs (A)........................... **410.00**

9¾" h, relief of hanging game birds and leaves (A) **82.00**

11¼" h, "Washington Taking Leave of his Mother," c1840–50s **365.00**

Plaque

6" d, relief of angel with two sleeping children and owl, pierced for hanging, Royal Copenhagen.................................. **30.00**

11⅜" d, allegorical figures of Day and Night, pierced for hanging, Royal Copenhagen, pr............................. **380.00**

Pot, Cov, 5⅞" h, body with molded bark tied with rope, cov with figural head of Gladstone, Robinson & Leadbeater (A)............... **225.00**

Roundel, 13⅜" h, smear glaze, modeled with St. George and the dragon fighting by the seashore, framed and glazed, c1850–70 (A).... **527.00**

Syrup Pitcher, 5¾" h, emb figure of George Washington, pewter lid (A)............... **38.00**

Tea Service, pot, 4½" h, creamer, 4½" h, sugar, 4" h, tray, 14½" l, cup and saucer, raised leaf design, Eng Reg marks **325.00**

Vase, 6¼" h, 5½" l, figural fox with dead rabbit under paws, bark textured fan vase in ground, oval base, unmarked.............. **55.00**

Wall Bracket, 10½" h, Triton and mermaid supporting shell form bracket, late 19th C, pr (A) . **425.00**

PATE-SUR-PATE (PASTE ON PASTE)

Austria, England, France, Germany c1860 to 1900s

History: During the early 1860s, several Sevres potteries attempted to copy the Chinese technique of pate-sur-pate. In pate-sur-pate the design exhibits a cameo-like decorative motif achieved by using tinted parian as the

background and adding layers of white parian slip that then are carved into the design before the firing. When fired, the layers of white parian slip become semi-translucent and vitrified. The dark ground shows through the thinner parts.

Marc Louis Solon, who trained at Sevres, brought the Victorian pate-sur-pate process to England in 1870 when he began employment at Minton. At first he depicted tall, thin classical female figures in diaphanous drapery. Later he expanded his repetoire to include children and cupids. Each creation was unique and signed.

Solon enjoyed a great reputation for his pate-sur-pate pieces. Since the painstaking pate-sur-pate technique was exceptionally slow and the market demand was great, Solon trained a series of apprentices while at Minton, the most talented of which were A. Birks and L. Birks. Solon worked at Minton until 1904. After retirement, he worked free lance until he died in 1913.

Not all pate-sur-pate examples were made at Minton. Royal Worcester, Grainger-Worcester, the Crescent Potteries of George Jones, and several other firms manufactured pate-sur-pate pieces. F. Schenk produced many examples for Crescent Pottery at Stoke. These pieces were inferior and repetitive when compared to those made at Minton and Worcester.

Meissen, Berlin, and Vienna on the Continent were known for the production of pate-sur-pate. Pieces from these factories lacked the finesse of Solon's works and tended to be heavy and Germanic in style.

Reference: G.A. Godden, *Victorian Porcelain,* Herbert Jenkins, 1961.

Museums: National Collection of Fine Arts, Smithsonian Institution, Washington D.C.; Victoria & Albert Museum, London, England.

Collecting Hints: Collectors should be aware that some George Jones wares are being sold as Minton products in today's marketplace.

Bonbonniere, 5" d, white enamel on pink ground, portrait bust medallion of young girl with hair tied in ribbon, scrolling foliage borders in yellow, green, blue, and pink, late 19th C, Meissen, underglaze "blue X'd swords" mark (A)................................ **3179.00**

Box

4½" l, 4" w, white medallion of Cupids with lyre in clouds, blue ground, Limoges **185.00**

Plaque, 7¾" h, 5" w, white slip design on charcoal black ground, c1900–10, "Limoges France" mark, $225.00

6" d, white slip design of nude sitting on river bank, cobalt ground, sgd "GOL" in design, blown out shape, gold beading, "F.M. Barbotine, Limoges, France" mark. **895.00**

Dish

9¹⁄₂" d, white slip design of maiden stringing hearts, green grass, brown ground, gold key border with green half mons on white ground, gilt dentil rim, c1880, sgd "L. Solon," Minton (A) **2505.00**

12" d, female with veil standing on marble terrace, reclining against celestial globe mounted on pedestal, beaded gilt border, pale green, yellow, and pink interlaced border with applied gilt tendril and flowerhead sprays, applied gilt stars, c1885, underglaze "blue scepter, iron-red KPM and orb" (A) . **7584.00**

Garniture, Vase, Cov, 13" h, 2 ewers, 11" h, sheer white relief with maidens, cherubs, and Cupid at play reserved within oval roundels on brown ground, reverse decorated with trophies and floral garlands, oval panels joined by pale blue bands decorated with scrolling foliage and classical vases, yellow ground, fluted socle and sq foot, c1893, sgd "A. Birks, imp "MINTONS," 3 panels with "AB," date code, printed crowned circle, shape no.1914 (A). . **8653.00**

Jardinaire

5" h, lobed body, sheer white relief with Cupids catching butterflies in nets, dark green ground, light green and gilt ribbon handles, c1890, "George Jones" mark (A) **1425.00**

7" h, circ panel of white slip design of seated Cupid as sculptor with hammer and chisel before bust on tan ground, reserved on white ground with gilded scroll borders, reverse with circ panel of pendant foliage, scrolls, cornucopia, and birds on tan ground, c1900, sgd "Birks, imp MINTON" mark (A). **2050.00**

Lamp, 12¹⁄₄" h, white slip design of putti flying amongst ferns and plants, fitted with oil lamp burner and base, late 19th C, England (A). . . **412.00**

Letter Holder, 6¹⁄₄" l, 4³⁄₄" h, woman playing card game with three female children, tree on left, blue ground, brass Art Nouveau frame . **575.00**

Moon Flask

10" h, circ panel of white slip design of young boy giving bouquet to young girl, well and garden on olive green ground, raised gilt border, overall blue ground, restored neck, c1890, A. Birks, "gilt crown and globe" mark. **600.00**

10¹⁄₄" h, white slip design of dancing maiden holding bunch of grapes, reverse with pink, brown, and gilt scrolling, dark green ground, c1900 . . . . **250.00**

Pilgrim Vase, 7³⁄₄" h, white lilies on green ground on each side, pink sides, white and gold handles, Grainger **420.00**

Plaque

6" h, 5" w, rect, white slip decoration of maiden kneeling and crying in bucket, standing Cupid turning wheel, green ground, framed, c1900, sgd "Miles' (A). . . **1480.00**

6¹⁄₄" h, 9¹⁄₄" l, rect, white slip relief of classical maidens and Cupids with emblems and spears, standing on balcony, c1890, sgd "L. Solon," Minton **2000.00**

7" d, circ, classical figure upon chariot drawn by four horses, Limoges (A) **140.00**

9" h, 4³⁄₄" w, rect, white slip decoration of maiden standing on plinth sweeping crown on to floor, blue-black ground, c1900, incised "MLS" mark. **950.00**

9¹⁄₂" h, 6¹⁄₄" w, white slip decoration of scantily clad maiden holding bunch of flowers, black ground, dtd 1886 (A). **910.00**

10¹⁄₄" h, 6¹⁄₄" w, rect, white slip design of scantily clad female holding flower, walking in forest, blue ground, c1870–90, Limoges (A). **960.00**

10⁵⁄₈" h, 6" w, domed rect, white slip allegorical maiden in long sheer robes with chained cherub on one side, kneeling cherub on other, entitled "Oratio, Redemptio, and Consolatio," border in green, blue, and brown with gilding, c1870, sgd "Paris," framed (A) **3643.00**

10³⁄₄" h, 6³⁄₈" w, rect, white slip design of woman holding vase, cherubs ascending to sky from whirlwind, brown ground, "L. Solon" on front (A). **2000.00**

11¹⁄₂" h, 7" w, rect, white slip design of five cherubs blowing trumpets into heart of maiden, green ground, sgd "L. Solon' (A) . **4212.00**

13³⁄₈" l, 9⁷⁄₈" h, white cameo of cattle, donkeys, and goats in wooded meadow, green ground, c1860–70, pr **1500.00**

20¹⁄₂" h, 8" w, oval, white slip design of angels with wreaths in clouds, cherubs on ground near fountain, black ground, c1890, "George Jones" mark, pr (A) **2505.00**

Plate

8³⁄₄" d, putto sketching companion, seated on billowing clouds, gray-green ground, white ground border with three maroon panels, overall gilt foliate details, c1878–1900, sgd "Julius Heintze," underglaze "blue scepter, printed orb and scepter" marks (A) **8025.00**

8⁷⁄₈" d, white slip design of nymph piper seated on branch of prunus tree, gilded floral borders between yellow band, c1885, Limoges. **1100.00**

9" d

Cherub seated on throne, woman kneeling offering heart, pierced border molded with scrolls accented in gold and pink, c1896, imp "Mintons" mark **475.00**

Maiden pouring water from vase over fleeing cherub in central circ medallion, pierced borders molded with scrolls and gilded, c1895, sgd "L. Solon, Minton, printed crowned globe" marks (A) **1309.00**

White slip design of wild rose, salmon pink ground, gold tracery and edge, unmarked **175.00**

9¹⁄₂" d

Center in white slip with muse in classical int attempting to read book while teasing cherub covers her eyes from behind, central lilac ground medallion, raised gilt borders, pale ivory ground, c1900, sgd "Marc Louis Solon," imp amd gilt printed marks, Minton (A). **1063.00**

Classical female in sheer white robe, holding staff, hound seated at side, reserved on pink ground, pierced border gilt with interlocking ovals centered by tiny florets in relief, c1880, Meissen, underglaze "blue X'd swords" mark (A). **3643.00**

Gilt center panel of etched scrolls, white slip design of coupled dolphins swimming through water, scrolled tails connected with acanthus leaves and vines, light gray ground, pierced gilt rim on white ground, gilded foot rim, c1918, Minton, set of 10 .... **3500.00**

Sheer white relief with cherubs at various pursuits on chocolate ground within waved cartouche edged in coral slip, white ground with star and dot design, 1876–78, imp "Mintons" and date codes, Retailer's marks for A.B. Daniell and Son, 16 Wigmore Street, London, set of 6 (A) **4326.00**

10³/₄" d, three rect panels of classical maidens and cherubs in sheer white robes on slate blue grounds, divided by cream and gilded floral panels, c1920, decorated by A. Birks, imp "MINTONS, gilt crowned circle," printed retailer's mark for Birks-Ellis-Ryrie Ltd, Toronto, set of 12 (A) **4000.00**

13" d, Art Nouveau style opaque white maidens in waves with fish and bird, swirling celadon green and pink ground, scalloped edge, sgd "Killer" **500.00**

Vase

4¹/₂" h

Florals with gold threads, black marbled ground, K.P.M.-Berlin **375.00**

White nude with veils on blue ground, Germany **145.00**

5³/₄" h, oviform body, oval panel in white with putto holding staff over celadon ground within tooled gilt frame over deep blue ground further gilt with leafy branches tied at bottom with ribbon, short flaring cylindrical neck, slender circ foot, sq base, c1880, Meissen, underglaze "blue X'd swords" mark (A) **3415.00**

6" h, white cupid chasing butterfly on black ground, George Jones **550.00**

6¹/₄" h, ovoid body, sheer white relief of cupids among ferns, gilded neck and foot, c1900, George Jones (A)............... **1050.00**

8¹/₂" h, woman in light gown holding basket over head, green ground............... **375.00**

9¹/₂" h, white slip design of two doves on base with branch arbor overhead, floral motif on reverse, slate blue ground, light blue neck with gilt accents and green swags, ring and acanthus leaf handles, c1877, imp "MINTON" mark (A).................. **1820.00**

10" h, slip decorated birds on turquoise, green, and gold ground, Royal Worcester, no.1684............................ **295.00**

10¹/₂" h

Ovoid body, sheer white relief with profile portrait of classical maiden, reserved within heart shaped scrolling panel in green, brown, and blue, on light green ground, two ringed lion mask handles in gilt, c1890, Limoges, printed mark, script numerals 177 (A) **800.00**

White flowers, green leaves, dark blue ground, gold handles, clover shaped top and base, unmarked................... **295.00**

12" h, semi-opaque enamels with angel fleeing two cherubs, flared neck and foot in gilding and brown, beading and foliage in raised white enamel, olive-green body, restored, c1900, Doulton (A)............. **300.00**

13" h, conical, green, brown, and gilt strap handles, woman in thin gown, cherub, shooting stars on front, cherub kneeling on cloud with stars on reverse, bright blue ground, sides with green and white stylized flowers, base with black and gold zig-zag design on light blue ground, c1872, imp "MINTON, MLS" mark (A)............. **9350.00**

15¹/₂" h, shouldered cylindrical body, white slip on brown ground with Venus sieving small hearts through basket with Cupid by side holding sickle, reverse with young child standing on dandelion leaves, flared neck and foot with formal floral design in pale blues and greens, gilded details, scroll handles, c1893, sgd "L. Solon, Minton, crowned globe" mark and date code (A) . **2821.00**

17¹/₂" h, stoneware, birds perched on branches in green and brown slip, Art Nouveau bands of foliage at top and base, c1890, Doulton Lambeth **1000.00**

21¹/₂" h, Chinese style white slip design of flying cranes over reeds, slate blue ground with scrolling gilt foliage, two small handles on neck with applied prunus, c1880, Minton, pr (A)............................ **7508.00**

38¹/₂" h, sheer white relief with jungle scene, crocodile, tiger, and panther in dense foliage, monkey swinging and seated in trees above, restored rim, c1860–70, Limoges (A)................. **4012.00**

Vase, Cov

10¹/₂" h, tapering cylindrical body, lobed and quatrefoil panels, two panels on brown ground before buildings or two swallows in flight above bridge, four smaller panels on slate blue ground with landscape scenes, cross-hatched ground with pate-sur-pate flowers and foliage, domed cov with fruit finial, gilt bronze mts, c1863, printed "S63" and incised mark (A) **2163.00**

14¹/₈" h, shield shape, white slip design of Venus and Cupid on light gray ground, molded and painted acanthus leaf gilt borders on gray ground, applied snake twist handles, leaf molded cov, circ foot on sq base, repaired, c1878–1900, "blue X'd swords" mark (A) **3860.00**

21" h, tall cylindrical neck, ovoid body, white slip on slate blue ground, crowned classical female holding presentation vase with cupids flying around holding hearts, reverse with two children seated on branches, formal gilt borders at neck and foot, inner gilt rim, coiled scroll handles, c1875–1890, sgd "Marc Louis Solon, printed globe mark, imp MINTONS" and date code (A) **15,048.00**

PEARLWARE

English
c1780–c1865

History: Pearlware, a variation of white creamware body, has a slightly bluish tint due to the addition of a small quantity of cobalt to the glaze. Pearlware is closer in general appearance and whiteness to porcelain than creamware. Wedgwood first made pearlware about 1779.

Pearlware was made mostly in tablewares. Among the

leading Staffordshire manufacturers were Herculaneum, Phillips Longport, Davenport, Clews, T. Mayer, Enoch Wood, Rogers, and Stubbs. Potteries at Leeds and Swansea also produced pearlware.

Polychrome floral decorations on pearlware became popular about 1800 and continued for approximately twenty years. These designs, usually in yellow, green, orange, or on silver luster resist were most commonly found on pitchers and jugs. Mocha decoration also was used on pearlware bodies.

Vast quantities of pearlware were shipped to the United States between 1790 and 1830. Some firms, such as Enoch Wood, produced pearlware specifically for the American market. Shell edge plates were decorated with the American eagle and shield in polychrome; other plates depicted prints of American ships with polychrome flags. Later blue transfer prints of American landmarks were applied to pitchers, plates, and chamber pots.

Museum: Victoria & Albert Museum, London, England.

Bowl
    10" d, 4¾" h, blue oriental decoration of pagoda flanked by trees and foliage, crisscross inner rim, hairline (A)............. **412.00**
    12¾" d, 4½" h, green feather edge, imp "Stevenson" mark (A) **250.00**

Bowl, 5" sq, red and green enameled floral border, early 19th C, unmkd, $150.00

Figure, 10½" h, dress with orange florals and green circles, gilt trim, green stained ground, white base, mid 19th C, (A) $200.00

Charger
    13¼" d, blue and white oriental pagoda in center, cross-hatch inner border, blue feather edge, practice painting on reverse, c1800, Staffordshire **1250.00**
    14" d, blue floral center, floral sprigs on border, blue and white, feather edge, c1790, Leeds **680.00**
Chocolate Pot, 6¾" h, cobalt and rust oriental garden scene, dbl entwined handle, flower finial outlined in blue, c1785 .... **1625.00**
Churn, Cov, 9¾" h, enameled entwined ribbon and laurel, restored, c1860, Wedgwood (A)..................................... **498.00**
Coffee Pot, 13½" h, blue and white, circ panels with blue leaf designs, 1810–20 .... **850.00**
Creamer
    3½" h, gaudy blue and red florals, emb leaf handle (A)............................ **40.00**
    4¼" h, emb and polychrome enameled floral decorations in medallions, repaired (A) ... **72.00**
    4¾" h, emb body with scattered polychrome enamel florals, ringed base (A).......... **275.00**
    5¾" h, red band on shaped rim, polychrome floral decoration, wishbone handle (A) ... **71.00**
Cup and Saucer, blue, green, pink, and yellow florals on cup and border of saucer, purple luster edge, c1830 .... **85.00**
Cup and Saucer, Handleless
    Polychrome rose decoration, hairline (A).... **22.00**
    Two cartouches of three classical figures in brown and white, mustard, blue, and green florals, c1810 .... **325.00**
Cup Plate, 4½" d, polychrome enameled rose decoration, emb rim (A)................... **44.00**
Dessert Service, Part
    Fruit stand, 12" l, lozenge shape, 2 dishes, lozenge shape, 10 plates, transfer printed in dark iron-red with overall pattern of evergreen sprigs beneath brown edged rim, 1810–15, brown enamel painter's triangle marks, fruit stand with "1507" mark, 13 pcs (A)................................ **1100.00**
    Six plates, 9" d, 2 shaped oval dishes, painted sprays of summer flowers and foliage in bright enamels, gilt line borders, early 19th C (A) **410.00**
Dish, 4¾" l, leaf shape with branch handle, molded green glazed veins and edge, three stub feet, late 18th C (A)................. **55.00**
Figure
    3⅜" h, seated pug, tan body with eyes, brown whiskers and mouth, brown collar, seated on grass green rect cushion molded at corners with tassels, repaired c1820 (A) **550.00**
    4¼" h, recumbent lion with mottled brown mane and ochre body, mottled brown base, restored, c1790, Yorkshire (A) **330.00**
    6⅜" h, swan with head on breast, white with blue wings, legs, and head, mound base washed in green (A)................... **2520.00**
    9" h, bust of Newton with brown hair, iron-red and green lined cloak, shaped waisted rect base with black, yellow, and iron-red marbleing, imp "Newton," c1830 (A)........ **965.00**
    9¼" h, bust of Handel in floral gown with orange trim over red-brown jacket, marbled waisted rect socle base, c1800 (A)....... **1010.00**
    10½" h, standing woman in orange flowered classic gown and blue edge, bird perched

on hand, green stained mound on white sq base with gold band (A) **209.00**

17 1/8" l, 11 7/8" h, setter, blue-tinged brown curly coat, gray muzzle and eyes, blue collar, standing on chamfered rect base sponged in light blue, streaked in brown, banded in blue on sides, crackled glaze, repaired, 1825–35 (A).................... **6050.00**

Flask, 6 1/4" h, circ, inscribed for "Thos. Tapper" on one side, reverse with chinoiserie island scene, 1788 (A)........................ **350.00**

Frog Mug, 4 1/2" h, blue floral decoration, yellow frog, early 19th C **495.00**

Jug
4 1/2" h, "The Good Samaritan," brown transfer, beige ground, purple luster band on top, c1820–30............................ **325.00**

6 3/8" h, ovoid shape, one side with farming implements thrust through wheatsheaf, reverse with spray of wild flowers, verse beheath spout "The Farmer's life . . . ," neck with continuous rustic scene, scrolling handle, c1800 (A) **2105.00**

6 3/4" h, bulbous shape, green, amber, blue, brown, and yellow pendant leaf and floral designs, cream ground (A) **66.00**

9" h, dogs and deer in pink and green, black accents **250.00**

Ladle, 10 1/2" l, green feather edge (A) **250.00**

Mug
3 1/8" h, "Hannah Isabella Dove" in black with rose ribbon and border, raised dotted base and top, blue and green leaves, c1820 ... **280.00**

4 3/8" h, cylindrical, ochre with band of molded blue and white stripes, rim and foot with brown stars, loop handle (A)........ **432.00**

4 5/8" h, blue leaf design, blue floral panel border at top, c1810 .... **295.00**

4 3/4" h, oriental bridge in brown, blue, yellow, green, and mustard florals, floral border on top and int, floral handle, c1810......... **650.00**

5" h, cylindrical, inscribed in red with verse to "Joseph and Sufanna Oddy," flanked by branches, formal border on top, crack in handle, 1803 (A)...................... **374.00**

5 1/4" h, molded satyr's mask with blue and green vines in hair, yellow horns and brown beard, hairline, c1780, Staffordshire (A)... **440.00**

5 3/4" h, cylindrical shape, seed pods on branches in amber, yellow, blue, green, and brown, ovoid shapes on rim, cream ground, base repaired........................ **250.00**

Pitcher
5 1/2" h, sanded body, brown band with yellow, green, and gilt florals............... **285.00**

6 1/4" h, polychrome stylized flowerheads on neck, Farmer's Arms on one side, verse on other, black view of cottage and "Henry Rielly/1809" under restored spout (A).... **385.00**

6 1/2" h, cartouche of Napoleon making out will, transfer decorated, early 19th C (A).. **360.00**

6 5/8" h, bulbous body, cylindrical rim, yellow, green, brown, and blue flowers and leaves, cream ground, blue rim and borders, Staffordshire (A)........................... **330.00**

6 3/4" h, green, yellow, brown, and blue beehive and florals, cream ground, brown outlined spout (A)........................ **1760.00**

7 1/4" h, blue florals and raised gold with green leaves, floral border around top, olive green lines, c1810...................... **795.00**

7 1/2" h, bulbous body, yellow, blue, amber, green, and olive flowers and trailing vines, cream ground (A) **550.00**

8" h, bulbous body, yellow, green, blue, amber, and brown stylized florals, cream ground, brown trimmed handle and rim (A) **550.00**

9" h
Applied enamel decoration of sprays of exotic flowers and leaves on sides, vine and berried band on neck, "Nathanial Moxom.Robert Mead.Fenny Stratford and A Fool and his money Are Soon parted" under spout (A)...................... **770.00**

Painted spray of flowers, reverse with bunch of grapes, blue band on shoulder, neck with band of scrolling vines, brown and green lined rim, c1780–1800, imp "Wedgwood" mark **900.00**

Plate
6 1/2" d
Polychrome floral and emb designs, luster trim (A) **55.00**

Pots of flowers in polychromes in red border with vining foliage, set of 6 (A) **214.00**

7 5/8" d, green and black floral decoration, green feather edge, imp "WEDGWOOD" mark (A) **150.00**

8 1/8" d, "Peony" pattern, blue and white florals, blue rim, c1820–40, imp "WEDGWOOD and blue Peony" mark.......... **65.00**

9 1/8" d, purple floral center, raised floral border, gilt rim, 1780, Staffordshire.......... **380.00**

9 1/2' d, green feather edged, scalloped, pr.. **295.00**

Platter
9" l, 7 1/2" w, blue transfer of oriental house scene, woods on right, clouds overhead, pierced-type border, scalloped rim, pr (A). **385.00**

18" l, 14 1/2" w, scalloped blue edge, imp "WOOD" mark...................... **275.00**

Plaque, 9 1/2" d, circ, relief molded, seated toper drinking a toast, encircled by smaller figures, reverse incised "1829," pierced for hanging, self framed (A)........................ **262.00**

Punch Bowl, 10 1/8" d, blue and white Orientals in a fenced garden on ext, sunburst on int, crack (A) **225.00**

Puzzle Jug, 7 1/4" h, ovoid shape, relief molded classical figures and acanthus leaves in blue, green, and brown, divided by horiz band inscribed in brown "If we slip as sure the best may err were still supported by Almighty care, 1791," handle molded as a winged angel blowing a trumpet which forms sucking spout, some restoration (A)...................... **1215.00**

Sauceboat, 7 1/2" h, swan shape, white, molded with plumage in relief, necks curved over to form handle, one restored, late 18th C, pr (A) **950.00**

Sugar Bowl, 5" h, yellow, brown, and blue Leeds type floral decoration (A).................. **72.00**

Tankard
5" h, polychrome florals in blue, mustard, olive and yellow **425.00**

5 7/8" h, black printed coat of arms of Free Masons, strap handle (A)............. **265.00**

Tea Caddy
5" h, shaped rect, figures of George III and Queen Charlotte in relief, blue floral on sides and shoulders, blue-gray ground.... **500.00**

5 1/8" h, rect, each side has winged putto draped with a garland of flowers or holding

bird and nest, top inscribed "Sarah Ralph 1793" in cobalt blue, 1793 (A) **561.00**

5¼" h, cylindrical shape, printed with flower head and scroll pattern (A) **225.00**

6½" h, rect, sides with applied figures of winged putti, shoulder and cov with busts of putti, blue accents, screw cov, late 18th C (A) **651.00**

Teapot, 6¼" h, swirled ribs and purple enameled delicate flowers and stripes (A) **115.00**

Tea Service, teapot, cov sugar with saucer, waste bowl, 4 cups, yellow overglaze decoration, enamel banding above an underglaze cobalt border of pendant husks, flower inside cups, 1830, Staffordshire **1250.00**

Teapot

3¼" h, multicolored scattered florals, repair to spout (A) **150.00**

5¾" h, New Hall type decoration of polychrome florals and hanging swags, lion finial, restored (A) **502.00**

6½" h, helmut shape, oriental scene with bridge in mustard, blue, and green, brown lines on rims.......................... **625.00**

6¾" h, blue oriental design of house by river with plants at sides (A).................. **500.00**

Toast Rack, 7" H-H, 4¼" h, overall floral pattern, c1820, Staffordshire.................. **625.00**

Tray

7¾" l, 6" w, center scene of oriental pagoda next to river with boat, blue transfer, basketweave and pierced loop border (A) **88.00**

10¼" l, oval shape, blue oval center with raised design, basketweave body, reticulated edge........................... **225.00**

Vase

7¼" h, 3 finger shape, blue and white designs, two dolphin base, molded drapery on top **850.00**

7⅞" h, five finger, blue and white floral design, vert ribbing on fingers, blue outlined rims, pr (A) **1800.00**

11½" h, oviform, two applied roudels of Hercules fighting the Nemean lion on blue ground, puce drapery, iron-red, green, and yellow striped body ground, flared foot, marbleized base, cov missing, c1775, Leeds (A).................................. **220.00**

Waste Bowl, 5⅞" d, red, pink, and green rose decoration, emb ribs with scalloped rim (A) . **33.00**

PIANO BABIES

England and Germany
19th Century

History: Piano babies, primarily in bisque, ranged in size from two to twelve inches long. They were popular additions to Victorian parlors, usually found on the top of a piano.

Piano babies were produced in a variety of poses from crawling, sitting, lying on their stomachs, to lying on their backs playing with their toes. Some babies were dressed; some were nude.

The most popular manufacturer was Heubach Brothers

4½" h, 11" l, bisque, aqua blanket, gold accents, yellow nighty, flesh body, unmkd, (A) $150.00

of Germany. Other identified makers include Hertwig and Company and Royal Doulton.

3½" h, sitting child in white gown with blue trim, brown wig, brown dog licking face, unmarked................................. **165.00**

3½" l, child reclining on stomach, imp "Heubach sunburst" mark **175.00**

4¼" h, sitting in white and green gown, white bonnet with pink trim, arms extended, unmarked................................. **100.00**

4½" h, sitting, arms raised **65.00**

5¼" h, seated baby, hands holding foot, white gown, turquoise trim, imp "orange Made in Germany" mark........................ **275.00**

6" l, baby lying on elbow, intaglio eyes, Heubach................................. **145.00**

6½" h, baby sitting, reaching for toes, Heubach................................. **285.00**

6¾" l, baby lying on stomach

Long bib with cat peeking out, dog on back **100.00**

Raised up on arms, one foot up, white gown, turquoise trim, imp "Heubach" mark..... **345.00**

7" l, baby lying on back playing with toes, intaglio eyes, wearing bonnet and gown, Heubach................................. **350.00**

7½" l, baby lying on back, holding foot, white gown, blue trim, imp "Heubach" mark **495.00**

8" l

Baby on stomach in nightie with green bow, bonnet with green ties................. **225.00**

Baby on stomach holding puppy, unmarked. **145.00**

Baby lying on back with hand holding toe, white nightie with blue ribbon, imp "Heubach sunburst" mark **395.00**

Crawling baby in white gown, kicking feet, Heubach............................. **420.00**

8¼" h, baby seated, holding foot, white gown, blue trim, imp "Heubach" mark **475.00**

9" h

Baby sitting on crossed leg, one hand up, other on chest, 55.00

Baby sitting, reaching for toes, unmarked **225.00**

10" l

Baby lying on stomach in colors **175.00**

Baby on stomach with pug dog............ **135.00**

10½" l, baby reclining on stomach, leaning on elbows, foot raised, white gown, turquoise trim, imp "Heubach sunburst" mark........ **495.00**

11" l

Baby half reclining, holding foot, unmarked . **165.00**

Lying on stomach, floral romper, black and
white kitten.......................... **300.00**
12" h
Girl with hand to her mouth (A) **55.00**
Seated boy holding apple (A)............. **55.00**

HILDITCH & SON
1822-1830

PITCHER AND BOWL SETS

English/Continental 19th and Early 20th Centuries

History: Pitcher and bowl sets or washstand china were popular during the 19th and early 20th centuries. A typical set consisted of a pitcher (ewer) and basin, soap dish, sponge dish, toothbrush tray, and slop pail. Additional specialized pieces, e.g., hair receivers and comb box, also were available. Wash sets allowed an individual to complete the washing up procedure in the privacy of the bedroom. The availability of piped water put an end to the Victorian and Edwardian jug and basin sets.

The list of manufacturers of washstand china was large. Principal English manufacturers include Minton, Wedgwood, George Jones, Doulton, Clarice Cliff, and Ridgway. Many Continental companies also made washstand china.

Collecting Hints: Not every set has the same number of pieces. Many sets featured only the pitcher and bowl.

Miniature
1 3/4" h, pitcher, 2 3/4" d, bowl, large red roses
and green leaves, cream ground, pink luster
trim (A) **110.00**
4 1/4" h, pitcher, 4 1/4" d, bowl, pink roses
with pink luster trim **200.00**

Pitcher, 7" h, bowl, 10" d, basketweave molded bodies, mint green band with gold trim, c1865, raised English Reg mark, $95.00

6" h, pitcher, 5 1/4" d, bowl, blue transfer with
floral cartouches, gold accents, "Hammersley & Co. China, England" mark **85.00**
Two Piece
9 3/8" h, pitcher, 12 5/8" d, bowl, dark brown
Adam's type open flowers, dark brown
leaves, c1840......................... **275.00**
10 1/4" h, pitcher, 14 1/4" d, bowl, "Homestead" scene, thatched cottage, multicolored flowers, blue band around base, top,
and handle, black line rim, cream ground,
imp "Cottage, Made in England" mark ... **225.00**
10 1/2" h, pitcher, 14 1/2" d, bowl, "Watchman What if the Night" design in colors,
brown figure on pitcher, buildings on int of
bowl, tan ground, c1902–22, "Royal Doulton" mark **775.00**
10 1/2" h, pitcher, 17" d, bowl, "Campion,"
flow blue with molded leaves and flowers,
molded handle, scalloped rim, Grindley
mark................................. **895.00**
11 1/4" h, pitcher, 13 1/4" d, bowl, brown
transfer of irises with leaves on white
ground, Eng Reg mark **225.00**
11 1/2" h, pitcher, 13 1/2" d, bowl, earthenware, border of rust and green geometric
design, cream ground, "Silvers France FN"
mark................................. **142.00**
11 3/4" h, pitcher, 14 1/2" d, bowl, black veining design on white ground **265.00**
12" h, pitcher, 15 1/4" d, bowl
Majolica, molded lily pads and flowers in
colors, c1859, Minton (A)............. **1650.00**
Shakespeare Series, Falstaff, Rosalind, and
Orlando figures in bowl, Katherine on
pitcher, green borders, yellow ground,
c1902–22, "Royal Doulton" mark **775.00**
12" h, pitcher, 16" d, bowl, ivory ground with
incised gold arrows and lines, cobalt stones,
c1910 Jugenstil **1300.00**
12 1/4" h, pitcher, 16" d bowl, raised pink
florals with yellow centers, turquoise leaves,
gilt lines, raised florals on rim, white ground,
English **395.00**
13" h, pitcher, 15 1/2" d, bowl, "Manhatten"
pattern, blue and white flow blue, c1890,
Johnson Brothers....................... **950.00**
13" h, pitcher, 16" d, bowl, black and white
band with pink roses, small floral sprays, gilt
rims, white ground, "T.R. & C. England"
mark................................. **375.00**
13 1/2" h, pitcher, 12" d, bowl, "Roselle" pattern, blue transfer, ironstone, paneled sides,
Eng Reg mark, "J. Mew & Son".......... **325.00**
14" h, pitcher, 16 1/2" d, bowl, "Primula" pattern, blue and white flow blue with gilt trim,
c1900, Dunn Bennet & Co. **550.00**
15" h, pitcher, 16 3/4" d, bowl, "Arundel" pattern, yellow and red flowers on top and
bottom, green drape, green and tan shaded
ground, "F.W.& Co." mark **225.00**
15" h, pitcher, 17" d, bowl, hp multicolored
floral basket cartouche, blue ribbon swags
on pitcher, bowl with alternating basket
with flowers and cartouches with flowers,
green rim shaded to white, white ground,
"NHP Made in England" mark.......... **250.00**
17" h, pitcher, 16 1/2" d, bowl, orange and
yellow florals, geometric shapes, gilt edges,
int rim of bowl with yellow florals, green
border bands, cream ground **235.00**

Three Piece
  16 1/2" h, pitcher, 14" d, bowl, 6" l soap with
    drainer, cov, Gaudy Ironstone, cobalt, pink,
    and yellow florals, rust and mustard bor-
    ders, bowl with shaped edge, c1840, "T.J.&
    J. Mayer, Longport" mark **2000.00**
Four Piece
  11 1/2" pitcher
    14" d, bowl, cov soap dish, cov toothbrush
      tray, purple stenciled flowerheads with
      brown stems on tan shaded ground,
      overall white ground, Hungary **175.00**
    14 1/2" d, bowl, soap dish, small bowl, lime
      green (A). **90.00**
    14 3/4" d, bowl, cup, soap dish, large brown
      flowers and leaves, white ground with
      molded swirls. **165.00**
Five Piece, 11 1/2" h, pitcher, 15 1/2" d, bowl,
    cup, soap dish, chamber pot, "Melbourne"
    pattern, blue floral and leaf design, Meakin .   **475.00**
Seven Piece
  11" h, pitcher, 14 3/4" d bowl, 7" h, pitcher,
    cup, waste bowl, toothbrush holder, cov
    slop jar, large red tulips with green leaves,
    white ground, spattered gold rims and han-
    dles. **385.00**
  11 1/4" h, pitcher, 15 1/4" d, bowl, 6 1/2" h,
    pitcher, 13" h, cov waste bowl, 5" h, vase,
    6" d, cov soap, 3 1/2" h, mug, yellow and
    red floral decoration, green curvilinear bor-
    ders (A) **500.00**
Eight Piece
  11 3/4" h, pitcher, 16 1/2" d, bowl, cov slop jar,
    cov chamber pot, small cylindrical pitcher,
    toothbrush holder, small curved pitcher, cov
    soap dish, scattered red and blue flowers
    and ribbons, green buckle at rim, white
    ground, late 19th C, England **1275.00**
  12" h, pitcher, 16" d, bowl, 5 1/2" d, cov soap,
    5 1/2" d, cov dish, waste bowl, 6" h, vase,
    small pitcher, cup, rose pattern, green rib-
    bon border, pink rim (A) **625.00**
  15 1/2" h, pitcher, 12" d, bowl, 10 1/2" h,
    chamber pot, 6 3/4" h, pitcher, cov soap,
    5 1/2" h, vase, 13" H-H, waste bowl, raised
    scrolls, pink centered yellow flowers, gilt
    trim, pink bow **1250.00**

PORTRAIT WARE

English/Continental
Mid 19th C to 1900

History: Plates, vases, and other pieces with portraits and
busts on them were popular during the mid-19th century.
Male subjects included important historical figures, such
as Napoleon, Louis XVI, and James Garfield. However,
most portraits featured beautiful women, ranging from the
French Empress Josephine to unknown Victorian ladies.
  Many English and Continental firms made portrait ware.
Makers include Royal Vienna, Limoges, Schumann, and
MZ Austria. Most examples were hand painted and often
bear an artist's signature. Transfer prints supplemented the
hand painted pieces.

Bowl
  7 1/2" d
    Bust of "Clementine," maiden with long
      hair and crown of leaves, pearl luster ext

Vase, 7 1/4" h, blue and violet bust with magenta
flower in hair, green ground, raised gilt flowers
on rim and ft, Royal Bonn, (A) $110.00

      and int border with raised medallions,
      three feet, Dresden. **320.00**
    Transfer of blonde woman with rose in hair,
      veiled bosom, "Victoria, Austria" mark .   **50.00**
    13" l, portrait of woman with long brown hair,
      pink and gilt, Oscar Schlegelmilch. **225.00**
  Box, Cov, 6" d, circ, center gilt ground cartouche
    of female portrait holding music, raised gold
    dot border, green and gold inner border, co-
    balt blue and gilt trim, white int, "Royal Vienna
    beehive" mark **240.00**
Plaque
  10" d, blue transfer of Von Hindenburg, open
    latticework border (A) **110.00**
  17 1/4" h, 14 1/2" w, bust of young girl in
    brown dress and white blouse, long brown
    hair, brown hat with green feathers, white
    ground with leaves and berries, gold rim,
    c1881, sgd "G. Landgraf," Crown Derby .   **5000.00**
Plate
  8" d, bust of "Amorosa" in colors, maroon
    border with gold tracery, "gold beehive"
    mark. **53.00**
  8 1/4" d, Victorian lady in blue gown, red
    flowers in hair, gold border, Limoges **95.00**
  9 1/2" d
    Bust of Josephine in colors, green border
      with gold tracery, "Z.S.& Co. Bavaria"
      mark. **70.00**
    Center painted with bust of young girl with
      long blond curly hair, red lace trimmed
      dress, blue border with gilded scrolling
      foliage, late 19th C, "blue beehive and H.
      Schmiechen Wahlifs, Wien" mark **725.00**
    Queen Louise in colors, gold starred band
      on forehead, blue-green border with gold
      trim, shaped rim, "Z.S.& Co. Bavaria"
      mark. **99.00**
  9 3/4" d
    Bust of "Constance" with turquoise and
      gold trim, "blue beehive" mark **95.00**
    Portrait of lady with large hat and pink bow,
      gold rococo scalloped and emb edge,
      cornflower blue border, marked **90.00**
    Young lady in large plumed hat, scrolled and
      scalloped lavender and gold border, dtd
      1905, Germany (A). **100.00**
  11 5/8" d, multicolored portrait of Gaines-
    borough-type woman in center, sapphire

blue border with gold trim, etched gold
floral rim, "Wallendorf Bavaria" mark.....   **75.00**
12¾" d, seated smiling woman in brocade
robe, playing dulcimer, pastel ground, gold
rim, pierced for hanging **110.00**
13¼" d, gypsy portait in center in white
blouse trimmed in gold, striped head scarf
with attached gold coins, turquoise blue
ground with gold design overlay, "Vienna
Austria crown" mark **475.00**
Soup Bowl, 9" d, Josephine Bonaparte in center,
fuchsia, green, and gold trim, "Carlsbad,
Austria" mark (A)........................   **18.00**
Vase
4½" h, bust of young woman with long
flowing blond hair, shaded dark brown
ground, scalloped open handles, ruffled rim,
"Austria" mark.........................   **38.00**
8" h, lady with peacock in colors, maroon and
gold ground with turquoise accents, "Royal
Windsor" mark **350.00**
11½" h, bust of girl in blue and tan dress,
gold chains and earrings with blue stones,
blue flowers in hair, green, tan, and yellow
shaded ground, gold vert handles, "crown
Austria" mark.........................   **150.00**

1824 – PRESENT

PORTUGAL—GENERAL

Ilhavo, Portugal
1824 to Present

History: Jose Ferreira Pinto Basto established a factory to
make porcelain at Vista Alegre in 1824. Soft paste porcelains and earthenwares, based on English models, were
made until 1832. Anselmo Ferreira, a modeler from Lis-
bon, and Joseph Scorder from Germany helped develop
the factory. In the early 1830s the ingredients to manufacture hard paste porcelains were found in the region.

Vista Alegre's golden period began in 1835 when Victor
Chartier-Rousseau, a French artist, arrived. He remained
until his death in 1852. During his tenure, an improved
hard paste porcelain became the standard product. Sevres
forms replaced the earlier English influenced pieces. Classical, Gothic, and Rococo Revival influences can be found
among Vista Alegre's products. Gustave Fortier served as
artistic director from 1851 to 1856 and from 1861 to
1869. French influences continued. The factory prospered.

During the late Victorian period, when the Portuguese
Joaquim de Oliverra (1870–1881) was head painter, the
factory experienced financial difficulties. These continued
under head painters da Roche Freire (1881–1889) and
Jose de Magalhaes (1889–1921). De Magalhaes was responsible for ornamental plates with high relief decorations that featured vibrant themes and Art Nouveau characteristics.

In 1924 the factory was reorganized. An emphasis was
placed on the production of classical patterns. Some contemporary designs were introduced.

**Fruit Bowl, 10½" l, 5½" h, blue and gilt out-
lined open basketwork, green and pink florals
with gold leaves on base, gold feet, "VA Portugal, Made in Portugal" mark, (A) $20.00**

The factory still is controlled by the descendants of the
original owner Jose Basto. The "VA" mark in blue has
been maintained. A laurel wreath and crown symbolizing
the royal patent of 1826 were added, but later abandoned.

Museum: Vista Alegre Museum, Ilhavo, Portugal.

Candlestick, 3⅜" h, modeled as coiled snake
with leafy sconce from mouth, natural colors,
early 20th C (A)........................   **220.00**
Charger, 17" d, Palissy-type with central modeled toad surrounded by snake, figural frogs
on border, grass ground, multicolored,
c1900....................................   **1200.00**
Garniture, two spill vases, 10¼" h, jardinaire,
figural reserves in colors, marked (A) **220.00**
Plaque, 15½" d, circ, Palissy type lobster with
shellfish, border with lizards, cricket, and beetle, tufted green grassy ground, imp factory
mark (A).................................   **1100.00**
Teapot, 8¾" h, modeled as monkey sitting on
back of snake, head forms spout, tail forms
handle, natural colors, tin glazes, restored, late
19th C **750.00**
Vase, 7" h, Palissy-type, applied bugs to body,
snake handles, natural earth colors, c1900 (A)   **500.00**

F&R. PRATT & Co
349
FENTON
1850

POT LIDS, AND
RELATED WARES

Staffordshire, England
c1840–1900

History: Pot lids are defined as under the glaze, chromatic,
transfer printed Staffordshire pot covers. The pots were
containers designed to hold food stuffs, delicacies, and
cosmetics, such as potted meats, relishes, fish paste,
sauces, rouge, lip salve, hair pomades for women, and

bear's grease for men. First sold about 1840, they reached their popularity in the Victorian era. They were priced according to size. There were five basic sizes ranging from the smallest (under 1 3/4" diameter) to the largest (5 1/2 to 8 1/2" diameter).

The finest pot lids were made between 1850 and 1870. Production continued to the end of the 19th century. Although at least eight firms made pot lids, Pratt & Company was the major manufacturer.

In 1836 George Baxter patented his process to make an oil color printing from a number of plates and blocks. Ten years later the process was applied to ceramics. Pratt's 1847 "Grace Before Meals" was the first full chromatic transfer printed under the glaze on a pot lid. T. J. & J. Mayer followed suit in 1851. Chromatic transfer printing first involved painting a watercolor. Next a key plate was engraved. Prints from the key plate were then transferred to three other plates that held the three prime colors.

Pratt's master artist-engraver was Jesse Austin. His key plate color was brown. From 1852 to 1869 Austin engraved plates that portrayed portraits of royalty and famous people on pot lids. Between 1864 and 1873 eleven different views of London on pot lids were made. In addition to his own original watercolors, Austin also reproduced in miniature forms the paintings of famous artists.

Early Pratt lids frequently were flat topped. Shapes varied. The glaze had a bluish tint, especially before 1870. In the 1870s the glaze was more gray-blue in tone. The glaze also featured fine crazing. Forty-seven pot lids had the line and dot border design. Large Pratt pot lids made before 1863 show three stilt marks on the underside. Pratt's chief competitor from 1856–1862 was Cauldon Place Pottery.

References: A. Ball, *The Price Guide to Pot-Lids & Other Underglaze Multi-colored Prints on Ware,* 2nd ed., Antique Collectors' Club, Ltd., 1980; H. G. Clarke, *The Pictorial Pot Lid Book,* Courier Press, 1960; Ronald Dale, *The Price Guide to Black & White Pot Lids,* Antique Collectors' Club, 1978; Cyril Williams-Wood, *Staffordshire Pot Lids & Their Potters,* Faber & Faber, 1972.

Museums: County Museum, Truro, England; Fitzwilliam Museum, Cambridge, England. (Collection seen by appointment only.)

Collecting Hints: Full color lids are the most popular among collectors. Pot lids with broad gold bands that were either produced for display at trade exhibits or showrooms or as souvenirs for families and friends of the master potter are most prized.

Box, 3" l, 1 7/8" w, hunter on horse with dead rabbit, donkey at side, polychrome transfer . **75.00**

Lid, 3 1/4" d, black transfer, c1890, $35.00

Vase, 6 1/4" h, "The Battle of the Nile" and "Persuasion," multicolored transfers, green ground, gold trim, c1840s, "F. & R. Pratt" mark, $295.00

Lid
3" d
"The Bear Pit," multicolored transfer **215.00**
"The Bride," multicolored transfer, "F.& R. Pratt" mark (A) **88.00**
3 1/4" d, "Cherry Tooth Paste, Patronized by the Queen," bust of Queen Victoria in center (A) **66.00**
4" d
"A Square in Strasburg," polychrome transfer **135.00**
"Dr. Johnson," polychrome transfer (A) **30.00**
Fishing scene, man and three children at water, polychrome transfer, F.& R. Pratt (A) **30.00**
"Pegwell Bay, Established 1760," polychrome transfer, Bates, Brown-Westhead, Moore & Co. (A) **35.00**
"Shakespeare's House, etc," polychrome transfer, stains (A) **65.00**
"The Late Prince Consort," multicolored transfer, c1862 (A) **88.00**
4 1/8" d
"No by heaven I exclaim-if ever I plant in that busom a thorn," multicolored transfer of two lovers **135.00**
"The Village Wedding," multicolored transfer (A) **88.00**
4 3/4" d, "The First Appeal," multicolored transfer, 3rd issue (A) **80.00**
4 1/2" d
"Dr. Johnson," c1850 (A) **55.00**
"Embarking to the East," multicolored transfer (A) **32.00**
"Garibaldi," multicolored transfer (A) **35.00**
"Landing the Fair," c1850 (A) **55.00**
"Seashells," c1850 (A) **55.00**
"Ship," c1850 (A) **55.00**
5" d, "Pegwell Bay-Lobster Fishing," multicolored transfer, "T. J.& J. Mayer" mark (A) . . **90.00**
"A Pair," card playing scene **95.00**
"A Race," horse race at fair **125.00**
"Landing the Fare," sailor carrying lady from water **135.00**
"The Enthusiast," man with gout fishing in pail **125.00**
"The Skewbald Horse" **85.00**
"The Wolf and Lamb," boys fighting **85.00**

Jar and Lid

1 3/4" d, "Golden Eye Ointment-Timothy
Whites & Taylor Ltd," black transfer 38.00
2 1/8" d, "Woods Cherry Tooth Paste," red
transfer. 115.00
2 3/16" d, "Calverts Carbolic Tooth Paste,"
black transfer 45.00
2 1/2" d, "Woods Areca Nut Tooth Paste,"
black transfer 35.00
2 3/4" d, "Oriental Tooth Paste," black transfer. 45.00
3" d
"Bears in School," multicolored transfer, chip
in rim 85.00
"Cherry Tooth Paste, John Cosnell," bust of
queen in center, polychrome transfer..... 75.00
3 1/4" d, "Dr. Bowditch Dentifrice," black
transfer. 48.00
3 3/8" d, "Burgess Anchovy Paste," black
transfer. 32.00
3 1/2" d
"Charge of the Scotish Greys at Balaclava,"
multicolored transfer (A) 55.00
"The Battle of Alma," multicolored transfer
(A). 75.00
"The Fall of Sabastopol," multicolored transfer
(A). 55.00
4" h, "The Boar Hunt," blue glazed earthenware, potted meat jar................... 38.00

Plate

8 5/8" d, "A Square in Strasbourg," multicolored transfer, "F.& R. Pratt" mark (A)..... 45.00
8 3/4" d, center scene of "Strathfieldsaye the
Seat of the Duke of Wellington," salmon
border, yellow and black rim 95.00

PRATT WARE

Staffordshire, Shropshire, and other English pottery centers c1785–1840

Scotland 1750–1840

History: Pratt ware is relief decorated, high temperature fired, under the glaze, cream colored earthenware and pearlware that was made between 1785 and 1840. William Pratt headed a family of potters who worked at Lane Delph and Fenton. William was the first of six generations of Pratts to make Pratt ware. Felix, John, and Richard, William's sons, managed the pottery after their father's death in 1799.

Jugs with relief molded designs of sporting and bucolic scenes or commemorative subjects featuring naval or military heroes or royal figures were the most popular forms. Tea caddies, plaques, flasks, teapots, dishes, mugs, cow creamers, busts, and other forms also were produced.

The body usually was white or a pale cream color. The glaze consisted of lead oxide tinged with blue. The wares were decorated with relief designs pressed from intaglio molds. Colors used for the decorations included: yellow, orange, ochre, green, cobalt blue, brown, black, and mulberry. The under the glaze color technique that protected the colors under a transparent glaze retained the brilliance of the pieces.

The majority of Pratt's jugs were unmarked. Other pot-

ters that imitated the wares from Pratt's factory included Wedgwood, Leeds, E. Bourne, T. Hawley, and R. M. Astbury. Under the glaze colored figures of animal groups, toby jugs, tall case clock money boxes, and watch stands appeared. Classical scenes were featured in relief decoration under the glaze on jugs. A number of relief decorations on Pratt ware duplicated the intaglio patterns found on jasper ware.

The Scottish East Coast Potteries made Pratt ware style jugs and other forms from the mid-1700s until 1840. Some pieces contained motifs with a distictive Scottish flavor.

Reference: John & Griselda Lewis, *Pratt Ware 1780–1840*, Antique Collectors' Club Ltd., 1984.

Museums: City Museum & Art Gallery, Stoke-on-Trent, England; Fitzwilliam Museum, Cambridge, England; Potsdam Public Museum, Potsdam, N.Y.; Royal Pavilion Art Gallery & Museum, Brighton, England; Royal Scottish Museum, Edinburgh, Scotland; Victoria & Albert Museum, London, England; William Rockhill Nelson Gallery of Art, Kansas City, Mo.

Bank

5" h, figural house with slot in roof, male figure on one end, female on other, faces in
windows, typical colors, repaired (A) 600.00
6 1/2" h, modeled as semi-detached gothic
cottage, blue tiled roof, ochre and blue windows and doors, base speckled in ochre
and black, c1815 (A) 756.00
Bough Pot, 7 1/2" h, D shape, pearlware, three
panels of house in landscape, rim molded with
satyrs' heads and oak branches, three semi-
circ feet (A)............................. 486.00
Bowl, 4 1/4" h, molded cartouche of "Apollo The
God of Music" on front, reverse cartouche
"Subdued by Reason," female in blue, green,
and mustard, brown bands, c1790 .... 625.00
Box, 2" h, figural recumbent spaniel with orange
and blue dots on rect cushion on cov, circ
screw base with painted flowers, c1800 (A). 2100.00
Candle Snuffer, 3 3/4" h, figure of seated man
with dog in lap, typical colors............. 95.00
Creamer
4 3/4" h, emb scenes of children at play in
heart shaped cartouches, typical colors (A) 250.00
4 7/8" h, emb hunt scenes, hanging leaves
from rim, typical colors (A) 175.00
Figure
2 3/4" h, recumbent cat on pillow base, typical
underglaze colors, repairs (A)........... 605.00

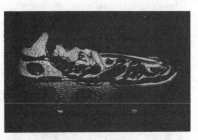

Figure, 8" l, 4 1/4" h, brown hair, mustard rim, blue, mustard, and yellow accented gown and blanket, mustard circles with yellow ints, c1790, $1250.00

3″ l, recumbent animals with long curling tail, brown scale-like coat, blue, green, and dark ochre oval mound base, c1800 (A) **2244.00**

3 1/2″ h, recumbent lion with tawny coat, muzzle dotted in brown, brown eyes and eyebrows, green grassy oval, canted plinth molded with plants, brown line, c1790 ... **2450.00**

5 1/4″ h, "Apollo," blue and yellow draperies, holding a lyre, books beside him, sq base, late 18th C (A)........................ **300.00**

5 1/2″ h

"Flora," ochre spotted robe, holding cornucopia of fruit, sq base, late 18th C (A)........ **300.00**

Shepherd and shepherdess with rams with curling horns, crook resting on base, he with recumbent dog by feet, she with pair of resting lambs, cobalt blue, ochre, and black, green topped oval rect base with sponged border, restored, early 19th C, pr (A)............................. **5236.00**

6 1/8″ l, ram, mustard horns and hoofs, green base **950.00**

6 3/4″ l

Recumbent ram, large curling yellow horns, brown hoofs, rocky mound spotted overall in blue, yellow, green, and ochre, late 18th C (A) **1200.00**

Standing lion in natural colors, right paw on globe, tongue hanging out, tail over back, rect plinth molded with blue, yellow, and ochre accented stiff leaf border, c1800 (A) **7125.00**

7 1/2″ h, "Cupid," blue drapery, brown hair, mustard, brown, and blue base, c1790 ... **700.00**

8 1/4″ h to 9 1/8″ h, "The Four Seasons," dressed in spotted yellow draperies, holding respective attributes, leaf molded sq plinths sponged in blue and ochre, "Winter" restored, late 18th C (A) **1850.00**

8 5/8″ h

Cavalry officer mounted on prancing horse, blue jacket, yellow sash and epaulettes, yellow breeches, brown boots, helmet embossed "GR," brown horse with orange saddle and reins, kit bag draped across horse behind rider, textured green mound base with ochre trim (A)....... **3780.00**

Young shepherd in manganese hat, ochre coat and breeches, spotted shirt, sheep over shoulder, sponged tree stump and sq blue line base.................... **475.00**

9 1/8″ h, classical lady in light yellow gown with aqua trim, red-brown hair, white flowered undergarment, holding jug, sq base, c1790–1810 (A) **286.00**

9 1/4″ h, "Cymon" and "Iphigenia" painted in green, brown, blue, orange, and ochre, youth with knee breeches undone, maid holding fruit in apron, arm repaired, c1790 .... **4950.00**

9 7/8″ h, St. George in blue and orange helmet, manganese tunic, slaying brown washed dragon, two females in yellow and orange flowered gowns at sides (A)...... **1100.00**

10″ h, man in blue coat, gray jacket, yellow breeches, orange hurdy-gurdy under arm, washed green mound molded sq base ... **475.00**

10 1/4″ h, Bacchus with grapes in hair wearing blue and ochre drapery, standing on oct base with tree stump covered in vines, sq

pedestal molded with reclining putto between brown lines, missing cup and staff, c1800 .... **200.00**

Flask

4 1/4″ l, molded as a scallop shell, brown, ochre, and blue, c1790 .... **2600.00**

4 3/4″ h, oval shape, molded classical figures on sides, typical colors (A) **300.00**

Jar, 1/2″ h, for fish paste, "The Continental Fish Market No. 11," multicolored scene, c1840s................................. **155.00**

Jug

4 3/4″ h, globular body, transfer printed in blue with bust portrait of "Admiral Lord Nelson" and "The Victory" on reverse, inscription below spout listing titles and victories, early 19th C (A)............................. **595.00**

4 7/8″ h, rustic cottage with hex walls, thatched roof with vines, gnarled stem forming handle, accented in black, blue, green, and ochre, c1810 (A)................... **234.00**

5″ h

Molded mask body in mustard, blue, brown, and green, yellow frog inside, ribbed base, scroll handle, c1790–1800...... **595.00**

Two cartouches of molded man in brown hat, mustard jacket, blue trim, 1800–20 **575.00**

5 1/8″ h, "Admiral Lord Duncan" on front and back, reverse in green, brown, blue, and ochre, c1800–20...................... **825.00**

5 1/4″ h, molded with men and hounds in landscape, one shooting bird, another with rabbit, reverse with hunter and hound, green leaf border, c1800 (A) **385.00**

5 1/2″ h, relief molded Tory with underglaze polychrome enamels in green, blue, yellow, brown, and ochre, c1770–90........... **1200.00**

6″ h, "Patriotic," relief of spray of rose and thistles under shamrock border, raised scrollwork on handle and spout, typical colors, early 19th C (A).................... **1012.00**

6 1/4″ h, flattened baluster, one side molded "Mischievous Sport," reverse with "Sportive Innocence," within heart shaped line and leaf garland cartouches, green, mustard, and blue, cream ground, c1795..... **840.00**

6 1/2″ h

Basketweave body, waisted neck, molded fruiting vine, two satyr heads on lip, typical colors (A) **320.00**

"The Sailor's Departure and Return," molded in green, mustard, ochre, and blue, c1790–1820.................... **950.00**

6 5/8″ d, yellow, blue, and ochre sprays of flowers, inscribed "W M N 1782" (A).... **532.00**

7 3/4″ h, "Lord Gervis," relief of Admiral in ochre tunic, blue cloak and breeches, sailing ships at sides, green and yellow stiff leaves top and base, blue outlined spout, green banded rim, hairline, c1795 (A).......... **340.00**

9″ h, Martha Gunn, seated holding flask and beaker on canted sq base, dress painted with colored sprays of green, blue, and orange flowers, yellow details and brown rim, rim and beaker restored, c1800 (A) **2226.00**

10″ h, ovoid body, "Tracey forever at Omberfly Court," within husk border medallion below spout, chinoiserie island scene on either side, cell diaper border, looped handle, restored spout, late 18th C (A) **1309.00**

Mug

3½" h

"Grey Goose" nursery mug, relief of Old Mother Slipper-Slopper in blue cloak, releasing brown spotted dogs, John in blue coat, black hat, orange breeches, dark green vine and stiff leaf border with blue grapes, hairline, c1800 (A)....... 335.00

Modeled satyr's head with beard, fruiting vine crown, multicolored, repairs, c1790 (A) 315.00

Pipe, 10" l, modeled as dbl looped serpent, scaled body, head and open mouth holding bowl, molded cottage figure on stem behind bowl, blue, yellow, brown, and orange, c1800 (A)..................................... 2860.00

Pitcher

4½" h, oval form relief grape and vine banding, early 19th C (A).................... 245.00

4¾" h

Emb fox hunting scene with red, brown, light blue, aqua, green, and black accents, pink luster rim 175.00

Portrait medallion of a gentleman, early 19th C (A) 300.00

5" h

Allegorical reserves of fall and spring, early 19th C (A) 250.00

Baluster shape, relief decorated with Admiral Duncan, early 19th C (A) 305.00

6" h, baluster shape, relief decorated with a couple and woman taking leave, early 19th C (A) 357.00

7⅛" h, seated man in cobalt jacket, yellow vest, holding foaming mug, reverse with classical scene, green trees and ground... 750.00

7¼" h, relief scenes of children in medallions, "Sportive Innocence" and "Mischievous Sport," polychrome enamels (A) 250.00

7½" h, relief busts and floral decorations in typical colors (A)....................... 400.00

8" h, relief design of tavern drinking scene, hanging swags from rim, vert stiff leaves at base, typical colors (A)................. 165.00

Plaque

7" l, relief with Bacchus and nymphs carousing in wooded setting, typical colors, molded blue frame, pierced for hanging, c1800 (A) 675.00

8" h, 6½" w, relief of two white putti holding torch, ochre leaves in ground, black, green, and yellow accents, blue ground, early 19th C (A) 605.00

8¾" h, oval, "Judgment of Paris," within blue and yellow laurel leaf frame with molded scrollwork above and below, c1790...... 1700.00

10¾" l, relief of two recumbent lions in blue, green, and brown, striped rim (A)........ 1115.00

Plate

8⅜" d, multicolored transfer, "Interior View of Independence Hall, Philadelphia, Kerr's China Hall is Opposite the Above," green border, gilt rim, made for American market, c1850 .... 105.00

8⅝" d, profile head of George IV wearing gray-green laurel wreath and naval uniform, rim molded with three panels of crown, rose and thistle, divided by basketweave molding in blue and ochre (A) 725.00

Punch Bowl, 11⅜" d, commemorative Battle of Camperdown, int with central circ medallion of crowned anchor and "Glorious 11th October, 1797" within formal rim border, ext with diaper border, restored (A) 1050.00

Sauceboat, 7¾" l, molded as duck with plumage, head forming handle, blue, green, brown, yellow, and ochre, late 18th C (A)... 1295.00

Spill Vase

6¼" h, bagpiper with peaked cap of blue, white, brown, and green bands with ochre tassel, striped coat, white waistcoat, ochre breeches, large white and brown stump, applied vine of green leaves and dark blue grapes, rocky base with large blue and white blossoms with yellow centers, repairs, c1790 .... 1950.00

7¹⁵⁄₁₆" h, triple, modeled as brown bull terrier baiting brown and ochre spotted bull with lowered head, black eyes, green tree mottled in brown behind them, open central trunk, flanking branches edged in ochre, green grassy rect base, brown band border, c1790 (A) 2475.00

Spirit Barrel, 6⅛" h, barrel shape, broad panel of flowers and leaf sprays between concentric ribbing, inscribed "Seaman," two blue lined holes................................. 250.00

Sugar Bowl, Cov, 5¾" h, almond shape with relief medallion of woman and child, swan finial, polychrome enamels (A)............. 400.00

Tea Caddy

4¾" h, rect, sides with relief of "macaroni" figures of lady wearing headdress, man with large wig and tricorn hat, maid and companion in blue, ochre, and green, neck restored, c1790 .... 275.00

5" h, raised figures on front and back in blue with mustard florals, blue circle decoration on shoulders, gray ground 325.00

5¾" h, relief classical figures on sides in ochre, blue, and ochre-orange, vert bands of ochre-orange at corners, early 19th C (A)........ 385.00

Teapot, 7" h, boat shape, center panel with chinoiserie landscape, other "A Trufle Shews Respect," panels divided by floret molded strips, dolphin finial, acanthus decorated handle and spout, stiff leaves around cov, shoulder, and base, repaired, c1790............. 2600.00

Tea Tile, 7¼" d, "The Red Bull Inn," multicolored scene, reclining cows in center cartouche, white band, gold color edge in classical design, c1840s................................. 110.00

Vase, 7" h, five vert fingers, emb leaves and flowers on fingers, typical colors, pr (A)..... 950.00

Wall Pocket, 9⁵⁄₁₆" h, cornucopia shape, molded with brown haired putto wearing a brown and blue heightened quiver of arrows suspended from yellow, blue, brown, and green floral garland at hips, "Winter" holding flaming urn, "Autumn" clutching wheat, each beneath green husk swag suspended from blue flowerheads, rope molded and green acanthus edged rim, pierced for hanging, repairs, c1805, pr (A)...................... 3300.00

Watchstand

8½" h, male and female on either side in green, mustard, blue, and brown, watchholder in mustard and blue, trimmed in green, minor restorations, 1780, Ralph Wood................................. 1650.00

11¼" h, longcase clock molded at front with classical figures framed with stiff leaf borders, flanked by boy and girl wearing draperies leaning against pedestals, blue, ochre, green, and mustard, sponged brown flat rect base, two knobs missing, 1820–26, Dixon, Austin & Co (A) **1650.00**

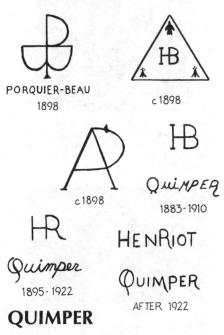

PORQUIER-BEAU
1898

c 1898

c 1898

QuiMPEɊ
1883-1910

HENRIOT

Quimper
1895-1922

Quimper
AFTER 1922

QUIMPER

**Quimper, Brittany, France
1600s to Present**

History: Quimper faience derives its name from the town in Brittany, in the northwest corner of France, were the potteries were located. Three of the major 17th and 18th century centers of French faience strongly influenced the early Quimper potters: Nevers, Rouen, and Moustiers.

Jean Baptiste Bousquet settled in Quimper in 1685 and started producing functional faience wares using Moustiers inspired patterns. Pierre, his son, took over in 1708. In 1731 Peirre included Pierre Bellevaux, his son-in-law, in the business. He introduced the Chinese inspired blue and white color scheme, the Oriental subject matter, and intertwining border pattern of leaves and flowers, and the use of the rooster as a central theme.

From Rouen, Pierre Clement Caussy brought to Quimper many important features such as "decor rayonnant," an intricate pattern of stylized leaves and florals on the outer border and lacy designs that resembled wrought iron trellises. By 1739 Pierre Clement Caussy had joined with Bousquet. He became the manager of the faiencerie and expanded the works.

Francois Eloury opened a rival factory in 1776 and in 1778 Guillaume Dumaine opened a second rival factory. Thus, there were three rival faience factories operating in Quimper producing similar wares by 1780.

Through marriage, Antoine de la Hubaudiere became the manager of the Caussy factory in 1782. The factory's name became the Grande Maison.

After the beginning of the 19th century, the essential Breton characteristics began to appear on the pottery - the use of primary colors, concentric banding in blue and yellow for border trims, and single stoke brushing to create a flower or leaf. Toward the end of the 19th century, scenes of everyday Breton peasants became popular decortive motifs. Artists such as Rene Quillivic joined Grande Maison in 1920 and produced figures.

Concurrently, the Eloury factory passed to Charles Porquier and later to Adolphe Porquier. In 1872 Alfred Beau, a master artist, joined the firm and produced Breton scenes and figures.

In 1884 Jules Henriot took over the Dumaine factory. He added the Porquier factory to his holdings in 1904. Mathurin Meheut joined the Henriot factory in 1925 and introduced patterns influenced by the Art Deco and Art Nouveau stylistic trends. Other noted artists at Henriot were Sevellec, Maillard, and Nicot. During the 1920s the HB concern introduced the Odetta line that utilized a stoneware body and decorations of the Art Deco period.

The Henriot factory merged with the Grande Maison HB in 1968, each retaining its individual characteristics and marks. Production ceased in the early 1980s. An American couple purchased the plant and renewed the production of Quimper.

Quimper pottery was made in a tremendous number of shapes and forms among which are utilitarian pieces, all types of figures and decorative articles, and in fact, just about everything imaginable.

References: Sandra V. Bondhus, *Quimper Pottery: A French Folk Art Faience,* published privately, 1981; Millicent S. Mali, *French Faience,* United Printing, 1986; Millicent Mali, *Quimper Faience,* Airon, Inc., 1979; Marjatta Taburet, *La Faience de Quimper,* Editions Sous le Vent, 1979, (French Text).

Museums: Musee de Faiences de Quimper, Quimper France; Victoria & Albert Museum, London, England; Villa Viscaya, Maimi, Florida.

REPRODUCTION ALERT: A line of pottery called "museum quality" has appeared on the market. These pieces feature a brownish wash over a crazed glaze surface. The marks are generally in brown as opposed to the blue or black factory marks of the earlier period. Originally these reproductions had paper labels, but the labels are removed easily. The reproductions sometimes are sold as old pieces.

The Blue Ridge Pottery and several Japanese firms have produced wares with peasant designs similar to those of Quimper. These are easily recognizable.

Peasant pottery similar in style and feel to Quimper has been produced by the Malicorne factory, near Paris. These pieces carry a Malicorne "PBx" mark. Examples have appeared on the market with the "x" removed and sold as genuine Quimper.

Modern Quimper pottery still is made and marketed in major department stores, such as Neiman-Marcus and Marshall Fields, and in china specialty shops.

An American couple now owns the Quimper factory. Many of the older patterns are being reproduced for an eager market. New pieces of Quimper are much lighter in weight than older examples.

Collecting Hints: Most Quimper available to the collector comes from the late 1800s to the mid-1920s. Since so much was made, the collector should focus on pieces that are in very good or better condition. Missing covers to sugar bowls, teapots, inkwells, etc., greatly reduce the value of these pieces and should be avoided. Small flakes in the glaze are inherent in the nature of the pottery, and, for the most part, do not detract from their desirablilty.

Pieces from the Odetta period (c1920) are less desirable because of the emphasis on Art Deco designs rather than the country motif associated with the more traditional Quimper pottery.

Marks: The "HR" and "HR Quimper" marks are found on Henriot pieces prior to 1922. The "HenRiot Quimper" mark was used after 1922. The "HB" mark covers a long span of time. The addition of numbers or dots and dashes refers to inventory numbers and are found on later pieces. Most marks are in blue or black. Consignment pieces for department stores such as Macy's and Carson Pirie Scott carry the store mark along with factory mark. These consignment pieces are somewhat less desirable in the eyes of the collector.

Newsletter: Quimper Faience, Inc., 141 Water Street, Stonington, CT 06378. Subscription: $10 for three years.

Ashtray, 4" h, 5½" l, two figural sailors at head of ashtray in dark blue suits, brown tray, "Henriot Quimper J.E. Sevellec" mark (A). **165.00**
Basket, 9¼" l, 5¼" h, seated peasant couple in meadow, scalloped blue and yellow decor riche border, int with painted basket of flowers, dbl rope twist handles joined by rod, "Porquier-Beau Quimper" mark (A) **1045.00**

Figure, 13¾" h, cream pantaloons, green jacket, lt blue vest, chips on base, glaze flakes, late 19th C, unmkd, (A) $495.00

Inkstand, 10½" l, 4½" h, Brittany coat of arms, scene of Quimper on front panel, couple in center, molded seashell and waves in blue and orange, "Henriot Quimper" mark, $850.00

Plaque, 18" h, 15" w, relief molded center tavern scene in terra cotta, blue, green, cream, brown, black, and cream border, French sayings top and bottom, Porquier-Beau mark, (A) $1800.00

Teapot, 5⅛" h, 8¼" l, multicolored florals, peasant, criss-cross top design, "Quimper France" mark, $270.00

Bell, 4¾" h, figural peasant woman in pink apron and black dress, holding green umbrella and gold purse, "Henriot Quimper" mark. . . **125.00**
Beverage Set, tray, 12½" d, pitcher, 7½" h, 8 cups, 3" h, half busts of male peasants playing instruments, female peasant, horiz stripes, brown and gold with orange and yellow accents, cream ground, "HB Quimper" marks (A)150.00
Bookends, 7" h, 7" l, Art Deco style bagpipers in colors on luster green bases, "HB Brion, Quimper" marks **385.00**
Bottle, 11" h, figural Breton woman in blue, pink, green, and brown costume, "Henriot Quimper" mark (A) **198.00**
Bowl
   5⅝" d, paneled shape, man in center with rust pants and blue coat, scalloped edge, gray ground, blue intertwined border, four dots and a la touche strokes inside and out, "HB" mark **175.00**
   10½" d, 3" h, scalloped body, center scene of blue and orange rooster with multicolored tail, green, blue, and orange florals, stylized sun in yellow and orange, blue, orange, and dark blue single stroke border, blue outlined scalloped rim, pierced for hanging, "Henriot Quimper" mark (A). . . . **550.00**
   12" H-H, 3¾" h, center scene of man with

flute, another with bagpipe, blue decor riche border, green sponged handles and foot, "blue Henriot Quimper" mark **495.00**

Bud Vase, 5" h, female peasant, typical flowers, blue and yellow banding, blue sponged lip, "HB Quimper" mark **70.00**

Butter Pat, 4 1/2" l, 3 1/2" w, female peasant in center, cobalt border, "Henriot Quimper France" mark (A). **10.00**

Candlestick, 9" h, triangular base with shells of peasants or flowers, dolphin feet, hex stem with dark blue, orange, and green criss-cross design, molded green serpent on stem, "HR Quimper France" mark, pr (A) **1430.00**

Cheese Dish, Cov, 9" d, figural star shaped, orange and blue criss-cross pattern, peasants, "HR" mark **365.00**

Chamberstick

5 1/2" d, female peasant with florals, ring handle with blue dashes, "Henriot Quimper France" mark. **230.00**

6 1/4" l, 5" w, 2 3/4" h, leaf shape outlined in blue dashes, male peasant on base with scattered flowers on each side, blue and orange criss-cross and floral spray hex nozzle, "HR Quimper France" mark **250.00**

Charger, 11 1/2" d, typical male and female peasant design in terra cotta, yellow, violet, rose, and green, terra cotta and green single stroke floral border, blue and yellow banded rim, "HB Quimper" on front (A) **405.00**

Cider Jug

6" h, dark blue and rust orange florals, blue sponged spout, handle, and top strap handle, yellow bands on top and base, "HB mark (A) **65.00**

6 1/4" h, stoneware, cobalt circles joined with swags lined in soft black, mottled brown glaze, cobalt handles, "HB Quimper Odetta" mark (A) **132.00**

Clock, 9 1/2" h, molded swirls on edge in blue and gold, painted florals above clock, walking peasant man with cane below, florals on sides, four curved feet, "HB Quimper" mark on front (A). **3200.00**

Coquille Dish, 4" d, matching spreader, shell shape with molded orange bow at top, female peasant in center, black, orange, yellow, and brown serrated border, male peasant on spreader handle, 1925, "Henriot Quimper" mark. **42.00**

Cream and Sugar, peasant decor, blue and yellow border banding, "Henriot Quimper France" marks **142.00**

Cup and Saucer

Hex shape, panels of seated male and female peasants, criss-cross designs and flowerheads on remaining panels, wishbone handle, "Henriot Quimper France" mark (A) . **187.00**

Oct shape, panels of seated male and female peasants, large size, yellow ground, "HB Quimper" mark. **67.00**

Orange Celtic designs, red dashes, blue and red criss-cross design, orange and black banding, "HB Quimper" mark **85.00**

Dish

4" d, gold, yellow, dark red, green, and black geometric center, gold and green banded border, ivory ground, c1925, "Henriot Quimper" mark **25.00**

5" d, shell shape, female peasant with flowers, "HB Quimper" mark **52.00**

8" d, frontal view of male or female peasant, blue sponged thumbprint rolled borders, "HR Quimper" marks on front, pr **750.00**

8 1/2" d, multicolored old lady peasant and child, green and gold shaped border with ermine tail crest at top, "Porquier-Beau Quiminirn" mark (A). **1210.00**

13 1/2" l, center with female peasant, flowers, and four dot design, blue shaped feather edge, overhead branch handle. **195.00**

Dish, Cov, 5" l, attached undertray, peasant woman on lid, pink ground, "Henriot Quimper France" mark **95.00**

Egg Server, 10 1/2" d, 5 1/2" h, molded circles and ovals with blue, mustard yellow, and green, male or female in two ovals, blue striped handle, shaped rim, "Henriot Quimper France" mark (A). **385.00**

Epergne, 11" h, 17 1/4" d, scalloped basin supported by blue, green, yellow, purple, and orange figural dolphins, tails pierce basin supporting central vase with medallion of peasant woman standing at fence or man with bagpipe, multicolored seashells and scattered flowers in basin, blue sponged border, repairs, "HR Quimper" mark (A) **2420.00**

Ewer

17" h, painted dancing couple on front, bouquet of multicolored flowers on reverse, figural pink and blue bow handle, blue, terra cotta, and green decor riche borders, yellow scale neck, "Henriot Quimper" mark (A). **2860.00**

22 1/2" h, frontal view of peasant couple in colors, florals on reverse, blue decor riche rim, center band, and foot, crest of Brittany or Quimper on neck, loop handle, "HR" mark, pr. **1400.00**

Figure

3 1/2" h, 4" h, female in green apron, purple bodice, yellow spotted scarf, black sleeves, white quaff, male in gray pants, black jacket and hat, blue vest, sgd "Sevellec, HenRiot Quimper," pr **135.00**

5" h, seated child in aqua gown with rose and green sprigged flowers, white cap with green dots, "B. Savigny, HB Quimper" mark (A). **465.00**

5 3/4" h, St. Anne with child, multicolored, "Henriot Quimper" mark **125.00**

6" h, Breton boy holding stick, dark blue jacket, green vest, yellow pantaloons, dark purple hat and gaiters, green base with "YANNIK" on front, "Henriot Quimper France" mark **450.00**

8 1/2" h, seated basket maker in blue pants, white shirt, black vest and hat, yellow and brown basket, "HB Quimper" mark (A) . . **255.00**

11 1/2" h, pair of bagpipe players in black and yellow jackets with blue and green accents, green trousers, sgd "Micheau-Vernez, Henriot Quimper" mark (A). **110.00**

15" h, St. Anne in yellow dress with ermine tails, blue cloak, Mary in blue, both reading scroll, "Henriot Quimper" mark **725.00**

Flower Holder, 7 1/2" h, Art Deco figural peasant woman in mauve apron spread over garnet skirt, large yellow and gold basket upheld with pink flowerhead openings, "Henriot Quimper" mark (A)............................ **715.00**

Hanging Box, 3 1/4" w, 4 1/4" h, rect, box with male peasant and florals on front, criss-cross design on sides, backplate pierced with starburst, "HB Quimper, France" mark......... **185.00**

Holy Water Font, 9 1/2" h, peasant man kneeling before cross, "Henriot Quimper" mark **330.00**

Ice Cream Set, tray, 12 plates, male and female peasants, arched square shape, sgd "J. LeTanneur, Henriot Quimper" mark **1150.00**

Inkwell

   3" w, 2" h, heart shape, red rose decor on top, blue border, yellow glaze ground, "Henriot Quimper" mark **159.00**

   4" d, 3 1/4" h, star shape, pale blue and terra cotta florals, seated peasant man playing horn, white ground, "Henriot Quimper France" mark (A)....................... **300.00**

   5" w, 3 1/4" h, heart shape, dark brown, blue, green, and pink flowers on cream ground, "Henriot Quimper France" mark (A) **165.00**

   7" l, quarter moon shape, male and female peasant reclining on each side of well, blue decor riche border with ermine tail crest in center, decor riche banding on well and cover, "Porquier-Beau Environs de Quimper" mark (A)......................... **2090.00**

Jardiniare

   8" h, 11" l, figural swan, blue feathers, blue sponging with gold dots, feet, beak, and eyes outlined in gold, cartouche of seated male peasant, "Henriot Quimper France" mark (A) **605.00**

   9"h, 18" l, front panel of four boys playing marbles, reverse panel with florals, blue decor riche border with yellow-gold rim, figural dragon handle, "Henriot Quimper" mark (A) **1100.00**

Knife Rest, 5" l, Art Deco reclining figure of male or female peasant in bright colors, "Maillard, Henriot Quimper" mark, pr (A) **225.00**

Match Holder, 3 1/4" h, 4" w, attached undertray, male and female peasants and flowers, "Henriot Quimper, France" mark **75.00**

Menu, 6 1/2" h, shield shape, molded crest of Brittany at upper left corner, painted peasant man in lower left corner, blue chain outlining shape, "HB" mark on reverse (A) **467.00**

Picture Frame, 11 1/4" h, 8 3/4" w, orange, blue, and green molded rococo border, male peasant with horn on left, female peasant on right, scattered loose florals, "HR Quimper" mark (A)................................... **2310.00**

Pipe Rack

   6" h, 10" w, fan shape, terra cotta, blue, green, and yellow geometrics, holes for pipes, pierced for hanging, "HB" mark (A) **467.00**

   9" h, 8 1/2" w, fleur-de-lys shape, male peasant with horn on right, female with distaff on left, scattered flowers, center hanging hole, soft colors, "HR" mark (A) **825.00**

Pitcher

   3" h, stoneware, cream and brown diamonds outlined in gray, dark blue ground, "Odetta, HB Quimper" mark **50.00**

   5" h, bust of male peasant lighting pipe, blue jacket, red vest, black hat, "Henriot Quimper A.G." mark (A) **121.00**

   6" h, lg open red flowerheads, green foliage, small blue and yellow flowers, white

ground, wide blue band at neck, "HB Quimper, France" mark................. **100.00**

   7" h, center band of impressed blue Celtic designs on cream ground, gray glaze, crimped handle, Odetta (A) **33.00**

   7 1/2" h, large open yellow and terra cotta flower with blue dot center, cream glaze, 19th C (A)............................. **88.00**

   8" h, Art Deco style bust of peasant woman holding pitcher in blue, black, and yellow on white ground, reverse with horiz and vert stripes, "HB Quimper" mark (A)......... **61.00**

   8 1/2" h, female peasant holding flowers, white ground, "HB Quimper mark **175.00**

Plaque, 18 1/4" , 15" w, oct, relief molded center of two drunken peasants in cream, brown, green, and blue, brown, black and cream geometric border, glaze skips and chips, Porquier-Beau................................... **1100.00**

Plate

   6 1/2" d, bust of male or female peasant in blue, yellow, and purple on cream ground, blue and tan Breton broderie raised enamel border, "HB Quimper" mark, pr (A)..... **73.00**

   7 1/4" d, floral center and border, pink ground, "Henriot Quimper France" mark........ **40.00**

   7 1/2" d, center motif of male or female peasant with florals, yellow, red, and green single stroke border, "HR Quimper" mark, pr (A) **220.00**

   8" d

      Male peasant in center, yellow and blue ring border, "Henriot Quimper France" mark (A) **20.00**

      Multicolored basket of open flowers in center, rose sponged border (A) **50.00**

   9" d, black line drawing of peasant woman with flowers, oyster ground, "Henriot Quimper, Claude Sanson" mark **15.00**

   9 1/4" d, central crest of Brest in colors, green decor riche border with yellow-gold rim line, Porquier-Beau (A).................. **1320.00**

   9 1/2" d, center with two peasant women kneeling and praying before roadside shrine in red, orange, blue, green, and yellow, blue stylized floral border, shaped rim, "Porquier-Beau" mark (A).................... **495.00**

   9 5/8" d, center armorial crest in colors, border of yellow shape fleur-de-lys, blue-green stylized leaves and ermine tails, shaped rim, "Porquier-Beau" mark (A).............. **137.00**

   11" d, oct, peasant woman in center, pink ground, "Henriot Quimper France" mark . **75.00**

Platter

   14 1/2" l, 11" w, oval, center with Breton couple dancing, yellow and black inner band, yellow and black sponged border, "Henriot Quimper" mark....................... **240.00**

   19 1/2" l, 14" w, center scene of four women at well, two male peasants playing instruments, yellow and blue decor riche border, restored border, "HB Quimper" mark (A). **2200.00**

Porringer

   5" d, multicolored floral int, pierced for hanging, sgd "Quimper" **27.00**

   6" d, bust of male or female peasant in center in brown shades, Breton broderie enameled ext, tab handles, "HB Quimper" mark, pr (A)................................... **70.00**

Powder Jar, 5 1.2" h, figural peasant girl in yellow and orange striped jumper, blue striped dress, blond hair with blue cap trimmed in yellow and gold, "Henriot Quimper" mark (A).................................... **330.00**

Puzzle Jug, 6" h, yellow ground with motto, open work at rim, blue handle............. **200.00**

Quintel

5" h, Mayflower motif on front in colors, green floral sprays and blue dots, five vert fingers, "Henriot Quimper France" mark (A)..................................... **187.00**

5½" h, typical peasant and floral decor, pink ground, "Henriot Quimper France" mark . **235.00**

Salt

3½" l, dbl, figural Dutch shoes attached at center, peasant in one, flowers in other, typical colors............................ **65.00**

5½" l, dbl, oct, man in one well, floral in other, blue sponge handle, "HenRiot Quimper, France" mark...................... **140.00**

Salt and Pepper Shakers, 3⅜" h, oct, stoneware, overall gray glaze, "HB Quimper France" marks (A)........................ **35.00**

Serving Dish, 10½" d, trefoil shape, modeled swan handle, male, peasant or large open flower in basket in each section, three small feet, hairline on rim, "HR Quimper" mark (A)................................ **440.00**

Snuff Bottle, book shape, Breton woman on front, rooster on reverse, French sayings, blue edge, unmarked (A)...................... **440.00**

Sugar Bowl

3⅜" h, bust of peasant woman on frint in brown shades, Breton broderie enameled trim, "HB Quimper" mark (A)........... **35.00**

3½" h, peasant woman, pink ground, "Henriot Quimper France" mark............. **65.00**

5½" h, female peasant in mustard, blue, yellow, and green, mustard sponged borders and dbl handles, scattered florals, cream ground, "HR Quimper" mark (A)........ **176.00**

Teapot

8" h, yellow, blue, and orange exotic bird on side panel, florals on reverse, florals and criss-cross design on side panels, blue dot and dash handle and spout, yellow, blue, and green butterfly and criss-cross pattern on lid, repaired finial, "HB Quimper France" mark (A)............................. **148.00**

8½" h, stoneware, dark brown, gray incised Celtic band outlined in blue on base, "HB Quimper France" mark............. **88.00**

Tobacco Jar, 4½" h, stoneware, relief decoration of flowers on sides, beaded band on rim and base, brown glaze (A)................ **148.00**

Tray

10¼" l, 7¾" w, oct, stoneware, two light brown stylized deer in center, star pointed panel, dark brown glaze, "HB Quimper Odetta" mark (A)..................... **520.00**

11½" l, dancing peasants, crest of Brittany, blue bow, tan bagpipe, yellow and blue decor riche border, repaired, "HR" mark front and back........................ **375.00**

12" l, 8½" w, peasant man with horn, female with flower, single stroke flowers on sides, blue and gold semi-circle and dot border, green twist handles, four small feet, "Henriot Quimper France" mark (A)......... **415.00**

13½" l, 9" w, center scene of male peasant fishing, female with basket, multicolored scattered flowers, molded rococo border in green, blue, and gold, crest of Brittany at top, crest of Quimper at base, open handles, pierced for hanging, repair to handle, "HR Quimper" mark (A)............... **880.00**

Vase

4" h, bust of male peasant, orange-yellow medallion, rose and blue chains of flowers, blue sponged rim, "Henriot Quimper" mark................................. **90.00**

4¾" h, squat shape, female peasant on front, mustard, rose Art Deco type florals on reverse, blue sponge borders and handles, tan ground, "Henriot Quimper" mark........ **185.00**

4¾" h, 7¾" w, ftd, open fan shape, female peasant and florals in terra cotta, blue, and green, reverse with florals, criss-cross design on end, "Henriot Quimper France" mark (A)............................. **385.00**

6" h, sq shape, two male peasants playing instruments in dark blue, orange, yellow and green, sides and back with pink, yellow, green, and blue scattered flower sprays, bamboo sides and feet, repaired corners, "HB" mark (A)........................ **495.00**

7½" h, brown, yellow, and black bust of male or female peasant, white ground, wide brown bands with black edges, "HB Quimper" mark, pr......................... **275.00**

8½" h, pink, green, and blue peasant man on front, pink, yellow, and blue florals on reverse, "HB Quimper" mark (A)......... **175.00**

9" h, female peasant on side, blue, red, and green florals, blue and yellow banding on neck, two blue pierced handles, "Henriot Quimper" mark....................... **250.00**

13½" h, tricorn shape, male peasant on front, red and green dashes on necks, yellow and blue banding, "HB Quimper" mark............................... **1050.00**

14¼" h, Art Deco geometric designs, light blue, mustard, orange, green, and blue, cross-hatch designs in rose, c1925, "HB Quimper" mark....................... **470.00**

16½" h, ewer shape with wide looping handles, painted scene of Breton couple with church in ground, pink and green florals, black ermine tails on sides, yellow and green botanical on reverse, leaf and decor riche foot, "HB Quimper" mark (A)...... **935.00**

Wall Pocket

7¼" h, bagpipe shape, molded blue bow and yellow horn, male peasant, scattered flowers and four dot design, white ground, "HB Quimper" mark (A)..................... **88.00**

7½" h, bagpipe shaped, blue bow at top, peasant decor, "HB" mark............. **185.00**

12¼" h, bellows shape, multicolored center panel of two peasant musicians with farm ground, blue and yellow decor riche borders outlined in gold and green sponging, "Henriot Quimper" mark (A)........... **880.00**

RELIEF MOLDED JUGS

England
1820–1900

History: During the 1820s in England, a new type of jug that was molded in one process with no additional decorations was made at numerous potteries. The main center was in the Staffordshire Potteries, but some relief molded jugs were made elsewhere.

The earliest jugs had hunting scenes, but by the mid 1800s, there was a wide range of designs including historical and commemorative subjects, classical figures, naturalistic patterns, biblical stories, religious architecture, scenes from literature and wildlife, and others. The best jugs were made during the 1840s and 50s. After that time, cheaper mass produced jugs resulted in a lesser quality product with mostly floral or geometric patterns.

Jugs were an essential part of everyday life in the Victorian era and were used for ale, water, cider, milk, wine, and toddy. Some were made with lids of Britannia metal, some had relief molded pottery lids, and some had strainers in the spout to feed invalids. There was a range of sizes, and some were made in sets. Jugs were produced in huge numbers, and the variety in shape, style, quality, size, decoration, and subject matter was vast.

To produce the master model for a relief molded jug, the modeler carved the original design, often in a block of alabaster. Casts were then made from the master to form reversed master molds. Further casts produced cases. Final castings resulted in the working molds. Approximately 25 jugs could be made from a master, and then a new mold was necessary.

At first jugs were buff colored, then pastel blues and green were used. White became the standard color. Jugs also were made in beige, gray and brown. Some makers used enamel colors for highlighting certain aspects of the designs. After c1845 colored grounds increased in popularity.

Many relief molded jugs are marked with either impressed, printed, molded, or applied marks. Applied marks are the most common on relief molded jugs. They were formed separately and then attached to the body using slip. Applied marks were used mostly in the 1830s and 40s, and molded marks were used in the 2nd half of the century. Printed marks were used in the 40s and 50s. Some marks included publication dates which indicated when a design was first introduced. These were either applied or impressed. The diamond shape registration mark was used from 1842 until 1883. This mark designated when a design was registered, not necessarily when it was made. Registration marks provided protection for makers against copying by other makers. After the Patents, Designs and Trade Marks Act of 1883, marks were either "Rd." or "Rd. No."

There were numerous makers of relief molded jugs. William Ridgway and Company's most famous jug Tam O'Shanter was based on scenes from a Robert Burns poem. He worked with James Leonard Abington from 1831–1860 mostly at the Church Works in Hanley. At least twenty-six different designs were made during this thirty year period in a wide range of subjects.

Another prolific maker of jugs was Herbert Minton who used model numbers on relief molded jugs to identify the designs. Charles Meigh's first relief molded jug was made in 1835. His famous Apostle jug was produced in huge quantities. This jug set the standard for others who made these jugs. William Taylor Copeland's first jug was "The Vintage Jug" made in 1844. After 1849 all his jugs were registered. Another important maker was William Brownfield who made a wide range of designs, mostly in naturalistic motifs to appeal to mid-Victorian tastes.

Additional makers included Ashworth, Doulton, Mason, Worcester, Wedgwood, Samuel Alcock and Company, and Mayer.

Reference: R.K. Henrywood, *Relief-Moulded Jugs 1820-1900*, Antique Collectors' Club Ltd, 1984.

Musuems: City Museum & Art Gallery, Hanley, Stoke-on-Trent, England; Potsdam Public Museum, Potsdam, NY; Victoria & Albert Museum, London, England; Wadsworth Atheneum, Hartford, CT.

4" h, ornate relief of "THE KILL" on body, applied blue enamel swags on neck (A)	44.00
4⅝" h, Bust of Lord Hill or Lord Wellington highlighted in red, yellow, green, and black, early 19th C (A)	220.00
6" h	
Blue syrup, molded leaves, high gloss finish, pewter lid	200.00
Raised applied mask, white cherubs, "Worthington & Green" mark	225.00
6⅝" h, white relief portraits of Distin family, buff ground, dark brown streaks at top, mask lip (A)	150.00
6⅞" h	
Busts of Napoleon on sides, two gold luster bands of relief leaves at top and base, mid 19th C (A)	110.00
Drab stoneware, relief with scenes of Battle of Plessey (A)	55.00
7" h, stoneware, with strainer spout, two relief scenes of putti under trees, emb band of grapes and vines around neck, imp "SPODE" mark (A)	55.00
7½" h	
Blue stoneware, relief of Arms, lion, and unicorn commemorating Crimean War, imp "May They Be United' (A)	135.00
Brown, relief of peasant figures and drinkers, vine decoration on neck, England (A)	40.00
Drabware, one side with soldiers bidding farewell and "Home," reverse with English and French soldiers standing over Russian bear and "Abroad' (A)	250.00
7⅞" h, relief bust of Wellington in wreath flanked by martial items on sides, relief of oak leaves in flowing blue, mid 19th C (A)	209.00
8" h	
"Apostle," white with pewter lid, c1842, Charles Meigh	525.00
Dark blue enamel band on neck, relief of fox hunt scene around body, weave band around base, Turner (A)	204.00

6" h, buff stoneware, "Tam O'Shanter and Souter Johnnie," c1830, unmkd, $500.00

Leaves, molded in white relief 120.00
Nelson in front of martial devices, angel
holding medallion portrait of King George,
Victory under full sail on each side, applied blue enamel border, restoration to
spout (A) 412.00
Relief of Tam O'Shanter on horse with ban-
shee and man around fireplace, gray salt
glaze, Ridgway 175.00
"Tulip" pattern, blue relief, Britannia lid signed
"Booth," c1870 . . . .   165.00
Warrior scene in tan relief, molded leaves at
top, pewter lid, imp and raised "Nov. 1,
1830, Published by C. Meigh" mark 300.00
8⅛" h, standing Crimean War soldier under
tree in gray, black, green, and pink luster, rifle
handle (A) 110.00
8¼" h
"Donatello," white, pewter lid, designed by
William Brown, raised "BR" mark 175.00
Drab stoneware, relief of battle scenes of Sir
Sidney Smith (A) 180.00
"The Archery Lesson," inverted grass border,
white, brown wash on neck, c1795, Turner
(A) 247.00
8½" h
Relief on sides of two boys playing, brown
body (A) 35.00
Silenius in green, c1840 . . . .   425.00
White ribbed, relief of band of putti with gar-
lands, shiny glaze, applied florals at base,
Brit Reg mark 95.00
9" h
"Apostle," tan, pewter lid, 1842 . . . .   575.00
Blue stoneware, relief of Garibaldi on horse-
back, imp "Wood & Challinor" mark (A) . .   125.00
Deer running, leaves on border, light blue, as
is 65.00
"Vintage," white, c1833–47, applied ribbon
mark above "COPELAND & GARRETT" . .   600.00
9¼" h, "Dancing Arimorini," blue-green color,
³/₁₀/1845 . . . .   625.00
9½" h
"Bacchus," white-gray color, pewter lid 650.00
Green flowerhead design, serpent on handle,
pewter lid, unmarked 185.00
Green stoneware, relief of three soldiers
crushing Imperial Eagle, dtd 1855, imp
"Ridgway" mark (A) 610.00
Pedestal base, handle formed from molded
head and body of Pan with pipes, four Bacchus heads and scrollwork body, grape and
vine border, putty color, glazed int, c1840,
Ridgway 350.00
Wheat design, white salt glazed body (A) . . .   65.00
9¾" h, "Apostle," eight sided, apostles in
arches, tan body, salt glaze, pewter top, "T.
Booth, Hanley" mark 265.00
10" h
"Bacchus," Charles Meigh 675.00
"Hecate," c1849, Walley 275.00
Soldiers and sailors with bust of Queen in cen-
ter, "Our army and navy brave volunteers"
around bottom, 1860 on spout, white, Brit
Reg mark," 225.00
"Three Soldiers," c1855, Ridgway & Abing-
ton 950.00
10½" h,
Green relief of putti playing tug of war, leaves
hanging, as is, Brit Reg mark 140.00
White relief of battles of Peninsular Campaign

with English dispatching French and Arabs,
lavender ground, white glazed int, mid 19th
C (A) 330.00
White relief of leaves, syrup, pewter lid 245.00
11" h
"Bacchanalian Dance," dark tan, c1844,
raised applied "Charles Meigh" mark 475.00
Ewer shape, white, relief of sheaf of wheat and
large scattered florals and wheat, stippled
ground, salt glaze finish (A) 71.00
11½" h
Bust of Josiah Wedgwood on one side, coronet topped by lion on other, imp "BORN
1730/DIED 1795" and figures depicting
science, art, and commerce 220.00
"Prince Albert" in cartouche in profile, white,
pewter lid, 1862, Brit Reg mark 1000.00
12" h, "Birdsnesting," relief white moldings,
brown ground, c1843, T.J.& J. Mayer mark . .   400.00

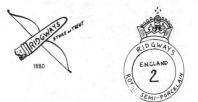

RIDGWAY

Shelton, Staffordshire, England
c1808–1855

History: Job Ridgway trained at the Swansea and Leeds
potteries. In 1808 he took John and William, his two sons,
into partnership at his Cauldon Place Works at Shelton. At
first the company only made pottery. Later porcelains
were added to supplement the earthenware line.

The early porcelain pieces usually were unmarked. A
few pieces done before Job Ridgway's death in 1813 are
impressed "Ridgway & Sons." After 1813 the two brothers separated. John retained the Cauldon Place factory
and made porcelains. William produced earthenwares at
the Bell Works.

John Ridgway specialized in the production of fine porcelain tablewares, mostly tea and dessert services. He was
appointed potter to Queen Victoria. Very few ornamental
pieces were made. Most pieces remained unmarked.
Hence, his wares are often attributed to other factories by
scholars and collectors.

William Ridgway expanded the scope of his operation
until he eventually owned six factories at Hanley and Shelton. Their principal production was utilitarian earthenwares, with a tinted bluish-mauve body. The earthenware
products that were made between 1830 and 1845 had no
mark, only a painted pattern number.

After 1856 there were a series of different partnerships with varying names. By 1962 the porcelain division of Cauldon was carried on by Coalport China Ltd.

The Ridgways used a distinctive system of pattern numbering, which is explained in G. Godden's *British Porcelain.*

Reference: G. A. Godden, *The Illustrated Guide to Ridgway Porcelains,* Barrie & Jenkins, 1972.

Museums: Cincinnati Art Museum, Cincinnati, Ohio; Potsdam Public Museum, Potsdam, N.Y.

Beverage Set, pitcher, 9½" h, 6 mugs, 4" h, tray, 12½" d, Coaching Days designs, black coaching scenes on caramel ground, silver luster trim **300.00**
Bowl
   8⅞" d, band of flowers and foliage in Imari colors, no.21138 (A) **300.00**
   9½" d, Coaching Days and Ways, "Henry VIII and the Abbot" in black and caramel brown **40.00**
Cup and Saucer, scene of boy fishing on lake with boats **25.00**
Cup and Saucer, demitasse, "Tuberose" pattern **10.00**
Dessert Plate, 8⅞"-9" d, "Harlequin" pattern, molded scalloped rim edge with gilt edge border of white beadwork with four clusters of gilt white blossoms, painted with assorted flowers and fruit, c1830, iron-red nos., 19 pcs (A) . . . **2750.00**
Dessert Service, Part
   Circ fruit stand, 9⅞" d, 5 plates, large floral spray in center, narrow fluted border, rim with border of lily patterned cobalt blue stripes alternating with gilt diamond and scrolls, gilt dentil edged cobalt blue band at edge, c1845, "iron-red 9171," 6 pcs (A) . . **770.00**
   Circ fruit stand, 13 3/16" w, cov circ sauce tureens, stands, 4 rect dishes, 3 sq dishes, oval dish, 20 plates, center in naturalistic shades with sprig of fruit within gilt edged panel reserved on blue-green ground, shaped rim feathered in gold, foliage scrolls, gilt pierced handles molded with roses and scrolling foliage, cov with rose blossom knob reglued, 1840–42, "iron-red 4990," 33 pcs (A) **1400.00**
   8 plates, 7¾" d, 2 tureens and lids, 8" l,

Plate, 9½" d, blue transfer of bird in sq, florals and banded design, gold rim, "blue quiver" mark, $48.00

basket and stand, 8¾" l, 4½" h, compote, 13" H-H, 3 serving dishes, 8" l, multicolored florals on white ground, raised berries and leaves in border, raised gilt berries and leaf on handles, scalloped edges trimmed in gilt, c1820, unmarked **7500.00**
18 plates, 9¼" d, 4 low ftd dishes, 2 med ftd dishes, 2 high ftd dishes, central roundel painted with basket of summer flowers and fruit on marble table, cobalt borders reserved with scrolling foliate orange and gilt designs, c1835, John Ridgway (A) **10,020.00**
19 plates, 8½" with scalloped edge, 4 rect sweetmeat dishes with pierced handles, 11" l, 3 round plates with pierced handles, 9½"l, oval plate with pierced handles, 11" l, cov sauce tureen with underplate and floral finial, 8½" h, small tureen, pedestal compote, 7" h, variety of fruit centers on white ground with wide blue-green band, white and gilt trims, gilt center border, c1860, 33 pieces **5500.00**
Dinner Service, cov soup tureen and stand, soup ladle, 3 cov sauce tureens and stands, 2 sauce ladles, 3 cov vegetable dishes, 18 soup plates, 27 dinner plates, 12 side plates, 15 dessert plates, 2 pudding dishes, fruit bowl, cheese dish, dish strainer, 2 serving dishes, "Fancy Stone China," underglaze blue and colored enamels with spray of flowers within border of further blooms on scrolled ground below gadroon rim, c1830, printed mark with title and initials, no. 1289, 101 pcs (A) **4605.00**
Dinner Service, Part, 2 cov circ vegetable dishes, 12" w, cov circ sauce tureens and stands, ftd circ bowl, oval platters, 16⅝" l, 14⅝" l, 12¾" l, 10⅝" l, 9¾" l, 12 plates, 9" d, ironstone, "Japan" pattern, printed in maroon, painted in underglaze blue, iron-red, salmon, blue, yellow, green, and gold with butterfly above oriental flowering plants within gilt edged underglaze blue roundel, brown edged scalloped rim, c1840, "maroon Royal Arms and IRONSTONE CHINA,'Sharpus & Co, 13 Cockspur St. London, 3/549, imp REAL IRONSTONE CHINA," 24 pcs (A) **2200.00**
Ice Pail, Cov, 13" h, horiz band of gilt edged orange feathery scrollwork reserved on pale yellow ground, above acanthus leaf molding, rope twist handles with trailing vine leaf terminals, cov with finials modeled as rhytons brimming with fruit, finial repaired, c1840, "red no.3564" (A) **3347.00**
Meat Platter, 18½" l, 15½" w, molded well and tree, "Tyrolean" pattern, light blue transfer, "William Ridgway" mark **195.00**
Mug
   4" h, Boating Days, "New Haven" and "Eton," brown body, silver luster trim **40.00**
   4⅛" h, Coaching Days, "Down the Hill on a Frosty Morning," caramel ground, silver luster top **21.00**
Pitcher
   4⅛" h, Coaching Days, black coaching scene on caramel ground, silver luster handle and rim **45.00**
   4¼" h, red transfers of family scenes on cream ground in roundels, reserved on cobalt ground, c1890, "Humphrey's Clock and William Ridgway" mark **195.00**

6", 7", 7³/4" h, overall gold oriental leaf and branch design, black ground, set of 3 .... **384.00**

6³/4" h, "Juvenile Sports" design in red, green, yellow, blue, and ochre, serpent handle restored (A) **55.00**

9¹/2" h, salt glaze, molded peak design, entwined rope twist handle, c1835, unmarked............................... **120.00**

9³/4" h, emb tavern scene painted in yellow, green, purple, red, pink, brown, and black, thistle border on neck, molded arm and hand handle, c1838–48 (A) **242.00**

Plaque, 12" d, Coaching Days, "In A Snow Drift," black transfer on yellow ground **130.00**

Plate

Cartouche of The Houses of Parliament surrounded by flowers and birds, ivory ground, c1830, set of 6 (A) **121.00**

8¹/2" d, oriental type florals in rose, rust, and purple with yellow centers, gray-green branches, raised, ribbed, scalloped edge, white ground, c1830, no.2004.......... **60.00**

9¹/2" d, "Indus" pattern.................. **20.00**

Platter

13" l, 10¹/2" w, Dickensware, "Bachelor Watches Nell and Grandfather," green on cream ground....................... **120.00**

13" l, 11" w, "Asiatic Palaces," dark blue transfer, "William Ridgway, Son & Co." mark................................. **158.00**

16" l, 18¹/2" d, no.2004, c1830 .... **495.00**

16¹/2" l, 11¹/4" w, small pink blossoms, green leaves, scalloped border with relief scrolls, gold trim and rim, "London, Ridgways England, Semiporcelain" mark **32.00**

17" l, "Oriental Sports," blue transfer, c1840, "J. Ridgway" mark................... **265.00**

18" l, "Devonshire" pattern, brown and white birds in oriental style (A) **50.00**

Sauce Tureen, Cov, 7" H-H, 5¹/2" h, hex shape, no.2004........................... **165.00**

Sauce Tueen, Cov, Fixed Stand, 6¹/2" h, gilt scroll edged panels of colored flowers on pale yellow ground, dark blue borders with rows of dots and dashes in gilding, scroll molded rim, pierced handles, c1825–30, "red no.1285" (A).................................. **2871.00**

Soup Plate, 10" d,

"India Temple" pattern, blue and white, 1814–30, "J.W.R." mark **75.00**

"View in Mesopotomia" pattern, blue and white, c1830 .... **70.00**

Teabowl and Saucer, oriental fishing scene, med blue transfers **65.00**

Teapot

5" h

Coaching Days, black scene on caramel brown ground, silver luster trim on handle and top, "Old English Coaching Days by Permission of McMillan & Co." mark **88.00**

"Royal Vistas" pattern, black transfer of sailing ships, green-yellow overglaze, copper luster trim **185.00**

6" h, 6" l, brown and white whooping cranes and foliage, emb leaves, dtd 1877, "Ridgway" mark **95.00**

Tea Service, Part, hex teapot, 6⁷/8" h, hex milk jug, 5 teacups, 5 coffee cups, 10 saucers, gilt palmettes beneath yellow ground border of demilunes with swags of gilt bellflowers and

scrolls below sunbursts, molded rim with gilt gadrooning, cobalt blue ground, 1825–30, "iron-red ²/₁₅₁₀" mark, 22 pcs (A)......... **550.00**

Tray

9¹/2" l, 7¹/2" w, Pickwick design, silver luster trim, scalloped rim, open handles **45.00**

11" l, scalloped triangle shape, classical urn on burnt orange shelf with green leaves in center gilt cartouche, wide beige border with brown designs, cobalt blue open handle with gilt, gilt rim, white ground, imp "Ridgway" mark **165.00**

Vase

7¹/4" h, squat globular body, painted landscape panel on molded and gilded turquoise ground, swans' head handles terminating in scrolls, flared quatrefoil foot, c1830–40, no.4290, pr (A)............. **710.00**

10¹/4" h, named view of "Abbey Church St. Albans, Herts" and "Episcopal Palace, Wells," reverse with named botanical specimens between wide gilt foliate scrolls on claret ground, flared neck and foot with molded gilt scrolling foliage, entwined branch handles, one piece repaired, c1840, script titles and no.5595, pr (A).......... **940.00**

Waste Pot, Lid, 11" h, 10" d, "Chester" pattern, floral design, pink glaze, Ridgway mark (A).. **70.00**

Rockingham Works
Brameld
c1826-1830

ROCKINGHAM

Swinton, South Yorkshire, England
Pottery 1745–1842
Porcelain 1826–1842

History: The Rockingham factory was located on the estate of Earl Fitzwilliam, Marquis of Rockingham, near Swinton in Yorkshire. The first pottery was manufactured in 1745. The factory continued production under various owners who concentrated on brown and yellow wares, blue and white dinner, tea and coffee services, and white earthenwares. In 1806 John and William Brameld took over the business and used the name "Brameld Co." They made pottery from 1806 to 1842.

Brown ware is the best known variety of Rockingham pottery. Its common forms include teapots, coffeepots, jugs, and cadogans (a pot from which liquid will not spill). The thickly applied glaze was intense and vivid purple brown when fired. The interior of pieces often was left white. Sometimes the brown exterior was decorated with gilding, enamel colors, or classical figures in relief. During the 19th century many companines copied the "Rockingham" glaze of a rich brown stained with manganese and iron.

The Bramelds introduced porcelain porduction in 1826. Rockingham bone china porcelain has a glaze somewhat prone to fine crazing. During the next sixteen years, until

1842, many ornamental wares and some utilitarian wares were made. Rockingham tea and coffee services in both simple and ornated decoration remained a mainstay of production. Finally the company also manufactured animal groups featuring dogs, cats, squirrels, rabbits, hares, deer, or sheep. Vases, ewers, baskets, scent bottles, candlesticks, desk pieces, trays and pieces for the dressing table constituted the principal ornamental forms.

The red griffin mark was used from 1826 to 1830 and the puce griffin mark from 1831 to 1842.

References: Alwyn Cox & Angela Cox, *Rockingham Pottery & Porcelain 1745–1842*, Faber & Faber, 1983; Arthur A. Eaglestone & Terence A. Lockett, *The Rockingham Pottery*, David & Charles, 1973, rev. ed.; D. G. Rice, *Ornamental Rockingham Porcelain*, Adam, 1965; D. G. Rice, *Rockingham Pottery and Porcelain*, Barrie & Jenkins, 1971.

Museums: City Museum, Weston Park, Sheffield, England; Clifton Park Museum, Rotherham, England; Rotherham Museum, Rotherham; Victoria & Albert Museum; Yorkshire Museum, York.

REPRODUCTION ALERT: Rockingham brown glaze was copied extensively throughout the 19th century by many factories.

Basket
  7½" h, helmet shape, applied colored flowers, gilt edged dbl acanthus foot, gilt rims, applied overhead handle, c1831–42, "puce griffin" mark (A)...................... **1180.00**
  9¼" l, center painted with titled rect scene of "Clifton," framing band of gilt vine leaves, applied flower border with gilt accents, entwined twig handle, c1830–37, "puce griffin" mark (A) **1795.00**
Box, Cov, 5" l, modeled as a white rose with yellow center, laying on bed of four veined leaves, cov perforated, hairline to base, c1830–40, "puce griffin and C.1" mark (A)....................................... **1673.00**
Candlestick, 7⅛" h, neck molded with white enameled ivy branches with gilt, green enamel ground, circ base molded with leaves, c1831–42, "puce griffin" mark (A) **365.00**
Compote, 9" l, 4" h, gilt design center on white ground, three floral panels, multicolored, purple, and rose, greenleaf border edged in gilt with gilt rim, white and gilt handles with raised leaf and berries, scalloped edge............ **325.00**
Cup and Saucer
  Enamel painted tulip and poppy, white

Pitcher, 7¼" h, 9¾" l, Turner body, engine turned bottom, c1810–25, "chrysanthemum pad" mark, $525.00

ground, barbed rims, c1826–30, "iron-red griffin, Tulipa and Papaver" marks (A) **536.00**
Gilt lined panel of painted exotic seashells and seaweed, green ground, restored, c1831–42, "puce griffin and no.743" marks (A).. **600.00**
Shell shape ribbed body painted with sprigs and sprays of summer flowers, mauve ground, gilt borders, iron-red handle, c1831–42, "puce griffin" mark (A) **1180.00**
Dessert Dish, 9¾" l, lobed, center painted with basket with colored flowers, shaded ground, border of gilt and green scrollwork, shaped handle enriched with gilding, c1826, "red circ griffin" mark, pr (A)...................... **1480.00**
Dessert Set
  2 fruit bowls, 11½" H-H, 2½" h, 2 compotes, 8½" d, 5¾" h, large compote, 12½" H-H, 7" h, large open painted flowers, raised blue and gold honeycomb borders, molded and scalloped gilt rims, unmarked (A) **1100.00**
  2 trays, 9½" H-H, cov sugar, 6½" h, waste bowl, 6½" d, 10 tea cups, 7 coffee cups, 11 small plates, green and gilt pattern border, white ground (A)........................ **400.00**
Dish
  9½" d, molded circ form with painted tulip in center, c1826–30 (A).................. **450.00**
  11½" l, oval, center painted with two spoon billed birds in marsh, gilt oval frame, gilt C scroll molded rim, matte green border, c1835 (A) **536.00**
Figure
  2⅜" h, seated black cat with gilt collar, sq green cushion base with gilt tassels, restored, c1826–30 (A).................. **1394.00**
  2¾" h, hare in white, black facial markings, gilt collar, crouching on oval gilt line base encrusted with foliage, restored, 1826–30, incised no.110, imp "ROCKINGHAM WORKS BRAMELD", iron-red cl.1 marks (A)................................. **340.00**
  3¹³/₁₆" l, recumbent great dane, white coat, black eyes, gray nose, iron-red mouth, salmon inner ear, gilt collar, rect base sponged in green, gilt band border, 1826–30, imp "griffin and ROCKINGLAM WORKS BRAMELD" marks, pr (A) **3575.00**
  3¾" h, standing peacock with outstretched tail feathers, gilt accents, green sponged base, c1825–30, incised no.136, imp "ROCKINGHAM WORKS BRAMELD" mark (A) **1600.00**
  4⅜" l, group of cat with three kittens, recumbent cat wearing gilt collar surrounded by three kittens with black markings, base marbled in black and splashed in blue, c1830–40, incised "model no.107" (A) **1253.00**
  6¼" h
    John Liston as "Billy Lackaday," mauve jacket, frilled shirt, white trousers, pink topped pedestal support, green base with titled gilt border, restorations, c1826, "red griffin," incised no.8" marks (A) **2953.00**
    Seated sherpherdess in puce bodice, long white skirt, broad brimmed hat with lilac ribbon, lamb in lap eating from bowl, rocky base with encrusted flowers,

c1826–30, incised no.4, imp "griffin and ROCKINGHAM WORKS BRAMELD" marks (A) **2038.00**

Ice Pail, 15" h, panels of domestic scenes reserved on blue ground, honeycomb raised gilding, gilt rustic handles with fruiting vine, berried holly stem, splayed foot with wintry panels, c1830–37, "puce griffin" marks, views named in red (A) **26,796.00**

Inkstand, 4¼" h, modeled as standing elephant, castle on back on shell molded shaped oval stand, blue enamel saddle cloth, gilt details, repair, crack, c1826–30, "iron-red printed griffin and script mark' (A) **750.00**

Inkwell, 3¾" h, bulbous shape, everted rim, pierced top, encrusted multicolored flowers, flower knob, c1831–40, "puce griffin" mark (A) **515.00**

Milk Jug, 4⅛" h, tooled gilt floral sprigs reserved on med blue ground, gilt handle and feet terminating in applied white blossoms, restored, c1830–35 (A) **385.00**

Mug, 1½" h, miniature
Painted scene of young girl holding wheat sheaf, landscape ground, reverse with trees, gilded rim and handle, c1830, "red griffin and ROCKINGHAM WORKS BRAMELD" mark (A) **1100.00**
Painted with sprays of flowers, gilt line rim and base (A) **360.00**

Plate
6⅜" d, pheasant and floral tree, Greek key border, brown-black transfer with polychromes, "Brameld" mark (A) **72.00**
9" d, painted center with exotic bird in landscape, raised C scroll border with gilt and painting, "puce griffin and green no.700" marks (A) **320.00**
9¼" d
Center painted with man fishing in boat, village church in ground, gray and blue border with gilt scrolling foliage, molded C scroll border, c1831–42, "puce griffin" mark (A) **645.00**
Named view of "Woodnook, Wentworth Park, Yorkshire," man holding game bird with dog by side, riverbank in woodland setting, wide band of scrolling vine and scattered insects, 1826–32, puce title (A) **490.00**
Painted center with rose and bluebells, border reserved with four panels painted with summer flowers on dark blue ground, painted in green and yellow with landscape vignettes, c1826–40, "iron-red griffin" mark (A) **500.00**
Painted vase of flowers overflowing onto marble table, med blue ground, gilt line band, shark's tooth and S scroll border, c1831–42 (A) **860.00**
9⅝" d
Center painted with named "Noble Liverwort," scattered insects, gilt chain border, shaped rim, c1831–42, iron-red named view on reverse (A) **645.00**
Fruit and flowers in center, med blue border with gilt foliate scrolls and shark's tooth, S scroll molded rim, c1826–30, "iron-red griffin and no.551" mark.............. **250.00**
Painted flowers in vase on marble table,

wide gilt leaf shaped cartouche, white and gilt primrose leaf molded border, pr (A) **1800.00**

Potpourri Vase, 4⅜" h, waisted rect shape, painted front and reverse with river landscape between gilt formal borders, four paw feet, pierced cov with acorn knob, dbl handles, c1826–31, "iron-red griffin" mark (A) **900.00**

Sauce Tureen, Cov, 7½" h, waisted body with leaf handles, painted panels of flowers on green ground, seaweed gilding, acorn finial, c1835, no.684 (A) **257.00**

Scent Bottle
5⅜" h, hex body, applied flowers with gilt branches, painted insects, repairs, c1831–40, "puce griffin" mark, pr (A) **600.00**
6" h, onion shaped body, applied garden flowers, gilt line rims, c1831–40, printed "puce griffin" mark (A) **450.00**
6⅛" h, painted with two panels of summer flowers between gilt scroll borders, apple green ground, repaired stopper, c1831–42, "puce griffin" mark (A) **800.00**

Tea Service, miniature, teapot, 4" d, milk jug, cov sugar bowl, rustic spouts and handles, four foliate feet, 2 cups and saucers, sides with applied trailing colored flowers in relief, c1831–42, "puce griffon" marks **1275.00**

Vase
4¼" h, flared form, painted bird perched in landscape in gilt line border, apple green ground, c1831–42, "iron-red griffin" mark (A) **5363.00**
4⅜" h
Cylindrical shape, continuous panel of ripe fruit on periwinkle blue ground, overhanging lips, traces of erased "red" marks, "C, No, 9 CL," pr (A) **324.00**
Flared shape, painted view of "Larington Yorkshire" with figures and sheep, wide gilt border, dark blue ground, restored, c1826–30, "iron-red griffin and painted title" **400.00**
5⅞" h, flared, painted cottage in landscape in sq gilt line border, apple green ground, c1826–30 (A) **600.00**
6½" h, flared hex shape, painted sprays of colored garden flowers alternating with blue ground panels of gilt scrolls, c1831–42, "puce griffin" mark (A) **800.00**
13¼" h, painted view of "Radford Folly" or "Chatsworth" in gilt scroll border, med blue ground, ribbed flared neck with molded vert lines, two figural stork handles, acanthus leaf molded quatrefoil feet, c1835, pr (A) **3647.00**

Vase, Cov
11⅜" h, multicolored floral basket in gold cartouche, tan ground, gold accented scroll handles and finial, perforated body and cov, c1830, "puce Manufacturers to the King" mark, pr (A) **220.00**
23⅝", 24" h, hex baluster shape, enameled parrots and butterflies perched on branches, oriental river scene with pagodas and pavilions, cov with painted oriental scene and gilt rose knob, gilt bands on foot, neck, rim, and cov rim, repairs, c1826–30, "iron-red Griffin and Rockingham Works Bramed" mark, pr (A) **24,200**

c1884

c1878

RORSTRAND

Near Stockholm, Sweden
1726 to Present

History: Rorstrand, established in 1726 near Stockholm, is the oldest porcelain factory in Sweden. Although formed for the production of tin-glazed earthenware, porcelain was the ultimate aim of the founder. A succession of German managers directed the production during the early years. The company made little impact on the ceramic world.

When Anders Fahlstrom became manager in 1740, the company began to flourish. Elias Ingman assumed control in 1753. The company immediately undertook to imitate the successful Sevres and Meissen wares. The company continued to prosper. Rorstrand absorbed the rival Marieberg factory in 1782.

Bengt Jeijer became manager in 1798. In the early 1800s the fortunes of Rorstrand were altered by two major events - the introduction and popularity of Wedgwood's creamware and the ban on the exportation of English clay. Rorstrand tottered on the brink of bankruptcy. Eventually the clay ban was relaxed. Workers from Stoke-on-Trent were imported. Rorstrand's products now had a finer clay body and strong English influence.

In the mid-1870s a limited company was formed. Production flourished due to the infusion of the fresh ideas of talented Scandinavian artists employed at the factory. Between 1895 and 1914 Rorstrand's art director and designer was Alf Wallander. He produced a wide range of tablewares and decorative pieces in the Art Nouveau style using delicate, sculptural modeling of figures and flowers, often in deep relief. Tonal qualities included delicate greens, pinks, and violets on a grayish off-white back-

ground. Wallander also used pale flower decorations contrasted with black grounds.

Following World War II, the entire factory was moved to the port city of Gothenburg, its present location.

The company has used the mark of three crowns of Marieberg with "RORSTRAND" since 1884.

Bowl, 8" w, heart shape, white	**45.00**
Lamp, 13" h, molded Cupid heads around stem, geometrics and swirls, tin glazed colors	**300.00**
Plaque, 13 3/8" h, 10" w, rect, "Vestalin," painted young woman in gauze dress tied with blue sash, veil on head, holding oil lamp, c1884	**3000.00**
Table Top, 23" l, 16 3/4" w, faience, blue painted center cartouche of kneeling Virgin Mary at altar and Angel of Annunciation with inscribed "Ava Maria Gratia Plena" staff, seeded latticework, shell, and foliage border, c1740 (A)	**9570.00**
Vase	
6 1/2" h, 7 1/4" l, ftd, rect, dark maroon and indented blue-green shapes with black, cream ground, "Rorstrand Made in Sweden" mark	**145.00**
8" h, stoneware, sgrafitto design	**350.00**
10" h, cylinder shape with flared neck, blue painted house in landscape with flowering plants, white ground, rim with paneled diaper and floral border (A)	**950.00**
13" h, reticulated creamy white body, blown out grapes and green leaves form top, marked	**375.00**
20 1/2" h, cut out friezes of flying ducks in shades of pink, blue, and green on gray ground, c1910	**2400.00**
Vase, Cov, Stand, 70" h, ovoid body, Renaissance style, molded with winged angels, masks, strapwork, hanging fruit, and garlands, Bacchus head scrolling handles, stand modeled as Corinthian capital on cylindrical column, molded acorns and foliage, stepped base with Bacchus heads, color accents with eggshell luster glaze, c1880 (A)	**2790.00**

1922

Rosenthal

1900-53

R. C.

KRONACH - BAVARIA
1901-33

ROSENTHAL

Selb, Bavaria, Germany
1879 to Present

History: The Rosenthal factory was located in Selb, Bavaria. Philip Rosenthal started initially by purchasing whiteware from Selb's other potter, Lorenz Heutschenreuther, decorating it, and selling it from house to house. Rosenthal established his own factory in 1879.

Rosenthal's factory flourished, providing quality figurals and tableware that was decorated tastefully. Simplicity of

Vase, 9" h, burgundy glaze, c1900, "Rorstrand Made in Sweden" mark, $675.00

designs and high quality workmanship made Rosenthal a household word.

Several additional factories were constructed. Production rose steadily. Designers of dinnerwares included Theodor Karner, Karl Himmelstoss, Ferdinand Liebermann, Philip Rosenthal, and Walter Gropius. "Darmstadt," "Donatello," and "Isolde" originally were produced in plain white between 1904 and 1910. Later heart-shaped motifs in the Art Nouveau manner were added to "Darmstadt." "Donatello" was decorated with underglaze pate-sur-pate, painted cherries, or a geometric pattern.

Figures made during the 1920s and 1930s were shaped and decorated in the Art Deco style. Many were signed by the artists. Following World War II, most of Rosenthal's assets were destroyed or outmoded. Sources for raw materials, mainly from the Eastern Block countries, were terminated.

Philip Rosenthal II assumed control, formed Rosenthal Porzellan AG, and began the restoration of the works. Many of the older designs, except for "Maria Weiss," 'Moss Rose," "Sans Souci," and "Pompadour" were abandoned in favor of fresh ideas originated by designers familiar with the modern tastes, among whom were Tapio Wirkkala from Finland, Jean Cocteau form France, and Bela Bechem from Germany.

The U.S. market was the major goal. Raymond Loewy was hired to design medium priced dinnerware for the American market. Under Philip's supervision, Rosenthal regained its prestigious position and flourishes today.

Bowl
| 9" d, grape design in colors | 32.00 |
| 10" d, multicolored classical woman with paint brush and easel, cobalt rim, marked. | 30.00 |

Bowl, Cov, 7½" h, hp florals with gilt on ivory ground, artist sgd ... 85.00

Cake Plate
| 11" d, child and two lambs in center, green florals on border, white ground, gold accents, c1901 (A) | 15.00 |
| 12" H-H, hp three color grapes, scalloped ruffled edge, open ruffled handles | 65.00 |

Candlestick, 9½" h, Art Deco woman holding candlestick ... 275.00

Cracker Jar, red and yellow roses on light green ground, c1901 (A) ... 180.00

Cream and Sugar, "pate-sur-pate" type blue cherries design ... 85.00

Cup and Saucer, "San Souci" pattern, white... 12.00

Cup and Saucer, Demitasse, "Maria" pattern .. 18.00

Figure, 9¼" h, 6¼" l, blue dress, gold trim, green frog, gray base, sgd "Ferd. Liebermann", (A) $350.00

Figure
| 3½" h, 4" l, sitting deer | 135.00 |
| 4¼" h, brown and white kitten playing with tail, imp "Prof. T. Karner" | 125.00 |

6" h
| Clown | 225.00 |
| Lady seated on bench with basket, dog at side, white with gilt highlights, no.K560 (A) | 175.00 |

6½" h
Little nude boy carrying goat, white, c1910, sgd "Fritz"	225.00
Two leaping deer, imp "H. Meisel"	315.00
7" h, 5½" w, girl holding flowers in front of deer	325.00
9" h, ram in mottled gray	195.00
10½" h, fairy queen, "L. Friedrich-Granau"	325.00
14" h, clown playing guitar, dog at feet (A)	775.00
14½" h, standing nude in classic pose, right hand above head, matte finish, sgd "R. Kaesbach"	150.00
16" h, white, lady with fish, sgd "Eva Mosbach"	600.00

Lamp, 9½" h, hp yellow and white daisies ... 85.00

Planter, 7½" l, 4" w, tree bark textured surface, knot holes front and back, unglazed white ext, glazed int. ... 90.00

Plate
6½" d, hp portrait of woman	55.00
8" d, "Moss Rose" pattern, set of 6	85.00
9⅞" d, panel painted with head and shoulder portrait of lady, pale yellow and white ground, jeweled with pseudo-hardstones in green, turquoise, blue, and red (A)	342.00
10" d, multicolored scene of girl and lamb	34.00
10½" d, gold "Maria" pattern	35.00
10¾" d, gold and green berry and leaf border, set of 12 (A)	176.00
13" d, yellow, pink, and white roses on light green border, gold rim, c1901 (A)	25.00

Platter
12" l
Roses on ivory ground, sterling rim	55.00
"Shadow Rose" pattern	25.00
15" l, "Greenblume" pattern	48.00

Urn, 15" h, ovoid form, one with floral design, one with Madonna and Child, gilt scrolled handles, white ground, pr (A) ... 1000.00

Vase
6" h
Bag shaped, Studio Line, white glaze, artist sgd	80.00
Black cats on front, white ground	40.00
Ewer shape, silver overlay on orange and gray-blue ground, "Kunstabteilung-Selb" mark	275.00
6½" h, dancing nude in colors, artist sgd	80.00
7¼" h, violet cameo of Greek god, cream ground, gold bead trim, c1930, pr	95.00
7½" h, multicolored fisherman with basket on back, beach and sea in ground, c1900, sgd "Hubel"	395.00
9⅞" h, polychrome floral bouquet in center, banded top and base, vert ribbed body, "Rosenthal" mark (A)	50.00
11" h, hp roses in colors	118.00
13½" h, tapered shape, girl with flower basket in green design beside flowering bush, gold trim, "crown RC" mark	250.00

Vegetable Bowl, Cov, 10¾" H-H, "Maria" pattern **65.00**

pink roses on light green shaded ground, "E.& O.G. Royal Austria" marks **115.00**

c1903

ROYAL AUSTRIA

**Altrohlau, Bohemia, now Czechoslovakia
1889 to Present**

History: In 1899 Oscar Gutherz joined with Edgar Gutherz, the former manager of the New York and Rudolstadt Pottery, to manufacture household, table, and decorative porcelains, mainly for export to the United States. The mark used was "O & EG" and "Royal Austria" until 1918.

The Austrian Porcelain Industry combine acquired the factory, named it Opiag, Branch Altrohlau, and operated it from 1918 until 1920. Between 1920 and 1945 the factory was called Epaig, Branch Altrohlau. It produced household and decorative porcelains, gift articles, and souvenir items. After World War II the company was nationalized.

Celery Dish, 12" l, pink roses with yellow and green centers, shaded pastel ground, gold rim **20.00**
Cream and Sugar, overall yellow and red carnations with green leaves, gold rims, handles, and three ball feet, "blue O.& E.G. Royal Austria" marks **40.00**
Dresser Set
Tray, 11¼" l, 8" w, bottle, 5¼" h, ring dish, 2¼" h, 3⅞" d, figural gold hand, ftd cov powder jar, 5" d, red roses, green leaves, shaded pink to cream ground, gold trim, "green O.& E.G. Royal Austria" marks **185.00**
Tray, 2 cov boxes, 2 candlesticks, ring tree, red roses on lime green and white ground, "Royal Austria" marks **145.00**
Plate, 9½" d, red center floral design, gold trim, "O.& E. G." mark **8.00**
Salt Dip, pink with gold ruffled edge, set of 6. . **60.00**
Tea Service, teapot, creamer, sugar bowl, 2 cups, ·

Plate, 9¾" d, multicolored floral center and panels, cobalt ground, gilt overlay, (A) $30.00

ROYAL BAYREUTH

**Tettau, Bavaria
1794 to Present**

History: Wilheim Greiner and Johann Schmidt established a porcelain factory at Tettau in 1794. They also maintained an association with the Volkstedt and Kloster Veilsdorf factories in Thuringia. The factory survived numerous wars, financial difficulties, and many changes in ownership until a great fire in 1897 destroyed most of the molds and early records. A more modern factory was built and operated until World War I.

The company operated under the name, Porcelain Factory Tettau, from 1902 until 1957. In 1957 the company adopted the name, Royally Priviledged Porcelain Factory Tettau GMBH, which it still uses today.

Animal and floral forms along with other unusual figural shapes were made at Tettau between 1885 and World War I. Designs included fruits, vegetables, lobsters, tomatoes, and people. Shapes ranged from ashtrays to vegetable dishes. Individuals often bought them as souvenir and novelty items because of their inexpensive cost. Much of the production was exported.

Today the firm produces dinnerware and limited edition collectibles. The name, "Royal Bayreuth," is used in the United States to identify the company's products.

ROSE TAPESTRY

Rose tapestry, similar in texture to needlepoint tapestry and called "matte finish" china, was made in the late 19th century. Rose tapestry has a rough effect that feels like woven cloth. It was made by wrapping the article in coarse cloth and then firing. The cloth was consumed in the firing, and the tapestry effect remained.

Decoration was added over the glaze. It varied from floral to scenic to portrait. The floral motifs included "rose tapestry," the most popular and prevelant design. The roses shaded from a pale pink to deeper red colors.

Occasionally pale yellow or white roses were combined with the pink or red roses. Rose tapestry also can be found in an apricot and deep orange-gold shade. The rarest rose tapestry is "sterling silver." The roses are deep gray to a pale silver gray shaded into white.

The background of rose tapestry is off-white or has a grayish or greenish tinge. Pale green leaves and small faintly tinted flowers complete the decoration.

Floral, scenic, and portrait tapestries were made in plates, pitchers, cups and saucers, vases, pin boxes, trays, bells, and many other shapes.

SUNBONNET BABIES

Molly and Mae, the Sunbonnet Babies, were created by Bertha L. Corbett, an American artist, in the early 1900s.

Corbett had no confidence in her ability to draw faces so she hid them under the large bonnets. The Sunbonnet Babies were drawn to develop good character traits and teach children their daily chores, e.g., washing ironing, sweeping, dusting, mending, baking, fishing, and going to church.

Variations identified as Beach Babies and Snow Babies also were made.

References: Joan & Marvin Raines, *A Guide to Royal Bayreuth Figurals*, privately printed, 1973; Joan & Marvin Raines, *A Guide to Royal Bayreuth Figurals*, Book 2, privately printed, 1977; Virginia & George Salley, *Royal Bayreuth China* privately printed, 1969.

BABIES

Bell, Beach babies, blue mark	295.00
Bowl, 6″ d, Snow babies	325.00
Cake Plate, 10¼″ d, Sunbonnet babies washing	400.00
Candleholder, shield back, Sunbonnet babies cleaning	350.00
Creamer, Snow babies, gold trim	90.00
Cream and Sugar, Sunbonnet babies fishing and sweeping	300.00
Cup and Saucer	
Beach babies	200.00
Sunbonnet babies	
Cleaning	120.00
Fishing	225.00
Ironing and sweeping	295.00
Cup and Saucer, Demitasse, Sunbonnet babies cleaning	275.00
Dish	
6″ d, Sunbonnet babies	
Cleaning, blue mark	120.00
Fishing, blue mark	135.00
Ironing	65.00
Mending, fluted gold trimmed rim	140.00
7″ d, Sunbonnet babies washing	135.00
7½″ d, Sunbonnet babies washing	85.00
8″ d, Sunbonnet babies ironing	
Ruffled edge, blue mark	165.00
Scalloped edge, ftd, blue mark	175.00
9″ d, Sunbonnet babies washing	225.00
Feeding Dish, 7¼″ d	
Sand babies	150.00
Sunbonnet babies	
Fishing, blue mark	235.00
Mending	225.00
Ferner, 5¾″ d, ftd, Sunbonnet babies washing and ironing, mending, sweeping, and cleaning, emb gold shells on rim, blue mark	795.00
Fruit Bowl, 9¾″ d, Sunbonnet babies, washing and hanging	90.00
Inkwell	
Sand babies skipping rope, blue mark	325.00
Sunbonnet babies running, blue mark	325.00
Jug, 4¼″ h, Sunbonnet babies cleaning, blue mark	235.00
Mug	
3¼″ h, Snow babies sledding, blue mark	80.00
3½″ h, Sunbonnet babies	
Cleaning, blue mark	245.00
Fishing, blue mark	165.00
Mustard Pot, Sunbonnet babies sweeping, blue mark	395.00
Pin Tray, 10″ l, 7½″ w, Sunbonnet babies fishing, blue mark	295.00
Plant Holder, 4½″ h, Sunbonnet babies watering	75.00
Posy Pot, Snow babies	50.00
Shoe, Sunbonnet babies cleaning, blue mark	625.00
Stamp Box, 2½″ l, 2″ w, Sunbonnet babies washing and ironing, blue mark	195.00
Tankard, 7″ h, Sunbonnet babies ironing	500.00
Teapot, 4″ h, Sunbonnet babies, babies fishing	495.00
Tea Tile, 6″ d	
Snow babies, blue mark	90.00
Sunbonnet babies cleaning, blue mark	210.00
Toothpick Holder, 3¼″ h, Sunbonnet babies cleaning, three small handles, SS rim	395.00
Tray, 7¾″ l, 4¼″ w, Sunbonnet babies sewing, dbl handles, blue mark	195.00
Tumbler, 3½″ h, Sunbonnet babies cleaning	375.00
Vase	
4″ h, Sunbonnet babies sweeping, blue mark	275.00
5½″ h, Snow babies	145.00

GENERAL

Ashtray	
4½″ w, triangular, riding to the hounds scene in colors, gold trim	85.00
6″ l, figural red lobster, blue mark	42.00
Bell, 3½″ h	
Dutch girl and boy standing on dock, boat in ground, unmarked	185.00
Nursery rhyme, "Ring around the rosey', circle of children dancing	295.00
Bowl	
6″ d, tavern scene in colors	95.00
10½″ d, pink and red roses on deep pink ground, ivory center	185.00
11″ d	
Molded stalks and leaves on flared light blue and white top, five figural gold bows on outer rim, circle of pink roses, green leaves and ferns, scattered roses on green bottom, blue mark	110.00
Red, white, and pink roses on light green ground, gold highlights, fluted and puffed rim (A)	100.00
Cake Plate	
10″ d, roses in center in colors, gold leaf border and handles	60.00
10½″ d, multicolored scene of hunter with gun and dog, pierced handle, blue mark	250.00
11″ d	
Mountain goats in colors, blue mark	125.00
Pink roses on cream ground, ornate gold handles, blue mark	95.00
Candlestick, 6″ h, hp pink and white roses, ivory ground, open work on sides, handled, blue mark	125.00
Candy Dish, 7″ d, devil and cards	125.00
Celery Tray, 12½″ l	
Figural red lobster, blue mark	245.00
Goose girl in colors	150.00
Chamberstick	
4″ h, Goose girl in colors, blue mark	80.00
4½″ h, Corinthian ware, enameled Grecian figures, black ground	55.00
Cheese Dish, 2¾″ l, 2″ w, 2″ h, miniature, farmer with turkeys design, slanted top with handle, ruffled edge on base	110.00
Chocolate Set, pot, 3 cups, figural red poppies	700.00

Cream and Sugar
Corinthian, classical figures on black ground   75.00
Figural tomato and lettuce leaf, blue marks..   65.00

Creamer, 3½" h, orange-red figural poppy, green handle, blue mark, (A) $121.00

Creamer
Figural
Alligator.............................   285.00
Apple................................   325.00
Bear.................................   575.00
Bird of Paradise......................   231.00
Chimpanzee..........................   495.00
Cockatoo.............................   210.00
Coral Shell...........................   65.00
Dachshund...........................   224.00
Devil, red............................   325.00
Duck.................................   203.00
Eagle................................   182.00
Fish Head............................   165.00
Frog, green body......................   135.00
Grapes, purple.......................   135.00
Horsehead...........................   750.00
Ladybug, blue mark...................   295.00
Lemon...............................   210.00
Lobster and leaf......................   140.00
Maple Leaf...........................   210.00
Monkey..............................   350.00
Mountain Goat.......................   250.00
Orange..............................   185.00
Owl.................................   350.00
Pansy...............................   185.00
Parakeet.............................   173.00
Perch................................   189.00
Poodle
Black.............................   135.00
Gray..............................   210.00
Robin...............................   175.00
Rooster
Black.............................   210.00
White.............................   210.00
Rose, blue mark......................   265.00
Snake...............................   595.00
Tomato..............................   40.00
Water Buffalo........................   155.00
3¾" h
Devil and cards design................   185.00
Figural clown in red with black buttons, blue mark................................   125.00
4" h
Devil and cards, blue mark.............   175.00
Figural black cat......................   185.00

Figural cow in red-brown, white, and gray, blue mark...........................   95.00
Figural crow.........................   185.00
Figural elk, blue mark.................   65.00
Figural moose, blue mark..............   60.00
Figural seal, blue mark................   245.00
Figural strawberry....................   165.00
Sheep grazing, multicolored, pinched spout, blue mark..........................   90.00
Three men in sailboat, blown out sides...   60.00
4¼" h
Corinthian, band of black and white key trim........................   65.00
Pheasant and bird, ruffled and stylized border of sky and buildings, blue mark....   55.00
4¾" h, tankard type, pinched spout, Dutch figures..............................   85.00
Cup and Saucer, tavern scene in colors.......   90.00
Dish
5¼" d, ruffled red poppy, green handle, blue mark...............................   50.00
5½" H-H, Arab and camel scene in center, riders and palm in ground, dark green ext, rolled edge, unmarked..................   55.00
8¼" d, shell shape
Gray tint, unmarked..................   25.00
Green tint, unmarked.................   25.00
Dresser Tray, 9¼" l, 7" w, colonial couple in colors, blue mark........................   185.00
Gravy Bowl, Cov, 8" l, 5¼" h, with underplate, gold Greek key design, white ground, blue mark................................   89.00
Hair Receiver, 3" h, pink roses on blue and white ground, three gold feet, blue mark........   78.00
Hatpin Holder
Courting couple in colors, cutout base with gold, blue mark........................   395.00
Oct, mother of pearl luster finish, scalloped rim, gold scroll trim, blue mark.........   115.00
Humidor, 6¾" h, sailing ships and windmills in blue, two handles on rim, blue mark.......   275.00
Inkwell, 4" sq, children on sled design........   135.00
Master Salt, devil and cards.................   325.00
Mug, 5¾" h, tavern scene.................   125.00
Pitcher
3½" h, mountain scene with five goats, gold handle.............................   65.00
4" h
Hunting scene in colors................   70.00
Pastoral scene of girl with three geese in colors.............................   65.00
Pastoral scene of three cows with trees, green ground........................   65.00
4¼" h, three bears playing in brown, yellow, green on cream ground, gold handle, blue mark................................   95.00
5" h
Corinthian, black and red, bands of yellow flowers, classical figures..............   95.00
"Face," leaf molded body, light gray matte finish, gold outlines...................   148.00
5½" h, elk head.......................   210
6" h, fisherman trio in boat, blue mark.....   135.00
7¾" h, orange-red figural lobster, green handle................................   175.00
8" h, multicolored hunt scene, apple green ground, blue mark.....................   100.00
12" h, Corinthian, red ground, pinched spout   225.00
Plate
6¼" d, musicians design................   60.00

6½" d, "Jack and the Bean Stalk" design, blue mark 145.00
7" d, modeled poppy, pearlized finish, blue mark 90.00
7½" h
  Devil and cards design, blue mark 485.00
  "Little Bo Peep" design, blue mark....... 85.00
9" d, roses design with gold tracery, blue mark 42.00
Relish Dish, 8" l, rooster and hens in colors... 175.00
Rose Bowl, 3½" d, 4" h, man fishing in wooded setting, blue mark 55.00
Salt and Pepper
  3½" h
    Corinthian, black satin ground with mytho-logical scenes, blue marks............. 110.00
    Figural purple grapes, green leaf bases, blue marks.............................. 135.00
    Figural lobster......................... 125.00
Salt Shaker
  Devil and cards 95.00
  Figural elk 225.00
Sugar Bowl, 3½" h, figural tomato, blue mark 55.00
Tea Set, teapot, 4½" h, creamer, 2½" h, open sugar bowl, 1⅛" h, cup and saucer, farmland and horses designs in colors............... 265.00
Toothpick Holder,
  Corinthian, three handled 95.00
  Pastoral scene 175.00
Vase
  2" h, two girls in red coats, sterling rim, pr.. 280.00
  3" h, girl with turkeys in colors 110.00
  3⅛" h, multicolored coaching scene at top, green base, dbl handles, blue mark....... 65.00
  3¼" h, two Arabs with horses, pastel blue, yellow, and pink ground, SP top, tab handles, blue mark 50.00
  3½" h, scene of peasant ladies with sheep in natural colors, silver rim, three handles, blue mark................................. 50.00
  3⅝" h, Dutch lady carrying basket, blue and cream ground, silver rim, dbl handles, blue mark................................. 45.00
  3⅞" h, large yellow rose on green, blue, and pink ground, gold trim, dbl handles, blue mark................................. 50.00
  4" h, mixed flower bouquet in colors, reticulated top 85.00

Vase, 5" h, Corinthian ware, Greek figure on each side, yellow bands, black matte ground, orange int rim, blue mark, (A) $77.00

4¼" h
  Five pink and yellow roses, cobalt ground 45.00
  Multicolored donkey and boy design..... 95.00
4½" h, Corinthian, bands of yellow flowers, classical figures 75.00
5¼" h, portrait medallion of bust of woman in period hat, gold incised leaf design frame, enamel trim 170.00
6" h, orange and black sunset cottage scene 210.00
6½" h, tavern scene, two handles 210.00
7" h
  Corinthian, urn shaped, blue mark 75.00
  Elk and doe in colors, dbl handled 225.00
  8" h, tavern scene in colors, two handled .. 120.00
8½" h, scene of deer in meadow with trees, temple in ground, shaded tan to burnt orange ground, blue mark................. 90.00
9" h, Corinthian, green ground 295.00
10" h, roses in colors, twisted handles on sides................................. 250.00
Wall Pocket, 9" h, yellow figural grapes with green leaves, blue mark.................. 210.00

TAPESTRY

Basket
  3¾" h, rose tapestry, green mark 400.00
  5" h, rose tapestry, braided handle, scalloped rim 450.00
  6" h, 5" l, 3¾" w, three color roses, circle of pink roses and white ferns around top, bouquets of yellow and white roses at base with open handle, pink roses on int, wishbone handle with gold trim, blue mark........ 395.00
Bonbon Dish, palette shape, three color roses, bouquet of pink, yellow and white roses in center, pink and white roses at edge, fancy handle, blue mark 195.00
Bowl, 10½" d, rose tapestry, pink and yellow roses................................... 675.00
Box
  3½" l, 2" w, 2" h, oval, Christmas cactus design 275.00
  3¾" l, 2" w, courting couple in colors, blue mark.................................. 235.00
Cache Pot, 2¾" h, 3¼" d, rose tapestry, ruffled top, gold handles................... 200.00
Charger, 12" d, rose tapestry............... 1150.00
Creamer
  3½" h, cavaliers design, blue mark........ 150.00
  3¾" h, tankard shape, pinched spout, rose tapestry, three color roses.............. 250.00
  4" h, pinched spout, rose tapestry, three color roses, blue mark 150.00
Ewer, 3½" h, multicolored scene of two ladies at pond, blue and green ground, gold trim, unmarked 135.00
Figure, 5" l, woman's slipper, red lace, blue mark................................... 335.00
Flower Pot, 4" h, with drain, three color roses, blue mark 550.00
Hair Receiver, rose design, blue mark........ 165.00
Hatpin Holder, saucer base, scene of swimming swans at sunset, blue mark............... 245.00
Nappy, clover shape with gold ring handle, rose tapestry, three color roses, blue mark....... 295.00
Nut Dish, 3¼" d, 1¾" h, rose tapestry, three color roses, gold feet, green mark......... 160.00
Pin Tray, Cov., 4½" d, pastoral scene with goats.................................. 165.00

Pitcher
  3¾" h
    Rose tapestry, ewer shape, ruffled top, gold
      handle 225.00
    Scene of three sheep in colors 295.00
  5¾" h, rose tapestry, pink roses 420.00
Plate
  6" d, rose tapestry, three color roses, blue
    mark 145.00

1887-1920

Bonn
1920

Plate, 9¾" d, Rose tapestry, pink roses, gilt rococo rim, blue mark, (A) $210.00

11¼" d, hp scene with woman bathing
  before a castle, curvilinear gilt highlighted
  border, tapestry ground, blue mark (A) . . .   100.00
Ring Box, 3" l, triangular, puffy cov, rose tapes-
  try, blue mark 295.00
Tankard, 4" h, pink roses with yellow ferns, gold
  beading and handle, blue mark 165.00
Teapot, Japanese chrysanthemums design, blue
  mark 695.00
Tray
  7¾" l, 4¼" w, rose tapestry, three color
    roses, dbl handles, blue mark 225.00
  9¼" l, courting couple in colors, blue mark   475.00
  9½" l, 7" w, rose tapestry, three color roses,
    blue mark 350.00
  11" l, 8" w, yellow and white daisies, pink,
    yellow, and white dogwood, blue mark . . .   425.00
Trinket Box, 3½" d, colonial couple in colors,
  blue mark 235.00
Vase
  3" h, woodland scene with dogs, multicol-
    ored 200.00
  3½" h, two swans on lake, natural ground,
    multicolored, unmarked 135.00
  3¾" h, scene of forest and gazebo in col-
    ors 220.00
  4" h, castle scene in colors 165.00
  4¼" h
    Violets design, blue mark 325.00
    Woodland scene in colors 125.00
  4½" h
    Courting couple in colors 165.00
    Polar bear design, gold handled, blue
      mark 250.00
  5¼" h, rooster and turkey fighting 260.00
  7" h, multicolored soccer scene, blue mark .   295.00
Wall Matchholder, bust of woman shading eyes
  with hand, blue mark 395.00

ROYAL BONN

Bonn, Germany
1836–1931

History: Franz Anton Mehlem founded a factory in the Rhineland in 1836 to produce household, decorative, technical, and sanitary earthenware and porcelain. Between 1887 and 1903 the factory reproduced Hochst figures in both porcelain and earthenware using the original molds from the defunct Prince-Electoral Mayence Manufactory in Hochst. Villeroy and Boch from Mettlach bought the factory in 1921 and closed it in 1931.

Royal was added to the mark in 1890. After that, products were marketed under the name, "Royal Bonn."

Biscuit Jar, 7½" h, pink, blue, rose, and orange
  flowers outlined in gold, beige and cream
  ground, embossed gold swirls, satin finish, SP
  top, rim, and handle 125.00
Bowl
  8" d, 2 decorative panels with roses, gilt curvi-
    linear and foliate design, burgundy ground,
    entwined handles, "Royal Bonn Germany"
    mark (A) 325.00
  11" d, hp purple, fuchsia, yellow, and blue
    portulaca, ribbed rim, c1880 (A) 13.00

Ewer, 12½" h, multicolored florals and raised gilt trim, gilt serpent handle, satin finish, "Franz Mehlem Bonn" mark, (A) $80.00

Cheese Keep, hp flowers on acorn, leaf, and swirl relief molded body, twig handle, "Bonn-Rhein" mark (A)............................ 38.00

Egg Server, hp florals, butterflies, and birds, swirl pattern, gold trim (A) 28.00

Cup and Saucer, lustered flowers in relief, marked................................ 30.00

Ewer
  12" h, multicolored enameled flowers, gold twist lizard handle..................... 245.00
  12 1/2" h, hp bird, orchids, and dragonfly, gold lizard handle around body 175.00

Jardinaire, 13" l, 9 1/2" w, large hp chrysanthemums front and reverse, blue-green ground, gold rim, marked 200.00

Plate
  7 1/2" d, red roses and green leaves in center, tan, green, and cream pearlized ground (A) 10.00
  8 1/2" d, red and white roses with green leaves, earthtone ground, crazing, c1900 (A)................................... 15.00
  10 1/4" d, earthtone colors of fisherman in river with trees and cliffs, relief scrollwork on border, c1860 (A).................. 13.00
  11 1/4" d, cottage scene on pale fuchsia and tan ground, crazing, "Bonn-Rhein" mark (A)................................... 10.00

Sardine Box, hp vert florals and gold, figural fish knob, "Bonn-Rhein" mark (A) 55.00

Tea Tile, 7" d, hp pink, yellow and purple pansies, white ground, green border, "Bonn-Rhein" mark (A)....................... 25.00

Tray, 12" l, birds and moon in colors........ 65.00

Vase
  4 1/2" h, bulbous shape, red and green roses, ivory and gold colors, pr 145.00
  6" h, bulbous shape, hp iris 75.00
  7 1/4" h, four magenta roses on front, shaded yellow to rust ground, single rose on reverse, "Royal Bonn" mark.............. 225.00
  7 1/2" h, purple and yellow irises, two gold handles, serrated rim 135.00
  8" h
    Bulbous shape, multicolored scattered iris design, gold trim, pr.................. 225.00
    Gold and orange flowers on brown and yellow ground......................... 95.00
    Hp bust of woman surrounded by flowers, reverse with fence, mountains and sky . 200.00
  8 1/4" h, profile portrait of lady with wreath of pink and cream roses, brown hair, cream dress, shaded brown and gold ground, emb gold design top and bottom, sgd "G. Muller" 550.00
  8 3/4" h, white roses on shaded green ground, flared top 95.00
  9 1/4" h, bulbous shape, enamel decorated portrait of young woman, molded scalloped rim, small gilt shaped handles, c1900, sgd "Dingendorf," pr (A) 770.00
  9 1/2" h, reserve of multicolored flowers on red ground, gold trim, small handles at neck................................. 175.00
  10 1/2" h
    Multicolored flower insert, oval bottom, narrow neck, dbl pierced handles, marked 225.00
    Portrait of woman in purple dress and scarf, light brown hair, shaded brown and gold

ground, emb gold top and base, dbl handles on shoulder, sgd "G. Muller" 550.00

12" h, bird and iris design in colors 85.00

12 1/4" h
  Art Nouveau, glazed exotic flowers on textured black matte ground............. 450.00
  Snowballs, shaded green ground, gold trim, pr 290.00

14" h, pear shape, hp rose and leaf design on cream ground, two animal head handles terminating at base, two additional base supports, round base, "FM" mark.......... 350.00

15" h, long, thin neck, overall flower design outlined in gold, crown mark........... 100.00

c1889   c1923

ROYAL COPENHAGEN

Copenhagen, Denmark
c1760 to Present

History: During the 1760s the Danish royal family was interested in discovering the Chinese secret for white hard paste porcelain. Louis Fournier, a French ceramist, came to Denmark to conduct experiments in hopes of uncovering the porcelain formula.

In 1772 Franz Muller, a Danish pharmacist and chemist, produced the first genuine hard paste porcelain. Muller with the Queen's suppport, founded the Danish Porcelain Factory in Copenhagen in 1775. By 1779 financial difficulties forced Muller to relinquish his hold to the Danish crown. The Dowager Queen Julianne Marie was the chief patron. Under her influences, the Copenhagen trade mark of three wavy lines was established. Each wave represented a waterway from Kattegat to the Baltic.

Royal Copenhagen's Flora Danica, decorated with the native plants of Denmark, is a famous 18th century service begun in 1790. A total of 1802 pieces were painted. The dinnerware was intended originally as a gift for Catherine The Great of Russia, but she died six years before its completion. All botanical illustrations were done free hand; all perforations and edges were cut by hand. The service still remains in the possession of the Danish crown. Flora Danica is still being produced today. Each piece is done entirely by hand by an individual artist who signs his work.

Royal Copenhagen's most famous pattern, Blue Fluted, was created in 1780. It is of Chinese origin and has three edge forms, smooth edge, closed lace edge, and perforated lace edge. It was copied by many other factories.

Although the quality of the porcelain kept improving during the early 19th century, and their was strong popular approval for the company's figures, vases, and accessory pieces in all pottery and porcelain compostions, the factory was not a financial asset for the crown. A. Falch, a private owner, purchased the factory in 1867. A condition of purchase was his right to continue to use the term "Royal" in the monogram. Philip Schou purchased the works from Falch in 1882 and moved to the present location at Smalzgade. Arnold Krog, who was appointed Art Director in 1885, was responsible for revitalizing Royal Copenhagen. The under the glaze painting technique was perfected under his control. Muller's early creations were reproduced as the "Julianne Marie Porcelain" line.

Dinner services, under the glaze painted figures, and vases were among the principal forms being made at Royal Copenhagen when Dalgas took over in 1902. The first Christmas plate was made in 1908. As at the Bing and Grondahl factory, the molds were destroyed each year after the holiday season to prevent restrikes in hopes of preserving the value of each plate for the collectors. During Dalgas' tenure, there also were experiments with stonewares and the renaissance of the overglaze painting tecniques.

References: Pat Owen, *The Story of Royal Copenhagen Christmas Plates,* Viking Import House, Inc., 1961; H.V.F. Winstone, *Royal Copenhagen,* Stacy International, 1984.

Museums: The Bradford Museum, Niles, Illinois; Rosenborg Castle, Copenhagen, Denmark.

Collecting Hints: Royal Copenhagen dinnerware sets are eager sought by collectors because of their high quality. The blue and white limited edition plates remain popular with collectors.

Bone Dish, 11 1/2" l, oval shape, fish in center, blue crabs applied at end, raised molded edge, "Royal Copenhagen with crown and Denmark" mark............................ **575.00**
Bouillon Cup and Saucer, 6 5/8" w, 6 3/4" d, "Flora Danica," botanical specimen below pink and gold molded beadwork border fluted gilt foliate band at rim edge, dentil edged rim of saucer, green and ochre entwined twig handles at sides, black botanical identification, underglaze "blue triple wave, green circ ROYAL COPENHAGEN, 20 3612" marks, set of 12 (A).................................... **6325.00**
Bowl
10" w, 4" h, scene of Cupid on chariot pulled by three maidens..................... **375.00**
10 3/4" d, Kauffmann type portrait in center, white and irid fuchsia, gold decor, 1900 (A)................................. **65.00**

Vase, 14 1/2" h, frieze of stampeding bulls, relief molded border of cows with horns forming ring handles, blue and white, "Royal Copenhagen and waves" mark, (A) $1540.00

Butter Pat
"Half Lace" pattern..................... **17.50**
"Symphony" pattern, set of 6............ **18.00**
Butter Plate, 6 3/4" d, "Flora Danica," botanical specimens, molded gilt beadwork, gilt foliate edge, black botanical identifications, underglaze "blue triple wave, green circ ROYAL COPENHAGEN, 203551" marks, set of 12 (A)................................... **2475.00**
Butter Server, 5 1/4" l, blue and white plain lace pattern, 1894.......................... **75.00**
Candlestick, 9" h, blue floral on white ground, bisque lion heads, floral garlands, no. 1/15, pr **150.00**
Casserole, Cov, 11 1/4" H-H, 7" h, blue and white plain lace pattern, strawberry finial.... **250.00**
Coffee Can and Saucer, "Flora Danica," botanical specimen below pink and gold molded beadwork border, band of gilt leafage at end of rim, serrated rim on saucer, black botanical identification on cups, underglaze "blue triple wave green circ ROYAL COPENHAGEN, 20 3512 and 20 3513" marks, set of 12 (A) ... **4125.00**
Cup and Saucer
"Blue Flute Full Lace" pattern, #1130...... **15.00**
"Flora Danica" pattern, set of 12 (A)....... **7150.00**
"Quaking Grass" pattern................... **10.00**
Decanter, 9 3/4" h, with stopper, Rosenburg Castle, blue and white **48.50**
Dinner Service
10 dinner plates, 12 soup bowls, 11 salad plates, 6 bread and butter plates, 13 tea cups and saucers, small tureen, soup tureen, sauce boat, undertray, 2 serving plates, teapot, 2 pitchers, cov sugar, 5 tumblers, 6 sweetmeat dishes, 4 ash trays, seagull on blue ground, 76 pcs (A)................. **825.00**
13 dinner plates, 14 salad plates, 11 bread and butter plates, 12 dbl handled soup bowls, 12 tea cups and saucers, 14 dessert plates, 4 salt cellars, 2 scallop shaped dishes, 7 1/2" d, gravy boat with plate, blue floral design, white ground, dinner and salad plates with pierced borders, "three waves and Royal Copenhagen Denmark with crown" marks, 96 pieces (A) **1050.00**
Dish, 20 1/2" l, "Flora Danica," pastel shades with named botanical specimen, rim edged in gilding within band of gilt molded beadwork, 20th C, script botanical identification in black, underglaze "blue triple wave, green DENMARK below crown" marks, pr (A) **2323.00**
Figure
3 3/4" h
Faun on stump, no.1738............... **165.00**
Three penquins standing in semi-circle, no.1284...................... **190.00**
4" h, peasant girl holding floral wreath, polychrome (A)........................... **330.00**
4" l, Scottie dog with green slipper in mouth, no.3476............................. **85.00**
4 1/2" h
Elephant, gray, no.2998................ **185.00**
Group of four fish swimming, no.2962 ... **75.00**
5" h, seated mother with blue dress, child with white and tan shorts. no.1568........... **155.00**
6" h
Elephant, gray, no.1771................. **250.00**
Girl seated on bench holding flower, blue dress, white apron, no.2298.......... **175.00**

6¼" h, boy in gold cloak holding umbrella (A)..................................... **80.00**

6½" h, cat, seated, gray and white, no.2452............................... **125.00**

6¾" h, girl knitting, white skirt, gray top with blue dots, no.1314.................... **350.00**

7" h

Elephant, white, no.21517.............. **225.00**

Girl holding rabbit, no.5653............. **175.00**

"Little Mermaid in Wintertime," cobalt and white.............................. **150.00**

7¼" h, girl with goose.................. **165.00**

7½" h

Boy with blue raincoat and umbrella..... **245.00**

Young boy whittling, polychrome (A)..... **125.00**

8" h

Girl with duck (A)..................... **220.00**

Two school children holding books and pretzel, polychrome (A).............. **100.00**

8½" h

Choir Boy, no.1624 .... **150.00**

Seated hunter with gun and dog, multicolored............................. **265.00**

9" h

"Eared Seal," no.1441 .... **115.00**

"Goose Girl," no.527................... **225.00**

Mermaid on rock, cream figure on gray base, no.4431 .... **850.00**

9½" h, girl carrying jug and lunch box, no.815............................ **150.00**

10" h, parian, boy feeding eagles, imp "Eneret"................................ **425.00**

11⅞" h, bisque, Byron seated on sarcophagus with feet resting on overturned column (A)........................... **750.00**

12¼" h, "Falster," peasant woman in polychrome (A).......................... **450.00**

21" h, stoneware, woman with sari........ **1200.00**

Fruit Basket, 9" w, "Flora Danica," circ, reticulated, int with spray of red currants below gilt dotted panel border, ext applied with two pastel flowering vines entwined with upright staves between pink and gold molded beadwork borders, twig handles shaded from brown to green, rim with gilt foliate dentil border, black botanical inscription, underglaze "blue triple wave, green circ ROYAL COPENHAGEN, green enamel 20 3534"marks (A) . **880.00**

Inkwell, 8¾" l, 6¼" w, rect, blue and white plain lace pattern, center square inkwell with lid **275.00**

Jardiniere, 18¾" h, gray and green toned cows grazing on island, white ground, flared foot with green and blue waves, c1912, sgd "Th. Fischer, Royal Copenhagen and three wave" marks.................................. **4500.00**

Lazy Susan, 11½" l, 4½" h, blue and white plain lace pattern, center handle, 1894, "Royal Copenhagen" mark....................... **295.00**

Mug, 4½" h, florals, 1905 Christmas design.. **140.00**

Pickle Dish, 6¼" l, leaf shape, central botanical specimen within pink and gold molded beadwork border, gilt foliate dentil edge on rim, gilt edged angular handle, black botanical identifications, underglaze "blue triple wave, circ green ROYAL COPENHAGEN 20 3542" marks (A)........................... **1100.00**

Pickle Tray, 9" l, "Half Lace" pattern, "three waves" mark........................... **68.00**

Plaque, 4¾" h, oval, painted hunting scene over scrollwork, molded frame with applied flowers and puce ribbon, c1770, "blue wave" mark, pr (A) **850.00**

Plate

6" d, blue and white full lace pattern, 1926–31 .... **45.00**

6½" d, blue and white plain lace pattern, 1786, "three waves" mark **45.00**

8½" d, "Basket of Flowers" pattern....... **15.00**

9" d, "Flora Danica," pastel shades with named botanical specimen, scalloped rim with pierced border edged in gilding within band of gilt molded beadwork, dentil edge with gilt foliate border, script botanical identification in black, underglaze "blue triple wave, green ROYAL COPENHAGEN, circ marks, imp 3554, script 2-/3554" marks, 20 pcs (A)..............................**13,094.00**

10" d

"Flora Danica," painted specimen flower, named on reverse, shaped pierced border accented in gilt, "blue wave" mark (A)............................... **440.00**

Goura Victoria bird painted in colors, perched on branch, named on reverse, shaped pierced border with gilding **750.00**

13¾" d, Kauffmann type scene in center, gold on gold design, white ground, c1900 (A)................................ **70.00**

Platter

12" d, "Blue Flute Plain" pattern.......... **50.00**

13" d, "Flora Danica," specimen flower in center, named on reverse, shaped pierced border accented in gilt, "blue wave" mark (A)................................ **550.00**

13¾ l, 11" w, blue and white plain lace pattern, 1923, "three waves" mark **195.00**

Sauceboat and Stand

9" l, oval, "Flora Danica," botanical specimen below pink and gold molded beadwork borders, gilt foliate edged rim, handle formed as brown and green shaded twig, blue and purple floral terminals, black botanical identification, underglaze "blue triple wave, green circ ROYAL COPENHAGEN, 20 3556 marks (A) **1210.00**

9¼" l, oval, with attached stand, fish design, two applied handles, gray ground, Royal Copenhagen, "three blue waves" mark... **395.00**

10" d, specimen fish in colors, named on reverse, branch handle terminating in flowerheads, serrated border accented in light green and gilt, "blue wave" mark (A)..... **400.00**

Soup Tureen, Cov, and Stand, 11⁹⁄₁₆" w, stand 13⅛" d, "Flora Danica," each with different botanical specimen within pink and gold molded beadwork border, gilt dentil rim, stem form handles shading from brown to green, black botanical identifications, underglaze "blue triple wave, green circ ROYAL COPENHAGEN, 20 3542 and 20 3563" marks (A) . **3300.00**

Teapot, 10" h, blue and white underglaze design of flowers and palmetto leaves on white ground, acorn finial (A) **55.00**

Tray, 10" l, "Blue Flute" pattern **58.00**

Tureen, Cov, 14" l, "Flora Danica" pattern, marked (A) **2540.00**

Vase

2¾" h, blue and white full lace pattern, 1935................................ **95.00**

5¼" h, blue and white plain lace pattern,
1926. . . . .   **55.00**
6" h
  Coral and gray crackle glaze. **40.00**
  Floral decor, crackle glaze. **100.00**
6⅞" h, open purple violets with green leaves,
white ground **165.00**
7" h
  Blackberries and blossoms design. **50.00**
  Crackleware with cactus design,
no.⁴⁴⁹/₂₇₈₂ **85.00**
  Red, white, and gray flowers **85.00**
7½" h, ovoid, white dogwood blossom,
leaves, and branch, blue ground, hairline,
c1900, marked. **750.00**
8" h, baluster shape, painted white daisies and
foliage, blue ground, c1900 . . . .   **775.00**
9½" h
  Ovoid, painted with two pink dogwood
blossoms and branch, reverse with butterfly, blue ground, c1900, "SK and no.
2636 and 1049" marks. **850.00**
  White florals on blue ground (A). **70.00**
10" h, ovoid, blue painted windmill in hilly
landscape, c1900 . . . .   **800.00**
17¾" h, ovoid form, sides painted with pen-
dant bellflowers and leaves in shades of
dusty blue, gray, and beige, 1917, sgd in
underglaze "gray Jenny Meyer, underglaze
"blue JM/1917" and factory marks (A) . . .   **1650.00**
18" h, fish design on shaded blue ground . .   **750.00**
22½" h, tapering cylindrical form, each side
with large residence between bullrush and
vines cartouches climbing wicker frame,
shoulder with Venus riding on two dolphins with attendants, flared neck with
"VM" below crown, circ foot on sq base,
dolphin handles, bright colors and gilding,
hair crack to handles, 1885, underglaze
blue mark (A). **4675.00**
Vegetable Tureen, Cov, 6½" h, 6¼" l, oval,
flowers and fish design, two applied gray handles, gray ground, Royal Copenhagen, "three
waves" mark. **525.00**

c1947

c1912

ROYAL DUX

**Dux, Bohemia (now Duchow,
Czechoslovakia)
1860 to Present**

History: In 1860 E. Eichler established the Duxer Porcelain
Manufactory in Dux, Bohemia. The factory was noted for
its portrait busts and lavishly decorated vases. Much of the
production was exported to America. After the turn of the
century, the Art Nouveau style was used for large porcelain figures and vases.

Shortly after the conclusion of World War II, the factory
was nationalized. The newly formed company produced
household, decorative, and table porcelains, plus coffee
and tea sets.

Figure, 8½" h, 17" l, blue body, green head,
white base, repaired, "raised pink triangle and
green Made in Czechoslovakia" marks, (A)
$137.00

Bowl, 13" h, 19" w, Art Nouveau style olive and
orange flowers with gilt, two maidens seated
on rim (A) **700.00**
Centerpiece
7¾" h, 11" w, Art Deco style, two nude
women with brown hair, kneeling before
cobalt, cream, and gold vase, imp "Royal
Dux Bohemia-Czechoslovakia, raised pink
triangle" marks. **375.00**
20" h, modeled maiden and two cherubs
holding shell dish on shoulders, gold-green
costumes, gray and gold wavy base, "pink
triangle" mark **1250.00**
Dish, 20" l, oblong, figural man, woman, and
child with flute in pastoral clothes and two
sheep on ext of bowl, early 20th C (A) **495.00**
Dresser Tray, 15" l, 12" h, figure of young girl
holding infant aloft, cat at feet, pond forms
tray, wood styled base with rocks, multicol-
ored satin finish, "pink triangle" mark **775.00**
Ewer, 4½" h, gold leaves and fruit on dark to
light green shaded ground. **185.00**
Figure
6" h
  Seated nude, white.   **85.00**
    8" l, two boys standing next to boat,
matte ivory finish with black outlines,
gold trim, "pink triangle Bohemia"
mark. **175.00**
6½" h, Art Deco style
  Bust of young woman with flat hat, "pink
triangle" mark **215.00**
  Horse in black matte finish. **75.00**
7" h, elephant in white (A). **45.00**
8" h
  Elephant, upturned trunk with celluloid
tusks, gold finish, "pink triangle" mark. .   **185.00**
  Sitting nude lady in colors, "pink triangle"
mark. **145.00**
8½" h
  Two children with basket in pink, beige, and
gold, "pink triangle" mark. **395.00**
  Woman with basket holding child, soft col-
ors, raised "pink triangle" mark. **395.00**
9" h
  Art Deco style Spanish lady in cobalt and
white **350.00**
  Bust of Caesar, gold shirt with floral pink
toga, green laurel wreath on head, circ
base, "pink triangle" mark **350.00**

Lady with gold-brown dress and pink wrap-around sash, holding flower, or man in gold-brown toga holding palette and ewer, brown sandals, "pink triangle and E" mark, pr........................ 350.00
10" h

Art Deco lady in soft blue-green dress, tam, and gloves, gold accents, sgd "Strobach"........................ 275.00

Roman woman in light colors, "pink triangle" mark........................ 200.00

11¼" h, woman with head scarf, jug in right hand, beige and tan.................... 400.00

11½" h

15½" l, mare with feeding foal, brown, tan and ivory shade, raised "pink triangle" mark.................................. 750.00

Peasant boy with sack over shoulder or girl sowing seeds from apron, pink, green, flesh, and gold satin finish, "pink triangle" mark, pr........................... 550.00

12" h, tiger in natural colors, chip on hind paw, "pink triangle" mark.............. 165.00

12½" h, 10¾" l, standing man in classical clothes holding scroll, woman seated on bench, soft green and brown tones, gold trim, "pink triangle" mark.............. 1120.00

13" h

14" l, young boy with fishing pole and dog, matte earthtone colors, glossy face, hands, and feet, c1925, "pink triangle" mark............................. 195.00

Seated mother wearing cap feeding baby, standing father drinking from jug, green, gold, cream, and pink satin finish, c1860–90, "pink triangle and E" mark 550.00

13½" h, lady seated on conch shell, gold-tan on off-white........................ 400.00

14" h, 10" l, "Tom Sawyer," young boy in blue-gray trousers, gray shirt, feathered hat, stick over shoulder, dog at side.......... 225.00

15½" h, cockatoo in natural colors, raised "pink triangle" mark.................... 155.00

16½" h, woman dressed in Art Deco style dress, right hand on chest with fan, leaning on pillar, "Royal Dux" mark............ 750.00

17" h, "Rebecca at the Well," holding jug, flower vase at rear, greenish gold dress, "pink triangle" mark.................... 950.00

18½" h, woman in gown, resting on wall, playing mandolin, satin beige, cream, and tan, sgd "Hamdel," unmarked........... 275.00

19½" h, boy or girl sheaving wheat in coral and green, c1910, "pink triangle" mark, pr 750.00

21" h, "Harvester & Wife," cobalt blue and white with gold trim, man with sickle and sheath of wheat, woman with sheath of wheat in right hand and in her apron, c1930–40, paper label, "pink triangle" mark, pr........................... 850.00

27" h, modeled as three nymphs in flowing robes, around inverted seashell on spiralled column of leaves and foliage, domed circ base, bronze green, cream, and pink, early 20th C, "pink triangle" mark...... 2300.00

Jardinaire, 10¼" h, figural boy and girl at each end, hanging drapery from bowl, polychrome matte finish, figure repaired (A)............ 250.00

Powder Jar, 6½" h, 6½" w, seated lady on top in cobalt and gold, "pink triangle" mark 595.00

Vase

7¼" h, rect, beige satin ground, modeled figure of oriental man or woman in pink and green clothing on front, raised "pink triangle" marks, pr 245.00
9" h

Hourglass shape, pink and green florals, marked 110.00

Light blue and cobalt flowers in white panels, gold trim (A).................... 120.00

10" h, oyster white front panel of boating scene, relief of Art Nouveau motifs, gilded whiplash handles outlined in black, "pink triangle" mark 225.00

12" h, girl in greenish gold costumes, one with jug, one with large water lily, baroque floral top, "pink triangle acorn E" mark, pr 1250.00

13" h, molded flowers and woman's head on each side, fluted body, matte green, ivory, and pink, gold dbl handles, "pink triangle" mark.................................. 350.00

15½" h, porcelain, classical maiden climbing tree trunk 450.00

25" h, sq tapered body, applied grape leaves and fruits hanging over maiden in clinging green dress, head turned from bird, base cut out and molded with cherubs, sgd "Thom" (A)................................... 900.00

Wall Pocket, 8" h, open purple and orangle blossoms modeled on front, blue and yellow and orange and yellow birds modeled on rim, green branch hanger, white to green shaded ground, "Royal Dux Czechoslovakia" mark . 185.00

1749 -1864

ROYAL VIENNA

Vienna, Austria
1864 to Present

History: After the Imperial Porcelain Factory closed in 1864, some of the artists and workers established their own small shops. They produced the same forms and followed the same decorative motifs that they used at the Imperial Porcelain Factory. The quality of the pieces varied from shop to shop. Some were overdecorated; some cheaply done. Many of the pieces imitating the earlier Vienna porcelains were marked with the beehive mark.

The Vienna Porclain Factory Augarten, that was established in 1922, considers itself the successor to the Imperial and Royal Porcelain Manufactory of Vienna which closed in 1864. This factory still makes decorative porcelain and figures.

A company started by Josef de Cente in 1793 as a tile and stove factory made copies of the porcelain and figures from the Imperial Vienna factory after it closed in 1864. De Cente bought many of the original molds and used them. His reproductions always were marked with "de Cente," mostly impressed in the base. In 1902 the Alexandria Porcelain works in Turn-Teplitz bought the molds from the de Cente factory.

Plaque, 18¼" h, multicolored, "blue beehive" mark, $750.00

Plate, 9¾" d, multicolored classical scene of "Mark Anthony's Death," gold filigree on maroon border, raised gold beading on inner and outer rim, "blue beehive" mark, (A) $55.00

Bowl, 9" sq, hp flowers and panels of birds in colors, iron-red ground. **125.00**

Box, 4½" h, 6¼" d, hp scene of lady on lavender couch, three girl attendants, one with mirror, red ground, "blue beehive" mark **350.00**

Cabinet Tray, 14" d, large rect panel with young man kneeling before maiden in boat, full moon lights waves, mountains in distance, claret ground, pink and blue circ and sq panels, white and gilded foliage, c1880–1900, "black enamel shield" mark, script title "Des Meeres und der Liebe Wogan' (A) **1400.00**

Centerpiece, 14½" h, bisque, maiden pushing wheelbarrow with child seated on top, multicolored (A) **275.00**

Charger

12" d, multicolored scene of couple in pastoral setting, gold trim, "blue beehive" mark   **125.00**

14¾" d, brightly painted with titled scene of "Wotan and Brunnhilde," reserved between yellow border painted with canted rect and circ panels, c1890, "blue shield, imp 247," gilt title. **1350.00**

15" d, reserved with rect panel painted with scene of Venus, Augustus, and Helen on burnished gilt and dark blue ground,

c1890–1900, "blue shield, imp 247," gilt script title **1000.00**

16¾" d, center painted with Mary Queen of Scots, red border with gilt accents, gilt rim, c1900, "blue beehive" mark **1430.00**

18½" d, int scene from Othello between canted rect border, burnished gilt ground, oval and sq panels, scrolling foliage, c1880, "blue shield" mark, script "Othello' (A) . . . **4118.00**

Coffee Service, cov coffee pot, 9½" h, cov sucrier, cov hot milk jug, 5 cups and saucers, classical females, children, and putti at festive pursuits, leisurely and artistic activities, gilt ground, dark blue borders, foliate scrolls and formal bands, late 19th C, sgd "Seller," underglaze "blue shield" marks, 16 pcs (A) **6584.00**

Cup and Saucer

Demitasse, scenic semi-nude cherub and cow in blue, pink, red, and gold, three lion paw feet, entwined serpents handle, "blue beehive" mark **225.00**

2¾" h, cylinder shape, painted obelisk shapes and floral scrolls divided by gilt bands, cobalt ground, "blue beehive" mark. **100.00**

3" h, conical shape, painted scene of Shakespeare's Cymbeline, Act III, Scene 3, named on base, cobalt ground with gilt scrolling, "blue beehive" mark **350.00**

4¼" h, female portrait on int, green with magenta ground, raised gold trim, two handled, 1890–1918, "blue beehive" mark. **295.00**

Cup and Saucer, Cov, reserve of neoclassical maidens on a jeweled ground, late 19th C (A)   **88.00**

Dish, 14" d, Germanicus confronting four female warriors grouped around table, polychome enameled and gilt border, c1880, underglaze "blue shield" mark, script titles (A). **2006.00**

Ewer, 8" h, compressed globular body, painted with en grisaille cherubs amd gilded foliage on multicolored ground, foot reglued, late 19th C, underglaze "blue shield" mark (A) **282.00**

Ewer and Stand

11½" h, painted with panel of classical figures reserved on burnished gilt ground between raised gilded borders, mauve and purple ground, c1880, underglaze "blue shield" mark, one inscribed "Hochzeitsfest' (A). **2112.00**

11¾" h, panel of classical figures between raised gilded borders on blue, mauve, and pink ground, stand with gilded foliate panels of classical urns and scrolling foliage, late 19th C, underglaze "blue shield" mark (A) **2163.00**

Figure

6" h, seated woman, man leaning over kissing her, multicolored, "blue beehive" mark . . . **175.00**

7¾" d, Apelles, Alexander the Great, and Campaspe, paneled border with gilding and painted panels, late 19th C, underglaze "blue beehive" and script title marks (A). . **243.00**

8" h, seated spaniel with brown patch markings, eyes and mouth with red details, c1880, imp "shield" and numerals marks (A). **941.00**

8½" h, standing Napoleon in green and red uniform with arms crossed, "blue beehive" mark. **95.00**

Ginger Jar, Cov, 9½" h, ovoid body, reserved with circ panels of figures on horseback before buildings enclosed within gilded ribbon borders on dark blue ground, domed cov with rect panels with sprays of summer flowers, late 19th C, "blue beehive" mark, pr (A). **2163.00**

Jardinaire, 9⅝" h, flattened oval form, two children, one in red suit and wide ruff, other with wide white collar, reserved within tooled gilt borders on red ground, band of beaded gilding in turquoise, lobed lip, four scrolling foliate feet, late 19th C, printed mark (A). **2244.00**

Kettle, Cov, 7¾" h, globular body, painted with children at play on matte gilt ground band against green ground, gilt metal mtd handle in dolphin form, late 19th C, painted "Werbug Tanz, painted shield" mark (A). **950.00**

Plaque

9⅞" h, 7" w, maiden seated on woodland river bank in flowing white dress, owl flying by side, late 19th C, sgd "F.H. Thallmayer," script title "Das Marchen" Copy after C. v Bodenhausen, Munich, framed (A) **1776.00**

16½" d, circ, Rudolf von Habsburg standing by the corpse of the dead King of Bohemia, in clearing with other wounded soldiers seated on ground, hills in distance, cloudy sky, framed within gilt rim, c1880, underglaze "blue beehive," imp numerals, title and "red 1278" marks **1500.00**

19" d, int of Bavarian house, guests dressed in traditional festive costumes, framed within gilt ogee band, purple ground scrolling gilt acanthus panels, pink ground interlaced gilt border, c1880, painted "shield" mark and script titles (A) **8448.00**

Plate

8⅜" d, multicolored center scene of woman and child with birdcage, child holding bird, red border with gold accents, "blue beehive and Austria" mark. **125.00**

8¾" d, multicolored center scene of girl with vase of apple blossoms, cobalt and aqua border with raised gold florals and swags, silver buds, "Apfelbluten and blue beehive" mark. **400.00**

9" d, "The Angelus" design in colors, gold trim, "blue beehive" mark. **38.00**

9½" d

Center scene of Madonna surrounded by floral shield medallions, brown border with gold heart shaped medallions, "blue beehive" mark. **475.00**

Cupid int with vignette of Roman maiden, cobalt and gilt border, shaped rim (A). . **121.00**

"Ersten Kirschen," young German farm girl holding cherries in apron, tooled gold border with cartouches of florals (A) . . . **1300.00**

Philemon and Baucis receiving Mercury and Jupiter inside a cottage, raised gilded border, blue ground, late 19th C, underglaze "blue beehive" and imp numerals mark (A) **475.00**

"Poesic," center portrait of dark haired woman with wreath in hair, border of gold geometrics, oval green jewels, ruby pendants, sgd "Wagner, blue beehive" mark (A) **1320.00**

"Ruth in a Cornfield," standing in meadow with sunset sky beyond, claret and blue border with gilt scrolling foliage, c1890, underglaze "blue beehive, Ruth" mark (A) **956.00**

Young lady standing against clouded sky, red borders with panels in yellow, blue, and gilding, c1890–1900, printed factory marks, pr (A) **2163.00**

9⅝" d

Diana and Cupid firing crossbow between formal borders painted with landscapes in gilding alternating with classical vase motifs, late 19th C, underglaze "blue beehive" and script title "Diana u. Silen" marks (A) **243.00**

Transfer printed and painted, views of Venus and Cupid with attendants on wooded and floral riverbank, dark blue and gilded borders, c1900, underglaze "blue shield" marks, pr (A) **1478.00**

9¾" d, portrait of blond woman, gold tracery surrounds head and shoulders, tinted ground, turquoise-green border with formal gold tracery decor, sgd "Constance, Made in Austria and blue beehive" mark **110.00**

9⅞" d

Portrait bust of young woman with dark hair and lilacs, dark green border with gold design, "blue beehive" mark **225.00**

Turbanned woman on one, other with young lady, claret and gilded ground, late 19th C, underglaze "blue beehive" mark, script titles, pr (A) **1881.00**

10" d

Center scene of maidens and cherubs in colors, aqua blue ground, gold trim **79.00**

"Echo," portrait of young woman with flowing hair, burnished gold floral border, sgd "Wagner' (A) **1450.00**

11" d, boy with horn, three maidens, tambourine, green trailing leaves, beaded gold crisscross panels on magenta, green and gold border **295.00**

12" d, center scene of maiden with goblet and garlands, cobalt and gold border, "blue beehive" mark (A) **25.00**

Platter, 14" l, 10" w, overall geometrics and flowers red, blue and green with gold accents on yellow ground, c1880, "blue beehive" mark (A). **18.00**

Tankard, Cylinder Shape

6¼" h, classical figures, reserved on dark blue ground with gilt details, "blue beehive" mark (A) **2600.00**

6¾" h, classical figures between gilt border on pink, blue, yellow, and red sectioned ground with gilding, cov with Leda and Swan, gilt metal mtd hinged cov, late 19th C, underglaze "blue beehive" mark (A). . . **3386.00**

Tea Caddy, Cov, 4⁶⁄₈" h, two panels of classical scenes with Perseus and Aeneas, red ground with gilded foliage, cov damaged, late 19th C, underglaze "blue beehive" mark, script titles (A). **464.00**

Tete-a-Tete Set

Tray, 12⅞" l, 2 coffee cans and saucers, cov coffee pot, cov milk jug, cov sucrier, Diana holding a bow, attendant by her side, hounds in rocky landscape, other pieces with head and shoulder portraits of ladies in 18th C dress, each panel reserved in gilded floral ground, horiz landscape and animal panels, c1900, sgd "Gisi Zepper, underglaze blue beehive" marks, 11 pcs (A) . . . **6758.00**

Tray, 15" l, cov coffee pot, cov cream jug, 2 coffee cans and saucers, cov sucrier, classical and mythological scenes within raised gilt borders on ruby ground, yellow, brown, and purple sections with gilt and white floral tracery, c1880, painted by F. Christy, underglaze "blue beehive" mark, imp marks and iron-red scene descriptions, 11 pcs (A) ... **5643.00**

Tray, 17¼" l, oval shape, 2 cups and saucers, teapot, cov milk jug, 2 handled cov sucrier, tray with oval portrait of young maiden in low white chemise, orange headband centered by six pointed star, framed by tooled gilt band over cream ground, claret border gilt with elaborate foliate scrollwork interspersed with medallions containing urns and floral devices, within pale blue rim gilt with band of acanthus leaves, other pieces with various portraits of young girls, c1900, sgd "Wagner, blue beehive, orange 3168" marks, 11pcs (A) **1366.00**

Tray
13⅝" l, oval, center scene of lion and lioness at river with palm trees, reserved between wide burnished gilt borders, open handles (A)................................... **1590.00**
17½" l, oval, painted colored flowers and foliage overflowing glass bowl onto table, red and gilt formal borders, late 19th C (A) . **2790.00**

Urn, Cov
11" h, panels of nymphs and cherubs in colors outlined in pink and gold florals, maroon ground, acorn finial, "blue beehive" mark **280.00**
14½" h, two central hp reserves of ancient festivals, red ground with gilt accents, small curved hp handles, sq base, pr (A)....... **2000.00**
30" h, baluster shape, reserves of Roman warriors before battle, cobalt ground, gilt foliate scrolled decoration, dbl mask and ring handles, late 19th C (A) **3960.00**
44" h, center reserve of "Europa and the Bull" or wounded man and maiden, cobalt ground with gilt band of scrolling foliage, cov with gilt floral swags, pineapple finial, late 19th C (A)........................ **9900.00**

Vase
3½" h, overall pink roses, "blue beehive" mark................................ **65.00**
3¾" h, bulbous shape, panel of girl holding candle in holder, cobalt ground with gold scrolls, "blue beehive" mark............ **60.00**
6¼" h, hp center scene of girl with bird, raised gold designs on burgundy ground, "blue beehive" mark **150.00**
7" h, "Exhibit," portrait of young woman in colors on lustered green body (A) **975.00**
7½" h, "Schwertlilie," scene of young woman with bouquet of irises, sgd "Rommler, blue beehive" mark (A)....... **200.00**
8½" h
Center medallion of bust of woman in red hat, yellow off shoulder gown, named "Una Gitana" on base, raised gold medallion with enameled white and blue flowers extended to reverse, maroon ground, "blue beehive" mark.......... **275.00**
Ovoid form, painted with "Aida," sheer white robe, colored jacket, cobalt blue ground with gilding, late 19th C, script title and imp numerals (A) **630.00**

12" h, ovoid, portrait of maiden in colors on purple ground (A)...................... **345.00**
12½" h, ovoid body, reserved with oval panel of maiden holding an amphora, pale green ground with complex gilded and colored panels, c1890, sgd "Kray," painted shield, script title "Wasser tragerin" marks (A)................................... **1935.00**
15⅜" h, ovoid body, maiden allegorical of "Night" in red, yellow, amd blue robe holding burning torch, other allegorical of "Day" in sheer white robe, waisted neck and foot, applied with laurel swag handles, sq plinth base, late 19th C, printed "shield" mark, script title (A) **2244.00**
21⅜" h, "The Triumph of Venus," dressed in white robes, surrounded by female attendants with cherubs above, reverse with maiden pouring water from urn with cupids looking on, flared neck and foot, raised gilded foliate motifs, foot restored, c1860–70, "blue beehive" and script titles (A) ... **6019.00**

Vase, Cov, Stand
11¾" h, shield shaped body, painted with various mythological scenes, Ariadne and Cupid, Naxos and Apelles, Alexander the Great, and Campaspe, mauve ground reserved with pink and blue gilded panels, late 19th C, underglaze "blue beehive" mark, pr (A)................................... **1215.00**
17¾" h, urn shape body, painted on either side with titled circ panel depicting classical figures in various pursuits, within tooled gilt frame over deep blue ground gilt with foliate scrollwork and bands of beadwork, two angular gilt handles, c1880, underglaze "blue beehive," titles in brown script (A) . **7286.00**
22½" h, ovoid body, band of classical figures reserved on burnished gilt ground between red borders, raised scrolling gilt foliage, c1870–90, underglaze "blue beehive, incised 96, Austria" mark, pr (A)........... **4400.00**

Whimsey and Cov, 5½" h, classical romantic cartouche on front outlined in raised dotted gold, gold designs on reverse with gilt birds, blue trim on snail topped cov, two handled, raised gilt trim, 19th C **235.00**

c1876-1891   1891

ROYAL WORCESTER

Worcester, England
1862 to Present

History: (see Worcester for early history) In 1862 Worcester Royal Porcelain Company Ltd. was formed by Kerr and Binns. Limoges style enameled porcelains, figures, and many dessert services were manufactured. Vases and other ornamental pieces were painted with figure subjects. Among the factory's popular wares was Ivory porcelain, a glazed parian ware.

During the 1870s, magnificent porcelains in the Japanese style were produced. Many were modeled by James Hadley, one of the finest ceramic modelers. Hadley left Royal Worcester in 1875 to freelance, but almost all his work was bought by Worcester.

In 1889 Thomas Grainger's factory was bought by the Worcester Royal Porcelain Company. Grainger had started his own factory in 1801 at St. Martin's Gate. After having several different partners, George, his son, eventually took over.

James Hadley started his own factory in 1896 to produce ornamental art pottery. It was located near Royal Worcester's main factory. By 1905 the Hadley firm was absorbed by the Royal Worcester Company. Binns retired in 1897 and Dyson Perrins took over.

Royal Worcester continues to make ordinary bone china patterns in the 20th century. Colored floral borders or blue and white transfer prints in the "Willow Pattern," "Royal Lily," and "Broseley Dragon" were most popular. Ornamental wares with a parian body are part of the product line.

During the 1920s and 1930s, the company maintained its fine quality wares in a depressed world market with some degree of success. Around 1924 luster wares were introduced, inspired by Wedgwood's dragon and fairyland lusters. In 1928 an electrical decorating tunnel kiln was installed, causing a great improvement in firing decorated wares and raising the standards of china production.

World War II restrictions forced china manufacturers to cut back on their production. Rich ornamental and decorated wares came to an end.

Worcester carried on production of some wares, especially the Doughty Birds for the United States market as part of the war effort involved with lend-lease. Dorothy Doughty's bird figures were absolutely correct in size and color and even the foliage on which they were modeled. Other figures also were produced during the war years including dogs by Doris Linder, Gwendoline Parnell's "London Cries," Miss Pinder-Davis's "Watteau" figures, and Eva Soper's series of small birds and children in wartime Britain.

After World War II, things began to return to normal. A great number of young painters apprenticed to Royal Worcester. In 1948 Doris Linder modeled the first limited edition, equestrian model featuring Princess Elizabeth on Tommy. It has become the most sought after of Worcester's equestrian models.

In 1950 the biscuit kilns were replaced by gas-fired tunnel kilns which produced even finer quality ware. The founding of the Dyson Perrins Museum at Worcester in 1951 marked the bicentenary of the Worcester Porcelain Company.

During the 1960s Doris Lindner's equestrian models achieved great success. In addition to limited edition figures Worcester produced tea, dinner and oven-to-table wares using both old traditional patterns as well as new ones. Demands for Royal Worcester porcelain continuously increased. A new factory opened in 1970. Much of the current porcelain decoration still is done by hand. Hard porcelain ornamental wares are part of the product line. Royal Worcester commemorative pieces include mugs, jugs, and trays.

References: Geoffrey A. Godden, *Victorian Porcelain*, Herbert Jenkins, 1961; Stanley W. Fisher, *Worcester Porcelain*, Ward Lock & Co. Ltd., 1968; Henry Sandon, *Royal Worcester Porcelain*, Barrie & Jenkins, 1973.

Museums: Dyson Perrins Museum, Worcester, England; Roberson Center for the Arts and Sciences, Binghamton, NY.

REPRODUCTION ALERT. Both Austria and Rudolstadt made copies of Royal Worcester wares.

Biscuit Jar, 7" h, cobalt leaves on white bamboo ground **355.00**
Bowl
  8 1/2" d
    Int with pheasants before waterfall in wooded clearing, ext peach and gilt, c1926, sgd "James Stinton, crowned circle" mark, date code (A) **2100.00**
    Molded sq shape, reticulated basketweave, burnt orange, yellow, rose, olive green, blue florals and leaves, gilt int, gilt border, marked **775.00**
Bowl, Cov, 4 1/2" H-H, multicolored florals on ivory ground, dtd 1862 .... **75.00**
Bowl, 6 3/8" d, dbl walled, ext reticulated with pale blue honeycomb and shield motifs between two shaped oval panels of stork and honeybee amongst bamboo and exotic trees, all below pale pink ribbon border encircled with white and blue jeweling, c1878, printed "crowned circle" mark (A) **1496.00**
Butter Dish, 5 3/4" h, 7 1/4" d, with drain, multicolored florals on beige ground, dtd 1890 .. **595.00**
Candlestick, 10 1/2" h, figure of Kate Greenaway type boy leaning on candlestick, dtd 1887, sgd "Hadley" **450.00**
Candy Dish, 10" h, majolica glazed parian ware, girl in turquoise coat, pink skirt, holding two baskets, pedestal base, pale pink int, turquoise ext **995.00**
Comport, Figural, 8" h, rustic boy and girl carrying baskets, white glaze with gilding, c1898, printed and imp "crowned circle," date letter, incised nos.962 and 963, applied Eng Reg mark, pr (A) **2534.00**
Cream and Sugar, molded leaves form body and handles, ivory color **50.00**
Creamer
  2 7/8" h, wren in leaves, twig handle, sgd "Powell" **35.00**

Pitcher, 8 1/2" h, rose and yellow oriental florals, gold trim, cream satin ground, horn handle, purple mark, (A) $66.00

4" h, ribbed body with scalloped mouth, multicolored flowers with gilt accents........   **120.00**

Cup and Saucer
"Doreen" pattern **25.00**
Pink, yellow, and blue flowers, beige satin finish, gold trim, dtd 1906.................   **95.00**

Cup and Saucer, Demitasse, hp sheep design, artist sgd **275.00**

Dessert Service, 12 plates, 9" d, 2 shaped oval dishes, 2 shaped sq dishes, ripe fruit and flowers between dark blue and pink tooled gilt swag and shell motif borders, c1912–13, printed "crowned circle," imp date codes, gilt no.W8346 marks, 16 pcs (A)..............   **9715.00**

Dinner Service, 12 dinner plates, 12 salad plates, 12 bread and butter plates, 12 dbl handled soup cups and saucers, 12 teacups and saucers, gravy, oval serving platter, 17" l, "Chantilly" pattern, 86 pieces (A)...............   **950.00**

Dish
3⅞" d, yellow and pink zinnias, gilt rim ...   **6.00**
9¼" l, 9¾" w, modeled as maple leaf with turned up sides, veined molded cream ground, hp multicolored flower clusters, gold and chocolate brown rim band, dtd 1887..   **175.00**

Ewer
6¼" h, ribbed body, hp flowers in colors, burnished gold trim, dtd 1888...........   **285.00**
6½" h
Compressed oviform body, flying swans amongst green reeds, blue ground, reserved with single swallow, scroll handle, everted lip, gilded details, c1903, sgd "C. Baldwyn," printed "crowned circle" mark, no.789 (A).....................   **2618.00**
Pink Cyclamen and other flowers on ivory ground, branch handle................   **150.00**
6⅝" h, purple flowers and green leaves on beige ground, gold band at base, beige figural shell design at top, purple mark, c1889 ....   **235.00**
7" h
Ovoid body, hp large floral sprigs on cream ground, gold molded rib handle, dtd 1885, pr **350.00**
Painted florals on cream ground, bulbous body with narrow neck, gold dragon handle **145.00**
9" h, blue flowers and tan leaves outlined in gold, cream satin ground, salamander handle, dtd 1887........................   **435.00**
11½" h, gourd shape, flowering branches enhanced with gilt, ivory matte ground, gold molded salamander handle circling body (A)....................................   **250.00**

Figure
5" h
"Burmah," sgd "F.G. Doughty," no.3068 .   **150.00**
Monk in colors.......................   **45.00**
5½" h, lady kneeling holding urn, no.637, c1900 ....   **400.00**
6½" h, group with brother and sister in pastel colors, F.G. Doughty, "Royal Worcester Bone China" mark (A).................   **165.00**
6¾" h, modeled nautilus shell on coral branches, peach and light yellow, c1909. .   **325.00**
7" h, "The Yankee," Countries of the World series, beige and brown, c1881.........   **300.00**
8½" h
Anne Boleyn in blue gown, gold trim high fan collar, holding fan, marked.........   **350.00**

Kate Greenaway boy with basket in cream and satin beige, pink and blue trim, dtd 1893 ....   **495.00**
Mary Queen of Scots in lavender and gold gown, puffed cape and hood, string of beads and cross, marked..............   **350.00**
9⅞" h, "Joy" and "Sorrow" modeled as standing women in light yellow gown with small pink and blue flowers, gold trim, dtd 1894, pr **850.00**
10½" h, ballerina in pastel colors, D. Charol, "Royal Worcester Bone China" mark (A) .   **330.00**
13½" h, gardener modeled as standing Egyptian woman in green and rust robe with gilt details, leaning on spade, rock molded base, dtd 1912, printed "crowned circle and 1606" marks (A)....................   **875.00**
19¼" h, Cairo water carrier, traditional costume, holding large amphora, folded ivory cloak, green, red, and blue floral border, c1887, printed "brown circle" mark (A) ..   **1689.00**

Gravy Boat, 7" h, blue and white oriental scene, gilt trim on handle, "Royal Worcester Vitreous England" mark **95.00**

Ice Pitcher, 9¾" h, cantalope molded body, large molded melon leaves on neck in cream and gold, painted multicolored flowers, gold melon vine handle, dtd 1889 ....   **360.00**

Jardinaire, 9" w, 7½" h, gold palm leaves on royal blue ground **595.00**

Jug
7½" h, multicolored castle scene, cobalt ground, reticulated, gem studded, gold cov   **550.00**
11½" h, painted owl on branch, moonlit sky, gold serpent handle, dtd 1885...........   **925.00**
16" h, maidens on rocks or waves, pink or orange flowers, green foliage, ivory ground, c1893, printed "crowned circle," date code mark, pr (A) **2112.00**

Pitcher
3½" h, blue, pink, and purple flowers outlined in gold, heavy gold on handle, mask spout, dtd 1895.......................   **60.00**
5½" h, floral design on cream ground.....   **75.00**
8" h, ewer shape, everted spout, painted flowers with gilt accents, ivory ground, elephant head handle **250.00**
8¼" h, large floral sprays on beige ground, large gilt loop handle **300.00**
10" h, 5½" d, purple and gold flowers, green and gold leaf, gold handle, bulbous bottom, cream ground, "Crown Royal Worcester" mark................................   **250.00**
11¾, 12" h, male piper or female guitar player, colored in green and gilt, c1912–14, pr (A)..................................   **1200.00**
13½" h, "Persian" shape, flying butterflies and bees in colors, reticulated neck, c1880   **725.00**

Plate
7⅜" d, hp multicolored flowers, cream ribbed ground, scalloped gold rim, dtd 1889, pr **100.00**
8¾" d
Botanical plate with purple and pink florals, olive green leaves, raised gold dots on border, c1872 ....   **125.00**
Two jays perched on branches, gilded borders, 1921, sgd "C.H.C. Baldwyn, printed crowned circle" mark and date code (A)   **475.00**
9¼" d, vein molded cream ground, hp multicolored florals, ruffled gold rim, c1887–88   **300.00**

9½" d, hp sprays of flowers, dtd 1880 .... **48.00**

10½" d

Brown transfer of Dr. John Wall with alternating medallions of old English buildings and pears on border **38.00**

Gold dot center with eight petal blue flower, cobalt and gold border, red mark, set of 10 .... **150.00**

Platter, 18" l, oval, small scattered multicolored flowers on satin cream ground, hp gold rim, c1900 (A) **160.00**

Potpourri Vase, Cov, 7½" h, lobed ovoid body, two sheep in mountainous landscape, pierced cov, neck, and foot gilded, 1919, sgd "E. Barker, printed crowned circle" mark and no.1312 (A) **1402.00**

Ring Tree, 4½" l, 2½" w, 2¾" h, oval dish with three prong holder, pink and yellow flowers on beige ground, c1898 .... **145.00**

Salad Bowl, 9" d, 4½" h, cream ext molded with grape leaves on basketweave ground, int with hp multicolored flower sprigs, open loop rim, dtd 1884 .... **335.00**

Salt, 2" h, sq, yellow, pink, blue, and red florals, salamander on side, dtd 1892, purple mark **350.00**

Scent Bottle, 4" h, pheasant in highland landscape, silver hinged cov, c1918, sgd "Jas Stinton, printed crowned circle" mark, no.1661, date code (A) **840.00**

Serving Dish, 10¾" d, 2¾" h, three sections, overhead handle, pink, yellow, and blue flowers on beige satin ground, gold trim, dtd 1905 .... **235.00**

Spill Vase, 4⅞" h, tapering cylindrical form, bulbous base, colorful Kingfisher and Bullfinch, beaded rim in white, three molded foliate and paw feet, c1870 (A) **255.00**

Tea Caddy, 4" h, hp bluebells, sgd "Sedgley" . **95.00**

Urn, 8¼" h, red and blue florals, cream ground, gold banding, figural face handles, int hairline, 1889................................... **225.00**

Vase

4" h, hp pheasants, sgd "Stinton," pr **895.00**

4⅛" h

Ftd, flowers and rasberries in colors, dtd 1909 .... **235.00**

Peacock in natural colors, gold trim, dtd 1909, sgd "A. Watkins". **200.00**

4½" h, luster finish, green, brown, and gold forest scene, 1921 .... **175.00**

6½" h, ftd, cylinder shape, scroll base, black faced sheep on front, dtd 1891.......... **275.00**

7" h, blue tree branches with two white parakeets................................. **195.00**

7¼" h, pierced outer wall with white cranes, bamboo, and prunus, light blue inner wall, dtd 1880 (A) **440.00**

7½" h, trumpet shape, two pheasants in wooded landscape, burnished gilt borders, c1926, sgd "J. Stinton' (A) **750.00**

7¾" h, flattened ovoid body, cream glazed basketweave design, modeled as branch extending into body terminating in iron-red and gilt flowers and foliage, woven design on dbl gilt handles, Greek keyfret on neck, four gilt feet **450.00**

7⅞" h, ovoid, spray of colored wild flowers heighted in gold, blush ivory ground,

pointed gilt handles, no.1766, date code for 1904 (A) **324.00**

8" h, pitcher form, orange magnolias, purple chrysanthemums and thistles, ivory ground, loop handle, gold rim, foot, and handle **350.00**

8½ " h, dry ivory ground overdecorated in white enamel geometrics, polychrome enameled frog hanging from branch with gilt highlights, dull gold with lustered gold floral designs at top and neck, no.636, dtd 1879 (A) **715.00**

8⅞" h, trumpet shape, ripe fruit and foliage on woodland bank, c1928, sgd "Ricketts, printed crowned circle," date code, no.G923 mark (A)..................... **802.00**

9" h

Tusk shape, poppies, butterfly, dragonfly, and fuchsia on tan ground, dtd 1890 .... **365.00**

Urn shape with narrow neck and pedestal foot, blue flowers and leafy stems on ivory ground, gold lug handles......... **250.00**

9⅝" h, orchids and blue forget-me-nots outlined in raised gold, beige satin ground, dtd 1896..................................... **325.00**

10" h, cylindrical form, molded overall with lightly concave and convex shells, some painted and gilt with landscape vignettes, others with bronzed and gilt markings, cream ground, key pattern borders, 1873, molded and printed "crowned circle" marks, printed date code, pr (A) **3542.00**

11" h, trumpet shape, gilt designs on magenta ground.............................. **250.00**

12" h

Blue, pink and orange wildflowers accented in gilt, ivory ground, elephant head handle, gilt rim, neck, and foot........... **225.00**

Ivory ware, floral motif, scrolled handles (A) **150.00**

Sabrina ware, blue-green color, c1896, marked **750.00**

13" h

Bottle shape, narrow neck, enameled flowers with gilt leaves trimmed and accented in raised gold, gilt scroll handles, four leaf feet, late 19th C (A) **1027.00**

Multicolored scene entitled "Natural Bridge, Virginia," cream matte glaze with gilt accents, pedestal foot, applied scroll handles (A)......................... **180.00**

Vase, Cov

6" h, egg shape on three hoof feet, open work on cov and body, c1910............... **560.00**

16" h, ovoid body, two views of Alnwick Caste with river and trees in front, reserved between molded border in matte green and pink, shoulder applied with lion mask terminals on scroll supports, floral knob, gilded details, c1903, sgd "H. David, printed crown and circle" mark, date code, no.1764 and script title (A)............ **897.00**

19¼" h, oval panels of fruit and foliage or summer flowers on table with tied curtain on one side, raised gilded borders on green and gilt ground, griffin scroll handles applied at shoulder, circ foot molded with satyr masks and acanthus leaves, c1897, sgd "Hawkins, printed crowned" mark, no.2419, no.369944, pr (A) **17,952.00**

c1885

ROZENBURG

The Hague, Holland
1884–1914

History: W. van Gudenberg established an earthenware and porcelain factory at The Hague in 1885.

Rozenburg is best known for a line of exceptionally thin earthenware that was made during the late 19th and early 20th century in the Art Nouveau style. The delicate, translucent body had over the glaze decorations of flowers, foliage, and birds derived from the design of Japanese batik-printed fabrics from the Dutch East Indies, now Indonesia. Mauve, yellow ochre, orange, and shades of green were some of the vivid enamel colors used on the white ground. The decoration on later examples was stiffer and had less delicate colors. Shapes featured elongated handles and spouts contrasted with the curved and flat surfaces of the body.

S. Juriaan Kok became director of the company from 1895 to 1913. He was responsible for a series of extraordianry Art Nouveau shapes. J. Schellink was employed as a painter who decorated his works with stylized flowers in brick-red, black, purple, green, and yellow on a bottle-green ground. He also used sea horses and spiked leaves in his motifs. Schellink painted in a series of tense, nervous, spots and lines with subtle color combinations. The eggshell thin porcelain that Schellink used was unique to Rozenburg. M. N. Engelen, the firm's chemist, developed it. Production stopped with the beginning of World War I.

Pieces were marked "Rozenburg/den Haag" along a stork, that was copied from the mark of the 18th century porcelain factory at The Hague, and a crown.

Vase, 12" h, "Tall Trees" design, mustard, mauve, green, and brown florals, brown tortoise shell base, lt green and tan int, c1895, $2800.00

Jug, 7" h, butterflies and flowers in Art Nouveau
style, green and blue ground, high gloss, stork
mark (A). 500.00
Plaque, 7⅝" h, 18¾" w, painted Dutch farm
scene in colors, artist sgd, framed (A). 650.00
Pot, 5" d, 5½" h, multicolored butterflies,
marked. 120.00
Vase
2½" h, bulbous shape, polychrome enam-
eled leaf design, c1900 (A). 300.00
4¼" h, polychrome enameled stylized leaf
design, turned rings on rim, c1900 (A) . . .   310.00
4¾" h, bulbous shape, narrow neck, Art
Nouveau style pomegranates in high gloss,
"Rosenburg den Haag" mark (A) 200.00
10¼" h, rust nasturtiums and green leaves
on navy blue ground, gold color top and dbl
handles with small black dots, marked. . . .   695.00
12" h, ovoid with arched overhead handle,
brown, ochre, blue, and green painted
dragon, c1900, marked (A). 1400.00
19¾" h, blue, green, brown, and ochre over-
all foliage design, c1900 (A). 1685.00
21" h, earthenware, multicolored flowers on
dark green ground, mtd on wooden base.   1600.00

c1924   c1918

RUDOLSTADT

Thuringia, Germany
1720 to Present

History: Macheleid, with the patronage of Johann Friedrich von Schwartzbrug-Rudolstadt, established a Rudolstadt factory about 1720. During the factory's peak period, 1767–1797, the firm was leased to Noone. The arrangement lasted until 1800. Rococo style tableware and large vases were made. After 1800 the firm was sold to the Greiners. A series of partnerships followed.

Ernst Bohne Sons made decorative porcelain, coffee and tea sets, and figures between 1854 and 1920. Many products were similar to R. S. Prussia pieces. After 1920 the factory became a branch of Heubach Brothers.

Lewis Straus and Sons in New York were co-owners of the New York-Rudolstadt Pottery between 1882 and 1918. This firm received the right to use the Royal Rudolstadt designation. The firm porduced household, table, and decorative porcelains and served as importers for the U.S. market.

The Rudolstadt-Volkstedt Porcelain Factory was nationalized in 1960.

Berry Set, master bowl, six serving bowls, roses
design, artist sgd 150.00
Bowl
10" d, hp purple and blue violets with green
leaves on light green ground, gold accents,
artist sgd (A). 20.00

Cream Pitcher, 4⅝" h, beige molded shell body, satin finish, gold serpent handle, "RW shield" mark, $25.00

11" l, oblong, dainty blue and yellow florals on light cream satin ground, gold trim, reticulated edge, handled (A) **10.00**
12" d, purple violets and white lily of the valley in four panels on pearlized ground, gold trim (A) **40.00**
Chocolate Pot
9¾" h, large and small yellow roses, green leaves, maroon branches, cream ground, gold handle, finial, and trim **88.00**
10" h, pink rose design, green and white flowers, gold trim **275.00**
Chocolate Set, pot, 4 cups and saucers, white open roses with green and gold trim **495.00**
Cup and Saucer, black silhouette of children playing, pink bands **35.00**
Dresser Tray, 10" l, six Kewpies in colors, sgd "R. O'Neill" **280.00**
Ewer
6½" h, gold outlined flowers and leaves, beige pebble ground **45.00**
15" h, multicolored scattered flowers on body, molded lion heads on neck, two small ornate gold handles (A) **150.00**
Figure
4¾" h, boot with blue and gold florals, gold beading and buckle **135.00**
5½" h, hunchback wearing brown hat, blue trousers, red cloak, floral vest, c1880, "Crown N" mark...................... **125.00**
8½" h
Bust of Queen Louise in colors, c1880 ... **140.00**
White, woman seated on bench with jug and applied flowers, embraced by standing man on base.................... **175.00**
12" h, girl and boy sitting on bench, brick wall behind in cream and gold............... **195.00**
14" h, girl holding fish, white dress with gold trim.................................. **85.00**
Pitcher, 13½" h, reticulated top, floral motif in colors, pr (A)........................... **55.00**
Plate
8" d, seven Kewpies design.............. **150.00**
8½" d
Center portrait of George Washington, gold trim............................... **45.00**
Copper red poinsettias, greenish yellow and beige ground, gold tracery **48.00**
Large hp roses **30.00**
9½" d, peach flowers, beaded gold border **65.00**
Relish Dish, 8" l, flowers in center, gold border . **28.00**

Tea Set, teapot, creamer, sugar bowl, overall orange luster finish **45.00**
Tray, 9¾" d, eleven Kewpies on grass, sgd "R. O'Neill" **100.00**
Urn, 13" h, white and gold flowers in gold outlined panels, shaded blue ground, gold panels, pr **575.00**
Vase
9¼" h, dbl walled body, reticulated front and back in pale pink with gold center design, satin cream ground with small purple flowers, dbl gold handles **150.00**
9¾" h, two large birds back-to-back, light blue enameling **230.00**
11½" h, lavender and coral flowers, beige ground, scalloped top, ornate floral and branch handles, gold trim, satin finish **145.00**
12" h
Center medallion of pre-Raphaelite style woman in colors, matte yellow biscuit glaze on body, gilt accents, modeled winged dragon handles (A)........... **300.00**
Enameled flowers on cream ground, flared reticulated mouth, ornate gold handles . **60.00**
13¾" h, pierced neck, purple flowers on cream ground, dbl handles.............. **195.00**
14" h, 9" d, multicolored floral panels, gold tracery front and back, two semi nude maidens form handles, baroque base, cream ground, flaring gold rim................. **550.00**

ВРАТЬЕВЪ

Baterin's factory
1812-1820

Заβода
SПКУЗНЕЦОВА
63 Rus5
c1835

КорНИЛОВЬIХЪ

Korniloff's factory
c1835

RUSSIA—GENERAL

Early 1800s to Present

St. Petersburg, now Leningrad, Russia 1744 to Present

History: The Kuznetsov family established a factory to manufacture porcelain and faience at Novocharitonowka in 1810. Their sons, trading as the Brothers Kuznetsov, managed the factory until the 1870s. They also operated other factories around Russia.

These factories produced powder boxes, vases, and toilet sets in blue and pink porcelain that was often enameled and gilded. Figures in biscuit porcelain were painted with regional costumes and other decorative motifs. Products from these Russian factories were exported to other Europeon countries, the Far East, and India.

In 1891 the firm acquired the Francis Gardner factory near Moscow. Marks usually incorporated "Ms. Kuznetsov" along with the place of manufacture.

Native Russian porcelains developed during the 1800s

due to the high duty on imported porcelains. The Kornilow Brothers established a factory to manufacture utilitarian wares in St. Petersburg in 1835.

The Yusupov Factory near Moscow operated from 1814 to 1831. White porcelain blanks for decoration were purchased from Sevres, Limoges, and Popov. Articles made at the factory were used as gifts for the members of the Tsar's family or for the friends and relatives of the Yusopovs.

The Popov Factory, established in 1806 at Gorbunovo, made dinner services, tea sets, and porcelain figures for an urban middle-class clientele. Popov's figures of Russian craftsmen, peasants, and tradesmen, are eagerly sought by collectors. The factory closed in 1872.

Initially the Imperial St. Petersburg porcelain factory enjoyed only limited success. Catherine the Great was associated with the factory by 1762. Her imperial patronage helped insure success.

Most of the wares were basically French in form, but often were painted with Russian views. When Jean-Dominique Rachette became head of the modeling workshop in 1779, he increased the sculpture output by making porcelain statues, groups in bisque, and portrait busts.

Enormous dinner services were made for the Tsar's palace and the nobility of the court, e.g., the "Arabesque Service" of 973 pieces in 1784 and the "Cabinet Service" of 800 pieces. The War of 1812 disrupted production at the factory somewhat. Portraits of heroes and military motifs appeared on the porcelains during and immediately following the war.

Reorganization took place in 1901. The Art Nouveau style was utilized. About 1907 soft paste porcelains were developed. A series of figures entitled "Peoples of Russia" was designed by P. Kamensky and issued beginning in 1907. The factory's work continued after World War I and during the Civil War. The revolution inspired designs for porcelains reflecting industrialization of the country.

The factory was renamed Lomonosov Factory in 1925 in honor of M. Lomonosov, the Russian scientist. Production continues today.

Marks changed many times. Until 1917 the cypher of the reigning monarch was used.

References: R. Hare, *The Art & Artists of Russia,* Methuen & Co., 1965; L. Nikiforova, compiler, *Russian Porcelain in the Hermitage Collection,* Aurora Art Publishers, 1973; Marvin Ross, *Russian Porcelains,* University of Oklahoma Press, 1968.

Museums: Hermitage, Leningrad, Russia; Russian Museum, Leningrad, Russia.

Bowl
  6 1/2" d,
    Front and back with circ plaques in white and rasberry with irid orange leaf and tendril designs, white ground, light green outer glaze, c1900, large "red Imperial eagle and Made in Dulev by company of M.S. Kuznetsov" 195.00
    Top half with rasberry ground and repeating aquamarine half-moon shapes with irid yellow leaf designs, outlined in ornate gilt patterns, gilt edge, c1900, large "red Imperial eagle and Made in Dulev by Company of M.S. Kuznetsov" 225.00
  7 1/4" d, 3 1/2" h, porcelain, pastel enameled floral decoration (A) 70.00
  9" d, porcelain, enameled floral sprays, cobalt banding, beaded gilt border, late 19th C (A) 110.00

Dish, 8" d, multicolored, children's sayings on border, "Kuznetsov" mark, $275.00

Creamer, 4" h, plaque with arrangement of wild flowers in red, green, and yellow, royal blue glaze, white plaque edged in gold, gilt highlights, c1890, "red Imperial eagle and Company of M.S. Kuznetsov-Made in Dulev".... 155.00
Cup and Saucer
  Empire style, white and gilt fluting, leaf and key fret borders, leaf terminal to scroll handle, Popov (A) 760.00
  Gilt scrolling and green banding, J. Kornilov Bros (A) 360.00
  Light blue and gilt paneled decoration (A)... 33.00
  Random pattern of stylized wild flower designs in brown, pink, yellow, blue, and green on cup, tendril shape white handle, saucer with yellow flowers on rim with interlaced orange-brown and green flowers, underglaze "green cipher of Alexander III, and 1892, blue Soviet hammer and sickle" marks, 1922 and inventory nos 495.00
  Scrolled gilt motif on light green and pink ground (A) 55.00
Dish, Cov
  6" l, 2 3/4" w, 4 1/2" h, ram figure, body embossed to simulate curly wool with glazed black patches, legs tucked under body, horns and eyes with gilt highlights, white ground, c1860s, "blue Imperial eagle with Company of M.S. Kuznetsov-Made in Dulev," 645.00
  6 1/2" l, 3 3/4" w, 5" h, duck figure, dark browns to simulate plumage of female duck, gilt bill, white ground, c1840s, underglaze "blue crowned star burst with Company of I.E. Kuznetsov in Volkov," mark......... 695.00
  7 1/2" l, 5" w, 5 1/4" h, pear figure, glazed in shades of light yellow and pale pink, top has large gilt twig handle with yellow miniature pear and green leaves, bottom base in leaf shape glazed in shades of green with vine like stem forming handle in gilt, c1860s, "blue Imperial eagle with Company of M.S. Kuznetsov-Made in Dulev," mark (A)..... 385.00
Figure
  2 3/4" h, bisque, standing black and straw colored dog, stump support, oval green base with marbled edges (A) 275.00
  4 1/4" h, porcelain, Mujik, traditional dress,

carrying teapot and cup, damaged, late 19th
C (A) **55.00**
Plate
6" d, border of crests in rust, cobalt, and
green, white ground, "Kornilow Bros Made
for Tiffany" mark....................... **65.00**
8¼" d, painted multicolored spray of roses,
pansies, and primulae, pink border with gilt
lyres and wreaths, gilt rim, Popov (A)..... **950.00**
9½" d, gilt, puce, and green floral border on
blue ground, late 19th C (A) **440.00**
10⅜" d, floral centers edged in gold, rim with
dark blue fretwork design, white ground,
crenulated outer rim with burnished gold
rim, reverse with blue imperial eagle with
script below in Russian "Of the Brothers
Kornilov in St. Petersburg," c1850s, pr ... **295.00**
Teacup and Saucer
Alternate panels of geometric designs and
flower and tendril designs in orange and
light gray with gold, gilt edges with large gilt
band inside of cup, tendril and flower design handle with gilt, bottom of cup with
alternating pierced patterns of diamonds
and circles, c1870s, underglaze "blue Imperial eagle and Company of M.S. Kuznetsov,
Made in Dulev," marks **245.00**
Wild flower arrangement of white, yellow, purple and green around cup, int with three
concentric gilt bands at top, ext with fluted
vert columns with light pink translucent
base, gilt rims and handle, c1870s, underglaze "blue Imperial eagle and Company of
M.S. Kuznetsov-Made in Dulev" **255.00**
Vase, 18⅞" h, ovoid shape, painted panel of
Indian girl with arrow, Spanish soldier and Indian in ground with mountains and clouds,
reserved on black ground with gilt foliage, gilt
dbl handles, sq base, Safronov (A) **725.00**

SALT GLAZED STONEWARE

Staffordshire, England
1671 through the 19th C

Rhineland, Germany
1500s to Present

History: Stoneware is pottery that is fired at such high
oven temperature that the body has vitrified and become
impervious to liquids. A salt glaze is achieved by throwing
salt into the high temperature oven causing the salt to
volatilize. The sodium in the salt combines with the
alumina and silica in the clay to form a thin vitreous coating on the surface of the stoneware. The glaze layer also
is impervious and has minute pitting.

ENGLISH

In the late 17th century potters in north Staffordshire
around Stoke-on-Trent began experimenting in hopes of
producing a purely English style of salt glazed stoneware.
John Dwight is credited with discovering the technique. In
1671 Dwight was granted a patent for the manufacturing
of salt glazed stoneware.
Six villages comprised "The Potteries" in Staffordshire.

The greatest concentration of potters was in Burslem.
Their salt glazed stoneware pieces were thin, lightweight,
and made to compete with porcelain. A brown salt glaze
stoneware was developed in the second half of the 18th
century and used for beer jugs, tankards, flasks, and industrial wares.
With the advent of mold making and slip casting, more
complicated shapes could be made. A wide range of utilitarian and decorative articles were produced. Few pieces
contained factory marks.
The Burslem families of Wedgwood and Wood manufactured salt glaze stoneware beginning in the late 17th
century. They trained a succession of master potters.
Enameled stoneware was introduced in the Staffordshire potteries about 1750. Enameled wares required a
second firing, at a considerably lower temperature than
the salt glaze oven, to "fix" the color to the pot. European
and Oriental porcelain decorative motifs were enameled
on salt glaze pieces. Transfer printing also was done on
white salt glazed stoneware.
The first salt glazed figures were animals. These were
not marked and rarely dated. Most salt glazed figures
were made by pressing slabs of moist clay into a two piece
mold and then uniting the halves using a slip.
Groups of figures required the process of press-molding
combined with hand modeling. A wide variety of salt glaze
bird and animal figues were made between 1725 and
1755. Usually the figures were ornamental, but cow
creamers and beer baiting jugs were useful exceptions.

GERMAN

Salt glazed wares were being manufactured in Germany
by the early 16th century to fill the demand for drinking
vessels for taverns. These brown salt glaze wares were
also exported to England for more than two hundred
years.

References: J. F. Blacker, *The ABC of English Salt-Glaze
Stoneware from Dwight to Doulton,* Stanley Paul & Co.,
1922; Arnold R. Mountford, *The Illustrated Guide to Staffordshire Salt-Glazed Stoneware,* Barrie & Jenkins, 1971;
Louis T. Stanley, *Collecting Staffordshire Pottery,* Doubleday & Co., 1963.

Museums: American Antiquarian Society, Worcester,
Mass.; City Museum, Stoke-on-Trent, England; British Mu-
seum, London, England; Colonial Williamsburg, Williams-
burg, Virginia; Fitzwilliam Museum, Cambridge, England;
Museum of Art, Rhode Island School of Design, Provi-
dence, Rhode Island; Victoria & Albert Museum, London,
England; William Rockhill Nelson Gallery of Art, Kansas
City, Mo.

German: Kunstgewerbemuseum, Cologne, Germany;
Metropolitan Museum of Art, New York; Rheinisches
Landesmuseum, Bonn, Germany.

ENGLISH

Bottle, 6¾" h, globular form, polychrome,
enamel vignettes of chinoiserie maidens
among fruiting and flowering trees, short cylindrical neck with lattice and flowerhead border,
c1750 (A) **7084.00**
Butter Tub, Cov, 4¹³⁄₁₆" l, press molded with
foliate scroll cartouches of dot and star diaperwork alternating with panels of basketwork,
grass molded upright tab handles, cov pierced
in diapered panels, recumbent cow knob, ear
repaired, 1760–70 (A) **1650.00**

Dish, 12" d, shaped rim with lattice work cartouche, basketweave border, c1760, $350.00

Tankard, 6" h, raised white ferns, olive green ground, pewter top, 19th C, $60.00

Cache Pot, 6½" h, 7½" d, taupe, applied classical decoration, c1830 . . . . **400.00**

Caster
  4¾" h, ogee shape with molded basketwork panels, top and foot with gadrooned rims, mid 18th C (A). **2100.00**
  10¼" h, baluster shape, pierced domed cov, splayed foot, screwed pewter mounts, finial restored, mid 18th C, Staffordshire (A). . . . **4250.00**

Coffee Pot
  Bird on branch with flower spray and springs painted in colored enamels on shaped oval reserves, purple handle and spout, blue ground, repaired, c1750–60, Staffordshire (A). **680.00**
  5¾" h, conical, pastel enamels with flowering peony and cherry trees, acorn knob, c1740 (A) **10,980.00**
  8⁷/₁₆" h, flaring cylindrical body, applied vine with grape clusters, leaves, blossoms, and a pear, squirrel near bird vignette, cov with perched squirrel, grape clusters, and leaves, top shaped knob, oct serpent spout, reeded S scroll handle, repaired, c1760 (A) **7700.00**

Cornucopia, 10½" h, molded in relief with bust of Plenty set in scroll panel, reserved on flower and foliage ground in shades of turquoise, green, pink, and yellow, sides pierced with six holes, Staffordshire (A) **684.00**

Creamer, 3⁷/₈" h, Eros in center circle, emb floral design, cobalt line trim (A) **125.00**

Cream Jug
  3" h, silver shape, relief of flowers and foliage of blue-stained clay, scalloped rim, grooved handle, pinched terminal, mask and spreading paw feet, c1735 . . . . **3300.00**
  3⅓" h, white glaze, two pecten shells raised on three paw feet, grooved strap handle, molded with snails below lip (A) **990.00**

Cream Jug, Cov, 5" h, molded pectin shells with human faces on each side, notched handle, shell molded cov, c1750 (A). **2100.00**

Dish
  8⁷/₈" l, quatrefoil shape, white, molded with seeded panels divided by panels of florets, applied two upright C scroll handles, raised on tripod feet, upturned shaped rim, mid 18th C (A). **900.00**
  10¼" d, center molded with herringbone sqs, panels of star and dot diapering within feathered cartouches separated by basketry, rim pierced, c1750 . . . . **1400.00**
  10¾" l, oval, cress center with scalloped oval panel press molded with pattern of foliate scrolls, pierced with circ drainage holes, scalloped sides with feather edged panels molded with two large leaves, three tapering feet, 1750–60 (A). **1100.00**
  14" d, circ, white, border of scroll edged diaper panels on basketwork ground, shaped rims, mid 18th C, pr (A). **925.00**

Ewer, 5⅛" h, blue and black criss-cross bands, pewter lid (A) **82.00**

Figure
  3⅛" h, seated cat, large ears, wide grin, oval base molded with patterned border, mid 18th C, Staffordshire (A) **1309.00**
  3⅝" h, gentleman, large tricorn hat, lightly patterned greatcoat, knee breeches, grassy mound base, 1745–55 (A) **2750.00**
  3¾" l, group of ewe and lamb press molded with lamb nestling against its recumbent mother, shaped oval mound, cream colored clay striated in chocolate brown, mid 18th C (A). **750.00**
  4⅝" h, lady wearing elaborate dress, braided hair hanging in ringlets at sides, staff in one hand, nosegay in other, wide-brimmed hat, dog at feet, rect base, repair to bottom of skirt, mid 18th C (A). **7050.00**
  4¾" h, seated cat, brown and gray solid agate body with thin blue glaze wash, c1745 (A) **2356.00**
  5" h, shepherdess wearing skirt molded in diaper pattern and flounced overskirt, holding a staff in one hand, flowers in other, standing in sq plinth with small dog beside her, dog reglued, tail repaired, c1735. . . . . **5200.00**
  5¾" h, seated monkey holding piece of fruit, collar around neck, two long ties hanging down back, fruit, ears and eyes in dark brown slip, brown raised dots on head, tie restored, c1740 . . . . **7500.00**
  6¼" h, chained lion seated on haunches, incised chain forms collar around neck, eyes and tongue in dark brown slip, c1740. . . . **4500.00**
  14" h, white cockatoo, Minton, pr **95.00**

Flask, 7¼" l, fox head, rounded face, molded

ridged collar, impressed "J. Bull Railway Tavern New Cross," c1830, Lambeth (A) **841.00**

Jar, Cov, 3 1/8″ h, pear shape, cov with flattened knob, hairline, c1755 .... **3300.00**

Jelly Mold, 3 7/8″ d, sun face, press molded with face within sixteen pointed circle simulating rays, 1750–60 (A) **1320.00**

Jug

3 1/8″ h, baluster shape, scratch blue, incised and picked out with simple stylized wild rose spray, rim restoration, c1760 (A) **673.00**

5 1/8″ h, baluster shape, three shell and paw feet, restored **500.00**

5 1/2″ h, paneled, mask spout, "The Union," c1846, imp "Copeland Garrett, Late Spode" mark **175.00**

7″ h, "Silenus," gray, c1840, Minton, raised mark no. 16 .... **575.00**

8 1/4″ h, stoneware, gray and tan salt glaze surface, two dark brown blobs, England (A) **27.00**

9 1/2″ h, bear shape, seated with front paws outstretched, collar and paws in olivebrown slip, clay chip fur, cov, damaged, c1740, Staffordshire (A)................ **3542.00**

9 5/8″ h, white, four emb wreathed medallions of people and animals from America, Africa, Asia, and Europe, two medallions of maps, branch handle **295.00**

Loving Cup, 4 1/4″ h, white raised seal of great US on front with two gold initials, Britannia on reverse, two handles outlined in blue, hairline, Castleford **225.00**

Milk Jug, 4 5/16″ h, pear shape, press molded with sixteen panels decorated in relief with vignettes of the hunt and various floral motifs, c1745 (A) **880.00**

Mug, 2 3/4″ h, painted with trailing flower sprays in colors, loop handle (A) **645.00**

Pepper Caster, 5 9/16″ h, pear shape, molded in four panels with vert rows of basketwork, star, and dot diaperwork beneath integral domed top, spirally reeded border, c1760 (A) **1100.00**

Pickle Dish, 4 1/8″ l, heart shape, press molded with assorted designs, foliate scrolls, and vines, 1745–55, pr (A)........................ **1375.000**

Pistol, 8 1/2″ l, large ball grip handle, incised details, c1840, imp "Stephen Green Lambeth" mark (A)................................ **225.00**

Pitcher

4 7/8″ h, white, emb hunt scenes with red-tan rim band, imp "Copeland" mark (A) **30.00**

7″ h

Caneware, foliate handle (A) **44.00**

Pleat design with emb foliage scrolls, putty color, imp "W. Ridgway & Co, Oct 1, 1835" (A)........................ **55.00**

7 7/8″ h, white, emb cattails, unmarked (A).. **55.00**

8″ h, brown grapes and leaves with branches entwined to form handle................ **375.00**

8 1/8″ h

Baluster shape, scenes of "The Sailor's Farwell" and "The Sailor's Return," broad strap handle, sealed hairline, c1760 .... **17500.00**

Brown and white with emb scenes of Falstaff, trees, and basket, rings on neck, imp "Turner" mark (A).................... **143.00**

9 1/2″ h, molded figural decoration commemorating Robert Burns, mid 19th C (A) **176.00**

Plate

8″ d, tan, molded open flowerhead in center,

stylized florals, grapes and leaves on border, shaped rim **125.00**

8 1/2″ d

Emb and reticulated border, shaped rim (A) **550.00**

Oct, polychrome, center landscape with seated lady in scarlet and blue holding yellow fan, conversing with strolling musician with mandolin across back, border of scarlet and green diapering with flowerheads, scarlet dot and diaper ground border with feathered cartouches, c1760.. **3700.00**

8 5/8″ d, oct, "The Sailor's Farewell" in enamels, star and dot diapered border in bright colors, c1760........................ **6800.00**

9 1/8″ d, armorial, center printed in puce with Royal Arms, scalloped rim molded with alternating panels of dot and star diaperwork divided by foliate fronds, c1760 (A) **3575.00**

9 3/4″ d, emb diaper and reticulated border, shaped rim (A)........................ **300.00**

Platter, 16 3/4″ d, molded diaper work panels, scalloped rim, flake, 18th C (A) **200.00**

Puzzle Jug, Globular Shape

7 1/2″ h, pierced cylindrical neck, tubular handle, rim with three nozzles, reddish-brown dip, c1740, London (A) **2992.00**

7 3/4″ h, brown glaze, neck pierced with wheel and leaf motifs, medallion molded in relief with shipping in harbor, entitled "Porto Bello, 17=41 and Jos=Puttock," handle applied with florettes, triple nozzle rim, London (A) **5220.00**

Sauceboat

3 1/8″ l, oval, molded relief of diaper, ozier, and scrolling panels, loop handle (A) **370.00**

5 5/8″ w, molded cartouches of diaper and basketweave edged in blue enamel scrollwork, c1765, Staffordshire (A) **1540.00**

6″ l, dbl lipped, molded with shells and foliage, dbl ribbed handles, pinched terminals, scrolled rim, splashed blue glazing, c1750 **2200.00**

6 7/8″ l, press molded body decorated in relief on either side with naked Chinese body kneeling amidst blossoms and leaves, three lion's mask and paw feet, reeded S scroll handle, hairlines, c1750 (A) **1925.00**

7″ l, white

Oval body molded with silver pattern panels and key fret borders, two reeded strap handles, dbl lipped, mid 18th C, Staffordshire (A) **1480.00**

Scroll edged panels of diaper and basketwork, molded, looped handle, curled terminal, mid 18th C, Staffordshire (A) **730.00**

Scent Flask, 2 3/4″ h, shield shape, design of hearts, flower heads and scattered asterisks, inlaid in dark brown slip, impressed zig-zag border, threaded aperture, repaired, c1725 (A)................................ **748.00**

Soup Tureen, Cov

11 13/16″ l, lozenge shape, press molded with foliate scroll edged cartouches of dot and star diaperwork alternating with panels of basketwork, handles and knob formed as layered scrolls, three grotesque mask and paw feet, repaired, 1740–50 (A) **660.00**

12 1/2″ l, 10 1/2″ h, panels of "rice-molded" design separated by basketweave scrolls, flame finial, gargoyle masks over four paw feet (A) **1045.00**

Spoon, Demitasse, 3³⁄₈" l, "Fiddle Thread and Shell" silver pattern, c1755, Thomas and John Wedgwood............................ **3675.00**

Spoon Tray, 5⁷⁄₈" l, center molded with pinwheels, scrolls, and foliage, lobed panel sides, c1745, Thomas and John Wedgwood...... **2950.00**

Strawberry Dish, 11¼" l, 9" w, 2³⁄₄" h, ftd, pierced body, scalloped rim, dbl handles, diapered panels, 18th C (A)................... **990.00**

Sweetmeat Dish

4⅝" l, fluted oval shape, white with Chinaman walking before a pavilion in garden in center, border of flowering plants, molded, mid 18th C, Staffordshire (A)............ **625.00**

7¼" d, two separate heart shaped trays conjoined, molded with shells and scrollwork, hairline, c1745....................... **4200.00**

Tankard, 2³⁄₄" h, miniature, bell shape, oriental landscapes painted in enamels, grooved handle with pinched terminal, c1760.......... **1500.00**

Tea Cannister, 4³⁄₈" h, sq body, molded with four key fret ground panels, two of bearded Chinese sage, two with chinoiserie maidens, mottled gray glaze with touches of manganese and green, c1760 (A)..................... **2037.00**

Teapot

2³⁄₄" h, globular body, miniature, white, decorated in relief with flowering plants, applied handle, plain spout, repair to handle, c1750, Staffordshire (A)................. **1214.00**

3³⁄₄" h, globular, curved spout, ear shaped handle, restored, mid 18th C, Staffordshire **500.00**

4¼" h, flowers in iron-red, rose, and green within cartouches of blue and yellow scrolls, crabstock handle and spout, turned knob, rose ground, hairline on body, c1760 .... **7500.00**

4½" h

"House" shape, two story mansion, one side with pseudo Royal Arms above door, with rampant lion and fleur-de-lys, spout molded as hand clasping serpent's head and with mask on either side, molded lamprey handle, c1750, Staffordshire (A) **6545.00**

Lobed baluster form, each lobe molded with seeded ground panel of armorial bearing above heraldic beast, foot with paneled border, domed cov with borders of stylized foliage, rim and foot restored, c1740 (A).......................... **2302.00**

4⅝" h, globular shape, Dutch style floral and scroll decoration in red, green, yellow, black, and gold, cracks, Staffordshire (A).. **1430.00**

4³⁄₄" h

Globular, white with gentleman wearing turquoise jacket over pink waistcoat, yellow breeches, seated in chair, playing horn, lady in pink dress, turquoise underskirt, playing mandolin, reverse with building in landscape, green knotted crabstock handle and spout, restored, c1760, Staffordshire (A) **2240.00**

Polychrome panel of titled "FRED. PRUSSIA REX," Prussian eagle, ribbon and shield on reverse, ermine tail ground, branch handle, spout, and finial, damages, c1760 (A) **1430.00**

5⅛" h, ovoid, stylized rose, bud, and foliage, crabstock spout, turned knob, faceted handle molded with rect and diamonds, chocolate ground, hairline, c1760 .... **4800.00**

5¼" h, molded on both sides with scallop shell flanked by dolphins and leafy vines, fluted spout with grotesque animal head at base, scaly dolphin handle, lozenge shaped foot molded with arched fluting, cov molded with four scallop shells, recumbent lion knob, 1740–45 (A)................. **3850.00**

5³⁄₈" h, modeled as kneeling camel fitted with foliate scroll edged harness and saddle belted across pleated saddle blanket, scaly dolphin handle, cov with top shaped knob molded with pleats, c1745 (A)........... **7700.00**

5½" h, spherical, mold applied reliefs of Tudor roses, anthemion, and scrolls, crabstock handle and spout, bird finial, mask and paw feet, c1740 .... **6500.00**

5³⁄₄" h, Georgian mansion, tiled roof, doorway surmounted by royal arms, vines on ends, serpent spout, notched handle, finial restored, c1750................... **6500.00**

6" h, hex pear shape body, enameled, iron-red, brown, yellow, rose, and blue scene of small building in landscape in molded green edged oval surmounted by bearded grotesque mask, crabstock spout, molded floral sprigs on back, cov molded with foliate scrolls, repaired, 1760–70 (A) **3025.00**

6½" h

Castleford type, emb and applied classical figures and acanthus leaves, cobalt line trim (A) **275.00**

Globular, painted with two flower bouquets and scattered flowerheads on pink ground, brown crabstock handle and spout, repaired crack, c1755 (A)....... **4180.00**

6½" l, applied scenes with figures in classical dress, cobalt trim, emb spout, woman and child finial, hairlines (A) **175.00**

6³⁄₄" w, globular, enameled famille rose style with flowering branches, green diaper border edged in pink, crabstock handle and spout, button knob, c1765, Staffordshire.. **900.00**

7³⁄₄" h, figural seated camel with relief molded buckled saddlecloth and howdah with molded standing figure of camel and tree, scaly fish handle, fluted cov (A)..... **4370.00**

9³⁄₄" h, applied classical scenes, cobalt line trim, child and woman finial, fancy handle with cobalt trim, repairs (A) **700.00**

Teapot Stand, 5³⁄₈" d, circ, rim with mold applied reliefs of bell, crown, leopard, high flared foot pierced with hearts and groups of three circles, c1730 .... **3500.00**

Tobacco Box, 5⁹⁄₁₆" h, brown, modeled as hex toll house with trees framing door and windows (A) **325.00**

Tureen, Cov, 9" h, white, press molded with dot and diaper, star and diaper basket patterns in scroll bordered panels, scroll finial, three grotesque mask feet (A)..................... **432.00**

Wall Pocket

8" h, dolphin's head with flying fins flanked by bands of scrollwork above, beared satyr's head encircled with ivy vine below, scalloped rim C scrolls in side, repaired crack, c1760, pr **2800.00**

11½" h, white, cornucopia form molded in relief with bust of "Plenty" within scrolling cartouche, top damaged, c1760, Staffordshire (A)................................ **2125.00**

GERMAN

Centerbowl, 13 1/2" w, stoneware, four applied grotesque masks and two female masks below crenelated rim, flower swags and putti between masks, incised hatchwork ground, lion's head at each end, gadroons, husks, and blossoms on base, four lion's paw feet, applied coat of arms on underside, c1885, Westerwald (A).............................. 1320.00

Figure, 2" l, whistle in cat shape, blue cat on gray base 500.00

1845

SAMSON

Paris, France
1845–1964

History: Samson made reproductions and copies of porcelains from famous manufacturers in hard paste porcelains. Some of the items they copied were originally only made in soft paste.

Edme Samson bought the Tinet factory in Paris. Until 1873 he decorated porcelains produced by other factories. Pieces he decorated had over the glaze marks, often duplicating the mark of the original factory.

Emile, his son, was the first in the family to make reproduction of decorative porcelains and figurals of the famous factories in England and the Continent. He started in 1873. The reproductions also contained a copy of the original mark under the glaze. Sometimes a small Samson mark was added over the glaze.

The Samsons owned over 20,000 originals of Meissen, Sevres, Chelsea, Capodimonte, Chinese, and Japanese porcelains. They made molds from these originals to produce their copies. Frankental, Ludwigsburg, Furstenburg, Vienna, Derby, Bow, Worcester, Chantilly, Tournay, Vincennes, Mennecy, and Copenhagen pieces also were copied, as was the tin glazed earthenwares of Rouen, Sinceny, and Marseilles.

The company was operated by the Samson family until 1964 when C. G. Richarchere took over.

From about 1845 to 1905 the original marks were imitated on the pieces they copied. The company registered some trademarks after 1900 and used them underglaze after about 1905.

REPRODUCTION ALERT: Overglaze marks are removed easily. There is evidence that a large number of Samson marks have been removed so that the pieces would appear to be from the original manufacturers.

Candelabra, 11 1/2" h, gentleman and lady in 18th C dress seated in front of bocage, seascroll and shell base, two naturalistic candle arms, damaged, 19th C, pr (A)............. 715.00

Chocolate Pot, 7 32/8" h, cylindrical body, Meissen style, gilt edged quatrefoil panel with colorful figures, barrels, boats, and buildings in river landscape, gilt edged spout,

Urn, Cov, 13" h, rose, purple, and green floral clusters, rust diapering on body, sq base, gilt trim, late 19th C, (A) $495.00

central stirring aperture, metal bail handle, small floral sprigs between gilt bands, puce ground, late 19th C, underglaze "blue dashed-X" mark (A) 715.00

Cup and Saucer, oriental type floral panels in rose, green, blue, and gold, gold handles, matte gold rim, black and white border at top, gold ground with dark red overlay, c1840, Paris, pr 495.00

Figure

7 1/8" h, seated young woman, maid looking at baby in yellow cradle, shaped rect base (A)................................. 465.00

8" h

Bow style, girl in flowered skirt, turquoise top, yellow apron, pink hat, holding dog, man in pink pants with black spots, circ design top holding dog with black hat, standing on pink and green ground, turquoise, white, and gilt scrolled ftd base, c1865, unmarked, pr 1500.00

Recumbent cat with gray markings, yellow eyes, oval scroll molded foliate base, ormolu mtd, late 19th C (A)............. 1683.00

8 5/8" h, Pagoda, Meissen style, seated cross-legged, counter-balanced head, tongue, and hands, loose florally painted robe, armorial to front, late 19th C (A) 1122.00

9 1/2" h, Bow style, bacchic children, two putti, goat, and kid, other with sheep and lamb, pierced scrolling bases, c1900, pr (A) 935.00

10 1/2" h, classical woman standing next to plinth with vase, dog at feet, polychrome, sq base (A)................................ 193.00

10 5/8" h, "The Continents," classical ladies in flowered robes, animal at feet, puce and blue accented scroll bases, set of 4 (A)... 1700.00

11 1/2" h

Cat, seated with tail curled around body, glazed in shades of ivory and rose, black and pink details, green glass eyes, one ear restored, c1900 (A) 450.00

Man in multicolored outfit playing bagpipe, black and white dog, applied florals on bocage in ground, white and gilt scroll base, woman in multicolored outfit playing mandolin, salmon and white dog at side, c1880, unmarked, pr **1200.00**

12" h, Meissen style, sportsman holding two leashed hunting dogs leaping at prey, natural colors, molded base painted with flowers, late 19th C **725.00**

13"-15" h, four seasons, multicolored maidens with spring flowers, sheaf of corn, grapes, or fire, base with gilt edged rococo scrolls, pseudo Derby mark, set of 4 ..... **1500.00**

20⅞" h, Meissen style, monkey seated on tree stump holding an apple, face and ears in peach and white, brown and white fur, one arm and foot restored, c1880, underglaze "blue cross" (A) **1000.00**

Ginger Jar, Cov, 11½" h, ovoid body, famille rose enamels with flowers and foliage, late 19th C, pr (A).......................... **1028.00**

Mug, 5" h, famille rose floral design (A) **105.00**

Plate

7½" d, oct, "Hob in the Well" pattern, painted Chinese boy rescuing another from large water jar by striking jug with rock, ground of bamboo, peony, and flying birds, border with painted scrolling peony, chrysanthemum, and fern, brown rim, "blue shield" mark, set of 8................... **850.00**

9¾" d, "Hot Spice Ginger Bread," man pushing cart, lady, two children, and dog surrounding him, dark blue gilded border, late 19th C, sgd "H. Desprez, pseudo crown, X'd batons, D" mark, script title (A)...................................... **200.00**

Punch Bowl, 13½" d, 5⅝" h, Chinese Export style of flowers, and eagle, hairlines (A)..... **137.00**

Tankard, 7⅜" h, cylindrical body, Meissen style, puce, iron-red, rose, brown, black, green, and gold with continuous scene of Chinaman bringing bouquet of flowers to lady seated at table being coiffed by attendant in garden, footrim with gilt band, handle with gilt trimmed foliate terminal, mtd with silver cov applied with repousse parcel gilt border of animal medallions and trees encircling central silver coin commemorating William Tell, int engraved "Troll Troll the Bonnie Brown Bowl," late 19th C (A).......................... **1760.00**

Tea Caddy

4¼" h, oriental type design in blue, orange, and gilt, blue borders with gilt, marked ... **175.00**

5½" h, crest on front molded in body cartouche, scattered flowers and berries in molded cartouche, gilt sterling lid, c1850, Paris.................................. **595.00**

Toothpick, 2½" h, blue with figural of classic lady, gold metal on top and three legs...... **145.00**

Urn, Cov, 13" h, lobed baluster body with rose and green florals and gilt, rust diaper banding, lobed cov with knob finial, sq base with rose and purple florals (A) **450.00**

Vase, 10" h, baluster shape, Chinese Export style design, late 19th C, pr **500.00**

Vase, Cov

7" h, ovoid, Meissen style, painted scene of merchants and ships in harbor, gilt scroll borders, domed cov, gilt metal mts, c1870, "blue X'd swords" mark, pr (A)......... **1800.00**

17" h, baluster shape, Chinese style, painted with precious objects and vases of flowers in famille rose enamels, lapet-shaped panels

on shoulder and domed cov, late 19th C, pr (A)...................................... **1985.00**

Wine Cooler, 7¼" h, 5¼" d, cylinder shape, armorial crest of Coarroach and Trevor on front in blue and white, lion and rooster in salmon, black, and rust, 2 floral panels on side, gilt trim and border, 18th C **625.00**

c1770

SARREGUEMINES

Lorraine, France
c1770 to Present

History: The Sarreguemines faience factory, one of the most important manufacturers of French faience, was established in Lorraine about 1770 by M. Fabray and Paul Utzscheider.

During the 19th century pottery and stoneware in the English style were manufactured. Transfer decorations were used frequently. Imitations of Wedgwood's cream colored earthenware, black basalt, cane, cameos, wall tiles, agate, and marbled wares were made in addition to biscuit figures and groups. Mocha ware and majolica also were manufactured.

Modern production includes faience and porcelain wares.

Museums: Museé Regional de Sarreguemines, Lorraine, France; Sevres Museum, Sevres, France.

Basket, "Rose and Leaf" pattern, no.4710, Sarreguemines (A)........................... **240.00**

Bowl, 8" l, majolica, fish shape, multicolored .. **30.00**

Dish, 8⅜" d, ftd, multicolored center scene of two dancers, black "Kochersberg Environs de Strasbourg" below, multicolored crest and vine border............................... **100.00**

Figure, 18" h, griffin with shell form bowl..... **200.00**

Plate, 7" d, black transfer of hunter, molded basketweave border, $28.00

Oyster Plate, 9½" d, six gray and coral wells,
"Sarreguemines France" mark **155.00**
Pedestal, 41" h, majolica type, emb and painted
floral column with molded leaves on base and
under platform, hairline, c1880 . . . .   **2500.00**
Pitcher
8½" h, face, c1890, Sarreguemines (A). . . .   **225.00**
9" h, happy and sad face on each side in
bright colors, tree leaf trim **109.00**
Plate
7½" d
"Cadet Reusselle" music theme in colors,
marked **28.00**
Majolica, leaves and fruit centers in olive
green and mustard, scalloped leaf
shaped edge, imp "Sarreguemines"
mark, set of 6 . . . .   **265.00**
Napoleon scenes: "Tomorrow You Will
Sleep in Toulon," "Never Fear, The Cannonball That Will Kill Me Has Not Been
Made," and "There is Honor and Courage, Unfortunate One!" black transfer,
scalloped edge, c1830, marked, set
of 3 . . . .   **165.00**
7⅝" d
"Les Greve," black transfer of animals and
hunter, c1820, marked **75.00**
"Nouvelles Questions," black transfer, blue
floral border, scalloped edge, c1830,
"H.B.& C." mark **55.00**
8¾" d, multicolored transfer of "DIE WAL-
KURE," bust of Wagner, music score,
marked. **25.00**
9" d, pencil outlined flowers and birds in blue,
red, yellow, and green, yellow outlined
shaped rim **95.00**
Platter
10" l, molded fruit on gold leaves **55.00**
12" d, majolica, fruits and leaves in colors,
marked. **60.00**
Teapot, 4¾" h, brown glaze, imp "Sarregue-
mines" mark. **22.00**
Toothpick Holder, figural swan in colors **26.00**
Vase
7" h, crystalline-silver crystals on blue-gray
ground, marked **100.00**
9⅛" h, majolica, olive green brick pattern,
two handles, turquoise int, imp "Sarregue-
mines" mark, pr. **295.00**
Wall Pocket, 4" w, 9½" h, beatle, blue, green,
and brown irid finish **200.00**

c1890

SCHAFER AND VATER

Thuringia, Germany
1890–1962

History: The Schafer and Vater Porcelain Factory was established in 1890 at Rudolstadt, Thuringia. The factory
produced many decorative pieces, figures, dolls, and novelty ware in hard paste porcelain. They also were decorators of white ware blanks.

Records of the company ceased in 1962.

Ash Receiver
3" h, 3½" l, white figural naked cherub . . .   **105.00**
3½" h, open mouthed lady juggling apple on
nose, unmarked. **58.00**
4¼" h
Scotsman seated on bench, swinging feet,
"Waiting For the Tide" on base. **175.00**
Welsh figure sitting on bench, large black
hat, black shoes, green skirt, orange
shawl, nodding feet, "A Welsh H' Attrac-
tion" on base. **175.00**
5¼" h, bald man with holes in head and
open mouth, "Keep hair" on base **145.00**
Basket, 4½" h, 2" w, white cameo bust of lady
on pink jasper ground **55.00**
Bottle
5" h, man sitting on keg with "What we
want". **95.00**
5½" h, "Old Scotch, Little Scotch," marked   **130.00**
7" h
Modeled pink and yellow roses, gray-green
ground, pink rose stopper, imp mark . . .   **55.00**
White cameo of cavalier and maiden drink-
ing in window, Cupid with banjo above,
"Prosit" below, green jasper ground, imp
mark. **69.00**
9½" h, man holding pig in blue, repaired . .   **150.00**

Schafer and Vater: Bottle, 7½" h, tan shading, stopper on reverse, imp mark, $235.00; Creamer, 5¾" h,
orange coat, black and white face, green handle, imp mark, $250.00

Box, 3" sq
  3 1/4" h, two wide-eyed boys in oval tub on
    cov, natural colors, marked............   **125.00**
  5 1/2" h, figural cov with girl in black skirt,
    gold bonnet, bodice, and apron, basket of
    flowers on arm, base with black scrolled
    front................................   **90.00**
  6" h, figural pink pig playing fife, "Pig 'n Whis-
    tle" on front, marked..................   **185.00**
Bisque, relief of Sphinx on sides, white with color
  accents, tan ground, Sphinx knob..........   **135.00**
Chamberstick, 5" l, gray cameo bust of woman
  on dark blue jasper ground, pink jasper base,
  imp mark...............................   **110.00**
Creamer
  3 1/2" h
    Figural clown with mandolin, multicolored   **135.00**
    Figural devil in colors...................   **85.00**
    Maid with jug and keys, multicolored.....   **95.00**
  3 3/4" h, Dutch girl with basket on back and
    keys, blue...........................   **60.00**
  3 7/8" h, smiling apple, multicolored........   **85.00**
  4" h, maid with jug and keys, blue.........   **85.00**
  5" h, girl with jug and black pocketbook ...   **70.00**
Cup and Saucer, shaped rect, two raised cartouches on woman's head outlined in white
  on lavender ground, saucer with raised white
  designs, matte finish, imp mark **149.00**
Figure
  3 1/4" h, wide-eyed sitting boy in blue hat,
    brown dog at side, marked..............   **75.00**
  3 3/4" h, girl with jug and black bag........   **50.00**
  4" h, bisque, two doves, two rabbits, "Every-
    body's Doing It" on base **70.00**
  4 1/8" h, bisque
    Boy whispering in girl's ear, "Don't Tell Any-
      one" on base......................   **85.00**
    Lady in green skirt, red blouse, yellow
      bonnet, sitting on stoop reading book,
      mkd............................   **95.00**
  4 1/4" h, short man in old fashioned blue swim
    suit, sitting on bench, large bare feet swing
    on base.............................   **175.00**
  4 3/8" h, bisque, girl in full skirt and feathered
    bonnet, holding twp large slippers **110.00**
  5 1/4" h, Scotsman in blue tam, green shirt,
    multicolored kilt, bending over, "Mind your
    own business" on base, "Of course I've
    pants ye fool" under kilt **130.00**
Hatpin Holder
  4 1/2" h, oriental woman sitting with fan in
    lavender and green jasper, gold trim **145.00**
  5" h, gray medallion of woman's head on
    dark blue ground, pink body, gray scrolls,
    jasper................................   **165.00**
  5 1/4" h, white emb seated pig on front, "You
    may push me, You may shuv, But I'm
    hanged if I'll be druv" **125.00**
Inkwell, 3 1/2" h, figural nodding child sitting on
  well, multicolored **138.00**
Jam Jar, 5 1/2" h, white cameos of classical
  figures, blue jasper, slot for spoon, imp
  mark..................................   **54.00**
Match Holder
  2 1/2" h, Chinese woman lying next to holder,
    orchid color **85.00**
  4" h, seated bald man in black coat with over-

sized feet and hands, fingers open at end,
  "How much-on dis" on base............   **145.00**
Match Striker, 3 1/2" h, bisque, fat man bending
  over, boy with bat behind, "Scratch Your
  Match On My Patch"....................   **95.00**
Mug, 3 1/4" h, molded deer in shades of brown,
  matte finish, white int, imp mark..........   **59.00**
Napkin Ring, Japanese geisha................   **75.00**
Pin Tray, 5" l, black skeleton holding wreathed
  open coffin, side with "Brockton Fair, If You
  Please," 1912..........................   **150.00**
Pitcher
  3 1/8" h, grinning Chinaman holding large
    bird.................................   **95.00**
  5" h, grotesque black woman, marked **165.00**
  5 1/2" h, Mother Goose, blue bonnet and
    shawl **85.00**
  6" h, figural monkey on back of man, green
    jacket and black hair, open mouth forms
    spout, brown monkey with tail forming han-
    dle, imp mark........................   **118.00**
Powder Box, 3" h, 3 3/4" d, cameo of woman's
  face on lid, pink jasper with lime green and
  gold highlights **105.00**
Tobacco Jar, Cov, 5 3/4" h, cartouche with raised
  female figure outlined in gilt, pink luster bottom, raised cartouche on cov with child, tan
  ground, c1900, imp mark **85.00**
Vase
  3 1/2" h, triangular shape, white scene of
    French couple on green jasper ground, pink
    jasper body with white scrolls **45.00**
  4" h, jewel cameo of two women, lavender
    jasper ground, marked.................   **65.00**
  4 1/8" h, boy facing wall, multicolored, base
    with "I'm so discouraged" **125.00**
  4 1/2" h, center cartouche of woman's head
    blowing horn in white on blue ground, blue
    jewel, pink jasper ground, imp mark......   **118.00**
  5" h, four Cupid musicians in relief on pink
    jasper ground, lower section with irid finish
    with four jewels, marked................   **55.00**
  6" h, medallion of two women with jewel
    decor on pink jasper ground, two handles   **145.00**

SCHLEGELMILCH PORCELAINS

History: The manufacturing of R. S. Prussia hard paste
porcelains began when Erdmann Schleglemilch founded
his porcelain factory at Suhl, Thuringia in 1861. Reinhold
Schleglemilch, Erdmann's brother, established his porcelain factory at Tillowitz, Upper Silesia in 1869. These two
factories marked the beginning of private ownership of
porcelain factories in that region.

    The founding of these factories coincided with the time
when porcelain items were experiencing a big demand,
especially in the United States and Canada. The peak
exporting years were from the mid-1870s until the early
1900s. The brothers were able to supply large quantities of
porcelains by utilizing new industrial production methodology and the availabiltiy of cheap labor.

c 1900 - MID 1920s

c 1900 -1920s

c 1870s - 1880

TILLOWITZ
Silesia
c 1920-1930s

c 1870s - 1914

E. S. GERMANY

Suhl, Thuringia
c1900 to c1925

Erdmann's factory at Suhl was associated with the E. S. marks. Some of the marks incorporated "Prov. Saxe," '1861," or "Suhl" in the mark.

The style and decoration of the porcelains were different in shape and decor form the "RSP" examples. Changes reflected fashions of the times. The porcelains had the elegant, flowing lines of the Art Nouveau period rather than the convoluted rococo shape between 1895 and 1905. A great number of "ES" pieces were totally hand painted. After 1905 the porcelain decoration returned to more classical and mythological themes and to simplier forms. Many of the transfers were in the style of Angelica Kauffmann.

c 1910 -1956

R. S. GERMANY

Tillowitz, Upper Silesia

The forms and decorations of "R. S. Germany" were molded more simply, had more subtle decorations, and reflected the Art Deco period.

Reinhold concentrated on tablewares. Many examples were hand painted. Reinhold used a mark similar to the "RSP" mark at his Upper Silesia factory, except that "Germany" was included instead of "Prussia." The mark was usually under the glaze as opposed to the overglaze "RSP" mark. A number of large American department stores had special patterns created just for their use. Many of the porcelain blanks used for home decorating contain the "RSG" mark. Some exported blanks were decorated professionally by Pickard, a decorating studio for china in Illinois.

R. S. PRUSSIA

Erdmann Schlegelmilch
Suhl, Thuringia
1861–1920

Reinhold Schlegelmilch
Tillowitz, Upper Silesia
1869–1956

Both Erdmann and Reinhold used the "RSP" mark. The famous "Red Mark" first appeared in the late 1870s and was used until the beginning of World War I. Decorative objects and tablewares were back stamped with the trademark featuring the initials "R. S." inside a wreath, a star above, and the word "Prussia" below.

There was a tremendous quantity of items produced with the "RSP" trademark. In addition to art objects, dresser sets, a large variety of tablewares (including complete dinner sets), and cake, chocolate, tea and coffee sets were all manufactured.

An endless number of "RSP" molds were made. Identical shapes were decorated differently; the same shape was made in a variety of sizes. Many molds produced pieces in the rococo style, including ornately fashioned scrollwork and flowers as part of the design of the blank. Some blanks were exported to the United States for the home decorating market.

Most "RSP" marked porcelains were decorated by transfer or a combination of transfer and enameling or hand applied gilt. Decoration were applied over the glaze. A few pieces were hand painted.

Decoration themes on "RSP" porcelains include: animals, birds, figural, floral, portrait, and scenics. Many pieces incorporate more than one theme. Floral themes are the most common; animal and fruit themes are the scarcest.

Background colors were part of the decorating scheme and not the finish or the glaze. These colors were applied over the glaze by the transfer method to highlight the central theme.

A variety of finishes such as glossy, iridescent, luster, matte, pearl, satin, etc., were used to complete an "RSP" piece. Gilt trim often was utilized on borders, bases, handles, feet, or to outline a particular design.

The Suhl factory stopped producing R. S. Prussia marked porcelains in 1920, unable to recover from the effects of World War I. The Tillowitz factory was located in a region where political boundaries kept changing. It finally came under the Polish socialist government control in 1956.

c 1945-1956

R. S. POLAND

Poland
1945–1956

R. S. Poland pieces have predominately classical decorations or simple designs rather than the ornate or rococo decorations and designs of "RSP" porcelains. Art objects, such as vases and jardinieres, dominated production over common tablewares. After World War II, little export business was done. R. S. Poland examples are quite rare.

Reinhold Schlegelmilch's factory came under control of the socialist government in Poland in 1956.

References: Mary Frank Gaston, *The Collectors Encyclopedia of R. S. Prussia & other R. S. & E. S. Porcelains,* Collector Books, 1982; George W. Terrell, Jr., *Collecting R. S. Prussia, Identification and Values,* Books America, 1982; Clifford S. Schlegelmilch, *Handbook of Erdmann and Reinhold Schlegelmilch, Prussia-Germany & Oscar Schlegelmilch, Germany,* privately printed, 3d edition, 1973.

Collectors' Club: International Association of R.S. Prussia Collectors, Inc., Mary McCastin, 22 Canterbury Drive, Danville, IN 46122. Membership: $20.00.

REPRODUCTION ALERT: Since the 1960s, R. S. Prussia collecting has grown rapidly. "RSP" pieces are being reproduced. There is a fake RSP red mark in the form of a decal which can be applied, glazed, and fired onto a piece of porcelain. This mark has an overall new apperance when compared to the old mark.

Japanese porcelain imports try and imitate "RSP" porcelains in type, decor, and mold. There are marked and unmarked examples. Most pieces initially have a paper "Made in Japan" label, but it is removed easily. The Lefton China Company manufactures reproductions.

' There are many ways to spot the reproductions. The reproductions and Japanese imports are fairly thick. The scallops, scrolls, and lattice are clumsy rather than delicate. Often the decoration is too bright. The background colors are not subtle, and the transfers are applied poorly. The gold trim lacks patina. These porcelains are sold in gift shops and flea markets.

Collecting Hints: Not all "RSP" is marked. Examples usually can be identified by studying the mold and the decor of an unmarked piece to see if it matches a known mold or design.

E.S. GERMANY

Basket, 6 3/8" l, lady with child in center, pearl
 luster finish, gold fancy handle, "Royal Saxe"
 mark................................... **125.00**
Bowl
 6 1/2" d, diamond shape, scene of man in boat
  in water with trees in red, green, and brown,
  "E.S. Germany Prov. Saxe" mark........ **50.00**
 9 3/4" d
  Multicolored scene of three ladies, "E.S.
  Germany Prov. Saxe" mark **100.00**

Portrait of "Lady with Rose" in center, irid
 gold with gold tracery **225.00**
 11" l, oval, woman holding bunch of flowers,
  pearl luster, jewel mold **90.00**
Cake Plate, 11 1/4" H-H, lady holding two roses
 in oval medallion, lustered pearlized ground
 with gold tracery **200.00**
Chocolate Cup and Saucer, multicolored scene
 of woman with daisy crown, "E.S. Prov. Saxe"
 mark..................................... **15.00**
Chocolate Set, pot, 5 cups and saucers, pink and
 yellow chrysanthemums, light green shaded
 ground, unmarked....................... **325.00**
Nut Bowl, 7 1/2" l, 6" w, multicolored windmill
 scene, four feet, "E.S. Germany Prov. Saxe"
 mark..................................... **75.00**
Plate
 6 1/2" d, center scene of classical maidens in
  colors, pearlized border, "Royal Saxe"
  mark, pr............................... **325.00**
 9 1/2" d
  Center scene of yellow, orange, and blue
   Bird of Paradise on gold branch, blue and
   gray ground, green swirl molded border
   with gold leaves, "E.S. Germany Prov.
   Saxe" mark.......................... **125.00**
  Roses and lily of the valley design, "Prov.
   Saxe" mark.......................... **27.00**
 12" d, multicolored windmill scene, "E.S. Germany, Prov. Saxe" mark **95.00**
Tray, 10" d, sectional, figural peasant in center,
 gold design, "Prov. Saxe E.S. Germany" mark. **45.00**
Trinket Box, 3" d, basket of flowers in colors on
 lid, "E.S. Prov. Saxe" mark............... **30.00**
Vase
 6" h, portrait of lady with swallows, small pink
  roses, irid green ground, dbl handles **395.00**
 7 1/2" h, gold man of the mountain on sides,
  center with portrait of lady and child, wine
  red ground, gold tracery, "E.S. Germany,
  Royal Saxe" mark **86.50**
 8 3/4" h, panel of lady and two girls on bench
  in landscape, cobalt ground, gold trim, "R.S.
  Suhl" mark **175.00**
 9" h, yellow, pink, and white chrysan-

Urn, 13 1/2" h, rose, yellow, and green shades,
raised gold trim, magenta base, gold handles, irid
int, "E.S. Germany, Prov. Saxe" mark, $650.00

themums, green leaves, gold tracery, tur-
quoise ground, "E.S. Prov. Saxe" mark. . . .   **120.00**
10" h, woman with holly crown, "E.S. Prov.
Saxe" mark. **150.00**
14" h, large roses on pearlized ground, dbl
handles, marked **145.00**

R.S. GERMANY

Berry Set, ruffled bowl, 10" d, 6 bowls, 9" d, pink
magnolia, luster finish.   **255.00**
Bowl
5³/4" w, white flowers with gold stems, wide
gold band **38.00**
6¹/2" d, white and pink flowers on tan ground .   **35.00**
7¹/2" d
Cabbage mold with yellow and orange
tulips, beige int, orange tulips on dark
beige ext, gilt trim. **125.00**
Pink and yellow flowers, pale green border,
gilt trim, pierced handles. **48.00**
9¹/4" d, large white flowers in center, green
ground, "R.S. Tillowitz" mark **45.00**
9¹/2" d
Cottages and trees in colors on green to cream
ground, ruffled gold rim, green mark . . .   **100.00**
Large white hp blossoms and green leaves
on light green ground, gold lily of the valley overlay, "Reinhold Schlegelmilch-Til-
lowitz" mark (A) **23.00**
10" d, hp multicolored iris, tan border. **45.00**
13" l, 7¹/2" w, variegated pink, orange, and
white multipetaled large floral blending into
ground, green leaves and stems, gold trim,
pierced ends, green mark **68.00**
Candy Dish, 7" d, hydrangea in shades of gray
and pink, green mark **45.00**
Celery Dish, 9¹/2" l, oval shape, hp with pink,
yellow, and purple florals in panels, white center, pierced cutouts in edge, gold rim and trim,
red ink mark **125.00**
Cheese and Cracker Dish, 10" d, lavender violet
bouquets, fancy gold handle. **100.00**
Condensed Milk Holder, 5" h, multicolored
florals on white ground, gold band on neck
and underplate. **195.00**
Creamer, 3¹/2" h, ribbed body, orchid flowers,
cream to green shaded ground, gold scalloped
rim **65.00**
Dish
6¹/4" l, 5¹/2" w, oval, four feet, large white
hydrangeas on beige ground, gold trim,
beaded and scrolled bottom, blue mark . .   **32.00**
Handled
6¹/4" l, red berries and green leaves, matte
gold handles and border, artist sgd. **22.00**
9¹/2" l, 4¹/2" w, large peach and pink rose
spray, gold and tan stylized floral rim,
gold trim, loop handles, green mark. . . .   **32.00**
Ferner, 7" l, 3³/4" h, five petaled yellow flower
with begonia leaves outlined in gold, gold rim,
blue mark, "red Reinhold Schlegelmilch Tillo-
witz Germany" mark **40.00**
Hatpin Holder, 4¹/2" h, Art Deco style straight
line designs on shaded green ground, rose
panels, artist sgd **95.00**
Mustard Pot
3" h
Azalea pattern **75.00**
Floral design, with spoon. **85.00**

**Hatpin Holder, 4¹/2" h, yellow roses, green
leaves, pearlized ground, green mark, (A) $45.00**

Pitcher, 6" h, figural clown, pearlized glaze . . .   **95.00**
Plate
6¹/4" d, lg red and yellow roses on green and
tan shaded ground, heavy gold trim. **15.00**
8" d, dogwood blossoms on maroon ground.   **18.00**
8¹/4" d
Clusters of violets on shaded green ground,
gold rim. **35.00**
"Cotton Plant" design, blue mark **85.00**
8¹/2" d
Clusters of violets and foliage on pastel
green ground, gold trim, blue mark **25.00**
White orange blossoms on muted green
and rose ground **25.00**
9" d, pastel manor house in rural setting,
"green R.S. Germany and gold Hand-
painted R.S. Germany" marks **185.00**
Relish Dish, 9³/4" H-H, pink poinsettias, ivory
green ground, "R.S. Tillowitz" mark **50.00**
Salt and Pepper, 2¹/4" h, pink and gray floral
border, white ground, gilt top and trim,
marked, pr. **25.00**
Talcum Shaker, 5" h, floral design, gold trim,
pearlized skirt. **185.00**
Tankard, 11" h, poppy and berry design, "R.S.
Germany" mark. **185.00**
Tray, 11¹/2" H-H, 7¹/4" w, rect, multicolored
sheepherder and mill scene **255.00**
Vase
4" h, portrait of Madame Henriette as Flora in
colors. **300.00**
4¹/4" h, shaped sq, purple, pink, and yellow
florals, gilt and white ground **28.00**
6" h, multicolored "Nightwatch" scene,
"green R.S. Germany" mark. **350.00**

R.S. POLAND

Candlestick, 6¹/4" h
Pink and peach roses, brown trim, pr. **195.00**
Tulips in shades of brown, gold trim, pr. **195.00**
Cream and Sugar, light peach colored roses on
brown and green ground. **150.00**
Cup and Saucer, ftd, pink roses, white ground
with cream top band, gold trim, blown out
mold. **125.00**
Dresser Set, tray, 12¹/2" l, 9" w, stickpin holder,
ring tree, cov jar, 4" d, cov jar, 3¹/4" d, large
yellow roses with gold trim, white ground. . .   **540.00**

Berry Dish, 5" d, 3 pale green roses in center, lt green ground, gold outline, mkd, $45.00

Planter, 6 3/4" h, 6 1/2" l, band of pink flowers,
   gold accents **230.00**
Serving Dish, 11" d, 8" h, lavender and pink
   roses, gold trim, shaped rim, center handle. . **515.00**
Tray, 13" l, 8" w, floral design in colors, pierced
   handles **125.00**
Urn, Cov, 11 1/2" h, pink and white roses,
   shaded brown ground **800.00**
Vase
   3 1/2" h, crowned crane design **800.00**
   3 5/8" h, yellow roses on tan ground **105.00**
   4" h, "Nightwatch" scene of four men and
     woman on blue-green ground **305.00**
   4 1/4" h, single rose on brown ground,
     marked, pr **105.00**
   8 1/4" h, pale pink roses, cobalt ground, pr. . **275.00**
   10" h, multicolored cottage scene with
     woman and sheep in foreground, gold han-
     dles, gold ornate rim **640.00**

R.S. PRUSSIA

Basket, 7" l, 2 5/8" h, oval, white flower on green
   ground, freeform edge, ornate handle **75.00**
Bell, 3 1/4" h, green bridal wreath trim, white
   ground, unmarked. **195.00**
Berry Dish, 5" d, white Easter lilies on light green
   ground, gold trim, set of 4 (A) **5.00**
Berry Set, master bowl, 9 1/2" d, 5 bowls, 5 1/2"
   d, roses design with gold and green irreg
   edges, red marks **260.00**
Bowl
   4" d, six ivory, six green panels, center with
     pink roses and snowballs, gold trim, red
     mark. **325.00**
   6" d
     Medallion mold, three feet, swallows decor,
       red mark **250.00**
     Reflected poppies and daisies, satin finish,
       mold #155, three ftd **395.00**
   9 1/4" d, yellow and pink roses in center, green
     border with gold tracery, pie crust edge,
     mold #23, unmarked **110.00**
   9 3/4" d, "Melon Eaters" design, mold #82,
     red mark **1200.00**
   10" d
     Blown out iris mold, cobalt blue, gilt trim,
       red mark. **375.00**
     Farm yard scene of two turkeys, emb gold
       flowers and tracery, unmarked **775.00**
     Grape and leaf border, eight blown out sec-

tions with small flowers, large roses in
   'center, red mark **475.00**
Madame Recamier in center, blown tied
   bows on rim. **850.00**
Pink and ivory poppies, beige and green
   ground, unmarked **175.00**
Yellow and pink roses, white lilies, raised
   gold accents, luster finish, red mark **159.00**
10 1/4" d
   3" h, pink poppies in center, cobalt, green,
     and brown floral border, mold #95, un-
     marked **865.00**
   Pink roses in center, pearl luster finish, co-
     balt and lavender border, gilt trim. **410.00**
10 1/2" d
   Large yellow roses, red mark **195.00**
   Lebrun portrait of Countess Anna Potocka,
     gold Tiffany type ground with gold flow-
     ers, unmarked **1295.00**
   Pink and yellow roses, pale pink ground,
     gold trim, lily mold **130.00**
   Pink roses, raised gold trim, scalloped edge,
     red mark **250.00**
   Small and large snowball florals, light green
     ground, four reticulated areas on rim,
     c1880 (A) **160.00**
   Small purple and white lilacs on int and ext,
     pale green to white shaded ground, dbl
     flared sides, puff-molded, ftd, c1892
     (A) **225.00**
   10 3/4" d, satin finish pink roses on white
     ground, green and gold trim, mold #213. **435.00**
   11" d, "Old man of the mountain" design,
     medallion mold, red mark **900.00**
   11 1/2" d, 3" h, pink poppies on shaded blue
     ground, carnation mold **400.00**
Box, Cov, 2 3/4" h, 4 3/4" d, barn with mill scene,
   pale green shading to darker green, gilt trim,
   red and green marks. **695.00**
Bun Tray
   13" l, light yellow iris and green leaves, white
     ground, mold #26 (A). **80.00**
   14" l, 6" w, three Lebrun and one Recamier
     portraits, cobalt ground, Medallion mold. . **875.00**
Butter Pat, dogwood blossoms, green pearlized
   luster finish **35.00**
Cake Plate
   10" d
     Baskets of flowers in autumn colors, open
       handles, icicle mold, red mark **195.00**
     Multicolored swallows, chickens, and ducks
       beside water and lilies, swag and tassel
       mold. **1010.00**
   10 1/2" d
     Basket of roses, pearl luster finish, medallion
       mold, red mark **275.00**
     Melon Boy, white pearl button finish, gold
       trim, red mark **975.00**
   10 3/4" d, swans and lily pads, icicle mold,
     open handles, red mark. **450.00**
   11" d
     Hydrangeas on shaded green ground, un-
       marked **75.00**
     Large yellow roses
       Blown out lily mold, unmarked **110.00**
       With cherries, open handles, unmarked **75.00**
     Peach, pink, and white roses in basket,
       cream ground, plume mold with gold and
       brown trim, red mark. **295.00**
     Roses and snowballs in center, opal jewel-
       ing and beading on rim. **195.00**

Three swans and evergreens, open handles,
  unmarked 195.00
11½" H-H
  Pink roses on green irid ground, red mark   85.00
  Swan scene in colors, satin finish 550.00
12" d, lilies of the valley design, satin finish,
  open handles 250.00
Celery Dish, 12" l, 5½" w, roses in center,
  green border with gold stenciling, stippled
  floral mold, unmarked 125.00

**Celery Tray, 13" l, pink and white roses, green
leaves, molded floral border, gilt trim, red and
green mark, (A) $242.00**

Chocolate Pot
  8½" h, ftd, pink roses with green panels, red
    mark 335.00
  9" h, rasberry mold, emb berries, swan design,
    satin finish, berry finial 495.00
  10½" h, snowballs and leaf design, light
    green ground, mold #521, red mark 325.00
  11" h, lush pink roses, green ground, red
    mark 125.00
Chocolate Set
  Pot, 12" h, 4 cups and saucers, yellow and
    lavender flowers, red mark 575.00
  Pot, 6 cups and saucers, "Melon" Boy decor,
    red mark 5000.00
Cider Pitcher, 6" h, floral design, vert ribbing, red
  mark 275.00
Cracker Jar, 6" h, 9" l, hex shape, three color
  roses, gold scrolls, gold and jeweled scalloped
  rim, fancy finial and handles, red mark 350.00
Cream and Sugar
  Pink roses, green leaves, satin finish, red
    mark 200.00
  Purple and gray flowers, green leaves, ivory
    ground, gold trim 75.00
Creamer
  2½" h, ftd, Rocky Cove pattern, red mark .   95.00
  Portrait of Princess Potocka, gold and red
    ground, scalloped bottom and top, applied
    flower spout, red mark 170.00
Cup and Saucer, pink and white roses, shaded
  tan ground, red mark 145.00
Cup and Saucer, Demitasse
  Farmyard scenes, three scenes of swallows,
    swan, and pheasant and pine tree, red
    mark 395.00
  Painted dainty flowers 85.00
  Pink flowers, green leaves, gilt trim, red mark   125.00
Dresser Tray
  11" H-H, shaped rect, roses with blue ground,
    raised dotted border, gilt trim, pierced han-
    dles 250.00
  11" l, 7" w, swans in colors, swag and tassel
    mold 475.00
  11½" l, 7½" w, floral design on pearl luster

ground, blown out carnation mold, red
  mark 295.00
11¾" l, 7½" w
  Five yellow and white lilies in center, cobalt
    ground, unmarked 750.00
  Forest scene in cobalt and green with white
    clouds in sky, gold trim, unmarked 275.00
  Icicle mold, "Reflecting Poppies and Dai-
    sies" design, red mark 300.00
  Lily mold, dark green and gold flowers, trac-
    ery on edge, bouquet of pink and orchid
    flowers in center, handled 150.00
Mustard Pot, white flowers on soft green ground,
  satin finish, original ladle 185.00
Pitcher, 6" h, pink roses, shaded green ground,
  gold trim, four feet, red mark 225.00
Plaque, 11¼" d, mill scene on green ground,
  yellow and lavender shaped border, un-
  marked 710.00
Plate
  6" d
    "Dice Throwers," jewel and ribbon mold .   525.00
    "Spring Season," satin finish, blown out iris
      mold, red mark 495.00
  8¼" d, castle scene in dark orange, purple,
    green, and blue, unmarked 275.00
  9" d, scattered flowers, jewels decorated as
    opals, mold #82, red and green wreath
    mark 300.00
  11" d, painted roses. 85.00
Relish Dish
  9½" l, snowballs, tulips, florals and jewels,
    satin finish, emb floral rim and handle 95.00
  10¼" d, "Snowbirds" design, icicle mold . .   650.00
  12" l
    Icicle mold, blue peacock with long feath-
      ers, white ground, red mark 695.00
    Yellow, pink, and white roses in center, four
      emb irises, ivory and turquoise ground,
      mold #25, red mark 245.00
Snack Set, pink and orange flowers, gilt trim, pale
  green edge 195.00
Sugar Shaker, 4¾" h, small pink roses, gold
  garlands, marked 260.00
Tankard
  10" h, Ribbon and Jewel mold, "Melon Eat-
    ers" pattern (A) 2700.00
  13" h, Blown out poppy mold
    "Fall Season" pattern (A) 6500.00
    "Summer Season" pattern (A) 6400.00
  14" h, "Melon Eaters" pattern, mold #643,
    unmarked (A) 7100.00
Teapot, 6½" h, 8⅝" l, mold #507, pale
  green, white florals, red centers, gold dentil
  rim, gold trim, satin finish, sgd, red mark 600.00
Tea Set
  Teapot, creamer, sugar bowl, dogwood blos-
    soms in green, yellow, and white, gold en-
    crusted trim, leaf mold and pedestal foot,
    "gold crown and Royal Vienna" marks . . .   350.00
  Teapot, creamer, cov sugar bowl, spooner,
    mold #507, irid Tiffany finish at top, clus-
    ters of pink roses on satin base 615.00
Tray, 11½" H-H, large pink and red flowers in
  center, raised molded design, shaded green
  ground, red mark 125.00
Vase
  4½" h, castle scene in colors, unmarked . .   295.00
  6" h, cobalt blue florals, raised gilt trim, pale
    cream ground, steeple mark 495.00
  7½" h, bunches of pink roses on gold Tiffany

type ground, gold tracery, dbl handles, ornate pedestal base, unmarked **275.00**

8³⁄₄" h, dice throwers on one side, child eating fruit with dog on opposite, blown out puffed neck trimmed with opal jewels, beaded rococo handles, scalloped molded foot with opal jewels, red mark **2000.00**

9" h

Portrait of Lady Racamier in red garment with white bodice, shaded green ground, gilt trim **495.00**

Small pink roses, gold tracery, elongated gold handles to base, satin finish, "Royal Vienna" dbl marks **325.00**

10¹⁄₄" h, multicolored scene of two ladies with fruit and flowers, green ground, gold trim, gold dbl handles, "Lebrun" on base . **495.00**

11" h, beaded center medallion of "Winter Lady," pearl luster finish, gold handles and scalloped base with dbl gold reticulated handles, tulip pointed rim, red mark **1250.00**

11¹⁄₂" h, multicolored animals in barnyard, red mark **950.00**

c 1793-1804

1778

Jevres 25

1825

SEVRES

DECORATOR MARK 1873

Paris, France
1738 to Present

History: The Dubois brothers started a small soft paste porcelain factory for the production of decorative flowers at Vincennes in 1738. Encouraged by Madame Pompadour, the factory found favor with Louis XV who became the chief shareholder in 1753. Louis XV controlled most of the products manufactured at Vincennes as well as throughout the rest of France. Gilding and the use of colored grounds were reserved for his pet projects. The familiar interlaced "L" mark was used during his reign to signify his participation.

In 1756 the factory was moved to Sevres, coming under the watchful eye of its chief benefactor Mme. de Pompadour. The first products were soft paste porcelain pieces decorated in the Oriental style. The soft paste porcelain lent itself well to the elaborate Rococo style favored by the king and his court. In addition to decorated soft paste, exquisite biscuit porcelain figures were produced, much to the delight of Madame Pompadour.

After the late 1760s hard paste porcelain gradually replaced the soft paste variety. Styles fell loosely into categories which had taken the names of the benefactors. The period of 1753 to 1763 was known as "Pompadour," 1763 to 1786 was "Louis XV," and 1786 to 1793 was "Louis XVI." The products of these periods ranged from small scent bottles to enormous dinner services to vases and urns of monumental size and decoration. The neoclassical styles was heavily favored. Jeweled or heavily enameled pieces first appeared about 1780.

Several directors influenced strongly the products from Sevres. During the directorship of Jean Hellot, about 1745 to 1766, several colors were introduced that have become associated with Sevres porcelain. The earliest ground color was gros bleu (1749) followed by bleu celeste (turquoise, 1752), rose pompadour (pink, 1756), and bleu roi (clear blue, 1763). The use of these colors during specific periods helped date Sevres porcelain.

Following the French Revolution, the company fell into disfavor and did not flourish again until the Napoleonic years. Alexandre Brogniart was appointed director by Lucien Bonaparte in 1800. The Empire style and scenics depicting Napoleon's campaigns and victories dominated the designs during the period. After 1804 soft paste was no longer made. Eventually the factory re-established itself as a leading producer of European hard paste porcelain.

A new range of colors was developed. Ground colors included dark blue, a pale blue called agate, and chrome green. These were seen most frequently in the First Empire Period, 1804 to 1815. Gilding was used extensively during this period. Painters were employed by Brongniart to paint miniature portraits on porcelain shapes that were modeled carefully by artists such as Theodore Brongniart and Charles Parcier.

Between 1800 and 1830 Sevres products included plaques, vases, table services, sculptures, and some very large special pieces. Porcelain plaques, made between 1818 and 1848, imitated oil paintings or frescoes. Some vases were made in a Neo-classical style that imitatied cameos. Napoleon revived the tradition of ordering large table services for his own use or for diplomatic gifts. Post-Revolution monarchs had France glorified as the subject matter for services. Coffee, tea, or breakfast services also were made between 1800 and 1830.

The reign of Louis-Phillipe, 1830 to 1848, saw few changes at Sevres. Brongniart continued with the styles he was using from the early 1800s. White backgrounds were used more frequently for everyday table services. Decorations lessened. Decorations were printed, especially when gilding was used.

Brongniart died in 1847. Jules Dieterle became artistic director from 1852 to 1855; Joseph Nicolle took over from 1856 to 1871. Most of the output of the Sevres factory from 1852 onwards was for imperial residences and diplomatic gifts.

The most important decorative technique of this period was the pate-sur-pate process. This type of decoration was very popular in France and in England. The pate-sur-pate process ended at Sevres in 1897. (See: Pate-sur-Pate.)

The Second Empire style at Sevres provided a complete break with the preceding period. This was an eclectic period, 1850 to 1870, utilized the Pompeian style to imitate decoration on classical vases with classical subjects. A return to the Rococo forms and decorations of the Louis XV times also occurred during this period.

The Third Republic period, 1870 to 1940, began with difficult conditions at the factory. The factory moved to its present location by the Park of Saint-Cloud. In 1876 the sculptor A. Carrier-Belleuse became artistic director. He remained until his death in 1886.

Many experiments were carried out with different porcelain bodies. Flambe glazes were developed and became popular. During the Carrier-Belleuse period, many different decorating techniques, e.g., painted decoration, pate-sur-pate decoration, and copper glazing, were used.

When Alexandre Sandier became director from 1896 to 1916, the factory was reorganized completely. He initiated new shapes and decoration techniques. Sinuous shapes were developed. The human figure was replaced as a decorative motif by painted vegetables, florals, and insects in the new Art Nouveau style. Winding tendrils appear on vases and plates. Stoneware bodies often were used for the Art Nouveau decorated pieces. Sculpture regained prominence in biscuit porcelain as many bust were modeled.

References: Carl Christian Dauterman, *Sevres,* Walker & Co., 1969; Carl Christain Dauterman, *Sevres Porcelain, Makers and Marks of the Eighteenth Century,* The Metropolitan Museum of Art, 1986; W. B. Honey, *French Porcelain of the 18th Century,* Faber & Faber, 1950; Egan Mew, *Royal Sevres China,* Dodd, Mead & Co., George Savage, *Seventeenth & Eighteenth Century French Porcelain,* Hamlyn Publishing Co., Ltd., 1969.

Museums: Art Institute of Chicago, Chicago, Illinois; British Museum, London, England; Frick Collection, New York, N.Y.; Gardiner Museum of Ceramic Art, Toronto, Canada; J. Paul Getty Museum, Malibu, California; Metropolitan Museum of Art, New York, New York; Musee des Arts Decoratifs, Paris, France; Musee du Louvre, Paris, France; Musee Nationale de Ceramique, Sevres, France; Victoria & Albert Museum, London, England; Wallace Collection, Hertford House, London, England; Walters Art Gallery, Baltimore, MD.

Marks: For most of the 18th century, painted marks on Sevres porcelain consisted of the royal cipher(interlacing L's), the date mark, and the identifying insignia of painters and gilders. Marks usually were blue, but could be brown or purple. Initials below the mark indicate the artist. Artists signed their own works as a means of quality control. The Sevres crown is never seen in soft paste examples.

From 1753–1793 date letters appeared within the crossed L's. For example, A=1753. R=1st letter date used on hard paste. Any letter before R cannot be hard paste Sevres porcelain. From 1793–1800 the monogram of the Republic of France (RF) was used with Sevres and a painter's mark to replace the royal cypher. No letter dates were used. The marks were continually changing after that.

Reproduction Alert: A high percentage of pieces with the Sevres marks are fake or questionable. There are some clues to look for to help establish an authentic piece from a fake or reproduction. 19th century Sevres examples had more decoration and more gold than 18th century pieces. Sevres examples were never marked on the lids. A marked lid indicates a fake. Many fakes had chateau marks. Soft paste was more often faked than hard paste since it is more valuable. Some Sevres white blanks were decorated by factory artists at home or at Paris porcelain dealers such as Peres and Ireland. Some blanks were decorated in England by Baldock and Mortlock.

There should be a hole underneath the rim in plates and saucers caused by the support used in the kiln with a black dot from iron oxide. If so, the piece dates from 1752–1803 or 4 and was fired in the kiln at Sevres. If there are two marks, the piece was refired. If one sees black paint in a hole or a hole with no purpose, then the example is a fake.

The incised mark on a piece must date the same or earlier than the decorator's mark. If the mark on a blank was cut later, the piece was considered a "second" and never decorated at the Sevres factory. Check painter's

sign or symbol to see if it agrees with the letter date. Many Sevres painters produced fakes at home after stealing colors from the factory for decorating. Restorers in France reduced the value of huge quantities of Sevres and Vincennes pieces by regilding chips.

Many colors used on soft paste produced surface bubbles that look like holes, such as in purple due to the gum content. The turpentine used in making hard paste left carbon dots, and there was no bubbling in the colors. One can see scratches in the glaze if pieces of soft paste were used. If the scratches are molten out, the piece has been refired and is worthless.

Jewelled specimens with any date before 1780 are fakes. 'Jewelled Sevres" has transparent raised enamels laid on gold that appeared like inlaid jewels on the surface of the porcelain.

Many Sevres copies were made by Samson. His mark was made to look like two L's. His glaze was yellowish, not white like Sevres soft paste.

Bowl, Circ
  8¹⁵⁄₁₆" d, center with shades of green and brown with branch of oak leaves within gilt edged blue roundel decorated with gilt foliate vine, lobed int and ext rim encircled by oak leaf vine between blue and gold foliate vine and band borders repeated around lower body, gilt banded foot, "blue enamel interlaced L's, PP for 1793, LG for Louis-Antoine Le Grand, incised 3I" marks, pr (A) **1100.00**
  10³⁄₈" d, scalloped, center with scattered floral sprigs, int and ext rim with floral garland suspended from rose, purple, and blue bowknots pendent, berried floral wreaths, gilt dotted band at gilt rim edge, "blue enamel interlaced L's, hh for 1785, LB, # for Michel-Barnabe Chauveaux, incised 25" marks (A)........................... **660.00**
  10⁹⁄₁₆" d, lobed, int and ext with gilt edged cabbage leaves feathered in blue, painted within large floral sprays, center int with floral sprays and sprigs, ext with rim edged in gilt feathering, c1759–65, "blue enamel interlaced L's, G, incised fi" marks (A).... **1100.00**
Box, 11" l, 6½" w, 5³⁄₄" h, enameled turquoise reserves of fruits, courtly lovers in country, or Bacchic cherubs dancing with musical instruments, bordered by white and gilt enameled beading, acanthus leaf and foliage

Vase, 12" h, hp multicolored florals and butterflies, 1922, "Decor Sevres" mark, $5500.00

ormolu mts, bun feet and acanthus support, sgd "E. Poitevin" **10,000.00**

Cache Pot, 6⅞" h, hp roses and pansies on front, rose sprig on reverse **375.00**

Charger, 17½" d, center in gray, black, and yellow with "Le heron hupe" on green and brown grassy plateau amidst rose and blue flowering plants before distant trees, gilt bands at inner and outer edges, "blue enamel interlaced L's, PP for 1792–93, D.T. for Dutanda," ornithological information marks (A) **24,200.00**

Chocolate Cup, Cov, trembleuse saucer, painted scattered sprays of flowers in blue line and gilt dash borders, gilt dentil rim, 1792, "blue interlaced L's and OO" mark (A). **275.00**

Coffee Can and Saucer
    Brown urns filled with puce flowers and green leaves, blue foliate scrolls, iron-red rose sprigs, gilt edged bright yellow ground, foot of cup with gilt berried vine border, center of saucer with spray of pink roses and green leaves within gilt roundel, 1786, "blue enamel interlaced L's, ii, P," incised 46 on cup, 41 on saucer (A) **4180.00**

Cup with tooled gilt edged oval with "La Pipee," couple seated on hummock tending bird trap, center of saucer with "La Belle Dormeuse," youth spying on sleeping shepherdess, reserved on turquoise ground patterned with gilt trelliswork enclosing foliate wreaths, gilt dentil edged rim, ear shaped handle with gilt blossom motifs, "blue enamel interlaced L's, P for 1768, k for Charles-Nicolas Dodin, cup incised jc and 8" marks (A) **13,200.00**

Coffee Cup and Saucer, scattered forget-me-nots under band of red scrolls and border of cornflowers, gilt bands, yellow ground, 1787, "blue interlaced L's and JJ" mark (A) **660.00**

Cream Jug, 3½" h, painted in enamels with three bunches of flowers, gilt dentil rim, branch handle, three crabstock feet with flowering terminals with gilding, c1770, incised "GP' (A) **740.00**

Cup and Saucer
    Conical, scattered floral sprays and sprigs, gilt dentil edged rim, gilt edged scroll handle, unglazed bases, "blue enamel interlaced L's, i for 1761, L for Denis Leve, cup incised s" marks (A). **660.00**

    Girl in lavender dress and rose skirt, leaning on hummock, blowing bubble on front of cup, saucer with boy in russet jacket, blue waistcoat, yellow breeches, seated on hummock, both within cartouches edged in tooled gilt foliate scrolls, diapered panels and floral sprays, bleu lapis ground, gilt dentil edge rim, gilt edged handle with chain of husks and dots, "blue interlaced L's, L for 1764, dot and painter's mark for Andre-Vincent Vielliard" marks (A). **5775.00**

    Overall scalloped roundels painted with roses in gilt line and bead edged reserves, green ground, 1768, "blue interlaced L's" mark (A). **880.00**

    Reserve of garden implements in landscapes, pale blue and gilt ground, trailing foliage and tiny flowerheads extending to entwined branch handle, c1766, "interlaced L's, painter's, letter date, incised 6" marks (A) **3700.00**

Cup, Cov, Stand, blue enamel putti in clouds reserved with gilt scrolled panels, cov with

birds, bleu lapis ground, 1756, "interlaced L's, letter date D, painter's arrow" marks (A). . . . **2165.00**

Dish, 9¾" d, central floral design with fruit in colors, border reserved with oval panels painted with floral groups bordered by gilt floral sprigs and scrolls, green ground, gilt edged rim, c1750 . . . . **175.00**

Ecuelle, Cov, swags of flowers, gilt berried branch knob, handle restored, hair crack, c1765, "interlaced L's, painter's letter date, incised DU" marks (A) **1200.00**

Ecuelle, Cov, Stand
    7⁷⁄₁₆" d, front and reverse in pink, blue, lavender, yellow, cream, gray, green, and brown with mythological scene with Cupid kissing Venus's hand or presenting golden apple on bowl, cov with Cupid seated and holding golden apple or white dove, stand with Cupid supported by two maidens or Europa seated, blue ground, border of tooled foliate scrolls, foliate scroll handles tied with gilt bowknots, "blue enamel interlaced L's, jj for 1787, star mark for Antoine Caton, incised 13 and 37cc on bowl, 13 and 31 on stand" marks (A). **6050.00**

    8⅞" d, wreath of pink roses and green leaves intersecting with one of blue cornflowers tied with lavender bowknot in gilt edged oval panel, panels flanked by garlands of oak leaves and acorns, cov with gilt berried green leafy branch knob, rims with gilt dentil edge, green ground, "blue enamel interlaced L's, O, 3 dot mark, incised DU and O" on ecuelle, "d" on stand (A) **2200.00**

    9⅞" d, kidney shaped panels with gilt scroll, trellis and floral border, light blue ground, domed cov with fish and shell finial, 18th C, "blue enamel interlaced L's' (A) **4012.00**

Ewer and Basin, 8¾" h, 11¾" l, ovoid body, gilt foliate vine beneath gilt dentil edged rim, loop handle feathered with foliations, shaped oval basin with gilt dentil edged rim, 1760–70, "blue enamel interlaced L's, incised da" on ever, "Jh" on basin (A). **385.00**

Figure
    6¼" h, biscuit, girl in full skirted dress with laced bodice resting elbow on basket of grapes on tree stump, stroking small dog, grassy rock base, c1760, incised "F' (A) . . **3846.00**

    6½" h, allegorical figure of Winter with putti at fire, C scrolled base, mid 18th C (A) . . . **470.00**

    8" h, period lady in plumed hat, floral bodice, and yellow skirt holding reticulated basket, man in pink floral waist coat holding bouquet of flowers, oval pedestal, c1795 . . . . **495.00**

    11" h, woman in blue trimmed floral dress and yellow floral cape dancing with man in green trousers, white floral vest and purple coats, marked. **1650.00**

Fruit Cooler, Cov, 8" h, circ body, shaded pink rose sprigs with green, turquoise, and ochre leaves, repeated within gilt edged oval panels, reserved on border of gilt centered rose and green flowerheads within gilt bands around rim of cooler, angular handles, dbl scroll knob, three bun feet in gilding, repaired, "blue enamel interlaced L's, Y for 1776, Kn" marks (A). **990.00**

Glass Cooler, 5" h, oval body, scattered bouquets of flowers, foliate scroll handles feathered in blue, scalloped gilt rims, c1775, "blue

enamel interlaced L's, X'' and painter's marks
(A)..................................... **1683.00**
Ice Pail, Cov, Liner, 8¼" h, bucket shape, scattered sprays of summer flowers, three bun feet, angular handles, entwined scroll handle on cover, blue feathered gilt line rims, c1770 (A)..................................... **5760.00**
Jardinaire
   10⅛" l, D-shape bombe body, multicolored oval panels on front with two children in rural setting playing, panels flanked by concave columns reserved with gilt edged panels of floral swags within bands of gilt bellflowers above scroll molded feet, white foliate scroll handles, turquoise ground, "blue enamel interlaced L's, l for 1761 painter's mark for Andre-Vincent Vielliard, incised mm" on one, incised "IP" on second, pr (A) **19,800.00**
   Lobed oval form, vignettes of exotic birds in parkland, flanked by swags of flowers, gilt scrolling leaf handles, c1765, "blue interlaced L's, letter date" marks............. **5340.00**
Medallion, 2¹⁵⁄₁₆" d, white biscuit portrait of Louis XVI with profile of King with bare neck, within molded circ self frame glazed and edged with gilt bands, pierced for hanging, 1777–79 (A)........................... **550.00**
Milk Jug, Pear Shape Body,
   3³⁄₁₆" h, pink and green rose sprigs within gilt foliate roundels, gilt molded floral sprays, branch form handle, three short feet, gilt dentil edge rim, "blue enamel interlaced L's, P for 1768" mark (A).................. **660.00**
   4¾" h, blue, rose, iron-red, gray, yellow, green, and brown with parrot perched on branch of small tree in wooded landscape within cartouche edged in gilt band, bead, and reel border, rich blue ground, gilt dentil edge rim, branch form handle, three feet with gilding, c1770, unmarked (A) **990.00**
Planter, 6½" d, oval, reserve painted with two young lovers in country setting, gilt border, four ormolu feet, cobalt ormolu scrolling handles (A) **330.00**
Plaque
   12¾" h, 11⅝" w, 12⅞" h, 11½" w, hp bouquet of summer flowers in dbl handled vase on gray marble ledge, framed, dtd 1804, sgd "Micaud Pinx," pr (A)....... **27,500.00**
   16½" h, 12⅛" w, rural Dutch scene of horse and cart and other figures outside tavern, church and other animals set in wooded landscape in distance, c1880, sgd, "blue interlaced L's," framed (A)........ **6147.00**
Plate
   Catherine D'Estes cipher on white ground, dbl gold and green geometric and star border, c1840, 23 pcs (A)..................... **550.00**
   8¼" d, armorial crest surrounded by floral vining, peach border, early 19th C **275.00**
   9³⁄₁₆" d to 9⁹⁄₁₆" d, named botanical specimen in pink, rose, or purple within gilt foliate vine border on white ground, blue marbleized rim with gilt scallop and dot bellflower border, black enamel botanical inscriptions, "SEVRES, star and date marks for 1832 and 1833 within milled circle in blue," set of 8 (A)..................................**12,100.00**
   9⅜" d, hard paste, gold and platinum chinoiserie of two Orientals seated in gar-

den, one with bird perched on hand, other with fan, three chinoiserie scenes on border, black ground, c1790–95, "interlaced L's, crown and iron-red LG painters" marks (A)................................. **4753.00**
   9½" d
   Half portrait of Madame de Lamballe in puce period dress, floral border, turquoise and gold rim, "chateau" mark .. **295.00**
   Painted exotic bird in landscape, three bouquets in gilt open oval cartouches, gilt dentil rim, 1776, "blue interlaced L's and Y" mark, pr....................... **600.00**
   9⁹⁄₁₆" d, center with shaded pink and green rose spray against deep claret ground within gilt edged roundel encircled by border of gilt scallops and dots with pink, blue, and green flowers, inner rim edge with gilt band and pink gilt dotted ribbon beneath claret ground reserved with wide border of flower filled gilt ovals, "blue enamel interlaced L's, KK for 1788, p, 2000 for Henry-Francois Vincent jeune in gold, incised 24" marks (A)............. **2200.00**
   9⅝" d, sprays of summer flowers enclosed within molded scroll borders in blue and gilding, 18th C, "interlaced L's," 9 pcs (A) **4224.00**
   9¾" d, shaped form, central cluster of flowers, apple-green rim tooled in gilding with scrolls, foliage, and garlands enclosing three reserves of floral sprays, c1771, "blue interlaced L's with S, St. Andrews cross" marks (A)..................................... **7854.00**
   9⅞" d, colorful center with two peaches amidst cluster of flowers, gilt edged bleu celeste ground rim with three floral sprays within oval panels bordered in tooled gilt trellis diaper vignettes, foliate scrolls and floral sprays, "blue enamel interlaced L's, L for 1764, painter's mark for Guillaume Noel, incised L" marks (A)................... **1800.00**
   10" d, cabinet, courting couple, one with gilt decorated border, other with floral reserves on blue ground, 3rd qtr 19th C, pr (A) ... **110.00**
Platter, 13¼" l, oval, reserve of painted military camp scene with men and women at leisure, scrolling gilt border, cobalt scalloped rim (A) **605.00**
Potpourri Vase
   6½" h, 11⁹⁄₁₆" l, oval, colorful scene of two men checking ledger on barrel before mast of ship on front, reverse with Italianate river scene with small figures and boats, within tooled gilt oval, blue ground, gold and white husk-molded foliate loop handles, pierced border of arches and circlets forming neck, cov missing, repairs, 1775–80, "blue enamel interlaced L's" mark (A).............. **3850.00**
   9½" h, ogee form, scene of body and dog standing next to horse returning from hunt on front, reverse with flower arrangement, within gilt-tooled flower garlands, gros-bleu ground, pierced shoulders, twin tied acanthus handles, short stem, domed circ foot, ormolu mtd, c1763 (A) **2805.00**
Salad Bowl, 9" d, center floral spray, sprays alternating with leaves edged in gilt on border, green ground, c1758, " blue interlaced L's, painter's, letter date, incised FP" marks, pr (A)........**14,800.00**
Soup Plate, 9½" d, scattered flower sprigs, three kidney-shaped flower panels within apple-green border with gilt tooled floral gar-

lands, c1775, "blue and gray enamel interlaced L's, S" marks, set of 6 (A)........... **1400.00**

Sucrier, Cov

3⅝" h,

Ogee shape, floral garlands and purple shaded blue drapery pendent from three pairs of gilt stippled shaded pink oval panels beneath rose shaded blue crescents decorated with gilt trellis diaperwork, enclosing gilt shaded purple bellflowers, gilt dentil edged rim, gilt dashed bright blue border, c1765, unmarked (A)......... **990.00**

Trailing flowers along poles, gilding, domed cov with flower knob, puce ground, c1756, "blue enamel crowned interlaced L's and date code D" marks (A)....... **1275.00**

4¼" h, painted garlands of pink roses, laurel and gilt palm fronds in blue oeil-de-perdrix ground, restored fruit finial, 1777, "red interlaced L's and Z" mark (A)............ **385.00**

4⅝" h, front and reverse in rose, blue, purple, yellow, iron-red, and green with floral spray within white oval panel edged in tooled gilt foliate scrolls and floral sprays, reserved on blue ground, gilt dentil edge rim, cov with ranunculus sprig knob, c1760, unmarked (A)................................. **4675.00**

Teacup and Saucer

Bird perched on cream and brown ledge beside cluster of fruit below purple drapery, saucer with brown and yellow urn filled with colorful flowers and two melons, tooled gilt borders of floral swags, foliate scrolls, berry vine, and panels of scalework, gilt dentil edge, loop handle with gilt husks, "blue enamel interlaced L's, Z for 1777, L," incised with potent cross marks (A)...... **4950.00**

Blue, rose, yellow, green, brown, and black on front of cup with bird perched on tree in landscape, saucer with bird standing between flowering plant and tree, each in gilt edged oval panel, blue ground, gilt berried vine panels, gilt dentil border, entwined foliate handle, "blue enamel interlaced L's, L for 1764, N" for Francois Aloncle, incised OO on cup, 2 on saucer (A)............ **3300.00**

Ogee shape, straw hat in center with horn and torch, saucer with fruit filled cornucopia, sheaf of wheat, rake, sickle, spray of cornflowers tied with rose ribbon, within gilt roundels reserved on trelliswork ground of gilt-stippled diamond shaped panels with blue and black flowerheads separated by rose foliate vines, gilt edged rim, bolder of blue bellflowers against gilt striated border, "blue enamel interlaced L's, O for 1767, S, incised F" on cup marks (A)............ **4950.00**

Rose, blue, purple, yellow, and green floral spray within panel edged in gilt foliate scrolls and tooled floral sprays on cup and saucer, rose pompadour ground, gilt feathered handle, "blue enamel interlaced L's, H for 1760, incised OO on cup, 2 on saucer" marks (A)............................ **1430.00**

Urn shape, painted panel with courting couple, saucer has two panels with landscapes, gilt swag design, brown ground, "interlaced L's with S' (A)........................ **150.00**

Teapot

4⅝" h, ovoid, duck within gilt borders of

scrolls and flowers, bright colors, cov with gilt floral garland and flower knob, ear handle, c1763, "blue enamel interlaced L'S, K and N" marks (A)..................... **1589.00**

5¼" h, painted scattered roses between berried laurel borders and gilt dentil rims, scroll spout, and handle, dome cov with flower finials, c1775, "blue interlaced L's" mark (A)............................ **528.00**

Tray

5⅞" w, sq, center with cruciform floral garland pendent in sea green outlined in black, gilt dashed sea green and black band at edge, pierced rim with gilt edged white scrolls and black edged sea green bellflowers, repaired, "blue enamel interlaced L's, N for 1766, eighth-note for Antoine-Toussaint Cornailles, incised J.f and S.C." marks (A). **1100.00**

6⅞" l, oval, center in brown, green, purple, rose, blue, yellow, gray, and iron-red with basket of fruit behind primroses near spade against wheelbarrow, hilly river landscape, within gilt edged oval panel, white ground patterned with mustard, yellow, and green trelliswork, gilt rim, c1767, "blue enamel interlaced L's, painter's mark for Andre-Vincent Vielliard" marks (A)............... **3025.00**

9" d, circ, ftd, center with roundel painted in shades of rose, blue, yellow, iron-red, and green with floral cluster within tooled gilt foliate scrolls and floral sprays, scalloped low rim and foot with gilt band borders, wide blue band, "blue enamel interlaced L's, Q for 1769, painter's mark for Guillaume Noel' (A)...................... **1100.00**

11⅞" l, oval

Floral bouquets and sprays in center, gilt dentil edged rim painted with floral sprays between gilt dashed blue bands, gilt trimmed foliate scroll handles, 1753–60, "blue enamel interlaced L's centering a dot above painter's mark, incised 35 and 17" marks (A)................... **660.00**

Int painted with sprigs of rose centered blue cornflowers, green and yellow leaves, center edged with gilt band, gilt dentil edged rim, gilt trimmed foliate scroll handles, "blue enamel interlaced L's, vt, incised 34A" mark (A) **500.00**

Tureen, Cov, 10½" h, bouquets of fruits and flowers within blue feathered borders, cluster of artichoke and onion finial, four scroll feet, gilt foliate handles tied with blue ribbon, crack in base, knob restuck, c1765, incised "square" mark (A)................................. **1122.00**

Urn

6⅝" h, named tropical birds perched on branches in mountainous landscapes within reserves of gilt ribbon tied bulrushes and flower trails separated by flower swags on blue celeste ground, c1767, "blue enamel interlaced L's" and date letters, purple descriptive inscriptions, pr (A)............ **36,366.00**

14" h, baluster form, reserves of courting couple, landscape on reverse, yellow ground with gilt, scrolled handles, 19th C, pr (A).. **1760.00**

15½" h, gray painted winged nymph and lion on iron-red ground in diamond shaped gilt decorated medallion, gray painted chimeras and acanthus trimmed in gilt, sq plinth, pr.. **600.00**

Urn, Cov
8" h, medallion of lady in period clothes, dark green ground, ormolu mounts, artist sgd. . **295.00**
16½" h, oval shape, floral reserves, gilt trellis pattern, mask handle, artichoke finial on domed lid, lavender ground, repaired (A) . **600.00**
20½" h, cartouche of period dressed figures in landscape, flowers on reverse, azure blue ground, ormolu salamander handles, base, collar, and finial, sgd "G. Poitewin" (A) ... **1540.00**
22" h, center band of pastoral scene in soft colors, cobalt ground with gilt overlay, caryatid handles, late 19th C (A)........ **1760.00**
Vase
6¼" h, ovoid shape, band of stylized fabrics and geometric motifs in shades of puce, sea green, and pale lavender between gilt dot bands at the shoulder, 1926, red enamel factory marks, "black enamel LJM" for Louis-Jules Mimard (A)................. **660.00**
6¾" h, vert ribbed body, sang-de-boeuf dark red and crimson glaze, gilt metal base, c1885 (A)........................... **1500.00**
8⅝" h, tulip form, two panels painted with rural figures and animals in landscapes within gilt scroll and floral border, flared foot tooled with flower wreath, rims with gilt feathering, turned-over foliate handles, bleu lapis ground, c1756, restored, "blue interlaced L's with D, caduceus mark, 2 dots, incised 3," pr (A)..................... **5610.00**
11" h, lobed ovoid form, earthenware, streaked cobalt blue and turquoise glaze, neck with gilt bronze collar cast as berried leafage, foot with gilt bronze ring turned rim, c1900, "MP/SEVRES" within beaded circle, underglaze "black V" marks (A) ... **1375.00**
12" h, baluster shape, shaded light to dark blue glaze, c1900 .... **150.00**
13" h, four circ medallions molded with athletes either boxing, wrestling, throwing the javlin, or discus, blue ground gilded with laurel leaves and berries, flared neck with bi-planes against gray ground, printed "mar Decore a Sevres, S 1924 DN, MADE IN FRANCE< O D.V.GUILLONNET, BRACQUEMOND, INV SC, incised 2-7-24" marks (A)........................... **6584.00**
14⁵⁄₁₆" h, cylindrical shape, pale yellow sides incised with whiplash tendrils, central band molded in low relief with stylized flowers and leaves between dbl gilt borders, 1925, red enamel factory marks, "black enamel Leon-Charles Peluche' (A).............. **3025.00**
26³⁄₈" h, ovoid body, flared neck and feet, classical maidens surrounded by cherubs in gilded bordered cartouches on marbled blue gound, gilded rims, c1863–66, sgd "S. Jadelot, printed mark, S63," incised numerals, pr (A) **7285.00**
35⁷⁄₈" h, ovoid body, painted with continuous scene of Venus, Cupid, maidens, and cherubs at play in woodland setting, reserved on light blue and gilt ground, gilt metal mts, gilt wood foot, c1860, "blue interlaced L's" mark (A) **6375.00**
Vase, Cov, 8¾" h, colored cartouches of classical figures, instruments, and animals between dark and light brown border on yellow ground, highlighted in gilding, cracked, c1880,

one panel sgd "DT, AB" for Alexander Blanchard, "Decore a Sevres 82, S80," incised potter's marks............................. **600.00**
Wine Cooler, sprays of flowers, entwined ribbon borders, blue and gilt shell and scroll handles, c1764, "interlaced L's, painter's, letter date, incised DU" marks (A).................. **1400.00**

c1908

SHAVING MUGS

Austria, England, France, Germany c1850–1920

History: Many shaving or barber's mugs were manufactured of pottery or porcelain. Most mugs were shaped like coffee mugs; others had soap drainers and other features incorporated into the designs. Scuttles had double spouts. One spout was used for the razor, and the other for the shaving brush.

Many barber supply companies in the United States imported blank shaving mugs from Linoges and Sevres in France, from Victoria Carlsbad and Imperial Crown China in Austria, from C. T. Germany and Felda China Company in Germany, from A. J. Wilkinson and Goddard in England, and other scattered sources.

The imported, plain white, unadorned pottery or porcelain mugs were decorated in the suppliers' workshops. Shaving mugs were not meant to be ornamental. They were designed for the owner's personal use at his favorite barber shop where he went for a daily or weekly shave. Some people viewed their private mug a status symbol; others felt it was more hygenic for each man to have his own mug reserved for his personal use.

FRATERNAL

Fraternal shaving mugs bear symbols of the various fraternal orders such as Masons, Elks, Moose, etc. In addition, the Industrial Revolution furnished an incentive for American laborers to unite in national organizations, e.g., the Noble Order of the Knights of Labor and the Grand International Brotherhood of Locomotive Engineers. Symbols of these labor organizations found their way on to shaving mugs just as did the symbols of fraternal groups.

GENERAL

Shaving mugs appeared in quantity after the Civil War and flourished during the Victorian age. One style of mug featured a photograph of the owner or his family or a favorite painting. It was made by adding a photographic emulsion to the ceramic body and then burning in the resulting image in a kiln.

Simple mugs with the owner's name added to a stock floral design were produced by all the decorating workshops. Scenes of the popular sports of the day also found their way onto shaving mugs.

Mugs with simply a number in gilt were used in hotel barber shops. The number corresponded to the hotel room numbers. Decal decorated mugs from Germany contained reproductions of either important people, such as Napoleon or Sitting Bull, well known works of art, or animals, e.g., horses, dogs, etc.

Character shaving mugs, introduced into the United States about 1900, were manufactured in Austria and Bavaria until the start of World War I. Animal and fish heads were among the popular forms. Some mugs also advertised shaving products, e.g., Wildroot.

Barber shop shaving declined after World War I. Safety razors had been invented and perfected. Returning soldiers had learned to shave themselves. In addition, the Blue Laws forced barber shops to close on Sunday, a popular pre-war shaving day. By 1930 shaving at the barber shop was nearly at an end.

OCCUPATIONAL MUGS

Occupational mugs, indicating the owner's type of work, exist for almost every business, profession, or trade. The mug has a picture featuring the owner's occupation and his name in gold, either above or below the illustration. Lettering was usually in the old English style. Both indoor and outdoor trades were depicted. Some mugs had a scene portraying the owner working at his trade; others illustrated the working tools or emblem of the tradesman.

Collecting Hints: Many collections have been assembled that contain mugs representing over six hundred occupations. Uncommon jobs, such as deep sea diver, are difficult to locate. Mugs picturing obsolete occupations are prized highly by collectors. An occupational mug depicting a profession such as doctor or lawyer are harder to find since professionals were less likely to advertise themselves than were tradesman or neighborhood merchants.

References: Robert Blake Powell, *Antique Shaving Mugs of The United States,* published privately, 1978; W. Porter Ware, *Price List of Occupational & Society Emblems Shaving Mugs,* Lightner Publishing Corporation, 1949.

Collectors' Club: National Shaving Mug Collectors' Association, E. Maxine Cook, 818 S. Knight Ave., Park Ridge, IL 60068. Membership: $15.00, *Newsletter* quarterly.

Museums: Atwater Kent Museum, Philadelphia, Pa.; Fort Worth Museum of Science & History, Fort Worth, Texas; The Institute of Texas Cultures Museum, San Antonio, Texas; Lightner Museum, St. Augustine, Florida; The New York Historical Society, New York, New York.

REPRODUCTION ALERT: New shaving mugs are manufactured frequently as "replicas" of the past, but these should be recognized easily. Since they were used frequently, old shaving mugs should show definite signs of wear along the handle and the top and bottom rims. Currently Japanese companies are making reproduction "occupational" mugs in heavy porcelains similar to the earlier examples. Reproduction mugs from France and Germany appear to be hand painted but actually are printed by the silk screen process. An experienced collector can spot the difference.

FRATERNAL

Brotherhood of Railroad Trainmen, railroad lantern with wheel inscribed "B of R.R.T." with crossed red and green flags, multicolored flowers at sides, gold name (A) **60.00**
Foresters of America, multicolored emblem of two American flags, deer's head in center with "Liberty, Unity, Benevolence, and Concord"

in circle, worn gold name, "T & V Limoges France" mark (A) **60.00**
Fraternal Order of the Elk, eagle holding two American flags flanked by gold sprigs, "gold F.O.E." and name (A) **35.00**

3½" h, gold Masonic emblem with blue "G" in center, blue and gold flowers, gold "N. WEBB," gold base and trim, unmkd, $110.00

Jr O.U.A.M., emblem of arm holding hammer, inscribed "Virtue, Liberty, Patriotism 23 Jr O.U.A.M." eagle on top of emblem, two American flags and gilt sprigs at sides, worn gold name (A) **90.00**
Knights of Pythias, gold name, knicks on rim . .   **135.00**
Knights of Tented Macabees (K.O.T.C.) hp emblem and florals, gold name, "T & V Limoges" mark **110.00**
Knights Templar, gold crown with red cross through middle, gilt decorations, gold name (A) **170.00**
Large gold eye with lashes and eyebrow, bible, sword, and name, I.O.O.F. **125.00**
Loyal Order of the Moose, multicolored transfer of moose head with gold wreaths, gold name, "P Germany" mark (A) **130.00**
Masonic, design in black, purple and Sunderland luster **300.00**
Odd Fellows
    Gilt emblem of three interlocking rings, gold band at rim and base, gold name (A) **35.00**
    Seeing eye, three interlocking circles, bible, and sword in colors, gold name, "Alpha, T & V Limoges France" mark (A) **25.00**
Shield with two crossed swords and K G E F H V, cross and crown, eye with three interlocking rings below, multicolored, gold script name, "Leonard, Vienna, Austria" mark (A). **450.00**
Wheel, calipers and "T" sq, "gold I.A.M." **110.00**
Woodsmen of the World,- tree stump marked "Dum Tacet Clamat," ax and hammer in front of stump, ax blade in top of stump, dove with sprig in flight, multicolored, "GOA France" mark (A). **130.00**

GENERAL

Arched red brick bridge over stream with mountains in ground, reverse with panoramic view of meadow, trees, fence, and red roofed barn, Gold name in banner, "Leonard, Vienna, Austria" mark (A). **230.00**
Bakery van in blue, black, red, and brown, pulled by two white horses, man sitting inside, "286

Genesee St. Lorenz Bakery, Genesee, Gra-
nacher, 286 Street" on van, gold name and
trim (A) **800.00**
Baseball player running to next base, coach in
ground, multicolored, gold trim (A) **60.00**
Bird dog with bird in mouth flanked by purple
and green cattails, gold name and rim (A). . .   **150.00**

4" h, gold "L.W. Eldred," rose ground, c1880,
"H. & Co." mark, $45.00

Black and white scene of girls sitting on brick wall
reading paper, gold name **95.00**
Blue painted ground with multicolored flowers
and gold "Lenzii Carmine" in diagonal banner
(A). **100.00**
English fox hunt scene in colors, "Germany"
mark. **85.00**
Fishermen, one seated in boat, other holding
string of fish, trees and rocks in ground, black
back, gold name in medallion (A) **500.00**
Floral decal with raised swirls **39.00**
Floral wreath with John R. Beisel in center, "T &
V Limoges" mark. **22.00**
Flow blue "Triumph" pattern **65.00**
Flowers, 3 1/2" h, raised flowers and leaves, mint
green and cobalt, Germany **40.00**
Flying eagle in front of Statue of Liberty, railroad
engine and steam boat in ground, fuchsia re-
verse, gold name in arch (A). **210.00**
Four emb irises, red, pink, and yellow poppies,
blue and ivory ground, "red R.S. Prussia" mark .   **295.00**
Gold name "Planner" in large black rect (A) . .   **25.00**
Gray horse, white horse in green meadow, light-
ning bolt in stormy sky, gilt floral decorations,
gold name (A) **310.00**
HP yellow roses with red centers, incised "Ger-
many" mark **39.00**
Irid with classical figure on green ground **49.00**
Lady's size, hp florals on body, handles, and
brush **95.00**
Large pink roses with green stems, gold name, "T
& V Limoges" mark (A) **50.00**
Multicolored pansies on blue ground, gold name
in white and yellow ribbon, black reverse (A)   **60.00**
Orange flowers, green leaves, yellow and green
ground, "C.T. Germany" mark **45.00**
Painted horse's head. **85.00**
Patriotic design, spread winged eagle holding
two American flags on top of globe, light blue
ground, interwoven framework and pink roses
surround eagle, gold name in banner, "1190 T
& V Limoges, France" mark (A) **160.00**
Pheasant and evergreens on white ground, "red
R.S. Prussia" mark **395.00**

Pink luster, relief of lily of the valley and leaves on
oct body, pierced soap shelf with gilt flower
spray, scrolled base, twig handle **40.00**
Portrait of woman in white and brown gown, hat
with red ribbon and white plumes **65.00**
Red roses and gilt swirls, unmarked (A) **25.00**
Robin in flight to nest with three eggs, large pink
flower on reverse, yellow ground with gilt
squiggles, diagonal band with gold name,
"KPM Germany" mark (A) **170.00**
Scuttle
2 1/8" h, portrait of long haired maiden, cream
and turquoise ground. **115.00**
3 1/2" h, small purple asters, brown leaves and
vines, white ground **45.00**
Norwich coat of arms on front. **65.00**
Pink fish with open mouth **115.00**
Small red roses, R.S. Germany **135.00**
Spread winged owl sitting on tree branch, cres-
cent moon on blue ground, gold name, "T &
V Limoges" mark (A) **140.00**
State seal of PA, two black horses rearing on
each side of cartouche with sailboat, eagle and
"Virtue, Liberty, and Independence," 'H &
Co." mark (A). **40.00**
Tea leaf ironstone, 3 1/8" h, "Bamboo" pattern,
c1800s, Grindley **110.00**
Two blue birds sitting on branch of flowering
bush, blue-green ground, gold name and trim,
"T & V France/ME Waite, Barber Supplies,
Utica, N.Y." mark (A) **140.00**
Two Section
Polychrome scene of water mill near flowing
stream, mountains in ground (A) **5.00**
Scattered florals with molded dots and swirls
(A). **10.00**
White ironstone, "Block Optic" pattern **60.00**

OCCUPATIONAL

Artesian Well Driller, name and wreath in gilt,
hairline (A). **110.00**
Artist, paint palette in colors, intertwined initials .   **350.00**

3 1/2" h, railroad engineer, multicolored transfer
of Michigan Central Railway, "green Limoges,
France" mark, $525.00

Baker, man placing two loaves of bread in red
brick oven, shelf of bread and tools in ground,
flour barrel, water bucket, firewood, and stool
on floor, gold name, "CFH GDM" mark (A).   **375.00**
Barber, three barbers in white coats with clients
in chairs, side wall with bottles and mirrors,
back wall with door marked "Bath Room,"

mug rack and pictures, three men seated waiting for barbers, gilt name, "T & V Limoges, France" mark (A).......................... **700.00**

Bartender, multicolored scene of bartender putting money in register, four patrons at bar, mirrored ground, gold name, "Vienna, Austria" mark (A).......................... **170.00**

Beef Grower, brown and white steer standing in green pasture, gold name (A).............. **90.00**

Bricklayer, man in white apron with trowel standing in front of salmon colored brick wall, bricks and mortar on ground, gold name, "D & C" mark (A)................................. **300.00**

Brick Maker, man in apron and hat stands in front of brown workbench with pile of bricks, wooden building and shed roof in ground, gold name, "D & C" mark (A)............. **650.00**

Broommaker, cartouche of broom flanked by flowers and gold name, royal blue ground, "Germany" mark (A) **410.00**

Buggy Driver, multicolored scene of gentlemen driving buggy, gold "HOMER H. CONN"... **475.00**

Butcher, multicolored cow head and butcher tools, gold name **200.00**

Cabinet Maker, man sawing board in shop with tools on floor, wall, and bench, nail keg in foreground, border of red, yellow, blue, and green florals, gold name, repaired base (A).. **130.00**

Cashier, man standing behind ornate counter with bars marked "Cashier," man in top hat and coat stands in front of cashier, gold vining (A)....................................... **700.00**

Cattleman, man in top hat and coat leading white blanketed steer by rope, brass caps on horns, green foreground, gold name, repaired chip on base (A)................................. **370.00**

Chauffeur, man in gray uniform and hat driving red convertible with green tufted seats, blue and green ground, gold name (A)......... **1300.00**

Coachman, multicolored scene of closed coach, seated driver in top hat, blanket on lap, two horses, gold name........................ **595.00**

Delivery Man, man driving black delivery truck with green stake bed, brown floor, black top, gold name, hairline (A)................... **750.00**

Dentist, man in smock working on patient in chair, table of instruments, "Dentist" sign on wall with colored bottles, mint green ground, gold name and trim (A) **1500.00**

Distiller, barrel marked "Whiskey," brown foreground, gold name (A)................... **260.00**

Doctor

Multicolored scene of horse and buggy with doctor emerging carrying bag, "gold R.D.K." in green panel................. **385.00**

Sitting in chair next to patient in bed taking pulse with watch, curtained window with top hat on table to left, oriental rug and patterned green floor, "gilt D.F. Shea, MD/ Physician & Surgeon," amber reverse (A) . **7600.00**

Dog Trainer, black dog with show stance, trade sign in mouth with man's name........... **495.00**

Duck Hunter, brown and white dog with duck in mouth, crossed shotgun and oar in front of dog, two men in boat shooting ducks in ground, multicolored, gold name, repaired chip on base, "Limoges France" mark (A)... **250.00**

Farmer, man plowing green pasture with two brown horses, fence and farm buildings in ground, blue sky, "gilt 4" on sides, gold name (A)....................................... **500.00**

Farrier, man in brown pants, yellow apron and red shirt shoeing Appaloosa horse in shop with plank floor, stone forge and red-brown brick walls, horseshoes, forge, and anvil in ground, gilt floral border, gold name, "Limoges, France" mark (A) **450.00**

Fireman

Driving gold-brown steam pumper pulled by gray horses, fireman on rear of pumper, traces of gilt and name, crack in handle and base (A)................................ **420.00**

Man in fire coat and helmet next to horse-drawn hook and ladder marked "Gilchrist H.& L. No.1," ladders on wagon, twelve helmets hanging from top rail and ropes from rear, two horses in front, black vining trim, gold name, "T & V" mark (A)........... **900.00**

Furniture Manufacturer, Eastlake parlor suite with purple, red, and green upholstery, gilt floral decoration and name (A) **475.00**

Gambler, multicolored horseshoe and four leaf clover, gold "James P. Diamond" **135.00**

Glass Blower, multicolored scene of one man blowing glass, one man rolling glass, gold name **1250.00**

Grist Mill Operator, two brown barrels marked "Flour," gilt border, fuchsia reverse, gold name (A)................................. **1400.00**

Haberdasher, black derby surrounded by pink roses and blue flowers, gold name (A)...... **320.00**

Hotel Clerk, clerk behind desk, gold "Edw. J. Sanders" **595.00**

Lighthouse Keeper, multicolored scene of lighthouse on rocks, three sailboats and birds in ground, yellow and purple flowers on side, gold name in banner (A) **210.00**

Lineman

Telephone pole with two crossed arms with insulators and lines, multicolored sky, gold name, "Limoges W.G.& Co. France" mark (A)................................... **425.00**

Wire cutting pliers in colors, gold name, "T & V Limoges" mark...................... **365.00**

Locomotive Engineer

Multicolored scene of engine,(faded), gold "R.G. Rackley"........................ **65.00**

Transfer with gilt trim, "M.D. Colbert, Limoges, France" mark **225.00**

Machine Operator, multicolored, Germany.... **750.00**

Medical Student, red and green pennant with "M.C." gilt sprigs, gold name (A).......... **320.00**

Milkman, red, green, and beige wagon marked "Pure Milk" pulled by brown horse, driver in blue suit getting milk from wagon, shaded blue, yellow, green, and salmon ground, reverse in blue, gold name, "Felda China EST Germany" mark (A) **525.00**

Musician, yellow cornet outlined in amber, flanked by gilt sprigs, gold name, "Fred Dolle W.G. Co./France" mark (A)................ **200.00**

Oil Well Driller, multicolored panoramic view of three well derricks in field, cabin with smoking stack, pump, storage barrels, ground of trees, rail fence, mountains, and field, gold name, "GDS France" mark (A).................... **525.00**

Painter, man in white overalls sitting on hoist with bucket of paint, painting house wall with windows, gilt sprigs on sides, gold name and trim, spider cracks (A)..................... **160.00**

Pharmacist, mortar and pestle in colors, gold name **50.00**

Pianist, man sitting on stool playing upright piano, wooden floor, light green walls, gilt sprigs, gold name, imp "Germany" mark (A) **1200.00**

Piano Maker, multicolored scene of Victorian grand piano marked "Blasius" with white and gray lined ground and floor, gold name, large chip of base, "Leonard" mark (A) **250.00**

Plumber, multicolored scene of Victorian bathroom, gold name **195.00**

Pretzel Maker, large pretzel on side, gold name and trim, chip on rear base (A) **140.00**

Printer, multicolored printer and cabinet, gold name **200.00**

Sailor, multicolored scene of battleship Indiana with sailors on deck, ships, birds and mountains in ground, gold name, "V & D Austria" mark (A). **2900.00**

Salesman, multicolored scene of arm with calling card, hairline. **295.00**

Shoe Salesman, multicolored scene of lady sitting in chair, man fitting shoe, brown counter, shelves with boxes in ground, gold name, chip on side, "KPM Germany" mark (A) **200.00**

Tailor, man sitting at table sewing blue garment, ground with ruler, measuring tape, and window, iron and ironing board under table, gold name, chip on rim, "CFH GDM" mark (A) . . **130.00**

Telegrapher, black telegraph key with yellow knobs, brown stand, gold name, "T & V Limoges" mark (A) **260.00**

Tinsmith, shears, hammer, and soldering iron crossed in middle, mint green ground, reverse with gilt vining, gold name, crack on side (A) **120.00**

Trainman, red box car with open door, blue-green ground, gold name, "Koken Barber Supply Co. St. Louis, Limoges France W.C.& Co." mark (A). **370.00**

Trolley Car Conductor, multicolored scene of trolley, passengers, and conductor, gold name **250.00**

Typesetter, man standing at table sorting type dressed in colonial clothes, tricorn hat on wall, gold name (A) **350.00**

Watch Salesman, gold pocket watch marked "Waltham," gold name, "T & V Limoges France" mark (A). **300.00**

1890-1910   1925-1945

SHELLEY

Longton, England
Mid-18th Century to Present

History: Members of the Shelley family manufactured pottery at Lane End beginning in the middle of the 18th century. In 1872 Joseph Shelley formed a partnership with James Wileman of Wileman & Co., operator of the Foley China Works. For the next fifty years the firm used the name Wileman & Co. Percy, Joseph Shelley's son, joined the firm in 1881. Percy became an excellent potter. During his fifty years as head of the firm, he developed the lasting reputation of Shelley china.

During the 1880s only average quality china was made. Pieces featured one color and poor quality transfers. Percy hired artists to produce dinner services with more elaborate decorations that were intended for the export market. During the 1890s the wares were more varied, featuring finer patterns and better colorations.

When Joseph died in 1896, Percy assumed complete control. The artist Rowland Morris modeled "Dainty White," the company's most successfully produced shape until 1966. The shape also was used for many pieces of commemorative ware.

Frederick Rhead, who trained under Solon at Minton and worked at Wedgwood, was employed as artistic director. Rhead introduced Intarsio, Spano-Lustra, Urbato, Primitf, and Pastello wares, a series of effects used on earthenwares. Intarsio was the most popular. A large number of patterns and styles were made.

Although the firm was still called Wileman & Co. in 1910, the mark utilized the Shelley family name enclosed in an outline shield shape. The art director now was Walter Slater who had been an apprentice at Minton and spent twenty years working at Doulton.

A new series of Intarsio ware that reflected Art Nouveau motifs was introduced in 1911. Flamboyant ware with flambe glazes and Cloisello ware followed. Under Slater's direction, bone china was developed. Before World War I, Shelley's china dinner services were very popular in the American market.

After the war, Percy's three sons were involved in the firm. By 1922 miniature objects, heraldic and coat of arms, souvenir china and earthenware with engraved views of places of interest, and Parian busts of military figures were produced in quantity. During the 1920s, many styles of teawares were made. "Eggshell china" refered to the thinness of the china. In 1925 the firm's name was changed to Shelley's. Nursery wares decorated by Hilda Cowham and Mabel Lucie Atwell came to the forefront along with "semi-porcelain" domestic china.

Percy retired in 1932. The delicate teawares of the 1920s and 1930s established Shelley's reputation. The Queen Anne octagonal shape is one of the best known forms. More modern shapes such as Vogue and Mode were introduced during the Art Deco period.

After World War II, earthenwares were discontinued. China dinnerwares remained in production. Lithographic techniques replaced the "print and enamel" decorations.

In 1965 the firm was renamed Shelley China Ltd. It was acquired by Allied English Potteries in 1966. The family connection with the firm finally ended. Allied merged with the Doulton Group in 1971.

References: Chris Watkins, William Harvey, and Robert Senft, *Shelley Potteries,* Barrie & Jenkins, 1980.

Ashtray

3½" d, Harebell pattern **20.00**

4" d, Stocks pattern, six flutes **25.00**

5" d, Begonia pattern. **15.00**

Bouillon Cup and Saucer

Pink Paisley pattern. **40.00**

Shades of rust on white, Wildman. **38.00**

Butter Dish, Cov, with drain, blue Greek key with pink roses, gold trim. **80.00**

Candy Dish, 4½" d, Crochet pattern, white with blue trim **25.00**

Casserole, Cov, red flowers and green berries, black leaves **40.00**

Cup and Saucer, "Dainty Blue" design in blue and white, $75.00

Cereal Bowl, 6 1/4" d
Blue Rock pattern 30.00
Melody pattern, green trim 40.00
Coffee Pot
6 1/2" h, Blue Rock pattern, six flutes 175.00
7 1/2" h, vert flowers, gold handle and foot, six
flutes 150.00
8 1/4" h, roses with gold leaves 175.00
Coffee Set, Demitasse
Pot, 7" h, cream and sugar, 6 cups and sau-
cers, beige with gold rims, handles, and
feet.................................. 200.00
Pot, cream and sugar, plate, 7" d, plate, 8 1/4"
d, 6 cups and saucers, Blue Phlox pattern,
Regent shape, #W070 .... 425.00
Cream and Sugar
Begonia pattern 30.00
Blue Rock pattern, six flutes 50.00
Daffodil Time pattern 35.00
Pale yellow shaded to pink, gold trim....... 50.00
Primrose pattern, six flutes 40.00
Regency pattern........................ 30.00
Spurge pattern, gray and green flowers with
yellow centers, green handles and border,
white ground, #012391 .... 30.00
Small yellow flowers with green leaves, gold
trim................................ 50.00
Stocks pattern, six flutes 45.00
Cream Pitcher, faience, one side with two boats,
reverse with sailboats, brown and green, Wild-
man 45.00
Cup and Saucer
Begonia pattern, six flutes 38.00
Blue Rock, six flutes 45.00
Bridal Rose, six flutes 45.00
Daffodil Time pattern 35.00
Dainty Blue pattern, six flutes.............. 38.00
English Lakes pattern, gold trim, #13788 ... 38.00
Indian Peony pattern, green peonies with dark
gray leaves, white ground, #13216...... 35.00
Lily of the Valley pattern
Six flutes 38.00
Fourteen flutes....................... 38.00
Old Mill pattern, blue handle, notched gold
rim 38.00
Pink roses and buds with yellow and blue
flowers, #2500....................... 40.00
Primrose Chintz pattern, pink trim.......... 38.00
Regency pattern, six flutes................ 30.00
Rose Pansey FMN
Six flutes 38.00
Fourteen flutes....................... 38.00
Rose Sprays pattern 30.00
Stocks pattern......................... 30.00
Summer Glory pattern 48.00

Tapestry Rose, yellow with gray flowers,
#13125 .... 40.00
Wild Anemone pattern, fourteen flutes 50.00
Cup and Saucer, Demitasse
Begonia pattern, sixteen flutes............. 38.00
Blue Rock pattern, sixteen flutes 38.00
Celandine pattern, six flutes 38.00
Daffodil pattern 38.00
Heather pattern 38.00
Lily of the Valley pattern, six flutes 38.00
Melody pattern
Blue trim, gold rim 38.00
Green trim 40.00
Primrose Chintz pattern, pink handle and
trim................................. 38.00
Red flowers and green berries, black leaves. 35.00
Rose and Red Daisy design, sixteen flutes .. 38.00
Rosebud pattern, sixteen flutes 40.00
Rose Spray pattern, sixteen flutes 38.00
Queen Anne shape, white and gold........ 38.00
Regent shape, green and beige 38.00
Stocks pattern, pink and green border, green
foot and handle...................... 38.00
Violet pattern, sixteen flutes 38.00
Woodland pattern, blue handle, gold trim... 38.00
Egg Cup
Harebell pattern........................ 40.00
Primrose pattern, six flutes 50.00
Regency pattern, six flutes................ 50.00
Rose and Red Daisy pattern, six flutes...... 60.00
Rose Spray pattern, six flutes 50.00
Mustard, Cov, six flutes
Rose and Red Daisy pattern 65.00
Wild Anemone pattern................... 40.00
Nappy
Begonia pattern, six flutes 25.00
Rose and Red Daisy pattern, six flutes...... 25.00
Plate
5 1/2" d, orange and yellow asters 15.00
5 3/4" d, Melody pattern, green trim........ 20.00
6" d
Begonia pattern, six flutes............... 25.00
Dainty White pattern, six flutes 25.00
DuBarry pattern........................ 25.00
Harebell pattern........................ 25.00
Indian Peony pattern, green peonies with
dark gray leaves, white ground,
#13216 .... 25.00
Primrose pattern, six flutes 25.00
Regency pattern, six flutes 25.00
Rosebud pattern, six flutes 25.00
Rose and Red Daisy pattern, six flutes.... 25.00
Rose Pansey FMN, six flutes............. 25.00
6 1/2" d
Meissenette pattern, six flutes 25.00
Rose and Red Daisy pattern, six flutes.... 25.00
7" d
Aqua, rust, and green small flowers, fluted 20.00
Red flowers with green berries, black
leaves.............................. 25.00
Rose and Red Daisy pattern, six flutes.... 30.00
Wildflower pattern, six flutes 25.00
7 1/2" d, Dainty Brown pattern, six flutes ... 40.00
8" d
Begonia pattern, six flutes............... 30.00
Bouquet of flowers on rim 25.00
Chain of blue flowers, dark blue trim, six
flutes 35.00
Crochet pattern #13303 .... 25.00
Dark rose with white roses and gray leaves. 30.00

Maytime pattern	30.00
Morning Glory pattern, six flutes	30.00
Pink with small gold stars	30.00
Rosebud pattern, six flutes	24.00
Tapestry Rose pattern, yellow and gray, #13125	30.00
9" d, sheet aqua pattern, Wildman	25.00
9½" d, Rosebud pattern, six flutes	50.00
10" d, green floral border, fluted gold trim, Wildman	40.00
10¾" d	
Begonia pattern, six flutes	60.00
Rosebud pattern, six flutes	55.00
White with silver trim, six flutes	50.00
11" d, Spring Bouquet pattern	40.00

Platter

12" l, Rose Spray pattern, six flutes	85.00
14" l, 12" w, DuBarry pattern	50.00
15" l, 12" w, Harebell pattern	85.00
16½" l, 13½" w, yellow flowers, gray leaves, white ground, #1227x	50.00

Pudding Mold, 5" h, 7" d, overall white glaze.	65.00
Ring Holder, Blue Calico pattern	50.00
Serving Plate, 8" d, violet flower border, Wildman	35.00
Tea and Toast Plate, 8" d, Violet pattern, six flutes	60.00
Teapot, 4½" h, Wildflower pattern	125.00
Toilet Set, bowl, pitcher, chamber pot,(missing lid), toothbrush holder, jar,(missing cov), cov soap dish, 2 cov boxes, ring holder, vase, and tray, Roself pattern	975.00

Trio, Cup, Saucer, Plate

Begonia pattern, six flutes	65.00
Blue Rock pattern	60.00
Crochet, plate, 6" d, #13303	40.00
Crocus pattern, plate, 7" d	55.00
Dainty White pattern, demitasse cup and saucer, plate, 5" d, six flutes	40.00
Dark pink flowers on pink ground, gold trim, notched rims	65.00
Duchess pattern	68.00
English Sprig pattern	65.00
Eve shape, yellow tulips and pansies, c1931.	125.00
Heather pattern	60.00
Maytime pattern, gold trim, plate, 8" d	70.00
Melody pattern, plate, 6" d	55.00
Primrose pattern	60.00
Rust red and black enameled flowered borders, gold trim, plate, 7" d, Wildman	50.00
Queen Anne shape, Tall Trees pattern, c1929	125.00
Spurge pattern, plate, 7" d, green and gray flowers with yellow centers, white ground, green border and handles, #012391	40.00
Wildflower pattern, plate, 6" d	50.00

Vase

3¼" h, black with multicolored bird, orange int	60.00
5" h	
Black base with pink, orchid, and blue flowered border	45.00
Multicolored drip glaze	50.00
6½" h, shaded light green to orange, pr	55.00
7" h, Intarsia, long legged birds with wide wings in flight, orange ground	45.00

Vegetable Bowl

Cov, 9" d, Harebell pattern	100.00
Open, 9¼" d, Harebell pattern	85.00

c1902   c1887

SITZENDORF

**Thuringia, Germany
1845 to Present**

History: A small porcelain factory was founded in 1845 in Thuringia. The Voight brothers managed the factory from 1850 until about 1900. They produced decorative figures and porcelains in the Meissen style.

At the turn of the century, the factory was called Alfred Voight AG. Within a few years the name was changed to Sitzendorf Porcelain Manufactory, its earlier designation. In 1923 earthenware were added.

The company was semi-nationlized in 1957 and completely nationlized in 1972. The current name is VEB Sitzendorf Porcelain Manufactory.

Candelabra, 14½" h, two children seated on baroque base, floral panel, four candle arms, c1850, "Voight" mark	375.00
Candlestick, 15" h, cherub with arm around candlestick, flower decorated base, marked	350.00
Center Bowl	
12½" l, 6½" h, open basketweave bowl, small painted flowers in inside and out, two figural standing cherubs at ends	675.00
17" l, 15" w, 10" h, three figural cherubs supporting conch shell with applied primroses in pink, blue, green, and yellow, chips	750.00

Figure, male in yellow jacket, green striped pants, black hat, female in turquoise jacket, basket of fruit, floral bases, "blue crowned S and dashes" mk, pr, (A) $154.00

Figure
4½" h, girl holding baby with cradle in colors 50.00
6" h, monkey band set, each in colorful costume playing a different instrument, 9 pcs, base marked......................... 850.00
8" h, hunting man or woman with dogs and rifles in colors, pr...................... 300.00
9" h, man in blue coat with tan trousers and a watering can, woman in white floral dress with basket of flowers, pr 325.00
9½" h
Man sowing seeds in colors, marked 100.00
Young man on ladder picking apples from tree, girl below with apples in apron, dog under ladder, multicolored 650.00
10" l, 9" h, lady seated on couch in white floral dress trimmed in pink and green, man standing at end in red coat holding hat with bow, two Russian wolfhounds in front of lady................................... 850.00
15" l, seated Roman lady in red toga, man in blue toga standing behind table on balcony, maidens serving wine, three girls in front, one riding chariot pulled by cheetahs 1950.00
17" l
Man in blue coat seated in chair looking at painting on easel, artist in ground flirting with his wife, oval plinth with flowers, base marked....................... 850.00
Slave trader presenting girl to Roman noble, slave and two dogs at side and back, two slave girls in rear, multicolored, full mark on base.......................... 1250.00
Mirror Frame
17¼" h, oval shape, molded and brightly colored florets and foliage, surmounted by two winged putti holding garland, two putti on sides, base with two scroll sconce supports, late 19th C, pr (A)..................... 467.00
33" h, waisted rect shape, surmounted by smaller mirror, applied cupids, flowers, and foliage in bright colors, gilded, base with three scroll candle holders and sconces, c1880, underglaze "blue crowned S" mark (A).................................. 1800.00
Perfume Bottle, 5" h, figural girl in blue luster dress with two black bows in front, flowers on side of skirt, holding pink feather on shoulder, brown hair, "crown" mark 60.00
Plaque, 12" d, seated girl and goat in high relief, blond hair with beaded headdress and gold floral leaf decor around rim, cream ground, c1885, Voight......................... 550.00
Powder Box, 5¼" h, figural girl in faded green luster dress with purple trim, fan and feather in white wide brim hat, "crown" mark 60.00
Vase, 8" h, 7" d, maiden scene with floral multicolored panels, three handles, large paw feet, 1830, "Voight" mark 225.00
Vase, Cov
8" h, panel of classic maidens, two panels of flowers, three handles, three paw feet, c1850, Voight Bros. 175.00
16" h, reserve of printed classical woodland scene framed in multicolored flowers, applied putto with raised cups and flowers on foot, pierced cov with putti raising flowers, pr 550.00

SLIPWARE

Staffordshire, England
Continental
17th C to Present

History: Slip is powdered clay that is mixed with water until a cream-like consistency is achieved. The slip then can be used to decorate pottery in a variety of ways such as trailing, marbling, combing, feathering, and sgraffito.

Trailing is decorating by means of extruding slip or glaze through a nozzle onto the surface of the piece.

Marbling is achieved by trailing different colored slips onto a form that is then either shaken or twisted to produce the pattern.

Combing is done by applying slip and then wiping over the piece with a toothed or pronged instrument or by using the fingers.

Feathering occurs by trailing a line of slip onto a wet ground of a contrasting color. The tip of a feather or another flexible, thin point is then drawn back and forth across the trailed line.

Sgraffito is achieved by cutting, incising, or scratching away a slip coating to reveal the contrasting slip or body underneath.

Colored slips are made by adding a small amount of various oxides to the slip. Slip was an early method to embellish ordinary clay-colored pottery. After the slip decorations were done, the vessel was covered with a lead glaze in order to make it non-porous and to produce a shiny surface. Slip decoration was used from the 17th century until the present time.

Slipware was made mainly at Wrotham in Kent in Staffordshire. Other manufacturing centers include Essex, Sussex, Somerset, and Devonshire. The earliest piece from Wrotham is dated 1612.

Between 1670 and 1710 the most spectacular pieces of slipware made in Staffordshire were large chargers made by the Tofts, John and William Wright, George Taylor, William Taylor, and Ralph Simpson. Favorite subjects included royal scenes, portraits of popular figures, and cavaliers. Coats of arms, mermaids, Adam & Eve, and the Pelican in her piety were used. Borders usually had a trellis pattern. Human figures had minimal anatomical details and were painted in a naive fashion. Forms that were slip decorated include tygs, teapots, cradles, baking dishes, puzzle jugs, posset pots, whistles, etc.

Potteries in Devon made large harvest jugs using the sgraffito technique. Decorations included coats of arms, lions, unicorns, ships, mariners' compasses, and floral designs.

Wrotham slip decorated wares continued to be made until the end of the 18th century. Fleur-de-lis, roses, crosses, stars, and masks were frequent motifs. Tygs, posset pots, two-handled mugs and cnadlesticks were made. A distinctive feature of Wrotham ware was handles made by weaving different colored clays together.

Reference: R. G. Cooper, *English Slipware Dishes 1650–1850*, Tiranti, 1968.

Museums: County Museum, Truro, England; Gardiner Museum of Ceramic Art, Toronto, Canada; Kansas City Art Museum, Kansas City, Missouri; Plymouth City Museum, Plymouth, England; Royal Albert Museum, Exeter, England; Sheffield City Museum, Sheffield, England.

Baking Dish
11" l, rect, creamy yellow slip on brown ground, inscribed "BEEF," 19th C (A)..... 510.00

Sweetmeat Stand, 6⅝" d, buff ground, lt yellow slip between bowls, dk brown dashes, late 17th C, (A) $560.00; 8¼" d, buff ground, straw colored slip between bowls, dk brown slip outlined bowls and lug handles, late 17th C, (A) $1310.00

13¼" l
  Circ, cream colored slip with checker pattern on dark brown ground, late 18th C (A) 1200.00
  Rect, dark brown body with cream squiggles, notched rim, late 18th C (A)...... 1300.00
  16½" d, circ, center with embossed "I.B." skeletal design in cream slip, uneven brown ground, notched rim, mid 18th C (A)..... 4675.00
  16¾" l, rect, three triple line squiggles in cream slip, dark brown ground, late 18th C (A)................................. 1190.00
  16⅞" l, 15⅛" w, cream slip geometrics on dark brown ground, England 2000.00
Bowl
  6¾" d, brown-black dip and runny glaze, int with vert trails of cream slip, ext with band of slipped motifs, applied small looped handle, int base with hollow spike, early 18th C, chips (A) 1600.00
  7¼" d, 2¾" h, redware body, yellow slip scroll design (A)...................... 33.00
  8½" d, redware body with yellow slip design (A)................................. 33.00
  13" d, redware body, coggled rim, 2 line yellow slip decoration (A)................. 38.00
  13½" d, redware with sieve holes, comb decorated yellow slip, coggled rim, incised repaired hairline, "B.A. 1752" (A)........ 1400.00
  14" d, redware body, yellow slip int with brown slip polka dot bird, repaired (A) ... 2300.00
Collander, 11" d, yellowware body with green glaze rim (A).......................... 22.00
Creamer, 3¾" h, redware body, leaf design in yellow slip, European (A)................. 50.00
Dish
  7¼" d, redware, yellow slip designs (A) ... 125.00
  10¼" d, cream slip trellis pattern, dark brown ground, England....................... 350.00
  11¼" d, press molded, center with figure of stag in dark brown slip, molded initials "I C," concentric borders of linked triangles and lozenges, cockle shell rim, pierced for hanging, early 18th C, Staffordshire (A) 21,054.00
  12½" l, yellow glazed ground carved with stylized peacock enclosed by large trailing flowering plant and inscription "1:7:9:3:H;R:," brown and green, German (A)................................... 555.00
  13¾" d, brown slip stylized bird and "1790,"

dots and squiggles, cream ground, dark brown pie crust rim (A)................11,100.00
16¾" d, glazed redware body decorated in high relief with scene of "The Sacrifice of Isaac" in heightened yellow, green, and dark brown slip beneath 1773, yellow edged rim with meandering yellow vine of stylized oak leaves and acorns heightened in green, reverse unglazed, North German (A)................................. 2750.00
Egg Stand, 7¼" d, cylindrical body, dark brown body, sq openings, domed top with round openings, dbl fleur-de-lys in cream slip, int with central warming dish, early 18th C (A) . 3000.00
Figure
  4½" h, overall creamy slip and yellowish lead glaze seated cat, chocolate brown squiggles, brown slip eyes, rect base, 18th C, Staffordshire (A)....................... 1575.00
  5" h, brown-red seated cat with mouse in mouth, yellow slip swirls, restoration to ears and base, late 18th C (A) 360.00
  6" h, seated cat with tan slip body and brown splashes and streaks, oval base, restored, late 18th C (A)....................... 605.00
  8" l, cradle, redware body, inlaid white slip stylized floral blossoms, repaired, "1733" (A)................................. 1540.00
  9¼" h, bird-whistle marbled in brown and yellow slip, holding strawberry in beak, circ base, late 18th C-early 19th C (A)......... 2618.00
Harvest Jug, 10½" h, ovoid body, cream slip on chocolate brown ground, "I:A" and "May 1:1816" above friendship verse, one side with cockerel, pewter repair to handle, crack (A)................................. 600.00
Honey Pot, 5⅜" h, globular body, combed brown design under honey colored glaze, molded feathery scrolls on center and neck, small ribbed handle, England (A).......... 1235.00
Jar, 10" h, ovoid body, redware, tooled lines on shoulder, brown splotches on red ground, applied handle (A)....................... 357.00
Jar, Cov, 11" h, urn shape, dark brown glaze, cream slip "MS and 1785" and stylized leaves and flowers, cracks, England (A) 1250.00
Jug
  3⅞" h, dark brown body with agate marbling, cream slip overlay incised with dice pattern, ear shaped handle, c1760 (A).... 950.00
  4" h, ovoid, panels on runny chocolate brown, tan, and cream slip on light brown slipped ground, green glazed horiz ribbed rim, c1760 (A) 950.00
  7" h, globular body, creamy slip splashed with horiz band of runny chocolate-brown spots below a line, looped strap handle, cylindrical neck, pulled spout, late 17th C, Staffordshire (A)......................... 2165.00
Loaf Pan, 16¾" l, 12" w, 3" h, redware body, three line yellow slip decoration, coggled edge (A)................................. 1540.00
Loving Cup, 7⅝" h, brown slip inscription for birth of Prince Edward in 1894, reverse with geometrics and florals in colors, cream ground (A)................................. 380.00
Milk Bowl
  11" d, redware body, yellow slipware star design in center, yellow slip swirls (A) 10.00
  12" d, redware body with yellow slip int (A) 11.00

13 1/2" d, redware body, bands and wavy lines in yellow slip, green and brown glaze (A). **1200.00**

Mug

3 1/4" h, thistle form, feathered chocolate brown squat body, flared neck inscribed "IT LT 1679," beaded brown line borders, honey ground, looped handle with row of brown dashes, rim repaired, 1679, North Staffordshire (A)...................**16,450.00**

7 1/4" h, cream slip of date "1721" and "Stephen Shaw," neck with beaded circ motifs, dark brown ground, yellow lead glaze, repaired handle, England (A) **1923.00**

Owl Jug, Cov, 8 3/4" h, globular body, decorated with combed brown and cream plumage, wings outlined with cream beaded dark brown trails, saucer eyes dotted in dk brown, cir med browm base, applied claws, loop handle at back, restored, c1700 (A) **48,620,00**

Pie Plate, 8" d, redware body, coggled rim, three line yellow slip crow's foot design (A) **220.00**

Pitcher

6" h, redware body, leaf and dot design in yellow slip, sgd "Rdo de Alba' (A) **20.00**

7" h, redware body, yellow slip zig-zags and swirls, green accents (A) **66.00**

7 1/2" h, redware body, yellow slip and brown splotches, applied rib handle (A)......... **1100.00**

8" h, redware body, yellow slip flowers, dots, and zig-zags (A)....................... **35.00**

9 1/2" d, 2 1/2" h, redware body, yellow slip design of pentagon in center with swirls, crimped rim, European (A) **15.00**

Plant Pot, 8 1/2" h, "1837" flanked by growing flowers, reverse with horiz squiggles, overhead rope twist handle, fixed stand (A)..... **510.00**

Porringer

4 5/8" d, buff color, cream slip ground decorated with brown striations below flared rim, small loop handle, hairline glaze cracks, 1700, Staffordshire (A)................... **1480.00**

5 1/2" d, redware body, upper part with streaky brown glaze, decorated with looped trail and spots of cream slip, looped handle, 18th C (A)........................... **975.00**

Puzzle Jug

6 3/4" h, inscribed with drinking verse and dated below, pierced cylindrical neck, five sucking spouts, 1876 (A)............... **513.00**

7 1/2" h

Molded decorations in relief, pierced neck, scalloped rim, brown slip on top section **250.00**

Pierced cylindrical neck, five sucking spouts, inscribed with drinking rhyme, dated below, 1860 (A)............... **374.00**

8 1/2" h, globular body, pierced cylindrical neck, creamy yellow slip, speckled brown ground with stylized flowers and scrollwork, damage, dated "1778" on one side, tubular handle, (A) **750.00**

Salt Container, 11 3/4" h, redware body, white slip design of stylized flower with blossom around opening, damage, England (A) **27.00**

Saucer

7 1/8" d, dark brown body with wavy lines of cream colored slip, late 18th C (A)....... **890.00**

8" d, dark brown body decorated with triple line cream squiggle, notched rim, late 18th C (A) **1122.00**

Sweetmeat Stand

6 5/8" d, triple, buff earthenware compartments joined by honey colored slip, rims and lug handles trailed with dashes of chocolate brown slip, restored, late 17th-early 18th C, (A) **561.00**

8 1/4" d, quadruple, buff earthenware compartments joined by straw colored slip, rims and lug handles trailed with lines of chocolate brown slip, early 18th C (A) **1300.00**

Tureen, Cov, 7 5/8" d, redware body, brown glaze, foliate scroll handles with cream and yellow accents, cov with molded blue grapes, yellow and manganese pears, pomegranates, flowers and green leaves, int with cream slip with sgraffiato floral sprays accented in yellow, brown, and green, early 19th C, Germany (A)..................... **880.00**

Whistle, 3" h, redware body, seated dog with tail forming whistle, yellow and dark brown slip, oval base (A) **1100.00**

SOFT PASTE

English/Continental
17th to 19th Centuries

History: Soft paste, or artifical porcelain, was made during the 17th and 18th centuries in Europe by using glass or a glass substitute that was ground up and mixed with clay. Over the years, the ingredients of soft paste varied.

The glaze was added in the second firing. This glaze was soft. It scratched and chipped easily. If the potter was careless, the glaze could wilt in the kiln and become uneven. The soft paste process was abandoned gradually during the early 19th century when the formula for hard paste porcelain became better understood.

Soft paste porcelain had the translucency of hard paste. It simply was softer and more porous. Since the melting temperatures of soft paste glazes and the colored enamels are similar, the overglaze enamel sinks into the glaze and softens the outline of painted decoration. Essentially pigment and surface are melded together.

Soft paste was made in France at Rouen, St. Cloud, Chantilly, Mennecy, Vincennes, and Sevres. English factories making soft paste include Chelsea, Bow, Derby, Worcester, and Liverpool. Most European countries produced soft paste porcelain before switching to hard paste porcelain production.

Bowl, 10 1/4" d, blue and white oriental motif with two men in landscape, stylized floral border, ext with landscape scenes (A) **80.00**

Charger, 12" d, peafowl with sponged trees in colors, blue feather edge (A) **990.00**

Cream and Sugar, creamer, 5 1/8" h, cov sugar bowl, 6" h, sprig design of bluebells and green leaves across middle, early 19th C **95.00**

Creamer

3" h, Leeds type decoration with floral band in four colors (A) **72.00**

3 1/8" h

Brown transfer of florals and birds, repaired chips (A)............................. **30.00**

Floral band and three color stripes, emb leaf handle (A)............................. **115.00**

3 1/4" h, fruit on vine in colors, blue border (A)................................... **231.00**

Basket, 11" l, multicolored center florals, cream ground, green trim, rope handles with floral terminals, Continental, pr, (A) $358.00

3³⁄₈" h, multicolored tulip design (A) **500.00**
3¹⁄₂" h, Leeds type blue and white oriental
  design (A) **225.00**
3⁵⁄₈" h
  Gaudy floral design in and light and dark
    yellow, ribbed handle with emb leaf ends
    (A) **250.00**
  Multicolored Leeds type floral design (A) . **137.00**
  Multicolored peafowl in tree (A) . . . **500.00**
Cup and Saucer, Handleless
  Black, blue, and dark orange emb vining foli-
    age and ribbing (A) **94.00**
  Blue, yellow, and ochre gaudy flowerheads
    with swags (A) **159.00**
  Gaudy floral decoration in colors, mismatched
    (A) **115.00**
  Large open floral with gaudy leaf design in
    colors (A) **202.00**
  Peafowl design in red, blue, green, black, and
    ochre (A) **220.00**
  Ribbed body, gaudy Leeds type floral design in
    colors (A) **260.00**
Cup and Saucer, miniature, blue and pink florals,
  green petals, c1800 . . . . **70.00**
Cup Plate, 4" d, black transfer of "Flower Gath-
  erers," boy and girl with basket and trees,
  raised flower and chain border, early 1800s. **85.00**
Jug, 5⁵⁄₈" h, oriental style flowers and urns in
  pink, yellow, green, and blue, mask spout (A)
  . . . . **75.00**
Mug
  2" h, overall blue glaze, c1800 . . . . **90.00**
  4⁷⁄₈" h, gaudy floral design in colors with
    chain, emb leaf handle (A) **313.00**
  6" h, blue and white, cross-hatch design with
    dots and florals, c1820–40 . . . . **295.00**
Pitcher
  6" h, bulbous shape, flared spout, pink roses
    with yellow, blue, brown, green, and red leaf
    and floral designs, cream ground, spout re-
    stored (A) **44.00**
  6⁵⁄₈" h, multicolored wheat sheaf and farm
    tools, repairs (A) **440.00**
  7" h, "Cockney Sportsman," man in rust coat,
    yellow breeches, horses in ground on one
    side, shooting scene on reverse, brown out-
    lined rims, c1800, Liverpool, England **1300.00**
  7¹⁄₂" h, gaudy Leeds type floral design in col-
    ors (A) **379.00**

7⁷⁄₈" h, farmer's tools, horse, cow, pig, grain,
  and "James Farr 1803" in colors (A) **2600.00**
Plate
  6¹⁄₂" d, polychrome enamel open rose with
    leaves in center, emb foliage border, luster
    trim (A) **33.00**
  6⁵⁄₈" d, oct, multicolored floral design, green
    feather edge (A) **140.00**
  7¹⁄₈" d, blue, green, and mustard scrolling
    leaves and flowers (A) **100.00**
  7¹⁄₄" d, gaudy tulip design in colors, floral
    wreath border (A) **357.00**
  8" d, oct, multicolored peafowl in tree, green
    feather edge (A) **650.00**
  8¹⁄₈" d, multicolored peafowl in green
    sponged trees, green feather edge (A) **400.00**
  8¹⁄₄" d, multicolored Leeds type floral design,
    brown striped scalloped rim (A) **165.00**
  8⁷⁄₈" d, central rooster in blue-green and
    brown, circ scalloped rim with blue border
    (A) **104.00**
  9¹⁄₄" d, multicolored peafowl in tree, green
    sponged tree, blue feather edge (A) **550.00**
  9³⁄₄" d, sunflower on leafy stem in green,
    brown, blue, and ochre, cream ground (A) **200.00**
  10" d, central rooster in blue, yellow, amber,
    and green, continuous vine and berry bor-
    der in blue and amber, cream ground, Staf-
    fordshire (A) **200.00**
  11" d, leaf shape, center scene of milkmaid
    and horse, white ground, molded basket-
    weave border (A) **10.00**
Platter, 13³⁄₄" l, central rooster with large tail in
  blue, green, and amber, black border with
  blue, green, and amber leaves (A) **71.00**
Shaker, 4¹⁄₂" h, blue feather edge, unmarked
  (A) **150.00**
Sugar Bowl, Cov, 6¹⁄₂" h, rose and blue florals,
  green leaves, scalloped shape, footed, as is . **50.00**
Teabowl and Saucer
  Black transfer of mill with mustard yellow rim
    (A) **65.00**
Teapot
  3³⁄₄" h
    Gaudy Leeds type floral design in colors
      (A) **350.00**
    Light green bands with dark brown stripes
      (A) **125.00**
  5" h, blue and white chinoiserie decoration, lst
    qtr 18th C (A) **275.00**
  5¹⁄₂" h, black transfer of oriental scenery with
    yellow ochre edges (A) **400.00**
  6" h, Leeds type floral design in colors, un-
    marked (A) **200.00**
  6¹⁄₄" h, blue, gold, and yellow gaudy floral
    and swag design (A) **462.00**
  6⁷⁄₈" h, multicolored Leeds type floral design,
    emb leaf handle (A) **575.00**
  8¹⁄₂" h, large open flowerhead in leaf medal-
    lion, multicolored, repairs (A) **220.00**
  9¹⁄₂" d, gaudy foliage swag with basket of
    flowers in colors, blue feather edge (A) . . . **379.00**
  10⁵⁄₈" h, Leeds gaudy floral decoration in col-
    ors, repairs (A) **125.00**
  11" l, helmet shape, florals, green leaves,
    c1820 . . . . **250.00**
Toddy Plate, 5⁵⁄₈" d, center design of spread
  winged eagle in colors, green feather edge
  (A) **1000.00**
Vase, 7¹⁄₂" h, five finger type, scattered floral

sprays in colors, feather edge openings, repairs (A) **302.00**
Waste Bowl, 5½" d, 2¾" h, gaudy polychrome floral band, hairline (A) **247.00**

EARLY 19ᵀᴴ CENTURY   1760-1804

SPAIN—GENERAL

Alcora, Province of Valencia
1726–1858

Count Aranda, assisted by Joseph Olerys of Moustiers and other French workers, established a faience factory in 1726. The original success of this factory was due to the skill of the French painters and the use of French models. The tin-glazed pottery that it produced was quite popular throughout Spain.

By 1737 all the workers were Spanish. Biblical or mythological scenes on large dishes or plaques were among its best pieces. The Count died in 1749. His son took over. A succession of Dukes of Hija owned the factory. When the factory was acquired by private owners, Francois Martin started to produce hard paste porcelain in imitation of Wedgwood's creamware in 1858.

Buen Retiro, near Madrid
1760–1812

King Charles III of Spain established Buen Retiro, near Madrid, using workers from Capodimonte in 1760. Soft paste porcelains were manufactured into services, tea sets, vases, bowls, and figures similar to Capodimonte wares. The factory also specialized in the porcelain tiles that were used to decorate palaces.

By the end of the 18th century, biscuit groups in the Sevres styles and medallions and plaques in the Wedgwood style were made. From 1765 until 1790 Giuseppe Gricci was the chief modeler. After his death, Spanish artists influenced the decorations.

Only hard paste wares were made at Buen Retiro after 1800. In 1808 the factory was transformed into a fortress that was destroyed by Wellington in 1812. In 1817 the factory was rebuilt at Moncloa in Madrid and remained in operation until 1850.

Hispano-Moresque, Valencia & Malaga
End of 13th Century to Present

Hispano-Moresque is white enamel, tin-glazed earthenware that is usually decorated with copper or silver metallic lusters. Moorish potters came to Spain, settled in Valenica, Manises, and Paterna, and made their lustered pottery.

Early luster colors were pale and filmy. Later pieces utilized a golden luster and deeper blue tones. As time progressed, the luster became more brassy and metallic in appearance.

Hispano-Moresque flourished for about three hundred years. By the end of the 16th century there was a steady decline, but the technique still continues today in Valencia. All sorts of vases, drug pots, pitchers, covered bowls, large dishes, and wall tiles are made.

Talavera
15th Century to Present

Talavera pottery is decorated in a peasant-like style with birds, animals, or busts in a blue and dusty-orange motif outlined in purplish-black. Talavera wares were popular with all levels of Spanish society into the 17th century. Monastic coats of arms and the cardinal's hat were decorated in yellow, orange, and green. Shapes included large bowls and two handled jugs featuring sporting scenes, bullfights, buildings, trees, figures, and animals.

During the mid-18th century Talavera adopted the styles used at Alcora which had copied the French style of Moustiers. Today only ordinary earthenwares are made.

Reference: Alice Wilson Frothingham, *Tile Panels of Spain: 1500–1650*, Hispanic Society of America, 1969.

Museums: Cleveland Museum of Art, Cleveland, Ohio; Hispanic Society of America, New York, New York; Musee Nationale de Ceramique, Sevres, France; Museo Arquelogical Nacional, Madrid, Spain; Seattle Art Museum, Seattle, Washington; Victoria & Albert Museum, London, England.

Albarello
  9⅝" h, manganese, green, and yellow with crowned dbl headed eagle and armorial bearing of Aguilar of Castile, minor haircracks, late 17th C (A) **957.00**
  11" h, 11½" g, waisted bodies in luster with foliage within line borders on blue ground, cracks, 16th C, Hispano-Moresque, pr (A) **1028.00**
  12¼" h, 12½" h, slender waisted body, dark blue with animals and figures in landscapes flanking diagonal drug labels inscribed "Se. Foeniculi" or Se Litri," cylindrical neck with flowering plants within line borders, one hair crack, mid 18th C, Catalan, pr (A) **2500.00**
Barber Bowl, 15½" d, painted with winged cherub mask in elaborate landscape, foliate borders, ext with landscape scene, damaged, c1670, Talavara (A) **652.00**
Basin, 16½" d, int painted with stylized carnations, ext with scrolling foliage, thumb print everted rim, 17th C, Hispano-Moresque (A). **1683.00**

Dish, 14½" d, copper luster with blue accents, luster splashes on reverse, c1580s, Andalusian, $275.00

Bowl, 10" d, circ, majolica, int painted in yellow, green, brown, and blue with hare leaping amidst trees, ext with continuous landscape, Talavera (A)............................ 270.00

Bowl, Cov, 15¾" d, manganese, yellow, ochre, blue banding of jumping hares and dogs alternating with flower sprays within a marbling border, finial of bird perched on crowned vase, cracked, early 19th C, Talavera (A)........ 1122.00

Charger

12½" d, center in yellow luster with flower within borders of scrolling foliage, hair crack, 17th C, Hispano-Moresque (A).... 1000.00

18" d, copper luster, central armorial shield of rampant lion, conical rim with arched molding enclosing panels of stylized foliage and molded studs, reverse with bands of scrolling palm leaves, restored, late 15th C, Hispano-Moresque (A) 2880.000

Dinner Service, Part, cov tureen, 12" H-H, urn shape, 12 plates, 10" d, red, blue, green, and gilt, curvilinear designs, dbl handled, fruit finial, white ground, Iberia mark (A)............. 600.00

Dish

9¼" l, copper luster with concentric bands of formal motifs and pseudo incriptions, reverse with concentric circles, pierced for hanging, 16th C, Hispano-Moresque (A).. 708.00

12" d, majolica, dark blue stylized rabbit in landscape, broad border of stylized foliage, pierced for hanging, mid 17th C (A)...... 984.00

12½" l, copper luster with central flower within formal leaf and whorl borders, restored, 17th C, Hispano-Moresque (A) ... 954.00

13½" d, gold luster painted center flowerhead boss, pseudo character inscription, border of stylized foliage on whorl ground, cracks, 16th C, Hispano-Moresque (A) ... 775.00

14¼" d, blue, ochre, and manganese with semi-heraldic rampant lion lifting forepaw, rim with stylized flowering plants, damaged, rim restored, 17th C, Talavera (A)........ 1440.00

14½" l, conical form, stylized cockerel among flowering bushes, scattered flowers within a whorl and line border, copper luster, 17th C, Hispano-Moresque (A)....... 650.00

15" d, dark copper luster painted stylized flowers in resist around spiral boss, molded palm leaves on border, cracked, late 16th C, Hispano-Moresque (A)................. 1325.00

15¼" d, blue, green, yellow, and manganese painted grotesque figures and animals in scattered flowering plants with insects, c1735, "blue Causda" mark (A) 1730.00

15½" l, stylized flowerhead within broad border of shaded foliage, wide rim molded with leaves and luster foliage, reverse with sketched foliage, pale copper luster, early 17th C, crack, Hispano-Moresque (A) 950.00

20½" d, central well with bird amongst stylized foliage within concentric borders of birds among dense foliage and flowers, reverse decorated with stylized palm leaves, restored, 16th C, Hispano-Moresque (A).. 1543.00

Figure

8¼" h, girl in white matte robe, brown hair, playing violin, "NAO, Made in Spain" mark.................................. 65.00

12" h, hunter with tan duck, blue pants, white shirt, tan vest, gray hat, gray-green base,

shiny glaze, "Ponceval Made in Spain" mark (A)................................... 18.00

Jardinaire, 4½" H, tapered sq shape, basket molded body with painted flower spray and single blossoms, molded shell and scroll on rim, four scrolled feet, c1760, "blue fleur-de-lys" mark, Buen Retiro 5100.00

Jug, 10½" h, polychrome large dog on hind legs in forest, blue, yellow, and manganese line borders, washed manganese strap handle, cracks, late 17th C, Talavera 450.00

Plaque, 18⅞" l, 12⅞" h, pottery, painted shepherdess in scarlet headscarf, holding lamb in arms, sheep at side, woodland setting, c1891, Seville................................ 725.00

Planter, 6½" l. figural lady's 20th C shoe, pointed toe, gray body with tan panels and gray geometric swirls on sides, "Made in Spain" mark 55.00

Vase, 9½" h, slender ovoid shape, copper luster with two bands of scrolling foliage, 17th C, Hispano-Moresque, Valencia, pr (A)........ 1337.00

Wine Glass Cooler, 10⅜" l, lobed oval shape, sides painted in rose, iron-red, blue, yellow, and green with floral swag from rose or blue bowknot, scalloped rim edged in gold and blue, female mask handle with skin in flesh tones, head enclosed in gilt edged rose drapery, blue and gilt edged scallop shell, 1765–70, "blue enamel fleur-de-lys" on one, other with incised "interlaced C's" mark, Buen Retiro, pr (A)..........................13,200.00

SPATTERWARE

Staffordshire, England
c1800–1850s

DESIGN

History. In design spatter there are small, shaped areas of spots or dots instead of large continuous overall spattered areas. Some design spatter is done with a stencil or template. Design spatter also is referred to as "structural spatter."

Colors used for design spatter were red, blue, green, and purple. Spatter techniques were combined with hand painted decoration motifs. Decorative center motifs include: Adams Rose, Columbine, Dogwood, and Pansy.

Known makers of design spatter are: T. W. Barlow, Elsmore and Forster, and Harvey.

GENERAL

History. Spatterware is a decoration that appeared on a variety of body compositions including soft paste, creamware, pearlware, and ironstone. It appealed to "popular" tastes because of inexpensive price and its cheery, colorful, and bright appearance. It was made primarily for export.

Spatter is a stippling or all-over design of color. One or more colors can be used. The color was applied in parallel stripes or concentric bands leaving a center of white for decoration. With spatter as a border, the center design could be either hand painted or transfer printed.

There were eight basic colors used for spatter: black, blue (the most common), brown, green, pink, purple, red, and yellow (the rarest). Most popular patterns were: Cannon, Castle, Peafowl, Pomegrante, Schoolhouse, and Thistle.

Few pieces of true spatter bear identifying manufacturer's marks. Among the known makers of spatter are: Adams, Cotton and Barlow, Harvey, and J. & G. Meakin.

References: Kevin McConnell, *Spongeware and Spatterware*, Schiffer Publishing Co., 1990; Carl F. & Ada F. Robacker, *Spatterware and Sponge*, A. S. Barnes & Co., 1978.

Museum: Henry Ford Museum, Dearborn, Michigan.

REPRODUCTION ALERT: "Cybis" spatter is an increasingly collectible ware made by Boleslow Cybis of Poland. The design utilizes the Adams type peafowl and was made in the 1940s. Some pieces are marked "Cybis" in an impressed mark; some examples are unmarked. The principal shape was cup plates. The body of the ware is harder than true spatter, and the glaze appears glassy rather than soft.

Many contemporary craftsmen also are reproducing spatterware examples.

DESIGN

Bowl, 6⅝" d, large open red rose on side, black line, green leaves, small blue flowerheads, dark red int band, "Staffordshire England" mark **65.00**
Coffee Pot, 10" h, thistle and lily of the valley design, red spatter loops, emb grape finial, mismatched lid (A) **165.00**
Creamer
  2½" h, green spatter band of flowerheads, red striped rim and middle, black striped handle (A) **82.00**
  3½" h, columbine, rose bud, and thistle in red, green, blue, purple, and black, green spatter chain of flowerheads on rim, red stripe (A) **165.00**
  4¼" h, open flower in green, yellow, black, and purple on sides, red spatter band of flowerheads on rim, blue line edge (A) . . .   **77.00**
Cup and Saucer, Handleless
  Green band of circles and fans (A) **40.00**
  Miniature, red, green, and black stick spatter flower (A) **82.00**
  Primrose in red, green, and, black, blue spatter band of flowerheads (A) **220.00**
  Three geometric bands in black, green, and red, hairline on saucer (A) **110.00**
Plate
  4½" d, green leaves with rust and yellow centers on border, black edge, cream ground, c1853–71, imp "Elsmore & Forster, Tunstall" mark **75.00**
  5¼" d, green center, raised floral border in orange, blue, and purple, copper luster rim, c1850 . . . .   **45.00**
  6" d
    Red and green flowers and leaves on border, "Staffordshire, England" mark **36.00**
    Small red stick spatter flowers and green dotted leaves on border, "Staffordshire, England" mark **42.00**
  6½" d, center with columbine, rose bud, and thistle in red, green, blue, black, and purple, green spatter chain of flowerheads on border, red rim stripe (A) **75.00**
  6¾" d, center open flower in green, yellow, black, and purple, red spatter band of flowerheads on border, blue striped rim (A) . . .   **28.00**

8½" d
  Maroon open rose and leaves in center, green, brown, and maroon leaves on border, maroon chain rim, unmarked **75.00**
  Primrose in red, green, and black, border of purple loops (A) **45.00**
  Red and blue simple florals (A) **25.00**
  Small purple stick spatter flowers with large red and blue flowers, Villeroy and Boch   **72.00**
8⅝" d, stick spatter inner border of leaf chain, outer border of floral and leaf chain in blue, red, green, and black, "Elsmore & Forster" mark, set of 12 (A) **620.00**
8¾" d
  Rose and bird in red, blue, green, and black in center, blue spatter leafy band on border, blue rim stripe (A) **82.00**
  Rose design in red, green, and black in center, blue and green spatter border (A) . .   **100.00**
  Stick spatter with center single rose with black, blue, and green leaves, border of blue-green flowers and black leaves, black line rim **68.00**
9¼" d, gaudy rose design on border in red, green, blue, and black (A) **75.00**
9½" d, center open rose in red with blue and green leaves, border with band of small green roses and red leaves (A) **99.00**
9¾" d, thistle and lily of the valley, red spatter swirls on border (A) **137.00**
9⅞" d
  Polychrome florals, "Auld Heatherware" mark (A) **38.00**
  Twelve sides, thistle and lily of the valley, red swirl spatter, heavy wear (A) **33.00**
10" d, gaudy floral polychrome center, blue rim, hairline (A) **25.00**
10¼" d, stick spatter design of large cobalt and green leaves with iron-red open flowers with yellow centers on border, 19th C, English mark **75.00**
10⅝" d, stick spatter center of three fruits with leaves, blue spatter leaf border (A) . .   **159.00**
Platter
  13½" l, oct, ironstone, multicolored floral design in center, blue spatter border (A) **165.00**

Platter, 11¾" l, blue, green, yellow, and rose center florals, rose floral border, "Auld Heather Ware Scotland" mark, $198.00

14³/₈" l, oval, large green, yellow, black, and purple open flower in center, blue border chain of open flowerheads, red rim stripe (A)...................................... **165.00**

Soup Plate

10³/₈" d, polychrome floral center, blue rim with red stripes (A)...................... **168.00**

10⁷/₈" d, polychrome floral center, sawtooth border, "Made in Belgium" mark (A)..... **50.00**

Sugar Bowl

4" h, polychrome floral chain on body, criss-cross chain on rim (A).................. **132.00**

4¹/₈" h, columbine, rose bud, and thistle in red, green, blue, black, and purple on sides, green spatter chain of flowerheads, red stripe rim (A)...................... **110.00**

6³/₄" h, gaudy florals in blue and white spatter, "Allertons" mark (A)................ **176.00**

7¹/₂" h, primrose in red, green, and black, purple loops at intersections of panels (A) **137.00**

Teabowl and Saucer

Floral design in three colors (A)............ **20.00**

Primrose in red, green, and black, purple loops between flowers and saucer boder (A)... **37.00**

Thistle and lily of the valley, red swirls on body and saucer border (A).................. **127.00**

Teapot

6" h, roseate pattern with blue floral centers in spatter (A)........................... **220.00**

8³/₈" h, green, yellow, black, and purple open flower on sides, red spatter open flower border, blue striped rims, domed cov (A). **330.00**

8³/₄" h, primrose in red, black, and green, purple loops at panels, handle and lid (A). **220.00**

Vegetable Bowl, Open, 8⁵/₈" l, stick spatter inner chain of leaves, chain of florals and leaves on border in blue, green, purple and black, "Elsmore & Forster" mark, pr (A)..... **143.00**

Waste Bowl

5¹/₂" d, gaudy floral design in polychrome enamels, "Adams Tunstall, England" mark (A)...................................... **93.00**

5³/₄" d, 3¹/₂" h, columbine, rose bud, and thistle in red, green, blue, purple, and black, green spatter band of flowerheads, red rim stripe (A)............................. **192.00**

GENERAL

Bowl

13" d, "Peafowl" pattern in blue, green, and red on branch with green leaves, blue spatter paneled border, "Adams" mark (A) ... **550.00**

13¹/₂" d, "Fort" pattern in black, gray, and red with green trees, blue spatter, hairline restored (A) **247.00**

Box, 8" l, figural dove in blue and pink spatter (A)....................................... **330.00**

Centerbowl

6¹/₄" h, 10" d, oct, ftd, eagle and shield, black transfer, center and sides, blue spatter rim and foot, two scroll handles (A).......... **523.00**

11" d, oct, "Rose" pattern in red and green on sides, borders and ext banded in blue spatter (A) **495.00**

Coffee Pot

8" h, oct paneled, "Tulip" pattern in red with green leaves, yellow spatter (A)......... **2310.00**

9¹/₄" h, Indians hunting bison, brown transfer, green spatter body, repairs (A) **88.00**

10³/₄" h, scrolled handle, overall blue spatter (A)..................................... **330.00**

Creamer

3³/₈" h, "Cluster of Buds" pattern in red and green, red and blue spatter body (A)..... **220.00**

3¹/₂" h

"Acorn" pattern in brown with green leaves, red spatter body (A).......... **385.00**

"Fish" pattern in green, red, and black on two sides, rim and base in brown line, yellow spatter body (A).............. **715.00**

Paneled, blue spatter (A)............... **138.00**

Red and green rainbow spatter, leaf emb handle ends (A)..................... **358.00**

3³/₄" h, red, blue, and green rainbow spatter, stains (A)........................... **220.00**

4" h

"Peafowl" pattern in blue, yellow, red, and black, red, blue, and green thumbprint spatter (A)........................... **150.00**

Red and green four part flower, red and blue spatter (A)..................... **275.00**

Red dots, blue spatter (A).............. **170.00**

"Rose and Bud" pattern in red, blue, green, and black, blue spatter (A) **200.00**

"Schoolhouse" pattern on two sides in red, blue, and yellow, blue spatter rim and spout (A)........................... **467.00**

"Windmill" pattern in red, blue, and yellow on sides, blue spatter on rim and spout (A) **143.00**

4¹/₂" h

"Rooster" pattern in yellow, blue, and pink, blue spatter rim and spout (A)........ **220.00**

"Spatter Dot" pattern in purple on two sides, purple spatter rim (A)........... **55.00**

4³/₄" h, oct paneled, "Tulip" pattern in red with green leaves, yellow spatter, "James Edwards" mark (A) **990.00**

5¹/₈" h, oct, ftd, "Umbrella Flower" pattern in purple and blue with green leaves, blue spatter on body (A) **467.00**

5¹/₂" h, sq oct shape, swirling red, green, black, and yellow rainbow stripes, handle repaired (A) **770.00**

6¹/₈" h, "Fort" pattern in black, green, and red, blue paneled spatter (A) **800.00**

Cup

2³/₄" h, "Two Men on a Raft" pattern in green, blue, and red, purple spatter rim (A)...................................... **250.00**

3¹/₄" h, "Peafowl" pattern in blue, red, yellow, and black, "George," green spatter, repairs (A).............................. **1150.00**

Cup and Saucer

Handleless

Miniature

Green, black and red rose, blue spatter (A) **135.00**

Overall red spatter (A)................ **33.00**

"Peafowl" pattern in blue, red, green, and black, green spatter **350.00**

Rainbow spatter

"Peafowl" pattern in blue, yellow, red, and black, red and green spatter (A) **300.00**

Red and blue, hairline in cup (A) **220.00**

"Tulip" pattern in red, green, and black, blue spatter (A).................... **175.00**

Blue spatter

"Fort" pattern in colors (A).............. **125.00**

"Peafowl" pattern in green, yellow ochre, red, and black, hairline on cup (A) **197.00**
"Schoolhouse" pattern in red, yellow, black, and green (A). **690.00**
Brown and black spatter, hp rose **250.00**
"Fish" pattern in red, green, and brown, red spatter body, set of 5 (A) **39,600.00**
Green and red rainbow spatter, red, blue, green, and black tulip pattern (A) **825.00**
Red spatter
Blue band with black foliage (A) **28.00**
"Peafowl" pattern yellow, blue, green, and black, hairline on cup (A) **257.00**
"Thistle" pattern in blue, green, and black (A) **82.00**
"Tulip" pattern in red, green, and black, hairline on cup (A) **137.00**
"Thistle" pattern in red and green, yellow spatter (A) **275.00**
Cup Plate, 4 1/8" d, "Peafowl" pattern in red, yellow, green, and black, blue spatter border, "Stoneware, E.W.& Co." mark (A). **690.00**
Dish
6 1/2" l, oct, "Primrose" pattern in purple and yellow with green leaves, red spatter border (A). **880.00**
8 7/8" d, "Tulip" pattern in yellow with green, blue, and brown leaves, black inner band, blue spatter rim, deep well (A). **247.00**
Honey Pot
5 1/4" h, "Pineapple" pattern in purple, black, and green, blue spatter body (A). **5830.00**
5 1/2" h, "Schoolhouse" pattern in red and yellow, green tree, blue spatter body, two small handles (A). **6820.00**
Jug, 7 1/4" h, hex, red tulip on one side, pink tulip on reverse, green leaves, yellow spatter body, spout repaired (A) **880.00**
Mug
2 1/2" h, "Peafowl" pattern in blue, red, black, and green, blue spatter (A). **467.00**
4 3/4" h, cylindrical shape, "Peafowl" pattern in red and blue, green leaf, inscribed "A Present From Alma for Paul," red and blue spatter lip, handle, and base (A) **55.00**
5" h, blue spatter, stains (A). **302.00**
5 1/8" h, cylindrical shape, "Peafowl" pattern in red, yellow, and blue in green spatter tree, blue spatter panels, cream ground, yellow rims (A) **660.00**
Pitcher
5" h, blue spatter (A) **187.00**
8 1/2" d, oct, central red "Tulip" pattern with green leaves on sides, yellow spatter body (A). **1650.00**
8 5/8" h, paneled, "Rose" pattern, red spattered body, stains (A). **125.00**
8 7/8" h, oct, red, green, blue, and yellow swag spatter, blue spatter handle and base (A) . **2530.00**
Plate
4" d, "Peafowl" pattern in blue, green, and rose, rose spatter border **155.00**
4 1/8" d, "Thistle" pattern in red with green leaves, yellow spatter border (A) **1540.00**
5" d, "Peafowl" pattern in blue, yellow, and red, allover yellow spatter (A). **1540.00**
7 1/4" d, "Parrot" pattern in red and green, blue spatter border (A) **743.00**
7 3/8" d, "Tulip" pattern in green, black, red, blue, and yellow ochre, red spatter (A) ... **850.00**

7 5/8" d, "Peafowl" pattern in blue, red, black, and yellow, red spatter, repairs (A) **55.00**
8" d
"Pineapple" pattern in purple, black, and green, blue spatter border (A) **2970.00**
"Rose" pattern in red and green, red, blue, and green rainbow spatter (A). **425.00**
"Rooster" pattern in yellow-ochre, red, blue, and black, red spatter (A) **230.00**
8 1/8" d
"Peafowl" pattern in blue, yellow, green, and black, red spatter border, stains (A) **330.00**
"Schoolhouse" pattern in red, green, black, and yellow, blue spatter border, "Pearl Stoneware, P.W.& Co." mark (A) **104.00**
8 1/4" d
Bird in yellow, blue, and brown on fence with green trees, two black inner bands, blue spatter border (A) **1045.00**
"Peafowl" pattern in blue, green, and red, red, blue, and purple spatter border (A) **1870.00**
"Rainbow" pattern in puce, yellow, green, and black, unmkd, (A) **235.00**
"Vine and Berry" pattern in red and yellow, green spatter (A). **385.00**

Plate, 8 1/2" d, brown and beige "Fort" pattern with green trees and grass, blue spatter border, unmkd, $790.00

8 3/8" d
Blue spatter, rim chips (A). **20.00**
"Christmas Balls" pattern as negative star in green spatter with triangular red and yellow dots (A). ...., ... **880.00**
"Dahlia" pattern in red, blue, and green, blue spatter (A) **400.00**
"Rainbow" pattern in blue and green spatter (A) **775.00**
Red, green, and black floral sprig in center, red and blue festooned spatter (A). **1072.00**
"Schoolhouse" pattern in red, green, and brown, red spatter (A) **1000.00**
8 1/2" d
"Fort" pattern in yellow with green trees, blue and red spatter border, "St. Clement" mark (A). **495.00**
"Peafowl" pattern in colors, blue spatter, "P.W.& Co." mark **175.00**
8 5/8" d, "Primrose" pattern in red, green, black, and yellow-ochre, blue spatter, surface pitting (A). **77.00**

8³/₄" d
"Peafowl" pattern center
Blue, mauve, and red rainbow border, unmarked, (A) **235.00**
Red spatter (A) **425.00**
Purple transfer of eagle in center, blue stick
spatter border, "R. Hammersley" mark
(A) **192.00**
"Tulip" pattern center in red with green
leaves, yellow spatter border, pr (A).... **605.00**
9" d
"Bird in Tree" pattern with blue and yellow
bird on green and black tree, two black
inner bands, blue and green spatter border (A)............................. **715.00**
"Reindeer" pattern on red ground, green
trees, blue spatter border (A)......... **990.00**
9¼" d
"Peafowl" pattern in blue, yellow-ochre,
green, and black, red spatter (A)....... **495.00**
Twelve petaled flower in blue, blue spatter
border (A).......................... **264.00**
9³/₈" d
"Acorn and Leaf" pattern in green, black,
teal blue, and yellow, blue spatter (A) .. **605.00**
"Acorn" pattern in brown, black, and green
shades, purple spatter (A)............. **800.00**
"Peafowl" pattern in blue, yellow, red, and
black, red spatter (A) **440.00**
"Rose" pattern in red, black, and green,
blue spatter border, rim repair (A) **302.00**
Six pointed star in red, green, and yellow
ochre, blue spatter (A)................ **605.00**
9½" d
"Bull's Eye" pattern center
Blue and green rainbow spatter (A) **660.00**
Red and green rainbow spatter (A) **297.00**
"Clover" pattern in green and red spatter
on black stems (A) **880.00**
"Fort" pattern in green, yellow, red, and
black, blue spattered paneled border (A) **82.00**
"Peafowl" pattern
Blue, yellow, and red, overall yellow spat-
ter body (A)....................... **3850.00**
Red, blue, yellow ochre, and black, blue
spatter ground, stains (A) **550.00**
"Pomegranate" pattern in purple, green,
blue, and black, blue spatter border (A) **550.00**
"Schoolhouse" pattern in green, red, and
brown, red spatter, rim repairs (A) **175.00**
Six pointed star in red, yellow, and green,
blue spatter border (A) **633.00**
"Thistle" pattern in red with green leaves,
yellow spatter border (A) **660.00**
"Vine and Berry" pattern in green and rust
with yellow enamels, unmkd, (A) **235.00**
9⁵/₈" d
"Fort" pattern in brown and red, green trees
and grass, blue spatter border (A)...... **880.00**
"Peafowl" pattern in red, yellow ochre,
green, and black, blue spatter (A)...... **475.00**
9³/₄" d
"Bull's Eye" pattern in red and green, rainbow spatter (A)..................... **605.00**
"Criss-Cross" pattern in blue and red spatter, blue and red spatter border (A).... **825.00**
"Fort" pattern in black, green, and red, blue
spatter, rim hairline (A) **650.00**
Paneled body, overall red, green, yellow,
black, and blue rainbow spatter (A) **2090.00**

"Peafowl" pattern in red, green, and yellow
ochre, blue spatter, repairs (A)........ **225.00**
"Thistle" pattern in red with green leaves,
yellow spatter border (A) **990.00**
9⁷/₈" d, red "Tulip" pattern with green leaves,
blue spatter border (A) **495.00**
10" d, "Peafowl" pattern in purple, green,
black, and yellow, red spatter (A) **295.00**
10³/₈" d
"Schoolhouse" pattern in red with green
tree and grass, green spatter border (A) **2860.00**
"Umbrella Flower" pattern in purple, green,
and blue, blue spatter border, faceted
edge (A) **2090.00**
10½" d, "Peafowl" pattern in tree in red,
green, blue, and black, blue spatter border,
imp "Adams" mark (A) **575.00**
10⁷/₈" d, "Peafowl" pattern in red, yellow,
and green on blue spatter ground, blue
spatter border (A)..................... **990.00**
11" h, oct paneled, central "Fort" pattern in
gray, black, and red with green trees, ob-
verse with green tree, blue spatter body
(A).................................. **1870.00**
Platter
13½" l, oct, capture of wild bull in center, red
transfer, blue spatter border (A)......... **121.00**
13³/₄" l, oct, "Tulip" pattern in red and blue
with green leaves, red and green striped
spatter border (A) **385.00**
14½" l, oct, "Thistle" pattern in red with
green leaves, yellow spatter border (A) ... **8360.00**
15½" l, eagle and shield in center, blue transfer, purple spatter border (A) **275.00**
17³/₄" l, Oct
Eagle and shield, blue transfer, red spatter
border (A)........................... **550.00**
"Pinwheel" pattern in purple, blue spatter
border (A)........................... **220.00**
18" l, oct, "Tulip" pattern in blue and red with
green leaves, red and green striped spatter
border, imp "anchor" mark (A) **4840.00**
Serving Dish, oct, "Thistle" pattern in red with
green leaves, yellow spatter border
9¹/₈" l (A)............................. **3080.00**
10³/₈" l (A) **1035.00**
Soup Plate, 10³/₄" d, blue, red, and green rainbow spatter, imp "Adams" mark (A) **675.00**

**Sugar Bowl, 5" h, blue spatter, gray ground,
$265.00**

Sugar Bowl
5¹/₈" d, faceted body, "Tulip" pattern in red
with green leaves, yellow spatter body (A) **935.00**
5½" d, "Tulip" pattern in blue and red, green

leaves, black-green and purple striped spatter (A) **358.00**

Sugar Bowl, Cov,

3¾" h, alternating black and yellow vert spatter stripes (A) **7860.00**

4" h, 4 color rainbow spatter (A) **75.00**

4⅛" h, red and green four part flower, red spatter, stains (A)......................... **220.00**

4¼" h, "Two Men on a Raft" pattern in green, blue, and red, blue spatter on shoulder, lip, and lid (A) **990.00**

4½" h

"Cluster of Buds" pattern in red and green, blue spatter body, lid repaired (A) **110.00**

"Dove" pattern in blue and yellow, red spatter on shoulder and lip (A) **220.00**

4⅝" h, "Rooster" pattern in blue, yellow, red, and black, red spatter, reglued chip (A)..................................... **75.00**

4¾" h, "Rose" pattern in red, green, and black, red spatter (A) **150.00**

4⅞" h

"Peafowl" pattern in blue, red, green, and black, red spatter, hairlines on lid (A)... **175.00**

Red, blue, and green rainbow spatter (A) **440.00**

5" h

"Beehive" pattern in yellow on green dot spatter on two sides, blue spattter on rim and lid (A).......................... **522.00**

"Rooster" pattern in blue, gold and red, rose spatter base and borders, repairs.. **650.00**

6" h, brown transfer of Crystal Palace, brown spatter on lid and rim, cream ground, lid repaired (A) **110.00**

6¼" h, blue spatter (A)................... **40.00**

6½" h, globular, "Parrot" pattern in red and green on sides, blue spatter body (A) **990.00**

7½" h, oct, "Peafowl" pattern in red, amber, and green on two sides, blue spatter body (A)....................................... **825.00**

8" h, hex, red "Thistle" pattern with green leaves, yellow spatter body, two lug handles (A)..................................... **3630.00**

8½" h, "Fort" pattern in black, green, and red, blue paneled spatter, chips, stains, repairs (A)............................... **275.00**

Teabowl, black and green spatter (A) **83.00**

Teabowl and Saucer

Bowl with blue and red striped spatter, saucer blue, red, and green six pointed star, blue and red striped spatter (A) **413.00**

Brown transfer of flying eagle, purple spatter (A)..................................... **75.00**

Center blue shield and stars, red spatter body (A)................................... **1100.00**

Floral spray in purple, green, blue, and black, green spatter, chip on cup rim (A) **15.00**

Gooney bird in blue, green, and purple, on black branch, blue spatter body (A) **800.00**

Miniature, blue spatter (A)................. **38.**

Purple spatter (A) **30.00**

Red and green spatter (A)................. **35.00**

"Thistle" pattern in red with green leaves, yellow spatter body, set of 4 (A) **1210.00**

Teapot

4" h, "Townhouse" pattern in black and blue, trellis on each side, striped red and purple spatter on body (A) **2310.00**

5½" h, blue-green spatter, hairline on bottom (A) **93.00**

6" h

"Rose" pattern in red, green, and black, purple and red spatter (A) **385.00**

"Schoolhouse" pattern on two sides in red, blue, and yellow, red spatter shoulder, lid, and rim (A)......................... **1100.00**

6¼" h

"Dove" pattern on two sides in blue, yellow, and green, blue spatter shoulder, rim, and lid (A) **413.00**

Paneled body, overall blue spatter (A).... **715.00**

6¾" h, red, blue, and green rainbow spatter (A)..................................... **577.00**

7⅝" h, "Tulip" pattern in red, blue, and black, green paneled spatter, repaired (A). **1040.00**

8½" h

Oct, "Schoolhouse" pattern on two sides in red and yellow with brown and green tree, green spatter body (A)........... **357.00**

Paneled, "Peafowl" pattern in blue, green, red, and black, blue spatter, hairline (A) **220.00**

"Peafowl" pattern in blue, red, green, and black, red spatter, damaged and repaired (A) **100.00**

9" h

Paneled body, red "Schoolhouse" pattern with green trees on sides, blue spatter body, repair to lid (A)................ **3410.00**

"Peafowl" pattern in rose, blue, and green, rose pink spatter handle and spout **575.00**

10½" h, oct faceted body, red "Rose" pattern with green leaves on sides, blue spatter body, handle and lid restored (A) **550.00**

Tea Set, teapot, 4⅜" h, creamer, 3¼" h, cov sugar bowl, 4" h, "Fort" pattern in green, black, and red, blue spatter ground (A) **3437.00**

Tureen, Cov, 8" h, oct, "Fort" pattern in yellow, brown, and red with green trees and grass, blue spatter lid and int, dbl handles (A)..... **4620.00**

Vegetable Bowl, open, 8⅜" l, "Thistle" pattern in red and green, blue spatter, 577.00

Waste Bowl, 6¾" d, 3⅜" h, red, blue, and green rainbow spatter (A) **408.00**

Stone-China
1805-30

1815-27

SPODE

Shelton, Staffordshire, England
c1797–1833

History: Spode is best known for two important contributions to the ceramic repertoire: the perfection of under the glaze transfer printing on earthenware and the introduction of the bone china formula. Josiah Spode I benefited from a five year apprenticeship with Thomas Whieldon. By 1770 he was an established master potter at Stoke-on-Trent at the factory where his successors continue today. Josiah Spode II, 1755 to 1827, opened a showroom and warehouse in the City of London in 1778.

The perfection of transfer printing in blue under the glaze on earthenware enabled Spode to copy, at reasonable prices, Chinese blue painted porcelain. These new examples provided replacements and additions for services that had become increasingly difficult to obtain from Chinese sources.

Earlier English porcelain manufacturers had failed to make large dinner plates and platters with straight enough edges to be commercially saleable. By July 1796 Spode was selling dinnerware that he called "English China" at prices well below those of his established competitors. By 1800 a bone china porcelain containing up to forty percent calcined ox bone had emerged. The credit for perfecting this formula is shared jointly by the two Spodes. Josiah I developed the initial formula, and Josiah II refined it. Josiah Spode II marketed products made with the new formula with such success that within ten years bone china became standard English china.

Josiah II's successful promotion of bone china was achieved in part through the on glaze decorating of Henry Daniel. The engraving techniques improved greatly. The zenith was reached in 1816 when, two years after the Tower pattern appeared, the pattern Blue Italian was introduced. Both patterns remain popular to the present day.

In 1813 Spode, responding to the demand for replacement pieces for polychrome Chinese porcelain services, adopted a stone china formula that was patented by J. & W. Turner in 1800. Turner's formula provided a superior body on which to decorate the more costly painted and gilded patterns. The body also matched the delicate gray color of the original Chinese porcelain. Over the years the formula was improved further and appears in today's market as Spode's Fine Stone China.

When Josiah II moved to Stoke in 1797 upon the death of his father, he left the management of the London business in the hands of William Copeland, who began his employment with Spode in 1784. Copeland worked with Spode as an equal partner. When Spode retired in 1812, Copeland assumed sole charge of the London house. His business acumen, augmented with the help of W. T. Copeland, his son, in 1824, contributed immensely to the success of the Spode enterprise.

(See: Copeland-Spode for a continuation of the company's history.

References: Robert Copeland, *Spode's Willow Pattern & Other Designs After the Chinese*, Blanford Press, 1990; D. Drakard & P. Holdway, *Spode Printed Wares*, Longmans, 1983; Arthur Hayden, *Spode & His Successors*, Cassell, 1925; Leonard Whiter, *Spode: A History of the Family, Factory & Wares, 1733–1833*, Random Century, 1989; Sydney B. Williams, *Antique Blue & White Spode*, David & Charles, 1988.

Museums: Cincinnati Art Museum, Cincinnati, Ohio; City of Stoke-on-Trent Museum, Hanley, England; Spode Museum, Stoke-on-Trent, England; Victoria & Albert Museum, London, England.

Collectors' Note: Although there is no collectors' club, inquiries about Spode Factory wares may be sent to: Historical Consultant, Spode, Stoke-on-Trent, ST4 IBX, England. All inquiries should contain good, clear photographs and full details on the marks.

Bowl, 10" d, castle design, med blue transfer, c1805, imp "SPODE" mark, $350.00

Basket, 8¹³⁄₁₆" d, circ, reticulated, center with floral bouquet and two floral sprigs, openwork sides and scalloped rim decorated with green and gilt bands, three green and gilt dbl foliate scroll handles flanking rose blossom, pairs of paw feet, "gray Spode" and incised potter's mark, pr (A) **1980.00**

Beaker, 2⁷⁄₈" h, botanicals painted in puce, yellow, and green with primula plant with stem of blossoms and buds, reverse with gilt floral spray, gold and white bead and reel border on rim, gilt band borders on footrim and int rim, c1815 (A) **1320.00**

Bowl, Ftd, 10¼" d, "Imperial" pattern with chinoiserie decoration, c1860 (A) **175.00**

Chamberstick, 2³⁄₄" h, gilt birds in branches on claret ground, beadwork and scroll border, gilt ring handle, early 19th C, no.3993 (A) **200.00**

Chocolate Cup, Cov
4³⁄₄" h, with stand, waisted body, painted with large pink cabbage roses, green foliage and gilt accents, domed cov with butterfly finial, winged caryatid handles, gilt line rims, c1820, script "Spode and no.2182" mark (A) **1254.00**
5⅛" h, with stand, painted birds in marshland with flowers in gilt edged panels, green ground, scrolling gilt handles, gilt knob, early 19th C (A) **2100.00**

Coffee Can and Saucer, painted chinoiserie figures at various pursuits in rustic landscapes, gilt key pattern borders, puce script "Spode and no.1579" marks (A) **2090.00**

Cream Pitcher, 4⅛" h, basalt, fluted body (A)   **128.00**

Cup, 2³⁄₄" h, modeled tulip blossom, dark red striped petals, gilt edged sq green base, canted corners, restored, "SPODE" mark (A) **765.00**

Cup and Saucer
Pink roses and gilt, ext with gilt leaves, 1823   **200.00**
Roses on cobalt ground, 19th C, 6 pcs (A) . .   **143.00**

Dessert Service
6 plates, 8" d, 2 shell shaped dishes, oval dish, fruit stand, printed and painted with oriental style design of two birds, flowering peony and other plants amongst rockwork against patterned ground, one cracked, c1820, printed and imp marks, no.4079A) **673.00**
12 plates, 9" d, 4 waisted rect dishes, 4 shell

shaped dishes, 3 sauce tureens, 2 covs, 2 stands, painted with named landscape views, blue and gilded ground, c1800, script titles and "Spode" marks, 27 pcs (A).... **10,560.00**

Dessert Service, Part

Rect fruit stand, 11 1/2" l, 2 circ baskets, 2 shell shaped dishes, 7 dessert plates, 4 dinner plates, "Peacock" pattern, printed in black and enameled in rose, green, turquoise, blue, iron-red, salmon, brown, purple, yellow, gray, and ochre with pair of peacocks perched on rockwork amidst peonies and other oriental flowering plants within border of floral sprays between yellow or ochre spearhead and fretwork bands, brown edged rims, 1815–20, imp "SPODES NEW.-STONE," no.2118, 17 pcs (A) **800.00**

Scalloped lozenge shaped fruit stand, 14 3/16" l, lobed oval sauce tureen, stand, scalloped sq dish, 2 shell shaped dishes, 2 oval dishes, 12 plates, wide border of underglaze blue panels decorated with gold floral motifs, alternating with gilt edged campaniform panels in iron-red and gilding with stylized bamboo and blossoms, gilt edged iron-red borders around center and rim edge, 1805–10, "iron-red SPODE" on sauce tureen, no.715, 20 pcs (A) **3575.00**

Dessert Plate

8 3/16" d, "Peacock" pattern, printed in black and enameled in rose, blue, yellow, iron-red, salmon, ochre, gray, and shades of green with pr of peacocks perched on rocks amidst peonies and other oriental flowering plants within ochre spearhead roundel, rim with four floral sprays in ochre fretowrk and blue cloud panel border at brown edge, c1815, "black SPODE Stone China fret" marks, 2118 in yellow or iron-red, set of 12 (A). **880.00**

8 3/8" d, "Famille-Rose" pattern, transfer printed in black and enameled in rose, green, yellow, iron-red, blue, brown, and gold with pair of Mandarin ducks with lotus and flowering aquatic plants, rim with pink trellis diaper border with panels of objects alternating with flowerheads within gilt band at edge, c1820, "black Spode, iron-red 2975" marks, set of 6 (A) **990.00**

Dinner Service, 2 sq cov tureens, 9 3/4" l, 2 oval cov tureens, 10 1/2" l, sauce tureen with platter, 7 1/2" l, 5 " h, 2 gravy boats, 2 platters, 11 1/4" l, 11" w, 2 oct vegetable bowls, 11 1/2" l, 9" w, blue and white "Oriental" pattern 1815–25, "blue Spode Stone China" mark, service for 12 .... **9600.00**

Dish, 10" l, 7" w, "Flower Cross" pattern, blue and white, blue border on reverse, worn gilt edge, c1810–20. .... **290.00**

Dog Dish, 7 1/16" h, rect shape with canted corners, blue printed "Queen Charlotte" pattern of chinoiserie landscape with two figures on bridge near pagoda, (A). **575.00**

Garniture of Vases, 6 1/8" h-7 1/2" h, painted bouquets of flowers on gilt scale blue ground, white beaded rim and foot, gilt loop and lion mask handles, c1820, no.1166, set of 3 (A) . **4600.00**

Ice Pail, Cov, 11" h, with liner, painted white and yellow lily of the valley and ranuculus, rim molded with entwined dolphins and stylized

acanthus leaves, cov with ring handle and three scroll feet, gilt rims and side handles, repairs, c1820, "iron-red script Spode and #1875" mark, pr (A). **3344.00**

Jug, 1 1/2" h, underglaze blue, iron-red, and gilding with "Imari" pattern of stylized flowers and foliage, loop handle, c1825, painted mark, no.2214 (A) **322.00**

Matchpot, 4" h, "Japan" pattern with flowering shrubs in fenced garden between borders and white beading, early 19th C, "SPODE" and no.967, pr (A). **2488.00**

Mug, 4 1/2" h, ironstone, oriental floral design in Imari enamels, c1820 (A). **412.00**

Mustard Pot, 3 3/4" h, white stoneware, relief of children, blue enamel banding, SP rim and cov (A). **55.00**

Pastille Burner, Cov, 6 1/4" h, oct summerhouse with pointed brown roof, edged with trellis work in gilding, applied colored mosses and flowers, gothic windows in blue and yellow, orange brick ground, winding steps flanked by flowering plants, 1815–27, puce printed mark (A). **2057.00**

Pitcher

4 1/4" h, Rosso Antico, enameled floral design, molded serpent handle (A). **55.00**

5 3/4" h, drabware, relief of children, grapes and vine border (A) **60.00**

Plate

7 1/8" d, "Italian" pattern, blue and white, c1784–1805, imp "Spode and blue Spode" mark. **165.00**

7 1/4" d, "Gothic Castle" pattern, blue and white, reticulated border, c1815 .... **375.00**

8 1/4" d

"Italian" pattern, blue and white, c1784–1805, imp "Spode and blue Spode" mark. **185.00**

"Tiber" pattern, oriental boating scene with villas and temple, med blue transfer (A) **132.00**

8 3/8" d, sq, English rural view in green, brown, blue, gray, yellow, and iron-red, within gilt roundel, cobalt blue ground, encircled by gilt scrollwork and patterned cartouches, notched rim, gilt scrollwork border, 1815–25, view identifications and "black Spode" mark, set of 5 (A) **1320.00**

9 1/8" d, "Temple Landscape" pattern, blue and white, 1805–20, imp "New Stone China" mark. **225.00**

9 3/4" d, "Net" pattern, blue and white, oriental scenes in cartouches, shaped edge, c1820 .... **385.00**

10" d, felspar, painted flower spray, apple green border, white and gilt gadrooned rim, "puce Spode and no.3034" marks, set of 6 (A). **875.00**

Platter

14 1/2" l, 11 3/4" h, blue Japanese type branches with shades of pink, blue and iron-red leaves, panels of blue with red and iron-red leaves on border extending to rim, c1820, "blue Spode Stone China" mark .. **350.00**

19" l, 14 1/2" w, two exotic birds on gray rock formations, large open dark pink flower, multicolored open flowers, garden flower sprays on border, orange and blue geometrics on rim, orange cavetto inner border, c1820, imp "Spode" mark **550.00**

20½" l, 15¾" w, blue transfer, classical ruins in foreground, castle in ground, c1820 .... **500.00**

20½" l, canted rect shape, underglaze blue, multicolor enamels, gilding with scrolling foliage, stylized flowers, c1825, imp "New Stone" mark (A) **1346.00**

Potpourri Basket, 4⅛" h, molded basketweave body, green painted sprigs of flowers and fruits, gilded borders, entwined handles, c1820, pr (A) **1045.00**

Potpourri Jar, Cov, 8¼" h, oct panel of shells on lilac ground, reverse with gilt urn and arabesques, gilt borders, gilded griffin handles and dragon finial, c1820 (A).............. **4114.00**

Punch Bowl, 12½" d, famille rose enamel painted ducks swimming with peonies, trellis border with precious objects, c1815–20, "Stone China," gilt no.360 (A)............. **3200.00**

Sauce Tureen, Cov
8" l, 4⅝" h, undertray, 10¼" l, iron-red, pink, cobalt, and gilt Imari type open flowers, green leaves, gilt veined handles and handle on cov, floral ladle, imp and "blue printed SPODE no.3277" marks, pr..... **1675.00**

8½" l, with undertray, "Royal Jasmine" pattern, brown transfer (A)................ **50.00**

10¼" d, with undertray, lobed bombe shape, "Japan" pattern of large peony, bamboo tree, and other flowers in fenced garden in elaborate border of gilt whorl panels, Imari palette, brown rim, gilt handles, c1820, "red Spode and no.967" mark (A)........... **900.00**

Soup Plate
9¼" d, "Queen Charlotte" pattern, blue and white, shaped rim in gold, dtd 1885...... **127.00**

9½" d, "Tiber" pattern, blue and white, rust rim, c1820 .... **235.00**

10" d, "Castle" pattern, blue and white, scalloped edge, c1805, imp Spode mark..... **350.00**

Sweetmeat Dish
7¾" l, molded rect shape, pink, rose, green, yellow, and rust floral center, oriental type border in blue, gilt, rust, and light blue, handle, c1810.......................... **695.00**

9¼" l, pink florals with rust florals on border, blue edged outlined border with brown and white circles with florals on border, scalloped and paneled, brown and white raised cupped handle, c1825, imp "Spode" mark **425.00**

Teapot
3¾" h, miniature, sides with applied trailing colored flowers, gilded accents, rustic handle and spout, c1830, "script Spode" mark (A)................................... **800.00**

4¾" h, molded tree trunk form, oak leaf relief decoration, brown glaze (A)............ **55.00**

Tray, 10⅜" l, rect
"Long Eliza" pattern, blue and white, shaped border, c1810–20, imp "Spode" and printed mark....................... **330.00**

Ruins in ground, couple with sheep near water in foreground, blue transfer, "blue Spode" mark............................... **160.00**

Vase
4½" h, flared cylinder shape, painted satirical scene of man drinking or man mending fishing net in gilt frame, yellow ground, reverse with flower spray and four gilt mons,

white molded beadwork and gilt on rim and base, c1810, "red Spode" mark, pr (A)... **1345.00**

10" h, Imari design in underglaze blue with polychrome enameling and gilt (A)....... **330.00**

10³⁄₁₆" h, ovoid shape, underglaze blue, iron-red, green, salmon, and gold, front and reverse with oriental fenced garden within floral, foliate and patterned panel borders, gilt edged flaring neck, underglaze blue scroll handles patterned with gilt scalework, 1810–15, "iron-red SPODE, 967" mark (A)........................ **3025.00**

15⅛, 15¼" h, multicolored enameled with large and small sprigs of iris, tulips, morning glories, and daffodils on dark blue ground, gold shell and seaweed clusters, gilt edged rim, c1820, "SPODE no.3419" mark, pr (A) **3850.00**

SPONGEWARE

Staffordshire, England
Continental
c1840 to c1900

History: Spongeware, a cut-sponge stamped pattern decoration used on earthenwares and everyday tablewares, was achieved by dipping a sponge in color and applying it to the ware to produce a stamp of the pattern. A single dip of color produced about a dozen impressions. This accounts for the variation in shades.

The stamping technique was invented in Scotland and brought to England about 1845. It was a time-saving device used in decorating inexpensive china that was made mostly for export.

Cut-sponge border patterns included a variety of florals, leaves, scrolls, stars, triangles, hearts, and chains. Some borders supplemented the cut-sponge decoration with hand painting. The center motif also included combinations of cut-sponge and painted decorations.

William Adams and Son of Tunstall was one of the largest English producers of cut-sponge decorated pieces. W. Baker and Company of Fenton; Edge, Malkin and Company of Burslem; and Britannia Pottery of Glasglow were other leading manufacturers of spongeware.

Petrus Regout and Company in Holland, and Villeroy and Boch, in Germany were among the principal Continental manufacturers.

References: Kevin McConnell, *Spongeware and Spatterware,* Schiffer Publishing Co., 1990; Earl F. & Ada F. Robacker, *Spatterware and Sponge,* A. S. Barnes & Co., 1978.

Collecting Hints: Cut-sponge work can be identified by the uneven strength of the color in repeated motifs. Remember, the color supply lessened in the sponge as the pattern was repeated. An uneven interval or space between decorative motifs also indicates spongeware. Border motifs may overlapped. A smudged effect often occurs because of too much pigment or a worn stamp. If a stamp has a defect in its design, it will be repeated throughout the pattern.

Bowl
7" d, bulbous shape, blue sponging........ **140.00**

8½" d, green and brown sponging on tan ground................................. **45.00**

Soup Plate, 9" d, "Bete und Hebrite" in red and black center, lt blue floral border, $35.00

c1722

c1680-1700

ST. CLOUD

Seine-et-Oise, France
c1690–1773

History: About 1675 Pierre Chicanneau established a factory for the production of faience and soft paste porcelain at St. Cloud. Shortly after Chicanneau's death in 1678, Berthe, his widow, assumed control of the works.

St. Cloud porcelain was thickly potted with a yellowish color to the body. The glaze was very glassy with a somewhat orange peel texture to the surface. The pieces were decorated in strong polychromes or in the simple blue motifs similar to the faience examples from Rouen, especially in the use of the Baroque diapering pattern. Many forms featured plain white and relief patterns. Fish scale-type embellishments were used as the method of decoration.

The variety of wares produced was quite large, exhibiting applied decoration. Accessory pieces, e.g., knife and cane handles, and novelty pieces, some of which were silver mounted, were made. Many of the designs incorporated elements from silverware such as reeding or gadrooning.

Family squabbles plagued the St. Cloud pottery. In 1722 Berthe Coudray died. Henri-Charles Trou II, backed by the sponsorship of the Duc d'Orleans, took control. The St. Cloud factory ended its operations about 1773.

References: W. B. Honey, *French Porcelain of the 18th Century*, 1950; George Savage, *Seventeenth & Eighteenth Century French Porcelain*, Hamlyn Publishing Co., Ltd., 1969.

Museums: J. Paul Getty Museum, Malibu, California; Victoria & Albert Museum, London, England.

9½" d, brown sponging on cream ground, unmarked	30.00
Bread and Milk Set, dark blue overall sponging on white ground, unmarked	225.00
Cup and Saucer, blue flower in cup	55.00
Cuspidor, 7¾" d, blue sponging on white ground, rim chip (A)	22.00
Milk Pitcher, 7½" h, black sponging on white ground	185.00
Mug, 5" h, baluster shape, pale grey body, coated on ext with cobalt-stained dip, looped handle with pinched terminal, c1775, cracks (A)	1589.00
Pitcher	
8½" h, tankard shape, blue sponging on white ground	165.00
9" h, blue sponging on white ground (A)	187.00
9½" h	
Blue and brown sponging, gilt trim, crazing (A)	30.00
Blue and white sponging (A)	145.00
10" h	
Barrel shape, green, gold, and brown sponging	95.00
Beige and blue sponging on white, hairlines (A)	137.00
10½" h, blue sponging on white ground, ftd oct base (A)	150.00
11" h, blue and brown sponging, hairline on handle (A)	60.00
Plate	
3¼" d, blue peacock center with rose color tail, rose sponge border, c1800, pr	225.00
9½" d	
Blue-gray sponging with areas of green, late 18th C (A)	336.00
Center flower in red, green, and black, red and green sponge border (A)	192.00
Platter, 14¼" l, 11¼" w, brown sponged border with cut sponged small red and blue flowers, green leaves, brown circle in center, cream ground, unmarked	550.00
Soup Plate, 9" d, blue and white sponging (A)	33.00
Vegetable Bowl, 8½" l, 6" w, dark blue sponging on white ground, c1820	225.00
Waste Bowl, 5⅝" d, overall red sponging (A)	71.00

Beaker, blue lacework scrolls and lambrequins, c1730, "blue sun in splendour" mark (A)	2000.00
Bonbonniere, 2" h, duck form, white, cov molded with flowering wild cherry branch, silver mts (A)	2211.00

Bonbonniere, 2" h, white, cov molded with flowering cherry branch, silver mts, c1730, (A) $2000.00

Coffee Cup and Saucer, trembleuse saucer, blue painted lambrequins above vert reeding, c1730 .... **484.00**

Egg Cup, 3¼" h, white, baroque metalwork form, fluted bowl on fluted knobed stem, conical foot, c1730 .... **1245.00**

Figure, 6¼" h, 6⅝" h, white chinoiserie, lady and man in frilled conical hats, belted short coat, ornamental collar, loose sleeves, long skirt, low base, c1735, pr (A) **4950.00**

Jar, 6¾" h, painted on sides with oriental figures in garden, reverse with three boys in fishing boat and island pavilion, gilt accents, lion mask handles accented in red, yellow, and brown, c1735 (A) **34,595.00**

Mustard Pot, 2⅜" h, painted iron-red, green, brown, and gilt band of flowering foliage between two ribbed bands, ring handle, cracks, c1740 (A) **550.00**

Potpourri
  5½" h, white, baluster vase shape, pierced shoulder with applied flowering branches, rockwork base, cov missing, c1745 (A) ... **786.00**
  7¼" h, white, dbl ogee shape with molded gadroons on lower section, pierced shoulder with applied festoons of flowers, rockwork base (A) **375.00**

Teapot, 4¼" h, ovoid body, molded around shoulder and base with fluted bands between underglaze blue zig-zag borders at mid-section, trellis diaper and flowerhhead borders on neck and foot, crested beast spout and handle, cov missing, cracks, 1725–35, "St. Cloud" mark (A) **330.00**

Wine Cooler, 7¹/₁₆" h,-7³/₁₆" h, molded on front and reverse with pink and yellow chrysanthemums and pink shaded green leaves growing behind white pierced rock between borders of molding fluting on rim, lower body, and foot, grotesque mask handles, open mouths with protruding tongues, turquoise ground, cracks, c1735, incised marks, pr (A)   **2475.00**

STAFFORDSHIRE—BLUE AND WHITE

England
End of 18th C–1880s

History: Blue and white transfer printed earthenwares came to the Staffordshire district of England by the end of the 18th century. The transfer printing process was first used by Thomas Turner at Caughley in Shropshire.

At first patterns reflected Chinese porcelain designs and the willow pattern was featured prominently in many examples. As the technique improved, scenics featuring abbeys, houses, castles, rivers, and exotic travel destinations were printed on wares. A tremendous export market developed since Americans were eager for scenes of American towns, sites, and historical events of interest.

Florals, birds, and animals also found their way to earthenwares as did literary illustrations from prominent authors such as Sir Walter Scott and Charles Dickens.

Another area where blue printed wares were utilized was in childrens feeding bottles, pap boats, and feeding cups for use with invalids.

All blue printed wares are underglaze. Many makers used the same designs since there were no copyright laws to protect designs. Wares that are not marked are very difficult to attribute to a particular maker.

With the Copyright Act of 1842, copying of designs became much more difficult. Original designs were now registered to protect from copying for three years and then there was a renewal option. Makers could no longer copy engraving from literary works or other books. Since new sources were needed, designers turned to romantic scenes which were then quite popular.

By the 1880s, there were relatively few new patterns in use. White dinner services with printed borders became popular. Brightly colored dinnerwares also came into vogue.

References: Arthur Coysh, *Blue-and-White Transfer ware 1780–1840*, David and Charles, 1970; A.W. Coysh and R.K. Henrywood, *The Dictionary of Blue and White Printed Pottery 1780–1880, Vol. II*, Antique Collectors' Club, 1989.

Collectors' Club: Friends of Blue, Ron Govier, 10 Sea View Road, Herne Bay, Kent CT 6 6JQ, 8 pounds sterling, quarterly bulletins.

Museum: Wellcome Museum, London, England

Platter, 14¾" l, stoneware, pagoda below patna on the Ganges river, floral border, med blue transfer, mid 19th C, "I. Hall & Sons" mark, $250.00

Soup Tureen, 12" h, reserves of Turk and camel, foliate decoration on diamond pattern ground, mid 19th C, "I. Hall" mark, $1000.00

Teabowl, 3 1/4" h, hounds surrounded by scrolling foliage, c1850, unmkd, $45.00

Berry Basket and Undertray, 10" H-H, 3 1/2" h, oct, oriental pattern, blue transfer, reticulated, c1790–1800 . . . . **595.00**

Berry Bowl, 6 1/2" d, Creamer, 5" h, blue and white urn in center with florals, swags with blue panels, blue florals int and ext, c1822–30, Hilditch & Son **225.00**

Bowl, 10 1/2" d, Quadrupeds Series, "Lion in center, four medallions of Deer, Zebras, Horses, and Goats," beaded edge, cracked, Hall (A) **330.00**

Bowl and Undertray, 12 3/8" l, dark blue transfer of fisherman and family, reticulated sides, repair to tray (A) **605.00**

Coffee Pot, 12 1/4" h, creamware, chinoiserie landscape of three figures standing by pagoda, floral and botanical band borders, strap handle, domed cov with ball finial (A) **380.00**

Creamer

5" h, dark blue transfer of basket of fruit, "Stevenson" mark (A) **137.00**

5 7/8" h, English scene of boy fishing (A) **220.00**

Cup Plate

3 1/2" d, man flying kite, English buildings on right, light blue transfer (A) **93.00**

4 1/8" d

Seashells, dark blue transfer, imp "Stubbs" mark (A) **185.00**

House in country scene, floral border (A) . **115.00**

"Youth and Old Age," transfer, child flying kite, old man looking at tombstone **135.00**

Dish, 5 3/8" d, four putti with goat and tree, leaf and grape border, light blue transfer, red line inner border, purple luster rim, unmarked . . . **75.00**

Egg Holder, 8" l, 5 1/4" w, 4 1/2" h, "Elephant" pattern, dark blue transfer, lion's head finial, six egg cups, hairline, c1830 "John Rogers & Son" mark **350.00**

Gravy Tureen, 7 1/2" h, with undertray, Quadrapeds Series, "Dog and Rabbit, Fox and Rooster," dark blue transfers, hairlines and repairs, Hall (A) **605.00**

Jug, 7" h, "Giraffe" pattern, two standing camels, one lying down, two arabs in dress, flowers and scroll border **150.00**

Meat Platter

16 7/8" l, "Italian Ruins" pattern of classical buildings by river with bridge, hop border, med blue transfer (A) **228.00**

19 5/8" l, "Greek" pattern of figures in circ cartouches on key fret and anthemion border, center figures, combed ground (A) . . . **285.00**

20 1/4" l, center scene of man on elephant,

birds on sides, floral, scroll and butterfly border, med blue transfer, c1820 . . . . **1200.00**

20 1/2" l, oct, "Hospitality" pattern, farmer's wife with children, blind and lame traveler, border of flowers and leaves (A) **900.00**

Mug

5 1/4" h, 5" d, floral and bird pattern, blue transfer, blue floral int rim, blue transfer on handle, c1820–40 . . . . **295.00**

5 1/2" h, cylinder shape, chinoiserie decoration, med blue transfer, loop handle, late 18th C (A) **295.00**

Pap Boat, 7 1/2" l, blue and white florals, c1850 . . . . **650.00**

Pitcher, 5 1/2" h, oriental scene, blue transfer, c1848, Eng Reg mark **225.00**

Plate

6 3/4" d, birds and fruit pattern, dark blue transfer, c1820 . . . . **150.00**

7 1/8" d, mother and child, med blue transfer (A) **45.00**

7 5/8" d

Game birds scene, dark blue transfer (A) . **95.00**

"Semi China Nankeen," paneled border, handled, 1816–30 . . . . **850.00**

8 1/2" d, dk blue transfer, oriental scene, gold trim, c1860 . . . . **150.00**

8 5/8" d, shell design in dark blue transfer, imp "Stubbs" mark (A) **148.00**

9" d, shepherd in med blue transfer, crazing (A) **22.00**

9 1/4" d, hunter with dog, cottage, and thatched roof cottage, med blue transfer, hairlines (A) **65.00**

9 1/2" d, elephant and attendant in oriental scene, Rogers **45.00**

9 3/4" d, oct, center mill scene, floral border, med blue transfer, unmarked **125.00**

10" d

"Greenwich" pattern, med blue transfer (A) **66.00**

Large fruit and flowers in center, floral border, dark blue transfer, c1790, Stubbs . . **325.00**

"The 1st Thanksgiving," scalloped edge, Crown Ducal **25.00**

"The Spirit of 76," scalloped edge, "Made for R.H. Stearns Co. Boston, Mass." on reverse, Crown Ducal **25.00**

10 1/8" d, center scene of scattered fruit in dark blue transfer, open flowers in border, scalloped rim, imp "radiating star" mark . . **150.00**

10 1/4" d

"Palestine," dark blue transfer, c1810, "Ralph Stevenson" mark **450.00**

"Quadrupeds," dark blue transfer, hairline (A) **100.00**

10 1/2" d

"Costumbres Espanole," Spanish dancers, bull fighters, bull ring scene in center, medallions on rim, imp "Geo. Jones" mark **65.00**

Garden whimsey scene in light blue transfer (A) **18.00**

Platter

12 1/4" l, 9 1/4" w, "Elephant and Howdah," dark blue transfer, 1798–1801, imp "Wedgwood & Co." mark **550.00**

12 3/4" l

"Chinese Pagoda and Bridge," light blue transfer (A) **55.00**

Vase of flowers, dark blue transfer, hairline . **285.00**

15" l, country squire and hunting dogs in forest setting (A) 300.00
15½" l, 13¾" w, "India Flowers" pattern, purple, orange, and pink flowers, ribbed bottom, c1830, semi- china 375.00
16½" l, 12¾" w, "Vue Du Temple De La Philosophie ER Memonville," dark blue transfer, c1825, imp "WOOD" mark..... 675.00
16⅝" l, "Cromwell Dismissing the Long Parliment," med blue transfer, "Jones & Son" mark................................ 550.00
16¾" l
12½" w, classic scene with two cows, river and bridge, floral border, c1825, "Thomas Lakin" mark 750.00
Oriental harbor scene, floral and leaf border, med blue transfer, c1820 .... 750.00
17" l, 13" w, "Beehive and Vases" pattern, dark blue transfer, c1825, R. Stevenson & Williams.............................. 985.00
17½" l, overall floral and butterfly decoration, 3rd qtr 19th C (A)................ 143.00
18" l, 13¾" w, Shipping Series, "Day Sea Battle," shell border, dark blue transfer, unmarked............................... 2200.00
19" l, blue transfer, center with floral bouquet and butterfly, floral border, 3rd qtr 19th C (A).................................. 467.00
19¼" l, 14¾" w, "Wreath," blue transfer, c1840, Dimmock....................... 525.00
20" l, 16" w, "Peruvian Hunters," light blue transfer (A) 175.00
20½" l, 16¾" w, "The Girl Musician," blue transfer, "J.& R. Riley" mark 250.00

Sauce Tureen, 6½" h, fluted baluster shape, "Flora" pattern of still life of fruit and roses, ribbon border, med blue transfer, leaf handles, cabbage rose knob, John Meir (A) 285.00

Serving Dish
11¾" l, oval, oriental scenes in dark blue transfer, imp "WOOD" mark (A) 300.00
17¾" l, Shipping Series, "Day Sea Battle', med blue transfer (A).................. 495.00

Slop Pail, 12" h, baluster shape, "The Gleaners" pattern, med blue transfer, shell handles (A). 1710.00

Soup Plate
8½" d, Oriental Sports, "Common Wolf Trap," med blue transfer, Challinor (A) ... 93.00
9" d, "Old English," gilt edge, Corona ware, c1902, "C.H.& Co." crown mark 17.50
9½" d, "Elephant" pattern, med blue transfer, Rogers........................... 95.00

Soup Tureen
10" h, blue transfer of Indian landscape scene, mid 19 C (A) 605.00
15½" l, 13½" h, "The Font," floral border, c1830 .... 2100.00

Sugar Bowl, Cov
5" h, continuous river scene by castle ruins, sea shell handles, floral border (A) 242.00
5½" h, vase of fruit on sides, floral swags, "TAMS, ANDERSON & TAMS" mark (A) . 115.00
6⅜" h, wide open florals, med blue transfer, floral knob, Stevenson 350.00
7" h, overall floral design, dark blue transfer (A).................................. 150.00

Teabowl and Saucer
Girl milking cow in meadow, border of flower blossoms, med blue transfers........... 125.00
Open flowerheads and leaves, saucer with border of dashes, med blue transfers..... 95.00
Romantic sailing scene in front of castle, dark blue transfers, unmarked............... 165.00

Teapot
7" h, rect, overall floral design, domed cov with bird finial (A)...................... 100.00
11¾" h, country scene with fishermen at waters edge, florals on upper portion, med blue transfer, unmarked................. 565.00
13" h, open flowers in basket, scattered large and small flowers, dark blue transfer, c1780 .... 1000.00

Toast Rack, 8" H-H, blue flowers, buildings on dividers, c1830........................... 675.00

Tray, 10¼" l, rect, "Classical Ruins" pattern, shaped edge, c1810–17, Thomas Lakin..... 385.00

Tureen and Tray, 9" l, paneled ovoid form, dbl scroll handles, blue border, eagle perched on globe clutching arrows, cream ground, repaired, c1846, T.F.& Co. (A) 99.00

Vase
3¾" h, three cows and couple on riverbank in front of mansion, dark blue transfer (A) 231.00
6" h, bulbous base, cylinder neck with wide flaring rim, circ foot, English manor house behind lake, floral border, vert handles, repairs, unmarked (A) 302.00

Vegetable Dish, Cov, 12" l, 8" w, 5½" h, "Weir" pattern, med blue transfer, c1908, "F.& Sons, Burslem" mark................. 118.00

STAFFORDSHIRE FIGURES

Staffordshire, England c1740–1900

History: During the eighteenth century, Staffordshire figures in salt glazed stoneware and Whieldon type earthenwares with translucent colored glazes were made by the family of Ralph Wood. (See: Ralph Wood)

Obadiah Sherratt's figures from the late 1820s display the rustic realism of true peasant art with humor, pathos, and brutality. The modeling is bold and crude; enamel colors are bright. Many figures are quite large. Usually Sherratt's figures are mounted on a table base. The name for the piece often is written on the front. Among his most famous pieces are "The Bull Baiting Group" and "Remus and Romulus." Sherratt also did classical and religious figures.

With the accession of Queen Victoria in 1837, simplicity of design appeared as well as restraint in the coloring of figures. Nineteenth century earthenware Staffordshire figures were made in a simple, uncomplicated manner, often mass produced at low cost for the cottage rather than for the stately home.

The figures featured a flat back, were compact in design, and were mounted on an oval base that was part of the figure. Figures were displayed on mantles, window ledges, bookcases, or Welsh dressers. Only the fronts were visible so decorations were restricted to the front of the figure. About 1840 potters made mantlepiece ornaments in under the glaze colors in great quantity. Cottage ornaments depicted the homely scenes characteristic of the people that bought them.

The most distinctive color used was the rich, dark, glossy cobalt blue. Additional colors included pink, green, orange, black, and some gold. After 1860 more colors were utilized including a pale flesh pink shade. The pottery was harder and whiter than in earlier pieces.

Both human and animal figures were molded. Just about every Victorian kitchen featured a pair of spaniels on either side of the kitchen clock. Greyhounds, poodles, dalmations, cats, and even zebras were memorialized in Staffordshire figures. Topical events, heroes and heroines of the times, members of the Royal Family, and theatrical characters appeared. Churches, cottages, and castles were popular. A unique form was the Victorian watch stand. Few figures were marked with a maker's mark.

Sampson Smith was the most prolific maker of the flat-backed figures and Staffordshire dogs. He worked from about 1847 to 1878. Others continued to use his molds to make figures long after his death. In addition to his famous dogs, Sampson Smith is known for figures of castles, churches, cottages, jockeys, Dick Turpin, toby jugs, politicans, and royalty, including Queen Victoria.

References: T. Balston, *Staffordshire Portrait Figures of the Victorian Age,* Faber & Faber, 1958; J. Hall, *Staffordshire Portrait Figures,* Charles Letts & Co., Ltd., 1972; Reginald S. Haggar, *Staffordshire Chimney Ornaments,* Phoenix House, Ltd., 1955; B. Latham, *Victorian Staffordshire Portrait Figures for the Small Collector,* Tiranti, 1953; A. Oliver, *The Victorian Staffordshire Figures: A Guide for Collectors,* Heinemann, 1971; P. D. G. Pugh, *Staffordshire Portrait Figures & Allied Subjects of the Victorian Era,* rev. ed., Antique Collectors Club, Ltd., 1987; H. A. B. Turner, *A Collector's Guide to Staffordshire Pottery Figures,* Emerson Books, Inc., 1971.

Museums: American Antiquarian Society, Worcester, Massachusetts; Brighton Museum, Brighton, England; British Museum, London, England; City Museum and Art Gallery, Stoke-on-Trent, England; The Detroit Institute of Arts, Detroit, Michigan; Fitzwilliam Museum, Cambridge, England, Victoria & Albert Museum, London, England.

REPRODUCTION ALERT: Lancaster and Sandlands are reproducing some of the old Staffordshire models, especially the animal and cottage figures. The colors march the old Staffordshire cobalt blue quite well.

Arbor Group, 13 1/2" h, Highland boy and girl in flesh, brown, gold, and white, flat back, hairline (A) **110.00**

Atlas, 11 1/4" h, kneeling muscular figure with drapery tied around waist, supporting spheri-

Farmer and Wife, 10" h, multicolored, rounded bk, c1865, unmkd, $255.00

Spill Vase, 12" h, "The Rivals", cobalt, orange, green, and pink, orange int, c1855, $500.00

cal potpourri holder pierced with holes and printed in black with flowers, black washed sq base, early 19th C (A) **450.00**

"Auld Lang Syne," 8 1/2" h, men seated at table in drinking group, two in blue coats, one in orange, c1860 .... **825.00**

Baby in Cradle, young girl standing at side, multicolored, rect base **125.00**

Bear, 2 1/4" h, long fur painted black, white collar around neck, standing on sponged green mound, c1830 .... **1450.00**

Bird, 3 1/4" h, whistle, with topknot, perched on green stump, glazed in translucent, brown and ochre, c1780 .... **1250.00**

Birds in Branches, 6 3/8" h, porcelain, two yellow birds nesting in gnarled tree with ivy, rocky mound base encrusted with flowers and vegetation, c1830 (A) **475.00**

Bottle, 6" h, man or woman with basket of flowers, multicolored, pedestal base, cork stopper, repairs, c1830, pr **350.00**

Boy with Sheep, 7" h, boy standing next to brick wall with sheep standing on ledge, green, gold, and brown accents, white ground (A) **143.00**

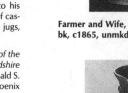

Cottage, 5" h, umbrella-type, salmon walls, white roof encrusted with multicolored florals, dk orange door, gold line on base, unmkd, $450.00

Bull-Baiting Group, 8" l, bull with head lowered, harassed by snapping terrier, rocky shaped oval mound, restored, early 19th C (A) **1378.00**

Bust of Washington, polychrome enamels with blue underglaze (A) **460.00**

Castellar Church, 14" h, central tower with clock face on one side, surrounded by bowed wall with battlements and central studded doors, flanked by round towers, brown washed over simulated stonework, white details, brown windows, repaired, early 19th C, (A) **5236.00**

Cat
3 3/4" h, seated, white body with black sponged markings, late 19th C (A) **137.00**

6 7/8" h, seated, splotched polychrome enameling, hairlines, pr (A) **770.00**

7" h, seated on cushion, striped black and orange body, c1800, pr (A) **633.00**

Charity, 7 1/4" h, center female holding child, child at each side, one with cross, overglazed polychromes, hairline (A) **220.00**

Children with Windmill, 9 3/4" h, crusted florals, c1850 .... **675.00**

Circus Group, 8 1/2" h, trainer in brightly painted costume, holding chain of standing bear, oval grassy base with scrollwork at front, flowering bocage, repairs, early 19th C (A) **2680.00**

Cobbler's Wife, 6 5/8" h, pouring from pitcher, orange, lavender, light yellow, blue, black, green, and blue (A) **198.00**

Cockerel, 8 1/2" h, overall in cobalt blue glaze, c1800 (A) **1295.00**

Cottage
5 1/4" h, money box, house sponged in black with purple, two faces peering from upstairs window, flanked by two figures, buff ground, c1810 (A) **650.00**

5 3/4" h, 6 1/2" w, three turreted castle with clock tower, salmon, blue, purple, and green, 19th C (A) **220.00**

6 1/2" h
5 1/4" w, blue shingled roof, center turret, red chimney, 19th C (A) **165.00**

6 1/2" w, two wings and dbl staircase, salmon, red, and yellow, 19th C, Rockingham **150.00**

7 1/8" h, two story decorated in orange, green, red, yellow, and blue **375.00**

7 3/8" h, 6" w, castle with drummer boy molded into side, orange, yellow, brown, green, and pink, 19th C (A) **242.00**

8" h, crusted flowers around first and second floors, orange pillars, gilt trim, gilt (A) **485.00**

8 1/4" h, 8 1/2" w, "TRINITY COLLEGE" with ivy covered walls in salmon, red, lavender, and yellow, restored, 19thC (A)......... **220.00**

Cybele, 9 7/8" h, holding long cornucopia filled with flowers, red, blue, pink, rust, and yellow coloring, late 18th C (A) **242.00**

Dalmation, 5 1/4" h, white with blue spots, cobalt blue base with gilt trim, gilt leash, c1830–50 **495.00**

Dancing Bear, 8 3/8" h, trainer in Turkish cap, fur trimmed cape, checked coat, holds muzzled dancing bear by a stout rope, between them is small dog done as a lion, scrolled base, leafy tree, repairs, c1825 .... **8750.00**

Dandy, 8 3/8" h, standing next to bocage, seashells on rect base, brown, yellow, and green, attrib to Obadiah Sherratt (A) **820.00**

Darby and Joan, 11 1/8" h, flesh faces, pink, blue, and black trim, marked on base **350.00**

Deer, 4" h, recumbent, natural colors, late 18th C (A)................................... **155.00**

Dick Turpin, 11 1/2" h, on horseback, multicolored (A)................................. **245.00**

Dogs, 9" h, rust and white, one sitting on white base, one sitting on tan keg, c1860 .... **485.00**

Donkey, 6 1/2" h, with basket of flowers, polychrome, repairs (A)...................... **137.00**

Duke and Duchess of Edinburgh, 14" h, 12 2/3" h, brightly colored, Duke in uniform with sashes over both shoulders, right hand on pedestal, holding plumed cocked hat, Duchess with full length dress with bow on each shoulder, waisted oval bases, c1874, pr (A)**654.00**

Duke of Cambridge, 13 1/2" h, on horseback, multicolored (A)......................... **385.00**

Equestrian
8" h, Mr. Wells as John Gilpin, polychrome enamel, man mounted on horse facing right, tricorn hat, riding jacket, waistcoat, breeches, and knee boots (A) **342.00**

9" h, 9 3/8" h, lady and gentleman each riding a white rearing steed with black patches, he wearing green jacket, yellow breeches, black topper and boots, she with green mantle, pink hat, colorful rect bracket base, horse with tree-stump support, restoration, c1830, pr (A)......................**16,269.00**

12" h, Lord Raglan, orange jacket, white trousers with yellow stripe, sleeve pinned to chest, holding baton in left hand, Thomas Parr (A) **1890.00**

Faith, 9" h, standing figure holding jug, rust, yellow, left blue, and green, sq base, restorations **200.00**

Falstaff, 6 7/8" h, seated plump figure, green, pink, yellow, orange, and purple (A)....... **198.00**

Fisherman and Woman, 13 1/2" h, standing man resting on basket and brick wall, woman in apron and brick wall, yellow, gold, tan, blue, black, and lavender, flat back, pr (A) **360.00**

G. Gordon, 16 1/2" h, standing figure in uniform, orange, gold, red, and black highlights, white ground, flat back, mid 19th C (A) **250.00**

Harlequin, 5 3/8" h, green, black, yellow, red, and lavender diamonds on costume, bocage missing (A) **1100.00**

Harvest, 11" h, woman holding cornucopia in polychrome enamels (A) **275.00**

Hen on Nest
9 1/2" l, white, unmarked (A) **165.00**

7" l, 6" h, 5 3/8" w, bisque, white hen with red comb, green grass, brown woven base ... **245.00**

10 3/4" l, hen with chicks on basketweave base, polychrome colors, unmarked (A)... **400.00**

Highlander, 16 1/2" h, cobalt jacket, plaid kilt, orange flag and drum trim, green and yellow leaves **550.00**

Highland Piper and girl, 14" h, sitting on archway with clock below, white with orange, green, brown, and lavender accents, flat back (A).. **209.00**

Hound, 7" h, 6 1/2" w, standing hound with dead rabbit at feet, orange, black, red, and green, 19th C (A) **245.00**

Hunter over Lion, 16" h, multicolored (A)..... **440.00**

Ice Skater, 7 1/2" h, man in period clothes on skates, black, light green, light blue, brown, and pink, bocage missing, 19th C **225.00**

Inkwell
3¾" h, 4¾" w, reclining whippet in brown
and gold on blue base (A) 110.00
4" h, 3¾" w, nesting swan in green, orange,
and gold 100.00
5" h, 7" l, whippet in tan, rust, and white,
cobalt base, gilt trim, rust "1851 SPRING"
mark................................... 650.00
King Charles Spaniel, 12½" l, recumbent animal with brown markings, on rect cushion in
green, yellow, and pink, 2nd half 19th C (A) 1250.00
Lady Archer, 7½" h, standing, feathered hat,
long dress, bow and arrow in hands, target on
tree, damaged, c1830 (A) 607.00
Leopard, 3⅝" h, head turned, paw raised, orange-brown with black spots, grassy oval base
with applied flowers and foliage, early 19th C
(A)................................... 1590.00
Little Red Riding Hood, 8¾" h, orange cloak
and cap, floral dress, dog, green and brown
base 535.00
Lion
2½" h, recumbent, cream glaze with green
spots, hairlines (A)..................... 303.00
2¾" h, seated, yellow and black coloring,
rect base, crack in base, 19th C 100.00
5¼" h, yellow lion with band about his middle, standing on shaped base before a
bocage with red and blue flowers, repair to
bocage tips, c1825 .... 2500.00
8" h
12" l, recumbent on rect plinth, allover
brown and yellow striped glaze (A) 220.00
Standing lion with front paw on ball, caramel brown, rect base, pr.............. 350.00
9" h, standing lion with teeth showing, front
paw on ball, yellow glaze, rect base with
painted flowers, c1825, pr (A).......... 1375.00
10" h, 13" l, seated, brown and gold coat,
black muzzle, yellow glass eyes, mottled
green base, late 19th C, pr (A)........... 110.00
10¾" h, 13¾" l, standing, brown coat, red
mouth, black muzzle, gold accents, glass
eyes, late 19th C, pr (A) 247.00
Lion and Lamb Group, 8½" h, orange and
black, seated facing to left and right, recumbent lamb at feet with brown markings,
molded oval bases with brown and green
markings c1848, pr (A).................. 2633.00
Man, 7¼" h, yellow tunic, brown hat, holding
nosegay, brown staff, hair in ringlets, brown
washed sq base, crack, late 18th C (A) 2050.00
Man and Woman
6½" h, man leaning on cane, woman with
basket in front, period clothes, multicolored,
pr (A)................................. 220.00
8½" h, seated with painted clock and border
surrounding them, man in blue top, green
and rust striped pants, woman in orange
bodice, rose, green, and white skirt 295.00
9½" h, each holding basket of grapes in colors flanking pseudo clock............... 200.00
Marat, 8¼" h, brown unbuttoned jacket, white
waistcoat, yellow breeches, wig and shoes
glazed in olive-brown, seated on tree stump,
hands resting on knees, olive-brown and
green rocky base, damage to left hand,
1793–94 (A)........................... 5340.00
Men, 9" h, man in beige coat and lantern, an-

other in rust coat with jug, black hats, white
and rose scroll base 795.00
Milkmaid with Cow, 7½" h, girl in floral skirt,
orange bodice, orange and white cow, crusted
flowers on base, c1860 .... 585.00
Minerva, 8" h, with helmet, torch, quiver, instruments of war on base, polychrome enamels
(A)................................... 355.00
Mountain Goat, 8⅛" h, long curving horns and
full beard, standing on rocky rect mound with
central rock support, animal glazed in yellow
and pale brown, base in turquoise and brown,
mid 19th C (A)......................... 1360.00
Musicians
5½" h, courtly players seated on Queen
Anne chairs, she with small dog in lap, plays
lute, he plays a flute, lute case and pile of
books beneath chair, blue neoclassical
bases, repair, c1800, pr 1850.00
8¼" h, man playing a bagpipe in feathered
hat, woman playing lute in feathered hat,
sitting on rocky ledge before a bocage,
small dog, two sheep at feet, waterfall at
base, repair, c1825 .... 2650.00
Napkin Ring, 2" d, two applied figures, one
draped in pink, one in blue, white ring,
c1840................................. 87.50
New Marriage Act, 7¼" h, young couple standing arm in arm on rocky mound with parson
and clerk to one side, plaque with inscription
attached to flowering tree support, multicolored enamels, marbled rect base, c1825 (A) 1417.00
Old Age, 10½" h, man on crutches, wife holding basket and walking stick, before flowering
tree, mound base with shredded vegetation
and colored scrollwork, restoration, early 19th
C (A)................................. 205.00
Parrot, 4¼" h, orange, purple. pink, rose, green,
sitting on white perch, gilt trim, green crusted
florals, c1820–40...................... 395.00
Pastille Burner
3¾" h, castle shaped, polychrome (A)..... 75.00
5⅜" h, 4¾" w, cottage shape with two
wings in tan, gray, red, black, and green,
19th C............................... 650.00
5½" h, cottage shaped, crusted florals
around roof, two orange chimneys, c1860 485.00
8½" h, oriental pavilion, three windowed
cupolas with umbrella roofs, three applied
multicolored floral bouquets, gilding,
c1820 .... 3300.00
Pekinese, 7½" h, creamware, white body with
gilt hair accents and collar, 19th C, pr (A)... 330.00
Persuasion, 8" h, lovers sit on a bench, she in
sprigged gown, he in swirled blue coat, pro-
poses and holds out a gold ring, potted plant,
small dog, umbrella, and hat rest on scrolled
base, repair, c1825 .... 9950.00
Phrenology Bust, 11" h, cranium printed with
brain segments, "PHRENOLOGY by L.N.
Fowler" on base, late 19th C (A)......... 815.00
Pigeon, 3¾" h, feathers sponged in pale and
med blue, sits on brown next, applied shredded grass, repair, c1820 .... 450.00
Poodle, 5½" h, white and cream, seated on
cobalt base, pr......................... 37.50
Popery, 9" h, holding book and scroll, polychrome, unmarked (A).................... 30.00
Preacher, 11" h, flanked by cherubs, multicolored, late 19th C (A) 200.00

Prince Albert, 16" h, wearing kilt, standing with flag, drum, and rifle, "WAR" on base, polychrome 150.00

Prince and Princess of Wales
11½" h, multicolored (A) 220.00
15" h, prince in green coat and black hair, holding top hat, princess in gold flowered dress with pink ribbons 390.00

Princess Louise, 12" h, multicolored (A) 88.00

Pug, 4½" h, tawny coat, studded black collar, seated on quilted green cushions with tassels, alert expression, c1810, pr 3800.00

Putti, 5⅞" h, holding bunches of flowers, bocage in ground, imp "WALTON" in scroll on back of base (A) 237.00

Queen Victoria, 17" h, wearing crown and veil, draped with an ermine trimmed cape (A) ... 220.00

Rabbit, 2⅜" h, white and black, green and brown mottled base 430.00

Red Riding Hood, 10½" h, spill vase at side, multicolored 250.00

Rhino, 9" l, black, standing, oval molded green and blue base, small green snake on either side, c1870 (A) 2244.00

Roaring Lion, 9⅜" h, forepaw resting on ochre globe, tongue flicked out, tail curled over back, green topped rect base edged with trellised ochre border, tail restored, early 19th C (A)..................................... 1309.00

Romeo and Juliet, 10½" h, Juliette seated under tree, Romeo kneeling at feet, blue, yellow, light green, orange, purple and black accents, tree restored, 19th C (A) 187.00

Tithe Pig Group, 6¼" h, parson looking at farmer and wife who offer baby instead of piglet, basket of eggs, wheat sheaves and three piglets at feet, scroll molded shaped oval mound base, some damage to tree support, early 19th C (A)....................... 525.00

Sailors, 10½" h, one standing with foot on cannon, another seated loading muzzle, oval base, polychrome 350.00

Scottsman 15" h, leaning on tree trunk, polychrome and white (A) 110.00

Spaniel
4" h, pink luster splotches, white ground, pr (A).................................... 187.00
4¼" h, white dog with rust spots, black nose, with basket, c1860 .... 195.00
5" h, white and rust, cobalt base, gilt trim, gilt leash, c1830–40 .... 525.00
6¼" h, white and rust dogs, c1860, pr 595.00
8" h, one black and white dog, one rust and white dog, cobalt blue base, c1850, pr ... 2950.00
8½" h, copper luster spots, ears, paws, and chains, pr............................. 250.00
9¾" h, white and green luster, detached paws, c1860, pr....................... 750.00
12½" h, black and white, c1870, pr....... 1250.00
13" h, black muzzle, red mouth, gold collar, yellow and black enamel eyes, white ground, pr (A) 302.00

Spill Vase
5" h
Boy in blue jacket, pink pants, girl in orange jacket, floral skirt, two sheep, brown and green base, c1847 .... 395.00
Girl in blue bodice, white floral skirt, dog, kennel with pink roof, crusted flowers, c1845 .... 550.00

5¾" h
Children, crusted florals, orange int on spill, c1850, pr 500.00
Milkmaid in flowered dress, milking red-brown spotted cow, small flower encrusted base........................ 375.00
Reclining shepherdess in blue jacket, white skirt with colored bands, lamb, c1850.. 165.00
6" h, milkmaid in blue bodice, pink and floral skirt, white and rust cow, brown and green base with crusted flowers, c1850........ 425.00
7" h, sheep and lamb on hill, tree stump vase on back flanked by bocage, imp WALTON" in scroll, 19th C (A) 440.00
7⅞" h, triple, two green dolphins supporting three entwined gray cornucopiae with brown edged rims, shell molded base, restoration, c1780 (A)...................... 510.00
9" h, white and orange mottled cow, milkmaid in white coat, yellow hat, green pail, green and brown enameled base, mid 1800s ... 575.00
9¼" h, dbl, church in salmon, crusted florals on front and sides, 1850............... 475.00
9⅞" h, naked boy asleep before gnarled tree stump, head resting on basket of flowers, recumbent lamb to each side, green wash base molded with rockwork, red flower and squirrel seated in branches above, hairline, early 19th C (A)..................... 1020.00
10" h, man, woman, two dogs, coleslaw trim.................................. 225.00
10½" h
Cow with red-brown markings, gilt horns, green and brown base............... 575.00
Girl in orange hooded cloak, white dress with florals, rust dog, crusted flowers, white base, orange int on spill........ 295.00
11" h, cow, horses, birds, gilt on base, orange int on spill............................ 495.00
11½" h, running stag being chased by hound, tree trunk vase, dark green, orange, yellow, green, and gold (A)............. 110.00
12" h, white dog with gilt accents, mottled green, yellow, and brown base, brown int on spill, c1870...................... 495.00
12½" h, dog trainer beside spill vase, tree trunk in colors, late 19th C........... 175.00

Stag and Doe, 6⅝" h, red-brown coats, recumbent on grassy mounds, repair, c1800...... 2800.00

Terrier, 12½" h, rust and white with polychrome details, glass eyes, gilt trim, chips on base, pr (A)............................. 295.00

The Flight to Egypt, 9¼" h, Mary seated on the back of a donkey holding Jesus in her arms, Joseph leading the way, shaped base, flower strewn bocage, repairs, c1825 .... 4200.00

Tithe Pig, 6" h, peasant couple offering pigs, eggs, and wheat to parson, lady holding baby, rocky base, bocage ground, multicolored, repairs, c1815 (A)........................ 440.00

Tom King, 10½" h, riding salmon horse with black mane, cobalt jacket, orange tie, white breeches 650.00

Uncle Tom and Little Eva, 8" h, seated black man with child sitting in lap.................... 450.00

Walton Group, 8½" h, "Friendship," two boys with dog, green bocage, c1820........... 3700.00

Watch Stand
8" h, boy and girl musicians and recumbent lion, draped watch holder, polychromed.. 400.00

12 1/4" h, youth and maid in grape arbor, polychrome enameling (A) **305.00**
Widow, 9 1/2" h, woman in multicolored dress
leaning on barrel, marked "Widow" on base
(A). **150.00**
Widow and Child, 9" h, seated woman in multi-
colored dress, child at side, barrel at other
side, "Widow" on base (A). **300.00**
William Wallace, 17" h, standing figure in kilt,
holding sword and shield, titled on base,
c1870 (A) **82.00**
Winter, 7 3/8" h, man with arms folded in ice
skating stance, polychrome enamels (A) **225.00**
Youth, Maid and Rabbit, 6 3/8" h, polychrome
enameling (A). **220.00**
Zebra, 8 7/8" h, 8 1/2" w, black and white body,
green grass base, pr (A). **187.00**

TURNER
c1784

WALTON
1818-35

HAMMERSLEY & Co
LONGTON
STOKE-ON-TRENT
ENGLAND
1912-1939

PATTERN
W H GRINDLEY & Co ENGLAND
c1880-1914

ROYAL CORONAWARE
J HANCOCK & SONS
STOKE-ON-TRENT
ENGLAND.
1912-1937

TRADE MARK
ADDERLEY
1906-1926

STAFFORDSHIRE— GENERAL

1700s to Present

History: In the Staffordshire district of England, numerous
pottery factories were established that produced a wide
variety of wares including figures, flow blue, transfer
printed wares, historic blue, and ornamental pieces.

Samuel Alcock and Company established a pottery in
Burslem about 1828 that was known for its Parian figures,
jugs, and decorative wares in the Classical style. The pottery also made a wide range of blue-printed earthenwares
and bone china. Sir James Duke and Nephews took over
the firm in 1860.

John and Edward Baddeley produced earthenwares at
Shelton between 1786 and 1806. The company manufactured a wide range of tablewares, often enameled in red
and black on a creamware ground.

Charles Bourne of Foley Pottery made bone china tablewares between 1807 and 1830. His factory equalled
those of Spode, Coalport, and Davenport. Pieces can be
identified by the pattern numbers and the initials "CB."

The Lane End factory of **Hilditch and Son** made teawares in under the glaze blue from 1822 until 1830.

Elijah Mayer established a pottery at Cobden Works,
Hanley about 1705. In 1805 the name changed to Elijah
Mayer and Son. Production continued until 1834. The
Mayers manufactured black basalt wares, tablewares in
cream colored earthenware, cane wares, and drab stone-
wares.

Humphrey Palmer was located at Church Works, Hanley in 1760. He produced wares popularized by Wedgwood such as black basalts, cream colored and agate ware
vases, and seals and cameos that frequently were modeled by J. Voyez. Most of Palmer's wares were decorative.
The pottery went out of business in 1778.

A. J. Wilkinson Ltd. was a Staffordshire pottery firm that
operated several factories in the Burslem area beginning in
the late nineteenth century. In 1885 Wilkinson took over
the Central Pottery. The plant made white granite ware for
the American market. Wilkinson introduced the use of
gold luster work on granite ware.

Wilkinson operated the Churchyard Works from 1887
until the early twentieth century and the Royal Staffordshire Pottery from c1896 until the present day. About
1900 Wilkinson gained control of Mersey Pottery, a sub-
sidiary of Newport Pottery. The factory remained in production until the 1930s. Highly glazed stonewares, some
of which were designed by Clarice Cliff, were made.

References: P. D. Gordon Pugh, *Staffordshire Portrait Fig-
ures & Allied Subjects of the Victorian Era*, rev. ed., Antique
Collectors Club, Ltd., 1987; Bernard Rackham, *Early Staf-
fordshire Pottery*, Faber & Faber, 1951; Louis T. Stanley,
Collecting Staffordshire Pottery, Doubleday, 1963; John
Thomas, *The Rise of the Staffordshire Potteries*, Adams &
Dart, 1971.

Museums: City Museum & Art Gallery, Stoke-on-Trent,
England; Everson Museum of Art, Syracuse, New York;
The Henry Francis DuPont Winterthur Museum, Winter-
thur, Delaware; William Rockhill Nelson Gallery of Art,
Kansas City, Mo.

Biscuit Jar, 6 3/4" h, pottery, aqua, mauve, and
yellow florals and leaves, gold trim, cream
ground, tapestry finish, SP lid, rim, and handle,
"Tunnecliffe & Sons" mark **110.00**

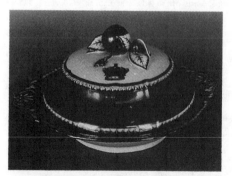

**Serving Dish, Cov, 11" d, apple green ground,
gilt trim, domed cov with plum finial, crest, "H.
& R. Daniel" mark, $350.00**

Bowl

5" d, "Countryside" pattern, blue transfer, "Wedgwood & Co." mark 5.00

8½" d, hex, multicolored large florals on int and ext, cream ground, Crown Ducal, A.G. Richardson (A). 18.00

10" d, 4" h, flying bird chasing butterflies in colors, gilt on blue ground, c1890, "Wiltshaw and Robinson" mark 325.00

14" H-H, oblong, "Dickens Days" pattern, horses and coach scenes, light tan, blue and yellow on ext, light green on int, black trim, c1900, "H.& K. Tunstall" mark (A) 23.00

Cake Plate

10" H-H, black and white oriental scene in center, oriental border scenes, c1840, "G.W. Turner & Sons" mark. 60.00

13" d, center scene of farmer sowing seeds in field, hills in ground, bird in tree, tree and berry border, imp "Brown, Westhead, Moore & Co. Fables" mark. 40.00

Candlestick, 6⅞" h, streaked white, yellow, and cream on black ground, 19th C, pr (A) 850.00

Chestnut Basket, 9" l, oval, chinoiserie landscape, lattice body, sprig handles, 2nd qtr 19th C (A). 275.00

Chocolate Set, tray, 16" d, pot, creamer, sugar, 6 cups and saucers, overall sepia and white flowers, "Brown, Westhead & Moore" marks 400.00

Coffee Pot, 9¾" h, baluster shape, body engine turned with fine wavy lines, female mask molded spout, finely grooved handle, cov with wavy lines, c1770 . . . . 2950.00

Compote, 8½" h, 4½" l, 4" w, five whooping cranes in center, gothic design border, brown and white, dtd 1877, "James Edwards & Sons" mark 65.00

Creamer

2⅜" h, gaudy floral design in red, green, and black (A) 60.00

3¼" h, river scene, red transfer, "Crown Staffordshire" mark. 5.00

3½" h

Gaudy floral design in red, blue, green, and black (A) 39.00

Gaudy vintage design in red, green, blue, and black, emb leaf handle (A) 61.00

4" h, emb polychrome scenes of two men seated on barrels with tankards (A) 25.00

4½" h, agate ware, blue and brown clay, strap handle, three lion mask and paw feet, mid 18th C (A). 1020.00

Cream Jug, 3¼" h, agate in white, brown, and blue clays, shaped rim, tapered handle, mask and paw feet, one foot restored, c1745 . . . . 4600.00

Cup and Saucer

Brown, tan, and cream agate design, cream rim, cream applied handle, late 18th C (A) 225.00

Large red roses, buds, and leaves on white center, wide green band on int, gold trim, scalloped rim, "Hammersley & Co., Bone China, Made in England" mark 14.00

Mini, Chinese figural motif, mauve transfers. 50.00

"Sporting Scenes," dog and bird, brown tones with gold trim, "J.F. Wileman" mark. 48.00

Cup and Saucer, Demitasse, hp flowers and insects, bamboo borders, c1872, "E.F. Brodley" mark. 100.00

Cup and Saucer, Handleless

Gaudy floral design in polychromes (A). 50.00

Luster, red, and green sunflower design, gaudy florals and leaves (A) 55.00

Cup Plate, 4" d, center urn in garden, floral paneled border, red transfer, unmarked (A). 31.00

Dessert Plate, 10¼" l, botanical specimen in polychrome, cobalt with underglaze border, gold highlights, scalloped edge, 1830, Staffordshire 200.00

Dessert Service

Cake plate, 9" d, 2½" h, triangular base with molded ball and claw feet, 6 plates, 9" d, multicolored transfers of different flowers, insects, birds, or butterfly and London scene, cream ground, "Powell, Bishop & Stonier" marks. 725.00

12 plates, 9" d, large comport, 2 med comports, 2 small comports, botanical, each painted with brightly colored specimen between gilded borders, c1880, "iron-red no.B/1684" mark, 17 pcs (A). 2700.00

12 plates, 9" d, 4 low comports, 2 tall comports, center with gilded medallion, transfer printed and painted with sprays of flowers, lime green wavy rim, c1868, "Brown, Westhead, Moore & Co., Eng Reg, no.B4342" marks, 18 pcs (A) 1820.00

Dish

4½" d, lady in magenta dress with peach underdress, playing banjo, lady in magenta dress holding music, man in lavender classic dress conducting, gold rim, "Fragonard-Royal Standard, Fine Bone China" mark . . 10.00

8" d, enameled seated oriental people in blue, yellow, green, and rose, flower bower overhead, c1820. . . . . 120.00

12" d, checker pattern circ panel in center, green glazed with scrolling panels of basketwork and diaper pattern, scrolling rim, hairline, c1760 (A). 2150.00

Dish, Cov, 10" l, 12 multicolored birds of paradise, blue and brown band, gold trim, c1900, "H.& K. Tunstall" mark (A) 8.00

Dresser Set, tray, 13" l, orange poppies in center, scalloped edge, 2 candlesticks, 5½" h, 2 powder boxes, 2½" d, pin tray, 4½" l, fluted and gold brushed design, "Stoke on Trent" marks (A) 225.00

Figure, 4¾" h, seated bagpiper in brown and cream clay covered in green, ochre, and brown glazes, seated on brown base, c1745, Astbury (A) 7920.00

Flask, 5" h, pottery, molded half figure of man smoking pipe and holding cup on each side, wide leaf border and knob handles, overglazed enamel colors, hairlines, early 19th C (A). 360.00

Hatpin Holder, 5" h, gold and cobalt butterflies with green and cobalt accents, gold fronds, pearl luster ground, gold rope trim on rim and base, c1895 . . . . 295.00

Inkstand, oval, modeled as alligator with head at one end and curled tail as handle at other end, green enamels and gilded, int painted with sprays of summer flowers, four feet, hair crack, c1830 (A) 600.00

Jam Jar, 4" h, polychrome floral decoration, silver rim on tray, "Royal Winton" mark (A). . . 40.00

Jewel Box, 5¼" h, 7½" H-H, applied florals, burnished gold handles, twisted handles on top, white lined surface, "E.J.D. Badley" mark. 250.00

Jug

5 1/2" h, molded manganese face, green raised frog spout with open mouth, green base and handle, c1760, Whieldon type .. **1250.00**

6" h, paneled

Gaudy Imari style with flower basket in iron-red, orange, cobalt and gilt, serpent handle, "Allerton" mark.................. **140.00**

Printed transfer design of urns, birds, and florals in green, pink, brown, blue, and ochre, brown lion's head spout (A) **55.00**

7" h

Paneled, printed flowers and overglazed in green, yellow, and blue, aubergine lion's head spout (A)...................... **44.00**

White and purple open flowers and leaves, cream ground, gold luster trim (A) **357.00**

8 1/2" h, titled "Spring" and "Langan Boxing Match" on two sides, black transfers, floral rim and handle, hairlines, c1825 (A)...... **412.00**

9" h, "How Lucky's My Lot" figure in large cartouche on front, pastoral scene on reverse in brown, white, and green, brown rim c1790, signed "Aynsley"................ **1700.00**

10 1/4" h, Bacchus mask molded with a grinning bearded and horned head crowned with fruiting vine, another mask flanked by goats' heads on the spout above, gad-roomed foot with flowers and fruit, handle modeled with a caryatid, glazed in blue, green, brown, and touches of ochre, restoration to spout, c1780, (A) **680.00**

Loving Cup

4 3/4" h, 8" w, "Farmer's Arms" transfer on front with "In God We Trust" and "The Husband's Diligence Provides Bread," back motto "Industry Produceth Wealth" and poem transfer, accents of rust and gold, two yellow frogs on int **550.00**

5" h, 8 1/2" l, rose decoration with dark green leaves, two salamanders inside in mustard with black dots **625.00**

5" h, floral cartouche in white, red, blue, and violet, outlined in gold, reverse cartouche "Edmund Brown Born Dec 28 1828" in gilt, pink ground, two white and gilt twisted handles, flower frog, Staffordshire **280.00**

5 1/4" h, 7 1/2" l, yellow frog inside with brown spots, multicolored floral decoration on front, gray crazed surface, blue lines aroung base, rim, and handle.................... **525.00**

Match Striker, 3" l, 1 1/4" h, girl in white dress with blue dots, hugging white dog, green trees, brown ground, white ribbed base **115.00**

Mug

2 1/4" h, raised purple luster, rose, and green flowers................................ **55.00**

2 3/4" h, vignettes of Orientals in yellow, blue, and green, blue and red ground (A)...... **50.00**

2 7/8" h, porcelain, "CRESCENT" and "A PRESENT FROM BUXTON," scene of town, green transfer........................ **50.00**

3 1/8" h, black transfer of parrot and two prs of men and women accented in green, blue, and red, criss-cross band on int lip (A) ... **55.00**

3 1/2" h, brown transfer of tennis scene, brown designs on rim int and handle, c1880 .... **295.00**

4" h

Molded Bacchus head, fruiting vine on fore-

head, brown ochre, yellow, and green, int with yellow frog, late 18th C (A)....... **510.00**

Gaudy pattern with alternating rust and cobalt blue stripes, brown and green band, leaf sprigs, tan frog int with red eyes ... **450.00**

4 1/4" h, figural bust of Lord Rodney, ochre face, brown hair, orange vest, blue jacket, "SUCCESS TO LORD RODNEY" on rim, restored, late 18th C (A) **275.00**

4 1/2" h

Molded Bacchus head, fruiting vine on forehead, shell molded base, translucent brown and green glazes, late 18th C... **500.00**

Molded beared satyr's head, pointed ears, horned brow with grape vine, green, brown, and ochre translucent glazes, c1780, Wood family type **1200.00**

Religious message by N. Shields in black framed by green leaves with brown ribbon, olive green frog int with rust eyes and mouth, tan ground, early 19th C... **510.00**

4 3/4" h, black and white transfer "View of the Cast Iron Bridge" with green, orange, and yellow, black frog int with magenta trim, black and white floral transfer inside, purple luster trim on rim and handle........... **495.00**

5" h,

Domino, molded mask surrounded by hood, polychrome spots, early 19th C (A) **500.00**

Mechanics Union black and white transfer, brown frog int, purple luster trim **475.00**

Sailor's Farewell poem in black and white transfer with green, yellow, and magenta, Crimea transfer on reverse, luster decoration on rim and handle, brown frog int, mid 19th C........................ **495.00**

5 1/8" h

Black and white mariner's verse transfer with magenta, blue, and green, leaf border, off white ground, brown frog int with black spots, magenta panels on sides of poem.............................. **395.00**

Paul Pry, man with cream hat, orange face, green tie, purple coat, brown handle, c1820 .... **450.00**

Nappy, 5" d, three floral sprays, dark red rim panel surrounded by gold scrolls, "Myott" mark.................................... **3.00**

Pipe, 8 1/2" l, coiled and twisted stem with green, dark red, and blue underglaze sponge design, modeled bust head bowl, early 19th C (A).. **1210.00**

Pitcher

3 1/4" h, white, emb eagle, shield, and star design **225.00**

5 1/4" h, "Gaden Arms," black transfer with polychromes, orange luster, chip on spout (A)................................. **45.00**

6 3/8" h, hex, polychrome cottage design of door and windows with leafy branches, branch handle (A)...................... **71.00**

6 1/2" h, pottery, emb animals on body, brown glaze, silver swags on border, figural lion handle, Arthur Wood.................. **50.00**

7" h, Portobello type, chinoiserie design, yellow transfer, dark brown glazed ground (A).................................. **1540.00**

8" h, Gaudy floral design in red, blue, green, and black on sides, shaped rim, scroll handle (A)................................. **110.00**

8¼" h, underglaze blue and red, green, and black enameled gaudy floral design (A)... **190.00**

8¾" h, gaudy floral pattern in polychromes, hairline (A) **30.00**

9" h, Gaudy floral decoration in underglaze blue, and red, black, and green enamel (A). **200.00**

Plaque

12½" d, pottery, Oliver Twist in blue jacket with bowl in hand asking for porridge from man in green jacket, "Old Foley/WC/England" mark **250.00**

12⅔" d, Art Deco style orange, tan, gray, and black geometrics, satin metallic luster, pierced for hanging, Charlotte Rhead..... **225.00**

13" h, 10⅞" w, porcelain, young girl in grassy meadow running into mother's arms, tall trees and fenced bank behind them, c1883, sgd "H.B. Hill," dtd, framed (A)... **2006.00**

Plate

6" d

Center scene of two women and mule, black transfer, emb and polychrome floral rim with luster (A).................... **70.00**

Woman spinning and "Fly Pleasure and it will follow you . . .," blue transfer, emb and polychrome floral rim with luster trim (A) **70.00**

6⅞" d, gaudy floral border in red, green, yellow, purple, and black, small flower in center, pr (A) **99.00**

7" d

John Wesley, black transfer with polychrome accents, emb floral rim (A) **55.00**

Oct

Sheet marble design, mulberry transfer, unmarked........................ **15.00**

Windsor Castle, black transfer with polychrome enamels and purple luster, emb daisy border (A).............. **25.00**

7½" d, Chelsea grape design, Adderleys... **13.00**

7⅝" d, red, blue, green, black, and yellow gaudy floral in center, wide border band of gaudy florals (A) **20.00**

7¾" d

Bramble pattern in green transfer with red and green enameling (A)............. **18.00**

"Sacred History of Joseph . . .," black transfer with polychromes, emb daisy border (A) **25.00**

Sunflower design in red, yellow, black, green, and blue in center, border chain of buds on border, scalloped edge (A).... **75.00**

7⅞" d, loose bouquet in center, border with gaudy flowerheads and leaves, red and green (A)........................... **55.00**

8" d

Gaudy pansy type florals in blue, yellow, green, red, and black, scalloped border (A) **95.00**

Red, blue, green, and black gaudy florals on border, set of 6 (A).................. **82.00**

8⅛" d, bird hunters, purple transfer with polychrome enameled emb floral rim (A) . **45.00**

8½" d, oriental scene, black transfer, c1834, "P.W.& Co." mark................... **50.00**

8⅞" d, gaudy floral border in red, green, and black, scalloped rim (A)............. **60.00**

9¼" d, gaudy floral design in center in green and pink, green and pink rim stripes, set of 4 (A)............................... **110.00**

9½" d, Portobello type, center open flowerhead, floral design on border, yellow transfer, dark brown ground

10" d

Gaudy design of flowers in polychromes in center, border of leaves and flowers, imp eagle mark (A)...................... **95.00**

Green feather edge (A) **71.00**

10" sq, hp purple pansies on brown and orange splashed ground, "H & K" mark **95.00**

10⅜" d, "Calcutta" pattern, "Brown, Westhead" mark.......................... **15.00**

10½" d

Center florals with enameled highlights on white ground, multicolored florals on light cream and blue border, Crown Ducal (A) **20.00**

Gaudy cabbage design on border in colors, shaped rim, set of 5 (A).............. **715.00**

Large gaudy open flowers and leaves in purple, black, and green on border, small open flower in center (A)............. **50.00**

Small center flower in red, blue, and green, emb scalloped border with green and red stripes (A)......................... **55.00**

10¾" d, "Commerce-Free Trade," black transfer on cream ground.............. **65.00**

Platter

12" d, hp border of blue flowers, brown brambles, green leaves on green border, "W.H. Grindley leaf" mark.................... **20.00**

12" l, 9" w, large cobalt flowers outlined in gold, white ground, open handles, chip on back, "pearl China Hanley" mark **75.00**

12¾" l, gaudy floral design in polychromes, leaf and floral border, imp "eagle" mark (A)................................. **300.00**

14¾" l, oct, center gaudy floral design in red, blue, green, and black, small florals and leaves on border (A)................... **82.00**

15" l

Blue feather edge, imp "Hall" mark (A)... **80.00**

"Mersey" pattern, gray transfer, crazing, "W.H. Grindley" mark............... **25.00**

18¼" l, 14¼" w, "Loretta," pattern, blueblack transfer, Alcock.................... **225.00**

19¾" l, "Sidon" design, red transfer (A)... **250.00**

20½" l, 16½" w, multicolored florals in rose, blue, light blue, green, rust, butterflies, gadrooned border, scalloped edge, 1825–29, "R. Stevenson & Williams" mark **950.00**

Potpourri Vase, Cov, 28½" h, ovoid body, painted with sprays of colorful flowers on apple-green ground, waisted neck, bud knob and loop handles in dark blue and gilt, c1860 (A).................................... **1350.00**

Punch Pot, 6¼" h, tapered ovoid shape, polished redware, oriental figures with birds, bands of engine turning and mold applied scrollwork, scrolled spout, sea serpent handle, c1765... **2950.00**

Puzzle Jug, 9½" h, "A Knock Down Blow" and "The Death," animal scenes, dancing figures in white, black, green, and rust, c1835...... **595.00**

Sauceboat

4½" h, blue feather edge (A)............. **70.00**

5⅞" l, dbl, solid agate, body molded with shells, white, brown, and blue clays, shaped rim, dbl handles, handle restored, c1745.. **4600.00**

Sauceboat, Stand
6½" l, oval form, hp floral banding, c1820
(A).................................... **165.00**
7³⁄₁₆" l, 6" l, silver shape, solid agate, va-
lanced rim, cream colored marbleized in
chocolate-brown and teal-blue, S scroll handle, stepped oval foot, quatrefoil shape
stand, restored, c1745 (A)............... **7150.00**
Sauce Tureen, 7³⁄₄" l, with undertray, "Venetian
Gardens," brown transfer, hairlines (A) **40.00**
Shaker, 3⅞" h, gaudy floral garland in red and
green with black stripe (A) **185.00**
Sugar Bowl
4⅞" h, gaudy floral design in red, blue, and
green, emb shell handles (A) **77.00**
5⅝" h, gaudy floral design in red, green, black,
and blue, two wishbone handles (A) **105.00**
Teabowl and Saucer, "Bower" design, red transfer (A)................................... **20.00**
Tea Caddy, 5⅞" h, rect, tortoise shell ware,
trellis patterned cartouche on front and reverse with florette, edged with foliate scrolls
with flowerheads, fruiting grapevines, and palmettes, chamfered corners glazed in gray,
1755–60 (A)........................... **880.00**
Teapot
2³⁄₄" h, spherical shape, redware, sheep grazing beneath tree, mold applied decoration,
loop handle, straight spout, c1765 .... **3500.00**
4½" h, compressed spherical shape, solid
agate, dark red, light and dark brown clays,
curved spout, loop handle, pinched terminal, turned knob, knob reglued, c1735 ... **5800.00**
4⁵⁄₁₆" h, spherical, tortoise shell ware, steaky
brown, green, and faint blue glaze, body
with applied fruiting rope twist grapevines
between two perched birds, crabstock
spout and handle, cov with grape cluster
and two leaves surrounding bird form knob,
restored, c1760 (A).................... **770.00**
5" h, center band of gaudy floral design in red,
black, blue, and green (A)............... **126.00**
5¼" h, molded pectin shell sides and cov,
serpent spout, lamprey handle, lion knob,
blue, brown, and ochre solid agate on
cream ground, c1750 (A) **5500.00**
6" h, cauliflower shape, molded with green
glazed leaves, curved spout, loop handle,
3rd qtr 18th C....................... **650.00**
6½" h, marbleized agate streaks of yellow on
red-brown ground, 19th C (A).......... **187.00**
7" h
Black stripes and blue, green, red, and black
sprig design, handle reglued (A) **30.00**
Red striping with polychrome enameled
florals, repaired finial (A)............. **104.00**
7½" h
Figural Princess Charlotte in yellow and gold
dress, brown hair, "H.J. Wood, Burslem,
England" mark...................... **110.00**
Globular body, redware, molded reliefs of
flowering branches with birds, flocks of
sheep grazing below, handle and spout
formed as gnarled branches, c1765 (A). **374.00**
8½" h, polychrome floral decoration on panels (A) **137.00**
9½" h, bulbous shape, ochre, brown, and
green flowers, continuous leaf and vine borders, cream ground, blue trimmed spout,
handle, and borders, restored (A) **247.00**

Teapot Stand, 5⅝" d, unglazed redware, center
panel with teapot with crown above, press
molded with oriental motifs set in panels of
diapering, c1760 .... **1400.00**
Tea Service, Part, teapot, 4¼" h, cov sugar
bowl, 3" h, 6 teabowls and saucers, brown
transfers and ochre enameled floral designs
with classical cartouche, early 19th C (A) ... **357.00**
Tea Set, pot, 9" h, cov sugar, creamer, brown
transfers of classical scenes, finial reglued (A) **105.00**
Toddy Plate
5⅞" d, "A Token of Affection," children at
bedtime with prayer, black transfer with
polychrome enamels, emb daisy rim (A) .. **55.00**
6⅜" d, black transfer and polychrome "Robinson Crusoe' (A) **33.00**
Toothpick Holder, 3½" h, 4" l, black and white
begging dog, multicolored pastel basket with
apllied flowers, "Wade, England" mark **16.00**
Trivet, 8" d, emb red and yellow flowerheads,
brown and green leaves, orange rippled
ground, c1930, "James Kent" mark **85.00**
Tumbler, 4" h, red and brown florals, gold trim,
c1900, "Ralph Wedgwood" mark.......... **5.00**
Tureen and Cov, 7³⁄₄" l, nesting pigeon form,
mauve plumage, nest colored and applied
with shredded vegetation, early 19th C (A).. **740.00**
Vase
6" h, pilgrim shape, white relief of Cupid on
black ground, "George Jones".......... **495.00**
6⅛" h, porcelain tulip formed as a lilac and
puce striated blossom, green stem above
another smaller tulip, both flanked by green
leaves, rising from green moss on gilt edged
shaped oval base, repaired, c1840 (A).... **880.00**
8" h, "Trellis" pattern, orange and yellow lustered flowers on upper section, brown tubing on lower section, beige ground, gold
trim, Charlotte Rhead.................. **185.00**
9" h, pottery, Art Nouveau figure of young
male hunter, black stylized vines, gilt accents, Forester & Sons.................. **145.00**
11" h, band of multicolored flowers on orange irid glaze, "Royal Staffordshire Pottery"................................. **45.00**
Waste Bowl, 6⅝" d, 3³⁄₈" h, gaudy floral design in red, purple, black, and green shades
(A)..................................... **71.00**
Whistle
3" l, 2" h, figural hen sitting on brown nest. **45.00**
Figure of child riding bicycle.............. **195.00**

STAFFORDSHIRE— HISTORIC

ENGLISH AND AMERICAN VIEWS 1818–1860

History: By 1786 there were eighty diferent potteries established in the Staffordshire district of England, the center
of the English pottery industry. By 1800 the number had
grown to almost two hundred. The pottery district included the towns of Burslem, Cobridge, Etruria, Fenton,
Foley, Hanley, Lane Delph, Lane End, Longport, Shelton,
Stoke, and Tunstall.

After the War of 1812, transfer printed Staffordshire
pottery that depicted American historical events, views of

cities and towns, tombs of famous individuals, portraits of heroes and other famous people, buildings of important institutions, patriotic emblems, and American landscapes were made for the American market. These historic view pieces allowed the British potters to recapture their dominance of the American market almost immediately upon the end of hostilities. Views were adopted from engravings, paintings, and prints by well-known artists of the period.

Dark blue pieces were favored between 1820 and 1840. This color was inexpensive, easy to secure, covered flaws in the wares, withstood the high temperatures of the kiln, and retained its deep coloration. During the 1830s and 1840s, lighter colors of pink and blue along with black, sepia, and green became popular. Wares made included tea services, dinner services, sets of plates, jugs, etc. Canadian views also were manufactured.

Numerous potteries made the historic blue wares. Each firm had its own distinctive border design and characteristics. The border design is the chief means of identifying a specific maker of an unmarked piece.

English views also were popoular. Transfers featuring old and famous castles, abbeys, manor houses, cathedrals, seats of the nobility, famous beauty spots, coastal subjects, English colleges, and London were used on the wares.

c 1816-1830

c 1828-1830

c 1845-1858

1802-1828

FENTON

T. G

1847-1859

Rural Scenery

J&WR

JOHN & WILLIAM RIDGWAY - c 1814-1830

William Adams and Enoch Wood were the first manufacturers to produce the English views. Enoch Wood took the lead with the American views. Factories that were established after 1820 concentrated on American views.

WILLIAM ADAMS

Stoke, 1827–1831
Tunstall, c1834 to Present

William Adams of Stoke was one of four potters with the name William Adams in the Staffordshire district. In 1819 a William Adams became a partner with William Adams, his father. Later his three brothers joined him. When the father died in 1829, William became the factory's manager. The firm operated as William Adams and Sons and controled four potteries at Stoke and one at Tunstall.

Initially English views, with a foliage border and the name of the scene on the back, were made. Two blue views were manufactured at Stoke. Views done at Tunstall have a border of baskets of roses. The Tunstall plant produced American views in black, light blue, sepia, pink, and green between 1830 and 1840.

William Adams died in 1865. All production was moved to Tunstall. The firm still operates today under the name, William Adams & Sons, Ltd.

CAREY AND SONS

Lane End, 1818–1847

Thomas and John Carey operated the Anchor Works at Lane End between 1818 and 1842. The firm changed names several times during its history. The factory produced English views, some of which were based on Sir Walter Scott's poem "Lady of the Lake."

JAMES AND RALPH CLEWS

Cobridge, 1819–1836

James Clews took over the works of Andrew Stevenson in 1819. Ralph, his brother, joined the firm later. In 1836 James came to the United States to establish a pottery in Troy, Indiana; but, the venture was a failure. Clews returned to England but never re-established himself as a potter.

Clews made both English and American views. The company made a variety of borders, the most popular having festoons that contained the names of the fifteen existing states.

THOMAS GODWIN

Burslem Wharf, 1829–1843

Thomas Godwin produced both American and Canadian views in a variety of colors. His borders included nasturtium and morning glories.

THOMAS GREEN

Fenton, 1847–1859

Thomas Green operated the Minerva Works in Fenton from 1847 until his death in 1859. His American view pieces contained variations of William Penn's 1683 Treaty with the Indians. The border was a simple, stenciled design. His printed wares were in green, pink, brown, black, and blue. After his death, his wife and sons managed the firm using the name M. Green & Co. It later became the Crown Stafforshire Porcelain Company.

RALPH HALL

Tunstall, 1822–1849

At the conclusion of a partnership with John Hall, Ralph Hall operated the Swan Bank Works in Tunstall. The firm exported many blue-printed wares to America.

JOSEPH HEATH

Tunstall, 1829–1843

Joseph Heath and company operated a factory at New Field in Tunstall between 1829 to 1843. The company's border design was composed of large roses and scrolls with a beaded band and white edge.

HENSHALL AND COMPANY

Longport, 1790–1828

The firm consisted of a series of different partnerships with the only recorded mark being that of Henshall and Company. Both English and American views were made. The border motif comprised fruit and flowers.

J. AND J. JACKSON

Burslem, 1831–1843

Job and John Jackson operated the Churchyard Works at Burslem between 1831 and 1843. Many of their American views were not copied by other manufacturers. Their border designs included sprays of roses, a wreath of fine flowers, a beaded band, and a white margin. Their transfer colors were black, light blue, pink, sepia, green, maroon, and mulberry.

THOMAS MAYER

Stoke, 1829–1838

In 1829 the Mayer brothers, Thomas, John, and Joshua, purchased the Dale Hall Works from Stubbs when he retired. Thomas produced the "Arms of the states" series at Dale Hall Works while the other brothers worked at Cliff Bank. Each factory produced fine ceramics.

MORLEY AND COMPANY

Hanley, 1845–1858

Until 1845 Morley was the sole owner of a pottery firm in Hanley. After that date the firm experienced a succession of owners. Between 1847 and 1858 it was called Francis Morley and Company. Both American and Canadian views were manufactured.

J. AND W. RIDGWAY AND WILLIAM RIDGWAY AND COMPANY

Hanley, 1814–1830

John and William Ridgway, sons of Job Ridgway, took charge of the Bell Bank works in 1814 when George

Ridgway retired. The brothers produced the "Beauties of America" series in dark blue with the rose leaf border. Their English views featured a border with flowers and medallions of children.

In 1830 the partnership was dissolved. John continued to operate Cauldon Place, Job's old manufactory, and William took charge of Bell Bank. John Ridgway continued the Cauldon Place Works from 1830 until 1858. In 1855 T. C. Brown-Westhead, Moore & Co. purchased the works.

William Ridgway and Company managed the Bell Bank Works from 1830 until 1859. Edward John, his son, joined the firm. By 1843 he was operating six potteries, mostly in Hanley. "American Scenery" and "Catskill Moss" were two series that were based on Bartlett's etchings. These series were issued in colors of light blue, pink, brown, black, and green.

JOHN AND RICHARD RILEY

Burslem, 1802–1828

John and Richard Riley operated at Nile Street between 1802 and 1814 and at the Hill Works in Staffordshire between 1814 and 1828. Mostly they made English views and blue printed dinner services with a border of large leaf-like scrolls and flowers.

JOHN ROGERS

Longport, 1815–1842

John and George Rogers operated two factories in Longport in 1802. When George died in 1815, John took Spencer, his son, into the firm. The name changed to "John Rogers and Son," a designation used even after the father died. Rogers produced four American views, three of which featured the Boston State House with a floral border. English views also were made.

ANTHONY SHAW

Burslem, 1850–1878

Anthony Shaw founded Mersey Pottery at Burslem in 1850. He specialized in views of the Mexican War period.

ANDREW STEVENSON

Cobridge, 1808–1829

One of the pioneers among English potters to make blue historical, transfer printed ware with American scenes was Andrew Stevenson. W. G. Wall, and Irish artist, went to the United States and supplied the drawings for Stevenson. Stevenson's pieces had a flower and scroll border. English views were made with roses and other flowers on the border.

RALPH STEVENSON

Cobridge, 1815–1840

Ralph Stevenson used a vine and leaf border on his dark blue historical views and a lace border on his transfers in lighter colors. British and foreign views were made.

Pieces from the works of Ralph Stevenson and Williams (R.S.W.) featured the acorn and oak leaf border design or the vases of flowers and scrollwork design. Williams was the New York agent for Stevneson.

JOSEPH STUBBS

Burslem, 1790–1829

Joseph Stubbs established the Dale Hall Works in Burslem in 1790. When he retired in 1829, he sold his pottery to the Mayer brothers. His American views used a border design of eagles with widespread wings among scrolls and flowers. Views included scenes in New Jersey, Boston, New York, and Philadelphia, Stubbs also made English views with a border of foliage and pointed scrolls.

ENOCH WOOD AND SONS

Burslem, 1819–1846

Enoch Wood, sometimes called the "Father of English Pottery," made more marked historical American views than any other Staffordshire manufacturer. In 1819 his firm operated as Enoch Wood and Sons. Enoch died in 1840. Enoch, Joseph, and Edward, his sons, continued the firm with their father's name. The sons sold the firm to Pinder, Bourne, and Hope in 1846.

The company's mark had several variations, but each included the name "Wood." The shell border with the circle around the view was used most frequently, though Wood designed several other unique borders. Many of the views attributed to unknown makers probably were made at the Wood factory.

Enoch Wood and Sons also made British views, including "English Cities" series, the "London Views" series, the shell border series, and the grapevine border series.

In addition, they produced French views such as ceramic portrayals of Lafayette and his home in France, and "Italian Scenery" Series, and views of Africa and India. Many of the foreign scenes were copied from engravings after water colors by traveling artists such as William Henry Bartlett.

In addition to views of places, Enoch Wood made other designs including a Scriptural Series of biblical scenes, a Sporting Series of hunting scenes, and a Cupid Series showing a variety of cherubs.

William Adams did an Animal Series. Scriptural subjects were done by Adams, Mason, Jackson, Ridgway and others.

References: David and Linda Arman, *Historical Staffordshire: An Illustrated Check List,* privately printed, 1974, out of print; David and Linda Arman, *Historical Staffordshire: An Illustrated Check List, First Supplement,* privately printed, 1977, out of print; Ada Walker Camehl, *The Blue China Book,* Tudor Publishing Co., 1946; Elizabeath Collard, *The Potters' View of Canada,* McGill Queen's University Press, 1983; A. W. Coysh and R. K. Henrywood, *The Dictionary of Blue & White Printed Pottery, 1780–1880,* Antique Collectors' Club, 1982; Ellouise Baker Larsen, *American Historical Views on Staffordshire China,* Dover Publications, Inc., Third Edition, 1975; N. Hudson Moore, *The Old China Book,* Charles E. Tuttle Co., 1974.

Museums: American Antiquarian Society, Worcester, Massachusetts; City Museum & Art Gallery, Stoke-on-Trent, England; Henry Ford Museum, Dearborn, Michigan; The National Museum of History & Technology, Washington, DC; Wellcome Institute of the History of Medicine, London, England; Worcester Art Museum, Worcester, Massachusetts; Yale University Gallery of Fine Arts, New Haven, Connecticut.

AMERICAN VIEWS

Adams
Cup and Saucer, "New York," red transfer
  (A) 209.00
Plate
  8" d, "Shannondale Springs, Va." pink
    transfer 95.00
  9 1/8" d, "Near Conway N. Hampshire,
    U.S." American Views series, red transfer
    (A) 66.00
Platter, 19 1/2" l, 15 1/2" w, "Landing of Columbus," four outer scenes in medallions separated by florals, light blue transfer, "W.A.& S." mark 495.00
Vegetable Dish, Cov, 12 1/2" l, "Lake George, U.S." pink transfer, "W. Adams & Sons" mark 50.00
Clews
Cup and Saucer
  "LaFayette at Franklin's Tomb" 295.00
  "LaFayette at Washington's Tomb," marked 295.00
Cup Plate
  3 7/8" d, Hudson River series, "View near Sandy Hill," dark brown transfer, imp "Clews" mark (A) 93.00
  "Landing of General LaFayette at Castle Garden, New York," dark blue transfer, imp "Clews" mark 500.00
Plate
  6 3/4" d, "A Winter View of Pittsfield, Mass," imp "Clews" mark (A) 375.00
  7 5/8" d, "States of America," dark blue transfer, imp "Clews" mark 375.00
  7 3/4" d, "American and Independence," dark blue transfer, imp "Clews Warrented Staffordshire crown" mark 410.00
  8" d, Picturesque Views, "West Point, Hudson River," black transfer (A) 30.00
  8 1/4" d, "Battery, New York," red transfer (A) 50.00
  8 1/2" d, "Winter View of Pittsfield, Mass' (A) 90.00
  8 3/4" d
    "America and Independence-University Building," imp "Clews" mark (A) 165.00
    Picturesque Views, "Near Fort Miller, Hudson River," brown transfer (A)... 30.00

Pitcher and Bowl Set, pitcher, 9 1/4" h, bowl, 12 1/4" d, "Boston State House," blue transfers, imp "Rogers and blue eagle" marks, (A) $1600.00

"Winter View of Pittsfield Mass." imp "Clews" mark (A) **165.00**

8⅞" d, "Peace and Plenty," dark blue transfer, imp "Clews" mark (A) **302.00**

9" d

"Landing of General LaFayette at Castle Garden, N.Y." imp "Clews" mark (A) **275.00**

Picturesque Views, "Baker's Falls, Hudson River," dark brown transfer (A) .. **71.00**

"Quebec," 'Neff Warton & Co. Louisville" retailers label (A) **297.00**

"States" series, "University Building' (A) **85.00**

10¼" d

"Landing of General LaFayette at Castle Garden, New York," floral border, imp "Clews Warrented Staffordshire" mark............................. **250.00**

"Peace and Plenty," imp "Clews" mark (A) **467.00**

10⅜" d, Picturesque Views, "Near Fishkill, Hudson River," dark brown transfer, imp "Clews" mark (A) **105.00**

10½" d

"Custom House," States border, dark blue transfer, imp "Clews" mark..... **75.00**

"Near Fishkill, Hudson River," brown transfer **70.00**

"Pittsfield Elm," med blue transfer, scratches (A) **412.00**

10⅝" d, Picturesque Views, "Near Fishkill, Hudson River," black transfer (A) **30.00**

11" d, "Landing of General LaFayette at Castle Garden, New York," imp "Clews" mark (A) **138.00**

Platter, 15½" l, "Newburgh on Hudson River".............................. **265.00**

Soup Plate

9⅞" d

"A Winter View of Pittsfield, Mass." ... **325.00**

"Landing of General LaFayette at Castle Garden, New York," imp "Clews" mark (A) **275.00**

"Table Rock, Niagara Falls" **295.00**

Sugar Bowl, Cov, "Landing of General Lafayette at Castle Garden, New York"..... **600.00**

Toddy Plate

4⅝" d, "A Winter View of Pittsfield, Massachusetts," no figures in foreground, imp "Clews" mark (A) **520.00**

4¾" d, "America and Independence" with states, imp "Clews" mark (A).......... **435.00**

Davenport

Plate, 8¼" d, printed portrait of Captain Hull, blue border (A) **1155.00**

Edwards, J.& T.

Pitcher, 5¾" h, "Boston Mail-Gentlemens Cabin," light blue transfer (A)........... **412.00**

Heath, J.

Plate, 8½" d, "Ontario Lake Scenery," 1845–53 .... **75.00**

Platter, 15" l, 12" w, oct, "Ontario Lake Scenery," med blue transfer, imp "HEATH" mark................................. **150.00**

Henshall

Plate, 10" d, "The Dam and Water Works, Philadelphia," Fruit and Flower Border series, dark blue transfer (A)............... **467.00**

Jackson, J.& J.

Plate

7¾" d, "Battery & C, New York," black transfer, "J.& J. Jackson" mark **35.00**

9" d, "The Water Works Philadelphia," brown transfer, "J.& J. Jackson" mark .. **25.00**

10¼" d, "The President's House, Washington," brown transfer, "J.& J. Jackson" mark............................... **38.00**

10½" d, "View of the Catskill Mountain House," purple transfer, rim chip (A)... **38.00**

Maker Unkown

Cup Plate, 3½" d, "Holiday Street Theatre, Baltimore," hairlines, unmarked (A)...... **170.00**

Dish, 5" l, leaf shape, "St. Paul's Chapel, N.Y." unmarked (A)........................ **3850.00**

Jug

4⅜" h, Sunderland luster, cream body overglazed with lime green, oval reserve of "The Enterprise & Boxer," reverse with "The United States and Macedonian," pink luster trimmed neck, spout, handle, and borders (A)..................... **1980.00**

5¾" h, cream body with lime green overglaze, cream reserves of Major General Brown at Niagara, reverse with Captain Hull of the Constitution, brown transfers, pink luster trimmed rim, spout, and handle (A)............................ **3300.00**

6¼" h, cream body, transfers of "The Wasp boarding the Frodic," reverse with "The Constitution's Escape after a Chase of Sixty Hours," copper luster trimmed spout, rim, handle, and borders (A) **2090.00**

6¾" h, cream body, yellow overglaze, transfers of Pike in oval, reverse with Captain Hull of the Constitution, pink luster trimmed rim, spout, handle, and borders (A) **3410.00**

Milk Pitcher, 7½" h, "LaFayette at Franklin's Tomb," blue transfer................... **1250.00**

Mug

2⅜" h, "San Francisco California Gold Rush," ships at anchor in bay with buildings, red transfer, unmarked (A) **330.00**

2½" h, "To Washington The Patriot of America," floral cartouche, eagles on shell, purple transfer (A) **132.00**

Pitcher

8¼" h

"Boston State House," med blue transfer, c1830 (A)...................... **660.00**

"Esplanade and Castle Garden," reverse with "Boston Almshouse," blue transfer, leaf and branch border (A) **880.00**

9" h, Sunderland luster, transfers of first and second views of Commodore Perry's victory, Independence insignia under spout, restored (A) **1210.00**

9¼" h, Commodore Perry in navel dress with "We have met the enemy, and they are ours!" reverse with "Second View of Com. Perry's Victory," black transfers, cream ground (A) **3520.00**

9½" h, inscribed scene of "Com. MacDonough's Victory on Lake Champlain, Sept. 11th, 1814," reverse with "Second View of Com. Perry's Victory," tan ground, copper luster banded spout, rim, and handle, small acanthus leaf handle on front (A) **4400.00**

Plate

7¼" d, "General Jackson The Hero of New Orleans," black transfer, three pink luster bands (A)..................... **220.00**

7½" d

"American Villa," fruit and foliage border,
dark blue transfer **75.00**
"William Penn's Treaty," brown transfer **55.00**
8" d, "Hancock House Boston," dark
brown transfer, hairline (A) **82.00**
8¼" d, printed portrait of Decator, blue
border, cream ground, unmarked (A)... **1555.00**
8⅝" d, "Baltimore, Court House," unmarked (A) **467.00**
9" d

"Boston Mails Series-Gentleman's
Cabin," black transfer **95.00**
"Main Street Bridge, Richfield Springs,
N.Y." dark blue transfer............ **850.00**
"Quebec," dark blue transfer, made for
Neff Warton, Louisville **465.00**
10" d

"Independence Hall," blue transfer **10.00**
"Landing of LaFayette," dark blue transfer
(A) **258.00**
"Philadelphia Dam and Water Works,"
blue transfer...................... **700.00**
"State House Boston," blue transfer ... **325.00**
10⅛" d, "LaFayette and Washington and
eagle," red transfer, emb blue rim, unmarked (A) **770.00**
10½" d, "Alleghany Scenery," center
scene of canal boat and town, floral border, black transfer **120.00**
Platter

19½" l, 15½" w, "New Haven, Connect-
icut," black transfer **55.00**
24" l, "Fairmount Near Philadelphia," blue
transfer **2950.00**
Teapot, 8½" h, ironstone, faceted surface,
"Arms of Pennsylvania" transfers, white
ground (A) **467.00**
Waste Bowl, 4¾" h, 8½" d, "LaFayette at
Franklin's Tomb," blue transfer........... **5000.00**
Mayer, T.

Platter, 14¾" l, 12½" w, state seal of Maryland in center, floral border, dark blue transfer, pierced for hanging **850.00**
Ridgway, J.

Soup Plate, 10" d, "Log Cabin-Side View, Man
Plowing With Two Horses," light brown
transfer **110.00**
Ridgway, J.& W.

Plate

8⅛" d, "Beauties of America Series,
Staughton Church" Philadelphia, blue
transfer, "J.& W. Ridgway" mark **525.00**
8¼" d, "Library Philadelphia," medium
blue transfer (A) **247.00**
9⅞" d, "New York, City Hall," medium
blue transfer (A) **247.00**
10" d, "City Hall, New York," 'J.& W. Ridgway" mark **175.00**
Platter, 11" l, "Little Falls, N.Y.," Catskill Moss
series, light gray transfer (A)............. **467.00**
Soup Dish, 8¼" d, "Beauties of America
Series, Staughton Church Philadelphia,"
blue transfer, c1814–30, "J.& W. Ridgway" mark **520.00**
Rogers, John & Son

Bowl, 10¼" d, "Boston State House," flower
and leaf border, med blue transfer (A).... **345.00**
Meat Dish, 18⅞" l, 13" w, with drain, "Boston State House," floral border, med blue
transfers, imp "Rogers" marks (A)........ **1180.00**

Pitcher and Bowl, pitcher 11" h, bowl 12" d,
"Boston State House and Commons," blue
transfer, c1816–40, "blue eagle" mark ... **2850.00**
Plate, 10" d, "Shannon," the Shannon frigate,
sprays of flowers, leaves, and mottled seashells on border, med blue transfer **325.00**
Stevenson, R.

Cup Plate, 3¾" d, "Battery New York," hairline, unmarked (A) **275.00**
Plate

7⅞" d, "Battery New York," dark blue
transfer, imp "Stevenson" mark (A) **275.00**
8⅞" d, "Hospital Boston," dark blue transfer, imp "Stevenson" mark (A)......... **275.00**
10" d, "American Villa," dark blue transfer. **450.00**
Toddy Plate, 5" d, "American Museum," imp
"Stevenson" mark (A) **900.00**
Stevenson & Williams

Plate

6½" d, "Columbia College, New York,"
Acorn and Oak Leaves Border series,
dark blue transfer, "RSW" mark (A) **467.00**
7½" d, "Columbia College, New York,"
Acorn and Oak Leaves Border series,
dark blue transfer, repaired hole, "RSW"
mark (A) **330.00**
8½" d, "City Hotel, New York," 'RSW"
mark............................... **85.00**
10" d

"Capital, Washington," dark blue transfer
(A) **335.00**
"Park Theatre, New York," Acorn and
Oak Leaves Border series, dark blue
transfer (A)........................ **330.00**
10⅛" d, "Harvard College," dark blue
transfer (A) **330.00**
Stubbs

Cup Plate, 3⅛" d, "Woodlands Near Philadelphia," partial spread eagle border, dark
blue transfer (A)....................... **264.00**
Wood, E.

Cup Plate, 3¾" d, black transfer of LaFayette
and Washington, imp "Wood" mark (A).. **600.00**
Plate

5½" d, "Boston State House," med blue
transfer, imp "E. Wood & Sons" mark.. **95.00**
7" d, "Monte Video, Connecticut, U.S." red
transfer (A).......................... **65.00**
7½" d, "America Independence" series,
"The Landing of the Fathers at Plymouth
Dec 22 1620," medallion of "Washington Born 1732 Died 1799" at bottom,
c1819–46, "Enoch Wood & Sons Bur-
slem" mark......................... **325.00**
7⅝" d, "View of Trenton Falls," regular
shell border series, dark blue transfer
(A) **176.00**
8⅜" d, "Falls of Montmorenci Near Quebec," dark blue transfer, imp "E. Wood &
Sons" mark (A) **330.00**
9¼" d, "Commodore MacDonnough's
Victory," imp "Wood" markA) **275.00**
9½" d

"Baltimore and Ohio Railroad," med blue
transfer (A)........................ **170.00**
"LaFayette at Washington's Tomb," floral
border, dark blue transfer, imp "Enoch
Wood & Sons" mark............... **150.00**
"Marine Hospital, Louisville, Ky," dark
blue transfer, "Enoch Wood & Sons"
mark (A) **138.00**

10" d

"America Independent July 4, 1776," Enoch Wood & Sons, Burslem **175.00**

"Boston State House," floral border, med blue transfer, c1818, "Enoch Wood & Sons" mark **475.00**

"Cadmus," seashell border, dark blue transfer, imp "Enoch Wood & Sons, Burslem, England" mark **175.00**

"Landing of General LaFayette at Castle Garden, New York," floral border, dark blue transfer, "Enoch Wood & Sons, Burslem, England" mark **175.00**

"Landing of the Fathers at Plymouth" .. **350.00**

"Table Rock, Niagara," shell border, "Enoch Wood & Sons, Burslem, England" mark **150.00**

"Union Line," 'Enoch Wood & Sons" mark **375.00**

10¼" d

"Baltimore & Ohio," seashell border, imp "E. Wood & Sons Warrented Semi China" mark (A) **467.00**

"Commodore MacDonnough's Victory," 'E.W.& Sons" mark **365.00**

10½" d

"Baltimore and Ohio Railroad," med blue transfer (A) **170.00**

"Union Line," seashell border, hairline, imp "Wood" mark **200.00**

Platter, 18¾" l, 14⅝" w, "Castle Garden, Battery, New York," seashell border, med blue transfer, "Enoch Wood & Sons" mark (A) **1320.00**

Soup Plate, 10¼" d, "Table Rock, Niagara," dark blue transfer, rim chips, imp "E. Wood & Sons" mark (A) **192.00**

Soup Tureen, 6½" h, "Passaic Falls, State of New Jersey," dark blue transfer, imperfections **150.00**

Sugar Bowl, 6⅞" h, "Commodore MacDonnough's Victory," finial reglued (A) **385.00**

ENGLISH VIEWS

Adams

Plate

6¾" d, "Melrose Abbey, Roxburghshire," dark blue transfer **125.00**

9" d, "Villa in Regent's Park, London,', Re-

Platter, 15½" l, "Windsor Castle," med blue transfer, unmkd, $500.00

gent's Park series, dark blue transfer (A) **110.00**

Platter, 19¼" l, 15" w, "Cornwall Terrace, Regents Park," dark blue transfer, imp "Adams" mark (A) **1850.00**

Clews

Plate, "St. Catherine's Hill, near Guildford," med blue transfer, imp "Clews" mark (A). **85.00**

Toddy Plate, 6⅛" d, "Remains of the Church Thornton Abbey," dark blue transfer, imp "Clews" mark (A) **82.00**

Undertray, 9¾" l, "English Scenery," ship in ground, three people in foreground, dark blue transfer (A) **132.00**

Hall, R.

Cup Plate, 4" d, "Worcester Cathedral," Select View series, dark blue transfer (A) **176.00**

Pitcher, 6¾" h, titled portrait of "Fayette" or "Washington," eagle under spout, verse "Republicans Are Not Always Ungrateful" on rim, black transfers, cream ground, c1825 (A) **1320.00**

Plate

8" d, "Gunton Hall, Norfolk," foliage border series, dark blue transfer (A) **55.00**

8½" d, "Fulham Church, Middlesex," blue transfer, "R. Hall's Picturesque Scenery" mark (A) **94.00**

8⅝" d, "Warleigh House, Sommersetshire," blue transfer, "R. Hall's Select Views" mark (A) **94.00**

10" d

"Biddulph Castle Staffordshire," blue transfer **250.00**

"Plains Hill, Surrey," dark blue transfer . **275.00**

Miscellaneous Makers

Basket, 10¼" H-H, 4¼" h, "Village Church," med blue transfer, diamond pierced sides, Wild Rose border, repaired with staples (A) **104.00**

Plate

6½" d, "Lakes of Killarney," dark blue transfer, pr (A) **154.00**

8½" d, "Irish Scenery-Fonthill Abbey, Wiltshire," red transfer, "Elkins & Co." mark **25.00**

9" d, "Richard Jordon's Birthplace," purple transfer, "Heath" mark **195.00**

10" d, "Vale House," fruit and flower border, dark blue transfer (A) **250.00**

10¼" d, "Blenheim, Oxfordshire," Flower and Leaves Border series, dark blue transfer, knife scratches (A) **148.00**

Serving Dish, 8½" H-H, "The Village Church," roses on handles, med blue transfer, pr (A) **935.00**

Soup Plate, 10" d, "Guy's Cliff, Warwickshire," med blue transfer, unmarked (A) .. **66.00**

Toddy Plate, "Windsor Park," dark blue transfer, unmarked (A) **25.00**

Ridgway, J. & W.

Plate, 9¾" d, "Christ Church, Oxford," classical border, med blue transfer, set of 6 (A) **440.00**

Sauce Tureen, 6½" h, with undertray, "Christ Church, Oxford" and "Trinity Hall, Cambridge," med blue transfers, "J.& W. Ridgway" mark (A) **385.00**

Riley, J. & R.

Basket, "Bretton Hall, Yorkshire," open lattice work border, dbl handles, med blue transfer, repaired (A) **440.00**

Plate

7" d, "The King's Cottage-Windsor Park,"
med blue transfer, "J.& R. Riley" mark. .   **125.00**

8¾" d, "King's Weston Gloustershire,"
floral border, med blue tansfer, "J.& R.
Riley" mark. **250.00**

10" d, "Hollywell Cottage, Cavan," dark
blue transfer, Large Scroll Border Series,
imp "RILEY" mark. **75.00**

Soup Plate, 8¾" d, "The Rookery, Surrey,"
Large Scroll Border series, dark blue transfer
(A). **121.00**

Stevenson & Williams

Platter, 18½" l, 14¾" w, "Windsor Castle
Aqueduct, Bridge at Rochester," blue trans-
fer. **250.00**

Stevenson, Ralph

Plate, 10¼" d, "Clifford Hall, Suffolk," dark
blue transfer, imp "Stevenson" mark **85.00**

Undertray, 8½" l, "Bedgrave Hall," Wild
Rose border, dark blue transfer, hairline
(A). **60.00**

Tams

Teapot, 12" h, Foliage Border Series, London view, dark blue transfer, chip on finial
filled. **685.00**

Wood, E.

Gravy Boat, "Sproughton Chantry, Suffolk',
Grapevine border, dark blue transfer (A). .   **121.00**

Plate

6½" d, "Shirley House, Surrey," Grapevine border Series, dark blue transfer
(A). **143.00**

7½" d, "Gunton Hall, Norfolk', Grapevine
border, med blue border. **85.00**

8" d, "Marlborough Hall, Derbyshire," dark
blue transfer. **75.00**

9¼" d, "Hanover Lodge Regents' Park,"
London Views series, dark blue transfer
(A) **99.00**

9¾" d, "Guy Cliff Warwickshire," med
blue transfer, imp "Enoch wood & Sons"
mark. **100.00**

10" d

"View of Liverpool," blue transfer, "E.
Wood & Sons" mark (A). **330.00**

"Wardour Castle Wiltshire," Grapevine
border, blue transfer, c1818–46, imp
"Enoch Wood Burslem" mark **195.00**

10½" d, "Taymouth Castle, Perthshire,"
Grapevine border Series, dark blue trans-
fer, "Enoch Wood" mark **90.00**

Sauce Tureen, Underplate, 7½" H-H, 6" h,
"Cokethorpe Park Oxfordshire," Grapevine
border Series, dark blue transfer, "Enoch
Wood & Sons" mark **525.00**

Undertray, 8¾" l, "Thornton Castle, Staffordshire, Grapevine border, dark blue
transfer, hairline, repairs (A) **71.00**

OTHER VIEWS

Hall, R.

Platter, 19½" l, "Church of St. Charles and
Polytechnic School, Vienna, Germany," foli-
ate and fruit border, dark blue transfer, "R.
Hall" mark (A) **495.00**

Toddy Plate, 6⅝" d, "The Hospital Near
Poissy France," dark blue transfer, "R. Hall's
Select Views" mark (A) **40.00**

**Soup Plate, 10" d, "Parisian Chateau," med blue
transfer, "R. Hall" mark, $98.00**

Maker Unknown

Compote, 6¼" h, 11½" H-H, pierced,
"Views in Mesopotamia," black transfer,
med blue enamel ground, applied sprays
and gilt highlights, black transfer of floral
sprays on ext, spirally fluted column (A) . .   **357.00**

Meat Dish, 21⅛" l, pearlware, "Pashkov
House, Moscow," blue transfer, elaborate
floral border (A). **1820.00**

Plate

6" d, "Oriental Scenery-Ancient Tomb at
Boghepore," light blue transfer **25.00**

10" d, "Batalha Portugal," med blue trans-
fer. **110.00**

10¼" d, "Italian Scenery-Bridge of
Lucano," med blue transfer **100.00**

Platter, 11¼" l, 9¾" w, "Muhlbrunn Colonnade and Karlsbad," acorn band, med blue
transfer. **65.00**

Rogers, John & Son

Meat Dish, 21¼" l, rect with canted corners,
"Oriental Scenery-Gate Leading to a
Musjed at Chunar Ghur," geometric border,
med blue transfer, imp "Rogers" mark (A)   **570.00**

Wood, E.

Gravy Tureen, 6½" h, "Italian Scenery-
Terni," dark blue transfers, repaired finial
(A). **302.00**

Plate

9¼" d, "LaGrange, The Residence of the
Marquis LaFayette," med blue transfer .   **195.00**

9½" d, "East View of La Grange, the Residence of the Marquis LaFayette," dark
blue transfer, imp "Wood" mark. **98.00**

10" d, "Italian Scenery-Ponte Rotto," dark
blue transfer (A) **55.00**

Platter

16½" l, "Cape Coast Castle on the Gold
Coast, Africa," med blue transfer, "Enoch
Wood & Sons" mark **800.00**

16⅞" l, "Italian Scenery-Ponte del
Palazzo," dark blue transfer, "Enoch
Wood & Sons" mark (A). **425.00**

Toddy Plate, 6½" d, French series, "Maison
de Raphael," dark blue transfer, imp
"Wood" mark (A).   **93.00**

Undertray, 8" l, "Italian Scenery-Chatteau De
Chillon," dark blue transfer (A) **302.00**

STAFFORDSHIRE— ROMANTIC

England
1830–1860

History: Between 1830 and 1860 the Staffordshire District potters produced a tremendous number of useful dinnerwares intended for everyday dining that featured romantic transfer printed designs.

Romantic wares were printed in blue, red, green, black, brown, purple, and yellow. Some patterns were issued in only one color, while some were produced in a variety of colors. Within each color group, there was a great deal of color variation. Blues ranged from the darkest navy to a pale powder blue to shades of turquoise.

Designs used for romantic wares reflected the tastes of the Victorian age. Scenes with castles, Alpine mountain peaks, and rivers evoked a fascination with European travel. Oriental scenery expressed the infatuation of the common man with dreams of far away places. English scenes were used, but they depicted homes of the nobility, castles, and other important locations.

Floral designs featured realistic flowers, leaves, fruits, and birds that reflected the English love of gardens. Some scenes added insects or butterflies in imitation of the Chinese patterns.

The Victorians loved the architectural and decorative styles of the past. Gothic elements, French designs from the Louis XV and XVI periods, and even Grecian and Roman designs became part of romantic transfer patterns. Classical designs often showed urns or vases in a garden setting. Some pieces contained allegorical stories.

Oriental designs utilized Chinese and Japanese flowers, baskets, exotic birds, flowering trees, pagodas, and urns. East Indian motifs depicted mosques, minarets, desert scenes, and men and women in Arabian or Turkish clothes. Elements of fantasy in these patterns reflected the love of far off, romantic places, unseen by the common English resident.

Scenic designs were popular. Pastoral scenes showing the typical English countryside featured rolling fields, domestic farm animals, groves of trees, brooks, and ponds. Figures placed in these scenes usually wore Medieval, Elizabethan, or Empire clothing. Greyhounds were a common decorative element.

Although the names of rivers, countries, cities, or towns often were used as titles for these romantic views, the scenes themselves were imaginary. Most of the scenes appeared rather dreamlike in conception. Tall trees, rivers, castles, arched bridges, gazebos, ruins, or fountains were included in the scenes. Borders were either floral, geometric, or featured reserves with landscape scenes.

Some scenes showed local people in their roles as farmers, fishermen, warriors, dancers, etc. In these cases, the scenic background was less prominent. The figures were most important. Other romantic subjects included zoological, religious, moralistic, botanical, marine, or geometric transfers.

In many instances, the designers of the transfers were not known. Many pottery firms purchased their transfers from engraving companies such as Sargeant and Pepper of Hanley. The firm designed the printed patterns and also engraved the copper plates necessary for printing the wares. Popular designs were used by more than one pottery manufacturer.

Romantic transfers were made by many factories. The best known were Adams, Clews, Davenport, Dillon, Dimmock, Hall, Hicks and Meigh, Meigh, Ridgway, Rogers, Spode, Wedgwood, and Wood.

Backstamps were used that reflected the romantic expressions of these Victorian potters. The backstamp was part of the sheet that contained the transfer pattern. When placed on the back of a piece, it indicated the pattern used.

References: Petra Williams, *Staffordshire Romantic Transfer Patterns,* Fountain House East, 1978; Petra Williams & Marguerite R. Weber, *Staffordshire II,* Fountain House East, 1986.

Museums: City Museum & Art Gallery, Stoke-on-Trent, England; Henry Ford Museum, Dearborn, Michigan.

Bone Dish, "Grecian," green transfer, "Ridgway" mark 7.00
Bowl
  6" d, "Brussels," red transfer 75.00
  6 1/4" d, "Chinese Pattern," polychrome with luster, Ashworth....................... 23.00
Bread and Butter, 6" d, "Venus," gray transfer with polychromes, "P.W.& Co." mark 18.00
Candy Dish, 5 3/4" d, "Tessino," light blue transfer, seven sides 38.00
Chamber Pot, "Florentine," light blue transfer . 120.00
Charger, 15" d, "Aesop's Fables-Lion and Fox," brown transfer, "Copeland & Garrett" mark. 100.00
Compote, 8 1/4" d, 5 1/2" h, "Hong," brown transfer with polychrome enamels (A) 45.00
Cup Plate
  "Aurora," light blue transfer, "Beach & Hancock" mark.......................... 25.00
  "Canova," black transfer 40.00
  "Union," blue transfer, "Venables & Co." mark.................................... 75.00
  "Warwick Vase," brown transfers, "P.W.& Co." marks 48.00
Cup and Saucer, Handleless
  "Garden Scenery," pink transfer 40.00
  "Peruvian Horse Hunt," brown transfers (A) 22.00
Dinner Service, Part
  7 piece, teapot, 8" h, plate, 9" d, 2 plates, 8 1/4" d, 2 handleless cups and saucers, cup plate, "Flensburg," black transfer center of flowers and eagle with polychromes, blue border (A)............................. 374.00
  17 piece, 6 plates, 9 1/2" d, 4 plates, 8 1/2" d, 6 handleless cups and saucers, bowl,

Plate, 9 1/4" d, "Tuscan Rose," dk brown transfer, "JWR" mark, $28.00

10¾" d, "Zamara," red transfers, repairs
(A). 358.00
Dish, 5¾" l, 4¾" w, shaped rect, "Gondola"
scene, blue transfer, 1857–72, Clyde Pottery
Co. Scotland. 200.00
Gravy Boat, "The Sower," purple transfer 60.00
Meat Platter, 15¾" l, 12½" w, "Athena," car-
touche border, med blue transfer, "Bishop &
Stonier" mark. 200.00
Milk Pitcher, 7" h, "Amoy," blue transfer, "Dav-
enport" mark 250.00
Pate Dish, 5" l, "Humphrey's Clock" Series, blue
transfer, c1830, W. Ridgway & Son 98.00
Pitcher
   5½" h, "Maryland," pink transfer 80.00
   8" h, oct, "Vista," dark gray with poly-
   chromes 145.00
   9¼" h, oct, "Florentine," brown transfer, "T.
   Mayer" mark 135.00
Plate
   5" d, "Friburg," blue transfer, Davenport . . .   15.00
   6" d, "Isolabelle," blue transfer, "W. Adams &
   Son" mark. 25.00
   6½" d, "Slamat," polychrome with luster, un-
   marked. 25.00
   6¾" d, "Millenium," red transfer (A) 85.00
   7" d, "Tyrolean," green transfer 24.00
   7⅛" d, "Pekin," polychrome with luster,
   "WEC" mark 25.00
   7¼" d, "Wild Rose" pattern, blue transfer,
   reticulated plate, c1815, Courtensay, Ox-
   fordshire 395.00
   7½" d
      "Columbus," brown transfer. 50.00
      "Eton," brown center, purple border 35.00
      "Texian Campaigne," pink transfer, An-
      thony Shaw 25.00
      "Tyrolean," pink transfer 24.00
   8" d
      "Acropolis," purple transfer 40.00
      "Ontario," blue transfer, "J. Heath" mark .   25.00
      "Zoological Gardens," purple transfer,
      "Clews" mark 65.00
   8¼" d
      "Berzoni" pattern, red transfer (A) 26.00
      "Bologna," red transfer, c1820s 25.00
      "Feather," green transfer, red and yellow
      enameling, scalloped rim (A) 10.00
      "Sena," sepia transfer with luster 25.00
   8½" d
      "Columbia," light blue transfer, "William
      Adams & Sons" mark. 24.00
      "Siene," blue transfer. 38.00
      "Sydenham," blue transfer 40.00
   8¾" d
      "Asiatic Pheasants," blue transfer 25.00
      "Buda," red transfer 16.00
      "Palestine," pink transfer, Adams 25.00
      "Parisian Chateau," brown transfer, "R.
      Hall" mark 18.00
   8⅞" d, "Swiss Scenery," brown transfer. . .   26.00
   9" d
      "Castle," dark blue transfer, gadrooned bor-
      der, Stevenson. 95.00
      "Grecian," green transfer, "Davenport"
      mark. 15.00
      "Lake," blue transfer. 42.00
      Oct, "Ontario Lake Scenery," blue transfer,
      "J. Heath" mark.   40.00
      "Sicilian," brown transfer. 29.00

Ten sides, "Mycene," blue transfer, c1853–
68, "Hulse Nixon & Adderly" mark 40.00
9¼" d
   "Abbey Ruins," blue transfer, c1836–1838,
   "T. Mayer" mark.   140.00
   "Canova," brown transfer 25.00
   "Pileau," brown transfer 29.00
   "Rural Scenery," red transfer, "Heath"
   mark. 62.00
   "Spanish Convent," purple transfer. 28.00
   "Verona," brown transfer with underglaze
   blue, polychrome enamels and luster,
   "Wood & Sons" mark (A). 225.00
9⅜" d
   "Belzoni," green transfer, "E.W.& S." mark
   (A) 22.00
   "Palestine," brown transfer, imp "ADAMS"
   mark. 32.00
9½" d
   Fourteen sides, "Marino," pink transfer, "G.
   Phillips" mark. 35.00
   "Seasons," red transfer, imp "Adams"
   mark. 66.00
   "Texian Campaigne," med blue transfer,
   Anthony Shaw 40.00
9¾" d
   "Belvoir Castle," blue transfer, floral border,
   Duke of Rotlands castle, c1830, Staf-
   fordshire 195.00
   "Bosphorus," brown transfer, c1875, "J.
   Marshall & Co." mark 18.00
   "Buda," red transfer 18.00
   "Eton," brown center, purple border 55.00
   "Tree of Life," polychrome with luster, un-
   marked 30.00
9⅞" d, "Bamboo," blue transfer (A) 75.00
10" d,
   "Crusaders," blue transfer. 65.00
   "Oriental"
      Light blue transfer, "Ridgways" mark . . .   29.00
      Red transfer 14.00
   "Pagoda," green transfer, Allerton. 26.00
   "Priory," blue transfer 37.00
   "Texian Campaigne," brown transfer, An-
   thony Shaw 575.00
   "Tuscan Rose," purple transfer, hairline
   (A) 35.00
10¼" d
   "American Villa," dark blue transfer 225.00
   "Andalusia," pink transfer 36.00
   "Archery," brown transfer. 50.00
   "Olympic Games, The Discus," brown
   transfer, "T. Mayer Stoke on Trent"
   mark. 175.00
10⅜" d
   "Lusanne Villa," mulberry transfer, scal-
   loped edge 25.00
   "Oriental," red transfer (A). 66.00
   "Valencia," blue and black transfer (A) . . .   60.00
10½" d
   "Acroplis," blue transfer 65.00
   "American Marine," blue transfer, Mason. .   25.00
   "Antiques," blue transfer. 65.00
   "Canova'
      Black transfer. 45.00
      Green transfer, Mayer 40.00
   "Millenium," green transfer (A) 30.00
   "University," blue transfer. 40.00
10¾" d
   "Acropolis," blue transfer 58.00

"Antiques," blue transfer............... 58.00
"Columbus," light blue transfer, imp
   "Adams" mark...................... 71.00
"Crusaders," blue transfer.............. 58.00
Platter
  13" l
    "Grecian," green transfer, "Davenport"
     mark.............................. 35.00
    "Oriental," blue transfer, Ridgway........ 90.00
  13½" l, 10" w, "Panama," blue transfer, "Ed.
    Challinor & Co." mark 75.00
  14" l, "Jenny Lind," pale yellow, brown, olive
    and rust polychrome transfer, "Royal Staf-
    fordshire Pottery, England" mark......... 60.00
  15" l, "Cleopatra," pink transfer with poly-
    chromes 175.00
  15½" l, 12" w, "Panama," blue transfer, "Ed
    Challinor & Co." mark 95.00
  15½" l, 12⅓" w, "Wild Rose," blue trans-
    fer, floral border 600.00
  15¾" l, "Mesina," blue transfer, "Wood &
    Challinor" mark 130.00
  16" l, 12½" w, "Lucerne," blue-gray transfer,
    "J.W.P.& Co." mark 300.00
  16½" l, 12¾" w, "Venetian Scenery," floral
    border, med blue transfer, c1830 .... 550.00
  16¾" l, "India Temple" pattern, blue trans-
    fer, 1814–30, John and William Ridgway.. 565.00
  17¼" l, "Acropolis," brown transfer....... 195.00
  20¼" l, "Canova," purple transfer, "T.
    Mayer" mark (A)...................... 250.00
Sauceboat and Stand, "Fibre," green transfer.. 100.00
Sauce Dish, 5" d, "Chinese," polychrome with
  luster, Adams 15.00
Sauce Tureen, with undertray, "Polish Views,"
  blue transfer 215.00
Soup Plate
  9¼" d
    "Warwick Vase," blue transfer, "J. Dim-
     mock" mark....................... 12.00
    "Wild Rose," green transfer, c1840 ...... 185.00
  9⅜" d, "Rhine," dark blue transfer, "J.F.W."
    mark................................ 23.00
  9½" d, "Chinese" pattern, polychrome with
    luster, "B.W.& Co." mark 30.00
  10⅜" d, "Chusan" pattern, black transfer
    with polychromes, set of 5 (A)........... 250.00
  10½" d, "Canova," pink transfer, Mayer... 55.00
Sugar Bowl
  5" h, "Belzoni," purple transfer........... 55.00
  7" h, "Malta," blue transfer, "W.H. Grindley"
    mark................................ 75.00
  7⅞" h, oct, "Gypsey," blue transfer....... 95.00
Teabowl and Saucer, "Abbey" pattern, brown
  transfer, "T. Mayer" mark 25.00
Teapot
  9" h, paneled, "Columbia," blue transfer
    (A)................................. 50.00
  9¾" h, oct, "Gypsey', blue transfer 245.00
  "Canova," blue transfer 200.00
Tea Set, teapot, creamer, cov sugar bowl,
  "Canova," blue transfers 525.00
Vegetable Dish, Cov, 11" l, "Palestine," blue
  transfer, hairline, chips on base (A)........ 45.00
Vegetable Tureen, Cov
  13" H-H, "Caledonia," purple transfer...... 325.00
  13½" H-H, 8½" h, "Olympic Games, The
    Sling," brown transfer, scalloped shape, de-
    sign in int, c1830, T. Mayer mark 550.00
  "Grecian," green transfer, "Davenport" mark 35.00

1892 -1921

STEINS

Germany
1840s to Present

History: A stein is a drinking vessel with a handle and an attached lid that is made to hold beer and ale. The use of a lid differentiates a stein from a mug. Steins range in size from the smallest at ³⁄₁₀ liters or ¼ liters to the larger at 1, 1½, 2, 3, 4, and 5 liters, and even 8 liters in rare cases. A liter is 1.05 liquid quarts.

GENERAL

The finest steins have proportional figures with intricate details that make them appear real. The decorations are made in a separate mold and applied to the body of the stein, giving the piece a raised effect. Etched steins, with the design incised or engraved into the body of the stein, are the most desirable and expensive steins. Artisans used black paint to fill in the lines and then other colors to complete the motif.

The simplest steins to produce were the print under glaze (PUG). A decal or transfer printed scene was applied by the transfer method, the body was covered with an additional coat of transparent glaze, and the piece was refired.

Character or figural steins depicted life-like creations of Indians heads, skulls, animals, Satans, vegetables, buildings, and people. Ernst Bohne's firm produced fine quality figural steins with realistic expressions.

Occupational steins were steins with a decoration or shape that depicted the owner's occupation. A slogan or the owner's name also may appear on the stein.

Thumblifts also came in a variety of designs on steins. Steins designed specifically for export to the United States had a United States shield as the thumblift. Other designs included a monkey, owl, jester, lyre, bust of a figure, twin towers, eagle, Munich maid, lion and shield, dwarf, or huntsman.

METTLACH STEINS

The most prolific period in the history of stein production occurred in the second half of the 19th century, coinciding with the peak of Mettlach stein manufacture.

Chromoliths made by Mettlach were molded. The designs appear to be etched by hand. Although the designs seem three-dimensional, they are smooth to the touch.

Mettlach's cameos or phanoliths have portraits or small scenes in a translucent white clay set against a green or blue background. Even though these are three-dimensional, the relief portions are blended into the background without showing seams.

When fire destroyed the abbey where Mettlach steins were produced in 1921, the company gave up production of chromoliths and cameos. Mettlach's stein competitors included Merkelbach and Wick, Albert Jacob Thewalt, Simon Peter Gerz, and the Girmscheid factory.

REGIMENTAL STEINS

During the reign of Kaiser Wilhelm II, 1888 to 1918, German reservists frequently purchased souvenir steins that had information such as the owner's name, unit, garrison town, service dates, and rosters of comrades inscribed on the them. Munich was the regimental stein capital. Most of the regimental steins date from the early 1890s.

Other European armies also issued regimental steins after the 1890s. A great variety of transfer scenes, finials, stein bodies, and lids were used for regimental steins. Lid varieties that include the finial type, screw off, fuse, flat, prisms, steeple or spindle, helmet, or crown have been identified. The thumblift on the stein usually represented the unit's state of origin or branch of service. Stein body size was usually the standard ½ liter. Maker's marks usually are found on pottery steins. Porcelain steins were rarely marked by the maker.

Mettlach military steins were only made in pottery. They were marked on the bottom with an incised stock or mold number and usually were dated.

References: J. L. Harrell, *Regimental Steins,* The Old Soldier Press, 1979; Gary Kirsner, *The Mettlach Book,* Seven Hills Books, 1983; Gary Kirsner & Jim Gruhl, *The Stein Book, A 400 Year History,* Glentiques, 1990; Dr. Eugene Manusov, *Encyclopedia of Character Steins,* Wallace Homestead, 1976; Dr. Eugene Manusov & Mike Wald, *Character Steins: A Collectors Guide,* Cornwall Books, 1987; R. H. Mohr, *Mettlach Steins & Their Prices,* Rockford, rev. 4th edition, 1972; R. H. Mohr, *Mettlach Steins,* privately printed, 9th edition, 1982; James R. Stevenson, *Antique Steins, A Collectors' Guide,* Cornwall books, 1982; Mike Wald, *HR Steins,* SCI Publications, 1980.

Collectors Club: Stein Collectors International, SCI Treasurer, Walt Vogdes, P.O. Box 4096, Rockville, MD 20850. Membership: $20.00. *Prosit,* quarterly.

Museum: Milwaukee Art Center, Milwaukee, Wisconsin.

REPRODUCTION ALERT: For more than twenty years, several German firms have reproduced regimental type steins. The reproductions, usually made only in porcelain, have different physical characteristics and historical inaccuracies. The firms used only the finial type of lid and tapered bodies as opposed to the straight bodies on original regimentals. Smooth transfers appear on the reproductions. Lids on the reproductions are stamped from a single piece mold and have no seam line.

Collecting Hints-Regimental Steins: Collectors favor steins with inlaid lids. The inlay is a decorated stoneware disk that is set into a pewter rim. The design in the lid is an extension of the colors and designs on the main body of the stein. A few steins did come without lids or with an all pewter lid in a variety of designs. Steins with missing lids are generally reduced 50 percent in value.

After the destruction caused by World War II, locating regimental steins, became difficult. Occasionally some do surface from German attics or barns.

DESIGN

¼ L, porcelain, blue cornflower on white ground, inlaid lid (A) **248.00**
⁴/₁₀ L, Hacher-Brau, Munchen print over glaze on front, pewter lid with crossed axes, "Gebr. Allmann, Munchen" mark (A) **301.00**

Devil head, ½ L rust brown with gold earrings, red lips, white horns, imp "anchor" mark, Ernst Bohne, (A) $375.00

1 L, relief molded glazed earthenware, Bacchanalian scene in brown, tan, and beige, "Colln Meissen", (A) $160.00

Regimental, ½ L, porcelain, Bruder Stolst Die Glaseran Reserve, 1910–12, officer lithophane, (A) $950.00

½ L, #590, PUG tavern scene, (A) $125.00

½ L

Art Nouveau style flowers growing from heart
and beer stein with bird, sgd "F.R.9" mark 150.00
Raised stylized trees on sides, brown glaze,
stoneware, pewter lid, "R. Merkelbach,
#2121" mark (A)...................... 138.00
8/10 L, blue incised design of two goats with front
hooves on barrel, pewter lid, Merkelbach &
Wick (A) 173.00

1 L

Blue incised and relief of XII Deutsches Bun-
desschieben on gray stoneware, "Reinhold
Merkelbach" mark (A) 248.00
Brown glaze over yellow glaze, incised floral
design, German sayings above and below,
pewter lid and base, Wetterau (A) 4620.00
Cobalt incised curved branches, horiz lines
above and below, pewter band and lid,
c1800 (A) 440.00
Oval raindrops, brown glaze, stoneware, pewter lid, "Reinhold Merkelbach, #2314"
mark (A) 156.00
Raised dark brown whirls at base, med brown
ground, stoneware, pewter lid (A)......... 178.00
Reserves of blue and yellow flower with green
leaves on purple ground, cobalt with yellow
and blue stylized flowers separate reserves,
faience, pewter lid and foot, Bayreuth,
"B.F.& S." mark (A).................... 1040.00

FIGURAL

¼ L, skull, porcelain, E. Bohne (A).......... 289.00
3/10 L, gray funnel with black and orange German saying, orange and black clown handle,
"Musterschutz Nurnberger Trichter" mark .. 495.00
½ L

Bear smoking pipe, tyrolean hat, porcelain,
feather damage, Schierholz (A) 2591.00
Bismark Radish in gray, porcelain, repair to leaf
tip, Schierholz (A) 446.00
Blue Hopps Lady, blue and white, porcelain,
Schierholz (A)......................... 1575.00
Happy Radish in gray, pewter rim, porcelain, engraved "Peter Karnz," repairs,
Schierholz (A)........................... 387.00
Monk, red-brown robe, full color face and
hands, lithophane of monk placing necklace
on lady, porcelain (A)................... 231.00
Munich Maid, lithophane of statue of Bavaria
and Hall of Fame (A) 282.00
Newspaper Lady, black cap, brown striped
shawl, black skirt with white clovers, porcelain, Schierholz (A) 3586.00

Pixie in shades of brown with white flower ring
on forehead, porcelain, Schierholz (A).... 992.00
Rooster in shades of brown, gray jacket,
glasses on beak, porcelain, Schierholz (A). 1386.00
Sad Radish, pewter mounts with insert of radish leaves, porcelain, Musterschutz....... 325.00
Stack of pretzels, pretzel handle and lid, Mettlach, #2388 (A) 397.00

METTLACH

#702/1909, ½ L, PUG, "King Gambrinus Lead-
ing a Parade" (A)....................... 275.00
#1005, 1 L, relief decorated with grape arbor
surrounding drink scenes, pewter lid with
figural thumbpiece (A) 385.00
#1108/1526, 1 L, PUG, celebration of opening of
new keg of Bock beer, pewter lid (A)....... 353.00
#1143/1526, 1 l, PUG, tavern scene, pewter lid,
rim fracture, sgd "Schlitt" (A) 243.00
#1452, ¼ L, mosaic, blue and beige floral de-
sign, inlaid lid, ... 300.00
#1476, ½ L, etched, gnomes tying grape
vines to stakes, grapes on inlaid lid, gnome
thumblift 350.00
#1526, ½ L, PUG, scene of man playing musi-
cal instrument to lady, dtd 1919 .... 195.00
#1863, ½ L, etched, Scene of Stuttgart, inlaid
lid 595.00
#1909/1113, ½ L, PUG, comic tavern scene,
sgd "Schlitt", V.& B. mark 300.00
#1995, ½ L, etched, St. Augustine, scenes of
Fort Marion and the Old City Gate, inlaid lid,
alligator handle (A) 618.00
#2035, etched, Bacchus party scene, inlaid lid
½ L (A)............................... 446.00
1 L (A)............................... 616.00
#2038, 4L, buildings in Black Forest, molded
foot, pewter mounted hinged lid mounted
with German castle (A) 2500.00
#2052, ¼ L, etched, Munich maid design, in-
laid lid of cherub drinking (A)............. 404.00
#2057, ½ L, etched, happy peasants dancing
and drinking beer, inlaid lid (A) 491.00
#2123, 3/10 L, drinking knights, inlaid lid, sgd
"H. Schlitt" (A)......................... 416.00
#2140, ½ L, enameled transfer of student
crest, crest on pewter lid with duelling marks,
dtd 1901 (A)........................... 144.00
#2192, ½ L, etched, figures dressed in cos-
tumes in brown and black on cream ground,
pewter lid, late 19th C, imp marks (A) 785.00
#2230, ½ L, etched, man and barmaid, inlaid
lid, 1910, plain base (A) 400.00
#2270, 2 L, PUG, young woman with soldier,
pewter lid (A).......................... 800.00
#2278, ½ L, white cameo of men in sporting
contests, rust ground, pewter lid (A) 300.00
#2402, ½ L, etched, "The Courting of Sieg-
fried," inlaid lid (A) 716.00
#2715, ½ L, white cameo, three panels of cou-
ples dancing, blue ground, brown floral medallions (A) 578.00
#2755, ½ L, white relief, three panels of figures
seated drinking and smoking, within floral borders, matte green ground, pewter lid, late 19th
C, imp marks (A)........................ 1271.00
#2880, ½ L, etched, tavern scene, brick base
and top, inlaid lid (A) 414.00
#2922, ¼ L, etched, two hunters drinking at
campfire, inlaid lid....................... 300.00

REGIMENTAL

½ L

1st Pioneer Battallion, 1st Company Ingol-
stadt, 1907–09, lithophane base, figural
pewter lid and thumbrest (A) 350.00

2nd Guard, Ulan Berlin 1903–06, pottery ... 600.00

3rd Inf. Reg. Augsburg, 1897–99, pottery,
steeple lid, remounted thumblift (A) 173.00

7th Bavarian Infantry Regt. Bayreuth,
1907–09 .... 450.00

11th Feld Art. Reg. Kassel, 1908–10, porcelain,
cannon finial, eagle thumblift (A) 520.00

12th Infantry Regiment, 9th Company, Neu
Ulm, 1900–1902, pewter lid with soldier
and lions, lithophane of soldiers letter home
(A) 275.00

15th Bayr. Inf. Reg. Neuburg, 1904–06, stoneware, lion and soldier finial (A) 300.00

16th Bayr. Inf. Reg. Passau, 1910–12, porcelain, lion and soldier finial, lion and shield
thumblift with stanhope glass eye (A) 318.00

23rd Infantry, 8th Company, Saargemund,
1903–05, pewter lid with soldier and lion,
lithophane of soldier's farewell (A) 300.00

109th Inf. Reg. Karlsruhe, 1903–05, porcelain,
seated soldier finial (A) 403.00

111th Inf. Reg. Rastatt, 1898–1900, porcelain,
seated soldier finial (A) 352.00

118th Inf. Reg. Worms, 1896–98, porcelain,
seated soldier finial (A) 260.00

1 L, Naval, S.M.S. Turingen, 1911–14, pottery,
standing sailor with flag finial, glass stanhope
under arm (A) 1337.00

SCENIC

½ L

Etched

Five musicians in colors, pewter lid, Merkelbach & Wick (A) 173.00

Knight receiving stein from maiden in tavern
window, German verse, pottery, "HR"
mark (A) 386.00

Hp front panel of two ladies watching man
play stringed instrument, sides with
threaded relief on pebble ground, pewter
lid, "HR" mark (A) 165.00

Relief

B.P.O.E. fraternal, elk with fallen man, pewter top 90.00

Bowling scene in colors, pottery, pewter lid,
"HR" mark (A) 275.00

Scene of Alpine tavern group watching
dancer, pottery, pewter lid (A) 148.00

¾ L, Capodimonte classical figures in wine harvest, mythological winged nude handle, pewter lid and base added at later date (A) 549.00

1 L

Etched, mtd cavaliers being served beer at tavern, pewter lid, holes for music box, "HR"
mark (A) 312.00

Stoneware, six molded men with beer stein
bodies in brewery, pewter top inscribed
"General Gaslight Company Atlanta,"
music box base, Germany 255.00

2 L, etched, scene of Heidelburg and castle, German verse, lid with inlaid relief of castle tower
(A) 693.00

4 L, multicolored raised figures of two lovers,
Cupid, knight, and lady, Gerz 235.00

STIRRUP CUPS

Staffordshire, England
c1770–1990

History: Whieldon make the first earthenware stirrup
cups. They date about 1770 and were in the shape of fox
masks. Later animal shapes included deer, stag, hare, and
bear heads.

The Staffordshire potters made a wide variety of stirrup
cups and they were rarely marked. Until 1825 the earthenware stirrup cups were well modeled and colored in naturalistic tones. After that date, quality decreased.

During the last quarter of the 19th century, stirrup cups
were made in soft past porcelain by Derby, Rockingham,
and Coalport. In addition to wild animal heads, bull dog,
bull terriers, setters and dalmatian heads were manufactured.

Bacchus Head, 4⅝" l, molded toothy smile
with beard, applied scrolled handle, restored,
Staffordshire 115.00

Dalmation Head, 4⅜" l, black dots and ears, tan
ground, early 19th C, Staffordshire, pr (A) 6090.00

Fox Head

3½" l, porcelain, brown fur, gilt collar, black
snout and ears, c1820 (A) 1100.00

3¹⁵⁄₁₆" l, dark red brown markings, light muzzle, gilt "TALLY HO" on collar (A) 530.00

4¼" l, pearlware, simulated agate, brown
transfer over buff, hairlines, early 19th C,
England 450.00

4⅝" l, creamware, iron-red ears, mauve
glaze with iron-red and black accents, late
18th C (A) 1715.00

4¾" l

Pottery, molded details, green glaze, late
18th C (A) 2285.00

Rounded head, long snout, reddish brown
and black, green eyes, late 19th C, German (A) 300.00

5" l

Creamware, white glaze, chip on rim, late
18th C (A) 765.00

Porcelain, orange, apricot, and brown simulated fur, gilt dcollar with script "Tallyho'
(A) 1485.00

**Hound Head, 5½" l, porcelain, black and
white, dk red mouth, c1820, $4000.00**

Rounded face, slender snout, brown fur, black details, gilded white collar, late 19th C, Staffordshire, pr (A) 654.00
5 1/8″ l, creamware, brown fur with black details to ears and snout, iron-red collar with black dots, inscribed "Talli:O', late 18th C (A). 2150.00
5 1/8″ l, pottery
Brown, black, and rust glazes, restored, England (A). 275.00
Iron-red fur, black snout
Gilt band on neck, c1840 (A) 715.00
Luster band on neck, c1850 (A) 400.00
5 1/2″ l, creamware
Translucent brown, ears laid back, tongue poking out, hairline, late 18th C (A). . . .   1950.00
White with brown glazed collar, c1800 (A) 1650.00
5 3/4″ l, porcelain, brown tones, eyes, nose, and mouth accented in black, gilt collar with "TALLY HO," Stevenson & Hancock . .   1500.00
6 1/4″ l, parian, molded details, chip on ear, c1860 . . . .   350.00
Hare Head, 6 5/8″ l, painted in shades of tawny brown, cup with gilded fluting between the ears, c1810, "red crown, crossed lines with dots and D" mark. 4200.00
Hound Head
4 1/8″ l, black spotted with gray muzzle, black nose, brown eyes, gilded band around rim, c1810 . . . .   1850.00
4 3/4″ l, gray snout, black nose, light brown patch markings, yellow collar, 19th C, Staffordshire (A) 448.00
5″ l
Brown patches, black nose and whiskers, gilt bordered yellow collar, cracks (A) . .   995.00
Porcelain
Black nose and spotted coat, white ground, pink luster collar 950.00
Brown markings, "JUNO" on collar, c1800 (A). 2420.00
5 1/2″ l
Brown markings, gilt collar, c1820 (A) 770.00
Brown patch markings, iron-red eyes and mouth, black details, large ears meeting under neck, hair crack to rim, early 19th C. 1683.00
Liver colored markings, gilt collar, c1820 (A) 770.00
7″ l, white ironstone, modeled face with imp "POWELL" on collar, hairlines, England. . .   350.00
Pug Head, 5 1/8″ l, black enamel markings, yellow eyes, bright orange collar, 2nd half 19th C, Staffordshire (A). 265.00
Stag Head
4 5/8″ l, creamware, tufts of curls between ears and antlers, splotched in brown, c1780 (A). 1100.00
5″ l, creamware, features outlined in runny green and manganese-brown glazes, laid back ears, crack (A) 4595.00
Trout Head
4″ l, green and white skin, mouth and gills in iron-red, eyes tan, gilded rim, c1900, German, pr (A). 748.00
5″ l, porcelain, natural colors, blue eyes, red and black mouth, cracked, late 18th C . . .   875.00
Whippet Head, 5 7/8″ l, brown mottled glaze (A). 1760.00

STONEWARE

London and Staffordshire, England
c1670 to Present

History: Stoneware, made from clay to which some sand had been added, was fired at a higher temperature than ordinary earthenwares and became partly vitrified and impervious to liquids. Often it was glazed by throwing salt into the kiln at full heat. (See: Salt Glaze.)

Stoneware was first made in England in 1672 when John Dwight founded Fulham Pottery and received a patent. He started by making copies of German wine jugs called "greybeards" and also modeled portrait busts, jugs, mugs, and red clay teapots. Dwight died in 1703. Fulham Pottery was carried on by his family. Dwight's examples were unmarked.

In Staffordshire John and Philip Elers made red stonewares and also introducted salt glazing and other improvements. Stoneware was made by firms throughout the Staffordshire Potteries district. Most stoneware was utilitarian in nature, but some of the useful wares were given a decorative treatment.

The Morleys made brown salt glazed stonewares in Nottingham between 1700 and 1799. Doulton & Watts were the best known and largest manufacture of commercial stonewares. English stoneware still is made, especially by present day studio potters like Bernard Leach, Charles Vyse, and Michael Cardew.

References: J. F. Blacker, *The A. B. C. of English Salt Glaze Stoneware from Dwight to Doulton,* Stanley Paul & Co., 1922; Adrean Oswald, R. J. C. Hildyard & R. G. Huges, *English Brown Stoneware 1670–1900,* Faber & Faber, 1982.

Museums: British Museum, London, England; Cincinnati Art Museum, Cincinnati, Ohio; County Museum, Truro, England; Victoria & Albert Museum, London, England.

Basket, 5 1/2″ h, shades of brown and tan, basketweave pattern, center handle, c1848–60, Derbyshire, imp "S.TT. Briddon" mark 675.00
Bear Jug, Cov, 7 1/2″ h, brown, seated with forelegs extended, simulated fur covering, ears, eyes, snout, tongue, claws, and teeth in cream slip, repaired, 18th C, Nottingham (A) 9451.00
Bleeding Bowl, 4 1/2″ d, iron-red dip, flared rim, molded lug handle pierced with heart, repaired, early 18th C, Nottingham (A) 535.00

Jar, Cov, 11″ h, 9″ H-H, incised cobalt designs on brown ground, "Germany" mark, (A) $70.00

Coffee Pot, 10¼" h, baluster shape, applied
reliefs of classical maidens, blue line borders,
domed cov with widow finial, early 19th C (A)   350.00
Dish, 5½" d, "Tiger" colored glaze, late 17th C,
London (A) 900.00
Drug Jar, 4¾" h, cylindrical, inscribed "MEL
ANG." on raised foliage edged label above
relief molded Royal Arms, upper part with
iron-red dip, japanned metal cov, c1830, imp
numeral (A) 300.00
Ewer, 9" h, applied grapevine and figures, brown
glaze, England (A) 18.00
Fern Pot, Cov, 8¹/₁₆" h, white, sq tapered shape,
four modeled veiled heads on corners, oval
relief molded medallions of classical figures on
sides, four lion paw and ball feet, pierced pyramid cov, basalt base, imp "Turner" mark (A) 2850.00
Figure
8½" l, brown recumbent lions, iron-red
washed manes, rect bases, early 19th C, pr
(A). 1000.00
9" h, white, bust of Earl Grey, waisted socle   145.00
9½" h, brown, bust of Disraeli, waisted socle,
c1888 (A) 680.00
Flask
5¼" h, flattened ovoid body, short neck incised with birds and stag among formal
flowers, initials "AMMB" below handle,
loop handle, zig-zag border on neck, blue
washed ground, late 18th C, Westerwald
(A). 598.00
6¼" h, each side and corner applied with
foliate motif within chained oval panel,
shoulder with four rosettes, 17th CA) 453.00
7" h, brown glaze
Figural gin maiden. 175.00
Modeled as Lord John Russell holding scroll,
inscribed "The True Spirit of Reform (A)   722.00
9⁷/₈" h, powder flask shape, relief of game
dog on each side, c1840, Stephen Green
(A). 85.00
11⁷/₈" h, hex body, diagonal bands of incised
borders and imp beetles on blue ground,
shoulders with radiating stamped borders,
pewter mtd, 18th C, Westerwald (A) 1954.00
Flip Can, 11" h, cylindrical body, applied rect
panel in relief with milking scene below
masked straining spout, flanked by classical
figures and tree above stag hunting scene,
studded borders, cov hinged at top of angular
handle, upper part reddish-brown, underside
inscribed "W.J. White Fecit, Decr 8. 1800,"
heart   shaped   handle   terminal   with
"W:W,1800," repair to hinge, Fulham (A) . . . 9350.00
Jar
6⅜" h, applied figures in period clothes,
pewter stopper and lid, unmarked (A) 155.00
7½" h, ovoid, cobalt stylized floral design,
open handles (A). 44.00
Jug
3⁷/₈" h, dbl walled depressed globular body,
brown glaze, carved with flowering plants,
banded cylindrical neck, Nottingham (A). .   432.00
7¼" h, reddish-brown dip, pewter mounted
rims, cov incised "G.F.Q. and 1696," Saxon
(A). 1645.00
7½" h, brown glaze, modeled head of Duke
of Wellington, Stephen Green 145.00
8" h, ovoid, blue glazed body with applied
rosettes, c1700, Westerwald (A) 425.00

8½" h, globular body, incised with trailing
stems and applied with flowerheads glazed
in manganese on blue glazed ground, pew-
ter mtd, late 17th C, Westerwald (A) 782.00
9¼" h, molded frieze of couples dancing in
row of arcades, inscribed "GERHET DU
MUS DAPER BLASEN SO DANSSEN DI
BUREN ALS WEREN SI RASEN EIS VF SPRI
BASTOR ICH WER DANS D KAP KOR,"
date 1597, neck with scrolling foliage and
grotesque masks, Raeren, imp "E" on han-
dle (A) 1050.00
9½" h, salt glaze, tan, horiz molded ridges,
c1575–1600, Seiberg (A). 550.00
10" h
Cylindrical Body
Applied frieze of peasant dancers under
arched colonnade, paneled sloping
shoulders stamped with foliate motif,
band of Renaissance foliage, birds, and
portrait medallions on neck, pewter
mtd, late 16th C (A). 1215.00
Molded frieze of prs of figures dancing in
row of arches above continuous descriptive verses, and 1598, scrolling
motigs incised on shoulders and tapering foot, neck applied with grotesque
mask, pinched spout, pewter mtd (A) 1645.00
Ovoid, gray ground with stylized cobalt
flower, loop handle (A) 38.00
10⅜" h, ovoid shape, applied florets on
flared stems, stenciled ground divided by
vert bands, manganese accents, pewter
mtd, early 19th C, Muskau (A). 500.00
10¾" h, globular body, blue geometrical foliate motifs in divided by vert bands of applied flowers, trailing border on neck,
pinched spout, 18th C, Westerwald (A). . .   700.00
11⅜" h, bulbous body, slender neck, applied
coat of arms on front, carved flowers on
stems, pewter cov, c1680, Westerwald (A) 1346.00
13¾" h, Bellarmine, bulbous body, three
oval medallions with arms of Cannoy of
Flanders and 1613, blue splash border
around central medallion, applied grinning
mask on neck, blue and manganese mark-
ings (A) 5236.00
15⅝" h, ovoid body, applied central row of
figures of Christ and twelve Apostles between borders, flared neck with pinched
spout with coat of arms bearing Adam and
Eve, handle with lion's mask and stylized
foliage, pewter mtd, mid 17th C (A). 1400.00
17½" h, Bellarmine, baluster shape with C
form handle, applied bellflower, royal
badge, "GR" and dtd 1789, pewter lid, late
18th C (A). 2090.00
Jug, Cov
6½" h, pear shape, molded bust of nobleman in dark brown spirally molded ground
with stylized flowers, blue, red, white, yellow, and gilt formal borders, pewter lid and
thumbpiece, c1670, Annaberg (A) 2442.00
10" h, applied center band of peasant dancers
under colonnades, paneled sloped shoulders stamped with stylized foliates, neck
band of Renaissance foliage, birds, and portrait medallions, pewter lid and knob, late
16th C, Germany 1575.00
10¾" h, brown, applied fox hunting scene

below windmill, trees, and cottage, upper part with dark iron dip, hinged metal cov, c1800 .... **500.00**
Krug, 10½" h, deep incised leaves and circlets in cobalt, gray body, pewter top, Westerwald................................. **950.00**
Milk Jug, Cov, 3¾" h, enameled yellow and iron-red flowerheads with zig-zag patterned bands in silver line borders, engine turned base and cov with foliate sprigs, blue body, c1790–1800, Samuel Hollins (A).......... **275.00**
Mug
5" h, applied pub scene, brown glaze, England (A)................................... **18.00**
6¾" h, globular body, cylindrical neck, loop handle, late 16th C, Germany **150.00**
Pitcher
6" h, "GR" and crest on front, incised cobalt flower petals, incised horiz brown lines, yellow ground, Westerwald **600.00**
6¼" h, blue-gray band on middle and neck, white relief of classical scenes of putti and goat, hairline on handle (A) **82.00**
10¾" h
Applied white figures of hunters with dogs, light blue ground, white fish shaped spout and handle, ochre "JOHN WOOD ESQ/Ankerton/1855," ochre rim, unmarked (A)........................ **275.00**
Cobalt outlined incised flowers, gray incised twists on sides, gray ground, Westerwald **1000.00**
Punch Set, 13" h, 12" w, hex shape, six panels of German buildings, two vine handles, cherub finial, cobalt ground, 13 pcs **350.00**
Schnelle, 9¾" h, cylindrical body, molded vert panels of crowded coat of arts of France above date 1574 and "H.H." arms of Spain and Orania with chain of Golded Fleece, sgd and dtd "Hans Hilgers' (A) **2000.00**
Storage Jar, 14½" h, ovoid body, thick brown glaze, folded neck, four lug handles, mid 17th C, Dutch (A).......................... **350.00**
Tankard
4⅜" h, white relief plaques of putti and classical figures, blue enamel ground, molded basketweave band around base, Turner (A)........................... **104.00**
8½" h, central applied band of circ medallions of Austrian dbl headed eagles flanking angels and dragon heads, grooved borders, blue glaze, pewter mtd, cov incised "L.W.," hair crack, early 18th C, Westerwald (A).. **700.00**
11" h, pear shape, incised and glazed in blue with checker pattern within blue borders, pewter mt damaged, 18th C, Oberhessen (A)................................. **300.00**
11⅜" h, cylindrical shape, stamped with rosettes on blue glazed ground between applied trailing borders, pewter mts, 18th C, Westerwald (A) **1028.00**
Applied design of figures at table and huntsmen and hounds, rim with "John Speller," incised "1757" on foot, salt glaze finish, hairlines, Fulham (A)................... **1760.00**
Teapot
3⅜" h, globular body, red, molded with flowering and fruiting gold leaf decorated pomegranate branches growing from modeled crabstock handle, short spout in form

of a blossom, floret shaped cov, parrot knob, 2nd half 17th C, Dutch (A) **935.00**
4¾" h, globular body, red, molded with stylized scrolling foliage, cov applied with cloud scrolls, silver-gilt mts with putto, cockerel, and turk's head finials, 2nd half 17th C, Dutch, imp "running fox" mark (A) **1954.00**
5¼" h, incised design of dianthus flower spars and leaves, curved spout, loop handle, c1750–60, Westerwald (A)............. **1520.00**
7" h, red, horiz bands of diamonds and wavy engine turning, molded handle, acorn knob, repairs, c1770 (A)...................... **357.00**
9¾" h, oval shape, white with blue line borders (A)............................... **200.00**
10½' h, oval shape, applied with reliefs of classical maidens, brown line borders, galleried rim, early 19th C (A)............. **300.00**

STRAWBERRY CHINA

Staffordshire, England
1820–1860

History: Strawberry china ware, a soft earthenware produced by a variety of English potteries, was made in three design motifs: strawberry and strawberry leaves (often called strawberry luster), green feather-like leaves with pink flowers (often called cut-strawberry, primrose or old strawberry), and the third motif with the decoration in relief. The first two types are characterized by rust red moldings. Most examples have a creamware ground and are unmarked.

Coffee Pot, 10½" h, vine border, domed cov, repair to spout (A)....................... **165.00**
Creamer
3⅜" h, lustered, "Leeds Pottery" mark **175.00**
3½" h, vine border, figural dolphin type handle, four small feet (A) **330.00**
4¼" h, scattered strawberries, solid border, hairline (A) **30.00**
Cup and Saucer, Handleless
Light green scattered leaves, iron-red vines and rims, large red strawberries, unmarked **185.00**
Red strawberries with yellow seed dots,

Jug, 8½" h, molded red strawberries, rose outlined flowers, green outlined foliage, copper luster rim, unmkd, $350.00

shades of green leaves, iron-red border, dark floral in int of cup, same design on ext, c1820 .... **185.00**

Vine strawberry border design (A)......... **302.00**

Dish
  5½" d, strawberry luster design (A) **100.00**
  6½" d, solid border strawberry pattern (A). **34.00**

Pitcher, 5⅝" h, pink luster strawberries, vining, and florals (A)........................... **82.00**

Plate
  7½" d, polychrome floral and strawberry design, pink border (A)..................... **187.00**
  8¼" d, stick spatter strawberry design in polychromes (A) **20.00**
  8¾" d, vining strawberries red, purple, green, and black on border, scalloped rim (A) ... **95.00**
  10" d, solid border strawberry pattern (A) .. **34.00**

Sugar Bowl, Cov, 6⅝" h, vine border, ruffled rim, small dbl scroll handles (A)............ **77.00**

Teapot
  5½" h
    Pink, red, yellow and green strawberries and vines, cream ground, blue borders, "Davenport" mark (A).................... **55.00**
    Red, pink, brown, and green relief of strawberries and vines, molded body, tip of spout missing (A) **45.00**
  6½" h, raised strawberry pattern, damage (A)................................ **40.00**
  6¾" h, overall strawberry and leaf design in colors, emb feet and flower finial (A)..... **1650.00**
  6⅞" h
    Solid border, cream ground with circ design of strawberries, leaves and vines (A) ... **440.00**
    Vine border, cream ground with flowers and strawberries on vines, repairs to lid, lip, and spout....................... **150.00**
  7" h, overall strawberry and leaf design, molded leaves on spout, repaired (A) **385.00**
  7¾" h, vine strawberry design and leaves in colors, open flowerhead on spout, hairlines (A)................................ **705.00**
  9¾" d, central basket of strawberries and leaves, strawberry and flower border, Staffordshire (A)........................ **247.00**

Waste Bowl, 6¼" d, 3⅛" h, vine strawberry border in colors (A)..................... **495.00**

A
SUSIE COOPER
PRODUCTION
CROWN WORKS.
BURSLEM
ENGLAND
c1932

SUSIE COOPER

Burslem, Staffordshire, England
1932 to Present

History: Susie Cooper studied at the Burslem Art School in Staffordshire in 1922. She made jugs, bowls, and vases in stoneware with Art Nouveau style incised designs. When Cooper finished her studies, she became a designer for A. E. Gray & Co., Ltd. at Hanley, Staffordshire in 1925.

She founded Susie Cooper Pottery, Burslem in 1932. Cooper designed and manufactured functional shape, earthenware tablewares with bright floral and abstract designs. Cooper introduced the "can" shape for the coffeepot, the straight sided shape that has become a universal design. Art Deco designs of bright oranges, greens, and browns are found on her later wares.

Susie Cooper eventually became part of the Wedgwood Group. Her patterns now decorate fine bone china tableware with the Wedgwood-Susie Cooper Design backstamp. The "can" coffeepot shape still is used.

References: Ann Eatwell, *Susie Cooper Productions,* Victoria & Albert Museum, Faber & Faber, 1987; Reginald G. Haggar, *Century of Art Education in the Potteries,* 1953.

Museum: Victoria & Albert Museum, London, England.

Breakfast in Bed Set, Kestral shape, mushroom glaze, 17 pcs **175.00**

Charger, 11½" d, sgraffito design, hp multicolored leaves, c1930s **135.00**

Cream Soup and Liner, multicolored pastel rings, set of 4 .... **35.00**

Cup and Saucer, Demitasse
  Light blue bands on beige ground.......... **15.00**
  Orchid design............................ **25.00**
  Roses design............................. **15.00**

Dinner Service, Kestral Shape
  Leaping deer on brown ground, for 6 ...... **850.00**
  Light brown, gray, and sky blue bands, for 12.................................... **850.00**

Dish
  8¾" d, ftd, black slip spiral design on white ground............................... **175.00**
  10⅝" d, "Parrot Tulip" design in green, purple, blue, red, and yellow **10.00**

Dish, Cov, 9⅞" d, "Parrot Tulip" design **65.00**

Pitcher, 5" h, earthenware, carved floral design on brown body, herringbone rim.......... **275.00**

Plaque, 13" d, large spray of large flowers on sky blue ground, "Handpainted Gray's Pottery" mark.................................... **950.00**

Plate, 10" d, green, tan, and gray bands, marked.................................. **10.00**

Tea Set
  Teapot, 5½" h, underplate, sugar, creamer, turquoise body with white dots, white handle and spout, cov has reverse design,

Sugar Bowl, cov, 4½" h, Kestral shape, blue and orange banding, cream ground, $45.00

creamer and sugar are white with turquoise int, "Susie Cooper, Bone China England" mark...................................... **195.00**
Teapot, creamer, sugar bowl, "Clematis" design in colors **195.00**
Vase
4½" h, dark blue feather design on med blue ground, orange and blue dots **575.00**
6" h, three handled, purple, brown, and orange orchids, pale green band on neck with brown dots........................... **375.00**
9½" h, black and brown swirls on gray body, c1935 .... **475.00**
12" h, earthenware, carved design on surface, green body......................... **575.00**

CAMBRIAN POTTERY
c 1783 - 1810

DILLWYN & CO. SWANSEA
c 1811 - 1817

BEVINGTON & CO.
c 1817 - 1824

SWANSEA

Wales
c1814 to Early 1820s

History: Swansea potters produced a large variety of earthenwares during the 18th and 19th centuries. Their porcelains, like those of Nantgarw, are very translucent, have fine glazes, and feature excellent floral painting.

After experiencing a lack of funds in 1814, Billingsley and Walker came from Nantgarw to work with Lewis Dillwyn at Swansea. Billingsley and Walker made fine porcelains between 1814 and 1817 at Swansea and then returned to start again at Nantgarw. Production continued at Swansea until the early 1820s. Many Swansea wares are artist decorated.

Swansea Welsh porcelain blanks were quite popular with London decorators.

References: W. D. John, *Swansea Porcelain,* Ceramic Book Co., 1958; Kildare S. Meager, *Swansea & Nantgarw Potteries,* Swansea, 1949; E. Morton Nance, *The Pottery & Porcelain of Swansea & Nantgarw,* Batsford, 1942.

Museums: Art Institute of Chicago, Chicago, Illinois; Glynn Vivian Art Gallery, Swansea, Wales.

REPRODUCTION ALERT: Swansea porcelain has been copied for many decades in Europe and England. Marks should be studied carefully.

Bowl
6⅜" d, four idyllic landscape vignettes within gilt cartouches, gilt line borders, c1815, painted by William Billingsley, "red Swansea" mark (A)........................ **740.00**
8⅝" d, blue printed profile of George III and Queen Charlotte, inscribed "A King revered, a Queen beloved" and "Long may they live," ext with chinoiserie scenes (A). **285.00**

Cow Creamer, 6½" h, 7½" l, iron-red and purple luster spots, luster horns, green base, c1825–40, "Glymorgan Pottery-Wales" mark, $475.00

Breakfast Cup and Saucer, central floral motif, diaper and pendant leaves, border of gilt foliate scrolls, 1814–22 (A)................... **325.00**
Cabaret Set, teapot, milk jug, slop bowl, open sugar bowl, tray, 13" sq, painted sprays of colored flowers, repairs, c1814–17, imp "DILLWYN & CO. SWANSEA" marks (A) ... **3432.00**
Cabinet Cup and Stand, multicolored bouquets, turquoise border edged with gold foliage and hung with colored sprays, three paw feet (A) **234.00**
Chamberstick, 2⅝" l, miniature, central nozzle, ring handle, band of trailing flowers and strawberries, c1815–20, "Swansea" mark (A) **740.00**
Cup and Saucer, white int, ribbed ext of cup, gold fluted border, gilt handle, c1820 ...... **150.00**
Dessert Dish
11" l, lobed rect shape, Imari style with peony flower and border scrolls in blue, red, and gold, twig handles with leaf terminals, "red stencil" mark (A)...................... **306.00**
11¼" l, oval, center painted with single sprig, border with four panels of painted roses on white ground, four panels of butterflies reserved on apricot ground with cruciform gilding, c1820 (A) **1500.00**
11⅜" l, shaped rect form, three painted floral sprays, shaped gilt rim, two gilt twig handles, c1814–22 (A)........................ **925.00**
Dessert Service, Part, 2 oval dishes, 11"l, 2 oval dishes, 9⅞" l, dish, shell shape, 8⅜" l, 8 plates, 7⅛" d, pearlware, each painted in center with different botanical specimen, brown edged rim, 1802–10, painted by Thomas Pardoe, brown botanical identifications, 6 imp "SWANSEA" marks, 13 pcs (A). **4675.00**
Dish
8¼" l, shell shape, border painted with continuous arrangement of bluebells, roses, primroses, and other garden flowers, lobed edge decorated with gilding, c1820, "iron-red script" mark (A)......................... **2257.00**
8¼" sq, painted center spray of flowers in green and gilt frame, flaring border painted with single sprigs of flowers and fruit, relief molded foliate scrollwork, shaped gilt rim, c1820–22, "red Swansea" mark (A)...... **635.00**
Figure, 5½" l, two running pointers with brown markings, molded green and turquoise grass

and floral ground, pink gilt lined stepped base, c1811–17, Dillwyn & Co. (A) **1825.00**
Inkstand, 4″ d, waisted shape, inkwell with raised collar liner, sand pot and cov with knob finial, separated by pr of intertwined dolphins forming handle, pots with scattered pink roses, gilding, 1814–22 (A) **1599.00**
Inkstand, Liner, Cov, 4″ d, scallop shell form, continuous arrangement of bluebells, roses, primroses, and other garden flowers, shell shaped pen holder, body and domed shell with gilded lines and gilded shell finial, c1814–22, body crack, "red stencil" mark (A). **1411.00**
Meat Dish, 12⅝″ l, rect with canted corners, center painted with summer flowers in basket on column, dark blue border with gilt rim, c1814–22 . . . . **2725.00**
Mug, 3⅞″ h, cylindrical, earthenware, molded with rect panel inscribed in gilt "Susan Carthew-Liskeard-1822," heart and lozenge shaped panels on pebbled ground painted with flowers and insects, ear shaped handle (A). **450.00**
Plate
6¼″ d, purple printed bust of Prince Albert and name, molded floral border, Dillwyn (A). **495.00**
7⅞″ d, center with concentric gold circles, three groups of leaves in green colors, imp "Swansea and trident" mark (A) **234.00**
8″ d, "Mandarin" pattern, black transfer printed and painted in colored enamels with gilding with oriental figures seated outside house with river in ground, border of gilt scroll panels reserving birds in branches, c1817–20 (A). **648.00**
8⅛″ d
Spray of three pink roses, two green leaves, dentil rim, border with scattered sprays of flowers, 1814–22 (A) **658.00**
Various birds perched on branches, enclosed by gilt rims and central florette, shaped rim with foliate scrollwork, 1814–22, "red stencil" mark (A). **452.00**
8⅜″ d, painted sprays of flowers and foliage reserved on white ground, gilt diaper and scroll border hung from green and gilt foliate pendants, c1820 (A) **1450.00**
8⅝″ d, wide border of iron-red rose hips and florets with gilt foliage reserved on khaki ground, no. 782, c1814–22 (A). **125.00**
9″ d, painted botanical center, gilt border with linked urns and scrolls, c1815–20. . . . . **1500.00**
9⅛″ d, center with armorial crest and motto, border of green urns with garden flowers linked by scrolling foliage, beaded rim, c1815–20 (A). **1715.00**
Service Plate
8″ d, "Marino Ballroom Service," colored enamels with stylized floral sprigs, c1817–22 (A) **225.00**
9¼″ d, "Burdett-Coutts Service," basket brimming with flowers within seeded gilt scroll border, gilt dentil edged rim painted with two moths, c1818 (A). **475.00**
Teacup and Saucer
Band of inter-connecting summer flowers above dark blue ground with pendant gilt flower heads, gilded dbl scroll handle, c1825–30, "red stencil" mark (A). **1505.00**

Continuous pattern of delicate trailing sprays of gilt and foliage urns and pink roses, 1814–22, "red script" mark (A) **325.00**
Sprays and sprigs of dog roses, primroses, lily of the valley, wild strawberries, and other wild flowers below border of gilt foliate scrolls, diaper and pendant leaves, 1814–22 (A). **1411.00**
Tea Service, teapot, 8⅛″ h, stand, cream jug, cov sugar bowl, slop bowl, 2 cake plates, 12 teacups, 12 coffee cups, 12 saucers, Imari style pattern of floral panels reserved on blue ground with gilt and iron-red stylized chrysanthemum, cups and covs with flowers growing behind a fence, teapot and cup interiors painted with oval reserves of flowers on blue ground with gilded foliage, cracks, c1814–22, "red Swansea and 219," 48 pcs (A). **9350.00**
Tea Set, teapot, sugar, creamer, terracotta, circ tapered form with enameled Etruscan motif band, c1840 (A). **121.00**
Tureen, 6⅝″ h, painted sprays of colored flowers and gilt scrollwork, plain gilt borders, dbl handles, gilt finial of three ram's heads, c1820 (A) **1530.00**
Vase
6¾″ h, painted center band of flowers, gilt borders, gilt bordered flared base with painted flowers, applied bee handles, restored, c1815–20, imp "SWANSEA and trident" mark, pr (A). **4720.00**
12½″ h, ovoid form, applied with relief pendant biscuit garland flowers, reserved on ground of pink roses and dots in gilding, circ foot, sq base, flared neck with baskets of flowers, two scroll handles terminating in ram's heads, gilding c1815 (A). **3179.00**
13⅜″ h, center panel of natural flowers and overturned basket, urn on column, hills in ground, gilt canted sq frame, reserved on light pink ground with gilt foliate scroll medallions and horiz bands, dbl scroll gilt handles with foliate terminals, sq foot, c1830. **1275.00**

c1760 - 1766   1910 -1940

SWEDEN—GENERAL

Marieberg, near Stockholm, Sweden 1758–1788

History: In 1758 Johann Ehrenreich established a factory at Marieberg, near Stockholm with the intention of making porcelain, but wound up producing faience instead. Pierre Berthevin, a porcelain expert, came to the factory and became director in 1766. Berthevin was the first in Sweden to make porcelain of the soft paste type. Pieces were decorated in the Classical design. Forms included cream jars, pitchers, small vases, and figures. Faience continued to be made and was decorated utilizing the transfer printing technique.

Henrik Sten took over in 1768. Hard paste porcelain was introduced during this period. Only small forms were made; no dinner services were produced. Custard cups, cream pots, and teapots were the most popular shapes. The decoration included both Classical and Rococo styles. Some figures in Swedish Rococo style costumes were made. Faience manufacturing continued. Strasburg faience was imitated in a table service for Baron Liljencrantz, the factory's owner. Around 1770 attempts were made to duplicate Wedgwood's creamware.

Marieberg was sold to Rorstrand in 1782. Sten resigned. Schumer took over until the works closed in 1788.

Marieberg's faience and porcelain pieces were marked.

GUSTAVSBERG

Island of Farsta, Sweden
1827 to Present

The Gustavsberg factory was established on the island of Farsta in 1827. The factory first produced faience and later made transfer printed creamware in the English style.

Samuel Gidenius enlarged and modernized the factory during the 1850s. Wilhelm Odelberg took control in 1869. During the 1860s, decorative majolica and bone porcelain were introduced. Parian was made from the 1860s until the late 19th century. After William Odelberg died in 1914, his two sons took over.

Between 1897 and 1914 G. Wennerberg was the artistic director. He made pottery decorated with simple floral designs in the sgraffito technique. In 1937 the firm was called AB Gustavsberg Fabriker.

The dinnerwares featured simple designs. "Blue Flower" has been made since 1870. "Allmoge" was introduced in 1905 and continues to the present day. "Elite" was very popular. "Amulet" in red, blue, or gray was designed by Stig Lindberg, the company's leading artist. Wilhelm Koge, another designer, modeled "Argenta" with silver and green backgrounds inspired by Persian wares. He also created "Pyro," "Praktika II," and "Carrara." Other sets included "Gray Bands" and "Marguente" in the Art Nouveau style.

Museums: American Swedish Institute, Minneapolis, Minnesota; Gustavsberg Ceramics Center, Island of Varmdo, Sweden.

Urn, Cov, 16¾″ h, irid aged green copper surface, gold trim, c1937, Gustavsberg, $4800.00

Bowl, 7″ d, silver overlay pattern, marked.....   **140.00**
Dish, 8½″ d, ftd, silver overlay slim fish, mottled green ground, Gustavsberg...............   **325.00**
Figure, 10½″ h, milkmaid in white bodice, apron, flowered skirt, yellow jacket, milk pail held on head, dairyman in spotted kerchief, plum colored breeches, yellow jacket, milk pail on head, another held at side, dog on sq scroll molded base, damage, c1775–80, pr (A)....   **1415.00**
Plate
   9⅝″ d, black transfer of classic buildings in landscape, three birds in trees on shaped border, crack, c1770, Marieberg........   **700.00**
   12½″ d, hp tree and mountain scene in blue shades, two blue bands on border.......   **35.00**
Pot, 4″ d, sgraffito, dark blue band of leaves on light blue ground, dtd 1912 ....   **38.00**
Sauceboat, 7½″ l, painted sprays of flowers, scattered sprigs and moth, twin scroll handles on sides, baroque molded spouts, handle crack, c1760, "black S" mark..............   **500.00**
Tray, 6″ l, 3″ w, steamship motif, sterling overlay, white ground, Gustavsberg...............   **55.00**
Vase
   5½″ h, stoneware, mottled green glaze, silver overlay floral bouquet design, "Gustavsburg Argenta" mark **795.00**
   5″ h, silver fish with stream of bubbles overhead, mottled green ground, Gustavsberg   **325.00**
   7¼″ h, earthenware, sea green glaze with silver overlaid florets, "GUSTAVSBERG KAGE 940" mark **1000.00**
   7½″ h, bottle shape, dark blue and green incised floral design, light blue ground, Gustavsberg mark (A) **90.00**
   8¼″ h, oviform, stoneware, sea green glaze with silver overlaid mermaid, "GUSTAVSBERG KAGE" mark (A) **800.00**
   8½″ h, stoneware, turquoise glaze with silver overlaid dragon, silver around neck, Gustavsberg "Argenta" mark...............   **495.00**
   15¹³⁄₁₆″ h, silver overlaid stoneware, glazed in mottled matte sea green, thin silver bands at lip and foot framing stylized rampant lion, c1935, printed overglaze "GUTAVSBERG/ARGENTA/A27/Made in/Sweden.............   **900.00**

1763-1897   SUISSE LANGENTHAL 1906-Present   NYON 1780-1860

SWITZERLAND

Zurich
1763–1790

Nyon
1781–1813

History: Two porcelain factories were established in Switzerland-one at Zurich and the other at Nyon.

Jacob Dortu from Berlin along with Ferdinand Muller, his father-in-law, founded the Nyon factory in 1781. Porcelain tablewares were made in the Louis XVI Parisian style until 1813. Delicate decoration was done with subtle colorations and good quality gilding. English-style stonewares were made and marked "Dortu & Cie."

Between 1763 and 1790, porcelain and faience were made at Zurich under the direction of Adam Spengler. From 1765 Spengler produced beautiful tablewares in rococo forms. Painted pieces were decorated with scenes of typical Swiss landscapes, florals in the Meissen style, and oriental style flowers. Tablewares decorated with the "onion" or "aster" pattern under the blue glaze were quite popular.

Soft paste porcelain pieces were made for a very short time and are exceedingly rare. These pieces were marked with either a painted under-the-glaze-blue or incised "Z."

Museums: National Museum, Zurich, Switzerland; Sevres Museum, Sevres, France

REPRODUCTION ALERT: Many imitations having cruder decorations and bright blue marks were made at German factories and sold to travelers in Swiss towns.

Coffee Service, Part, coffee pot, 8 1/8" h, cov sugar bowl, 12 coffee cups and saucers, ribbed shape, oriental flower sprays in shades of purple and gilt, one cup restored, c1770, underglaze "blue Z, imp K, incised C, NV, I, and D" marks (A) 4070.00
Custard Cup, Cov, 3 1/8" h, bulbous body, scattered blue cornflowers with green stems, white ground, gilt accented scroll handle, pine cone knob, gilt dentil rim, c1790, "blue fish Nyon" mark, set of 11 (A) 850.00
Ewer, 13" h, ovoid body, earthenware, applied and trailed spray of flowers and "A.K. and 1866," strap handle, ribbed neck (A) 2000.00
Figure, 4 3/4" h, boy garderer in flowered cloak and linen shirt, holding hat to chest, rake leaning on tree stump, c1770, underglaze "blue Z" mark, Zurich (A) 650.00

TEA LEAF IRONSTONE

Staffordshire, England
c1856 to Present

History: The tea leaf pattern started about 1856 when Anthony Shaw of Burslem began decorating his white ironstone with three copper luster leaves. At first it was called "Lustre Band and Sprig." Later names were "Edge Line and Sprig" and "Lustre Spray." The sprig eventually was viewed as a tea leaf, thus giving the pattern its name.

Tons of English tea leaf pattern ironstone china was sent to the United States where it greatly appealed to the American housewife. It was durable, white, and had a simple elegance.

Over thirty English potteries in Staffordshire manufactured wares decorated with the tea leaf pattern. The most prolific were Alfred Meakin Potteries and Anthony Shaw. The tea leaf pattern also was utilized at W. H. Gridley, Alcock Potteries, William Adams, Mellor, Taylor & Co., Wedgwood, and many others. Each company used a slight variation of the tea leaf copper luster pattern. Since all decoration was applied by hand, no two designs are exactly alike, adding to the charm of the ware. Powell & Bishop and Bishop & Stonier also did the design in gold luster.

References: Annise Doring Heaivilin, *Grandma's Tea Leaf Ironstone*, Wallace-Homestead, 1981; Jean Wetherbee, *A Look at White Ironstone*, Wallace-Homestead, 1980.

Museums: Lincoln Home, Springfield, Illinois; Sherwood Davidson House, Newark, Ohio; Ox Barn Museum, Aurora, Oregon.

Collectors Club: Tea Leaf International, P.O. Box 904, Mount Prospect, Illinois 60056. Membership: $20.00., *Tea Leaf Readings*, bi-monthly publication.

REPRODUCTION ALERT: Some recent reproductions are noted for their poor coloration, uneven copper luster decoration, and lower weight. Original ironstone examples are much heavier than newer ceramic pieces.

Apple Bowl, Pedestal
    4 3/8" h, 10 1/2" d, "Meakin" mark 435.00
    6 1/2" h, 9 3/4" d, "Wilkinson" mark 475.00

Figure, 4 3/4" h, gardener, flowered cloak, linen shirt, rake leaning on tree stump, chips, c1770, "blue Z" mark, Zurich, (A) $650.00

Tray, 12" H-H, "Anthony Shaw Opaque Stone China England" mark, $95.00

Bacon Rasher, "W.H. Grindley" mark......... **35.00**

Baker, 10½" l, 7½" w, oval, "Thomas Furnival" mark.. **55.00**

Bone Dish, Crescent Shape

    6¼" l, 2⁵⁄₁₆" d, "Wilkinson" mark........ **50.00**

    6⁵⁄₈" l, 3⅛" d, "Meakin" mark........... **50.00**

Bowl

    6", 7", 8½" d, piecrust edge, set of 3..... **95.00**

    6¾" sq, "Alfred Meakin" mark........... **30.00**

    7½" sq, "Alfred Meakin" mark........... **35.00**

    8" sq, "Alfred Meakin" mark............. **56.00**

    8½" sq, "Alfred Meakin" mark........... **55.00**

    9½" sq, "Alfred Meakin" mark........... **75.00**

Bread Plate, 12" l, oval, "Mellor, Taylor" mark. **55.00**

Butter Dish, Cov

    4" h, liner, sq shape, "Bamboo" pattern, 1883, "Meakin" mark....................... **125.00**

    4⅜" h, liner, "Daisy" pattern, c1880s, "Anthony Shaw" mark.................... **225.00**

Butter Pat

    2⅝" sq, "Meakin" mark................. **5.00**

    2⅞" d, unmarked..................... **8.00**

    3" d, "Alfred Meakin" mark............. **12.00**

Coffee Pot, 8¾" h, "Fish Hook" pattern, c1870s, "Meakin" mark................... **110.00**

Compote

    9" d, 3½" h, "Shaw"................... **400.00**

    9½" d, 4" h, ftd, six sided, "Sunburst" pattern, "Anthony Shaw" mark............ **450.00**

Creamer, 5⅛" h

    "Bamboo" pattern, "V" shape lip, 1883, "Meakin" mark..................... **115.00**

    "Burgess" mark...................... **85.00**

Cup and Saucer

    Pepper leaf variant, "Elsmore and Forster" mark.................................... **42.00**

    Single morning glory motif, Portland Shape, late 1850s, "Elsmore & Forster" mark.... **75.00**

    Slant front, "Meakin".................. **69.00**

    Squatty Shape, "Meakin" mark.......... **50.00**

    Straight sided, "Alfred Meakin" mark...... **75.00**

Cup and Saucer, Handleless

    Chinese shape, dtd 1856, "Anthony Shaw" mark, set of 12...................... **935.00**

    Niagara Shape, 1856, "Walley" mark....... **65.00**

    Pepper leaf variant, "Elsmore and Forster" mark.................................... **50.00**

    Pomegranate variant on int of bowl, center of saucer, copper luster band on int, two luster bands on ext, unmarked................ **40.00**

Cup Plate

    3½" d, set of 12...................... **465.00**

    3⅝" d, unmarked, England............. **34.00**

    3⅞" d, "Niagara Fan," "Anthony Shaw" mark................................ **55.00**

    4½" d, Chinese shape, dtd 1856, "Anthony Shaw" mark........................... **55.00**

Donut Dish, 8⅞" sq, 5⁷⁄₁₆" h, "Burgess & Leigh" mark........................... **450.00**

Gravy Boat, "Alfred Meakin" mark........... **50.00**

Milk Pitcher, 8" h, Wilkinson.............. **150.00**

Mug, 2½" h, miniature................... **150.00**

Nappie

    5¹⁄₁₆" d, Chinese shape, dtd 1856, "Anthony Shaw" mark........................... **45.00**

    5⅜" d, pepper leaf variant, No.2 shape, "Elsmore & Forster" mark, set of 4.......... **135.00**

    5⅝" l, rect shape, "Wilkinson" mark...... **22.00**

Oyster Bowl, 6¼" d, "Alfred Meakin" mark.. **45.00**

Pickle Dish, 8½" l, "Wedgwood & Co." mark.................................... **32.00**

Pitcher

    7" h, "Lily of the Valley" pattern, c1860s, "Anthony Shaw" mark.................... **295.00**

    7¾" h, "Square Ridged" pattern, "Wedgwood" mark.......................... **140.00**

    8" h, bulbous shape, "Acanthus Leaf" pattern, c1880s, "Wilkinson" mark............ **250.00**

    9" h, "Square Ridged" pattern, "Mellor Taylor" mark.......................... **180.00**

    11½" h, blown out flowers and leaves, fluted collar, scalloped rim, "Burgess" mark..... **245.00**

    12½" h, "Burgess" mark................ **175.00**

    13" h, "H. Burgess" mark............... **200.00**

Pitcher and Bowl Set, bowl, 14⅝" d, pitcher, 11½" h, "Square Ridged" pattern, hairline to bowl, 1886, "Burgess and Eng Reg" mark.................................... **315.00**

Plate

    6" l, rect, 2 small handles................ **20.00**

    6¾" d

        "A.J. Wilkinson" mark................. **10.00**

        "W.H. Grindley" mark................. **12.00**

    7½" d, pepper leaf variant, "Elsmore & Forster" mark.......................... **18.00**

    7¹¹⁄₁₆" d, Chinese shape, dtd 1856, "Anthony Shaw" mark, set of 6............ **120.00**

    8" d, "Alfred Meakin" mark............. **12.00**

    8¼" d, Wedgwood.................... **14.00**

    8½" H-H, Alfred Meakin................ **18.00**

    8¾" d

        "Alfred Meakin" mark................. **14.00**

        Wedgwood........................ **14.00**

    9" d

        "Alfred Meakin" mark................. **15.00**

        "Anthony Shaw" mark................ **15.00**

    9⅛" d, "Arthur J. Wilkinson" mark........ **14.00**

    9½" d

        Morning glory...................... **24.00**

        Pepper leaf variant, "Elsmore & Forster" mark............................ **20.00**

    9⅝" d, Chinese shape, "Shaw".......... **25.00**

    9¾" d

        "Alfred Meakin" mark................. **18.00**

        "Anthony Shaw" mark................ **18.00**

        Portland shape, Morning glory motif, late 1850s, "Elsmore & Forster" mark...... **28.00**

    10" d

        "Alfred Meakin" mark................. **25.00**

        "Wedgwood & Co." mark.............. **25.00**

    11⅛" d, Portland shape, morning glory variant, "Elsmore & Forster" mark........... **105.00**

Platter

    8½" d, Meakin....................... **50.00**

    9¼" sq, Meakin...................... **50.00**

    10" l, 7¼" w, "Alfred Meakin" mark...... **30.00**

    11" l, 8" w, rect, "Alfred Meakin" mark.... **45.00**

    12" l

        8½" w, rect, "Alfred Meakin" mark...... **55.00**

        9½" w, "Mellor, Taylor & Co." mark.... **45.00**

    12½" l, oval, Meakin.................. **35.00**

    13" l, 9½" w

        "Alfred Meakin" mark................. **35.00**

        "Wedgewood & Co." mark (A).......... **10.00**

    13½" l, oval, Meakin.................. **50.00**

    13¾" l, 9¾" w, scalloped edge, Meakin. **55.00**

    14" l, 10¼" w, Wedgewood............. **55.00**

1859-97

15" d, "Burgess & Leigh" mark	40.00
15¾" l, 11½" w, "Alfred Meakin" mark	45.00
16" l, 12" w, "Alfred Meakin" mark (A)	8.00
17" l, 12" w, "Alfred Meakin" mark	55.00

Relish Dish
8¼" l, 4½" w, Meakin	35.00
Pepper leaf variant	125.00

Sauce Dish
4½" sq, Wedgewood	10.00
4¾" d, oct, "Anthony Shaw" mark	15.00
5" d, "Alfred Meakin" mark	20.00

Sauce Tureen, Cov
4⅞" h, underplate, ladle, rect shape, "Plain Square" pattern, c1870s, "Wedgwood" mark	425.00
6¾" h, underplate, oval shape, "Lily of the Valley" pattern, repair to lid, c1860s, "Shaw" mark	350.00

Service Tray, 9" sq, "Wedgewood & Co." mark ... 40.00

Soap Dish, Cov
3¾" h, with liner, "Square Ridged" pattern, 1886, "Burgess and Eng Reg" mark	175.00
3⅞" h, with liner, "Cable and Ring" pattern, "Anthony Shaw" mark	195.00

Soup Plate
8¾" d, "Wilkinson" mark	18.00
8⅞" d, "Wedgwood" mark	18.00
9" d, "Wedgewood" mark	18.00
10" d, Meakin	35.00

Sugar Bowl, 6¾" h, "Bamboo" pattern, 1883, "Meakin" mark ... 65.00

Sugar Bowl, Cov, 6¾" h, Niagara shape, large pomegrante finial, 1856, "Walley" mark 225.00

Teacup and Saucer, "Alfred Meakin" mark 75.00

Teapot, 8" h, 8½" w, "Wedgewood" mark .. 225.00

Tea Service, Children's, teapot, 4" h, sugar bowl, 3½" h, creamer, 2¾" h, cups and saucers, daisy type flower surrounded by fern type leaves, c1820s, unmarked, 13 pcs 395.00

Toothbrush Holder
"Alfred Meakin" mark	180.00
"Arthur J. Wilkinson" mark	165.00
"Mellor, Taylor & Co. England" mark	165.00

Tureen, Cov, 7½" d ... 90.00

Vegetable Bowl
5¼" sq, "Mellor, Taylor & Co." mark	50.00
6¼" l, 4¼" w, rect, Meakin	50.00
7⅝" sq, "Square Ridged" pattern, c1880s, "Wilkinson" mark	20.00
7¾" l, 5½" w, rect, Meakin	50.00
9½" l, 6¾" w, rect, Meakin	70.00
10½" l, 7¼" w, rect, Meakin	70.00

Vegetable Bowl, Cov
10" l, 5½" w, "Alfred Meakin" mark	150.00
11" l, 7" w, "Alfred Meakin" mark	125.00

Vegetable Tureen, Cov
5¼" h, rect shape, "Square Ridged" pattern, Wedgwood	95.00
5½" h, rect shape, six sided, "Sunburst" pattern, c1880s, "Shaw" mark	175.00

Wash Pitcher, 12" h, New York shape, teaberry variant, Clementson ... 450.00

Waste Bowl
5½" d, Chinese shape, tea leaf on int, copper luster rim, dtd 1856, "Anthony Shaw" mark	140.00
"Alfred Meakin" mark	50.00

TEPLITZ

Bohemia, Germany, now Czechoslovakia 1892–1945

History: Teplitz is a town in Bohemia. Several companies in the Turn-Teplitz area manufactured art pottery in the late 19th and early 20th century. Amphora was one of the companies.

Ernst Wahliss of the Alexandria Works in Teplitz manfactured and decorated pieces in the Art Nouveau style. In 1902 the factory bought six hundred molds from the Imperial and Royal Porcelain Manufactory in Vienna and made copies from them of earlier Vienna decorative porcelains and figures. After 1910 the firm manufactured faience wares. In 1925 the firm was called Ernst Wahliss AG. The plant ceased operation in 1934.

Additional Listing: Amphora.

Bowl
5½" d, multicolored enameled girl pulling rooster's tail, "Stellmacher" mark	55.00
6½" H-H, Art Deco style, lime green relief leaf swags, light to dark yellow ground, matte rust pierced handles, reeded band to foot, "dbl circle, 3 shield, and PD" marks	450.00
6¾" w, Art Deco style, four bouquets of white flowers from baskets, blue, green, white, and gold chains of flowers joining bouquets, cream glaze ground, gold accents on rim and foot, Alexandria Porcelain Works	650.00

13½" H-H, 7½" h, pedestal, twist body extends to form handles, flowers and stems twist from base in white and green enamels,

Ewers, 9" h, olive green base with molded sunflowers, gilt trim, tan neck, matte finish, "E W Turn Teplitz" mark, pr, (A) $260.00

Vase, 14 1/2" h, orange lobster with gold on gold-green base, "EST" under claw, Stellmacher, $12,000.00

Water Pitcher, 12 1/2" h, black and cream enamel swirls on green textured surface, "Stellmacher Turn-Teplitz Austria" mark, $1200.00

leaf tips accented in gold, "dbl circle, 3 red shield and PD" marks 950.00
Dish, Cov, 6 3/4" h, 5 1/2" w, Jugendstil ceramic, white with black line dots, paneled gilt rims, c1911, sgnd "E. Wahliss, red Vienna Turn Austria crown" mark 900.00
Ewer
    6" h, bulbous, large pink flowers and leaves, encrusted gold matte finish, twisted gold handle, "R.St.K." mark 65.00
    6 1/2" h, blue and gold florals, cream ground, frond type handle 50.00
    9" h, variegated purple poppies, gold bulbs, cream ground, molded flowers, applied front handle, "R.St.K." mark (A) 80.00
Figure
    7 1/2" h, bust of woman with pale green ruffled collar on shoulders, pink bow at waist, feathers in hair, "R.St.K." mark 525.00
    9" h, bust of young woman with flowers in green and irid lavender glazes, Ernst Wahliss (A) 300.00
    10" h, Art Nouveau bust of woman with

white rose in hair, green-gold finish, "E.W." mark 750.00
    15" h, bust of bare shouldered woman with blond hair tied in bun with green hibiscus in hair, light green eyes, collar necklace at throat, loose green garment on chest with gilt floral sprays, gilt crescent base, "Ed Stellmacher" mark 1100.00
    18" h, 19" l, two arabs riding camels in shades of brown and tan, early 19th C (A) 770.00
    21 1/2" h, woman with large hat in period dress, bird on each hand, two large open tulips and stems as vases on base, multicolored 1500.00
Pitcher, 8 3/4" h, green transparent forest scene, raised gold leaves on neck, brown branch handle, c1895, R.St.& K. 225.00
Urn, 10 1/2" h, hp woman with flowers, Wahliss mark 285.00
Urn, Cov, 6 1/2" h, natural roses and leaves on front with gold accents, reverse with single blossom with green stem, med brown handles, light yellow and gold accents on pierced foot, neck, and cov, "Alexandria Porcelain Works, Turn, Austria" mark 95.00
Vase
    3 1/2" h, light blue and white Kate Greenaway type girl bouncing ball, matte green ground, "Stellmacher, Teplitz" mark 75.00
    4" h, multicolored arab on horse, "Stellmacher" mark 85.00
    4 1/2" h, multicolored pirate on dark brown ground, "Stellmacher, Teplitz Austria" mark 100.00
    6 1/2" h, grove of blue cedar trees on cream ground, raised mushrooms with red caps and cream stems below, gray-green shaded foot, gold accents, "dbl circle, 3 shields and PD" marks 650.00
    7 1/2" h, center medallion of portrait of girl in mop cap, enameled circle of flowers with gold leaves on neck, green ground, reverse with bouquet of flowers, metallic blue foot with gold accents, matte gold pierced dbl handles and neck, "EW crown" mark 350.00
    7 3/4" h, squat shape with two loop handles, multicolored enameled arab on horse, olive green ground 295.00
    8" h
        Farm scene in colors, dbl handles, Stellmacher 95.00
        Painted reclining Venus reading to Cupid, white ground with small gold stars, c1900 .... 650.00
    9 1/2" h, modeled torso of Bacchus with right arm raised holding cup in gold with green highlights, gray glazed rock modeled ground, "Ernst Wahliss" mark 1150.00
    10" h
        Multicolored enameled cavalier on brown ground, dbl handles, Stellmacher 125.00
        Urn shape, gold scrolls in center with lavender lattice work, tan shaded to cream ground, dbl handles, "Turn Teplitz R.St.K. Bohemia" mark 95.00
    11" h
        Applied wolfhound, bronze finish, "Amphora, Turn Teplitz" mark 695.00
        Blue and gold flowers on cream ground .. 195.00
        Pink and green enameled applied flowers

with man's face, cream ground, sgl handle **225.00**
12" h, multicolored florals with gold beading,
two serpent handles, "R.St.K. Turn Teplitz"
mark............................... **350.00**
12½" h
Baluster shape with gilt everted rim, hp yellow roses and stems on green and cobalt
ground........................... **175.00**
Art Nouveau, Crown Oakwood style, sgd
"Klimt" **550.00**
13" h
Art Nouveau style head shape of woman in
shades of brown and green, clusters of
flower blossoms in central panel, gold accents, repairs, "Crown Oak, Turn Teplitz"
mark, pr.......................... **650.00**
Multicolored poppies and stems, green to
cream ground, gold trim, two handles .. **185.00**
14½" h, lower section with red and gold open
poppies, gold stems, upper section with
mauve tree trunks on gray ground, gold loop
handles on neck, gold shaped rim........ **1200.00**
15¾" h, trumpet shape, raised vert stems
with modeled berries at neck (A) **650.00**
17" h, shaded cobalt with blown out blue and
white flowers, molded gold serpent around
neck, "R.St.K." mark................... **650.00**
29" h, figural woman leaning on shell form
vase, set on three branch feet, overall encrusted florals, hairlines **750.00**
Vase, Cov, 6" h, large pink and white flowers on
front, reticulated neck, top, and dbl handles,
"Alexandria Turn Austria" mark........... **75.00**

c1880   c1875

c1872-1951

TILES

Bristol, Liverpool, London, England

Denmark, France, Germany, Holland, Italy, Spain, Portugal
1600s to Present

History: Tiles have been used for centuries on floors, walls, fireplaces, chimneys, and facades of houses, palaces, and castles. They even have been installed into furniture such as washstands, hall stands, and folding screens. Tiles clean easily and are quite decorative. Numerous pub-

lic buildings and subways use tiles to enhance their appearances.

The earliest of the **Dutch** tin glazed tiles featured polychrome figures, landscapes, flowers, and animals. Many used the fleur-de-lys motif in the corners. Additional subjects such as ships, sea monsters, mythical figures, fisherman, farmers, and biblical subjects appeared in the late 17th century. Tile pictures that were adapted from paintings and engravings of Dutch interiors or landscapes also were made.

Before 1629 at least twenty-five factories in Holland were making tiles with the Delft potteries the most prolific. After 1650 the Delft potteries became less important. However, all Dutch made tiles are generically called "Delft" tiles.

Even though the number of factories making tiles diminished during the 18th century, production increased throughout Europe. **Denmark, Germany, Portugal**, and **Spain** imitated Dutch tiles in their factories. The **Portugese** tiles featured motifs in two tones of cobalt blue or polychromes. Flemish workers came to **Spain** and introduced the majolica technique. They used a tin oxide glaze for their decorated tiles.

French tiles were influenced by both Italian and Dutch styles of decoration. In **Italy**, majolica tiles were made in centers such as Florence, Siena, and Venice.

Tiles made in **England** from the 16th through the first half of the 18th century generally followed the Dutch tiles in method of manufacture and design. Polychrome painting, blue and white motifs inspired by Chinese porcelains, birds, landscapes, and flowers all reflected the strong Dutch influence. Factories that produced tiles were centered in Bristol, Liverpool, and London.

In 1756 John Sadler from Liverpool produced the first transfer printed tiles and revolutionized the tile industry. The use of the transfer printing process on tiles allowed a far greater variety of designs and liberated the tile industry from the old Delft motifs. Transfer printing on tiles was responsible for the growth of the Victorian tile industry.

Herbert Minton was in charge of the production of tiles at Minton's. In 1828 he produced encaustic tiles with inlaid decorations, reviving a technique use in medieval Europe. Minton bought Samuel Wright's patent for encaustic tiles in 1830. Minton specialized in tiles for wall decorations in public buildings. Minton began transfer printing tiles in 1850. Minton's Kensington Studio, which was opened in 1871, employed such designers as Moyr Smith, Henry Stacy Marks, and William Wise who made painted or printed pictorial titles. Many of Smith's tiles were based in famous literary series.

During the 1870s decorative wall tiles were in use everywhere. By the 1880s over one hundred companies in England were producing tiles.

Decorative tiles were a major industry in the Ironbridge Gorge in the late 19th century. Tiles were produced by Maw and Craven Dunnill for church floors, shop counters, public buildings, facades, porches, and many other uses. Maw's factory at Jackfield was the largest decorative tile factory in the world in the 1880s.

The Craven Dunnill firm was formed in 1871 and built its new Jackfield works in 1875. Many encaustic tiles were made for use in new and restored churches. With the revival of the Gothic style, their reproductions of medieval tiles were in great demand.

George Maw and Arthur, his brother, bought the encaustic tile business of the Worcester Porcelain Company in 1850. In addition to floor tiles, they manufactured glazed tiles for walls, porchways, fireplaces, and washstands. Tiles were either hand painted, transfer printed, or stenciled. They also made ceramic mosaic tiles. The Benthall Works was added to the company in 1883.

In 1892 the Pilkington brothers established a pottery to manufacture tiles and other products at Clifton Junction, Manchester. Many experiments were done. The "Royal" prefix was granted to the company by King George V in 1913 and the company became known as "Royal Lancastrian."

Many designs used on tiles were copied from other fields of art. The Art Nouveau and Art Deco motifs were popular for tile designs.

References: Julian Barnard, *Victorian Ceramic Tiles*, N. Y. Graphic Society Ltd., 1972; Anne Berendsen, *Tiles, A General History*, Viking Press, 1967; C. H. de Jonge, *Dutch Tiles*, Praeger, 1971; Jonathan Horne, *English Tinglazed Tiles*, Jonathan Horne, 1989; Terence A. Lockett, *Collecting Victorian Tiles*, Antique Collectors' Club, 1979; Anthony Ray, *English Delftware Tiles*, Faber & Fabaer, 1973; Noel Riley, *Tile Art*, Chartwell Books, Inc., 1987; Hans Van Lemmen, *Tiles: A Collectors' Guide*, Seven Hills Books, 1985.

Collectors Club: Tiles & Architectural Ceramics Society, Reabrook Lodge, 8 Sutton Road, Shrewsbury, Shropshire SY26DD England. Membership: 18 pounds sterling. Bulletin and annual journal.

Museums: Boymans-van Beunigen Museum, Rotterdam, Holland; City Museum, Stoke-on-Trent, Hanley, England; Ironbridge Gorge Museum, Teford, England; Lambert van Meerten Museum, Delft, Holland; Victoria & Albert Museum, London, England.

Collecting Hints: Tiles are becoming increasingly more popular. They are difficult to identify as to manufacturer since they were mass produced and many were unmarked. Some firms only decorated tiles they received from another factory. The method of manufacture also may provide clues to the maker. Information on the back of a tile sometimes will indicate the manufacturer or the date that the tile was made.

Condition is an important factor in determining price. Bad cracks, chips, and scratches definitely lower a tile's value. Crazing in the glaze is not uncommon in a tile and usually does not affect the price if it does not detract from the tile's appearance.

3" sq, multicolored scenes of men at various
    occupations, Spain, lot of 7 . . . .   **35.00**
4 1/8" sq
    Art Deco stylized yellow and brown fish swimming over waves, moons overhead, white ground, "HB Quimper" mark **25.00**
    Fleur-de-lys in triangular floret border, yellow and green shades, c1875, imp "MINTON

8" sq, turquoise, rose, and cream crackle design, "Gien" mark, $160.00

HOLLINS & CO. No. 6" mark, set of 16
    (A) **585.00**
4 3/4" l, 3 1/2" w, Wedgwood calendar, brown transfer, Cunard Line Dock (new) Boston, 1912 calendar on reverse **125.00**
4 3/4" sq, center scene of peasant woman flanked by florals, blue border, "Henriot Quimper France" mark (A) **66.00**
4 7/8" sq, Delft
    Black printed scene of Chinese woman fishing or "Nancy Dancing the Hornpipe," Sadler, pr (A) **160.00**
    Painted bird in flight, standing on branch or tree stump, green, yellow, blue, red, and manganese, dbl blue circles, blue flowerhead corners, England, set of 24 (A) **4625.00**
5" sq
    Biblical scene in blue, 18th C **20.00**
    Blue scene of Chinese fisherman, in circ panel, reserved on manganese and blue ground, mid 18th C, English Delft (A) **720.00**
    Central rosette in blue, 3rd quarter 18th C, English Delft (A) **65.00**
    Dog and sheep in farm scene, black print, c1760 Liverpool (A) **242.00**
    European landscapes with ladies by trees, boatmen, rural buildings, castle, manganese tones, mid 18th C, London Delft, set of 12 (A) **750.00**
    Figures in landscapes in circ panels in tones of blue, mid 18th C, London Delft, set of 12 (A) **600.00**
    Floral sprays in center, blue trefoil corner motifs, restored, c1760–80, Liverpool Delft, set of 8 (A) **430.00**
    Flower basket in blue on diaper bracket, circle motif in corners, 3rd quarter 18th C, English Delft (A) **65.00**
    Gateway and avenue of trees leading to mansion in oct panel, powder blue ground, 3rd quarter 18th C, Liverpool Delft (A) **65.00**
    Girl and peddler resting under tree in black print, c1760 Liverpool (A) **285.00**
    Harbor, milking, fishing, or landscape scenes, blue painted, London Delft, set of 16 (A) .   **378.00**
    "Lad Being Apprehended Outside the Inn," gray print by Sadler and Green, c1760–75, Liverpool Delft (A) **125.00**
    Mrs. Yates in the character of Jane Shore, black print, trellis pattern border, c1780, Liverpool (A) **620.00**
    Mulberry scenic with man threatening other man stealing apples, 18th C, Delft **85.00**
    Scenes of milkmaid, man with basket on back, man with dog, cow in barn, barred oxhead corners, blue and white Delft, mid 18th C, London, set of 12 (A) **1851.00**
    Shepherd lovers with a dog, black print, c1760 (A) **285.00**
    "The Astrologer," printed in gray by Sadler and Green, c1760–75, Liverpool Delft (A) **125.00**
    "The Shearing of Sampson," blue scene in dbl line circles, mid 18th C, English Delft (A) . .   **95.00**
    "Two Girls Drinking Coffee," printed in black by Sadler and Green, c1760–65, Liverpool Delft (A) **175.00**
    "Two Young Gentlemen and a Girl Fishing," printed in black by Sadler and Green, c1760–70, Liverpool Delft (A) **75.00**

Various animals in shaped circ panels, blue painted, Dutch Delft, set of 12 (A) **285.00**

5⅛" sq

Blue oriental florals, white floral border, pale blue ground, 1780, Bristol Delft. **185.00**

Bowl of fruit in center, floral corners, polychrome enamels, Dutch, pr (A) **70.00**

Manganese colored pot of flowers in circ cartouche, dot and line rim, Dutch Delft (A) . **11.00**

Polychrome, central oct reserve of jardinaire of flowers in garden against bright blue ground, iron-red carnation at each corner, powder blue ground, London Delft, set of 3 (A). **531.00**

Shepherd and shepherdess figures at various pursuits in landscapes by trees, spider corner motifs, manganese, 18th C, Dutch Delft, set of 12 (A). **600.00**

Single flower and stem in manganese, Dutch Delft, set of 4 (A) **44.00**

5¼" sq

Boy with fishing pole seated on bank, multicolored, blue ground with dark blue geometrics at corners **95.00**

Figures in landscape with sponged trees, blue print, Bristol (A) **130.00**

Manganese biblical scenes, 18th C, Dutch Delft, set of 34 (A) **1720.00**

5½" sq, biblical scene in manganese, 18th C (A). **25.00**

5¾" sq, frontal view of peasant woman with basket, yellow and garnet rose outer rim, chipped corners, "HB Quimper" mark (A) . . **330.00**

5⅞" sq, white, brown, cocoa floral, leaves, stems, tan ground, "Semagres Made in Italy" mark. **10.00**

6" sq

Art Nouveau low relief of pink and green flowers, green ground, "MINTON" mark (A). **38.00**

Aqua ground with Art Nouveau style flower in pink, blue, and lime green, dust pressed, "ENGLAND" mark (A). **22.00**

Blue floral design, light yellow ground, dust pressed, "A.M. Ltd ENGLAND" mark (A) . **28.00**

Blue transfers of youths in settings of various titled months, Wedgwood, set of 12 (A) . . **880.00**

Caramel ground with Art Nouveau flower in pink and green, dust pressed, "MADE IN ENGLAND" mark (A). **33.00**

Cattle in stream, black transfer, white ground, Minton mark. **175.00**

Classic building on river bank, cows and figures in foreground, blue transfer, Minton . **70.00**

Daffodils in yellow with brown throats and blue stems, dark green ground, dust pressed, "ENGLAND" mark (A). **38.00**

Dark red flowers with green leaves, gray ground, dust pressed, Eng Reg mark (A) . . **28.00**

"Elaine," tan and brown transfer, sgd "Moyr Smith, raised Minton China Works, Stoke on Trent" marks. **75.00**

Flower with red petals and tan stem, shaded green ground, dust presssed (A) **33.00**

Flower with tan buds and green leaves, blue ground, dust pressed (A). **66.00**

"Fortunes of Nigel," hand tinted, blue-gray with black and tan, Sir Walter Scott Series, sgd "Moyr Smith". **75.00**

Four sqs, two with dark blue-green, two with

pale yellow with dark blue-green stylized tulips, dust pressed (A). **35.00**

"Gareth," tan and brown transfer, sgd "Moyr Smith, raised Minton China Works, Stoke on Trent" marks. **75.00**

Goats, black transfer, white ground, Minton mark. **175.00**

"Guy Mannering," hand tinted, blue-gray with black and tan, Sir Walter Scott Series, c1902, sgd "Moyr Smith". **75.00**

"Guinevere," tan and brown transfer, sgd "Moyr Smith, raised Minton China Works, Stoke on Trent" marks. **75.00**

Historic Boston in blue, circ cartouche, floral and ermine tail corners, late 19th C, set of 9 (A). **275.00**

"Isolit," tan and brown transfer, sgd "Moyr Smith, raised Minton China Works, Stoke on Trent" marks. **75.00**

Knight and lady design, Minton **45.00**

"Left Behind," multicolored scene of girl on pony with hunter in red coat in distance. . **195.00**

Light yellow ground with two large blue morning glories with purple buds and green leaves, dust pressed (A). **33.00**

Low relief of two stylized flowers in red on light green and tan heart, green ground, "England" mark (A). **33.00**

"Lynette," tan and brown transfer, sgd "Moyr Smith, raised Minton China Works, Stoke on Trent" marks. **75.00**

"Morte D'Arthur," tan and brown transfer, sgd "Moyr Smith, raised Minton China Works, Stoke on Trent" marks. **75.00**

"Old Mortality", hand tinted, blue-gray with black and tan, Sir Walter Scott Series, sgd "Moyr Smith, Minton and Buzley" mark . . **60.00**

"Pellas," tan and brown transfer, sgd "Moyr Smith, raised Minton China Works, Stoke on Trent" marks. **75.00**

Polychrome bird with nest, "Minton" mark (A). **20.00**

Red floral with green leaves, gray ground, dust pressed, "G.T. Ltd, ENGLAND" mark (A) . **33.00**

Sailing ship with man in water, hp in colors, English Reg mark (A) **77.00**

Sheep and barn, "Farmyard Series," black transfer, Minton mark. **150.00**

Sgraffito vegetables in colors, Pilkington (A) . **55.00**

Stag and Hound, black transfer, ochre ground, by William Wise, c1870, "Minton & Hollins" mark **175.00**

Stylized flower with three red and green buds in low relief, large blue-green leaf, lime green ground, "MINTON HOLLINS & CO." mark (A) **71.00**

Tan flowers with brown leaves on Art Nouveau flower, medium green ground, dust pressed, "ENGLAND" mark (A). **33.00**

Two lavender tulips and large central Art Nouveau motif, gray ground, dust pressed (A). **22.00**

Violets in purple on green shaded ground, dust pressed, unmarked (A) **44.00**

"Vivien," tan and black transfer, sgd "Moyr Smith, raised Minton China Works, Stoke on Trent" marks. **75.00**

Wildlife scene in colors, Villeroy and Boch . . **48.00**

Wreath enclosing Art Nouveau flower in yellow, med green, and tan, dark green ground, "ENGLAND" mark (A) **33.00**

Yellow-cream ground with red and tan center floral motif and four olive green leaves in corners, dust pressed, "Eng Reg and ENGLAND" mark (A) 33.00

Yellow daffodil with green leaves in low relief, dark green ground, "A.M. Ltd ENGLAND" mark (A) 35.00

6⅛" sq, polychrome scene of man fishing, wood frame (A)........................ 25.00

6¼" sq, Blue and white
Floral medallion, "De Porcelyne Fles" mark . 20.00
Harbor scene with lighthouse, "De Porcelyne Fles" mark........................... 30.00

6¾" sq, majolica, St. John kneeling before the Madonna and Child in stylized rocky landscape, blue, green, ochre, black, gilt ebonized frame, c1540, Urbino (A)................. 4140.00

7¼" sq, majolica, relief of birds building nest in center, leaf corners, multicolored, c1870, "Minton, Hollins & Co." mark (A)........ 137.00

7⅞" sq, cavalier holding dog by tail, beside stone building, multicolored enamels, sgd "F. Vogler," Montereau (A).................. 85.00

8" sq
Figure clutching a cross, captioned "B. ALFONSO DE LIGUORO," stylized palms in corners, dark colors, mid 18th C, Castelli (A).. 480.00
"Lysander," brown transfer, tan ground, raised "Wedgwood" mark 135.00
Majolica, molded yellow and ochre with sacred monogram within sunburst order of San Bernadino, incised stylized foliage, deep blue ground, mid 16th C, Urbino (A) 2244.00
"Oberon," brown transfer, tan ground, raised "Wedgwood" mark 135.00
Painted wading bird walking into water, c1870, Minton........................ 400.00
"Peasblossom," brown transfer, tan ground, raised "Wedgwood" mark 135.00
Polychrome transfer of coastal French city scene, c1870, "Creil et Montereau" mark (A).. 330.00
"Scorpio," Zodiac Series, raised "Minton and Hollingsworth" mark................... 100.00

11⅞" h, 6" w, raised profile of head with flowers in hair, orange and brown glazes, c1900, Frampton, pr..................... 450.00

13⅛" h, 15¹³⁄₁₆" l, faience, ochre horse pulling black roofed green and manganese carriage driven by man in manganese hat and ochre jacket, yellow ground, white sky, early 19th C, Spanish (A)...................... 1500.00

19¾" sq, stove, equestrian figure of Elector inscribed in relief "CURFFST MENTZ" within scroll cartouche, framed by arched arcade with two female saints, two putti, and angel's head, blue, manganese, yellow, and green, in wood frame, c1600, Nuremberg (A)........ 2200.00

41" h, 9" w, enamel decorated with portrait of man or woman in medieval style, bird in lower section, late 19th C, set of 5 (A) 1430.00

TILE PICTURES

16⅛" h, 10⅝" w, manganese painted rearing horse, small house in ground, Dutch Delft, set of 6 tiles (A) 380.00

19" h, 25" w, blue and white scene of fleet of sailing ships, mtd in oak frame, artist sgd, c1900, Holland, 12 tiles (A) 770.00

44½" h, 47" w, blue painted serving boy bringing chocolate to mistress in palace int, rococo border of shell scrolls and foliage in yellow, ochre, manganese, and green, marbled frieze, mid 18th C, Portuguese, mtd on two timber panels (A)........................... 5760.00

67¾" h, 40¾" w, "Little Jack Horner," boy seated in large chair holding plum, pie in lap, brown and gray paneled walls, multicolored accents, c1895–1905, "Doulton & Co." mark (A).. 6270.00

63¾" h, 38" w, Flemish hunting figures in 16th C costumes, wooded landscape, shooting pheasants, ochre, brown, and green shades, molded "Maw & Co. Broseley, Art Tiles, W.B. Simpson & Sons, imp W.B.S.& S." marks (A) 2508.00

TOBY JUGS

Staffordshire, England
1775 to Present

History: Toby Jugs, first made by English potters from Staffordshire in the 18th century, are drinking vessels. Although they were at the zenith of their popularity from 1775 to 1825, Toby jugs still are being produced today. After they became outmoded as drinking mugs, they survived as ornamental pieces.

Some of the earliest Toby jugs were made by Ralph Wood and Whieldon at their Burslem potteries in Staffordshire. Some claim the name "Toby" originated with the Uncle Toby character in Laurence Sterne's *Tristram Shandy*. This is subject to debate.

The typical Toby jug features a seated toper clasping a jug with both hands or holding a glass in one hand and a jug on a knee in the other. The seated figure is usually a male wearing a three cornered hat, each corner of which formed a spout. Figures were dressed in costumes of the period and usually have genial facial expressions. Toby jugs were designed for use in cottages and inns. Variations included standing figures and occasional female figures. Most are usually ten inches tall while miniatures, which are rarer, measure about three to six and one-half inches tall.

Some early Whieldon Toby jugs have the mottled and tortoise shell underglazed effect. The Ralph Wood jugs have a somewhat whiter body and softer, translucent glazes. After 1780 some overglaze enamels were used. Wedgwood, Pratt, and Davenport, along with other English potters, made Toby jugs.

References: Desmond Eyles, *'Good Sir Toby,'* Doulton & Co., Ltd., 1955; Bernard Rackham, *Early Staffordshire Pottery*, Faber & Faber, 1951; Vic Schuler, *British Toby Jugs*, 1st edition, Kevin Francis Publishing Ltd., 1986; C. P. Woodhouse, *Old English Toby Jugs*, Mountrose Press, 1949.

Museums: City Museum & Art Gallery, Stoke-on-Trent, England; Victoria & Albert Museum, London, England.

4" h, bisque, full figure seated man in pink vest, black boots, striped breeches, green hat spout, tan hair, holding yellow mug 125.00

4⅜" h, standing gentleman in blue coat, brown hat, ochre-orange breeches and green base, figural lyre handle, handle crack, early 19th C Yorkshire (A)........................... 1540.00

6″ h, brown hat, rust breeches, olive green jacket, Pratt-type, $2200.00

4⅝″ h, blue and light tan coat, striped vest, holding jug in left hand, glass in right hand, blue, mustard, black, and white, c1780, Prattware **1750.00**

5″ h, President Taft in colors, "Germany" mark **115.00**

6½″ h, seated man
Smoking, wearing blue jacket, ochre-gray breeches, holding ale jug on knee, some damage and repair of pipe, late 18th C (A) **748.00**
Wearing dark blue jacket, yellow breeches, holding foaming ale jug and beaker, heavy brows, restored, late 18th C, Ralph Wood type (A) **10235.00**

6¾″ h, "One Armed," seated man on chair holding foaming ale jug, white coat with ochre trim, olive green waistcoat, ochre breeches, brown shoes, canted sq base, late 18th C (A) **1045.00**

7¼″ h, seated man in green coat, holding mug and pipe, "Wood & Sons" mark **75.00**

7½″ h, pearlware, "Doctor Johnson," seated man with spotty face, black coat, gray stockings, iron-red chair, pouring from jug, yellow base and handle, early 19th C (A) **940.00**

7¾″ h, standing gentleman in blue coat, black and white hat, ochre-orange breeches and collar, red trim, early 19th C, Yorkshire (A) **1049.00**

8″ h
"Doctor Johnson," seated, black coat, breeches, and tricorn, black and white striped waistcoat, red, yellow, blue, and black marbled base, pouring jug of ale into lap, holding foaming beaker, restored, early 19th C (A) **560.00**
Seated full figure man in black, hat, blue coat, tan breeches, yellow shirt, holding mug . . . **350.00**

8⅞″ h, pearlware, gentleman in brown jacket, dark red waistcoat, yellow breeches, sitting on sheaves of corn, holding foaming ale jug in one hand, beaker in other, c1800, Staffordshire (A) **2917.00**

9″ h, seated man in black hat, blue coat, darker blue breeches, brown hair and shoes, c1770, Ralph Wood **5100.00**

9¼″ h
Blue jacket, yellow breeches, deep olive hat, holding jug of ale, pipe resting by right leg, spout repaired, early 19th C, Prattware (A) **496.00**

Souter Johnny, seated man in black hat, blue jacket, brown tunic, chartreuse breeches, gray hose, holding beer stein, Wm Kent . . **95.00**

9⅜″ h, seated gentleman
Jug on knee, semi-transparent colors with blue, green, yellow, and brown sponging, repair to hat (A) **300.00**
Lantern in hand, transparent green coat, brown sponging, repairs (A) **100.00**

9½″ h, thin man, seated
Blue faced mottled gray jacket, holding foaming brown jug, green glazed chair with crossed stretchers, restored, late 18th C (A) **1850.00**
Ochre and brown striped jacket, yellow breeches, dark brown tricorn hat and long hair, globular ale jug on knee, foliate molded handle, crossed stretcher on chair, restored, late 18th C, Prattware (A) **6170.00**

9⅝″h
Admiral Lord Howe, seated on barrel, green jacket, manganese waistcoat and breeches, dog and pipe at feet, foaming globular ale jug, hat restored, late 18th C (A) **3085.00**
Seated man wearing dark blue jacket, gray breeches, shoes and tricorn, holding empty brown ale jug, late 18th C, creamware (A) **875.00**
Seated man with warty face, holding empty ale jug, brown coat and breeches, pale yellow waistcoat, marbled canted sq base, rim restored, early 19th C, Staffordshire (A) **897.00**

9¾″ h, seated man
Blue coat and hat, purple breeches, green seat and tankard in lap, mid 19th C (A) **440.00**
Blue sponged jacket, purple gray breeches and shoes, waistcoat in yellow, foaming brown ale jug, keg between feet, pipe at side, late 18th C, creamware (A) **1120.00**
Green jacket, yellow waistcoat, ochre muffler, blue breeches, gray-brown boots, pipe resting on marbled base, restoration to hat and handle, late 18th C, Pratt-type (A) **2460.00**
Mottled manganese jacket, purple-gray breeches, keg at feet, foaming brown ale jug, late 18th C, creamware (A) **725.00**
Yellow jacket, orange-ochre cuffs and trim, blue hair, breeches, and shoes, holding jug on lap, Ralph Wood type, 18th C (A) **907.00**

9⅞″ h, "Spotty Face," seated man in brown coat, yellow waistcoat, tan breeches, gray stockings, holding full jug, pipe at side, blue lined canted sq base, rim repair, "Neale & Co." mark (A) **1254.00**

10″ h
Pearlware, seated man in green, blue, yellow, and black sponging, holding jug and pipe (A) **3350.00**
Seated man
Blue coat, yellow waistcoat, blue striped stockings, holding full jug of ale, brown lined canted sq base, repair to handle and rim, early 19th C, Prattware (A) **1028.00**
Blue sponged jacket, yellow waistcoat, purple breeches, keg at feet, foaming ale jug, restored, late 18th C (A) **905.00**
"Tax Collector," rust trousers, gold vest, blue jacket, black boots and hat, Staffordshire **395.00**
Toper holding brown jug, barrel between feet,

mottled blue coat, yellow waistcoat, gray hat and breeches, Ralph Wood (A) **720.00**

10" h, Cov

Seated gentleman with jug on knee in semi-transparent and sponged light yellow, green, blue, and brown, hairline on cov (A) **1050.00**

10¼" h, "Punch," white and rust striped clothing, green hat, c1890 . . . .   **265.00**

10½" h, seated cat as schoolmaster, iron-red coat, green spotted necktie, rim modeled as mortar board, circ green and brown sponged base, rope twist handle, c1850, Staffordshire (A) **320.00**

11¼" h

"Hearty Good Fellow," walking, wearing blue jacket, ochre waistcoat, yellow breeches, supported on green glazed base extending to form handle, restoration to hat and shoulders, c1800, Prattware **1020.00**

Majolica, standing man with hands in pockets, cobalt jacket, black breeches, tricorn hat, woman holding fan, blue blouse trimmed in pink, black shawl, yellow-orange skirt, c1868, imp "MINTON" mark, pr (A) **1870.00**

"Squire," green coat, dark blue waistcoat, manganese glazed tricon hat and long hair, foaming ale jug, corner chair, handle repaired, late 18th C (A) **6170.00**

11½" h, "Rodney's Sailor," dark blue jacket, checked trousers, foaming ale jug and beaker, anchor at feet, chair with chest beneath, green glazed base, crack, late 18th C, creamware (A) **2460.00**

11¾" h, "Winston Churchill" modeled as caricature of stateman as First Sea Lord of the Admiralty, seated on bulldog draped with Union Jack, c1940, designed by Clarice Cliff, Wilkinson Ltd, facsimile signature, printed mark, #47 (A) **1317.00**

1875-1901   1900-1909

c1958-1962

TORQUAY

Torquay District, South Devon, England
1870s–1962

History: G. J. Allen discovered red terra cotta clay on the Watcombe House grounds, just north of Torquay in 1869.

The pottery industry in Torquay owes its existence to this discovery.

Allen established the Watcombe Pottery. Charles Brock was appointed manager, and skilled workers were employed from Staffordshire. Watcombe Pottery was established during the peak of the art pottery movement, 1870 to 1900, and found a ready market for its products.

The appeal of the terra cotta wares was the natural color of the clay and the innovative shapes. A small amount of enamel decoration or gilt borders were added. At first, the style was classical, comprised of vases, figures, and busts imitating Greek and Roman originals. Later busts of contemporary and historical celebrities, vases, jars, architectural wares, garden ornaments, and tea services were made.

Watcombe Pottery also was known for its terra cotta plaques. Statues were made for advertising purposes. Enamel decoration of flowers, birds, and fish on ornamental wares was accomplished in a natural style on unglazed terra cotta.

In 1875 Dr. Gillow established the Torquay Terra-Cotta Company Ltd. at Hele Cross, just north of Torquay. Smaller decorative wares, such as statuettes, plaques, vases, figures, and busts were made. Some utilitarian examples also were produced. Products were similar to those made at the Watcombe Pottery.

Torquay Terra-Cotta Company declined. It closed in 1905 as a result of the decline in the Arts and Crafts movement and the shift to more modern styles. Enoch Staddon reopened the Torquay Pottery in 1908 to make pottery rather than terra cotta ware. The factory closed during WWII.

The Aller Vale Pottery, under the direction of John Phillips, started making terra cotta and other art wares in new forms and styles near Torquay in 1881. By 1890 the pottery was catering to holiday visitors who wanted something to take home as a souvenir. Designs were painted in thick colored slip on items prepared with a dip coat of slip of a uniform color. They were finished with a clear glaze. Usually rhymes or proverbs were scratched through the ground so the lettering showed up in the dark red color of the body. This "motto ware" gained tremendous popularity during the early 20th century, not only in resorts, but all over the country.

Watcombe Pottery combined with Aller Vale in 1901 to form the Royal Aller Vale and Watcombe Art Potteries. Watcombe started to manufacture the Aller type wares. One style of decoration showing the thatched cottage between trees was called "Devon Motto Ware" or "Cottage Ware." In addition to the motto, sometimes the place name was inscribed. Commemorative wares were made. The combined potteries eventually closed in 1962.

During the early part of the 20th century, several smaller potteries such as Longpark Pottery, Burton, and Daison were established in or near Torquay. Most were founded by men who had worked at one of the major potteries in the district. The designs tended to copy the styles used by Aller Vale and Watcombe. When Longpark closed in 1957 and Watcombe in 1962, the red clay pottery industry in Torquay ended.

References: Virginia Brisco, Editor, *Torquay Mottowares*, Torquay Pottery Collectors Society, 1990; D. & E. Lloyd Thomas, *The Old Torquay Potters*, Arthur H. Stockwell, Ltd., 1978.

Museums: Devonshire Museum, Devonshire, England; Exeter Museums, Exeter, England; Torquay Museum, South Devon, England.

Collectors Club: North American Torquay Society, Shelley Crawford, Rt.6, Box 9A, Oxford, MS 38655. Membership: $10.00. Quarterly magazine. Torquay Pottery Collectors' Society, 604 Orchard View Drive, Maumee, Ohio, 43537. Membership: $13.00. Quarterly magazine. Torquay Pottery Collectors Society, US/Canada Coordinator, Beth Pulsipher, Box 373, Schoolcraft, MI 49087. Membership: $22.50. Quarterly magazine.

Basket
    2¼" h, green, "Lynton," unglazed base ... **44.00**
    3½" h, pink rose on blue ground, "Lemon & Crute" mark **35.00**
Beaker, dbl handles, Normandy pattern, green glaze over white clay, Allervale **88.00**
Biscuit Barrel, 8" h, pink roses on streaky mauve ground, wicker handle, "Longpark Torquay" mark **150.00**
Bottle, 3¾"h, "Cornish Lavender". **40.00**
Bowl
    4¼" d, cottage, "May the Hinges of Friendship Never Go Rusty, Watcombe Torquay" mark **49.00**
    6" d, Crocus pattern, stamped "Longpark Torquay England" mark **78.00**
    7" d, kingfisher **68.00**
Cakestand, 5"h, 9" d, fruit pattern, "He is Well Paid Who is Well Satisfied" **95.00**
Candlestick
    6¼" h, white clay, multicolored scrolls, "Aller Vale" mark **90.00**
    7½" h, scandy, "Be the Day Weary or Be the Day Long at Last it Ringeth to Evensong," imp "Watcombe" mark **145.00**
    8" h, scandy, "Happy Be Thy Dreams"..... **96.00**
Chamberstick
    4" h
        Black cockerel, "Snore and You Sleep Alone," stamped "Longpark Torquay" mark. **78.00**
        Blue ground with white daisy design, imp "Aller Valle" mark. **104.00**
    4½" h, colored cockerel, "Many Are Called But Few Get Up, Longpark Torquay" mark **112.00**
    5½" h, scandy, "Be the Day Weary or Be the Day Long at Last it ringeth to Evensong".... **98.00**

Toast Rack, 4" h, 3½" sq, brown rack, cream base, imp "St Ives" and "Help Yourself to Toast" on base, imp "Watcomb Torquay England" mark, $75.00

Coffee Pot, 7" h, cottage, "May the Hinges of Friendship Never Go Rusty, Watcombe Torquay" mark........................... **104.00**
Compote, 5" h, 7" d, ftd, "Do Not Stain Todays Blue Sky With Tomorrows Coulds"........ **116.00**
Condiment Set, cottage, sugar bowl, "Speak Little Speak Well," pepper, "Good Examples Are Best Sermons," salt, "Actions Speak Louder Than Words, Watcombe Torquay" marks **120.00**
Creamer
    1¾" h, cottage, "Wookey Hole, Help Yourself to the Cream, Royal Watcombe Torquay" mark........................... **37.00**
    2" h, Cockington Church, "Cockington, Watcombe Torquay" mark.................. **42.00**
    2¼" h
        Black cockerel, "Straight From the Cow, Longpark Torquay" mark.............. **40.00**
        Cottage
            "From Lynmouth Fresh From the Dairy, Longpark Torquay" mark **32.00**
            "Put a Stout Heart to a Steep Hill, Made in England" mark **30.00**
        Scandy, "Stracht Frae the Cod," imp "Allervale" mark **45.00**
    2½" h, scandy, "Take a Little Milk, Watcombe Torquay" mark.................. **28.00**
    2¾" h
        Colored cockerel, "Be Aisy With Tha Crain, Longpark Torquay" mark.............. **39.00**
        Cottage, pedestal, "Take a Little Cream, Watcombe Torquay" mark.............. **53.00**
        3" h, Kerswell daisy, "Straucht Frae The Coo," imp "Aller Vale" mark **65.00**
    3½" h
        Cottage, "From Coniston Fresh From the Dairy, Longpark Torquay" mark........ **65.00**
        Scandy, scalloped edge, "Take a Little Cream" **49.00**
Cup and Saucer, black cockerel, "Dauntee' Be Fraid Au't Now, Longpark Torquay" marks .. **60.00**
Dish, 7" d, scandy, "There's More in the Kitchen"................................ **88.00**
Dresser Tray
    10½" l, blue Kingfisher, imp "Watcombe Torquay England" mark................. **128.00**
    11" l, scandy, "Vessels Large May Venture More Little Boats Must Keep the Shore," imp "Watcombe Torquay England" mark................................. **160.00**
Egg Cup
    1¾" h, cottage, "Fresh Today, Longpark Torquay' mark **32.00**
    2½" h, with saucer, black cockerel, "Fresh Today, Longpark Torquay" mark......... **45.00**
    3" h, with saucer, cottage, "Fine Words Will Not Fill, Watcombe Torquay" mark **39.00**
Fish Tray, 5¾" l, colored cockerel, "A Placice For Ashes, Longpark Torquay" mark........ **58.00**
Hair Tidy, 4" h, scandy, "Save While You Have-and Give While You Live, Watcombe Torquay" mark.............................. **95.00**
Inkwell, 2" h, scandy, "Wa'al Us Be Main Glad Tu Zee'e, Aller Vale" mark **33.00**
Jam Jar, 4¾" h, sailboat scene, "Southsea, Be Aisy With Tha Jam," stamped "Longpark Torquay England" mark **52.00**
Jardiniere, 5¼" h, relief of pheasant in colors,

blue ground, "black Royal Torquay Pottery England" mark 160.00
Mug
3" h
Cottage, "Fairest Gems Lie Deepest, imp "Royal Watcombe Torquay" mark 56.00
Scandy, "A Stitch in Time Saves Nine," two handles, imp "Watcombe Torquay" mark 68.00
5" h, cottage, "When Day Breaks Make the Most of the Pieces, Longpark" mark 112.00
Pen Tray, 9" l, scandy, "The Pen is Mightier Than the Sword," stamped "Longpark Torquay" mark 39.00
Pepper Pot, 2½" h, cottage scene, "Hot & Strong," Crown Dorset 26.00
Pitcher
2¼" h, sailboat design 30.00
3" h
Cottage, "Fairest Gems Lie Deepest, Watcombe Torquay" mark 28.00
Seagull in flight, blue ground, "Bigbury On Sea," stamped "Royal WQatcombe Torquay" mark 28.00
Shamrock, "The Green Immortal Shamrock, Aller Vale" mark 48.00
3½" h, Crocus pattern, stamped "Longpark Torquay England" mark 72.00
4" h
Green leaves, white flowers, imp "Watcombe Torquay" mark 75.00
"Portland Bill," lighthouse scene 40.00
Sailboat, blue, "Lands End, Watcombe Torquay" mark 25.00
Scrolled, "Stracht Frae the Cod," imp "Made in England" mark 76.00
4¼" h, cottage, "Still Waters Run Deep, Watcombe Torquay" mark 56.00
4½" h
Black cockerel, "Good Morning, Never Say Die Up Man and Try, Watcombe England" mark 68.00
Cottage, "Everything Has a Bright Side," stamped "Watcombe Devon Mottoware" mark 58.00
5¼" h, cottage, "To a Friend's House the Road is Never Long," stamped "Devon Mottoware" mark 64.00
6" h
Colored cockerel, "There Would Be No Shadows if the Sun Were Not Shining, Longpark Torquay" mark 150.00
Kingfisher pattern, "T.W. Lemon & Son, Wesuma Pottery" mark 95.00
Mottled blue ground, eight petaled flowers, stamped "Royal Torquay Pottery" mark 56.00
Plaque, 10" d, Cockinton Forge in colors 192.00
Plate
5" d
Black cockerel, "From Durham Tis Deeds Alone Must Win the Prize, Longpark Torquay" mark 58.00
Cottage
"Hope Well and Have Well," stamped "Royal Watcombe Pottery" mark 42.00
"No Road is Long With Good Company, Made in England" mark 40.00
Sailboat, "Torquay, Say Little But Think Much," stamped "Watcombe Torquay" mark 45.00
Scandy, "Truth Like a Cork Never Sinks," green rim 50.00
5¼" d, scandy, "We're Not the Only Pebbles on the Beach," blue rim, "Aller Vale" mark 38.00
5½" d, windmill scene in colors, stamped "Watcombe Torquay" mark 48.00
6" d, cottage, "A Thing of Beauty is a Joy Forever, Royal Watcombe Torquay" mark 45.00
6¼" d, cottage, "Time and Tide Wait For No Man, Watcombe Devon Mottoware" mark 45.00
6½" d, Cottage
"Better To Sit Still Than Rise To Fall, Watcombe Torquay" mark 48.00
"Kinds Words Are the Music of the World," stamped "Watcombe Torquay" mark .. 48.00
10" d, Cottage
"No Road Is Long With Good Company, Dartmouth Pottery" mark 74.00
"One Today is Two Tomorrow, Dartmouth Pottery" mark 74.00
Platter, 10" d, crain in colors, "Barton Pottery" 168.00
Pot
2½" h, two handles, three legs, Normandy, imp "Allervale" mark 35.00
3" h, scandy, "Vessels Large May Venture More. Little Boats Must Keep the Shore," imp "Aller Vale HH & Co." mark 69.00
3½" h, 2 story house, "If You Cant Fly Climb" 29.00
Puzzle Jug, 4" h, scandy, "Here I Am Filled With Good Cheer Come Taste Me If You Can" .. 112.00
Sauce Pan, 3½" d, scandy 56.00
Scent Bottle
2" h, "Devon Violets" 27.00
2½" h, "Devon Lavender" 27.00
Sugar Bowl
1¾" h, snow cottage, "Take a Little Sugar, Watcombe Torquay" mark 48.00
3" h, scalloped edge, cottage, "Elp Yerzel Tu Sugar, "Longpark Torquay" mark 57.00
Sugar Dish
1¾" h, colored cockerel, "From Rothbury, Be Aisy With Tha Sugar," stamped "Longpark Torquay" mark 45.00
2¾" h, black cockerel, "Good Morning, From Cheddar, Take a Little Sugar, Watcombe Torquay" mark 62.00
3" h, seagull scene on light blue ground, "Mousehole, Watcombe Torquay" mark .. 28.00
3¼" h, cottage, "Clevedon, 'Elp Yerzel Tu Sugar, Longpark Torquay" mark 57.00
Teapot
3½" h, 6½" l, green with brown handle and spout, imp "Watcombe Torquay" mark... 72.00
4" h, scandy, "'Elp Yerzels Cum Me Artiez" 79.50
4½" h
Cottage, "Take a Cup of Kindness From Auld Lang Syne," stamped "Made in England" mark 59.00
Primrose, "Now Ladies All I Pray Make Free and Tell Me How You Like Your Tea" .. 98.00
Sailboat scene, "Take a Cup of Tea Its Very Refreshing" 75.00
Tea Stand, Cottage
4½" d, "Take a Cup of Tea Its Very Refreshing," stamped "Watcombe DMW" mark . 48.00

5½" d, "He Also Serves Who Stands and Waits," stamped "Longpark Torquay" mark.................................. 49.00
Toast Rack, 3¼" sq, cottage, "Take a Little Toast, Royal Watcombe Torquay" mark..... 65.00
Tobacco Jar, 6" h, amber, "Tobacco You Are Welcome," Exeter....................... 96.00
Tray
4½" d, black cockerel, "Good Morning," imp "St. Mary Church England" mark 68.00
5" l, 3" w, "A Reminder of a Visit to the English Lake District," Coronation year 1937, stamped "Watcombe Torquay England" mark.......................... 68.00
Cottage
5" l, "A Stitch in Time Saves Nine, Watcombe" mark..................... 32.00
9" l, 3 section, "Do Noble Deeds Not Dream Them All Day Long, Watcombe Torquay" mark...................... 98.00
Vase
3" h
Normandy, green dripping on white clay, imp "Allervale" mark................. 33.00
Small flowers with white brush tip petals, blue-green ground, three twisted handles, "Longpark Torquay" mark........ 58.00
3¼" h, crain design, black ground, stamped "Daison Art Pottery Torquay" mark, pr ... 125.00
3½" h, black cockerel, "Du All Tha Gude Ur Kin in Every Wey Ye Kin," three handles, "Longpark Torquay" mark.............. 80.00
4" h, sailboat, "Weymouth, Say a Kind Word When You Can, Exeter" mark 38.00
4¼" h
White flowers, green leaves, terra cotta body, c1883–95, imp "Terracotta Works Longpark Torquay" mark............. 75.00
Windmill scene, "Never Say Die Up Man an Try," Crown Dorset 42.00
4½" h, scandy, "Isnt Your Life Extremely Flat. With Nothing Whatever to Grumble at," two handles, imp "Aller Vale Devon England" mark.......................... 68.00
5" h, kingfisher, "Never Prove False to a Friend, Royal Torquay Pottery" mark 46.00
6" h
Daffodil, three small handles, stamped "Longpark Torquay" mark 135.00
Tintern Abbey design, "Longpark Torquay" mark............................ 120.00
6½" h, butterfly, three handles, "Royal Torquay Pottery" mark.................... 85.00
7¾" h, relief of peacock on blue ground .. 65.00
8" h
Blue heather......................... 85.00
Scandy, "Life is mostly Froth and Bubble. Two Things Stand as Stone Kindness in Another's Trouble Courage in Your Own," dbl handles, "Watcombe" mark. 125.00
9½" h, applied leaves and flowers, two twisted handles, "Longpark Torquay" mark............................... 195.00
9¾" h
Diving Kingfisher with waterlilies, three handles, "Watcombe Torquay England" mark.......................... 220.00
Dbl handles, blue ground with peacock .. 140.00
10" h, peaches, black ground 125.00

DU PAQUIER
1720-30

c1760-1770

VIENNA

**Vienna, Austria
1718–1864**

**Du Paquier
1718–1744**

**State Factory
1744–1864**

History: the Vienna Porcelain Factory, founded in 1718 by Claudius Du Paquier, was the second European factory to produce hard paste porcelain. Meissen was the first. Du Paquier developed high quality white porcelain. The privilege to make porcelain was granted to Du Paquier by the Emperor Charles VI. The decorations of the Du Paquier period fall into three catergories: 1) 1725 in which the polychrome oriental theme was emphasized; 2) 1730–1740 in which polychromed scrolls, landscapes, and figurals in cartouches were dominant and black and gilt were used to highlight the themes; and 3) the final period which featured German florals or "Deutch Blumchen" designs similar to the Meissen treatment. The adoption of Meissen styles contributed to the rise of Vienna as one of Meissen's chief rivals. However, unlike Meissen, the Du Paquier factory did not produce a large number of figures.

Du Paquier sold his factory to the Austrian state in 1744. It became the Imperial Porcelain Manufactory and fell under the influence of Empress Maria Theresa. The quality of the porcelain reached its peak during this period, known as the State Period, 1744–1864. The Austrian coat of arms was used as the factory mark. Following the Seven Years' War, 1756–1763, which altered greatly the production at Meissen, Vienna porcelain assumed the undisputed leadership in European porcelain.

Between 1747 and 1784 Johann Niedermeyer, the chief modeler, contributed much to the success of the factory by creating rococo influenced figurals decorated in soft pastel colors. After 1765 the styles from Sevres greatly influenced the decorative styles at Vienna. Anton Grassi come to work at Vienna in 1778. He moved the factory's production away from Rococo styles into the Neo-classical influences.

Joseph Leithner concentrated on developing new background colors, especially a fine cobalt blue that was a match for Sevres' bleu roi. He introduced a special gold color. Leithner enhanced all the colors used at Vienna.

Under the management of Konrad Sorgenthal between 1784 and 1805, the factory produced richly ornamented dinner and tea services, vases, urns, and plates in the Neo-classical and Empire styles. Emphasis was placed on the reproduction of paintings by famous artists such as Angelica Kauffmann and Rubens onto porcelain vases, plates, and plaques that were surrounded by gilt frames that often included the painter's name.

Flowers were the principal decorative element used on Viennese porcelains. Seventeenth century Dutch flower paintings were adapted or copied on plates, cups, vases, or plate sets. Many pieces had black backgrounds to make the flowers stand out.

When the Congress of Vienna was held, numerous participants placed orders for services. After this period, the factory experienced a period of stagnation. Competition from the Bohemian factories started to take its toll.

After reaching the very pinnacle of success in the highly competitive porcelain field, the state porcelain factory was forced to close in 1864 due to financial difficulties.

The beehive mark was adopted in 1749. The year was stamped on pieces beginning in 1784.

References: W. B. Honey, *German Porcelain*, Pitman; George W. Ware, *German & Austrian Porcelain*, Crown Publishers, Inc., 1963.

Museums: Art Institute of Chicago, Chicago, Illinois; British Museum, London, England; Gardiner Museum of Ceramic Art, Toronto, Canada; Metropolitan Museum of Art, New York, New York; Osterreiches Museum fur Angewandte, Kunst, Vienna, Austria; Smithsonian Institution, Division of Ceramics and Glass, National Museum of American History, Washington D. C.; Woodmere Art Museum, Philadelphia, Pa.

Basket, 10½" l, oval, center painted in puce, iron-red, yellow, and green with floral spray and sprigs, open basketwork sides studded with yellow centered rose florettes, ropework foot, green twisted branch handles, 1765–75, underglaze "blue shield, incised 3" mark (A)   **440.00**

Beaker and Stand, 3½" h, underglaze blue, iron-red, and gilt sprays of oriental plants on each side, zig-zag borders, dbl handles, DuPaquier............................... **1000.00**

Beaker, Cov, and Stand, 3⅞" h, painted swags, bandelwork, and lambrequin borders in puce, blue, green, iron-red, violet, gilt, c1725–30 (A).......................... **5700.00**

Bowl, 10⅝" d, ext with multicolor scene on front with Lot being intoxicated by his daughters while Sodom burns in distance, reverse with angel drawing maiden into heavens, gilt edged oval panel, lilac ground borders of gilt foliate scrolls, central wider border of raised gilt bands alternating with blue bands, band on

Figure, 5" h, multicolored, "blue beehive" mark, (A) $165.00

int, underglaze "blue shield, imp date cipher 811, 55" marks (A)...................... **6600.00**

Cabinet Cup and Saucer, flared body with applied handle, rect painted bust of Diana with crescent crown and quiver of arrows, gilt ears of corn, c1818, "blue shield" mark (A) **882.00**

Cabinet Cup, Cov, Stand, panels painted with classical masks and figures, "Achelous and Hercules" and "Bacchus and Silenus," gilt blue and turquoise ground, "shield" marks (A)........ **684.00**

Chocolate Cup and Saucer, Cov, 3⅜" h, 5" d, fluted, cup with purple beribboned blossoms around rim, foot with scalloped line, handle with foliate sprigs, cov with blossom on top of ball knob, hatched dentil border at rim also on saucer rim, four floral sprays on saucer, c1725, Du Paquier (A)........................... **3300.00**

Coffee Can and Saucer
Mythological, Venus in iron-red drapery being pulled through gray clouds by two prs of white doves in gilt edged oval panel, gilt handle, spring green ground with gilt ovals, gilt foliate boughs and fretwork, gilt wheel device in center of saucer, underglaze "blue shield, 96 in gold for Anton Kothgasser, imp date cipher 802, 39 or 11" marks (A).... **3025.00**

Rect panel with four cherubs' heads with clouds, lilac-pink ground beneath pale yellow border or green, gold, and brown foliate motifs enclosed by gilt edged brown ribbon within gilt bands, angular handle edged in gilding, underglaze "blue shield, imp date ciphers 804, 39 or 11" marks (A)........ **770.00**

Coffee Cup and Saucer, 5⅛" d, 2¹³⁄₁₆" h, chinoiserie design in raised and washed gold on cup with two Chinamen conversing on rock before distant pavilion, another strolling, saucer with Chinaman seated on rock and fishing beneath willow tree, another standing by rock, gilt edged rim with black border, gilded handle, coral-red ground, underglaze "blue shield, imp date cipher 90, 16" marks (A)..................................... **3300.0**

Coffee Pot, 7⅞" h, pear shape, lady with fan taking walk through parkland with little daughter, reverse with lady seated in landscape, gilt scrolls on spout and handle, rim and cov decorated with border of parallel strokes in green, iron-red, and purple, fruit knob, c1785, underglaze "blue shield" mark, imp 7 (A)........ **740.00**

Cream Jug, 3⅛" h, pear shape, painted with two landscape scenes of figures at harbor, gilt scroll banded rim and handle, c1770, "blue shield" mark (A)......................... **242.00**

Cup and Saucer
Center panel with scene of buildings and street on cup, chartreuse ground with gilt designs, saucer in chartreuse and gilt, gilt int and handle, 1815, "blue shield" mark.... **3100.00**

Conical flaring shape, reserve of Place de St. Michael in gilt floral border, gilt palmettes at rim, c1820, imp "Roy a Vienne and blue shield" mark........................... **200.00**

Painted Cupid in cloud in Sevres style, green and gilt trailing borders and garlands, c1780, "blue shield" mark (A)........... **305.00**

Yellow and brown building, gold trim, c1820, "blue shield" mark **150.00**

Ecuelle, Cov, 7" w, shades of rose, iron-red, blue, purple, green, yellow, and black on front, reverse and int with floral sprigs, gilt banded flaring foot, cov with insects and florals, handles formed as green scaly dolphins with gilt heightened iron-red fins and tails, gilt rim, 1735–40, Du Paquier (A) **19,800.00**

Figure

White glaze

5" h, young boy seated on rock, monkey at side, "blue shield" mark **175.00**

5 1/2" h, monkey French horn player, horn broken, c1800, "blue shield" mark..... **375.00**

6 1/4" h, woodsman, black neckerchief, pink jacket, white striped iron-red sash, white shirt and apron, gray breeches, log in left hand, silver and tan ax above tan chopping block, green mottled base, c1760, underglaze "blue shield, imp O for Dionisuis Pollion, brown 13" marks (A) **880.00**

7" h, mother seated with child in lap, another at side, toys and cat on base, multicolored, incised "shield" mark................... **750.00**

7 1/8" h, white, equestrian group, nobleman in tricorn hat, long cloak, riding horse, rect mossy base, c1770, incised "shield and B" mark (A) **475.00**

7 5/8" h

"Geography" as young boy in white shirt, puce waistcoat and breeches, holding calipers to globe above map, companion in russet coat and breeches, peers through black telescope, brown monkey in yellow jacket and russet breeches, holding ball, green mottled mound base, gilt scroll border on foot, 1765–70, underglaze "blue shield" mark (A) **605.00**

Paris and Helena, seated on molded rocky base, holding apple for Amor standing in front of them, some restoration, tree missing, 1755–60, underglaze "blue shield" mark **555.00**

7 13/16" h, sausage seller, brown edged fur hat with gilt tassel, iron-red striped yellow neckerchief, dark mauve doublet over white shirt and apron, black breeches, leaning on brown basket of sausages on mottled brown tree stump, sheaf of yellow wheat, yellow blossoms and green leaves on gilt foliate scroll border, c1765, underglaze "blue shield, imp R, and brown 12" marks (A).................................. **990.00**

7 7/8" h, gallant and pug, man in long gray hair, white neckerchief, iron-red cloak, puce jacket and breeches, yellow chair with black tricorn hat, gray and black recumbent pug, green mottled mound base, gilt scrolls, restored,c1770, underglaze "blue shield, incised E" mark (A) **1210.00**

7 15/16" h, seated spaniel, black and brown eyes, black nose, salmon shaded mouth open to show teeth, brown spotted curly white coat, repaired, imp "shield, date cipher 854, 86, incised 3" marks (A) **1100.00**

8 3/8" h, barometer bearer, youth in dark brown tricorn, iron-red striped white neckerchief, turquoise green lined yellow jerkin, white shirt, yellow sashed russet breeches, brown barometer in tan basket, puce strap over shoulder, resting on brown tree stump, pale green washed mound base, c1760, underglaze "blue shield, imp P" mark (A) ... **880.00**

11 1/4" d, shepherd group, two pairs of lovers, gilt scrolls on base, c1760, underglaze "blue shield" mark.......................... **1870.00**

17 3/4" h, Saint Gregory, gray beard, iron-red mouth, brown eyes, gold and white papal tiara, gilt edged stole decorated with cross, robe tasseled at back, edged with border of gilt arches and trefoils, sq base with concave sides, repairs, 1765–75 (A).............. **2475.00**

Ice Pail, Cov, 7 7/8" h, sprigs and sprays of flowers, angular handles, scroll knob in puce, c1770, underglaze "blue shield, iron-red A/62"mark (A).......................... **670.00**

Plate

8 3/4" d, four shaped cartouches of putti and emblems of love among clouds within trelles and flower cartouches in two shades of gold against dark blue and gilt ground, c1800, "blue shield incised JS,3," marks, set of 6 (A) **4000.00**

9 1/4" d, center with green frog, green stemmed purple grapes, puce rose, and other flowers, scalloped rim with sprig of forget-me-nots, iron-red strawberries, and two insects, c1740, Du Paquier (A) **7150.00**

9 1/2" d

Famille rose style flowering plants and insects, border with four groups of emblems and flowers, c1750, pr **1850.00**

Magenta, yellow, blue, and pink florals and shells in center and four arrangements on border, white ground, c1875, "blue shield" mark....................... **2400.00**

Neoclassical, center with pale salmon ground reserved with purple luster roundel decorated in raised gold, border of leaves, bands, and beadwork, three large fan shaped panels with mythological figures on pale green ground, alternating with three groups of four smaller panels with mythological beasts on orange ground, edged in gilding, purple luster ground rim with wide border of gilt floral and foliate scrolls, underglaze "blue shield, imp date cipher 94, and 32" marks (A) **2475.00**

Painted bird on perch above rose, tulip and peony, burnished gilt border etched with scrolling foliage, c1816, sgd "J. Fischer, blue shield" mark (A)................. **5432.00**

Parrot perched on branch, emerald green, turquoise, yellow, blue, and crimson plumage, orange border, burnished gilt bands, c1828, imp "shield, 1828, 46 for Kanter, script mark L'Amazone femelle' (A) **3500.00**

9 9/16" d, allegorical, "The Three Fine Arts," three classically draped maidens: "Painting, Architecture, and Sculpture," before low wall and large trees, gilt edged rim with narrow pink bands and beadwork, gilt border of neoclassical urns, underglaze "blue shield, 96 in gold, imp date cipher 98, and 32" marks (A) **1100.00**

10" d

Baroque reserves of two multicolored birds, birds and butterflies in small reserves on border, green ground, gold frames, c1890, "X'd V's Josel Vater" mark, pr .. **250.00**

Delicate floral decoration in blue and green,

reticulated border, blue rim, early 1800s,
pr **550.00**
12" d, center scene of Psyche and her sisters,
cobalt ground border with eight roundels of
putti and gilt foliage (A) **1045.00**
Snuff Box, Cov, 2⅝" l, oval, ext with rococo
cartouches painted in shades of green, brown,
puce, iron-red, turquoise, black, and blue on
front with gentleman smoking pipe, reverse
with seated child with another holding domino
mask to her face with other children, ext of cov
with couple conversing by garden monument,
int of cov with mother supporting daughter,
1760–70, underglaze "blue shield" mark on
int of box, gold mounting (A) **10,500.00**
Soup Plate, 9⁹⁄₁₆" d, puce, iron-red, yellow, and
green peony bouquets, white ground, ozier
molded border, c1780, "blue shield" mark, set
of 5. . . . . **400.00**
Soup Tureen and Cov, 9⅝" h, shaped circ
body, clusters of German blossoms below
molded trellis border, cov with rose finial,
flared foot, two scroll handles and shell terminals, 1744–49, imp "shield" mark (A) **2775.00**
Tea and Coffee Service, Part, coffee pot, 9⅝" h,
hot water jug, 6 teacups, 6 saucers, 2 coffee
cups and trembleuse saucers, colored flower
spray and scattered sprigs, 1790–1800, 'blue
shield" marks (A) **1300.00**
Teabowl and Saucer
Bowl painted with travelers in landscape, saucer with poacher and wife carrying game,
gilt rims, c1755–60, "blue shield" mark . . . **450.00**
Bowl with black continuous scene of soldiers
laying siege to town, int with armorial tro-
phy, saucer with fighting soldiers on
horseback, gilt highlights, c1735, Du
Paquier (A) **10,527.00**
Teapot
3⅞" h, painted chinoiserie of Orientals
fighting dragon, reverse with tea ceremony, animal spout, wishbone handle accented in gilt, restored, c1750, "blue
shield" mark (A) **2850.00**
7½" h, underglaze blue birds in flight over
chinoiserie garden, c1760, "blue shield"
mark. **250.00**
Tete-a-Tete Set, Part, oval tray, 16⅜" l, cylindri-
cal coffee pot, cov hot milk pot, 2 coffee cans
and saucers, shades of brown, tan, gray, green,
iron-red, lilac, and pale blue with sheep and
goats, tray also with cattle in mountainous
landscape within panel edged raised gilt border of palmettes, arches, and bellflowers, reverse of cups with gilt diamonds centering
blossoms and foliate scrolls, leaf sprays, and
grapevines repeated as border between gilt
beadwork bands on rim, gilded mushroom
knobs, gilded rim edges, 1798–99, underglaze
"blue shield" marks, 7 pcs (A) **40,700.00**
Tray, 15" l, oct, puce ground, tooled gilt center
floral rosette, tooled acanthus and foliate borders with green lines, trellis pierced rim,
c1801, "blue shield" mark (A) **1765.00**
Tureen, Cov, 7¼" h, globular shape, multicol-
ored enamels and gilt bouquet of Indian
flowers, birds, and insects, iron-red and gilt
lambrequin and zig-zag border, scroll handles
accented in puce, silver rim, domed knob,
c1720–25, Du Parquier **13,750.00**

1874 - PRESENT

METTLACH
VB

1885 - PRESENT

VILLEROY AND BOCH

Mettlach, Germany
1836 to Present

History: Johann Franz Boch founded a dinnerware factory
in 1809 in an old Benedictine abbey in Mettlach. This
factory merged with the Nicholas Villeroy plant in Waller-
fongen, Saar in 1836 to form the Villeroy and Boch company. The Luxembourg factory founded in 1767 by the
Boch brothers also was included in this merger. Eventually
there were eight Villeroy and Boch factories in other cities
in addition to the main factory at Mettlach. August von
Cohausen was the director who instituted the use of the
old abbey tower as the factory's trademark.

Stonewares, original in both design and production
techniques, were produced starting in the 1840s and were
the most famous of the Villeroy and Boch wares. In addition to steins, punch bowls, beakers, wall plaques, beverage sets, drinking cups, hanging baskets, and vases were
made.

Chromolith, colored stonewares, utilized two colors of
clay worked side by side but separated by a black intaglio
line. Raised decoration was done by applying the design
and fusing it to the body of the stoneware pieces. This
process was known as etched, engraved, or mosaic inlay.

Motifs included Germanic scenes depicting peasant
and student life and religious and mythological themes.
Punch bowls featured garlands of fruit, while steins were
adorned with drinking scenes, military events, folk tales,
and student life scenes. About 1900 Art Nouveau decorations appeared on plaques, punch bowls, vases, steins,
umbrella, and flower stands.

Planolith stoneware plaques were given an initial coating of a delicate green matte color, glazed, and then fired.
Figures to decorate the plaques were formed separately,
applied to the pre-fired background, and then fired again.
These applied decorations were ivory colored and stood
out in relief against the green ground. Motifs on plaques
included scenes from Greek mythology and Germanic
legends.

Cameo stonewares had raised ivory colored decorations set on light blue or light green backgrounds. There
was a less fluid quality to these applied decorations. The
stoneware was more dense.

The pinnacle of stoneware production was between
1880 and 1910. Prominent artists at Mettlach were Christian Warth, Heinrich Schlitt, Fritz Quidenus, Mittein, and
Johann Baptist Stahl.

Terra cotta for architectural use was made from 1850;
mosaic tiles were made from 1852. Cream colored earthenwares for domestic use were produced at factories in
Dresden from 1853 and in Schramberg from 1883.
Around 1890 artists at Mettlach manufactured plates and

vases decorated in the Delft style and the faience style of Rouen.

Around World War I business had lessened due to unfavorable economic conditions and the lack of unskilled labor. In 1921 a major fire destroyed all molds, formulas, and records of the factory.

Although the factory continued to produce tiles, dinnerwares, and plumbing fixtures, almost fifty years lapsed before the factory revived the production of steins and plaques.

Reference: Gary Kirsner, *The Mettlach Book,* Seven Hills Books, 1983.

Museums: Keramik Museum, Mettlach, Germany; Museé de l'Etat, Luxembourg; Munchner-Stadtmuseum, Munich, Germany; Rijksmuseum, Amsterdam, Holland; Sevres Museum, Sevres, France; Villeroy & Boch Archives & Museum, Mettlach, Germany.

Beaker
  1/4 L, PUG
    Alpine couple, multicolored, #$^{1135}/_{2327}$
    (A) **122.00**
    Couple at feast, multicolored, #$^{1134}/_{2327}$
    (A) **110.00**
  1/4 L, white cameo of dancers on blue ground
    in floral medallion, #2815 (A).......... **318.00**

Tumbler, 5" h, PUG, multicolored on tan ground, #2327, "Mercury and Mettlach, Made in Germany" mark, (A) $40.00

Vase, 11" h, etched, swans in forest setting in tan, brown, steel blue, and ecru, #2609, "castle" mark, (A) $975.00

Beer Pitcher, 13" h, 7" d, middle band on white on blue of dancing people with German phrases, six bottom frieze panels in tan relief of flower and bird design, 4 L, "Villeroy & Boch, Mettlach 171" mark..................... **450.00**
Charger, 15 1/2" d, gentleman on horseback, signed "Stocke," #2142 (A) **600.00**
Clock, 11 1/2" h, steeple shape, blue and white, flowers on sides and top, pastoral scene on front, "Villeroy & Boch Wallerfangen-Made in Saar-Basin" mark........................ **375.00**
Ewer, 17 3/4" h, central frieze of festive beerhall, band playing while couples dance and drink, neck and foot with formal panels between leaf molded borders, subdued tones, c1884, Mettlach, imp shape number, production number, and date codes (A)..................... **900.00**
Garniture Set, Bowl, 16 3/4" l, 2 vases, 16 3/4" h, Art Nouveau style etched large flowing gold leaves, green foliage on gray ground, gold and green handles, #2414, 2415, dtd 1898, "castle" marks............................. **1595.00**
Mug, 5" h, "Join Health and Cheer, Drink Hires Root Beer, tan ground, "Mettlach Made in Germany" mark........................ **145.00**
Pitcher
  6 1/2" h
    Etched, scene of couples dancing, #1513 **305.00**
    Hp plums and green leaves **165.00**
  8 1/2" h
    Cameo of girl in pigtails on blue ground .. **195.00**
    Relief of green leaves on gray ground, birch handle, c1890 .... **250.00**
  10 1/2" h, relief of two men playing cards on overturned basket, mask spout, scroll handle, white **85.00**
  12 1/2" h, cylindrical body, figures by the sea, stamped and #2893, hinged pewter lid, Mettlach (A)......................... **198.00**
Plaque
  8" sq, white cameos of Cupid standing on urn, lady next to tree, green jasper ground, dtd 1907, #7074........................... **375.00**
  10 1/4" d, blue and white scene of two boats in harbor, #1532, Mercury mark (A)..... **65.00**
  11" d, etched, Autumn Season design, woman carrying baskets of fruit, blue-gray ground, brick red edge, #1607, dtd 1885, "castle" mark........................ **525.00**
  12" d, PUG multicolored Johannskirche in Stuttgart, #$^{1044}/_{3718}$.................... **100.00**
  14 1/2" d, incised multicolored enameled battle scene, #1769, "W.S." mark.......... **650.00**
  16" d, etched
    Black and white scene of king on throne with attendants, brown, blue, and cream geometric border, gold rim, #1048-11, "castle" mark...................... **525.00**
    Gnome sitting in tree drinking from goblet or holding wine bottles, relief gold border, #2112, 2113, sgd "H.S. Schlitt," pr (A) **1800.00**
  17" d, etched, castle on the Rhine scene in colors, gold edge, #1108, dtd 1895, "castle" mark............................ **850.00**
  17 1/2" d
    Delft, blue and white Dutch port scene with boats and people, c1897, #5080 ..... **425.00**
    PUG, wine bottle, glass, and fruit, c1880, Mettlach **395.00**

18" d
  Polychrome scene of geese in flight with
    wildflowers, Mettlach #1044 (A) 350.00
  White cameo of Grecian soldiers in boat,
    satin green ground, sgd "Stahl, castle"
    mark 1250.00
  20³/4" d, white cameos of man riding dol-
    phin, two seated females in rushes, flying
    mallards in foreground, c1900, Mettlach
    #7048 (A) 2504.00
Punch Bowl
  15" h, 14" d, underplate, band of blue and
    dancing people, neptune loop handle, floral
    relief lid, fish finial, oval floral panels on un-
    derplate, German names and places, 8 liter,
    "V & B Mettlach, 2087" mark 1250.00
  16" h, 15½" H-H, scenes of clas-
    sical women and children, blue ground,
    "Mettlach #3149 castle" mark 850.00
Toothpick Holder, incised floral design, #1461,
  Mettlach (A) 60.00
Tureen, Cov, 14" H-H, 10" h, shaped hex, rose
  colored leaves and florals on white ground,
  raised border with circles outlined in rose,
  scroll finial and handles, "Villeroy and Boch
  Paris" mark 95.00
Vase
  11" h, arabesques on blue ground, #1897,
    "castle" mark 345.00
  12½" h, etched, four scenes of boy in tree,
    boy shooting arrow, picking flowers,
    #1591 . . . .   470.00
  14" h, etched, panels of cherubs as four sea-
    sons, blue ground, dtd 1897, #1537, pr .   650.00
  15" h, ovoid body, two panels of children at
    rustic pursuits on blue ground, tall spirally
    molded cylindrical neck, flared fluted foot,
    lustrous brown and blue, two handles, late
    19th C, imp marks and numeral (A) 375.00
Vase, Cov, 20" h, young couple among elabo-
  rate scrolling foliage on gray ground, other has
  gentleman talking to young maid, waisted circ
  foot, applied and molded with various strap
  and scroll motifs, late 19th C, imp signature,
  #1735 and 2066, pr (A) 1496.00

Francois Gravant took over and appointed Charles
Adams the director. The king granted many concessions
to Adams. The factory entered a period of prosperity.

Vincennes products made between 1745 and 1756 are
prized by collectors. Jean-Jacques Bachelier took charge
of painting and modeling in 1747. He introduced the use
of biscuit porcelain for figure modeling. A Vincennes factory specialty was artificial flowers, popular in Paris around
1750.

In 1753 the king issued an edict giving the exclusive
privilege of porcelain making in France to Adams. He
sanctioned the use of the royal cypher, a pair of interlaced
"L's."

The porcelain works were removed from the Chateau of
Vincennes to a new building at Sevres in 1756. The firm
became the Royal Porcelain Factory of Sevres.

Pierre Antoine Hannong, a Strasbourg potter, established a factory for hard paste porcelain in the vacated
buildings at Chateau Vincennes in 1767. He was granted
the right to produce porcelain as long as he did not in-
fringe on the Sevres factory's designs. Only a small quantity of porcelains were made. In 1774 the factory was
purchased by Seguin whose patron was the Duc de
Chartes. Seguin used the title "Royal Factory of Vincennes." His products duplicated those of many French
factories.

Reference: George Savage, *Seventeenth & Eighteenth
Century French Porcelain,* Spring Books, 1969.

Museums: British Museum, London, England; Gardiner
Museum of Ceramic Art, Toronto, Canada; J. Paul Getty
Museum, Malibu, California; The Frick Collection, New
York; Victoria & Albert Museum, London, England; Wads-
worth Atheneum, Hartford, CT.

Bowl, 8³/4" d, circ, colorful central small floral
  sprays surrounded on angular panels of rim
  with larger floral sprays, gilt edged rim, "blue
  enamel interlaced L's, C for 1755, T for Binet"
  marks (A) 440.00
Coffee Cup and Saucer
  Painted birds in colors in gilt palm and floral
    borders, bleu lapis ground, gilt dentil rims,
    repaired saucer, 1754, "blue interlaced L's
    and B" marks (A) 660.00

c1753

VINCENNES

Chateau of Vincennes, Paris, France
1738–1772

History: Gilles and Robert Dubois brought soft paste porcelain manufacturing to the royal chateau at Vincennes in
1738. They were assisted by Orry de Fulvy, Councillor of
State and Minister of Finance. After two years, the Dubois
brothers failed.

**Coffee Cup and Saucer, gilt sprays of garden
flowers in cartouche of palm fronds and sprays,
border of seeded scale and diaper panels, bleu
lapis ground, gilt dentil rims, gilt laurel swags on
reverse of saucer, c1752, "blue interlaced L's"
mark, (A) $2575.00**

Sprays of garden flowers within cartouche of flower sprays and palm fronds, border of scrolling foliage enclosing seeded scale and diaper panels, gilt dentil rims, bleu lapis ground, c1752, cup with underglaze "blue interlaced L's" mark (A)................ **2555.00**

Cup, Cov, 4³/₄" h, gilt shield shaped reserves of flower trails and flower borders, gilt flower knob, c1750–52, "blue interlaced L's" mark. **925.00**

Cup and Saucer

Painted birds in flight in gilt tooled foliate borders, reserved on bleu lapis ground, dtd 1750, "blue interlaced L's and E" marks (A) **2442.00**

Puce painted and gilded figures working beside lake setting, leaf scroll and drapery vignettes, scattered flowers, insects, and bird, c1754, "blue interlaced L's and B" mark (A) **3663.00**

Trails of flowers and foliage suspended from ribboned pole in gilt and puce, gilt dentil rims, c1752, "blue interlaced L's" mark... **750.00**

Cup and Saucer, Cov, 3⁵/₈" h, 5⁵/₈" d, panel edged in tooled gilt grasses and floral sprays tied with bowknot with tooled gilt floral cluster against white ground, gilt dentil edged rims, ear shape handle, ranunculus sprig knob, bleu lapis ground, c1753, underglaze "blue interlaced L's" mark (A) **4125.00**

Dish, 9¹⁵/₁₆" l, lozenge shape, painted in shades of rose, purple, yellow, blue, green, and gray with sprays and sprigs of Meissen style flowers within molded rim edged in gilding, c1750, "blue enamel interlated L's with central dot" mark (A)............................... **2090.00**

Ecuelle, Cov, Stand

7⁷/₈" l, quatrefoil bowl, oval stand, rose color with gilding, birds on grassy areas between fruiting grapevines, int of bowl with small bird in flight above branch, entwined rose foliate scroll and gilt grapevine handles, cov with fish, shell, and seaweed knob, gilt edged rim, c1752, "blue enamel interlaced foliate L's" mark (A) **4950.00**

10" l, painted flower garlands, birds, and butterfly, gilt line rims, dbl entwined gilt handles, figural marine knob, c1750, "blue interlaced L's and dot" mark (A)........ **24,420.00**

Figure

6³/₄" l, sleeping boy on white drapery forming hood over head, left elbow resting on high stone of rocky mound base, c1752 (A)...............................**12,100.00**

8¹/₈" h, white glazed reclining water nymph in rushes, arm resting on overturned urn, knarled tree stump in ground (A) **20,645.00**

8¹/₂" h, white bisque, "The Grape Eaters" modeled as girl leaning on lap of young man who feeds her grapes from basket, dog and hat on base, c1752, incised "B and H" mark (A)...............................**16,296.00**

Liqueur Bottle Cooler, 12¹/₄" l, oval, ext with multicolor clusters of flowers and fruit with floral sprays between gilt dashed blue bands at gilt dentil edged rim and gilt edged foot, blue and gilt feathered foliate scroll handles, int with gilt dashed blue band at rim, "blue enamel interlaced L's, C for 1755, B for Boulanger pere, incised H. and T." marks (A) ... **1760.00**

Milk Jug, Pear Shape Body

3⁵/₈" h, multicolored floral spray on white within oval panel edged in gilt grasses and flowers on both sides, gilt dentil border, gilt scroll spout and foliate scroll handle, turquoise body, cov missing, "blue enamel interlaced L's, B for 1754, bird mark for Boucher (A) **3300.00**

4⁵/₈" h, front with blue and flesh tones with shepherd boy seated beneath tree near two sheep within cartouche edged in gilt rococo scrollwork, diapered panels, floral sprays, reserved on beu lapis ground, white branch form handle, three molded blue feet with gilding, "blue enamel interlaced L's, C for 1755, K for Charles-Nicolas Dodin" marks (A)................................... **6050.00**

Mustard Pot and Cov, 3³/₈" h, gilt foliate scroll panel painted with two exotic birds in flight, one carrying flowering branch, flat cov with gilt flower knob and gilt border, gilt dentil rims, bleu lapis ground, c1753, "interlaced L's with letter date A, 4 dots, incised 3" marks (A) .. **1850.00**

Pitcher and Basin, 9¹/₄" l, painted scattered bouquets, gilt dentil rims, silvered mts, replaced cov, dtd 1754, "blue interlaced L's and date" mark (A)..................................... **1100.00**

Potpourri Vase, Baluster shape

6¹/₂" h, applied climbing multicolored roses, rocky base with tree stump, some damage, c1750 (A)............................. **1200.00**

12" h, painted bouquets and scattered flowers, pierced shoulder edged with molded gilt foliage, pierced cov with puce flower finial, dtd 1754, "blue interlaced L's" and date mark (A)......................... **15,400**

Saucer, 5¹/₂" d, center in blue, iron-red, rose, and black with two birds in flight within roundel of gilt floral and leaf sprays, bleu lapis ground rim with gilt dentil edge, underglaze "blue interlaced L's, C for 1755" blue enamel painter's diamond mark, incised mark (A) ... **1430.00**

Sucrier, Cov, 3³/₄", front reserve in rose, green, blue, yellow, iron-red, gray, and brown with pr of birds on bowl, single bird on cov, within shaped oval panel edged in tooled gilt grasses and floral sprays against white ground, gilt dentil edge rim, iron-red tipped white ranunculus sprig knob with gilt stem and leaves, bleu lapis ground, "blue interlaced L's, B for 1754, V for Mutel" marks (A) **3850.00**

Tray, 11" l, oval, Cupid amidst cream, gray, and lavender clouds against white ground in two B shape panels edged in gilt grasses and flowering vines at each end, sides with triangular panels with either rose drums and yellow cornet or quiver of arrows, edged in gilt flowering vines, gilt dentil edge rim, turquoise ground, "blue enamel interlaced L's, B for 1754, K for Charles-Nicolas Dodin" mark (A).......... **5500.00**

Vase, 2¹/₂" h, urn shape, painted flowering branches in colors, gilt line rim, c1752, "blue interlaced L's and dot" mark, pr (A)........ **1540.00**

Wine Glass Cooler, 4⁵/₁₆" h, cylindrical body, shades of rose, green, blue, yellow, purple, brown, and black with sprays and sprigs of Meissen style flowers beneath gilt bands on upper and lower rims and foot, gilded lady's mask handles, c1750, "blue enamel interlaced L's enclosing dot" mark (A)..............**13,200.00**

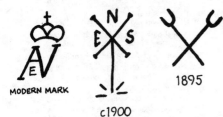

MODERN MARK

1895

c1900

VOLKSTEDT

Thuringia, Germany
1760 to Present

History: The Volkstedt porcelain factory was started about 1760 under the patronage of Johann Friedrich von Schwartzburg-Rudolstadt. The peak of its fame occurred between 1767 and 1797 when the factory was leased to Christian Fonne. A succession of owners followed.

Until 1800 the factory produced mostly ordinary tablewares. These were usually massive in design and decorated in the rococo style. Some fine vases decorated in rococo or formal styles were made. Decorative motifs included small portraits, landscapes, and ornamental maps.

Between 1898 and 1972 Karl Ens occupied one portion of the Volkstedt factory. The firm made decorative porcelains, figures, and gift articles. The company was nationalized in 1972 and named VEB Underglaze Porcelain Factory.

During the 20th century, Volkstedt manufactured tablewares, vases, and figures in the Meissen style.

Museum: Victoria & Albert Museum, London, England.

Cabaret Set, tray, 17¼" l, teapot, cov hot water jug, cream jug, 2 cov chocolate cups, stands, scenes of children at play in rural landscapes, gilded wreath borders, c1880, underglaze "blue X'd swords" mark, 13 pcs (A) **3198.00**

Compote, 8⅝" h, 9" d, figural, two children leaning on tree stump base, applied florals on base and bowl rim, hp roses on bowl int, autumn colors with gold trim **225.00**

Figure
2½" h, Spring as a farmer's wife with yellow

Figure, 11" h, 18½" l, off-white feathers, cobalt top, greenish body, pink legs and face, "green Karl Ens" mark, (A) $140.00

tled bonnet, black jacket, flower sprigged blouse and skirt, holding basket of vegetables, base with puce scrolls, from series of Four Seasons by Desoches, c1770, underglaze "blue F, X'd swords, star" incised marks (A) **790.00**

3½" l, 5½" h, girl in white lace dress with applied flowers, brown hair with comb, brown ballet shoes **160.00**

4⅛" h-6¾" h, monkey band, drummer, trumpeter, violinist, cellist, hurdy-gurdy player, bassonist, french horn, player, flutist, conductor, bright costumes, gilt scroll edged base, some restoration, late 19th C, underglaze "blue X'd swords" mark, 9 pcs (A) **1400.00**

6" h, "Canova Beauty," young girl in lavender floral dress with top, torch in left hand, lamp in right hand **140.00**

6½" l, 6½" h, girl in red dress seated on bench having flowers handed to her by crouching man in blue coat, "crown N" mark **450.00**

7" h, raven in natural colors **125.00**

7½" h, group of exotic ostriches in pink, gray, and blue, "Karl Ens" mark **125.00**

7⅞" h, two cherubs holding floral garlands, towing shell-shaped chariot, multicolored enamels, flat oval base, late 19th C (A) ... **247.00**

8½" l, 9" h, boy in red coat, girl in floral dress standing by baluster rail watching two swans **550.00**

9" l, period woman and man seated at chess table in colors **850.00**

9" l, 9½" h, woman in gold floral dress seated playing a lute, man standing at side in red coat holding music book **1050**

9½" h, standing woman in hat and robe holding fan, white, c1910 .... **110.00**

9⅞" h, young man in orange jacket and yellow breeches in tree with nest in hand, girl in orange bodice and puce skirt holding apron, birdcage on brown and green washed base, c1775 (A) **6283.00**

27½" h, exotic bird with sculpted feathers in colors, perched on white tree stump with green, brown, and purple applied vines, leaves, and grapes, c1921 (A) **5200.00**

30½" h, girl seated on tree stump, holding birdcage with parrot, white dress, yellow collar, white shoes with blue bows, purple bow in brown hair, c1922 (A) **1300.00**

Lamp Base, 9" h, figural lady holding basket of flowers in colors **135.00**

Milk Jug, 5⅞" h, painted silhouette of gentleman, reverse painted coat of arms in puce, gilt medallions, flanked by ribbon-tied floral swags, replaced lid (A) **1178.00**

Plate
9½" d, Vienna style, "Cornelia Vetterlein" in brocaded velvet dress, coiled plaited hair embellished with pearls, woodland landscape, castle in distance, dark green ground gilded with scrolling foliage and exotic birds, 1907–23, script title, printed mark (A) **1589.00**

11" d, center portrait bust of period woman in hex medallion, gilt shaped rim, c1800s, "Beyer and Bock" mark **150.00**

Potpourri Vase, Cov, 8½" h, pierced rococo form, two cartouches painted with clusters of fruit or flowers, molded shells, scrolls, and foli-

age, domed pierced cov with flower knob,
c1765, underglaze "blue X'd swords" mark
(A)...................................... **2430.00**
Vase, 24⅝" h, ovoid, applied colored flowers
and foliage, white ground, late 19th C...... **1900.00**

c1759-1769

WEDGWOOD
c1900

WEDGWOOD

**Burslem, near Stoke-on-Trent, England
1759–1769**

**Etruria factory, England
1769–1940**

**Barlaston, near Stoke-on-Trent, England
1940 to Present**

History: By 1759 Josiah Wedgwood was working in Burslem, Staffordshire manufacturing earthenware. A partnership with Bentley was formed shortly after he moved to his new factory in Etruria in 1769. The partnership lasted until 1780.

BLACK BASALT

Black Basalt was fine grained, unglazed black stoneware made between 1767 and 1796. This term was coined by Josiah Wedgwood to describe a refined version of "Egyptian black." In his 1787 catalog, Wedgwood described his ware as "a black porcelain biscuit (that is unglazed body) of nearly the same properties with the natural stone, striking fire from steel, receiving a high polish, serving as a touchstone for metals, resisting all acids, and bearing without injury a strong fire - stronger indeed than the basalts itself." "Egyptian Black" was used for utilitarian wares and for large relief plaques, vases, busts, medallions, seals, and small intaglios. It was a black clay body that resembled bronze when unpolished. Both historical and mythological figures and faces were produced.

BONE CHINA

When Josiah II took over, he introduced the manufacture of bone china in 1812. Production continued until 1828. Josiah II was not satisfied with the product, so it was discontinued. Bone china was not manufactured again until 1878.

The forty year period from 1840 to 1880 was one of modernization. Solid jasper was reintroduced. Parian ware, a fine white body resembling marble, was produced. When Wedgwood introduced majolica in 1860, the company was the first to use a white body and semi-transparent colored glazes.

When Wedgwood began to manufacture porcelain again in 1878, the products were of very high quality in texture, color, glaze, and decoration. The printed mark with the Portland vase was used on this porcelain.

Fourth and fifth generations of Wedgwoods continued to operate the firm into the 20th century. An interest in late 18th century design was revived. Commemorative wares were made for the American market.

CREAMWARE

Wedgwood's creamware utilized a Cornwall clay that created a lighter, stronger body of a more uniform texture. It became designated "Queensware" after Wedgwood supplied a breakfast set for Queen Charlotte in 1762.

JASPER

Jasper, probably Josiah Wedgwood's best known product, was started in 1774. Known as a "dry body" because it as non-porous and unglazed, this vitreous fine stoneware was made in several shades of blue, green, lilac, yellow, maroon, black, and white. Sometimes more than one color was combined. "Solid" jasper had the body colored throughout; white jasper "dip" was a white jasper body with the color laid on the surface. Raised figures and ornaments in white adorned the tremendous variety of jasper shapes. Classical motifs were most prominent. Wedgwood's replica of the Barberini or Portland vase was considered a high point in the production.

PEARLWARE

Pearlware, introduced by Wedgwood in 1779, was whiter than Queensware. Cobalt oxide was added to the glaze, reacting like a laundry blueing that whitens clothing.

After Bentley's death in 1780, Wedgwood worked alone until 1790 when his sons and Thomas Byerley became his partners. From 1769 until 1780 the firm was called "Wedgwood and Bentley." It was simply "Wedgwood" in the decade from 1780 to 1790. The name became "Wedgwood Sons and Byerley" between 1790 and 1793 and "Wedgwood & Sons & Byerley" between 1793 and 1795. Josiah Wedgwood died in 1795.

REDWARES

Other "dry bodies" or redwares made that were manufactured between 1776 and 1870 included a) cane ware (pale buff colored stoneware); b) rosso antico (dark red to chocolate colored unglazed stoneware); c) terra cotta (light red stoneware); d) drabware (olive gray stoneware); and, e) white stoneware (pure white biscuit). Both utilitarian and decorative wares were made.

WEDGWOOD LUSTERS

Wedgwood lusters were formed by applying iridescent or metallic films on the surface of the ceramic wares. The effect was obtained by using metallic oxides of gold, silver, copper, etc. Lusters were applied as embellishments to an enamelled object or as a complete or near complete covering to duplicate the effect of a silver or copper metallic object. The lusters were decorated by the resist method.

From 1915 to 1931 Wedgwood produced fairyland lusters from the designs of Daisy Makeig-Jones. Fairyland lusters were made in Queensware plaques and bone china plates and ornamental pieces, such as vases and bowls. The designs combined the use of bright underglaze colors, commercial lusters, and gold printing, often with fantastic and grotesque figures, scenes, and landscapes.

Pattern numbers were painted on the base of fairyland luster pieces by the artist who decorated them along with the Wedgwood marks.

A new factory was built at Barlaston, six miles from Etruria. Firing was done at Barlaston in six electric ovens. Production started at the new factory in 1940. Etruria eventually was closed in June 1950.

On May 1, 1959, the company commemorated its bicentenary. During the 1960s, Wedgwood acquired many

English firms such as Coalport, William Adams & Sons, Royal Tuscan, Susie Cooper, and Johnson Brothers. Further expansion in the 1970s brought J. & G. Meakin, Midwinter Companies, Crown Staffordshire, Mason's Ironstone, and Precision Studios into the fold. Each company retained its own identity. The Wedgwood Group is one of the largest fine china and earthenware manufacturers in the world.

References: M. Batkin, *Wedgwood Ceramics 1846–1959,* Richard Denis Publications; David Buten, *18th Century Wedgwood,* Methuen, Inc. 1980; Alison Kelly, *The Story of Wedgwood,* The Viking Press, 1975; Wolf Mankowitz, *Wedgwood,* Spring Books, 1966; Robin Reilly, *Wedgwood,* 2 vols., Stockton Press, 1989; Robin Reilly & George Savage, *The Dictionary of Wedgwood,* Antique Collectors' Club, Ltd, 1980; Geoffrey Wills, *Wedgwood,* Chartwell Books, Inc., 1989.

Collectors Club: The Wedgwood Society, The Buten Museum of Wedgwood, 246 N. Bowman Avenue, Merion, Pa. Membership: &10.00.; The Wedgwood Society, The Roman Villa, Rockbourne, Fordingbridge, Hents. SP6 3 PG, England. Membership: 7 1/2 pounds. Wedgwood Data Chart, semi-annual newsletter; The Wedgwood Society of New York, 5 Dogwood Court, Glen Head, New York, 11545. Membership: $22.50, Ars Ceramic Magazine.

Museums: Birmingham Museum of Art, Birmingham, Alabama; The Brooklyn Museum, Brooklyn, NY; Buten Museum of Wedgwood, Merion, Pennsylvania; City Museum & Art Gallery, Stoke-on-Trent, England; Henry E. Huntington Library & Art Gallery, San Marino, California; R. W. Norton Art Gallery, Shreveport, Louisiana; Victoria & Albert Museum, London, England; Wedgwood Museum, Barlaston, England.

REPRODUCTION ALERT: Two marks are currently in use on Wedgwood pieces. If neither of these marks appear on a piece, it is probably not Wedgwood.

BASALT

Bowl
2 3/8" h, 4 3/8" d, classical scenes, imp "WEDGWOOD" mark (A) 50.00
4 3/8" h, 4 7/8" d, classical scenes and garlands (A) 160.00
Box, Cov, 4" h, 3 1/2" d, round, black with white cameo design of servants carrying dishes of fruit, cherubs 75.00
Bust
1 7/8" h, classical female, wood base decorated to simulate Wedgwood, late 18th C (A) 440.00
9 3/4" h, Newton, imp Wedgwood and Bentley mark (A) 2600.00
11 1/2" h, Prior, circ base, "WEDGWOOD" mark 750.00
14" h, John Bunyan on raised circ base, imp "WEDGWOOD" mark (A) 1210.00
14 1/2" h, Shakespeare, imp Wedgwood and Bentley mark (A) 4200.00
15 1/2" h, Marcus Aurelius, head turned to right, wearing cloak, imp "MARCUS AURELIUS" on waisted circ socle, circ ebonized wood base, 1774–80, imp "Wedgwood & Bentley" mark (A) 3575.00
18" h, Mercury, imp "WEDGWOOD" mark (A) 1000.00
Candlestick
7 3/4" h, classical figures and scroll designs (A) 100.00

8 1/4" h, modeled dolphin on rect base with seashells, upturned tail terminating in leaf molded sconce, repairs, late 18th C, pr (A) .   1430.00
Creamer, 3 1/8" h, helmet shape, engine-turned checkerboard pattern 300.00
Figure
2 7/8" h, 4 5/8" l, bulldog, imp "WEDGWOOD" mark (A) 250.00
3 1/2" h, 4 3/4" l, elephant, imp "WEDGWOOD" mark (A) 310.00
3 1/2" h, 5" l, walking elephant, yellow glass eyes, white jasper tusks, c1919, "Wedgwood, Made in England" mark 425.00
4 1/2" h, seated raven on oval base, tail repaired, imp "WEDGWOOD" mark (A) . . .   165.00
4 1/2" l, figure of nude sleeping child on blanket, rect base, imp "WEDGWOOD" mark (A) 935.00
4 3/4" l, modeled walking bear, c1913, "WEDGWOOD" mark (A) 825.00

Figure, 7" h, 9" l, sgd "Skeeping," imp "WEDGWOOD" mark, $895.00

7 1/4" h, bison in standing pose, molded grass between legs, irreg rect base, c1927, sgd "Skeaping' (A) 880.00
Inkstand, 3 3/4" h, urn shape quill holder with dbl handles ending in dbl sided stand, circ inkwell and sander with molded shell motif on cov, late 18th C, "Wedgwood" mark (A) 1870.00
Jar, Lid, 3" h, 4 1/4" d, classical figures, imp "WEDGWOOD" mark (A) 80.00
Medallion, 2 3/4" , 2 1/4" w, relief of Marius facing left, titled below, self framed, c1775, Wedgwood and Bentley (A) 220.00
Oil Lamp
5 1/2" h, Rosso Antico applied leaves, handle and sunburst, molded beaded trim, early 19th C (A) 522.00
6 1/2" h, four shell molded wick holders on rim, cov with knob, circular waist on sq base, late 18th C (A) 990.00
Pitcher, 7 3/8" h, classical figures and putti, imp "WEDGWOOD" mark (A) 160.00
Plaque
4" h, 5" w, lavender and white oval, three putti with globe, imp "WEDGWOOD" mark (A) 350.00
7 3/8" h, 5 1/2" w, oval shape, Hercules and the two headed bull, imp "WEDGWOOD" mark (A) 400.00
8 1/2" h, 8" w, "The Beloved of the Great

Enchantress," gilded panel of King Tut and Queen Ankhesenamun, wood frame, 1974 (A) **465.00**

Potpourri Vase, Cov, 12" h, globular body with molded trailing vines, three figural fish supports from waisted triangular foot, pierced lattice cov, c1900, pr (A) **6000.00**

Sucrier, Cov, 4¹/₈" h, framed medallion of classical scenes in relief, molded stiff leaf border, imp "WEDGWOOD" mark (A) **302.00**

Tankard, wide band of acorns, branches, and leaves in relief on wide center band, late 18th C, imp "WEDGWOOD" mark (A) **410.00**

Teapot
  4¹/₂" h, globular shape, cane pattern, c1820, imp "WEDGWOOD" mark **695.00**
  7³/₄" d, squat shape, "Capri" enamel floral decoration (A) **128.00**

Tea and Coffee Service, Miniature, teapot, brazier for kettle, cov tea caddy, cov sucrier, milk jug, slop bowl, 3 coffee cups, 5 tea bowls, 3 saucers, late 18th C, 20 pcs (A) **2337.00**

Tea Service, Part, teapots, 8¹/₂" l, 8" l, glazed floral designs, 2 saucers, 1 cup, 1 handleless cup, imp "WEDGWOOD" mark, 6 pcs (A) **100.00**

Tray, 10¹/₈" l, 7¹/₂" w, oct, raised classical scene, raised leaf border, mid 19th C, imp "WEDGWOOD" mark.................... **375.00**

Urn, 7" h, ovoid shape with neoclassical design, three down curving legs, shaped base, late 19th C, pr (A) **385.00**

Vase
  6¹¹/₁₆" h, dbl spouted, relief decorated, front with "Sportive Love," sides with ram's head masks, body surmounted with putto seated between two spirally fluted spouts, 19th C, imp "WEDGWOOD and W" marks (A) .. **1650.00**
  7" h, relief of Seasons on each side, fluted neck, acanthus molded loop handles, sq base, c1775, Wedgwood and Bentley (A). **1320.00**
  7³/₈" h, ram's head and swag design, imp "WEDGWOOD Made in England" mark (A)................................. **110.00**
  7¹/₂" h, putti and garlands design, imp "WEDGWOOD" mark (A) **130.00**
  7¹/₂" h, 5³/₈" d, flared lip, geometric and rams head design, imp "WEDGWOOD" mark (A) **130.00**
  11¹/₂" h, canopic-modeled head of Egyptian, fluted neck, sq base, c1775, Wedgwood and Bentley (A) **6050.00**
  11³/₄" h, decorated in relief with swags of drapery suspended between two smiling masks, shoulder with Greek key border below molded scales surmounted by fish tail handle, sq base with panels, 1770–80, imp "WEDGWOOD & BENTLEY:ETRURIA. circ mark," pr (A) **14,300.00**
  13" h, ovoid shape, matte orange-brown with classical bearded man and lady flanking an altar, key fret border, dbl handles, c1800, imp "WEDGWOOD' (A)................ **2871.00**

Vase, Cov
  6³/₄" h, classical female reliefs to sides, serpent handles terminating in male masks, fluted neck, sq base, restorations, c1775, Wedgwood and Bentley (A)............. **2420.00**
  9¹/₄" h, raised scenes of children, zodiac border with beaded trim, loop handles, sq base, c1775, Wedgwood and Bentley (A)...... **2640.00**

  12" h, medallion of "The Three Graces" on front, sq base, female head handles hung with garlands, beaded rim, cov with sibyl knob, c1775, imp "WEDGWOOD & BENTLEY:ETRURUA.circ mark' (A)............. **2750.00**
  15¹/₂" h, dbl ogee body, swags of drapery pendant from four goats' head handles, knobed domed cov, repaired, c1770–80, "WEDGWOOD & BENTLEY" mark (A) ... **3053.00**

GENERAL

Baking Dish, 11¹/₂" l, yelloware, applied vintage and vegetables, glazed insert, imp "Wedgwood" mark (A)......................... **214.00**

Bough Pot, Lid, 14³/₄" h, ironstone, "Eastern Flowers" pattern, blue floral motif, gilt trim, yellow ground, pierced lid, restorations, pr (A)...................................... **600.00**

Bowl, 3⁵/₈" h, 7" d, drabware, basketweave pattern, flared lip, imp "WEDGWOOD" mark (A) **200.00**

Candlestick, 9¹/₂" h, modeled dolphin with upright tail terminating in leaf molded sconce, rect base bordered with shells, pink glaze, hairlines on base, c1869, pr (A) **770.00**

Chop Plate, 12¹/₂" d, "Kutani" pattern **75.00**

Cream and Sugar, "Old Vine" pattern **20.00**

Creamer
  2¹/₂" h, 5" w, drabware, light brown, c1840 . **175.00**
  2³/₄" h, Rosso Antico, applied grape and vine decor (A)............................. **175.00**

Cup and Saucer, encaustic, rust enamel trim, spiral handle (A) **175.00**

Dinner Service, Part, oval platter, 16⁵/₈" l, 6 oval platters, 10¹/₂" l, 30 dinner plates, 9⁷/₈" d, pearlware "Water Lily" pattern, transfer printed in sepia with shades of salmon and gold with lily and two lotus plants in pond, gilt edged rim, 1808–11, imp "WEDGWOOD" mark, 37 pcs (A) **5500.00**

Dish
  9³/₄" l, bone china, oval shape, view of "Cottage at Pinxton" within gilt rim, c1815 (A)................................... **486.00**
  12¹/₂" d, Turkish figures by mosque, wide floral border, blue transfer, deep well, c1830 (A) **451.00**

Game Pie Dish, Cov, Liner, 8¹/₂" h, oval shape, caneware, leaf, vine, and floral decoration with dead game, crouching rabbit finial, c1870, imp "Wedgwood" and date code (A) **280.00**

Game Pie Pot, 10" l, 6¹/₂" h, oval shape, pale red clay, molded animals, hare handle, c1865................................... **850.00**

Honey Pot, 4" h, attached underplate, beehive shape, white stoneware (A)............... **130.00**

Milk Pitcher
  6¹/₄" h, 4¹/₂" d, light olive green with encircling Grecian garden scene with floral band above and below, "Wedgwood/England" mark................................... **150.00**
  6³/₈" h, hex, bone china, Imari colors, c1880 .... **225.00**

Pitcher
  6³/₈" h, drabware, six panels with relief of ladies and scrollwork **195.00**
  6¹/₂" h, copper grapes on cream ground... **42.00**

Plaque
  4¹/₄" h, 3¹/₂" w, Rosso Antico, bust of Tibe-

rius with underglazed white and black speckles on face, 18th C, imp "WEDG-WOOD/TIBERIUS" mark (A) **900.00**

15⅛" d, pottery, blue and white bust of lady holding fan, ribbon in hair or bust of lady with morning glories in hair, butterfly on hand, pierced for hanging, dtd 1877, pr . .   **495.00**

Plate

7" d, glazed drabware, gold lines, c1830 . . .   **70.00**

8⅝" d, Queen's Ware, enameled, each with different large and small floral and foliate sprigs within feather molded rim edged in purple, shades of purple on deep cream colored body, 1769–77, set of 6 (A) **1320.00**

8¾" d, Ivanhoe series, "Urfried Relating Her Story to Cedric," cobalt transfer on white ground **40.00**

9" d, "Horticultural," blue and white transfer, c1840, imp "WEDGWOOD" mark **225.00**

9¼" d, blue and white transfer of Bunker Hill Monument **25.00**

9½" d, Ivanhoe series, "Rebecca Repelling the Templar," blue transfer **80.00**

9¾" d, Queensware, "Nautilus" design, Guy Green pattern 83, green shell edge, c1777–8, imp "WEDGWOOD" mark **375.00**

10" d

Boston Library, blue transfer, c1900 . . . . . .   **40.00**

Ivanhoe series, "Wamba and Gunch the Swine Herd," black and caramel brown   **40.00**

10½" d, "Month of May," polychrome scene of Kate Greenaway type children . .   **135.00**

Platter

12¾" l, pearlware, "Argyle" pattern, border of green-yellow leaves, turquoise ground, gold accents, c1860, imp "WEDGWOOD" mark **110.00**

17" l, stoneware, blue transfer scene of cows (A) **175.00**

18" l, "Kutani" pattern **75.00**

Potpourri, 8¾" h, 7" d, 10" w, caneware, grape vine patterning on sq base, imp "WEDGWOOD" mark (A)650.00

Punch Bowl, 12" d, Harvard Tercentenary in red transfer. **275.00**

Soup Plate, 9¾" d, "The Festoon" pattern, river scene with columned structures behind fishing boats, border of draped floral garlands, blue transfer, gilt trim, c1872, set of 6 (A) . . .   **185.00**

Sugar Bowl, Cov, 4½" h, 4" d, caneware, cherubs, imp "WEDGWOOD" mark (A) **230.00**

Tea Caddy, 4½" h, black transfer of man with sheep, man and woman on bench in landscape on reverse, c1770, imp "WEDGWOOD" mark **550.00**

Teapot

4" h, caneware, pentagonal body molded as cluster of bamboo stalks, inset cov with coiled bamboo sprig knob, 1775–80, imp "Wedgwood & Bentley' (A) **2750.00**

4¼" h, caneware, beehive effect, molded with horiz bands of bound reeds and applied with raffia bound scroll handle and tapering spout, handle repaired, c1800 (A)   **1000.00**

5¾" h, globular, bands of colored chintz like pattern extending over inset cov, small iron-red and black ladybird motifs continuing over handle, leaf molded spout, pierced knob, c1770 (A) **4500.00**

10⅜" w, white glazed stoneware, molded

Vase, Cov, 7½" h, diceware, white cameos of "Pegasus cared for by Nymphs," "Bellerophon watering Pegasus at the Sacred Spring," "Ulysseus staying the Chariot of Victory," and "Aurora in her Chariot," green ground, diceware on blue ground on base and cov, early 19th C, (A) **$1520.00**

stylized floral pattern, gilt trim, finial shaped as spaniel seated on pillow, c1820 (A) . . .   **130.00**

Urn, Cov, 11" h, pink diapering with gilding on white ground, early 19th C (A) **990.00**

Vase, 5½" h, bulbous shape, Queensware, everted rim, circ base, molded floral and leaf decoration, hp dot and floral fields, printed "WEDGWOOD ETRURIA ENGLAND, Ovington Brothers" mark (A). **715.00**

Vase, Cov, 11¼" h, decorated in relief with border of bow-tied drapery swags, body marbleized in tones of brown, gray, apricot, and ochre, green int, cov with ball knob, creamware handles, black basalt base, repaired, c1775, imp "WEDGWOOD & BENTLEY: ETRURIA.circ mark' (A). **1210.00**

Vegetable Bowl, Cov, "Patrician" pattern **55.00**

JASPER

Biscuit Box, 7¾" h, 5" d, yellow with SP rim, lid, and handle, imp "WEDGWOOD" mark (A).   **300.00**

Biscuit Jar

6" h, 5¼" d,

White cameos of classical women, dark blue ground, SP top, rim, and handle, "WEDGWOOD ENGLAND" mark. **150.00**

White classic cameos on yellow ground, "WEDGWOOD ENGLAND" mark. **575.00**

6¼" h, white cameos of classic figures and trees on sage green center band, lavender bands top and base, SP cov, "WEDG-WOOD" mark. **695.00**

6¾" h, 4¾" d, white cameos of classic women and cupids on dark blue ground, SP top, rim, handle, and ball ftd base, "WEDG-WOOD" mark. **150.00**

9" H-H, lavender bands at top and bottom,

white classic cameos on sage green ground, SP handle and rim............... **925.00**

Bowl, 4³⁄₈" d, white cameos of mythological figures on dark blue ground, "WEDGWOOD" mark.................. **70.00**

Cache Pot, white classical figures on med green ground, restored, "WEDGWOOD/ENGLAND" mark, pr (A)................ **75.00**

Candlestick

  6" h, white classical cameos on olive green ground, "WEDGWOOD ENGLAND" mark **75.00**

  10¹⁄₂" h, figure of Ceres or Cybele in white jasper holding green jasper cornucopia terminating in leaf molded sconce, green jasper circ base on sq base with applied stiff leaves, c1800, "WEDGWOOD" marks, pr (A)............................ **1540.00**

Chimney Piece Tablet, 22¹⁄₂" h, 5³⁄₄" w, 10¹⁄₄" h, 5³⁄₄" w, white jasper relief, one with bow tied ribbon suspending classical ewer and scabbard hung with floral wreath, other with flaming pedestal hung with floral swags, green body, framed and glazed, late 18th C (A)......................... **4250.00**

Cheese Dish, Cov, 9¹⁄₄" d, white classical cameos on dark blue ground, domed cov, imp "WEDGWOOD ENGLAND" mark (A)...... **220.00**

Chocolate Pot, 6" h, white classical cameos on dark blue ground.................. **135.00**

Clock, 9¹⁄₄" h, 6³⁄₄" w, white classic cameos on light green ground, "WEDGWOOD" mark............................. **795.00**

Coffee Can and Saucer, 2¹⁄₂" h

  White cameos of trophies, ram's heads, and floral garlands, lilac medallions on light blue ground, imp "WEDGWOOD" marks (A) . **880.00**

  White relief with festoons of fruit pendant from ribboned ram's heads enclosing trophies and green ground medallions with putti at various pursuits, blue dip ground, 19th C, imp "WEDGWOOD" mark (A) .. **605.00**

Hair Receiver, 3¹⁄₂" h, white cameos of classical figures in cartouches, hearts, flowers, and leaves on cov, dark blue ground, "WEDGWOOD" mark...................... **145.00**

Jam Jar, 3⁷⁄₈" h, 3¹⁄₂" d, black cameos of garlands of grapes and leaves joined to lion's heads with ring in mouth, gold ground, SP lid and spoon, imp "Wedgwood, England" mark............................. **295.00**

Jar, Cov, 3" h, white cameos of classical figures in medallions, stiff leaves on cov, dark blue ground, "WEDGWOOD ENGLAND" mark . **95.00**

Jewel Box, 4¹⁄₂" l, 2" h, white cameos of grapes and vines on green ground, "WEDGWOOD, MADE IN ENGLAND" mark.............. **60.00**

Jug

  6³⁄₈" h, tankard shape, white cameos of classical women, Cupids, and grapes on dark blue ground, "WEDGWOOD" mark **135.00**

  6¹⁄₂" h, blue and white with pewter lid, classical figures and putti, imp "WEDGWOOD" mark (A) **180.00**

Medallion

  1⁷⁄₈" h, 1¹⁄₂" w, white cameo bust of Frederick William II on dark blue ground, brass frame, Wedgwood and Bentley (A)...... **605.00**

  3¹⁄₂" h, 2⁷⁄₈" w, white and rose portrait of Princess Elizabeth, imp "WEDGWOOD" mark (A) **270.00**

4¹⁄₂" h, 2³⁄₈" w, blue and white portraits of Benjamin Franklin and Lafayette, imp "WEDGWOOD" mark, pr (A).......... **130.00**

Milk Pitcher, 6" h, white cameos of maidens, peacock, cherubs, trees, and floral bouquet, light blue ground........................ **150.00**

Pin Tray, 1¹⁄₂" l, 1" w, lavender with relief of Cupids and chariot being pulled by lions, floral relief.................................. **40.00**

Pitcher

  2¹⁄₂" h, white cameos of classical figures on crimson ground, c1920, imp "WEDGWOOD, MADE IN ENGLAND" mark (A). **605.00**

  6" h, bulbous shape, white mythological figures on dark blue ground, "WEDGWOOD ENGLAND" mark **125.00**

  6¹⁄₄" h, white classic cameos on dark blue ground, "WEDGWOOD" mark.......... **125.00**

  7¹⁄₂" h, white cameo medallions of Franklin and Hamilton, olive green ground, "Wedgwood, England" mark................... **350.00**

  8¹⁄₄" h, white classical cameos on olive green ground, rope twist handle, imp "WEDGWOOD ENGLAND" mark (A).......... **220.00**

Plaque

  2" h, 6⁷⁄₈" w, white cameos of two classical figures with bows amid scroll motif, blue ground, imp "WEDGWOOD" mark (A) .. **250.00**

  2" h, 3" w, oval, yellow, white, and blue, two classical figures within scrolled border (A) **450.00**

  3¹⁄₂" h, 8⁵⁄₈" w, white cameos of five classical figures in theatrical setting, black ground, imp "WEDGWOOD" mark (A) .. **250.00**

  4" d, white cameo of "Pegasus," light blue ground, imp "WEDGWOOD" mark...... **125.00**

  4¹⁄₄" h, oval, white relief with portrait of Duke of York in military uniform, blue ground, imp "Wedgwood," incised "Duke York' (A)... **378.00**

  5³⁄₄" h, 11¹⁄₂" w, white cameos of "Dancing Hours', blue ground, imp "WEDGWOOD" mark (A) **700.00**

  5⁷⁄₈" h, 8¹⁄₄" w, white cameos of marriage of Cupid and Psyche, blue ground (A) **650.00**

  6¹⁄₄" h, 20³⁄₄" l, white cameos of Achilles in Scyros among the daughters of Lycomedes, blue ground, imp "WEDGWOOD" mark (A)................................ **1330.00**

  8¹⁄₂" d, white cameos of Cupids around border, green ground, "Wedgwood, England" mark............................... **235.00**

  9³⁄₈" h, 6³⁄₈" w, oval, white cameos of standing classical figures of women, blue ground, imp "WEDGWOOD" mark, pr (A)....... **400.00**

  9¹⁄₂" h, 26" w, blue, "Sacrifice to Love," decorated with figures bringing ox and flowers to Cupid on altar, imp "WEDGWOOD" mark (A) **2300.00**

  12" l, 6" h, center panel of white cameos of "Dancing Hours" on light blue ground, white leaf border, green outer border, c1840, imp "WEDGWOOD" mark (A)... **1650.00**

  13¹⁄₂" l, 6" w, white cameos of seven graces on light blue ground................... **495.00**

Ring Tree, 2³⁄₄" h, post in center, panels of white cameos of classic ladies and border of flowers on blue ground, "WEDGWOOD" mark............................... **145.00**

Tea Caddy, 5³⁄₄" h, white and black classical figures on yellow ground, "WEDGWOOD ENGLAND" mark **1575.00**

Teapot

3⅞" h, cylindrical shape, white festoons of fruit hanging from rams' heads, panels with trophies and oval medallions of classical vignettes on lilac ground, solid blue ground, imp "Wedgwood' (A)................. **1224.00**

4½" h, 7½" l

White classical cameos on blue ground, acanthus leaves on lid................ **350.00**

White classical cameos on dark olive green ground........................... **150.00**

Tea Set

Teapot, 7¾" l, cov sugar bowl, creamer, white classical cameos on dark blue ground, late 19th C, "WEDGWOOD, ENGLAND" marks (A)........................... **275.00**

Teapot, 8" l, sugar, creamer, white classical figures on sage green ground, 1890 imp "WEDGWOOD" mark **375.00**

Urn

7⅞" h, blue and white, handles decorated with classical figures (A) **425.00**

8" h, 5⅝" d, yellow with black foliage pattern, imp "WEDGWOOD" mark (A) **450.00**

Urn, Cov

7" h, white cameos of "Dancing Hours" on green ground, repaired, "Wedgwood, Made in England" mark, pr............. **450.00**

8¼" h, four white medallions with garlands and rams heads, green ground, "WEDGWOOD" mark........................ **695.00**

9½" h, white classical figures and leaves on lavender ground, dbl handles, sq base, "WEDGWOOD" mark **1190.00**

Vase

3½" h, beaker shape, white classical figures in landscape, black ground, "Wedgwood, Made in England" mark................ **75.00**

5⅛" h,

White cameos of four seasons on blue ground, "WEDGWOOD ENGLAND" mark, c1892–1915.................. **88.00**

White cameos of Cupids, man, and girl with dogs on dark blue ground, pr, "WEDGWOOD" marks...................... **175.00**

6½" h, cylinder shape, white classic cameos of ladies, black ground, white floral border, "WEDGWOOD" mark **175.00**

Bowl, 7" d, Dragon luster, gold dragon and phoenix birds, blue-green ext, mottled lt green int, #Z4831, "gold Portland vase, Wedgwood, Made in England" mark, $500.00

7½" h, blue, green, and white, with SP lip, classical figures on horseback, imp "WEDGWOOD" mark (A) **375.00**

7¾" h, Portland, white relief on dark blue ground, imp "ENGLAND" mark (A) **465.00**

9½" h, copy of Portland, black with white glazed design, classical figures in garden setting, imp "WEDGWOOD" mark (A)... **400.00**

9⅞" h, Portland, blue with white relief of classical figures in Arcadian setting, base with Phrygian head, handles strung with masks, 19th C, imp mark (A) **1215.00**

LUSTER

Bowl

3½" d, 2" h, Butterfly, Z4830........... **65.00**

4" d

Dragon, man on camel in gilt on int, dragon ext, blue scale ext, gold int border, printed "WEDGWOOD" mark **225.00**

Oct, Flame Fairyland, int with "Elves and Bell Branch" design of elves on shaded green ground, ext with "Poplar Trees" pattern on Italianate views, printed "Wedgwood, Made in England" mark (A) **300.00**

5" d, Hummingbird **148.00**

5½" d, 3" h, Dragon luster, orange mottled ext, blue int, gold dragon in center, #Z4825, "Portland vase" mark **325.00**

6½" d, Butterfly, flame ext, cobalt int **375.00**

Teapot, 6" h, 7" l, stoneware, white body, recumbent spaniel on lid, c1817, $1000.00

7½" d, oct panels, Fairyland, "Castle on a Road" on ext, "Bird in a Hoop" on int, #Z25125, c1920 (A).................... **3300.00**

8¹⁄₁₆" d, Fairyland, ext painted in tones of pink, green, magenta, black, yellow, and brown with "Garden of Paradise," int with "Jumping Fawn" in tones of green, blue, yellow, and red-violet, foot painted with "Flaming Wheel" border on blue ground, c1920, "gold-over-brown-printed Portland Vase WEDGWOOD MADE IN ENGLAND Z4968, Z in black" marks (A) **3300.00**

8⅛" d, Fruit, int with gold outlined multicolored grapes and peaches in center, fruits on sides, mottled red-orange luster ground, ext with gold outlined fruit, mottled blue luster ground, "Portland vase" mark **550.00**

8¼" d, center cartouche with yellow tiger

with black stripes, hunter with umbrella, black and white border, white ext, impressed and printed "WEDGWOOD and DM Jones" marks **295.00**

8½" d, Oct

Dragon, int with large gold dragons on mottled blue luster ground, ext with large gold dragons on mottled orange-red luster ground, #Z4825, "Portland vase" mark **450.00**

Fairyland, "Moorish" ext, "Smoke Ribbons" on int **2710.00**

8⅝" d, Butterfly, orange speckled int with gold butterflies, border with cartouche with oriental pagoda in rust, ext with pale irid blue butterflies, gold printed "WEDGWOOD" mark **895.00**

8⅞" d, Fairyland, int with "Elves and Bell Branch" pattern, little folks and fairies amongst cobwebs, ext with "Poplar Trees" pattern against dark green ground, gilt details, 1920s, printed "urn mark Z 4966" (A) **1496.00**

9" d, Oriental, orange, green, and pink with black and gold highlights, "Wedgwood, Made in England" mark (A) **575.00**

9⅛" d, Dragon, blue ext, pale turquoise int with orange and gilt dragons, int border cartouche with pagoda, gold printed "WEDGWOOD" mark **995.00**

9½" d, Fairyland, "Poplar Trees" on ext, "Woodland Elves III-Feather Hat" on int, #Z4968, c1920 (A) **3300.00**

10⅝" d, Fairyland, int with "Woodland Bridge" pattern, central circ medallion with mermaid holding mirror, ext with "Poplar Trees" pattern, 1920s, printed "Portland mark, Z4968" (A) **1683.00**

11½" d, oct, Fairyland, "Boxing Match" on int, "Castle on a Road" on ext. **4000.00**

Box, Cov, 6" d, fire eating tigers in gilt, pale irid int with geometric designs, red woman finial, green luster ground. **995.00**

Cup and Saucer, Fairyland, "Leapfrogging Elves," Z4968 . . . . **750.00**

Dessert Dish, 10¼" l, shaped oval, Moonlight, paneled rim, c1805, imp "WEDGWOOD" mark **850.00**

Dessert Plate, 8¼" d, shell shape, Moonlight, c1810, imp "WEDGWOOD" mark **1250.00**

Dessert Service, Part, fruit comport and stand, 8½" h, 12 dessert plates, 6 shaped dishes in sizes, Moonlight, molded pectin and nautilus shell forms, purple, orange, and gray-green splashes, repairs, c1810–20 (A) **9000.00**

Dish, 13" l, shell form, Moonlight, c1810 . . . . . **525.00**

Jug, 5½" h, Moonlight, shades of purple with touches of orange, imp "WEDGWOOD" mark **750.00**

Melba Cup, 3" h, 4¼" d, Fairyland, "Leapfrogging Elves" design, #Z4968 . . . . **750.00**

Pitcher

2" h, bulbous blue ext, red int lip **260.00**

4" h, Moonlight, purple and orange shades, imp "WEDGWOOD' mark **750.00**

5⅛" h, Moonlight, blue line decoration around rim and handle, imp "WEDGWOOD" mark **795.00**

Plaque, 10⅞" l, 10⅞" w, Rect, Fairyland "Elves in a Pine Tree" design, little folks at

leisurely pursuits in pine tree, spider in cobweb, wide blue ground and gilt border, 1920s, printed "Portland vase mark and Z5154" (A) **4488.00**

"Torches," scene of steps illuminated by fairy lights rising from lake to easter palace, overhung with tall tree entwined by serpent and supporting bird's nest, branches hung with Chinese lanterns, several pixies and elves at play, mother-of-pearl luster border, 1920s, sgd "S.M. Makeig-Jones," printed urn mark, Z5331 (A) **4862.00**

Plate, 10⅝" d, Fairyland, "Boys on a Bridge," light green bat over boy in boat near bridge, orange border with gilt flowers and leaves, printed "Portland vase mark and W558" (A) **2375.00**

Punch Bowl, 11" d, 6" h, Butterfly, white pearl ext, coral int, large gold butterflies, #Z4832, "Portland vase" mark **995.00**

Tumbler, 2¼" h, orange and black ext, green int with gold creatures **255.00**

Tray, 13¼" d, Fairyland, int painted with "Fairy Gondola," ext printed with "Flight of Birds" and "Pebble and Grass" borders on green and blue mottled ground, c1920, gold printed "Portland Vase, WEDGWOOD MADE IN ENGLAND, Z49468 and red arrow" marks (A) **3630.00**

Urn, Cov, 11¼" h, Dragon, magenta and gilt, "WEDGWOOD" mark **895.00**

Vase

4⅜" h, Hummingbird, multicolored hummingbirds outlined in gold, bands of gold geese, mottled blue luster ground, mottled orange-red luster int, "Portland vase" mark **195.00**

5" h, Butterfly, four multicolored butterflies on ivory luster ground, orange int, gold neck. **175.00**

5¼" h, dragon and cricket on blue luster ground, #Z4829 . . . . **305.00**

7⅞" h, Fairyland, "Butterfly Woman," winged maidens seated in flowering branches, midnight blue ground, flared rim with pixies and birds, c1920s, #Z4968 . . **550.00**

8¼" h, "Rainbow Landscape" design, "Portland Vase" mark **2395.00**

8½" h

Butterfly, med blue ext, irid int, multicolored butterflies int and ext, ftd, printed "WEDGWOOD" mark **795.00**

Butterfly, orange ext, green int, pedestal base **995.00**

Dragon, blue ext, mottled green int, pr . . . **1200.00**

Fairyland

"Candlemas" design, #Z5157, c1920 (A) **2640.00**

"Goblins" design, brown fairies with orange wings, multicolored ground, #Z5367 . . . . **1600.00**

8⅝" h, Fairyland, black, orange, green, blue, pink, and gilt Chinese pagodas, bridges, and "Chinese Lighthouse," three tree trunks, Chinese lanterns and foliage on shoulders, Z5300, "Portland vase" mark (A) **2150.00**

9" h

Hummingbird, green and orange hummingbirds on speckled blue ground, gilt accents, orange luster int (A) **900.00**

Ovoid shape, Argus Pheasant luster pattern in red and gold, mottled blue ground,

flared lip, "Portland vase and Z5486"
mark (A) **2470.00**
11½" h, cylindrical body, Flame Fairyland,
"Torches" pattern incorporating steps leading to palace lit by torches, serpent and little
fork with tree nearby, flared foot and rim
with "Flaming Wheel" border, 1920s, sgd
"S.M. Makeig-Jones," printed "urn mark,
Z4968, 3177" (A) **2057.00**
Vase, Cov, Fairyland
8⅜" h, ovoid form, elephants and attendants
beneath birds and giraffes crossing bridge
behind festooned pillars, domed cov with
foliage, 1920s, printed "Portland vase mark,
2351, Z5266" (A) **1940.00**
11" h, "Jeweled Tree" design with "Copper
Trees" and "Cat and Mouse" panels on lustrous mauve ground, domed cov with button finial, 1920s, gilt "Portland vase mark,
Z4968, 2046" marks (A) **2618.00**

WHIELDON WARE

Fenton Vivien, Stoke-on-Trent, England
1740–1780

History: Thomas Whieldon founded his earthenware factory at Little Fenton in 1740. He began potting small items
such as boxes, cutlery handles, chimney pieces, and teapots. Whieldon introduced various metallics into the clay
to alter the color of the earthenware body.

Whieldon experimented with colored glazes, attempting to imitate tortoise shell. Most Whieldon ware is either
mottled brownish or greenish in tone.

Several noted potters apprenticed with Whieldon. Josiah Spode is probably the most famous. In 1754 Whieldon took Josiah Wedgwood as a partner. While working
for Whieldon, Wedgwood invented a green glaze which
was used to decorate fanciful wares in the shapes of pineapples and cauliflowers. Together Whieldon and Wedgwood continued to make marbled, agate, and tortoise
shell pieces. Wedgwood left in 1759. Whieldon continued
producing the variegated wares until the demand for these
pieces diminished. He retired in 1780.

No Whieldon pieces are marked. Many earthenware
potteries copied Whieldon's tortoise shell wares between
1740 and 1780. Since no pieces are marked, it is impossible to attribute a piece to a specific factory. The term
"Whieldon ware" is now generic.

Reference: F. Falkner, *The Wood Family of Burslem*, Chap-
man & Hall, 1912.

Museums: City Museum, Stoke-on-Trent, Hanley, En-
gland; Fitzwilliam Museum, Cambridge, England; Museum
of Art, Rhode Island School of Design, Providence, Rhode
Island; Sussex Museum & Art Gallery, Brighton, England;
Victoria & Albert Museum, London, England; William
Rockhill Nelson Gallery of Art, Kansas City, MO.

Canister, 4⅜" h, rect, arched shoulder, molded
rope-edged sqs with stars and dots, cream,
brown, and green glazes, c1760 (A) **1060.00**
Cradle, 4" l, green glazed, interlocking circles on
body, interlocking ovals and band of overlap-
ping oak leaves on hood, c1770 . . . . **950.00**
Cream Jug
3½" h, baluster shape, cauliflower, scrolled

**Plate, 9" d, brown tortoise shell glaze, ribbed
rim, c1760, unmkd, $150.00**

foliage handle, silver shape rim, cauliflower
florets, dark green leaves, c1760, Whiel-
don/Wedgwood/Greatbatch **2150.00**
3⅝" h, brown and green tortoise shell glaze,
scalloped lip, ribbed handle (A) **495.00**
Cup, 3" h, green and ochre stripes, flared rim,
scrolled handle, two thumb rests, multiple
rows of tiny indentations, c1760, part of Whi-
eldon/Wedgwood/Greatbatch melon service **3500.00**
Dish
14" l, molded border with scrolls and panels
of basketwork and trellis pattern, shaped
rim, tortoise shell glaze, hairline, c1760
(A). **1500.00**
15" d, six knotted wood molded panels,
shaped hexafoil rim, mottled brown glaze,
c1770 (A) **715.00**
Figure
2¼" h, recumbent pig, green translucent
glaze, oval base with concave sides, c1760,
Whieldon/Wedgwood/Greatbatch type . . . **1250.00**
2½" h, pug seated on flat rect base, coat in
manganese patches, eyes with brown slip,
tail restored, c1775 (A) **2226.00**
3½" h, gray cat with cobalt ears and black
lines, cobalt splashes, restored, c1750 . . . . **1800.00**
4½" h, cobbler in brown apron, seated on
glazed redware stump, pale translucent
green and blue-gray splashes, eyes dotted in
brown, damage to tools, c1750, Astbury-
Whieldon (A) **23,628.00**
4⅞" h, seated cat with white body, green
and brown splotches, 19th C (A) **550.00**
5⅛" h, seated bagpiper in splashed green,
brown, and gray jacket and breeches,
brown slip eyes, seated on brown stump,
c1740–50, Astbury-Whieldon (A) **4235.00**
5⅞" h, press molded figure of standing lady,
mottled brown gown, blue bodice, mid
18th C (A). **8140.00**
6¾" l, deer in manganese brown and gray,
flat shaped oval base applied with florets
and leaves in green, ochre, and blue-black,
damage, c1750 (A) **18,700.00**
7" h, hawk perched on domed rect base,
cream slip with brown and green streaked
glaze, applied brown eyes, late 18th C (A) **9000.00**
8" h, bust of Empress Maria Theresa, cream
body with translucent gray-blue and brown
glaze, blown slip eyes, waisted socle, mid
18th C (A). **7400.00**

8 1/4" h, Falstaff in open purplish-gray jacket with yellow and green underneath, belted, buckle on left arm applied with large bird in relief, sword in right hand, dark brown boots and hat, circ base with flowers and foliage, restored, c1755 (A) **20,570.00**

Jug, 3 3/8" h, baluster shape, runny green and manganese-brown glaze, restored rim (A) . . . **345.00**

Loving Cup, 4 1/2" h, brown, yellow, and blue splashes, incised rings on base, dbl handles, unmarked **525.00**

Milk Jug, Cov, 4 3/4" h, brown tortoise shell glaze, sparrow beak spout, ribbed handle, flower finial, three mask and paw feet, c1760 . . . . **1650.00**

Plaque, relief molded half portrait of Marie Squires as a gypsy in wide brimmed hat, or Sara Malcolm, cartouche shaped rim with shells, ochre, green, and manganese wash, restored, c1765, pr (A) **14,300.00**

Plate

7" d, brown, green, and blue tortoise shell glaze (A) **357.00**

8 1/2" d, oct

Dark brown tortoise shell glaze in flame effect, raised milled border, c1760 . . . . **400.00**

Spattered tortoise shell decoration, c1770 **695.00**

8 3/4" d

Oct, dark brown, tan, and yellow tortoise shell glaze, molded diaper border **350.00**

Yellow fruits and green leaves, gray-green diapered ground dotted in manganese brown, scalloped rim of twigs, c1760 . . . . **400.00**

9" d

Green and yellow patches on brown mottled ground, ozier and diaper molded panels on border, wavy rim (A) **245.00**

Mottled brown with yellow and green accents, molded feather edge, late 18th C, England (A) **250.00**

Oct, brown tortoise shell glaze, emb rim (A) **450.00**

9 1/8" d

Brown tortoise shell glaze with blue, green, and amber splashes, emb and shaped rim (A) **520.00**

Oct shape with tortoise shell glaze in black with spots of brown, blue, and green (A) **550.00**

9 1/4" d

Black and brown tortoise shell glaze with green, blue, brown, and yellow splashes, emb diaper border (A) **575.00**

Dark green glaze, rim molded with melon vines, c1760, Whieldon/Wedgwood/ Greatbatch **1600.00**

9 3/8" d

Green and yellow patches on brown mottled ground, wavy gadrooned rim (A) . . **266.00**

Mottled brown glaze, shaped piecrust border, restored, late 18th C, England (A) . . . **165.00**

Oct, brown tortoise shell glaze, emb rim (A) **400.00**

Tortoise shell brown with green accents, scalloped border with molded rim, hairline, late 18th C, England (A) **275.00**

9 1/2" d

Black tortoise shell glaze with green, blue, and brown splashes, emb diapered border (A) **375.00**

Brown tortoise shell glaze with green and

amber splashes, emb and shaped rim (A) **495.00**

Mottled brown and tan ground with green spots, knife scratches **300.00**

9 3/4" d, oct, tortoise shell glaze in black, with spots of brown, blue, and green (A) **475.00**

10" d, multicolored tortoise shell glaze, emb scalloped rim (A) **600.00**

10 1/4" d, dark green, brown, ochre, and cream glaze, pierced trellis rim, fruit, foliage and basketry outlined by rococo scrolling, c1760, Whieldon/Wedgwood/Greatbatch **3600.00**

Soup Plate, 9 1/4" d, black tortoise shell glaze with green, blue, brown, and yellow splashes, emb diapered rim (A) **500.00**

Tea Caddy

4 1/8" h, cauliflower shape, emb leaves and head in dark green and white, hairline, 18th C (A) **220.00**

4 3/4" h, rect, molded overlapping green leaves with cream flowers, c1760 (A) **290.00**

4 7/8" h, rect, molded panels of chinoiserie figures splashed in green, brown, and blue, restored, c1760 (A) **528.00**

Teapot

3 1/4" h, pineapple shape, translucent ochre and green glaze, leaves rising upward from the base and around foliage molded finial, finely grooved spout and handle, c1760, Whieldon/Wedgwood/Greatbatch **9850.00**

3 5/8" h, creamware, gray glazed, applied trailing stems of cream Tudor roses and green and yellow leaves, crabstock handle, spout, and finial, c1755–60 (A) **1730.00**

3 7/8" h, globular shape

Crabstock handle and spout, three lion mask and paw feet, applied leaves and flowers, splashed managanese-brown glaze, restored, c1760 (A) **861.00**

Emb vining design in brown tortoise shell glaze, repairs (A) **1375.00**

4" h, white and green emb cauliflower design, repair to spout, unmarked (A) **525.00**

4 1/4" h

Cauliflower shape, grooved scroll handle, split terminal molded with slightly curving leaves, cauliflower spout and knob, repaired, c1760, Whieldon/Wedgwood/ Greatbatch **4800.00**

Globular shape, grapevines with corkscrew tendrils and cluster of grapes, overlapped dbl and triple leaves, crabstock handle and spout, turned knob, cov applied with blossoms and foliage, tortoise shell glaze in browns, gray-blues, green, and cream, repaired spout, c1750 . . . . **2500.00**

4 3/4" h, molded globular green and yellow striped melon, raised surface veins, reeded handle with floret and leaf, pineapple molded leaf spout, restored, c1760 (A) . . .**10,175.00**

5" h

Cauliflower shape, green glazed upright leaves, foliate spout, scroll molded lamprey handle, finial repaired, c1765, Wedgwood/Whieldon type (A) **2429.00**

Globular, applied trailing prunus branches, splashed runny managanese, gray-blue, and green glaze, three mask and paw feet, crabstock handle and spout, asparagus tip finial, c1760 (A) **5700.00**

Melon shape, translucent green and ochre glaze, foliage molded spout and handle, flower finial with applied flower and leaf issuing from handle, c1765, Whieldon/ Wedgwood/Greatbatch.............. **9500.00**

5¼" h, globular body, black glazed, modeled with trailing gourd branches with gilding, gilt flying bird knob, crabstock handle and spout, triple mask and paw feet, c1755 (A)........................... **1771.00**

5⅜" h

Modeled tree stump with fruiting vine and moss, applied crabstock handle and spout, shell finial, translucent brown, green, and gray glaze, repaired, c1770 (A) **4210.00**

Molded pectin shell body with solid marbled gray, brown, and cream ground, lamprey handle, bird head spout, poodle finial (A) **3250.00**

5½" h

Molded overlapping green leaves with cream flowers, curved green spout, scroll handle, cracks, restorations, c1760..... **500.00**

Spherical shape, grape vines, brown tortoise shell glaze, gilding of leaves, grapes, and masks, crabstock handle and spout, bird finial, mask and paw feet, c1760 ...... **3500.00**

6" h, globular shape, molded overlapping green glazed leaves, light green top, curved spout, loop handle, 19th C, ... **700.00**

Tea Service, Part, teapot, 4½" h, cov, ftd milk jug, sugar bowl, waste bowl, 4 cups and saucers, Tudor roses, grapes, vines, and foliage, glazed in grayish tortoise shell with splashes of green, ochre, brown, and blue, teapot with crabstock spout and handle, bird finial, three mask and paw feet, repairs, c1760 ....**25000.00**

Tray, 9" l, 8" w, black tortoise shell glaze with green and yellow splashes, emb floral scalloped edge (A)........................... **1375.00**

Wall Pocket, 6¼" h, molded as bracket with shaped crown moldings supported by putto's head flanked by C scrolls, baroque scrollwork at bottom, putto's face in dark cream with brown eyes, rest in tortoise shell glazes of greens, ochres, dark grays, and brown, repaired crack, c1755 .... **2400.00**

Wall Vase, 12" l, cornucopia shape, molded with trailing hops and vines enclosing central scrolling medallion with bust of Flora, pierced shell molded border, splashed with green, blue, manganese, and ochre glazes, rim restored, c1760 (A) **1682.00**

WILLOW WARE

English/Continental
1780s to Present

History: Blue willow china is the English interpretation of hand painted blue and white Chinese porcelain that was exported to England from China in the 16th century. The transfer method of decoration and the under the glaze decorating techniques introduced after 1760 provided the methodology to produce willow ware in large quantity.

The first English willow pattern is attributed to Thomas Minton at his Caughley Pottery in Staffordshire in the 1780s. The pattern was called Willow-Nankin.

Josiah Spode developed the first "true" willow pattern in the 1790s. Spode made three different willow patterns. The standard pattern developed in 1810 by Spode is the one that is considered the "true" willow pattern. It differs from the first two patterns in border design and the method by which the transfer pattern was engraved.

Spode's willow pattern has a willow tree in the center leaning over the bridge. A tea house with three pillars forming the portico and located near a large orange tree is behind the center willow tree. There is a bridge with three figures crossing towards an island. A boat with a man is on the lake. Two birds are flying towards each other at the top enter. Finally, a fence crosses the foreground. The outer border features several scroll and geometic designs. The inner border consists of geometric designs that frame the center pattern.

Many manfacturers used transfers that were variations of the Spode willow pattern. Some produced their own original blue willow versions. By 1830 there were more than two hundred makers of willow pattern china in England. English firms still producing blue willow pattern china are Booth's by Royal Doulton, Burleigh, Coalport, Johnson Brothers, Meakin, and Wedgwood.

During the 20th century other countries making willow ware included Belgium, France, Germany, Holland, Ireland, Mexico, Poland, Portugal, and Spain. Potteries in the United States and Japan also make pieces decorated with the blue willow pattern.

A tremendous variety of shapes were made in the blue willow pattern. Many pieces were not marked by the manufacturers, especially during the early period.

The color of the transfer varies with manufacturer. During the 1820s, a pale blue was fashionable. A whole spectrum of blues was used during the Victorian era. Although the most common color is blue, pieces can be found in black, brown, green, pink, yellow, and polychrome.

References: Robert Copeland, *Spode's Willow Pattern and other designs after the Chinese*, Rizzoli International Publications, Inc., 1980; Mary Frank Gaston, *Blue Willow: An Identification and Value Guide*, Collector Books, second ed., 1990; Veryl Marie Worth, *Willow Pattern China*, privately printed, revised 2nd edition, 1981.

Collectors' Club: International Willow Collectors, Eva Lee Revels, Corres. Sec., P.O. Box 14331, Arlington, TX 76094-1331. $5. The Willow Society, 359 Davenport Road, Suite 6, Toronto, M5R 1K5 Canada. Membership: $15.00. *The Willow Transfer Quarterly, The Willow Exchange,* and *The Mandarin's Purse* (price guide).

Banana Boat, 12½" l, 7¾" w, blue, c1775, Caughley **750.00**

Berry Bowl, 4¾" d, blue, "Royal Pottery, Staffordshire, Burslem" mark.................. **8.00**

Bone Dish, 5"l, 2¾" w, two temples, garden, water, bridge and fence, lady on bridge, man in garden, gold touches on rim, blue, c1937, pr . **55.00**

Bowl

5" d, blue, "Johnson Bros." mark **4.00**

5½" d, blue, "Maastricht" mark **5.00**

6" d, blue, "Johnson Bros." mark **5.00**

8¼" d, blue, "Johnson Bros." mark **25.00**

9½" l, 7½" w, blue, "Staffordshire" mark **35.00**

Butter Boat, 3" l, leaf shape, twig handle, blue willow border int and ext **195.00**

Butter Pat, 3¼" d, center scene of small house with garden and tree, blue, c1920, "Willow,

Platter, 15½" l, 12½" w, blue, imp "crown" mark, $135.00

Woods Vitrified Ware. Mfd by Wood & Sons England" mark **35.00**
Cereal Bowl, 6" d, blue, Ridgway **10.00**
Charger, 13" d, pink, "Allerton" mark **75.00**
Cream and Sugar, blue, "Copeland's China England" mark (A).......................... **200.00**
Creamer
  3½" h, blue design on handle, Ridgway ... **12.00**
  3¾" l, blue, leaf design on int **80.00**
  Ftd base, blue, "John Steventon & Sons, Burslem" mark........................... **45.00**
Cup and Saucer
  Blue
    "Johnson Bros." mark **8.00**
    "Two Temples II" pattern with butterfly border on inner scalloped edge, c1870–89, Grainger & Co. **35.00**
    Worcester pattern variant, bone china... **18.00**
  Oversize, brown, "Two Temples II" pattern, "England" mark....................... **48.00**
Cuspidor, 6" h, blue, "Ridgway Semi-China" mark................................. **350.00**
Dish
  8" l, 7¾" w, handled, blue, c1770, Caughley **250.00**
  9" d, pea green, c1920, "Manufacture Imperial Royal Nimy-Made in Belgium" mark .. **45.00**
  9¾" l, blue, "Made in England" mark (A).. **40.00**
Egg Cup, 5½" h, pink, "Made in England" mark **22.00**
Egg Hoop, 2½" h, open at both ends, blue, c1810................................. **125.00**
Grill Plate, 11" d, blue, "Maastricht" mark **10.00**
Infant Feeder, 6½" l, open top, blue, unmarked.............................. **35.00**
Knife Rest, 3¾"l, blue, unmarked, pr **175.00**
Ladle, 6" l, blue, bow knot border, imp "WEDGWOOD" mark......................... **50.00**
Milk Pitcher, 6½" h, blue, unmarked **85.00**
Mug
  3" h, blue, red, yellow, and green, c1912... **95.00**
  3½" h, straight sides, blue, unmarked **15.00**
  4" h, earthenware, blue, c1870, unmarked.. **125.00**
Pickle Dish, 5¼" l, 4¼" w, leaf shape with tab handle, blue, c1850 .... **55.00**
Pitcher
  3½" h, pink, "Allerton" mark.............. **75.00**
  4" h, blue, unmarked..................... **55.00**
  5¾" h, blue, "C.T.M." mark (A)........... **25.00**
  11¼" h, ironstone, blue, serpent handle, Mason **525.00**
Pitcher and Bowl, bowl, 6⅝" d, pitcher, 5⅞"

h, blue, "Two Temples II" pattern, Grainger & Co. **250.00**
Plate
  4¾" d, light blue, c1920, "Willow over crown" mark **40.00**
  4⅞" d, brown, c1873–90, Edge Malkin.... **30.00**
  5¾" d, blue, "Allerton" mark............. **5.00**
  6" d, dark cobalt blue, two temples with butterfly border, c1915, "Greene Co. Ltd. Gresely, England" mark................. **10.00**
  6¼" d
    Mulberry, c1920, "Britannia Pottery Co. Ltd. Glascow, Made in Great Britain" mark . **35.00**
    Simplified center design, ornate scroll and trailing flower border, blue, unmarked.. **25.00**
  6¾" d, blue, polychrome accents, "Ashworth Hanley" mark.................... **40.00**
  7" d
    Dark blue, "John Steventon & Sons, Burslem, England" mark.................. **7.00**
    Medium blue, c1920, Wedgwood **15.00**
    Pink, pale green, light blue, lavender, and peach design on border, gold rim, c1920, "Myott Son & Co. England" mark..... **30.00**
    Polychrome design, Ashworth **35.00**
    Scalloped edge, blue, "Allerton" mark.... **15.00**
  7½" d, blue, "Burslem, England" mark **8.00**
  8" d, blue
    Border willow pattern, c1936, Myott Sons & Co. **12.00**
    "Johnson Bros." mark **5.00**
  8¼" d
    Blue, "Two Temples II" pattern, "Semi-China Warrented" mark **65.00**
    Red, "WR Midwinter England" mark **14.00**
  8½" d, blue, gold rim, c1805–20, "Davenport Stone China" mark................. **145.00**
  8¾" d, gold, light blue, and orange "Two Temples II" pattern on blue ground, c1914–41"Paladin China" mark **100.00**
  9" d, Blue
    "Johnson Bros." mark **12.00**
    "Ridgway" mark **25.00**
    Scalloped edge, "Allerton" mark........ **18.00**
  9⅛" d, blue, "Maastricht" mark **15.00**
  9¼" d, blue **20.00**
  9½" d
    Blue, Villery & Boch **8.00**
    Navy blue and brown transfer, Ridgway .. **45.00**
  9¾" d, blue
    "Shelton, Stoke on Trent" mark **10.00**
    "W.S.& Co.'s Wedgewood" mark (A) **28.00**
  10" d
    Blue
      Fluted edge, "Allerton" mark **20.00**
      "Myott & Son England" mark **50.00**
      "Olde Alton Ware" mark **30.00**
      "Ridgway" mark **25.00**
    Pea green, c1937, "Willow Ware by Royal China" mark......................... **25.00**
  10½" d, blue, "WA Adderly & Co." mark . **25.00**
Platter
  9½" l, blue, "WA & Co. Staffordshire" mark................................. **55.00**
  11½" l, blue, unmarked.................. **65.00**
  12" l
    9¼" w, dark blue **80.00**
    9½" w, blue, "Johnson Bros. England" mark............................... **35.00**
  13½" l, 11" w, blue, "Allerton" mark **70.00**

13¾" d, blue (A)........................ 65.00
14" l, blue
"Allerton" mark....................... 55.00
"Johnson Bros." mark 25.00
14½" l, blue, "Myott & Son England" mark 50.00
15" l, blue, Allerton 90.00
15" l, 11½" w, rose, "Mandarin Spode,
Copeland England" mark............... 150.00
15½" l, 12½" w, blue.................. 55.00
15¾" l, blue, "Allerton" mark (A)........ 45.00
16" l, 13" w, blue 150.00
16½" l, blue, well and tree.............. 225.00
17¼" l, 14" w, blue.................... 125.00
17¾" l, blue, "R.H.& Co." mark (A)....... 95.00
19½" l, 12½" w, blue, combed back, Staffordshire Stone China................... 250.00
21¾" l, blue, tree and well, "Staffordshire"
mark (A) 125.00
Pudding Mold, 4½" w, blue, red, green, and
peach transfer, unmarked 45.00
Salt and Pepper, 4⅝" h, blue, imp "England"
marks.................................... 60.00
Sauce Boat, 6" l, blue, "Ridgway Semi-China"
mark.................................... 60.00
Sauce Tureen
6⅞" l, with ladle and undertray, blue, chip on
rim (A).................................. 225.00
7" H-H, 5" h, blue, c1820, unmarked...... 325.00
Serving Dish, 8" d, blue, "Ridgway bow and
quiver" mark............................ 35.00
Soap Dish, 6½" l, with drain, blue, Maling ... 165.00
Soup Bowl
6½" d, with saucer, blue................ 85.00
7⅜" d, blue pattern with green, yellow, and
orange overpaint........................ 50.00
7¾" d, red, "WR Midwinter, England"
mark.................................... 18.00
8" d, pink, "Swinnerton" mark 6.00
8½" d, blue with gold trim, "Burleigh Ware,
Burslem, England" mark................. 24.00
Soup Plate, 10¼" d, blue, worn gilt rim, "Burleigh Ware" mark (A) 23.00
Teapot, 5" h, miniature, blue, gold trim, gold
finial, "Sadler, England" mark 125.00
Tea Service, teapot, open sugar, creamer, dish, 6
cups and saucers, shaded rose, pink, yellow,
and peach on black matte ground, gold outlines, "Royal Winton, Grimwades, England"
marks.................................... 475.00
Toothbrush Holder, 5" h, blue, dagger border,
c1891–1902, Minton 75.00
Tray, 9½" l
6½" w, blue, "Allerton" mark 55.00
7½" w, deep well, blue.................. 45.00
Trinket Box, 2¾" d, 1¾" h, dark blue, un-
marked.................................. 125.00
Trivet, 6" w, blue "Two Temples II" pattern,
Gresley mark 60.00
Tumbler, 5½" h, blue, unmarked........... 20.00
Tureen, 12" l, 8" w, 5½" h, blue, dbl handles,
"Allerton England" mark 135.00
Vase, Bud, 2¼" h, blue, unmarked......... 25.00
Vase
10" h, dark blue with gold and enameled wil-
low pattern legend on base, c1912, John
Tams Ltd................................ 375.00
12" h, blue with green, red, white, black and
gold enamels, gold border with red and
black.................................... 475.00

Vase, Cov, 15½" h, ironstone, blue, Mason
(A)..................................... 302.00
Vegetable Bowl
8½" l, blue, Meakin 35.00
9½" l, 7½" w, blue, "Allerton England"
mark.................................... 85.00
10" l, 7" w, blue, fluted edges, c1925, "Globe
Pottery, Cobridge, England" mark....... 60.00
10" H-H, handled, blue, "Ridgway Semi-
China" mark............................ 65.00
Vegetable Bowl, Cov, 11" l, 9" w
Blue, "Allerton" mark................... 60.00
Pink, "Allerton" mark................... 79.00
Vegetable Dish, 8¼" l, 6" w, twelve sided rect,
pale blue ground, imp "Ashworth Real Stone
China" mark............................ 80.00
Vegetable Tureen, Cov, 11" H-H, 6½" h, blue,
c1891, John Tams, Longton 145.00
Wash Bowl, 16" d, blue................... 325.00
Water Pitcher, 8" h, black with gold trim, c1930,
Royal Doulton 160.00

ENOCH WOOD & SONS BURSLEM STAFFORDSHIRE

1818–1846

BURSLEM

1818–1846

WOOD, ENOCH

**Fountain Place Pottery, Burslem,
Staffordshire, England
c1784–1840**

History: Enoch Wood came from an important pottery
family that included Aaron Wood, his father, Ralph Wood,
his cousin, and William Wood, his brother. After he completed his apprenticeship, Enoch entered a partnership
with Ralph in 1784. They made enamel colored figures
and toby jugs using the new over the glaze decoration
technique.

In 1790 Enoch wood entered into a partnership with
Caldwell. The company's mark was Wood & Caldwell.
Enoch bought out Caldwell in 1819 and formed a new
partnership with Enoch, Joseph, and Edward Wood, his
sons. The firm became known as Enoch Wood & Sons.

The company made under the glaze blue transfer
printed dinnerware, much of which was exported to
America. In addition to the blue historic wares, many romantic wares were printed in pink, purple, black, sepia,
green, or mulberry. Views used include British, French,
Italian, and American scenes. Although views were the
most popular designs, biblical scenes, hunting scenes, and

cherub motifs also were made. Many of the printed designs have the title marked on the back.

Marked pieces are impressed "WOOD."

References: A. W. Coysh & R. K. Henrywood, *The Dictionary of Blue & White Printed Pottery 1780–1880*, Antique Collectors' Club, 1982; vol. 2, 1989.

Museums: Cincinnati Art Museum, Cincinnati, Ohio; Fitzwilliam Museum, Cambridge, England; Potsdam Public Museum, Potsdam, New York.

Bowl, 10″ d, red and pink cherries with green stems on white ground, wide cobalt and gold border, c1900, "Wood & Sons" mark (A).................................... **25.00**

Centerpiece, 8″ d, bowl set in branches on tree stump, boy standing at side with painted Christmas cactus extending to sides of bowl, gold stencilled base...................... **395.00**

Cup Plate, 4⅝″ d, scene of two sailboats and rowboat, two men on shore, shell border, dark blue transfer, hairlines, imp "Wood & Sons" mark (A)................................ **181.00**

Plaque, 7⅞″ l, oval, relief molded half figure of man holding wine glass and jug, old lady behind with paper in hand, buff stoneware, imp mark................................... **175.00**

Plate
6½″ d, center rust brown transfer of "A TRIFLE FOR MARGARET" in lozenge, enameled floral border, imp "Wood and Sons" mark (A)............................ **265.00**

7″ d, "Elyse" pattern, blue transfer, festooned rim, "Wood & Sons" mark.............. **8.00**

7¼″ d, pearlware, red transfer of turkey in center, relief of red, green, and blue flowers on border, brown line rim, imp "Enoch Wood & Sons" mark................... **275.00**

7½″ d, transfer of soldiers sitting in front of building, emb border, c1820–40........ **85.00**

9¾″ d, "Seaforth" pattern, blue transfer, shaped edge........................ **15.00**

10″ d
"English Scenery" pattern, blue transfer... **28.00**

Meeting House, Old Sturbridge Village, blue transfer...................... **25.00**

"Niagara Falls," blue and white, "Wood & Son, Burslem, England" mark........... **14.00**

Pearlware, green feather edge, imp "Enoch Wood & Sons" mark (A)............. **104.00**

"Zoological Series-Deer," dark blue transfer (A) **165.00**

10¼″ d
"European Scenery," brown transfer, shaped rim......................... **35.00**

Farmyard scene with beehive, med blue transfer, "Enoch Wood & Sons" mark (A).............................. **135.00**

10¾″ d, imprisoned Cupid design, dark blue transfer, "Wood & Sons" mark (A)....... **85.00**

Platter
14¾″ l, blue feather edge, imp "Wood" mark (A) **61.00**

17″ l, rect, center chinoiserie scene, floral border, med blue transfer, mid 19th C (A) ... **275.00**

17⅛″ l, "Corfu" pattern, dark brown transfer of boating scene in center, yellow-brown border with dark brown flowers **460.00**

Sauce Dish
4¼″ d, castle in ground, two fishermen in foreground, dark blue transfer, imp "Wood & Sons" mark..................... **175.00**

4½″ d, landscape scene, dark blue transfer, imp "Wood & Sons" mark (A).......... **175.00**

Soup Plate, 10¼″ d, scene of hunter and dog, med blue transfer, "Enoch Wood" mark (A). **95.00**

Toby Jug, Charles Dickens characters, multicolored, "Wood and Sons" marks, set of 12 (A)............................... **150.00**

Toddy Plate, "Cadmus" pattern, dark blue transfer, imp "Wood & Sons" mark (A) **150.00**

Toothbrush Holder, 5¼″ h, "Marlborough" pattern, iron-red open flowers, cobalt hanging chains, "Wood & Sons" mark **78.00**

Tureen, Cov, Underplate, 13″ H-H, 14″ l, oblong, purple transfer, "Castles" pattern, Hinchingbrooke on tureen, Bodiam Scene in platter, cov with twisted branch handle, "Wood and Sons England" mark (A).............. **90.00**

Ra WOOD
BURSLEM
c.1770 - 1801

WOOD, RALPH

near Stoke-on-Trent, England

Ralph Wood the Elder
1754–1772

Ralph Wood the Younger
1760–1795

History: Ralph Wood and Ralph, his son, were the most important makers of earthenware figures and toby jugs during the second half of the eighteenth century.

After his apprenticeship, Ralph Wood, initially worked for Thomas Whieldon, making salt glazed earthenware and tortoise shell glazed ware. Eventually, he founded his own firm. during the 1750s Ralph Wood started making figures in cream colored earthenware with metallic oxide

Teabowl and Saucer, bowl, 3¾″ h, saucer, 5⅝″ d, sea urchins and flowers, dk blue transfers, c1825, $175.00

stained glazes. He kept the colors separate by painting them on with a brush. The modeling of his figures was quite lively. Ralph's figures gained a reputation for portraying the mood and attitude of the character exactly.

Ralph the Younger was a skilled figure maker and joined with his father during the 1760s. Ralph the Younger continued the tradition established by his father and eventually produced even more figures than Ralph Wood the Elder. Since Ralph the Younger used many of his father's molds, it is impossible to assign a particular figure to the father or the son with certainty. Later in his career, Ralph the Younger switched to using enamel colors on figures.

Subjects included equestrian figures, contemporary portrait figures, some satyrical groups, classical figures, allegorical figures, and many different animals. All the molded human figures had large hands and well defined, bulging eyes. Ralph Wood also is credited with introducing the toby jug form. These were very successful and copied by dozens of potters. (See: Toby Jugs.)

In addition to figures and toby jugs, Ralph Wood's factory also made plaques. John Voyez, a modeler, produced the plaques. Characteristic of Voyez's work are figures with bulging eyes, thick fleshy lips, slightly flattened noses, and a sentimental inclination of the head.

The Woods were the first figure makers to mark their wares with an impressed company mark and sometimes mold numbers. However, some were not marked. "R. Wood" was the mark of Ralph the Elder. "Ra Wood" was the younger's mark.

References: Capt. R. K. Price, *Astbury, Whieldon & Ralph Wood Figures and Toby Jugs,* John Lane, 1922; H. A. B. Turner, *A Collector's Guide to Staffordshire Pottery Figures,* Emerson Books, Inc., 1971.

Museums: British Museums, London, England; Cincinnati Art Museum, Cincinnati, Ohio; City Museum, Stoke-on-Trent, Hanley, England; Fitzwilliam Museum, Cambridge, England.

Figure
    4³/₄", 6⁶/₈" h, model of stag or doe at lodge, fawn colors, oval grass base, pr **1600.00**
    5¹/₂" h, violinist in runny green translucent glaze, gray-blue hair, brown clay violin,

Figure, 10¹/₄" h, pearlware, "The Widow," lady with floral dress, rose cape, boy with rust outfit, pale green base, marbled pedestal, Ralph Wood the Younger, $1000.00

    seated on light manganese mound, restored, c1770 (A) **3053.00**
    5⁷/₈" h, Admiral Rodney, open coat and uniform washed in green enamel with manganese dots, emblems of war at feet, tree stump behind him molded with his name, hand of sheathed sword, restored, c1780 (A). **921.0**
    6³/₄" h, recumbent deer, pale fawn translucent glaze, green bases with hummocks of shredded clay, repaired, c1785, Wood family, pr **2750.00**
    8¹/₂" h, winged Cupid in blue drapery with telescope, astride gray-brown standing lioness, oval mound base, rect plinth, wing missing, c1780 (A) **3845.00**
    8⁵/₈" h
      Diana, figure in blue bodice and yellow drapery reaching for quiver on shoulder, spotted hound at side, green and brown rockwork base with sq plinth, bow missing, restorations, c1760, imp "RA. Wood Burslem" mark (A) **1320.00**
      Shepherdess wearing gray jacket over brown bodice, green bustle and pale brown overskirt, recumbent sheep on scroll molded green base, repairs, c1780 . . . . **1100.00**
    8⁷/₈" h, Apollo, green and blue classical drapery, holding green lyre, standing on shaped green and pale brown base, applied shredded clay grass, c1780, Wood family **3400.00**
    9" h, pearlware, bust of Milton in pink and puce drapery cloak, black coat and brown hair, waisted socle, c1790, imp "Ra. Wood 81" mark **900.00**
    9¹/₄" h, pearlware, bust of Handel in brown wig, green lined puce drapery and blue coat, waisted socle, repainted, c1785, imp "80 Ra. Wood Burslem" mark (A) **990.00**
    9³/₄" h, "Vicar and Moses," dozing vicar in white vestments, Moses in purple jacket, manganese pulpit, restored, c1780, imp "Ra. Wood, Burslem" mark (A) **750.00**
    10⁷/₈" l, standing lion facing left, paw resting on white ball, brown translucent glaze, white classical base with translucent green top, restored tongue and tail, c1760 . . . . . **3200.00**
    12¹/₄" h, Chaucer wearing crimson lined flower sprigged cloak, jacket and pale yellow breeches, arm on scroll supported by two books, resting on marbled pedestal, rect marbled base, late 18th C, imp "Ra. Wood/Burslem, no.155" marks (A) **2670.00**
    13¹/₄" h, bust of Plato with black hair and beard, maroon toga with yellow-ochre sash, black plinth, cracked (A) **203.00**
    14³/₄" l, brown spotted greyhound supported on tree stump with dead rabbit under paws, oblong base streaked in green and ochre, hairline, c1770 (A) **5500.00**
Mantel Vase, 9³/₄" h, molded with Bacchic putti, shell molded ogee body flanked by twin winged dragon handles, acanthus molded foot, canted rect base, green and manganese glazes, c1790 (A). **354.00**
Spill Vase, 10³/₈" h, seated shepherd and shepherdess with sheep, gnarled tree with three openings in ground, rocky mound base, restored, late 18th C **1000.00**

c1807-1813

c1852-1862

FBB

c1813-1840

c1792-1807

c1755-1775

c1755-1790

WORCESTER

Worcester, England
1751–1892

History: The Worcester pottery was established in 1751. The pieces from the initial years of operation have decorations characterized by a strong dependence on Oriental themes in under the glaze blue and on the glaze enamel. Production concentrated primarily on making excellent utilitarian wares, mostly tea and dessert sets. Very few purely ornamental pieces were made. The china was symetrical and featured a smooth glaze. This initial period, 1751 to 1776, was known as the "Dr. Wall" period, named after one of the original stockholders.

After 1755 transfer printing was used extensively. By 1760 most of the best pieces had the typical Worcester deep blue cobalt under the glaze background, done either in a solid or scale motif. Panels were painted with beautiful birds, flowers, and insects.

The factory was managed by William Davis, one of the original partners from the Dr. Wall period. Davis died in 1783; Thomas Flight then purchased the factory. The middle period, also known as the Davis-Flight period, lasted from 1776 to 1793. Neo-classical designs were emphasized. Many of the whiteware blanks used for decoration were purchased from France. There was a limited quantity of fine clay for porcelain production in the area of the Worcester plant. The company received a Royal Warrant from George III in 1789.

Martin Barr joined the works in 1793. The period from 1793 to 1807 is designated the Flight & Barr period. Patterns continued to be rather plain. Barr's son joined the firm in 1807, resulting in the Barr Flight & Barr period between 1807 and 1813. Decorative motifs from this era were quite colorful and elaborate.

Martin Barr Sr. died in 1813. The time from 1813 to 1840 is called the Flight Barr & Barr period. Patterns continued to be quite colorful, finely painted and gilded. The quality of porcelains made during the early 19th century was very high. Pieces were richly painted, often featuring gilt trim on a well potted body with a perfect, craze-free glaze.

In 1840 Flight Barr & Barr merged with the Chamberlain factory and took the name of Chamberlain and Company. The plant moved to Diglis. Quality of production declined during this time.

Kerr and Binns bought the firm in 1852. During the Kerr & Binns period, 1852 to 1862, the factory enjoyed a great artistic recovery. In 1862 R. W. Binns formed the Worcester Royal Porcelain Company Ltd., a company whose products then carried the "Royal Worcester" designation.

References: Franklin A. Barret, *Worcester Porcelain & Lund's Bristol*, Faber & Faber, 1966, revised ed.; Lawrence Branyon, Neal French, John Sandon, *Worcester Blue & White Porcelain, 1751–1790* Barrie & Jenkins, 1981; F. Severne Mackenna, *Worcester Porcelain: The Wall Period & Its Antecedents*, F. Lewis Ltd., 1950; H. Rissik Marshall, *Colored Worcester Porcelain of the First Period*, Ceramic Book, 1954; Dinah Reynolds, *Worcester Porcelain 1751–1783: An Ashmolean-Christie's Handbook*, Phaidon-Christie's, 1989; Henry Sandon, *Flight & Barr: Worcester Porcelain 1783–1840*, Antique Collector Club, 1978; Henry Sandon, *The Illustrated Guide to Worcester Porcelain*, Herbert Jenkins, 1969.

Museums: Art Institute of Chicago, Chicago, Illinois; British Museum, London, England; City Museum, Weston Park, Sheffield, England; Dyson Perrins Museum, Worcester, England; Gardiner Museum of Ceramic Art, Toronto, Canada; Henry Ford Museum, Dearborn, Michigan; Seattle Art Museum, Seattle, Washington; Sheffield City Museum, Sheffield, England; Victoria & Albert Museum, London, England.

REPRODUCTION ALERT: At the end of the 19th century, Samson and other continental artists copied 18th century Worcester examples. Booths of Turnstall reproduced many Worcester designs utilizing the transfer method. These reproduction pieces also contain copies of the Royal Worcester mark. Even though an earthenware body instead of porcelain was used on the Booth examples, many collectors have been misled by the reproductions.

Basket
5″ l, miniature, shaped rect body, named Yellow Hammer and Goldfinch reserved on gilt seaweed ground, gilt piecrust molded rim and overhead handle, c1825, "Flight, Barr

Can, 5½″ h, cylinder shape with loop handle, parrot with fruit and insects, blue transfer, c1770, "blue crosshatched crescent" mark, $500.00

Inkwell, 4½" h, 5¾" l, painting of Edgar Tower Worcester in center panel, multicolored butterflies on reverse, gold monograms on side, gold trim, cracked cov, "script Flight, Barr and Barr" mark, (A) $412.00

Jug, 12" h, blue transfer of floral design on ovoid cabbage leaf molded body, mask spout, c1770, "blue crosshatched crescent" mark, $2000.00

Junket Bowl, 10" d, "Pine Cone" pattern, blue transfer, molded border with raised sides and molded with shells, c1775, "blue crosshatched crescent" mark, $850.00

and Barr, Royal Porcelain Works, Worcester, London House, 1 Coventry Street" mark (A) 1600.00

5⅜" l, rect, colored flowers on light green ground, gilt gadrooned rim, gilt overhead handle, c1820–30, Flight, Barr and Barr (A). 1435.00

6¼" d, circ, "Pine Cone" pattern, blue printed florals and fruit, pierced rim with applied florets, c1775, underglaze "blue crescent" mark (A) 1235.00

8⅝" d, circ, int with floral spray on deep blue ground in gilt edged panel, ext applied with puce and green florettes, two handled, pierced sides, c1770, "crescent" mark (A) 792.00

8¾" l, oval, int with spray of flowers reserved in gilt scroll edged panel on blue scale ground, pierced sides with flowers, ext wash in pale yellow and applied with green centered pink florets, twig handles with flowering terminals, c1765–70 (A) 1822.00

9⅜" l, "Pine Cone" pattern, blue printed florals, fruit and pine cones in center, pierced sides with applied florets on ext, handles ending in flowering terminals, c1775, "blue crescent" mark (A)........ 1110.00

Beaker, 3¾" h, cylindrical shape, painted in sepia within gilt roundel, one with "VALOUR" seated and holding mane of lion beside him, other with female "IMPARTIALITY" standing and holding scale and nest of birds, flaring rim and foot with gilt band borders, c1805, "Flight & Barr, Wor. Manufacturers to their Majesties," pr (A)............................. 605.00

Bottle, 4½" h, hex, "Wheatsheaf" pattern, bamboo and prunus behind wheat sheaves in Kakiemon colors of iron-red, turquoise, blue, green, yellow, and black, flowering plant on reverse, blossoms on sides, two blue centered flowerheads on rim, c1753–56 (A) 5500.00

Bough Pot, Cov, 8½" l, D shape, six natives and horse in "The Bridge & Great Cataract at Alata" in green, brown, purple, and gray, gold and white borders, sides have rect views, gilt spirally banded pilasters, bun feet, panels of gilt vermiculation on ground and cov, three rows of pierced openings on cov, gilt artichoke knob with six leaves, c1805, "Chamberlains Worcester" mark (A)................ 7700.00

Bowl

5⅞" l, "Kempthorne" pattern, Japanese style painted flowering plants in blue, iron-red, and green on ext, demi- floret and gilt hatched border on int, c1770, "blue pseudo seal" mark (A) 957.00

6⅛" d, blue floral int and inside rim, blue florals and butterflies ext. 1785–99, "blue crescent "mark 400.00

7⅛" d, lobed circ form, colorful Chinese style with flowering wild cherry, peony, and prunus plants issuing from pierced rocks, c1753, incised barbed "T" mark (A).....12,397.00

7¼" d, center with blue printed summer flowers, lattice border with applied flowers on ext, Dr. Wall period (A) 700.00

8" l, 3½" h, blue and white embossed and painted with Crane decoration, oriental scene with man fishing in bowl's center, raised ext with blue decoration, blue rim, Dr. Wall 1st Period 1200.00

10" l, lobed lozenge form, blue fruit and floral cluster center, beehive border, 1st Period (A).. **467.00**

11½" d, 5" h, blue and white printed "Pine Cone" design, blue geometric border on int, pine cones on ext, c1770–80, shaded "blue crescent" mark................... **3800.00**

11¾" d, fluted, "Old Mosaick Japan" pattern, underglaze blue, iron-red, and gold with prunus branch within gilt flowered iron-red border beneath fan shaped panels in underglaze blue and gilding, or iron-red, rose, green, and turquoise with floral sprays or diaperwork, mons and rim edged in gilding, ext with four underglaze blue and iron-red peony sprays, repaired, 1765–70, underglaze "blue pseudo Chinese 4-character" mark (A)................... **1100.00**

Butter Boat

3¼" l, leaf shape with stem handle, int painted with iron-red, rose, yellow, turquoise-green, and sepia flowering branches, c1756–58 (A) **1430.00**

3½" l, geranium leaf molded, painted with sprays of flowers in underglaze blue, c1760, underglaze blue workman's marks (A).... **190.00**

Butter Cooler, Cov, 5½" w, oval shape, wooden tub form raised on four scroll feet with apple finial, sprays and sprigs of colored flowers, yellow accents, c1757 (A) **720.00**

Butter, Cov, Stand, 7" H-H, 3¾" h, oval shape, blue printed rose design, tray, butter, and cov with applied handles, damaged, c1770–80, "blue crescent" mark.................... **625.00**

Candlestick, 6¾" h, two modeled yellow canaries perched on pink apple blossom bocage above scroll molded base with puce and gilt accents, scrolling handle on reverse, repairs, c1770 (A) **18,700.00**

Caudle Cup, Cov, 4¹¹⁄₁₆" h, "Old Japan Fan" pattern, underglaze blue, iron-red, green, and gilding with stylized fans, iron-red and green floral sprig knob, gilt rims, cup int with central iron-red, green, and gilt chrysanthemum blossom, 1768–72, underglaze "blue pseudo Chinese character" mark (A).................. **525.00**

Centerpiece

8" h, three tiers of pink and gilt edged molded shells, painted florals on int, set on molded rocky mound with shells and coral, restored, c1770 (A) **5740.00**

15" l, elliptical form, painted on both sides and center with oval panel of shells, within wide orange border with stylized holly leaves and key fret designs, flared foot, 1792–1807, incised "B" mark (A) **3553.00**

Charger, 14¾" d, blue and white printed "Pine Cone" pattern, scalloped edge, c1770–80, shaded "blue crescent" mark............. **3200.00**

Chestnut Basket, 7½" l, blue and white "Pine Cone" pattern, basketweave body joined by applied flower heads, dbl twig handles joined with floral clusters, c1775, 1st Period (A)................................... **1930.00**

Coffee Can, 2½" h, cylindrical, "L'Amour," transfer printed in black, reverse with balustraded garden, grooved loop handle, c1760–65 (A)................................. **650.00**

Coffee Can and Saucer, painted moonlight classical ruins scene in yellow and black, gilt scroll

panel, dark blue ground, c1807–13, incised "B, Barr, Flight and Barr" mark, pr (A) **4290.00**

Coffee Cup and Saucer

"Dragon in Compartments" pattern, fluted, dbl entwined handle, c1770, underglaze "blue fretted square" mark (A) **650.00**

Mirror shaped panels with exotic birds, insects, and floral sprigs, blue scale ground, c1785–90 (A)......................... **468.00**

Coffee Pot, Cov, 9" h, pear shape, "Mansfield" pattern in underglaze blue, upright spout, scrolling handle, c1765–70, underglaze "blue crescent" mark (A) **510.00**

Cottage Night Light Holder, Cov, 6¾" h, gothic style building, pointed arched windows, timber framed gables, dormer window, thatched roof in brown with two chimney stacks, base molded with steps, painted with flowers, mounted with candle receptacle, restored, 1815–20, painted "Flight, Barr & Barr, Royal Porcelain Works Worcester, London House, Coventry Street" mark (A)................ **2057.00**

Creamboat

3½" h, molded, painted with narcissus and trailing flowers, foot molded with shells and leaf border, lamprey handle, entwined dolphin molded spout, c1765, script "W" mark (A).. **2460.00**

4" l, hex form, colorful flower sprays and scattered sprigs, sides molded with scrolls and leaf spout, dbl scroll handle, 1753–55 (A). **2037.00**

Cream Jug

2⅞" h, sparrow beak, "The Tea Party," transfer printed in black, reverse with "Maid and Page," c1760–65 (A) **530.00**

3¼" h, molded and colored overlapping shells, pr of entwined green dolphins below spout, green lamprey handle, c1765–70 (A)......................... **950.00**

Cress Dish, 9" d, blue and white painted "Pine Cone" pattern, with holes, scalloped edge, c1775–80, shaded "blue crescent" mark ... **1200.00**

Cup, fluted, blue floral design, florals on int rim, c1775................................. **65.00**

Cup and Saucer

2¹³⁄₁₆" h, fluted, center of saucer with gilt edged roundel, bleu celeste ground, gilt edged barbed rim, entwined foliate scroll handle dotted and feather edged in gilding, c1772, underglaze "blue pseudo seal" mark (A) **440.00**

"Japan" pattern, fluted, panels of prunus and chrysanthemum divided by radiating blue ground panels with gilding, iron-red mons, pierced scroll handle, c1770, underglaze "blue fretted squares' (A) **607.00**

3⅜" h, ovoid, painted domestic oriental scenes, c1765–70 (A) **950.00**

Cup and Saucer, handleless, blue and white, c1770, "blue crescent" mark............. **120.00**

Cuspidor, globular, underglaze blue with "Three Flowers" pattern, wide flared neck, c1775, underglaze "blue crescent" mark (A) **785.00**

Dessert Service, Part, center dish, 13¹⁵⁄₁₆" l, cov sauce tureen, stand, 4 oval dishes, 4 sq dishes, 4 shell shape dishes, 20 plates, iron-red, gold, and black stylized blossom with blue buds and gilt veined iron-red leaves with central gilt oval or roundel, gilt edged rim with wide border of exotic birds with flowers and

foliage in rose, iron-red, green, yellow, and
gold, 1800–04, incised "B or 1B" marks, 34
pcs (A)...................................**19,800.00**
Dinnerware, plate, 9½" d, rimmed soup, 9½"
d, underglaze cobalt decorations with gilt embellishments, center circle in cobalt and gilt,
circles on border with feathered leaves, gilt
scalloped rim, c1780–1800, 14 pcs **3400.00**
Dish
3¾" l, shell shape, blue and white, "Two
Peony Rock Bird" pattern, rim with scrolls,
c1755, underglaze blue workman's mark
(A)....................................   **567.00**
4¾" l, leaf shape pickle, "Two Peony Rock
Bird" pattern, molded on int with veining
and two small buds and leaves issuing from
short gnarled stem handle, insects above
bird on rock, peonies and other flowering
plants, rim with six leaf scroll devices,
c1756, underglaze blue workman's mark
(A)....................................   **880.00**
5¹/₁₆" l, oval potted meat, "Leaning Rock
Fisherman" pattern, basketwork body
molded on either side with rococo scroll
edged cartouche in underglaze blue, one
with fisherman near rock, willow, and
gazebo, other with small Chinaman in
fenced garden, ends with scroll edged quatrefoil panels of floral sprays repeated in
center of int, cov missing, 1758–60, underglaze blue workman's mark (A).......... **1320.00**
5⅜" d, shell shape, underglaze blue with arrangement of mushrooms, peapods, and
other vegetables, blue border, feather
molded rim, c1775, underglaze "blue crescent" mark (A).......................   **374.00**
7¼" d, shell shape, blue and white, c1770,
Dr. Wall period, "blue crescent" mark....   **600.00**
7½" w, cushion shape, painted floral spray
centered by four floral bouquets, shaped sq
rim with gilt accented cobalt band, c1770,
"blue crescent" mark..................   **150.00**
8" d, painted seashells in burnished gilt oct
panels, gray marbled ground, leaf chain border, c1807–13, incised "B, Barr, Flight and
Barr" mark, pr (A)....................**13,943.00**
8⅜" l, cabbage leaf shape, molded in center
with purple veining extending to curling
stem handle, crimped edge shaded in
green, 1760–65, pr (A) **800.00**
9" l, leaf shape, sprays and springs of flowers
in underglaze blue, overlapping leaves with
blue edges, stalk handle, c1765–70 (A)... **1430.00**
9⅜" w, shaped sq, "Bishop Sumner" pattern,
center with iron-red edged roundel painted
with phoenix in flight in fenced garden,
eight panels of deer or birds with shrubbery
in iron-red, green, blue, yellow, turquoise,
and purple, brown enameled edge, 1770—
75, "gold open crescent" mark (A).......   **990.00**
10⅜" d
Heart shape, "Old Mosaick" pattern, continuous flowering prunus branch within
paneled border reserving mons, c1770,
underglaze "blue pseudo character"
marks (A) **1540.00**
Lozenge shape, "Fan" pattern, stylized
chrysanthemums and mons in Imari style,
c1770, underglaze "blue cresent" mark
(A) **985.00**

10⅝" d, "Flying Fox" pattern, Kakiemon
style with fox in flight above squirrel along
trailing vine between two banded hedges,
brown edged lobed rim, hairlines, c1752,
"red anchor" mark (A)................ **3475.00**
10¾" d
"Lady in a Pavilion" pattern, fluted, tasseled
curtains, song bird perched on cage, blue,
pale turquoise, iron-red, gilding, scalloped rim, c1750–52 (A)............. **3400.00**
Leaf shape, black scene of Chinaman holding sunshade and bird perched on hand,
vase of flowers on table in fenced garden,
rim with border of scrolls and diaper panels, c1756–60 (A) **1558.00**
11⅞" l, oval, spray and sprig of colored
flowers in center, pale yellow honeycomb
basketwork ground, molded vine stock and
green leaf handles, arcaded basketwork rim
painted with flowers, c1765 (A) **10,829.00**
14⅞" l, canted, rect, sprays of colored flowers in vase and mirror shaped gilt scroll
edged panels, gilt line border on rim, blue
scale ground, c1770, underglaze "blue fretted square" mark (A) **4675.00**
Egg Cup, 2¼" h, "Queen Charlotte" pattern,
conical bowl supported on flared foot, c1800,
Flight & Barr, incised "B" mark (A) **1230.00**
Ewer, 11½" h, white relief flowers and foliage
on pink ground, gilt accented lip, scroll handle
with mask terminal, c1870–89, Grainger.... **1200.00**
Ewer and Basin, 3½" h, miniature, ovoid body,
spray of summer flowers between gilt scroll
borders, blue ground, gilded borders, snake
handle, wide lip, same on basin, c1840, Chamberlain's script mark on ewer (A)........   **654.00**
Ice Pail, Cov, 8¾" h, Kakiemon colors of "Jabberwocky" pattern in shaped turquoise and
gilt C scroll borders, cov with scrolling handle,
cracks, c1770 (A) **1760.00**
Inkstand, 10" l, rect, dolphin handle, urn shaped
pots, pen channels, salmon and white marbled
and gilt veined molded base, Barr, Flight and
Barr (A) **1430.00**
Inkwell
5¹⁵/₁₆" l, ingot shape, front and ends with
sepia ground border painted with colorful
blossoms, reverse with gilt stippled panel of
gilt foliate scrolls with quiver shaped pen
holders, gilt entwined serpent handle, two
circ inkwells with gilt bordered covs, ball
knob, applied beadwork bands, gilt band
borders, repaired, 1807–13, "crown and
Prince of Wales feathers above BARR
FLIGHT & BARR Royal Porcelain Works
WORCESTER/London-House FLIGHT &
BARR Coventry Street" within brown ovals
(A)................................... **1100.00**
8¾" l, shaped rect form, view of Worcester
from river, gilded scrolling foliage, orange
ground, recesses containing pounce pot
and two liners, restored, c1840, Chamberlain's (A) **673.00**
Jug, Mask
5⅝" h, baluster shape, underglaze blue with
flower sprays, scrolling handle, c1765–70,
underglaze "blue crescent" mark (A).....   **374.00**
7½" h, Cabbage leaf
Blue "Pine Cone" pattern, late 18th C (A)   **605.00**
Gilt edged circ panel showing Worcester

cathedral from the Severn, gilt monograms "RR" between underglaze blue borders, scrolling handles, c1795, Flight & Barr Worcester, underglaze "blue crescent" mark (A)...................... **2337.00**

8" h, leaf molded globular body, cylindrical neck, naturalistic flower sprays in underglaze blue, scrolling handle, c1770, script "W" mark (A) **575.00**

8¼" h, cabbage leaf, c1765, Dr. Wall period, "blue crescent" mark................... **2100.00**

11⅝" h, cabbage leaf, c1770............. **3000.00**

Junket Bowl

10" d, blue transfer of floral and fruit clusters, ext with clusters of fruit, molded border over raised sides molded with shells, c1775 (A)................................... **550.00**

10¹⁄₁₆" d, "Old Japan Fan" pattern, scalloped, central chrysanthemum blossom enclosed by underglaze blue and white flowering vine border, int with underglaze blue and iron-red, green and gold stylized fans and mons, ext with two underglaze blue trailing branches with iron-red blossoms and buds, gild edge rim, 1768–72, underglaze "blue pseudo Chinese characters" mark within dbl circle (A) **1210.00**

Ladle, 5⁷⁄₁₆" l, boat shaped, "The Maltese Cross Flower" pattern, dark underglaze blue, sides of ext with two floral sprays, flowerhead terminal highlighted in blue, 1770–75, underglaze "blue open crescent" mark (A) **990.00**

Mug

2½" h, blue painted and iron-red Chinese man with satchel on pole over shoulder, crossing bridge between islands, stylized rock and tree, grooved loop handle, hairline, c1754–56 (A)........................ **1980.00**

3¼" h

Baluster, black transfer printed with titled portrait of Frederick the Great pointing to trophies of war and Fame blowing two trumpets, dtd 1757, sgd "RH Worcester' (A) **1476.00**

Cylindrical, view of Worcester cathedral, c1795, Flight & Barr Worcester (A)..... **2711.00**

Bell Form

3⅜" h, black transfer printed "The Doll" and "Bubbles" divided by two butterflies, each child seated on ornamental scroll, ribbed loop handle, c1760–65 (A) **5049.00**

3½" h, colored floral sprays and sprigs in gilt scroll edged vase and mirror shaped panels, grooved loop handle, blue scale ground, c1770, underglaze "blue crescent" mark (A)...................... **3553.00**

3⅝" h, baluster shape, blue painted "Willow Root" pattern of oriental lady by fenced garden with bird, tree from rockwork, S scroll handle with dbl whorl design, small leaf terminals, c1752–55 (A)................. **13,200.00**

4¾" h, baluster shape

"Quail" pattern, painted Kakiemon style quail with gnarled prunus tree and flowering shrub, iron-red and gilt floret border, grooved loop handle, c1770 (A) **1150.00**

Underglaze blue with sprays of naturalistic flowers, grooved loop handle, c1765–70, underglaze "blue crescent" mark (A)... **1215.00**

5" h

Cylindrical, blue and white "Gardener" pattern of Chinese scholar and attendant beside low table on fanciful island, c1770, "crescent" mark (A)................. **2302.00**

Enameled and gilt with sprays and sprigs of colored flowers, turquoise line border at top, grooved loop handle, c1775 (A)... **561.00**

"Japan" pattern, vert panels of prunus and crysanthemums divided by orange bands with gilt diapering and mons, grooved loop handle, c1770 (A)...................... **1050.00**

5½" h, blue rose centered spray group pattern, florals on handle, c1765–75, "blue crescent" mark **850.00**

5¾" h, Baluster shape

Lilac purple painted scene of classical ruins in Italianate landscape, reverse with ruins, reeded loop handle, c1756–60 (A)..... **2475.00**

Underglaze blue with sprays of naturalistic flowers, grooved loop handle, cracks, c1765–70 (A)........................ **475.00**

Mustard Pot, 5³⁄₁₆" h, black transfer of rooster and hen with three chicks on grassy plateau, domed cov with turnip knob, c1760 (A).... **3025.00**

Mustard Pot, Cov, and Spoon, 3½" d, cylindrical form, blue and white "Mansfield" pattern, cov with flower knob, spoon with scroll molded handle, sprig on inside of bowl, molded scrolled handle, c1770, underglaze "blue crescent" mark (A)................. **1736.00**

Patty Pan, 4¾" d, circ, peony spray attracting winged insect, formal border, c1770, underglaze "blue script W" mark (A) **325.00**

Plaque

5" d, head and shoulders portrait of William Pitt, brown coat, white waistcoat and cravat, within gilt linked hearts border, framed, c1830, Chamberlain's (A) **800.00**

5¾" h, 4¾" w, idyllic rural scenes of "Part of Warwick Castle" and "Water Mill, Westmoreland," gilt wooden frames, 1820–30, imp "crowned FBB, Flight, Barr & Barr" mark (A) **5200.00**

Plate

5¾" d, "Blind Earl" pattern, molded int with budding rose twig and center spray of flowers, scrolling gilt edged turquoise border, gilt edged fluted rim, c1765–70 (A).. **1619.00**

6¼" d, "Marchioness of Huntly" painted with swirling swags of colored flowers suspended from gilt scroll edged border, scalloped rim, c1770 (A) **514.00**

7" d, "Old Japan Fan" pattern, Imari palette, scalloped rim, c1770, underglaze "blue pseudo character" marks (A) **390.00**

7½" d

"Blind Earl" pattern molded budded rose sprig in green, brown, and pink, painted insects in gilt lobed rim, c1770 (A)..... **1000.00**

Sprays and sprigs of brightly colored flowers within vase and mirror shaped gilt scroll edged panels, scalloped rim, blue scale ground, c1770, underglaze "blue crescent" mark (A)...................... **840.00**

7⅝" d

"Bengal Tiger" pattern, dragons in compartments and antiques, scalloped rim, cell diaper border, c1770, underglaze "blue fretted square" mark (A).............. **822.00**

"Old Mosaick Japan" pattern, center with continuous flowering prunus branch, radiating decorative panels, gilt edged scalloped rim, c1770, underglaze "blue pseudo character" marks, pr (A) **1074.00**

8½" d
Blue, red, and green overall flower design, Chamberlain (A) **30.00**
Blue and white floral sprays, lobed basket-weave border, c1775, 1st Period (A) . . . **165.00**
"Brocade" pattern, radiating diaper panels, prunus branches, writhing dragons and mons, fluted rim, c1765–70, "gilt crescent" mark (A). **607.00**
Cluster of plums in center, radiating purple C scrolls, pink diaper and berried leaves border, c1775 (A) **1650.00**
Scene of bull baiting watched by crowd on one, other with pointer putting up a game bird, apricot ground rim with gilt foliate scrolls, c1815, imp "crown and FBB" mark, pr (A) **1063.00**
Transfer printed in black with classical ruins and statuary, pendant floral sprays on gilt edged fluted rim (A). **950.00**
8⅞" d, puce drapery swags with gilt tassel edge, gilt dentil rim, c1770 (A) **198.00**
9¼" d, blue and white printed "Pine Cone" pattern, scalloped edge, c1775–80, shaded "blue crescent" mark, set of 6. . . . . **3400.00**
9⅞" d, arms of East India Company in center, rim gilded with flowers and foliage, apricot ground, 1817, printed name and New Bond Street address mark **1850.00**
10½" d, floral center, reticulated border, three small feet, Grainger **755.00**
Platter, center Boar's head heraldic crest, blue and gilt palmette rim, Chamberlain, pr (A). . . **850.00**
Potpourri Basket, Cov, 3⅝" h, sprays of summer flowers on flared base, rim and cov molded with blossom and berries, branch loop handle, gilded details, blue ground, 1815–25, Chamberlain's script mark to cov (A) **425.00**
Sauceboat
5½" l, raised floral cartouches with blue florals, blue floral int and lip, c1770–80, Dr. Wall Period, "blue crescent" mark **325.00**
6¼" l, painted exotic birds in branches, gadrooned borders accented in purple, molded split scroll handle with gilt trim, c1765 (A) **1245.00**
6½" l, press molded, four ext panels in cartouche pattern, oriental blue scenes in panels, int designs, fluted dbl ends, two monkey handles, c1755–60 . . . . **2500.00**
7¾" l, underglaze blue with oriental island scenes within scroll molded cartouches, int with flowering plants attracting winged insect, c1755, painter's marks (A). **2337.00**
8¼" l, chinoiserie island scene on int in underglaze blue, ext with molded foliate cartouches with painted scenes, two scrolling handles applied with monkey head thumb pieces, dbl lipped, restored, c1755–60, underglaze blue painter's mark (A) **1130.00**
8¾" l
"The Fringed Tree" pattern, Chinese fisherman on ext in underglaze blue between small bridge and gazebo, reverse with Chinaman between two small island pavi-

lions, second Chinaman in sampan, int with island pavilion beneath floral sprays, insects, and trellis diaperwork on rim and spout, 1755–60, underglaze blue workman's mark (A) **385.00**
Silver shape, four vignettes of ladies and gallants, rim with scrolls and stylized foliate, dbl lipped, dbl handled, molded with scrolling foliage around vignettes, c1760 (A) **1860.00**
Saucer Dish
6¹³⁄₁₆" d, "Walk in the Garden" pattern, underglaze blue with two birds flitting above Chinese lady watching small body holding pole with bird, rim with trellis diaper border with four floral panels, c1760, underglaze blue workman's mark (A) **550.00**
7⁹⁄₁₆" d, "Old Japan Fan" pattern, scalloped, iron-red and green centered gilt chrysanthemum blossom encircled by underglaze blue roundel reserved with flowering vine and surrounded by underglaze blue, iron-red, and green fan and moms devices patterned with gilt trelliswork, gilt edged rim, 1768–72, underglaze "blue crescent" mark (A) . **1100.00**
Sauce Tureen, Cov
6⅜" l, oval, "Bishop Sumner" pattern, iron-red, green, blue, yellow, turquoise, and purple with six panels of birds or deer with flowering shrubbery, brown edged rim with flowering vine border, shell form handles, bud sprig knob, gilding, 1770–75, "gold open crescent" mark (A). **1210.00**
6½" H-H, sprays of flowers and sprigs of colored flowers in gilt and scroll edged shaped panels, two shell handles, cov with foliate bud finial, blue scale ground, c1770, underglaze "blue script W" mark (A). **2150.00**
6⅞" h, shield shape, three shells and seaweed in brown, iron-red, yellow, ochre, purple, rose, and black, against shaded brown ground in gilt-edged oval panel, gilt griffin's head and ring handles, gilt ground, sq base with gilt top and sides, cov with gilt flame form knob, c1810, imp "crowned BFB" mark, cov with "crown, Price of Wales feathers above brown BARR FLIGHT & BARR Royal Porcelain Works WORCESTER/London-House No,1 Coventry Street," pr (A) .**12,100.00**
Scent Bottle, Stopper, 6¾" h, pear form, printed and painted with named view of Worcester within gilt scroll reserved on green ground, c1830, Chamberlain's script mark (A) **785.00**
Soup Plate
9⅝" d, lobed, "Earl Manvers" pattern, center painted with cluster of plums within feathered gilt medallion, encircled by radiating purple scrollwork hung with berried foliage within border of pink diaper and berried leaves, c1770–75 (A) **2362.00**
9¾" d, center with iron-red bouquet in circ reserve, blue scale ground, border with three cartouches of iron-red houses in landscapes, rim restored, c1770, "blue sq seal" mark. **750.00**
Soup Tureen, Cov, Stand, 10¼" h, circ, purple and gold with sprays of stylized flowers, berries, and leaves, flowerhead knob, foliated scroll handles, molded leafs around lower

gilded body, gilt bands on rims, c1825, imp "crowned FBB" mark (A).................. **770.00**

Spittoon, 4" h, blue printed flower sprays and moth, rim with lattice and lambrequin border, c1780 (A)............................. **460.00**

Spoon Tray, 6" l, hex, romantic figures seated on mounds with trees, man playing instrument, lady with arm outstretched in gilt scroll edged shaped panels, smaller panels with floral sprays, blue scale ground, c1770, "blue fretted square" mark (A)........................ **3292.00**

Sucrier, 7½" h, elliptical form, bat printed band of seashells and seaweed between gilt line borders, bifurcated foliate handles, c1807–13, imp "Barr, Flight and Barr" mark (A)........ **125.00**

Sucrier, Cov
4⅛" h, "Japan" pattern in Kakiemon colors and gilt panels of chrysanthemums and prunus branches alternating with gilt accented cobalt panels reserved with iron-red flowerhead, domed cov with yellow and iron red flower finial, c1770, "blue seal" mark (A)............................. **475.00**

4½" h, "The Tea Party," "The Fortune Teller," and "Maid and Page," black transfers, cov with classical ruins and flower finial, c1760–65 (A)........................ **897.00**

4¾" h, exotic birds in parkland, winged insects within gilt scroll edged base and mirror shaped panels, cov with open flower finial, blue scale ground, c1770, underglaze "blue fretted square" mark (A)................ **2337.00**

"Jabberwocky" pattern, fluted, bright colored beasts on flowering branches, flower finial on cov, c1770 (A).................... **1337.00**

Tankard, Cylindrical
3¾" h, Lord Henry Thynne series, circ cartouche on front with landscape of castle on lake with turquoise and black husk border, sides with clusters of fruits, insects, and moths, blue bands with gilt dentils and interlocked C scrolls with flowerheads, c1770, "open crescent" mark.................. **2500.00**

5¹⁵⁄₁₆" h, "The Cracked Ice Ground" pattern, underglaze blue prunus blossoms, panel of Long Eliza on either side beside beaker of flowers or seated on rockwork beneath bamboo, 1765–70, underglaze "blue crescent" mark (A)........................ **1980.00**

Teabowl
4⅝" d, blue floral int, blue oriental scenes on ext, blue inside rim, c1780, "blue crescent" mark............................... **230.00**

Fluted, Kakiemon style with dragon with clouds and two crabs by flowering plants, int with iron-red and gilt rim border, 1758–60 (A)....................... **740.00**

Teabowl and Saucer
Idyllic scenes, saucer with "The Signal Tower," small cracks in saucer, c1760–65 (A)..... **550.00**

"Sir Joshua Reynolds" pattern, fluted, Kakiemon palette of iron-red, yellow, turquoise, and blue with four panels with Chinese pheasant perched on rock with peonies, or flowering peony branches separated by underglaze blue panels with peony roundels within gilt foliations, blue and white vine border, c1770, underglaze "blue pseudo seal" marks........................... **400.00**

Teabowl, Coffee Cup, Saucer, 4¾" d, "Floral

Queen's" pattern, underglaze blue, ext with two rows of petal shaped panels centering floral sprig, teabowl and saucer with floral sprig in center, c1770, underglaze blue script "W" within rect marks (A)............... **770.00**

Tea Caddy, 6" h, ovoid body, blue and white florals, domed cov with floral finial, c1775, 1st Period (A)............................. **715.00**

Teacup and Saucer
Famille rose style scattered puce, gray, and brown flower sprays and bouquets accented with gilt, ochre line rims, c1775... **200.00**

Fluted body, "Old Japan Fan" pattern in iron-red, green, blue, and gold, c1770, "blue oriental four character" mark in dbl circle (A) **660.00**

"Japan" pattern, fluted, prunus and chrysanthemum divided by radiating underglaze blue panels reserving iron-red mons, c1770, "fretted sq" mark (A).................. **250.00**

Oval cartouches painted in rose, purple, iron-red, yellow, and green with exotic birds and leafy branches within gilt scrolls, center with cluster of fruit in rose and green, gros bleu ground, gilt rims, 1772–75, underglaze "blue crescent" mark (A) **935.00**

"Root" pattern, blue scattered flowering branches, c1758 .... **300.00**

Teapot
4¾" h, globular, sprays of colored flowers in gilt edged scroll reserves, apple green ground, restored, c1770 (A)............ **1122.00**

5¹⁄₁₆" h, cucumber, parsnip, and flowers in rose, yellow, iron red, green, blue, purple, and gray, striated tulip and sprigs on reverse, oct faceted spout, domed cov with floral knob, loop handle, c1758–60 (A)... **6600.00**

5½" h, Globular
Blue and white cartouche of chinoiserie figures, domed cov with floral finial, c1775, 1st Period (A)................. **770.00**

Exotic birds in parkland, cov with winged insects, c1770–75 (A) **1335.00**

"Imari" pattern, panels of flowering branches divided by gilt hatched blue bands reserving florets (A) **1378.00**

5½" h, spherical, "Kempthorne" pattern, underglaze blue, iron-red, green, turquoise, and gold with oriental flowering plants between underglaze blue bands with gilt herringbone design, iron-red demi-flowerhead panels around shoulder, foot, and cov rim, floral sprig knob, spout and handle with rose flower spray, c1770, underglaze "blue pseudo seal" mark (A).................. **605.00**

5¾" h, globular, black transfer of "L'Amour" and "Comedie Italienne," cov with classical ruins and flower finial, c1760–65 (A)..... **935.00**

6" h
Globular, oriental family around table, printed and painted, iron-red loop and dot border, cov with flower finial, c1770 (A) **925.00**

Spherical, "Mandarin" pattern, two panels of figures on river bank in conversation with boatman, reserved on pink diaper ground with bamboo vignettes, cov with floral knob, c1775 (A) **885.00**

6¼" h
Fluted body, dry blue painted floral sprays, dbl entwined handle, cov with flower

finial and gilt dentil border, repaired finial, c1770, "blue pseudo seal" mark (A) ... **1110.00**

Globular shape, "Queen Charlotte" pattern, rose and iron-red whorled bands of stylized flowers alternating with floral bands in underglaze blue with gilding, shoulder and gilt edged cov rim with iron-red flowering vine border, cov with iron-red and green floral sprig knob, c1770, underglaze "blue pseudo seal" mark (A) **1760.00**

Globular Shape

6 1/2 " h, multicolored Japanese scene, rust borders also on spout and handle, c1788, Dr. Wall period **395.00**

9" h, underglaze blue "Plantation" pattern of fenced garden and buildings on both sides, spout and cov with trailing flower sprays, cov with knobbed finial, restored, c1765 (A) **775.00**

Teapot, Cov, Stand, 10 5/8 " h, oval body, vermicular design enclosed by diamond border, scroll handle, everted thumb piece, gilding c1830, Chamberlain's (A) **425.00**

Tray, 13 1/4 " l, painted view of Windsor Castle in gilt edged rect panel reserved on green ground with raised gilt accents, scroll molded rim accented with gilt, c1840, "Chamberlain & Co. and named view" mark (A) **1915.00**

Tureen, Cov, 6 7/8 " h, quarterlobed oval, printed in black, classical ruins and floral sprays, rustic handles with flowering terminals, cov with gilt gadrooned edge, cov missing handle, c1770 (A) **539.00**

Urn, 3 11/16 " h, 3 3/4 " h, cylindrical body, gold and white foliate scroll edged panel on front with various London views, gilt bands and white beadwork borders, flaring rim, int border of gilt palmettes and bellflowers, three gilt lion's paw feet, triangular base, c1820, brown script topographical inscriptions, "Flight Barr & Barr Worcester & No 1 Coventry St London," imp "crowned FBB" marks, pr (A) **3575.00**

Urn, Cov, 7 9/16 " h, shield shape, summer flowers on gilt edged wide drab green band below band of white molded beadwork, lower body and cov with apple green ground, gilt flame form knob, three gilt dolphin supports on base, trefoil base, c18200, imp "crowned FBB" mark (A) **2750.00**

Vase

4 3/4 " h, hex, enameled oriental woman with parasol on front, man with staff on reverse, flowering branches on sides, paneled diaper and floret border, c1753 (A)........ **7650.00**

5" h, baluster shape, rose, yellow, iron-red, blue, green, brown, and gray floral bouquet with scattered sprigs and insects, c1758–60 (A)................................... **1375.00**

5 1/4 " h, campana shape, painted peacock in parkland in gilt edged panel, claret ground, applied gilt caryatid handles, gilt gadrooned rim, c1820–30, Flight, Barr and Barr (A) .. **1725.00**

6" h, conical shape, scene of three cows in hilly meadow before distant town in shades of green, yellow, brown, blue, and slamon, within gilt band and foliate bordered oval panel, gilt and foliate dot and dash bands, gilt bands on rim, ankle, and foot, gilded molded ring handles, c1800, incised "B,

purple Flight & Barr Worcester Manu. to their Maj" (A)......................... **1100.00**

6 5/8 " h, "Warwick," front and reverse painted with colorful floral clusters, pale yellow ground cartouches edged in raised gilt scrollwork, reserved on green ground above band of white molded beadwork, gilt band borders, gilt entwined grapevine handles, gilt gadrooned rim, green circ foot, gilt stippled sq base, c1825, imp "crowned FBB" mark (A) **2200.00**

Vase, Cov, 15 1/4 "h, hex, alternate panels on tree peony and long tailed birds perched among flowering trees in underglaze blue, shoulders and domed covs painted with panels of chinoiserie landscapes reserved on ground of scrolling flowers within diaper borders, repaired, c1760, underglaze "blue X'd swords" marks, pr (A)........................... **14,400.00**

Wall Pocket

10" h, 10 1/8 " h, cornucopia shape, spirally molded, painted in shades of iron-red, purple, blue, green, yellow, and black with insects with oriental flowering branches and scattered blossoms, bulbous rim with similar flowers and leaves, pierced for hanging, 1753–55, pr (A)....................... **8250.00**

11" l, "The Cornucopia Prunus" pattern, molded body, c1757–60, 1st Period, Dr. Wall, "blue pseudo Meissen X'd swords" marks, pr............................. **9500.00**

Waste Bowl

4 3/4 " d, ext black penciled quail walking with another perched on rock, iron-red, blue, yellow, rose, and green enameled flowering plants, scalloped rim with iron-red border and gilt scrolls and dots (A) **660.00**

5 15/16 " d, ext penciled and enameled in green, blue, iron-red, and salmon with Chinese river landscape with man bearing parcels behind another on horseback before fisherman, opposite bank has man in window of pavilion, int with four small floral sprigs beneath rose trellis diaper border with three panels of gilt flowers at rim, c1760 (A) **7150.00**

6" d, black penciled continuous scene of oriental fishermen, island and pavilions on ext, rocky island on int, c1756–58 (A)........ **660.00**

Wine Taster, 3" l, peach form, molded with blossoming branches extending across basketwork ext from gnarled twig handle, floral border around int rim, c1760–65 (A) **2775.00**

YELLOW-GLAZED EARTHENWARE

Staffordshire, Yorkshire, Liverpool, England/Wales c1785–1835

History: English yellow-glazed earthenware is creamware or pearlware featuring an overall yellow glaze. The principal period of production was between 1785 and 1835. The color varied from a pale to a deep yellow. Yellow-glazed earthenware also is known as "canary" or "canary luster" ware.

Most of the yellow-glazed wares were either luster painted, enamel painted, or transfer printed. Sometimes two or three techniques were used on the same pieces. Silver luster was combined the most often with the yellow ground.

Enamel painting on yellow-glazed wares exhibited a wide range in subject matter and technique. The most popular enamel decorative motif was floral. Most flowers were stylized rather than naturalistic. Much of the decoration had a "primitive" or naive feel to the depictions. Iron-red and greens were two of the most popular colors. Pastoral landscapes and geometric patterns also were used for enameled decorations.

Transfer printed yellow-glazed wares had the printing done over the glaze. Most patterns were in black, but brown and red were used occasionally. Landscape scenes were the most popular motifs, followed by scenes with birds and animals. Other themes included politics, historical events, sporting scenes, and some mythological figures. Sometimes the transfer prints were over painted in enamel colors.

Yellow-glazed earthenwares were made in nearly all shapes and forms except for complete dinner services. Jugs and pitchers were the most popular forms made.

Yellow-glazed eathenware figures of animals and birds enjoyed great popularity. Some utilitarian pieces such as children's mugs were made in quantity.

Most yellow-glazed earthenware does not contain a maker's mark. Among the identified Staffordshire Manufacturers that made the ware are Josiah Wedgwood, Josiah Spode, Davenport, Enoch Wood & Sons, and Samuel Alcock & Co. Rockingham Pottery in Yorkshire made yellow wares; Leeds followed suite in the North. The Sunderland Pottery made yellow-glazed wares in addition to its more famous pink luster wares. Several potteries in New Castle and Liverpool contributed examples.

Cambrian and Glamorgan, two Swansea potteries, made a considerable number of yellow-glazed pieces. Another Welsh pottery, South Wales in Llanelly also made yellow wares.

Reference: J. Jefferson Miller II, *English Yellow-Glazed Earthenware*, Smithsonian Institution Press, 1974.

Museums: Art Institute of Chicago, Chicago, Illinois; City Museum & Art Gallery, Stoke-on-Trent, England; National Museum of American History, Smithsonian Institution, Washington, D.C.; Nelson-Atkins Museum of Art, Kansas City, Missouri; Rose Museum, Brandeis University, Waltham, Mass.

Bowl
   4³/₄" d, black transfer of mother and child, black rims, hairline **450.00**
   5" d, ftd, green and red flowers with brown berries and stems, brown outlined serrated rim **875.00**
   6" d, 3" h
     Adam Buck type, ladies with children, rust transfer, rust border (A) **385.00**
     Silver luster pennants, rust rim on base, silver feather border on white ground, Staffordshire **750.00**
   6³/₄" d, 3⁵/₈" h, slant sided, ftd, wide band of florals in red, green, rust, and pink luster, 19th C (A). **440.00**
Creamer
   3³/₄" h, bulbous body with flared spout, ftd,

Pitcher, 5" h, silver luster overlay, yellow ground, restored, c1830, unmkd, (A) $285.00

   iron-red, green, and brown cabbage roses and leaves (A) **715.00**
   3⁷/₈" h, fluted body, iron-red and green flowers and leaves (A) **413.00**
Cup, 2³/₈" h, black transfer of three goats on int, sailboat with church scene on one side, castle and valley on other, unmarked. **125.00**
Flower Pot, 4" h, pink luster design of panoramic view of house with landscape, 19th C (A). . .   **275.00**
Gravy Boat, 2¹/₂" h, miniature, red, brown, and green applied enamel flowers and leaves, canary ground, imp "WEDGWOOD" mark (A)   **550.00**
Jug
   4³/₈" h, silver luster bands of stylized foliage, angular handle, c1815 (A). **535.00**
   4¹/₂" h, brown printed side commemorating death of Lord Nelson in 1805, reverse with portrait of Duke of Wellington, canary ground (A) **418.00**
   5" h, transfer of Tom Cribbs and Tom Molinaux in wreath, poem on reverse, iron-red transfers (A) **2090.00**
   5¹/₄" h, black bat printed with two scenes of figures in boats with country mansion, silver luster line border, spout chip, c1815 . . . .   **350.00**
   5¹/₂" h, black printed panels of rural landscapes, silver luster borders, angular handle **95.00**
   6¹/₂" h, Charity and Hope, gray transfers, silver luster roundels, rim, spout, handle, and borders (A) **495.00**
Loving Cup, 5" h, ftd, silver resist design of grapes and vines, dbl loop handles (A) **440.00**
Mug
   2" h, Miniature
     "A Trifle For Eliza" on front, yellow ground. **275.00**
     Silver luster bird panel, silver rim **750.00**
   2¹/₄" h
     "A Trifle for Fanney" in leafy cartouche, canary ground (A) **385.00**
     "Boys Balancing," transfer printed in red, c1820 . . . .   **950.00**
     Solid canary Staffordshire child's, crack sprayed, c1830 . . . .   **195.00**
   2³/₈" h, red transfer of "A Harp For Elizabeth," luster body, emb leaf handle (A). . .   **375.00**
   2¹/₂" h
     "A Present for My Dear Girl," brown transfer, c1820. . . . .   **525.00**
     Black transfer of monkey gazing at mirror

surrounded by cartouche with "The Gift is But a Little Treat/But My Regard for You is Great/Mimicry," spider on int (A) **660.00**

Blue and rust florals, brown rim.......... **325.00**

Floral decoration in rust, green, and brown, hairline (A) **145.00**

Polychrome enameled flower, emb leaf handle, hairline (A) **190.00**

Rust transfer of girl with farm scene, c1820 .... **425.00**

2³/₄" h

Floral band in iron-red and silver luster, c1815 (A) **175.00**

Pink luster house design (A) **175.00**

Rust transfer of woman with basket and dog............................... **435.00**

3¹/₂" h, red transfer of woman slopping hogs, black edge stripes, emb leaf handle (A)... **275.00**

Pitcher

2³/₄" h, side pouring spout, applied green and brown ribs outlined in light orange, canary ground (A) **385.00**

4¹/₂" h

Motto "I Do Not Know What Man To Trust" on front, fortress on reverse, panels outlined in silver luster, silver luster trim on rim, top, and handle, c1820.... **1025.00**

Silver resist design of leaves and tendrils, wide luster band on rim, spout and handle, 19th C (A)...................... **390.00**

4³/₄" h, "The Farmer's Creed," black transfer with red enameling, silver luster rim (A)... **440.00**

4⁷/₈" h

Canary luster with orange flowers and leaves, c1820....................... **650.00**

"The sun of Old England" and "The determined enemy of corruption," black transfers, polychrome enamel rim with brick red striping, glued repair to spout (A) .. **275.00**

Two different English manors, black transfers, silver luster border (A) **440.00**

5¹/₂" h, canary yellow with iron-red florals and silver luster leaves, rim, and lines on handle, c1820 .... **1150.00**

5⁵/₈" h

Black transfers of farming scene in silver luster roundels, silver luster bands and trim **595.00**

Overall silver luster body with canary fern leaves and bands of curlicues (A) **192.00**

5³/₄" h, front with molded Satyr face in orange and black, black scrolls and large orange roundels, canary ground (A)........ **495.00**

6" h, cartouches of Charity and Hope with silver luster, c1820 .... **1250.00**

6¹/₂" h, molded swirl fluted body, iron-red grapes, green leaves, brown lip and rim (A)................................. **715.00**

7" h, large cabbage roses in iron-red, green and brown leaves (A)................... **1375.00**

Plate

6³/₄" d, central rose in iron-red, green, and brown, molded border with floral chain (A) **1100.00**

8¹/₄" d, black transfers of history of Rome, stylized vine borders, canary ground, c1810, Montreau, set of 8 (A) **1100.00**

10" d, molded border with cabbage rose pattern in iron-red, green, and brown (A).... **3410.00**

Sauce Tureen, Cov, and Stand, 8¹/₈" h, oval, trailing red outlined flowers and resist silver

foliage, lustered handles, canary yellow ground, early 19th C, pr (A) **4594.00**

Spill Vase, 4¹/₂" h, center panel with iron-red, blue-green florals, leaves, and lines, brown rim and lines around base, wide brown rim inside, canary yellow ground, c1830, Staffordshire, pr **950.00**

Sugar Bowl, 5¹/₂" h, 6¹/₂" w, Castleford type, band of molded classical figures under arches around body, florals and circles on shoulder, orange-ochre, blue, green, brown, and red (A)........................... **2530.00**

Teabowl and Saucer, "Tea Party', black transfers, imp "SEWELL" mark (A)................... **220.00**

Teapot

3¹/₂" h, round body with tapered cylindrical spout, iron-red, green, and brown cabbage roses and leaves (A)................... **853.00**

3⁵/₈" h, Adam Buck type, woman playing piano, black transfer on each side, hairline, 19th C **350.00**

Toy, 2⁵/₈" h, 4¹/₂" w, hooded cradle with emb geometrics around body, crack on rim, 19th C (A)................................. **440.00**

Urn, 3³/₄" h, brown stripes, c1830 .... **385.00**

Vase

5" h, 4¹/₂" w, 2" d, moon shaped, multicolored bird and flower decoration, gilt and white handles, round gilt feet, restoration to rim, 1878, crown printed and incised marks, pr **2200.00**

7¹/₂" h, garniture type, brown, rust, green, and blue overall floral design, vert stiff leaves from base, scalloped rim, sq base (A)................................. **1040.00**

ZSOLNAY

c 1828 - 1900

Pecs, Funfkirchen
1862 to Present

History: Vilmos Zsolnay established a Hungarian earthenware pottery at Pecs, Funfkirchen in 1862. Initially utilitarian earthenwares were the main product. Ornamental wares decorated in Persian motifs were added to the line. The factory also produced reticulated and pierced highly decorative ornamental vases similar to those by Fischer. Enamel was used to paint designs onto porcelains and were fired at high temperatures.

At the turn of the century vases and bowls with Art Nouveau decorations and boldly colored glazes were made. Many of the patterns were designed by J. Rippl-Ronai about 1900. An experimental workshop under the direction of V. Wartha produced some luster decorated pieces between 1893 and 1910. Vases in billowing, folded shapes decorated in shades of green, yellow, and blue lusters or in motifs of plants and cloud-like designs were manufactured. Zsolnay porcelains in fountains, sculptures, and tiles were used to decorate public buildings all over the old Austro-Hungarian empire.

Porcelain figurines were added to the line about 1900. These are in great demand today.

The factory is called the Alfoldi Porcelain works today and produces Herend and Zsolnay porcelains.

The Zsolnay factory is still in business today. It produces figures with an iridescent glaze.

The company's mark is a stylized design representing the five churches of Zsolnay. Sometimes the word "Pecs" also appears.

Museum: Zsolnay Museum, Pecs, Hungary.

Bowl, 6" sq, reticulated Persian design in gold, burgundy, and blue...................... **95.00**
Box, Cov, 4½" l, 5½" d, encircling chariot scene, green-gold color, round shape, marked................................ **90.00**
Compote, 11" d, ribbed dish on center pedestal, four caryatids modeled as angels as supports, blue-green irid glaze..................... **1000.00**
Cup, 7" h, cream skull with brown eyeholes, gold crown, set on bulbous plant and green crackle luster circ foot, marked **450.00**
Dish, 8½" w, fan shape, cream and gold with rolled sides **165.00**
Figure
  3¼" h, seated figure of young girl in large bonnet, holding small open dish, green-gold irid glaze............................. **145.00**
  3½" h, girl with basket in irid green-gold glaze.................................. **145.00**
  4" h, 3½" l, French poodle, head and tail erect, green-gold color, rect base **50.00**
  4¼" h
    3¼" l, Dachshund in green-gold color, rect plinth, marked **45.00**
    5¼" l, standing "Puli," Hungarian sheep dog, beige coloring................... **95.00**
  4½" h, handpainted chickadees, green Hungary mark **85.00**
  4¾" h
    Girl with chicken, irid purple glaze, rect base, marked...................... **158.00**
    Seated dog in irid green-gold finish **65.00**
  5" h
    3½" l, boxer dog in reclining position, green-gold color, marked **45.00**
    4" l, spaniel in seated position, sad expression, long ears, green-gold color, marked **50.00**
  7½" l, two bears in green-gold color, raised plinth, marked **125.00**
  6" h
    Billy goat with kid, gold and blue irid, sgd "Sinko" **250.00**
  6" l
    Sleeping deer, gold and blue irid, sgd "Sinko" **250.00**
  6½" h, 3½" l, eagle in perched position, wings folded, detailed feathers, green-gold color............................ **75.00**
  7½" l, giraffe with head and neck erect, green-gold color, small plinth............ **45.00**
  8" l, two polar bears on rock, green irid **300.00**
  10¼" h, woman pulling dress up over head, draped cloth, green-gold color, vase, pedestal at side, marked...................... **250.00**
  10½" h, greyhound, irid glaze........... **90.00**

Jardinaire, 16" l, ovoid, multicolored florals, protruding pierced roundels, cream ground, "blue steeple" mark, (A) $413.00

Vase, 16" h, enameled rust and iron-red flowers and butterflies on chocolate oriental bark ground, dtd 1896, "Millenium Zsolnay" mark, $25,000.00

Pitcher
  8" h, green and gold irid glazes, "blue tower" mark................................. **150.00**
  9" h, figural duck, reticulated, dbl walled, marked.............................. **165.00**
Plate, 12" d, pink and blue flowers on light yellow center, reticulated gold trimmed border extending to rim, Zsolnay, Pecs mark....... **245.00**
Puzzle Jug, 8" h, flowers and insects on ornate yellow ground, five reticulated medallions, large beads, loop handles, "PECS HUNGARY" mark.................................. **369.00**
Vase
  3" h, squat, globular, crackled red shading to yellow irid (A)......................... **440.00**
  4½" h, baluster form, mottled blue and green irid **300.00**
  5½" h, red irid crackle glaze **100.00**
  6" h, Grecian figures around body, irid green and gold, "gold castle" mark **175.00**
  6½" h, relief of bacchanalian ladies, green-gold irid.............................. **100.00**
  8" h
    Blue and green irid, six handles (A) **800.00**
    Compressed bulbous shape, Persian type design in irid orchid, pink, purple, and

white, gold enhancing, "gold tower" mark............................... **160.00**

8½" h, peach colored floral reticulated casing over body, petal shaped top **375.00**

8¾" h, blue irid, "Zsolnay Pecs" mark (A). **250.00**

9¼" h, sq shape, reticulated in blue, orchid, tan, and cream glaze with flowers and leaves, two upright handles, four claw feet **495.00**

9½" h

Maiden with long hair in front, green-gold color, bulbous shape, straight neck, flaring rim, marked...................... **150.00**

Sq, reticulated blue, orchid, green, tan, and cream glaze with flowers and leaves, two upright handles, four claw feet, "brown tower" mark........................ **415.00**

Tapered, red textured crackle glaze (A)... **100.00**

9¾" h, pastel flowers on cream glaze, reticulated body, two upright handles, four claw feet................................... **450.00**

10" h, reticulated, gilt Persian motif, cream with gilt trim, glass liner, c1880, "steeple" mark................................. **295.00**

11¾" h, cylindrical contour, three dark olive frogs sitting under water, one expelling bubbles against mottled purplish spotted irid ground, c1900, imp factory marks (A).... **5500.00**

12" h, puzzle type, pink with Art Nouveau style flowers outlined in gold, crown top, four handles, repaired **125.00**

13" h, green irid pebble ground, raised gold medallion on neck, twp gold handles with red jewels **650.00**

14" h, baluster shape, white spider webs on black ground (A)...................... **60.00**

Vase, Cov, 11⅜" h, ovoid body, blue and red lustrous flowers, green lustrous foliage, same on domed cov, monogram for "Julia Zsolnay, dated 2, VIII 1926," script decorator's marks (A)..................................... **2100.00**

APPENDIX

BRITISH REGISTRATION MARKS
1843 - 1883

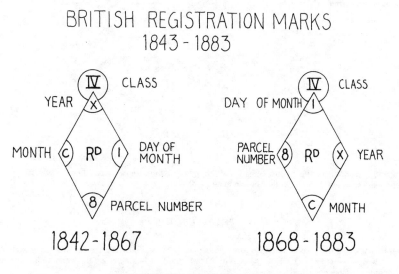

1842-1867   1868-1883

THE BRITISH REGISTRY MARK

The British Registry mark or diamond is found on ceramics manufactured in Great Britain or handled by British agents for foreign manufacturers. The mark was used first in 1842 and continued in use in this form until 1883. The mark is usually found impressed or raised on the ceramic body and indicates that the shape or material was registered or printed when the decoration or pattern was registered.

Through registration of the shape or pattern, the manufacturer was protected from infringement for a period of three years before renewal was necessary. By examining and deciphering this device, the collector can determine the earliest date that a piece was registered, then place it in its proper time frame.

Deciphering the mark is not difficult. All ceramics are classified number IV as seen at the top of the diamond. Both examples bear this identification.

The 1842–1867 diamond is deciphered in the following manner: the top semicircle designates the year, the left one indicates the month, the right one indicates the day of the month, and the bottom one indicates the parcel number that identifies the manufacturer. The following is a list that corresponds to the semicircles in the 1842–1867 diamond:

Year	Month for Both Devices
1842—X	January—C or O
1843—H	February—G
1844—C	March—W
1845—A	April—H
1846—I	May—E
1847—F	June—M
1848—U	July—I
1849—S	August—R and September 1–19th, 1857
1850—V	September—D
1851—P	October—B
1852—D	November—K
1853—Y	December—A
1854—J	
1855—E	
1856—L	
1857—K	
1858—B	
1859—M	
1860—Z	
1861—R	
1862—O	
1863—G	
1864—N	
1865—W	
1866—Q	
1867—T	

From this chart, it can be determined that the sample diamond on the left dates the registration of the shape or decoration on January 1, 1842.

In 1868, the British Registry mark was altered slightly to the form on the right. The following list corresponds to the diamond used from 1868–1883:

Year

1868—X	1877—P
1869—H	1878—W from March 1–6
1870—C	1878—D
1871—A	1879—Y
1872—I	1880—J
1873—F	1881—E
1874—U	1882—L
1875—S	1883—K
1876—V	

The diamond mark on the right dates January 1, 1868. In 1888, the diamond-shaped device was replaced with the complete registration number filed in the London Patent Office.

PHOTO CREDITS

We wish to thank all those dealers and collectors who permitted us to photograph their antique pottery and porcelain. Unfortunately we are unable to identify the sources of all our pictures; nevertheless, we are deeply appreciative to all who have contributed to this price guide.

Connecticut: Lee Cizek, Avon; Maria & Peter Warren, Wilton. **Florida:** Pascoe & Co., Miami Beach.

Illinois: Beaux Arts Gallery, Chicago; Fly-By-Nite Gallery, Chicago; Freidarica Ltd., Highwood; Heather Higgins, Wilmette; Terrie Kempe, Riverside; Longfield's Keep, Chicago; Jeffrey Najjoum, Chicago; Remember When, Libertyville; Rusnak's Antiques, Berwyn; Old Smith & Co., Mossville; Stocker Antiques, Westmont; Bonnie & Floyd Wombles, Summer Hill.

Indiana: David O'Reilly, Ft. Wayne. **Kansas:** Fine Americana, Shawnee Mission. **Maryland:** Barry & Lisa McAllister, Clear Spring; Deborah Dohd, Owings Mills. **Massachusetts:** Ellipse Antiques, Dennis: John Hunt Marshall, Blandford.

Michigan: Fancy-Full Antiques, Livonia; Margaret Durkin Antiques, Grosse Pointe; Old Lyon Antiques, Inc., Milan; Onion House Antiques, Okemos; The Ragman, Portland; Windsor House Antiques, Royal Oak.

Minnesota: C.L. Nelson, Spring Park. **New York:** Knightsbridge, Inc., New York City; Frances Wisniewski, Syracuse; Yesterdays, New York City.

Ohio: Antiques at the Log House, Liberty Center; Barbara Bako, North Canton; Far Hills Antiques, Dayton; June Greenwald Antiques, Cleveland Heights; D L Zelinameyer, Lakewood.

Oklahoma: The Antiquary, Tulsa. **Pennsylvania:** Rosalyn Quill Antiques, Pittsburgh. **Virginia:** Malcolm Magruder, Millwood; Turn of the Century, Newport News. **Wisconsin:** Charmaine's English Antiques, Lake Delton; B. Issod, Wausau; Pierce & Pierce, Wisconsin Rapids.

Sotheby's in London must be given an extra special thanks for providing photographs from their auction catalogues for rarer categories.

SPECIAL CREDITS

Our gratitude must go to the following people for exceptional help with either data for this book and/or photographs. Without their generous help, we would have been unable to write this second edition.

A Little Bit Antiques, Ltd., Glenview, Illinois; Mardee & Kim Chandler, Sturgis, Michigan; Margaret Durkin, Grosse Pointe, Michigan; Fly-By-Nite Gallery, Stuart & Tom Tomc, Chicago, Illinois; Knightsbridge Antiques, Winnetka, Illinois; Malcolm Magruder, Millwood, Virginia; C.L. Nelson, Spring Park, Minnesota; Mary and Dudley Pierce, Wisconsin Rapids, Wisconsin; Raven and Dove Antiques, Randi Schwartz, Wilmette, Illinois; Wynn A. Sayman, Richmond, Massachusetts; Seekers Antiques, Inc., Columbus, Ohio; Taylor B. Williams, Chicago, Illinois; Maria & Peter Warren, Wilton, Connecticut.

AUCTION HOUSES

The following auction houses cooperated with us by providing complimentary subscriptions to their catalogues for all pottery and porcelain auctions. In addition, Sotheby's in London provided photographs for our use. Their cooperation is appreciated greatly. Without this help, it would have been impossible to produce this price guide.

Armans
P. O. Box 3239
Newport, RI 02840

William Doyle Galleries
175 East 87th St.
New York, NY 10028

Garth's Auction, Inc.
2690 Stratford Rd.
P. O. Box 369
Delaware, OH 43015

Gene Harris Auction Center
203 So. 18th Ave.
P. O. Box 476
Marshalltown, IA 50158

Hanzel Galleries, Inc.
1120 South Michigan Ave.
Chicago, IL 60605

Leslie Hindman Auctioneers
215 West Ohio St.
Chicago, IL 60610

Phillips
406 East 79th St.
New York, NY 10021

Phillips-London
101 New Bond Street
London W1Y OAS
United Kingdom

Robert W. Skinner, Inc.
Bolton Gallery, Route 117
Bolton, MA 01740

Sotheby's
1334 York Ave.
New York, NY 10021

Sotheby's-London
34–35 New Bond Street
London W1A 2AA

Wolf's Auction Gallery
1239 West 6th Street
Cleveland, OH 44113

Additionally, catalogues from these listed auction houses were used for data for this book.

Christie's
502 Park Avenue
New York, NY 10022

Christie's East
219 East 67 Street
New York, NY 10021

Christie's London
8 King Street, St. James
SW1Y GQT

Dunning Auction Service
755 Church Road
P.O. Box 866
Elgin, IL 60121

ADDITIONAL NOTES ON MARKS

Bisque: see Heubach and Sevres for marks.
Creamware: see Leeds and Wedgwood for marks.
Crown and Royal Crown Derby: Year ciphers were incorporated in some marks.
Delft: see Bristol and Liverpool for additional marks.
Flow Blue: see Staffordshire General for additional marks.
Majolica: See Keller and Guerin, Minton, and Sarreguemines for additional marks.
Minton: Year ciphers were incorporated in some marks.
Mulberry China: see Flow Blue and Staffordshire General for marks.
Parian: see Copeland-Spode and Minton for marks.
Pate-Sur-Pate: see Minton and Sevres for marks.
Pearlware: see Clews, Davenport, Ridgway, Staffordshire General, Wedgwood, and Enoch and Ralph Wood for marks.
Piano Babies: see Heubach for marks.
Pitcher and Bowl Sets: see Staffordshire General for additional marks.
Royal Worcester: Year ciphers were incorporated in some marks.
Samson: no identifiable marks recorded. Used marks simulating those of Chelsea, Meissen, and Sevres.
Sevres: Year ciphers were incorporated in some marks.
Staffordshire Blue and White: see Staffordshire General and Historic marks.
Tea Leaf Ironstone: see Ironstone marks.
Tiles: see Minton and Wedgwood for additional marks.
Toby Jugs: see Pratt and Enoch and Ralph Wood for marks.
Wedgwood: Year ciphers were included in some marks.
Willow Ware: see Staffordshire General for marks.

GLOSSARY

Applied. Parts or ornaments attached to the body by means of liquid clay (slip). Also called sprigging.

Anthemion. A formal type of decoration in the shape of stylized honeysuckle flowers and leaves.

Bail Handle. Arched fixed or movable overhead handle.

Baluster Form. Bulbous center with narrow top and bottom usually with flared ends.

Bargeware. Earthenware of narrow proportions for use on canal boats and barges. These pieces were decorated with florals and luster. Larger pieces featured modeled teapots on the covers or handles.

Bat Printing. The transfer of a design by means of glue-like slabs. Most often used on glazed surfaces.

Bellarmine. Stoneware jug or bottle featuring bearded mask and coat of arms under neck.

Bell-Toy Pattern. Oriental pattern featuring child holding toy composed of stick with bells. Popular pattern at Worcester.

Bird or Sparrow Spout. Modeled spout in form of open bird beak. These were closely associated with examples fabricated in silver.

Blanc de Chine. French term referring to a translucent white or ivory porcelain covered in thick glaze. Produced by several English and French companies after Chinese originals.

Bleu Lapis. Streaked or veined bright blue ground color often found in combination with gold accents. Used at Vincennes.

Bleu Persan. Dark blue ground color used on Nevers faience often in conjunction with white or yellow ornamentation.

Blind Earl Pattern. Low relief design of rosebuds, leaves, and insects which covers entire surface. Designed for the blind Earl of Coventry in 1755. The pattern was used at Worcester and Chelsea.

Bocage. Modeled foliage, branches, and flowers which form arbor or canopy background for figures. A method of covering unfinished backs of figures.

Bonbonniere. French term for small covered sweetmeat container.

Cachepot. Ornamental container designed to hold utilitarian flowerpot.

Cartouche. A method of framing or outlining a design, usually with elaborate borders. (See Laub-und-Bandelwerk)

China. Term frequently used to refer collectively to pottery and porcelain, but correctly applies only to porcelain.

Chinoiserie. European decoration utilizing pseudo-Chinese figures, pagodas, and landscapes. Used extensively in early 18th century England and the Continent.

Crabstock. Modeled in form of branch of crab apple tree. Found on handles, spouts, and feet.

Dentil. Border treatment of small rectangular blocks giving appearance of teeth. Usually in gilt.

Diapering. Diamond or lozenge type pattern that is usually repetitive and connected.

Ecuelle. French term for small, covered shallow bowl with double parallel handles. Used for serving soup.

Engine-Turned. Machine-applied design that cuts into the surface of the clay.

Etched. Method of decoration using an acid-resistant covering in which the design is cut, exposed to hydrofluoric acid and pigment added to the etched recesses.

Famille Rose. Chinese-style design which incorporates opaque pink or rose-colored enamels.

Flambe. French term for red shaded glazes derived from reduced copper.

Fuddling Cup. Group of cups joined together internally and externally, usually with multiple handles.

Gadrooned. Continuous pattern of reeding or fluting used mainly as a border treatment. Inspired from silver examples.

Grisaille. French term for printing in gray shades on porcelain to give the effect of relief.

Hausmalerei. German term for ceramic decorators who literally worked at home. They purchased whiteware from factories such as Meissen and Vienna or finished partially decorated pieces.

Imari. Japanese style using designs based on native Japanese textiles. Colors of red and dark underglaze blue predominate.

Istoriato. Italian term for mythical, biblical, or genre historical scenes that were painted in polychromes on earthenwares. These paints often cover the entire surface of the object.

Kakiemon Style. Based on the Japanese decorations of the Kakiemon family. The main features include asymmetrical patterns of florals, birds, and Orientals in iron-red, yellow, and shades of blue utilizing large masses of white ground in the color scheme. Popular on 18th century Meissen, Chantilly, Chelsea, Bow, and Worcester.

Lambrequin. French term for a scalloped border pattern that consists of hanging drapery, lace and scrollwork, and leaves. This pattern reached its zenith at Rouen.

Laub-und-Bandelwerk. German term meaning leaf and strapwork. This elaborate type of design was used extensively in the cartouche borders at Meissen and Vienna.

Mon. Japanese inspired form representing circular stylized florals. Frequently incorporated in European interpretations of Oriental designs.

Ozier. German term which describes a molded or painted woven basket-type treatment. Many variations exist including continuous and interrupted patterns.

Posset Pot. Multi-handled pot with center spout designed to hold mixture of wine or ale and milk.

Potpourri Vase. Designed to hold liquid, flower petals, and herbs. Pierced shoulder or cover allows for the escape of the aromatic scents.

Prunus. Plum blossom-type decoration which is based on the Chinese symbol for spring.

Putto. Italian term referring to nude or semi-nude young boy. Frequently used as accessory decoration.

Quatrefoil. Shape or design divided in four equal lobes or sections.

Reserve. An area of a design without ground color designated to receive a decorative panel.

Sheet Design. Repetitive design from border to border.

Silver Shape. Copies in porcelain and pottery of existing silver pieces. These usually were reserved for borders, spouts, and handles.

Transfer Printing. The transfer of a design from prepared copper plates by means of tissue paper. The design, once cut into the copper plates, was prepared with color. A thin sheet of tissue transferred the design to the dry ground of the piece prior to glazing.

Trembleuse. French term used to describe a well or vertical projections found on saucers that were devised to keep the accompanying cups from shifting on the saucers. They were designed specifically for those with unsteady hands.

Additional glossary terms can be found in the following books: Louise Ade Boger, *The Dictionary of World Pottery & Porcelain*, Scribners, 1971; George Savage & Harold Newman, *An Illustrated Dictionary of Ceramics*, Van Nostrand Reinhold Company, 1974.

BIBLIOGRAPHY

The following is a listing of general reference books on English and Continental Pottery and Porcelain that the reader may find useful. A list of marks books is also included.

CONTINENTAL REFERENCES

Paul Atterbury, General Editor, *The History of Porcelain,* Orbis Publishing, 1982; John Cushion, *Continental China Collecting for Amateurs,* Frederick Muller, 1970; Hugo Morley-Fletcher and Roger McIlroy, *Christie's Pictorial History of European Pottery,* Prentice-Hall, Inc., 1984; Reginard Haggar, *The Concise Encyclopedia of Continental Pottery and Porcelain,* Hawthorn Books, Inc., 1960.

ENGLISH REFERENCES

G. A. Godden, *British Porcelain,* Clarkson N. Potter, 1974; G. A. Godden, *British Pottery,* Clarkson N. Potter, Inc., 1975; G. Bernard Hughes, *Victorian Pottery & Porcelain,* Spring Books, 1967; Griselda Lewis, *A Collector's History of English Pottery,* 4th ed, Antique Collectors Club, 1987; G. Willis, *English Pottery & Porcelain,* Guiness Signatures, 1968.

GENERAL REFERENCES

Emmanuel Cooper, *A History of Pottery,* St. Martins Press, 1972; John P. Cushion, *Pottery & Porcelain Tablewares,* William Morrow & Co., Inc., 1976; Antoinette Fay-Halle and Barbara Mundt, *Porcelain of the Nineteenth Century,* Rizzoli, 1983.

MARKS REFERENCES

W. Chaffers, *Marks & Monograms on European & Oriental Pottery & Porcelain,* William Reeves, 1965; J. P. Cushion, *Pocket Book of British Ceramic Marks,* Faber & Faber, 1984; J. P. Cushion and W. B. Honey, *Handbook of Pottery & Porcelain Marks, 4th Edition,* Faber & Faber, 1981; G. A. Godden, *Encyclopedia of British Pottery & Porcelain Marks,* Barrie & Jenkins, 1977; M. Haslam, *Marks & Monograms of the Modern Movement,* Lutterworth Press, 1977; Robert E. Rontgen, *Marks on German, Bohemian & Austrian Porcelain, 1710 to the Present,* Schiffer Publishers, 1981.

INDEX